George T. Wolz

St. Charles College

August 6, 1955

THE JEWISH COMMUNITY

ITS HISTORY AND STRUCTURE TO THE AMERICAN REVOLUTION

In Three Volumes

VOLUME THREE

Professor Morris Loeb, of New York, the distinguished chemist, scholar and public worker, who died on October 8, 1912, by his last Will and Testament, created a Fund under the following terms: "I give and bequeath to the Jewish Publication Society of America the sum of Ten Thousand Dollars as a permanent fund, the income of which alone shall, from time to time, be utilized for and applied to the preparation and publication of a scholarly work devoted to the interests of Judaism."

The present work is the fourth issued under this Fund. The first, SAADIA GAON — HIS LIFE AND WORKS, by Henry Malter, was published in 1921. The second, THE PHARISEES — THE SOCIOLOGICAL BACKGROUND OF THEIR FAITH, by Louis Finkelstein, was published in 1938. The third, THE JEWS IN SPAIN — THEIR SOCIAL, POLITICAL AND CULTURAL LIFE DURING THE MIDDLE AGES, by Abraham A. Neuman, was published in 1942.

THE MORRIS LOEB SERIES

THE JEWISH COMMUNITY

ITS HISTORY AND STRUCTURE TO THE AMERICAN REVOLUTION

BY

SALO WITTMAYER BARON

Jur. D., Ph. D., Pol. Sc. D., Rabbi

PROFESSOR OF JEWISH HISTORY, LITERATURE AND INSTITUTIONS ON THE MILLER FOUNDATION, COLUMBIA UNIVERSITY

VOLUME THREE

PHILADELPHIA

THE JEWISH PUBLICATION SOCIETY OF AMERICA

1942–5702

PRINTED IN THE UNITED STATES OF AMERICA
PRESS OF THE JEWISH PUBLICATION SOCIETY
PHILADELPHIA, PENNA.

PREFACE

A FEW brief explanations in regard to the method employed in the preparation of this Volume may be of use to many readers.

The Notes, as indicated by their length, are intended not only to give references to sources, but also to treat of some additional aspects which for one or another reason could not be dealt with in the text. They thus combine features of footnotes and of excursuses. In view of their physical separation from the text, however, it was deemed expedient as a rule to lump together the documentation of an entire paragraph in the text, so as not to necessitate constant reference to Vol. III. The sources usually follow the order of the discussion in the text, except insofar as they happen to be included in the same publication, all pages of which are listed at its first mention. The careful reader ought to experience no difficulty in locating the source of each statement. The frequent cross references to other notes ought to facilitate consultation of some related discussions not only in these notes but also in the text to which they are appended. For obvious reasons in our elaboration of some significant aspects the chronological *terminus ad quem*, the American Revolution, was even less strictly adhered to here than in the text.

The only purpose of the Bibliography is to furnish fuller data for books and articles in either text or notes. It is not a *bibliographie raisonnée* nor does it attempt to list all sources and secondary literature dealing with the various aspects of the ancient and medieval Jewish community. It merely records for the reader's convenience in alphabetical order works cited by the author. It also indicates which publications (about a dozen in all) were not directly accessible to him, but were used only through more or less reliable quotations in other sources or monographs.

The Index, finally, tries to give full guidance to the subjects, persons, localities and sources treated in the text and the notes. In the absence of a separate index of biblical, talmudic and other passages, the reader will find under the entries Bible, Talmud and the individual authors sufficient data to enable him to locate, without undue hardship, a particular passage dealt with in this book.

S. W. B.

CONTENTS

VOLUME THREE

PAGE

ABBREVIATIONS ix

NOTES 1

I. Quest for New Forms, 3; *II.* The Palestinian Municipality, 6; *III.* Synagogue, 10; *IV.* Graeco-Roman Association, 13; *V.* Talmudic Consolidation, 21; *VI.* Protected Community, 34; *VII.* European Corporation, 51; *VIII.* Supercommunity, 65; *IX.* Local Society, 88; *X.* Membership and Elections, 98; *XI.* Lay and Ecclesiastical Officers, 118; *XII.* Religious Guidance, 142; *XIII.* Education and Public Enlightenment, 160; *XIV.* Law Enforcement, 172; *XV.* Public Finance, 183; *XVI.* Social Welfare, 197; *XVII.* Crucible of Capitalism and Enlightenment, 219.

BIBLIOGRAPHY 225

INDEX 339

ABBREVIATIONS

(Biblical books and Talmudic tractates are cited in the customary abbreviations).

Bab.	Babylonian Talmud.
Ḥ. M.	Ḥoshen Mishpaṭ (a section of Jacob b. Asher's *Ṭurim* and Joseph Karo's *Shulḥan 'Aruk*).
HUCA	Hebrew Union College Annual.
Israel	La Rassegna mensile di Israel (New Series, unless otherwise stated).
JGJC	Jahrbuch für Geschichte der Juden in der Čechoslovakischen Republik.
JJLG	Jahrbuch der jüdisch-literarischen Gesellschaft in Frankfurt a.M.
JQR	Jewish Quarterly Review (New Series, unless otherwise stated).
M.	Mishnah.
MGJV	Mitteilungen der Gesellschaft für jüdische Volkskunde.
O. Ḥ.	Oraḥ Ḥayyim (a section of Jacob b. Asher's *Ṭurim* and Joseph Karo's *Shulḥan 'Aruk*).
PAJHS	Publications of the American Jewish Historical Society.
REJ	Revue des études juives.
Tos.	Tosefta.
Yer.	Palestinian Talmud (Yerushalmi).
Y. D.	Yoreh De'ah (a section of Jacob b. Asher's *Ṭurim* and Joseph Karo's *Shulḥan 'Aruk*).
ZGJD	Zeitschrift für die Geschichte der Juden in Deutschland (New Series, unless otherwise stated).
ZGJT	Zeitschrift für die Geschichte der Juden in der Tschechoslovakei.

NOTES

VOLUME ONE

NOTES TO CHAPTER I

QUEST FOR NEW FORMS

[1] The differences of significance and function associated with the term community have been subjected to numerous analyses, as in Ferdinand Tönnies's *Gemeinschaft und Gesellschaft*; Robert M. McIver's *Community*; and E. C. Lindeman's *Community*. A fairly good review of the various approaches to the problem is given by George Simpson in his *Conflict and Community: A Study in Social Theory*, pp. 71 ff.

[2] Cf. H. S. Linfield's study of "The Jewish Communities in the United States," *American Jewish Year Book*, XLII (1940–41), 217, 225. Cf. also the same author's previous essays ibid., XL (1938–39), 61–84; XLI (1939–40), 181–86; and his remarks explaining the general method of research employed in these investigations in his *State Population Census by Faiths*, and his *Communal Census of Jews: Methods Used in Recent Years.* These methods have often been criticised, however. Morris R. Cohen, in particular, who, as chairman of an advisory committee, collaborated with Dr. Linfield during the last census, has declared that the figures given for the larger part of American Jewry are "only guesses with an unknown margin of error." Cf. his review of the *American Jewish Year Book*, XLII in *Jewish Social Studies*, III (1941), 231 f. Accepting, therefore, Dr. Linfield's absolute figures with considerable reserve, the present author feels, nevertheless, that the main trends revealed by a comparison with the preceding censuses are far more likely to stand the test of more exact researches.

[3] The failure to recognize fully these aspects of congregational life has lent a somewhat distorted emphasis to Maurice J. Karpf's otherwise highly instructive description, *Jewish Community Organization in the United States.*

[4] The main champions of the *Volksgemeinde* were recruited from among those diaspora-nationalists in Russia who, headed by the "bourgeois" historian Simon M. Dubnow and by the "proletarian" publicist Chaim Zhitlowsky, envisaged the future of world Jewry as that of a permanent

national minority living a culturally sheltered life under constitutional safeguards of minority rights. The Socialist *Bund*, hampered by its Marxist internationalism, and the Zionist parties, hindered by their early exclusive pro-Palestinian orientation, followed rather reluctantly. In the period of the Russian revolution of 1905, however, they joined hands in sponsoring a more or less unified, if not altogether clear, program.

The fullest discussion of the pertinent problems viewed from the standpoint of Jewish communal history is given in Dubnow's *Pisma o starom i novom evreistvoie* (Letters on Old and Modern Judaism). First published in *Voskhod* in the years 1897 to 1907, this volume is available also in a partial German translation by E. Hurwicz and a complete Hebrew translation, from a thoroughly revised manuscript, by Abraham Lövinson. Zhitlowsky's ideas are best available in his collected Yiddish essays, *Gezamelte Shriften*. Cf. also Oscar I. Janowsky, *The Jews and Minority Rights, 1898–1919*, pp. 51 ff.; Kurt Stillschweig, *Die Juden Osteuropas in den Minderheitenverträgen;* idem, "Die nationalitätenrechtliche Stellung der Juden in den russischen und österreichischen Nachfolgestaaten während der Weltkriegsepoche," *MGWJ*, LXXXII (1938), 217–48 (supplemented by a similar essay on post-War Czechoslovakia in *Historia Judaica*, I [1938], 39–49); and further literature listed in Salo W. Baron's *Social and Religious History of the Jews*, III, 163 ff., nn. 13 and 16.

[5] The attitude of the Reform leaders to the problems of Jewish community organization, sometimes historically and theologically rather equivocal, would bear further investigation.

[6] The literature on the modern Jewish community in different countries is very large, though far from satisfactory. Despite the superabundance of primary source material for certain areas of Jewish settlement and despite a few worth-while scholarly monographs, the evolution of the modern community has never been subjected to close scholarly scrutiny. The present author anticipates considerable progress in this direction to be made by two detailed studies, of the New York community to the Civil War and of the Russian community to 1844, undertaken by two of his pupils (Hyman B. Grinstein and Isaac Levitats respectively), both nearing completion. Before long he also expects to be able to submit a general analysis of the community in the nineteenth and twentieth centuries, similar to that of the pre-Emancipation community presented here. The listing of even a selected group of available books and essays on the

modern community would far transcend the bounds of this introductory statement. The interested reader may find some guidance in the bibliography to the article "Gemeinde" in the *Encyclopaedia Judaica*, VII, 210 ff.; the pertinent notes to S. W. Baron's aforementioned *History*, Vol. III and his *Bibliography of Jewish Social Studies, 1938–39*, especially pp. 135 ff., 242 f.

[7] Cf. below, Chap. IV.

[8] Cf. Chap. VII.

[9] Many of these adverse effects came to the fore in the extensive debates which preceded the adoption of the so-called *Austrittsgesetz* in Prussia in 1876, which enabled a Jew to secede from the community, "on account of religious scruples." This law, passed after vigorous agitation by professed agnostics and the extreme orthodox, was subsequently condemned by Bismarck and his associates. In his reply of 1884 to the Austrian government which, engaged in the preparation of a new Jewish community law, sought information on the effects of the decree of 1876, the German Chancellor emphasized the results of an inquiry especially instituted by the Prussian administration which had shown that the alleged "religious scruples have been used as a rule as a mere subterfuge to conceal the real reason for the secession — the desire to get rid of the obligatory contributions." More consistently, the Weimar Republic in the early weeks after the Armistice dropped the requirement of "religious scruples," making secession without conversion to another faith a matter of sheer formality. Cf. S. W. Baron, "Freedom and Constraint in the Jewish Community," *Essays and Studies in Memory of Linda R. Miller*, pp. 9–23.

[10] Cf. the pertinent remarks, reflecting both theoretical insight and extensive practical experience, in Leo Baeck's essay, "Gemeinde in der Grossstadt," reprinted in his *Wege im Judentum*, pp. 288 ff.

[11] For detailed illustrations cf. below and, more generally, in S. W. Baron's "Historical Critique of the Jewish Community," *Jewish Social Service Quarterly*, XI (1935), 44–49.

[12] Apart from a few more or less extensive encyclopaedia articles (such as that mentioned above, n. 6) the nearest approach to such synthetic treatment is L. Venetianer's Hungarian work, *A zsidóság szervezete* (Jewish Community Organization in European Lands). Besides its relative inaccessibility to non-Hungarian readers and the fact that it appeared more

than forty years ago, its scope is limited to a rather cursory survey of the history of the European communities. Despite its indubitable pioneering merits, it has little to offer to a contemporary student. The vast monographic output, on the other hand, has thus far been rather askew. For example, an enormous literature is available — and is steadily growing — on the Jewish community in early modern Poland. Very little, however, has been written about the next largest community, that of the Ottoman Empire, in the same period. While the communal efforts of medieval German Jewry have been closely investigated, those of the even greater center of Spanish Jewry have been treated more perfunctorily, and those of neighboring Italy practically not at all. How much do we know about Jewish communal life in the vast areas of Islam, except for the Babylonian and Palestinian centers during the geonic era? Many of these lacunae in our knowledge of the ancient and medieval community may perhaps be excused on the ground of the paucity of sources. But what excuse can be offered for the neglect of scholarship in treating adequately Jewish communal life in the nineteenth and twentieth centuries, for which we have a superabundance of records? A really satisfactory solution of these difficulties will be found only when, through a large collective effort, a gigantic *corpus* of Jewish communal records covering all countries and periods is made accessible to general research. Such a *corpus* would open up, not only the vast material scattered in innumerable publications in a variety of languages, but also the enormous amount of sources still slumbering in manuscript form in the world's major libraries and archives.

NOTES TO CHAPTER II

THE PALESTINIAN MUNICIPALITY

[1] Josh. 13 ff.; I Chron. 4.33. For the literary and archaeological evidence showing the existence of such 400 small townships in close proximity to one another, cf. S. W. Baron, "Israelitic Population under the Kings" (Hebrew), *Abhandlungen* in memory of H. P. Chajes, pp. 95 ff., 112 ff. For other aspects of Palestine's historical geography, cf. George Adam Smith, *Historical Geography of the Holy Land*, 25th ed.; F. M. Abel, *Géographie de la Palestine*; and Valentin Schwöbel, *Die Landesnatur Palästinas*. Cf. also H. D. Kallner and E. Rosenau, "The Geographical

Regions of Palestine," *Geographical Review*, XXIX (1939), 61–80; and in general, Peter Thomsen, *Systematische Bibliographie der Palästina-Literatur.*

[2] The "king's mowings" (*gizze ha-melek*), mentioned in Amos 7.1, although probably reminiscent of the wool tax collected in Babylonia and elsewhere, is too incidental to constitute conclusive evidence. The abuses of the publicans, who undoubtedly were responsible for the rise of the agricultural tithe to one-third and more of the crop, had aroused popular enmity even in Babylonia under Hammurabi. Cf. Bruno Meissner, *Babylonien und Assyrien*, I, 122 ff. It is also notable that in the Israelitic cities we hear nothing of royal prefects such as were common in Babylonia or Egypt. Even the *sarim*, who had become royal officers in Egypt by the time of the eighteenth dynasty, retained in Israel their original chief function of self-governmental executives. Cf. A. Moret, "L'administration locale sous l'ancien Empire égyptien," *Académie des inscriptions ... Comptes rendus*, 1916, pp. 378–86; Auguste Baillet, *Oeuvres diverses*, I, 135–44. The juxtaposition of "the princes of Judah, and the princes of Jerusalem" by Jeremiah (34.19) need not refer to any but municipal executives of capital and provinces. Cf. the "elders of Judah and of Jerusalem," recorded in the same period, II Kings 23.1 and II Chron. 34.29. The evident paucity of references to royal slaves and eunuchs — the biblical '*ebed ha-melek* is a free Israelite — in the higher and lower ranks of the Israelitic administration is likewise revealing.

[3] Gen. 18.25; II Sam. 15.3; I Kings 3.16–28; II Kings 8.1–6, 14.5; Isa. 11.4, 5; 16.5; Ps. 72.1. Hans Zucker's contention (in his *Studien zur jüdischen Selbstverwaltung im Altertum*, pp. 10 f.) that the Deuteronomic injunction, "judges and officers shalt thou make thee in all thy gates," (16.18) is addressed to the king, is clearly disproved by the tenor of the entire book and by such passages as Deut. 17.8 ff., 14 ff., etc.

[4] Cf. Martin Noth, *Das System der zwölf Stämme Israels.*

[5] The supreme importance of the provinces has been easily overlooked because of the one-sided orientation of sources. The ancient historians, whether writing at royal courts or any other focal point, were, of course, interested primarily in describing national events and personalities of nation-wide influence. Prophets, too, even when addressing themselves to the masses, found it convenient to speak before large gatherings at the central sanctuary of Bethel or to crowds on the streets of Jerusa-

lem. There they were also likely to encounter many provincials, visiting one or another center for business, pleasure or edification, and likely to carry the prophetic message to distant cities and hamlets. It seems, moreover, that transcripts of prophetic addresses were circularized in the provinces, thus reaching countless thousands beyond the voice of the prophets.

[6] Most Israelitic cities were surrounded by walls even at a time when the monarchy had provided a measure of security against Bedouin raids. Sennacherib's boast of having conquered 46 "fortified cities" in Judah, which had one-third of the area and about one-quarter of the population of all Israel, may be regarded as a historical fact. That conditions underwent a great change during the Second Commonwealth may be seen from the usual talmudic division into *kerak* (large city), *'ir* (town) and *kefar* (village), of which only the first seems to have possessed walls. Cf. the passages discussed in Samuel Krauss's essays on the "City, Town and Village" (Hebrew), *He-'Atid*, III (2d ed. 1923), 1–50; idem, "Ueber Siedlungstypen in Palästina in talmudischer Zeit," *MGWJ*, LXXXII (1938), 173–90; Paul Romanoff, "Onomasticon of Palestine," *Proceedings of the American Academy for Jewish Research*, VII (1936), 154 ff. The change may well have been brought about by the prolonged peace under Persian domination and the reluctance of the imperial administration to grant the right to fortify cities when even Persian cities were satisfied with a mere citadel. Since fortifications naturally would have made the suppression of the frequent irredentist revolts more arduous, prolonged negotiations preceded the erection of a wall around Jerusalem (Ezra 4; Nehem. 2 ff.). The distinction between closed and open cities in the operation of the law of the Jubilee Year, established by the so-called Holiness Code (Lev. 25.30–31), although using the basically pre-exilic terminology of *'ir* and *ḥaṣer*, may already refer to the new situation in which the walled city is an exception rather than the rule.

[7] Ex. 24.9; Num. 11.16, 25; Judg. 9.2; Ezek. 8.11, etc.

[8] Eduard Meyer and Bernhard Luther, *Israel und seine Nachbarstämme*, p. 504. Max Weber in his renowned essay on the social ethics of the Israelitic religion (*Gesammelte Aufsätze zur Religionssoziologie*, III) supported this thesis of an early oligarchy of big landowners with keen argument and great erudition. He pointed out, in particular, how widespread such oligarchic systems were in the ancient Mediterranean basin. Little

wonder that lesser scholars followed, often uncritically, the lead of Meyer and Weber. It seems to the present author, however, that they overlooked a few fundamental factors, such as the exceptionally small size of most Palestinian townships, their predominantly agricultural character, their political and economic self-sufficiency and their local popular assemblies.

[9] I Sam. 11.15; II Sam. 5.3; I Kings 12.6; 20.7–8; II Kings 12.17; 21.24; 23.1–2, 30. Two of these passages (I Kings 20.7–8; II Kings 23.1) refer to elders and people working in unison.

[10] Baron in *Abhandlungen Chajes*, pp. 91 ff.

[11] Since the absorption of the Canaanites had not been completed under Solomon, his recorded census of the *gerim* and their total of 153,600 (II Chron. 2.17) may well be historical. The *gerim* would thus amount to about 10 percent of the total Israelitic population according to the chronicler's version of the results of David's census (I Chron. 21.5), which is a likely proportion.

[12] Ludwig Köhler, "Die hebräische Rechtsgemeinde," *Bericht der Universität Zürich*, 1930–31, pp. 3–23. Cf. also Abram Menes, "Prophets and Popular Assembly" (Yiddish), *Yivo Bleter*, IX (1936), 199–217.

[13] Deut. 13.6; 17.7–8; Isa. 10.1 ff.; Jer. 8.8. Cf. Abram Menes, *Die vorexilischen Gesetze Israels*, pp. 88 ff.

[14] Deut. 4.1 ff.; 8.10; 26.3 ff.; 31.10–12; II Kings 19.4 ff.; 20.2; Jer. 10.23 ff.; 11.14; 12.1; 14.7. Louis Finkelstein, elaborating a theory advanced by Leopold Löw, has made seem plausible certain pre-exilic antecedents of the synagogue. He has shown that already under the long reign of Menasseh the pious men of Jerusalem could not possibly participate in the idolatrous worship at the Temple with its "graven image of the grove" (II Kings 21.7), but had to resort to private conventicles whose main feature was prayers. Cf. his "Origin of the Synagogue," *Proceedings of the American Academy for Jewish Research*, I (1928–30), 49–59; and his *Pharisees*, II, 562 ff. Julius Wellhausen, too, has keenly sensed the connection between the *bamah* and the synagogue but, due to his general tendency to postdate biblical developments, sought it in the Restoration period. Cf. his *Israelitische und jüdische Geschichte*, 4th ed., pp. 196 f. The resumption of worship by pious homecoming groups at desecrated shrines appears unlikely, however, unless we postulate its continuation, in a non-sacrificial manner, by the Judeans who had been left behind. The evidence, even in this case, appears very dubious. Cf.

also S. W. Baron, *A Social and Religious History of the Jews*, III, 26 f., notes 17–18; his review of Finkelstein's *Pharisees* in the *Journal of Biblical Literature*, LIX (1940), 65 ff.; Mendel Silber, *The Origin of the Synagogue*; Bernard J. Bamberger, "Factors in the History of the Synagog," *Yearbook of the Central Conference of American Rabbis*, XLVIII (1938), 218–37.

NOTES TO CHAPTER III

SYNAGOGUE

[1] Judg. 5.17; I Kings 20.34; Bruno Landsberger, *Assyrische Handelskolonien in Kleinasien aus dem dritten Jahrtausend*, p. 9. Cf. also Georg Eisser and Julius Levy, *Die altassyrischen Rechtsurkunden vom Kültepe*.

[2] Deut. 17.16; Jer. 3.12–18; 30–31; 44.1; Ezek. 3.4, 17; 12.10; 37. The inscriptions of Sargon and Sennacherib are available in English translation in George A. Barton's *Archaeology and the Bible*, 6th ed., pp. 465 ff.

[3] Mal. 1.11. The growth of the diaspora has clearly been shown by Charles C. Torrey in his *Ezra Studies*, pp. 294 ff. and by Antonin Causse in *Les dispersés d'Israël*. For the depopulation of Palestine after 586, cf. William F. Albright, *Archaeology of Palestine and the Bible*, 3d ed., pp. 169 ff., 218 ff.

[4] Ezek. 6.13; 11.16; 20.40–41; 43.10–17. Since the days of the talmudic rabbis (Meg. 29a) this "little sanctuary" has often been identified with the synagogue. Although the general talmudic view that the synagogue dates back to Moses, the patriarchs, or to an even earlier period, is evidently unhistorical, this particular tradition seems to embody a kernel of truth. Cf. also Johannes Jeremias, "Hesekieltempel und Serubbabeltempel," *Zeitschrift für die alttestamentliche Wissenschaft*, LII (1934), 109–12.

[5] A. Menes, in his "Tempel und Synagoge," ibid., L (1932), 268–76, makes it plausible that we have in Josh. 22.9–34 an exilic defense of the new institution against the adherents of the old type of worship. Cf. also Ps. 40; 51; 69.31 ff.

[6] M. Sanh. I, 6; Susannah 1.4; Nehem. 1.1–8. Cf. also Bernhard Luther, "Ḳahal und 'edah als Hilfsmittel der Quellenscheidung im Priester-Kodex und in der Chronik," *Zeitschrift für die alttestamentliche Wissenschaft*, LVI

(1938), 44–63; and, in general, Leonhard Rost, *Die Vorstufen von Kirche und Synagoge im Alten Testament.*

[7] Jer. 39.8; Shabbat 32a; Mark Lidzbarski, *Das Johannesbuch der Mandäer*, 18.67 (II, 75 f.); Ps. 74.8. The other explanations of the term in Jeremiah, cited by S. Krauss in his *Synagogale Altertümer*, pp. 54 f., are far less plausible.

[8] Samuel Daiches, *The Jews in Babylonia in the Time of Ezra and Nehemiah according to Babylonian Inscriptions.*

[9] Hans Heinz Schaeder, *Ezra der Schreiber*; R. de Vaux, "Les decrêts de Cyrus et de Darius sur la réconstruction du Temple," *Revue biblique*, XLVI (1937), 29–57; Cowley, *Aramaic Papyri*, no. 21 (unfortunately the largely restored text is not altogether dependable).

[10] Nehem. 3.8, 31–32. For the guild organization in the ancient Near East, cf. now I. Mendelsohn's "Gilds in Babylonia and Assyria," *Journal of the American Oriental Society*, LX (1940), 68–72; and "Guilds in Ancient Palestine," *Bulletin of the American Schools of Oriental Research*, 80 (Dec. 1940), 17–21.

[11] Without wishing to press this hypothesis, the present author is inclined to believe that it explains more difficulties than others hitherto suggested. Regnant opinion, since Meyer's *Entstehung des Judentums*, has seen members of the former landowning class in clan units, while the formerly landless exiles were counted in local units. There are, however, very serious objections to this theory: 1) We have no evidence whatsoever for the assumption that Israelites who had lost their land — for instance, Hananel, Jeremiah's cousin (32.6 ff.) — also lost clan membership. 2) There were no local units among those returning with Ezra. 3) Clan units were much more populous than local units. A "local" membership ranging from 42 to 743 (for three combined localities) is fully understandable in the light of the small size of the Israelitic township, but a combined membership of over 9000 men for the four largest groups of aristocratic landowners appears hardly likely. 4) How can this theory explain the combination of two or three localities? 5) How does a local group, such as the Tekoites, have "nobles" (Nehem. 3.5)? These and other questions seem largely answered by our hypothesis.

The 3,630 or 3,930 "children of Senaah," in whom Meyer sees the residue of the formerly landless population of Jerusalem, were much more likely a third group, outside both the clan and local congregations. That is why they are enumerated after these congregations and just before other special groups (priests, levites, etc.). It may, perhaps, be suggested that they were the remainder of both pre-exilic and Babylonian *gerim*, insofar as they had not yet been absorbed by the other groups. The existence of a large number of such "strangers" in the exilic community is attested by Ezek. 14.7; 47.22, etc. Since such a conglomeration of *gerim* would normally embrace stray members of various tribes, there is no difficulty in accepting the reputed descent of some members from the tribe of Benjamin (cf. I Chr. 9.7). Other members may have been descendants of disestablished priests who had moved to other localities, a fact which, incidentally, might help explain the confusion in the genealogy of R. Eleazar b. Zadok (cf. *Tosafot* on 'Er. 41a s. v. *mi-bene*) better than either the Tosafists' assumption of the tannaite's maternal descent from Sanaa, or L. Finkelstein's hypothesis of "the forcible entry of a lay family into the priesthood." Cf. his *Pharisees*, II, 511. Cf. also Zeeb Jawitz, *Toledot Israel*, 3d ed., VI, 281 f. Many of these "strangers" in the Babylonian Exile, however, as well as members of *Landsmannschaften*, must gradually have joined the more renowned clan congregations through "covenant" or other forms of admission.

[12] II Kings 25.27–30. According to a tradition which, although recorded only by Sherira Gaon and Benjamin of Tudela in the tenth and twelfth centuries respectively, is not necessarily unhistorical, Jehoiachin and his successors founded a synagogue in the vicinity of Nehardea, which city served as the residence of the exilarchs for centuries. Cf. the sources cited by Krauss, op. cit., pp. 214 ff. The "prince" in Ezekiel's constitution may already have reflected the position of these early semi-secular and semi-religious leaders. Cf. also Chap. V, n. 30.

[13] Cowley, op. cit., no. 15. Cf., however, ibid. no. 14 where, according to Halévy's interpretation, the community refused to recognize Mibtaḥiah's previous marital venture with an Egyptian, Pi. But this marriage very likely was preceded by the bride's (temporary) conversion to her husband's creed, whereas Asḥor seems to have taken the religion of his wife who had speedily reverted to Judaism.

[14] Ibid., nos. 10, 13, 15, 17, 18. Cf. also no. 45 which appears likewise to have been written by either Nathan b. Ananiah or his son. The predominantly religious-minded later biblical and rabbinic sources have misled modern scholars into believing that the primary function of the

"scribe" (*sofer*, *safra*, *grammateus*) was to serve as an expert in scriptural law. Schraeder, op. cit., pp. 39 ff., has demonstrated, however, that Ezra himself apparently had also been a Persian chancery official. Not only had earlier Israelitic kings employed "scribes," such as David's uncle Jonathan and Hezekiah's, perhaps alien-born, secretary Shebna, but, as we shall see, the later community councils, Jewish as well as Greek, also had influential permanent officials bearing this designation.

[15] Cf. the evidently exilic Prayer of Solomon, I Kings 8.46–50 and Dan. 6.11. Examples of the new devotional and commemorative psalms may be found, for instance, in Ps. 106 and 137. Cf. also Zech. 7.5–7.

NOTES TO CHAPTER IV

GRAECO-ROMAN ASSOCIATION

[1] Viktor Tscherikower, *Die hellenistischen Städtegründungen von Alexander dem Grossen bis auf die Römerzeit.*

[2] The Greek term *presbyteros* (elder), used in the Letter of Aristeas, stands for as great a variety of functions as its Hebrew equivalent, *zaken*, which the Septuagint, indeed, usually so translates. *Hegoumenos*, originally used for a head of a village or a professional association, was soon widened to include all persons in authority, presidents of religious associations, etc. Cf. Colin Roberts, Theodore C. Skeat and Arthur Darby Nock, "The Gild of Zeus Hypsistos," *Harvard Theological Review*, XXIX (1936), 45. The Septuagint usually translates the biblical term *nagid*, referring to Israelitic kings, by *hegoumenos*, a title adopted also by Simon, the Maccabean. Cf. Zucker, *Studien*, pp. 10 n. 1, 43.

[3] Salomon Reinach, "La communauté juive d'Athribis," *REJ*, XVII (1888), 235–38; Krauss, *Synagogale Altertümer*, pp. 261 ff.; Roberts *et al.*, op. cit., pp. 55 ff., 62 ff., 69, where reference is also made to another, rather dubious, Jewish inscription of 29 B. C.E. whereby the synagogue in Fayyum was likewise dedicated to the Most High.

[4] Strabo, quoted by Josephus, *Antiquities*, XIV, 7, 2.115; Tos. Sukkah IV. 6, ed. Zuckermandl, p. 198; Yer. V, 1, 55ab; Bab. 51b. The large-scale immigration of the Jews to Egypt is evidenced by Claudius' famous epistle to the Alexandrians (published by H. Idris Bell in his *Jews and Christians in Egypt*) in which the emperor warned the Jewish litigants

"not to introduce or invite Jews who sail down to Alexandria from Syria or Egypt, thus compelling me to conceive the greater suspicion," and by the increase of the Jewish quarters from one mentioned by Strabo, to two in the days of Philo. Cf. note 14, A. Segré's "Note sullo *status civitatis* degli Ebrei nell'Egitto tolemaico e imperiale," *Bulletin de la Société royale d'archéologie d'Alexandrie*, N. S., VIII (1933), p. 169 n. 1; V. Tscherikower, "On the History of the Jews of Fayyum during the Hellenistic Period" (Hebrew), *Magnes Anniversary Book*, p. 202.

[5] *Antiquities*, XIII, 3, 1.62–68. Cf. in general S. A. Hirsch, "The Temple of Onias," *Jews' College Jubilee Volume*, pp. 39–80; Joshua Brand, "The Temple of Onias" (Hebrew), *Yavneh*, I (1939), 76–84.

[6] In the ancient communities of Egypt were also found curious survivals of the old clan congregation, under the Greek name *phyle*. When Philo, apparently commenting on Num. 36.7–9 (*De legibus specialibus*, II, 16.128), states that an heirless estate reverts to the deceased man's *phyle*, "for the *phyle* is also a sort of family on a larger and more complete scale," he seems to reflect real practice. A *phyle* of "Macedonian" Jews is indeed recorded by Josephus (*Against Apion*, II, 4.36; cf. also *Antiquities*, IV, 7, 5.175). The passage in Strabo's description of the situation of the Jews in Cyrene may likewise have originally contained this term. Cf. Juster, *Les Juifs dans l'Empire Romain*, I, 417; II, 12 n. 2. But whatever significance this clan-group may have had for the civic status of Jewry, it did not interfere with the cohesiveness of the new territorial community which united all older and newer arrivals.

[7] The location of only three ancient synagogues has been tentatively identified. Cf. Hermann Vogelstein and Paul Rieger, *Geschichte der Juden in Rom*, I, 48. All were outside the boundaries of the inner city, the *pomerium*. But it is doubtful whether these three institutions are identical with those known from the inscriptions, many of which may well have been erected in the city proper. For the ancient Roman synagogues in general, cf. now the inscriptions assembled by J. B. Frey in his *Corpus inscriptionum Judaicarum*, I, and Frey's introduction thereto; idem, "Les communautés juives à Rome aux premiers temps de l'Eglise," *Recherches des sciences religieuses*, XX (1930), 269–97; XXI (1931), 129–68; Arnaldo Momigliano, "I nomi delle prime sinagoghe romane e la condizione giuridica delle communità in Roma sotto Augusto," *Israel*, VI (1931–32), 283–92. Much may also be learned from a comparison with the con-

temporary status of the Christians for which cf. the recent study of Arthur Stapylton Barnes, *Christianity at Rome in the Apostolic Age*.

[8] David Ḳimḥi, *Commentary* on Gen. 1.31. Barnes (op. cit., pp. 85 ff.) argues with some force that at least two of these synagogues (those of the "Hebrews" and of the "Olive Tree") belonged to Judeo-Christian rather than Jewish congregations. Much more evidence, however, is needed for verification of this hypothesis.

[9] Juvenal, *Satires*, III, 296.

[10] I Macc. 10.25 ff. (v. 34 emphasizes the religious safeguards for the Jews of the whole Empire); 13, 35 ff. For the chronology cf. now Elias Bickermann's *Der Gott der Makkabäer*. According to Josephus (*War*, VII, 3, 3.44) the later Seleucidae even returned some of the Temple objects carried away by Antiochus IV to the synagogue in Antioch. Cf. also Carl H. Kraeling, "The Jewish Community of Antioch," *Journal of Biblical Literature*, LI (1932), 130–60; Isaak Heinemann, "Wer veranlasste den Glaubenszwang der Makkabäerzeit?" *MGWJ*, LXXXII (1938), 146–72.

[11] Krauss, op. cit., pp. 199 ff.; *Codex Theodosianus*, XVI, 8, 4: "hiereis et archisynagogis et patribus synagogarum et ceteris qui in eodem loco deserviunt" refers back to the immediately preceding decree of 321. Cf. Julius Aronius, *Regesten zur Geschichte der Juden im fränkischen und deutschen Reiche*, no. 2, where these titles are incorrectly translated, however; Adolf Kober, [*History of the Jews in*] *Cologne*, pp. 5 f.

[12] E. L. Sukenik, *The Ancient Synagogues of Palestine and Greece*, pp. 37, 80; Frey, *Corpus*, I, No. 694. Cf. also A. Marmorstein, "The Synagogue of Claudius Tiberius Polycharmus in Stobi," *JQR*, XXVII (1936–37), 373–84.

[13] Theodore Reinach, *Textes d'auteurs grecs et romains relatifs au Judaisme*, p. 20.

[14] Philo, *In Flaccum*, 8.55; *Legatio*, 20.132 ff.; Josephus, *Ag. Apion*, II, 4.33 ff.; *War*, II, 7.488; 8.495; *Antiquities*, XIV, 10, 24.260–65. Cf. also Strabo's *Geography*, XVII, 9, 794; Carl Wessely, "Das Ghetto von Apollinopolis Magna," *Studien zur Palaeographie und Papyruskunde*, XIII (1913), 8–10; Segré, l.c.

[15] Philo, *De vita Mosis*, II, 5.41–42.

[16] Philo, *Quod omnis probus liber*, 12.81; Yer. B.B. IV, 6, 14c; Bab. B.M. 24a. For the much debated relation between the terms *synagogé*

and *proseuché*, cf. now also the quotation from an unpublished Ryland papyrus: . . . *συναγωγῆς ἐν τῆ προσευχῆ*, communicated by Roberts *et al.*, op. cit., p. 72.

[17] Josephus, *Life*, 54.277; Acts 23.19; II Macc. 3.10; Ovid, *Ars amatoria*, I, 75; Ber. 8a with reference to Deut. 11.21.

[18] Quoted from the lost *Hypothetica* by Eusebius in his *Praeparatio evangelica*, VII, 7, ed. by E. H. Gifford, 360a, and translated into English by Gifford (III, Pt. 1, pp. 389 f.) and by C. D. Yonge in *The Works of Philo Judaeus*, IV, 217 f. The alleged first public reading of the Septuagint is described in the Letter of Aristeas, 308.

[19] Men. 28b; Hugo Gressmann, "Jewish Life in Ancient Rome" *Jewish Studies in Memory of Israel Abrahams*, pp. 170–91; Sukenik, op. cit., pp. 47 ff., 70; S. Klein, "Das Fremdenhaus der Synagoge," *MGWJ*, LXXVI (1932), 545–57, supplemented ibid., pp. 603–4; LXXVII (1933), 81–84; *Preliminary Report on the Synagogue of Dura.*

[20] Abot de R. Nathan, ed. by S. Schechter, XXXV, p. 106. Cf. also in general the literature listed in Baron's *History*, III, 51 n. 15; 70 n. 17, 20.

[21] Philo, *Legatio ad Caium*, 16.115; *B. G. U.* (*Berliner griechische Urkunden, Aegyptische Abteilung*), IV, 1040; Bell, op. cit., p. 29; Salomon Reinach, "Les Juifs d'Hypaepa," *REJ*, X (1885), 74. Reinach's and Juster's explanation of the Hypaepa inscription as referring to an association of *Neoi* (I, 487 n. 3) is much more convincing than the other interpretation suggested by Reinach and accepted by Krauss (op. cit., pp. 231, 395 ff.) that the term merely described the seating order in the synagogue. For the Jewish educational system in Alexandria cf. also Wilhelm Bousset's *Jüdisch-christlicher Schulbetrieb in Alexandreia und Rom*; and Raphael (Ralph) Marcus's "Main Educational Teachings of Philo Judaeus" (Hebrew), *Touroff Anniversary Volume*, pp. 223–31.

[22] *B. G. U.*, IV, 1131, 1151. W. Judeich *et al.*, *Altertümer von Hierapolis*, No. 212. Although Palestine, like Elphantine Jewry, must long before have possessed archives (see above), it now adopted for it the Greek loan-words *arché* and *archeion*. Cf. the references in the talmudic dictionaries of Jastrow and Levy, and Chapter V, n. 10.

[23] Johannes Asiaticus, *Historia ecclesiastica*, cited by F. Nau in *Revue de l'Orient chrétien*, II (1897), 462 n. 2; Salomon Reinach, "Inscription grecque de Smyrne," *REJ*, VII (1883), 161 ff. The division of the fine between the government and the community, found also in a Jewish (?)

inscription of Hierapolis (Krauss, op. cit., pp. 234 f.), was a fairly common provision of the Hellenistic associations. For the famous Jewish catacombs in Rome, their relation to the Palestinian ossuaries and their influence on Christian burial, cf. the literature cited in Baron's *History*, III, 53 and George La Piana's "Foreign Groups in Rome in the First Centuries of the Empire," *Harvard Theological Review*, XX (1927), 364 f. Cf. also below n. 34.

The other communal activities in the diaspora, such as the administration of justice and of charities, economic regulation, and so forth will be discussed in the next chapter in conjunction with similar functions of the Palestinian communities about which our information is much more extensive and reliable.

[24] Yer. Meg. I, 6, 70b; III, 2, 74a, etc.; Josephus, *Antiquities* XIV, 10, 8.216; John of Antioch in the fragments ed. by Theodor Mommsen, *Hermes*, VI (1872), 332; *Mitteilungen des kais. deutschen archaeol. Instituts*, Athen. Abteilung, XXII (1897), 484; Lampridius, *Alexander Severus*, 45, 6 ff. in *Scriptores Historiae Augustae*, with an Engl. transl. by David Magie, II, 270 f. Cf. also below n. 26; Roberts *et al.*, op. cit., p. 72; Meg. 28 ab.

[25] M. Meg. IV, 2, 6, contrasted with Tos. IV, 11, 226; Philo, *De legibus specialibus*, III, 31.171.

[26] Cowley, *Aramaic Papyri*, no. 30, 22; Ḳid. 73a; Yer. Yeb. VIII, 2, 9b. The Damascus sect actually had this fourfold division. Cf. *Fragments of a Zadokite Work*, ed. by Solomon Schechter, XIV, 5–6.

[27] M. Ber. V, 4; Giṭ. V, 8, etc. Cf. Ismar Elbogen, *Der jüdische Gottesdienst in seiner geschichtlichen Entwicklung*, 3d ed., pp. 67 ff., 172 f.

[28] Ḳid. 32b; Yer. Pe'ah VIII, 7, 21a; Philo, *In Flaccum*, 10.74 ff.; *De legibus spec.*, III, 14.80.

[29] The Berenice inscription, often republished (e. g. by Juster, op. cit., I, 438 n. 4 and, in German, by Krauss, op. cit., pp. 265 f.) has given rise to endless discussions since the publication, two centuries ago, of Peter Wesseling's monograph, *Diatribe de Judaeorum archontibus ad inscriptionem Berenicensem*. For meetings of the "full council" (*pasa gerousia*), cf. Philo, *De leg. spec.*, III, 14.80; Acts 5.21. The Domnos inscription is found in Frey's *Corpus*, I, no. 494. The time limits usually set for elective officers in Rome may also have influenced the Palestinian authorities in the only appointment of a judge in that community (Judah b. Titus)

recorded in the Talmud. Unlike their colleague of Gaza, he and the judge appointed to Tyre were to return after the expiration of their term. Cf. Yer. Bik. III, 3, 65d. For the general problem of patriarchal control over the leadership of the diaspora communities, cf. below, Chap. V.

[30] La Piana, op. cit., p. 361.

[31] Luke 13.14; Acts 18.17; Justin Martyr's *Dialogue*, 137, 2; Flavius Vopiscus, *Vita Saturnini*, VIII; St. Ambrose, *In Lucc.* 6.54 (on Luke 8.14); Pes. 49b; Sukenik, op. cit, pp. 40 ff. The Talmud (B. B. 11a) expects at least the supervisors of the charities to make up budgetary deficiencies personally. Juster's theory concerning the salaried, rabbinic function of the archisynagogus (op. cit., I, 450 ff.) has been effectively refuted by Krauss (op. cit., pp. 119 ff.) and others.

[32] In Greek associations, too, the position of the *hyperetes* varied greatly. Often a menial servant, he sometimes held a position second only to that of the president. In the recently published papyrus of an Egyptian guild, dating from 69–58 B. C. E., we find the members binding themselves "to obey the president and his servant [*hyperetou*] in matters pertaining to the corporation." Roberts *et al.*, op. cit., pp. 41 f., 50, 79 f. The title *ḥazzan*, too, if related to the Assyrian *khazana* or chief of a city, would seem to indicate a dignified rank. Cf. Meissner, op. cit., I, 132 and Ismar Elbogen, "Eingang und Ausgang des Sabbats," *Festschrift Israel Lewy*, p. 177 n. 6. The later reduction of the office to that of a reader is first recorded in the Muslim period in Pirke de R. Eliezer, XII, etc. Cf. Louis Ginzberg's *Genizah Studies*, II, 253 f., 548 n. 20.

[33] For local autonomy in Egypt, cf. Pierre Jouguet, *La vie municipale dans l'Egypte romain*; William L. Westermann, "Ptolemies and their Subjects," *American Historical Review*, XLIII (1938), 270–87. The special Jewish tax in Ptolemaic Egypt is discussed by Juster, op. cit., II, 281 f. The much debated position of the ethnarch and the contradictory statements concerning the policy of Augustus in Philo, *In Flaccum*, 10.74 (the emperor substituted, in 11 B. C. E., a *gerousia* for an ethnarch) and Josephus, *Antiquities*, XIX, 5, 2.283 (Claudius declared that Augustus had not forbidden the Jews to have an ethnarch of their own) have again been discussed, but by no means definitely disposed of, by Fuchs, *Juden Aegyptens*, pp. 91 ff., and V. Tscherikower, *Ha-Yehudim ve-ha-Yevanim* (Jews and Greeks in the Hellenistic Period), pp. 303 n. 5, 402 f. For the alabarch cf. Jean Lesquier, "L'arabarchès d'Egypte," *Revue*

Archéologique, Ser. V, Vol. VI (1917), 95–103 (not alabarch but tax-administrator and chief of customs); M. I. Rostovtzeff and C. B. Welles, "A Parchment Contract of Loan from Dura Europus on the Euphrates," *Yale Classical Studies*, II (1931), 49 ff. (distinguishes between arabarches, chief of the Arab tribes and, occasionally, governor-general of southern Egypt, and alabarches, "closely connected with special taxes paid by the Jews.")

[34] For Theudas, cf. Yer. M. Ḳ. III, 1, 81d; Bab. Pes. 53ab. The embassies sent from other communities to Rome, with or without the permission of the local Roman officials, are frequently mentioned by Philo, Josephus and the rabbinic sources, listed by Juster, op. cit., I, 435 n. 4, and Zucker, *Studien*, pp. 149 ff. The case made by Berliner, Juster, Krauss and others for a united leadership of Roman Jewry is not altogether weakened by Frey's recent arguments to the contrary in his essay and *Corpus*. Juster's hypothesis, however, concerning the "little patriarchs" (I, 402 ff.) has not been accepted by other scholars.

[35] Suetonius, *Divus Julius*, 42; idem, *Augustus*, 32; Josephus, *Antiquities*, XIV, 10, 8.214–15. Cf. also Erich Ziebart's *Das griechische Vereinswesen*, pp. 128, 130 f.

[36] Ever since the eighteenth century, there has been a constant outcropping of denials of the legal recognition of the Jewish community as a *politeuma* by the Romans after the fall of Jerusalem. These denials were principally supported by the decree of Caracalla, dated in 213 C. E. (taken over by the *Code of Justinian*, I, 9.1) which read: *Quod Cornelia Salvia universitati Judaeorum qui in Antiochensium civitate constituti sunt, legavit, peti non potest.* No lesser authorities than Savigny and Giercke saw in this imperial refusal to recognize the validity of an individual legacy in favor of the community of Antioch an implied non-recognition of the community as such. As late as 1937, Ernst Schönbauer, invoking this decree, contended that the *Constitutio Antoniana* of the preceding year had granted the Jews constitutional equality of rights but not the status of a "community in public law" (*öffentlich-rechtlicher Verband*). Cf. his stimulating essay on the meaning of that constitution, entitled "Reichsrecht, Volksrecht und Provinzialrecht," *Zeitschrift für Rechtsgeschichte*, LXX (1937), 342 f. He seems, however, to have overlooked the weighty and, to the present author, fully convincing argument that the decree of 213 represents a singular deviation from an otherwise thoroughly

attested recognition of the public status of the Jewish community. Cf. Juster, op. cit., I, 432 ff. and the literature cited there.

[37] Josephus, *War*, II, 12, 2.229 ff.; *Antiquities*, XVI, 6, 2.162; 4–5.168–70; A. Momigliano, "Severo Alessandro Archisynagogus" *Athenaeum*, XXII (1934), 151–53.

[38] Josephus, *Antiquities*, XIV, 10, 17.235. For the extremely complex problem of the Jewish *status civitatis* under the Roman Empire, cf. the literature listed in Baron's *History*, III, 46 ff. n. 3–4, 6, and especially Juster's standard work. Unfortunately our information concerning the operation of the Roman laws with respect to Jewish communal activities is very meager. We know little, for instance, about the Jewish administration of justice in the dispersion. There is no doubt that, like Paul, most Jews insisted on the exclusivity of their own courts of justice. They were met half way by the widespread conviction concerning the legitimacy of such group jurisdiction, as evidenced by Aristotle's classical exposition in his *Politics*, IV, 16, 1300b. Many Hellenistic associations, too, had provisions that no member should summon another member to court for offenses committed within the association. That is why there is nothing intrinsically wrong in Erwin R. Goodenough's attempt to reconstruct *The Jurisprudence of the Jewish Courts in Egypt.* His failure, emphasized by critics such as Isaak Heinemann and Norman Bentwich (*MGWJ*, LXXIV, 1930, 363–69 and *JQR*, XXI, 1930–31, 151–57) is largely due to the fact that Philo's work on *Special Laws* is, like his other writings, not "one of the most comprehensive pictures of legal practice which we have of any people from that period" (Goodenough, p. 255) but a current free commentary on the Pentateuch with theory and practice inextricably intertwined. Through ingenious interpretation, however, he as well as Bernhard Ritter (in *Philo und die Halachah*) before, and G. Allon (in his Hebrew "Studies in Philonic Halakah," *Tarbiz*, V–VI, 1933–35) and Samuel Belkin (in *Philo and the Oral Law*) after him have succeeded in uncovering numerous vestiges and hints of details of legal practice in the mass of purely theoretical law. For the functioning of a Jewish court in Alexandria, cf. also Tos. Pe'ah IV, 6, 23; Ket. III, 1, 263.

[39] In the *Theodosian Code*, XVI, 8, where most of the anti-Jewish legislation of the Christian Empire was recodified, we find no record of this prohibition before the decrees of 423 addressed to the Eastern Empire (XVI, 8, 25–27). Its existence before that time has been made plausible

by Juster, however, on the basis of a decree of 415 and a passage in a fourth-century Christian work. Don Isaac Abravanel's reference (in his *Ma'ayene ha-Yeshu'ah* [Commentary on Daniel], XI, 5, also quoted by Krauss, op. cit., p. 419 n. 4) to such a prohibitive decree of Constantine, supposedly abrogated by Constantius and Julian, may be mentioned here for what it is worth.

[40] *Theodosian Code*, XVI, 8, 9; St. Ambrose, *Epistles* XL–XLI (Migne, *Patrologia latina*, XVI, 1148 ff.). For St. Ambrose's general leadership of the anti-Jewish orientation in the Church, cf. J. R. Palanque, *St. Ambroise et l'Empire Romain*, pp. 205 ff., 523 ff. (the epistles were written in Dec. 388 C. E.).

[41] *Theodosian Code*, II, 1.10; *Code of Justinian*, I, 9, 8.

NOTES TO CHAPTER V
TALMUDIC CONSOLIDATION

[1] These distinctions between the Palestinian and diaspora communities and the great disparity in the latter have hitherto received but scanty attention. Tscherikower (*Ha-Yehudim*, p. 305) simply assumes that "in matters of inner organization all Jewish communities resembled one another." Krauss (op. cit., p. 139) declares that it is "unthinkable" that, for instance, the synagogue council should be a new creation of the diaspora and not merely an adaptation of models from the mother country. M(oritz) Friedlaender goes to the other extreme in his theory that the synagogue, with all that it stood for, was altogether a diaspora institution and that Palestinian leadership consistently opposed it. He devotes to this untenable theory his otherwise brilliant monograph *Synagoge und Kirche in ihren Anfängen*. Only detailed studies of individual regions, such as those undertaken by Schürer, Berliner, La Piana and Frey for the city of Rome, may more fully establish these regional and local peculiarities.

[2] Sanh. 17b; Tos. B. M. XI, 23, 396.

[3] Acts 7.9; Samuel Klein, *Jüdisch-Palästinensisches Corpus inscriptionum*, pp. 36 ff.

[4] The evolution of the synagogue in general is fully described in Elbogen's *Gottesdienst* and A. Z. Idelsohn's *Jewish Liturgy and its Development*. The Palestinian triennial cycle, the *haftarot* and the midrashic homilies thereto have been the subject of Jacob Mann's recent (unfortunately

incomplete) investigation in his *The Bible as Read and Preached in the Old Synagogue*, I. For the change in the recitation of the Decalogue, cf. George Foot Moore's *Judaism*, III, 95 f. As pointed out by Moore, the date of this change and the particular heresy which caused it, are still in doubt. Although the oldest recorded authority for it, R. Nathan the Babylonian (Ber. 12a), lived in the second century, the Talmud (ibid.) records two attempts by third and fourth century Babylonian sages to reintroduce this recitation in the great centers of Babylonian learning (Sura and Nehardea-Pumbedita). Nor, apparently, was Palestinian Jewry altogether unanimous on the subject, as is possibly intimated in the obscure and much-debated story recorded in Yer. Meg. IV, 5, 75b. According to Samuel Klein's correct interpretation of this passage, the dismissal of R. Simon the Scribe by the community of Tarbane was due to his refusal to interrupt the recitation of the Decalogue for the benefit of the children. Cf. Klein's Hebrew essay in *Minḥah le-David* (*The David Yellin Jubilee Volume*), pp. 96 ff. It is not likely, however, that the interruption demanded was to be during the reading of the Torah, as Klein assumes. Nor is a difference of opinion between the Sepphoris and the Tiberian leaders as to the propriety of such an interruption at all probable. It appears far more reasonable to relate all such disputes to the daily recitation of the Decalogue as a prayer, in public as well as private worship, where more consideration could be given to both the requirements of school children and local custom.

The debate on this change, in the face of the people's tenacious reverence for this supreme Sinaitic revelation, has not ceased even in modern times. While Ḥayyim Benveniste, as well as Isaac Luria, objected to the recitation of the Ten Commandments in private worship, Ibn Adret and Karo tried to encourage it, prohibiting only congregational recitation. Solomon Luria, on the other hand, allowed even public recitation provided it was done outside the central liturgical section of Shema' and the preceding and concluding blessings. He even ordered the reader in his academy's place of worship to recite the Decalogue aloud before *Baruk she-amar*. Cf. Solomon ibn Adret, *Responsa*, I, 184; Jacob b. Asher, *Ṭur*, O. Ḥ. no. 1, and Joshua Falk's commentary thereon; Benveniste, *Keneset ha-gedolah*, ibid.; Solomon Luria, *Responsa*, no. 64; Ḥayyim J. D. Azulai, *Ṭub 'ayyin* (A Juridical Treatise), no. 10.

[5] M. Meg. I, 8; II, 1, etc.; Justinian's *Novella* 146. J. S. Zuri's observa-

tion that itinerant preachers were common in Palestine but not in Babylonia, although partly controverted by the speaking tours of Rab and Mar Zutra, confirms the general impression that the mobility of commercial as well as intellectual travelers in the Hellenistic and early Roman Empires was greater than in more feudal Persia. Cf. Zuri's *Toledot ha-mishpaṭ ha-'ibri ha-ṣibburi* (A History of Hebrew Public Law), I, 285.

[6] Tos. Meg. IV, 41, 228 f.; Yer. Ḥag. I, 1, 75d; Bab. Pes. 49b. Neither must one imagine (as does Krauss, op. cit., pp. 171, 175) that the general congregation was reduced to a passive role, interrupted at most by a few "responsoria." Ancient congregations, if perhaps with more decorum, prayed no less loudly than have the modern East European orthodox Jews. They recited so loudly, indeed, as to induce the mild Pope, Gregory the Great, to decree in 591 that, if the *vox psallentium* should disturb services in a neighboring church, the synagogue be removed to another place (*Epistolae*, II, 6). Evidently, for the same general reason, the Council of Narbonne, in 589, forbade the Jews to chant funeral psalms (Canon 9). Cf. also the references from St. Jerome's and other works in Juster, op. cit., I, 368, notes 2–3. For the ancient interpreters cf. S. J. Glücksberg, "The *Meturgemanim* in the Talmudic Period" (Hebrew), *Sinai*, II, Pt. 1 (1938), 218–21.

[7] M. Abot, I, 2; Meg. 27a.

[8] Philo, *Works*, ed. Mangey, VI, 204; Josephus, *Against Apion*, II, 18.175; Ḳohelet Rabbah on 7.28. According to the talmudic tradition, reported by Rab at the beginning of the third century, the great educational reform was undertaken by Joshua b. Gamala and his associates. Previously R. Simon b. Sheṭaḥ had established schools for young men of sixteen and seventeen in the larger cities (B. B. 21a–22a). Arguing that it is unlikely that such a vital reform was put into effect by a high priest with Sadducean leanings shortly before Jerusalem's fall, Wilhelm Bacher suggested an emendation of the text to read: R. Joshua b. Peraḥiah instead of b. Gamala, and Simon the Just instead of b. Sheṭaḥ. This would put the two reforms back to the second and first pre-Christian centuries, respectively. Cf. his essay, "Das altjüdische Schulwesen," *Jahrbuch für jüdische Geschichte und Literatur*, VI (1903), 48–81. This emendation has not been accepted by other scholars, however. For the use of the term *yeshibah* in Ecclesiasticus 51.29, cf. below, Chap. XIII n. 3. The manifold aspects of talmudic education are treated, with much repetition in B.

Strassburger's *Geschichte der Erziehung und des Unterrichts bei den Israeliten*; Towa Perlow's *L'éducation et l'enseignement chez les Juifs à l'époque talmudique;* Nathan Morris's *The Jewish School from the Earliest Times to the Year 500 of the Present Era;* S. J. Tcharno's *Le-toledot ha-ḥinnuk be-Israel* (A Contribution to the History of Education in Israel), Pts. I-II; and Nathan Drazin's *History of Jewish Education from 515 B. C. E. to 220 C. E.*

[9] Yer. Yeb. XII, 6, 13a. A similar combination of offices was offered by Busrah, in Transjordan, to another candidate who was to be designated by R. Simon b. Laḳish (Yer. Sheb. VI, 1, 36d). The translation here given, of *sofer* as scribe, seems more justified than that traditionally accepted as Bible teacher. Cf., e. g., Moore, op. cit., I, 290; Zucker, op. cit., pp. 183 f. Elementary instruction would more likely have been included in the office of *ḥazzan*, whereas a regular secretary (and perhaps notary) was more likely to be needed. Cf. also Krauss, op. cit., p. 151 for variants in the text.

[10] Yer. B. Ḳ. IV, 3, 4b; Sifre on Deut. 16; Mekilta on Ex. 21.1; Giṭ. 88b; M. Giṭ. I, 5 and the talmudic comments thereon. Paul, too, voiced his grief over a brother going to law with a brother, "and that before the unbelievers" (I Cor. 6.6). The more liberal minority opinion of R. Simon b. Yoḥai, in M. Giṭ. I, 5, is best understood in the light of the Hadrianic suppression of civil Jewish jurisdiction in his days (Yer. Sanh. VII, 2, 24b) which undoubtedly affected also the Jewish archives. The latter's importance under the Second Commonwealth is dramatically illustrated by Josephus' description of the initial stages of the Jewish revolt (*War*, II, 17, 6.427 ff.). The French Revolution started with the burning of a prison, the Jewish rebellion with that of a repository for legalized records of economic exploitation.

[11] Yer. Pe'ah, I, 1, 15d; Bab. Sanh. 5 ab, 33a; B. Ḳ. 82a; Shabbat 139a. In Palestine there were different degrees of ordination which, increasingly treated as a patriarchal prerogative, generally included such an authorization. In Babylonia, where the ordination, always conferred by individual rabbis, was of a lower order, the main emphasis lay upon the exilarchic authorization, which was supposedly valid even for Palestine. The complex problems of the two institutions are analyzed by A. Epstein in his "Ordination et autorisation," *REJ*, XLVI (1903), 197–211. Cf. also H. J. Bornstein, "The Rules of Ordination and its History" (Hebrew), *Hatekufah*, IV (1919), 393–426. The general, none too ample, data concerning the talmudic courts of justice have been critically examined by

H. P. Chajes in his "Les juges juifs en Palestine de l'an 70 à l'an 500," *REJ*, XXXIX (1899), 39–52. Cf. also Juster, op. cit., II, 93 ff.

[12] Aelius Spartianus, *Hist. Aug. Pescennius Niger*, VII, in *Scriptores historiae Augustae*, ed. by D. Magie, I. The following pathetic elucidation of an old advice may serve as an illustration of both the growing complaints and the dangers of cooperation: " 'Thou shalt not become acquainted with the authorities' (Abot, I, 9). In what fashion? It teaches you that no one should try to gain a [good] name with the authorities, because . . . sooner or later they place their eyes upon him, kill him and confiscate his property. . . . It [also] teaches you that no one should contend, 'I am the prefect of the city,' or 'I am his deputy,' because they rob Israel" (Abot de R. Nathan, XI, pp. 46 f.). Cf. also A. Gulak, "The Method of Collecting Roman Taxes in Palestine" (Hebrew), *Magnes Anniversary Book*, pp. 97–104; idem, "Boulé and Strategia" (Hebrew), *Tarbiz*, XI (1939), 119–22.

[13] Juster, op. cit., I, 206 n. 12; Philo, *De leg. spec.*, IV, 193–96; Yer. B. B. V, end, 15ab; Bab. B. B. 89a; B. M. 49 ff.; *Theodosian Code*, XVI, 8, 10; *Code of Justinian*, I, 9, 9. The exceedingly complicated rabbinic economic theory and practice still await elucidation. Some of the problems and the literature thereon are discussed in S. W. Baron's study of "The Economic Views of Maimonides" in his *Essays on Maimonides*. Only partially modifying the teachings of the Talmud, these Maimonidean views reflect both the ancient doctrines and their adaptation to the medieval Muslim environment.

[14] Ecclesiasticus 7.10, 32, etc.; Tobit, 4.3–19, etc.; Job 31.16–22; Josephus, *Against Apion*, II, 29.211. Although it has been plausibly shown that this formulation of Josephus, as well as the related, more expanded statement in Philo's *Hypothetica* (preserved in Eusebius' *Praeparatio evangelica*, ed. by E. H. Gifford, VIII, 358d) were strongly influenced by the "Bouzygian Imprecations" which had attained wide circulation throughout the Graeco-Roman world (cf. Hendrik Bolkenstein's essay, "Een geval van sociaal-ethisch syncretisme," *Mededeelingen van den Kon. Akademie van Wetenschapen*, Section *Letters*, LXXII [1931], 1–52) it must be borne in mind that this Hellenistic collection of curses was itself the result of fusion of Greek and Oriental ethical teachings. Philo and Josephus, both of whom chiefly addressed Gentile audiences, may simply have used a formula familiar to a majority of their readers, to

show them that these basic ethical postulates had already been included in the Mosaic legislation. Whether or not they wished to imply that the Greek collection owed its origin to Jewish prototypes, which would have been quite in line with their frequent assertions of Hellenism's general indebtedness to Jewish culture, they undoubtedly were right in assuming Judaism's historic priority in this particular attitude toward the poor.

[15] For details cf. M(agnus) Weinberg, "Die Almosenverwaltung der jüdischen Ortsgemeinden im talmudischen Zeitalter," *Israelitische Monatsschrift* (supplement to *Jüdische Presse*), 1893, nos. 1–3, 5, 6, 9; Joseph Lehmann, "Assistance publique et privée d'après l'antique législation juive," *REJ*, XXXV (1897), pp. I-XXXVIII; Kaufman Kohler, "Zum Kapitel der jüdischen Wohltätigkeitspflege," *Festschrift. . . A. Berliner*, pp. 195–203; idem, "The Historical Development of Jewish Charity" (1890), in *Hebrew Union College and Other Addresses*, pp. 229–52; Aart van Iterson, *Armenzorg bij de Joden in Palestina van 100 v. Chr.— 200 n. Chr.* Cf. also, in general, Hendrik Bolkenstein's noteworthy study of *Wohltätigkeit und Armenpflege im vorchristlichen Altertum.*

[16] Shab. 118b; Josephus, *War*, II, 20, 5.570–71; M. Meg. I, 3; Prov. 21.9; 25.24. For the ten *baṭlanim*, cf. the extensive literature cited by Schürer, op. cit., II, 515; and Krauss, op. cit., pp. 103 ff. The *ḥeber ha-'ir* is treated by J. Horovitz in a revised reprint from the *Festschrift Jakob Guttmann*, in favor of an individual, and by Krauss in *JJLG*, XVII (1926), 195–240, favoring a collective group. (Cf. also Horovitz's reply, ibid., pp. 241–314). The latter contention is supported by a Ras Shamra text, first published by Ch. Virolleaud in *Revue des études sémitiques*, I, Pt. 1 (1934), p. IX.

[17] Ḳid. 76b.

[18] Yer. M. Ḳ. II, 3, 81b; Pes. 112a, 113a; Shab. 114a; Adolf Büchler, *The Political and the Social Leaders of the Jewish Community of Sepphoris in the Second and Third Centuries.* The author has clearly demonstrated the existence of a bitter conflict between the rabbis and the official leaders of Sepphoris (Diocaesarea) whom the former accused of oppressing and exploiting the masses, of negligence in the performance of their duties, of insufficient consultation of the people or, at the other extreme, of yielding too readily to public clamor. The wealthy leaders reciprocated in kind and accused the rabbis of corruption, venality, immoral life, and so forth. Büchler's thesis, although frequently supported by speculation and

arbitrary interpretation of the sources rather than by direct evidence (cf. especially pp. 22 f., 43 ff.), well illustrates the resistance encountered by the rabbis in their drive for power. In the settlement of these conflicts, Sepphoris Jewry was little hampered by outside interference, inasmuch as it seems that the city's population was then entirely Jewish. Despite Hadrian's attempt to impose local pagan rule, as evidenced by the second-century coins struck in the city, we learn from Epiphanius that under the reign of Constantine "no pagan, Samaritan nor Christian" was allowed to live there. Cf. his *Adv. Haer.* XXX, 11, in Migne's *Patrologia graeca*, XLI, 425; A. H. M. Jones, *The Cities of the Eastern Roman Provinces*, pp. 277 f. For R. Joḥanan's advice concerning the *boulé*, cf. also the study of the "Economic Conditions of Galilean Jewry" in that period by A. Marmorstein in *Festschrift Jakob Freimann*, Hebrew section, pp. 82 ff., 92; and above, n. 12.

19 Sifre Deut., 48. The available sources unfortunately do not enable modern investigators to answer the intriguing question as to the extent to which electoral "democracy" prevailed in the talmudic community. Zacharias Frankel in his essay, "Die Gemeindeordnung nach talmudischem Rechte," *MGWJ*, II (1853), 294 n. 9, observed that the statement in the Babylonian Talmud (Meg. 26ab) about the "seven best men of the city [acting] in the presence of the city's inhabitants," is rendered in the Palestinian Talmud (III, 2, 74a) with the omission of this significant qualification. He drew therefrom the conclusion that the Babylonian community was more "liberal." In fact, the opposite is more likely to have been true, since the traditions of the ancient Israelitic *Rechtsgemeinde* must have been doubly powerful in the original homeland, and since, indeed, the tannaitic sources rather frequently refer to majority decisions of the community as a whole (Tos. Sanh. II, 13, 418; Mishnah, X, 4, etc.). Nevertheless, the rabbis refrained from regulating the electoral methods and rights. They may have been discouraged from such an undertaking by the enormous diversity of diaspora constitutions, or they may have distrusted the voting masses who often, as in Sepphoris, followed the lead of their patrician opponents. More likely, they simply left such regulation to the particular community. Their main program, after all, had been to establish a different, non-electoral democracy of scholarship.

20 M. B. B. VI, 7; Bab. B. B. 7b; Yer. Pe'ah VIII, 6, 21a.

21 *Theodosian Code*, XVI, 8, 2–4.

[22] Soṭah 20a; 'Er. 13a; Giṭ. 60b; B. B. 22a; Jerome, *Adversus Vigilantium*, 13 end, and *Adv. Jovinianum*, I, 25 (Migne, *Patrologia latina*, XXIII, 245, 350). The poverty of the scholars, which the Romans often derided, and their need of public support is attested also by many talmudic passages. Cf. Yer. Pe'ah VIII, 8, 21b; Bab. B. B. 75a, etc.

[23] M. B. M. II, 11; Sanh. 110a; Ḳid. 32b; Suk. 38b; M. Soṭah IX, 15; Giṭ. 62a.

[24] *Antiquities*, XIV, 10, 2 ff., 191 ff.; Juster, op. cit., I, 391 ff.; Zucker, op. cit., pp. 148 ff. Zucker overlooks, however, the fact that the first outsider to mention the office, Origen, uses the titles of ethnarch and patriarch interchangeably (*Epistola ad Africanum*, 14; *De principiis*, IV, 3; *Comm. on Psalms*, Introd., in Migne's *Patrologia Graeca*, XI, 82 ff., 348; XII, 1056). The inscription of the Stobi synagogue, cited above, contains the provision that for any change in construction a large fine shall be paid "to the patriarch." Written about 165 C. E., this is the first dated reference to a Jewish official bearing this title. His identity with the Palestinian *nasi* is the more likely, as the adoption of this unusual designation by a provincial leader, as suggested by Frey, *Corpus*, no. 694, at this early date would seem highly improbable. For the Old Testament use of the term *nasi*, cf. Noth, *System*, pp. 151 ff. "The Sources concerning Hillel's Elevation to the Nesiut" are analyzed in a Hebrew essay by Israel Goldberger in *Ha-Zofeh*, X (1926) 68–76, but this designation is used here, of course, in the looser terminology of the later rabbinic tradition.

The date of the Roman recognition of the patriarchate is uncertain. Without knowledge of the Stobi inscription, Juster has advanced reasonable arguments for the assumption that it was granted by Antoninus Pius as one of the means of appeasing the indomitably rebellious mood of Jewry. The spread of the patriarchal influence to the Balkans by 165 makes it doubly probable that this recognition was extended to Simon b. Gamaliel II, as intimated in several talmudic sources (Tos. Sanh. XII, 5–6, 416 f.: Simon's failure to mention his colleagues; Hor. 13b; Yer. Bik. III, 3, 65c) rather than to his youthful son, Judah I, who at the time of the Stobi provision was only about 30 years old (Ḳid. 72b, etc.). Cf. also below, n. 27; Zucker, op. cit., pp. 99 f., 135, 153 f.

Signs of such recognition multiply under Judah's regime. To be sure, the fact that he was offered a Roman escort during journeys, a rather burdensome honor which he gladly declined (Gen. Rabbah 78, ed. Theodor-Albeck, p. 935) need not be conclusive. Origen, too, although holding no such official position, was given a guard of honor. But the text of the letter addressed, in the scribe's first attempt, "From thy servant Judah to our master, King Antoninus" (ibid., 75, p. 883), bears all the earmarks of authenticity. The very precedence of the name of the sender before that of his superior, although unusual in the official Graeco-Roman epistolary style, is borne out by the Palestinian usage, even among Roman officials, recorded in Acts 23.26. For the much-debated problem of the identity of Judah's "friend" on the imperial throne, cf. now Luitpold Wallach's essay "The Colloquy of Marcus Aurelius with the Patriarch Judah I," *JQR*, XXXI (1940–41), 259 ff.

The complex relationships between the patriarchs and the Sanhedrin and the highly contradictory nature of our evidence for the period before the fall of Jerusalem become somewhat less puzzling if we assume a clean-cut distinction between the royal council functioning in Jerusalem before 70 C. E., and the scholarly academy established by R. Joḥanan b. Zakkai in Yabneh, and invested with manifold legislative and judicial powers, which subsequently moved to other Palestinian localities. Both these institutions are designated in the sources by the same term, Sanhedrin. Cf. Elias Bickermann, "The Sanhedrin" (Hebrew), *Zion*, III (1938), 256–60. For the patriarchate in general, cf. also Israel Lévi's "L'origine davidique de Hillel," *REJ*, XXXI (1895), 202–11; XXXIII (1896), 143–44; and Zuri, op. cit.

[25] Giṭ. 59a; Gen. 49, 10; Libanius' *Epistolae*, no. 1251 (in *Opera*, ed. by Richard Förster, XI, 327) in M. Schwabe's interpretation in his Hebrew essay on "The Letters of Libanius to the Patriarch of Palestine," *Tarbiz*, I, Pt. 2 (1929–30), 85–110; Pt. 3, 107–21; Yer. Ḥag. I, 7, 76c. For the term and function of the apostles, cf. Hermann Vogelstein, "Die Entstehung und Entwicklung des Apostolats im Judentum," *MGWJ*, XLIX (1905), 427–29; idem, "The Development of the Apostolate in Judaism and its Transformation in Christianity," *HUCA*, II (1925), 99–123.

[26] Yer. Bik. III, 3, 65d; Sanh. II, 6, 20d; Ber. III, I, 6a. Of course not all Diaspora Jews need have readily accepted this additional burden. Hence there is no denying the possibility that Julian the Apostate's famous epistle "To the Community of the Jews" (*Epistolae*, ed. Bidez, no. 204; ed. Wright, no. 51) was forged by a Jewish objector to this patriarchal impost. This hypothesis has recently been advanced by Joseph

Vogt in his *Kaiser Julian und das Judentum*, pp. 47 n. 2, 64 ff. A very good case has been made, however, and, despite Bidez's and Vogt's arguments, can still be made in favor of the authenticity of this epistle. Cf. the recent Hebrew essays by Mordecai Heck, "Is Julian's Declaration a Forgery?," *Yavneh*, II (1939–40), 118–39; and J. (Hans) Levy, "Emperor Julian and the Rebuilding of the Temple at Jerusalem," *Zion*, VI (1940–41), 27 ff.

[27] R. H. 20b; Ḥul. 95b; Yer. Ned. VI, 8, 40a; Sanh. I, 2, 19a. The date of the patriarchal intervention against Ḥananiah, the nephew of R. Joshua, is very uncertain. The text of the Palestinian Talmud reads: Rabbi, i. e. R. Judah I. Graetz, arguing that this event must have taken place soon after the Bar Kocheba revolt, assumed that the patriarchal author of the three epistles must have been Judah's father, Simon b. Gamaliel. But in order to do so, he had to resort to the desperate expedient of emending the text to: Rabbi Simon. Cf. his *Geschichte*, IV, 4th ed., p. 443. More circumspectly, Isaac Halevy in his *Dorot ha-rishonim* (Jewish History), II, 199 f., presents the intervention as a collegiate action, without naming the patriarch or giving a definite date, but placing it generally at about that time. He, too, however, must emend the words שלח ליה רבי to read שלחו ליה. This interpretation is accepted by many scholars e. g., Jawitz (op. cit., VI, 143 f.). That it is possible, however, to retain the reading of the original source by dating the correspondence in about 160 C. E., has been argued with some success by Zucker, op. cit., pp. 161 f.

[28] *Theodosian Code*, XVI, 8; Jerome, *Epistolae*, 57, 3, in Migne's *Patrologia latina*, XXII, 570; Julian, *Epistolae*, no. 204 (Cf. above n. 26). Cf. also, in general, Juster, op. cit., I, 391 ff.; Zucker, op. cit., pp. 148 ff.

[29] Yer. 'Er. III end, 21c. The date of Hillel II's promulgation, long accepted as 358–59 C. E., was put back by some 15 years by Eduard Mahler in his *Handbuch der jüdischen Chronologie*, pp. 416 ff. Zucker, however, (op. cit. pp. 168 f.) has plausibly argued for the restoration of the older chronology. The opinion of the rabbinic authorities concerning the observance of two holidays is well summarized in later geonic responsa (by Hai and Joseph Rosh ha-seder), ed. by B. M. Lewin in *Ginze Kedem*, IV (1930), 33 ff.

[30] I Chr. 3.16 ff.; Ad. Neubauer, *Medieval Jewish Chronicles*, I, 70 f., 74 f.; Judah ibn Kuraish, quoted in the anonymous *Commentary* on

I Chr. 3, ed. by Raphael Kirchheim, p. 16. It may be noted that on a tombstone discovered in Alexandria was found the name, Aḳabiah b. Alyoini, analogous to I Chr. 3, 24. This tombstone dates from the third pre-Christian century; cf. S. Klein's remarks in *MGWJ*, LXXVII (1933), 192 f. The strongest argument usually adduced against the exilarchic tradition, namely the failure of Josephus to mention this significant office, is even less conclusive than most *argumenta ex silentio*. Addressing himself primarily to Greek readers, Josephus rarely discussed the inner life of the Jewish community except insofar as it impinged upon the political and legal status of the Jews under their Hellenistic and Roman rulers. Were it not for an incidental citation from Strabo and a decree of Claudius (*Antiquities*, XIV, 7, 2. 117; XIX, 5, 2.283) he might have passed over in silence the ethnarchs, the highest officers of Egyptian Jewry, although the general history of the latter is treated by him in far greater detail than that of their Babylonian coreligionists. Even adding the information preserved in the extant local records, including the works of Philo — no such body of material has come down to us from Babylonia before the third century C. E.— our knowledge of this important office or that of the alabarch is extremely scanty. Cf. also Chap. III, n. 12; IV, n. 33. The reference of the distinguished Arabian historian, Ṭabari, to an exilarch in the days of Jesus may, however, be altogether legendary. Cf. his *Annals*, ed. Leyden, I, 741 and Ignaz Goldziher, "Renseignements de source musulmane sur la dignité de resch-galuta," *REJ*, VIII, (1884), 121.

31 Shebu. 6b; Yer. Soṭah VII, 6, 22a.

32 Sanh. 17b; B. B. 70b, etc.; B. Ḳ. 58b; B. B. 55a. The term, *dayyane di baba* (judges of the exilarchic court), though recorded only in the post-talmudic period, was probably in use as early as Sassanian Persia. Witness the designation of the exilarchic court as the *baba di-resh galuta* in B. B. 65a.

33 B. M. 73b; B. B. 54b–55a; Ṭabari, *Geschichte der Perser und Araber*, transl. by Th. Nöldeke, p. 241. Cf. in general, the analysis of the pertinent talmudic sources in J. Newman's *Agricultural Life of the Jews in Babylonia*, pp. 161 ff. Neither are apparently the contemporary Parsee and Christian accounts sufficiently articulate and explicit to allow a clear reconstruction of the Persian fiscal administration. The active participation of the Jewish community and its head, the exilarch, however, is clearly indicated in various talmudic passages (e. g. R. Huna's amusing, though hardly histor-

ical advice to an exilarch on how to reduce a sudden impost, Yer. Soṭah, V, 5, 20b) and is also borne out by outside sources. Cf. for instance, the story reported by a Christian chronicler of what happened to Simon the chief of the Christians (the counterpart to the Jewish exilarch) when his arrest was ordered by Shapur II. "You will not release him," the King is reported to have enjoined the Persian official, "until he has signed this document and agreed to collect for payment to us a double poll tax and double tribute from the whole people of the Nazarenes which is in the country of the godhead and dwells on our territory. For our godhead has only the troubles of war, and they have only rest and pleasure! They dwell on our territory and share the sentiments of Caesar, our enemy!" Quoted (from the Syriac *Acta Martyrum et Sanctorum*, ed. by P. Bedjan, II, 136 ff.) by Clément Huart in his *Ancient Persia and Iranian Civilization*, pp. 156 f. While the suspicion of pro-Roman sentiments would have been unjustified in the case of the Jews, the argument that the Parsees bore the brunt of war and military service and that, hence, non-Parsees should carry the main burden of taxation was applicable to Jews as well, notwithstanding their sporadic participation in the country's defense against the Romans. Cf. Baron, *History*, I, 254; III, 66 f.

[34] 'A. Z. 9b; Ṭabari, *Geschichte*, pp. 241 ff. The complicated chronology of these events is given here in accordance with the investigations of Funk in his *Juden in Babylonien*, II, 143 ff. Graetz (*History*, III, 3 f.), followed by Bacher (*Jew. Encycl.*, V, 289 f.), and others date Mar Zutra's rebellion in the years 511–18. Mar Zutra's title in Tiberias is likewise controversial. It seems that he and his descendants were not the only ones to be distinguished by the title *rosh ha-pereḳ*. This office, known to Byzantines as that of *archipherekitai*, is mentioned also in the discriminatory *Novella 146* of Justinian, and seems to have been held by other Jewish exegetes of Scripture. At any rate, in the Muslim period the title seems to have been given to such scholarly synagogue readers who had no connection with an academy. Cf. Jacob Mann, *The Jews in Egypt and in Palestine under the Fatimid Caliphs*, I, 58 n. 1, 269 f. For the general history of the exilarchate, cf. Felix Lazarus's monograph *Die Häupter der Vertriebenen;* and J. S. Zuri's more specialized treatment of the period 320–55 C. E., op. cit., III (Period of Rab Nachman bar Jizchak).

[35] Sanh. 5ab; Yer. Kil. IX, 4, 32b.

[36] The objections raised by Zucker (op. cit., p. 135 n. 3) against Frankel's and Graetz's identification of the *ḥakam* as a special officer, rather than an ordinary member, are not weighty enough to alter the evident and simple meaning of the sources (Tos. Sanh. VII, 8, 426; Ḳid. 32b, etc.). There is an enormous literature concerning the life and work of individual rabbis and various activities of the ancient academies, but we have no full monographic treatment of their organization, legal status under the two empires, relations to the central offices and to one another, and so forth. Cf. especially, A. Marmorstein, "La réorganisation du doctorat en Palestine au troisième siècle," *REJ*, LVI (1913), 44–53; Zuri, op. cit.; Samuel K. Mirsky, "On the Organization of the Babylonian Academies in the Talmudic Period" (Hebrew), *Ḥoreb*, III (1936), 109–24; and the two Hebrew studies of the main seats of Jewish learning in Babylonia by M. D. Judelowitz, "The Town of Sura," *Sinai*, I-II, and *Ḥayye ha-Yehudim bi-zeman ha-Talmud* (Jewish Life in the Talmudic Period; on Pumbedita).

[37] Tos. Oholot XVIII, 17, 617; Miḳva'ot VII, 11, 661; Sifre on Num., 124; Soṭah 21a; Meg. 28a; Yer. M. Ḳ. III, 1, 81d. There is even some indication that friendly Roman rulers, apart from granting tax exemptions to scholars, helped support them directly. It has been suggested that a recorded gift of fields in the Gaulanitis to the patriarch was made for that purpose. Cf. Graetz's *History*, II, 482.

[38] Ber. 28a, 37a; Meg. 5a.

[39] Yer. Sanh. I, 2, 18c, 19a; R. H. II, 6, 58ab; Bab. Hor. 13b. For the duration of the patriarchal ordination cf. Jawitz, op. cit., VII, 107 n. 3.

[40] Gen. Rab. 16 (ed. by Theodor and Albeck, p. 145); 'A. Z. 19b (implied); Ber. 24b; Sanh. 12a, 38a. While there is general agreement as to the sort of gathering which went under the name of *kallah*, its origin and etymology are still obscure. The more recent explanations offered by Jacob Z. Lauterbach (in *Hebrew Union College Jub. Vol.*, 1925, 211–22) as an abbreviation for *keneset lomde torah* (gathering of Torah students), by S. Krauss (in *Livre d'hommage... Poznanski*, pp. 142 ff.) as derived from *kalal* and meaning the reviewing of the traditional law, and by E. Hildesheimer (in *Festschrift Jakob Freimann*, Hebrew section, pp. 62 ff.) as the equivalent of a gathering, derived from the same root, merely reveal the usual perplexities inherent in institutions reaching back to remote antiquity.

NOTES TO CHAPTER VI

PROTECTED COMMUNITY

[1] *Seder Eliyahu rabbah*, XX; ed. Friedmann, pp. 113 f. Cf. also ibid., X, p. 54. V. Aptowitzer has made it plausible that the compiler of this work lived in Babylonia in the ninth century. Cf. his "Seder Elia," *Jewish Studies in Memory of George A. Kohut*, pp. 5–39.

[2] Yakub abu Yussuf, *Livre d'impôt foncière*, French transl., pp. 187 ff.; Yakubi, *Tariḥ*, II, 279, quoted by Emile Tyan in his *Histoire de l'organisation judiciaire en pays d'Islam*, I, 121 f.; A. Harkavy, "Neṭira and his Sons," *Festschrift A. Berliner*, Hebrew section, pp. 36, 39. A similar intervention of a Spanish-Jewish grandee two centuries later elicited a poem of praise by Yehudah Halevi. Cf. his *Diwan*, ed. by H. Brody, I, no. 20. On the other hand, when taxation became altogether unbearable, the Jews occasionally resisted by force, as when Lucena Jewry rebelled against their sovereign, Abd Allah of Granada. Cf. E. Levi-Provençal, "Les 'Mémoires' de 'Abd Allah, dernier roi Ziride de Granade," *Al-Andalus*, IV (1936–39), 113 ff. Cf. also H. Schirman, "The Life of Yehudah Halevi" (Hebrew), *Tarbiz*, IX (1937-38), 45 f.

[3] Joseph ibn Megas quoted by Maimonides in his *Commentary* on M. Abot, IV, 5. Cf. also Ibn Megas' clearer definition of this privilege in his *Ḥiddushim* (Novellae) on B. B. 8a. For eleventh-century Lucena, the predominant position of the Jewish community, which had shut out the Muslim population from the interior of the city, and the former's claim that the city had originally been built by Jewish exiles from Jerusalem, cf. the Arabic and Hebrew sources cited by D. Kaufmann in his *Gesammelte Schriften*, II, 105 n. 2. Cf. also above, n. 2.

This general tax exemption for scholars, clearly formulated by Naḥshon Gaon of Sura (874–82; *Teshubot ha-geonim*, ed. by Harkavy, no. 537) and often reiterated in juristic literature of both Muslim and Christian lands, was reinforced by frequent detailed communal enactments. For example, in the early 1500's the Egyptian *nagid*, Isaac ha-Kohen Sholal, issued a general ordinance to this effect. It was supported by the Jerusalem rabbinate with severe bans and curses against "the men, women, family or tribe" which would break it and impose upon the scholar "whether poor or rich" any impost, except the capitation tax. Quoted from Joseph Sambari and

Mordecai ha-Levi by S. A. Rosanes, in his *Dibre yeme Israel be-Togarma* (A History of the Jews in Turkey), I, 2d ed., pp. 199 f. Cf. also Chap. XV n. 36.

[4] Al-Mawardi, *Al-Aḥkam al-sultaniyya*, ed. Cairo, p. 62 quoted by Ben-Zion Dinaburg in his *Israel ba-golah* (Israel in Dispersion; a Source Book) I, 16, and by Tyan in his *Organisation judiciaire*, I, 125, 240. For the right of establishing *waqfs* and inheriting heirless estates, cf. Omar II's decree cited by Ibn Sa'ad in his *Biographien Muhammeds, seiner Gefährten . . . bis zum Jahre 230 der Flucht*, V, p. 262; and, in general, Georges Vajda's "Juifs et Musulmans selon le hadiṭ," *Journal asiatique*, CCXXIX (1937), 57–128; A. Mez's *Die Renaissance des Islam*, (in English transl. in *Islamic Culture*, II–VII, 1928–33); Reuben Levy's *Introduction to the Sociology of Islam*; and Philip K. Hitti's, *History of the Arabs*.

[5] Most of the sources, largely Muslim, are quoted by I. Goldziher in his "Sa'id b. Hasan d'Alexandrie," *REJ*, XXX (1895), 6 ff.; Martin Schreiner in his "Contributions à l'histoire des Juifs en Egypte," ibid., pp. 212 ff.; and Richard J. H. Gottheil in his "Dhimmis and Moslems in Egypt," *Old Testament and Semitic Studies in Mem. of William R. Harper*, II, 351–414. The latter article includes also the text and translation of an interesting document of 1456. For the legislation of the Mameluke sultans and, especially, for the extensive decree of 1354, cf. L. A. Mayer, "The Status of the Jews under the Mamelukes" (Hebrew), *Magnes Anniversary Book*, pp. 161–67.

[6] The obvious attempt of Aleppo Jewry to persuade the Muslim authorities of the antiquity of their synagogue as antedating Islam, may well have been responsible for its reading the date of the oldest inscription therein as referring to 342 rather than to 833 C. E. Cf. M. Sobernheim and E. Mittwoch, "Hebräische Inschriften in der Synagoge von Aleppo," *Festschrift . . . Jakob Guttmann*, p. 279. Cf. also J. L. Porter, *Five Years in Damascus*, 2d ed., p. 235; Mann, *Jews in Egypt*, I, 72 f.; II, 72 f.; Solomon Munk, *Palestine*, p. 644; Ibn al-Nakas quoted by Dinaburg, op. cit., II, 113; Jacob Moses Toledano, "Ancient Synagogues in Alexandria and its Environs" (Hebrew), *HUCA*, XII–XIII (1937–38), 701–14; S. Krauss, "Ancient Synagogues in Palestine and the Near East" (Hebrew), *Yerushalayim* (in Memory of A. M. Luncz), pp. 221–49; I. Shohet, "The Synagogue on the Tomb of the Prophet Samuel" (Hebrew), *Bulletin of the Jewish Palestine Exploration Society*, VI (1938–39), 81–86 (with addi-

tional notes by S. Assaf *et al.*, ibid., pp. 141–44; VII, 40); David S. Sassoon, "The History of the Jews in Basra," *JQR*, XVII (1926–27), 410 ff., 454 ff.; *The Occident* (Philadelphia), XVIII (1860–61), 199 f.; and Chap. XII, n. 4.

In Abraham Galanté's *Documents officiels turcs concernant les Juifs de Turquie*, pp. 51 ff. we find two interesting Turkish decrees in French translation, dated in 1694 and 1837 respectively, which well illustrate the complicated procedure required for permits to rebuild or repair synagogues. In the later decree, the Sultan, after a long recitation of the testimony offered and the officials who had taken part in the proceedings and quotation of an affirmative responsum (*fatwa*) of the ecclesiastical chief of Islam, gave the Jews permission to re-erect the synagogue "under the condition that it should not exceed its former size by even a palm or finger in length, height or width." The slow and extremely complicated procedure in obtaining a permit to replace a burned synagogue is well illustrated by Moritz Levy's description of such attempts by the community of Sarajevo in the years 1794–1813 in his *Die Sephardim in Bosnien*, pp. 112 ff.

The influence of the Byzantine legislation is evident. Less so is that of Sassanian Persia. There, too, occasional prohibitions of new religious structures for non-Parsees are recorded, but at least in the treaty concluded by Chosroes I with Justinian in 563, the Persian monarch promised to allow his Christian subjects to erect new churches. Cf. Eduard Sachau, "Von den rechtlichen Verhältnissen der Christen im Sassanidenreich," *Mitteilungen des Seminars für orientalische Sprachen zu Berlin*, X, Pt. 2 (1907), 77 ff. The relative absence of talmudic complaints on this score — the recurrent complaints of the destruction of synagogues need not refer to allegedly new buildings — may in part be due to the greater antiquity and perhaps also lesser missionary efforts of the Persian Jewish communities in the more intolerant period of the later Sassanian regime. In part, however, it must be ascribed to the feeling among Jews that all measures against the synagogue were only part of a large anti-Jewish campaign expressed in oppressive taxation, if not in expulsions or massacres. That is also why Jewish sources contain so few specific references to legal or illegal attacks on synagogues under Christian Rome, Islam or in medieval Europe.

[7] *Sha'are ṣedeḳ* III, 6, 7, fol. 24a; B. M. Lewin, *Otzar ha-Gaonim*, VII, 113 f.; *Teshubot geone mizraḥ u-ma'arab*, ed. by Joel Müller, no. 42; *Sha'are*

teshubah, nos. 23, 86; Simḥah Pinsker, *Lickute kadmoniot*, Addenda, pp. 31 f.; *Seder Eliyahu*, XVIII, p. 106. Violation of the Sabbath rest commandments for economic reasons must have been so frequent as to justify a special formula for action against it. Cf. Mann's *Texts and Studies in Jewish History and Literature*, I, 587 (the editor considers the entire collection as early geonic). The numerous complaints of leaders against disobeying members are well illustrated by Zadok ha-Levi's letter, published by Mann in his *Jews in Egypt*, II, 182 f. Cf. in general also, Raphael Mahler, "On the National-Social Character of the Karaite Movement in the Early Period" (Yiddish), *Yivo Bleter*, VIII (1935), 304–22, continued ibid., IX (1936), 31–62; and for numerous parallels in the Muslim environment, Tyan, *Organisation judiciaire*, I, 428 ff., 447 ff., 473 ff.

[8] Louis Ginzberg, *Genizah Studies* (*Ginze Schechter*), II, 504–73; B. M. Lewin, "Genizah Fragments" (Hebrew), *Tarbiz*, II (1930–31), 385; Hartwig Hirschfeld, "Some Judaeo-Arabic Legal Documents," *JQR*, XVI (1925–26), 279–86; Stephan Gerlach der Aeltere, *Tage-Buch der von zween ... Römischen Kaysern ... an die Ottomanische Pforte ... abgefertigten Gesandtschafft*, pp. 49, 174. Cf. also Graetz, *Geschichte*, IX, 28 n. 1. Characteristic of the feeling of superiority in Babylonia is a distinction drawn by a Babylonian gaon (Kohen Zedek?) stating that if a man from North Africa settle in Palestine for over 12 months and there take a wife, he is to be considered ritualistically as a full-fledged resident, even though he intends to return to his native country. Not so in the case of a Babylonian visitor who, after several years, must still regard himself as a non-resident and comply with the regulations and customs of both countries. *Teshubot geone mizraḥ u-ma'arab*, no. 39. Cf. also S. Assaf's "Palestine in the Responsa of the Babylonian Geonim" (Hebrew), *Ṣiyyon*, I (1926), 21–30.

[9] *Sha'are teshubah*, no. 34 (Naṭronai); Zedekiah b. Abraham 'Anav, *Shibbole ha-leḳeṭ*, ed. by Solomon Buber, II, 150 (Hai); Maimonides, *Mishneh Torah*, Sanhedrin, XIX; V. Aptowitzer, "Formularies of Decrees and Documents," *JQR*, N. S. IV (1913–14), 26 f., 42 ff. Cf. also I. H. Weiss, *Dor dor ve-doreshav* (A History of Halakah), IV, 6th ed., pp. 97 f. The penalties at the disposal of medieval Jewish authorities are treated by S. Assaf in his *Ha-'Oneshin aḥre ḥatimat ha-talmud* (Criminal Jurisdiction since the Conclusion of the Talmud); H. Tykocinski, *Die gaonäischen Verordnungen* (*Taḳḳanot*); and Jacob Mann in his "Historical

Survey of Capital Jurisdiction at the Present Day" (Hebrew), *Ludwig Blau Jub. Vol.* (*Ha-Zofeh*, X), pp. 200–8. Mann postulates, on the basis of admittedly meagre evidence, the exercise of such jurisdiction by the Jewish judges of Muslim Spain, beginning with Ibn Megas of Lucena. Cf. also Chap. XIV, nn. 12 ff.

[10] Mann, *Jews in Egypt*, I, 261 f.; *Teshubot geone mizraḥ u-ma'arab*, nos. 179, 199; *Teshubot ha-geonim*, ed. by Harkavy, no. 278; Hai's responsum, ed. by S. Assaf in *Ginze Kedem*, I (1922), 77. Cf. also Mann, "The Responsa of the Babylonian Geonim as a Source of Jewish History," *JQR*, X (1919–20), 140 ff.; Tyan, *Organisation judiciaire*, I, 428 ff.

[11] Ibn al-Nakas quoted by Dinaburg, op. cit., II, 117; Rosanes, op. cit., I, 9; Mann, *Egypt*, I, 30 ff. Personal payment of the tax was demanded by the government, in 1229, also from the Gaon Ibn al-Shuwaich in Bagdad. Cf. Walter J. Fischel, *Jews in the Economic and Political Life of Mediaeval Islam*, p. 130. There, too, the exceptional nature of this measure is demonstrated not only by taxation of a leading scholar, but also by the insistence that the payment be made at the Diwan in broad daylight.

[12] *Teshubot geone mizraḥ u-ma'arab*, no. 205 (the author, Nathan the Babylonian, or a North-African scholar by the same name, seems to indicate here the practice of his native country); Rosanes, op. cit., I, 8; *Toratan shel rishonim*, II, 58, no. 7; *Sha'are teshubah*, no. 195. Some communities, forced to pay the assessed total amount even in periods of famine, had to borrow money. Cf. A. Cowley, "Bodleian Genizah Fragments," *JQR*, O. S. XIX (1906–7), 108. For this reason the Cairo community had to sell (about 1409) three pieces of real estate of its *waqf* (*heḳdesh*). Cf. Mann's *Texts*, I, 427 ff.

The method of assessing taxes within the community is well illustrated by a few tax lists published by Richard Gottheil and William H. Worrell in their *Fragments from the Cairo Genizah in the Freer Collection*, pp. 66 ff., and by Mann in his *Egypt*, II, 245 f.; and his *Texts*, I, 468. Cf. also the interesting formula for a mutual agreement among community members included in Judah b. Barzilai's *Sefer ha-Sheṭarot* (Book of Deeds), ed. by S. J. Halberstam, pp. 137 f. Although the author frequently adopts models from similar collections by Saadia and Hai, this particular formula seems to mirror the more "democratic" methods prevalent in Muslim

Spain rather than the practice under the more authoritarian regime in Babylonia.

[13] The accusation of venality, although supported by the great authority of Sherira's *Epistle* (ed. by B. M. Lewin, p. 92) is not borne out by the actual history of exilarchic succession. The ceremonies accompanying the installation of a new exilarch are fully described in the famous report of Nathan, the Babylonian, who seems to have attended the installation of David b. Zakkai in 920. This report, apparently written in Arabic, is preserved only in Hebrew translation, best available in Adolf Neubauer's *Medieval Jewish Chronicles*, II, 83 ff. Cf. Israel Friedländer, "The Arabic Original of the Report of R. Nathan Ha-Babli," *JQR*, O. S. XVII (1904–5), 747–61; Alexander Marx, "Der arabische Bustanai-Bericht und Nathan ha-Babli," *Livre d'hommage . . . Samuel Poznanski*, pp. 76–81. Another description of the installation, possibly dating from an even earlier period, is preserved in Solomon ibn Verga's *Shebet Yehudah*, ed. by M. Wiener, no. 42, pp. 84 ff. The decree of appointment of an exilarch is referred to in *Diwân al-Insha*. Cf. E. Fagnan, "Arabo-Judaica," *REJ*, LIX (1910), 228. However, a similar decree issued in favor of a Bagdad gaon and dated in 1209 has been published in Arabic, with Ignaz Goldziher's German translation, by Poznanski in his *Babylonische Geonim im nachgaonäischen Zeitalter*, pp. 37 ff. For an English translation cf. Fischel, op. cit., pp. 128 f. The somewhat analogous decree of appointment of the Egyptian *rais al-yahud* (*nagid*) by the Mameluke rulers after 1301 is preserved, in part, in the writings of Al-Umari and Al-Kalkashandi and given in Hebrew translation by A. N. Pollak in his Hebrew essay on "The Jews and the Egyptian Treasury in the Times of the Mamelukes," *Zion*, I (1935–36), 34 f. Cf. also Gottheil in *JQR*, O. S. XIX, 527 ff. A decree of appointment of a Nestorian *catholicos*, dated 1139, has been published with an abridged German translation by Alfred von Kremer in his "Zwei arabische Urkunden," *Zeitschrift der deutschen morgenländischen Gesellschaft*, VII (1853), 219–23, and revised with an English summary, by H. F. Amedroz in his "Tales of Official Life from the 'Tadhkira' of Ibn Hamdun," *Journal of the Royal Asiatic Society*, 1908, pp. 447 ff., 467 ff. Cf. also Tyan, *Organisation judiciaire*, I, 262 ff., 447 ff.

[14] Ibn Laḥia quoted by Ignaz Goldziher in *REJ*, VIII, 124 f.; S. Pines, "Une notice sur les Rech Galuta chez un écrivain arabe de IXe siècle,"

REJ, C (1936), 71–73; Alexander D. Goode, "The Exilarchate in the Eastern Caliphate, 637–1258," *JQR*, XXXI (1940–41), 163 n. 3; Benjamin's *Itinerary*, ed. by Marcus N. Adler, pp. 40 f., Hebrew text, p. 41a n. 29 (from Ms. Rome).

[15] Michael Syrus, *Chronique*, IV, 519, ed. with a French translation by J. B. Chabot, III, 68 f.; Nissim of Marseilles, *Ma'ase nissim*, quoted by J. H. Schorr in *He-Ḥaluṣ*, VII (1865), 110. For the importance of this argument in the eleventh-century Judeo-Christian controversy, cf. Parkes, *Community*, p. 31. Sometimes exilarchs called themselves metaphorically "kings." Cf. Mann, *Texts*, I, 338 n. 82.

Arabian folklore often attached superhuman features to the Jewish prince, some Muslims believing, for instance, that his hands must touch his knees. One may note also the complaint of the Jacobite patriarch to the caliph, that the Magian and Jewish chiefs were temporal sovereigns, whereas Christian patriarchs had only spiritual authority. In 912 the patriarch was, indeed, forbidden to take up his residence in Bagdad, a privilege early extended to both the exilarch and the catholicos. Cf. Mez in *Islamic Culture*, II, 262 ff. Cf. also W. Fischel, "The 'Resh Galuta' in Arabic Literature" (Hebrew), *Magnes Anniversary Book*, 181–87; Ismar Elbogen, "Unbekannte Huldigungsgedichte für einen Nasi," *MGWJ*, LXXVI (1932), 334–38 (referring to Exilarch Josiah, probably of eleventh-century Mosul); and, in general, the careful chronological survey of the succession of the individual exilarchs in Goode's aforementioned essay.

[16] St. Jerome, *Commentary* on Isaiah 3.4 (Migne, *Patrologia latina*, XXIV, 64), echoing Eusebius.

[17] The eight extant versions of the story of "Bustanai, the Exilarch" have been carefully analyzed by H. Tykocinski in his Hebrew essay, under this title, in *Debir*, I (1923), 145–79. Version V (cf. George Margoliouth in *JQR*, O. S. XIV, 303 ff.; E. J. Worman, ibid., XX, 211 ff.), to which special reference has been made here, was apparently composed at the end of the tenth century. Cf. Marx, l. c.

[18] Levy, *Sociology*, I, 292; Pinsker, *Lickute*, Addenda, p. 103; Gregory Abulfaraj Bar-Hebraeus, *Chronicon ecclesiasticum*, ed. by J. A. Abbeloos and T. J. Lamy, I, 366 f.; S. Assaf, "Letters of R. Samuel b. 'Ali and his Contemporaries" (Hebrew), *Tarbiz*, I, Pt. 2 (1929–30), 66 f. Felix Lazarus, in his "Neue Beiträge zur Geschichte des Exilarchats," *MGWJ*, LXXVIII

(1934), 279–88, points out that, like the Christian chiefs, the Jewish leaders must have remonstrated against the decree. We possess, however, no record of its revocation or modification. On the pretender, Daniel the Karaite, cf. the reference in Amram Gaon's *Seder*, ed. by A. L. Frumkin, II, 206 f. and Isaak Markon's "Wer ist der in einem Responsum des Naṭronai Gaon II erwähnte Karäer Daniel?" *Festschrift Moritz Schaefer*, pp. 130–36. The abrupt legal change is, nevertheless, reflected in the statement of a contemporary Muslim writer, Al-Jaḥiẓ, that the catholicos and the exilarch functioning in Muslim countries had no right to condemn a person to prison or flagellation; they might impose only ecclesiastical censures and prohibit intercourse with the culprit. On the other hand, Ibn Ḥazm's contention that "the prince of captivity wields no power whatsoever over Jews or any other persons; he merely bears a title which carries with it neither authority nor prerogatives of any kind" (quoted by Goldziher in *REJ*, VIII, 125 ff.) grossly exaggerates the decline of the exilarchate in the author's day (early eleventh century) and is explicable only by his Muslim as well as Spanish biases.

[19] S. Assaf, "Letters of Babylonian Geonim" (Hebrew), *Tarbiz*, XI (1939–40), 152 ff. (publishing an interesting letter of Exilarch Hezekiah written in 1036, two years before his assumption of the office of Gaon of Pumbedita); Neubauer's *Chronicles*, II, 85 ff.; C. Duschinsky, "The Yekum Purkan," *Livre d'hommage . . . Poznanski*, pp. 182–98; B. M. Lewin, "Ancient Fragments from a Maḥzor of the Academy in Pumbedita" (Hebrew), *Ginze Kedem*, III (1925), 50–56; S. Assaf, "Portions of a Benediction for the Exilarch Ḥisdai b. David" (Hebrew), ibid., IV (1930), 63–64; Sherira and Hai, *Responsum*, ed. by S. Assaf ibid., I (1922), 73 ff. (drawing a distinction between the רבנן דמתיבתא visiting in Adar and Ellul and the רבנן תנאי permanently affiliated with the Academy).

[20] Mann, *Texts*, I, 75 ff., 83 ff., 109 ff., 147 ff., 204, 237; Assaf in *Tarbiz*, I, Pt. 2, 61 f.; ibid., XI, 146 ff.

[21] Maimonides, *Commentary* on M. Abot, IV, 5. Maimonides objected with equal vehemence to scholars deriving their main livelihood from the exilarchic chest. In dissuading his favorite pupil, Joseph ibn ʿAḳnin, from accepting the presidency of an academy in Bagdad, he emphasized the fact that, with the increase of his educational burdens, Joseph would see himself forced to reduce his mercantile activities. "I should not advise you," he added, "to accept anything from them, for I prefer one dirhem

which you may earn from weaving, tailoring or carpentry to whatever you may obtain through the authorization by the exilarch." Recorded by Abraham Maimonides in his *Birkat Abraham* (Responsa), *Zikronot*, no. 2; and S. Poznanski in *Babylonische Geonim*, pp. 30 f., 56 ff.

[22] Neubauer, *Chronicles*, II, 87 f.; *Teshubot ha-geonim*, ed. Lyck, no. 56. For the chronology of the individual geonim, cf. the list compiled by S. Assaf in *Encycl. Jud.*, VII (1931), 271 ff. and the literature cited therein. Cf. also Simon Eppenstein, "Beiträge zur Geschichte und Literatur im gaonäischen Zeitalter," *MGWJ*, LII–LVII (1908–13).

Perhaps the greatest achievement of the academies, the geonic responsa, can be mentioned here only in passing. For a fuller discussion, cf. Baron, *History*, III, 81 n. 8 and the literature cited there. Cf. also below, n. 33, and for Muslim parallels, Tyan, *Organisation judiciaire*, I, 323 ff. Of special interest, from the organizational point of view, are the activities aiming at the unification of Jewish liturgy by the compilation of standard prayer books. We know of at least four such attempts: by Naṭronai, Zemaḥ, 'Amram (or rather his assistant Zemaḥ) and Saadia. Saadia's prayer book, recently published in Jerusalem, will undoubtedly shed much new light on this important phase of Jewish communal control.

The orderliness of correspondence depended, of course, on the keeping of regular records. That the archives, however, could not always be maintained in the desired state of effectiveness may be seen from the occasional complaints of the geonim that they were unable to check their own or their predecessors' replies. Cf. e. g. *Sha'are ṣedeḳ*, IV, 8, 6, fol. 94b.

It may also be mentioned that, while it became a rule for priests coming from another locality to prove their genealogical claim (cf. e. g., Mann's *Egypt*, I, 172; II, 205 f.), 'Amram and Naṭronai insisted, for the purposes of communal peace, that even an unlearned priest should be first called to the Torah in preference to a "prince in Israel" (quoted by Jacob b. Asher in his *Ṭur*, O. Ḥ. 135). Cf. however, the scathing remarks allegedly addressed to the overbearing priests of Ifrikiya by Hai Gaon, published by B. M. Lewin in *Ginze Ḳedem*, IV (1930), 51–56.

[23] Cf. M. Auerbach's "Der Streit zwischen Saadja Gaon und dem Exilarchen Dawid ben Sakkai," *Jüdische Studien Joseph Wohlgemuth ... gewidmet*, pp. 1–30, where the blame is more equitably distributed between the two protagonists than in the previous literature, which was much more partial to Saadia.

[24] Ginzberg, *Genizah Studies*, II, 158; Mann, *Texts*, I, 90, 105, 148 ff.

[25] Assaf in *Tarbiz*, I; Mann, *Texts*, I, 230 ff., 394 f. Cf. also below, n. 30. It must be borne in mind, however, that Maimonides' high estimate of the exilarchic office may in part have been influenced by his active dislike of Samuel b. 'Ali, for which cf. now also the Hebrew transl. of his "Responsum to His Disciple Joseph ha-Ma'arabi," ed. by A. H. Freimann in the *Lewin Jubilee Volume*, pp. 27–41.

[26] Jacob b. Elijah's *Letter*, ed. by Joseph Kobak, *Jeshurun*, VI (1868), 29 (cf. Mann's remarks in *REJ*, LXXXII, 1926, 374, and the discussion between A. Z. Schwarz and Mann thereon in *Alim*, I, 1934–35, pp. 37, 75–77); Mann, "The Exilarchic Office in Babylonia and its Ramifications at the End of the Geonic Period" (Hebrew), *Livre d'hommage . . . Poznanski*, pp. 18–32; his *Texts*, I, passim; Goode in *JQR*, XXXI, 168; Fischel, *Jews in . . . Mediaeval Islam*, pp. 126 ff.; Adler, *Jewish Travelers*, p. 86.

[27] Elkan N. Adler, "The Installation of the Egyptian Nagid," *JQR*, O. S. IX (1896–97), 717 ff.

[28] Ginzberg, *Geonica*, II, 86 ff. and, more fully, in B. M. Lewin's ed. in *Ginze Kedem*, II (1923), 33 ff.

[29] Abraham ben Nathan ha-Yarḥi, *Sefer ha-Manhig* (On Jewish Laws and Customs), ed. by J. M. Goldberg, fol. 32ab, no. 58; *The Chronicle of Ahimaaz of Oria*, ed. by Marcus Salzmann, pp. 21 (text), 97 (transl.). For a recent discussion of the Mar Uḳba episode and the conflicting testimony of Nathan and Sherira thereon, cf. Mann's Hebrew essay "Varia on the Gaonic Period," *Tarbiz*, V (1933–34), 148 ff. A good deal of information concerning these provincial officers during the thirteenth century is now available in Abraham Maimuni's *Responsa*, ed. by A. H. Freimann and S. D. Goitein. Cf. also Chap. V, n. 24.

[30] Rosanes, op. cit., I, 123 ff.; IV, 491 ff. (with reference to the *Chronicle* of Joseph Sambari); Mann, *Egypt*, I, 256 f.; Ibn abi Zimra, *Responsa*, II, no. 622. The office of *nagid* in the Yemen, hitherto known only from a somewhat cryptic statement of Benjamin of Tudela (*Travels*, ed. by Adler, p. 47) is now fully attested by a Rainer papyrus containing a letter addressed by the Jewish leaders of Aden (including Ḥalfon, the *Nagid*) to Egypt in 1153 and published by E. Strauss in *Zion*, IV (1938–39), 217–31. Cf. also J. L. Fishman, "The Institution of *Nagid* in Israel" (Hebrew), *Ha-Tor*, VII (1924), nos. 6, 8, 11–17; and S. Assaf, "Contributions to the

Lives of the *Negidim* Jonathan and Isaac Sholal" (Hebrew), *Zion*, II (1936–37), 121–24 (referring to two of the last Egyptian princes). D. Neustadt in "Some Problems concerning the *Negidut* in Egypt during the Middle Ages" (Hebrew), ibid., IV (1938–39), 126–49, has subjected the sources concerning the rise of that institution to renewed close scrutiny and shown the serious contradictions inherent in the accepted interpretation. Thus far his arguments are purely negative. Their validity will be tested only by his forthcoming attempts at positive reconstruction which will show whether a new theory might solve more difficulties than does the regnant hypothesis.

The *negidim* did not wholly repudiate the authority of the exilarch. Abraham Maimonides, himself a *nagid*, admitted that the contemporary exilarchs, like the heads of the Palestinian academies, were entitled to the privileges of biblical or talmudic princes (*nesiim*). Cf. his *Responsa*, nos. 4–5; *Ḳobeṣ teshubot ha-Rambam*, ed. by Lichtenberg, I, no. 250. In periods of weakness in the Egyptian leadership (about 1161) we find the energetic exilarch, Daniel b. Ḥisdai, authorizing Nethaneel ha-Levi "in the presence of our chiefs and patricians with the people assenting" to serve as the head of the school in Fustat. As such he is to officiate as "the High Court for all the cities of Egypt and all the provinces, he is to teach, judge and appoint courts in every district, and all the scholars, chiefs and the rest of the holy nation are to listen to him, obey his commands and assist him in truth and rectitude" (Assaf in *Tarbiz*, I, Pt. 3, pp. 68 f.). But such direct action was quite exceptional and for the most part, during the last two centuries of its existence, exilarchic supremacy appears to have been purely nominal.

This is possibly also the meaning of the phrase בית דין הקבוע מפי נשיאנו ראש גלויותינו in the aforementioned letter from Aden in 1153. Although addressing themselves principally to the Egyptian leaders, the Yemenite Jews neither severed their connections with Bagdad, nor foreswore their allegiance to the exilarchic family. Even a few decades later we find some of the most ardent admirers of Maimonides, the unofficial leader of Egyptian Jewry, address their inquiries on the troublesome problems of resurrection to both the sage of Fustat and his antagonist, Samuel b. 'Ali in Bagdad, thereby creating a somewhat embarrassing situation for Maimonides and giving him the final stimulus for the composition of his renowned treatise on resurrection. Cf. A. Harkavy, "Fragment einer

Apologie des Maimonidischen מאמר תחית המתים," *Zeitschrift für hebr. Bibliographie*, II (1897), 125–28, 181–88; Joshua Finkel, "Maimonides' Treatise on Resurrection" in S. W. Baron (ed.), *Essays on Maimonides*, pp. 116 ff. Cf. also the "Letters of a Babylonian Gaon to the Yemen" (Hebrew), ed. by B. M. Lewin in *Ginze Ḳedem*, III (1925), 14–23. It is quite possible that the communities in Yemen continued to pay lip service to exilarchic hegemony, as in fact did the Egyptian Jews themselves (see the document cited above, n. 27), while enjoying to all intents and purposes a fully autonomous leadership of their own.

[31] Justinian's *Novella* 146. The differences in custom come clearly to the fore in the recently recovered fragments of the *Sefer ha-Ma'asim*, the Palestinian provenance of which has unjustifiably been doubted by some scholars. It really seems to have been but "a direct continuation of the Palestinian Talmud and was written there in the Palestinian style." Cf. Saul Liebermann in *Ginze Ḳedem*, V (1934), 177 ff.; Mann in *Tarbiz*, V, 300 f. These distinctions were so manifold and persistent that a large collection of "Differences in Customs between the Jews of Palestine and of Babylonia" was compiled in the geonic period and attained a fairly extensive circulation. First published by Joel Müller (Vienna, 1878), this treatise has been republished with notes by B. M. Lewin in *Sinai*, I–II (1937–39). Cf. also Mordecai Margulies's edition of the *Ḥilluḳim she-ben anshe mizraḥ u-bene Ereṣ Israel* (The Differences Between Babylonian and Palestinian Jews).

[32] Ginzberg, *Geonica*, II, 49 ff.; Ḥayyim Y. Bornstein, "The Controversy between Saadia Gaon and Ben-Meir" (Hebrew), *Sefer ha-Yobel* (Jubilee Volume in honor of) *Nahum Sokolow*, pp. 19–189; Henry Malter, *Saadia Gaon; His Life and Works*, pp. 69 ff., 351 ff., 409 ff.; Mann, *Egypt* I, 50 ff.; idem, *Texts*, I, 232; idem in *Tarbiz*, V, 157 ff., 273 ff. Saadia retorted to Ben-Meir's accusation by claiming descent from Shela, the third son of Judah. Tradition had it that among his ancestors also was Ḥanina b. Dosa. But those legendary claims may well have been fabricated in order to take the edge off Ben-Meir's attack. Cf. Malter, op. cit., pp. 31, 107, n. 230.

[33] Jacob Mann has furnished reasonable grounds for the dearth of extant inquiries addressed to the Palestinian academies. Cf. his note in *Tarbiz*, V, 289. Apart from a few weak links in his argument, however, he has altogether failed to explain the extreme paucity of quotations from such

responsa in the later rabbinic letters as contrasted with their innumerable references to decisions by Babylonian geonim.

[34] Noble descent undoubtedly carried great weight in academy circles, too. Cf. M. Ḳid. IV, 5. In the second century the patrician, R. Eleazar b. Azariah, was given precedence over the great R. Akiba. A century later the young Davidian, R. Huna, was elected head of Sura against several distinguished candidates. Sherira, having stressed this point, boasts of his own Davidic descent from a line better than Bustanai's (*Epistle*, ed. by Lewin, pp. 92 f.). Nevertheless, David b. Zakkai, after a period of hesitation, appointed Saadia, a complete outsider of undistinguished parentage, to the supreme office in Sura. To appreciate this move fully, one must bear in mind the general aversion of the population of the Caliphate to the appointment of non-native chiefs. Cf. Tyan, *Organisation judiciaire*, I, 249 f. A few decades later, Samuel b. Ḥofni, of priestly, non-Davidic lineage, enjoyed full equality with Sherira's son, Hai. Cf. George Margoliouth, "Some British Museum Genizah Texts," *JQR*, O. S. XIV (1901–2), 308 f. Heredity also played a rôle in Babylonia and more in Palestine. Most Babylonian geonim belonged to some six or seven families, but only Hai immediately succeeded his father. It took Naḥshon b. Zadok 53 years, and Dosa b. Saadia, aged nine at his father's death, fully 71 years before they reached the supreme position in the academy. In Palestine, on the other hand, direct hereditary succession was much more frequent. Cf. Assaf, *Encycl. Jud.*, VII, 274, 280.

[35] Elijah Capsali, *Debe Eliyahu*, in the excerpts ed. by Moses Lattes, pp. 8 f. New light upon the activities of the first Turkish *ḥakam bashi* has been thrown by S. Assaf's recent edition, from a Ms. Sassoon, of "Responsa and Letters by Moses Capsali" (Hebrew), *Sinai*, III, Pt. 1 (1939), 149–58.

[36] Ḥayyim Benveniste, *Keneset ha-gedolah*, *Eben ha-'ezer*, 28, fol. 59d–60a. Although the origin of this regulation went back to the talmudic requirement that the "bridegroom's benediction" be recited in the presence of ten men (Ket. 8b), the leading medieval jurists had declared valid marriages performed without the benediction, demanding only that it be recited later. In the sparsely populated Jewish communities of Germany, rabbis, including Isserlein, were ready to waive the requirement altogether where ten men were not available. Only Karo, perhaps under the influence of the Turkish custom, following Capsali's enactment (which

he fails to mention, however), advised prospective bridegrooms to abstain from marrying until they might secure the required quorum. Cf. Maimonides' *Mishneh Torah*, Ishshut, X, 5–6, and Jacob b. Asher's *Ṭur Eben ha-'ezer*, 62, as well as the commentaries thereon. Abraham Maimuni well summarized the regnant opinion when he decided that only the presence of two witnesses is essential "for the sake of testimony. But the presence of all those attending a wedding is neither necessary nor harmful; it is neither an obligation nor a disadvantage." Cf. his *Responsa*, no. 92.

A similar ordinance had been enacted in thirteenth-century Spain, but Ibn Adret had doubts as to its legality (cf. his *Responsa*, I, 1206). Indeed, Capsali was sharply attacked on this, as well as on other scores, by the Italian rabbi, Joseph Colon (cf. his *Responsa*, Root 73). Nevertheless, Colon's Italian countrymen, confronted by similar problems arising from the mass migrations of the sixteenth century, adopted precisely the same ordinance (they mentioned only Ibn Adret) in their synodal resolutions at Ferrara in 1554. Cf. also Louis Finkelstein's *Jewish Self-Government in the Middle Ages*, pp. 75, 302, 305 ff., 364. The communities of Candia, as well as the distinguished rabbis of Salonica passed analogous measures in 1440, 1504 and 1567. Cf. David Solomon Sassoon, *Ohel Dawid, Descriptive Catalogue of the Hebrew and Samaritan Manuscripts in the Sassoon Library, London*, I, 353; Abraham Danon, "La communauté juive de Salonique au XVIe siècle," *REJ*, XLI (1900), 256 f. It was placed ahead of all other regulations in the famous collection of ordinances adopted by the "Castilian" community in Fez and published by Abraham Ankava in his *Kerem ḥemer* (A Juridical Collection), II, 2 ff. For another recension of these ordinances, cf. Ms. Sassoon, no. 715 in Sassoon's *Catalogue*, I, 357 ff.

[37] Elijah Mizraḥi, *Responsa*, no. 15. The life and works of this distinguished leader of Turkish Jewry have been the subject of a recent Hebrew biographical sketch by A. Ovadiah in *Sinai*, III (1939–40).

[38] Four *bérats* in favor of central or provincial chief rabbis are given in French translation in Galanté's *Documents*, pp. 36 ff. Another, confirming, for the first time, the election of Moses Perera (styled Mussa Effendi) as *ḥakam-bashi* of Sarajevo in 1840, has been translated into German by Moritz Levy, op. cit., pp. 67 ff. Still another, of 1842, confirming the election of Abraham Ḥayyim Gagin as chief rabbi of Jerusalem, may be found in Hebrew translation in A. M. Luncz's Hebrew essay on "The

Ḥakam-bashi in Turkey," *Yerushalayim*, IV (1892), 186–217. The six texts reveal both characteristic similarities and divergences. The failure of Gagin's three successors to secure an imperial confirmation was very likely due to the exorbitant "gift" of some 30,000 piastres paid by this first *ḥakam-bashi* of Jerusalem after Palestine's return to direct Turkish suzerainty. The actual submission of the Jews to their regional chief rabbis is well illustrated by the resolution adopted in 1804 by the members (*yeḥidim*) of the community of Philippopolis pledging unswerving obedience to the chief rabbi of Adrianople "in both secular and religious matters." Cf. the text republished by Rosanes, op. cit., V, 389 ff., containing also a brief sketch of the general history of the chief rabbinate of Adrianople.

Although transcending the chronological limits set for the present study, the above documents have been cited here, because of the significant light they shed also on the earlier history of the Turkish chief-rabbinate. For the same reason, a brief sketch of more recent developments and an analysis of the noteworthy constitutional reform of 1864, sponsored by the progressive anti-rabbinical party, may also usefully be appended to this note. The new constitution, issued as an imperial decree of April 1, 1864 (available in French translation by Galanté, op. cit., pp. 10 ff., and in David Yellin's Hebrew rendering in Luncz's aforementioned essay), was soon emulated by many local statutes throughout the Empire. It prescribed that the community of Constantinople be governed by a general assembly of representatives, by a lay executive council, an ecclesiastical council and the *ḥakam-bashi*. The general assembly, consisting of 60 lay and 20 rabbinical members, was to be elected, according to an ordinance of 1914, for a period of ten years, with biennial elections of one-fifth of its lay membership. The general electorate, whose qualifications are not legally specified here, was to vote by secret ballot in the various quarters of the city. It could choose, however, only from a list of candidates previously approved by the rabbi and notables of the quarter. The 60 lay members elected were to co-opt 20 rabbinical colleagues. All eighty subsequently were to elect, for a two-year term, the executive council of nine lay members in charge of the general, and especially the financial, affairs of the community. The ecclesiastical council, likewise to be elected by the general assembly, was to consist of seven permanent members and four annual associates. The former could be deposed only if impeached and convicted by a joint committee of the two councils presided over by the chief rabbi. The prerogatives of the ecclesiastical council are vaguely described by injunctions such as that the council must not allow preachers "to excite the public to act contrary to the opinions and wishes of the government; it must not permit rabbis to interfere with such Jewish affairs as are outside of their range of activity; it must not prevent the publication of books nor the cultivation of arts and sciences among their people, unless they be prejudicial to the government, to the people or to religion" (Art. 23).

For the election of a *ḥakam-bashi*, the general assembly was to be augmented by 40 representatives of the large provincial communities of Adrianople, Brussa, Smyrna, Salonica, Bagdad, Cairo, Alexandria and Jerusalem. The interests of the capital, in which the newly elected officer was to serve also as provincial chief rabbi, were safeguarded by its majority of two-thirds. The assembly, moreover, although allowed to vote secretly, was restricted in its choice to a list of five candidates previously agreed upon by the lay and ecclesiastical councils of Constantinople. The necessary qualifications of each candidate are described as follows:

> The chief rabbi is the head of the entire Jewish nation inhabiting the Ottoman Empire; it is he who will execute the orders of the imperial government. Consequently, he ought to enjoy confidence and trust on the part of both the government and the people, be endowed with good qualities, be a Turkish subject and a descendant of parents and grandparents who were Turkish subjects. He ought to have irreproachable antecedents, have served with loyalty and abnegation in his previous functions and beversed in administrative and religious affairs. He must not be less than thirty nor more than seventy years of age (Art. 1).

In the face of this high-sounding introduction, the actual prerogatives of the office appear rather vague. The legislator does not conceal his intent to delimit the powers of the rabbinic organs in favor of the lay council, whose rights alone are clearly and unequivocally defined. An energetic person in the chief rabbi's office, supported by a sympathetic government, still could make extensive use of the broad powers vested in him by virtue of the specific decrees of confirmation. But on the whole, the *ḥakam-bashi* was now reduced from a supposedly authoritarian leader of all Ottoman Jewry to a chief ecclesiastical officer of the metropolis, functioning side by side with three independent communal bodies. The post-war diminution of Turkish territory, the transfer of the capital to Angora, the final abolition of the caliphate, the totalitarian and nationalist policies of the Kemalist government and its disregard of the internationally guaranteed minority rights of the Jews, have robbed the chief rabbi of the last vestiges of his imperial authority.

39 Benjamin's *Itinerary*, transl. by Adler, p. 39; R. Gottheil, "An Eleventh-Century Document," *JQR*, O. S. XIX (1906–7), 500, 527; Maimonides, *Commentary* on M. Bek. IV, 4; idem, *Responsa*, ed. by Freimann, no. 13; Abraham Maimuni *Responsa*, no. 4 (Lichtenberg's *Ḳobeṣ*, I, no. 250); Mann, *Egypt*, I, 268 ff., 277 ff.; idem, *Texts*, I, 215, 258 ff. According to Mez, op. cit., pp. 78 f., 132 ff. (*Islamic Culture*, II, 441 ff.; III, 571 ff.) the mania for titles spread in Islam from about the tenth century on. About that time we also find increasing evidence of its contagious effects among the Jews. Cf. also Mayer in *Magnes Anniversary Book*, p. 166.

40 *Teshubot ha-geonim*, ed. by Harkavy, no. 180; Lewin, *Otzar*, IV, 24; Neubauer, *Chronicles*, II, 85 f.; Fischel, *Jews in Mediaeval Islam*, p. 128. The paucity of pertinent Jewish sources for the first two centuries of Muslim rule makes it impossible to trace the origin of the appointment of individual judges by exilarchs and geonim and the extent to which this evolution paralleled that under Islam, for which cf. Tyan's *Organisation judiciaire*, I, 134 f., 169 f.

41 Bertinoro, *Epistles*, in Abraham Kahana's *Sifrut ha-historia* (Jewish Historical literature), II, 42; Isidore Epstein, *Responsa of Rabbi Simon b. Zemaḥ Duran*, pp. 60 f. For a similar official in Tunis in 1774, cf. below, Chap. XIII, n. 29.

42 *Sha'are ṣedeḳ*, IV, 7, 4, fol. 84b; *Teshubot ha-geonim*, ed. by Harkavy, no. 233; Mann in *JQR*, X, 340 ff., 363 f.; idem, *Texts*, I, 451 f.; Judah b. Barzilai's *Sefer ha-Sheṭarot*, pp. 7 f., 131. The conflict between the eastern and western communal administration is well illustrated in the responsa of Isaac b. Sheshet Profet and Simon b. Zemaḥ Duran, Spanish rabbis who, after 1391, took over the management of the Algerian communities. Cf. the vivid description of the ensuing clashes in Epstein, op. cit. Somewhat analogous were the differences between Muslim Andalusia and the eastern caliphates. While the doctrine that, in the absence of an *imam*, the people have the right to choose their own *cadi* was fairly universal, it was in Spain alone that the judges, whose tenure of office was generally

rather short, were early assisted by collegiate bodies of laymen. Cf. Tyan, *Organisation judiciaire*, I, 222, 339 ff., 461 ff.

[43] Simon b. Zemaḥ Duran, *Sefer ha-Tashbeṣ*, III, 45; Rosanes, op. cit., II, 17; David b. Ḥayyim ha-Kohen, *Responsa*, XIII, with reference to Yeb. 13b–14a; Emmanuel, *Israélites de Salonique*, I, 72. The various complicated methods of harmonization, varying with each changing situation or personal bias, are well illustrated by the authorities cited in a responsum of Mordecai Bassano (about 1700) published by S. W. Baron in his Hebrew essay on "A Communal Conflict in Verona," *Sefer ha-Yobel . . . Shemuel Krauss* (Samuel Krauss Jubilee Volume), pp. 217–54. Cf. also Chap. X, n. 15.

NOTES TO CHAPTER VII

EUROPEAN CORPORATION

[1] Vogelstein and Rieger, *Rom*, I, 220.

[2] Joseph Jacobs, *Jews in Angevin England*, p. 14; Asher b. Yeḥiel, *Halakot* (Juristic Commentary) on B. B. 8a. The feeling of superiority of the Jews arriving from Muslim regions even in the Christian parts of Spain is well illustrated by numerous poems of Moses ibn Ezra and others. Cf. Salo W. Baron, "Yehudah Halevi: An Answer to a Historic Challenge," *Jewish Social Studies*, III (1941), 250 f.

[3] Solomon ibn Adret, *Responsa*, I, 769; Finkelstein, *Jewish Self-Government*, pp. 41 f., 153 ff. Finkelstein seems to overstress decidedly the difference of opinion between Gershom and Jacob Tam as to the full authority of the individual community, Gershom comparing it with the ancient Sanhedrin, while Tam wished to reserve full authority for an outstanding leader in each generation. Cf. pp. 50 ff., and D. M. Shohet in his *Jewish Court in the Middle Ages*, pp. 130 ff. For the varying degrees of the prohibition to appeal to Gentile courts, cf. the sources cited by S. Assaf in his *Bate ha-din*, pp. 11 ff. A few illustrations will be given below.

In considering rabbinic insistence upon a Jewish judiciary, one should not wholly discount the vested interests of lay and rabbinic courts in fees and fines. The Jews were not always able to prevent rapacious governments from appropriating all or part of the fines imposed by Jewish judges, but they certainly did not wish to renounce them on principle. Cf., however, Asher b. Yeḥiel's *Responsa*, XXI, 9.

4 Maimonides, *Ḳobeṣ*, I, no. 140, fol. 26c; Ibn Adret, *Responsa*, cited by Karo on *Ṭur*, Ḥ. M. 26 end. It appears that, although "France" evidently was included by Maimonides in his generalization concerning "all the Jews in Christian countries," he laid special stress upon the Byzantine suppression of Jewish civil jurisdiction. "Roumania" is actually mentioned at the end of the epistle. There, indeed, the Jews enjoyed but limited judicial autonomy, and under Manuel Comnenus had been placed entirely under the authority of the ordinary courts. Cf. Joshua Starr, *The Jews in the Byzantine Empire, 641–1204*, pp. 222 f. no. 172; 241, no. 194. Cf. also below, n. 17.

5 Rashi, *Commentary* on Giṭ. 9b; Karo on *Ṭur*, Ḥ. M. 369, quoting Naḥmanides and Meir Abulafia as opposed to Maimonides and Asheri. There is great need of fuller investigation of medieval views concerning the "law of the kingdom." A few general remarks will be found in Leopold Löw's essay in his *Gesammelte Schriften*, III, 347–58; Shohet, op. cit., pp. 105 ff.; A. N. Z. Roth, "The Law of the Kingdom is Law" (Hebrew), *Ha-Soker*, V (1937–38), 110–26 (with notes by D. S. Löwinger).

6 The influence of the Church upon the status of European Jewry has recently been stressed, perhaps with a somewhat exaggerated emphasis, by James Parkes in his "Christian Influence on the Status of the Jews in Europe," *Historia Judaica*, I (1938), 31–38. This is also the main theme of the same author's major series on the *History of Anti-Semitism* of which there have appeared two volumes, *The Conflict of the Church and the Synagogue* and *The Jew in the Medieval Community*. Further light on the subject may be expected from the third volume, to be devoted entirely to the relations between the Catholic Church and the Jews during the European Middle Ages.

7 Emmanuel Rodocanachi, *Le Saint-Siège et les Juifs*, pp. 139 f., 156 f., 201 ff.; Vogelstein and Rieger, *Rom*, I, 222, 229 f., 263, 316; II, 33 f.; Solomon Grayzel, *The Church and the Jews in the XIIIth Century*, nos. 5, 118. For the greeting with the scroll Gregory XIV and his successors substituted an obligation of the community lavishly to adorn Titus' Arch (in commemoration of the fall of Jerusalem) and the Coliseum through which the papal procession passed.

[8] Gregory's *Epistles*, I, 34; II, 6; VIII, 25; IX, 38, 195, in *Monumenta Germaniae Historica, Epistolae*, I, II; Nathan b. Yeḥiel, *'Aruk*, concluding poem, ed. by Alexander Kohut, VIII, 301; Vogelstein and Rieger, *Rom*, I, 135, 231, 286; Solomon Katz, "Pope Gregory the Great and the Jews," *JQR*, XXIV (1933–34), 121 ff.

[9] Grayzel, op. cit., nos. 50, 123; Amador de los Rios, *Historia social, politica y religiosa de los Judios de España y Portugal*, II, 637 f.; Fritz Baer, *Die Juden im christlichen Spanien*, I, Pt. 1, no. 513; Pt. 2, no. 283; Bartolomeo and Giuseppe Lagumina, *Codice diplomatico dei Giudei di Sicilia*, II, Pt. 1, no. 533; Majer Balaban, *Zabytki historyczne Żydów w Polsce* (Historical Remains of the Jews in Poland), pp. 54 ff.; Armand Mossé, *Histoire des Juifs d'Avignon et du comtat Venaissin*, pp. 107 ff. The frequency of the conversion of synagogues into churches is illustrated by the inclusion in the Sacramentary of the Roman Church of a special "oration and prayer in dedication of this place, where there had previously been a synagogue." Cited from *Codex Assemani* by Parkes in his *Conflict*, p. 401. Cf. also M. Schorr, *Żydzi w Przemyślu* (Jews in Przemyśl to the End of the Eighteenth Century), pp. 138 ff., giving the text of King Władysław IV's decree of 1638 concerning the erection of new synagogues; and Ben Zion Katz, *Le-Ḳorot ha-Yehudim* (Excerpts to the History of the Jews in Russia, Poland and Lithuania in the 16th and 17th Cent.), p. 8, illustrating through two rabbinic responsa the difficulties besetting the Polish Jews because of this Canonical prohibition. That the suppression of synagogues was tantamount to withdrawal of toleration from Jews, was clear to the lawmakers. Yet the ducal decree of 1622 outlawing synagogues throughout Hannover was coupled with the injunction that the Jews, still considered as such, should regularly attend Church services under the penalty of one thaler per person for failure to comply. In 1689 preachers were ordered to invite the Jews once a year and to enlighten them on the tenets of the Christian faith. Cf. Hildebrand Bodemeyer, *Die Juden*, p. 33.

[10] Gedaliah ibn Yaḥya, *Shalshelet ha-ḳabbalah* (Chronicle), ed. Amsterdam, 1697, fol. 94ab; Nicholas Eymeric, *Directorium inquisitorum*, ed. Venice, 1607, fol. 353b.

[11] A. Bertolotti, "Les Juifs à Rome aux XVIe, XVIIe et XVIIIe siècles," *REJ*, II (1881), 287; Emanuel Hecht, "Kinderraub," *MGWJ*, X (1861), 399 f.; Vogelstein and Rieger, *Rom*, II, 240, 253; Baer, *Spanien*, I, Pt. 2,

pp. 484 ff.; Cecil Roth, "Forced Baptisms in Italy," *JQR*, XXVII (1936–37), 117–36.

[12] Lagumina, *Codice*, II, Pt. 1, no. 558; A. Berliner, *Geschichte der Juden in Rom*, II, 92 ff., 106 ff.; M. Mortara, "Die Censur hebräischer Bücher in Italien und der *Canon purificationis*," *Hebräische Bibliographie*, V (1862), 75; A. Z. Schwarz, "Letters Concerning the Confiscation of Books in 1553" (Hebrew), *Alim*, II (1935–36), 49–52; and, in general, William Popper, *The Censorship of Hebrew Books*; N. Porges, "Censorship," *Jewish Encyclopedia*, III, 642–50. Cf. also Chap. XI, n. 48; XIII, nn. 29–31.

[13] J. D. Mansi, *Sacrorum conciliorum nova et amplissima collectio*, II, 8 ff. (Elvira, Canons 16, 49–50, 78); XIX, 788 (Cuyacense, 1050, Can. 6: *ut . . . cum Judaeis non habitent, nec cibum cum eis sumant*); XXII, 231 (III Lateran C. 26); XXIII, 1176 ff. (Breslau C. 12); Baer, *Spanien*, I, Pt. 2, No. 8; Aronius, *Regesten*, nos. 310, 724; Vogelstein and Rieger, *Rom*, II, 191 f.; Antonio Ciscato, *Gli Ebrei in Padova (1300–1800)*, pp. 247 ff.; A. Pesaro, *Memorie storiche sulla communità israelitica ferrarese*, pp. 39 ff.

[14] Vogelstein and Rieger, *Rom*, I, 319, 493.

[15] The question of special Jewish taxation in the Byzantine Empire is answered affirmatively by F. Dölger in "Die Frage der Judensteuer in Byzanz," *Vierteljahrsschrift für Sozial und Wirtschaftsgeschichte*, XXVI (1933), 1–24 and, to a certain extent, by M. A. Andréadés in "Les Juifs et le fisc dans l'empire byzantin," *Mélanges Charles Diehl*, I, 7–29; and in the negative by Starr, *Byzantine Empire*, pp. 11 ff.

[16] Justinian's *Codex* I, 5, 21; 9, 2, 8–9; *Nov.* 37, 8; 45; 131, 14; 146; Juster, op. cit., I, 250 f.; II, 103 ff.

[17] Parkes, *Conflict*, pp. 232, 246 ff.; S. Krauss, *Studien zur byzantinisch-jüdischen Geschichte*, pp. 55 ff., 63, 87 ff., 94; Starr, *Byzantine Empire*, pp. 1 ff., 18 ff., 37 ff., and the sources cited therein; *Teshubot ha-geonim*, ed. by Harkavy, no. 255. Cf. also above, nn. 4, 9.

[18] R. Straus, *Die Juden im Königreich Sizilien unter Normannen und Staufen*, pp. 20 nn. 23, 24, 45, 54, 59; O. Senigaglia, "La condizione giuridica degli Ebrei in Sicilia," *Rivista italiana per le scienze giuridiche*, XLI (1906), 75–102. Cf. below, Chap. VIII, n. 10.

[19] Cf. especially Lagumina, *Codice*, II, Pt. 1, nos. 534, 537, 620; Nicola Ferorelli, *Gli Ebrei nell' Italia meridionale dell'età romana al secolo XVIII*, pp. 100 f., 173 ff., 181 f. The designation and treatment of the Jews as *cives* was not altogether exceptional; it occurred also in the southern

French cities of Arles and Marseilles. Cf. P. Hildenfinger, "Documents relatifs aux Juifs d'Arles," *REJ*, XLI (1900), 72 n. 5; Adolphe Crémieux, "Les Juifs de Marseille au moyen age," ibid., XLVI (1903), 3 ff. Cf. also Baron, *History*, III, 101 n. 10, 105 n. 14, and below, n. 56.

[20] Baer, *Spanien*, I, Pt. 2, no. 167.

[21] Baer, *Studien zur Geschichte der Juden im Königreich Aragonien*, p. 40 n. 106; *Ordenaçoens do Senhor Rey D. Affonso V* (a collection of laws dating from the reign of Affonso II to that of Duarte, 1211–1438), II, 74, 14, pp. 445 ff.; Baer, *Spanien*, I, Pt. 1, nos. 198 (1332), 224a (after 1346), 25 Art. 16, 35 (1354), 432 (1391); Pt. 2, nos. 97 (1291), 275 Art. 16 (1412), 318 Art. 119 (1465); Grayzel, op. cit., no. 17. The Church, nevertheless, did not remain empty-handed. Apart from numerous transfers of Jews or Jewish revenue to territorial lords, including bishops, we find, for instance, the record of a decree issued in 1302 by Ferdinand IV of Castile, enjoining the Jews of the bishopric of Segovia to pay 30 dineros annually to the bishop and chapter of that city "in commemoration" of the Jewish part in the crucifixion of Jesus. Although the authenticity of this motivation is subject to doubt, the payment of this tax over a period of 90 years (1321–1412) is attested by records preserved in the cathedral of Segovia. Cf. Baer, *Spanien*, I, Pt. 2, no. 116.

[22] David Kaufmann, "Jewish Informers in the Middle Ages," *JQR*, O. S. VIII (1895–96), 217–38; supplemented by S. J. Halberstam, ibid., pp. 527 f.; Baer, *Spanien*, I, Pt. 1, nos. 307, 317; Pt. 2, no. 205, 11; *Ordenaçoens . . .Affonso*, II, 71 pp. 432 f.; 81, 3–4, pp. 476 ff., also cited by M. Kayserling, in his *Geschichte der Juden in Portugal*, p. 16. For certain legal restrictions of the general principle, however, cf. *Ordenaçoens*, II, 77, pp. 457 ff.; 82, pp. 491 ff.; 84, pp. 497 ff.; 89, pp. 507 ff.; 96–98, pp. 521 ff. Cf. also Isidore Epstein, *The "Responsa" of Rabbi Solomon ben Adreth of Barcelona (1235–1310) as a Source of the History of Spain.*

[23] *Ordenaçoens . . . Affonso*, II, 90, pp. 508 f.; Kayserling l. c.; *Las Siete Partidas*, VII, 24, 5 (ed. Madrid, 1807, III, 671 f.) and in the English transl. by E. H. Lindo in his *History of the Jews of Spain and Portugal*, pp. 99 f.; Baer, *Spanien*, I, Pt. 1, nos. 91 Art. 5 (1239, demands also the release, under bail, of Jewish prisoners from Friday afternoon to Monday morning), 147 (beginning of 14th cent.), 175 Art. 1, 10 (1320), 249 (1352), p. 1042 Art. 8; Pt. 2, nos. 58 (*Fuero de Ledesma*, Art. 393), 60 (*Fueros de Castile*, Art. 220 prescribing various fines for the violation of the Sabbath

by the Jews), 61 (*Fuero real*, IV, 2, 17), 63 (*Siete Partidas*), 21 (Martinez, 1378), 227 (1380), 235 (1386), 247 (Martinez, 1390).

[24] Lagumina, *Codice*, I, no. 15; Fidel Fita and Gabriel Llabres, "Privilegios de los Hebreos mallorquines en el Códice Pueyo," *Boletín de la Real Academia de la Historia*, XXXVI (1900), 132 f. no. 24, 280 ff. nos. 60–61; Isaac b. Sheshet, *Responsa*, I, 52, 107; Baer, *Studien*, pp. 62, 88 ff.; idem, *Spanien*, I, Pt. 1, nos. 317 (1377), 367 (1384); Pt. 2, nos. 227 (1380), 275 Art. 7 (1412), 330 (1476). The translation given here from the latter decree is a variation of Lindo's translation, op. cit., p. 198. Cf. also Epstein's *Adreth*, pp. 46 ff. and his *Duran*, pp. 42 f., 65. Of special interest is the petition of some south Italian Jews for the right to appeal to the ordinary Christian courts in lieu of the superior tribunals in Naples, and that they also be allowed, if they felt "aggrieved in any cause," to revert to Jewish judges even while a case was pending in the Christian court. This request was granted by Ferdinand in 1481. Cf. Ferorelli, *Italia meridionale*, pp. 180 f.

[25] Baer, *Studien*, pp. 41, 75 ff. (p. 80 n. 24: excerpt from *Privil. Valent.* fol. 34 of 1283); idem, *Spanien*, I, Pt. 1, pp. 1037 ff. (reprinting and analyzing the *Fuero* of Teruel of 1176, etc.); and nos. 343, 586 Art. 1, 12 (concerning adherence to the Maimonidean Code); Lindo, op. cit., pp. 147 f.; *Ordenaçoens . . . Affonso*, II, 88 (7–9), 92, 93 (1–2), pp. 502 ff.; Kayserling, *Portugal*, pp. 14 ff.; Lagumina, *Codice*, I, no. 34; Ferorelli, *Italia meridionale*, p. 182. Cf. J. E. Scherer, *Die Rechtsverhältnisse der Juden in den deutsch-österreichischen Ländern*, p. 275. Cf. also Chap. XI, nn. 62 ff.

[26] Baer, *Spanien*, I, Pt. 2, no. 181, Pet. 68; Kayserling, l. c.

[27] J. M. Rigg, *Select Pleas, Starrs and other Records from the Rolls of the Exchequer of the Jews (1220–1284)*, p. XLIX; Amulo, *Contra Judaeos*, 44, in Migne's *Patrol. lat.*, CXVI, 172. Cf., in general, also A. Lukyn Williams, *Adversus Judaeos*, pp. 358 ff.

[28] E. J. Laurière and D. F. Secousse (eds.), *Ordonnances des roys de France de la troisième race*, I, 75 (1254, Art. 32–33); III, 480 (1361, Art. 24); D'Blossiers Tovey, *Anglia Judaica*, pp. 110 (1241), 200 ff. (1275); H. P. Stokes, *Studies in Anglo-Jewish History*, pp. 33, 83 ff. Cf. also Chap. VIII, n. 13.

[29] M. Wiener, *Regesten zur Geschichte der Juden in Deutschland während des Mittelalters*, I, pp. 12 f., nos. 74–75; 91, no. 82; Otto Stobbe, *Die Juden in Deutschland*, p. 26; Laurière and Secousse, op. cit., I, 53; III, 475 (Art.

3); Scherer, *Rechtsverhältnisse*, pp. 79 ff., 82 f., 94 ff., 114 n. 1, 243 ff.; Parkes, *Medieval Community*, pp. 119 ff., 252 f., 396 ff. Cf. also Chap. XIV, nn. 22–23.

[30] Mansi, op. cit., XXII, 231, Can. 26; Jacobs, *Angevin England*, p. 63; Tovey, op. cit., pp. 216 ff.; A. Francis Steuart, "Jews in Rome, 1704," *JQR*, O. S. XIX (1906–7), 398–99 (citing an excerpt from a manuscript *Journal* by Charles Talbot, Duke of Shrewsbury); Maimonides, *Mishneh Torah*, Naḥlot, I, 3.

[31] Aronius, *Regesten*, nos. 171, 280, 496; Frank I. Schechter, "The Rightlessness of Mediaeval English Jewry," *JQR*, IV (1913–14), 139 f. (on the basis of two writs dated in 1242, the author makes it plausible, but by no means certain, that Jewish judicial autonomy had previously been severely restricted).

[32] R. Hoeniger, "Zur Geschichte der Juden Deutschlands," *ZGJD*, O. S. I (1887), 136 ff.; Scherer, *Rechtsverhältnisse*, pp. 256 ff., 261 ff., 277 f., and the sources cited there; Herbert Fischer, *Die verfassungsrechtliche Stellung der Juden in den deutschen Städten während des dreizehnten Jahrhunderts*, pp. 123 ff., 167 ff.; Jacobs, *Angevin England*, pp. 135, 212, 331, 372 f.; *Calendar of the Plea Rolls of the Exchequer of the Jews* (*1218–1277*), edited by J. M. Rigg and H. Jenkinson. Cf. also Guido Kisch, "The Jewry Law of the Medieval German Law-Books," *Proceedings of the American Academy for Jewish Research*, VII (1936), 61–145; X (1940), 99–184; Berthold Altmann, "Studies in Medieval German Jewish History," ibid., X (1940), 5–98.

[33] Scherer, *Rechtsverhältnisse*, pp. 162 ff., 252, 291 ff., 299 ff., 305 ff., and the sources cited there; Laurière and Secousse, op. cit., I, 216; Jacobs, *Angevin England*, pp. 156 ff.; Grayzel, op. cit., pp. 58 n. 78, 106. For a discussion of the complex problems concerning the oath *more judaico* and the extensive literature thereon, cf. below, Chap. XIV, n. 31. Cf. also Chap. XI, n. 62.

[34] Salomon Ullmann, *Histoire des Juifs en Belgique jusqu'au 18e siècle*, pp. 35 ff., 64 ff.; idem, "Geschichte der Spanisch-portugiesischen Juden in Amsterdam im XVII. Jahrhundert," *JJLG*, V (1907), 19 ff.; Siegmund Seeligmann, *Bibliographie en Historie. Een Bijdrage tot de geschiedenis der eerste Sephardim in Amsterdam*; Jacob Zwarts, "De eerste Rabbijnen en Synagogen van Amsterdam naar archivalische Bronnen," *Bijdragen en Mededeelingen . . . Joodsche Wetenschap in Nederland*, IV (1928), 147–

271; Herbert I. Bloom, *The Economic Activities of the Jews of Amsterdam in the Seventeenth and Eighteenth Centuries*, pp. 3 ff. Cf. also Kopel Libermann, "La découverte d'une synagogue secrète à Anvers à la fin du dix-septième siècle," *REJ*, XCIX (1935), 37 n. 3, 41 ff.; Ernest Ginsburger, *Les Juifs de Belgique au XVIIIe siècle.*

[35] *Resolution Vroedschap* of May 1612, cited by Ullmann in *JJLG*, V, 27 (the municipal authorities threatened to tear down any synagogue constructed by the Jews); Zwarts, op. cit., p. 266 (extract from the Protocol of the Church Council of June 12, 1614); Abraham b. Joseph ha-Levi, *'Ein Mishpaṭ* (Responsa), IV, no. 45 (on the author and his responsum cf. the comments by [Lazar] Grünhut in *Zeitschrift f. hebr. Bibliographie*, IX, 1905, 97 f.; H. J. Zimmels, *Die Marranen in der rabbinischen Literatur*, pp. 155 ff.; I. Maarsen, "De Responsa als Bron voor de Geschiedenis der Joden in Nederland," *Bijdragen en Mededeelingen*, V, 1933, 120 ff.); H. J. Koenen, *Geschiedenis der Joden in Nederland*, p. 146; J. S. da Silva Rosa, *Geschiedenis der Portugeesche Joden te Amsterdam (1593–1925)*, pp. 10 ff.; Arthur K. Kuhn, "Hugo Grotius and the Emancipation of the Jews in Holland," *PAJHS*, XXXI (1928), 173–80; Fred Oudschans Dentz, *De kolonisatie van de Portugeesch Joodsche Natie in Suriname*, p. 41 (Art. VII). Cf. also Hendrik Brugmans and A. Frank (eds.), *Geschiedenis der Joden in Nederland*, I (particularly the essays by J. D'Ancona, D. M. Sluys and Jac. Zwarts on various phases of communal history).

Some Dutch cities, such as Alkmaar (1604), Haarlem (1605), Rotterdam (1610), actually anticipated the action of the Amsterdam municipal organs. Cf. S. Seeligmann, "Het Marranen-Probleem uit oekonomisch Oogpunkt," *Bijdragen en Mededeelingen*, III (1925 = L. Wagenaar Jubilee Volume), pp. 109 ff. Cf. also such local monographs as Helena Poppers, *De Joden in Overijsel van hunne vestiging tot 1814*, pp. 10 f., 27 ff., 69 ff.; Jac. Zwarts, *De joodsche Gemeente van Amersfoort, Gedenkschrift*, pp. 41 ff.; J. H. Buzaglo, *Bijdragen t. d. geschiedenis d. Portugeesche Israelieten en hunne gemeenten te 's-Gravenhage van plm. 1690 tot plm. 1730.* In Brazil on the other hand, the opposition of the populace and the *classis* (the Dutch church council), apparently stimulated by recurrent scandals arising from anti-Christian utterances and blasphemies of individual Jews, brought about the closing of the two Jewish houses of worship in 1638. An official report of the following year stated that "the Jews were censured for conducting their services too publicly and for some time past have been quiet." Nevertheless, the Jews of the leading community of Recife, in particular, continued to organize their congregation *Tszur Israel* along the lines of the united Spanish-Portuguese community of Amsterdam. In the regulations which they adopted in 1640 they even exceeded the exclusivity of their Amsterdam model; they demanded that there be no other Jewish congregation in the city, and that, except for the already established synagogue on the island of Antonio Vaz, no other congregation be organized throughout the colony without the permission of the Recife elders. Cf. Herbert I. Bloom, "A Study of Brazilian Jewish History, 1623–1654," *PAJHS*, XXXIII (1934), 55 ff., 69 ff. Incidentally, these regulations, extant in photostats and in English translation in the Oppenheim collection in the Library of the American Jewish Historical Society in New York, would seem worthy of publication by a competent scholar. For New Amsterdam and Cayenne, cf. below.

36 Lucien Wolf, "Jews in Elizabethan England," *Transactions of the Jewish Historical Society of England*, XI (1929), 1–91; Wilfred S. Samuel, "The First London Synagogue of the Re-Settlement," ibid., X (1924), 1–147; idem, "The Jewish Oratories of Cromwellian London," *Miscellanies* of that Society, III (1937), 46–55; Moses Gaster, *History of the Ancient Synagogue of the Spanish and Portuguese Jews*, pp. 14, 34. The Ashkenazic settlers, unaffected by the prohibition of 1703, slowly organized their own congregation, beginning with the acquisition, in 1696–97, of a separate cemetery at Alderney Road abutting "south partly on a piece of ground called the Jews' Burial Place." Cf. Cecil Roth's *Archives of the United Synagogue*, p. 44. Contrary to a widespread belief that there had also existed an Ashkenazic house of worship in the days of the Commonwealth, it is now assumed that the synagogue followed, rather than preceded, the cemetery and that hence, "hitherto the United Synagogue has adopted a phantom as its spiritual ancestor!" Samuel in *Miscellanies*, III, 55.

37 Idem in *Transactions*, X, 3, 49 ff. (reprinting Greenhalgh's letter); James Picciotto, *Sketches of Anglo-Jewish History*, pp. 32 ff., 39 f.

38 Elkan Nathan Adler, *London*, pp. 100 ff.; Nathan Osterman, "The Controversy over the Proposed Readmission of the Jews to England (1655)," *Jewish Social Studies*, III (1941), 301–28; H. S. Q. Henriques, *The Jews and the English Law*, pp. 147 ff.

39 Ibid., pp. 53 ff. The legal status of the Jewish community in the

eighteenth century was well summarized by Lord Hardwicke, the Chancellor on the occasion of the litigation which arose, in 1744, from Elias de Paz's much-debated bequest in favor of a *Yeshibah.* Reviewing the existing legislation, including the Toleration Act, the Chancellor declared: "This renders those religions [of the Christian Dissenters] legal, which is not the case of the Jewish Religion, that is not taken notice of by any law, but is barely connived at by the legislature." And Hardwicke was personally rather pro-Jewish and a sponsor of the *Jew Bill* of 1753. Cf. ibid., pp. 19 ff., 241.

The early statute (*ascamot*) of the Spanish-Portuguese congregation in English translation is now available in Lionel D. Barnett's *El libro de los acuerdos: Being the Records and Accompts of the Spanish and Portuguese Synagogue of London from 1663 to 1681.* The *takkanot* of the Ashkenazic Great Synagogue, adopted on the occasion of its dedication in 1722, are evidently an elaboration of an unknown earlier set of rules; the manuscript is in the synagogue's archives. These regulations, first published in 1761 and 1771 (cf. Cecil Roth's *Magna Bibliotheca Anglo-Judaica*, p. 297), were thoroughly revised on the occasion of the consecration of the new building in 1790. The new statute is published in full by Moses Margoliouth in *The History of the Jews in Great Britain*, III, 234 ff.

40 Cecil Roth, "The Portsmouth Community and its Historical Background," *Transactions of J. H. S. E.*, XIII (1936), 158; Stokes, *Studies*, pp. 120 f., 227, 231; Charles P. Daly, *The Settlement of the Jews in North America*, pp. 11 f., 21 ff.; Samuel Oppenheim, "The Early History of the Jews in New York, 1654–1664," *PAJHS*, XVIII (1909), 9 ff., 21 ff., 75 f.; Lee M. Friedman, *Early American Jews*, pp. 49 ff. In 1658 the courts of New York recognized the Jewish Sabbath as a legitimate reason for Jacob Barsimson's failure to appear and refused to enter a default judgment against him (ibid., p. 24). The Jewish burial ground, however, long considered to have been established in 1656, was not purchased until 1682. Cf. below, Chap. XII, n. 40.

41 Daly, op. cit., pp. 25 ff.; Albion Morris Dyer, "Points in the First Chapter of New York Jewish History," *PAJHS*, III (1895), 46 ff.; Max J. Kohler, "Civil Status of the Jews in Colonial New York," *PAJHS*, VI (1897), 89 ff.; David de Sola Pool, *The Mill Street Synagogue (1730–1817) of the Congregation Shearith Israel*, pp. 4 ff. The original regulations of the Shearith Israel Congregation of 1705–6 are not extant, but it may

be assumed that they did not materially differ from those of 1726 which were expressly adopted in order "to Revive the same with some amendments and additions." Cf. "The Earliest Extant Minute Books of the Spanish and Portuguese Congregation Shearith Israel in New York, 1728–1786" (Jacques Judah Lyons's transcript checked against the original), *PAJHS*, XXI (1913), 1 ff.

[42] Max J. Kohler, "The Jews in Newport," *PAJHS*, VI (1897), 65 ff.; Morris A. Gutstein, *The Story of the Jews of Newport . . . 1658–1908*, pp. 31, 36 ff.; N. Darnell Davis, "Notes on the History of the Jews in Barbados," *PAJHS*, XVIII (1909), 129 ff.; Cardozo de Bethencourt, "Notes on the Spanish and Portuguese Jews in the United States, Guiana and the Dutch and British West Indies during the Seventeenth and Eighteenth Centuries," ibid., XXIX (1925), 7–38; Wilfred S. Samuel, "Review of the Jewish Colonists in Barbados, 1860," *Transactions of J. H. S. E.*, XIII (1936), 1–111; Samuel Oppenheim, "The Jews in Barbados in 1739," *PAJHS*, XXII (1914), 197 f.; George Fortunatus Judah, "The Jews' Tribute in Jamaica," ibid., XVIII (1909), 149–77. The oldest extant piece of British legislation concerning Jewish liberty of conscience and freedom of worship seems to be the enactment issued in 1665 by the Governor, Council and Assembly of Surinam. Cf. Great Britain, Foreign Office, *Handbooks Prepared under the Direction of the Historical Section*, CXXXVI: Dutch Guiana, p. 10 n. 1; and the text in Dutch in Dentz, op. cit., pp. 45 f.

[43] Théophile Malvezin, *Histoire des Juifs de Bordeaux*, pp. 177 ff., 207 ff., 222 ff. The anti-Jewish bias of the report of 1734 is best characterised by the following manifestly absurd generalization: *Ils ont pour domestiques de jolies paysannes, qu'ils rendent enceintes pour servir de nourrices à leurs enfants; et font porter ceux dont ces jeunes paysannes accouches à la boëte des enfants trouvés.* Ibid. p. 182. Before the acquisition of their cemetery in 1728, the Jews had to bury their dead in a section of a local convent cemetery. According to a contemporary visitor, this section presented a picture of great neglect in 1749. It is undoubtedly due to the great secrecy with which the Jews of Bordeaux performed their synagogue services that an interested visitor, the Benedictine monk, Dom Martenne, wrote in 1715 that "the Jews of Bordeaux have neither a synagogue nor any distinguishing mark." Cf. Ad. Detcheverry, *Histoire des Israélites de Bordeaux*, pp. 110 ff. Cf. also L. Cardozo de Bethencourt

"Le Trésor des Juifs Sephardim," *REJ*, XX (1890), 287–300; XXV (1892), 97–110, 235–45; XXVI (1893), 240–56; G. Cirot, "Les Juifs de Bordeaux. Leur situation morale et sociale de 1550 à la Revolution," *Revue historique de Bordeaux*, II–XXXII (1909–39, 14 instalments).

[44] Henry Léon, *Histoire des Juifs de Bayonne*; Ernest Ginsburger, "Les Juifs de Peyrehorade," *REJ*, N. S. IV (1938), 36 f., 45 ff.; Léon Kahn, *Histoire de la communauté israélite de Paris: Le Comité de bienfaisance, l'hôpital, les cimetières*; Paul Hildenfinger, *Documents sur les Juifs à Paris au XVIIIe siècle: Actes d'inhumation et scellés*; Robert Anchel, "Les Juifs à Paris au XVIIIe siècle," *Bulletin de la Société de l'histoire de Paris*, LIX (1932), 9–23; Jacques Decourcelle, *La condition des Juifs de Nice aux 17e et 18e siècles*; Jacqueline Rochette, *La condition des Juifs d'Alsace jusqu'au décret du 28. septembre 1791*; Nathan Netter, *Vingt siècles d'histoire d'une communauté juive* (*Metz et son grand passé*).

[45] Abraham Cahen, "Les Juifs de la Martinique au XVIIe siècle," *REJ*, II (1881), 99 ff.; idem, "Les Juifs dans les colonies françaises au XVIIIe siècle," ibid., IV (1882), 127 ff.; V (1882), 81 ff., 267 ff.; Oppenheim in *PAJHS*, XVIII, 17 n. 18 (citing a French traveler, Antoine Biet, who found in 1654 that the Jews of Martinique "were permitted in the Island to Judaise, and in the sight of all the world to exercise their religion and observe their Sabbath"); J. Rennard, "Juifs et Protestants aux Antilles françaises au XVIIe siècle," *Revue d'histoire des missions*, X (1933), 436–62; Charles Woolsey Cole, *Colbert and a Century of French Mercantilism*, I, 351, 362, 394; II, 42 (in 1670 Colbert writes that Jews "must not be driven out" from the colonies).

[46] Philipp Bloch, *Die Generalprivilegien der polnischen Judenschaft*, pp. 102 ff.: Art. 9, 36, 37; *Volumina legum* (Polish Statutes), I, 270 (550); Josef Meisl, *Geschichte der Juden in Polen und Russland*, I, 245 ff. Cf. also in general Moses Schorr, *Rechtsstellung und innere Verfassung der Juden in Polen*.

[47] Majer Balaban, "Jewish Communal Structure in Poland in the 16th–18th Centuries" (Polish), *Kwartalnik poświęcony badaniu przeszłości Żydów w Polsce*, I, Pt. 2 (1912), 21; idem, *Żydzi lwowscy na przełomie XVIgo i XVIIgo wieku* (The Jews of Lwów about 1600 C. E.), pp. 231 ff., 282 ff., Appd. nos. 37, 50, 103; Bloch, *Generalprivilegien*, l. c., Art. 10, 11, 21, 22, 41; Mathias Bersohn, *Dyplomataryusz dotyczący Żydów w dawnej Polsce* (Collection of Documents Concerning Jews in Old Poland, 1388–1782),

no. 57 (1551); David Bencionas Teimanas, *L'autonomie des communautés juives en Pologne aux XVIe et XVIIe siècles*, pp. 44, 49. For the penalty for disregarding a ban, cf. Chap. XIV, n. 21.

[48] Bersohn, l. c.; Meisl, op. cit., I, 231; II, 113; Teimanas, op. cit., pp. 43 ff., 46; Simon M. Dubnow, *History of the Jews in Russia and Poland*, I, 190. Cf. also below, Chap. VIII, n. 17.

[49] Bloch, *Generalprivilegien*, pp. 95 ff., 102 ff., Art. 1, 7, 23, 24, 26, 30, 40; Meisl, op. cit., I, 225 f.; II, 214; M. Balaban, "Die Krakauer Judengemeinde-Ordnung von 1595 und ihre Nachträge," *JJLG*, X (1913), 297; Stanisław Kutrzeba, "The Judiciary over Jews in the Cracow Palatinate" (Polish), *Przegląd prawa administracyjnego*, XVI (referring to mixed Judeo-Christian litigations); Z. Honik, "Court Jurisdiction over Lithuanian Jewry after the Union of Lublin" (Yiddish), *Yivo Bleter*, XIV (1938), 316–34 (with special reference to the judicial reforms of 1566, but important also for the understanding of the entire legal status of Lithuanian Jewry).

[50] Teimanas, op. cit., pp. 40, 49 f.; Meisl, op. cit., I, 245. For further details cf. Chap. XV.

[51] Cecil Roth, *Venice*, pp. 131 f.; Umberto Cassuto, *Gli Ebrei a Firenze nell' età del Rinascimento*, pp. 196 ff., 213 ff.; Perugini, "L'inquisition romaine et les Israélites," *REJ*, III (1881), 96 f. no. 11, 106 no. 46.

[52] Jacobs, *Angevin England*, p. 141; B. L. Abrahams, *The Expulsion of the Jews from England in 1290*, p. 20; J. M. Rigg, *Select Pleas*, p. XLIX. Cf. in general also Parkes, *Community*, pp. 220 ff.

[53] J. C. Ulrich, *Sammlung jüdischer Geschichten . . . in der Schweiz*, pp. 14 f.; Heymann Chone, "Zur Geschichte der Juden in Zürich im 15. Jahrhundert," *ZGJD*, VI (1936), 198–209; Karl Hegel, *Chronicon Moguntinum*, p. 20; J. S. Menczel, *Beiträge zur Geschichte der Juden von Mainz im XV Jahrhundert*, pp. 34 ff.; Robert Hoeniger and Moritz Stern, *Das Judenschreinsbuch der Laurenzpfarre zu Köln*; Adolf Kober, *Grundbuch des Kölner Judenviertels, 1135–1425*; idem, *Cologne*, pp. 71 ff., 353 n. 12; Artur Goldmann, *Das Judenbuch der Scheffstrasse zu Wien* (1389–1420); Max Ephraim, "Histoire des Juifs d'Alsace et particulièrement de Strasbourg depuis le milieu du XIIIe jusqu'à la fin du XIVe siècle," *REJ*, LXXVII (1923), 145 ff.; Salo Baron, *Die Judenfrage auf dem Wiener Kongress*, pp. 39 ff., 87 ff., 101 ff., 193 ff. (for Bremen and Lübeck); Franz Loewy, "Wie eine jüdische Gemeinde entstand. Zur Geschichte

der Gemeinde Glatz," *Jahrbuch für jüdische Geschichte und Literatur*, XXXI (1938), 208–22; and, in general, Stobbe, op. cit., pp. 19 ff., 140 ff.; Fischer, op. cit. passim; idem, "Judenprivilegien des Goslarer Rates im 14. Jahrhundert," *Zeitschrift für Rechtsgeschichte*, LVI (1936), 89–149.

[54] Fita and Llabres, op. cit., pp. 302 ff., nos. 75–76; Baer, *Studien*, pp. 51 ff.; Gunnar Tilander, "Documento desconocido de la aljama de Zaragoza del año 1331," *Studia neophilologica*, XII (Uppsala, 1939–40), 23 ff.

[55] Ferorelli, *Italia meridionale*, pp. 100, 104 n. 2, 169 ff., 182; *Consuetudines Palermitanae*, Art. 15, cited by R. Straus, *Sizilien*, p. 102. The memorial of the city of Palermo, dated July 11, 1492, following that of high government officials, dated June 20, 1492, against the decree of banishment issued in Sicily and Naples two days before, merely accentuates Ferdinand's arbitrariness in identifying the interests of the Spanish dependencies with his understanding of those of the Spanish mainland. Cf. Lagumina, *Codice*, II, Pt. 2, nos. 883, 894, 923; and above nn. 18–19.

[56] Stephen Batory's privilege of 1578 is included in the *Sumaryusz przywilejów nadanych Żydom polskim* (A Summary of the Privileges granted the Jews in Poland), published by M. Schorr in *Evreiskaya Starina*, II (1909), 97; Schorr, *Rechtsstellung*, pp. 7 f.; *Volumina legum*, V, 314 (643:1678); VII, 352 f. (755:1768); Honik in *Yivo Bleter*, XIV, 331; Wladyslaw Smolenski, *Stan i sprawa Żydów polskich w XVIII wieku* (The Status of the Jews and the Jewish Question in Poland in the Eighteenth Century), pp. 8 f. Cf. also Israel Klauzner, *Toledot ha-kehillah ha-'ibrit be-Wilno* (History of the Jewish Community in Wilno), I, 3 ff., graphically describing the centuries-long struggle of the Jews, often aided by the Crown and the nobles, against the Wilno burghers. The burghers were also the main promoters of literary anti-Semitism. One of the most radical denunciations of Polish Jewry, written by Sebastjan Miczyński under the outspoken title, *Zwierciadło Korony polskiej* (The Mirror [in the sense of the German *Spiegel*] of the Polish Crown: Heavy Insults and Vexations of Jews) was published in 1618 under the sponsorship of the municipality of Lwów. It was suppressed by royal order, after an interpellation in the Polish Diet. Cf. Filip Friedman's as yet unpublished *History of the Jews in Poland* (Polish). Cf. also A. N. Frenk, *Ha-'Ironim ve-ha-yehudim be-Polin* (The Burghers and the Jews in Poland); Elena Hekker, "Jews in Polish Cities during the Second Half of the Eighteenth

Century" (Russian), *Evreiskaya Starina*, VI (1913), 184–200, 325–32; J. Joffe, "The Struggle between Burghers and Jews in Curland during the Eighteenth Century" (Russian), ibid., IV (1911), 568–80 (with special reference to a memorandum of 1759); and Chap. X, n. 3.

NOTES TO CHAPTER VIII

SUPERCOMMUNITY

[1] The statute of 1402 is included in the *Ordenaçoens . . . Affonso*, II, 81, pp. 476 ff. It is well summarized by Kayserling, *Portugal*, pp. 9 ff. The preamble indicates that its renewal in 1440 was occasioned by the complaints of the *procuradores* of the community of Lisbon and other communities against Don Juda Cofem, *nosso Arraby Moor*. For other interventions of the Portuguese communities, often represented by that of Lisbon, see *Ordenaçoens*, II, 73, pp. 436 ff.; 90, pp. 508 f.

[2] Ibn Adret, *Responsa*, III, 411.

[3] The resolutions of the conference of 1354 are reprinted in Baer's *Spanien*, I, Pt. 1, no. 253 (cf. also the editor's notes thereto) and, with an English translation, in Finkelstein's *Self-Government*, pp. 328 ff. Cf., in general, also Baer's *Studien*, pp. 118 ff. Similar conventions of Castilian Jewry for the purpose of tax distribution and communal regulation are mentioned in several records of the fourteenth and fifteenth centuries. Cf. Asher b. Yeḥiel's *Responsa*, VI, 15; Baer's *Spanien*, I, Pt. 2, nos. 134, 143, 287, 329, 358. The most famous of these gatherings was the "synod" of Valladolid in 1432 (see below). The choice of this locality also for the *juntas* of 1476 and 1486 is not surprising, because since John II Valladolid had served as the royal capital and the foremost seat of the Cortes.

[4] Baer, *Spanien*, I, Pt. 2, nos. 70 (1255), 241 (1388), 244 (1389), 258 (1395), 264 (1401).

[5] Ibid., p. 52 and nos. 230 (1383–84), 287 (IV, 1), 307 (Doc. 5, 1465), 329 (1476), 347 ff. (1485), 352 (3), 355 (1486), 358, 365 ff. (1488), 373 (1491), 379 (1492).

[6] Ibid., Pt. 1, nos. 104 (1271), 153 (Doc. 5, 1304–5), 601–3 (after 1391); idem, *Studien*, pp. 126 f.; idem in *Debir*, II (1923), 316 f. (on Alconstantin); Assaf, *Ha-'Oneshin*, no. 74; Kayserling, *Die Juden in Navarra, den*

Baskenländern und auf den Balearen, pp. 88 f. It is interesting to note that when, in 1369, the Castilian city of Molina surrendered to the Aragonese troops, Don Samuel Abulafia, appearing as the representative of the Jewish community, included in the stipulations a provision that he continue to exercise in the city those rabbinic and judicial functions which were formerly his "as rabbi of the court of the King of Castile." The King promised not only to keep Don Samuel in office for life, but also to reserve his post for those descendants "who shall prove capable." Baer, *Spanien*, I, Pt. 1, no. 292.

[7] The conspiracy of silence on the part of contemporary Hebrew writers with respect to their chief rabbis is too uniform and consistent to be the effect of an accident. Even Ḥasdai Crescas, a prolific author and influential jurist, philosopher and apologist, is known to us as Aragonese chief rabbi primarily through a chance remark of a Christian debater at Tortosa (*qui fuit Rabi vel magister omnium vestrum*), an inconclusive reference in a Hebrew letter of 1401 ("chief and judge over us and over all Israel" could not possibly have had the technical meaning of chief rabbi in the writer's locality, Navarre), and a somewhat dubious note in another Hebrew letter of 1411 concerning the "late" Ḥasdai's successor in the chief rabbinate (according to Baer, *Enc. Jud.* V, 696 ff., Ḥasdai died in 1412). Cf. Baer's *Studien*, p. 127 n. 12; idem, *Spanien*, I, Pt. 1, p. 1001; Isidore Loeb, "Josef Haccohen et les chroniqueurs juifs," *REJ*, XVI (1888), 34. Indeed, Ḥasdai himself, writing in 1391, a year after his appointment by Queen Violante as chief trial judge for Jewish informers throughout the realm — the later decree conferring upon him the chief rabbinate seems irretrievably lost — apparently refrains from using any official designation. Cf. his epistle on the French controversy, reproduced in Isaac b. Sheshet's *Responsa*, no. 269, and his description of the massacres, in Solomon ibn Verga's *Shebeṭ Yehudah*, ed. by M. Wiener, pp. 128 ff.

[8] S. Schechter, "Notes sur Messer David Léon tirées de manuscrits," *REJ*, XXIV (1892), 135 = *Kebod Ḥakamim* (A Polemical Work) by Messer David Leon, ed. by S. Bernfeld, p. 64. The barb is evidently aimed at Seneor rather than at Paul of Burgos.

[9] Baer, *Studien*, p. 29 (referring to the appointment of Don Pedro Fenollet, Viscount de Illa); idem, *Spanien*, I, Pt. 1, no. 253 (9), 283; Pt. 2, no. 287 (III, 7).

[10] Leopold Zunz, *Zur Geschichte und Literatur*, pp. 510 f.; Lagumina, *Codice*, I, nos. 87 (Palermo, 1392), 123 (1396), 124, 130, 137, 148 (1397), 158 (1399), 174 (1402), 186 (1403), 193, 203 (1405), 211 (1406), 218, 222 (1408), 238 (1413), 247 (1414), 256 (1415), 272 (1416), 285 (1418), 293 (1420), 296, 297, 300 (1421), 301, 305 (1423), 325 (1429), 332 (1431), 336 (1432), 337 (1433), 359 (1438), 360 (1439), 364 (1440), 366, 371–75 (1446–47), 378–80 (1447), 382 (1448); II, Pt. 1, nos. 554 (1474), 601 (1477), 777 (1490), 813, 846 (1491); Ferdinando Lionti, "Le magistrature presso gli Ebrei di Sicilia," *Archivio storico siciliano*, N. S. IX (1884), 332 f., 347 ff. Zunz identifies the *dienchelele* with *bet din kelali* (supreme court). In view of the spelling *de ancheleli*, *enhalali*, *diencalili*, etc., in the sources and the fact that it invariably refers to a single officer, the identification with *dayyan kelali* (supreme judge, the Hebrew equivalent of *iudice universale*), would seem decidedly preferable. Cf. David Kaufmann's review of Güdemann's work reprinted in his *Gesammelte Schriften*, II, 240; Isidore Loeb, "Règlement des Juifs de Castille en 1432 comparé avec les règlements des Juifs de Sicile et d'autres pays," *REJ*, XIII (1886), 208 f., 215 f.

[11] Lagumina, *Codice*, I, nos. 151 (1399), 182 (1403), 332 (1430–31). The office of the Sicilian chief justice has been discussed here at somewhat greater length because of the considerable confusion in the available literature on the subject. Unfortunately, the few extant documents do not allow a complete reconstruction of its history. We cannot even tell whether these chief judges were rabbinically trained scholars. The exercise of the medical profession by most of them would rather favor such an assumption, as would their authority in "spiritual" matters mentioned in the sources, the title *rabi* or *reab* given to Joshua and the phrase referring to Abenafia "and four other rabbis, experts in Jewish law" ibid., nos. 193, 371, 373. The story Isaac b. Sheshet told about an itinerant French scholar in Cagliari who approached the Sicilian chief rabbi and, through the use of superior French dialectics, tried "to put him to shame and to controvert him in the presence of the congregation, but failed," would also seem to imply rabbinic training of that chief justice. Cf. Isaac's *Responsa*, no. 171. Cf. also below, n. 30.

[12] Agobard's writings in Migne's *Patrol. lat.*, CIV, 70, 105, 112, 178; Alain de Boüard, *Actes et lettres de Charles I, Roi de Sicile, concernant la France* (*1257–1284*), nos. 215, 958–59; also summarized by Willy Cohn in

his "Die Judenpolitik König Karls I von Sizilien in Anjou und in der Provence," *MGWJ*, LXXIV (1930), 429–37.

[12a] L. Lazard, "Les revenus tirés des Juifs de France dans la domaine royale (XIII s.)," *REJ*, XV (1887), 239 f.; Laurière and Secousse, *Ordonnances*, III, 471, 487; IV, 496, 532; V, 498; Isaac b. Sheshet, *Responsa*, nos. 268–73. Cf. also Scherer, *Rechtsverhältnisse*, pp. 252 ff., 261 ff. The *conservateur*'s office persisted, however, in Provence, where Jews were allowed to remain until 1500. Its functioning is recorded in various years from 1403 on. Cf. Léon Bardinet, "Condition civile des Juifs du Comtat Venaissin (1409–1513)," *REJ*, VI (1882), 16; and Émile Camau, *La Provence à travers les siècles*, [1928], pp. 327 ff.

Office and title were taken over by neighboring Savoy-Piedmont, where, in 1554, Marco Antonio Bobba, Bishop of Aosta, was appointed *conservator degli Ebrei*. In 1572 a ducal decree provided for the appointment of three conservators for Savoy, Nice and Piedmont, respectively. Another decree of 1620 limited the appointment to men of senatorial rank. As in France the conservator soon appointed *subconservators* in all major cities. Cf. *Privilegi e concessioni di S.S. R. M. e i suoi reali predecessori a favore dell' Università Generale degli Ebrei del Piemonte*, pp. 14 f., 79 ff., 88, 145 ff.; M. Lattes, "Documents et notices sur l'histoire politique et littéraire des Juifs en Italie," *REJ*, V (1882), 227, 237; Jacques Decourcelle, *La condition des Juifs de Nice aux 17e et 18e siècles*, p. 216.

Despite efforts of several scholars, many phases in the brief history of the medieval French chief rabbinate are still obscure. Not even the position of an earlier regional chief, the hereditary *nasi* of Narbonne, mentioned in several Hebrew and French sources, emerges clearly from the mist of legend. Local Jewish tradition, largely accepted also by the Christian contemporaries, had it that, at the time of Charlemagne's conquest, the Jews obtained as a reward for their services one-third of the city's territory and the privilege of permanently continuing under the autonomous rule of their own "King" of the House of David. Cf. Israel Lévi, "Le roi juif de Narbonne et le Philomène," *REJ*, XLVIII (1904), 197–207, supplemented by his remarks, ibid., XLIX (1904), 147–50. The Jewish leader seems, on the whole, to have occupied a post analogous to that of a provincial *nagid* under Islam.

For the last great controversy about the chief rabbinate cf. the same author's "La lutte entre Isaie, fils d'Abba Mari, et Yohanan, fils de

Matatia pour le rabbinat de France à la fin du XIVe siècle," *REJ*, XXXIX (1899), 85–94. Ch. Lauer's more recent examination of the sources in his "R. Meir Halevy aus Wien und der Streit um das Grossrabbinat in Frankreich," *JJLG*, XVI (1924), 1–42, meritorious in many details, is vitiated by the author's spirited but hardly tenable defense of what appears to have been a wholly unwarranted interference of the Viennese rabbi with the inner affairs of French Jewry. Without reference to these extended discussions Solomon Zeitlin tries to explain the entire controversy by the divergent attitudes of the Spanish and the northern rabbis toward governmental appointment of communal officers. Cf. his recent essay on "The Opposition to the Spiritual Leaders Appointed by the Government," *JQR*, XXXI (1940–41), 288 ff.

[13] A full discussion of the available records for the six successive "archpresbyters" and of the "justiciars" of the Jews in England is found in Stokes, *Studies*, pp. 23 ff., 44 ff., 83 ff., 243 ff. It is effectively supplemented by Michael Adler's recent biography of "Aaron of York" (who held the English presbyterate in the difficult years 1236–43) in *Transactions of the Jewish Historical Society of England*, XIII (1936), 113–55. Cf., in particular, pp. 122 ff., 143. Cf. also Chap. VII, n. 28.

[14] Wiener, *Regesten*, pp. 58 f. no. 35; 65 f. nos. 75, 76, 80; 71 ff., 254 f.; Moritz Stern, *König Ruprecht von der Pfalz in seinen Beziehungen zu den Juden*, pp. XVIII f., XXVII, XXXIII, XLVIII ff. and nos. 1, 8 ff., etc.; idem, *Die israelitische Bevölkerung der deutschen Städte*: VII: Worms, Pt. 1: Die Reichsrabbiner des 15. und 16. Jahrhunderts; Heymann Chone, "Rabbi Joseph von Schlettstadt," *ZGJD*, VII (1937), 1–4 (referring to 1418); Richard Grünfeld, *Zur Geschichte der Juden in Bingen am Rhein*, p. 13; Adolf Kober, "Die deutschen Kaiser und die Wormser Juden," *ZGJD*, V (1935), 140 f.

[15] Ludwig Feilchenfeld, *Rabbi Josel von Rosheim*; Saul Pinhas Rabbinowitz, *R. Joseph Ish Rosheim* (Hebrew); H. Bresslau, "Aus Strassburger Judenakten," *ZGJD*, O. S. V(1892), 307 n. 2, 327 f., 330 ff. Cf. below nn. 25–26. The history of the German chief rabbinate, like that of the French, is still full of obscurities. Only Israel, Anselm and the two rabbis of Worms have found their careful investigator in Moritz Stern. The antecedents of the office, however, as well as its development after 1435 remain highly uncertain. The designation of Meir of Rothenburg as *supremus magister* in a decree of Emperor Rudolf I of 1288 (Wiener,

Regesten, pp. 13 f. no. 81) sounds suspiciously like that of an official head of German Jewry. His sudden, though unsuccessful, flight, his imprisonment and especially the detention of his corpse by the emperor's order for the satisfaction of an imperial claim, is also best explained by the hypothesis that he was personally responsible for some, possibly controversial, tax arrears of the German-Jewish communities. This impression is reinforced by the leading role played by his disciple Asher b. Yeḥiel, after his incarceration, and by the latter's emigration from Germany a few years later (1303). The designation "lord of the land" (*ish adone ha-areṣ*) given to Asher by his nephew Moses ha-Kohen, and his issuance of ordinances for all of Germany, likewise indicate, though they do not prove, some such official position. Cf. Alfred Freimann, "Asher b. Jechiel: Sein Leben und Wirken," *JJLG*, XII (1918), 249. Governmental appointment of Meir of Rothenburg is indeed asserted, on the basis of the rather equivocal Hebrew sources, by Jost, Graetz and, less positively, by Güdemann, but denied by J. Wellesz in his "Meir b. Baruch de Rothenbourg," *REJ*, LIX (1910), 47 f. H. J. Zimmels, in his *Beiträge zur Geschichte der Juden in Deutschland im 13. Jahrhundert* (with special reference to Meir's *Responsa*), pp. 2 f., refrains from taking sides in the controversy.

The assumption, too, that the chief rabbinate was never recognized by the Jewish communities, which has become a commonplace in Jewish historical literature, requires much more positive evidence, than is hitherto available. Israel's supposed resignation soon after 1407 is controverted by King Conrad's provision, in 1415, for a substitute in the event of death. Cf. Wilhelm Altmann, *Die Urkunden Kaiser Siegmunds (1410–1437)*, I, no. 1784; Stern, *Ruprecht*, p. LV n. 1 (Stern, incidentally, repudiates the identification of this Chief Rabbi Israel with a rabbinic author of the day by the same name whose residence or native place was Lower Austrian Krems or Moravian Kremsier, cf. Ad. Frankl-Grün, *Geschichte der Juden in Kremsier*, I, 14 f.). Cf. also M. Frank, *Ḳehillot Ashkenaz u-bate dinehen* (The Jewish Communities and Courts in Germany from the Twelfth to the End of the Fifteenth Century), p. 14 n. 11. Neither is it likely that the emperors should have continued appointing chief rabbis for another century and a half and that, as late as 1569, Maximilian II should have referred, as a matter of course, to the "rabbi whom we have ordained for the common Jewry in Germany" (G. Wolf, "Die Anstellung der Rabbiner und ihr Wirkungskreis" in his *Kleine historische Schriften*, pp. 139 f.; there is no indication in what connection, if any, this officer was with the delegates of German Jewry who, three years before, had appeared at the Diet of Augsburg and obtained from the Emperor the renewal of their privilege of 1544. Cf. Max Freudenthal, "Zur Geschichte der Judenprivilegien Kaiser Maximilians II auf dem Reichstag zu Augsburg 1566," *ZGJD*, IV, 1932, 83–100), if their appointees were consistently and effectively boycotted by their coreligionists.

The absence of specific references to these officials in the contemporary Hebrew sources is decidedly inconclusive. One may, perhaps, disregard in this connection the statement on the title-page of Bezaleel Ashkenazi's *Responsa*, first printed in Venice, 1595, in which the author's uncle, Isaac Bezaleel's, is designated as the "Chief Rabbi of all Germany." If the latter be identical with one of the founders of Polish rabbinic learning residing in Włodzimierz, his previous leadership in Germany may have contributed to the great reverence in which he was generally held by his rabbinic colleagues. Cf. Chaim Nathan Dembitzer, *Kelilat Yofi* (A History of the Lwów Rabbinate), pp. 48 ff.; A. L. Frumkin and E. Rivlin, *Toledot Ḥakme Yerushalayim* (A History of the Scholars of Jerusalem), I, 115 n. 1. Be that as it may, we certainly would have learned but little from Hebrew letters about the indubitably powerful chief rabbis of Portugal or Aragon. Cf. above nn. 1, 7. A minor indication of the actual effectiveness of these imperial decrees may perhaps be found also in the provision inserted in Charles IV's decree of 1348 and in that of Ruprecht in 1402 (Stern, *Ruprecht*, pp. XXXVI, XLVI f., no. 1) which, threatening with confiscation of property those Jews who would fail to extricate themselves from a ban within 30 days, seems to have exercised some influence upon the Polish decrees of 1527 and 1551 (cf. next note). Such acceptance by German emigrés to Poland of governmental support of the Jewish excommunication cannot easily be squared with their alleged boycott of all imperial centralizing efforts in their country of origin.

[16] Louis Lewin, *Die Landessynode der grosspolnischen Judenschaft*, pp. 22, 24, 26, 28 ff.; M. Balaban, *Dzieje Żydów w Krakowie i na Kazimierzu* (A History of the Jews in Cracow and Kazimierz), I, 60 ff., 265 ff.; idem, *Skizzen und Studien zur Geschichte der Juden in Polen*, pp. 77–96 (on Abraham and Michael Ezofowicz).

[17] Ph. Bloch, "Der Streit um den Moreh des Maimonides in der Gemeinde Posen um die Mitte des 16. Jahrh.," *MGWJ*, XLVII (1903),

349 ff., giving the text of the decree of 1527 which evidently influenced that of 1541 and was, in part verbatim, repeated in the significant privilege of 1551, as published in Bersohn's *Dyplomataryusz*, nos. 46 and 57. Cf. above, Chap. VII, n. 48.

[18] Lewin, *Landessynode*, pp. 29 ff.; Balaban, *Z zagadnień ustrojowych Żydowstwa polskiego* (Some Organizational Problems of Polish Jewry), passim. The latter essay emphasizes the growing difficulties of the Lwów chief rabbinate in the course of the eighteenth century, but offers also a good survey of similar conflicts in the other Polish provinces. The provincial chief rabbinate was, for a while, maintained also by the Austrian government after 1772, and extended over the entire province of Galicia. Cf. N. M. Gelber, "The Regional Chief Rabbinate in Galicia (1776–1786)" (Russian), *Evreiskaya Starina*, VII (1914), 305–17; idem, "Aryeh Leib Bernstein, Chief Rabbi of Galicia," *JQR*, XIV (1923–24), 303–27. A fuller investigation of the various Polish chief rabbinates not only on the basis of all extant governmental and communal records, but also by utilization of the considerable literary output of some leading chief rabbis, is likely to furnish new and highly valuable clues to the practical operation of the Jewish autonomous organs in Poland.

[19] Gregory's *Epistles*, I, 34, 45; VIII, 25; IX, 38 (*Monumenta Germaniae*, I, 47 f., 71 f.; II, 27, 67); Vogelstein and Rieger, *Rom*, I, 135, 212, 230, 233 f., 252; II, 35, 43 f., 253, 256 and the sources cited therein; Jacob R. Marcus, *The Jew in the Medieval World*, pp. 159–64 (giving the English translation of Reuchlin's letter); Cecil Roth, "Une mission des communautés du Comtat Venaissin à Rome," *REJ*, LXXXIV (1927), 1–14; idem, "The Forced Baptisms of 1783 at Rome and the Community of London," *JQR*, XVI (1925–26), 105–16; G[raetz], "Einige handschriftliche Briefe von Jonathan Eibeschütz," *MGWJ*, XVI (1867), 426 ff.; Israel Halperin, "The Council of Four Lands and Its Relations with the Outside World" (Yiddish), *Yivo Studies in History*, II (1937), 74 f.; Umberto Cassuto, "Una lettera di raccomandazione per un inviato degli Ebrei Polacci al Papa (1758)," *Rivista israelitica*, I (1904), 25–27 (a copy of this letter of recommendation to Cardinal Cavalchini was prepared for Rabbi Sabbato Fano in Rome. It may readily be assumed that this rabbi had a share in securing the letter from Cavalchini's nephew). Cf. also Ch. VII, nn. 11–12. Even private individuals seeking redress from the pope

against the local authorities frequently carried letters of recommendation to the community of Rome. One such letter, referring to a curious case of a Jewish family in Negroponte, then under Venetian domination, has been published by Carlo Bernheimer in *REJ*, LXV (1913), 224–30.

[20] A. Neubauer and M. Stern, *Hebräische Berichte über die Judenverfolgungen während der Kreuzzüge*, pp. 3, 47, 87 f., 169 f.; Aronius, *Regesten*, nos. 177–78; I. Loeb in *REJ*, XVI, 37, no. 38; D. Kaufmann, "L'incendie de Salonique du 4 Ab 1545," ibid., XXI (1890), 295; S. Z. H. Halberstam, *Ḳehillat Shelomoh* (a catalogue of his manuscripts), pp. 161 f.; Frankl-Grün, *Kremsier*, I, 97 ff.; Siegmund Seeligmann, "Ein Originalbrief der Vierländersynode nach Amsterdam aus 1677," *Livre d'hommage . . . Poznanski*, pp. 147–52; David Kaufmann, "David Carcassoni et le rachat par la communauté de Constantinople des Juifs faits prisonniers durant la persécution du Chmielnicky," *REJ*, XXV (1892), 202–16; Rosanes, *Togarma*, IV, 28; I. Maarsen, "The Council of Four Lands and the Communities of Amsterdam in the Seventeenth Century" (Hebrew), *Ha-Zofeh*, VIII (1924), 289–300; C. Roth, "An Association for the Redemption of Captives in the Seventeenth Century" (Hebrew), ibid., IX (1925–26), 232–35, supplemented by Simon Bernstein, ibid., XIII (1929), 355–57; Bernstein, "The Letters of Rabbi Mahalalel Halelujah of Ancona," *HUCA*, VII (1930), 505, 507 ff., 522; Leopold Löwenstein, "Zur Geschichte der Juden in Fürth," *JJLG*, VIII (1911), 184; Marcus, *Medieval World*, pp. 457 f.; Lewin, *Landessynode*, pp. 40 f. For the famous, though futile, attempt of the Levantine communities to boycott the harbor of Ancona in retaliation for the papal prosecution of Marranos who had found refuge in that city, cf. Graetz, *History*, IV, 577 ff.; Nehama, *Salonique*, IV, 96 ff.

[21] Joseph Sarachek, *Faith and Reason: The Conflict over the Rationalism of Maimonides*; Mann, *Texts*, I, 422 ff. (if Mann's interpretation of the obscure document is correct we have a *terminus ad quem* in the siege of Akko in 1291); Sassoon, *Catalogue*, I, 397 f. (recording a letter dispatched in 1298 in the anti-Maimonidean controversy by Jesse b. Hezekiah of Damascus, "the *nasi*, prince of the captivity of all Israel and his court"). Cf. also above, n. 17 and below, n. 29; Chap. IX, n. 8. David Kaufmann, "Zur Geschichte der Kämpfe Asarja dei Rossis" in his *Gesammelte Schriften*, III, 83–95; Mortimer J. Cohen, *Jacob Emden, A Man of Controversy*

(cf., however, the serious reservations made by S. W. Baron and G. Scholem in their reviews of this work in *Jewish Social Studies*, I, 1939, pp. 483–87; and *Kirjath Sepher*, XVI, 1939–40, pp. 320–38).

[22] Alexander Marx, "A Jewish Cause Celèbre in Sixteenth-Century Italy (the *Pesaḳim* of 1519)," *Abhandlungen . . . H. P. Chajes*, pp. 149–93; Josel of Rosheim's *Memoir* published by I. Kracauer in *REJ*, XVI (1888), 91 f., 99; H. J. Bornstein in *Hatekufah*, IV, 394–426 (giving the background for, rather than the story of, the Berab and Ibn Ḥabib controversy); Dob (Bernard) Revel, "The Renewal of the Ordination Four Hundred Years Ago" (Hebrew), *Ḥoreb*, V (1939), 1–26 (a fuller treatment of that controversy); Cecil Roth, *A Life of Menasseh ben Israel*, pp. 225 ff. Cf. also Bernhard Brilling, "Beziehungen des Vierländer-Parlaments zu Deutschland in 17. Jahrhundert," *ZGJD*, III (1931), 272–75 (referring to a decision of the Polish Council in a Hamburg controversy of 1664). Of course, sometimes such outside interventions were bitterly resented by the local leaders. Samuel di Medina sharply rebuked the Safed authorities for their meddling in the controversy over the appointment of a preacher in the Catalan congregation in Salonica. Cf. his *Responsa*, on Y. D. no. 86.

[23] Mann, *Texts*, I, 65 n. 7, referring to *Teshubot geonim ḳadmonim* (Responsa of the Early Geonim), ed. by David Cassel, no. 46 and *Teshubot ha-geonim mitok ha-genizah* (Geonic Responsa from the Genizah), ed. by S. Assaf, p. 46.

[24] *Close Rolls 1237–1242*, p. 464: *ne de cetero capitula teneant in Anglia*. A collection of most medieval Hebrew sources referring to synods is to be found in Finkelstein's *Self-Government*. The author's extensive comments are further clarified and corrected by Fritz Baer's criticisms and his reply thereto in *MGWJ*, LXXI (1927), 392–97; LXXIV (1930), 23–34; and by Selig Auerbach in *Die rheinischen Rabbinerversammlungen im 13. Jhd*. Cf. also Moritz Stern, "Der Hochverratsprozess gegen die deutschen Juden im Anfange des 17. Jahrhunderts," *Monatsblätter für Vergangenheit und Gegenwart des Judentums*, ed. by B. Koenigsberger, 1890–91, pp. 24–39, 80–90, 115–28, 154–62 (incomplete).

[25] Finkelstein, *Self-Government*, pp. 139, 149 ff.; Baer in *MGWJ*, LXXI, 392 ff.; Salo W. Baron, "Rashi and the Community of Troyes" in American Academy for Jewish Research, *Rashi Anniversary Volume*, pp. 47–71.

[26] Finkelstein, *Self-Government*, passim. The translation here given of the introduction to the synodal decisions of 1150 differs in several geographic identifications from that published by Finkelstein (p. 155). The rendering of Rheims instead of Rhine has already been suggested by Stern in *Monatsblätter*, p. 30. On philological as well as geographic and historical grounds the more important Châlons-sur-Marne appeared preferable to Châlon-sur-Saône, to which identification Finkelstein has been induced by Henri Gross's *Gallia judaica*, p. 592. Poitou rather than the capital Poitiers is clearly indicated in the sources. It is notable that the English, who at that time occupied Poitou, placed no obstacles in the way of the rabbis wishing to attend the synod. Cf. Vincent, *Les Juifs en Poitou au bas moyen âge*, p. 5. It is questionable, on the other hand, whether the decisions of this synod were confirmed by a conference of German rabbis of the same year. Cf. Auerbach, *Rabbinerversammlungen*, p. 13. Finkelstein, in his above discussion with Baer, has made plausible two independent synods in 1220 and 1223 respectively, but has been unable to marshal sufficient evidence for a synod immediately preceding 1220. Auerbach, still basing his entire discussion on the assumption of such an early synod, seems unaware of Baer's strong arguments to the contrary.

In addition to these northern synods, we also learn of frequent later gatherings of the southern French communities convoked primarily, like the organs of the Spanish *collectas*, for purposes of tax assessment. We possess the record of Count Louis d'Etampes' order of 1364 that such an assembly of all the Jewries of Languedoc be called together by Solomon de Moneurchan. Cf. Emile Azémard, *Étude sur les Israélites de Montpellier au moyen-âge*, pp. 108 ff. (also *REJ*, XXIII, 1891, 270 f.). Although Arles was separated from the other communities in 1385, it was required until 1402 to make contributions towards the liquidation of the common indebtedness. Having subsequently rejoined the provincial organization it served, for the most part, as the seat of these regional conferences. That held in 1419–20 was attended by nineteen delegates (7 from Marseilles, 4 from Arles, 3 from Aix, 2 from Apt, and 1 each from Salon, Tarascon, and Draguignan). Similar assemblies and conventions are also recorded for the years 1448 and 1459. Cf. P. Hildenfinger in *REJ*, XLI, 65 ff., 82 ff.; XLVII, 229 ff.; XLVIII, 66 ff. It may readily be assumed that the provincial *conservateurs*, possessing a personal interest in the fiscal proceeds, were, like the Count of Etampes before, their main initiators in the fifteenth century. Cf. above, nn. 12 and 12a.

[27] Cf. next note.

[28] The history of the German Jewish conferences in the crucial period, 1307–1659, has yet to be written. Even earlier there seems to have been a conference in Worms (?) in which Asher b. Yeḥiel participated and which adopted unanimous resolutions in certain controversial matters concerning inheritance laws. Cf. Asher's *Responsa*, LXXXIV, 3. His description of the widespread massacres which preceded seems to refer to the Rindfleisch excesses of 1298. Hence the meeting must have taken place between 1299 and 1303, the date of his departure for Spain. Cf. also Alfred Freimann in *JJLG*, XII, 248 f. Other records, often no less obscure, have been preserved of the following gatherings: 1) About 1307 in Mayence; cf. N. Brüll, "Synoden der deutschen Juden im Mittelalter," *Jahrbücher für jüdische Geschichte und Literatur*, VIII (1887), 61, with reference to Ḥayyim Or Zaru'a, *Responsa*, no. 110. Since Ms. Frankfort, however, reads the decisive passage הוצרכו ליתן מס גדול למלך [דודל] i. e. Emperor Rudolf of Hapsburg, confirming a previous suggestion by J. Wellesz, this conference must have taken place before the emperor's death in 1292, most likely some time between 1286 and 1291. Cf. Wellesz's study on "Hayyim b. Isaac Or Zaroua," *REJ*, LIII (1907), 74; LIV (1907), 102; and M. Liber's notes thereon, ibid., LIII, 268. — Finkelstein in his *Self-Government*, pp. 72 f. assumes that "somewhat later" there was a synod convened by Ḥayyim Or Zaru'a, referred to in Isserles's *Responsa*, no. 57. Isserles, however, here and in his *Commentary* on *Ṭur*, Ḥ. M. 17, quotes "communal ordinances enacted by R. H. [in some ed. of *Ṭur*: S.] of Vienna together with other leaders" in the name of Mordecai b. Hillel, who died a martyr's death in 1298. Although the printed texts of Mordecai contain no such reference in his comments on Sanhedrin I and Shebu'ot IV, it may readily be assumed that such a conference (if indeed the matter was not arranged by correspondence) took place toward the end of the thirteenth century. Should, however, the reading S. [=Shalom] of Vienna unexpectedly prove correct, and should the passage have been interpolated in Isserles' edition of Mordecai, the date would have to be moved forward to the second half of the fourteenth century.— 2) 1381 in Mayence; cf. Finkelstein, op. cit., pp. 74 ff., 251 ff.— 3) 1384–86 in Weis-

senfels; cf. Johann Jacob Schudt, *Jüdische Merckwürdigkeiten*, II, 80; Neufeld, *Die Juden im thüringisch-sächsischen Gebiete*, II, 67 f., 70; K. Burdach, *Vorspiel*, pp. 219, 226.—4) 1391 in Erfurt; cf. J. Caro, "Die Rabbinersynode zu Erfurt 1391," *Jüdisches Literatur-Blatt*, XI (1882), 110–11, 115; Yehudah Kaufmann, *R. Yom Tob Lipmann Mühlhausen* (Hebrew), p. 17 n. 52; Neufeld, l. c. Cf. also Theodor Kroner, *Die Geschichte der Juden in Erfurt*, p. 28.— 5) 1431 in Nuremberg; cf. I. Kracauer, *Geschichte der Juden in Frankfurt a. M., 1150–1824*, I, 166 f. It is likely that Jacob Weil's *Responsa*, nos. 101, 115, 147, refer to this gathering, in which many rabbis participated, rather than to the more obscure assembly of 1438, as suggested by Graetz, *Geschichte*, VIII, 426. — 6) 1434 in Basel; cf. Kracauer, *Geschichte*, I, 174 ff. Max Simonsohn in his *Die kirchliche Judengesetzgebung im Zeitalter der Reformkonzilien von Konstanz und Basel*, pp. 37 ff. makes no mention of this Jewish gathering or of its influence upon the deliberations of the Universal Council of the Church. The Council's decision of 1435 ordering the elders of Ratisbon to facilitate the collection of imperial taxes from the Jews (Wiener, *Regesten*, p. 194, no. 585) indicates, however, that Sigismund made good fiscal use of this occasion, as he did of that offered him by the preceding Universal Council of Constance. Cf. Simonsohn, pp. 22, 45, n. 1 and above, n. 14. — 7) 1438 in Nuremberg; cf. Graetz, l. c.— 8) 1453 in Rothenburg; cf. H. Bresslau, "Zur Geschichte der Juden in Rothenburg an der Tauber," *ZGJD*, O. S. III (1889), 316 n. 8. The appeal from Cracow for assistance in the difficulties occasioned by the incendiary sermons of John Capistrano, reported by Rabbi Meisterlein in Moses Menz's *Responsa*, no. 63, 5 — if indeed it was addressed to a German conference — may refer to this gathering which may have actually taken place in 1454. — 9) About 1456 in Bingen; cf. Graetz, *Geschichte*, VIII, 427 ff. — 10) 1471 in Ratisbon; cf. Moritz Stern, "Die Versammlung zu Worms," *ZGJD*, O. S. III (1889), 250 f. (the decree, dated Aug. 1, 1470, evidently convoked the conference for July 1, 1471); Kracauer, I, 226 f. — 11) 1476 in Nuremberg; cf. Graetz, *Geschichte*, VIII, 436, with reference to Joseph Colon's *Responsa*, Root 4.— 12) 1493 [or 1393] in Worms; cf. Brüll, op. cit., p. 62, with a slipshod reference to [J. P.] Ludewig's *Reliquiae Manuscriptorum*, I. — 13) 1513 in Worms (convoked by the decree of 1510); cf. Stern, in *ZGJD*, O. S. III, 248 f.; Bresslau, ibid., pp. 315 ff.; Feilchenfeld, op. cit., pp. 21 f.; Kracauer, *Geschichte*, I, 265 f. — 14–16) 1523 in Nuremberg, 1529 in

Günzburg (?) and 1530 in Augsburg; cf. Stern, *Bevölkerung*, VII, 19 f.; Feilchenfeld, op. cit., pp. 115 f., 153 ff. — 17–18) 1541 and 1542 in Worms; cf. Bernhard Ritter, "Aus dem Frankfurter Gemeindebuche," *MGWJ*, XXVIII (1879), 36 ff.; M. Horovitz, *Frankfurter Rabbinen*, I, 16 ff., 19 ff., 46 f.; Feilchenfeld, op. cit., pp. 33 f., 50 f.; Stern, *Bevölkerung*, VII, 24 ff. — 19–22) 1562, 1582, 1600, 1603, all in Frankfort; cf. Stern in *Monatsblätter*, pp. 155 ff.; M. Horovitz, *Rabbinen*, I, 25 ff., 36 ff., 40 n. 1, 47 ff.; idem, *Die Frankfurter Rabbinerversammlung vom Jahre 1603*; Finkelstein, op. cit., pp. 78 ff., 257 ff.; Kracauer, *Geschichte*, I, 330 ff.— 23) 1659 in Hanau (at the initiative of the Frankfort elders, two representatives each from Worms, Fulda, Würzburg, Mayence and Friedberg and three local leaders of Hanau met with them to consider ways and means of obtaining from the newly-elected emperor, Leopold I, the renewal of "all the liberties [privileges]" of German Jewry); cf. [Leopold] Löwenstein, "Eine jüdische Notabelnversammlung in Hanau im Jahre 1659," *Israelitische Monatsschrift*, 1897, p. 43 (I am indebted to Professor Alexander Marx for this reference). It is difficult to see, however, the connection between this assembly and the dispatch of its two leading Frankfort delegates to Vienna, where they succeeded in securing very favorable action by the imperial government. Cf. Kracauer, *Geschichte*, II, 74 ff.

[29] Hillel b. Samuel of Verona, *Iggeret* (Epistle) to Maestro Gaio (or Isaac b. Mordecai) in Eliezer Ashkenazi's *Ta'am zekenim* (A Collection of Manuscript Sources), fol. 72b, and reprinted in the Maimonidean *Ḳobeṣ*, ed. by Lichtenberg, III, 14d f. Cf. also Ismar Elbogen, "Hillel da Verona e la lotta per Mosé Maimonide," *Annuario di studi ebraici*, II (1938), 99–105.

[30] Lagumina, *Codice*, I, 302 (1421), 374–75 (1447), 385 (1451), 407 and 412 (1454: The communities of Messina, Marsala, etc., were forced to contribute to the expenses of that of Palermo incurred for a common cause), 429 (1455); II, Pt. 1, nos. 491 (1459), 494–98 (1467). Cf. also above, n. 10.

[31] Lagumina, ibid., nos. 520–21, 524–29; Ferorelli, *Italia meridionale*, pp. 151 ff., 162 ff.

[32] Lagumina, *Codice*, II, Pt. 1, nos. 751 (1489), 754–57, 759, 761, 772–73 (1490), 775–77, 795, 799, 841 (1491); Pt. 2, nos. 878–79 (1492), 890–92, 895, 906, 912, 956, 974–75.

[33] Vogelstein and Rieger, *Rom*, I, 318, 490 ff.; II, 162 f.; Vicenzo Forcella, *Catalogo dei manoscritti riguardanti la storia di Roma . . . nella Biblioteca Vaticana*, I, no. 249. For the Candia conferences, cf. the text of the resolutions and the comments thereon in H. Rosenberg's "Die Statuten der Gemeinden auf der Insel Candia," *Festschrift David Hoffmann*, pp. 267–80; and in Finkelstein's *Self-Government*, pp. 82 ff., 281 ff. A fuller text covering several sessions is available in Ms. Sassoon no. 407 and is extensively summarized in Sassoon's *Catalogue*, I, 349 ff. Some of these decisions, here reproduced, will be referred to below, but a comprehensive analysis of the workings of this noteworthy organizational experiment must await the publication of the entire manuscript which, it appears, Prof. Umberto Cassuto is now preparing for the *Mekize Nirdamim* Society in Jerusalem.

[34] Cf. next note.

[35] The history of the Italian conferences and synods is likewise still full of obscurities. The last general survey is to be found in I. Sonne's "I congressi delle communità israelitiche italiane nei secoli XIV–XVI ed il sinodo dei quattro paesi in Polonia," *L'Idea sionistica*, I, Pts. 11–12 (1931), pp. 5–9, whereas the sources cited by Finkelstein are very incomplete. Thus far the following assemblies have been established with a fair degree of certainty: 1) 1399 in Rimini; cf. E. S. Artom, "Notizie sugli Ebrei a Rimini e nelle Marche," *Miscellanea di studi ebraici . . . H. P. Chajes*, pp. 1–9; Sonne, l. c., with reference to Isaac b. Sheshet's *Responsa*, no. 127.— 2–5) 1416 in Bologna, 1418 in Forli, 1423 (?) in Perugia, 1428 in Florence; cf. Finkelstein, *Self-Government*, pp. 86 ff., 281 ff. and the sources cited there. The conference in Perugia, omitted by both Finkelstein and Sonne, seems to be clearly referred to in the *be-Perusha*, passed over in Finkelstein's paraphrase on p. 297; cf. Cassuto, *Firenze*, pp. 28 f.— 6–7) 1442–43 in Tivoli and Ravenna; cf. Vogelstein and Rieger, *Rom*, II, 11 f., 412. Cf. also Berliner, *Rom*, II, Pt. 1, 71 f.— 8) 1448, Recanati appeals to Ancona to call a conference; cf. David Kaufmann's "Correspondance échangée entre les communautés juives de Recanati et d'Ancone en 1448," *REJ*, XXIII (1891), 249–55. The appeal very likely was heeded. On Capistrano's fleet cf. Rodocanachi, *Saint-Siège*, p. 149 n. 1.— 9) 1469 in Pisa (rather than Piove del Sacco); cf. Sonne, l. c.— 10) 1510–20, Yeḥiel Trabotto of Macerata mentions a

prospective gathering of "patricians and rabbis" in his Ms. *Responsa*, nos. 31a and 73; cf. Sonne, l. c.— 11) 1530–32, Azriel Dayyena of Sabionetta apparently refers to a contemporary conference of the rabbis of Mantua, Ferrara, Bologna, the Marches and Lombardy; cf. Sonne, "Neue Dokumente über Salomo Molcho," *MGWJ*, LXXV (1931), 131, 135. On another occasion in 1535 (or 1518) the same rabbi suggested a more comprehensive all-Italian congress with one representative each from the Venetian republic, Mantua-Ferrara, Bologna-Romagna, the Marca-Rome, and the Kingdom of Naples which, by imposing a property (?) tax of ½ to 1 per cent upon the Jews throughout Italy, would assemble the necessary funds for the redemption of captives and generally coordinate all efforts in this direction. Cf. the excerpt published by S. Assaf from the Jerusalem Ms. of Dayyena's Responsa in *Kirjath Sepher*, XIV (1938), 544, 548 f. It is unlikely, however, that this large assembly should actually have been convoked without leaving further traces in historical records. — 12) 1554 in Ferrara; cf. Finkelstein, *Self-Government*, pp. 92 ff., 300 ff.— 13) 1559 (?) in Rome; cf. Sonne, l. c., rather questionable.— 14–15) 1563, two deputies are sent by the Italian communities to the Council of Trent; 1585–86 conference of Padua; cf. Mortara in *Hebr. Bibliographie*, V, 72 ff., 96 n. 17; Vittore Colorni, "Le magistrature maggiori della comunità ebraica di Mantova (Sec. XV–XIX)," *Rivista di storia del diritto italiano*, XI (1938), 70, 74 f.; Vogelstein and Rieger, *Rom*, II, 163, 179 f.— 16) 1676, under the presidency of Moses Zacuto, delegates of the communities in the Duchy of Mantua, enact a series of regulations concerning legal procedure. Cf. Zacuto's *Shudda de-dayyana* (The Judge's Discretion) and Assaf's *Bate ha-din*, pp. 130 ff.— 17) 1758 in Busseto near Parma, a conference of representatives of the communities in the principality, threatened with sudden expulsion. Cf. Ephraim E. Urbach, "Aus der Geschichte der Juden in Italien im 18. Jahrhundert," *MGWJ*, LXXX (1936), 275–81. The latter two conferences evidently were merely of local importance.

Surveying the development of the north-central Italian conferences, Sonne postulates a certain regularity in their meeting every ten years, and sees therein a close parallel to the Polish councils. This theory seems very far-fetched. Even if the periodicity of these meetings were more clearly demonstrated, the resemblance between the conference of communal representatives from many states in Italy (not only the Papal States) and the regular "Diets" in Poland and Lithuania, with their numerous compulsory features, is rather remote.

[36] Finkelstein, *Self-Government*, p. 163; Rodocanachi, *Saint-Siège*, p. 227, no. 2; Stern in *Monatsblätter*, l. c.; Kracauer, *Geschichte*, I, 357.

[37] Lewin, *Landessynode*, pp. 20 f., 27 f.; *Russko-evreiskii arkhiv*, ed. by Sergey A. Bershadskii *et al.*, I, 192 f.; I. Schipper, "The Composition of the Council of Four Lands" (Yiddish), *Yivo Studies in History*, I (1929), 77; Raphael Rabbinovicz, Introduction to his *Diḳduḳe sopherim* (Variae lectiones in . . . Talmud Babylonicum), I, 61 ff.

[38] Simon M. Dubnow, *Pinḳas ha-medinah* (The Minutes of the Lithuanian Council of Provinces), 278 ff.; idem, "The Council of Four Lands in Poland and its Attitude toward the Communities," *Sefer ha-yobel* (Jubilee Volume in honor of) *Nahum Sokolow*, 250–61; I. Schipper, "The Warsaw Committee; A Contribution to the History of Jewish Autonomy in Poland" (Polish), *Księga jubileuszowa* (Jubilee Volume in honor of) *Markus Braude*, pp. 145–55; and, in general, M. Balaban, "Vierländersynode," *Jüdisches Lexikon*, V, 1213 ff.; Teimanas, op. cit., pp. 89 ff. The following twelve districts represented separate fiscal units within the Polish Council, and their debts had to be separately liquidated after the Council's dissolution in 1764: Greater Poland, Cracow-Sandomierz, Przemyśl, Lublin, Chełm-Bełz, Zamość, Red Russia-Bracław, Ostrog, Włodzimierz, Volhynia-Kiev, Podole, Węgrów.

[39] Of the original protocols of the Polish council, only 6 leaves seem to have been preserved, unless one could locate the source for I. T. Eisenstadt's quotations in his *Da'at Kedoshim, Materialien zur Geschichte der Familien . . .*, I, 99, 124. Since 1894 these leaves have been in the possession of S. M. Dubnow and undoubtedly were recently transferred, with the bulk of Dubnow's archives, to the Yiddish Scientific Institute in Wilno. Cf. *Yivo Studies in History*, I (1929), 699; II (1937), 565 ff. Many transcripts of the Council's proceedings and resolutions, however, have been incorporated into the minute books of the communities of Poznań, Cracow, Lwów, Żółkiew and so forth, and in the works of contemporary writers. The state archives in Warsaw also contain a number of pertinent records. Much of this material is still unpublished, but a great many documents have been made accessible to research. Cf., in particular, A. Harkavy, *Ḥadashim gam yeshanim* in the Appendix to the Hebrew translation of Graetz's *Geschichte*, Vol. VII; Louis Lewin,

"Neue Materialien zur Geschichte der Vierländersynode," I–III, *JJLG*, II (1904), 1–26; III (1905), 79–130; XI (1916), 141–208; S. Dubnow, "Records of the Jewish Crown Diet or the Va'ad of the Four Lands" (Russian), *Evreiskaya Starina*, V (1912), 70–84, 178–86, 453–59 (publishing 28 Hebrew records dated in 1621–99 from the Tykocin Collection); I. Schipper, "Polish Regesta to the History of the Council of Four Lands" (Yiddish), *Yivo Studies in History*, I (1929), 83–114; N. M. Gelber and I. Halperin, "The Council of Four Lands in the Years 1739, 1753" (Hebrew), *Zion*, II (1937), 153–84, 331–46; D. Weinryb, "From the Communal Minute Books in Cracow" (Hebrew), *Tarbiz*, VIII (1936–37), 185–207, supplemented by S. H. Kuk, ibid., p. 368. For some time past, Israel Halperin has been preparing for the press a collection of all extant pertinent material.

The protocol of the Lithuanian Council has been edited from three manuscripts (though not sufficiently explained) by Dubnow in his *Pinkas ha-medinah*, which also includes 7 records of decisions concerning the conflict between the two councils in the years 1633–81. The Council's "legislative activity," as reflected in this *Pinkas*, has been fairly well summarized in Yiddish by I. Sosis in the Minsk *Zeitshrift*, II–III (1928), 1–72. A considerable number of *Tosaphot u-milluim* (Addenda and Supplements) to these *Minutes* have been published by Israel Halperin. In his "Beginnings of the Lithuanian Jewish Council and its Relations with the Council of Four Lands" (Hebrew), *Zion*, III (1937–38), 51–57, Halperin has also tried to reaffirm Harkavy's long discarded theory concerning the early separation of the two Councils. Unfortunately the single incomplete document which he publishes, probably dating from the 1560's, offers no conclusive evidence. It may simply refer to a Lithuanian provincial council, similar to that of Greater Poland and the other provinces (despite the plural of *medinot Lita*), which dispatched representatives to the common central council, meeting in Lublin. For the relations between the Wilno community and the Council cf. Klauzner, *Wilno*, I, 138 ff.

Schipper in his aforementioned article on the "Composition of the Council of Four Lands," *Yivo Studies in History*, I, 78–82, has advanced a theory that the Polish Council consisted of 3 groups: 1) a tribunal of 7 rabbis; 2) an executive committee of 23 members, similar to the Lesser Sanhedrin; 3) an additional membership of 40 at the plenary sessions, making a total of 70 (not 71!), in conscious emulation of the Great Sanhedrin and, one might add, of the Babylonian academies during the geonic period. Schipper's ingenious, but highly artificial, reconstruction of the few available sources has been successfully refuted by Halperin in his "Zur Frage der Zusammensetzung der Vierländersynode in Polen," *MGWJ*, LXXVI (1932), 519–22. While the stray records concerning the activities of the Polish Council do not yet enable us to give the exact dates of its numerous sessions, we find in Dubnow's and Halperin's editions fairly reliable data for the following sessions of the Lithuanian Council; 1623, 1626, 1627, 1628, 1631, 1632, 1634, 1637, 1639, 1644, 1647, 1649, 1650, 1651, 1655, 1659, 1661, 1664, 1665, 1667, 1670, 1673, 1676, 1679, 1683 (Jan. and Oct.), 1687, 1691, 1694 (June and Nov.), 1697, 1700, 1702, 1705, 1713, 1714, 1717, 1719–20, 1721, 1724, 1726, 1730 (two sessions), 1739, 1740, 1748, 1751, 1761.

The Lithuanian Karaites seem to have been stimulated by their Rabbanite compatriots to meet in similar general assemblies. In view of the early date of their first assembly (1553), however, independent origin from similar fiscal exigencies is likewise possible. Cf. Mann's *Texts*, II, 590 ff. The great preponderance of Troki over the other Karaite settlements, in any case, largely obliterated the difference between a general and a local assembly.

[40] Joshua Falk Kohen, *Ḳuntres* [*ha-ribbit* or *ha-taḳḳanot*] (A Compilation on Usury *or* of Ordinances); Harkavy, *Ḥadashim*, pp. 13, 35 ff.; Dubnow in *Yivo Studies in History*, I, 702; Klauzner, *Wilno*, I, 134 f.

[41] Jacob Emden, *Torat ha-ḳanna'ut* (The Lore of Zeal), fol. 61a. Cf. also I. Halperin, "The Council of Four Lands and the Hebrew Book" (Hebrew), *Kirjath Sepher*, IX (1932–33), 367–94; idem, "Approbations of the Council of Four Lands in Poland" (Hebrew), ibid., XI (1934–35), 105–16, 252–64, supplemented, with respect to the provincial councils, ibid., XII (1935–36), 250–53; and above, notes 19–20.

[42] Lewin, *Landessynode*, passim.

[43] Ibid., pp. 29, 69 f.; Moses Zacuto, *Iggerot ha-Remez* (Epistles), no. 30; David Kaufmann, "Die Schuldennot der Gemeinde Posen während des Rabbinates R. Isak b. Abrahams (1668–1685)," *MGWJ*, XXXIX (1895), 94 f. Neither the date nor the place of Moses Zacuto's birth is known, but he himself reminisces on Poznań "as I have known and esteemed it and from whose sources I have drawn at the time of its glory."

[44] Dubnow, *Pinkas*, p. 14, no. 72.

[45] Perugini in *REJ*, III, 105 f.

[46] Lewin, *Landessynode*, pp. 59, 61; J. Landsberger, "Schulden der Judenschaft in Polen," *JJLG*, VI (1909), 252–79; I. Schipper, "The Financial Ruin of the Central and Provincial Autonomy of the Jews in Poland (1650–1764)" (Yiddish), *Yivo Studies in Economics*, II (1932), 1–19. In 1666, while contracting one of their early debts, the leaders of the Council of Four Lands recognized the right of the creditor "to seize all Jews, both the provincial chiefs and the ordinary Jews in their respective localities . . . and to imprison them . . . , to take away the property of all Jews in the realm, to close the synagogues, to confiscate the Jewish houses in the Jewish towns and hamlets and to transfer them to Christians or to whomever else. . . ." Cited by Schipper in *Yivo Studies in History*, I, 85. These harsh provisions evidently were repeated in many contracts and caused endless tribulations in the period of growing insolvency. Cf., e. g., the letter of solicitation sent out by the community of Lublin in 1709 and published by A. Lewinsky in *MGWJ*, XLVI (1902), 170–76. It is interesting to note that, among other creditors of the central and provincial councils, the Jesuits and Dominicans carried some loans over a period of nearly a century. The Church's share in the 2,501,581 fl. indebtedness of the Polish councils amounted to nearly 35 per cent, that of nobility to nearly 30 per cent. Cf. Schipper, "Financial Ruin," p. 17. A good analysis of a typical budget of the Council adopted in 1726 is given by Raphael Mahler in his Yiddish essay "A Budget of the Council of Four Lands in the Eighteenth Century," *Yivo Bleter*, XV (1940), 63–86. Cf. also below, Chap. XV, n. 31.

[47] Balaban, *Z zagadnień ustrojowych*, pp. 11 f., 23 f.; Ignaz Schipper, "Beiträge zur Geschichte der partiellen Judenlandtage in Polen um die Wende des XVII und XVIII Jahrhunderts," *MGWJ*, LVI (1912), 456–77, 602–11, 736–44; idem, in *Yivo Studies in History*, I, 109 f.; Lewin in *JJLG*, II, 20. Cf. also Lewin, *Landessynode*, passim, supplemented by his "Nachträge" thereto in *Festschrift . . . Simon Dubnow*, pp. 124–35; R. Mahler, "Hebrew Documents relating to the Provincial Councils in Old Poland" (Yiddish), *Yivo Studies in History*, II (1937), 639–49. Of course, the withdrawal of government recognition enabled opponents to denounce the legitimacy of new enactments by the two Councils after

1764, but such opposition was easily silenced or disregarded. Cf. Klauzner, *Wilno*, I, 144 f.

48 As a matter of fact, the provincial synods did not entirely disappear even after the partitions of Poland. According to Maria Theresa's ordinance of July 16, 1776, the Galician chief rabbinate was to be permanently supported by a council of twelve elders elected for the entire country. The Prussian administration, too, convoked in 1793 and 1797 a Jewish diet in the newly occupied territories. Cf. Gelber in *JQR*, XIV, 303 ff.; Lewin, "Ein Judenlandtag aus Süd- und Neuostpreussen," *MGWJ*, LIX (1915), 180–92, 278–300.

49 This German translation was published by Gerson Wolf in *Die alten Statuten der jüdischen Gemeinden in Mähren samt den nachfolgenden Synodalbeschlüssen*, but the Hebrew text still awaits critical publication. Only the articles referring to the judiciary have thus far been published from a Bodleian Hebrew manuscript by S. Assaf in his *Bate ha-din*, pp. 124 ff. Cf. the next note.

50 Marx in *Abhandlungen . . . Chajes*, p. 170; Brüll in *Wiener Jahrbuch für Israeliten*, N. S. III (1867–68), 188; A. Frankl-Grün, "Das Landesrabbinat in Kremsier," *MGWJ*, XLIII (1899), 360–70, 425–32; Emmanuel Baumgarten, "Maria Theresa's Ernennungsdekret für den mährischen Landesrabbiner Gerson b. Abraham Chajes," ibid., XLIV (1900), 76–80 (the appointment was made in 1780); Willibald Mueller, *Urkundliche Beiträge zur Geschichte der mährischen Judenschaft im 17. und 18. Jahrhundert*, pp. 103 ff., 157 ff.; Hugo Gold (editor), *Die Juden und Judengemeinden Mährens in Vergangenheit und Gegenwart* (especially the articles by Alfred Willmann, with notes by Heinrich Flesch, on the chief rabbinate, pp. 45–52; by Hugo Meissner on the *Landesmassafond*, pp. 67–72; and by Alois Hilf on the new Union, pp. 72–74). G. Wolf mentions (in his *Kleine historische Schriften*, p. 149) that in 1789 Joseph II agreed with the main Austrian governmental body, the Court Chancery, that "as was done in Galicia, the appointment of a provincial chief rabbi for the Moravian lands be discontinued." The will of the Jews to maintain their old institution prevailed, however. Cf. also Max Freudenthal, "David Oppenheim als mährischer Landesrabbiner," *MGWJ*, XLVI (1902), 262–74; and the next note.

51 Tobias Jakobovits, "Jüdisches Gemeindeleben in Kolin (1763-1768)," *JGJC*, I (1929), 336 ff.; idem, "Die Erlebnisse des Oberrabbiners

Simon Spira-Wedeles in Prag (1640–1679)," ibid., IV (1932), 253–96; idem, "Das Prager und Böhmische Landesrabbinat Ende des siebzehnten und Anfang des achtzehnten Jahrhunderts," ibid., V (1933), 79–136 (p. 130: Oppenheim's order of 1717); idem, "Die Erlebnisse des R. Berl Jeiteles als Primator der Prager Judenschaft," ibid., VII (1935), 421–36; G. Wolf, "Gemeindestreitigkeiten in Prag 1567–1678," *ZGJD*, O.S. I (1887), 309–20. Cf. also Bernhard Brilling, "Eine Eingabe der böhmischen Judenheit vom Jahre 1560," *ZGJT*, V (1938), 59–62; S. H. Lieben, "David Oppenheim," *JJLG*, XIX (1928), 1–38; C. Duschinsky, "Rabbi David Oppenheimer, Glimpses from his Life and Activity," *JQR*, XX (1929–30), 217–47.

[52] Horovitz, *Frankfurter Rabbinerversammlung*, pp. 21 f.; Finkelstein, *Self-Government*, pp. 258 f.

[53] L. Munk, "Die Constituten der sämmtlichen hessischen Judenschaft im Jahre 1690," *Jubelschrift . . . I. Hildesheimer*, pp. 69–82 and Hebrew section pp. 77–85; idem, "Die Judenlandtage in Hessen-Cassel," *MGWJ*, XLI (1897), 505–22; idem, "Aus dem Constituten-Buch der sämtlichen hessischen Judenschaft," *Festschrift . . . Salomon Carlebach*, pp. 339–50; L. Horwitz, "Landrabbiner und Landschreiber in Kurhessen," *MGWJ*, LIV (1910), 513–34. Cf. also J. Lebermann, "Das Darmstädter Landrabbinat," *JJLG*, XX (1929), 181–252 (chiefly dealing with the nineteenth century); and the general remarks of Fritz Baer on the western German councils and chief rabbinates in his "Gemeinde und Landjudenschaft," *Korrespondenzblatt des Vereins zur Gründung . . . einer Akademie für die Wissenschaft des Judentums*, II (1921), 16–29; and in *Das Protokollbuch der Landjudenschaft des Herzogtums Kleve*, Vol. I: *Die Geschichte der Landjudenschaft*, pp. 79 ff. Baer seems unduly to minimize, however, government pressure in the formative stages of most of these organizations.

[54] Munk in *MGWJ*, XLI, l. c.

[55] Baer, *Kleve*, I, passim. Vol. II, which was to contain the original minute-book for the years 1690–1807, has thus far remained unpublished. In the meantime there has been discovered an even more valuable minute book of the provincial community of Paderborn, a study of whose Jewish communal structure has been undertaken by Berthold Altmann. Dr. Altmann has kindly placed at the present author's disposal his preliminary essay on *Die Juden im ehemaligen Hochstift Paderborn zur Zeit des 17. und 18. Jahrhunderts*, submitted in 1924 as a dissertation in

typescript to the University of Freiburg i. B. Cf. also the same author's recent study of "The Autonomous Federation of Jewish Communities in Paderborn," *Jewish Social Studies*, III (1941), 159–88; and Hildegard Kraft's "Die rechtliche, wirtschaftliche und soziale Lage der Juden im Hochstift Paderborn," *Westfälische Zeitschrift*, XCIV, Pt. 2 (1938), 101–204.

[56] For these and other councils cf. Leopold Moses, *Die Juden in Niederösterreich*, pp. 78 f., 105 f.; A. Eckstein, *Geschichte der Juden im ehemaligen Fürstbistum Bamberg*, pp. 61 ff., 153 ff.; D. Kaufmann, "The Minute Book of the Community of Bamberg" (Hebrew), *Ḳobeṣ al yad*, XII–XIII (1896–97), pp. 14 ff., 30 ff., 38; Carl Rixen, *Geschichte und Organisation der Juden im ehemaligen Stifte Münster*, pp. 33 ff., 41; Felix Lazarus, "Judenbefehlshaber, Obervorgänger und Landrabbiner im Münsterland," *MGWJ*, LXXX (1936), 106–17; LXXXI (1937), 444–45; idem, "Die Judenbefehlshaber im Münsterland (Vorort Coesfeld)," *ZGJD*, VII (1937), 240–43; L. Donath, *Geschichte der Juden in Mecklenburg von . . . 1266 bis . . . 1874*, pp. 115 f., 124 ff., 128 ff., 321 ff.; S. Freund, *Ein Vierteljahrtausend Hannoversches Landrabbinat, 1687–1937*; Bernhard Wachstein, "Das Statut der jüdischen Bevölkerung der Grafschaft Wied-Runkel (Pinkas Runkel)," *ZGJD*, IV (1932), 124–49; idem, "A Jewish Community in the Eighteenth Century: Pinkas Runkel" (Yiddish), *Yivo Bleter*, VI (1934), 84–116; VIII (1935), 187 (giving the original of that minute-book); M. Brann, "Geschichte des Landrabbinats in Schlesien," *Jubelschrift . . . H. Graetz*, pp. 218–78; idem, "Etwas von der schlesischen Landgemeinde," *Festschrift . . . Jakob Guttmann*, 225–55; J. Landsberger, "Zur Biographie des R. Baruch Wesel (Bendix Ruben Gumpertz), ersten schlesischen Landrabbiners, ca. 1690–1754," *JJLG*, V (1907), 182–205; VI (1909), 416; VII (1910), 380.

For the intercommunal cooperation in the electorate of Trèves cf. Ph. Bloch, "Ein vielbegehrter Rabbiner des Rheingaues, Juda Mehler Reutlingen," *Festschrift . . . Martin Philippson*, pp. 114–34 (pp. 122, 127 mention an assembly of delegates and the appointment of a rabbi by the united communities of Koblenz, Trèves and environs); Adolf Kober and Elisabeth Moses, *Aus der Geschichte der Juden im Rheinland*; Jakob May, "Die Steuern und Abgaben der Juden im Erzstift Trier," *ZGJD*, VII (1937), 156–79 (a more detailed study of their organization was planned by the author). An indication of the control exercised by the elders of

Mayence over the communities of the entire bishopric may be found in the question addressed by them to Ḥayyim Joseph David Azulai, a visiting rabbi from Palestine, probably in 1754–55. They asked whether they could, as of their own right, change provisions in an ordinance enacted long before for "Mayence and the districts," or whether they had to obtain the consent of a plenary assembly of all members. Azulai favored the latter procedure. Cf. his *Ḥayyim sha'al* (Responsa), I, 30, and, for the date, his itinerary *Ma'agal tob ha-shalem*, p. 25. Cf. also the sources cited in Baer's *Kleve*, p. 80 n. 2.

It is noteworthy that the Alsatian communities incorporated into France likewise had a provincial organ to deal with the common taxes. Delegates met annually in plenary session in Obernai, settled accounts, regulated imposts and elected three syndics to serve as a permanent executive committee under the supervision of a royal intendant. The last session took place on November 10, 1788, a few months before the outbreak of the Revolution. Cf. I. Loeb, "Les Juifs de Strasbourg de 1349 à la Révolution," *Annuaire de la Société des études juives*, II (1883), 139–98; Julien Weill, "Contribution à l'histoire des communautés alsaciennes au XVIIIe siècle," *REJ*, LXXXI (1925), 169–80; M. Ginsburger, "Un emprunt de la nation juive d'Alsace,' ibid., pp. 83–86 (referring to a decision of the Alsatian Council of 1778 to negotiate a loan of 40–50,000 livres in Paris); idem, "Samuel Sanvil Weil, Rabbin de la Haute et Basse-Alsace (1711–1753)," ibid., XCV–VI (1933), 54–75, 179–98; Robert Anchel, *Napoléon et les Juifs*, pp. 7 f., 52 (Trèves, 1805–6).

NOTES TO CHAPTER IX

LOCAL SOCIETY

[1] Emmanuel, *Israélites de Salonique*, I, 104 ff., 284 ff.; Joseph Nehama, *Histoire des Israélites de Salonique*, II, 63 ff., 108 ff.; III, 103 ff.; Isaac b. Samuel Adribi, *Responsa*, no. 223 (ed. Sudzilków, 1833, fol. 68d); Rosanes, *Togarma*, IV, 144. The Salonica burial societies, however, seem to have been attached to individual congregations. Adribi regards, in fact, the maintenance of such a society, along with the election of officers, collections for charity and autonomous regulation of synagogue affairs, as the main criterion of congregational independence. Cf. his *Responsa*, no. 60.

[2] Even in Poland, where the active participation of women in any form of public life was more restricted than in the Mediterranean countries, they were often admitted to charitable and other associations. Cf. Raphael Mahler, "Women, Children and Adolescents as Members of By-Gone Associations" (Yiddish), *Di Zukunft*, XLIII (1938), 163–66; Klauzner, *Wilno*, I, 106 (referring to a *ḥebra de-nashim ṣadkaniot* constituting a special division of the Wilno burial society); and below, Chap. X, n. 31.

[3] Capsali's *Responsa*, ed. by Assaf in *Sinai*, III, Pt. 1 (1939), 155; Nehama, op. cit., pp. 55 ff.; David ibn Abi Zimra, *Responsa*, I, 292. Cf. also Chap. VI, n. 8.

[4] Ezekiel Landau, *Derushe ha-ṣelaḥ*, fol. 7b. This matter was so close to Landau's heart that he constantly reverted to it in his sermons. Cf. ibid., fol. 13c, 33ab, 36d, 38b, 47d, 48b. That the rise of ḥasidic sectarianism has, nevertheless, created serious disturbances within the Jewish community is emphasized by P. Marek in his Russian essay on "Ḥasidism and the Crisis in Jewish Self-Government," *Evreiskaya Starina*, XII (1928), 45–101. Cf. also above, n. 1 and Chap. XII, n. 6.

[5] Baer, *Spanien*, I, Pt. 1, no. 179; Tilander in *Studia neophilologica*, XII, 12 Art. 6; Epstein, *Adreth*, pp. 66 ff.; Nissim b. Reuben of Gerona, *Responsa*, nos. 1, 75; Asher b. Yeḥiel, *Responsa*, XIII, 12–13; Isaac b. Sheshet, *Responsa*, nos. 261, 466; M. Grunwald, "Aus Spanien und Portugal," *MGWJ*, LXXIII (1929), 366 f. Cf. also the somewhat dubious reference to a social affair held by the "holy association" of Vienna, dated about 1320, according to G. Wolf in "Die Einladung der Wiener Chebra vom J. 1320 und der Satzbrief vom J. 1329," *Hebräische Bibliographie*, VI (1863), 118 f.

[6] Gen. Rabbah 96, 5 (ed. Theodor and Albeck, p. 1196); Rashi on Gen. 47.29; Vogelstein and Rieger, *Rom*, II, 316 ff. (Rome was in general a city of many charitable associations, cf. Rodocanachi, *Saint-Siège*, p. 75 n. 2; Ludwig von Pastor, *The History of the Popes from the Close of the Middle Ages*, V, 66); Baer, *Spanien*, I, Pt. 1, nos. 296 (1369), 399 (before 1391), 508 (1414); Dubnow, *Pinkas*, no. 972. Cf. also M. Lipschutz, "Un livre de compte du XVIIe siècle de la Confrèrie des Purificateurs et Fossoyeurs de Carpentras," *REJ*, LXXXII (1926), 425–30; Ab. Cahen, "Le rabbinat de Metz pendant la période française (1567–1871)," ibid., VII (1883), 110 f. (first statute of confraternity *ḳabranim*, adopted in 1621, was revised in 1722 and 1751); L. D. Barnett, "The First Record of the

Hebra Guemilut Hasadim, London, 1678," *Transactions of the Jewish Hist. Soc. in England*, X (1921–23), 258–60; Heinrich Flesch, "Aus den Statuten der mährischen Beerdigungsgesellschaften," *JGJC*, V (1933), 157–74; J. Diamant and B. Glaser, "Statuten (Tekanoth) einer Chewra Kadischa für Jugendliche in Prag zu Ende des 18. Jahrhunderts," *ZGJT*, V (1938), 13–22; Bernhard Wachstein, *Die Gründung der Wiener Chewra Kadischa im Jahre 1763*; Simon Unna, *Gedenkbuch der Frankfurter Juden nach Aufzeichnungen der Beerdigungs-Bruderschaft*, I (for the period 1624–1680); *Festschrift zum 200-jährigen Bestehen des israelitischen Vereins für Krankenpflege und Beerdigung Chewra Kadischa zu Königsberg i. Pr. 1704-1904*; Klauzner, *Wilno*, I, 105 ff.; David Fränkel, "The Minute Book of the Ḥebrah Ḳadishah in Chorostków" (Hebrew), *Alim*, I (1934–35), 21–25, 44–46; Moses Feinkind, "The 'Ḥebra Ḳadisha' in Piotrków" (Yiddish), *Lodzer Visenshaftleche Shriften*, I (1938), 55-62. Fairly representative excerpts in German from statutes of various associations are assembled in Kurt Wilhelm's *Von jüdischer Gemeinde und Gemeinschaft.* Cf. also in general Ephraim Frisch, *A Historical Survey of Jewish Philanthropy from the Earliest Times to the Nineteenth Century*, pp. 143 ff. (p. 160 n. 51 enumerates 8 printed statutes of early modern associations).

It appears that early medieval Jewish burial societies primarily provided funerals for members. Whether or not the talmudic *ḥabburah* resembled in this respect the Greek *homotaphoi* and the more numerous Roman burial brotherhoods (M.Ḳ 27b favors such an assumption, except for the city of Jerusalem where difficulties arising from local requirements of purity necessitated greater specialization of burial societies, cf. *Treatise Semaḥot*, XII, 5, ed. by Michael Higger, pp. 195 f.), the Franco-German commentators took such a system for granted. Cf. Rashi's comments on M.Ḳ., l. c.; *Tosafot* on Ket. 17a bottom; Eliezer b. Joel ha-Levi, *Sefer Rabiah*, ed. by V. Aptowitzer, II, 561 ff. The impression of contemporaneity of these comments is reinforced by the inquiry submitted to Asher b. Yeḥiel by a Spanish brotherhood which refers to its statutes as to an agreement among its members providing for funeral services, if the family "of one of them happens to be in mourning." Cf. his *Responsa*, XIII, 12.

Fritz Baer, in his essay "Der Ursprung der Chewra," *Jüdische Wohlfahrtspflege und Sozialwissenschaft*, I (1928), 241–47, raises the intriguing question as to the relation of these medieval associations to their talmudic prototypes. Unfortunately, here, as in the oft-debated general problem of the historic continuity between the medieval guilds and fraternities and Graeco-Roman associations, no definite answer can be deduced from the meagre source material. For a good survey of the older theories advanced in historical literature in France and Germany cf. Walter Müller, *Zur Frage des Ursprungs der mittelalterlichen Zünfte*, pp. 1–18. Cf. also James W. Thompson, *An Economic and Social History of the Middle Ages (300–1300)*, pp. 788 ff.; Pier Silverio Leicht, *Corporazioni romane e arti medievali*. In Spain, for which we have the fullest records of medieval Jewish societies, the problem has been further complicated by the question of Muslim heritage. We know of the spread of the professional and other guilds under Islam from the ninth century on. Cf. Louis Massignon, "Enquête sur les corporations musulmanes d'artisans et de commerçants au Maroc (1923–24)," *Revue du monde musulman*, LVIII (1924), 61 ff., 149 ff. (asserting Jewish influences upon their evolution); supplemented by his two essays in *Revue des études islamiques*, I (1927), 249–86; his article on "Sinf" in *Encyclopaedia of Islam*, IV (1924), 436 f.; and Bernhard Lewis, "The Islamic Guilds," *The Economic History Review*, VIII (1937–38), 20–37. Cf. also Julius Klein's stimulating discussion of "Medieval Spanish Gilds" in *Facts and Factors in Economic History* (in honor of E. F. Gay), pp. 164–88. The author refrains, however, from a consideration of the non-professional associations, such as the *hermandad de la caridad* for the burial of the poor, said to have been founded in the eleventh century by the Cid Campeador, which has close affinities to the Jewish *ḥebrah ḳadishah*. Cf. Léon Lallemand, *Histoire de la charité*, III, 338.

[7] Baer, *Spanien*, I, Pt. 1, no. 320 (1378); Vogelstein and Rieger, *Rom*, II, 316 ff.

[8] G. Scholem, "Kabbala," *Encyclopaedia Judaica*, IX, 649 ff. (on the Provençal conventicles); Simon b. Zemaḥ Duran, *Sefer ha-Tashbeṣ*, II, 185 (briefly referring to a North African study group of *maskilim* for the reading of the works by Maimonides); S. Schechter, *Studies in Judaism*, II, 238, 244 f., 292 ff. (on Safed); Frumkin and Rivlin, *Toledot*, II, 135 ff.; XII, 47 ff. (on Padua and Jerusalem); Aron Freimann, "A Contribution to the History of the Shabbetai Zevi Movement" (Yiddish), *Yivo Studies in History*, II, 140–51; E. Tsherikover, "The Commune of the Jerusalem Kabbalists 'Love of Peace' [Ahavat Shalom] in the

Middle of the Eighteenth Century" (Yiddish), ibid., 115–39. Cf. also Simon Ginzburg, *The Life and Works of Moses Hayyim Luzzatto*, pp. 22 (including a reference to a similar brotherhood in Ferrara), 165 ff.; idem, *R. Moses Ḥayyim Luzzatto u-bene doro* (M. H. L. and his Generation, a Collection of Letters and Documents), pp. 8 ff., 407 f., 454 f. (both containing the text of the statute of the Padua association); I. Sonne, "Documents" (Hebrew), *Sefer ha-Shanah li-Yehude America* (American Hebrew Year Book), 5695 (1935), pp. 218–25; supplemented, ibid., 5698 (1938), 154–62.

Of considerable interest is also the text, recently recovered, of a pledge signed in 1575 by many disciples of Isaac Luria in Safed in which these mystics bound themselves for ten years to accept the undisputed leadership of Ḥayyim Vital Calabrese and not to reveal any of the Cabalistic secrets of their master without Vital's permission. Cf. the text, published from a private archive in the small town of Stolin in Poland, long a center of Karlinic ḥasidism, by Wolf (Zeeb) Rabinowitsch in his "Manuscripts from an Archive in Stolin" (Hebrew), *Zion*, V (1939–40), 125–32. This document is more fully analyzed by G. Scholem, ibid., pp. 133–60.

[9] Baer, *Spanien*, I, Pt. 1, nos. 362 note (Almunia 1384), 399 (Barcelona before 1391), 508 (Monzon 1414); Pt. 2, no. 281, Section I (Council of Valladolid 1432), etc.

[10] The text of these *Ḥukke ha-Torah*, first published by M. Guedemann, has been reprinted together with many other statutes and records pertaining to educational associations in Simḥa Assaf's *Mekorot le-toledot ha-ḥinnuk be-Israel* (Sources for the History of Jewish Education from the Beginning of the Middle Ages to the Haskalah Period). In his introduction to our text (I, 6 ff.), Assaf mentions the numerous theories as to its date and provenance advanced by his predecessors (northern France, Germany or Algiers in the 12th or 13th century, or Babylonia in the geonic period) and adds his own hypothesis that the document originated in Bohemia after the return of Petaḥiah of Ratisbon about 1190 C.E. to this his native land. The subject would deserve renewed investigation.

[11] Baer, *Spanien*, I, Pt. 2, no. 157; Hildenfinger in his aforementioned essays on Arles, *REJ*, XLI, 70 ff., 87 ff.; XLVII, 232 f.; XLVIII, 51 f.

[12] Roth, *Venice*, p. 69; Assaf, *Mekorot*, II, 205 f. The statutes of the Verona and Modena associations are published ibid., pp. 141 ff., 169 ff.

That of Modena is also given in a free German translation from another manuscript by M. Grunwald in *MGJV*, XXXVII-XL (1911), 63–71. Cf. also Chap. XIII, n. 5 and above, n. 1.

[13] The influence of the Crusades upon the formation of Christian brotherhoods and societies is stressed particularly by Max Heimbucher in his *Die Orden und Kongregationen der katholischen Kirche*, II, 571 ff. Their influence upon the evolution of Jewish philanthropy, however, is yet to be investigated.

[14] Jacob Weil, *Responsa*, no. 26 and, in general, the sources cited by Jacob b. Asher in *Ṭur*, Y.D. 256 and the commentaries thereon.

[15] Baer, *Spanien*, I, Pt. 1, nos. 351 (1382), 463 (1397: Introd.), 532 (1425) and the note thereto (1467); Pt. 2, nos. 76 (1266), 386 ff. (1492); Sancho Saral, *El gremio zaragozano*; Ad. Neubauer, "Zwei Klagelieder," *Israelitische Letterbode*, VI (1880–81), 36; reprinted in H. G. Enelow's edition of *Menorat ha-Maor* by Israel ibn Al-Nakawa, II, 450 f.

[16] Vogelstein and Rieger, *Rom*, II, 316 ff.; S. de B. [H. Sommerhausen], "Les Israélites néerlandais-Reminiscences," *Archives israélites*, VI (1845), 375 n. 1. Cf. also Hildenfinger in *REJ*, XLI, 69 f., 78 ff. (publishing a record of the reorganization of a society *l'ḥolim* in Arles in 1401); Amedeo Revere, "La confraternità israelitica 'Sovegno' di Padova," *Israel*, XII (1938), 277–86 (on the history of a charitable loan association since 1713); J. M. Hillesum, "Vereenigingen bij de Portugeesche en Spaansche Joden te Amsterdam in de 17de en 18de eeuw," *Jaarboek van den Vereeniging Amstelodamum*, I (1902), 167–83; E. Morpurgo, "Bibliografia della storia degli Ebrei nel Veneto," *Rivista israelitica*, VIII (1911), 25 ff. (listing 32 publications of Venetian confraternities); Alexander Marx, "Italienische Statuten," *Zeitschrift für hebräische Bibliographie*, XI (1907), 116 ff.; XV (1911), 143 ff. (describing statutes of various charitable organizations in Mantua and Venice); Balaban, *Żydzi lwowscy*, pp. 539 ff.; Klauzner, *Wilno*, I, 120 ff.; A. Sulzbach, "Ein alter Frankfurter Wohltätigkeitsverein," *JJLG*, II (1904), 241–66 (on *Rodfe Zedakah*, with statute of 1786).

[17] G. Uhlhorn, *Die christliche Liebestätigkeit seit der Reformation*, III, 278; Charlotte Koch, *Wandlungen der Wohlfahrtspflege im Zeitalter der Aufklärung*, pp. 60 ff.; Roth, *Venice*, p. 151; *Taḳḳanot me-ha-ḥebra ḳadisha de-biḳḳur ḥolim ḥadashah . . . Fiorda* (Statutes of the Society for the Visiting of the Sick . . . in Fürth).

[18] For the biblical and talmudic sources, cf. I Chr. 4.14, 21, 23; Nehem. 3.8; M. Demai, IV, 5; Ḥagigah 9b; B.Ḳ. 21b; B.M. 75a; and other references in I. Benzinger's *Biblische Archäologie*, 3d ed., pp. 150 ff.; Samuel Krauss's *Talmudische Archäologie*, II, 249 ff. I. Mendelsohn has made it plausible that the Jewish guilds of both Roman Palestine and Babylonia under the Sassanians and the ensuing anti-competitive regulations had roots in older associations reaching back to the Hammurabi period. Cf. his essays cited above, Chap. III, n. 10. For the Graeco-Roman and Byzantine guilds, cf. the Hierapolis inscription quoted by Juster, op. cit., I, 486 n. 3; *Codex Theod.*, XIII, 5, 18 (390). Cf. also Juster, ibid., II, 264 f., 305 ff.; Franz Poland, *Geschichte des griechischen Vereinswesens*; J. P. Waltzing, *Etude historique sur les corporations professionelles chez les Romains*.

[19] Edwin Hanson Freshfield, *Roman Law in the later Roman Empire, Byzantine Guilds, Ordinances of Leo VI*, in English transl.; Giorgio Zoras, *Le corporazioni bizantine*; Benjamin's *Itinerary*, ed. by Adler, pp. 11 ff.; Starr, *Byzantine Empire*, pp. 28 f. (especially with reference to Thebes, Salonica and Constantinople, where Jewish segregation within the corporative society seems to presuppose separate guilds for the numerous Jewish craftsmen).

[20] Massignon, op. cit. (in *Revue du monde musulman*, LVIII, 221 ff. the author summarizes a manuscript record of guild regulations adopted in 16th or 17th century Fez in Morocco against converted Jews); Georges Vajda, "Les corps de métiers en Turquie d'après deux publications de V. Gordlevskij," *Revue des études islamiques*, VIII (1934), 79–88 (stressing the religious elements in the Turkish guilds); Epstein, *Duran*, p. 64 n. 24. It is interesting to note, however, that the *ḥabburot* recorded in the geonic sources (cf. e. g. Ginzberg's *Genizah Studies*, II, 15; Mann's *Egypt*, I, 54 n. 2; his *Texts*, I, 25, 120, 338) are primarily schools or groups of scholars rather than professional associations.

[21] It is noteworthy that the Jewish guilds but rarely included associations of merchants. The reason for this outwardly paradoxical situation undoubtedly lay in the growing concentration of Jews on commercial endeavors, and their frequent need for new and unorthodox methods of marketing and distribution. Often the cause of friction with established Christian merchant guilds, these unorthodox methods and the general minority status of the Jewish "serfs" of the royal power, tended to create

in the Jewish street a somewhat "freer" economy, at least in the mercantile field, which counteracted prevailing trends toward commercial guild regulation. This aspect of Jewish associational history, however, would deserve much more careful investigation. So would, in fact, the entire history of Jewish guilds, particularly outside of Poland, which alone has thus far been the subject of several monographic studies. Cf. below, n. 24.

For an analysis of the main motives behind medieval guild formation cf. Georg v. Below's pertinent essay, reprinted in his *Probleme der Wirtschaftsgeschichte*, pp. 258–301. Below has rightly declined to subscribe to Schmoller's extreme opinion that "the guild system can in no way be explained by economic considerations" and pointed out that the numerous non-economic motives, which he does not minimize, never played more than a secondary role. In Jewish life, too, despite the preponderance of the religious and defence factors in the entire make-up of the people in dispersion, the primacy of the economic motivation for the organization of Jewish guilds, wherever such existed, appears undeniable.

[22] Julius Klein, op. cit., p. 179 n. 3 (without reference to the sources); M. Kayserling, "Ein Verein der jüdischen Schuhmacher in Saragossa," *Allgemeine Zeitung des Judentums*, LVI (1892), 438 (giving a German translation of an unpublished statute, or rather a fragment thereof, as confirmed by Pedro IV in 1336); Baer, *Spanien*, I, Pt. 1, nos. 279 (1367, 1370), 392 (1390, 1401), 402 (1391), 523 (1417 and note thereto; cf. also Bonafed's sharp satire published by Danon in *REJ*, XLI, 109 ff.); Pt. 2, nos. 275 (1412, Art. 20), 296 (1443), 356 (1486). From the above one can easily judge the faulty generalization in L. Rabinowitz's "The Medieval Jewish Counter-Part to the Gild Merchant," *Economic History Review*, VIII (1937–38), 180–85 based upon the alleged absence of both the "ban of settlement" and the Christian guild in medieval Spain. His basic view, however, that the *ḥerem ha-yishub* was the Jewish outgrowth of the medieval economic regimentation is doubtless correct. Cf. also Chap. X,, notes 2 and 3.

[23] Caro, *Sozial- und Wirtschaftsgeschichte der Juden*, I, 247 ff., 489 ff.; Lagumina, *Codice*, I, nos. 386–87; Ferorelli, *Italia meridionale*, pp. 125 ff; Vogelstein and Rieger, *Rom*, II, 117 f., 416 ff., 436 ff.; Berliner, *Rom*, II, Pt. 1, 101 f.; idem, "Aus schweren Zeiten," *Jubelschrift . . . Hildesheimer*, pp. 154–65 (the text is printed in the Hebrew section, p. 111); I. Schipper, *Yiddishe Geshichte* (An Economic History of Medieval Jewry), III, 96,

101 f. Cf. also M. Wischnitzer's remarks and bibliography in his article "Handwerk," *Encyclopaedia Judaica*, VII, 951 ff.; and for Holland the data assembled by Siegmund Seeligmann in his essay "De Gilden en de Joden," *De Vrijdagavond*, V (1928), 135–37 (with special reference to Elias Voet Jr.'s *Haarlemsche goud- en zilversmeden en hunne merken*).

For contracts between parents and master artisans in which the latter pledged themselves to teach a particular trade to an apprentice, cf. Berliner, *Rom*, II, Pt. 1, p. 102; Assaf, *Meḳorot*, III, 118; F. H. Wettstein, "Discourses on Ancient Matters" (Hebrew), *Ha-Zofeh*, IV (1915), 178 f. (from the Cracow minute-book). Of interest is also the ordinance enacted by the communities of Candia in 1363 forbidding Jewish customers to order garments from Gentile tailors, unless they were sewn in a Jewish house under close supervision. Cf. Sassoon's *Catalogue*, I, 351. This is but another instance of the encouragement given by the biblical taboo of *sha'atnez* to Jewish needle trades.

[24] A good general survey of the Polish Jewish guilds is to be found in Mark Wischnitzer's "Die jüdische Zunftverfassung in Polen und Litauen im 17. und 18. Jhd.," *Vierteljahrsschrift für Sozial- und Wirtschaftsgeschichte*, XX (1928), 433–51. This essay appeared also in Yiddish, with additional notes by the editors, in the Minsk *Zeitshrift*, II–III (1928), 73–88. It is supplemented by additional material and more recent bibliography in I. Halperin's "Jewish Artisan Guilds in Poland and Lithuania" (Hebrew), *Zion*, II (1937), 70–89; M. Kremer's "Study of Craft and Craft Guilds among the Jews of Poland in the 16th to the 18th Centuries" (Hebrew), ibid., pp. 295–325; idem, "The Participation of Jewish Artisans in Christian Guilds in the Old Republic of Poland" (Yiddish), *Bleter far Geshichte*, II (1938), 3–32; Klauzner's *Wilno*, I, 11, 34 f., 39, 123 ff.; and D. Weinryb's *Al yaḥsan shel ha-ḳehillot be-Polin le-ba'ale melakah u-le-po'alim* (On the Attitude of the Polish Communities to Craftsmen and Laborers).

The statutes of the Cracow barbers' guild, originally published by F. H. Wettstein in *Oṣar ha-sifrut*, IV (1892), 604 f. are cited here from the English transl. by J. R. Marcus in his *Medieval World*, pp. 446 ff.

[25] Baer, *Spanien*, I, Pt. 1, no. 362 (the decree speaks of *confratrias* and *elemosinarii*, but very likely included in its scope all Jewish associations); Balaban, *Żydzi lwowscy*, pp. 337, 533 f., App. 109; H. W. Margolies, *Dubno rabbati* (A History of the Dubno Community),

pp. 90 f.; Isaac Levitats, "The Pinḳas of the Dubno Community," (Yiddish), *Yivo Studies in History*, II, 102; P. Kon, "From the Wilno Archives" (Yiddish), ibid., pp. 608 ff. (shedding light on the social struggle in Minsk in 1777); and Michael M. Zarchin, "Tailors' Guild of Kurnik, Province of Posen," *JQR*, XXVIII (1937–38), 47–56. For Bohemia and Moravia, cf. Tobias Jakobovits, "Die jüdischen Zünfte in Prag," *JGJC*, VIII (1936), 57–141 and the sources cited there, especially in note 55. For the indebtedness of the Roman community in the seventeenth and eighteenth centuries, cf. Vogelstein and Rieger, *Rom*, II, 333 ff., 341 f., 427 ff.; and below, Chap. XV, n. 30. In some cases, as in bankrupt Wilno of 1792–93, the community argued that its synagogue, cemetery and bathhouse were owned by these semi-independent associations. Cf. Klauzner, *Wilno*, I, 100.

VOLUME TWO

NOTES TO CHAPTER X

MEMBERSHIP AND ELECTIONS

[1] Müller, *Beiträge*, pp. 8 f., 33 ff.; Theodor Haas, *Die Juden in Mähren*, p. 7; Baron, *Die Judenfrage auf dem Wiener Kongress*, pp. 192 f.; Munk in *MGWJ*, XLI, 515 f. Some Polish communities voluntarily restricted the admission of new members, declared that old members returning after a two-year absence should be treated as temporary sojourners, and limited the number of marriages. A Poznań ordinance of 1681 forbade the conclusion of more than four marriage contracts a year by persons with dowries of 400 fl. or less, if one party came from outside the locality, and of no more than two such contracts between natives. Persons of moderate wealth and, in the case of marriage, students of Jewish law were exempted. Cf. Michael M. Zarchin, "Studies in the Communal Records of the Jews in the Province of Posen during the Eighteenth and Nineteenth Centuries," *JQR*, XXIX (1938–39), 145 ff., 250, 309 ff.; Weinryb, *'Al yaḥsan*, pp. 9 ff. Undoubtedly the sharpest curtailment of Jewish immigration and the most effective bureaucratic control over new Jewish arrivals with the enforced cooperation of the Jewish elders were instituted by the Brandenburg-Prussian legislation under the "Great Elector," Frederick William, and his immediate successors. Cf. Selma Stern, *Der preussische Staat*, passim.

[2] B. B. 21b f. and the commentaries of the school of Gershom, of Rashi and the Tosafists thereon; L. Rabinowitz, "The Talmudic Basis of the *Ḥerem ha-yishub*," *JQR*, XXVIII (1937–38), 217–23; idem, "The Origin of the Canterbury 'Treaty' of 1266," *Miscellanies of the Jewish Historical Society of England*, III (1937), 76–79; idem in *Econ. History Review*, VIII, 180 ff.; Finkelstein, *Self-Government*, pp. 10 ff., 376 f.; Shohet, *Jewish Court*, pp. 23 ff. An interesting, though somewhat obscure, controversy over an early application of the ban of settlement is recorded by Jacob Tam in his *Sefer ha-yashar* (Responsa), ed. by F. Rosenthal, pp. 167 f. For a fuller discussion of the origin of the *ḥerem ha-yishub* and the meaning of early medieval rabbinic interpretations thereof cf. S. W. Baron's aforementioned essay in *Rashi Anniversary Volume*, pp. 62 ff.

[3] Dubnow, *Pinkas ha-medinah,* nos. 46–47 (1623), 202 (1628), 505, 516 (1655), 600 (1667), 642 (1670); Halperin, *Milluim,* no. 40 (1695). Of a different order is the prohibition for Jews to settle in the province of Mazovia (including the city of Warsaw) repeatedly enacted by the Council of Four Lands under pressure of local anti-Jewish opinion. In 1669 the Council, admitting that it had theretofore relaxed its surveillance, renewed this prohibition in view of the constantly deteriorating political status of Polish Jewry and imposed on executive organs the obligations to banish all transgressors without delay. "Should any of the monthly elders intervene with the community in favor of one or another individual, and try to obtain for him a merciful extension of time, such an elder shall pay a fine of 10 thalers without any discount, so that this ordinance be fully upheld." Three years later the Council re-enacted the prohibition in terms no less severe. Cf. Dubnow in *Evreiskaya Starina,* V, 80 ff., nos. 11 and 16. For the background of Mazovian intolerance and especially for the royal privilege *de non tolerandis Judaeis* of 1527, cf. Emanuel Ringelblum's *Żydzi w Warszawie* (Jews in Warsaw), I, 28 ff.

[4] A. N. Frenk, "A Contribution to the History of the *Ḥazakah*" (Hebrew), *Ha-Shiloaḥ,* II (1897), 240–47; Lewin in *Festschrift Dubnow,* p. 130; Kracauer, *Geschichte,* II, 45 f.; Müller, *Beiträge,* p. 71; Max Grunwald "Die Statuten der 'Hamburg-Altonaer Gemeinde' von 1726," *MGJV,* XI (1903), pp. 31 f., 39, 41 ff., 55 f., 58; Marcus, *Medieval World,* p. 216, Art. XVI; Wachstein in *ZGJD,* IV, 136, 146; Samuel b. David ha-Levi, *Naḥlat shibe'a,* Pt. II (Responsa), no. 3. Cf. also Chap. XV, nn. 15–20; XVI, n. 52. For the great local variations and the existence, even in Germany, of unrestricted localities, such as medieval Goslar, cf. H. J. Zimmels, *Beiträge zur Geschichte der Juden in Deutschland im 13. Jahrhundert,* pp. 37 ff.

The ban persisted, nevertheless, into the eighteenth century. The community of Fürth forced its overlord to insert a special article to this effect in his *Reglement* of 1719 and subsequently vigorously protested every infraction by the government authorities. Cf. Friedrich Neubürger, *Verfassungsrecht der gemeinen Judenschaft zu Fürth und in dessen Amt im achtzehnten Jahrhundert,* pp. 20 f. Discussing the matter from the ethical rather than the legal standpoint, the author of the famous medieval *Book of the Pious* direly threatened those responsible for the admission of persons causing damage to local Jews. To preserve family pride, he also advised his readers not to choose their residence in communities composed "of many families or of people hailing from different localities" (Judah b. Samuel, *Sefer ḥasidim*, ed. by J. Wistinetzki, 2d ed., nos. 1301, 1600).

Of course with their general weakness for the scholar the medieval rabbis attempted to secure exceptional treatment for scholars. Isaac Or Zaru'a succinctly declared that "a scholar whose learning is of service to the people, even if he comes from another country . . . and there is another scholar in town, must not be prevented" from settling there. This interpretation was frequently quoted with approval by later rabbis and was invoked in the famous controversy between Israel Bruna (of Brünn) and Anselm in Ratisbon. Cf. Jacob Weil's *Responsa*, nos. 118, 151, etc.; Isserles in *Shulḥan 'Aruk*, Y. D. 245 end. In order to insure the selection of the best-qualified person, as well as greater impartiality in the administration of the rabbinic office, some communities preferred outsiders, or even foreigners. The community of Poznań long expressed such a preference in a statute, as did Fürth (cf. Neubürger, op. cit., p. 34). The rabbinate of Sarajevo, up to 1781, as shown by the communal minute book, was held by a succession of "aliens." Cf. Levy, *Bosnien*, p. 29. With the growing professionalism of the rabbinate, however, the rights of established rabbis called for protection against outsiders. Cf. Moses Sofer, *Ḥatam sofer* (Responsa) on Y. D., no. 230. Cf. also Chap. XI, notes 33, 36.

[5] Baer, *Spanien*, I, Pt. 1, nos. 88 (1229), 93 (1241), 106 (1272), 137 (1294), 199 (1332); Isaac b. Sheshet, *Responsa*, no. 132. Governmental desire to attract wealthy Jewish settlers is well illustrated by James I's privilege of 1267 in favor of Astrug b. Vidal of Carcassonne. In return for his acceptance of the royal invitation to settle in Montpellier, Astrug was to enjoy complete immunity from all civil or criminal prosecution for past crimes or obligations. Cf. Francisco de Boffarull y Sans, *Los Judios en el territorio de Barcelona* (*siglos X al XII*), p. 72, no. lxiii (cf., however, ibid., p. 109, no. cxxxii, concerning Astrug's suicide seven years later). Such immunity, reminiscent of similar privileges later granted to Jews by some Italian merchant republics (cf. above, II, 11 f.), merely attested to the high evaluation of these Jewish settlers as economic and fiscal assets of their respective countries.

[6] *Privilegi . . . Piemonte*, pp. 7 f., 16; Colorni in *Rivista st. dir. it.*, XI, 101; Riccardo Curiel, "Gli Ebrei di Trieste nel secolo XVIII," *Scritti in onore di Dante Lattes* (=*Israel*, XII), pp. 245 f.

[7] Isaiah Sonne, "Contributions to the History of the Jewish Community of Bologna at the beginning of the XVIth century" (Hebrew), *HUCA*, XVI (1941), 51 f., n. 34 (Dr. Sonne kindly placed at the present author's disposal the proofs of this very informative article in advance of its publication); Elbogen in *Jewish Encyclopedia*, VII, 664 f.; Perugini in *REJ*, III, 96 f. no. 11, 106 no. 46; Abraham Berliner, "Antiquities," *Magazin f. d. Wiss. d. Judentums*, XII (1885), Hebrew section, pp. 13–14. Cf. also Abba Apfelbaum, "A Venetian Ordinance of 1636" (Hebrew), *Ha-Zofeh*, XII (1928), 268–70 with N. S. Libowitz's remarks thereon, ibid., XIII (1929), 88–90. Communal control of admissions did not seem irreconcilable with the right of Jews freely to choose their own residence. Even the outspoken champions of such freedom in the controversy which arose, about 1346, due to the removal of a Jewish family from Gerona to Perpignan, never denied the right of the elders of Perpignan to impose conditions on the settlers. Cf. Baer, *Spanien*, I Pt. 1, no. 224a. The sentiments voiced by these champions were shared, moreover, by the northern French Tosafists who evidently raised no serious objections to the *ḥerem ha-yishub*, although it may be that considerations of this nature induced Jacob Tam to limit the operation of that principle. Cf. above, n. 2, and below, n. 10. The greater liberality of the southern medieval communities was, nevertheless, clearly reflected as early as 1130 in the reply of the Roman sages to an inquiry from Paris concerning the application of this ban: "We are astounded about your request that we take sides in a matter which, not being customary in our country, is unfamiliar to us." Published by Samuel David Luzatto in his "Responsum of the Roman Scholars Addressed to the Scholars of Paris" (Hebrew), *Bet ha-Ozar*, I (1847), 57a–60a.

A different sort of communal problem arose from the operation in the modern period of the system of European "capitulations" in the Turkish possessions of the Near East. The more recent Jewish arrivals from the western countries, as well as many natives who in one way or another secured the protection of a privileged European power, naturally preferred extraterritorial status granted their compatriots by the international treaties. Extraterritoriality of this kind not only subjected such Jewish "Franks" to the jurisdiction of their respective consuls rather than to that of the local rabbis, but freed them from communal taxes. In most cases they voluntarily contributed sums appropriate to their generally favorable economic position, but they could be forced to pay only such imposts as rested generally on alien Jews. This status of permanent "resident aliens" enjoyed by a large section of the population necessarily became a constant source of intracommunal friction. For an analysis of conditions in the typical community of Aleppo in Syria, cf. Alexander Lutzky's recent Hebrew essay on "The 'Francos' and the Effect of the Capitulations on the Jews in Aleppo (from 1673 till the time of the French Revolution)," *Zion*, VI (1940–41), 46–79. Cf. also A. J. Braver, "Jewish Enjoyment of the Privileges of the Capitulations in Palestine" (Hebrew), ibid., V (1939–40), 161–69.

[8] Finkelstein, *Self-Government*, pp. 124, 137, 177, 185; Ibn Adret, *Responsa*, V, 277; Baer, *Spanien*, I, Pt. 1, no. 143, par. 10; Munk in *Jubelschrift Hildesheimer*, Hebrew section, p. 81; Levy, *Bosnien*, p. 24; Tilander in *Studia neophilologica*, XII, 16 f. Art. 16–18; Elbogen in *Jewish Encyclopedia*, VII, 665; Epstein, *Adreth*, pp. 26 f.; idem, *Duran*, pp. 13 ff. The problem of mutually assessing visitors led to a protracted legal controversy between the communities of Mantua and Verona in the eighteenth century; the majority of rabbis argued in favor of such discriminatory taxation. Cf. A. Marx's discussion in *Zeitschrift f. hebr. Bibliogr.*, XI, 112 n. 1; XV, 145. Not until 1616 did Pisan Jewish merchants obtain liberation from a tax imposed on all merchandise brought to neighboring Leghorn, although both cities had long been part of the same Grand Duchy of Tuscany. Cf. S. H. Margulies, "Dall' archivio dell' Università israelitica di Pisa," *Rivista israelitica*, V (1908), 72. Some communal associations in Italy, on the other hand, concluded regular treaties of reciprocity with similar associations in neighboring cities. The statute of the association *raḥmim* in Modena refers to such pacts with the community of Mantua and others. Cf. *Costituzioni della Compagna ebraica della misericordia della città di Modena*, 1791, pp. XVII f.

To reconcile these varying practices with the talmudic scale of duties, Josef Colon suggested that the talmudic law applied only to visitors, whereas newcomers settling for permanent residence were, from the outset, subject to the regular charitable and other imposts. Cf. his *Responsa*, Root, 17, 3, quoted with approval also by Joseph Karo on *Ṭur*, Y. D. 256. There were, of course, numerous cases of tax evasion, Jacob Weil, e. g., reporting one in which a woman, after prolonged sojourn, evaded fiscal responsibilities on excuse of illness. Cf. his *Responsa*, no. 106.

[9] Mossé, *Avignon*, p. 147; Decourcelle, *Nice*, pp. 220 f., 236; Baer, *Spanien*, I, Pt. 2, no. 132 (1312); Pt. 1, nos. 30a (1156), 74 (1210), 77 (1211), 78 (1212), 114 (1278); Finkelstein, *Self-Government*, pp. 149, 228, 243; Ḥayyim Or Zaru'a, *Responsa*, no. 80; Jacob Weil, *Responsa*, no. 38, etc. For further discussion of tax immunities in these and other countries, cf. Chap. XV.

[10] Isidore Loeb, "Statuts des Juifs d'Avignon (1779)," *Annuaire de la Société des études juives*, I (1881), 239 ff.; Mossé, *Avignon*, pp. 147, 158; Baer, *Spanien*, I, Pt. 1, nos. 143 (5), 163 (11), 224a; Ibn Adret, *Responsa*, III, 406; Tilander in *Studia neophilologica*, XII, 18 Art. 21–22; Perles in *MGWJ*, XVI, 344 ff.; Munk in *Jubelschrift Hildesheimer*, p. 77; *Tosafot* on B. Ḳ. 58a. Cf. also "The Ordinances of the Polish and Lithuanian Councils concerning Fugitives," analyzed by F. Dickstein in his Hebrew essay in *Ha-Mishpaṭ ha-'ibri*, I (1918–20), 29–76; the severe restrictions included in the Sicilian statutes approved by the government in 1451, 1455 and 1456 (Lagumina, *Codice*, I, nos. 385, 425, 432); in that of the Moravian communities Art. 206–8, 237, 307 (Wolf, *Statuten*, pp. 56 f., 64, 78); and in that of Hamburg of 1726, Art. 107, 117, 119, 120, 122, 214 (M. Grunwald in *MGJV*, XI, 39, 41 f., 43, 58; idem, *Hamburgs deutsche Juden bis zur Auflösung der Dreigemeinden, 1811*, pp. 42, 44 f.); Moses Menz, *Responsa*, no. 120 (scolding the community of Ratisbon for prematurely cancelling the right of sojourn of an absentee member); and the objections raised by Ḥayyim Ya'ir Bacharach (in his *Ḥavvot ya'ir* [Responsa], no. 80) against the imposition by a particular community of a higher departure levy than had been customary theretofore.

It undoubtedly was also in cooperation with the Jewish elders of Perpignan that Pedro IV gave, in 1365, his permission to three Jews to proceed to France "where they hope to pursue their trade with greater profit than in these lands," on condition that they leave their wives and children behind and furnish sufficient guarantees for their share of communal taxes. Cf. Pierre Vidal, "Les Juifs des anciens comtés de Rousillon et de Cerdagne," *REJ*, XV (1887), 51 n. 1. The privileges of Piedmontese Jewry of 1603 and 1609 provided that departing Jews should first arrange with their community for their share in the communal debt and prohibited the export of Jewish capital. Cf. *Privilegi . . . Piemonte*, pp. 83 f., 134 f. The popes imposed a heavy "flight tax" on Jews desirous to leave the Papal States. Cf. Rodocanachi, *Saint-Siège*, pp. 65 f. (referring to

Leo XII ?). The Jewish elders of Carpentras tried to collect, out of the possessions of Jews who departed because of a decree of expulsion, not only their share in the communal indebtedness but also a contribution toward the expenses incurred in obtaining the revocation of the decree of banishment. This procedure elicited the protest of Joseph Karo in Turkey. Cf. D. Kaufmann, "Une lettre de Josef Caro adressée aux Juifs de Carpentras," *REJ*, XVIII (1889), 133–36. The Jews, too, became so used to feudal overlordship that some elders spoke of one community having "sold" a member to another. Cf. e. g., Asher b. Yeḥiel's *Responsa*, VI, 15, which, incidentally, strengthens the conclusion that similar terminology in innumerable royal decrees is not to be taken too literally. Cf. Baron, *History*, II, 22 ff.; III, 100 ff.

Even northern rabbis, however, were inclined to treat leniently a Jew who had broken a residence oath given to his feudal overlord under compulsion provided that, at the time of taking the oath, he had made strong mental reservations. Cf. the sources quoted by Shohet in his *Jewish Court*, p. 14. As late as 1791, Rabbi Zeeb Wolf of Dubno signed a similar pledge to the city's overlord, Prince Michael Lubomirski: "I have taken upon myself, of my own will and under no compulsion or restraint, that during all the time of my occupancy of the rabbinic chair in the city of Dubno I shall not venture to move outside the walls of the city without the authorization of His Highness, the Prince. Neither shall I dispose of any of my property, be it in secret or in public, by myself or through others, so that it be removed from this city. . . ." Rabbi Wolf had then been in office for fourteen years, having succeeded his father who had officiated for a period of twenty years! Cf. Margolies, *Dubno*, pp. 15 f., 178. Cf. also above, n. 7 and Chap. VII, n. 19.

[11] Margoliouth, *History*, III, 239, 246 ff.

[12] Scipione Calabi, "Le confraternite della communione israelitica di Verona," *Educatore israelita*, XII (1864), 79 f.; *Statuto della Pia Opera di Misericordia Israelitica in Verona*, 1900. Cf. also *Costituzioni . . . Modena*, p. xvi. For an interesting record of personal influence and perpetual family control in the educational association of medieval Arles, cf. Chap. IX, n. 11. This hereditary system created many a complex legal situation. Upon the death of a Marrano who had joined the Amsterdam Society for the Marrying off of Orphan Girls, it was discovered that his eldest son had returned to Christianity, but that his grandson subsequently reverted to

Judaism. For the ensuing controversy and rabbinic decision, cf. Jacob Sasportas, *Ohel Ya'akob* (Responsa), no. 59.

[13] Klauzner, *Wilno*, I, 107; Wischnitzer in *Vierteljahrsschrift*, XX, 443 f.; Jakobovits in *JGJC*, VIII, 118 ff.

[14] Emmanuel, *Salonique*, I, 72, 149 f., 215 f., 293; Nehama, *Salonique*, III, 85 ff.; Danon in *REJ*, XL, 211, 215; XLI, 108 f.; Malvezin, *Bordeaux*, pp. 212 ff.; Grunwald, *Hamburg*, pp. 45 f.

[15] Decourcelle, *Nice*, pp. 218, 227 f., 281 f.; S. W. Baron in *Sefer ha-Yobel . . . Krauss*, pp. 217–54, supplemented by I. Sonne's "Materials to the History of the Jews in Verona" (Hebrew), *Zion*, III (1938), 123–69; continued in *Ḳobeṣ 'al-yad*, N. S. III (XIII), Pt. 2 (1939), 145–91; Vogelstein and Rieger, *Rom*, II, 24 f., 40, 128, 131 f. The difficulties often besetting the communal rabbis and other city-wide leaders in the face of such conflicts are well illustrated by the case of a Damascus rabbi to whom the native (*Mustarab*) congregation wished to forbid attendance at the synagogue of the Spanish refugees. Not even the rabbi's withdrawal from the city to a neighboring village enabled him to keep aloof from the controversy. Cf. Rosanes, *Togarma*, I, 114. Cf. also Chap. VI, n. 43.

[16] Baer, *Spanien*, I, Pt. 1, nos. 132 (1292), 187 (1327), 536 (1453); The Amsterdam statute of 1639 Art. 2–3 in D. H. de Castro's *De Synagoge der Portugeesch-Israelietische Gemeente te Amsterdam*, p. XXI; Salomon Ullmann in *JJLG*, V, 33 f.; Da Silva Rosa, *Geschiedenis*, pp. 45 ff.; Barnett, *El libro de los acuerdos*, p. 5 (Art. 7); Roth, *Archives*, p. 32, no. 1.

[17] Decourcelle, *Nice*, pp. 223 f.; Neubürger, *Fürth*, pp. 11, 19 f.; Dubnow, *Pinḳas*, no. 6; M. Schorr, *Organizacya Żydów w Polsce* (Jewish Communal Organization in Poland until 1772), p. 44; idem, *Żydzi w Przemyślu* (Jews in Przemyśl), pp. 141 f.; Balaban, *Żydzi lwowscy*, pp. 252 ff. Cf. also Lagumina, *Codice*, I, no. 46; Klauzner, *Wilno*, I, 146 ff. The provincial diet of Cassel, without consulting the Jews of the neighboring county of Schwarzenfels, resolved to force them into its jurisdiction. Cf. Munk in *Jubelschrift . . . Hildesheimer*, Hebrew section, p. 83. As late as 1794 the community of Kimpolung, in the newly annexed Austrian province of Bukovina, complained that the district community of Suczawa, the recipient of all the communal revenue, contributed only the ludicrous sum of 10 fl. to the maintenance of Kimpolung's local officials. Cf. Manfred Reifer, *Ausgewählte historische Schriften*, pp. 98 f. Cf. also Rudolf Wenisch, "Beziehungen Kommotaus zu den Juden der Umgebung im sechzehnten

und siebzehnten Jahrhundert," *JGJC*, VII (1935), 37–198; and, on a different plane, Meir of Lublin's *Responsa*, no. 40 (of 1601–2) in which the community of Hotzenplotz was told to pay its promised contribution of two-fifths toward a subsidy to prevent the expulsion of the Jews from Zülz, Silesia (the other three-fifths had been paid by the Polish, Moravian, and Prague councils, respectively). For the background of this decision cf. Israel Rabin, *Die Juden in Zülz*, pp. 8 ff. Cf. also Chap. VIII, nn. 18, 47.

18 Menz, *Responsa*, no. 63. There are a number of interesting medieval German illustrations of the effects of centralized control on the jurisdiction of the courts, and its breakdown under the influence of local transfers of sovereignty or the disaffection of the dependent Jewries. Cf. Frank's *Ḳehillot Ashkenaz*, pp. 85 ff.

19 Ibn Adret, *Responsa*, V, 222; Joseph of Trani, *Responsa*, no. 58; Ḥayyim Or Zaru'a, *Responsa*, no. 65. Elijah Capsali once characterized a meeting of twenty-five elders in Candia, who in 1546 introduced the perpetual celebration of a local holiday, as "the large assembly numbering twenty-five men." Cf. his "Memoir" published by A. Berliner in *Ḳobeṣ 'al yad*, XIX (1903), 19–26. For bachelor's and women's suffrage, cf. below, n. 31.

This is not the place to discuss the vast and complex problems of the size of the Jewish population during the medieval and early modern periods, however deeply its size, rise or decline in the various communities may have influenced the development of the communal organization. The following few points may suffice. The entire Jewish population of England at the end of the twelfth century seems not to have exceeded 2000, distributed over a considerable number of communities. Cf. Jacobs, *Angevin England*, pp. 381 f. In 1290, after sustained growth, the total number of Jews who left England was about 16,000, to which figure one may add, perhaps, a few more thousands of those who remained behind. Cf. B. L. Abrahams, *Expulsion*, p. 39. According to a recent estimate, Paris alone among the medieval northern French communities had a Jewish population exceeding 100 families. Cf. L. Rabinowitz, *The Social Life of the Jews of Northern France in the XIIth to the XIVth Centuries*, pp. 29 ff.; Baron in *Rashi Anniv. Vol.*, pp. 58 ff. A list of Jewish heads of families in Avignon who, in 1358, were called upon to take a civic oath of allegiance to the pope, included 210 names. This figure seems to indicate a Jewish population of well in excess of 1,000 persons. The number subsequently decreased to 85 families at the end of the papal regime in 1789, and to 25 families in 1810. Cf. M. de Maulde, *Les Juifs dans les états français du Saint-Siège au moyen âge*, p. 5. The important community of Augsburg enumerated in its tax lists of 1401 and 1437, seventeen and twenty-odd taxpayers respectively. The departing Jewish population of 1438 was estimated at over 300 persons. Cf. Fritz Leopold Steinthal, *Geschichte der Juden in Augsburg*, pp. 38, 50. Similarly, Nuremberg, then the most heavily assessed community in Germany, numbered in 1449 but 150 members [taxpayers?], which contrasts, however, with the number of 500 martyrs of 1349 recorded in the contemporary local martyrology. Erfurt, probably the largest German-Jewish community of the day, possessing four or five synagogues and four ritual slaughter houses, had in 1357–89 only 50–86 taxpayers. Cf. S. Neufeld, op. cit., II, 171 f. Cf. also M. Stern, "Zur Statistik der Wormser Juden im 15. Jahrhundert," *Israelitische Monatsschrift*, 1897, nos. 1–2, 9–11; Menczel, *Mainz*, pp. 65, 70 ff.; Wilhelm Grau, *Antisemitismus im späten Mittelalter*, pp. 18 ff. (on Ratisbon, biased); E. Dukesz, "Aus dem Archiv der Stadt Altona," *Jahrbuch für die jüdischen Gemeinden Schleswig-Holsteins*, I (1929–30), 131–34 (listing all Jews under governmental protection in 1664); Leopold Löwenstein, "Verzeichnis der israelitischen Einwohner von Karlsruhe im Jahre 1733," *Blätter für jüdische Geschichte und Literatur*, III (1902), 131–37, 154–57 (55 Jews enjoying the right of sojourn; with dependents and employees a total of 282 persons); A. Lewinsky, "Zur Statistik der jüdischen Bevölkerung in Stadt und Hochstift Hildesheim im 18. Jahrhundert," ibid., pp. 113–19, 150–53, 169–71; Jacob Jacobson, *Jüdische Trauungen in Berlin, 1723–1759*; and generally Pinthus in *ZGJD*, II, 204 f.

These figures may be contrasted with the 10–12,000 estimated Jewish population of Rome in the eighteenth century (cf. Rodocanachi, *Saint-Siège*, pp. 69 f.; Vogelstein and Rieger, *Rom*, II, 231) and with the 10,507 Jews living in Prague according to the official census of 1729 (after the eventful years of 1744–46 their number declined to 6,061; cf. Jakobovits in *JGJC*, VIII, 127 ff.). Even a middle-sized community like Verona grew from its foundation in 1404–5 to about 400 souls in 1600 and more than 1,000 in 1751, then constituting about 2⅛ per cent of the city's total population. Cf. Baron in *Sefer ha-Yobel Krauss*, pp. 222, 250 n. 26. For Venice, cf. C. Roth's *Venice*, pp. 106 f.; for Bologna, cf. Ermanno Loevinson, "Notizie e dati degli Ebrei entrati a Bologna nel sec. XV,"

Annuario di studi ebraici, II (1938), 125–73 (a detailed archival study); and for Frankfort, I. Kracauer, "Beiträge zur Geschichte der Frankfurter Juden im dreissigjährigen Kriege," *ZGJD*, O. S. III (1889), 130 ff.; Joseph Unna, *Statistik der Frankfurter Juden bis zum Jahre 1866*. Cf. also Roberto Bachi, "La demografia del Ebraismo italiano prima dall' emancipazione," *Israel*, XII (1938), 256–320. For medieval Spain, cf. especially Isidore Loeb's essay in *REJ*, XIV, 161–83, which, despite certain questionable methodological approaches, offers the relatively best estimates for the last decades of the Jewish settlement on the Peninsula. Further data are given in Marx' remarks in *JQR*, O. S. XX, 247 ff.; and in Baer's *Spanien*, passim.

The ratio of growth in most cities was far surpassed, for local reasons, by the phenomenal increase of the Jewish population in Metz under French domination. In 1624 the government reluctantly authorized 76 Jewish families. By 1718 it was gradually forced to raise the quota to 480 families. Cf. Roger Clément, *La condition des Juifs de Metz sous l'ancien régime*, pp. 33, 254 f., 268 ff., 278 ff. Cf. also the list of Jews in Metz in 1739 published by M. Ginsburger in *REJ*, L (1905), 238 ff. From that time on the population remained fairly stable until the events of 1789 which were followed by a sharp decline. According to official statistics, Metz had 550 Jewish families (3,025 persons) in 1789; 503 families (2,764 persons) in 1800, and 456 families (2,186 persons) in 1810. Cf. S. Posener, "Les Juifs sous le premier empire; les statistiques générales," ibid., XCIV (1933), 163 f. There is little doubt that the largest Jewish community in Christian Europe before 1800 was in Amsterdam, where it reached in 1795 a total of 2400 Sephardim and 21,000 Ashkenazim. Cf. Bloom, *Economic Activities*, pp. 203 ff. Figures for Poland and Turkey are, on the whole, less reliable, except for those derived from the Polish and Austro-Prussian censuses after 1764. These have been under close scholarly scrutiny in recent years. Cf. for instance, G. Kleczynski and Fr. Kluczycki, *Liczba głów żydowskich w Koronie z taryf roku 1765* (The Number of Jews in Poland on the Basis of the Assessments of 1765); Ch. Korobkow, "Jewish Population Statistics for Poland and Lithuania in the Second Half of the Eighteenth Century" (Russian), *Evreiskaya Starina*, IV (1911), 541–62; Raphael Mahler, "The Jewish Population in the Area of the Present Province of Lodz in 1764" (Yiddish), *Lodzer Visenshaftleche Shriften*, I (1938), 32–54; Klauzner, *Wilno*, I, 46 ff.

[20] Baer, *Aragonien*, p. 102 and the sources listed there; idem, *Spanien*, I, Pt. 1, no. 188; Pt. 2, no. 287 (iv, 7); Finkelstein, *Self-Government*, pp. 371 ff.

[21] J. C[assuto], "Aus dem ältesten Protokollbuch der Portugiesisch-Jüdischen Gemeinde in Hamburg," *JJLG*, XI (1916), 5 f. The statute of Sugenheim concluded with the provision that "in order that no householder may be able to excuse himself through ignorance, the communal chiefs shall have the cantor read this communal constitution to all the householders, publicly, word by word, in the synagogue right now, and then every year at the Pentecost and relate its entire contents exactly and without deviation." Marcus, *Medieval World*, pp. 220 f. The Great Synagogue in London, however, drew a curious distinction between "the alteration of any established law, or the enactment of any new one" which was to "be proclaimed in the Synagogue on the first Sabbath or festival day following, and be posted near the door of the Synagogue, for the space of fourteen days at least," and "cases when the whole code of Laws be made anew, or the old ones completely revised" in which the forwarding of a copy to each member was deemed sufficient. Cf. Margoliouth, *History*, III, 280 f. Perhaps the framers of the statute counted on general awareness of projected major constitutional changes.

[22] Joseph Karo, *Shulḥan 'Aruk*, Ḥ. M. 163, 3 and the remarks of Isserles and Joshua Falk Kohen thereon; Isserlein, *Terumat ha-Deshen* (Responsa), no. 344; Joseph Katz, *She'erit Yosef* (Responsa), no. 18; Samuel di Medina, *Responsa*, on Ḥ. M. no. 421; Krochmal, *Ṣemaḥ Ṣedeḳ* (Responsa), nos. 1, 18 (Krochmal's opinion is controverted, however, by Jacob b. Joshua Reischer in his responsa *Shebut Ya'akob*, I, no. 72); other sources cited by I. Sosis in his "Social Conflicts in the Jewish Communities of the Sixteenth and Seventeenth Centuries according to the Rabbinic Responsa" (Hebrew texts with Yiddish translation), *Zeitshrift*, I (1926), 225–38, and by Assaf in his *Bate ha-din*, pp. 44 ff.

[23] Vogelstein and Rieger, *Rom*, I, 342 f.; II, 40; *Taḳḳanot Ḳ. Ḳ. Hamburg be-London* (Statute of the Hambro Congregation in London), 1795, Art.32; Levy, *Bosnien*, p. 23; Baer, *Spanien*, Pt. 1, no. 146.

[24] Attilio Milano, "I capitoli di Daniel da Pisa e la Communità di Roma," *Israel*, X (1935–36), 324–38, 409–26; E. Rodocanachi, "La communauté juive de Rome au temps de Jules II et de Léon X," *REJ*, LXI (1911), 73 ff.; Colorni in *Riv. st. dir. it.*, XI, 66 f., 70, 73, 75, 79, 88 ff.,

91 f., 102, 108, 114. For the division into three electorial *curiae* cf. also below, notes 32–33. The exceptional right of a single member to object to the appointment of certain communal officials will be discussed below, Chap. XII, n. 52; XV, n. 37.

[25] Ḥayyim Or Zaru'a, *Responsa*, no. 222; Meir of Rothenburg, *Responsa*, ed. Prague, no. 968; Joseph Karo on *Ṭur*, O. Ḥ. 153 (quoting Eliezer b. Joel); Finkelstein, *Self-Government*, pp. 33 f., 49 ff., 107 f., 121, 132 f.; Baer in *MGWJ*, LXXI, 395; Zimmels, *Beiträge*, pp. 21 f.; Epstein, *Adreth*, p. 34; Isaac b. Sheshet, *Responsa*, nos. 457–61 (discussing intricate questions which arose from the delegation, by the community of Alcolea to a committee of twelve, of the authority to prepare a new statute); Adribi, *Dibre ribot* (Responsa), no. 224; Mossé, *Avignon*, p. 139; Maulde, *Etats français*, pp. 51 n. 1, 165 f. Art. LXXXV (in 1643 70 members of the community complained that the elders had introduced innovations by way of interpretation); Sonne in *HUCA*, XVI (1941), 56 ff. (the important Bologna ordinance of 1511 against outside bans was apparently adopted only by the rabbis and elders, but it was afterwards read on three successive occasions from the pulpit of the great synagogue, thus evidently giving the members an opportunity to raise objections); Jacob Reischer, *Shebut Ya'akob*, no. 72 (seven constitution makers); Grunwald, *Hamburg*, p. 41; idem in *MGJV*, XI, 35, 55; Margoliouth, *History*, III, 234, 280; *Takkanot* of the Hambro Congregation, Introd. and Art. 52, 56 (the congregation decided in 1794 to change its old statutes which had "no bearing whatsoever upon our time," and elected a committee of eleven to prepare a new draft); Decourcelle, *Nice*, pp. 229 ff. (from the document here published we may deduce that Moses Hağas or Hağis, the well-known cabalist, sojourned in Nice in 1738, evidently returning to Palestine from Altona, cf. Frumkin and Rivlin, *Toledot*, II, 133). Cf. on the other hand, Lagumina, *Codice*, I, no. 148 (in 1398 King Martin authorized the *prothi et universitas Judaeorum* together to adopt statutes and submit them for government approval), 302 (the statutes submitted by the united Sicilian communities for royal approval in 1421 mention only the *sapientes, scientes atque consultatores*, as empowered to issue local ordinances); Danon in *REJ*, XLI, 108 f. and Emmanuel, *Salonique*, I, 71 (three leading rabbis proposed the new statute, subject to the approval of the other rabbis of Salonica); Levi ibn Ḥabib, *Responsa*, nos. 30 (in Trikkala the community elected three *metakne takkanot*, but a controversy arose when

a copy of the ordinances prepared by them was torn), 99 (decision that the ordinance be valid only after confirmation by the rabbi). In the Moravian community of Gaya, a committee elected by lot from the entire membership revised, in 1688–89, the statute which had been in force since 1675. Cf. H. Flesch, "Die Takkanot der Gemeinde Gaya," in Gold's *Mähren*, p. 35. On the other hand, a substantial part, perhaps nearly one-half of the entire adult membership participated in the adoption in 1497 of a new statute for the community of Ratisbon. The ten members of the Council who then acted together with thirty-two other "best men of the community," as recorded in a contemporary document (cf. Raphael Straus's unpublished Appendix to his *Die Judengemeinde Regensburg im ausgehenden Mittelalter*, no. 676), may easily have amounted to a majority of direct taxpayers. Cf. also Kracauer, *Geschichte*, II, 182.

This fairly widespread uniformity should not blind us to the fact, however, that vestiges of ancient individualism survived also in this field. Particularly in the Balkan provinces of sixteenth-century Turkey, cross-currents generated by prevailing unrest and many-sided creativity, brought to the fore traditions which long seemed defunct. Joseph of Trani, for instance, insisted that communal agreements, like those among partners, should bind only persons present at deliberations, even if the latter acted unanimously. Cf. Trani's *Responsa*, I, 68. The case was exceptional, however, insofar as the agreement referred to was directed against the established communal authorities. The rabbi may here have felt justified in demanding more than the usual majority vote. For divergent interpretations of this responsum cf. the sources cited by Zuri in his *Ha-Mishpaṭ ha-ṣibburi*, I, 308 n. 25.

26 De Castro, *Synagoge*, p. xxi; Barnett, *El libro*, p. 3. For the permanent *difensori dei capitoli* in Rome, cf. Milano in *Israel*, X, 421 f., Art. 27. It is likely that the *'Omedim al tikkune ha-medinah* mentioned in the decisions of Valladolid in 1432 (Baer, *Spanien*, I, Pt. 2, no. 287, II, 1) refers neither vaguely to "those who look into the public needs" (Finkelstein, *Self-Government*, p. 351) nor to those who draft the statutes (Loeb in *REJ*, XIII, 200), but rather to their defenders.

While the term *takkanah* and *ḥerem ha-ṣibbur* were often used interchangeably, there was some legal difference between a communal ordinance invested with the sanction of a ban, and one not so fortified. Since any new ordinance was generally considered a deviation from accepted law, that issued without a ban was to be given as restricted an interpretation as possible. If subject to doubt, it was not to be applied at all. The ban, on the other hand, by introducing an element of ritualistic severity, enforced more rigid application. Even dubious cases had to be decided as falling under its sanction, lest perchance people legally subject to a ban have free intercourse with their neighbors. Cf. Asher b. Yeḥiel, *Responsa*, LVI, 5; Joseph ibn Leb, *Responsa*, II, 72. Cf. also Zuri, *Ha-Mishpat*, I, 307 ff. At the same time a community wishing to revoke an ordinance could rather informally withdraw its ban, according to a geonic decision in *Sha'are teshubah*, no. 33. Cf. also ibid., no. 139.

[27] Finkelstein, *Self-Government*, pp. 228, 232, 242 f., 251; Rashi on Shabu. 38b bottom; Meir of Rothenburg, *Responsa*, ed. Prague, nos. 184 (referring to a geonic responsum), 443, 712; Ḥayyim Or Zaru'a, *Responsa*, no. 2; Epstein, *Adreth*, pp. 71 ff. Cf. also Chap. XI, nn. 24, 35; XIV, n. 22.

[28] This practice of the *'ikkub tefillah* is extensively discussed and documented in Assaf's *Bate ha-din*, pp. 25 ff.; and Finkelstein's *Self-Government*, pp. 119, 128 f., 382. Its prevalence in Spain, doubted by these two scholars, is evidenced by documents published in Baer's *Spanien*, I, Pt.1, no. 74 (1210, cited above II, 14) and by J. Millas y Vallicrosa in his edition of *Documents hebraics de Jueus catalans*, no. XVIII (Hebrew text of 1262 on p. 71). Similarly the provision in the thirteenth-century statute of Candia mentioning the "frequent closing of the synagogues at the times of services [for slight reasons]" and forbidding "every Hebrew among us" to do so, very likely refers to such extralegal interruption of prayers, rather than to excommunication properly so-called. Cf. the text in Finkelstein, *Self-Government*, p. 274 (transl. p. 280) and David Kaufmann's remarks in his *Gesammelte Schriften*, II, 244 f. The Sassoon codex no. 407 contains also the record of a resolution passed by the Candia communities in 1527 and referring to "liturgy, bans and the closing of the synagogue." Cf. Sassoon's *Catalogue*, I, 349, 354. In view of the vast area for which this custom is attested, there is no longer reason to doubt its ancient Palestinian origin. Cf. also M. Horovitz, "A Responsum of 1469," *Magazin für die Wissenschaft des Judentums*, X (1883), Hebrew section, p. 5; L. Löwenstein, "Wormser Gemeindeordnungen," *Blätter für jüdische Geschichte und Literatur*, IV (1903), 149 Art. 34; Neubürger, *Fürth*, p. 24, n. 1; Dubnow, *Pinkas*, no. 1007 (1761).

[29] I. Kracauer, *Urkundenbuch zur Geschichte der Juden in Frankfurt a. M.*, I, no. 203 (for the general background, cf. idem, *Geschichte*, I, 50 f.); A. Epstein, "Der Wormser Judenrat," *MGWJ*, XLVI (1902), 157 f.; Frank, *Ḳehillot*, pp. 7 f.; G. Wolf, *Kleine hist. Schriften*, p. 139 n. 2 (with reference to Deut. 1.13); Balaban, *Żydzi lwowscy*, App. no. 50; Schorr, *Organizacya*, p. 26 n. 2 (both publishing texts of the oath of fidelity regularly taken by the Jewish elders); Balaban, *Dzieje*, I, 253 ff.; idem in *JJLG*, X, 314 f.; Selma Stern, *Der preussische Staat*, I, Pt. 1, nos. 229, 231, 234, 236–37, 246 (9), 250; Levi ibn Ḥabib, *Responsa*, no. 39.

[30] *Las Siete Partidas*, II, 20, 8; Baer, *Spanien*, I, Pt. 2, no. 63, and the note thereto; Vogelstein and Rieger, *Rom*, II, 312; Munk in *MGWJ*, XLI, 511 ff. In Arles in 1435, the two elders took an oath on the scroll of law "to behave well and in accordance with the law in the said office, to administer it according to the law and to observe the statutes. . . ." Cf. Hildenfinger in *REJ*, XLI, 63 n. 4. Cf. also Chap. XV, nn. 45–46.

Governmental inconsistency is well exemplified particularly in the official Sicilian records. On the one hand, the king appointed a rabbi (1283) or elders for life (1399–1403, 1422). On the other hand, he revoked a similar appointment and instituted free elections in Palermo and elsewhere (1397, 1399, 1422, 1476, etc.). In 1479 a royal order suddenly forbade Jewish communities to elect new officers until further notice, but in the following year the Viceroy warned the royal officials in Taormina not to interfere with the election of two Jewish *proti* according to custom. In separate decrees for the communities of eighteen districts he subsequently ordered free balloting. Soon after he suspended elections in Messina. In 1484 a new general suspension of elections was followed speedily by exemptions for many communities and various interventions in local voting. The ordinances adopted by the Jewish parliament in 1489, royal approval of which was obtained at a high price, provided for annual elections without government interference. But a year later the Viceroy appointed an elder in Catania, first until the next election, then for an indefinite period, since "for the time being" Jewish officers throughout the realm were not to be changed. He finally consented to replace this elder by another from among five candidates nominated by the Jews. Cf. Lagumina, *Codice*, I, nos. 33, 140, 158–59, 167, 184, 188, 292, 298, 302, 304, 381; II, Pt. 1, nos. 592, 599, 601, 634, 640, 667, 670, 676–77, 684, 688–89, 691, 705, 711, 716, 749–50, 757, 763, 768, 791, 797, 817–18, 820–23,

837, 849, 863, 867. Little wonder in the light of such instability of policy that the Jews strove with all means at their disposal to prevent government interference in their internal affairs.

[31] The rabbinic sources for the exclusion of women from communal suffrage are casuistically discussed, with a view to contemporary emulation, by A. S. B. Spitzer, in his Hebrew essay on "The Torah Must Be Obeyed; an Analysis of the Law Concerning Woman Suffrage," *Jakob Rosenheim Festschrift*, Hebrew section, pp. 1–43. Women were allowed, however, to be present in their special compartment at the imposition and dissolution of bans. Cf. Ibn Adret, *Responsa*, III, 329. Their rights as members of synagogues are well exemplified by the statutes of the Great Synagogue in London in Margoliouth's *History*, III, 247 f. For their activities as charity overseers cf. Vogelstein and Rieger, *Rom*, II, 316; Dubnow, *Pinkas*, no. 131; Margolies, *Dubno*, pp. 48, 164; Zarchin in *JQR*, XXIX, 157. Cf. in general also T. Lewenstein, "Über die rechtliche Stellung der jüdischen Frauen," *Nachalat Z'wi*, VI (1935–36), 159–75; and Chap. IX, n. 2.

The exclusion of bachelors from the plenary assembly and from electoral rights was expressly stipulated in some statutes, e. g. those of Carpentras of 1645. Cf. Mossé, *Avignon*, p. 142. The Jerusalem statute is included in the *Sefer ha-Takkanot ve-ha-haskamot . . .Yerushalayim* (The Book of Ordinances in Jerusalem), 2d ed., fol. 41 ab (cf. also the excerpts in the German transl. by Wilhelm, *Von jüdischer Gemeinde*, pp. 88 f.).

[32] Kracauer, *Geschichte*, II, 183, 200.

[33] Mossé, *Avignon*, pp. 142 f.; Jules Bauer, "Un commencement d'insurrection au quartier juif d'Avignon au XVIIe siècle," *REJ*, XXXVIII (1899), 123–36; Loeb in *Annuaire*, I, 204 f.; Baer, *Spanien*. I, Pt. 1, nos. 188 (1327), 480 (1408); idem, *Aragonien*, pp. 112 f.; Dubnow, *Pinkas*, nos. 919, 986, 1015 (these decisions of the Council were often disregarded, as may be seen by the example of Wilno, whose board of electors numbered 120 in 1750, and 196 in 1787; cf. Klauzner, *Wilno*, I, 90); Schorr, *Organizacya*, p. 90 Art. 2; Vogelstein and Rieger, *Rom*, II, 40, 128, 275; M. Balaban in *Kwartalnik*, I, 31 f.; Wolf, *Statuten*, pp. 26 f., 35 (subsequently modified), 81, 95 (with respect to emigrés from Vienna in 1670); idem, *Kleine hist. Schriften*, p. 149 n. 2 (3 classes in Prague); Müller, *Beiträge*, pp. 103 ff. The first statute of the united Italian and German communities in Ferrara, adopted in 1573, prescribed that every

person possessing 50 scudi or more be subjected to a tax and incidentally become a voter. Cf. Pesaro, *Memorie*, p. 31. In eighteenth-century Fürth the names of all voters who had enjoyed residence rights for twelve years (six, in cases of scholars distinguished by the title *ḥaber*) were placed in three ballot boxes according to wealth: the first contained the names of all possessing 6000 fl. and over, the second those of voters with a fortune of 2500–6000 fl., the third those of voters with 600–2500 fl. (*ḥaberim* in the possession of the title for twenty years or of residence rights for thirty years were included if they had property valued at 400 fl. or more). Cf. Neubürger, *Fürth*, pp. 27 ff. For the three-class system, which seems in some respects to date back to the geonic period (cf. Ginzberg, *Geonica*, II, 96, 104 f.) and which became very widespread in European electoral systems, and for the exclusion of relatives, cf. also Joseph Katz, *She'erit Yosef*, no. 30; Lagumina, *Codice*, II, Pt. 1, no. 140; Milano in *Israel*, X, 409 Art. 1; Baer, *Kleve*, pp. 105, 123; Selma Stern, *Der preussische Staat*, I, Pt. 1, p. 110; Weinryb in *MGWJ*, LXXXII, 253; above nn. 22–24; and the numerous references assembled by Loeb in *REJ*, XIII, 208; Grunwald, *Hamburg*, p. 42; Levitats in *Yivo Studies in Hist.*, II, 108 n. 39. In Frankfort it required many years of struggle and the intervention of the rabbis of Fulda, Hildesheim and Metz, acting as court of arbitration, to establish in 1618 the exclusion of close relatives from the main communal board as a constitutional principle. Cf. Kracauer in *ZGJD*, O. S. III, 346; IV, 25 ff.

[34] Wolf, *Statuten*, l. c.; Müller, *Beiträge*, l. c.

[35] Moses Menz, *Responsa*, no. 63, 3; M. Balaban in *JJLG*, X, 314 ff.; Margolies, *Dubno rabbati*, p. 40; Lewin, *Landessynode*, pp. 31 f., 62; Müller, *Beiträge*, pp. 103 ff., 157 ff. Cf. also Dubnow, *Pinkas*, no. 38 (1623) prescribing that, in Lithuanian communities whose deputies were elected during Passover week, nothing be undertaken in provincial questions without consulting these deputies. According to the agreement concluded between Lwów and the provincial communities in 1740, the respective strengths were to be: 2 delegates from the capital and 5 from the palatinate for matters of tax distribution; 6 and 12 in the provincial council; 2 each in the central council. This agreement did not prevent the complete elimination of Lwów representatives from the provincial council in 1762. Cf. Balaban, *Z zagadnień ustrojowych*, pp. 8 ff.

[36] Baer, *Spanien*, I, Pt. 1, no. 543; Elbogen in *Jewish Encyclopedia*, VII, 664 f.; Lagumina, *Codice*, II, Pt. 1, no. 817; Decourcelle, *Nice*, p. 232.

[37] Baer, l. c., nos. 186, 480; Teimanas, *Autonomie*, pp. 72 ff.; Balaban in *Kwartalnik*, I, 30 f.; idem, *Żydzi lwowscy*, pp. 259 ff.; Buber, *Ḳiryah nisgabah* (A History of the Jews in Żółkiew), pp. 96 ff., 100 ff.

[38] Balaban in *JJLG*, X, 314 ff. For the complex electoral procedure in Hamburg and extensive safeguards of honest ballotting, cf. Art. 37–59 of the statute, published by Grunwald in *MGJV*, XI, 13 ff. Cf. also Colorni, in *Riv. st. dir. it.*, XI, 104, 107.

There was no uniform election day in the Jewish communities. While in Poland the half-holidays of Passover were preferred, we find exceptions even there. For instance, in Kobylin elections were regularly held on the eve of the New Moon of Shebat. Cf. Wischnitzer in *Vierteljahrsschrift*, XX, 442 n. 26. The community of Hildesheim provided for regular elections during the Passover half-holidays but it allowed the elders, conjointly with the auditors, to postpone them until as late as Iyyar 18. Cf. A. Lewinsky, "The Communal Statute of Hildesheim [of 1706]" (Hebrew), *Ha-Eshkol*, VI (1909), 237. Other dates included the evening following the Feast of Tabernacles in Carpentras (Mossé, *Avignon*, p. 142); the Saturday following that festival in Marsala (Lagumina, *Codice*, II, Pt. 1, no. 705); May 1, or the first Wednesday in May in Palermo (ibid., no. 863); the 17th of Tammuz in Rome (Vogelstein and Rieger, *Rom*, II, 128); the 18th of Tammuz, later the middle of Ab, in Moravia (Wolf, *Statuten*, pp. 26, 79, 86). The London Sephardic *Mahamad* had to announce the elections on the Jewish New Year. Cf. Barnett, *El libro*, p. 4 Art. 3. The Great Synagogue also held its annual elections "immediately after the New Year," while the Hambro congregation was to be assembled for that purpose on the Sunday closest to the first of Nisan. Cf. Margoliouth, *History*, III, 240 Art. 38; *Taḳḳanot Ḳ. Ḳ. Hamburg*, Art. 11.

Electoral methods were sometimes adjusted to meet momentary needs. In Satanów, we learn from a rabbinic responsum, there was a custom for all members to congregate annually during the half-holidays of Passover and to choose electors by a majority vote. Around 1600 the voters were once "too lazy" to meet at the stated time. A week after Passover, the rabbi took the initiative and forced the community to assemble. A minority, evidently bent on obstructing the elections, protested because the usual ballot gave close relatives a chance to vote together. The rabbi, yielding in part, drew by lot several names and ordered these voters, under pain of 10 fl. fine, instantly to elect the communal officers. Cf. Benjamin Slonik, *Mase'at Binyamin* (Responsa), no. 7.

[39] Baer, *Spanien*, I, Pt. 2, no. 287 (II, 1, end); Finkelstein, *Self-Government*, pp. 357 f.; Dubnow, *Pinkas*, nos. 63 (1623), 160–61 (1628), 655 (1670), 720 (1676), 766 (1679), 895 (1694), 991 (1761); Klauzner, *Wilno*, I, 94; Stanisław Kutrzeba, *Zbiór aktów* (A Collection of Documents), no. 149. The short-lived "Polish" community of Amsterdam, largely composed of Lithuanian refugees, closely followed electoral and other customs of the mother country. Due to conflicts with the "German" community, it added, however, special qualifications for both the active and the passive franchise of persons who had temporarily joined the rival synagogue. Cf. Isaac Ber Markon's Hebrew publication of "The Statutes of the Polish Community in Amsterdam of the Year 432 [1672]," *Ṣiyyunim* in memory of J. N. Simhoni, pp. 168 ff. Cf. also D. M. Sluys, "Bijdrage tot de geschiedenis van de Poolsch-Joodsche Gemeente te Amsterdam," *Feestbundel . . . L. Wagenaar*, pp. 137–58; and Max Grunwald, "Altjüdisches Gemeindeleben," *MGJV*, XLI–XLIV (1912), 76 ff. (based upon the papers of Rabbi Samuel Joseph Steg of Warburg).

[40] Baer, *Spanien*, I, Pt. 1, nos. 140 (1297), 143 (Art. 11 = Ibn Adret, *Responsa*, V, 284; ca. 1300); idem, *Aragonien*, pp. 114 f.; Epstein in *MGWJ*, XLVI, 159 f., 161 f.

[41] Emmanuel, *Salonique*, I, 285 f.; Nehama, *Salonique*, III, 75 f.; Milano in *Israel*, X, 415 Art. 13; Vogelstein and Rieger, *Rom*, II, 128; Zbigniew Pazdro, *Organizacya i praktyka żydowskich sądów podwojewodzińskich* (Organization and Practice of the Jewish Palatinate Courts in the Years 1740–1772), nos. 65, 80–81. Cf. also Zunz, *Zur Geschichte*, pp. 510 ff.; Lagumina, *Codice*, II, Pt. 1, nos. 440, 599, 673; and Ferorelli, *Italia meridionale*, p. 105 for the growth of minority rule in Sicily and Naples.

Ḥayyim Or Zaru'a supplied a curious rationale for the perpetuation in office of worthy leaders and their claim to constant re-election, by referring to the hereditary principle of the biblical monarchy. Cf. his *Responsa*, no. 65. For successful revolts — rare phenomena — against attempts at fortifying minority control, cf. Baer, *Spanien*, I, Pt. 1, no. 552 (giving the royal decree of 1477 restoring a somewhat more liberal method of elections in Lerida); and Krochmal's *Ṣemaḥ ṣedeḳ*, no. 18 referred to above.

[42] Barnett, *El libro*, p. 4 Art. 4; Grunwald in *MGJV*, XI, 40 f., 46; Dubnow in *Evreiskaya Starina*, V, 74 no. 4; idem, *Pinḳas*, nos. 56, 152, 656. Many a perspicacious observer must have shared Rabbi Elijah b. Samuel of Lublin's observation that the excessive penalties on voicing dissent in these "corrupt generations" had led to the "absence of truth." Cf. his *Yad Eliyahu* (Responsa), no. 48.

Some unruly members thought that they might escape communal discipline by artificially creating conscientious objections. As far back as the eleventh century the issue was raised in the school of Rashi as to what was to be done with a member who, in anticipation of a communal ordinance, bound himself by an oath not to submit to it. The master decided that such an oath was to be classed as one taken "in vain" and that, if the offender was duly forewarned, he was subject to flogging of the biblical kind. Cf. Rashi's *Sefer ha-Orah*, ed. by Salomon Buber, p. 222, no. 139.

NOTES TO CHAPTER XI

LAY AND ECCLESIASTICAL OFFICERS

[1] Isaac b. Sheshet, *Responsa*, I, no. 228 (cf. Jacob Weil, *Responsa*, no. 106 and Baer, *Aragonien*, p. 114, n. 61); Justinian's *Novellae*, no. 146; Parkes, *Church and Synagogue*, pp. 392 f.; Epstein, *Adreth*, pp. 15 f., 35 f.

[2] Lewinsky in *Ha-Eshkol*, VI, 238 Art. 9; Klauzner, *Wilno*, I, 92; Jakobovits in *JGJC*, IV, 262; Nehama, *Salonique*, III, 89 f.; Rodocanachi, *Saint-Siège*, pp. 78 f.; Vogelstein and Rieger, *Rom*, II, 253, 312, 319 f.; Joel Sirkes, *Bayit ḥadash* (Responsa), O.S., no. 43; Hillel b. Naftali Hirz, *Bet Hillel*, on Y.D. no. 157; Katz, *Le-Ḳorot*, pp. 12 f.; Levy, *Bosnien*, p. 23. Cf. also Chap. XV, n. 30.

[3] Baer, *Spanien*, I, Pt. 1, no. 118; Mossé, *Avignon*, p. 144; Grunwald in *MGJV*, XI, 25; Levy, *Bosnien*, p. 25; Barnett, *El libro*, p. 7 Art. 13; William Flavelle Monypenny and George Earle Buckle, *The Life of Benjamin Disraeli Earl of Beaconsfield*, revised ed., I, 26 f. Cf. also below, n. 17.

The Great Synagogue of London had a graduated scale of fines ranging from at least half a guinea for failure to attend a meeting, to 25, 30 guineas and £40 respectively, for refusal to serve as Overseer, Treasurer or Warden (persons aged seventy years, those who had previously held the office or who had "been fined" over a period of years, were excused). Unwarranted resignation was punishable by double the original fine. In fact, any member informed by the Secretary in writing of election to office was expected to reply affirmatively within twenty-four hours, silence being "considered as a refusal to accept the office, and the party [to] be fined accordingly." Cf. Margoliouth, *History*, III, 241 ff., 249. Similar detailed provisions were included in the statute of the Hambro Synagogue of 1795, which, incidentally, also doubled the fine for unjustified resignations in the middle of a term. Cf. *Takkanot Ḳ. Ḳ. Hamburg*, Art. 8–9, 21. Prussian statutes, too, outlawed all resignations during the three-year term of office. Cf. Selma Stern, *Der preussische Staat*, I, Pt. 1, p. 110.

Even voluntary associations sometimes forced their members to attend meetings or hold office. The statute of one Berlin educational society, adopted in 1768, penalized failures by severe fines up to 1 ducat. Cf. M. Stern, "Das Vereinsbuch des Berliner Beth Hamidrasch 1743–1783," *JJLG*, XXII (1931–32), Hebrew section, p. II Art. 7–8. Cf. also *Costituzioni Modena*, p. 24 Art. XVIII; Wolf, *Statuten*, p. 13 Art. 50, 140 Art. 13; and Mordecai b. Hillel ha-Kohen's *Commentary* on B. B. no. 488, which states in terms of a legal norm that anyone elected a communal officer must accept. This opinion is quoted with approval by Isserles in his comments on Jacob b. Asher's *Ṭur*, Y.D. 256. Moralists, too, such as Israel ibn Al-Nakawa, often exhorted their readers "not to withhold participation in serving the needs of Israel." Cf. *Menorat ha-Maor*, IV, 209 f. For peculiar legal complications which arose when a member vowed not to accept office unless he received a stipulated sum from the community or, as in Hildesheim in 1696, unless some fellow-member were excluded from the board, cf. Menaḥem Azariah da Fano's *Responsa*, no. 48; Elyakim Götz, *Eben ha-shoham u-me'irat 'eynaim* (Responsa), no. 39. Acceptable excuses included those adduced in 1367 by Pedro IV of Aragon, when he exempted a Jew over fifty years old who was a student of the Law, and by the Sicilian viceroy in 1486, when he excused a barber of Malta so that he might undisturbedly pursue his calling for the benefit of nobles and burghers. In 1490 the viceroy excused an elder of San Marco because he had served two terms. Cf. Baer, *Spanien*, I, Pt. 1, no. 286; Lagumina, *Codice*, II, Pt. 1, nos. 631, 730, 791.

[4] Ibn Adret, *Responsa*, I, 617 (with reference to Yer. Pe'ah IV, 8, 21); Mordecai b. Hillel on B. M., nos. 457–58, and B. B., nos. 480, 482, 488; Karo on *Ṭur*, O.Ḥ. 153 and Y.D. 256; Finkelstein, *Self-Government*, pp. 52 f., 153, 156 f., 168 f.; Frank, *Ḳehillot*, pp. 2 f.; Shohet, *Jewish Court*, pp. 11, 37 f., 44.

As in the Graeco-Roman communities, the choice of titles was often arbitrary and it seems hopeless to try to attach each function exclusively to a particular title. The difficulty is aggravated by the extensive use of some titles, e. g. *parnas* and *gabbai*, as family names. It is often impossible to say whether a particular source refers to a communal officer or to a private citizen bearing such a name. Cf., e. g., Stokes, *Studies*, pp. 59 ff. On occasion, the ambiguity of designations caused extended legal controversies. In Bordeaux, for instance, the term *anciens* in the royal decrees of 1760 and 1763 was interpreted by some to refer to the oldest householders or to those settled in the city for the longest period, rather than to communal officers. This interpretation was naturally rejected by the French authorities in 1765–66. Cf. Malvezin, *Bordeaux*, pp. 217 ff. A careful compilation and examination of the terms used in all available medieval and early modern sources is, nevertheless, likely to shed new light on the communal structure.

[5] Epstein in *MGWJ*, XLI, 162 f.; Wolf Feilchenfeld, "Die innere Verfassung der jüdischen Gemeinde zu Posen im 17. und 18. Jahrhundert," *Zeitschrift der historischen Gesellschaft für die Provinz Posen*, XI (1896), 122–37.

The term "seven best men of the city" became a stereotype and was used generally in legal and historical sources without reference to the real number. While the declaration reported in 1118 by Joseph ibn Megas in the name of "the court, the elders and the seven best men of the city" (*Responsa*, no. 237) may have referred to a real figure, the recurrent use of the phrase in decisions of the Lithuanian Council (Dubnow, *Pinḳas*, no. 56, etc.) is a conscious archaism. To be sure, in some communities there were seven officers or a council of seven. Mention has already been made of the seven chiefs of the burial society of Huesca elected in 1323 by the seven sections of the association. In Moravia the old statutes called for the election of a board of eleven members in the larger communities, of seven in the smaller groups. Cf. Baer, *Spanien*, I, Pt. 1, no. 179; Wolf, *Statuten*, p. 51. Cf. also Frank, *Ḳehillot*, p. 3 n. 3, and Louis Lewin, *Geschichte der Juden in Lissa*, p. 84 n. 1. But this number had as little meaning as did those of six or twelve, which are much more frequent.

[6] Baer, *Spanien*, I, Pt. 1, nos. 189 (1327), 533 (1431), 543 (1459); Francisco Fernandez y Gonzalez, *Ordiniamento formado por los procuradores de las aljamas hebreas*, pp. 105 f. Cf. also, in general Loeb in *REJ*, XIII, 198 f., 208 ff.; Baer, *Aragonien*, pp. 110 ff.; Epstein, *Adreth*, pp. 15 ff., 33 ff.; Kayserling, *Navarra*, p. 75.

[7] *The Chronicle of Aḥima'az*, ed. by Salzman, especially pp. 15 (Hebrew), 86 (English); Starr, *Byzantine Empire*, pp. 37 ff.; Guedemann, *Geschichte des Erziehungswesens und der Kultur der abendländischen Juden während des Mittelalters*, II, 273 ff., 339 ff. (publishing the statute of Syracuse registered in 1363 and confirmed by the king in 1364, where, however, only one *proto* governed the community, aided by the council of twelve *elemosinarii*; the same statute is published also by Lagumina, *Codice*, I, no. 52 and by Lionti in *Archivio storico siciliano*, N.S. IX [1884], 200 ff.); Lionti, ibid., pp. 333 ff.; idem, "I ministri della religione presso gli Ebrei di Sicilia," ibid., X (1885), 130–36; Lagumina, *Codice*, I, nos. 302, 304; II, Pt. 1, no. 768; Ferorelli, *Italia meridionale*, pp. 105 ff.

[8] Vogelstein and Rieger, *Rom*, I, 220, 263, 342 f.; II, 6, 40, 128, 411 f.; Milano in *Israel*, X, 409 ff.; Rodocanachi, *Saint-Siège*, pp. 78 f. (emphasizing that the brevity of tenure in the Roman community was in keeping with the then prevalent practice of Italian cities).

[9] Elbogen in *Jewish Encyclopedia*, VII, 664 f.; Loevinson in *Bolletino storico livornese*, I; De Maulde, *Etats français*, pp. 138 ff.; Mossé, *Avignon*, pp. 121 ff. The Mantua offices are extensively discussed by Colorni in *Riv. st. dir. it.*, XI. Cf. also Riccardo Pacifici, "I regolamenti della Scuola italiana a Venezia nel secolo XVII," *Israel*, V (1930–31), 322–402; Edgardo Morpurgo, "L'università degli Ebrei in Padova nel XVI secolo," *Bolletino del Museo Civico di Padova*, XII (1909), 16–25, 65–75. For Corfù cf. J. A. Romanos, "Histoire de la communauté israélite de Corfou," *REJ*, XXIII (1891), 69.

[10] Kracauer, *Geschichte*, II, 178 ff.; idem in *ZGJD*, O. S. III, 347 f.; IV, 25 ff.; Grunwald, *Hamburg*, p. 51; idem in *MGJV*, XI, 18 ff., 26 f., 35 f.; Margoliouth, *History*, III, 235 ff. Cf. also *Taḳḳanot Ḳ. Ḳ. Hamburg*, Art. 10; Löwenstein in *Blätter für jüd. Geschichte und Literatur*, IV, 145 ff.

(on Worms); M. Ginsburger, "Rechte und Pflichten eines Judenvorstehers in der Grafschaft Rappolstein," ibid., pp. 64–70; Guido Kisch, "Entwicklung und Verfassung der jüdischen Gemeinde zu Halle," *Sachsen und Anhalt, Jahrbuch der historischen Kommission*, VI (1930), 306–36 (eighteenth century). For an interesting study of the council of elders in Cologne during the years 1255–1347, cf. the pertinent excursus in Robert Hoeniger's *Judenschreinsbuch der Laurenzpfarre zu Köln*, pp. 242 ff. Cf. also below, n. 73.

[11] Frank, *Ḳehillot*, pp. 5 ff.

[12] Balaban in *JJLG*, X, 316 ff.; Lewin, *Lissa*, pp. 75 ff.; S. M. Dubnow, "Communal Statutes from the End of the Sixteenth to the End of the Eighteenth Century" (Russian), *Voskhod*, 1894, Pt. 2, p. 96; Levitats in *Yivo Studies in Hist.*, II, 87 ff. Cf. also Klauzner, *Wilno*, I, 90 ff.; and, in general, Balaban in *Kwartalnik*, I, Pt. 2, pp. 23 ff. (giving also an interesting tabulation of officers in ten Polish communities); and Teimanas, *Autonomie*, 56 ff. For lively sketches of two eighteenth-century petty tyrants, Lewko Balaban of Lwów and Zelman Wolfowicz of Drohobycz, cf. Balaban's *Z historyi Żydów w Polsce* (Sketches and Studies in the History of the Jews in Poland), pp. 129 ff., 155 ff.

[13] B. B. 9a; Jacob b. Asher, *Ṭur*, Y. D. 249, 250, 257 and Karo's and Isserles's comments thereon; Jacob Weil, *Responsa*, no. 173; Shohet, *Jewish Court*, pp. 37 f.

[14] Baer, *Aragonien*, pp. 106, 110 f., 114 n. 61; idem, *Spanien*, I, Pt. 1, no. 543; Lagumina, *Codice*, I, nos. 319–21; II, Pt. 1, 494, 496, 498, 545, 601, 703, 722, 749–50, 758, 797, 844; Colorni in *Riv. st. dir. it.*, XI, 93 f.; Emmanuel, *Salonique*, I, 70; Flesch in Gold's *Mähren*, p. 34; Barnett, *El libro*, p. 8, Art. 16; Marcus, *Medieval World*, p. 217; Kracauer, *Geschichte*, II, 181; Grunwald in *MGJV*, XI, 29; Wachstein in *ZGJD*, IV, 140. For instances of irregularities in financial administration cf. the memorial prepared by a papal jurist in Avignon in 1417 and the decision of the Polish community of Schwersenz in 1760, published respectively by Maulde, *Etats français*, pp. 170 ff. and by Zarchin in *JQR*, XXIX, 152, 311 f. Cf. also Ezekiel Landau, *Noda' bi-Yehudah* (Responsa) on Y.D. nos. 156–57 and Chap. XV, nn. 45–46.

The provincial chief in the bishopric of Paderborn for several decades (until 1675) drew a salary of 60 thalers, received a 10 per cent commission on all taxes collected by him, was handsomely rewarded for special services and, although one of the wealthiest potential taxpayers, was permanently exempted from taxation. Some of these chiefs, such as the powerful Court-Jew Berend Levi, refused nevertheless to render accounts, claiming that their government appointment exempted them from the control of their "inferiors." Popular clamor grew so loud and it was so effectively supported by the rabbis in and outside the bishopric, that investigations were repeatedly made and Berend Levi as well as one of his successors in office, Heinemann, were convicted of embezzling communal funds and forced to resign. Cf. Altmann, *Paderborn* (Ms.). Cf. also idem in *Jewish Social Studies*, III (1941), 181. This lurid picture of communal autocracy, although springing from specific local conditions and temporary even there, reveals both the excesses of a governmentally sustained oligarchy and the measure of counterbalance offered by the rabbinate.

15 Simon b. Zemaḥ Duran, *Magen Abot* (Commentary on Abot), II, 9; Benjamin's *Itinerary*, ed. by Adler, p. 41; Shabbetai Donnolo, *Ḥakmoni* (Commentary on the Book of Creation), ed. by D. Castelli, p. 3; Rashi on M. Ḳ., 22b; Jacob Tam, *Sefer ha-Yashar*, ed. Vienna, fol. 81a; Isaac b. Moses, *Or Zaru'a*, II, nos. 42, 12; 418, 15; Baer, *Spanien*, I, Pt. 1, no. 88; Kayserling, *Portugal*, pp. 8 f.; Judah b. Barzilai, *Sefer ha-Sheṭaroṭ*, ed. by Halberstam, p. 132 (in our translation the emendation suggested there, n. 7, is disregarded); Boffarull y Sans, *Los Judios en el territorio de Barcelona*, p. 90, no. XCV; Hoeniger, *Judenschreinsbuch*, pp. 29 f., no. 117. Cf. also David Kaufmann, "Three Centuries of the Genealogy of the Most Eminent Anglo-Jewish Family before 1290," *JQR*, O.S. III (1891), 561; Zunz, *Zur Geschichte*, pp. 185 f.; idem, *Die Ritus des synagogalen Gottesdienstes geschichtlich entwickelt*, p. 158; Guedemann, *Geschichte*, III, 34 n. 1; Lauer in *JJLG*, XVI, 9 ff.; and, especially Simḥa Assaf, "Studies in the History of the Rabbinate in Germany, Poland and Lithuania" (Hebrew), *Reshumot*, II (2d impression, 1927), 259–300.

The statements in both text and notes were written before the publication of Solomon Zeitlin's recent essay on "Rashi and the Rabbinate," *JQR*, XXXI (1940–41), 1–58, in which the author contends that "Rashi was the founder of the Rabbinate in western and central Europe." However, the evidence submitted in favor of this far-reaching contention (especially, pp. 38 ff.) appears too arbitrary and inconclusive to warrant any change in our presentation.

16 Isaac b. Moses, *Or Zaru'a*, II, nos. 34, 43, 50, 78 (16); Guedemann,

Geschichte, I, 256 f.; II, 12 ff. Guedemann has dimly sensed the importance of the pre-literary centuries of North-European Jewish history for the formation of local customs and for the subsequent differences in the rabbinic recognition of custom. Further illustrations may be found in the sources listed by Finkelstein in *Self-Government*, p. 21 n. 1; S. A. Horodezky in *Leḳorot ha-rabbanut* (Biographical Sketches of Rabbis), especially pp. 117 ff.; N. S. Greenspan, "On the History of the Commandment concerning Phylacteries and of its Neglect" (Hebrew), *Ozar Hachaim*, IV (1927–28), 159–64, supplemented by Z. D. Grünberger, ibid., V (1928–29), 71–72; L. Rabinowitz, *France*, pp. 86, 176 ff. The broader implications of this problem, only hinted at here, deserve monographic treatment.

[17] Baer, *Spanien*, I, Pt. 1, nos. 107 (1273), 118, 121 (1280), 123 (1282). Of course, there were also rabbinic judges. In the Lerida document of 1270 mentioned above, n. 15, Ḥasdai Nasi, the rabbi, served also as chief judge, although he was assisted by two laymen of his own choice "de melioribus et sapientioribus dicte aliame." The latter were obliged to accept Ḥasdai's appointment, their only valid excuse being physical infirmity. Cf. Boffarull y Sans, l. c.

[18] Ibn Adret, *Responsa*, II, 290; Baer, *Spanien*, II, 287 (I, 2; II, 1); Finkelstein, *Self-Government*, pp. 354, 356.

[19] Baer, *Spanien*, I, Pt. 1, nos. 88 (1229), 127 (1284), 163 (1310–13), 307 (1371); Pt. 2, nos. 62 (Art. 88), 135 (1305–21), 338 (1483); idem, *Aragonien*, pp. 117 f.; Asher b. Yeḥiel, *Responsa*, CVII, 6; Maimonides, *Mishneh Torah*, Ḥobel u-mazziḳ, III, 5–6; Jacob b. Asher, *Ṭur*, Y.D. 243 and 340; Isaac b. Sheshet, *Responsa*, nos. 27, 61, 212, 220; David ha-Kohen, *Responsa*, no. 25; Samuel di Medina, *Responsa*, on O. Ḥ. no. 8 (objects only to the imposition of the ban on a Sabbath); on Y.D., nos. 82 (local ordinance against private bans), 145, 181. Cf. also above, nn. 15, 17; Chap. XI, nn. 19, 24, 35.

It appears that the shift in emphasis from the judicial to the ecclesiastical functions of the rabbinate was partly due to the change from Muslim to Christian rule. Under Islam, with its high evaluation of the juristic expert, the Jews could more readily follow their legalistic proclivities and entrust their own leadership openly to men distinguished by juridical learning. Under Christendom the ecclesiastical character of the clergy, although reinforced by the administration of Canon Law, emphasized the sacerdotal function. This fact to some extent colored not only state legislation concerning rabbis, but also some of the Jewish documents of the period. The statement in the *Seder Eliyahu rabbah* "and they have built themselves a synagogue and a schoolhouse and hired themselves a *ḥakam* and elementary teachers" (XI, ed. Friedmann, p. 54) may or may not have been written in early medieval Italy (cf. Chap. VI., n. 1), but phrases such as are contained in Pedro IV's decrees addressed to the community of Saragossa in 1342 and 1364, authorizing the excommunication of governmentally appointed "rabbis of the synagogue or slaughter-house" as contrasted with the *albedin*, and intervening in behalf of a rabbi who, like his ancestors, had served "in the great synagogue" of the city (Baer, *Spanien*, I, Pt. 1, nos. 215, 269) are decidedly a reflection of the new status. That this new emphasis, however, was not exclusive even for Aragonian royal decrees in that period, may be noted, e. g., in Pedro's pledge of 1339 addressed to the three rabbis (*deyanis sive judicibus*) of Huesca to protect them in the exercise of their judicial functions. Cf. also above, n. 15.

[20] Danon in *REJ*, XL, 216; Emmanuel, *Salonique*, I, 285; Nehama, *Salonique*, III, 84. The growing preponderance of the judicial element in the rabbinate of the Spanish exiles in the Ottoman Empire, perhaps once more stimulated by Islamic models, is reflected, for instance, in the above mentioned definition of a congregation or synagogue by Adribi (cf. Chap. IX, n. 1), in which rabbis appear to be no integral part of a synagogue, although they undoubtedly served as the chief communal leaders. These illustrations could easily be multiplied, but perhaps they sufficiently demonstrate the complexity of the evolution of the Sephardic rabbinate, a problem which requires further clarification.

[21] Starr, *Byzantine Empire*, pp. 37 ff.; Guedemann, *Geschichte*, II, 275 ff., 337 ff.; Lionti in *Arch. stor. siciliano*, N.S. X, 131 ff.

[22] Vogelstein and Rieger, *Rom*, II, 110, 127 ff., 416 f.; Cassuto, *Firenze*, pp. 213ff. (a community of 100–300 Jews including several wealthy bankers certainly could afford to maintain a rabbi, had it so desired); Colorni in *Riv. st. dir. it.*, XI, 103, 106; Finkelstein, *Self-Government*, pp. 301 f., 304 f.; Ludwig Blau (ed.), *Leo Modenas Briefe und Schriftstücke*, pp. 166, 171; Simon Bernstein (ed.), *The Divan of Leo of Modena*, pp. XXIV f., 113 ff.; Assaf, *Bate ha-din*, pp. 13, 90, 130 ff.

[23] Aronius, *Regesten*, nos. 170–71; Frank, *Ḳehillot*, pp. 1 ff.

[24] Shalom b. Isaac Sekel cited by Isserlein's disciple, Joseph b. Moses

in *Leket Yosher*, I, 118 f.; Isaac b. Sheshet, *Responsa*, no. 271 (with reference to the French chief rabbinate); Finkelstein, *Self-Government*, pp. 63 f., 222, 232, 251; Isserlein, *Pesakim u-ketabim*, nos. 241, 255; Jacob Weil, *Responsa*, nos. 129, 163; Colon, *Responsa*, Roots 163, 168. Karo and Isserles cite these divergent views in their comments on Jacob b. Asher's *Ṭur*, Y.D. 243 and 340, but in *Shulḥan 'Aruk*, ibid., they decide that "if testimony is offered that anyone insulted a scholar, be it only by words (and in the scholar's absence), the court shall excommunicate the offender and not release him without the latter's consent." They also accept a scholar's direct action in principle. Yet there is little evidence of this practice in northern countries after the fifteenth century. The community of Frankfort in 1606, nevertheless, deemed it wise to stipulate in its contract with a new rabbi, Isaiah Horowitz, that the latter "shall not excommunicate any objector (God forbid!) without calling together, within three days, the members of the Academy and the Council." Horovitz, *Frankfurter Rabbinen*, I, 59. Cf. also in general, M. Güdemann, "Die Neugestaltung des Rabbinerwesens und deren Einfluss auf die talmudische Wissenschaft im Mittelalter," *MGWJ*, XIII (1864), 68–70, 97–110, 384–95, 421–44; and above, n. 19.

[25] Jacob b. Asher, *Ṭur* and Joseph Karo, *Shulḥan 'Aruk*, Y.D. 243 and the commentaries thereon; Schorr, *Organizacya*, p. 90; Frank, *Ḳehillot*, pp. 23 ff. and the sources cited there. Cf. also Chap. VI, n. 3; XV, n. 36.

[26] Rudolf Geyer and Leopold Sailer, *Urkunden aus Wiener Grundbüchern zur Geschichte der Wiener Juden im Mittelalter* (includes numerous records of Meir ha-Levi's transactions in the years 1393–1406); Jacob Moelln, *Sefer Maharil* (Custumal), 1858, p. 153.

[27] Assaf in *Reshumot*, II, 273 ff., 282; David Kaufmann, *Samson Wertheimer, der Oberhoffaktor und Landesrabbiner (1658-1724) und seine Kinder*; Bernhard Wachstein, *Die Inschriften des alten Judenfriedhofes in Wien*, II, 350 ff.; J. Taglicht, *Nachlässe der Wiener Juden im 17. und 18. Jahrhundert*, pp. 132 ff. (the fl. 32.37 owed by Hirschl Jamnitz evidently were a part of Eskeles' rabbinic share in the sale of citrons).

Financial support was given not only to officiating rabbis, but also to those attached to synagogues and schoolhouses in a sort of "research" position. The aforementioned collection *Ḥukke ha-torah* (Laws of the Torah), provided (Art. 2) that "a school be established for saintly persons who take upon themselves the yoke of the Law . . . because just as one sets up readers to recite prayers in lieu of the [uneducated] multitude, so shall one set up students, permanently engaged in the uninterrupted pursuit of learning to substitute for the populace." Guedemann, *Geschichte*, I, 268; Assaf, *Mekorot*, I, 6 ff. Modern instances of communal support of such non-officiating rabbis, often going under the name *Klausrabbiner*, are fairly numerous. The Berlin *Beth Hamidrasch* association, for example, maintained in 1743 three, that of Mannheim in 1708 two such "rabbis." Cf. Stern in *JJLG*, XXII, p. VI; Isak Unna, "Die Verordnungen für die Lemle Moses Klausstiftung in Mannheim," ibid., XVII (1926), 134.

[28] Judah b. Asher's "Will" in Israel Abrahams' *Hebrew Ethical Wills*, pp. 180 ff.; Antonio Rubio y Lluch, *Documents per l'historia de la cultura catalana migeval*, II, no. 62; Baer, Spanien, I, Pt. 1, nos. 163, 210 (Art. 22: the judge is to receive 60 solidi annually); Pt. 2, no. 287 (I, 2); idem in *MGWJ*, LXIX, 55; Finkelstein, *Self-Government*, p. 354.

[29] Jacob Emden, *Megillat sefer* (Autobiography), p. 25; Leser (Eliezer) Landshut, *Toledot anshe shem u-peulatam be-'adat Berlin* (The Lives and Works of the Leaders of the Berlin Community from 1671 to 1871), pp. 78 ff.; C. Duschinsky, *The Rabbinate of the Great Synagogue, London, from 1756 to 1842*, pp. 29, 35 ff.; Lewin, *Landessynode*, pp. 29 ff., 67 f., 72 ff.; Schorr, *Organizacya*, p. 91; Balaban in *Kwartalnik*, pp. 32 ff.

[30] Isaac b. Moses, *Or Zaru'a*, I, no. 113; Isaac b. Sheshet, *Responsa*, nos. 268, 270; Loeb in *Annuaire*, I, 234 (Art. XVI).

[31] The Cracow statute, ed. by Balaban in *JJLG*, X, 331 ff.; idem, *Żydzi lwowscy*, pp. 291 ff.; Klauzner, *Wilno*, I, 96; Grunwald, *Hamburg*, p. 46; idem, in *MGJV*, XI, 50 ff.

[32] Wolf, *Statuten*, pp. 40 ff.; Baer, *Aragonien*, p. 117 n. 73; W. Müller, *Beiträge*, pp. 158 f.

[33] Solomon Ephraim b. Aaron Lentshits, *'Olelot Ephraim*, nos. 351 ff.; idem, *'Ammude shesh* (Sermons), ed. Leyden, 1772, fol. 24a; Horovitz, *Frankfurter Rabbinen*, I, 41 f., 58 ff. For other records concerning the emoluments of rabbis cf. De Castro, *Synagoge*, pp. xxvi f. Art. 22 (the salaries of the four rabbis of the united Sephardic Congregation in Amsterdam range from 150 to 600 fl.); Donath, *Mecklenburg*, pp. 134 f. (the salary of the newly elected chief rabbi is fixed in 1764 at 150 thalers, but is reduced to 100 thalers in 1767 when the entire amount due for three years remains in arrears); Rixen, *Münster*, pp. 39 f. (the chief rabbi's salary is raised from 100 fl. in 1771 to 150 fl. in 1790); Jakobovits in *JGJC*,

IV, 293 (Chief Rabbi Wedeles complains in 1668 that, while his predecessors had received an annual salary of 1000 fl., he is paid only 100–200 fl.); Duschinsky in *JQR*, XX, 227 (Chief Rabbi Oppenheim, although the recipient of a generous salary, may engage in business); Weill in *REJ*, LXXXI, 174 f. (an Alsatian rabbi receives 100 écus and numerous incidentals); Jules Bauer, "L'université israélite de Nice de 1785 à 1803," ibid., LXIII, 269 ff. (rabbi's salary reduced in 1787 from 50 to 25 louis); Gelber in *JQR*, XIV, 303 (Galician chief rabbi to receive 800 fl. annually and various emoluments). Some other data have been assembled by Assaf in his *Bate ha-din*, pp. 93 ff. and in *Reshumot*, II, 277 ff. Almost invariably a house or apartment rent-free, tax immunities and various gifts in kind, considerably increased the real wages of rabbis.

Although the principle of free competition among scholars was hallowed by old traditions, the rabbinical conferences of Ferrara and Frankfort, as well as the Polish and Lithuanian Councils, tried to protect the revenue of local rabbis against inroads by "interlopers." The Lithuanian Council decided in 1631 that no rabbi should officiate at weddings outside his community. This provision was fortified by local ordinances, such as that adopted in Dubno, forbidding couples to leave town to marry and thus deprive the local officials of their due. Cf. Finkelstein, *Self-Government*, pp. 263, 302, 304 f.; Horovitz, *Rabbinerversammlung*, p. 27; Dubnow, *Pinkas*, no. 226; Margolies, *Dubno*, p. 61. Cf. also Colon, *Responsa*, Root 169; and Chap. X, nn. 1, 10.

Other noteworthy data are given by the following authors: Guedemann, *Das jüdische Unterrichtswesen während der spanisch-arabischen Periode*, pp. 186 ff.; Zimmels, *Beiträge*, pp. 26, 89; Léon Gauthier, "Les Juifs dans les deux Bourgognes," *REJ*, XLIX (1904), 14; Schechter, ibid., XXIV, 127 ff. (about David Messer Leon's rabbinic career and vicissitudes); Alexander Marx, "Glimpses of the Life of an Italian Rabbi of the First Half of the Sixteenth Century (David ibn Yaḥya)," *HUCA*, I (1924), 605–24 (Ibn Yaḥya complains, among other matters, that the Naples community owed him a salary for services extending over twelve years including a contractual obligation of 100 gold scudi per annum for the last seven years); Grunwald, *Hamburg*, pp. 68 ff., 71 ff., 209 ff. (cf., however, the aspersions cast upon Katzenellenbogen's election by Jacob Emden in his *Autobiography*, pp. 125 f.); Kracauer, *Geschichte*, II, 274; Munk in *Jubelschrift Hildesheimer*, pp. 74, (Hebrew) 77; Baer, *Kleve*, pp. 108 f.; Lewin, *Lissa*, p. 75; Da Silva Rosa, *Geschiedenis*, p. 75 (from 1642 on Isaac Aboab received 1200–1600 fl. annually from the congregation of Recife, Brazil, the oldest Jewish community in the New World). Cf. also below, n. 70.

34 Baer, *Spanien*, I, Pt. 1, no. 63 (note); Wolf, *Statuten*, p. 75 (the rabbi may be elected for a period of more than one year); Grunwald, *Hamburg*, pp. 68 ff.; I. Zinberg "The Conflict between the Elders and the 'Last Rabbi' of Wilno" (Hebrew), *He-'Abar*, II, (1918), 45–74; idem, "The Feud between the Heads of the Jewish Community and the Rabbinate in Wilno in the Second Half of the 18th Century" (Yiddish), *Yivo Studies in History*, II (1937), 291–321; Klauzner, *Wilno*, I, 126 ff. (comparing the terms of Samuel b. Avigdor's contract with those, far less favorable, granted in 1708 to his less well connected predecessor, Baruch Rapaport); Teimanas, *Autonomie*, p. 67.

35 Sonne in *HUCA*, XVI, Hebrew section, pp. 39 f., 44 n. 13, 76 ff.; Dubnow in *Evreiskaya Starina*, V, 184 (on the decision of the Polish Council); Halperin, *Milluim*, nos. 22–26; Zinberg, l. c.; Klauzner, l. c.; Herbert I. Bloom, "The Dutch Archives, with Special Reference to American Jewish History," *PAJHS*, XXXII (1931), 12 f.; Roth, *Venice*, pp. 144 f. In Rome the *fattori* had the ultimate decision with respect to bans and the appointment of rabbis, cf. Milano in *Israel*, X, 414 Art. 11; 422, Art. 29; Vogelstein and Rieger, *Rom*, II, 128. According to the *capitoli* of Verona, published in 1769, the rabbi had to be re-elected every year by secret ballot by a majority of two-thirds of all votes. Cf. Roth, "Rabbi Menaḥem Navarra," *JQR*, XV (1924–25), 437. Cf. also *Kolbo* towards the end; Curiel in *Scritti . . . Lattes*, pp. 242 f., 246. The Frankfort rabbi was obliged to promulgate bans at the order of the council, was forbidden to correspond with rabbis of other cities, or to appear at a meeting in the community house without the elders' permission. Cf. Kracauer, *Geschichte*, II, 179, 275; Horovitz, *Frankfurter Rabbinen*, III, 42 (Art. 103 of the statute of 1754).

36 Dubnow, *Pinkas*, nos. 48 (1623), 171 (1628), 229 (1631), 726 (1676), 918 (1720); Moses Sofer, *Ḥatam Sofer* (Responsa), O. Ḥ. no. 206 with reference to *Shulḥan 'Aruk*, Ḥ. M. 333, 3 (which, however, speaks only of private employment); and Y. D. 334, 42 (referring to the excommunication of a scholar). For legal questions arising from attempted demotions of rabbis, cf. e. g. Isserles, *Responsa*, no. 50 (a community attempts to depose a

rabbi before he starts his ministrations), 153 (a rabbi appointed by the government); idem, on *Ṭur*, Y. D. 245 (citing authorities for the duty of keeping a rabbi in office despite the availability of a more prominent scholar); Bezaleel Ashkenazi, *Responsa*, no. 25 (a rabbi is being removed because of his alleged ignorance and failure to preach). Cf. also above, n. 33; Chap. X, n. 4; Chap. XIII, n. 5.

[37] Wolf, *Statuten*, pp. 18 f.; Assaf, *Bate ha-din*, pp. 89 ff., 126 f.; Jacob Abraham b. Raphael, *Naḥlat Ya'akob*, Preface; Jakobovits in *JGJC*, VIII, 123.

[38] Jacob Weil, *Responsa*, no. 146; Ezekiel Landau, *Derushe ha-ṣelaḥ* (Homilies), fol. 7b.

[39] Zinberg in *He-'Abar*, II, 65 ff.; Wolf, *Statuten*, pp. 29, 37 ff.; Leopold Löw, "Was war, was ist, was soll der Rabbiner sein?" in his *Gesammelte Schriften*, IV, 175 ff. Even in medieval Cologne, where the power of the "Jews' bishop" was buttressed by both governmental support and his relatively long tenure of office (despite annual elections), he signed on deeds first only if he happened to hold also the rabbinic office, as was sometimes the case. Otherwise the rabbi's signature appears first on all extant deeds. Cf. Hoeniger, *Judenschreinsbuch*, p. 244.

[40] N. D. Davis, *Sheṭarot, Hebrew Deeds of English Jews before 1290*, no. 180; Isaac b. Moses, *Or Zaru'a*, II, nos. 91, 329; Joseph b. Moses, *Leḳeṭ yosher*, II, 38; A. Marx, "On Joseph Arli's Demotion from, and Restoration to, the Rabbinate" (Hebrew), *Tarbiz*, VIII (1936–37), 171–84 (the date of this controversy is now given as 1532 by Sonne in *HUCA*, XVI, 73, n. 128); Kracauer, *Geschichte*, II, 276. The much-debated question of the origin of the title *morenu* has been brought closer to a solution by Ch. Lauer's careful analysis of sources and theories in *JJLG*, XVI, 1–42. The problem, however, of the connection, if any, between the new emphasis on rabbinic ordination and the practice of granting licenses and the *jus ubique docendi* to university graduates, which, conceived and propagated by Paris from 1291 on, spread to other European universities in the fourteenth century, would merit special examination.

[41] Nathan Neta Hannover, *Yeven Meṣulah* in Kahana's *Sifrut*, II, 314; Sonne in *Idea sionistica*, I, 7; Schorr, *Organizacya*, p. 91 (Art. 7); *Taḳḳanot Ḳ. Ḳ. Hamburg*, Art. 51; Finkelstein, *Self-Government*, pp. 79, 260 f., 263, 302, 304 f.; Horovitz, *Rabbinerversammlung*, pp. 24 Art. 5, 27 f. Art. 13. The antecedents of the Ferrara resolution may be found in a local ordi-

nance previously enacted by one of its leaders, Meir Katzenellenbogen, in his home community of Padua. The latter's son, Samuel Judah, more radically demanded that only the ordination by an outstanding rabbi be recognized, and actually demoted an unworthy title holder. Cf. Sonne in *HUCA*, XVI, 47 f., 75 (text). Some Italian communities altogether refused to recognize titles conferred by rabbis of another locality. For an extended controversy between Isaac Levi, the grandson of Leo of Modena, and the rabbinate of Venice which repudiated the title *ḥaber* obtained by him from outside rabbis, cf. his authobiographical account, *Medabber tahapukot*, ed. by L. Blau in *Ha-Zofeh*, II (1912), 169–86; III (1914), 45–54, 69–96. Cf. also Sonne in *Ḳobeṣ 'al yad*, XIII, Pt. 2, pp. 145 ff. (similar restriction in Verona). The communities of Candia decided in 1577 that "all ordinations conferred outside the island shall have no validity whatsoever." Cf. Sassoon, *Catalogue*, p. 356.

Several samples of writs of ordination, as well as contracts between rabbis and communities shedding light on the status of rabbis, have been reprinted or summarized by Assaf in *Reshumot*, II, 296 ff.; idem, *Meḳorot*, I, 160, 191; idem, *Ha-'Oneshin*, p. 18 n. 1; Zinberg, l.c.; M. Brann in his "Samson Wertheimers Rabbinats-Diplom aus Eisenstadt," *Festschrift . . . Adolf Schwarz*, pp. 499–508 (dated 1693); Graetz in *MGWJ*, XVI, 422 ff. (Eibeschütz's objections to the proposed contract in Metz); D. Kaufmann in his "Rabbinic Diploma whereby Ezekiel Landau was Invited to Serve as Chief Rabbi of Prague" (Hebrew), *Ha-Eshkol*, I (1898), 177–84 (dated 1754); B. Friedberg in his "Das Rabbinatsdiplom des R. Isaac ha-Cohen in Pinczów," *MGWJ*, XLIV (1900), 71–76 (dated 1773); L. Wreschner in his "R. Akiba Egers Leben und Wirken," *JJLG*, II (1904), 76; III (1905), 315 (dated 1791, 1809); Philipp Bloch, "Die ersten Kulturbestrebungen der jüdischen Gemeinde Posen unter preussischer Herrschaft," *Jubelschrift . . . H. Graetz*, pp. 203 ff.; idem in *Festschrift Philippson*, pp. 127 ff.; Israel Goldberger in his "Two Rabbinic Diplomas" (Hebrew), *Ha-Zofeh*, II (1912), 132–38; Heinrisch Flesch in his "Der Pinax von Austerlitz," *Jahrbuch für jüdische Volkskunde*, II (1925), pp. 580 ff.; and idem in his "Rabbinatsdiplome," *ZGJT*, I (1930–31), 109–15. Cf. also the contract of Abraham Chelm Segal of Emden as rabbi of Hildesheim, dated in 1766 (Ms. Adler, no. 3993) in Elkan Nathan Adler's *Catalogue of Hebrew Manuscripts*, p. 47.

While the choice of a rabbi was completely at the discretion of either the board or the plenary assembly, there were also vestiges of the hereditary principle. Meir of Rothenburg once counseled deferential treatment of a worthy son of a deceased rabbi. Cf. his *Responsa*, ed. Lwów, no. 110. One family, as we have seen, occupied the rabbinate of Toledo's great synagogue for several generations before 1364. Cf. also Joseph of Trani, *Responsa*, no. 31. The communal plutocracy undoubtedly resented the later independence of the rabbinic office and it was probably due, in part, to the opposition that some communities, such as Poznań or Worms, long insisted on candidates outside their own membership. Cf. Ḥayyim Ya'ir Bacharach, *Kelale eṣ ḥayyim*, Preface in his *Ḥavvot ya'ir*, fol. 230b. They thus revived a long-abandoned practice in some early French communities which had thus tried to forestall close family control. We learn, for instance, that the entire Jewish population of twelfth-century Orléans was related to each other within the legal impediments of propinquity for certain communal actions, with the sole exception of the rabbi, who had evidently been brought from another locality. Cf. Jacob Tam, *Sefer ha-yashar* (Responsa), no. 36. There was, of course, much less justification for such apprehensions in the far more populous modern communities. In Metz, this practice of electing only outside rabbis was partly checked by Louis XIV's decree of 1657, which demanded royal approval for the invitation of a foreigner, but this was merely a part of the general government surveillance over Jewish immigration. Cf. Cahen in *REJ*, VII, 105; Clément, *Metz*, pp. 93, 270.

[42] Jacob Weil, *Responsa*, no. 129, 163; Isserlein, *Pesaḳim*, no. 68; Zinberg in *Yivo Studies in Hist.*, II, 295; J. Perles, "Geschichte der Juden in Posen," *MGWJ*, XIV (1865), 87 ff.; idem in *MGWJ*, XVI (1867), 222 ff. In sixteenth-century Italy ordinations for money became so frequent as to result in mutual recriminations between rabbis and to evoke a public censure of this practice by Azriel Dayyena. Cf. Marx in *Abhandlungen Chajes*, pp. 170 f.; and Assaf in *Kirjath Sepher*, XV, 116 ff.

[43] Harkavy, *Ḥadashim* in the Appendix to Graetz-Rabbinowitz, *Dibre yeme Israel*, VII, 17 ff.; Dubnow, *Pinḳas*, nos. 839–40, 882; Klauzner, *Wilno*, I, 127 f.; Balaban, *Z zagadnień*, p. 12. For other illustrations, cf. Assaf in *Reshumot*, II, 269 ff. Cf. also Jacob Reischer's sweeping condemnation (in *Shebut Ya'akob*, II, 143) of the prevalent practice of German Jewish leaders of appointing even unqualified relatives and friends as judges, and his feeling that the preference given in Metz to lay courts

of arbitration need not be considered an evil. It goes without saying that, in addition to Jewish leaders, many influential government officials often had to be bribed. Particularly those officials who, like the Polish palatins, had authority to confirm communal elections expected substantial douceurs.

Another reflection of the rabbi's public law status was the requirement that he take an oath of fealty to the ruler. For several formulas of such oaths, generally very lengthy, cf. Munk in *Jubelschrift Hildesheimer*, pp. 76 f.; idem in *MGWJ*, XLI, 518; L. Horwitz, ibid., LIV, 521 f. (all referring to Hesse); Müller, *Beiträge*, p. 158 (Moravia). Cf. also Chap. X, n. 28.

[44] Solomon Ephraim Lentshits, *'Ammude shesh*, l. c.; Loew b. Bezaleel, *Netibot 'olam*, Section on Law, end (ed. Zhitomir, p. 95); Assaf, *Bate ha-din*, pp. 45 f. For various aspects of the early modern rabbinate cf., in addition to the literature cited in the preceding notes, also Jac. Zwarts, *De eerste Rabbijnen*; Löwenstein in *JJLG*, VI–VIII (on the Fürth rabbinate); M. Grunwald, "Altjüdisches Gemeindeleben," *MGJV*, XLI–IV (1912), 82 ff.; XLV–VIII (1913), Pt. 2, pp. 27 ff. (on Hamburg).

[45] Wolf, *Statuten*, p. 3, Art. 10; Horodezky, *Le-Ḳorot ha-rabbanut*, pp. 175 f.; [Bershadskii], *Russko-evreiskii Arkhiv*, III, no. 172.

[46] Leo of Modena, *The History of the Present Jews throughout the World* (English transl. by Simon Ockley from the Italian work, *Riti*), II, 1, 1, 5; III, 1, 20 (pp. 63 ff., 114); Nehama, *Salonique*, III, 84; Gaster, *History of the Ancient Synagogue*, p. 115; Ḥayyim Joseph David Azulai, *Ma'agal ṭob ha-shalem* (Itinerary 1753–1794), ed. by Aron Freimann, I, 61; Messer Leon, *Nofet ṣufim* (Rhetoric); Vogelstein and Rieger, *Rom*, II, 289, 310; Lellio della Torre, *Scritti sparsi*, II, 238 ff.; Roth, *Venice*, pp. 145 ff. Cf. also De Castro, *Synagoge*, pp. xxv f., Art. 19: sermons are to be delivered on every Sabbath and holiday; on three successive occasions by Saul Levy Morteira, on one by Menasseh ben Israel; Marx in *HUCA*, I, 613, 617 (David ibn Yaḥya claims that his sermons attracted many Christian friars).

[47] Jacob Moelln, *Sefer Maharil*, p. 7; B. H. Auerbach, *Geschichte der israelitischen Gemeinde Halberstadt*, p. 91; Margoliouth, *History*, III, 255 f.; Zedekiah Anav, *Shibbole ha-leḳeṭ ha-shalem* (Ritualistic Code), ed. by S. Buber, p. 160 (preferring this explanation of the term *shabbat ha-gadol* to that, more widely accepted, concerning that Sabbath's dis-

tinction through the miracles preceding the Exodus, cf. also David ibn Abudirham's *Commentary on Prayers*, ed. Venice, 1545, fol. 45c). Cf. also the sources cited by Weill in *REJ*, LXXXI, 175, which mention the unusual obligation of an Alsatian rabbi to preach once every three months.

[48] *Chronicle of Aḥima'az*, ed. by Salzman, pp. 5 f. (Hebrew), 67 ff. (English); Joseph Marcus, "Studies in the Chronicle of Ahima'az," *Proceedings of the American Academy for Jewish Research*, V (1934), 85–93; Zeraḥiah ha-Levi, *Ha-Maor ha-ḳaṭan*, on Alfasi 'Er. V to fol. 59a; Joseph of Trani, *Responsa*, I, 100; Jacob Reischer, *Shebut Ya'akob*, II, 149; S. Schweinburg-Eibenschitz, "Une confiscation des livres hébreux à Prague," *REJ*, XXIX (1894), 266–71, apparently overlooked by S. H. Lieben in *Soncino Blätter*, III (1929), 51 ff.; and by G. Kisch in *JGJC*, II (1930), 486, n. 30. Levi ibn Ḥabib sharply attacked the preachers who made it a habit to discuss mysteries of the Cabala before uninitiated audiences. Cf. his *Responsa*, no. 75.

[49] Dubnow, *Pinḳas*, nos. 130, 401, 596; Halperin, *Milluim*, no. 89; Soṭah 40a. Cf. also Meir Katzenellenbogen, *Responsa*, no. 71; Israel Bruna, *Responsa*, no. 231 (and the additional sources cited in the Index thereto, ed. Stettin, fol. 124c); Bezaleel Ashkenazi, *Responsa*, no. 25; Klauzner, *Wilno*, I, 132. When Polish rabbis after 1648 began occupying, in ever-increasing numbers, the rabbinic pulpits in most central and west European communities, criticism of their legalistic emphases was often coupled with resentment of their "alien" origin. Ezekiel Landau of Prague, for instance, although relatively a moralist among his fellow preachers, was often accused by the populace of stressing legal minutiae "in accordance with Polish customs." Cf. his *Derushe ha-ṣelaḥ* (Sermons), fol. 15c.

Since preaching was so popular with the masses it is not surprising that professional associations often maintained permanent preachers for their congregations. For Prague, cf. Jakobovits in *JGJC*, VIII, 134 n. 60. For the numerous rabbinic criticisms of preachers, on the other hand, and of their methods of interpreting talmudic legends, cf. Samuel Edels' introduction to his *Ḥiddushe aggadot* (Novellae on the Aggadah), appended to most recent Talmud editions. Cf. also in general J. D. Eisenstein's article "Maggid," *Jewish Encyclopedia*, VIII, 252 ff.; Israel Bettan's critical essays on several distinguished Jewish preachers (Anatoli, Baḥya b. Asher, 'Arama, Muscato, Figo, Lentshits and Eibeschütz) in his *Studies in Jewish Preaching: Middle Ages*; A. Marmorstein, "A Few Remarks on Seventeenth-Century Preachers" (Hebrew), *Alim*, II (1935–36), 37–41 (based upon a work by Abraham b. Eleazar ha-Kohen); and, especially, Leopold Zunz's *Die gottesdienstlichen Vorträge der Juden historisch entwickelt*, pp. 410–48.

[50] Synagogue audiences, as we have seen, often were exposed to harangues by Christian missionaries. James II of Aragon, for instance, decreed in 1299 that the famous preacher, Raymond Lull be allowed to preach in all synagogues of the Kingdom. Apart from disputing his arguments, if they so felt inclined, the Jews were not to obstruct him. Cf. M. Kayserling, "Notes sur l'histoire des Juifs en Espagne," *REJ*, XXVII (1893), 148 f. Lull wrote a handbook for the guidance of Christian preachers amongst Jews and Saracens and subsequently (in 1312) induced the Council of Vienne to recommend the establishment of missionary chairs for Hebrew at the Universities of Salamanca, Paris, Oxford and Bologna. Cf. Ewald Mueller, *Das Konzil von Vienne 1311–12*, pp. 155 ff., 636 ff., 693 ff.

[51] Rashi, *Sefer ha-Orah*, ed. by Buber, I, 12, no. 31; *Tosafot* on Men. 30a (concurrent reading); Nissim Gerondi, *Commentary* on Alfasi to Meg. IV, fol. 21b, and *Kolbo* no. 20 (the cantor reads aloud); Asher b. Yeḥiel, *Responsa*, VI, 1, cited with approval by his son, Jacob in *Ṭur*, Y. D. 251 and by Josef Karo on *Ṭur*, O. Ḥ. 53.

[52] Meir of Rothenburg, *Responsa*, ed. Cremona, no. 190; ed. Lwów, nos. 109, 111–12; ed. Prague, no. 137; Krochmal, *Ṣemaḥ ṣedeḳ*, no. 34 (quoting Hai Gaon and Karo on *Ṭur*, O. Ḥ. 53); Meir Katzenellenbogen, *Responsa*, nos. 42, 64; Zimmels, *Beiträge*, pp. 26 ff., 89 f.; *Or Zaru'a*, I, no. 114; Karo and Isserles on *Ṭur*, O. Ḥ. 53 (citing numerous authorities on the problem of unanimity); Abraham Gumbiner, *Commentary on Shulḥan 'Aruk*, O. Ḥ. 53, 20; Isserles, ibid., 581; Lagumina, *Codice*, I, 421.

[53] Mann, *Texts*, I, 454 f; Baer, *Spanien*, I, Pt. 1, nos. 215 (1340–42), 294 (1369), 542 (1458); Lauer in *JJLG*, XVI, 26. Cf. also Zunz, *Gottesdienstliche Vorträge*, pp. 411 ff. The incident in Cologne, first recorded by Meir of Rothenburg as having occurred "in the days of Abi-Ezri" (cf. his *Responsa*, ed. Prague, no. 137), is now ascribed to Eliezer b. Joel ha-Levi himself soon after his assumption of the rabbinic office in Cologne (about 1199). Cf. V. Aptowitzer *Mabo le-Sefer Rabiah* (Introduction to the Book Rabiah), pp. 16, 220 f., 428 f.; Kober, *Cologne*, p. 79. This

incident is cited by many subsequent authorities, including the Constantinople Chief Rabbi Moses Capsali in his *Responsa*, ed. by Assaf in *Sinai*, III, Pt. 1 (1939), 151 ff. In the same connection cf. also Sassoon, *Catalogue*, pp. 350 ff., referring to decisions by the communities of Candia in 1363 and 1458 aimed at the prevention of the selection of readers by the government or otherwise against the will of the majority of worshipers: "An accuser shall not become the mouthpiece for the defense."

[54] Israel Bruna, *Responsa*, no. 253; Asher b. Yeḥiel, *Responsa*, IV, 22; G. Wolf, *Kleine hist. Schriften*, p. 152 n. 1; Isaac b. Moses, *Or Zaru'a*, II, no. 42; Meir of Rothenburg, *Responsa*, ed. Lwów, no. 113; Frank, *Ḳehillot*, pp. 25 f.; Grunwald, *Hamburg*, pp. 44, 51; Isaac b. Sheshet, *Responsa*, nos. 475–77. We have, however, no European counterpart of the provincial "great *ḥazzan*," the "supervisor over the readers" in Babylonia, of whom Hai Gaon speaks in one of his letters. Cf. Mann, *Texts*, I, 113, 122, 151 f.

[55] De Maulde, *Etats français*, pp. 144 ff. (Art. 62–64); Ibn Adret, *Responsa*, I, nos. 215, 450 (preferring a salaried to an honorary reader); Karo and Isserles on *Ṭur*, O. Ḥ. 53; Y. D. 257; Solomon Luria, *Responsa*, no. 20; Jonathan Eibeschütz, *Ya'arot debash* (Sermons), I, 52c; Dubnow, *Pinḳas*, nos. 62, 645; Margolies, *Dubno*, pp. 172 f.; Zedekiah Anav, *Shibbole ha-leḳeṭ*, pp. 11; Jacob Moelln, *Sefer Maharil*, p. 156.

[56] J. Müller, *Mafteaḥ*, p. 67; Immanuel of Rome, *Maḥberot* (Makamas), XV; Margoliouth, *History*, III, 257 ff.; Alfasi, *Responsa*, no. 294. Cf. also Moses Menz, *Responsa*, no. 81 (claims to have regulated the relationships between the precentor and the community).

The question as to whether a reader, like the priest at the Temple, must be free of physical defects, such as blindness, was hesitatingly answered in the affirmative by Bacharach for cases where an alternate reader would be available. Cf. his *Ḥavvot ya'ir*, no. 176. He was evidently unfamiliar with the opposite view expressed by Yehudai Gaon, cf. Müller, l. c. Cf. also Anav, l. c. Bacharach's view (l. c., no. 140), that a reader may not resign in the middle of an agreed term, is likewise controverted by Jacob Reischer in his *Shebut Ya'akob*, I, 6.

For interesting disputes deeply affecting the reader cf. Finkelstein, *Self-Government*, pp. 60, 229, 244 f. (medieval Germany); Epstein, *Adreth*, p. 59; Isaac b. Sheshet, *Responsa*, no. 34 (both medieval Spain); Berliner, *Rom*, II, Pt. 2, p. 35 (Rome 1577 on the pronunciation of the priestly blessing); Boaz Cohen, *Ḳunṭres ha-teshubot* (Bibliography of Responsa), no. 33 (describing a correspondence published in London 1827). Cf. in general, also M. Schloessinger, "Hazzan," *Jewish Encyclopedia*, VI, 284 ff.; A. Z. Idelsohn, "The *Ḥazzan* in Eastern Europe" (Hebrew), *Ha-Toren*, XI (1924–25), 138–54; idem, "Kantoren," *Encyclopaedia Judaica*, IX, 888 ff.; Jacob Shatzky, "Cantors and Synagogue Music in Holland" (Yiddish), *Yivo Bleter*, XVII (1941), 146–56; and Chap. IV, n. 32.

57 Buber, *Ḳiryah nisgabah*, pp. 82, 87 f., 95 f., 111 Art. 50; Dubnow, *Pinḳas*, nos. 129, 157, 496; Klauzner, *Wilno*, I, 134 ff.; Baer, *Kleve*, p. 113; Lewin, *Landessynode*, pp. 51, 69, 109, 111 f.; Danon in *REJ*, XLI, 219; Güdemann, *Geschichte*, III, 95 (the *Schulklopfer* first mentioned in 1225). The Great Synagogue in London drew a distinction between the *Shamesh* or Clerk, charged with certain executive functions, and the beadle who had more menial tasks. Cf. Margoliouth, *History*, III, 259 ff. In many other communities the lesser official was called *untershammash*. For a description of their functions, cf. ibid. and the Avignon statute of 1779 (Art. XI), in Loeb's edition in *Annuaire*, I, 220.

58 Abraham Epstein, *Eldad ha-Dani*, p. 119, section 30 (text incomplete); Rashi and Tosafot on M. Ḥullin I, 1; Jacob b. Asher, *Ṭur* and Joseph Karo, *Shulḥan 'Aruk*, Y .D. 1, 1 and the commentaries thereon; Charles Duschinsky, "May a Woman act as Shoheteth?" *Gaster Anniversary Volume*, pp. 96–106. The communal aspects of Jewish ritual meat administration are now treated by Jeremiah J. Berman in his comprehensive monograph on *Sheḥita*.

59 Mossé, *Avignon*, p. 110 (showing how the papal bulls were often disregarded even under papal sovereignty); C. Ciavarini, *Memorie storiche degli Israeliti in Ancona*, pp. 22 f. (on the city statute of 1566); Crémieux in *REJ*, XLVI, 32 ff. (on the arrangements between the Jewish and the Christian butchers of Marseilles); Baer, *Spanien*, I, Pt. 1, nos. 160, 163, 272, etc.; Kayserling, *Portugal*, p. 14. Cf. also Chap. XII, nn. 35 ff.; XV, n. 12.

60 Rubio y Lluch, *Documents*, II, nos. 149, 175, 258 (contrasted with the appointment of cantors by elders according to Nissim Gerondi's *Responsa*, no. 65); Isaac b. Sheshet, *Responsa*, nos. 113, 497–500; Danon in *REJ*, XL, 218; XLI, 114 f.; Margolies, *Dubno*, pp. 135 f.

61 Finkelstein, *Self-Government*, pp. 231, 248, 260; Horovitz, *Rabbinerversammlung*, pp. 22 f.; Dubnow, *Pinḳas*, nos. 258, 359, 838, 960; Lewinsky

in *Ha-Eshkol*, VI, 240, Art. 20; Duschinsky, *Rabbinate*, pp. 17, 116 f., 264 ff. (giving also a list of 147 slaughterers authorized in London in the years 1822–45); Azulai, *Ma'agal ṭob ha-shalem*, I, 35 f. (the author, at the insistence of the local elders, examines all *shoḥetim* in Bordeaux, disqualifying several). For a typical rabbinic authorization of a slaughterer cf. the text cited, from a Jerusalem manuscript, by Gulak in his *Oṣar ha-sheṭarot*, p. 354.

There were, of course, numerous variations in detail. For example, while the communities of Kleve insisted upon triennial examinations of all slaughterers by the provincial chief rabbi, those of Cassel exempted holders of the degree *ḥaber*. Cf. Baer, *Kleve*, p. 108; Munk in *Jubelsschrift Hildesheimer*, Hebrew section, p. 78. There also were numerous local ordinances regulating in great detail the processing and sale of ritual meat. Cf. e. g. Margolies, *Dubno*, pp. 162 f. Especially complicated were the conditions in medieval cities which, in order to protect the monopoly rights of the Christian butcher guilds, compelled Jews to buy meat prepared by Jewish experts employed by non-Jewish butchers. Cf., e. g., Stobbe, *Deutschland*, pp. 65, 171, 271 f.; Cassuto, *Firenze*, pp. 218 f.; Klauzner, *Wilno*, I, 18 ff.

Notwithstanding these local differences Jews of one region did not, as a rule, hesitate to consume food prepared under the regulations prevailing in other districts. Even Ashkenazim and Sephardim were ready to overlook in this respect the ritualistic minutiae separating their respective groups. Local ordinances which discouraged the purchase of meat in butcher shops under the supervision of another congregation, had purely fiscal motives. Cf. the letter of R. Leb Norden of London, dated in 1755 and published by Duschinsky in *Rabbinate*, pp. 278 ff. Fiscal considerations determined also the singular participation of the Portuguese community of Hamburg in the meat taxes collected by its "German" coreligionists and the ensuing controversies over the respective shares in the years 1790 and 1852–56. Cf. Alfonso Cassuto, "Die historische Grundlage zur Beteiligung der Hamburger Portugiesisch-Jüdischen Gemeinde an der von der Deutsch-Israelitischen Gemeinde erhobenen Fleischabgabe (Schächtabgabe)," *Jahrbuch für die jüdischen Gemeinden Schleswig-Holsteins*, IV (1932–33), 32–38. Nevertheless such ritualistic differences often split East European communities in the early, revolutionary period of ḥasidism. The role played by the ḥasidic slaughterer as spearhead of anti-rabbinism would bear further investigation. Cf. also P. Marek's Russian essay cited above, Chap. IX, n. 4.

[62] Rigg, *Calendar*, I, 128; Stokes, *Studies*, pp. 31, 46 f.; Israel Abrahams, H. P. Stokes and Herbert Loewe, *Starrs and Jewish Charters Preserved in the British Museum*; F. Ashe Lincoln, *The Starra: Their Effect on Early English Law and Administration*.

[63] Baer, *Spanien*, I, Pt. 1, pp. 1044 ff. and nos. 82, 84, 215, 540 (the name, *notarius*, seems here to be used for an executive official), etc.; Pt. 2, no. 113; Kayserling, *Navarra*, p. 73 (Christian notaries for Jewish deeds); *Consuetudines Palermitanae*, c. 36 (in Wilhelm von Brünneck, ed., *Siciliens mittelalterliche Stadtrechte*, p. 27). Cf. also Lagumina, *Codice*, I, nos. 421, 460; II, Pt. 1, no. 473; Clément, *Metz*, pp. 207 ff. (the French government insists in 1670 on a French registry, and in 1733 on the certification of loan contracts by French notaries). For Aragon and Navarra, cf. especially the various collections of deeds published by José M. Millas y Vallicrosa.

[64] Assaf, *Bate ha-Din*, pp. 99 ff., 133 f. (giving much information from the Hebrew sources on communal scribes and witnesses, including excerpts from Moses Zacuto's report of the decisions of the Italian assembly of 1676); Isaac b. Sheshet, *Responsa*, nos. 304, 452, 511.

[65] Roth in *JQR*, XV, 438; *Takkanot K. K. Hamburg*, Art. 58; Schorr, *Organizacya*, p. 92 Art. 15; Dubnow, *Pinkas*, no. 54; Klauzner, *Wilno*, I, 132 ff.; *Teshubot ha-geonim*, ed. by Harkavy, nos. 231, 238; Asher b. Yeḥiel, *Responsa*, XIII, 18. For the numerous secretarial services rendered by rabbis in Italy, cf. Meir Katzenellenbogen, *Responsa*, no. 40 (describing functions of the rabbi of Otranto); Berliner, *Rom*, II, passim; Marx in *HUCA*, I, 617; Bernstein, ibid., VII, 522.

A fine, but unfortunately rare example of an archivist with scholarly interests was the secretary of the community of Mantua, Bonaiuolo Isaac Levi who, in the years 1782–1810, compiled a detailed register of archival documents under his supervision. This register in 11 volumes of 6000 pages has been utilized to good advantage by Colorni in *Riv. st. dir. it.*, XI. For the Hamburg community's strict safeguarding of the integrity of its archives, cf. Grunwald in *MGJV*, XI, 28. In Rome, probably at the instigation of the communal elders, the papal administration in 1668 ordered all Jews to surrender archival material to the community. Cf. Attilio Milano and Roberto Bachi, *Università israelitica a Roma. Storia e riordinamento del archivio col catalogo del archivio e un saggio bibliografico sulli Ebrei di Roma.* Cf. also Chap. VII, nn. 25, 49.

The functions of the private *libellarius,* on the other hand, were little regulated by communal ordinances. The Lithuanian Council, however, evidently prompted by both ritualistic and anti-competitive motives, adopted in 1687 and 1761 resolutions for communal supervision of the preparation and sale of phylacteries, *mezuzot* and scrolls of law, and authorizing only scribes licensed by a rabbi to ply the trade. Cf. Dubnow, *Pinkas,* nos. 447, 521.

[66] Isaac b. Sheshet, *Responsa,* no. 175 (mentioning arrears owed by the community on a teacher's salary); Baer, *Spanien,* I, Pt. 2, no. 287 (I, 2); Finkelstein, *Self-Government,* pp. 353 f.; J. Prener, "Contrat d'engagement du rabbin d'Avignon en 1661," *REJ,* LXV (1913), 315 ff.; Wolf, *Statuten,* p. 4 Art. 12, 15; Hildenfinger in *REJ,* XLVII, 228, 232 f.; XLVIII, 51 f.; Dubnow, *Pinkas,* nos. 832, 835; Munk in *Jubelschrift Hildesheimer,* pp. 76 f. Characteristically Mordecai b. Hillel in the thirteenth century discusses the appointment of a teacher by the community as an ordinary phenomenon. Cf. his *Commentary* on B. M. no. 457. Cf. also Assaf's *Mekorot,* passim; above, Chap. IX, nn. 10 ff.; and below, Chap. XIII, n. 13.

[67] *Costituzioni Modena,* pp. 6 ff. Art. II; Samuel Krauss and Isidor Fischer, *Geschichte der jüdischen Aerzte vom frühesten Mittelalter bis zur Gleichberechtigung*; Max Meyerhof, "Medieval Jewish Physicians from Arabic Sources," *Isis,* XXVIII (1938), 432–60; Abraham Galanté, *Médecins juifs au service de la Turquie*; L. Glesinger, "Beiträge zur Geschichte der Pharmazie bei den Juden," *MGWJ,* LXXXII (1938), 111–30, 417–22; Adolf Kober, "Rheinische Judendoktoren, vornehmlich des 17. und 18. Jahrhunderts," *Festschrift des Jüdisch-Theologischen Seminars Fraenckelscher Stiftung,* II, 173–236; three essays by D. E. Cohen on Dutch Jewish physicians in *Nederlandsch Tijdschrift voor Geneeskunde,* LXXI (1927), LXXIV (1930), LXXVIII (1934); Lewin, "Jüdische Aerzte in Grosspolen," *JJLG,* IX (1912), 367–420; J. Landsberger, "Zur Geschichte des Sanitätswesens der jüdischen Gemeinde in Posen," ibid., X (1913), 361–71; Balaban, "Jewish Physicians in Cracow and the Ghetto Tragedies (15th–17th Centuries)" (Russian), *Evreiskaya Starina,* V (1912), 38–53; idem in *Kwartalnik,* pp. 36 ff.; Klauzner, *Wilno,* I, 122, 137; Curiel in *Scritti Lattes,* pp. 246 (the newly elected rabbi of Trieste in 1767 was to serve also as treasurer, secretary, teacher and physician), 243 f.; Balaban, *Żydzi*

lwowscy, pp. 533 f. (Jewish musicians could, by agreement, perform at Christian ceremonies); Gaster, *Synagogue*, p. 21; Kracauer, *Geschichte*, II, 110 f., 182, 289, 291 f.; Israel Abrahams, *The Book of Delight and Other Papers*, pp. 287 ff., 314; Brann in *Jubelschrift Graetz*, p. 226; Max Grunwald, *Samuel Oppenheimer und sein Kreis*, p. 336 n. 5 (a Prague Jew applies in 1724 for the position of Jewish letter carrier in Breslau); Ezekiel Landau, *Derushe ha-ṣelaḥ*, fol. 49c (on Jewish postmasters violating the Sabbath); C[assuto] in *JJLG*, XIII, 67, 72 (Jewish letter carriers in Hamburg).

[68] Bacharach, *Ḥavvot ya'ir*, no. 206 (favoring the discretionary powers of the envoy against his opposition); Mossé, *Avignon*, pp. 151 f.; Lewin "Der Schtadlan im Posener Ghetto," *Festschrift ... Wolf Feilchenfeld*, pp. 31–39; Dubnow, *Pinḳas*, pp. 301 f.; Balaban, *Żydzi lwowscy*, pp. 337; Curiel in *Scritti Lattes*, pp. 254 f. (a Jewish guard employed to lock the ghetto gates from the inside); Manuel Serrano y Sanz, *Origenes de la dominacion española en America*, I, p. XXXI; Baer in *MGWJ*, LXIX, 60; Stokes, *Studies*, p. 46; Vogelstein and Rieger, *Rom*, II, 239, 314.

[69] Kracauer, *Geschichte*, II, 110 f., 113; Gabriel Hemmerdinger, "Le dénombrement des Israélites d'Alsace (1784)," *REJ*, XLII (1901), 264. Cf. also Chap. XII, n. 22.

[70] Abrahams, *Wills*, pp. 59 f.; Ibn Adret, *Responsa*, I, nos. 645, 1157; Menaḥem ibn Zeraḥ, *Ṣedah la-derek* (on law and ethics), I, 4, 19; Grunwald, *Hamburg*, pp. 42 Art. 152, 51; De Castro, *Synagoge*, pp. xxvi f., Art. 22 (giving the salaries of communal officials after the 1639 merger of the three Sephardic congregations); Vogelstein and Rieger, *Rom*, II, 311; Ernest Ginsburger in *REJ*, N. S. IV (1938), 56 f., 59 f. (in 1801 the reader and the teacher together received £32 12).

[71] Dubnow, *Pinḳas*, no. 50; Margoliouth, *History*, III, 256 f.; *Taḳḳanot Ḳ. Ḳ. Hamburg*, Art. 43, 47.

[72] Baer, *Kleve*, pp. 113 f.; Horwitz in *MGWJ*, LIV, 526 f. (in 1800 the scribe received 150 thalers plus incidentals). Cf. also above, n. 33.

[73] A good illustration of such stabilized oligarchic rule is offered by the community of Frankfort, where a single family, Kann (with its offshoots in the families Beer, Stern, Bing and Haas), held uninterrupted sway for over two centuries (1550–1754). Even the internecine feud between members of that clan, Abraham Drach and Isaak zur Kanne, which, dragging out for two decades (1669–86), sharply divided the

communal constituency and led to costly interventions by the city and imperial authorities, did not break the family's control over communal affairs. It was terminated only by another upheaval, when Beer Löw Isaak zur Kann, for thirty years the despotic ruler of the community, was sharply attacked by a faction led by four brothers Kulp, accused of embezzlement of 200,000 florins from communal funds and placed by the rabbi under severe excommunication. But his downfall and death in disgrace in 1764 were due to a very large extent to his business reverses and failure to collect debts owed him by the elector of Mayence, two landgraves of Hesse and many prominent nobles. Cf. Alexander Dietz, *Stammbuch der Frankfurter Juden*, pp. 62, 159, 163.

NOTES TO CHAPTER XII

RELIGIOUS GUIDANCE

[1] Baer, *Spanien*, I, Pt. 2, no. 222; Aronius, *Regesten*, no. 124. Cf. also above, Chap. IX, n. 4.

[2] Colon, *Responsa*, Root 113; Ludwig Geiger, *Geschichte der Juden in Berlin*, I, 21 ff.; Finkelstein, *Self-Government*, pp. 120, 130; Meir Katzenellenbogen, *Responsa*, no. 85; Karo and Isserles on *Ṭur*, O.Ḥ. 153. Cf. also Baer, *Spanien*, I, Pt. 1, no. 112 (p. 125); Lagumina, *Codice*, I, no. 124; Selma Stern, *Der preussische Staat und die Juden*, I, Pt. 2, nos. 51, 322, 323, 327, etc.

It goes without saying that unclarified legal situations often generated difficulties and conflicts. When the Catalan synagogue in Salonica, after the disastrous conflagration of 1545, was rebuilt by Baruch Almosnino from private funds, no one but some members of the Almosnino family regarded the new building as private property. Decades later, nevertheless, one of Almosnino's grandsons felt entitled to protest against some remodeling undertaken by the congregation, and it required all of Samuel di Medina's tact and ingenuity to obtain an agreement. Cf. his *Responsa*, on Ḥ. M. no. 30; Nehama, *Salonique*, III, 85.

[3] Maimonides, *Mishneh Torah*, Tefillah XI, 1; Jacob b. Asher, *Ṭur*, O. Ḥ. 150 and Joel Sirkes's comments thereon; Meir of Rothenburg cited by Mordecai on B. B., no. 478; Baer, *Spanien*, I, Pt. 2, no. 287 (I, end;

Baer's correction "or over" cannot be accepted); Finkelstein, *Self-Government*, p. 355; Henry Berkowitz, "Notes on the History of the Earliest German Jewish Congregation in America," *PAJHS*, IX (1901), 125 f.; Margolies, *Dubno*, pp. 51, 67 f., 108, 128, 144 f., 167. Elijah b. Samuel of Lublin denied, however, the obligation of an individual to attend congregational services if attendance involved monetary loss. Cf. his *Yad Eliyahu* (Responsa), no. 7.

Communal ordinances in Spain enforcing at least weekly attendance or directed against early departure of workingmen from morning services are recorded by Ibn Adret (*Responsa*, V, 222) and Isaac b. Sheshet (*Responsa*, no. 518), respectively. The Assemblies of Candia in 1238 and Valladolid in 1432 passed detailed resolutions concerning the congregational obligations of members. Cf. Finkelstein, op. cit., pp. 268 ff., 278, 355 f. The statutes of associations likewise frequently regulated the synagogue attendance of their members. Cf., for instance, that of the tailors' guild in Płock Art. 1–2, ed. by Ringelblum in *Yivo Studies in Economics*, II, 20 ff. For interesting pertinent controversies between members, cf. Isaac b. Sheshet, *Responsa*, no. 466; Meir of Lublin, *Responsa*, no. 34; Samuel b. David, *Naḥlat shibe'a*, no. 6.

[4] Mordecai on Meg. no. 819; Ibn Ḥabib quoted by Karo on *Ṭur*, O. Ḥ. 154; Jacob b. Asher, ibid., 151 and the commentaries thereon. It was perhaps due, in part, to the recognition of these more secular aspects of the synagogue by both the Jews and their rulers that we so seldom hear of it being granted the right of asylum. James I's privilege of 1265, addressed to Barcelona and all other Jewish communities of its *collecta* and ordaining that no official shall "seize anyone among you in your synagogues" (Boffarull y Sans, *Los Judios en . . . Barcelona*, p. 66, no. li), seems to be but one of the few exceptions proving the rule of general denial.

[5] L. Löwenstein, *Geschichte der Juden am Bodensee*, I, 69; Solomon Duran, *Responsa*, no. 285; Moses Menz, *Responsa*, no. 38.

[6] Raphael Joseph b. Aaron Ḥazzan, *Ḥikre leb* (on the *Shulḥan 'Aruk*), II, no. 10; Decourcelle, *Nice*, p. 283; Simon Adler, "Das Judenpatent von 1797," *JGJC*, V (1933), 207 f. Cf. also Buber, *Ḳiryah nisgabah*, pp. 115 f.; Reifer, *Schriften*, pp. 95 f. (penalties imposed by the Austrian administration in the Bukovina, in 1792–96, on unauthorized private worship adversely affecting also the ḥasidic congregation of Ḥayyim Tyror Tscher-

nowitzer); and above Chap. VI, n. 6; Chap. IX, n. 4. For the existence of a few smaller places of worship in the otherwise fairly well centralized community of London, cf. Cecil Roth, "The Lesser London Synagogues of the Eighteenth Century," *Miscellanies of the Jewish Historical Society in England*, III (1937), 1–7.

This system of private congregational worship, removing a significant phase of Jewish religious life from communal control, did not go unchallenged. According to Isaac b. Sheshet, the community of Teruel had a standing ordinance which prohibited the holding of religious assemblies of ten adult Jews in private houses, "in order that the entire populace frequent the synagogue." An exception was made only in favor of prisoners who, if their number reached four or more, were allowed to get together for semi-public worship. Cf. his *Responsa*, no. 331. The German community of Hamburg first levied 4 thalers monthly from each private synagogue and controlled the election of officers. An amendment adopted in 1715 suppressed all private houses of worship except those maintained by scholars of rank. Cf. Grunwald in *MGJV*, XI, 60 f. Cf. also idem, "Kleine Beiträge zur jüdischen Kulturgeschichte," ibid., XVI (1905), 159 f. (describing Rabbi Samuel Steg's effective intervention in 1789 against private synagogues in Warburg). In 1754 the rabbi and judges of Wilno renewed a strict prohibition of private gatherings for morning worship "in whatever fashion or intention" under the pain of excommunication and fine. Cf. Klauzner, *Wilno*, I, 98. In 1764 a member was arrested in Trieste for refusing to read a communal proclamation from the pulpit of his private chapel. Cf. Curiel in *Scritti . . . Lattes*, p. 245 n. 3.

[7] Alexander Kisch, "Das Testament Mardochai Meisels," *MGWJ*, XXXVII (1893), 29 ff.

[8] Baer, *Spanien*, I, Pt. 1, nos. 226, 585; Hildenfinger in *REJ*, XLVII, 228; XLVIII, 75 ff.; Asher b. Yeḥiel, *Responsa*, V, 3, 5, 7; Isaac b. Sheshet, *Responsa*, nos. 249, 253, 397–98, 501; Dubnow, *Pinkas*, nos. 173, 230; Balaban, *Żydzi lwowscy*, pp. 301, 509.

[9] Ibn Adret, *Responsa*, II, 52; De Castro, *Synagoge*, p. xxiv Art. 13. Cf. also Shohet, *Jewish Court*, pp. 60 ff.; Zimmels, *Beiträge*, pp. 23 ff., 122; Epstein, *Adreth*, pp. 61 ff. Some communities kept regular registers of synagogue seats, similar in all respects to the land records of municipalities. Such a register, still extant in Tobischau, Moravia, covers all entries for the years 1650–1730. Cf. H. Flesch, "Aus dem Pinax von

Tobischau," *JGJC*, III (1931), 257–73. The question of the right of pre-emption by neighbors in synagogue seats is answered in the affirmative by Abraham b. David and others quoted by Karo on *Ṭur*, Ḥ. M. 178, and in the negative by many authorities cited by Elijah b. Samuel in *Yad Eliyahu*, no. 72. Cf. also Aryeh Yehudah Löw b. Hirz's decision in *She'elot u-teshubot ha-geonim batra'e* (Responsa of More Recent Rabbis), no. 57. In fact, some modern Polish rabbis, such as David ha-Levi of Lwów (17th century) argued for the retention of ownership by the community, transferring to seat holders only permanent right of possession. Cf. his *Ṭure zahab* on *Shulḥan 'Aruk*, Y. D. 192. But there is no evidence for such "emphyteutic" relationships in either the extant synagogue ordinances or the older juristic literature. For interesting controversies arising from ownership in seats cf. e. g. Menaḥem Mendel Krochmal's *Ṣemaḥ ṣedeḳ*, no. 94 and Benjamin Aaron Slonik's *Mase'at Binyamin*, no. 4. Such protracted quarrels induced the community of Żółkiew in 1626 to issue an ordinance protecting the rights of seat holders. Cf. Buber, *Ḳiryah nisgabah*, pp. 88 ff.

[10] Ibn Adret, *Responsa*, I, 618, 642; Dubnow, *Pinḳas*, no. 305; Halperin, *Milluim*, no. 27; Israel Elfenbein's Hebrew edition of *Sefer Minhagim of the School of Rabbi Meir ben Baruch of Rothenburg by an anonymous Author (1220–1293)*, p. 14; Wolf, *Statuten*, p. 115; Grunwald in *MGJV*, XI, 8.

[11] M. Mortara, "The Text of Rabbi Nethaneel Trabotto's Will," *Magazin für die Wissenschaft des Judentums*, XIV (1887), Hebrew section, pp. 11–22; Rubio y Lluch, *Documents*, II, 303; Baer, *Spanien*, I, Pt. 1, no. 374; Meir of Rothenburg, *Responsa*, ed. Lwów, no. 113. Cf. also Zimmels, *Beiträge*, pp. 24 ff.; Jacob Moelln, *Sefer Maharil*, fol. 61a (discusses the reason for the sale of the function of removing the scroll from the ark and returning it thereto); Epstein, *Duran*, pp. 73 ff.; Menaḥem Azariah da Fano, *Responsa*, no. 64 (members in Milan are obliged to pay the entire annual amount despite an intervening decree of expulsion); Akiba Eger, *Responsa*, no. 12 (after the unification of a Polish and a German congregation, some members of the former still invoke their "acquired right" in conducting services on certain occasions; Eger rejects this claim). Isaac b. Sheshet (*Responsa*, no. 282) reports the case of a community which had to borrow money from a Gentile in order to redeem an ornature for a scroll. The Italian custom, cited with disapproval by Joseph Colon (*Responsa*, Root 159 end), of lending precious ornaments to the synagogue

while retaining ownership and the right of disposal, was severely condemned by Joseph Karo as contrary to talmudic law. Cf. his comments on *Ṭur*, Y. D. 259. Cf. also the extensive discussions in Samson Morpurgo's *Shemesh ṣedaḳah*, I, Pt. 1, 14, 15.

[12] Asher b. Yeḥiel, *Responsa*, V, 8; Finkelstein, *Self-Government*, pp. 123, 136 f.; Jacob Weil, *Responsa*, no. 64; Isserles on *Ṭur*, O. Ḥ. 154; Solomon Duran, *Responsa*, I, 143; Antonius Margharita, *Das ganze jüdische Glaub* (1530), quoted by Richard Krautheimer in his *Mittelalterliche Synagogen*, pp. 116 f.; Mossé, *Avignon*, pp. 148 f.; Margolies, *Dubno*, p. 76. In Rome two charitable associations specialized in providing private homes with materials for kindling lights on Sabbath and Ḥanukkah. Cf. Vogelstein and Rieger, *Rom*, II, 318.

[13] Morpurgo, *Shemesh ṣedaḳah*, I, Pt. 2, no. 20, fol. 67c; II, Pt. 2, no. 33; Vogelstein and Rieger, *Rom*, II, 145, 155; Baer, *Spanien*, I, Pt. 1, nos. 31 (p. 22), 575; Wiener, *Regesten*, pp. 49 no. 171, 90 no. 78, 96 no. 124, 97 nos. 130–31. Cf. also Balaban, *Żydzi lwowscy*, App. no. 51; and above, nn. 6–7.

[14] Baer, *Spanien*, I, Pt. 1, no. 455; David de Sola Pool, *The Mill Street Synagogue*, pp. 25 ff.; Isaac b. Moses, *Or Zaruʻa*, II, 385, with reference to Meg. 26a. The Polish and Lithuanian Councils often supported the erection of local synagogues and schools from their own funds and through appeals to the affiliated communities. Cf. Lewin in *JJLG*, III, 83 (1609 concerning a synagogue in Lublin, the Council's meeting place); Dubnow, *Pinḳas*, no. 98; and other sources cited by Mahler in *Yivo Bleter*, XV, 82 f.

[15] Meir of Rothenburg, *Responsa*, ed. Berlin, p. 134 no. 97; ed. Prague, no. 610; ed. Lwów, no. 496; Mordecai on A. Z., no. 840; Zimmels, *Beiträge*, pp. 66 f.; Krautheimer, *Synagogen*, pp. 20, 116 ff. Nevertheless these passages could be cited even by eighteenth-century Italian rabbis to prohibit the painting of gold stars on synagogue doors or walls. Cf. Joseph b. Immanuel Ergas, *Dibre Yosef* (Responsa), no. 8. Cf. also Moses Menz, *Responsa*, no. 76. For the attitude of some ancient rabbis, on the other hand, cf. the statement of R. Abun, in the Leningrad Ms. of ʻA. Z. 41d, published by Jacob Nahum Epstein in his "Additional Fragments of the Yerushalmi" (Hebrew), *Tarbiz*, III (1931–32), 20. Outstanding examples of illuminated Hebrew manuscripts are the Sarajevo and Darmstädter *Haggadahs*, published by David Heinrich Müller and Julius von Schlosser, and by B. Italiener, respectively. For the medieval and early modern synagogues cf. Krautheimer, op. cit.; idem, "Die Synagoge in Worms,"

ZGJD, V (1935), 87–99; Elie Lambert, "Les synagogues de Tolède," *REJ*, LXXXIV (1927), 15–33; A. S. Yahuda, "The Synagogue of Samuel [Abulafia] ha-Levi in Toledo" (Hebrew), *Bitzaron*, III (1940–41), 101–9, 251–58 (built in 1357); A. Breier, M. Eisler and M. Grunwald, *Holzsynagogen in Polen*; Alfred Grotte, *Synagogenspuren in schlesischen Kirchen*; "Die Altonaer Synagogen," *Jahrbuch für die jüdischen Gemeinden Schleswig-Holsteins*, VI (1934–35), 30–36 (an illustrated historical sketch of the period since 1647); Marvin Lowenthal, *A World Passed By*; Franz Landsberger, *Einführung in die jüdische Kunst*; and other literature cited in Baron's *History*, III, 51 ff. n. 15, 116 f. n. 2.

[16] Baer, *Spanien*, Pt. 2, no. 267; Meir ha-Kohen, *Haggahot Maimoniot* on *Mishneh Torah*, *Tefillah* XI, 1; Moses of Coucy, *Sefer ha-miṣvot*, Positive Commandments, no. 19; Karo and Sirkes on *Ṭur*, O. Ḥ. 150, with reference to Gen. 42.1; Grunwald, "Volkstracht, Hausbau u. ähnl.," *MGJV*, I (1898), 116. It is noteworthy that, although forced to give up the competition in height with the Church, the rabbis insisted on this visible sign of superiority of the synagogue over houses owned by Jews. Tam himself, finding that a relative in Troyes had raised his house above the synagogue, ordered that the synagogue be elevated. Cf. Karo on *Ṭur*, O. Ḥ. 150. Cf., however, Asher b. Yeḥiel's *Responsa*, V, 1, referring to the addition of a second story to the synagogue only in order to accommodate the school. Cf. also Isserles, *Shulḥan 'Aruk*, O. Ḥ. 150, 2; Elbogen, *Gottesdienst*, pp. 467 f., 471 ff., 596; Krautheimer, *Synagogen*, pp. 94 ff., 132 f.

[17] Baer, *Spanien*, I, Pt. 1, no. 351. The expression "synagogues of women" mentioned, ibid., no. 210, side by side with those of men in Huesca in 1340, both served by rabbis, may refer to either a woman's compartment or to a complementary structure. The latter may also be the meaning of no. 351.

The names of but a few Jewish architects (two from sixteenth-century Prague) and interior decorators have come down — undoubtedly the result of overwhelming communal control. Cf. Krautheimer, p. 142. A quaint illustration is given in Krochmal's *Ṣemaḥ ṣedeḳ*, no. 50. A talented artist in the Moravian community of Prossnitz, on his own initiative, replaced an ugly decoration on the doors of the ark by a beautiful one, and signed upon it his name. The irate elders, conceding the artistic merits of the new piece, forced him nevertheless to strike out his name, and were therein supported by Krochmal, the chief rabbi of the province. This characteristic attitude lends additional credence to Umberto Cassuto's reading of a Hebrew inscription in Trani which commemorated the erection of its main synagogue in 5007 A. M. (1247 C. E.): נבנת זאת הבירה על יד מבין נעים החבורה. The expert Jewish architect, though "the delight of the association" (a confraternity or the community at large), is not mentioned by name. Cf. Cassuto's "Iscrizioni ebraiche a Trani," *Rivista degli studi orientali*, XIII (1932), 178 ff. For the four synagogues of Trani cf. also Giovanni Carano-Donvito, "Gli Ebrei nella storia economica di Puglia," *Rivista di politica economica*, XXIII (1933), 838.

18 Finkelstein, *Self-Government*, pp. 231, 249; Meir Schiff, homily on *Ve-ethanan* appended to his *Ḥiddushe halakot* (Juristic Novellae), Pt. II, fol. 12b; Maimonides, *Responsa*, no. 38; *Tosafot* on Ber. 46a, 49b; Menaḥem ibn Zeraḥ, *Ṣedah la-derek*, I, 1, 33, 35; Simon Duran, *Tashbeṣ*, III, 98, 290, 320; Epstein, *Duran*, pp. 38, 72 ff.; A. Berliner, "The Memor Book of Worms" (Hebrew), *Ḳobeṣ al yad*, III (1882), 32; S. B. Nisenbaum, "Un manuscrit de la 'Gueniza' de Lublin," *REJ*, L (1905), 89 (about 1660); Balaban, *Żydzi lwowscy*, pp. 509 f. Cf. also Jacob Reischer, *Shebut Ya'akob*, I, 11 (a local prohibition to raise one's voice in the synagogue may be violated for the purpose of silencing derogatory remarks about a scholar); Ezekiel Landau, *Derushe ha-ṣelaḥ*, fol. 9bc (chatting in the synagogue is both a desecration of its sanctity and a disturbance to neighbors), 33c, 38a, 48b.

There is no record, however, of rabbis objecting to prayer *cum magno clamore*, which was often censured by medieval ecclesiastics such as Innocent III in 1205, on grounds of prestige rather than esthetics. Cf. Grayzel, *Church*, pp. 106 f.; Scherer, *Rechtsverhältnisse*, p. 52 n. 2; and above, Chap. V, n. 6. For the general problem of synagogue chants, which can be mentioned here merely in passing, cf. especially A. Ackermann's "Der synagogale Gesang in seiner historischen Entwicklung" in Jakob Winter and August Wünsche, *Die jüdische Litteratur seit Abschluss des Kanons*, III, 477–529; and A. Z. Idelsohn's *Jewish Music in Its Historical Development*. Cf. also above, Chap. XI, pp. 51–56.

19 Abraham Maimuni, *Responsa*, no. 62 (excessive prayers are not forbidden); Asher b. Yeḥiel, *Responsa*, IV, 13. Differences in ritual were sufficiently significant, however, to cause the formation of a separate con-

gregation, even where the two groups were forced to worship in the same synagogue. The *cinque scuole* in Rome are an example; so is the decree of the papal vicar general in Ferrara of 1532 allowing the German-Jewish settlers in the city to hold services in their own ritual in the communal synagogue, but refusing them permission to construct a new synagogue. Cf. Perugini in *REJ*, III, 95. Only exceptionally, as in Verona, did the local majority force a group of newcomers to adopt the local ritual. Cf. Sonne in *Zion*, III, 145 ff. The more usual rigid adherence of the Jews to *Landsmannschaft* rites is best illustrated by the behavior of the numerous Jewish visitors to the renowned fairs of Leipzig, who refused to worship together even during the short duration of a fair. According to the deposition of Cantor Wolff Ulmann of 1835, there existed, as a rule, during that period separate synagogues of Jews from Brody, Warsaw, Dessau, Wollstein, Breslau, Cracow and Halberstadt, each maintaining a reader of its own. Cf. Arno Kapp, "Elkan Herz," *ZGJD*, IV (1932), 200. For an interesting conflict between two Egyptian congregations over the possession of a synagogue, cf. Levi ibn Ḥabib, *Responsa*, no. 10.

Characteristically, rabbinic leadership favored local liberties rather than absolute conformity. In a typical instance, an oriental Jew was excommunicated by his rabbi because he ventured to deride the poem *Ḥad gadya* of the Ashkenazic Passover *Haggadah*. Ḥayyim Joseph David Azulai, consulted in this matter, fully endorsed the excommunication, "for the man is an overbearing sinner who makes fun of a custom observed by myriads of Jews in Poland, Germany and vicinity." Cf. his *Ḥayyim sha'al* (Responsa), no. 28.

The rabbis could afford to be the more tolerant of these minor disparities as they felt perfectly secure in the basic uniformity of world Jewry's ritual which had long before been definitely established by the talmudic sages. An example of how effective ancient Jewish leadership had been in staving off ritualistic influences of the environment may be found in "The Iranian Festivals Adopted by the Christians and Condemned by the Jews," as recently analyzed by S. H. Taqizadeh in the *Bulletin of the School of Oriental Studies* (*University of London*), X (1939–40), 632–53, with reference to 'A. Z. 11b and other talmudic sources discussed by Alexander Kohut in *REJ*, XXIV (1892), 256–71. No such menace ever seems to have confronted medieval or early modern Jewry.

[20] Cassuto, *Firenze*, p. 217. Cf. in general Cassuto's essay "Les traduc-

tions judéo-italiennes du Rituel," *REJ*, LXXXIX (1930), 260–80; with some corrections by Sonne in *HUCA*, XVI, 43 n. 12.

[21] Justinian's *Novella* 106; Baer, *Spanien*, I, Pt. 2, no. 227; Morpurgo, *Shemesh ṣedaḳah*, I, 6. The Prussian decrees of 1702–3, which prohibited the recitation of parts of the prayer *'Alenu* and instituted regular supervision of Jewish services by a government observer, were inspired by a combination of Christian apologetics and monarchical absolutism. Cf. the extensive description in Johann Balthasar König's *Annalen der Juden*, pp. 138 ff. Cf. also above, Chap. VII, n. 43.

[22] Barnett, *El libro*, p. 4 Art. 4; Aronius, *Regesten*, no. 711 Art. 15; Baer, *Spanien*, I, Pt. 1, no. 579; Meir of Rothenburg, *Responsa*, ed. Cremona, no. 35; ed. Lwów no. 206; Ḥayyim Or Zaru'a, *Responsa*, no. 157; Löwenstein, *Bodensee*, pp. 62 f.; Decourcelle, *Nice*, p. 280; Cassuto in *JJLG*, XI, 21; Güdemann, *Geschichte*, I, 243; Abrahams, *Jewish Life*, pp. 21 ff. The Żółkiew statute imposed a fine of one-half thaler for charity on any woman picking a quarrel in the synagogue. Cf. Buber, *Ḳiryah nisgabah*, p. 83. The Amsterdam German congregation, provoked by the disturbances in its services occasioned by the opposition to innovations of its new reader, Yeḥiel Michael b. Nathan of Lublin, forbade in 1700 all derisive imitations of the *ḥazzan*, derogatory gestures and disrespectful haste in congregational responsoria. Cf. Isaac Maarsen, *De Amsterdamsche Opperrabbijn R. Saul Löwenstam* (1755–1790) *en zijn Tijd*, pp. 13 f.; Shatzky in *Yivo Bleter*, XVII, 148.

It undoubtedly was the frequency of blows in the synagogue which, perhaps together with the example set by the Church, influenced Jacob Tam to raise the fine for assault and battery there from 25 to 50 denars. Cf. Finkelstein, *Self-Government*, pp. 177, 187; *Kolbo*, no. 116; L. Rabinowitz, "France in the Thirteenth Century," *Judaism and Christianity*, ed. by W. O. E. Oesterley, Herbert Loewe and Edwin I. J. Rosenthal, II, 207. This doubling of the fine was sometimes reflected in state legislation. For Osnabrück in 1309 cf. Albert Gierse, *Geschichte der Juden in Westfalen während des Mittelalters*, pp. 51, 72. Some early modern communal statutes (e. g. those of Hamburg and London) went further and included detailed provisions for the proper administration of synagogues and the maintenance of order and decorum in them. Cf. Grunwald in *MGJV*, XI, 1 ff. (Art. 1–32); Margoliouth, *History*, III, 257 ff.

The lack of decorum in the synagogue was often duplicated in the medieval churches. Berthold of Ratisbon's censure of those women who, while in church, "laugh and chatter as if they were at a fair," and St. Bernardino's denunciation of the "many ignorant folk who . . . come drunken from the taverns or wait outside the church," refer to abuses in Christian houses of worship similar to, or worse than, those practiced among the Jews. Cf. G. G. Coulton, *Ten Medieval Studies*, pp. 117 f. At the same time the greater awe inspired by Catholic priests, due to fundamental separation between laity and clergy, and the lesser share of the mass of worshipers in the divine services, may have contributed in other countries and periods to a somewhat more decorous behavior of the latter. Upon entering a church, Christian laymen must have been much more conscious than were their Jewish compatriots of entering the house of God rather than a "house of the people."

The terms *scola Judaeorum*, *Judenschule* (with its derivative verb *schulen*) and so forth, which seem first to occur in connection with a Roman synagogue in a record of 1111, have been variously explained. The frequent assumption that they are of non-Jewish origin is contradicted by a decree of Philipp II (Augustus) of 1183 and a statement of the bishops of Bordeaux of the end of the thirteenth century, both contending that it was the Jews themselves who introduced its use. Cf. Bouquet and Brial's *Recueil des historiens des Gaules et de la France*, XVII, 10; Vincent, *Poitou*, p. 10. Perhaps the Jews merely translated into European languages their well-accepted term, *bet ha-midrash*, for which, indeed, they claimed superior sanctity to that of their *bet ha-keneset*. Cf. Maimonides, *Mishneh Torah*, Talmud torah, IV, 6; Jacob b. Asher, *Ṭur*, O. Ḥ 151; Y. D. 246. The synagogue itself had, ever since talmudic and geonic times, served as the main schoolhouse. Solomon Duran in the fifteenth century comforted an inquirer that, "since from time immemorial teachers have instructed children in the synagogue," he need not worry over his occasional slumber there. Cf. Assaf's *Meḳorot*, II, 4 n. 8, 78 f. Cf. also ibid., III, 8, 27, 68, 85. A synagogue in Monzon, near Lerida, converted into a church in 1414, had, in fact, previously been called *midras* in Hebrew. Cf. Baer, *Spanien*, I, Pt. 1. no. 508. Cf. also ibid., no. 179 (p. 238). This usage seems not to have been universal in Spain, however. Cf. e. g. Ibn Adret, *Responsa*, V, 522: "an upper story close to the synagogue, called the *midrash.*" Cf. also D. S. Blondheim, *Les parlers judéo-romans et la Vetus Latina*, pp. 106 ff.; and Wachstein in *ZGJD*, IV, 135, n. 21.

[23] Ibn Adret, *Responsa*, I, 581; Krautheimer, *Synagogen*, p. 146; S. Saalfeld, *Das Martyrologium des Nürnberger Memorbuches*; M. Weinberg, "Untersuchungen über das Wesen des Memorbuches," *JJLG*, XVI (1924), 253–323; idem, "Memorbücher," *Menorah* (Vienna), VI (1928), 697–708; idem, *Die Memorbücher der jüdischen Gemeinden in Bayern*; Max Markreich, "Das Memorbuch der Judengemeinde in Emden," *Jahrbuch für die jüd. Gemeinden Schleswig-Holsteins*, V (1933–34), 24–36. For a related, though different, type of communal record, cf. Gustav Trexler's "Das Gödinger Maskir-Buch," *ZGJT*, V (1938), 28–36.

[24] Aronius, *Regesten*, no. 168; Baer, *Spanien*, I, Pt. 1, no. 578; Donath, *Mecklenburg*, pp. 23, 29 ff., 297, 308 ff.; Ginsburger in *REJ*, N. S. IV, 36, 38 f.; Nehama, *Salonique*, IV, 147 f.; Samuel Oppenheim, "The Jewish Burial Ground on New Bowery, New York, Acquired in 1682, Not 1656," *PAJHS*, XXXI (1928), 77–103; Gutstein, *Newport*, pp. 36 ff., 295 ff.; Roth, *Archives of the United Synagogue*, p. 44. Cf. also E. Nübling, *Die Judengemeinden des Mittelalters, insbesondere die Gemeinde der Reichsstadt Ulm*, pp. 39 ff.; Colorni in *Riv. st. dir. it.*, XI, 62 f.; Edmund H. Abrahams, "Some Notes on the Early History of the Sheftalls of Georgia," *PAJHS*, XVII (1909), 172 f.; Reba C. Strickland, *Religion and the State of Georgia in the Eighteenth Century*, p. 127 (the first Jewish cemetery in Savannah, Ga., was established on a private plot belonging to the DeLyon family. When burial there was refused to an outsider, Mordecai Sheftall in 1773 donated a five-acre tract of land which "shall be and forever remain to and for the use and purpose of a place of burial, for all persons *whatever* professing the Jewish religion, and to and for the purpose of erecting a synagogue or building for the worship of those of the said profession." This burial ground was used until 1850, the community having found some way of overcoming the opposition of the Protestant majority which had been vocal as late as 1769).

[25] Thomas, *Summa theol.*, II, 2, 32, 2; Raphael Meldola, *Mayyim rabbim* (Responsa), II, 65–66; Mordecai Judah Leb Sacks and Elijah Isaac Prissmann (eds.) *Shiṭah 'al Mo'ed Ḳaṭan* (Comments on M. Ḳ.) by a Disciple of R. Yeḥiel of Paris [Yedidiah of Nuremberg], in *Harry Fischel Institute Publications*, Section III, p. 98 and the notes thereto (cf.

also Menaḥem ha-Meiri's comments, ibid., p. 131); *Kolbo*, no. 112; Jacob b. Asher, *Ṭur*, Y. D. 367 (with reference to Giṭ. 61a) and 344 (with reference to M. Ḳ. 22b); and Karo's and Sirkes's comments thereon. The great importance attached to public mourning for deceased leaders in many communities is reflected in the anxious inquiry addressed to Azulai by a community which was confronted by a testamentary provision of its deceased rabbi asking that no public mourning be observed in his behalf. The congregation indignantly claimed "that it accrued to its honor to hold funeral services for the departed and that the name of the Lord may almost be desecrated thereby before the Gentiles and the general populace. Indeed one may fear the outbreak of factional strife in the community on this score." Azulai insisted that the rabbi's will be respected, particularly since he had not forbidden private rites and orations in his home. Cf. *Ḥayyim sha'al*, I, 34.

Some difficulties seem to have arisen in the case of relapsed converts to Christianity, at least insofar as their "repentance" was not considered complete by the Jewish leaders. When Benedict of York, baptized under the stress of the massacres of 1190, subsequently reverted to Judaism and soon thereafter died, he "was a stranger to the common burial ground of the Jews, even as of the Christians." Cf. the excerpt from Roger of Hoveden's "Chronicle" in G. G. Coulton's *Life in the Middle Ages*, III, 34. As a curious exception one may note the burial of Jewish corpses together with those of Christians in the district cemetery of Barrois in 1321–23. Cf. Emile Lévy, "Un document sur les Juifs du Barrois en 1321–23," *REJ*, XIX (1889), 246–58. For the meaning of the term *mi-pene darke ha-shalom* (for the sake of peace), frequently used by the rabbis, cf. Jacob Z. Lauterbach's essay on "The Attitude of the Jew towards the Non-Jew," *Yearbook of the Central Conference of American Rabbis*, XXXI (1921), 201 ff.

26 Bloom, *Amsterdam*, p. 207; Joḥanan Holleschau, *Ma'aseh rab* (a pamphlet on the London controversy, printed together with *Teshubot ha-geonim*), 1707; Adler, *London*, pp. 117 ff.; Wiener, *Regesten*, pp. 58 f.; Stobbe, *Deutschland*, p. 146; Meir of Rothenburg, *Responsa*, ed. Prague, end; Isserlein, *Pesaḳim*, no. 65; Frank, *Ḳehillot*, pp. 85 f.; Halperin, *Milluim*, no. 37. Cf. also Dubnow in *Evreiskaya Starina*, V, 72 f., no. 2 (the Polish Council decided in 1621 that the community of Zabludowo, possessing a synagogue, where it employs a reader, and a cemetery of its

own, is not obliged to contribute to the general taxes for the upkeep of the regional community of Tykocin, except such as are devoted to the maintenance of the regional rabbinate).

The early unity of the communities of Mayence and Worms may well have been cemented by the existence during the early part of the eleventh century of a cemetery in the former city only. That of Worms is first mentioned as such only about 1220 (cf. Aronius, *Regesten*, nos. 145, 185, 412, 736), although its earliest known tombstone inscription seems to date back to 1048. Cf. the full survey of these inscriptions in Max Grunwald's "Le cimetière de Worms," *REJ*, N. S. IV (1938), 71–112. That is perhaps why Rashi's famous teacher, Jacob b. Yakar of Worms, and the latter's father were buried in Mayence. Cf. Sali Levi, *Beiträge zur Geschichte der ältesten jüdischen Grabsteine in Mainz*, pp. 12 ff.; and in general the same author's "Die Verbundenheit zwischen den jüdischen Gemeinden Worms und Mainz im Mittelalter," *ZGJD*, V (1934), 187–91.

[27] Jacobs, *Angevin England*, p. 62; Rodocanachi, *Saint-Siège*, p. 30 n. 2 (cf., however, Berliner's *Rom*, II, Pt. 2, pp. 62 ff.); idem, "La communauté juive de Rome au temps de Jules II et de Léon X," *REJ*, LXI (1911), 76 ff.; M. A. Gerson, "Les Juifs en Champagne," *Mémoires de la Société academique d'agriculture . . . du Département de l'Aube*, LXIII (1899), 183; Louis de Grandemaison, "Le cimetière des Juifs à Tours," *REJ*, XVII (1889), 262–75 (with references to other French cemeteries); Salomon Kahn, "Documents inédits sur les Juifs de Montpellier," ibid., XIX (1889), 264; Vincent, *Poitou*, pp. 10, 46 f.; *Tosafot* on Shab. 139b; Alexander Pinthus, "Studien über die bauliche Entwicklung der Judengassen in den deutschen Städten" in *ZGJD*, II (1930), 124; Baer, *Spanien*, I, Pt. 1, nos. 175, 243; H. Baerwald, *Der alte Friedhof der israelitischen Gemeinde zu Frankfurt am-Main*; Lagumina, *Codice*, I, no. 433.

[28] Aronius, *Regesten*, nos. 313a, 547, 603; Scherer, *Rechtsverhältnisse*, p. 182 (Art. XIV), 225 f.; Bloch, *Generalprivilegien*, pp. 52, 110 (Art. XVIII); Regné in *REJ*, LXIII, no. 696; Berliner in *Jubelschrift Hildesheimer*, pp. 156 f.; Da Fano, *Responsa*, nos. 44, 56; Ibn abi Zimra, *Responsa*, I, 741. Cf. also L. A. Schiavi, "Gli Ebrei in Venezia e nelle sue colonie," *Nuova Antologia*, CXXXI (1893), 498 f., mentioning repeated desecrations of the Jewish cemetery in Candia; and Jacob Reischer's *Shebut Ya'akob*, II, 103, referring to thieves who confessed to having despoiled the Jewish cemetery in Brussels over a period of ten years.

[29] Isserlein, *Terumat ha-deshen*, no. 284; Weil, *Pesaḳim*, nos. 3, 49; Karo and Isserles on *Ṭur*, Y. D. 368; Ciscato, *Padova*, pp. 299 ff. Cf. also ibid., pp. 277 f., 301 f. A remarkable decree for the protection of all Jewish cemeteries and houses of worship was issued in 1455 by Henry IV of Castile at the instance of the Jewish communities in the realm, represented by a Christian *procurador*. This decree was confirmed by Ferdinand in 1479 and 1484. Cf. Baer, *Spanien*, I, Pt. 2, no. 316. For an earlier protective decree issued by James I in behalf of the synagogues and cemeteries of the *collecta* of Barcelona in 1267, cf. Boffarull y Sans, *Los Judios en . . . Barcelona*, p. 75, no. lxx.

The use of a cemetery as a quarantine for a Jewish leper, so that he might be kept in isolation even from Christian fellow-sufferers, is illustrated by means of an incident in Bourg in 1462 by Ernest Wickersheimer in his "Lèpre et Juifs au Moyen Age," *Janus, Archives internationales pour l'histoire de la médecine*, XXXVI (1932), 43–48. It is questionable, however, whether this singular record may be considered a sufficient basis for generalization. Were this practice very widespread, it very likely would have been recorded elsewhere, too, in view of the great prevalence of leprosy in the middle ages. Leprosy after the Crusades, says James J. Walsh, became "almost as much of a folk disease as tuberculosis came to be towards the end of the nineteenth century." Cf. his *History of Nursing*, p. 39. It may be noted, however, that ancient Israel seems to have been relatively free of that horrible disease and that its occurrence among Jews is attested only from the Hellenistic period on. Cf. A. Bloom's recent study, *La lèpre dans l'Ancienne Egypte et chez les Anciens Hébreux*. Even then, it appears, it never assumed the character of a mass disease among the Jews.

[30] Baer, *Spanien*, I, Pt. 2, no. 263; Aronius, *Regesten*, nos. 381, 440, etc.; Decourcelle, *Nice*, pp. 285 f.; Jacob b. Asher, *Ṭur*, Y. D. 363; Zdenka Münzer, "Die Altneusynagoge in Prag," *JGJC*, IV (1932), 63–105. Cf. also Ad. Neubauer, "Documents inédits. XV: Documents sur Avignon," *REJ*, X (1885), 94 (citing Ms. Ginzburg, no. 566) concerning the decision of the community of Avignon to bury their dead one on top of the other. Undoubtedly to forestall future difficulties, the community of Syracuse, Sicily, obtained in 1187 from the bishop of Cefalù a piece of ground for the extension of its cemetery in "emphyteutic possession." The pertinent Judeo-Arabic record, extant in the Royal Archives of Palermo, has been

published by Salvatore Cusa in *I diplomi greci ed arabi di Sicilia*, pp. 495 f. Cf. also Michele Amari, *Storia dei Musulmani di Sicilia*, 2d ed., I, p. xxxii; III, 298.

[31] Ferorelli, *Italia meridionale*, p. 103; Baer, *Spanien*, I, Pt. 1, no. 549 (p. 881); Pt. 2, no. 58 (Art. 314); Scherer, *Rechtsverhältnisse*, pp. 181 f. (Art. XIII), 223 ff.; *Kolbo*, no. 114; Leopold Löwenstein, *Geschichte der Juden in der Kurpfalz*, p. 32; Stobbe, *Deutschland*, pp. 42, 169 f., 217 f., 269 f.; S. Adler in *JGJC*, V, 207 f.; Kapp in *ZGJD*, IV, 199; Clément, *Metz*, p. 105 n. 1. Cf. also Balaban, *Żydzi lwowscy*, pp. 334, 542, App. no. 82; Klauzner, *Wilno*, I, 8; and for the legal difficulties encountered by many communities, Bernhard Brilling, "Der Streit um den Friedhof zu Ottensen," *Jahrbuch für die jüd. Gemeinden Schleswig-Holsteins*, III (1931–32), 45–68.

[32] Berliner, *Aus dem inneren Leben der deutschen Juden im Mittelalter* 2d ed., pp. 118 f.; Obermeyer, *Die Landschaft Babylonien im Zeitalter des Talmuds und des Gaonats*, pp. 321 ff.; Mann, *Texts*, II, 87 f.; Meir of Rothenburg, *Responsa*, ed. Lwów, no. 164; Graetz, *History*, III, 640. Cf. also Joshua Trachtenberg's *Jewish Magic and Superstition: A Study in Folk Religion*, passim.

[33] Zunz, *Zur Geschichte*, pp. 395 ff.; Aronius, *Regesten*, no. 66; Berliner, *Rom*, II, Pt. 2, pp. 62 f., 110 (Art. XI); Rodocanachi, *Saint-Siège*, p. 199; Vogelstein and Rieger, *Rom*, II, 237 f.; Mossé, *Avignon*, p. 111; Pesaro, *Memorie*, p. 54. The rigid prohibition of profane use of cemeteries and tombstones is often reiterated in rabbinic literature. Cf. Jacob b. Asher's *Tur*, Y. D. 367–68 and the commentaries thereon; Elijah b. Samuel's *Yad Eliyahu*, no. 94.

For Jewish funerary arts cf. the literature on medieval Jewish art generally (above, n. 15), and, especially Gustav Cohn, *Der jüdische Friedhof. Seine geschichtliche und kulturgeschichtliche Entwicklung*; Arthur Levy, *Jüdische Grabmalkunst in Osteuropa*; Sandor Wolf, "Die Entwicklung des jüdischen Grabsteines und die Denkmäler des Eisenstädter Friedhofes" in B. Wachstein's *Die Grabinschriften des alten Judenfriedhofs in Eisenstadt*; Alfred Grotte, *Alte schlesische Judenfriedhöfe* (*Breslau und Dyherrnfurth*); Max Diamant, *Jüdische Volkskunst* (principally in Rumania, 18th and 19th cent.). Cf. also the literature on individual cemeteries, such as B. Wachstein's *Inschriften . . . Wien*, supplemented by his additional "Randbemerkungen" in *Quellen und Forschungen zur*

Geschichte der Juden in Deutsch-Oesterreich, XI (1936); M. Horovitz, *Die Inschriften des alten Friedhofs der israelitischen Gemeinde zu Frankfurt a. M.* (including a sketch of the history of the Jewish tombstones); Julius Hülsen, *Der alte Judenfriedhof in Frankfurt a. M.* (popular); A. Nordmann, *Der israelitische Friedhof in Hegenheim in gesch. Darstellung*; D. Henriques de Castro, *Auswahl von Grabsteinen auf dem Niederl. Portug.-Israel. Begräbnissplatze zu Oderkerk an den Amstel*; Sh. B. Nisenbaum, *Evreiskie nagrobnyie pamiatniki goroda Liublina* (Jewish Tombstones of the City of Lublin, XVI–XIX Cent.); N. M. Gelber, "Aus dem Pinax des alten Judenfriedhofes in Brody (1699–1831)," *JJLG*, XIII (1920), 119–41; Israel Klauzner, *Ḳorot bet ha-'almin ha-yashan be-Wilno* (A History of the Old Cemetery in Wilno); and J. Szper, *Stary cmentarz żydowski w Łodzi* (The Old Jewish Cemetery in Lodz, nineteenth century).

34 S. Wigderman, "Donkey's Burial" (Hebrew), *Reshumot*, II (2d printing, 1927), 453; [Lyons] in *PAJHS*, XXI (1913), 66 f., 74 f.; Meir of Rothenburg, *Responsa*, ed. Prague, nos. 149, 176; Baer, *Spanien*, I, Pt. 2, no. 163 (p. 162); Naḥmanides and Nissim Gerondi on Alfasi, M. Ḳ. end; *Ṭur*, Y. D. 334, 340, 345 and the commentaries thereon. Cf. also Götz, *Eben ha-shoham*, nos. 13 (a Polish refugee in Germany demands in his will that he be buried in his native cemetery of Międzyrzecze), 44 (the rabbi strains his ingenuity to afford friendly treatment to a pious suicide); Samuel di Medina, *Responsa*, on Y. D. no. 128; and Leon Nemoy, "A Tenth-Century Disquisition on Suicide According to Old Testament Law,' *Journal of Biblical Literature*, LVII (1938), 411–20. The question as to whether a suicide committed by a Jewish prisoner, to forestall severe torture known to be practiced by his prosecutors, called for the usual abstention from mourning and other penalties, is answered in the negative by several authorities cited by Azulai in his *Ḥayyim sha'al*, I, 46.

Needless to say that the "donkey's burial" lent itself to exaggeration, abuse and often generated friction in the community. When in 1792 the community of Druya decided to punish one, Jacob the Surgeon, by burying him outside the range of graves, a protesting member invoked state aid and appeared with soldiers at the funeral, forcing the "holy association" to assign an ordinary grave. The rebel was thereupon excommunicated and threatened with the refusal of all ministrations in event of his death, or of that of any close relative, unless he obtained the pardon of each and every member of the association. Cf. Elyakim Druyanow, "Fragments from an Ancient Minute Book of the 'Holy Association' in Druya, Province of Wilno" (Hebrew), *Reshumot*, I (1918), 444 f., 448 f. and, in general, S. Assaf, *Ha-'Oneshin*, pp. 35, 118 f., 122, 138 f.

For a regular tariff on funerals according to the age of the deceased (children up to ten, those between ten and thirteen, and adults), cf. *Costituzioni Modena*, pp. 16 ff. Art. IX. An interesting problem confronted the leaders of the Polish Council in connection with the funeral charges of the communities in which it held its sessions. There seem to have been complaints that the cemetery administration in Jarosław was charging excessive fees to wealthy persons who visited the sessions of the Council and happened to die there. In 1699 the Council set a maximum fee of 60 fl. Cf. Isak Lewin, "Eine Urkunde der Vierländersynode aus dem Jahre 1699," *MGWJ*, LXVII (1933), 387–89. Cf. also Chap. IX, n. 6.

[35] Scherer, *Rechtsverhältnisse*, p. 44; Mossé, *Avignon*, p. 110; Vogelstein and Rieger, *Rom*, II, 188, 195, 237 f.; Ciavarini, *Ancona*, pp. 22 f.; Max Radin, "A Charter of Privileges of the Jews in Ancona of the Year 1535," *JQR*, IV (1913–14), 231, 242; Achille Nordmann, "Histoire des Juifs à Genève de 1281 à 1780," *REJ*, LXXX (1925), 27.

[36] Stobbe, *Deutschland*, pp. 65, 171, 271 f.; R. Straus, "Ein Landshuter Judeneid aus dem 14. Jahrhundert," *ZGJD*, V (1934), 44 ff.; Meir of Rothenburg, *Responsa*, ed. Prague, no. 90; Cassuto, *Firenze*, p. 218; *Privilegi . . . Piemonte*, p. 7; Clément, *Metz*, pp. 162 ff.

[37] Baer, *Studien*, pp. 25 f.; idem, *Spanien*, I, Pt. 1, nos. 21 (1135), 80 (1213), 160 (1306), 263 (1359), 272 (1364), 434 (1391), 587 (1409); Pt. 2, nos. 56–57 (13th century), 125 (1309), 163 (1337–47), 230 (1383–84), 233 (1385), 249 (p. 235:1386), 274 (1409); Epstein, *Adreth*, pp. 89 f.; Kayserling, *Portugal*, p. 14; idem, *Navarra*, p. 73; Ibn Adret, *Responsa*, II, 213; Pribram, *Urkunden*, I, 358 ff.; Bloch, *Generalprivilegien*, pp. 53, 110 (Art. XX); Georg Adler, "Das grosspolnische Fleischergewerbe vor 300 Jahren, " *Zeitschrift der histor. Gesellschaft f. d. Provinz Posen*, IX (1894), 209–372; Balaban, *Żydzi lwowscy*, App. no. 15; Klauzner, *Wilno*, I, 18 ff. Cf. also Boffarull y Sans, *Los Judios en . . . Barcelona*, p. 75, no. lxix (1268); Lagumina, *Codice*, I, nos. 340, 344, 395, 445, 464 (separate slaughterhouses and meat taxes in Sicily); Ciscato, *Padova*, pp. 274 f. (distinguishing signs for kosher meat); Aronius, *Regesten*, no. 571 (a tariff ranging from 1–24 denars to be paid by Jewish slaughterers was enacted by the city of Tulln, Lower Austria, in 1237), 724 Art. 1; Nübling, *Juden-*

gemeinden, pp. 47 ff.; Samuel di Medina, *Responsa*, on Y. D. 40 (on the conditions in Sofia, and the difficulties arising from the ritualistic differences between the natives and the "Ungaros" followed by the Sephardim).

[38] For a variety of communal ordinances in the field of *sheḥitah* cf. e. g., Isaac b. Sheshet, *Responsa*, no. 467; Hildenfinger in *REJ*, XLI, 64; Colorni in *Riv. st. dir. it.*, XI, 67; Joseph Katz, *She'erit Yosef*, nos. 11, 70; Samuel b. David, *Naḥlat shibe'a*, no. 70. Cf. also Chap. XI, nn. 58 ff.; XV, nn. 12–13.

[39] Stobbe, *Deutschland*, p. 171; Clément, *Metz*, pp. 140 ff.; Baer, *Spanien*, I, Pt. 1, no. 434; Vincent, *Poitou*, p. 10; Krochmal, *Ṣemaḥ ṣedeḳ*, no. 28; Morpurgo, *Shemesh ṣedaḳah*, I, Pt. 2, no. 14. Cf. also Jac. Zwarts, *Hoofdstukken uit de geschiedenis der Joden in Nederland*, pp. 247 ff. (on a guild of Jewish fish merchants in eighteenth-century Amsterdam). Concerning sturgeon and caviar cf. e. g. Pierre Belon, *Les observations de plusieurs singularitéz et choses mémorables trouvées en Grèce, Asie, Judée, Egypte, Arabie et autres pays éstranges*, 1553, fol. 71b, excerpted by Paul Grunebaum in "Les Juifs d'Orient d'après les géographes et les voyageurs," *REJ*, XXVII (1895), 126 f.; and the remarks of Leopold Löw on the preliminaries to the pertinent controversy between Aaron Chorin and Isaac Krisshaber at the end of the eighteenth century in his biographical sketch of Chorin reprinted in his *Gesammelte Schriften*, II, 260 ff.

[40] Rabinowitz, *France*, pp. 88 ff.; Maimonides, *Responsa*, nos. 369, 382 and Freimann's notes thereon; Finkelstein, *Self-Government*, pp. 225, 234 ff., 260.

[41] Horovitz, *Rabbinerversammlung*, pp. 13, 23 f.; Lagumina, *Codice*, I, nos. 395, 406; II, Pt. 1, nos. 536, 577, 623, 624, 666, 743, 764, 776; Isaac b. Sheshet, *Responsa*, no. 262; Epstein, *Adreth*, pp. 89 f.; Baer, *Spanien*, I, Pt. 1, no. 250; Pt. 2, no. 287 (III, 6); Finkelstein, *Self-Government*, pp. 98, 318, 325, 352, 366 f.

[42] Samuel di Medina, *Responsa*, on Y. D. no. 53; Grunwald in *MGJV*, XI, 40; idem, *Hamburg*, p. 70; Malvezin, *Bordeaux*, pp. 203 ff. For ritualistic measures adopted in 1539 to promote wine exports from Candia, cf. Sassoon, *Catalogue*, pp. 354 f.; Assaf in *Sinai*, III, Pt. 1, p. 158.

[43] Isserlein, *Pesaḳim*, no. 52; Baer, *Kleve*, p. 116 n. 179; Dubnow, *Pinḳas*, nos. 397, 436, 954, 1022; Halperin, *Milluim*, no. 53; idem in *Yivo Studies in History*, II, 71 f.

Shippers of *lulabs* from Germany to Italy are mentioned in a will written by a Veronese Jew in 1641 and published in Assaf's *Mekorot*, II, 139 f. Also of interest are the decisions by Joel Sirkes that contributions for the purchase of a communal citron be assessed partly per capita and partly in ratio to wealth (against the contrary opinions voiced by Jacob Moelln and Moses Isserles), and by Moses Menz that the destruction of a choice citron requires restitution of the market price of an ordinary one. Cf. Elijah b. Moses Gershon (ed.), *She'elot u-teshubot hageonim batra'e*, no. 37; Menz, *Responsa*, no. 112. Cf. also Chap. XI, n. 32; XV, n. 14.

[44] Meir of Rothenburg, *Responsa*, ed. Prague, no. 233; ed. Berlin, pp. 42, no. 289, 173 no. 53; Jacob b. Asher, *Ṭur*, Y. D. 201 ff. and the commentaries thereon; Ḥayyim Or Zaru'a, *Responsa*, no. 153; Judah Menz, *Responsa*, no. 7; Isaac Gershon (ed.), *Mashbit milḥamot*; Judah b. Moses Saltaro (ed.), *Mikveh Israel*; Moses b. Yeḥiel di Porto (ed.), *Palge mayyim* (all referring to the bath in Rovigo; cf. also Blau, *Leo Modenas Briefe*, I, 110 ff.).

[45] Margolies, *Dubno*, pp. 148, 174; Vogelstein and Rieger, *Rom*, I, 220; II, 132 (a beautiful bathhouse of the Spanish community); Baer, *Spanien*, I, Pt. 2, no. 23; Nübling, *Judengemeinden*, pp. 46 f.; Friedrich J. Hildebrand, *Das romanische Judenbad im alten Synagogenhofe zu Speier am Rhein* (twelfth century); E. Hirsch, "Das Judenbad zu Friedberg in Hessen," in F. Dreher's *Friedberg i. H. in Wort und Bild*, pp. 79–85 (about 1260); idem, "Glocke als Wetterzauber beim Friedberger Judenbad von 1260," *Festschrift Cimbria*, pp. 95–103; K. Walter, *Das Judenbad zu Offenburg* (fourteenth century); Krautheimer, *Synagogen*, pp. 148 f., 164 f., 188 f., 217 ff. For the medieval bathhouse in Montpellier, cf. Charles d'Aigrefeuille, *Histoire de la ville de Montpellier*, II, 548. Cf. also H. Flesch, "Der Judenbader zu Gaya," *MGWJ*, LXXIII (1929), 119–30.

NOTES TO CHAPTER XIII

EDUCATION AND PUBLIC ENLIGHTENMENT

[1] Maimonides, *Mishneh Torah*, Talmud torah, I, 8–10; II, 1; Jacob b. Asher, *Ṭur*, Y. D. 245–46. The translation of the term *medinah* in *Mishneh Torah*, II, 1, by "state," here given, is made necessary by the context as well as by Maimonides' general use of this term as the equiv-

alent of a Greek *polis*, i. e. a city or city state. Cf. Baron in *Essays on Maimonides*, p. 169.

[2] Assaf, *Meḳorot*, II, 52, 57, 81 ff.; Baer, *Spanien*, I, Pt. 2, no. 287 (I); Finkelstein, *Self-Government*, pp. 350 ff.

[3] Meir of Rothenburg, quoted by Meir ha-Kohen in *Haggahot Maimoniot* on *Mishneh Torah*, l. c., I, 8; Isserles on *Ṭur*, Y. D. 245, quoting German as well as Spanish authorities. The predilection for higher education had roots in remote antiquity when, long before the establishment of public elementary schools, the Palestinian community had maintained schools for boys of sixteen and over. Even the term *yeshibah* for such an advanced school seems to have been used already during the Second Commonwealth, as illustrated by the Hebrew original of Ecclesiasticus (51.29), if one pays no heed to various emendations suggested by modern scholars. Nevertheless the importance of elementary education and the communal responsibility for it were often stressed by such leaders as Ezekiel Landau, who once proclaimed the very survival of the community of Prague through the ages of ceaseless persecution to have been entirely due to the existence in its midst of a communal "school for children." Cf. his *Derushe ha-ṣelaḥ*, fol. 5b.

[4] *Mishneh Torah*, l. c., I, 6; *Ṭur*, l. c. and the commentaries thereon; Assaf, *Meḳorot*, I, 19, 209; II, 29; Israel ibn Al-Nakawa, *Menorat ha-Maor*, ed. by Enelow, IV, 142, with reference to Ḳid. 29b: An exceptionally bright son should be given precedence, however. For the importance of the quinquennial division in the ancient educational system, cf. Zuri's remarks in his *Toledot*, I, 327.

[5] Assaf, *Meḳorot*, I, 18, 22, 83, 137, 151 f., 189 f.; II, 148 ff., 159; Decourcelle, *Nice*, pp. 271 f.; Eibeschütz, *Ya'arot debash*, I, 11a; Meir of Rothenburg, *Responsa*, ed. Prague, no. 245. A medieval legend describes in picturesque detail the conclusion of a contract in which the father promised to pay a teacher 1,000 gold pieces for the tutoring of his son for a period of twenty-five years. Cf. Assaf, III, 115. Apparently here, as in public employment, the prohibition of signing contracts of more than three-years duration and thus excessively restricting one's personal liberty, which was specifically applied to private tutors by Meir of Rothenburg and others, was pushed aside. Cf. Chap. XI, n. 36. In fifteenth-century Rome, however, even wealthy fathers regarded it as a pious duty to coach their children. Cf. Vogelstein and Rieger, *Rom*, II, 109.

[6] Maimonides, *Mishneh Torah*, l. c., I, 11; III, 13; Joseph b. Moses cited Chap. XI, n. 24; I. Rivkind, "A Codex of Prague Ordinances" (Hebrew), *Reshumot*, IV (1926), 347 (cf. also Ezekiel Landau, *Derushe ha-ṣelaḥ*, fol. 52a); Assaf, *Meḳorot*, I, 5; II, 72; Kaufmann in his *Gesammelte Schriften*, II, 232; *Tosafot* on Ber. 11b; Moses of Coucy, *Sefer ha-miṣvot*, Positive Com. no. 12, quoted with approval in *Haggahot Maimoniot*, l. c. I, 8 and by Isserles on *Ṭur*, Y. D. 245. In one of his sermons, Jonathan Eibeschütz proffered a lengthy naturalistic explanation for the divinely ordained long winter nights which enable even busy traders and workingmen to devote several hours daily to study. Cf. his *Ya'arot debash*, I, 78d. Night study, moreover, had behind it the authoritative advice of several talmudic sages, quoted, together with other medieval sources, by Isaiah Horowitz in his *Shene luḥot ha-berit*, on Shebu'ot (ed. Amsterdam fol. 182a). Amatus Lusitanus, on the other hand, as a physician, tried to dissuade readers from study at night. In his noteworthy description of the treatment he had given to Azariah de' Rossi he declares that such study "is harmful and contrary to nature, and is therefore to be avoided. For it causes serious and grave disturbances to the body. . . ." Cf. his *Centuriae curationum medicinalium*, 4th Centuria, Curatio 42, in Harry Friedenwald's English translation in his "Two Jewish Physicians of the Sixteenth Century," *Medical Leaves*, 1941, p. 54.

[7] *Sha'are ṣedeḳ* (Responsa), III, 6, 29, fol. 26b; Assaf, *Meḳorot*, II, 95 f.; A. Berliner, *Persönliche Beziehungen zwischen Christen und Juden im Mittelalter*; Abrahams, *Jewish Life*, pp. 365 ff., 443 ff. Cf. also Isaiah Horowitz, l. c. (fol. 185a).

[8] Maimonides, *Mishneh Torah*, l. c. I, 13; *Ṭur*, Y. D. 245 and Isserles' comments thereon; Assaf, *Meḳorot*, I, 18, 21 f., 40, 59 f., 210 f.; II, 112; Isserlein, cited by Joseph b. Moses in *Leḳeṭ yosher*, II, 19; Simon Duran, *Tashbeṣ*, III, 78 (referring to a ritualistic decision by the wife of Joseph b. Joḥanan Treves of France); Kaufmann in *Gesammelte Schriften*, II, 247; Berliner, *Rom*, II, Pt. 1, pp. 39 f., 116 ff. (on Paula, a thirteenth-century copyist of Hebrew manuscripts). Solomon Ephraim Lentshits emphasized the importance of married state for the scholar, "for only if he takes a wife, shall she assume responsibility for the household, so that he may study the Torah of the Lord by day and night." Cf. his *'Olelot Ephraim*, no. 338. Cf. also, in general, Nahida Remy, *The Jewish Woman*; Michael Adler's essay on "The Jewish Woman in Medieval England"

in his *Jews of Medieval England*, pp. 15–45; A. M. Habermann, *Nashim 'ibriot be-tor madpisot* (Jewish Women as Printers, Compositors, Publishers and Patronesses of Authors) with the same author's additional remarks in *Kirjath Sefer*, XV (1938), 373–76.

[9] Rabbinic views on the extreme reverence due scholars and the master-pupil relationship are well summarized by Jacob b. Asher in his *Ṭur*, Y. D. 242–43, and the commentaries thereon. Samuel di Medina's opinion is given in his *Responsa*, on Ḥ. M., no. 1.

[10] For typical complaints of leading central European rabbis in the eighteenth century, cf. the frequent discourses on the subject in the sermons of Jonathan Eibeschütz and Ezekiel Landau (*Ya'arot debash*, I, 13b, 46c, 50a, 65c, 87bc [here the author extols his father-in-law, Isaac Spira, then deceased, for picking him, an impecunious orphan, as his daughter's mate in preference to many an eligible son of wealthy parents]; *Derushe ha-ṣelaḥ*, fols. 24c, 52a); and the sharp exhortation by Meir Schiff published in his *Commentary* on Giṭ., end. It is noteworthy that some early modern communities, such as the "Turkish" congregation in Vienna in 1778, felt prompted to adopt a statutory requirement of literacy for all candidates for public office. Cf. N. M. Gelber, "Contribution à l'histoire des Juifs espagnoles à Vienne," *REJ*, XCVII (1934), 123 f.; XCVIII (1934), 44 ff.

[11] Johannes Gerson, quoted by Coulton in his *Ten Medieval Studies*, p. 120; Assaf, *Meḳorot*, III, 114; I. Goldziher's article on "Education, Muslim" in Hasting's *Encyclopaedia of Religion and Ethics*, V, 201 f. For a general comparison with Muslim higher education during the first four centuries of the Muslim era, cf. also A. Tolas's recent study *L'enseignement chez les Arabs: La Madrasa Nizâmiyyâ et son histoire.*

[12] Meir of Rothenburg, *Responsa*, ed. Prague, no. 667; Ibn Adret, *Responsa*, VII, 516. The critique of the pre-emancipatory system of education, begun by the reformers of the Mendelssohn circle, particularly Hartwig Wessely, was later combined with much of the anti-Polish bias which characterized even such distinguished German Jewish writers of the nineteenth century as Steinheim and Graetz. Cf. especially Steinheim's *Moses Mendelssohn und seine Schule in ihrer Beziehung zur Aufgabe des neuen Jahrhunderts*; and M. Duschak's appendix to his *Schulgesetzgebung und Methodik der alten Israeliten*, pp. 105 ff. For a partial corrective cf. Isaak Markon's essay, "Etwas über den Einfluss der Wilnaer Emi-

granten auf das geistige Leben der deutschen Judenheit im XVII Jahrhundert," *Jahrbuch für die jüd. Gemeinden Schleswig-Holsteins*, I, (1929–30), 111–18.

[13] Rashi on Gen. 49.7 (although cited from the Midrash this statement has a contemporary sound); *Tosafot* on Ket. 63a; Vogelstein and Rieger, *Rom*, II, 109 f., 111 n. 2 (quoting Jacob b. David Provençale); Assaf, *Mekorot*, I, 18 f., 22, 140 f., 188 ff., 192 f.; II, 53, 67, 138. The interesting Nikolsburg statutes of 1676 and after (based on older regulations) have been published in the original mixed Hebrew and Yiddish, as well as in German translation, by Güdemann in his *Quellenschriften zur Geschichte des Unterrichts und der Erziehung bei den deutschen Juden von den ältesten Zeiten bis auf Mendelssohn*, pp. 255 ff. Cf. also P. Kon, "Organized Action of the Wilno Teachers Against Competition in 1822–23" (Yiddish), *Yivo Bleter*, IV (1932), 94 (not having obtained satisfaction from the communal elders, they appealed to the Governor-General, apparently likewise without success); Wachstein in *ZGJD*, IV, 136 (Art. 16–18, 20), 138 (Art. 32), 145 f.

It is noteworthy that a teacher in the Jewish school of Girgenti was exempted by the Sicilian viceroy in 1468 from the obligation of assuming any other communal office. Cf. Lagumina's *Codice*, II, Pt. 1, no. 514. For the financial status of the teachers and their protection during sickness, cf. the numerous references given in Zimmels, *Beiträge*, p. 63; Rabinowitz, *France*, pp. 217 f.; Balaban, *Żydzi lwowscy*, pp. 524 f.; and, especially, in Assaf's *Mekorot* as listed in the Indices s. v. *sakar*. The Nice ordinance of 1738 set a monthly tuition fee of 10 sous per pupil for well-to-do parents, 3–4 sous for parents of moderate means, and none for the needy. The basic rate was raised to 20 sous in 1761. In any case, however, the community supplemented the teacher's income and paid for an assistant out of its general funds. Cf. Decourcelle, *Nice*, pp. 271 ff. Exceptionally, however, as in eighteenth-century Wilno, private teachers were forced to pay 6.66 per cent of all their tuition fees toward the support of the local Talmud Torah school for the needy. Cf. Klauzner, *Wilno*, I, 119. Cf. also Chap. XI, nn. 66, 70.

The prevalent lack of regulation produced some rather queer phenomena. A father could claim that the tutor had proved incompetent and refuse to pay him his wages, unless the latter took an oath that he was really capable. The bitter feelings generated in the German community of London by the extended feud over a writ of divorce induced many fathers to demand in 1706 such an oath from all teachers. Cf. Meir of Rothenburg, *Responsa*, ed. Prague, no. 488; Assaf, I, 184 f.

[14] Lagumina, *Codice*, II, Pt. 1, no. 491 (for the use of the *studium generale* throughout Europe as the equivalent of "university" before the adoption of the latter term for Paris in 1219 and Oxford in 1245, cf. Arthur F. Leach, *Educational Charters and Documents 598–1909*, p. xxiii); Loeb in *Annuaire*, II, 185 ff. Art. XII, XV, XXIV; Ab. Cahen, "Enseignement obligatoire édicté par la communauté israélite de Metz," *REJ*, II (1881), 303–5; Finkelstein, *Self-Government*, pp. 230, 247 f.; Asher b. Yeḥiel, *Responsa*, XIII, 6, 14, the latter quoted with approval by his son, Jacob in *Ṭur*, Y. D. 259; Joseph of Trani, *Responsa*, nos. 116–17. In his frequent exhortations of the Metz congregation Jonathan Eibeschütz emphasized that support of needy scholars is more pleasing to the Lord than donations for the adornment of synagogues, and that people, who would readily give away their last shirt for the re-erection of the Temple in Jerusalem (perhaps an echo of the Shabbetian frenzy), should the more gladly part with their money for the establishment of an academy of scholars, which is of even greater importance. Cf. his *Ya'arot debash*, I, 13a, 46c.

Among the numerous legal questions which arose from changes in the original purpose of the endowment those reflected in the following two inquiries seem especially worthy of note. Samuel di Medina (*Responsa*, on Y. D. no. 167) was asked whether the legacy of a Salonican Jew for the benefit of a school in Hebron could be transferred to the Talmud Torah in Salonica if the school in Hebron went out of existence. The rabbi answered in the affirmative. Jacob Reischer, on the other hand, refused to sanction the stoppage of payments to an association of scholars made by a philanthropist when the majority turned out to be less worthy and pious than the donor had hoped. But even Reischer insisted only upon a preliminary formal absolution of the donor from his original vow. Cf. his *Shebut Ya'akob*, I, 72.

[15] *Sefer ḥasidim*, no. 1707; Assaf, *Meḳorot*, I, 16, 20, 104; II, 55 ff., 61; Baer, *Spanien*, I, Pt. 2, no. 157 (giving the text and attempted reconstruction of the Hebrew original of a deed endowing an academy in Ecija in 1336); Siméon Luce, "Catalogue de documents du Trésor de Chartes relatifs aux Juifs sous le regne de Philippe le Bel," *REJ*, II (1881), 17; Hildenfinger, ibid., XLI, 70 ff., 87 ff.; Vogelstein and Rieger, *Rom*, II,

301; Meir of Rothenburg, *Responsa*, ed. Cremona, no. 108. The endowment of a *studium ad opus scolarium Judeorum pauperum* by Juceffus Cohen of Tortosa through the bequest (?) of a house, many books and 1,000 solidi (about 1300 C. E.) is recorded in Rubio y Lluch's *Documents*, I, no. 71. Left to the administration of a son and two other trustees, the school was run for sixteen years by a surviving trustee alone; quite badly, according to the complaint of the testator's grandson.

    [16] Assaf, *Meḳorot*, I, 5, 73 ff.; II, 23 f.; Güdemann, *Geschichte*, III, 60 ff.; G. G. Coulton, *Life in the Middle Ages*, II, 119 ff.; Joseph b. Moses, *Leḳeṭ yosher*, I, 32b; II, 51a.

    [17] Munk in *Jubelschrift . . . Hildesheimer*, pp. 76 f.; Dubnow, *Pinḳas*, nos. 528, 709; Assaf, *Meḳorot*, I, 108 ff., 134 f. Cf. also Wachstein in *ZGJD*, IV, 138 (Art. 33), 149. The practice of extending hospitality in private homes to students, as well as that of granting direct academy subsidies, is recorded in southern Italy as far back as the thirteenth century in a manuscript of Isaiah of Trani's *Pesaḥim*. Cf. Sassoon, *Catalogue*, II, 739.

    Apart from supporting the students, some communities had to pay for them state sojourn-taxes. In 1586 the Frankfort elders had a hard time to persuade the city council that rumors concerning the large number of Jewish pupils from abroad ("there is too much vermin") were vastly exaggerated, and to prevent their wholesale expulsion. Cf. Kracauer, *Geschichte*, II, 279 f. By 1709, however, the number of foreign students had increased to 53. Cf. Salomon Adler, "Die Entwicklung des Schulwesens der Juden zu Frankfurt a-M. bis zur Emanzipation," *JJLG*, XVIII (1927), 157 f. (referring also to the extant ledgers of the Talmud Torah administration for the years 1772, 1780, 1793 which include numerous entries for expenses in behalf of students). Cf. also Moritz Stern, "Jugendunterricht in der Berliner jüdischen Gemeinde während des 18. Jahrhunderts," ibid., XIX (1928), 39–68; XX (1929) 379–80; Zwarts, *Hoofdstukken*, pp. 88 ff. (on the Amsterdam academy in the seventeenth century; cf. below, n. 33); G. Sonnino, "Il Talmud Torà di Livorno," *Israel*, X (1935–36), 183–96; Alfredo Toaff, "Il Collegio Rabbinico di Livorno," ibid., XII (1938), 184–95; S. H. Margulies, "Il Talmud Torà di Firenze," *Rivista israelitica*, V (1908), 14–24, 48–54; and Klauzner, *Wilno*, I, 118 f.

    [18] Assaf, *Meḳorot*, I, pp. XII f., XV; II, 79 f., 115 ff., 124; Pesaro,

Memorie, p. 56; Boaz Cohen, *The Responsum of Maimonides Concerning Music*; Leone da Sommi, *Trattato sull'arte rappresentativa* (cf. J. Schirmann, "Eine hebräisch-italienische Komödie des XVI Jahrhunderts," *MGWJ*, LXXV, 1931, 109 ff.); Moritz Steinschneider, "Die italienische Literatur der Juden," ibid., XLII–XLIV (1898–1900); M. Güdemann, "Ein Projekt zur Gründung einer jüdischen Universität aus dem 16. Jahrhundert," *Festschrift . . . A. Berliner*, pp. 164–75; Vogelstein and Rieger, *Rom*, II, 299 f. A remarkably varied program of instruction is recorded also by David ibn Yaḥya in his Memoir published by Marx in *HUCA*, I, 620 ff.

Jews in Mediterranean countries also participated, both as teachers and students, in general university life. The famous medical school of Padua attracted Jewish students even from distant Poland. Central European universities, however, began admitting Jewish students only in the era of Enlightenment. Cf. Louis Lewin, "Die jüdischen Studenten in der Universität Frankfurt a. d. Oder," *JJLG*, XIV (1921), 217–38; XV (1923), 59–96; XVI (1924), 43–86; Guido Kisch, *Die Prager Universität und die Juden*; and the literature listed there and in Baron's *History*, III, 94 n. 2., 142 n. 15. For training in manual crafts, under the direction of master artisans, and the pertinent guild regulations, cf. Chap. IX, n. 23.

19 Meier Spanier, "Der Spruchdichter Süsskind von Trimberg," *Jahrbuch für jüd. Geschichte und Literatur*, XXXI (1938), 124–36; Assaf, *Meḳorot*, I, 40 ff.; Kracauer, *Geschichte*, II, 99 ff.

20 Judah b. Asher's "Will" in Abrahams's *Wills*, II, 174; Coulton, *Ten Medieval Studies*, pp. 35, 120; Rashi on *Ḳid.* 30a; Jacob Tam in *Tosafot* ibid.; Jacob b. Asher, *Ṭur*, Y. D. 245–46 and Karo's and Sirkes's comments thereon; Maimonides, *Mishneh Torah*, l. c., I, 11–12 and Meir ha-Kohen's *Haggahot Maimoniot* thereon; Assaf, *Meḳorot*, I, 26, 80; II, 4, 68 f.; Jacob Emden, *Megillat sefer*, pp. 46 f.; idem, *She'elat Ya'aviṣ* (Responsa), no. 10.

21 Honorius IV's bull, *Nimis in partibus* of 1286, published in Maurice Prou's *Les registres d'Honorius IV*, no. 809 and quoted by P. [J.] Constant in his *Les Juifs devant l'église et l'histoire*, p. 46 n. 1; Profiat Duran, *Ma'ase efod*, Introd., pp. 18 ff. The problem of the relatively greater "strictness [in the observance] of the words of the Scribes than of those of the Torah" was a frequent subject of discussions between Jews and Christians. Eibeschütz records a rather humorous explanation which

he once gave to a powerful nobleman in Vienna by pointing out the difference between the noble and his own servant. If the noble would tell the rabbi to leave the room and upon refusal slay the visitor with his sword, he would be called to account by the king. But if the guard at the castle's gate in execution of his orders would fire upon a visitor disobeying the command to halt, he would receive praise as a zealous watchman. Cf. *Ya'arot debash*, I, 12b.

[22] Ibid., fol. 65b ("everyone styled a Jew is obliged to read every day, evening and morning, a few pages in the books of ethics, of which, thank God, many are available in print." A student of the much-praised encyclopaedic work *Shene luḥot ha-berit*, by Isaiah Horowitz, ought to pay more attention to its ethical than to its legalistic chapters.), 67c; Ezekiel Landau, *Noda' bi-Yehudah* (Responsa) on O. Ḥ. 35; idem, *Derushe ha-ṣelah*, fol. 8d (cf. also ibid., fol. 24c, 40d, 53b, 54a, which passages clearly reflect the inconsistencies of a rabbinic educator in the early Enlightenment period); Buber, *Ḳiryah nisgabah*, p. 106; Assaf, *Meḳorot*, Index s. v. *pilpul*.

The excesses of the pilpulistic method are well illustrated by Azulai's story of how he had once taken part in an extended juristic discussion with the scholars of Tunis (1774). He first successfully defended a certain point of view, but when he was shown that the same view and the arguments in its support had been expressed by a previous author, he feared that he might be accused of plagiarism. He therefore turned around and conclusively proved the opposite point of view. "And all the listeners were amazed to see that the Holy One Blessed be He has bestowed from His bounty upon the lowliest of the lowly." Cf. his *Ma'agal ṭob*, I, 61 f. Certain rather superficial parallels between Jewish and Jesuit dialectics are discussed by H. F. Stewart in his stimulating essay on "Casuistry" in *Judaism and Christianity*, ed. by Oesterley and Loewe, II, 299–331. The author, who had to rely upon Jewish second-hand information, does not seem to do full justice to Jewish *pilpul*, however. For an advanced rabbinic curriculum, mainly designed for *yeshibah* graduates continuing independent studies, cf. the "Will" of Jonah Landsofer, in Assaf's *Meḳorot*, I, 180 f. and in English translation in Emanuel Gamoran's *Changing Conceptions in Jewish Education*, p. 210.

[23] Maimonides, *Mishneh Torah*, l. c., II, 2; Jacob b. Asher, *Ṭur*, l. c.,

and the commentaries thereon; Assaf, *Meḳorot*, I, 11, 87, 116, 119, 134 f., 190, 249; II, 78; Horovitz, *Frankfurter Rabbinen*, II, 42.

[24] Ibn al-Nakawa, *Menorat ha-Maor*, IV, 139; Maimonides, l. c.; Assaf, *Meḳorot*, I, 189, 207; II, 59; Meg. 32a; Tos. Ḳid. I, 11; Bab. Ḳid. 30b.

[25] Assaf, *Meḳorot*, II, 114.

[26] Ginzberg, *Geonica*, II, 11 f., 119; Solomon Maimon, *An Autobiography*, pp. 34 f.; Profiat Duran, l. c.; Yehudah Halevi, *Kitab al-Khazari*, II, 79–80; *Allgemeine Zeitung des Judentums*, IV (1840), 180; Güdemann, *Spanisch-arabische Periode*, p. 181; Abrahams, *Jewish Life*, pp. 379 f. For the operation of the older Jewish schools, cf. several pertinent essays in L. Ginzberg's *Students, Scholars and Saints*. Although primarily treating of nineteenth century conditions, they also furnish a picture of the entire pre-emancipation school system. Cf. also Joshua Trachtenberg, "Jewish Education in Eastern Europe at the Beginning of the 17th Century," *Jewish Education*, XI (1939), 121–37.

Magic elements sometimes encroached on pedagogy as upon all other phases of medieval life. According to Zedekiah Anav it had been customary in his native Rome to abstain from castigating pupils with a cane or whip in the three weeks of national mourning, from Tammuz 17 to Ab 9, because of the prevalence of an evil spirit (*ḳeṭeb meriri*) in those days. An injury then inflicted, however slight, might have serious consequences. In Anav's day (before 1260, cf. Sassoon, *Catalogue*, II, 160) this self-restraint of parents and teachers was restricted to the hours of 4–9 P. M. Cf. his *Shibbole ha-leḳeṭ*, I, no. 263. Study as such, on the other hand, was considered the most effective defence against the demonic powers. Although Rashi voiced a widespread belief that "scholars require superior protection, for demons are more envious of scholars than of other men" (*Commentary* on Ber. 62a), it was generally agreed that they were entirely immune from attack during study periods. Cf. Trachtenberg, *Jewish Magic*, pp. 155, 297 f.

[27] Zunz, *Zur Geschichte*, p. 211; Finkelstein, *Self-Government*, pp. 178, 188, 213; Meir of Rothenburg, *Responsa*, ed. Cremona, nos. 104, 197; *Sefer ḥasidim*, no. 682; Elijah Menaḥem of London, quoted from a Ms. Sassoon by Isidore Epstein in his recent essay on "Pre-Expulsion England in the Responsa," *Transactions of the Jewish Historical Society of England*, XIV (1940), 194. As late as 1300–1347 grammar school boys in Oxford

had to pay 3d. for an ordinary copy of Donat's popular textbook on Latin grammar, as compared with 4–5d. which they paid to a teacher for a term's instruction. Cf. J. W. Adamson's essay on "Education" in C. G. Crump and E. F. Jacob (eds.), *The Legacy of the Middle Ages*, p. 260. For the alleged correlation between the increased output of parchment by the tanners of Troyes and the literary articulateness of the school of Rashi, cf. Baron in *Rashi Anniversary Volume*, pp. 50 f.

[28] Johs. Pedersen, "Masdjid" in the *Encyclopaedia of Islam*, III, 361 (giving valuable information on Arabian libraries); Abrahams, *Wills*, I, 80 ff.; Cecil Roth, "A Seventeenth Century Library and Trousseau," *Studies in Jewish Bibliography . . . in Memory of Abraham Solomon Freidus*, pp. 160–69; Profiat Duran, *Ma'aseh efod*, pp. 19 f.; *Sefer ḥasidim*, nos. 675 ff.; Joseph b. Moses, *Leḳeṭ yosher*, II, 59; Asher b. Yeḥiel, *Responsa*, VI, 25; XCIII, 3; Karo on *Ṭur*, Y. D. 245 end.

[29] Danon in *REJ*, XL, 228 f.; XLI, 264; Emmanuel, *Salonique*, I, 105; Nehama, *Salonique*, III, 111, 142; IV, 195 ff.; Barnett, *El libro*, p. 11 Art. 30; De Castro, *Synagoge*, p. XI, Art. 37. For actual cases of suppression of books by communal authorities, cf. the minutes of the Portuguese community of Hamburg rendered by C[assuto] in *JJLG*, VII, 181; XI, 27. In his *Itinerary* Azulai relates that in 1774 the learned and powerful Jewish cadi of Tunis, having had a quarrel with the local cabalists, imprisoned their leaders and confiscated all their cabalistic works "under the excuse that they read these books for self-glorification rather than for the sake of pure study." Cf. *Ma'agal ṭob*, I, 58. The influence of printing upon Jewish culture is briefly discussed by Abraham Berliner in his *Ueber den Einfluss des ersten hebräischen Buchdrucks auf den Cultus und die Kultur der Juden*. The subject deserves renewed investigation in greater detail.

[30] Lewin in *JJLG*, II, 16, no. 62; Buber, *Ḳiryah nisgabah*, p. 104 f.; Halperin in *Kirjath Sepher*, IX, 370; XI, 106; idem, *Milluim*, no. 82; Dubnow, *Pinḳas*, nos. 502, 528, 710, 739; Assaf, *Meḳorot*, I, 107 ff., 111 f., 136; Grunwald in *MGJV*, XI, 33 (Art. 85–86); Leopold Löwenstein in *JJLG*, VIII, 184; idem, *Index approbationum*, supplemented by B. Wachstein's "Bemerkungen," *MGWJ*, LXXI (1927), 123–33. The relations of the state and the Church toward Hebrew printing in Holland, long a main center of Hebrew typography, is discussed by Izak Prins in his essay, "De oud-hollandsche drukpersvrijheid ten opzichte van het

joodsche boek," *Bijdragen en Mededeelingen . . . Genootschap . . . Nederland*, V (1933), 147–76. Cf. also Simḥa Assaf's "The People of the Book and the Book" (Hebrew), *Reshumot*, I (1918), 292–316; Solomon Funk's "Der Schutz der geistigen Arbeit in der Halacha," *JJLG*, XVIII (1927), 289–304; and the four monographs on the *History of Hebrew Typography* by B. Friedberg. For interesting side-lights on the reasons which prompted various Hebrew authors to write their books, cf. Abraham Yaari's recent study *Be-ohole sefer* (In the Book-Realm). Certain aspects of the history of the Yiddish book production are treated by Max Weinreich in his *Di shvartse Pintelech* (The Black Dots). Much material of communal interest has also been assembled by Alexander Marx in his description of "Some Jewish Bookcollectors" which is scheduled to appear in his forthcoming volume of *Studies in Jewish History and Bibliography*.

31 Balaban, "Zur Geschichte der hebräischen Druckereien in Polen," *Soncino-Blätter*, III, Pt. 1 (1929), 42 ff.; Kracauer, *Geschichte*, II, 101 ff.; Emanuel Ringelblum in his Yiddish essays on the "Restrictions on the Importation of Jewish Books to Poland at the End of the Eighteenth Century," *Yivo Bleter*, IV (1932), 149–58; "The Stamp Tax on Jewish Books in Poland in the Eighteenth Century," ibid., V (1933), 123–36 (supplemented by B. Weinryb's remarks ibid., p. 408); "The Census of Jewish Books in Poland in 1776," ibid., pp. 333–45.

Of considerable interest are also the constant, though largely unsuccessful, efforts of the Jewish leaders to impede the dissemination of anti-Semitic writings. Cf., e. g., G. Wolf, "Der Prozess Eisenmenger," *MGWJ*, XVIII (1869), 378–84, 425–32, 465–73; L. Löwenstein, "Der Prozess Eisenmenger," *Magazin für die Wissenschaft des Judentums*, XVIII (1891), 209–40; M. Wiener, "Des Hof- und Kammeragenten Leffmann Berens Intervention bei dem Erscheinen judenfeindlicher Schriften," ibid., VI (1879), 48–63. Cf. also above, Chap. VII, n. 56.

32 Ibn al-Nakawa, *Menorat ha-Maor*, IV, 139; Isaiah Horowitz, *Shene luḥot ha-brith* on Shebu'ot, ed. Amsterdam, fol. 196 ab.

33 These practical aspects of their instruction were important for the students not only because many of them were trained for the rabbinate, in which position they were to pass judgment on all legal matters, but in some cases also while they were still at the academy. Especially those European schools of higher learning which, going beyond the celebrated Babylonian academies, allowed pupils to take part in discussions leading

to practical legal decisions given in replies to inquiries, greatly stimulated such active participation. The most renowned western *yeshibah* of modern times, the *Eṣ ḥayyim* of Amsterdam, allowed students to publish, from 1730 on, a scholarly series entitled *Peri eṣ ḥayyim*, in which they printed many responsa and legal decisions. A modern selection, in German translation, from the series which is nowadays extremely rare, was prepared a few years ago by Menko Max Hirsch under the title *Frucht vom Baum des Lebens*.

NOTES TO CHAPTER XIV

LAW ENFORCEMENT

[1] Lagumina, *Codice*, I, no. 419; II, Pt. 1, nos. 760, 806; Rashi on Giṭ. 10b; Selma Stern, *Der preussische Staat*, I, Pt. 1, p. 115.

[2] *Tosafot* on Sanh. 42a; Isserlein, *Terumat ha-deshen*, no. 227.

[3] Recanati quoted by Karo on *Ṭur*, Ḥ. M. 2; Asher b. Yeḥiel, *Responsa*, II, 17; Isserles, *Responsa*, no. 28. Isserlein considered it "self-evident" that rabbis are not entitled to permit anything forbidden in the existing literature, unless they have positive traditions of divergent local usage. Cf. his *Pesaḳim u-ketabim*, no. 241. For the extensive borrowings from custumals also in European law, cf. Paul Vinogradoff's essay on "Customary Law" in Crump-Jacob's *Legacy of the Middle Ages*, pp. 313 ff. Isserles was actually considered by the populace as one who had in part released it "from the yoke of the heavy burden resting upon its shoulders" as a result of the more exacting demands of his predecessors, according to a contemporary rabbi who rather stingingly referred in this connection to the title of Isserles' main juridical treatise, the *Torat ḥaṭat*. Cf. Ḥayyim b. Bezaleel's *Vikkuaḥ mayyim ḥayyim* (Polemical Notes on *Torat ḥaṭat*). Cf. also Jawitz, *Toledot*, XIII, 60 n. 1.

This problem of relatively strict or lenient attitudes of leading rabbis has been treated with undue emphasis in the Hebrew letters of the Enlightenment era. Such writers as Isaac Hirsch Weiss, in reviewing the history of Halakah, often distributed praise or blame in accordance with the alleged leniency or strictness. In their rationalist zeal, these *Maskilim* overlooked the profound conflicts of conscience often preceding an individual decision and, occasionally, the pressure of public opinion, which was more likely to condone errors arising from excessive piety than such as were due to apparent carelessness or indifference.

[4] Charles (J. K.) Duschinsky, "The Book *Ma'ase bet din* of the Frankfort Community of the Years 5529–59 [1769–99]" (Hebrew), *Ha-Zofeh*, X, 106–15 (incomplete); Ibn Adret, *Responsa*, III, 63; Jacob b. Asher, *Commentary* on Ex. 21.1, quoted also by Israel ibn al-Nakawa in his *Menorat ha-Maor*, IV, 185 (cf. the editor's note thereto); Isaiah of Trani, *Sefer ha-Makri'a*, no. 32 end; Jacob b. Asher, *Ṭur*, Ḥ. M. 1, 13, and the commentaries thereon; Mordecai Yafeh, *Lebush*, 14, 1; Grunwald in *MGJV*, XI, 34 (Art. 90). Much more comprehensive is the record of the Jewish judiciary in Prague which is still extant in 42 vols. covering the years 1682–1779. The contents of Vols. I A–B, insofar as they refer to the proceedings during 1682, are summarized by Simon Adler in his "Das älteste Judicial-Protokoll des jüdischen Gemeindearchivs in Prag (1682)," *JGJC*, II (1931), 217–56. The minute-books of the Jewish courts of Rome, Lwów and Przemyśl, likewise older than those of Frankfort and London, have been utilized extensively by Berliner in his *Rom*, Buber in his *Anshe shem*, and Schorr in his *Przemyśl.* Cf. in general Assaf's *Bate ha-din*, pp. 46–64; Frank's *Ḳehillot*, pp. 30 ff.

[5] Joseph ibn Ḥabib, *Nimmuḳe Yosef* on Alfasi, Sanh. III, beginning; Moses Menz, *Responsa*, nos. 74, 84; Isaac b. Sheshet, *Responsa*, no. 454; Jacob b. Asher, *Ṭur*, Ḥ. M. 15 and the commentaries thereon. The period of relative stability of rabbinic civil law after the great innovations by custom in Europe during the first millennium and before the new inroads of early capitalism in Italy, Holland and Germany — in eastern Europe these inroads began to be felt only in the nineteenth century — coincides with the rise of the professional rabbinate. In vain did Jacob Weil still protest that "no judge in our day is to be considered a public expert" competent to force parties to appear before him (*Responsa*, no. 146, quoted also by Isserles on *Ṭur*, Ḥ. M. 3). Rabbinic courts increasingly arrogated to themselves the compulsory powers of the ancient experts. This coincidence, or rather causal interrelation, of the modicum of stability and uniformity in Jewish law and the rise of a professional class of experts to expound and elaborate it, would bear further investigation.

In view of the general reliance of medieval Jewry on the authority of the Talmud, only a very careful examination of the changing views of rabbis with reference both to their personal tempers and experiences and to the variations in their social background may yield satisfactory results. One must also bear in mind the possibility of purely accidental decisions and the great power of the autonomous juristic technique as it evolved in the schools of Jewish law. In any case, such studies as Eduard Baneth's *Soziale Motive in der rabbinischen Rechtspflege*, offering a good summary of the varying interpretations of a tannaitic law (M. Ket. X, 4) throughout the ages, would become doubly meaningful if they were combined with sound, self-disciplined, sociological interpretation.

6 Leo Strauss, "On Abravanel's Philosophical Tendency and Political Teaching" in J. B. Trend and H. M. J. Loewe (ed.), *Isaac Abravanel: Six Lectures*, p. 127; Azariah de' Rossi, *Me'or 'eynaim* (Historical Studies), ed. by D. Cassel, p. 446; Salo Baron, "Azariah de' Rossi's Attitude to Life" in *Jewish Studies in Memory of Israel Abrahams*, p. 32. Cf. also Y. F. Baer, "Don Isaac Abravanel and his Relation to Problems of History and Politics" (Hebrew), *Tarbiz*, VIII (1936–37), 241–59; and Ephraim E. Urbach, "Die Staatsauffassung Don Isaac Abravanels," *MGWJ*, LXXXI (1937), 257–70. The three essays on Abravanel complement one another. Considerable material for a much-needed history of Jewish political thinking is stored away particularly in the ethical and homiletical literature. For example, Solomon Ephraim Lentshits devotes considerable space to a discussion of the relation between marriage and international peace, and argues for the nexus between the peace among nations and their common descent from Adam and Eve. Writing, however, in the overheated atmosphere of the Wars of Religion, he makes the significant concession that people of different faiths may war one upon another. Cf. his *'Olelot Ephraim*, no. 374.

7 Ibn Adret, *Responsa*, I, 729; Gershom quoted by Karo and Isserles on *Ṭur*, Ḥ. M. 2; Maimonides, *Mishneh Torah*, Sanhedrin, XXIV, 4–10.

8 Maimonides, *Commentary* on M. Sanh. III, 1; Isaac b. Sheshet, *Responsa*, no. 271; Sirkes on *Ṭur*, Ḥ. M. 3; Finkelstein, *Self-Government*, pp. 121, 132 f., 227, 240 f.

9 Mordecai b. Hillel on B. B. no. 522; Isserles on *Ṭur*, Ḥ. M. 4; Jacob Weil, *Responsa*, nos. 123–24; Menaḥem of Merseburg, *Nimmuḳim*, (appended to Weil's Responsa), fol. 63d; Asher b. Yeḥiel, *Responsa*, VII, 11. The history of Jewish public law with reference to the Diaspora community deserves monographic treatment. Cf. Samuel Eisenstadt's

programmatic essay on "The Investigation of Our Public Law" (Hebrew), *Ha-Mishpaṭ ha-'ibri*, I (Moscow, 1918–20), 8–28.

[10] Graetz, *History*, IV, 535; D. B. Revel in *Ḥoreb*, V (1939), 1–26.

[11] Isaac b. Sheshet, *Responsa*, nos. 234–39. Cf. also the few general remarks by Israel Ostersetzer in his interesting essay "On the Investigation of the Spirit of Jewish Law" (Hebrew), *Sefer ha-Shanah li-Yehude Polania* (Polish Jewish Yearbook), I (1937), 35–60.

[12] Maimonides, *Commentary* on M. Ḥullin I, 2; *Mishneh Torah*, Ḥobel u-mazziḳ VIII, 11; S. W. Baron, "The Historical Outlook of Maimonides," *Proceedings of the American Academy for Jewish Research*, VI (1934–35), 88 n. 170; Nehama, *Salonique*, III, 170 f.; Moritz Stern, "Aus Regensburg, Urkundliche Mitteilungen," *JJLG*, XXII (1931–32), 25 f. One need not take too seriously inquiries, such as that addressed to Azulai during his sojourn in Tunis in 1774, as to whether Jewish visitors from Leghorn who belonged to a masonic lodge should be put to death. Even the despotic Jewish cadi of the city had to be satisfied with denouncing them to the Muslim authorities which flogged and fined them. Cf. *Ma'agal ṭob*, I, 64. Neither is the frequently recorded employment of Jewish executioners in the eastern Mediterranean at all indicative of prevalence of the extreme penalty among Jews. It was particularly the Byzantine Empire and its successor states, such as the Venetian administration of Candia, which imposed upon the Jews the highly unpleasant duty of supplying officials for a post universally shunned by their Christian subjects. Cf. S. Assaf, "Jewish Executioners. A Contribution to the History of the Jews in Candia" (Hebrew), *Tarbiz*, V (1933–34), 224–26; Starr, *Byzantine Empire*, p. 202 and the same author's forthcoming essay on "Jewish Life in Crete under the Rule of Venice." Cf. also Chap. VI, n. 9; XVI, n. 56; and, in general, Assaf's *Ha-'Oneshin*; Palṭiel Dickstein, *Dine 'Oneshin* (Criminal Law: with Special Reference to Hebrew Law and the Actual Law of Palestine); and the older literature listed in Eisenstadt's *'Ein Mishpaṭ*, pp. 153 ff.

[13] Asher b. Yeḥiel, *Responsa*, VII, 11; XVII, 1, 8; XVIII, 4, 13; Simḥa Assaf, *Ha-'Oneshin*, pp. 18 ff., 22 and nos. 48–49, 66, 69, 87.

[14] Ibid., nos. 58, 110; *Teshubot ha-geonim*, ed. by Harkavy, no. 440 and p. 384; Isaac b. Sheshet, *Responsa*, no. 70; Maimonides, *Commentary* on M. Nazir, IV, 3; Rashi on Sanh. 7b; Menaḥem of Merseburg, *Nimmuḳim*, fol. 64c, 65c, 66b; Jacob Weil, *Responsa*, no. 147 fol. 37d f.; Solomon

Luria, *Yam shel Shelomoh* on B. Ḳ., VIII no. 49 (Isserles, although combatting these views as a matter of principle, must admit that it is left to the discretion of the court to convert physical into monetary punishment or vice versa; cf. his comments on *Ṭur*, Ḥ. M. 2); Balaban, *Żydzi lwowscy*, pp. 239, 292 ff.; Dubnow, *Pinḳas*, nos. 43, 144.

15 Baer, *Spanien*, I, Pt. 1, pp. 1059 ff.; Pt. 2, nos. 64, 174 (this usage under Alfonso XI was expressly maintained by Henry II in 1367 against the wishes of the Cortes, these privileges being frequently invoked thereafter. Individual debtors, however, were often forced to renounce their rights and consent to imprisonment. Cf. ibid., nos. 205 Art. 15, 288 pp. 301 f., 337 n. 3, 387 p. 426, 390 p. 431); Assaf, *Ha-'Oneshin*, pp. 25 f., 29 and nos. 41, 61, 69, 71–72, 84; Elkan N. Adler, "Provençal and Catalonian Responsa," *JQR*, O. S. XII (1900), 144; Epstein in *Trans. of the Jewish Hist. Society of England*, XIV, 195 n. 35. For the arrest of five distinguished citizens by the community of Prague in 1752 because, without securing communal authorization, they had addressed a letter to Amsterdam in the Emden-Eibeschütz controversy, cf. Salomon Hugo Lieben, "Handschriftliches zur Geschichte der Juden in Prag in den Jahren 1744–1754," *JJLG*, II (1904), 294, 321, 327 ff. Sometimes, as in Palermo in 1476 and in Termini in 1490, Jewish officials were arrested by the government for failing to meet the fiscal obligations of the community. Cf. Lagumina, *Codice*, II, Pt. 1, nos. 637, 783. Cf. also ibid., nos. 762, 799; Pt. 2, no. 931 (reproducing the government decrees of 1488–89 forbidding Palermo Jewish authorities to imprison Jews able to furnish bonds during the fifteen days before or after Jewish holidays; of 1490 restraining the Christian officials of Geraci from freeing Jews incarcerated by Jewish judges for spiritual transgressions; and of July 11, 1492 which, in execution of the general decree of expulsion, ordered the authorities to release all Jewish debtors ten days before their scheduled departure). For the arrest of Christian debtors by Jewish creditors in Germany and for the generally extensive criminal jurisdiction in the early German-Jewish communities, cf. *Ma'aseh ha-Geonim*, edited by A. Epstein and J. Freimann, no. 81; Stobbe's *Deutschland*, pp. 130, 159 ff., 255; Zimmels, *Beiträge*, p. 103 n. 224. Cf. also Chap. XI, nn. 1–2.

16 Baer, *Spanien*, I, Pt. 1, no. 175; Pt. 2, no. 287 (II, 6); Finkelstein, *Self-Government*, p. 361. Cf. also Lagumina, *Codice*, II, Pt. 1, nos. 648, 651.

17 Frank, *Ḳehillot*, p. 52 n. 2; Ferorelli, *Italia meridionale*, p. 183;

Balaban, *Żydzi lwowscy*, pp. 502 f.; Joseph ibn Ḥabib, *Nimmuke Yosef* on Alfasi B. Ḳ. VIII beginning.

[18] Aptowitzer in *JQR*, IV, 26 ff., 42 ff.; Epstein, *Adreth*, pp. 71 ff., 76; Maimonides, *Commentary* on M. Ḥullin I, 2; *Tosafot* on Makkot 11b.

[19] Flesch in Gold's *Mähren*, p. 33 Art. 22; Dubnow, *Pinkas*, nos. 277, 690; idem in *Evreiskaya Starina*, V, 453 ff., nos. 25 f.; Lewin in *JJLG*, III, 119 f. no. lxxx; Vogelstein and Rieger, *Rom*, II, 277; Jacob Sasportas, *Ohel Ya'akob* (Responsa), nos. 21–22, 24–25; Meir Katzenellenbogen, *Responsa*, no. 69; Wiener, *Regesten*, pp. 59 no. 41, 62 no. 60; Asher b. Yeḥiel, *Responsa*, III, 9.

[20] Zacharias Frankel, *Der gerichtliche Beweis nach mosaisch-talmudischem Rechte*, p. 430 n. (cf. also Hai's responsum in *Sha'are teshubah*, no. 41; and Jonathan Eibeschütz, *Ya'arot debash*, I, 11a, quoting the *Zohar*); Bauer in *REJ*, LXIII, 271 (the Nice community threatens with an automatic ban all slanderers of the deceased rabbi); *Kolbo*, no. 139 (the most widely accepted formula of the severe excommunication) and Appendix; *Regolamento fatto dall'università degli Ebrei di Reggio per la continuazione delli accordi in essa rinovati l'anno 1757*, p. 12 (giving a mild formula); L. Lewin, "Ein Bannfluch," *Festschrift David Hoffmann*, pp. 162–66 (dated 1691–92); S. Dubnow, "From My Archive" (Yiddish), *Yivo Bleter*, I (1931), 405 f. (the excommunication of a "rebel" in 1732).

[21] Finkelstein, *Self-Government*, pp. 227, 241 n. 2; Rigg, *Select Pleas*, pp. 87 f.; Colon, *Responsa*, no. 127; Stern, *Ruprecht*, pp. xxvi (Art. 1a), XLVI f.; Jacob b. Asher, *Ṭur*, Y. D. 345, 376 and the commentaries thereon; Assaf, *Ha-'Oneshin*, pp. 31 ff. and nos. 14, 49, etc.; idem, *Bate ha-din*, pp. 32 ff. Cf. also Chap. VII, n. 47. The extension of the effects of excommunication to a condemned man's wife and children elicited the protests even of such rigid pietists as Solomon Luria. Cf. his *Yam shel Shelomoh* on B. Ḳ., X no. 13. But these were little heeded even in Luria's own country. Cf. e. g. the text of the Poznań ban of 1692 published by L. Lewin in *Festschrift . . . David Hoffmann*, pp. 162–66. Similarly ineffectual, at least in legal theory, had been, centuries before, a gaon's insistence that "if a community excommunicates a person, we [nevertheless] circumcise his son and extend to him the privilege of burial." Cf. *Sha'are teshubah*, no. 40. In 1722 the elders and judges of Cracow deprived a swindler and his descendants of the passive franchise. Cf. Assaf's *Ha-'Oneshin*, nos. 157, 159.

Gradual relaxation of a stringent ban is illustrated by the procedure of the Prague rabbinate in the case of a local reader who had made offensive statements about Eibeschütz of Hamburg. Cf. Salomon Hugo Lieben, "Zur Charakteristik des Verhältnisses zwischen Rabbi Jecheskel Landau and Rabbi Jonathan Eibenschütz," *JJLG*, I (1903), 325 f. — For the related penalties of the loss of the "right of sojourn," the equivalent of exile from a city or country, and the milder forms of expulsion from synagogue, etc. cf. Assaf, *Ha-'Oneshin*, pp. 35 ff.; and above Chap. X, nn. 1–2.

[22] Wiener, *Regesten*, pp. 64 f., 74, 91, 95, 254; Stern, *Ruprecht*, pp. xlvi ff., liv f.; Güdemann, *Geschichte*, III, 46 ff.; Finkelstein, *Self-Government*, pp. 63 f., 228, 242 f.; Israel Bruna, *Responsa*, no. 188. For quaint illustrations of the abuses which had crept into the administration of the communal ban also in the near-eastern communities, cf. Abraham Maimuni's *Responsa*, nos. 4–8. Not only did individual scholars freely indulge in excommunicating private opponents, but they also charged substantial amounts for the ceremony of releasing culprits from the ban. In a curious litigation, an Egyptian Jewish judge actually accused the court of Alexandria of trespassing on his financial preserve because it had revoked an excommunication. Such gross misuse of this eminent means of enforcing social control induced many Egyptian and Palestinian communities of the thirteenth century to ordain that thenceforth only bans pronounced by at least three recognized leaders of a particular community should be legally binding. It is not clear to what extent these ordinances were influenced by western models. Cf. also Chap. XI, nn. 19, 24, 35.

[23] Baer, *Spanien*, I, Pt. 1, nos. 79, 88, 100, 317 (p. 464), 325; Scherer, *Rechtsverhältnisse*, pp. 242 f.; Parkes, *Medieval Community*, pp. 252 f.; Stokes, *Studies*, pp. 51 ff.; Milano in *Israel*, X, 422 Art. 29 (against the excessive use of the ban); Mossé, *Avignon*, p. 145; Ismar Freund, *Die Emanzipation der Juden in Preussen*, II, 53; Isserlein, *Terumat ha-deshen*, no. 276; Sasportas, *Ohel Ya'akob*, no. 76 (1683); Graetz, *History*, V, 44 f., 614 f.; idem, *Geschichte*, X, 3d ed., p. 414. In Brandenburg-Prussia attacks on the Jewish ban became very vocal in the early years of the eighteenth century and led to the decree of 1705 which voided all bans issued without previous royal approval. Cf. Selma Stern, *Der preussische Staat*, I, Pt. 1, p. 113; Pt. 2, nos. 274–76. Cf. also Chap. VII, n. 29.

In Venice, where in 1561 the patriarch allowed three rabbis in collaboration with five (of the seven) *capi* to excommunicate fellow Jews for whatever cause, this right was temporarily suspended in 1581 and 1606. The community, nevertheless, continued to exercise this jurisdictional power, even when, in 1671, state supervision was secularized and transferred from the patriarch to the *cattaveri*. The extant governmental "licenses" for Jewish bans issued in the years 1605–1794 fill two volumes in the Venetian archives. Cf. Roth, *Venice*, pp. 131 f. One must also bear in mind that the *ḥerem* was not only a penalty but a sanction, and that most communal ordinances were issued under threat of excommunication. Hence the term was often used as a synonym for *takkanah* or ordinance. Such usage penetrated even government privileges extended to Jewish communities. Cf. e. g. Lagumina, *Codice*, I, no. 199; II, Pt. 1, no. 744. Cf. also Chap. X, n. 26.

[24] Meir of Rothenburg, *Responsa*, ed. Prague, no. 904; Assaf, *Bate ha-din*, pp. 29 ff.; Frank, *Ḳehillot*, pp. 51 f., 55 f.; A. Berliner, "A Letter Addressed by the Roman Community to the Elders of Pesaro" (Hebrew), *Ḳobeṣ 'al yad*, XIX (1903), 68–71.

[25] Balaban in *JJLG*, XI, 90; J. Wellesz, "Die Dezisionen R. Isaks aus Corbeil," ibid., IX (1912), Hebrew section, p. 7 no. 64. The influence of early medieval laws may be discerned, for instance, in the decisions of R. Meshullam who rather frequently refers to cases of assault and battery among Jews. Whether or not the frequency of these decisions was due to an excessive truculence of southern French and Italian Jewry of that period, the system of fines advocated by the rabbi clearly reflects the prevailing trend in European laws. Cf. Ginzberg, *Ginze*, II, 271, 274.

[26] Dubnow, *Pinḳas*, nos. 172, 529, 788; Yom Tob Lipmann Heller, quoted by B. Z. Katz in his *Le-Ḳorot*, p. 27; Stern, *Ruprecht*, p. lvii; Mordecai b. Hillel on B. Ḳ., no. 152; Epstein in *Transactions of the Jewish Historical Society of England*, XIV, 194 (cf. also above, Chap. VII, n. 5); Wachstein in *ZGJD*, IV, 138 (Art. 30), 148 f. The community of Bologna placed violations of its ordinance of 1511 under the sanction not only of its own ban, but also of a fine of 100 gold florins to be paid to the sovereign ecclesiastical authorities in the city. Cf. Sonne in *HUCA*, XVI, 57.

[27] *Sha'are teshubah*, no. 41; Müller, *Teshubot geone mizraḥ u-ma'arab*, no. 217; Munk in *Jubelschrift Hildesheimer*, Hebrew section, p. 81; Judah b. Asher, *Responsa*, no. 61; Jacob Weil, *Responsa*, no. 157. Preachers often exhorted their audiences not to remain silent in the face of an

unlawful or immoral act, but to admonish severely transgressors or would-be transgressors. Jonathan Eibeschütz, in fact, contended that admonition by a neighbor is likely to prove far more effective than any amount of exhortation by a rabbi, whose high professional standards did not fully invite emulation. Cf. *Ya'arot debash*, I, 10a, 80a.

[28] Assaf, *Bate ha-din*, pp. 15 ff.; Sifre, Deut. XVI, ed. Friedmann, fol. 68b; M. Abot, V, 8; Dubnow, *Pinḳas*, no. 67; Maimonides, *Mishneh torah*, Sanhedrin, XXI, 6, taken over almost verbatim by Karo in *Shulḥan 'Aruk*, Ḥ. M. 16, 2; Yom Tob b. Abraham quoted by Isserles, ibid. and by Karo on *Ṭur*, ibid.

[29] Baer, *Spanien*, I, Pt. 2, no. 287 (II, 4); Finkelstein, *Self-Government*, pp. 72 f., 360; Meir of Rothenburg, *Responsa*, ed. Prague, nos. 357 (in the name of the Tosafist Isaac b. Samuel of Dampierre), 413; ed. Berlin, p. 155 no. 30; Assaf, *Bate ha-din*, pp. 95 ff., 132; Shohet, *Jewish Court*, pp. 100, 202 ff. For discussion of the legal implications of the *harsha'ah*, its growing economic function and its great social complexities, cf. Baron in *Essays on Maimonides*, pp. 202 ff. Rabbinic insistence, even under Islam, upon both personal appearance and oral transactions is doubly remarkable, as Muslim law had early stressed representation by attorneys and written briefs. Cf. Tyan, *Organisation judiciaire*, I, 315 ff., 390 ff. Cf. also Marx in *Abhandlungen . . . Chajes*, pp. 186 ff. (on change of venue).

[30] Mordecai on B. Ḳ., nos. 72 ff.; Isserlein, *Pesaḳim u-ketabim*, no. 62; Sonne in *HUCA*, XVI, 45 f., 75; Isaac b. Sheshet, *Responsa*, nos. 5, 179, 268; Finkelstein, *Self-Government*, pp. 72 f., 301 f., 304, 360. Cf. also Morpurgo, *Shemesh ṣedaḳah*, II, Pt. 2, no. 12; Grunwald in *MGJV*, XI, 34 Art. 91; Isserles on *Ṭur*, Ḥ. M. 17; idem, *Responsa*, no. 57; Joseph Ergas, *Dibre Yosef*, no. 13; Berliner, *Rom*, II, Pt. 1, p. 102; Lewin, *Landessynode*, p. 39 (a Roman merchant and a Polish nobleman apply to Jewish courts against Jewish defendants). For changes in the attitude of the Jewish public and the French government which had forced the community of Metz to revamp its judicial system in 1694 and again in 1709, cf. Ab. Cahen, "Le rabbinat de Metz pendant la période française (1567–1871)," *REJ*, VIII (1884), 257 f., 262 ff.; Jacob Reischer, *Shebut Ya'akob*, II, 143. Cf. also above, Chap. VIII, n. 26.

[31] For the oath *more judaico* cf. Lagumina, *Codice*, I, no. 74; II, Pt. 1, no. 759; Donath, *Mecklenburg*, pp. 10 f.; Balaban, *Żydzi lwowscy*, pp.

316 ff., App. nos. 33, 35; S. J. Fockema Andreae, "Der eed der Joden in Nederland onder de Republick," *Verslagen en Mededeelingen der Kon. Akademie van Wetenschapen*, Section Letters, 4th ser., X, Pt. 1 (1909), 3–19; and, generally, Baron's *History*, II, 96 f.; III, 118 n. 5; Guido Kisch, "Studien zur Geschichte des Judeneides im Mittelalter," *HUCA*, XIV (1939), 431–56; idem, "The Landshut Jewry Oath," *Historia Judaica*, I (1939), 119–20, supplemented by the same author's discussion with Raphael Straus, ibid., III (1941), 41–45. The formula of a fourteenth-century oath administered by the Jewish community of Mestre near Venice is given in Joseph b. Moses's *Leket yosher*, II, 36 f. Several later formulas are listed by Wachstein in *ZGJD*, IV, 142. In the early nineteenth century, when the oath *more judaico*, although under attack, had not yet been abolished even in post-emancipation France, some Jews wished to compel the opposing parties to use the solemn form of the Jewish oath. Akiba Eger rebuked one such litigant in his *Responsa*, no. 93.

The general history of the Jewish oath is still full of obscurities and would greatly merit monographic treatment. It has been pointed out, for example, that the oath on the Torah roll (*bi-nekiṭat ḥefeṣ*), though discouraged in the Orient during the geonic age and considered abolished "in our generations" by Rashi, was much in vogue in England and elsewhere in medieval Europe. Cf. Ginzberg, *Geonica*, II, 147; Rashi on Shebu'ot 38b; Moses of Coucy, *Sefer ha-Miṣvot*, Commandment 123; the commentaries on Maimonides' *Mishneh Torah*, Shebu'ot, XI, 13; H. P. Stokes, "Records of Mss. and Documents Possessed by the Jews in England before the Expulsion," *Transactions of the Jewish Hist. Society of England*, VIII (1918), 80 f.; Epstein, ibid., XIV, 198 n. 145.

[32] Finkelstein, *Self-Government*, pp. 105 f., 225 f., 237, 331 f., 339; Assaf, *Ha-'Oneshin*, pp. 15, 20, nos. 66, 87; idem, *Bate ha-din*, pp. 74 ff.; Shohet, *Jewish Court*, pp. 151 ff., 170 ff.; Baer, *Spanien*, I, Pt. 1, nos. 253 (Art. 8), 398; Isaac b. Sheshet, *Responsa*, nos. 234–35. In a famous eighteenth-century controversy which arose over the disqualification of a writ of divorce issued in Kleve by the rabbinic court of Frankfort, distinguished leaders elsewhere, e. g. Ezekiel Landau, took up the cudgels in the defense of the smaller community. Cf. Landau's *Derushe ha-ṣelaḥ*, fol. 43d.

The mutual discrimination against witnesses of another denomination likewise raised numerous procedural questions. On the eve of the expulsion a Jew of Murcia complained to Ferdinand and Isabella that Chief Rabbi Abraham Seneor had forced him to appear before a Jewish court, whereas he had only Christian witnesses. Cf. Baer's *Spanien*, I, Pt. 2, no. 379.

For the great informality (despite severe penalties for disobedience) of court summonses, which might be sent through any neighbor, and the great reliance placed in marshals in this and in other respects, cf. Jacob b. Asher, *Ṭur*, Ḥ.M. 8, 11, and the commentaries thereon.

[33] Isserlein, *Terumat ha-deshen*, no. 305; idem, *Pesaḳim*, no. 63; Samuel di Medina, *Responsa*, on Ḥ.M. no. 6; Meir of Rothenburg, *Responsa*, ed. Prague, nos. 410, 546; Jacob b. Asher, *Ṭur*, Ḥ.M. 2, 7, 13, 17 and the commentaries thereon.

[34] Alfred Glaser, *Geschichte der Juden in Strassburg*, p. 12; Lagumina, *Codice*, II, Pt. 1, no. 620; Aron Freimann, "R. David Lida and his Apologia in *Be'er 'Eshek*" (Hebrew), *Sefer ha-Yobel (Jubilee Volume) . . . Nahum Sokolow*, pp. 455–80; Sonne, in *HUCA*, XVI, 56 ff. (giving the text of the Bologna ordinance and of its motivation and defense by the local rabbi Abraham ha-Kohen); Finkelstein, *Self-Government*, pp. 263, 302, 304 f.; Wolf, *Statuten*, p. 59; Joseph Katz, *She'erit Yosef*, no. 40; Horovitz, *Rabbinerversammlung*, pp. 16, 27.

Regional communities, of course, exercised considerable jurisdiction over their sub-communities. In an interesting case affecting the small community of Zabłudowo, the Polish Council decided in 1654 that in civil litigations involving amounts up to 30 florins the inhabitants should use the local court. If the contested amount exceeded 30 florins both the plaintiff and the defendant had the right to refer the matter to the superior court of their regional community of Tykocin, which could also, on its own initiative, demand the submission of each such controversy to its final decision. In litigations arising from revenue farming or communal appointment, however, exclusive authority rested with the court of the regional community of Grodno. Cf. Dubnow in *Evreiskaya Starina*, V, 77 f., no. 7.

[35] Cf. the present author's further remarks in *Essays on Maimonides*, pp. 145 ff., 260 ff.

NOTES TO CHAPTER XV

PUBLIC FINANCE

[1] Berliner, *Rom*, II, Pt. 1, p. 100; Ibn Adret, *Responsa*, II, 213; Meir of Rothenburg, *Responsa*, ed. Lwów, no. 130; Munk in *MGWJ*, XLI, 537.

[2] Schipper in *Yivo Economic Studies*, II, 19; Bacharach, *Ḥavvot ya'ir*, no. 136. An interesting intercommunal controversy concerning the respective shares in a "gift" to be proferred to the sovereign on the occasion of the birth of a grandson engaged the attention of jurists at the end of the eighteenth century. Cf. Azulai's *Ḥayyim sha'al*, II, 18. Many taxes had the flimsiest justification. The fairly substantial "tent tax," for example, paid by many generations of Turkish Jews, is supposed to have originated from an altercation between a Muslim and a Jew on the subject of the future world. The Jew argued that Paradise would have room for Jews only, whereas Muslims would at best dwell in tents outside in order to guard the horses of the Jews. The Grand Vizier, upon learning of this debate, humorously decided that, since there is no money in Paradise, the Jews should pay in advance an annual fee to the government of their prospective guards. Cf. Nehama, *Salonique*, p. 113. Some rabbis, nevertheless, touched in the sensitive spot of their patriotic allegiance, put the blame upon the Jews rather than the governments. In the typically Jewish spirit of self-accusation, Ezekiel Landau explained the enormous tax load of Bohemian Jewry, which time and again he declared to be the most burdensome in the world, as due to divine retribution for the Jews' neglect of the Torah, rather than to the self-interest of the "benign and merciful" Empress Maria Theresa. Cf. his *Derushe ha-ṣelaḥ*, fol. 16a, 35b, 50d, 52a.

[3] Baer, *Spanien*, I, Pt. 1, nos. 210–11. For a similarly extensive ordinance enacted in Saragossa in 1331, but afterwards partially revoked, cf. Tilander's aforementioned essay in *Studia neophilologica*, XII (1939–40), 1–45. A comprehensive tax law in neighboring Portugal was made part of the royal code in the *Ordenaçoens . . . Affonso V*, II, 74, pp. 445 ff. Cf. also Kayserling, *Portugal*, pp. 54 ff.

[4] Lagumina, *Codice*, I, no. 385; Jacobs, *Angevin England*, pp. 320 ff.;

Jakob Schwalm, "Ein unbekanntes Eingangsverzeichnis von Steuern der königlichen Städte aus der Zeit Kaiser Friedrichs II, "*Neues Archiv der Gesellschaft für ältere deutsche Geschichtskunde*, XXIII (1897–98), 519 ff.; Isert Rösel, *Die Reichssteuern der deutschen Judengemeinden von ihren Anfängen bis zur Mitte des 14. Jahrhunderts*; Caro, *Sozial- und Wirtschaftsgeschichte*, I, 415 ff.; Baer, *Spanien*, I, Pt. 2, no. 334. Cf. also Stobbe, *Deutschland*, pp. 27 ff., 206 ff.; Nübling, *Judengemeinden*, pp. xxxvi ff., 241 ff., 435 ff.; A. Danon, "Etude historique sur les impôts directs et indirects des communautés israélites en Turquie," *REJ*, XXXI (1895), 52–61; Nehama, *Salonique*, II, 108 ff. The Jewish contributions to the maintenance of the London *domus conversorum* in the early years of its existence from 1232 to 1290 are treated by M. Adler in his extensive essay on that institution reprinted in his *Jews of Medieval England*, pp. 279 ff. For general aspects of medieval Jewish taxation, cf. Baron's *History*, II, 16 ff.; III, 99 nn. 6–7; and the literature listed there.

[5] Lagumina, *Codice*, I, nos. 36, 352; II, Pt. 2, no. 1038; Straus, *Sizilien*, pp. 26 f.; Stobbe, *Deutschland*, p. 31; Abrahams, *Life*, pp. 54 ff.; Ibn Adret, *Responsa*, V, 222; Baer, *Studien*, pp. 18 f.; idem, *Spanien*, I, Pt. 1, no. 129; Pt. 2, no. 96 (p. 88); Tilander in *Studia neophilologica*, XII, 11 Art. 2–3; Epstein, *Adreth*, pp. 13, 17, 101; Berliner, *Rom*, II, Pt. 2, p. 20; Mossé, *Avignon*, p. 161; Meir of Rothenburg, *Responsa*, ed. Lwów, no. 131.

[6] Balaban, *Żydzi lwowscy*, pp. 341 ff., App. nos. 20, 48, 89; idem in *Kwartalnik*, pp. 39 ff.; B. Weinryb, "Beiträge zur Finanzgeschichte der jüdischen Gemeinden in Polen," *MGWJ*, LXXXII (1938), 250 f., 252 f. (Dr. Weinryb has kindly placed at the present author's disposal a continuation of this essay in manuscript; it has since appeared in *HUCA*, XVI [1941], 187–214); Mahler in *Yivo Bleter*, XV, 67 ff.; Perles in *MGWJ*, XIV, 176 n. 18.

The censuses, which served as the basis for the capitation tax were extremely unreliable, particularly when they covered large communities or regions. Apart from the usual attempts at tax evasion, the Jews tried to dodge the census enumerators on account of their superstitious fear, nurtured from the biblical accounts of the untoward results of King David's early census, that counting must ultimately lead to diminution. That is why the figures accepted, as a compromise, by the Polish government (e. g. in the first decade after 1549, of slightly over 6,000 persons over eight years) are decided underestimates. The authorities of Anjou in 1271, on the other hand, imposed a poll tax for 1,000 Jews, even though the Jewish population was far less than this figure. Cf. Léon Brunschvicg, *Juifs d'Angers*, pp. 12 f. The Jews of Augsburg, too, beginning with 1429, paid an annual lump sum of 200 guilders. Cf. Wiener, *Regesten*, p. 190, no. 562.

Special difficulties arose where, as in Lithuania, the Rabbanite organs were responsible also for taxes paid by their Karaite compatriots over whom they had but limited jurisdiction. For an interesting analysis, cf. Isaac Lurie's "The Lithuanian Communities and the Karaites: The Assessment of Karaite Taxes and their Collection during the 16th and 17th Centuries" (Hebrew), *He-'Abar*, I (1918), 159–71.

[7] Margolies, *Dubno*, pp. 80 ff.; Levitats in *Yivo Studies in Hist.*, II, 96 ff., 112 f.; Wachstein in *ZGJD*, IV, 134, 143 f.; Baer, *Kleve*, pp. 123 f.; Mossé, *Avignon*, pp. 154, 161; Meir of Rothenburg, *Responsa*, ed. Prague, no. 941; Mordecai on B. B. nos. 475, 481; Finkelstein, *Self-Government*, pp. 12 f., 149; Frankel in *MGWJ*, II, 335; Rabinowitz, *France*, pp. 110 ff. (the objection on p. 113 n. 2 fails to explain why similar considerations of "simple justice" had no effect upon medieval governments or later Jewish scholars such as Isserlein, cf. *Terumat ha-deshen*, no. 342); Tilander in *Studia neophilologica*, XII, 11 ff., Art. 4–11, 14–15, 19–20; Ibn Adret, *Responsa*, III, 148; Baer, *Spanien*, I, Pt. 2, no. 170.

[8] Grayzel, *Church*, no. 63. One Ardingo "Judaeus" paid the tithe to the bishop of Modena in 1025, but it is not altogether certain that he was a Jew. Some scholars have argued that, by a strange coincidence, he may have belonged to a Christian family, Judaeus. Cf. Attilio Milano, "Gli Ebrei in Italia nei secoli XI° e XII°," *Israel*, XIII (1938), 28.

[9] Milano, "Documents pour l'histoire de la communauté juive d' Ancone," *REJ*, LXXXVII (1929), 173; Dubnow, *Pinkas*, no. 561 (cf. also nos. 4, 618, 750); Klauzner, *Wilno*, I, 159 f.; Elbogen in *Jewish Encyclopedia*, VII, 664 f.; Rodocanachi, *Saint-Siège*, pp. 223, 232 ff.; idem in *REJ*, LXI, 77 ff.; Vogelstein and Rieger, *Rom*, II, 125 ff., 217, 333 ff., 427 ff.; V. Franchini, "La congregazione 'De usuris' in Roma," *Economia*, N. S. VIII (1931), 418 f.; Milano, *Ricerche sulle condizioni economiche degli Ebrei a Roma* (1555–1848), passim.

[10] Meir of Rothenburg, *Responsa*, ed. Cremona, no. 228 (cf., however, the much lower rate indicated ibid., ed. Berlin, p. 204, no. 127); Wiener,

Regesten, p. 177, no. 497; Milano in *REJ*, LXXXVII, 167, 169, 171 (the figures given are somewhat contradictory); Mossé, *Avignon*, p. 161.

[11] Da Fano, *Responsa*, no. 43.

[12] Tilander in *Studia neophilologica*, XII, 18 ff. Art. 23, 25–27, 36; Berliner, *Rom*, II, Pt. 2, p. 79; Vogelstein and Rieger, *Rom*, II, 126 f., 188, 333, 335, 427; Dubnow, *Pinkas*, no. 474. Cf. also Jakobovits in *JGJC*, I, 348 f. (giving a detailed account of the Kolin meat tax and its administration in 1768); Danon in *REJ*, XXXI, 60 f. (Adrianople meat tax in 1784); Manfred Laubert, "Geleitszoll und Koscherfleischabgabe, zwei Sondersteuern der Posener Juden," *MGWJ*, LXVII (1923), 273–78; Moritz Stern, "Zur Geschichte der Fleischgebühren in der Berliner jüdischen Gemeinde," *Soncino-Blätter*, II (1927), 97–108; Victor Hofmann von Wellenhof, "Die Sonderbesteuerung der jüdischen Bevölkerung in Galizien und der Bukowina bis zum Jahre 1848," *Vierteljahrsschrift für Sozial- und Wirtschaftsgeschichte*, XII (1914), 404–48; Julius Hessen, "A Study in the History of the *Korobka* Tax in Russia" (Russian), *Evreiskaya Starina*, IV (1911), 305–47, 487–512. The emergency nature of the early *korobka* levies in Poland is further illustrated by the numerous data assembled by Weinryb in the continuation of his "Beiträge," *HUCA*, XVI, 187 ff. The community of Fez, Morocco, renewed in 1830–35 the ancient system of paying slaughterers directly from the income of the meat tax rather than allowing them to receive fees from butchers. Cf. *Ḳobeṣ pesaḳim* (Columbia University Manuscript X 893.19 K 79), fol. 102–3.

Exceptionally, Jewish slaughterhouses could be used directly by the governments to exact payments from the non-Jewish population. The privilege granted to the Jews of Salerno in 1121, stating that "no person shall dare to maintain abattoirs for the slaughtering of quadrupeds, except the aforementioned Jews," seems to indicate such use for a state monopoly. Cf. Straus, *Sizilien*, pp. 29 f.

[13] Jacob Shatzky, "Ducal Ordinances for the Jews of Sokołów" (Yiddish), *Yivo Economic Studies*, I (1928), 80–87; Schorr, *Organizacya*, p. 92; Balaban, *Żydzi lwowscy*, p. 338; idem in *Kwartalnik*, p. 45; D. [B.] Weinryb, "Studies in the Economic and Financial History of the Jews in the Polish and Lithuanian Cities in the Seventeenth and Eighteenth Centuries" (Hebrew), *Tarbiz*, X (1938–39), 95 (emphasizing the complexity of the term *korobka*), 101 f. The yield of all meat taxes (including the

revenue from hides and feathers) amounted to 78,900 florins in the Wilno community in the 1780's. Cf. Klauzner, *Wilno*, I, 162 f. It thus exceeded 53 per cent of its entire regular budgetary income. Distributed over the approximately 5,000 Jews then living in Wilno, the per capita yield was about 16 florins annually, but this amount was greatly increased by the administrative expenses and the profits of the tax farmers, all of which had to be carried by the consumers. This circumstance may perhaps best explain the discrepancy between the higher figures quoted by the complainants of 1786 and the actual communal revenue. Further difficulties confronting the Jewish butchers and meat-consuming public in the earlier period because of the monopolistic attempts of the Christian butcher guilds, as well as the ensuing protracted law-suits, are treated ibid., pp. 18 ff. Among the oldest recorded prohibitions on importing meat from neighboring communities is that enacted by the Candia communities in 1363 on both ritualistic and economic grounds. Cf. Sassoon, *Catalogue*, p. 350. For other interesting illustrations cf. the searching analysis of several Polish eighteenth-century community budgets in Weinryb's continuation of his "Beiträge." Cf. also Chap. XII, nn. 37–38.

[14] Ibn Adret, *Responsa*, II, 213; Colorni in *Riv. st. dir. it.*, XI, 67; Lagumina, *Codice*, II, Pt. 1, nos. 531, 764; Pt. 2, no. 932; Mahler in *Yivo Bleter*, XV, 72 f.; Baer, *Kleve*, p. 116 n. 179; G. Wolf, "Zur Geschichte der Juden in Böhmen," *ZGJD*, III (1889), 91; Salomon Hugo Lieben, "Die von Maria Theresia projektierte Esrogimsteuer," *MGWJ*, LIII (1909), 720–22. The Hamburg community, which annually ordered citrons from Italy, purchased a special consignment of 70 citrons, of which the first six were given to the synagogue of the city, two to the community of Wandsbek, and six to the elders in office. The remainder went to smaller congregations in the vicinity and to former communal officers. Distribution was by lot. Cf. Grunwald in *MGJV*, XI, 37. In the course of time the original pro rata payment for the use of citrons was replaced by a tax computed, as were most other imposts, on a mixed per capita and property basis. This became so general that the claim of a wealthy German widow to exemption, because women were not legally required to make ritualistic use of citrons, was clearly repudiated by Samuel b. David in his *Naḥlat shibe'a*, II, 34.

For a transfer tax on non-ritualistic objects, such as houses, cf. Klauzner, *Wilno*, I, 160. Cf. also the interesting responsum of Akiba Eger (no. 87): The community of Piła (Schneidemühl) belonging to a Polish nobleman, after Prussia's annexation of the city, arranged with the landlord to pay him an annual lump sum, to cover which it was to collect 2 per cent from each purchase or lease of real estate by a Jew, for a period in excess of ten years. Eighteen years later there arose a question as to whether an heir obtaining for cash his brother's share in an inherited house was subject to this levy; Eger decided in the negative. Cf. also Pribram, *Urkunden*, II, 446 ff.; and Chap. XII, n. 43.

[15] The two instalments of the Cracow ordinance have been published by F. Wettstein in his *Dibre ḥefeṣ mi-pinḳese ḳahal ḳadosh Ḳraka* (Excerpts from the Cracow Minute-Books), pp. 58 ff. (summarized in Polish by Balaban in *Kwartalnik*, pp. 46 ff.), and by Weinryb in *Tarbiz*, X, 208 ff., 224 ff.

[16] Lagumina, *Codice*, II, Pt. 1, no. 769; Nehama, *Salonique*, IV, 28 ff.

[17] Epstein, *Duran*, p. 16; Vogelstein and Rieger, *Rom*, II, 229, 275. Cf. also Chap. X, n. 4.

[18] Lagumina, *Codice*, I, nos. 73, 364; Emmanuel, *Salonique*, I, 215 f.; Elbogen in *Jewish Encyclopedia*, VII, 664 f.; Klauzner, *Wilno*, I, 27 f., 157 f.; Weinryb in *Tarbiz*, X, l. c. Cf. also Chap. XVI, n. 9. A complex problem of taxing property of alien Jews in Lwów was the subject of an inquiry addressed to Azulai. Cf. *Ḥayyim sha'al*, II, 20.

[19] Baer, *Studien*, pp. 26 f.; idem, *Spanien*, I, Pt. 2, no. 58; idem, *Kleve*, pp. 36, 126 f.; Stobbe, *Deutschland*, pp. 40 ff., 215 ff.; Donath, *Mecklenburg*, pp. 135 f.; Baron, *Wiener Kongress*, pp. 13, 18 f., 43; Laubert in *MGWJ*, LXVII, 273 ff. In their noteworthy application for release from the corporal tax, submitted to the "Great Elector" Frederick William in 1684, the representatives of Brandenburg Jewry argued only from the purely economic standpoint that such a tax would severely hamper their earning a living. The government acceded to their request after they had paid a lump sum of 400 thalers. Individual Jews, such as the Dutch trader Moses Jacobson in Memel, too, succeeded in wringing such concessions from the reluctant Prussian authorities only by pointing out the indubitable commercial advantages accruing to the state from their journeys. Cf. Selma Stern, *Der preussische Staat*, I, Pt. 2, nos. 49–50, 181–83, etc.

[20] Meldola, *Mayyim rabbim*, II, 61–64; Ergas, *Dibre Yosef*, nos. 30–36. Cf. also Chap. X, n. 26.

[21] I. Loeb, "Actes de vente hébreux originaires d'Espagne," *REJ*, X (1885), 117 f.; Isserlein, *Terumat ha-deshen*, nos. 342, 345–46; Meir of Rothenburg, *Responsa*, ed. Berlin, pp. 239 f. no. 240; ed. Prague, no. 104; *Tosafot* on B. B. 8b; Rabinowitz, *France*, pp. 100 f.; Finkelstein, *Self-Government*, pp. 230, 247 f.; Ibn Adret, *Responsa*, I, 617; V, 269; Epstein, *Adreth*, pp. 92 f.; Israel Bruna, *Responsa*, no. 176; Colon, *Responsa*, Root 128. Cf. also Jacob b. Asher, *Ṭur*, Y. D. 256, 259 and the commentaries thereon; Joseph of Trani, *Responsa*, no. 63 (allowing wide discretionary powers); Jacob Reischer, *Shebut Ya'akob*, II, 84 (voicing the same opinion in favor of victims of a pestilence raging in 1713). The administration of legacies and endowments often gave rise to controversies between executors and communal leaders. Cf. e. g. Baer's *Spanien*, I, Pt. 1, no. 397. Difficulties with the government are illustrated by the legacy of one Anello of Girgenti, cf. Lagumina, *Codice*, II, Pt. 1, nos. 584, 587, 591, 609–10; cf. also ibid., Pt. 2, no. 1010. To obtain income from endowments, communal administrators usually had to lend on interest, compromising with the anti-usury laws in accordance with the rabbinic interpretation. Cf. below, n. 44; and Chap. XIII, nn. 14–15. The Lithuanian Council expected a return of some 10–16.66 per cent on such investments. Cf. Dubnow, *Pinḳas*, nos. 287, 456–57. Cf. also Klauzner, *Wilno*, I, 121; and, more generally, Decourcelle, *Nice*, pp. 270 ff. (giving comparative data for the taxes enacted in 1738, 1761 and 1785).

[22] Maimonides, *Mishneh Torah*, Naḥlot I, 3.

[23] Baron, *History*, II, 20 f.; III, 99 f. n. 8; Parkes, *Medieval Community*, p. 261; D. Kaufmann, *Gesammelte Schriften*, II, 247. Cf. also *Privilegi Piemonte*, pp. 123 f. (1616), 286 f. (1744); Balaban, *Żydzi lwowscy*, pp. 335 f. Where billeting continued to be practiced it lent itself to the usual abuses. In Dubno, in 1804, Jacob the Sexton was condemned for accepting bribes from the rich and placing the entire burden on the middle class and the poor. Cf. Margolies, *Dubno*, pp. 146 f. Frequently military taxes, originally conceived as payment for release from personal service, were speedily converted into general imposts resting upon the Jewish community. In Bohemia the special Jewish military tax instituted in 1574 was at first levied only from men over twenty years of age, but from 1596 on it began to be collected indiscriminately from all Jewish families in the province. Cf. J. Rokycana, "Die militärische Dienstpflicht der böhmischen Juden," *ZGJT*, I (1930–31), 104–8.

[24] Krochmal, *Ṣemaḥ ṣedeḳ*, no. 19.

[25] De Castro, *Synagoge*, p. xxxi Art. 38; Gelber in *REJ*, XCVII, 124 f.; XCVIII, 46; Meir of Rothenburg, *Responsa*, ed. Berlin, pp. 209 f., no. 141.

[26] Ibn Adret, *Responsa*, V, 259.

[27] Samson Morpurgo, *Shemesh ṣedaḳah*, I, Pt. 2, no. 20 (fol. 67c). Cf. also ibid., no. 4.

[28] Mossé, *Avignon*, pp. 82 f.; Lewin, *Landessynode*, pp. 58, 63.

[29] Baer, *Spanien*, I, Pt. 1, nos. 170, 214, 472; Pt. 2, no. 209.

[30] Lagumina, *Codice*, I, no. 395; II, Pt. 1, nos. 536, 577, 592, 597, 615, 638, 714, 764 (Palermo in 1489 owed the large sum of 15,000 florins), 776, 780, 783, 789, 819, 827, 853; Pt. 2, nos. 891 ff., 901, 924; Rodocanachi, *Saint-Siège*, pp. 255 ff.; Vogelstein and Rieger, *Rom*, I, 347 n. 1; II, 125 ff., 229, 254, 342; Berliner in *Ḳobeṣ 'al yad*, XIX, 68 ff.; Jules Bauer, "Un document sur les Juifs de Rome," *REJ*, LI (1906), 137–49 (publishes a memorial addressed by the Roman community to Pius VI in 1787 graphically describing the unfortunate fiscal evolution which had caused communal debts to rise above 200,000 scudi); Franchini in *Economia*, N. S. VIII, 418 f.; Milano, *Ricerche* (gives detailed figures for the revenue and expenditure in 1696, 1721, 1740, 1744, and 1801 and shows how in 1801 the entire income covered less than 40 per cent of outlay). For the indebtedness of the communities of Arles, Nice, Venice and Verona, cf. Hildenfinger in *REJ*, XLVII, 224–29; XLVIII, 54 ff.; Decourcelle, *Nice*, p. 279; Roth, *Venice*, pp. 120 ff.; Azulai, *Ma'agal ṭob ha-shalem*, pp. 9 f. (describing in picturesque detail the difficulties he encountered in trying to collect in 1754 an old debt of the Venetian community to the poor relief of Hebron and how he ultimately obtained payment through direct intervention with the government); Baron in *Sefer ha-Yobel Krauss*, pp. 223 f. Cf. also E. Morpurgo in *Rivista israelitica*, VII, 228 (referring to a memorial of the Venetian community of 1691 concerning its debts and the annual contributions of the communities of Padua and Verona). In the Reglements of 1638–60 the community of Avignon obtained the unusual privilege exempting objects used in the synagogue and school from seizure by communal creditors and forbidding the arrest of elders on account of communal debts. Cf. Maulde, *Etats français*, p. 51 nn. 3–4. Other communities were less fortunate. Cf. Chap. XI, n. 2; Chap. XII, n. 13; Chap. XIV, n. 15.

[31] Wettstein, *Ḳadmoniot mi-pinḳesaot yeshanim* (Documents from

Ancient Minute-Books), no. 28; Perles in *MGWJ*, XVI, 110 f., 152 ff.; Lewin, *Lissa*, pp. 56 f.; Balaban in *Kwartalnik*, pp. 42 ff.; Pazdro, *Organizacya*, no. 70; Zarchin in *JQR*, XXIX, 251 f., 283 ff.; I. Galant, "The Indebtedness of the Jewish Communities in the Seventeenth Century" (Russian), *Evreiskaya Starina*, VI (1913), 129–32 (with special reference to Łuck); Margolies, *Dubno*, p. 57; Fünn, *Ḳiryah ne'emanah*, p. 19; Klauzner, *Wilno*, I pp. xii, 166 ff. (giving a very detailed account of the Wilno communal debts and the attempts to liquidate them in 1766 and 1793); Tsherikover in *Yivo Studies in Hist.*, II, 576 f.; Judyta Freylich, "The Problem of Liquidating the Debts of the Community of Kazimierz [Cracow] after the Third Partition (1795–1809) and under the Republic of Cracow (1817–1829)" (Polish), *Miesięcznik żydowski*, III, Pt. 1 (1933), 467–78; Manfred Laubert, "Die Schuldenregulierung der jüdischen Korporationen in der Provinz Posen," *MGWJ*, LXVIII (1924), 321–31 (beginning in 1835). Interesting illustrations of the per capita tax load of Polish Jewish communities have been drawn from communal budgets by B. Weinryb in *HUCA*, XVI, 209 ff., 213 f. Cf. also Filip Friedman, "Materials for the History of the Jews in Łęczyca" (Yiddish), *Lodzer Visenshaftleche Shriften*, I (1938), 242 (the community, re-established after the Swedish war in 1724, was forced to apply in 1732 for a ten-year moratorium on a debt of 5,660 florins owed to the Jesuits); Lewin in *Festschrift Dubnow*, pp. 131 ff. It was a sign of both financial stringency and great communal authority when, in 1628, the Lithuanian Council authorized provincial organs requiring funds for public expenditure to order any community or individual under their jurisdiction to endorse their notes. Cf. Dubnow, *Pinḳas*, no. 156.

A part of the indebtedness of the Polish Councils and local communities had a curious commercial origin. Since loans extended to individual Jewish merchants often depended on certification of good standing by the Jewish authorities, there was a great temptation for the elders to borrow directly from Christian creditors at the moderate rate of about 7 per cent and to lend to Jewish businessmen at rates up to 20 per cent. Cf. Friedman's unpublished volume on the history of the Jews in Poland. Similarly, according to the anonymous seventeenth-century author of some manuscript notes preserved in the Vatican Library and published by Rieger, the Jewish community of Rome borrowed "from Christians 236,000 scudi at 4 per cent and lent them on usury at 18 per cent." Cf.

Vogelstein and Rieger, *Rom*, II, 427. The protracted economic decline of both the Polish and the Roman Jews in the eighteenth century, resulting in endless bankruptcies, left the communal treasuries in the possession of numerous uncollectible loans for which they were responsible.

[32] S. Rothschild, *Die Abgaben und die Schuldenlast der Wormser jüdischen Gemeinde 1563–1854*; Kracauer, *Geschichte*, II, 203 f.; Baer, *Kleve*, p. 128; Grunwald in *MGVJ*, XLI–XLIV, 73 ff.; Joseph Katz, *She'erit Yosef*, no. 9 (on an inquiry from Moravia); Jakobovits in *JGJC*, I, 343 (on the community of Kolin persuaded by the government to contract a debt in 1755); Clément, *Metz*, pp. 102 ff. (including a tabulation of communal expenditures for the years 1605–10, 1650–60, 1700–14, 1715–35, 1765–70, 1785–89); Maurice Aron, "Liquidation des dettes de l'ancienne communauté juive de Metz," *Annuaire de la Soc. des études juives*, II (1883), 109–35; N. Netter, "Die Schuldennot der jüdischen Gemeinde Metz (1791–1854)," *MGWJ*, LVII (1913), 591–619; LVIII (1914), 63–80.

[33] Baer, *Spanien*, I, Pt. 1, nos. 114, 129, 174, 189, 199, 200, 215, 246, 274; Pt. 2, no. 137; Lagumina, *Codice*, I, nos. 30, 40, 46, 199, 238, 302, 355, 385, 386, 424 (Messina may tax sons of families engaging in business on their own accounts), 441; II, Pt. 1, nos. 470, 593, 617, 619, 704, 718, 749, 757 (Viceroy accepts without reservation the suggestion of the united communities of the realm that no one be exempted from the "gift" to the king, while other resolutions are merely recommended or deferred), 767, 771, 780, 789, 804, 807, 851, 856, 858, etc.; Ferorelli, *Italia meridionale*, pp. 154 f.

[34] Finkelstein, *Self-Government*, pp. 149, 228, 243, 283, 290, 368 f.; Baer, *Spanien*, I, Pt. 2, no. 287 (IV, 1); Tilander in *Studia neophilologica*, XII, 11 f. Art. 3, 6; Ibn Adret, *Responsa*, I, 967; V, 141–43, etc.; Meir of Rothenburg, *Responsa*, ed. Berlin, p. 69 no. 520; ed. Prague, no. 932; Asher b. Yeḥiel, *Responsa*, XIII, 20a; Ḥayyim Or Zaru'a, *Responsa*, no. 80; Isserlein, *Terumat ha-deshen*, nos. 341–42; Jacob Weil, *Responsa*, no. 38; Menaḥem of Merseburg, *Nimmuḳim*, fol. 63abc, 64ab; Götz, *Eben ha-shoham*, no. 32 (referring to a controversy in Hildesheim, 1691); further sources quoted in Jacob b. Asher's *Ṭur*, Ḥ. M. 163 and the commentaries thereon; and by Isaac Lampronti in his *Paḥad Yiṣḥaḳ* (A Legal Dictionary), s. v. *Ḳahal*; Frankel in *MGWJ*, II, 337; Epstein, *Adreth*, 33 ff., 105 f.; Danon in *REJ*, XL, 221; XLI, 250; Emmanuel, *Salonique*, I, 215 f.; Nehama, *Salonique*, IV, 28; Vogelstein and Rieger, *Rom*, II,

346; Milano in *REJ*, LXXXVII, 171; Mossé, *Avignon*, p. 161; Decourcelle, *Nice*, p. 236; Loeb in *Annuaire*, II, 186 Art. XIX; Baer, *Kleve*, pp. 121 f.; Kaufmann in *Ḳobeṣ 'al yad*, XII–XIII, 2 f. (the community of Bamberg in 1697 grants considerable tax privileges, but not full immunity, to orphans and widows, except women engaging in business); Grunwald, in *MGJV*, XI, 44; Wachstein in *ZGJD*, IV, 134, 143; Wolf, *Statuten*, p. 52 Art. 192; Dubnow, *Pinḳas*, nos. 166–67, 178, 491. When an unnamed German regional council asked Jacob Reischer about its claim on one of its wealthiest members who, enjoying a governmental tax immunity for thirty years, nevertheless voluntarily made contributions to the communal treasury, the rabbi counseled moderation and amicable settlement since "it is advisable not to be too pedantic with respect to wealthy leaders who have a name with the authorities and are able to intervene in emergencies." Cf. his *Shebut Ya'akob*, II, 181. Cf. also Chap. X, n. 9. These sources, fairly representative of the major countries of Jewish settlement and the various periods, could easily be multiplied in view of the almost universal practice of granting tax immunities of some sort to individuals, groups or institutions.

[35] *Teshubot ha-geonim*, ed. by Harkavy, no. 537; Maimonides, *Commentary* on M. Abot IV, 5; *Mishneh torah*, Talmud torah, VI, 10; Asher b. Yeḥiel, *Responsa*, XV, 7; Jacob b. Asher, *Ṭur*, Y. D. 243; Ḥ. M. 163 and the commentaries thereon; Meir of Rothenburg, *Responsa*, ed. Prague, no. 716; ed. Lwów, no. 131.

[36] Isserlein, *Terumat ha-deshen*, nos. 341–42; Israel Bruna, *Responsa*, no. 102 end; Meir Katzenellenbogen, *Responsa*, no. 55; Benjamin Slonik, *Mase'at binyamin*, no. 3; Abrahams, *Jewish Life*, p. 59; Baer in *MGWJ*, LXIX, 55; idem, *Spanien*, I, Pt. 1, no. 175; Milano in *REJ*, LXXXVII, 171 (on Ancona); Danon in *REJ*, XXXI, 58 ff. (on Turkey); Nehama, *Salonique*, IV, 27 f.; Levi ibn Ḥabib, *Responsa*, no. 141 (defining qualifications for exemption); Menczel, *Mainz*, p. 39; Grunwald in *MGJV*, XI, 61 f. (Hamburg); Dubnow, *Pinḳas*, nos. 189–90, 233, 532, 607, 660, 743, 778, 806; Schorr, *Organizacya*, p. 90; Margolies, *Dubno*, pp. 80 ff.; Weinryb in *Tarbiz*, X, 227; Wolf, *Statuten*, pp. 52 Art. 191; Klauzner, *Wilno*, I, 130. As late as 1832 the rabbinic court of Fez, Morocco, acknowledged the claim of a wealthy scholar to complete immunity from all regular and extraordinary taxes. Cf. *Ḳobeṣ pesaḳim* (Ms.), fol. 21. Cf. also Chap. VI, n. 3; XI, n. 25. In emergencies, however, even the provincial chief

rabbis of Lithuania had to pay a gold florin each (1771). Cf. Halperin's *Milluim*, no. 98. Another difficulty arose in the Enlightenment era when some qualified scholars joined the new movement and thus incurred the displeasure of the more orthodox leaders who still were in control of the community. Ezekiel Landau, though rather ineffectually insisting upon tax immunities for scholars in Prague, made the significant reservation that "we have no interest, however, in men who are capable of study but do not study and free themselves from the yoke of the Torah." Cf. his *Derushe ha-ṣelaḥ*, fol. 49d.

[37] Jacob b. Asher, *Ṭur*, O. Ḥ. 53, 55; H. M. 163 and commentaries; Joseph of Trani, *Responsa*, no. 69; Elyakim Götz, *Eben ha-shoham*, nos. 64–65; Joseph Katz, *She'erit Yosef*, nos. 18, 70; Krochmal, *Ṣemaḥ ṣedeḳ*, nos. 1, 18; Kracauer, *Geschichte*, II, 31 f.; Baer, *Spanien*, I, Pt. 1, no. 146; Pt. 2, no. 375; idem, *Kleve*, pp. 117 ff.; Lagumina, *Codice*, I, nos. 175, 358.

[38] Vogelstein and Rieger, *Rom*, II, 335; Weinryb in *MGWJ*, LXXXII, 255 f.; idem in *Tarbiz*, X, 94, 104; M. Balaban, "The Situation of the Cracow Community about the Year 1700" (Polish), *Miesięcznik żydowski*, II (1931), 413–28; Grunwald in *MGJV*, XI, 29; Wachstein in *ZGJD*, IV, 134, 142 f.; Sosis in *Zeitshrift*, I, 231 ff. Cf. also Chap. X, n. 22.

[39] Israel Bruna, *Responsa*, no. 268; Frank, *Ḳehillot*, pp. 15 f.; Wolf, *Kleine histor. Schriften*, p. 151; Baer, *Spanien*, I, Pt. 1, nos. 98 (a combination of methods in Saragossa, 1264), 124, 146, 163, 206 (also p. 283), 210, 343; Pt. 2, no. 136; Tilander in *Studia neophilologica*, XII, 15 ff. Art. 13, 17, 28; Epstein, *Adreth*, pp. 19 f.; Hildenfinger in *REJ*, XLI, 67; Mossé, *Avignon*, pp. 152 ff., 159 f.; Roth, *Venice*, pp. 124 f.; Zimmels, *Beiträge*, p. 30; Wachstein in *ZGJD*, IV, 134, 142; Finkelstein, *Self-Government*, pp. 52, 226, 238; Nissim Gerondi on *Alfasi* M. Ḳ., III, end; Mordecai, ibid., no. 936; Jacob b. Asher, *Ṭur*, Y. D. 345 and the commentaries thereon.

[40] Vogelstein and Rieger, *Rom*, II, 128, 217, 271, 314; Milano in *Israel*, X, 417 f. Art. 17; idem in *REJ*, LXXXVII, 172, 174 f.; Munk in *MGWJ*, XLI, 513; Asher b. Yeḥiel, *Responsa*, VI, 4; Isserlein, *Terumat ha-deshen*, no. 342.

[41] Baron in *Sefer ha-Yobel Krauss*, pp. 223 f., 226, 251 n. 37; Baer, *Spanien*, I, Pt. 1, no. 128 (tax chests, 1285); Roth in *JQR*, XV, 441 ff.; idem, *Venice*, p. 125; Morpurgo in *Rivista israelitica*, VII, 229 no. 43, 230 no. 49; Colorni in *Rivista st. dir. it.*, XI, 104, 118; Dubnow, *Pinḳas*,

no. 125. The relationship, if any, between the Polish *korobka* and the Italian *cassella* or its Spanish antecedents would bear further investigation. Not only is the former term derived etymologically from *krobia* = box, but e. g. the statute of Pinczów provided expressly for the closing of the box, in which the *korobka* money was to be deposited, with three keys, two of which were to be kept by citizens specially designated every week, while one key was to remain in the hands of the permanent *korobka* administrator. Cf. Weinryb's remarks in *HUCA*, XVI, 187 n. 1.

[42] Colon, *Responsa*, Roots 1, 6, 17, 127; Finkelstein, *Self-Government*, pp. 122, 135, 258 f., 264; Baer, *Spanien*, I, Pt. 1, nos. 97, 143, 146, 174, 175, 185, 207, 210, 273, 540, 543; Pt. 2, nos. 136, 140, 142, 210; Epstein, *Adreth*, pp. 13 ff.; Ferorelli, *Italia meridionale*, pp. 151 ff., 156 f., 160; Mossé, *Avignon*, pp. 155, 162; Decourcelle, *Nice*, p. 175; Morpurgo, *Shemesh ṣedakah*, I, Pt. 2, no. 24; Grunwald in *MGJV*, XI, 34 ff.; Flesch in Gold's *Mähren*, pp. 32 ff.; Horovitz, *Rabbinerversammlung*, pp. 11 ff., 21 f., 28 f.; Baer, *Kleve*, pp. 101 ff., 117, 144 ff. Cf. also Chap. XI, nn. 6 ff.

[43] Stern, *Ruprecht*, pp. xxx f., 6 ff.; Lewin, *Landessynode*, pp. 77 f.

[44] Abraham Maimuni, *Responsa*, no. 66 (discussing the related problem of placing orphans' funds in interest-bearing investments, with reference to the talmudic discussion, B. M. 70a) and the editor's comments thereon; Baron in *Essays on Maimonides*, pp. 213 ff.; Isaac b. Moses, *Or Zaru'a*, I, 30, fol. 18ab (objecting to Joel ha-Levi's prohibition of lending communal funds on interest to Jews, at least out of permanent endowments), quoted with approval by Menaḥem Recanati in his *Piṣke halakot*, no. 65; Isserles on *Shulḥan 'Aruk*, Y.D. 160,21; and with a discussion of numerous early modern sources by Azulai in *Hayyim sha'al*, II, 32; Lagumina, *Codice* I, nos. 199, 426; II, Pt. 1, nos. 523, 524, 751, 765, 780, 864; Nehama, *Salonique*, IV, 24 f.; F. H. Wettstein, "From the Minute-Books of the Cracow Community," *Gedenkbuch . . . David Kaufmann*, Hebrew section pp. 81 f.; Pazdro, *Organizacya*, no. 58 (Lwów decree of 1765); Jacob b. Asher, *Ṭur*, Ḥ. M. 2, 4, 7, 97, 183 and the commentaries thereon; Sasportas, *Ohel Ya'akob*, no. 4.

[45] Baer, *Kleve*, l. c.; Dubnow, *Pinḳas*, no. 493; Weinryb in *MGWJ*, LXXXII, 261; Friedman's history of the Jews in Poland. Cf. also P. Marek, "Tax Assessors (*Shammaim*) in the Lithuanian Communities of the XVII and XVIII Centuries" (Russian), *Evreiskaya Starina*, I (1909), 161–84. Where, as in Salonica, triennial or longer assessments were

customary, some rabbis objected to any alteration during the tax period. Cf. Joseph of Trani, *Responsa*, no. 57. Cf. also Jakobovits in *JGJC*, I, 338. In Mantua, before the establishment of the *cassella* in 1707, there were, in addition to the tax assessors and collectors chosen from the wealthier taxpayers, several "judges of assessment," selected from members paying less than the required minimum, to review cases under protest. The latter apparently were considered more impartial. Cf. the remarkable responsum by Emden (in *She'elat Ya'aviṣ*, no. 78) which sheds considerable light on the communal organization in Mantua (overlooked by Colorni, l. c.). Preachers, too, such as Ezekiel Landau, frequently attacked inequalities in the tax administration and tax evasions by the rich. Cf. *Derushe ha-ṣelaḥ*, fol. 35c. Cf. also I. Loeb, "Histoire d'une taille levée sur les Juifs de Perpignan en 1413–1414," *REJ*, XIV (1887), 55–79; *Regolamento Reggio 1757*, Articles 3 (elders entitled to impose surtaxes within the triennial tax period); 6 (members failing to pay on the exact date are publicly proclaimed to be sinners); 9 (communal creditors may not balance taxes against communal liabilities); 13 (2 *cassettes*); 17 (each member to submit a declaration, *biglietto d'oblazione*, 8 months before the expiration of the triennial term); A. Balletti, "Le istituzioni finanziarie nelle università israelitiche dell'Emilia," *Giornale degli Economisti*, 2d ser. XXVIII (1904), 359–69; and Asher Gulak, *Oṣar ha-sheṭarot*, nos. 373 (reprinting the formula of a tax reduction on account of impoverishment), 384 (publishing a deed of the communal charities which established a mortgage for a loan).

[46] Buber, *Ḳiryah nisgabah*, p. 82; Balaban in *JJLG*, X, 312, 349 ff.; Kracauer, *Geschichte*, II, 215 f.; *Regolamento Reggio 1757*, Art. 7, 14, 16; Roth, *Venice*, pp. 124 ff.; Grunwald in *MGJV*, XI, 33; Ibn Adret, *Responsa*, I, 680, 811; Asher b. Yeḥiel, *Responsa*, VI, 26; XIII, 20; Colon, *Responsa*, Roots 2, 70, 193; Jacob b. Asher, *Ṭur*, Ḥ. M. 7, 33, 37 and the commentaries thereon; David b. Raphael Meldola, *Dibre David* (Responsa), nos. 53–54; Morpurgo, *Shemesh ṣedaḳah*, II, Pt. 2, nos. 3, 5; Baer, *Spanien*, I, Pt. 1, no. 207 (Pedro IV acknowledges exclusive rabbinic jurisdiction); Lagumina, *Codice*, I, nos. 385, 425, 432; Ferorelli, *Italia meridionale*, p. 160; Zimmels, *Beiträge*, p. 35. Cf. also Chap. X, nn. 2, 4, 7, 10; XIV, n. 9. For intercommunal controversies, particularly with respect to contributions to a common undertaking or regionally assessed taxes, cf. Moses Menz, *Responsa*, no. 1; Ms. Adler no. 4095d in E. N.

Adler's *Catalogue*, p. 45 (referring to a dispute of Hungarian communities in 1761 over the incidence of Maria Theresa's "tolerance tax"); and Chap. VIII, nn. 19–20.

[47] It nevertheless was a rather unusual step for the Jewish public to seek redress from the government. Such was the case in Wilno, where a section of the lower classes, driven to despair by excessive taxation, and perhaps encouraged by a pertinent specific clause in the Palatin's ordinance of 1768, submitted in 1786 a long list of fiscal grievances to the governor's office. Cf. Klauzner, *Wilno*, I, 27 f., 156 ff. The ensuing protracted controversy, fully recorded in the local archives, will be dealt with by the same author in his as yet unpublished Vol. II.

NOTES TO CHAPTER XVI

SOCIAL WELFARE

[1] Clément, *Metz*, p. 117.

[2] Z. Frankel, "Ueber manches Polizeiliche des talmudischen Rechts," *MGWJ*, I (1852), 243–61; Jacob Jacobson, "Mosaiksteine zur Kultur- und Sanitätsgeschichte der Posenschen (grosspolnischen) Juden im 18. Jahrhundert," *Menorah*, VII (1929), 335 ff.; I. Löw, "Jardin et Parc," *REJ*, LXXXIX (1931), 147–63; Colorni in *Riv. st. dir. it.*, XI, 121 f.; Umberto Cassuto, "I più antichi capitoli del ghetto di Firenze," *Rivista israelitica*, IX (1912), 203–11; X (1913), 32–40, 71–80 (many provisions of these statutes of 1571–1611 refer to policing and maintaining cleanliness in the ghetto); Kayserling, *Navarra*, p. 74; Dubnow, *Pinḳas*, no. 142.

[3] Pesaro, *Memorie*, pp. 39 ff. For the establishment of the ghetto in Wilno by royal decree of 1633, the obligation assumed by the community to purchase, within 15 years, all Christian houses situated there, and the new tasks thenceforth resting upon it, cf. Klauzner, *Wilno*, I, 9, 42, 55 ff., 100 f.

[4] Hoeniger, *Judenschreinsbuch*, pp. 163 f., no. 365 (1335); Pinthus in *ZGJD*, II (1930–31), 297 f.

[5] Samuel di Medina, *Responsa* on Ḥ.M. 278 ("the entire subject of [real estate] *ḥazaḳot* hangs in the air and is based exclusively upon ordinances and [communal] enactments issued by our ancestors"); Finkelstein, *Self-Government*, pp. 31, 175 f., 181, 209, 265, 275 f., 302, 305; Baer,

Spanien, I, Pt. 2, no. 181; Nehama, *Salonique*, III, 156 ff.; Danon in *REJ*, XL, 226 ff.; XLI, 257 ff.; Vogelstein and Rieger, *Rom*, II, 163; Perugini in *REJ*, III, 95; Gulak, *Oṣar ha-sheṭarot*, nos. 382, 389. Cf. also Sasportas, *Ohel Ya'akob*, nos. 9–10 (a Leghorn *ḥazaḳah* of 1654); Moses Capsali, "Responsa" in *Sinai*, III, Pt. 1, pp. 156 f. (in two responsa the chief rabbi sharply denounces the practice of Spanish refugees in the Balkans of outbidding native Jews in leasing houses); Levi ibn Ḥabib, *Responsa*, no. 119 (discussing the implications of the Salonica ordinance which forbade the renting of a house or shop within three years after the departure of their former tenant); Bezaleel Ashkenazi, *Responsa*, nos. 34 (a house stands unoccupied for several months because of *ḥazaḳah*), 43 (the "great" community and the community Shalom of Rhodes sharing a *ḥazaḳah* acquired by bequest); Joseph of Trani, *Responsa*, no. 59 (a *ḥazaḳah* in a house which burned down and remained unoccupied for ten years); Azulai, *Ḥayyim sha'al*, I, 74 Section 1 (insisting on indemnity for the Jewish occupant of real estate recently acquired by a Jew from a Gentile and citing a pertinent ordinance of the Smyrna community); Eliezer Rivlin, "The *Ḥazaḳah* of Real Estate in Jerusalem" (Hebrew), *Festschrift Jakob Freimann*, pp. 149–62 (a historical survey); Moise Finzi, "Il diritto di hazakà," *Festschrift A. Berliner*, pp. 93–96 (with special reference to Italy).

The Jewish *ḥazaḳah* went much beyond anything known even in the regimented medieval economy. A number of guild statutes (e. g. those of the Basel furriers of 1226, butchers of 1248 and bakers of 1256) may have strictly forbidden members to outbid each other in hiring journeymen or leasing apartments. Cf. Below, *Probleme der Wirtschaftsgeschichte*, p. 290. But compared with the vast scope and ramifications of Jewish tenant protection, these guild regulations seem timid and half-hearted measures.

[6] A. Lewinsky, "Sulla storia degli Ebrei in Italia durante il secolo XVIII," *Rivista israelitica*, IV (1907), 148; Edmond About, *Rome contemporaine*, excerpted in English transl. in the *New York World* of Nov. 24, 1860 and reprinted therefrom in the *Occident*, XVIII (1860–61), 224; Rodocanachi, *Saint-Siège*, pp. 42 ff., 214 ff.

[7] Ibid., p. 269 (the capital value probably was computed on the basis of 6 per cent as in contemporary Ancona, cf. Milano in *REJ*, LXXXVII, 173); Vogelstein and Rieger, *Rom*, II, 334; Samuel di Medina, *Responsa*

on Y.D. no. 127; Ḥ.M., nos. 228, 296; Emmanuel, *Salonique*, I, 80; Nehama, *Salonique*, II, 85 ff.; III, 162 ff.; Morpurgo, *Shemesh ṣedaḳah*, II, Pt. 2, no. 10 (1725); Sasportas, *Ohel Ya'akob*, no. 65; Gross, *Gallia judaica*, p. 114.

[8] Loeb in *Annuaire*, I, 168; Buber, *Ḳiryah nisgabah*, p. 91; Dubnow, *Pinḳas*, nos. 79–80; Joel Sirkes, *Responsa*, O.S., no. 4; Kosover in *Yivo Studies in History*, II, 225 f.; Levitats, ibid., pp. 98, 110 n. 84; Margolies, *Dubno*, p. 46. Some German communities, further trying to reduce competition for the limited living space available, decreed that no one should lease more than one house. Jacob Weil, citing Isaac Or Zaru'a and others, argued in favor of exempting from this restriction scholars who required additional quarters for students. Cf. his *Responsa*, no. 118. Cf. also Jacob Reischer, *Shebut Ya'akob*, II, 156 (discussing the conflagration in Prague in 1713 and the ensuing controversies over the responsibility of tenants of lower stories for the repair of roofs).

[9] Ezekiel Landau, *Derushe ha-ṣelaḥ*, fol. 18a (probably all exported Vienna clothing came from non-Jewish shops rather than from those of the then very small number of *Toleranzjuden*); Wachstein in *ZGJD*, IV, 135, 137, 145 and the literature listed there; Samuel b. David, *Naḥlat shibe'a*, II, 2, 65–66; Da Fano, *Responsa*, no. 67.

[10] Finkelstein, *Self-Government*, pp. 49, 376 f.; Moïse Schwab, "Une supplique de la communauté de Rome à Pie V," *REJ*, XXV (1892), 113–16; Samuel di Medina, *Responsa*, on Y.D. nos. 117–18, 122, 124, 150, 155, etc. (communal ordinances concerning the trade in wool, skins, coins, meat and the attendance at fairs); Sasportas, *Ohel Ya'akob*, nos. 47, 56, 57; Emmanuel, *Salonique*, I, 72, 77; idem, *Histoire de l'industrie des tissus des Israélites de Salonique*, pp. 25 ff.; Nehama, *Salonique*, IV, 37 ff.; Jakobovits in *JGJC*, I, 337 n. 20; Baer, *Spanien*, I, Pt. 1, nos. 197, 218, 335; Grunwald, *Hamburg*, p. 211; idem, in *MGJV*, XI, 37 ff. For Poland-Lithuania, cf. e. g. Dubnow, *Pinḳas* under the entries listed in the index s. v. *ḥazaḳah*; Joseph Katz, *She'erit Yosef*, no. 17 (a controversial case decided by Solomon Luria and other rabbis in conflicting ways); Luria, *Responsa*, no. 35; Katz, *Le-Ḳorot*, pp. 18 f.; Balaban, *Żydzi lwowscy*, pp. 352 ff.; Tsherikover in *Yivo Studies in History*, II, 580; Zarchin in *JQR*, XXIX, 312 f. There also were cases of conflicting loyalties, particularly where governments were interested in the competitive bidding of Jews for the administration of state monopolies. Ezekiel Landau, confronted by such a situation,

could not entirely restrain newcomers from outbidding holders of a particular concession before its renewal. But he praised the local system of three-year leaseholds which at least reduced the competition to a triennial rather than the usual annual event. Cf. his *Derushe ha-ṣelaḥ*, fols. 9d, 13b.

A remarkable instance of communal control is reported by Isaac b. Sheshet in his *Responsa*, no. 178, referring to the agreement, under ban, of members of a community in Algiers not to ship wheat to a Christian country (evidently Spain) during one year. The members thereafter regretted this hasty action.

For communal statutes including a considerable number of extensive regulations affecting the economic life of members, cf. e. g. Ad. Frankl-Grün, "Die Gemeindeverfassung von Kremsier," *MGWJ*, XL (1896), 210 ff. (on a Jewish *berdon* of 1689, etc.); Grunwald in *MGJV*, XI, 34, 48 ff. Cf. also Chap. X, nn. 2–4.

[11] Baer, *Kleve*, pp. 36 f., 122 f.; Barnett, *El libro*, p. 10 art. 26; Wolf, *Statuten*, p. 55; Kaufmann in *Ḳobeṣ 'al yad*, XII–XIII, 9 ff. (Bamberg statutes on competition and the hiring of servants); Munk in *Festschrift Salomon Carlebach*, pp. 342, 347. Cf. also Gelber in *REJ*, XCVII, 123 f.; XCVIII, 144 (the Turkish community of Vienna excluded "domestics" from holding any communal office).

[12] Krauss, *Studien*, pp. 86, 93 n. 1 (based on Joseph ibn Leb's *Responsa.* I, 48; III, 107); Mordecai on B.B. no. 481. For the general rabbinic doctrine of communal price fixing and difficulties in achieving it cf. Baron in *Essays on Maimonides*, pp. 170 ff. Discussion, however cursory, of the vast amount of legislation concerning business ethics and commercial instruments would far transcend the bounds of the present chapter and must be relegated to future monographic treatment. In these domains, general rabbinic social theory and legal interpretations emanating therefrom were far more important than the enactments of local or regional communal organs.

[13] *Ma'aseh ha-geonim*, ed. by A. Epstein and A. Freimann, pp. 54 f. no. 61; Baer, *Spanien*, I, Pt. 1, nos. 175 (Art. 14), 329; Pt. 2, no. 181.

[14] Finkelstein, *Self-Government*, pp. 228, 243 f., 262 f., 285 f., 292 ff., 373 f.; Baer, *Spanien*, I, Pt. 2, no. 287 (V).

[15] Lagumina, *Codice*, I, no. 151; II, Pt. 1, no. 782; Nehama, *Salonique*, IV, 140 ff. (mentioning also the great jeopardy into which all Turkish Jewry was placed in 1595 by a feminine member who displayed a necklace

valued at 40,000 ducats or some $80,000 in gold before the irate Sultan Murad III); Colorni in *Riv. st. dir. it.*, XI, 87, n. 1; Rodocanachi, *Saint-Siège*, pp. 84 ff.; Attilio Milano, "La Pragmatica degli Ebrei romani nel secolo XVII," *Israel*, VII (1932–33), 176–88; idem in *REJ*, LXXXVIII (1929), 51–58 (publishing the text of the Ancona *pragmatica* of 1739); Cecil Roth, *Venice*, pp. 209 ff.; idem, "Sumptuary Laws of the Community of Carpentras," *JQR*, XVIII (1927–28), 357–83; Abr. Cahen, "Réglements somptuaires de la communauté juive de Metz à la fin du XVIIe siècle, 1690–1697," *Annuaire de la Société des études juives*, I (1881), 77–121.

[16] Schudt, *Merckwürdigkeiten*, IV, Pt. 2, pp. 83 ff.; Pt. 3, pp. 73 ff.; Kracauer, *Geschichte*, II, 243 ff.; Löwenstein in *JJLG*, VIII, 188 ff.; Wachstein in *ZGJD*, IV, 135, 138 f., 144, 147 f.

[17] Dubnow, *Pinkas*, nos. 199 ff., 309 ff., 339, 463, 470, 669 ff., etc.; Munk in *Festschrift Carlebach*, pp. 339 ff.; idem in *MGWJ*, XLI, 520 f.; David Fränkel, "Contribution to the History of the Jews in Constantinople" (Hebrew), *Alim*, I (1934–35), 110–12 (on the ordinance of 1725); Lewin in *JJLG*, II, 8 f., nos. 18, 21, 24; idem, *Landessynode*, pp. 71, 86 ff. Cf. also Eibeschütz, *Ya'arot debash*, I, 37ab (a typical rabbinic sermon against luxuries of any kind); Abrahan Galanté, *Histoire des Juifs de Rhodes, Chio, Cos, etc.*, pp. 65 f. (quoting the Rhodes prohibition of dowries and trousseaus exceeding 500 piastres in value which, first enacted in 1722, was renewed in 1752 and 1802); Grunwald in *MGJV*, XI, 9, 12 f., 52 ff., 56 f., 62 ff.; idem, "Luxusverbot der Dreigemeinden (Hamburg-Altona-Wandsbek) aus dem Jahre 1715," *Jahrbuch für jüd. Volkskunde*, I (1923), 227–34; Bernhard Wachstein, "The Prague Anti-Luxury Ordinances of 1767" (Yiddish), *Yivo Bleter*, I (1931), 335–54; Wolf, *Statuten*, p. 138; Balaban in *JJLG*, X, 360; XI, 103; idem, *Żydzi lwowscy*, pp. 532 ff.; Buber, *Ḳiryah nisgabah*, pp. 96, 116; P. Kon, "The Struggle of the Wilno Community Against Luxury in Dress in 1809" (Yiddish), *Yivo Bleter*, III (1932), 281–83; Ankava, *Kerem ḥemer*, II, 8ab (an anti-luxury ordinance of the Castilian community of Fez promulgated in 1688, because the actual practice was "detrimental to the poor"); and, more generally, J. R. Marcus, *Medieval World*, pp. 193 ff.; Wilhelm, *Von jüdischer Gemeinde*, pp. 73 f., 76 ff. (giving translations in full or in part of several communal ordinances); H. Flesch, "Mässigkeitsverordnungen," *ZGJT*, I (1930–31), 279–95 (with special reference to Moravia); Roth, "Sumptuary Laws,"

Jewish Chronicle Supplement, April 1934, pp. V f. and the literature listed by him (in *JQR*, XVIII), Flesch and Wachstein.

Rabbinic interpretation of these communal enactments often considerably increased their severity. Samuel di Medina, for instance, taught that a sumptuary and anti-dancing ordinance promulgated by the community of Patras must be observed also by Patras Jews residing in Lepanto. Cf. his *Responsa* on Y.D., no. 149. Of interest are also many provisions in state and municipal sumptuary laws, sometimes specifically referring to Jews. The Mannheim ordinance of 1716, for instance, emphasized the prohibition against the wearing of costly gold and silver ornaments by Jewish women. After 1748, every Jewess wearing skirt or coat adornments of gold or silver had to pay 3 fl. to the government. The Jewish community as such paid 50 fl. annually for the privilege of allowing women to wear gold or silver woven laces on headgear. Cf. Berthold Rosenthal, "Oberrabbiner Michael Scheuer als Kritiker seiner Zeit," *ZGJD*, III (1931), 73. For a notable example of anti-luxury legislation affecting household domains other than clothing and food, cf. the resolution, adopted by the Lithuanian Council in 1628, which forbade Jews paying less than a 4 groszy tax on their property to employ Gentile maids, and those on relief to employ any servants at all. Dubnow, *Pinḳas*, no. 146.

[18] Israel Bruna, *Responsa*, nos. 34, 165; *Ṭur* and *Shulḥan 'Aruk*, O.Ḥ. 2 and the commentaries thereon (especially that of Joel Sirkes); Judah b. Asher, *Responsa*, no. 20; Meir Zvi Weiss, "A Decision by R. Judah Muscato" (Hebrew), *Ha-Eshkol*, VII (1913), 202–7; Solomon Luria, *Responsa*, no. 72; Katz, *Le-Ḳorot*, p. 13 no. 10 (a seventeenth-century rabbi permitted even the taking of an oath with the head uncovered, to obviate which the community had been paying 100 florins to the authorities); Azulai, *Ḥayyim sha'al*, II, 35 Section I (cites numerous authorities permitting such recitation of a benediction; also contends, that, although a wig is considered the equivalent of a headgear, it is customary to place a hat on top of it before a benediction). Cf. also I. Kahan, "L'usage de se couvrir la tête," *REJ*, LXXXIV (1927), 176–78; A. Marmorstein, "L'acte de se couvrir la tête chez les Juifs," ibid., LXXXV (1928), 66–69. Questions also arose from the ancient biblical taboo on mixing linen and wool; cf. Ḥayyim Or Zaru'a, *Responsa*, no. 84.

[19] Wischnitzer in *Vierteljahrsschrift f. Sozial u. Wirtschaftsgeschichte*, XX. 450; Tsherikover in *Yivo Studies in History*, II, 589 f.

A related subject of communal regulation was the extent to which members were allowed to cut their hair or beard. Talmudic regulations being open to a variety of interpretations (cf. the older and more recent sources cited by Azulai in his *Ḥayyim sha'al*, I, 52; II, 27), regional differences often gave rise to conflicts. The leaders of Salonica once sought to force all Italian Jews in the city to grow long beards in accordance with the local custom, and threatened the disobedient with a ban or expulsion. Cf. Morpurgo's *Shemesh ṣedaḳah*, I, Pt. 2, no. 61. The community of Bayonne observed an age-old mourning custom of not cutting the hair between the first and the ninth of Ab. Some members balked at this observance which, they claimed, exposed them to the ridicule of their Gentile friends, but Raphael Meldola insisted on strict compliance except by individuals having dealings with the authorities, and in case of sickness or a joyous family celebration. Cf. his *Mayyim rabbim*, II, 67.

The wig (*sheitel*) which replaces the hair of a bride and which is today considered the height of orthodoxy, was viewed as a radical innovation two centuries ago. Zealous Jacob Emden prohibited its public display. Cf. his *She'elat Ya'aviṣ*, no. 9. Men, on the other hand, were often puzzled by the problem of showfringes. The community of Metz, for instance, was informed by Jonathan Eibeschütz that wearers of modern coats were legally bound to adorn them with ritual fringes, unless the latter's back vents (slits) were sewn up with silk thread which, indeed, Metz Jewry was told to do by communal ordinance. Cf. *Ya'arot debash*, 112a.

[20] Finkelstein, *Self-Government*, pp. 23 ff., 94 f., 139 ff., 302, 305 f., 317, 323; Baer, *Spanien*, I, Pt. 1, nos. 249, 406, 452; Lagumina, *Codice*, I, nos. 264, 302; II, Pt. 1, nos. 468, 649, 774; P. L. Bruzzone, "Les Juifs au Piémonte," *REJ*, XIX (1889), 141–46; Ankava, *Kerem ḥemer*, II 6 cd (1593, 1599); Epstein, *Adreth*, pp. 81 f., 87, 119 ff.; idem, *Duran*, pp. 88 ff.; Joseph of Trani, *Responsa*, no. 39; Joseph Ergas, *Dibre Yosef*, no. 43 (cf. also ibid., nos. 15–17); Morpurgo, *Shemesh ṣedaḳah*, II, 1 (the practical joke of a married man with children in Casale who, in 1710, betrothed a widow in the presence of witnesses, attracted wide rabbinic attention); Jacob Reischer, *Shebut Ya'akob*, II, 118–19; Akiba Eger, *Responsa*, nos. 44, 45, 55, 56, 58.

[21] Barnett, *El libro*, p. 12 Art. 37; Finkelstein, *Self-Government*, pp. 96 f., 317, 323; Buber, *Anshe Shem*, p. 222, nos. 1–2; Dubnow, *Pinḳas*, nos. 32, 42, 43, 185, 314, 361, 430, 461, 968, 1003. Cf. also Nehama, *Salonique*,

IV, 149. In Italy at least young men enjoyed considerable freedom in the selection of their mates and Joseph Colon, among others, argued against undue parental interference. Cf. his *Responsa*, Root 164. Samuel di Medina, too, overruled a father's strict orders that his son not marry a particular woman, although her station in life made her an appropriate mate. Cf. his *Responsa*, on Y.D. no. 95. A Balkan community could even question the validity of a legacy of 500 fl. in favor of the academy of Rhodes and the needy Jews of Safed bequeathed by an angry father in order thus to punish his son for marrying an orphan. Joseph of Trani felt compelled to acknowledge the legitimacy of the will. Cf. his *Responsa*, no. 46. In Germany, on the contrary, a wealthy father arranged for the marriage of his son to an equally wealthy widow without the son's knowledge. Cf. Götz, *Eben ha-Shoham*, nos. 1–5, referring to a typical case in Hildesheim in 1698. In Bayonne, too, an "ancient" ordinance, renewed in 1700–3, prohibited marriages performed in secret or without parental approval. A marriage concluded in contravention of this ordinance was once voided by two rabbis. These might have invoked the authority of the Tosafist, R. Yom Tob [b. Isaac] who, in twelfth-century England, ruled that any man who takes a wife without her relatives' consent shall be forced to divorce her, if need be through excommunication and the aid of government organs. Quoted by Epstein in *Transactions of the Jewish Historical Society of England*, XIV, 199, 50. Cf., however, the more hesitant opinion of David Meldola in his *Dibre David*, nos. 73–76.

It may also be noted that the communities of Candia ordered members in 1567 to refrain from giving daughters or other relatives in marriage to strangers who had not completed a year's residence. Cf. Sassoon, *Catalogue*, p. 355. As late as 1767 the community of Rhodes forbade its members to marry "aliens." Cf. Galanté, *Juifs de Rhodes*, p. 65. Cf. also Chap. X, n. 1.

[22] Baer, *Spanien*, I, Pt. 2, no. 287 (III, 3); Finkelstein, *Self-Government*, pp. 302, 305 f., 317, 323, 364 f.; Isaac b. Sheshet, *Responsa*, no. 15; Rosanes, *Togarma*, IV, 144. While the author of the *Book of the Pious* and others discountenanced marriages between old men and young girls, they considered the mating of an old woman and a young boy, which more surely precluded procreation, as more obnoxious. Cf. Azulai, *Ḥayyim sha'al*, I, 74 Section 48. Cf. also Solomon Ephraim Lentshits, *Olelot Ephraim*, no. 340; Jacob Emden, *She'elat Ya'aviṣ*, no. 14; Israel Lévi,

"Un recueil de consultations de rabbins de la France méridionale," *REJ*, XXXVIII (1899), 111, 120 f. (concerning a case of betrothal of a prostitute in jest); Morpurgo, *Shemesh ṣedakah*, II, 2 (a married childless Jew in Corfù exercises his duty as a levir, but his marriage is impugned on the ground of the rabbi's absence from the ceremony; Morpurgo decides in favor of its validity). An ordinance issued in 1680 by the communal board of Mantua with the approval of Rabbi Moses Zacuto and restated in 1694, ordered the attendance of the rabbi and an elder at all marriage ceremonies. Cf. Colorni in *Riv. st. dir. it.*, XI, 103. Cf. also Ankava, *Kerem ḥemer*, II, 6b (1592); Assaf, *Meḳorot*, II, 200; and Chap. VI, n. 36.

[23] Solomon b. Simon Duran, *Milḥemet miṣvah*, p. 14; Zimmels, *Marranen*, pp. 61 ff.

[24] Reischer, *Shebut Ya'akob*, II, 82; Baer, *Spanien*, I, Pt. 2, no. 60.

[25] Finkelstein, *Self-Government*, pp. 286 f., 294 f.; Baer, *Spanien*, I, Pt. 1, nos. 171 (p. 211), 203, 205, 317; Abraham Zacuto, *Sefer Yuḥasin ha-shalem* (Chronicle), ed. by Filipowski, fol. 225a; Ibn Verga, *Shebet Yehudah* (Chronicle), ed. Wiener, p. 95; Straus, *Judengemeinde Regensburg*, Appendix, nos. 44–47, 56, 168 (24). On the other hand, the literary theme of seduction of Jewish girls by Christians, frequently repeated from the days of Caesarius von Heisterbach (about 1170–1240), may well have reflected a modicum of reality. Cf. Fritz Aronstein, "Eine jüdische Novelle von Grimmelshausen," *ZGJD*, V (1934), 239.

[26] Abrahams, *Jewish Life*, pp. 84 f., 103 ff.; Isaac Arama, *'Aḳedat Yiṣḥaḳ* (an ethical treatise), I, 20 (ed. Lwów, 1868, fol. 162a). Cf. also Morpurgo, *Shemesh ṣedakah*, I, Pt. 2, no. 48; Roth, *Venice*, pp. 201 ff.

[27] Rivkind in *Reshumot*, IV, 349 ff.; Kracauer, *Geschichte*, II, 293; Bauer in *REJ*, LXIII, 273; Grunwald in *MGJV*, XI, 12 f., 49; J. Unna, "Oberrabbiner Michael Scheuer als Kritiker seiner Zeit," *ZGJD*, I (1929), 324 f.; Rosenthal, ibid., III, 72 f. (both discussing the sexual laxity in eighteenth-century Mannheim); Wolf, *Statuten*, pp. 72 f.; Dubnow, *Pinḳas*, nos. 88, 132–34, 259, 356, 947, 993, 1005, 1023; Götz, *Eben ha-shoham*, no. 43 (the community of Hildesheim forces a citizen to discharge his widowed maidservant, because of rumored intimacy, but in 1699 is prevented by Götz from forbidding him to marry the woman's daughter). The Prague decree of 1611 was subsequently amplified by an ordinance outlawing the employment of married women in households, except if their services were required as wet-nurses. Nevertheless, Ezekiel Landau,

the initiator of this enactment, testified to the considerable sexual laxity in the ghetto of Prague as well as in the Bohemian villages. Cf. his *Derushe ha-ṣelaḥ*, fols. 4a, 25d, 52b, etc.

[28] Finkelstein, *Self-Government*, pp. 271 f., 279, 316 f., 320 f.; Buber, *Anshe shem*, p. 232 no. 22. Early in his career as rabbi of Metz, Eibeschütz pledged himself to insist upon the inclusion in each contract of betrothal of a clause obliging the fiancés to abstain from any physical contact whatsoever until after wedlock. Later on he ordained that women visit the graves of their ancestors a day or two before the eves of the New Year and the Day of Atonement, the mornings before the holidays being reserved for male visitors. Cf. his *Ya'arot debash*, I, 18c, 75c. Various resolutions with respect to loose women, illegitimate children, the behavior of fiancés and the protection of the honor of Jewish girls were adopted by the communities of Candia also in 1363, 1477, 1526, 1568. Cf. Sassoon, *Catalogue*, I, 350, 352, 354 f. Cf. also Kosover in *Yivo Studies in History*, II, 240 ff., and Tsherikover's remarks thereto, ibid., pp. 246 f.

[29] Otto Kinkeldey, "A Jewish Dancing Master of the Renaissance (Guglielmo Ebreo)," *Studies . . . in Memory of Freidus*, pp. 329–72 (lived in fifteenth-century Pesaro); Moritz Steinschneider, "Miszellen," *Zeitschrift für hebräische Bibliographie*, IX (1905), 189 (on dancing teachers); Berliner, *Aus dem Leben*, pp. 121, 136; Meir of Rothenburg, *Responsa*, no. 118 (referring to the sale of a dance hall to a private citizen); Benjamin Ze'eb, *Responsa*, no. 303; Wachstein in *ZGJD*, IV, 139, 149 (with additional literature); Lagumina, *Codice*, II, Pt. 1, nos. 532, 671; Assaf, *Meḳorot*, II, 200, 239; Solomon Luria, *Responsa*, nos. 28, 59; Judah Menz, *Responsa*, no. 16. Cf. also Vogelstein and Rieger, *Rom*, II, 321; Rodocanachi, *Saint-Siège*, pp. 62 f.; Loeb in *Annuaire*, II, 187 Art. XXIII and XXVII, 193 f. Art. III (the Alsatian communities prohibit all dancing except in conjunction with weddings); Israel Bruna, *Responsa*, no. 76; Götz, *Eben ha-shoham*, no. 50 (boys dance and play instruments on half-holidays without interference); Eibeschütz, *Ya'arot debash*, I, 30a; Wachstein, *Eisenstadt*, p. 147 n. 5; Löwenstein in *JJLG*, VIII, 185 (as late as 1804 the community of Fürth threatened women dancing with men with public inscription of their names "in large letters" on the blackboard of the main synagogue). Many anti-luxury ordinances (e. g. of sixteenth-century Salonica) included provisions against dancing and gaming. Cf. Nehama, *Salonique*, IV, 142 ff.

The same puritanical motives inspired also the frequent prohibitions in northern countries, such as that enacted in Fürth in 1744, against Jewish attendance at theatrical performances. Cf. Löwenstein in *JJLG*, VIII, 184. Italian Jewry was more liberal, the pope in 1771 prohibiting only Christian attendance at comedies produced in the Jewish quarter. Cf. Lewinsky in *Rivista israelitica*, IV, 147. Cf. also I. Schipper, *Geshichte fun yidisher teaterkunst un drame* (A History of Jewish Theatrical Arts and Drama from the Beginning to 1750); Jacob Shatzky, "Drama and Theatre among the Sephardim in Holland" (Yiddish), *Yivo Bleter*, XVI (1940), 135–49; and, more generally, Baron, *History*, II, 42 ff., 112 ff.; III, 77 f., 108 f.

30 Viktor Kurrein, "Kartenspiel und Spielkarten im jüdischen Schrifttume," *MGWJ*, LXVI (1922), 203–11; Finkelstein, *Self-Government*, pp. 228, 242, 286, 291 f. Cf. also Baer, *Spanien*, I, Pt. 1, nos. 136, 163 (10), 179 (28), 304, 325; Isaac b. Sheshet, *Responsa*, nos. 171, 249; Güdemann, *Geschichte*, I, 60, 260 f.; III, 139; Steinschneider in *Zeitschrift f. hebr. Bibliographie*, IX, 186 ff. (on various ball games); Wellesz in *JJLG*, IX, Hebrew section, p. 6 Art. 62 (Isaac of Corbeil forbids the release of a Jew from an oath not to gamble); Israel Bruna, *Responsa*, no. 71 (permits attendance at horse races but uncertain about tournaments); Samuel di Medina, *Responsa*, on Y.D. no. 84 (opposes the revocation of a communal agreement against gaming); Morpurgo, *Shemesh ṣedaḳah*, I, Pt. 2, nos. 5, 25, 32; Rodocanachi, *Saint-Siège*, p. 128 n. 1 (reporting the legend of a Jewish pope who betrayed himself by winning a chess game and lost his throne); Sassoon, *Catalogue*, I, 355 (Elijah Capsali and his associates prohibit in 1533 any games on the Ninth of Ab); Israel Abrahams, "Samuel Portaleone's Proposed Restrictions on Games of Chance," *JQR*, O.S. V (1892–93), 505–15 (about 1630); H. P. Chajes, "Un *herem* di R. Mosè Zacuto contro il giuoco (1693)," *Rivista israelitica*, V (1908), 95–97; Roth, *Venice*, pp. 207 ff.; Grunwald in *MGJV*, XI, 50; Löwenstein in *JJLG*, VIII, 184 f.; Kracauer, *Geschichte*, II, 241 ff.; Jacob Reischer, *Shebut Ya'akob*, II, 79 (a local ban on gaming applies to foreign students of the academy, but not to other visitors); Wolf, *Statuten*, pp. 73 f.; Dubnow, *Pinḳas*, no. 51; Wachstein in *ZGJD*, IV, 137 ff., 147 (citing many other sources); Marcus, *Medieval World*, pp. 220 (Art. XXVIII: the community of Sugenheim in 1756 forbids all Purim masquerades and processions with torches), 418 ff. (English excerpts from Leo of Modena's youthful dialogue

on gaming entitled *Sur me-ra'* [Turn Away from Evil] written in 1584); and, in general, I. Rivkind, "Dice Tax in Connection with the Tax of Disgrace" (Hebrew), *Zion*, I (1935–36), 37–48; idem, "Contributions to the History of Gaming Among Jews; Its Influence on Family Peace" (Hebrew), *Ḥoreb*, I (1934), 82–91; idem, "The Laws concerning Gamblers" (Hebrew), ibid., II (1935–36), 60–66; Baron, *History*, III, 120 n. 7.

31 Finkelstein, *Self-Government*, pp. 43 ff., 56, 67, 69, 105, 160 ff., 166, 216 f.; [Alfred von Reumont], "Die Juden im Kirchenstaate und in Toscana," *Der Orient*, II (1841), 259; Jacob Joshua Falk, *Pene Yehoshu'a*, II, no. 63; Lagumina, *Codice*, II, Pt. 1, nos. 645, 709; Baer, *Spanien*, I, Pt. 1, pp. 1067 ff. (showing the influence of the Christian environment upon the ordinance of the French synod); Joseph Katz, *She'erit Yosef*, no. 52; Samuel b. David, *Naḥlat shibe'a*, II, 82; S. Assaf, "Differing Ordinances and Customs in Regard to the Husband's Inheritance of his Wife's Estate" (Hebrew), *Madda'e ha-yahadut*, I (1926), 79–94. For an example of the extensive communal ordinances regulating the financial status of wives, cf. the statute drafted by Simon Duran in 1394 and adopted by the Spanish community of Algiers in Duran's *Tashbeṣ*, II, 292, and Epstein's *Duran*, pp. 84 ff. Cf. in general also Louis M. Epstein's *Jewish Marriage Contract*, passim.

32 Meir of Rothenburg, *Responsa*, ed. Prague, no. 81; Finkelstein, *Self-Government*, pp. 216 f.; Abraham Maimuni, *Responsa*, no. 106; Assaf, "Documents of 1620–30" (Hebrew), *Reshumot*, VI (1930), 455; Dubnow, *Pinḳas*, nos. 34, 36; J. Wellesz, "Ueber R. Isaac b. Mose's 'Or Sarua'," *JJLG*, IV (1906), 90 (quoting medieval sources for the institution of the marriage broker and his fees); Mordecai on B.Ḳ., nos. 172–73 (citing different opinions of rabbis concerning these fees); Isserlein's *Pesaḳim*, no. 85 (reporting regional differences in payment of fees after the engagement or wedding); Grunwald in *MGJV*, XI, 49, Art. 159 (the marriage broker was to receive from each party 1 per cent of the bride's or bridegroom's dowry, depending on which was larger); Kaufmann in *Ḳobeṣ 'al yad*, XII–XIII, pp. 4 f. (the community of Bamberg fixes the fee at 2 thalers for the first 100 thalers and of 1–1½ per cent of any additional amount of the dowry; if two brokers claim credit for the match, the initiator is entitled to one-third of the fee, while two-thirds are to go to the man who successfully completes the negotiations); Balaban, *Żydzi lwowscy*, p. 529 (the broker's fee, originally fixed by the Polish Council at 2.5 per cent of the dowry in a local

marriage, and at 3 per cent if the couple lived at a distance of more than 45 miles, was reduced in 1747 to 1.6 and 2.4 per cent, respectively). Cf. also idem in *JJLG*, X, 334 f.; Kosover in *Yivo Studies in History*, II, 223 f.

[33] Maimonides, *Mishneh torah*, Matenot 'aniyyim, IX, 3; *Ṭur* and *Shulḥan 'Aruk*, Y.D. 250, 251, 256; Baer, *Spanien*, I, Pt. 1, no. 185 (the community of Lerida promises in 1326 to distribute annually 60 solidi worth of Passover flour to the poor from rent due to a Jewish creditor); Asher b. Yeḥiel, *Halakot*, on Pes., quoted in *Kolbo*, no. 47; Berliner, *Rom*, II, Pt. 2, 56 f.; De Maulde, *Etats français*, pp. 149 f. (Art. 67).

[34] Ibn Adret, *Responsa*, III, 380, 414; Balaban in *JJLG*, X, 342; Barnett, *El libro*, p. 9 Art. 24.

[35] Isaac b. Moses, *Or Zaru'a*, I, 11, fol. 15b; Judah Menz, *Responsa*, no. 7; Wachstein in *ZGJD*, IV, 136; Grunwald in *MGJV*, XI, 31 f., 45 ff. Cf. also *Regolamento Reggio, 1757*, p. 9 Art. 15; *Taḳḳanot Ḳ. Ḳ. Hamburg*, Art. 54–55; Wachstein, *Eisenstadt*, p. 183; Marcus, *Medieval World*, pp. 219 f. (Sugenheim); I. Loeb in *Annuaire*, II, 185 Art. XI (the Alsatian communities free newlyweds from *pletten* for one year). Needless to say that there also were frequent cases of evasion. Ezekiel Landau, who often censured the uncharitableness of the Prague community, contrasting it with the extensive philanthropies of the Polish community of Brody and seeing in it the ultimate cause for the inimical governmental legislation, also contended that "many rich men turn back the poor person despite his possession of a *plet*. The poor man is sent hither and thither while the supervisors have no power to enforce their will." Cf. *Derushe ha-ṣelaḥ*, fol. 9ab, 26d. Cf. also M. Horovitz, "Die Wohltätigkeit bei den Juden im alten Frankfurt," *Israelitische Monatsschrift*, XXVII (1896), 17–18, 21–22, 26–27.

[36] A. Marmorstein, "Sur un auteur français inconnu du treizième siècle," *REJ*, LXXVI (1923), 114; Dubnow, *Pinḳas*, nos. 78, 378, 597, 666, 880 (this decision and that of 1761 seem to conflict with Jonah Theomim's entry to no. 378 stating that the restriction was abrogated in 1677); Halperin, *Milluim*, nos. 1, 89.

[37] Hannover, *Yeven meṣulah* in Kahana's *Sifrut*, II, 316 f.; A. Heppner and J. Herzberg, *Aus Vergangenheit und Gegenwart der Juden und der jüdischen Gemeinden in den Posener Landen*, p. 79 n. *). Cf. also Buber, *Ḳiryah nisgabah*, p. 109 (Art. 30–31); Zarchin in *JQR*, XXIX, 156 f.

[38] Maulde, *Etats français*, p. 150 Art. LXVII; Loeb in *Annuaire*, I, 237 f. Art. XXX; Mossé, *Avignon*, p. 170.

[39] The Purim festival was universally observed by public and private collections for the poor. According to an ordinance issued by David ha-Levi in 1635, but apparently little observed even in his native Lwów, contributions collected in the synagogue on that day were to be disbursed immediately, one half to minor synagogue officials, the other to the needy. Cf. Abraham Judah (Ad.) Frankl-Grün, "The Ordinances of the [Author of] *Ṭure Zahab*" (Hebrew), *Ha-Zofeh*, III (1914), 188–90. Samuel b. David ha-Levi (in his *Naḥlat shibe'a*, II, 4–5) records the futile attempt of some members of a small community to induce the charity overseers to spend revenue derived from the sale of synagogue functions on ritualistic implements and of others to distribute their own payments for such functions to poor persons of their choice, including kinsmen. The rabbi upheld the authority of the communal administration. Cf. also Chap. X, n. 11; Maulde, *Etats français*, p. 149 Art. LXVII; Baer, *Kleve*, p. 116; Munk in *MGWJ*, XLI, 510, 519, and in general, Frisch, *Philanthropy*, pp. 101 ff.; Abraham Cronbach, *Religion and Its Social Setting*, pp. 99–133.

[40] Grunwald in *MGJV*, XI, 30 f., 44; Baer, *Kleve*, p. 123.

[41] Milano in *REJ*, LXXXVIII, 56, Art. XV; Dubnow, *Pinḳas*, nos. 603, 972; Roth, *Venice*, pp. 153 ff., 157. Cf. also Colorni, in *Riv. st. dir. it.*, XI, 121 (after 1591 Mantua included among its elected functionaries 3 elders in charge of all loans, in kind and money, to individuals and to the government). The Maimonidean eight degrees of charity are thoroughly analyzed and compared with those of Moses of Coucy (seven degrees), and Ibn al-Nakawa (five and nine degrees) by Abraham Cronbach in his recent essay on "The Gradations of Benevolence," *HUCA*, XVI (1941), 163–86.

[42] L. D. Barnett in *Transactions of the Jewish Historical Society in England*, X, 258–60; Koch, *Wandlungen der Wohlfahrtspflege*, pp. 15, 57 ff. The renowned Talmud Torah association of Salonica long accommodated indigent visitors in its premises. Cf. Nehama, *Salonique*, III, 107. Not all of these institutions were overcrowded, however. In 1765 the Wilno *heḳdesh* accommodated in addition to its personnel, only 18 patients and 3 persons on poor-relief. And Wilno's community was then the largest in Lithuania. Cf. Klauzner, *Wilno*, I, 45 ff., 121.

[43] De Maulde, *Etats français*, pp. 141 ff., 152; Loeb in *Annuaire*, I, 213 Art. IX. Cf. also Jules Bauer, "La peste chez les Juifs d'Avignon," *REJ*,

XXXIV (1897), 251–62; B. A. Fersht, "The Earliest Jewish Friendly Society in England, Rodphea Sholom," *Miscellanies of the Jewish Historical Society in England*, II (1935), 90–98 (the statute of 1767 calls for personal attendance at the bedside of a fellow member).

[44] Mordecai on 'A. Z. no. 799; Jacob b. Asher, *Ṭur*, Y. D. 249, 251, 258 and commentaries thereon; Alfasi, *Responsa*, no. 6; Joseph ibn Megas, *Responsa*, no. 207; Maimonides, *Mishneh Torah*, Matenot 'aniyyim, X, 7; idem, *Responsa*, ed. Freimann, no. 80; Moses of Coucy, *Sefer ha-miṣvot*, Positive Commandments no. 162; Meir of Rothenburg, *Responsa*, ed. Prague, no. 692; Ibn Adret, *Responsa*, III, 296; Joseph Colon, *Responsa*, Roots 128, 159; Aronius, *Regesten*, nos. 146, 361; Saalfeld, *Martyrologium*, pp. XV, 93, 304; Kracauer, *Geschichte*, I, 206; II, 227 f., 293, 424 f.; K. Baas, "Jüdische Hospitäler im Mittelalter," *MGWJ*, LVII (1913), 452–60; Frisch, *Philanthropy*, pp. 142 ff.; Baer, *Spanien*, I, Pt. 2, nos. 76, 287 (I, 2), 386, 390, 391; Loeb, "Les sacs des juiveries de Valence et de Madrid en 1391," *REJ*, XIII (1886), 239–47; idem, "Notes sur l'histoire des Juifs en Espagne," ibid., XIV (1887), 264 ff.; Lagumina, *Codice*, I, no. 418. Cf. also Kaufmann in *Ḳobeṣ 'al yad*, XII–XIII, 2 (a Bamberg statute of 1697 provides for medication of a sick stranger until he recovers and can be sent to another community); Grunwald in *MGJV*, XI, 38 (Art. 104: household help is entitled to the employer's contribution of 2 thalers for the costs of illness, the balance to be defrayed by the community); Wachstein in *ZGJD*, IV, 138 (Art. 31); Jacobson in *Menorah*, VII, 335 ff.

In a Barcelona court decision of 1292 the term, *heḳdesh*, seems still to be used in the generic sense, cf. David Fränkel, "A Court Decision Written in Barcelona in 1292" (Hebrew), *'Alim*, I (1934–35), 42–43. Similarly, when Samuel di Medina took pains to emphasize that the ancient laws concerning "sacrilege" do not apply to a contemporary *heḳdesh*, he had all current charities in mind. He reported in another connection, however, a decision of four Balkan congregations to erect a common hospice. In a subsequent controversy the rabbi decided in favor of the majority of three congregations against one. Cf. his *Responsa*, on O. Ḥ. no. 20; Y. D. nos. 207–9. Cf. also Baron in *Essays on Maimonides*, p. 152 n. 50.

[45] B. Weinryb, "Private Letters in Yiddish of 1588," *Yivo Studies in History*, II (1937), 44 f., 64 ff. (publishing two letters addressed to the Cracow elders in Olkusz); Jacob Zahalon, *Oṣar ha-ḥayyim* (A Medical

Treatise), fol. 22b–d; Berliner, *Rom*, II, Pt. 2, pp. 58 ff. Cf. also Karl Kassel, "Zwei Schriftstücke zur Geschichte der Aerzte und Apotheker in Fürth," *MGWJ*, LXVI (1922), 233–35; Klauzner, *Wilno*, pp. 120 ff.; Chap. IX, n. 15; XI, n. 67; XIII, n. 17; XV, n. 21.

[46] Horwitz in *MGWJ*, LIV, 522; Moses Menz, *Responsa*, no. 73; Dubnow, *Pinkas*, nos. 37, 351, 362; Grunwald in *MGJV*, XI, 54 f.

[47] Judah Menz, *Responsa*, no. 1; Emden, *She'elat Ya'aviṣ*, no. 3 (fol. 7, 18); Isserlein, *Pesaḳim*, no. 162, quoted with approval by Karo on *Ṭur*, Ḥ. M. 12; Isserles and Sirkes on *Ṭur*, Y. D. 248; Finkelstein, *Self-Government*, pp. 318, 324 f. Some communities went out of their way to protect minors. The important Bologna ordinance of 1511, often referred to in these pages, was enacted for the immediate protection of orphaned Yeḥiel Nissim da Pisa against outside creditors. Cf. Sonne in *HUCA*, XVI, 82, 86 f., 94.

[48] *Reglement voor de Broedershap von het Weesjongenshuis . . . Aby Jetomim;* Hugo Barbeck, *Geschichte der Juden in Nürnberg und Fürth*, pp. 113 f. Cf. also M. Kaufmann, "Die erste israelitische Kleinkinder-Bewahranstalt in Europa errichtet im Jahre 1835 in Prag," *ZGJT*, I (1930–31), 247–52; and, in general, Max Grunwald, "Jüdische Waisenfürsorge in alter und neuer Zeit," *MGWJ*, LXVI (1922), 3–29.

[49] David Kaufmann in *Ḳobeṣ 'al yad*, XII–XIII, 9 f.; Berliner, *Rom*, II, Pt. 2, 57 f.; Vogelstein and Rieger, *Rom*, II, 314, 316; Dubnow, *Pinkas*, nos. 41, 93, 119, 128, 366. Zechariah of Porto's will, which subsequently became the subject of protracted controversy among the Italian rabbis, is remarkable not only because of the large amounts involved, but also because of their allocation to various communities. Of the 4,000 scudi devoted to the redemption of captives, 2,500 were to be administered by two elders of the community of Leghorn, and 1,500 by two elders in Venice. The legacy for Palestine was to be equally divided between the necessitous Jews of Jerusalem and of the rest of the country. The endowment to provide dowries of 50 scudi each for dowerless brides was to be distributed as follows: Rome and Venice were to receive 3,000 scudi each; Ferrara 2000; Mantua 1500; Ancona, Florence, Modena and Reggio 1000 each; Urbino, Rovigo, Pesaro, Senigallia, Padua, Verona, Siena, Pisa and Leghorn 500 each. This division seems roughly to have corresponded to the size of the respective communities in the middle of the seventeenth century. Cf. the text of the will and the codicil in Meldola's *Mayyim rabbim*, IV, 33, and the discussions thereon ibid., 34–42; Shabbetai Beer,

Be'er 'eshek, no. 108. Cf. also Bernstein in *HUCA*, VII, 499 f.; idem, "A Dispute among Italian Rabbis of 1663" (Hebrew), *Ha-Zofeh*, XIV (1930), 198–203. The community of Carpentras provided native dowerless brides with 15 écus, strangers with only 3 écus. That of Avignon in 1779 disbursed up to 100 écus for a bride. Cf. Mossé, *Avignon*, p. 170; Loeb in *Annuaire*, I, 235 f. Art. XXII. Few communities or associations, however, could emulate the example of the renowned confraternity of the Ponentine congregation in Venice which distributed among its beneficiaries sums ranging up to 300 gold ducats. But this was largely a mutual benefit association. Cf. Roth, *Venice*, pp. 157 f. Cf. also Samuel di Medina, *Responsa*, on Y. D. no. 162 (a Ferrara widow departing for Venice wishes to transfer with her the fund bequeathed by her deceased husband for the benefit of dowerless orphan girls and secretive poor; the community of Ferrara successfully objects); Chap. IX, nn. 16–17; XV, n. 21.

50 Maimonides, *Mishneh Torah*, Matenot 'aniyyim, VIII, 10; Jacob b. Asher, *Ṭur*, Y. D. 252 and the commentaries thereon; Colon, *Responsa*, Root 5; Lagumina, *Codice*, I, nos. 182, 193. Acting in accordance with these juridical postulates the community of Candia in 1533 disposed of some of its synagogue equipment for the ransom of captives. Cf. Sassoon, *Catalogue*, p. 364. Cf. also Shalom (S. W.) Baron's Hebrew essay, "A Contribution to the History of Palestine Relief and Ransom of Captives," *Sefer ha-Shanah li-Yehude Amerika* (*American Hebrew Year Book*), [VI], 5702 (1942), 168–80.

51 Cecil Roth, "The Jews in Malta," *Transactions of the Jewish Historical Society of England*, XII (1931), 187–251; Baer, *Spanien*, I, Pt. 1, no. 276; Pt. 2, nos. 362 n. 2, 366, 367, 376; I. Loeb, "Un convoi d'exilés d'Espagne à Marseille en 1492," *REJ*, IX (1884), 66–76. Cf. also Marx in *HUCA*, I, 609 f., 613, 620.

52 Colorni in *Riv. st. dir. it.*, XI, 70 f., 97; Meldola, *Mayyim rabbim*, II, 61–63; Dubnow, *Pinḳas*, nos. 452, 503, 505, 542, 989; Halperin, *Milluim*, no. 15; Roth, *Venice*, pp. 158 ff.

53 Seeligmann in *Livre d'hommage . . . Poznanski*, p. 150; Joseph Katz, *She'erit Yosef*, no. 72; Augustine, *Epistles*, no. 11, 7–9 in Migne's *Patrol. latina*, XXXIII, 427; Luria, *Yam shel Shelomoh*, on Giṭ., VI, no. 66; Azulai, *Ḥayyim sha'al*, I, 35; Mann, *Egypt*, I, 87 ff., 244; II, 316 f.; *Texts*, I, 136 ff., 348 ff., 366 ff.; Baron in *Essays on Maimonides*, pp. 244, 246 f.;

Baer, *Spanien*, I, Pt. 1, no. 246 and the note thereto; Emmanuel, *Salonique*, I, 223 ff.; Nehama, *Salonique*, III, 121 ff.

[54] Belon, *Observations*, fol. 195 (Grunebaum, *REJ*, XXVII, 134).

[54a] Dubnow, *Pinḳas*, nos. 460, 484–85, 516. Non-Jewish captives, too, were often ransomed by Jews. Such liberal-mindedness was by no means self-evident at that time. We know that, for instance, the Catholic Order of Redemption, since its foundation in the late twelfth century the main Christian agency for the ransom of captives, often refused to include Protestants in its acts of charity. A case is actually recorded in the eighteenth century when the North African pirates, upon the receipt of 3,000 pieces for three Frenchmen, were willing to throw a Lutheran captive into the bargain, but the Redemptionists refused to take him. Cf. Stanley Lane-Poole and J. D. Jerrold Kelley, *The Story of the Barbary Corsairs*, p. 255. It is difficult to say, however, whether the individual Jewish efforts in behalf of Christian captives were made in fulfillment of the rabbinic commandment to dispense charity also to Gentiles "for the sake of peace," or in expectation of a reward. In at least one case mentioned in the sources (a Jew of Murcia ransoming two Christian captives of Almeria in 1490) the redeemer complained that he did not get back the ransom money. Cf. Baer, *Spanien*, I, Pt. 2, no. 387 (p. 424). The matter is less clear in the case of the Jew who, according to the testimony given in 1593 before Joel Sirkes, lost his life trying to ransom Polish nobles; cf. Sirkes's *Responsa*, O.S., no. 77. Such far-flung activities often required the services of professional agents. Meir of Lublin mentions in his *Responsa* (no. 89) a Jew who frequently traveled between Poland and Turkey in the regular business of ransoming captives. Cf. also Katz, *Le-Ḳorot*, pp. 43 ff.; Chap. VIII, nn. 19–20.

[55] Cf. I. Loeb, "Le nombre des Juifs de Castille et d'Espagne au moyen-âge," *REJ*, XIV (1887), 161–83.

[56] Buber, *Anshe shem*, pp. 222 ff.; Lewin in *JJLG*, III, 88 f., no. 14; Assaf, *Ha-'Oneshin*, no. 136a; Adler, *London*, pp. 151 ff.; Meir of Lublin, *Responsa*, nos. 15, 120; Bacharach, *Ḥavvot ya'ir*, nos. 139, 141; Katz, *Le-Ḳorot*, p. 14 no. 12; Colon, *Responsa*, Root 7; Balaban, *Żydzi lwowscy*, p. 506 App. no. 40; Heinrich von Boos, *Geschichte der rheinischen Städtekultur*, I, 28 no. 871; Lagumina, *Codice*, II, Pt. 1, no. 562. For a remarkable instance of diplomatic intervention in behalf of Jewish prisoners, cf. the 1554 correspondence between Suleyman the Magnificent and Pope Pius IV

published by Paul Grunebaum in "Une episode de l'histoire des Juifs d'Ancone," *REJ*, XXVIII (1894), 142–46. Jewish prisoners in state penitentiaries, moreover, often obtained communal aid in the satisfaction of religious needs such as ritual food and Sabbath rest. Cf. e. g. Baer, *Kleve*, p. 116; Vogelstein and Rieger, *Rom*, II, 316.

[57] Israel Bruna, *Responsa*, no. 77; Margolies, *Dubno*, pp. 149 f., 166 f.; H. J. Zimmels, "Erez Israel in der Responsenliteratur des späteren Mittelalters," *MGWJ*, LXXIV (1930), 44–64; Baer, *Spanien*, I, Pt. 1, no. 216; Pt. 2, no. 388 n. 1; Samuel di Medina, *Responsa*, on Y. D. no. 93; Lagumina, *Codice*, I, no. 432; II, Pt. 1, nos. 693, 709. Cf. also Isaac Ben-Zevi's recent edition of Moses Bassola's *Masa'ot Ereṣ Yisrael* (Pilgrimage to Palestine, 1521 C.E.) with the additional remarks thereon by N. Shalem, A. J. Braver and D. Benveniste in the *Bulletin of the Jewish Palestine Exploration Society*, VI (1939), 86–95, 100–1, 115–23 and by B. Lewis in the *Bulletin of the School of Oriental Studies* (University of London), X (1939), 179–84; Ursula Schwerin, *Die Aufrufe der Päpste zur Befreiung des Heiligen Landes von den Anfängen bis zum Ausgang Innozenz IV*.

[58] C. Roth, "An English Account of the Jews of Jerusalem in the Seventeenth Century," *Miscellanies of the Jewish Historical Society of England*, II (1935), 99–104.

[59] Roth in *JQR*, XV, 440 n. 25; idem, *Venice*, pp. 166 f.; Dubnow, *Pinkas*, nos. 53, 286, 348, 456–57, 462, 492, 523, 814; Wolf, *Statuten*, pp. 5 f.; Munk in *MGWJ*, XLI, 519. Cf. also Mann, *Egypt*, I, 162, 165; J. L. Fishman, "The First German Scholars in Palestine, I" (Hebrew), *Mizraḥ u-ma'arab*, II (1928–29), 50–57; Rosanes, *Togarma*, I, 43; IV, 144, 301, 304, 499; Sassoon in *JQR*, XVII, 449 f.; Levy, *Bosnien*, pp. 23 f.; De Maulde, *Etats français*, pp. 160 f.; Loeb in *Annuaire*, I, 236 Art. XXIII; Colorni in *Riv. st. dir. it.*, XI, 121 n. 3; Da Fano, *Responsa*, no. 103; Vogelstein and Rieger, *Rom*, II, 315, 317; Lewinsky in *Rivista israelitica*, VI, 56 ff. (reproducing a fantastic contemporary account of a messianic movement in Ferrara in 1721); Elija S. Artom, "La 'alijjàh d'un Ebreo modenese nel secolo XVIII," *Israel*, XI (1936–37), 44–49, with reference to letters by Abraham Ishmael Ḥayyim Sanguinetti published by J. Mann in *Tarbiz*, VII (1935–36), 74 ff.; Wettstein in *Gedenkbuch D. Kaufmann*, pp. 78 f. (a Nikolsburg Jew advances 600 florins to two Jews of Cracow who promise to send to him in Palestine his share in the profits); Buber, *Anshe Shem*, pp. xii f.; Balaban, *Żydzi lwowscy*, pp. 349 f.; Tsherikover in

Yivo Studies in History, II, 577 f.; Zarchin in *JQR*, XXIX, 262 f.; Auerbach, *Halberstadt*, p. 129; Lewinsky in *Ha-Eshkol* VI, 240 Art. 21 (Hildesheim, 1706); Katz, *Le-Ḳorot*, pp. 30 n. 3, 57 f.; De Castro, *Synagoge*, p. xxxi Art. 37; Barnett, *El libro*, p. 9 Art. 24.

It was natural for people to be particularly liberal in their offerings for Palestine in periods of great messianic excitation. Cf. e. g., David Kaufmann, "Don Joseph Nassi, Founder of Colonies in the Holy Land, and the Community of Cori in the Campagna," *JQR*, O.S. II (1889–90), 291–97, 305–10 (the whole community is ready to depart for Tiberias in 1564–65 and dispatches two delegates to collect money for that purpose). Another characteristic example is recorded by Samuel b. David in his *Naḥlat shibe'a*, II, 81. At the height of Shabbetian frenzy in 1666, even a German rabbi yielded to the blandishments of a Jerusalem messenger and vowed to pay 2 thalers annually for the rest of his life, an amount far in excess of his means. When calmer counsel prevailed, he retracted this pledge with the assistance of a messenger from Safed, obviously a rival of the former Shabbetian envoy. Pious vows for the Holy Land on the occasion of severe illness were also very frequent. Joseph of Trani once absolved guardians of a dying orphan for such a substantial offering, which had subsequently been attacked by the orphan's heirs. Cf. his *Responsa*, no. 127. There were, on the other hand, communities which, to preserve the local resources, limited the right of members to send contributions abroad. An Italian community which had fixed the maximum at 7 scudi sought to apply the ordinance to resident aliens (1704). Cf. the correspondence between Moses Ḥağis and Samson Morpurgo in the latter's *Shemesh ṣedaḳah*, I, Pt. 2, no. 19.

[60] Lieben in *JJLG*, XIX, 29 ff.

[61] Azulai, *Ma'agal ṭob ha-shalem*; E. Ginsburger in *REJ*, N.S. IV, 58 f.; Dubnow, *Pinḳas*, nos. 558–59; David Kaufmann, "Letters Referring to the History of Palestine" (Hebrew), *Yerushalayim*, III (1889), 110. Opposition to the wasteful system of dispatching messengers was voiced even earlier by the community of Corfù in its letter to the leaders of Jerusalem written in 1628 published by Baron in his aforementioned essay in the *Sefer ha-Shanah li-Yehude Amerika*. For Palestinian messengers intervening in legal controversies of Diaspora communities, cf. e. g. Shabbetai Beer's *Be'er 'esheḳ* (some responsa, including that cited above n. 49, are signed by the author as "the Jerusalem messenger and represen-

tative of Safed and Hebron"); Meldola's *Mayyim rabbim*, I, 41–42; II, 62 (David Melammed and Israel Cohen of Hebron, 1718, 1725), II, 34–55 (Raphael Israel Kimḥi of Safed, 1730); II, 61; III, 10 (Jacob Vilna of Jerusalem, 1725). Sometimes intervention in local affairs was forced upon the messengers against their will and good judgment. Cf. Azulai's description of how he was forced, after long resistance, to take drastic action against several Bordeaux *shoḥetim*, in his *Itinerary*, I, 35 ff. Cf., however, also ibid., p. 63 (Azulai speaks rather deprecatingly of the scholarship of most of his fellow messengers), 87 f. (about his conflict with the messenger from Safed), 89 (in 1777 he disqualifies, on his own initiative, the *shoḥet* in Gradisca).

62 At present cf. especially A. M. Luncz, "*Ḥalukkah*, Its Origins, History and Ramifications" (Hebrew), *Yerushalayim*, VII (1906), 25–40, 181–201; [O.] Eberhard, "Chalukah und Chalukareform," *Mitteilungen und Nachrichten des deutschen Palästina-Vereins*, XIV (1908), 17–29; Eliezer Rivlin, "The Statute of the *Ḥalukkah* of the Perushim District in Palestine of 1823" (Hebrew), *Ṣiyyon*, II (1926–27), 149–70; I. Sonne, "An Appeal from Reggio for the Support of the Jerusalem Talmudic Academy (1698)" (Hebrew), *Zion*, IV (1938–39), 86–88; David de Sola Pool, "Early Relations between Palestine and American Jewry," *Brandeis Avukah Annual* of 1932, pp. 536–48; Frumkin and Rivlin, *Toledot*; Samuel Klein, *Toledot ha-yishub ha-yehudi be-Ereṣ Israel* (A History of the Jewish Settlement in Palestine from the Conclusion of the Talmud to the Modern Colonization Movement), and other literature cited in Baron's *History*, III, 167 f. n. 17.

63 Abrahams, *Wills*, II, 192; Finkelstein, *Self-Government*, pp. 48, 91, 177, 185 f., 230, 247, 264, 358; Meir of Rothenburg, *Responsa*, ed. Prague, no. 74; Jacob b. Asher, *Ṭur*, Y. D. 248–51 and the commentaries thereon; *Tosafot* on Ket. 49b and B. B. 8b; Colon, *Responsa*, Root 128; *Takkanot Amsterdam*, Art. 18, 19, 61.

64 Grunwald in *MGJV*, XI, 29, 45 ff.

65 Marcus, *Medieval World*, pp. 218 f.; Wachstein in *ZGJD*, IV, 136.

66 Emmanuel, *Salonique*, I, 222 f. Abraham Maimuni, asked about the validity of a will bequeathing the deceased person's entire property to charity and completely disinheriting the children, answered bluntly, "The will stands, and the children receive nothing." Cf. his *Responsa*, no. 50

[67] Berliner, *Rom*, II, Pt. 2, p. 56; Vogelstein and Rieger, *Rom*, II, 335 ff. Cf. also Mossé, *Avignon*, pp. 149 f.; Dubnow, *Pinkas*, nos. 88, 482, 723; Halperin, *Milluim*, no. 27. In their communication to the community of Pesaro in 1696 the Roman elders complained with some exaggeration that they had but ten well-to-do families in a sea of 6,000 "barefooted and ragged paupers." Cf. Berliner in *Ḳobeṣ 'al yad*, XIX, 68 ff. The picture presented by a list of "protected" Jews in the young and prosperous community of Altona where only four Jews appear as public charges in 1664 was exceptional. Cf. E. Dukesz in *Jahrbuch für die jüdischen Gemeinden Schleswig-Holsteins*, I, 131 ff.

The ideas underlying the operation of communal and sub-communal Jewish charities in medieval and early modern times, and the details of their functioning and effects have never been examined with sufficient care. Source material is available in abundance in legal, homiletical and ethical documents as well as in communal records. The small community of Tobischau in Moravia, for one example, possesses in its archives a complete ledger of all entries of its *ṣedaḳah* for the years 1645–95. Cf. Flesch in *JGJC*, III (1931), 257 ff. For illuminating parallels rather than for rather dubious examples of reciprocal influences, studies of the general history of public welfare would also be used. Such an analysis would doubtless open new vistas on a major motivating force in Jewish communal survival.

[68] Jacob b. Asher, *Ṭur*, Y. D. 245, 257, and the commentaries thereon; Israel Bruna, *Responsa*, no. 276; Emperor Julian's *Epistles*, ed. by Bidez, no. 84 (I, Pt. 2, 430d; ed. by Wright, III, no. 22); Kohler in *Festschrift . . . Berliner*, p. 202; Lancelot Addison, *The Present State of the Jews (more particularly relating to those in Barbary)*, 3d ed., p. 212; Daly, *Settlement*, p. 9 n. 5; Samuel Oppenheim in *PAJHS*, VIII (1909), 4, 22, 50, 52; David M. Schneider, *The History of Public Welfare in New York State 1609–1866*, pp. 12 f.

[69] Mordecai on B. B. no. 488; Selma Stern, *Der preussische Staat*, I, Pt. 1, pp. 111 f.; Pt. 2, no. 323. Fränkel's action was, nevertheless, condemned by the authorities and he was forced to pay a fine of 25 thalers. Ibid., Pt. 1, p. 112 n. 1.

The manifold aspects of charity in both theory and practice often engaged the attention of jurists and moralists, and became the subject of an extensive specialized literature. The renowned preacher, Elijah b.

Solomon Abraham ha-Kohen of Smyrna, produced one of the bulkiest treatises on charity in any language, in his *Me'il ṣedaḳah* (The Mantle of Benevolence), first published in Smyrna in 1731. Its contents have recently been summarized by Abraham Cronbach in a series of three essays in *HUCA*, XI (1936), 503–67; XII–XIII (1937–38), 635–96; XIV (1939), 479–557.

Beginning with the eighteenth century, Jewish mendicancy and general problems of Jewish relief attracted more widespread attention in the outside world. There began to appear pamphlets, like Joseph Isaac's *Unmassgäbliche Gedanken über Betteljuden* (translated from Yiddish) and Christoph Voll's *Von dem Armenrechte der Juden an dem Kaiserlichen Reichskammergerichte*, which were published in Nuremberg, 1791 and Wetzlar 1787, respectively.

NOTES TO CHAPTER XVII

CRUCIBLE OF CAPITALISM AND ENLIGHTENMENT

[1] Cf. especially Helena Hekker, "Reform Projects of Jewish Life in Poland at the End of the Eighteenth Century" (Russian), *Evreiskaya Starina*, VII (1914), 206–18, 328–40; N. M. Gelber, "Die Juden und die Judenreform auf dem polnischen vierjährigen Sejm (1788–1792)," *Festschrift . . . Simon Dubnow*, pp. 136–53.

[2] An analysis of the respective laws may most conveniently be found in Stöger's *Darstellung der gesetzlichen Verfassung der galizischen Judenschaft*; Ludwig von Rönne and Heinrich Simon's, *Die früheren und gegenwärtigen Verhältnisse der Juden in den sämmtlichen Landesteilen des Preussischen Staates*; Count Nicholas Golitsyn's *Istoria ruskavo zakonodatelstva o Evreiach* (A History of Russian Legislation concerning Jews), I (covering the period of 1649 to 1825). Despite the respective biases of these authors and their frequently antiquated data, these works may still be used with great profit today. Cf. in general also Majer Balaban, *Dzieje Żydów w Galicyi* (A History of the Jews in Galicia and the Republic of Cracow, 1772–1868); S. M. Dubnow, *History of the Jews in Russia and Poland*, I, 309 ff.; and Levitats's forthcoming study mentioned above Chap. I, n. 6.

[3] Werner Sombart, *The Jews and Modern Capitalism*, p. 49. A fuller, though as yet far from adequate analysis of this significant chapter in modern history is to be found in Felix Priebatsch's "Die Judenpolitik des fürstlichen Absolutismus im 17. und 18. Jahrhundert," *Festschrift Dietrich Schaefer*, pp. 564–657. Hans Peter Deeg's *Hofjuden*, ed. by Julius Streicher, is, like other works promoted by this notorious Jew-baiter, of but pseudo-scientific value.

[4] I. Freund, *Die Emanzipation der Juden in Preussen*, II, 52 f. Characteristic is also the instruction given, as far back as 1709, to the court-Jew Marcus Magnus upon his appointment as *Oberältester* of Berlin Jewry. He was directed "to attend the meetings of the Jewish elders in the name of His Majesty, faithfully and diligently to safeguard His best interests and utility and to prevent His harm or damage, to adhere firmly to the ordinances hitherto proclaimed or yet to be proclaimed . . . ." Cf. Selma Stern, *Der preussische Staat*, I, Pt. 2, no. 305. Cf. also in general ibid., Pt. 1, pp. 102 ff.

[5] The complex problems of the history of Jewish Enlightenment have been briefly discussed by the present author in his *Social and Religious History of the Jews*, II, 205 ff. Cf. also the literature listed ibid., III, 138 ff. The semi-conscious political alliance between *Haskalah* and governments has been demonstrated, perhaps with a little overemphasis on this single factor, on the example of Galician Jewry by R. Mahler in his essay on "The Austrian Government and the Hasidim during the Period of Reaction (1818–1848)," *Jewish Social Studies*, I (1939), 195–240; and his recent volume on *Der Kamf tsvishn haskole un khsides in Galitsie* (The Struggle between Haskalah and Hasidism in Galicia in the First Half of the 19th Century). This ramified subject would still merit further comprehensive treatment.

[6] There is a vast, though as yet far from satisfactory, literature dealing with various aspects of the Jewish part in the rise of modern capitalism. Some of it, especially as it accumulated since the publication of Sombart's aforementioned much-debated work, has been listed by the present author in his *History*, III, 132 ff.; and his *Bibliography of Jewish Social Studies, 1938–1939*, pp. 146 ff., 244. The converse problem, however, of the effects of modern capitalism upon the Jews and their communal life, more directly relevant to our present investigation, has not yet been subjected to the much-needed searching and comprehensive analysis. A few brief remarks

will be found in the present author's forthcoming essay on "Modern Capitalism and Jewish Fate," which is to appear soon in the *Menorah Journal.*

[7] *Letters of Certain Jews to Monsieur Voltaire*, Engl. transl., pp. 37 f.

[8] Cf. above Chap. VII. It is hoped that these fascinating developments will be dealt with extensively in the present writer's work on the modern Jewish community, now in the early stages of preparation.

BIBLIOGRAPHY

BIBLIOGRAPHY

ABEL, FELIX MARIE, Géographie de la Palestine. 2 vols., Paris, 1933–38.

אבות דרבי נתן (Abot de-Rabbi Nathan). Ed. with an Introduction, Notes and Indices by Solomon Schechter. Vienna, 1887.

ABOUT, EDMOND, Rome contemporaine. Paris, 1861. Excerpted in English transl. in the *New York World* of Nov. 24, 1860 and reprinted therefrom in the *Occident*, XVIII (1860–61), 223–24.

ABRAHAM B. ELIEZER HA-KOHEN, ס' אורי וישעי (Ethical Treatise). Berlin, 1704.

ABRAHAM B. JOSEPH HA-LEVI, ס' עין משפט (Responsa). With a Foreword by J. Kubo and David Pisano. Salonica, 1896.

ABRAHAMS, B. LIONEL, The Expulsion of the Jews from England in 1290. London, 1895. Reprinted from *JQR*, O. S. VII (1894), 75–100, 236–58, 428–58.

ABRAHAMS, EDMUND H., "Some Notes on the Early History of the Sheftalls of Georgia." *PAJHS*, XVII (1909), 167–86.

ABRAHAMS, ISRAEL, "Samuel Portaleone's Proposed Restrictions on Games of Chance." *JQR*, O. S. V (1892–93), 505–15.

———, The Book of Delight and Other Papers. Philadelphia, 1912.

———, Jewish Life in the Middle Ages. 2d ed., Enlarged and Revised on the Basis of the Author's Material by Cecil Roth. London, 1932.

———, ed., Hebrew Ethical Wills. (Hebrew text with English transl.). 2 vols., Philadelphia, 1926. "Schiff Library of Jewish Classics."

———, H. P. Stokes and Herbert Loewe, eds., Starrs and Jewish Charters Preserved in the British Museum. 3 vols., Cambridge, 1930–32.

Abravanel, Don Isaac, ס' מעיני הישועה (Commentary on Daniel). Stettin, 1860.

Abu Yussuf, Yakub ibn Ibrahim, Kitab al-Kharaj (Le livre d'impôt foncière). French translation by E. Fagnan. Paris, 1921.

Ackermann, A., "Der synagogale Gesang in seiner historischen Entwickelung." *In* Jakob Winter and August Wünsche, Die jüdische Litteratur seit Abschluss des Kanons. 3 vols., Trier, 1894–96, III, 477–529.

Adamson, J. W., "Education." *In* Legacy of the Middle Ages, ed. by C. G. Crump and E. F. Jacob, Oxford, 1926, pp. 255–85.

Addison, Lancelot, The Present State of the Jews (more particularly relating to those in Barbary). 3d ed., London, 1682.

Adler, Elkan Nathan, "The Installation of an Egyptian Nagid." *JQR*, O. S. IX (1896–97), 717–20.

———, "Provençal and Catalonian Responsa." *JQR*, O. S. XII (1900), 143–49.

———, Auto de Fé and Jew. London, 1908.

———, Catalogue of Hebrew Manuscripts in the Collection of Elkan Nathan Adler. Cambridge, 1921.

———, [History of the Jews in] London. Philadelphia, 1930. "Jewish Communities Series."

———, ed., Jewish Travellers. With an Introduction. New York, 1931.

Adler, Georg, "Das grosspolnische Fleischergewerbe vor 300 Jahren." *Zeitschrift der historischen Gesellschaft für die Provinz Posen*, IX (1894), 209–372.

Adler, Michael, "Aaron of York." *Transactions of the Jewish Historical Society of England*, XIII (1936), 113–55.

———, Jews of Medieval England. London, 1939.

Adler, Salomon, "Die Entwicklung des Schulwesens der Juden zu Frankfurt a/M. bis zur Emanzipation." *JJLG*, XVIII (1927), 143–73; XIX (1928), 237–78.

Adler, Simon, "Das älteste Judicial-Protokoll des jüdischen Gemeindearchivs in Prag (1682)." *JGJC*, II (1931), 217–56.

———, "Das Judenpatent von 1797." *JGJC*, V (1933), 199–229.

Adribi, Isaac b. Samuel, ס' דברי ריבות (Responsa). Sudzilków, 1833.

Aegyptische Urkunden aus den königlichen Museen zu Berlin. Griechische Urkunden. Vols. I–IX, Berlin, 1895–1937. Usually abbreviated as B. G. U.

Affonso V (Portuguese king), Ordenaçoens do Senhor Rey D. Affonso V. 5 vols., Coimbra, 1792. Colleçaõ da legislaçaõ antiga e moderna do Reino de Portugal. Parte I: Da legislaçaõ antiga.

Agobard of Lyons (Archbishop), Opera Omnia. *In* Migne's Patrologia latina, Vol. CIV.

Aḥimaaz b. Palṭiel of Oria, ספר יוחסין (The Chronicle of Aḥimaaz). Edited and transl. into English by Marcus Salzman, New York, 1924.

Aigrefeuille, Charles d', Histoire de la ville de Montpellier depuis son origine, avec un abrégé historique de tout ce qui précéda son établissement, à laquelle on a ajouté l'histoire des jurisdictions anciennes et modernes de cette ville avec les statuts qui lui sont propres. 2 pts., Montpellier, 1737–39.

Albright, William F., The Archaeology of Palestine and the Bible. 3d. ed., New York, 1935.

Alfasi, Isaac b. Jacob, ס' הלכות (Halakic Commentary on the Talmud). Printed with the Wilno and other Talmud editions.

———, ס' שאלות ותשובות (Responsa). Leghorn, 1781.

Allgemeine Zeitung des Judentums, IV (1840), 180–81 (local correspondence).

Allon, Gedaliah, "Studies in Philonic Halakah" (Hebrew). *Tarbiz*, V (1933–34), 28–36, 241–46; VI (1934–35), 30–37, 230–33.

Altmann, Berthold, Die Juden im ehemaligen Hochstift Paderborn zur Zeit des 17. and 18. Jahrhunderts. Diss. in typescript. Freiburg i. B., 1924.

———, "Studies in Medieval German Jewish History." *Proceedings of the American Academy for Jewish Research*, X (1940), 5–98.

———, "The Autonomous Federation of Jewish Communities in Paderborn." *Jewish Social Studies*, III (1941), 159–88.

ALTMANN, WILHELM, Die Urkunden Kaiser Siegmunds (1410–1437). 2 vols., Innsbruck, 1896–1900.

"Die Altonaer Synagogen." *Jahrbuch für die jüdischen Gemeinden Schleswig-Holsteins*, VI (1934–35), 30–36.

AMARI, MICHELE, Storia dei Musulmani di Sicilia. 2d ed. revised by the Author and ed. by Carlo Alfonso Nallino. Vols. I–III, Pt. 1. Catania, 1933–37.

AMBROSE, ST. (Ambrosius of Milan), Opera omnia. *In* Migne's Patrologia latina, Vols. XIV–XVII.

———, Select Works and Letters, English translation. New York, 1896. *In* A Select Library of Nicene and Post-Nicene Fathers, Vol. X.

AMEDROZ, H. F., "Tales of Official Life from the 'Tadhkira' of Ibn Hamdun." *Journal of the Royal Asiatic Society*, 1908, pp. 409–70.

AMRAM GAON, סדר ר' עמרם גאון (Liturgy). Ed. by Aryeh Leb Frumkin. 2 vols., Jerusalem, 1912.

AMULO OF LYONS (Archbishop), Contra Judaeos. *In* Migne's Patrologia latina, Vol. CXVI.

ANAV, ZEDEKIAH B. ABRAHAM, ס' שבלי הלקט (Ritualistic Code). Ed. by Salomon Buber. Wilno, 1886.

ANCHEL, ROBERT, Napoléon et les Juifs. Paris, 1928.

———, "Les Juifs à Paris au XVIIIe siècle." *Bulletin de la Société de l'histoire de Paris*, LIX (1932), 9–23.

ANDRÉADÈS, M. A., "Les Juifs et le fisc dans l'empire byzantin." *Mélanges Charles Diehl. Études sur l'art et l'histoire de Byzance.* 2 vols., Paris, 1930, I, 7–29.

ANFOSSI, M. D., Gli Ebrei in Piemonte. Loro condizioni giuridico-sociali dal 1430 all' emancipazione. Turin, 1914.

ANKAVA, ABRAHAM B. MORDECAI, ed., ס' כרם חמר (A Juridical Collection). 2 vols., Leghorn, 1869–71.

APFELBAUM, ABBA, "A Venetian Ordinance of 1636" (Hebrew). *Ha-Zofeh*, XII (1928), 268–70.

APTOWITZER, VICTOR *or* AVIGDOR, "Formularies of Decrees and Documents from a Geonic Court." *JQR*, IV (1913–14), 23–51.

———, "Seder Elia," *Jewish Studies in Memory of George A. Kohut*, New York, 1935, pp. 5–39.

Aptowitzer, Victor *or* Avigdor, מבוא לספר ראבי"ה (Introduction to the Book of Rabiah by Eliezer ben Joel ha-Levi). Jerusalem, 1938.
Cf. also Eliezer b. Joel.

Arama, Isaac b. Moses, ס' עקדת יצחק (An Ethical Treatise). Lwów, 1868.

Aristotle, Politics. Ed. by Fr. Susemihl. Leipzig, 1894. Bibliotheca scriptorum graecorum et romanorum Teubneriana.

———, Politics, English transl. by Benjamin Jowett. *In* The Works of Aristotle translated into English under the editorship of W. D. Ross. Vol. X, Oxford, 1921.

Aron, Maurice, "Liquidation des dettes de l'ancienne communauté juive de Metz." *Annuaire de la Société des études juives*, II (1883), 109–35.

Aronius, Julius, Regesten zur Geschichte der Juden im fränkischen und deutschen Reiche bis zum Jahre 1273 . . . . Bearbeitet unter Mitwirkung von A. Dresdner und L. Lewinski. Berlin, 1887–1902.

Aronstein, Fritz, "Eine jüdische Novelle von Grimmelshausen." *ZGJD*, V (1934), 237–41.

Artom, Elija S., "Notizie sugli Ebrei a Rimini e nelle Marche." *Miscellanea di studi ebraici . . . H. P. Chajes*, Florence, 1930, pp. 1–9.

———, "La 'alijjàh d'un Ebreo modenese nel secolo XVIII." *Israel*, XI (1936–37), 44–49.
Cf. also Mann, Jacob.

Aryeh b. yehudah Löw b. Hirz, *see* Elijah b. Moses Gershon.

Asher b. Yeḥiel, ס' הלכות (Halakot, a Juristic Commentary on the Talmud). Printed with many editions of the Babylonian Talmud.

———, ס' שאלות ותשובות (Responsa). Venice, 1607–8.

Ashkenazi, Bezaleel b. Abraham, ס' שאלות ותשובות (Responsa). Venice, 1595.

Ashkenazi, Eliezer, .ed., ס' טעם זקנים (A Collection of Manuscript Sources). Frankfort, 1854.

Asiaticus, Johannes, *see* Nau, François.

Assaf, Simḥa, "The People of the Book and the Book" (Hebrew). *Reshumot*, I (1918), 292–316.

Assaf, Simḥa, העונשין אחרי חתימת התלמוד (Criminal Jurisdiction since the Conclusion of the Talmud). Jerusalem, 1922.

———, "Three Responsa by Sherira and Hai" (Hebrew). *Ginze Ḳedem*, I (1922), 73–80.

———, בתי הדין וסדריהם אחרי חתימת התלמוד (The Organization of the Jewish Courts after the Conclusion of the Talmud). Jerusalem, 1924.

———, מקורות לתולדות החנוך בישראל (Sources for the History of Jewish Education; from the Beginning of the Middle Ages to the Haskalah Period). 3 vols., Tel-Aviv, 1925–36.

———, "Differing Ordinances and Customs in Regard to the Husband's Inheritance of his Wife's Estate" (Hebrew). *Madda'e ha-yahadut*, I (1926), 79–94.

———, "Palestine in the Responsa of the Babylonian Geonim" (Hebrew). *Ṣiyyon*, I (1926), 21–30.

———, "Studies in the History of the Rabbinate in Germany, Poland and Lithuania" (Hebrew). *Reshumot*, II (2d impression 1927), 259–300.

———, תשובות הגאונים מתוך הגניזה (Geonic Responsa from the Genizah). Jerusalem, 1929.

———, "Letters of R. Samuel b. 'Ali and his Contemporaries" (Hebrew). *Tarbiz*, I (1929–30), Pt. 1, pp. 102–30; Pt. 2, pp. 43–84; Pt. 3, pp. 15–80.

———, "Documents of 1620–30" (Hebrew). *Reshumot*, VI (1930), 454–58.

———, "Portions of a Benediction for the Exilarch Ḥisdai b. David" (Hebrew). *Ginze Ḳedem*, IV (1930), 63–64.

———, "Geonim." *Encyclopaedia Judaica*, VII, 271–83.

———, "Jewish Executioners. A Contribution to the History of the Jews in Candia" (Hebrew). *Tarbiz*, V (1933–34), 224–26.

———, "Contributions to the Lives of the *Negidim* Jonathan and Isaac Sholal" (Hebrew). *Zion*, II (1936–37), 121–24.

———, "Responsa of R. Azriel Dayyena" (Hebrew). *Kirjath Sepher*, XIV (1937–38), 540–52; XV (1938–39), 113–29. With additional notes by S. H. Kook, I. Sonne and the author, ibid., XV, 136, 264–68, 389.

Assaf, Simḥa, "Letters of Babylonian Geonim" (Hebrew). *Tarbiz*, XI (1939–40), 146–59.
Cf. also Capsali, Moses.

Auerbach, B. H., Geschichte der israelitischen Gemeinde Halberstadt. Halberstadt, 1886.

Auerbach, Moses, "Der Streit zwischen Saadja Gaon und dem Exilarchen Dawid ben Sakkai." *Jüdische Studien Josef Wohlgemuth . . . gewidmet*, Berlin, 1928, pp. 1–30.

Auerbach, Selig, Die rheinischen Rabbinerversammlungen im 13. Jahrhundert. Würzburg, 1932.

Augustine (Augustinus Aurelius) of Hippo, St., Opera omnia. *In* Migne's Patrologia latina, XXXII–XLVII.

———, Works. Engl. transl. by Marcus Dodd. Vols. I–XIV. Edinburgh, 1872–76.

Azémard, Emile, Étude sur les Israélites de Montpellier au moyen-âge. Nîmes, 1924. Diss. Montpellier.

Azulai *or* Asulai, Ḥayyim Joseph David, ס' טוב עין (A Juridical Treatise). Leghorn, 1798.

———, ס' חיים שאל (Responsa). 2 vols., Tarnów, 1886.

———, ס' מעגל טוב השלם (Itinerary 1753–1794). Ed. by Aron Freimann. Jerusalem, 1934.

Baas, K., "Jüdische Hospitäler im Mittelalter." *MGWJ*, LVII (1913), 452–60.

Bacharach, Ḥayyim Ya'ir b. Samson, ס' חוות יאיר (Responsa). Frankfort, 1699. Includes כללי עץ חיים.

Bacher, Wilhelm, "Das altjüdische Schulwesen," *Jahrbuch für jüdische Geschichte und Literatur*, VI (1903), 48–81.

———, "Exilarch." *Jewish Encyclopedia*, V, 288–93.

———, "Gaon." *Jewish Encyclopedia*, V, 567–72.

Bachi, Roberto, "La demografia del Ebraismo italiano prima dell' emancipazione." *Israel*, XII (1938), 256–320.

Baeck, Leo, Wege im Judentum: Aufsätze und Reden. Berlin, 1933.

Baer, Fritz *or* I. *or* Yitzhak, Studien zur Geschichte der Juden im Königreich Aragonien während des 13. und 14. Jahrhunderts. Berlin, 1913. *In* Historische Studien, Heft 106.

Baer, Fritz *or* I. *or* Yitzhak, "Gemeinde und Landjudenschaft." *Korrespondenzblatt des Vereins zur Gründung . . . einer Akademie für die Wissenschaft des Judentums*, II (1921), 16–29.

———, Das Protokollbuch der Landjudenschaft des Herzogtums Kleve. Vol. I: Die Geschichte der Landjudenschaft. Berlin, 1922.

———, "Recent Books and Sources for the History of the Jews in Spain" (Hebrew). *Debir*, II (1923), 310–21.

———, "Zur Geschichte der Juden im christlichen Spanien." *MGWJ*, LXIX (1925), 54–61. A review of A. Rubio y Lluch's Documents per l'historia de la cultura catalana migeval and of Manuel Serrano y Sanz's Origenes de la dominacion española, I, Madrid, 1918.

———, "Review of L. Finkelstein's Jewish Self-Government in the Middle Ages." *MGWJ*, LXXI (1927), 392–97; supplemented by his "Nachwort zu dem Aufsatz von Finkelstein 'Zu den Takkanot des Rabbenu Gerschom.' " Ibid., LXXIV (1930), 31–34.

———, "Der Ursprung der Chewra." *Jüdische Wohlwartspflege und Sozialwissenschaft*, I (1928), 241–47.

———, Die Juden im christlichen Spanien. Erster Teil: Urkunden und Regesten. Vols. I–II, Berlin, 1929–36.

———, "Crescas, Hasdai." *Encyclopaedia Judaica*, V, 696–98.

———, "Don Isaac Abravanel and his Relation to Problems of History and Politics" (Hebrew). *Tarbiz*, VIII (1936–37), 241–59.

Baerwald, [H.], Der alte Friedhof der israelitischen Gemeinde zu Frankfurt am-Main. Frankfort, 1883.

Baillet, Auguste, Oeuvres diverses. 2 vols. Paris, 1905.

Balaban, Majer, Żydzi lwowscy na przełomie XVIgo i XVIIgo wieku (The Jews of Lwów about 1600 C. E.). Lwów, 1906.

———, Skizzen und Studien zur Geschichte der Juden in Polen. Berlin, 1911.

———, "The Jewish Communal Structure in Poland in the 16th–18th Centuries" (Polish). *Kwartalnik poświęcony badaniu przeszłości Żydów w Polsce*, I, Pt. 2 (1912), 17–54.

Balaban, Majer, "Jewish Physicians in Cracow and the Ghetto Tragedies (15th–17th Centuries)" (Russian). *Evreiskaya Starina*, V (1912), 38–53.

———, Dzieje Żydów w Krakowie i na Kazimierzu 1304–1868 (History of the Jews in Cracow). Vol. I (1304–1655), Cracow, 1913. A revised edition and Vol. II appeared in 1936, but were not accessible in New York.

———, "Die Krakauer Judengemeinde-Ordnung von 1595 und ihre Nachträge." *JJLG*, X (1913), 296–360; XI (1916), 88–114.

———, Dzieje Żydów w Galicyi i w Rzeczpospolitej Krakowskiej 1772–1868 (A History of the Jews in Galicia and the Republic of Cracow, 1772–1868). Lwów, [1914].

———, Z historyi Żydów w Polsce (Sketches and Studies in the History of the Jews in Poland). Warsaw, 1920.

———, "Vierländersynode." *Jüdisches Lexikon*, V, 1213–17.

———, "Zur Geschichte der hebräischen Druckereien in Polen." *Soncino-Blätter*, III, Pt. 1 (1929), 1–50.

———, Zabytki historyczne Żydów w Polsce (Historical Remains of the Jews in Poland). Warsaw, 1929.

———, "The Situation of the Cracow Community about the Year 1700" (Polish). *Miesięcznik żydowski*, II (1931), 413–28.

———, Z zagadnień ustrojowych Żydowstwa polskiego (Some Organizational Problems of Polish Jewry). Lwów, 1932. Reprinted from Bibljoteka lwowska, Vols. XXXI–XXXII.

Balletti, A., "Le istituzioni finanziarie nelle università israelitiche dell' Emilia." *Giornale degli Economisti*, 2d ser. XXVIII (1904), 359–69.

———, Gli Ebrei e gli Estensi. New ed., Reggio Emilia, 1930.

Bamberger, Bernard J., "Factors in the History of the Synagog," *Yearbook of the Central Conference of American Rabbis*, XLVIII (1938), 218–37.

Baneth, Eduard, Soziale Motive in der rabbinischen Rechtspflege. Berlin, 1922.

Barbeck, Hugo, Geschichte der Juden in Nürnberg und Fürth. Nuremberg, 1878.

Bardinet, Léon, "Condition civile des Juifs du Comtat Venaissin (1409–1513)." *REJ*, VI (1882), 1–40.

Bar-Hebraeus, Gregory Abulfaraj, Chronicon ecclesiasticum. Ed. and transl. into Latin by J. A. Abbeloos and T. J. Lamy. 3 vols., Louvain, 1872–77.

Barnes, Arthur Stapylton, Christianity at Rome in the Apostolic Age: An Attempt at Reconstruction of History. London, 1938.

Barnett, Lionel D., "The First Record of the Hebra Guemilut Hasadim, London, 1678." *Transactions of the Jewish Historical Society in England*, X (1921–23), 258–60.

———, El libro de los acuerdos: Being the Records and Accompts of the Spanish and Portuguese Synagogue of London from 1663 to 1681. Translated from the Original Spanish and Portuguese. Oxford, 1931.

Baron, Salo W., *or* Shalom, Die Judenfrage auf dem Wiener Kongress. Auf Grund von zum Teil ungedruckten Quellen dargestellt. Vienna, 1920.

———, "Azariah de' Rossi's Attitude to Life." *Jewish Studies in Memory of Israel Abrahams*, New York, 1927, pp. 12–52.

———, "The Israelitic Population under the Kings" (Hebrew). *Abhandlungen zur Erinnerung an Hirsch Perez Chajes*, Vienna, 1933, pp. 76–136.

———, "The Historical Outlook of Maimonides." *Proceedings of the American Academy for Jewish Research*, VI (1934–35), 5–113.

———, "An Historical Critique of the Jewish Community." *Jewish Social Service Quarterly*, XI (1935), 44–49. *Also* in *Jewish Education*, X (1936), 2–8.

———, A Social and Religious History of the Jews. 3 vols., New York, 1937.

———, "A Communal Conflict in Verona" (Hebrew). *Sefer ha-Yobel . . . Shemuel Krauss* (Samuel Krauss Jubilee Volume), Jerusalem, 1937, pp. 217–54.

———, "Freedom and Constraint in the Jewish Community. A Historic Episode." *Essays and Studies in Memory of*

Linda R. Miller, ed. by Israel Davidson, New York, 1938, pp. 9–23.

Baron, Salo W., "Review of Mortimer J. Cohen's *Jacob Emden*." *Jewish Social Studies*, I (1939), 483–87.

———, "Review of L. Finkelstein's *Pharisees*." *Journal of Biblical Literature*, LIX (1940), 60–67.

———, Bibliography of Jewish Social Studies, 1938–39. New York, 1941. Jewish Social Studies, Publications, no. 1.

———, "Rashi and the Community of Troyes." *In* American Academy for Jewish Research, Rashi Anniversary Volume (Texts and Studies, I), New York, 1941, pp. 47–71.

———, "Yehudah Halevi: An Answer to a Historic Challenge." *Jewish Social Studies*, III (1941), 243–72.

———, A Contribution to the History of Palestine Relief and the Ransom of Captives" (Hebrew). *Sefer ha-Shanah li-Yehude Amerika* (*American Hebrew Year Book*), [VI], 5702 (1942), 168–80.

———, "Modern Capitalism and Jewish Fate." *Menorah Journal*, XXX (1942), 116–38.

———, ed., Essays on Maimonides. An Octocentennial Volume. New York, 1941. Includes the editor's essay, "The Economic Views of Maimonides," pp. 127–264.

Barton, George A., Archaeology and the Bible. Pt. I: The Bible Lands, Their Exploration and the Resultant Light on the Bible and History; Pt. II: Translations of Ancient Documents which Confirm or Illuminate the Bible. 6th ed. Philadelphia, 1933.

Bassola, Moses, ס' מסעות ארץ ישראל (Pilgrimage to Palestine, 1521 C. E.). Ed. by Isaac Ben-Zevi. Jerusalem, 1939. Library of Palestinology, no. 11.

Bauer, Jules, "La peste chez les Juifs d'Avignon." *REJ*, XXXIV (1897), 251–62.

———, "Un commencement d'insurrection au quartier juif d'Avignon au XVIIe siècle." *REJ*, XXXVIII (1899), 123–36.

———, "Un document sur les Juifs de Rome." *REJ*, LI (1906), 137–49.

BAUER, JULES, "L'université israélite de Nice de 1785 à 1803." *REJ*, LXIII (1912), 269–75.

BAUMGARTEN, EMMANUEL, "Maria Theresas Ernennungsdekret für den mährischen Landesrabbiner Gerson b. Abraham Chajes." *MGWJ*, XLIV (1900), 76–80.

BEDJAN, P., ed., Acta Martyrum et Sanctorum. 7 vols., Leipzig, 1890–97.

BEJARANO, M. MENDEZ, Histoire de la juiverie de Seville. Madrid, 1922.

BELKIN, SAMUEL, Philo and the Oral Law: The Philonic Interpretation of Biblical Law in Relation to the Palestinian Halakah. Cambridge, Mass., 1940.

BELL, H. IDRIS, Jews and Christians in Egypt. London, 1924.

BELON, PIERRE, Les observations de plusieurs singularitéz et choses mémorables trouvées en Grèce, Asie, Judée, Egypte, Arabie et autres pays étrangers. Paris, 1553. Non vidi.

BELOW, GEORG VON, Probleme der Wirtschaftsgeschichte; eine Einführung in das Studium der Wirtschaftsgeschichte. Tübingen, 1920.

BENJAMIN OF TUDELA, The Itinerary of Rabbi Benjamin of Tudela. Transl. into English and ed. by A. Asher. Vol. I: Text, Bibliography and Translation; Vol. II: Notes and Essays. London, 1840–41. New impression, New York, n. d.

———, The Itinerary . . . . Newly edited and translated by M. N. Adler. London, 1907. Reprinted from *JQR*, O. S. XVI–XVIII (1904–6).

BENJAMIN ZEEB B. MATTATHIAS, ס' שאלות ותשובות (Responsa). Venice, 1539.

BENTWICH, NORMAN, "Philo as Jurist." *JQR*, XXI (1930–31), 151–57. A review of E. R. Goodenough's Jurisprudence of the Jewish Courts in Egypt.

BENVENISTE, DAVID, "Notes on the Map of Palestine of the Traveller Moses Bassola" (Hebrew). *Bulletin of the Jewish Palestine Exploration Society*, VI (1939), 115–23.

BENVENISTE, ḤAYYIM B. ISRAEL, ס' כנסת הגדולה (Juristic Treatise, arranged according to Jacob b. Asher's *Ṭurim*), 8 vols.,

Leghorn, 1658; Constantinople, 1711, 1716, 1729; Salonica, 1757; Smyrna, 1660, 1731, 1734.

Ben-Zevi, Isaac, ed., *see* Bassola, Moses.

Benzinger, Immanuel, Biblische Archäologie. 3d ed., revised, Leipzig, 1927. Angelos-Lehrbücher, Vol. I.

Bereschit Rabba, mit kritischem Apparat und Kommentar von J. Theodor. Nach dem Ableben des Verfassers bearbeitet und ergänzt von Ch. Albeck. 2 vols. and Index, Berlin, 1912–37.

Bergl, J., Geschichte der ungarischen Juden. Leipzig, 1879.

Berkowitz, Henry, "Notes on the History of the Earliest German Jewish Congregation in America." *PAJHS*, IX (1901), 123–27.

Berliner, Abraham *or* Adolph, Persönliche Beziehungen zwischen Christen und Juden im Mittelalter. Halberstadt, 1882.

———, "Antiquities." *Magazin für die Wissenschaft des Judentums*, XII (1885), Hebrew section, pp. 13–14.

———, "The Memor-Book of Worms" (Hebrew). *Ḳobeṣ ʻal yad*, III (1882), 1–62.

———, "Aus schweren Zeiten." *Jubelschrift . . . I. Hildesheimer*, Berlin, 1890, pp. 154–67; Hebrew section pp. 104–11.

———, Geschichte der Juden in Rom von der ältesten Zeit bis zur Gegenwart (2050 Jahre). 2 vols., Frankfort, 1893.

———, Ueber den Einfluss des ersten hebräischen Buchdrucks auf den Cultus und die Kultur der Juden. Frankfort, 1896.

———, Aus dem inneren Leben der deutschen Juden im Mittelalter. 2d ed., Berlin, 1900.

———, "A Letter Addressed by the Roman Community to the Elders of Pesaro" (Hebrew). *Ḳobeṣ ʻal yad*, XIX (1903), 68–71.

———, "A Memoir by R. Elijah Capsali" (Hebrew). *Ḳobeṣ ʻal yad*, XIX (1903), 19–26.

Berman, Jeremiah J., Shehitah. A Study in the Cultural and Social Life of the Jewish People. New York, 1941.

Bernheimer, Carlo, "Document relatif aux Juifs de Négrepont." *REJ*, LXV (1913), 224–30.

Bernstein, Simon, "Contributions to the History of the Ransom of Captives in Italy during the 17th Century (From a Manuscript)" (Hebrew). *Ha-Zofeh*, XIII (1929), 355–57.

———, "A Dispute among Italian Rabbis of 1663" (Hebrew). *Ha-Zofeh*, XIV (1930), 198–203.

———, "The Letters of Rabbi Mahalalel Halelujah of Ancona." *HUCA*, VII (1930), 497–536.

———, ed., The Divan of Leo of Modena. Philadelphia, 1932.

Bershadskii, Sergey A., *et al.*, eds., Russko-evreiskii Arkhiv (Russian-Jewish Archives; A Periodical). 3 vols., St. Petersburg, 1882–1903.

Bersohn, Mathias, Dyplomataryusz dotyczący Żydów w dawnej Polsce (Collection of Documents Concerning Jews in Old Poland, 1388–1782). Warsaw, 1910.

Bertolotti, A., "Les Juifs à Rome aux XVIe, XVIIe et XVIIIe siècles." *REJ*, II (1881), 278–89.

Bethencourt, L. Cardozo de, "Le trésor des Juifs Sephardim: Notes sur les familles françaises israélites du rit portugais." *REJ*, XX (1890), 287–300; XXV (1892), 97–110, 235–45; XXVI (1893), 240–56.

———, "Notes on the Spanish and Portuguese Jews in the United States, Guiana and the Dutch and British West Indies during the Seventeenth and Eighteenth Centuries." *PAJHS*, XXIX (1925), 7–38.

Bettan, Israel, Studies in Jewish Preaching: Middle Ages. Cincinnati, 1939.

B. G. U., *see* Aegyptische Urkunden.

Bickermann, Elias, Der Gott der Makkabäer. Berlin, 1937.

———, "The Sanhedrin" (Hebrew). *Zion*, III (1938), 256–60.

Blau, Ludwig, ed., Leo Modenas Briefe und Schriftstücke. 2 pts., Strasbourg, 1907.

———, "Isaac Levi's מדבר תהפוכות" (Hebrew). *Ha-Zofeh*, II (1912), 169–86; III (1914), 45–54, 69–96.

Bloch, Philipp, "Die ersten Kulturbestrebungen der jüdischen Gemeinde Posen unter preussischer Herrschaft." *Jubelschrift . . . H. Graetz*, Breslau, 1877, pp. 194–217.

Bloch, Philipp, Die Generalprivilegien der polnischen Judenschaft. Posen, 1892. Reprinted from *Zeitschrift der Historischen Gesellschaft für die Provinz Posen*, Vol. V.

———, "Der Streit um den Moreh des Maimonides in der Gemeinde Posen um die Mitte des 16. Jahrh." *MGWJ*, XLVII (1903), 153–69, 263–79, 346–56.

———, "Ein vielbegehrter Rabbiner des Rheingaues, Juda Mehler Reutlingen." *Festschrift . . . Martin Philippson*, Leipzig, 1916, pp. 114–34.

Blondheim, David S., Les parlers judéo-romans et la Vetus Latina. Paris, 1925.

Bloom, A., La lèpre dans l'Ancienne Egypte et chez le Anciens Hébreux. La lèpre dans la Bible. Cairo, 1938. Communication faite au Congrès International de la Lèpre au Caire, Mars 1938.

Bloom, Herbert I., "The Dutch Archives, with Special Reference to American Jewish History." *PAJHS*, XXXII (1931), 7–21.

———, "A Study of Brazilian Jewish History, 1623–1654: Based chiefly upon the Findings of the late Samuel Oppenheim." *PAJHS*, XXXIII (1934), 43–125.

———, The Economic Activities of the Jews of Amsterdam in the Seventeenth and Eighteenth Centuries. Williamsport (Pa.), 1937.

Bodemeyer, Hildebrand, Die Juden. Göttingen, 1855.

Bodenheimer, R., "Beitrag zur Geschichte der Juden in Oberhessen von ihrer frühesten Erwähnung bis zur Emanzipation." *ZGJD*, II (1931), 251–62; IV (1932), 11–30.

Boffarull y Sans, Francisco de, Los Judios en el territorio de Barcelona (siglos X al XIII) Reinado de Jaime I 1213–1276. Barcelona, 1910.

Bolkenstein, Hendrik, "Een geval van sociaal-ethisch syncretisme." *Mededeelingen van den Koninklijke Akademie van Wetenschapen*, *Afd. Letterkunde*, LXXII (1931), 1–52.

———, Wohltätigkeit und Armenpflege im vorchristlichen Altertum. Ein Beitrag zum Problem "Moral und Gesellschaft." Utrecht, 1939.

Bondy, Gottlieb, ed., Zur Geschichte der Juden in Böhmen, Mähren und Schlesien von 906 bis 1620. Hrsg. von G. Bondy, zur Herausgabe vorbereitet und ergänzt von Franz Dworský. 2 vols., Prague, 1906.

Book of the Pious, *see* Judah b. Samuel.

Boos, Heinrich von, Geschichte der rheinischen Städtekultur von ihren Anfängen bis zur Gegenwart, mit besonderer Berücksichtigung der Stadt Worms. 2d ed., 4 vols., Berlin, 1897–1901.

Bornstein, Ḥayyim Y., "The Controversy between Saadia Gaon and Ben Meir" (Hebrew). *Sefer ha-Yobel* (Jubilee Volume in honor of) *Nahum Sokolow*, Warsaw, 1904, pp. 19–189.

———, "The Rules of Ordination and Its History" (Hebrew). *Hatekufah*, IV (1919), 393–426.

Boüard, Alain de, Actes et lettres de Charles I, Roi de Sicile, concernant la France (1257–1284). Extraits des registres angevins de Naples. Paris, 1926.

Bouquet Martin, Michel-Jean-Joseph Brial, *et al.*, eds., Recueil des historiens des Gaules et de la France. Nouvelle édition, publiée sous la direction de M. L. Délisle. 24 vols., Paris, 1868–1904.

Bousset, Wilhelm, Jüdisch-christlicher Schulbetrieb in Alexandreia und Rom; literarische Untersuchungen zu Philo und Clemens von Alexandreia, Justin und Irenäus. Göttingen, 1915. Forschungen zur Religion und Literatur des Alten und Neuen Testaments, N. S. 6.

Brafman, Jacob, Kniga Kahala (The Book of the Kahal). 2d ed., 2 vols., St. Peterburg, 1882.

———, Das Buch vom Kahal auf Grund einer neuen Verdeutschung des russischen Originals hrsg. von S. Passarge. 2 vols., Leipzig, 1928.

Brand, Joshua, "The Temple of Onias" (Hebrew). *Yavneh*, I (1939), 76–84.

Brann, Marcus, "Geschichte des Landrabbinats in Schlesien." *Jubelschrift . . . H. Graetz*, Breslau, 1887, pp. 218–78.

———, "Etwas von der schlesischen Landgemeinde." *Festschrift . . . Jakob Guttmann*, Leipzig, 1915, pp. 225–55.

Brann, Marcus, "Samson Wertheimers Rabbinats-Diplom aus Eisenstadt." *Festschrift . . . Adolf Schwarz*, Berlin, 1917, pp. 499–508.

Braver, Abraham Jacob, "The Census of the *Ḥeders* in Lwów in 1782" (Hebrew). *Reshumot*, I (1918), 419–28.

———, "Ben-Zevi, A Pilgrimage to Palestine in 1521 A. D." (Hebrew). *Bulletin of the Jewish Palestine Exploration Society*, VI (1939), 100–1. Refers to Moses Bassola's *Pilgrimage*.

———, "Jewish Enjoyment of the Privileges of the Capitulations in Palestine" (Hebrew). *Zion*, V (1939–40), 161–69.

Breier, A., M. Eisler, and M. Grunwald, Holzsynagogen in Polen. [Vienna], 1934.

Bresslau, Harry, "Zur Geschichte der Juden in Rothenburg an der Tauber." *ZGJD*, O. S. III (1889), 301–36; IV (1890), 1–17.

———, "Aus Strassburger Judenakten." *ZGJD*, O. S. V (1892), 115–25, 307–34.

Bretholz, Berthold, Geschichte der Juden in Mähren im Mittelalter. Vol. I, Brünn, 1934.

———, Quellen zur Geschichte der Juden in Mähren vom XI. bis zum XV. Jahrhundert (1067–1411). Prague, 1935.

Brilling, Bernhard, "Beziehungen des Vierländer-Parlaments zu Deutschland im 17. Jahrhundert." *ZGJD*, III (1931), 272–75.

———, "Der Streit um den Friedhof zu Ottensen." *Jahrbuch für die jüdischen Gemeinden Schleswig-Holsteins*, III (1931–32), 45–68.

———, "Eine Eingabe der böhmischen Judenheit vom Jahre 1560." *ZGJT*, V (1938), 59–62.

Bromberger, S., Die Juden in Regensburg bis zur Mitte des 14. Jahrhunderts. Berlin, 1934.

Brugmans, Hendrik, and A. Frank, eds., Geschiedenis der Joden in Nederland. Vol. I, Amsterdam, 1940.

Brüll, Nehemias, "Zur Geschichte der Juden in Mähren." *Kalender für Israeliten* auf das Jahr 5628 (1867/68). Beilage zum *Wiener Jahrbuch für Israeliten*, N. S. III (1867–68), 181–220.

BRÜLL, NEHEMIAS, "Synoden der deutschen Juden im Mittelalter." *Jahrbücher für jüdische Geschichte und Literatur*, VIII (1887), 60–62.

BRUNA, ISRAEL B. ḤAYYIM, ס' שאלות ותשובות (Responsa). Stettin, 1860.

BRÜNNECK, WILHELM VON, ed., Siciliens mitteralterliche Stadtrechte, nach alten Drucken und Handschriften, mit einer Einleitung herausgegeben und dem Inhalt nach systematisch dargestellt. Halle, 1881.

BRUNSCHVICG, LÉON, "Les Juifs d'Angers et du pays Angevin." *REJ*, XXIX (1894), 229–44. Also reprint.

BRUZZONE, P. L., "Les Juifs au Piémont." *REJ*, XIX (1889), 141–46.

BUBER, SALOMON, קריה נשגבה (A History of the Jews in Żółkiew). Cracow, 1903.

BÜCHLER, ADOLF, The Political and Social Leaders of the Jewish Community of Sepphoris in the Second and Third Centuries. London, 1909. Jewish College Publications, no. 1.

BURDACH, KONRAD, Vorspiel. Gesammelte Schriften zur Geschichte des deutschen Geistes. Vol. I, Pt. 1: Mittelalter. Halle, 1925. Deutsche Vierteljahrsschrift für Literaturwissenschaft und Geistesgeschichte, Buchreihe, Vol. I.

BUZAGLO, J. H., Bijdragen tot de geschiedenis der Portugeesche Israelieten en hunne gemeenten te 's–Gravenhage van plm. 1690 tot plm. 1730. The Hague, 1939. Reprinted from the yearbook, *Die Haghe*, ed. by W. Moll, 1939. Non vidi.

CAHEN, ABRAHAM, "Les Juifs de la Martinique au XVIIe siècle." *REJ*, II (1881), 93–122.

———, "Enseignement obligatoire édicté par la communauté israélite de Metz." *REJ*, II (1881), 303–5.

———, "Réglements somptuaires de la communauté juive de Metz à la fin du XVIIe siècle, 1690–97." *Annuaire de la Société des études juives*, I (1881), 77–121.

———, "Les Juifs dans les colonies françaises au XVIIIe siècle." *REJ*, IV (1882), 127–45, 236–48; V (1882), 68–92, 258–72.

Cahen, Abraham, "Le rabbinat de Metz pendant la période française (1567–1871)," *REJ*, VII (1883), 103–16, 204–26; VIII (1884), 255–74; XII (1886), 283–97; XIII (1886), 105–26.

Calabi, Scipione, "Le confraternità della communione israelitica di Verona." *L'Educatore israelita*, XII (1864), 78–85.

Camau, Emile, La Provence à travers les siècles. Paris, 1908–30. Vol. IV, pp. 249–367: Les Juifs en Provence. This chapter appeared in 1928.

Capsali, Elijah, *see* Berliner, Abraham *and* Lattes, Moses.

Capsali, Moses, "Responsa and Letters" (Hebrew), ed. by Simḥa Assaf. *Sinai*, III, Pt. 1 (1939), 149–58.

Carano-Donvito, Giovanni, "Gli Ebrei nella storia economica di Puglia." *Rivista di politica economica*, XXIII (1933), 836–43.

Caro, Georg, Sozial- und Wirtschaftsgeschichte der Juden im Mittelalter und in der Neuzeit. 2 vols., Frankfort, 1908–20. Vol. I appeared in 2d ed., Frankfort, 1924.

Caro, J., "Die Rabbinersynode zu Erfurt 1391." *Jüdisches Literatur-Blatt*, XI (1882), 110–15.

Cassel, David, ed., תשובות גאונים קדמונים (Responsa of the Early Geonim). With an Introd. by S. J. L. Rapoport. Berlin, 1848.

Cassuto, Alfonso, "Die historische Grundlage zur Beteiligung der Hamburger Portugiesisch-Jüdischen Gemeinde an der von der Deutsch-Israelitischen Gemeinde erhobenen Fleischabgabe (Schächtabgabe)." *Jahrbuch für die jüdischen Gemeinden Schleswig-Holsteins*, IV (1932–33), 32–38.

C[assuto], J., "Aus dem ältesten Protokollbuch der Portugiesisch-Jüdischen Gemeinde in Hamburg." *JJLG*, VI (1909), 1–54; VII (1910), 159–210; VIII (1911), 227–90; IX (1912), 318–66; X (1913), 225–95; XI (1916), 1–76; XIII (1920), 55–118.

Cassuto, Umberto, "Una lettera di raccomandazione per un inviato degli Ebrei Polacci al Papa (1758)." *Rivista israelitica*, I (1904), 25–27.

———, "I più antichi capitoli del ghetto di Firenze." *Rivista israelitica*, IX (1912), 203–11; X (1913), 32–40, 71–80.

———, Gli Ebrei a Firenze nell' età del Rinascimento. Florence, 1918.

CASSUTO, UMBERTO, "Les traductions judéo-italiennes du Rituel." *REJ*, LXXXIX (1930), 260–80.

———, "Iscrizioni ebraiche a Trani." *Rivista degli studi orientali*, XIII (1932), 172–80.

CASTRO, D. HENRIQUES DE, De Synagoge der Portugeesch-Israelietische Gemeente te Amsterdam. The Hague, 1875.

———, Auswahl von Grabsteinen auf dem Niederl.-Portug.-Israel. Begräbnisplatze zu Oderkerk an den Amstel nebst Beschreibung und biographischen Skizzen. Leyden, 1883.

CAUSSE, ANTONIN, Les dispersés d'Israël, les origines de la Diaspora et son rôle dans la formation du judaïsme. Paris, 1929.

———, Du groupe ethnique à la communauté religieuse. Le problème sociologique de la religion d'Israél. Paris, 1937.

CHAJES, HIRSCH PEREZ, "Les juges juifs en Palestine de l'an 70 à l'an 500," *REJ*, XXXIX (1899), 39–52.

———, "Un *herem* di R. Mosè Zacuto contro il giuoco (1693)." *Rivista israelitica*, V (1908), 95–97.

CHONE, HEYMANN, "Zur Geschichte der Juden in Zürich im 15. Jahrhundert." *ZGJD*, VI (1936), 198–209.

———, "Rabbi Joseph von Schlettstadt: Zur Geschichte der Familie Treves." *ZGJD*, VII (1937), 1–4.

CIAVARINI, C., Memorie storiche degli Israeliti in Ancona. Ancona, 1898.

CIROT, G., "Les Juifs de Bordeaux. Leur situation morale et sociale de 1550 à la Revolution." *Revue historique de Bordeaux*, II–XXXII (1909–39), 14 instalments.

CISCATO, ANTONIO, Gli Ebrei in Padova (1300–1800). Padua, 1901.

CLÉMENT, ROGER, La condition des Juifs de Metz sous l'ancien régime. Paris, 1903.

Close Rolls of the Reign of Henry III preserved in the Public Record Office. Vol. IV, 1237–1242. London, 1911.

CODEX JUSTINIANUS, *see* Corpus Iuris Civilis.

CODEX THEODOSIANUS, Theodosiani libri xvi cum constitutionibus Sirmondianis et leges novellae ad Theodosianum pertinentes. Ed. by Th. Mommsen and P. M. Meyer. Berlin, 1904–5.

Cohen, Boaz, קונטרס התשובות (Bibliography of Responsa). With an Introduction on Their Importance for the History of Jewish Law. Budapest, 1930. Reprinted from *Ha-Zofeh*, XIV.

———, The Responsum of Maimonides Concerning Music. New York, 1935. Reprinted from the *Jewish Music Journal*, II, 2 (May–June, 1935), pp. 3–6.

Cohen, D. E., "De vroegere Amsterdamsche Joodsche Doctoren," *Nederlandsch Tijdschrift voor Geneeskunde*, LXXI (1927), 1385–1401.

———, "De Amsterdamsche Joodsche Chirurgijns," *Nederlandsch Tijdschrift voor Geneeskunde*, LXXIV (1930), 234–56

———, "De Joodsche Geneeskundigen in de noordelijke Nederlanden voor 1600," *Nederlandsch Tijdschrift voor Geneeskunde*, LXXVIII (1934), 533–43.

Cohen, Morris R., "Review of the American Jewish Year Book, XLII." *Jewish Social Studies*, III (1941), 231–32.

Cohen, Mortimer J., Jacob Emden, A Man of Controversy. Philadelphia, 1937.

Cohn, Gustav, Der jüdische Friedhof. Seine geschichtliche und kulturgeschichtliche Entwicklung. Mit besonderer Berücksichtigung der ästhetischen Gestaltung. Frankfort, 1930.

Cohn, Willy, "Die Judenpolitik König Karls I von Sizilien in Anjou und in der Provence." *MGWJ*, LXXIV (1930), 429–37.

Cole, Charles Woolsey, Colbert and a Century of French Mercantilism. 2 vols. New York, 1939.

Colon, Joseph, ס' תשובות (Responsa). Cremona, 1557.

Colorni, Vittore, "Le magistrature maggiori della communità ebraica di Mantova (Sec. XV–XIX)." *Rivista di storia del diritto italiano*, XI (1938), 57–126.

Constant, P. [J.], Les Juifs devant l'église et l'histoire. Paris, 1897.

Constitutio criminalis Carolina. Die peinliche Gerichtsordnung Kaiser Karls V. Kritisch hrsg. von J. Kohler und Willy Scheel. Halle, 1900. Die Carolina und ihre Vorgängerinnen, Vol. I.

Corpus Iuris Civilis, Ed. by Th. Mommsen, P. Krueger, B. Schoell, and W. Kroll. 3 vols., Berlin, 1928–29. I. Institutiones, ed. by P. Krueger; Digesta, ed. by Th. Mommsen. II. Codex Iustinianus, ed. by P. Krueger. III. Novellae, ed. by R. Schoell and W. Kroll.

Costituzioni della Compagna ebraica della misericordia della città di Modena. Modena, 1791.

Coulton, George Gordon, Life in the Middle Ages. Selected, Translated and Annotated. 4 vols., Cambridge, 1928–30.

———, Ten Medieval Studies. With Four Appendices. 3d ed., Cambridge, 1930.

Cowley, A., "Bodleian Genizah Fragments. III." *JQR*, O. S. XIX (1906–7), 107–8.

———, ed., Aramaic Papyri of the Fifth Century B. C. Edited, with Translation and Notes. Oxford, 1923.

Crémieux, Adolphe, "Les Juifs de Marseille au moyen âge." *REJ*, XLVI (1903), 1–47, 246–68; XLVII (1903), 62–86, 243–61.

Cronbach, Abraham, Religion and Its Social Setting. Cincinnati, 1933.

———, "The Me'il Zedakah." 3 pts. *HUCA*, XI (1936), 503–67; XII–XIII (1937–38), 635–96; XIV (1939), 479–557.

———, "The Gradations of Benevolence." *HUCA*, XVI (1941), 163–86.

Crump, C. G., and E. F. Jacob, eds., The Legacy of the Middle Ages. Oxford, 1926.

Curiel, Ricardo, "Gli Ebrei di Trieste nel secolo XVIII." *Scritti in onore di Dante Lattes* (=*Israel*, XII), Città di Castello, 1938, pp. 237–55.

Cusa, Salvatore, I diplomi greci ed arabi di Sicilia publicati nel testo originale . . . 2 vols. (in continuous pagination). Palermo, 1868–82.

Daiches, Samuel, The Jews in Babylonia in the Time of Ezra and Nehemiah According to Babylonian Inscriptions. London, 1910.

DALY, CHARLES P., The Settlement of the Jews in North America. Ed. with notes and appendices by Max J. Kohler. New York, 1893.

DANON, ABRAHAM, "Étude historique sur les impôts directs et indirects des communautés israélites en Turquie." *REJ*, XXXI (1895), 52–61.

———, "La communauté juive de Salonique au XVIe siècle." *REJ*, XL (1900), 206–30; XLI (1900), 98–117, 250–65.

DAVID B. ḤAYYIM HA-KOHEN, ס׳ שאלות ותשובות (Responsa). Salonica, 1803.

DAVID B. JUDAH OF MANTUA (Messer Leon), ס׳ כבוד חכמים (A Polemical Work). Ed. by Simon Bernfeld. Berlin, 1899.

DAVID B. SAMUEL HA-LEVI, ס׳ טורי זהב (Commentary) on Joseph Karo's *Shulḥan 'Aruk*. Printed with many editions of the latter work.

Cf. also Frankl-Grün, Adolf.

DAVIS, N. DARNELL, Sheṭarot, Hebrew Deeds of English Jews before 1290. London, 1888.

———, "Notes on the History of the Jews in Barbados." *PAJHS*, XVIII (1909), 129–48.

DECOURCELLE, JACQUES, La condition des Juifs de Nice aux 17e et 18e siècles. Paris, 1923.

DEEG, HANS PETER, Hofjuden. Ed. by Julius Streicher, Nuremberg, 1938. Juden, Judenverbrechen und Judengesetze in Deutschland von der Vergangenheit bis zur Gegenwart, I, No. 1.

DEMBITZER, CHAIM NATHAN, כלילת יופי (A History of the Lwów Rabbinate). Cracow, 1888.

DENTZ, FRED OUDSCHANS, De Kolonisatie van de Portugeesch Joodsche Natie in Suriname en de Geschiedenis van de Joden Savanne. Amsterdam, [1927].

DETCHEVERRY, AD., Histoire des Israélites de Bordeaux. Bordeaux, 1850.

DIAMANT, J., and B. GLASER, "Statuten (Tekanoth) einer Chewra Kadischa für Jugendliche in Prag zu Ende des 18. Jahrhunderts." *ZGJT*, V (1938), 13–22.

Diamant, Max, Jüdische Volkskunst, mit einer Note: Die Chazaren und die Ansiedlung der Ostjuden. Vienna, [1937].

Dickstein, Palṭiel, "The Ordinances of the Polish and Lithuanian Councils concerning Fugitives" (Hebrew). *Ha-Mishpaṭ ha-'ibri*, I (Moscow 1918–20), 29–76.

———, דיני עונשין (Criminal Law). With Special Reference to Hebrew Law and the Actual Law of Palestine. Tel-Aviv, 1938.

Dietz, Alexander, Stammbuch der Frankfurter Juden. Geschichtliche Mitteilungen über die Frankfurter jüdischen Familien von 1349–1849 nebst einem Plane der Judengasse. Frankfort, 1907.

Dinaburg, Ben Zion, ישראל בגולה (Israel in Dispersion; a Source Book). 2 vols., Jerusalem, 1926–36.

Dölger, F., "Die Frage der Judensteuer in Byzanz." *Vierteljahrsschrift für Sozial und Wirtschaftsgeschichte*, XXVI (1933), 1–24.

Donath, L., Geschichte der Juden in Mecklenburg von ältesten Zeiten (1266) bis auf die Gegenwart (1874); auch ein Beitrag zur Kulturgeschichte Mecklenburgs. Nach gedruckten und ungedruckten Quellen. Leipzig, 1874.

Donnolo, Shabbetai b. Abraham, ס' חכמוני (Commentary on the Book of Creation). Ed. by D. Castelli. Florence, 1880.

Drazin, Nathan, History of Jewish Education from 515 B. C. E. to 220 C. E. Baltimore, 1940.

Druyanow, Elyakim, "Fragments from an Ancient Minute-Book of the 'Holy Association' in Druya, Province of Wilno" (Hebrew). *Reshumot*, I (1918), 437–49.

Dubnow, Simon M., "Communal Statutes from the End of the Sixteenth to the End of the Eighteenth Century" (Russian). *Voskhod*, 1894, Pt. 2, pp. 90–107.

———, "The Council of Four Lands in Poland and its Attitude toward the Communities." *Sefer ha-Yobel* (Jubilee Volume in honor of) *Nahum Sokolow*, Warsaw, 1904, pp. 250–61.

———, Pisma o starom i novom evreistvoie (Letters on Old and Modern Judaism, 1897–1907). Revised ed., St. Petersburg, 1907.

Dubnow, Simon M., "Records of the Jewish Crown Diet or the Va'ad of the Four Lands" (Russian). *Evreiskaya Starina*, V (1912), 70–84, 178–86, 453–59.

———, History of the Jews in Russia and Poland. 3 vols., Philadelphia, 1916.

———, פנקס המדינה (The Minutes of the Lithuanian Council of Provinces.) A Collection of Enactments and Decisions from 1623 to 1761, from a Grodno manuscript, with additions, and variants from copies in Brześć and Wilno, ed. with introduction and notes. Berlin, 1925.

———, "Two Yiddish Proclamations by the Council of Four Lands in 1671 (A Page from the Lost Minute-Book)" (Yiddish). *Yivo Studies in History*, I (1929), 699–702.

———, "From My Archive" (Yiddish). *Yivo Bleter*, I (1931), 404–7.

———, מכתבים על היהדות הישנה והחדשה (Letters on Old and Modern Judaism). Revised ed., transl. into Hebrew by Abraham Lövinson with the author's collaboration. Tel-Aviv, 1937.

Dukesz, E., "Aus dem Archiv der Stadt Altona." *Jahrbuch für die jüdischen Gemeinden Schleswig-Holsteins*, I (1929–30), 131–34.

Duran, Simon b. Zemaḥ, ס' התשב"ץ (Responsa). 4 vols., Amsterdam, 1738.

———, ס' מגן אבות (Theological Treatise and Commentary on Abot). 4 pts., Livorno, 1762–85.

Duran, Solomon b. Simon, ס' מלחמת מצוה (Polemical Treatise). Leipzig, 1856.

———, ס' שאלות ותשובות (Responsa). Leghorn, 1742.

Duschak, Moritz, Schulgesetzgebung und Methodik der alten Israeliten, nebst einem geschichtlichen Anhange und einer Beilage über höhere israelitische Lehranstalten. Vienna, 1872.

Duschinsky, Charles *or* J. K., The Rabbinate of the Great Synagogue, London, from 1756 to 1842. London, 1921.

———, "The Book *Ma'ase bet din* of the Frankfort Community of the Years 5529–59 [1769–99]" (Hebrew). *Ha-Zofeh*, X (1926), 106–15 (incomplete).

Duschinsky, Charles *or* J. K., "The Yekum Purkan." *Livre d'hommage . . . Poznanski*, Warsaw, 1929, pp. 182–98.

———, "Rabbi David Oppenheimer, Glimpses from His Life and Activity, derived from His Manuscripts in the Bodleian Library." *JQR*, XX (1929–30), 217–47.

———, "May a Woman act as a Shoheteth?" *Gaster Anniversary Volume*, London, 1936, pp. 96–106.

Dyer, Albion Morris, "Points in the First Chapter of New York Jewish History." *PAJHS*, III (1895), 41–60.

Eberhard, [O.], "Chalukah und Chalukareform." *Mitteilungen und Nachrichten des deutschen Palästina-Vereins*, XIV (1908), 17–29.

Eckstein, Adolf, Geschichte der Juden im ehemaligen Fürstbistum Bamberg. Bamberg, [1898].

Edels, Samuel, חדושי אגדות (Novellae on the Aggadah). Appended to most recent editions of the Talmud.

Eger, Akiba b. Simḥa, ס' שאלות ותשובות (Responsa). Fürth, 1781.

Eibeschütz, Jonathan b. Nathan, ס' יערות דבש (Homilies). 2 vols. Karlsruhe, 1779–82.

Eisenstadt, Israel Tobiah, דעת קדושים (Materialien zur Geschichte der Familien welche ihre Abstammung von den im Jahre 1659 im litthauischen Städtchen Rushani in Folge einer Blutbeschuldigung als Märtyrer gefallenen herleiten). 2 pts., St. Petersburg, 1897–98.

Eisenstadt, Samuel, "The Investigation of Our Public Law" (Hebrew). *Ha-Mishpaṭ ha-'ibri*, I (Moscow, 1918–20), 8–28.

———, עין משפט. Repertorium bibliographicum litteraturae totius iurisprudentiae hebraicae. Jerusalem, 1931.

Eisenstein, Jehudah David, "Maggid." *Jewish Encyclopedia*, VIII, 252–54.

Eisser, Georg, and Julius Levy, Die altassyrischen Rechtsurkunden vom Kültepe. 4 pts., Leipzig, 1930–35.

Elbogen, Ismar, "Leghorn." *Jewish Encyclopedia*, VII, 664–66.

———, "Eingang und Ausgang des Sabbats nach talmudischen Quellen." *Festschrift . . . Israel Lewy*, Breslau, 1911, pp. 173–87.

Elbogen, Ismar, Der jüdische Gottesdienst in seiner geschichtlichen Entwicklung. 3d ed., Frankfort, 1931.

———, "Unbekannte Huldigungsgedichte für einen Nasi." *MGWJ*, LXXVI (1932), 334–38.

———, "Hillel da Verona e la lotta per Mosé Maimonide." *Annuario di studi ebraici*, II (1938), 99–105.

Elfenbein, Israel, ed., ספר מנהגים דבי מהר"ם ב"ר ברוך מרוטנבורג (A Costumal of the School of Rabbi Meir ben Baruch of Rothenburg) by an anonymous Author [1220–1293]. New York, 1938.

Eliezer b. Joel ha-Levi, ס' ראבי"ה (Sefer Rabiah, enthaltend Dezisionen, Novellen und Responsen zum Talmud). Ed. by V. Aptowitzer. Vols. I–III, Berlin, 1912–Jerusalem, 1935. With a volume of "Addenda et Emendationes" to Vols. I–II. Jerusalem, 1936.

Cf. also Aptowitzer, Viktor.

Elijah b. Moses Gershon of Pinczów, ed., שאלות ותשובות הגאונים בתראי (Responsa of More Recent Rabbis). Prague, 1816.

Elijah b. Samuel of Lublin, ס' יד אליהו (Responsa). Amsterdam, 1712.

Elijah b. Solomon Abraham ha-Kohen of Smyrna, ס' מעיל צדקה (The Mantle of Benevolence). Smyrna, 1731.

Cf. also Cronbach, Abraham.

Emden, Jacob b. Zevi, ס' שאלת יעב"ץ (Responsa). 2 pts., Altona, 1739–59.

———, ס' תורת הקנאות (The Lore of Zeal). Amsterdam, 1752.

———, מגלת ספר (Autobiography). Ed. by David Kahane. Warsaw, 1896.

Emmanuel, Isaac Samuel, Histoire de l'industrie des tissus des Israélites de Salonique. Paris, 1935.

———, Histoire des Israélites de Salonique. Vol. I: 140 B.C. to 1640 C.E. Salonica, 1936.

Encyclopaedia Judaica; das Judentum in Geschichte und Gegenwart. Ed. by Jacob Klatzkin, *et al.* Vols. I–X [A–L], Berlin, 1928–34.

Ephraim, Max, "Histoire des Juifs d'Alsace et particulièrement de Strasbourg depuis le milieu du XIIIe jusqu'à la fin du

XIVe siècle." *REJ*, LXXVII (1923), 127–65; LXXVIII (1924), 35–84.

EPIPHANIUS, ST., Opera omnia. *In* Migne's Patrologia graeca, XLI–XLIII.

EPPENSTEIN, SIMON, "Beiträge zur Geschichte und Literatur im gaonäischen Zeitalter." *MGWJ*, LII (1908), 328–43, 455–72, 591–620; LIV (1910), 189–205, 305–20, 452–61, 588–99; LV (1911), 64–75, 220–32, 317–29, 464–77, 614–28, 729–42; LVI (1912), 80–102. "Nachträge und Berichtigungen." Ibid., LVII (1913), 99–102.

EPSTEIN, ABRAHAM, אלדד הדני (Eldad ha-Dani) seine Berichte über die Stämme und deren Ritus in verschiedenen Versionen nach Handschriften und alten Drucken mit Einleitung und Anmerkungen, nebst einem Excurse über die Falascha und deren Gebräuche. Pressburg, 1891.

———, "Der Wormser Judenrat." *MGWJ*, XLVI (1902), 157–70.

———, "Ordination et autorisation," *REJ*, XLVI (1903), 197–211.

———, and JAKOB FREIMANN, eds., ס' מעשה הגאונים (Responsen und Dezisionen der Gelehrten aus Speyer, Worms und Mainz). Mit Einleitung und Anmerkungen von A. Epstein, ergänzt und redigiert von J. Freimann. Berlin, 1909.

EPSTEIN, ISIDORE, The "Responsa" of Rabbi Solomon ben Adreth of Barcelona (1235–1310) as a Source of the History of Spain. London, 1925.

———, The Responsa of R. Simon b. Zemaḥ Duran as a Source of the History of the Jews in North Africa. London, 1930.

———, "Pre-Expulsion England in the Responsa." *Transactions of the Jewish Historical Society of England*, XIV (1940), 187–205.

EPSTEIN, JACOB NAHUM, "Additional Fragments of the Yerushalmi" (Hebrew). *Tarbiz*, III (1931–32), 15–20.

EPSTEIN, LOUIS M., The Jewish Marriage Contract; a Study in the Status of the Woman in Jewish Law. New York, 1927.

ERGAS, JOSEPH B. IMMANUEL, ס' דברי יוסף (Responsa). Leghorn, 1742.

EUSEBIUS PAMPHILIUS OF CAESAREA, Opera omnia quae extant. 6 vols. *In* Migne's Patrologia graeca, Vols. XIX–XXIV.

———, Historiae ecclesiasticae libri X. Ed. by F. A. Heinichen. 3 vols., Leipzig, 1827–28.

———, The Ecclesiastical History. Greek text with English translation by K. Lake, 2 vols., London, 1926–32. "Loeb Classical Library."

———, Evangelicae praeparationis libri XV. Ed. and transl. into English by E. H. Gifford, 4 vols., Oxford, 1903. Vol. III in 2 pts. contains the English transl.

EYMERIC, NICHOLAS, Directorium inquisitorum. Ed. and annotated by F. Pegna. Revised edition, Venice, 1607.

FAGNAN, E., "Arabo-Judaica." *REJ*, LIX (1910), 225–30.

FALK KOHEN, JOSHUA B. ALEXANDER, ס' מאירת עינים (Commentary) on Joseph Karo's *Shulḥan 'Aruk*, Ḥ. M. Printed with many editions of the latter work.

———, ס' פרישה ודרישה (Commentaries) on Jacob b. Asher's *Ṭurim*. Printed with many editions of the latter work.

———, קונטרס [הרבית] (A Compilation on Usury *or* of Ordinances). Sulzbach, 1692.

FALK, JACOB JOSHUA B. ZEVI HIRSCH, ס' פני יהושע (Novellae on Talmudic Tractates). 3 pts., Lwów, 1860.

FANO, MENAHEM AZARIAH DA, ס' שאלות ותשובות (Responsa). Dyhernfurt, 1788.

FEILCHENFELD, LUDWIG, Rabbi Josel von Rosheim: Ein Beitrag zur Geschichte der Juden in Deutschland im Reformationszeitalter. Strasbourg, 1898.

FEILCHENFELD, WOLF, "Die innere Verfassung der jüdischen Gemeinde zu Posen im 17. und 18. Jahrhundert." *Zeitschrift der Historischen Gesellschaft für die Provinz Posen*, XI (1896), 122–37.

FEINKIND, MOSES, "The 'Ḥebra Ḳadisha' in Piotrków" (Yiddish). *Lodzer Visenshaftleche Shriften*, I (1938), 55–62.

FERNANDEZ Y GONZALEZ, Francisco, Ordiniamento formado por los procuradores de las aljamas hebreas. Madrid, 1886.

FERORELLI, NICOLA, Gli Ebrei nell'Italia meridionale dell'età romana al secolo XVIII. Turin, 1915.

FERSHT, B. A., "The Earliest Jewish Friendly Society in England, Rodphea Sholom." *Miscellanies of the Jewish Historical Society in England*, II (1935), 90–98.

Festschrift zum 200-jährigen Bestehen des Israelitischen Vereins für Krankenpflege und Beerdigung Chewra Kadischa zu Königsberg in Pr. 1704–1904. Königsberg, 1904.

FINKEL, JOSHUA, "Maimonides' Treatise on Resurrection: A Comparative Study." *In* Essays on Maimonides, ed. by S. W. Baron, New York, 1941, pp. 93–121.

FINKELSTEIN, LOUIS, Jewish Self-Government in the Middle Ages. With a Foreword by Alexander Marx. New York, 1924.

———, "The Origin of the Synagogue." *Proceedings of the American Academy for Jewish Research*, I (1928–30), 49–59.

———, "Zu den Takkanot des Rabbenu Gerschom." *MGWJ*, LXXIV (1930), 23–31. A reply to Baer.

———, The Pharisees: The Sociological Background of their Faith. 2 vols., Philadelphia, 1938.

FINZI, MOÏSE, "Il diritto di hazakà." *Festschrift A. Berliner*, Frankfort, 1903, pp. 93–96.

FISCHEL, WALTER J., Jews in the Economic and Political Life of Mediaeval Islam. London, 1937. Royal Asiatic Society Monographs, Vol. XXII.

———, "The 'Resh Galuta' in Arabic Literature" (Hebrew). *Magnes Anniversary Book*, Jerusalem, 1938, pp. 181–87.

FISCHER, HERBERT, Die verfassungsrechtliche Stellung der Juden in den deutschen Städten während des dreizehnten Jahrhunderts. Breslau, 1931.

———, "Judenprivilegien des Goslarer Rates im 14. Jahrhundert." *Zeitschrift der Savignystiftung für Rechtsgeschichte*: Germanistische Abteilung, LVI (1936), 89–149.

FISHMAN, JUDAH LEB, "The Institution of Nagid in Israel" (Hebrew). *Ha-Tor*, VII (1924), nos. 6–8, 11–17.

———, "The First German Scholars in Palestine, I" (Hebrew). *Mizraḥ u-ma'arab*, II (1928–29), 50–57.

Fita, Fidel, and Gabriel Llabres, "Privilegios de los Hebreos mallorquines en el Códice Pueyo." *Boletín de la Real Academia de la Historia*, XXXVI (1900), 15–35, 122–48, 185–209, 273–306, 369–402, 458–94.

Flesch, Heinrich, "Der Pinax von Austerlitz." *Jahrbuch für jüdische Volkskunde*, II (1925), 564–616.

———, "Der Judenbader zu Gaya." *MGWJ*, LXXIII (1929), 119–30.

———, "Rabbinatsdiplome." *ZGJT*, I (1930–31), 109–15.

———, "Mässigkeitsverordnungen." *ZGJT*, I (1930–31), 279–95.

———, "Aus dem Pinax von Tobischau." *JGJC*, III (1931), 257–73.

———, "Aus den Statuten der mährischen Beerdigungsgesellschaften." *JGJC*, V (1933), 157–74.

Fockema Andreae, S. J., "Der eed der Joden in Nederland onder de Republick." *Verslagen en Mededeelingen van den Kon. Akademie van Wetenschapen*, Section Letters, 4th ser., X, Pt. 1 (1909), 3–19.

Forcella, Vincenzo, Catalogo dei manoscritti riguardanti la storia di Roma che si trovano nella Biblioteca Vaticana. 4 vols., Rome, 1879–85.

Franchini, V., "La Congregazione 'De usuris' in Roma." *Economia*, N. S. VIII (1931), 413–23.

Frank, Moses, קהלות אשכנז (The Jewish Communities and Their Courts in Germany from the Twelfth to the End of the Fifteenth Century). Tel-Aviv, 1938.

Fränkel, David, "The Minute-Book of the Ḥebrah Ḳadishah in Chorostków" (Hebrew). *Alim*, I (1934–35), 21–25, 44–46.

———, "A Court Decision Written in Barcelona in 1292" (Hebrew). *Alim*, I (1934–35), 42–43.

———, "Contribution to the History of the Jews in Constantinople" (Hebrew). *Alim*, I (1934–35), 110–12.

Frankel, Zacharias, Der gerichtliche Beweis nach mosaisch-talmudischem Rechte. Berlin, 1846.

———, Ueber manches Polizeiliche des talmudischen Rechts." *MGWJ*, I (1852), 243–61.

Frankel, Zacharias, "Die Gemeindeordnung nach talmudischem Rechte. Eine historisch-rechtliche Skizze." *MGWJ*, II (1853), 289–304, 329–44.

Frankl-Grün, Adolf *or* Abraham Judah, "Die Gemeindeverfassung von Kremsier." *MGWJ*, XL (1896), 179–84, 209–19, 255–61.

———, Geschichte der Juden in Kremsier. 3 vols., Breslau, 1896–1901.

———, "Das Landesrabbinat in Kremsier." *MGWJ*, XLIII (1899), 360–70, 425–32.

———, "The Ordinances of the [Author of] *Ṭure Zahab*" (Hebrew). *Ha-Zofeh*, III (1914), 188–90.

Cf. David b. Samuel ha-Levi.

Freimann, Alfred, *or* Abraham Ḥayyim, "Asher b. Jechiel: Sein Leben und Wirken." *JJLG*, XII (1918), 237–317.

Cf. also Maimonides, Abraham *and* Moses; *and* Zacuto, Abraham.

Freimann, Aron, "R. David Lida and his Apologia Be'er 'Eshek" (Hebrew). *Sefer ha-Yobel* (Jubilee Volume in honor of) *Nahum Sokolow*, Warsaw, 1904, pp. 455–80.

———, "A Contribution to the Ḥistory of the Shabbetai Zevi Movement" (Yiddish). *Yivo Studies in History*, II (1937), 140–51.

Cf. also Azulai, Ḥayyim Joseph David.

Frenk, Azriel Nathan, "A Contribution to the History of the Ḥazakah" (Hebrew). *Ha-Shiloaḥ*, II (1897), 240–47.

———, העירונים והיהודים בפולין (The Burghers and Jews in Poland. A Historical Sketch). Warsaw, 1921.

Freshfield, Edwin Hanson, Roman Law in the later Roman Empire, Byzantine Guilds, Ordinances of Leo VI. In English translation. Cambridge, 1938.

Freudenthal, Max, "David Oppenheim als mährischer Landesrabbiner." *MGWJ*, XLVI (1902), 262–74.

———, "Zur Geschichte der Judenprivilegien Kaiser Maximilians II auf dem Reichstag zu Augsburg 1566." *ZGJD*, IV (1932), 83–100.

FREUND, ISMAR, Die Emanzipation der Juden in Preussen mit besonderer Berichtsichtigung des Gesetzes vom 11. März 1812. Ein Beitrag zur Rechtsgeschichte der Juden in Preussen. 2 vols., Berlin, 1912.

FREUND, S., Ein Vierteljahrtausend Hannoversches Landrabbinat, 1687–1937. Hannover, 1937.

FREY, JEAN-BAPTISTE, "Les communautés juives à Rome aux premiers temps de l'Eglise." *Recherches des sciences religieuses*, XX (1930), 269–97; XXI (1931), 129–68.

———, Corpus inscriptionum judaicarum. Recueil des inscriptions juives qui vont du IIIe siècle avant Jésus-Christ au VIIe siècle de notre ère. Vol. I: Europe. Paris, 1936. Vol. II is to contain the inscriptions of Asia and Africa.

FREYLICH, JUDYTA, "The Problem of Liquidating the Debts of the Community of Kazimierz [Cracow] after the Third Partition (1795–1809) and under the Republic of Cracow (1817–1829)" (Polish). *Miesięcznik żydowski*, III, Pt. 1 (1933), 467–78.

FRIEDBERG, BERNARD *or* ḤAYYIM DOBERISH, "Das Rabbinatsdiplom des R. Isaac ha-Cohen in Pinczów." *MGWJ*, XLIV (1900), 71–76.

———, תולדות הדפוס העברי בפולניה (History of Hebrew Typography in Poland). Antwerp, 1932.

———, תולדות הדפוס העברי באיטליה וכו' (History of Hebrew Typography in Italy, Spain, Portugal, Turkey and the Orient from Its Beginning and Formation about the Year 1472). Antwerp, 1934.

———, תולדות הדפוס העברי בערים האלה באירופה (History of Hebrew Typography of the Following Cities in Europe): Amsterdam, Antwerp, Avignon, Basle . . . Leyden, London, etc. From its Beginning in the Year 1516. Biographies of the First Printers, Their Assistants and Successors, with Bibliographical Enumeration of all Printed Works. Antwerp, 1937.

FRIEDENWALD, HARRY, "Two Jewish Physicians of the Sixteenth Century." *Medical Leaves*, 1941, 49–56.

Friedländer, Israel, "The Arabic Original of the Report of R. Nathan Ha-Babli." *JQR*, O. S. XVII (1904–5), 747–61.

Friedlaender, Moritz, Synagoge und Kirche in ihren Anfängen. Berlin, 1908.

Friedman, Filip, "Materials for the History of the Jews in Łęczyca" (Yiddish). *Lodzer Visenshaftleche Shriften*, I (1938), 239–46.

———, Historja Żydów w Polsce (History of the Jews in Poland). Typescript.

Friedman, Lee M., Early American Jews. Cambridge, Mass., 1934.

Friedmann, Meier, ed., ספרי (Sifre). On Deuteronomy. Vienna, 1864.

Frisch, Ephraim, A Historical Survey of Jewish Philanthropy from the Earliest Times to the Nineteenth Century. New York, 1924.

Frumkin, Aryeh Leb, תולדות חכמי ירושלים (A History of the Jerusalem Scholars from 1490 to 1870). Ed. with the author's biography, notes, additions and indices by Eliezer Rivlin. 3 vols., Jerusalem, 1928–30.
Cf. also Amram Gaon.

Fuchs, Leo, Die Juden Aegyptens in ptolemäischer und römischer Zeit. Vienna, 1924.

Funk, Solomon, Die Juden in Babylonien, 200–500. 2 vols., Berlin, 1902–8.

———, "Der Schutz der geistigen Arbeit in der Halacha." *JJLG*, XVIII (1927), 289–304.

Fünn, Samuel Joseph, קריה נאמנה (A History of the Jewish Community in the City of Wilno and Biographical Notes on Its Rabbis, Scholars, Writers and Benefactors). With additional notes by Mattathias Shtrashon and a biography of the author by Hillel Noah Steinschneider. Wilno, 1914.

Galant, I., "The Indebtedness of the Jewish Communities in the Seventeenth Century" (Russian). *Evreiskaya Starina*, VI (1913), 129–32.

GALANTÉ, ABRAHAM, Documents officiels turcs concernant les Juifs de Turquie. Recueil des 114 lois, réglements, firmans, bérats, ordres et décisions de tribunaux. Istanbul, 1931.

———, Histoire des Juifs de Rhodes, Chio, Cos, etc. Istanbul, 1935.

———, Médecins juifs au service de la Turquie. Istanbul, 1938.

GAMORAN, EMANUEL, Changing Conceptions in Jewish Education. New York, 1924.

GASTER, MOSES, History of the Ancient Synagogue of the Spanish and Portuguese Jews. The Cathedral Synagogue of the Jews in England situate in Bevis Marks: A Memorial Volume 1701–1901. London, 1901.

GAUTHIER, LÉON, "Les Juifs dans les deux Bourgognes. Étude sur le commerce de l'argent aux XIIIe et XIVe siècles." *REJ*, XLVIII (1904), 208–29; XLIX (1904), 1–17, 244–61.

GEIGER, LUDWIG, Geschichte der Juden in Berlin. 2 vols., Berlin, 1871. I: Als Festschrift zur zweiten Säkular-Feier im Auftrage des Vorstandes der Berliner Gemeinde. Nach den Akten des Geh. Staats-, des Ministerial-, des Stadt- und des Gemeinde-Archivs, nach gedruckten Quellen und den Materialien des Herrn L. Landshuth; II: Anmerkungen, Ausführungen und Urkundliche Beilagen.

GELBER, NATHAN MICHAEL, "The Regional Chief Rabbinate in Galicia (1776–1786)" (Russian). *Evreiskaya Starina*, VII (1914), 305–17.

———, "Aus dem Pinax des alten Judenfriedhofes in Brody (1699–1831)." *JJLG*, XIII (1920), 119–41.

———, "Aryeh Leib Bernstein, Chief Rabbi of Galicia." *JQR*, XIV (1923–24), 303–27.

———, "Die Juden und die Judenreform auf dem polnischen vierjährigen Sejm (1788–1792)." *Festschrift . . . Simon Dubnow*, Berlin, 1930, pp. 136–53.

———, "Contribution à l'histoire des Juifs espagnoles à Vienne." *REJ*, XCVII (1934), 114–51; XCVIII (1934), 44–49.

———, and ISRAEL HALPERIN, "The Council of Four Lands in the Years 1739, 1753" (Hebrew). *Zion*, II (1937), 153–84, 331–46.

Gerlach, Stephan, Tage-Buch, der von zween römischen Kaysern Maximiliano und Rudolpho, beyderseits den andern dieses Nahmens, an die Ottomannische Pforte zu Constantinopel abgefertigten Gesandtschafft. Frankfort, 1674. Non vidi.

Gerondi, Nissim b. Reuben, *see* Nissim b. Reuben of Gerona.

Gerson, M. A., "Les Juifs en Champagne." *Mémoires de la Société academique d'agriculture, des sciences, arts et belles-lettres du Département de l'Aube*, LXIII (1899), 173–261.

Geyer, Rudolf, and Leopold Sailer, Urkunden aus Wiener Grundbüchern zur Geschichte der Wiener Juden im Mittelalter. With a Preface by Otto Stowasser. Vienna, 1931. Historische Kommission der Israelitischen Kultusgemeinde in Wien, Quellen und Forschungen zur Geschichte der Juden in Deutsch-Osterreich, Vol. X.

Gierse, Albert, Geschichte der Juden in Westfalen während des Mittelalters. Naumburg a. S., n. d.

Ginsburger, Ernest, Les Juifs de Belgique au XVIIIe siècle. Paris, 1932. Reprinted from *REJ*, XC–XCI (1931).

———, "Les Juifs de Peyrehorade." *REJ*, N. S. IV (1938), 35–69.

Ginsburger, M., "Rechte und Pflichten eines Judenvorstehers in der Grafschaft Rappolstein." *Blätter für jüdische Geschichte und Literatur*, IV (1903), 64–70.

———, "Les Juifs de Metz sous l'Ancien Régime." *REJ*, L (1905), 112–28, 238–60.

———, "Un emprunt de la nation juive d'Alsace." *REJ*, LXXXI (1925), 83–86.

———, "Samuel Sanvil Weil, Rabbin de la Haute et Basse-Alsace (1711–1753)." *REJ*, XCV–VI (1933), 54–75, 179–98.

Ginzberg, Louis, Geonica. 2 vols., New York, 1909. I: The Geonim and Their Halakic Writings; II: Genizah Studies.

———, Students, Scholars and Saints. Philadelphia, 1928,

———, גנזי שעכטער (Genizah Studies in Memory of Dr. Solomon Schechter). 2 vols., New York, 1928–29. I: Midrash and Haggadah; II: Geonic and Early Karaitic Halakah. Texts and Studies of the Jewish Theological Seminary of America, Vols. VII–VIII.

GINZBURG, SIMON, The Life and Works of Moses Hayyim Luzzatto, Founder of Modern Hebrew Literature. Philadelphia, 1931.

———, ed., ר' משה חיים לוצאטו ובני דורו (R. Moses Ḥayyim Luzzatto and his Generation). A Collection of Letters and Documents. Tel-Aviv, 1937.

GLASER, ALFRED, Geschichte der Juden in Strassburg. Von der Zeit Karl d. Gr. bis auf die Gegenwart. Strasbourg, 1894.

GLESINGER, L., "Beiträge zur Geschichte der Pharmazie bei den Juden." *MGWJ*, LXXXII (1938), 111–30, 417–22.

GLÜCKSBERG, S. J., "The Meturgemanim [Interpreters] in the Talmudic Period" (Hebrew). *Sinai*, II (1938), 218–21.

GOLD, HUGO, ed., Die Juden und Judengemeinden Mährens in Vergangenheit und Gegenwart. Ein Sammelwerk. Brünn, 1929.

GOLDBERGER, ISRAEL, "Two Rabbinic Diplomas" (Hebrew). *Ha-Zofeh*, II (1912), 132–38.

———, "The Sources concerning Hillel's Elevation to the Nesiut" (Hebrew). *Ha-Zofeh*, X (1926), 68–76.

GOLDMANN, ARTUR, Das Judenbuch der Scheffstrasse zu Wien (1389–1420). Vienna, 1908. Historische Kommission der Israelitischen Kultusgemeinde in Wien, Quellen und Forschungen zur Geschichte der Juden in Deutsch-Österreich, Vol. I.

GOLDZIHER, IGNAZ, "Renseignements de source musulmane sur la dignité de resch-galuta." *REJ*, VIII (1884), 121–25.

———, "Sa'id b. Hasan d'Alexandrie." *REJ*, XXX (1895), 1–23.

———, "Education, Muslim." *In* Hasting's Encyclopaedia of Religion and Ethics, V, 198–207.

GOLITSYN, COUNT NICHOLAS N., Istoriia russkago zakonodatel'stva o Evreiakh (A History of Russian Legislation Concerning the Jews). Vol. I: 1649–1825. Petersburg, 1886.

GOODE, ALEXANDER D., "The Exilarchate in the Eastern Caliphate, 637–1258." *JQR*, XXXI (1940–41), 149–69.

GOODENOUGH, ERWIN R., The Jurisprudence of the Jewish Courts in Egypt; Legal Administration by the Jews under the Early Roman Empire as Described by Philo Judaeus. New Haven, 1929.

Gottheil, Richard J. H., "An Eleventh Century Document, concerning a Cairo Synagogue." *JQR*, O. S. XIX (1906–7), 467–539.

———, "Dhimmis and Moslems in Egypt." *Old Testament and Semitic Studies in Memory of William R. Harper*, 2 vols., Chicago, 1908, II, 351–414.

———, and William H. Worrell, eds., Fragments from the Cairo Genizah in the Freer Collection. New York, 1927.

Götz, Elyakim b. Meir, ס' אבן השוהם ומאירת עינים (Responsa). Dyhernfurth, 1733.

Graetz, Heinrich, Geschichte der Juden. 11 vols., Leipzig, 1853–76. Later editions of individual volumes were revised by Marcus Brann, Simon Eppenstein, etc.

———, History of the Jews (English transl.). 6 vols., Philadelphia, 1891–98.

———, ס' דברי ימי ישראל (Hebrew transl. by Saul Pinhas Rabbinowitz), Warsaw, 1890–99.

———, Einige handschriftliche Briefe von Jonathan Eibeschütz." *MGWJ*, XVI (1867), 421–30, 460–67.

Grandemaison, Louis de, "Le cimetière des Juifs à Tours." *REJ*, XVIII (1899), 262–75.

Grau, Wilhelm, Antisemitismus im späten Mittelalter. Das Ende der Regensburger Judengemeinde 1450–1519. With a Foreword by Karl Alexander von Müller. Munich, 1934.

Grayzel, Solomon, The Church and the Jews in the XIIIth Century. A Study of Their Relations During the Years 1198–1254, Based on the Papal Letters and the Conciliar Decrees of the Period. Philadelphia, 1933.

Great Britain, Foreign Office, Handbooks Prepared under the Direction of the Historical Section of the Foreign Office. Vol. CXXXVI. Dutch Guiana. London, 1920.

Greenspan, N. S., "On the History of the Commandment concerning Phylacteries and of its Neglect" (Hebrew). *Ozar Hachaim*, IV (1927–28), 159–64.

GREGORY (GREGORIUS) I, POPE, Epistolae. *In* Monumenta Germaniae Historica, Epistolae. Vols. I–II. Berlin, 1887–99.

GRESSMANN, HUGO, "Jewish Life in Ancient Rome," *Jewish Studies in Memory of Israel Abrahams*, New York, 1927, pp. 170–91.

GROSS, HENRI, Gallia Judaica; Dictionnaire géographique de la France d'après les sources rabbiniques. Paris, 1897.

GROTTE, ALFRED, Alte schlesische Judenfriedhöfe (Breslau und Dyherrnfurth). Berlin, 1927. Monographien zu Denkmalpflege und Heimatschutz.

———, Synagogenspuren in schlesischen Kirchen. Breslau, 1937.

GRÜNBERGER, Z. D., "On the History of the Commandment of Phylacteries and of its Neglect" (Hebrew). *Ozar Hachaim*, V (1928–29), 71–72. Refers to ibid., IV, 159–64.

GRUNEBAUM, PAUL, "Les Juifs d'Orient d'après les géographes et les voyageurs." *REJ*, XXVII (1893), 121–35.

———, "Une épisode de l'histoire des Juifs d'Ancone." *REJ*, XXVIII (1894), 142–46.

GRÜNFELD, RICHARD, Zur Geschichte der Juden in Bingen am Rhein. Bingen am Rhein, 1905.

GRÜNHUT, [LAZAR], "[Bibliographische Notiz über] Abraham Halevis Responsen." *Zeitschrift für hebräische Bibliographie*, IX (1905), 97–98.

GRUNWALD, MAX, "Volkstracht, Hausbau u. ähnl." *MGJV*, I (1898), 113–16.

———, "Die Statuten der 'Hamburg-Altonaer Gemeinde' von 1726." *MGJV*, XI (1903), 1–64.

———, Hamburgs deutsche Juden bis zur Auflösung der Dreigemeinden 1811. Hamburg, 1904.

———, "Kleine Beiträge zur jüdischen Kulturgeschichte." *MGJV*, XVI (1905), 144–75; XVII (1906), 14–38, 96–120.

———, "Die Statuten des Talmud Tora-Vereins in Modena um 1750." *MGJV*, XXXVII–XL (1911), 63–71.

———, "Altjüdisches Gemeindeleben." *MGJV*, XLI–IV (1912), 1–4, 73–88; XLV–VIII (1913), Pt. 2, pp. 27–31.

———, Samuel Oppenheimer und sein Kreis (Ein Kapitel aus der Finanzgeschichte Österreichs). Vienna, 1913. Historische

Kommission der Israelitischen Kultusgemeinde in Wien, Quellen und Forschungen zur Geschichte der Juden in Deutsch-Österreich, Vol. V.

Grunwald, Max, "Jüdische Waisenfürsorge in alter und neuer Zeit." *MGWJ*, LXVI (1922), 3–29.

———, "Luxusverbot der Dreigemeinden (Hamburg-Altona-Wandsbek) aus dem Jahre 1715." *Jahrbuch für jüd. Volkskunde*, I (1923), 227–34.

———, "Aus Spanien und Portugal. Bemerkungen zur Fritz Baer, Die Juden im christlichen Spanien." *MGWJ*, LXXIII (1929), 366–76.

———, "Le cimetière de Worms." *REJ*, N. S. IV (1938), 71–112.

Güdemann, Moritz, "Die Neugestaltung des Rabbinerwesens und deren Einfluss auf die talmudische Wissenschaft im Mittelalter." *MGWJ*, XIII (1864), 68–70, 97–110, 384–95, 421–44.

———, Das jüdische Unterrichtswesen während der spanisch-arabischen Periode. Vienna, 1873.

———, Geschichte des Erziehungswesens und der Kultur der abendländischen Juden während des Mittelalters und der neueren Zeit. 3 vols., Vienna, 1880–88.

———, Quellenschriften zur Geschichte des Unterrichts und der Erziehung bei den deutschen Juden von den ältesten Zeiten bis auf Mendelssohn. Berlin, 1891.

———, "Ein Projekt zur Gründung einer jüdischen Universität aus dem 16. Jahrhundert." *Festschrift . . . A. Berliner*, Frankfort, 1903, pp. 164–75.

Gulak, Asher, אוצר השטרות הנהוגים בישראל (Thesaurus of Deeds Frequently Used by Jews). Jerusalem, 1926. ספריה משפטית, ed. by Judah Junowicz, Vol. V.

———, "The Method of Collecting Roman Taxes in Palestine." (Hebrew). *Magnes Anniversary Book*, Jerusalem, 1938, pp. 97–104.

———, "Boulé and Strategia: A Contribution to the Roman Fiscal Administration in Palestine" (Hebrew). *Tarbiz*, XI (1939), 119–22.

GUMBINER ABRAHAM ABELE B. ḤAYYIM KALISCH, מגן אברהם (Commentary), on Joseph Karo's *Shulḥan 'Aruk*. Printed with many editions of the latter work.

GUTSTEIN, MORRIS A., The Story of the Jews of Newport: Two and a Half Centuries of Judaism, 1658–1908. New York, 1936.

HAAS, THEODOR, Die Juden in Mähren. Brünn, 1908.

HABERMANN, ABRAHAM MEIR, נשים עבריות בתור מדפיסות (Jewish Women as Printers, Compositors, Publishers and Patronesses of Authors). Berlin, 1933.

———, "Women Connected with the Printing of Hebrew Books: A Supplement" (Hebrew). *Kirjath Sefer*, XV (1938), 373–76.

HAGGAHOT MAIMONIOT, *see* Meir ha-Kohen.

HAI B. SHERIRA GAON, *see* Lewin, Benjamin Menasseh.

HALBERSTAM, SALOMON Z. H. *or* Z. J., קהלת שלמה (A Catalogue of His Manuscripts). Vienna, 1890.

———, "A Response of Solomon b. Aderet." *JQR*, O. S. VIII (1895–96), 527–28. Refers to David Kaufmann's "Jewish Informers in the Middle Ages."

Cf. also Judah b. Barzilai.

HALEVI, YEHUDAH B. SAMUEL (ABU'L-ḤASAN), Kitab al-Khazari (Sefer ha-Kuzari). Das Buch al-Chazari des Abu l'hasan Jehuda Hallevi, im arabischen Urtext sowie in der hebräischen Uebersetzung des Jehuda ibn Tibbon, hrsg. von Hartwig Hirschfeld. Leipzig, 1887.

———, ———, Das Buch Kusari des Jehuda ha-Levi nach dem hebräischen Texte des Jehuda Ibn-Tibbon herausgegeben, übersetzt und mit einem Commentar, sowie mit einer allgemeinen Einleitung versehen von David Cassel. Leipzig, 1853; 5th ed., Leipzig, 1922.

———, ———, Kitab al-Khazari, Translated from the Arabic with an Introduction by H. Hirschfeld. With a Preface to the new edition by M. M. Kaplan. 2d ed., New York, 1927.

———, Diwan. Nach Handschriften und Druckwerken bearbeitet und mit erklärenden Anmerkungen versehen von H. Brody (Hebrew). 4 vols. Berlin, 1894–1930.

Halevy, Isaak, דורות הראשונים; die Geschichte und Literatur Israels. 4 vols., Frankfort, 1918–22. Incomplete.

Halperin, Israel, "The Council of Four Lands and the Hebrew Book" (Hebrew). *Kirjath Sepher*, IX (1932–33), 367–94.

———, "Zur Frage der Zusammensetzung der Vierländersynode in Polen." *MGWJ*, LXXVI (1932), 519–22.

———, "Approbations of the Council of Four Lands in Poland" (Hebrew). *Kirjath Sepher*, XI (1934–35), 105–16, 252–64. Supplemented ibid., XII (1935–36), 250–53.

———, תוספות ומילואים ל״פנקס מדינת ליטא״ (Addenda to the Minutes of the Lithuanian Council of Provinces, edited by Dubnow). Collected and edited with Introduction and Indices. Jerusalem, 1935. Reprinted from *Ḥoreb*, Vol. II.

———, "Beginnings of the Lithuanian Jewish Council and its Relations with the Council of Four Lands" (Hebrew). *Zion*, III (1937–38), 51–57.

———, "The Council of Four Lands and Its Relations with the Outside World" (Yiddish). *Yivo Studies in History*, II (1937), 68–79.

———, "Jewish Artisan Guilds in Poland and Lithuania" (Hebrew). *Zion*, II (1937), 70–89.

Hannover, Nathan Neta, ס׳ יון מצולה (A Chronicle of the Massacres in 1648). Venice, 1652. *Also in* Abraham Kahana's Sifrut ha-historia ha-israelit, II, 295–318.

———, ———, In the Yiddish transl. by W. Latzky-Bertoldi, with a Supplement by I. Israelsohn and an Investigation concerning the Period of Chmielnicky by Jacob Shatzky. Wilno, 1938.

Harkavy, Abraham Eliyahu, "Fragment einer Apologie des Maimonidischen מאמר תחית המתים," *Zeitschrift für hebräische Bibliographie*, II (1897), 125–28, 181–88 (the second instalment appeared under a slightly changed title).

———, חדשים גם ישנים in the Appendix to the Hebrew translation of Graetz's Geschichte, Vol. VII, Warsaw, 1899.

———, "Neṭira and his Sons." *Festschrift . . . A. Berliner*, Frankfort, 1903, Hebrew section, pp. 34–43.

Cf. also Teshubot ha-geonim.

Ḥayyim b. Bezaleel, וכוח מים חיים (On Law, with Polemical Notes on Isserles's תורת חטאת). Amsterdam, 1711.

Hecht, Emanuel, "Kinderraub." *MGWJ*, X (1861), 399–400.

Heck, Mordecai, "Is Julian's Declaration a Forgery?" (Hebrew). *Yavneh*, II (1939–40), 118–39.

Hegel, Karl, ed., Chronicon Moguntinum bis 1406. Hannover, 1885. Die Chroniken der deutschen Städte vom 14. bis ins 16. Jahrhundert, Vol. XVIII.

Heimbucher, Max, Die Orden und Kongregationen der katholischen Kirche, 3d ed., revised. 2 vols., Paderborn, 1933–34.

Heinemann, Isaak, "Jüdisch-hellenistische Gerichtshöfe in Alexandrien?" *MGWJ*, LXXIV (1930), 363–69. A review of E. R. Goodenough's Jurisprudence of the Jewish Courts in Egypt.

———, "Wer veranlasste den Glaubenszwang der Makkabäerzeit." *MGWJ*, LXXXII (1938), 146–72.

Hekker, Elena, "Jews in Polish Cities during the second half of the Eighteenth Century" (Russian). *Evreiskaya Starina*, VI (1913), 184–200, 325–32.

———, "Reform Projects of Jewish Life in Poland at the End of the Eighteenth Century" (Russian). *Evreiskaya Starina*, VII (1914), 206–18, 328–40.

Hemerdinger, Gabriel, "Le dénombrement des Israélites d'Alsace (1784)." *REJ*, XLII (1901), 253–64.

Henriques, Henry Straus Quixano, The Jews and the English Law. Oxford, 1908.

Heppner, Aron, and J. Herzberg, Aus Vergangenheit und Gegenwart der Juden und der jüdischen Gemeinden in den Posener Landen. Bromberg, 1904–31.

Hessen, Julius, "A Study in the History of the Korobka Tax in Russia" (Russian). *Evreiskaya Starina*, IV (1911), 305–47, 487–512.

Higger, Michael, ed., מסכת שמחות Treatise Semaḥot and Treatise Semaḥot of R. Ḥiyya and Sefer Ḥibbut ha-ḳeber . . . Ed. from Manuscripts with an Introd., Notes and Variants. New York, 1931.

Hildebrand, Friedrich, J., Das romanische Judenbad im alten Synagogenhofe zu Speier am Rhein. Spires, 1920.

Hildenfinger, Paul, "Documents relatifs aux Juifs d'Arles." *REJ*, XLI (1900), 62–79; XLVII (1903), 221–42; XLVIII (1904), 48–81, 265–72.

———, Documents sur les Juifs à Paris au XVIIIe siècle: Actes d'inhumation et scellés. Paris, 1913.

Hildesheimer, Azriel, "A Contribution to the Study of the 'Kalla' in the Geonic Period." *Festschrift Jakob Freimann*, Berlin, 1937, Hebrew Section, pp. 58–71.

Hillel b. Naftali Hirz, בית הלל (Comments on Joseph Karo's *Shulḥan 'Aruk* Y. D. and Eben ha-'Ezer). With notes by his son, Moses. Dyhernfurth, 1691.

Hillesum, J. M., "Vereenigingen bij de Portugeesche en Spaansche Joden te Amsterdam in de 17de en 18de eeuw." *Jaarboek van den Vereeniging Amstelodamum*, I (1902), 167–83.

Hirsch, Emil, "Das Judenbad zu Friedberg in Hessen." *In* F. Dreher's Friedberg i. H. in Wort und Bild, Friedberg, 1925, pp. 79–85.

———, "Glocke als Wetterzauber beim Friedberger Judenbad von 1260." *Festschrift der philosophisch-historischen Verbindung Cimbria-Heidelberg zu ihrem 50-jährigen Bestehen*, Dortmund, 1926, pp. 95–103.

Hirsch, Menko Max, ed., Frucht vom Baum des Lebens. Ozer [!] Peroth Ez Chajim des Rabbinerseminars Ets Haim in Amsterdam. Zeitlich geordnet, ins Deutsche übertragen und in gekürzter Form herausgegeben. Berlin, 1937.

Hirsch, S. A., "The Temple of Onias." *Jews' College Jubilee Volume*, London, 1906, pp. 39–80.

Hirschfeld, Hartwig, "Some Judaeo-Arabic Legal Documents." *JQR*, XVI (1925–26), 279–86.
Cf. also Halevi, Yehudah.

Hitti, Philip K., History of the Arabs. 2d ed., London, 1940.

Hoeniger, Robert, "Zur Geschichte der Juden Deutschlands im früheren Mittelalter." *ZGJD*, O. S. I (1887), 65–97, 136–51.

———, and Moritz Stern, eds., Das Judenschreinsbuch der Laurenzpfarre zu Köln. Berlin, 1888. Historische Kommission für Geschichte der Juden in Deutschland, Quellen zur Geschichte der Juden in Deutschland, Vol. I.

Hoffmann von Wellenhof, Victor, "Die Sonderbesteuerung der jüdischen Bevölkerung in Galizien und der Bukowina bis zum Jahre 1848." *Vierteljahrsschrift für Sozial- und Wirtschaftsgeschichte*, XII (1914), 404–48.

Holleschau, Johanan, ס' מעשה רב (A pamphlet on the London controversy printed together with תשובות הגאונים). Amsterdam, 1707.

Honik, Z., "Court Jurisdiction over Lithuanian Jewry after the Union of Lublin" (Yiddish). *Yivo Bleter*, XIV (1938), 316–34.

Horodezky, Samuel Abba, לקורות הרבנות (Biographical Sketches of Rabbis). Warsaw, 1914.

Horovitz, Jakob, חבר עיר. Frankfort, 1915. Revised reprint from *Festschrift Jakob Guttmann*, Leipzig, 1915, pp. 125–42.

———, "Nochmals חבר עיר. Bemerkungen zu 'חבר עיר' des Herrn Prof. Krauss." *JJLG*, XVII (1926), 241–314.

Horovitz, Marcus, Frankfurter Rabbinen. Ein Beitrag zur Geschichte der israelitischen Gemeinde in Frankfurt a. M. 4 vols., Frankfort, 1882–85.

———, "A Responsum of 1469." *Magazin für die Wissenschaft des Judentums*, X (1883), Hebrew section, pp. 1–11.

———, "Die Wohltätigkeit bei den Juden im alten Frankfurt." *Israelitische Monatsschrift* (Supplement to *Jüdische Presse*), XXVII (1896), 17–18, 21–22, 26–27.

———, Die Frankfurter Rabbinerversammlung vom Jahre 1603. Frankfort, 1897.

———, Die Inschriften des alten Friedhofs der israelitischen Gemeinde zu Frankfurt a. M. Frankfort, 1901.

Horowitz, Chajim Meir, ed., בית נכות ההלכות *or* תורתן של ראשונים (A Collection of Geonic Sources, etc.). 2 pts., Frankfort, 1881.

Horowitz, Isaiah b. Abraham, ס' שני לוחות הברית (Ethical-kabbalistic treatise with a preface by Shabbetai Horowitz). Amsterdam, 1649.

Horwitz, L., "Landrabbiner und Landschreiber in Kurhessen." *MGWJ*, LIV (1910), 513–34.

Huart, Clément, Ancient Persia and Iranian Civilization. London, 1927.

Hülsen, Julius, Der alte Judenfriedhof in Frankfurt a. M. Frankfort, 1931.

Humann, Carl, Conrad Cichorius, Walther Judeich and Franz Winter, eds., Altertümer von Hierapolis. In *Jahrbuch des deutschen archäologischen Instituts*, Supplementary issue, no. 4, Berlin, 1898.

Ibn abi Zimra, David b. Solomon, ס' שאלות ותשובות (Responsa). 7 vols., Warsaw, 1882–83.

Ibn Abudirham, David b. Joseph, ס' אבודרהם (Commentary on Prayers). Venice, 1545.

Ibn Adret, Solomon b. Abraham, ס' שאלות ותשובות (Responsa). Vol. I, Bologna, 1539; Vols. II, III, V, Leghorn, 1657, 1778, 1825; Vol. IV, Salonica, 1808; Vols. VI–VII, Warsaw, 1868. Also Responsa ascribed to Naḥmanides, edition Constantinople, 1519.

Ibn Ḥabib, Joseph, ס' נמוקי יוסף (Commentary on Alfasi's Halakot). Printed with many editions of the latter work.

Ibn Ḥabib, Levi b. Jacob, ס' שאלות ותשובות (Responsa). Venice, 1565.

Ibn Leb, Joseph b. David, ס' שאלות ותשובות (Responsa). 4 parts, Amsterdam, 1762.

Ibn Megas, Joseph, ס' חדושים על בבא בתרא (Novellae on the Tractate Baba batra). Amsterdam, 1702.

———, ס' שאלות ותשובות (Responsa). Salonica, 1791.

Ibn Saad al Zuhri, Muhammad, Biographien Muhammeds, seiner Gefährten . . . bis zum Jahre 230 der Flucht. Vols. I–IX. Ed. by Ed. Sachau, Leiden, 1905–1940. Includes V: Biographien der Nachfolger in Medina. Ed. by K. V. Zettersteen. Leiden, 1905; VI: Biographien der Kufier. Ed. by K. V. Zettersteen. Leiden, 1909.

Ibn Verga, Solomon, ס' שבט יהודה (Judah's Rod, A Chronicle). Ed. and transl. into German, with additions by M. Wiener. 2 vols., 2d impression, Hannover, 1924.

IBN VERGA, SOLOMON, ס' שבט יהודה, La Vara de Juda. Spanish transl., with an "Estudio preliminaro" by F. Cantera Burgos. Granada, 1927.

IBN YAḤYA, DAVID, *see* Marx, Alexander.

IBN YAḤYA, GEDALIAH B. JOSEPH, ס' שלשלת הקבלה (The Chain of Tradition, A Chronicle). Amsterdam, 1697.

IBN ZERAḤ, MENAHEM B. AARON, ס' צדה לדרך (On Law and Ethics). Lwów, 1859.

IDELSOHN, ABRAHAM ZVI, "The *Ḥazzan* in Eastern Europe" (Hebrew). *Ha-Toren*, XI (1924–25), 138–54.

———, "Kantoren". *Encyclopaedia Judaica*, IX, 888–902.

———, Jewish Music in Its Historical Development. New York, 1929.

———, Jewish Liturgy and its Development. New York, 1932.

IMMANUEL B. SOLOMON OF ROME, ס' המחברות (Makamas). Ed. by J. Wilheimer, with a note in German by M. Steinschneider. Lwów, 1870.

ISAAC B. MORDECAI GERSHON, ed., ס' משבית מלחמות (A Collection of Rabbinic Decisions). Venice, 1606.

ISAAC B. SHESHET (Profet, Perfet *or* Barfat), ס' שאלות ותשובות (Responsa). Constantinople, 1547.

ISAAC, JOSEPH, Unmassgäbliche Gedanken über Betteljuden. Nuremberg, 1791. Translated from Yiddish.

ISAIAH OF TRANI, ס' המכריע (Decisions). With Novellae on the Tractate Ta'anit. Munkacs, 1900.

ISSERLEIN, ISRAEL B. PETAḤIAH, ס' תרומת הדשן (Responsa). Ven ce, 1546.

———, ס' פסקים וכתבים (On Law). Venice, 1546.

Cf. also Joseph b. Moses.

ISSERLES, MOSES B. ISRAEL, ס' ההגהות or מפה (Glosses on Joseph Karo's *Shulḥan 'Aruk*). *In* most editions of that Code.

———, ס' דרכי משה (Commentary on Jacob b. Asher's *Ṭurim*). Printed with many recent editions of the latter work.

———, ס' תורת חטאת (Juridical Treatise). Cracow, 1569.

———, ס' תורת העולה (On the Temple ritual, astronomy and philosophy). Prague, 1569.

———, ס' שאלות ותשובות (Responsa). Cracow, 1640.

Italiener, Bruno (in collaboration with Aron Freimann, August L. Mayer, and Adolf Schmidt), ed., Die Darmstädter Pessach-Haggadah. Codex Orientalis 8 der Landesbibliothek zu Darmstadt aus dem vierzehnten Jahrhundert herausg. und erläutert. Mit einer Gesammtbibliographie der illustrierten Haggadah. Leipzig, 1927.

Iterson, Aart van, Armenzorg bij de Joden in Palestina van 100 v. Chr.–200 n. Chr. Leiden, 1911.

Jacob Abraham b. Raphael, ס' נחלת יעקב (Homilies on the Pentateuch). Amsterdam, 1722–24.

Jacob b. Asher, ארבעה טורים (Ṭurim; The Four Pillars). 4 parts, with numerous commentaries. Piove di Sacco, 1475, and in many later editions. A code of Jewish law. The four parts have the following subtitles: Oraḥ Ḥayyim (abbreviation, O. Ḥ.); Yoreh Deah (Y. D.); Eben ha-'Ezer; Ḥoshen Mishpaṭ (Ḥ. M.).

———, פירוש על התורה (Commentary on the Pentateuch). In the Horeb Pentateuch ed., New York, 1928, and other editions.

Jacob b. Elijah of Valencia (Venice), "A (Polemical) Letter" (Hebrew). Ed. by J. Kobak. *Jeschurun*, VI (1868), 1–34.

Jacobs, Joseph, The Jews of Angevin England. Documents and Records. From Latin and Hebrew Sources, Printed and Manuscript, for the First Time Collected and Translated. London, 1893.

Jacobson, Jacob, "Mosaiksteine zur Kultur- und Sanitätsgeschichte der Posenschen (grosspolnischen) Juden im 18. Jahrhundert." *Menorah*, VII (Vienna, 1929), 335–59.

———, Jüdische Trauungen in Berlin, 1723–1759. Berlin, 1938.

Jakobovits, Tobias, "Jüdisches Gemeindeleben in Kolin (1763–1768)." *JGJC*, I (1929), 332–68.

———, "Die Erlebnisse des Oberrabbiners Simon Spira-Wedeles in Prag (1640–1679)." *JGJC*, IV (1932), 253–96.

———, "Das Prager und Böhmische Landesrabbinat Ende des siebzehnten und Anfang des achtzehnten Jahrhunderts." *JGJC*, V (1933), 79–136.

Jakobovits, Tobias, "Die Erlebnisse des R. Berl Jeiteles als Primator der Prager Judenschaft." *JGJC*, VII (1935), 421–36.

———, "Die jüdischen Zünfte in Prag." *JGJC*, VIII (1936), 57–141.

Janowsky, Oscar I., The Jews and Minority Rights, 1898–1919. With a Foreword by Julian W. Mack. New York, 1933.

Jastrow, Marcus, A Dictionary of the Targumim, the Talmud Babli and Yerushalmi, and the Midrashic Literature. 2 vols., London, 1886–1903.

Jawitz, Zeeb (Wolf), ס' תולדות ישראל (A History of the Jews: Revised on the Basis of Original Sources). Vols. I–XIII. Jerusalem, 1932–37. Vols. I–VIII in 3d and 4th eds., IX–XIII posthumously ed. from the author's Ms. by B. M. Lewin.

Jeremias, Johannes, "Hesekieltempel und Serubbabeltempel," *Zeitschrift für die alttestamentliche Wissenschaft*, LII (1934), 109–12.

Jerome (Hieronymus), St., Opera omnia. 11 vols. in 9. *In* Migne's Patrologia latina, Vols. XXII–XXX.

———, "Letters and Select Works" (English transl.). New York, 1890. *In* A Select Library of Nicene and Post-Nicene Fathers of the Christian Church, Vol. VI.

Jewish Encyclopedia. A Descriptive Record of the History, Religion, Literature and Customs of the Jewish People from the Earliest Times to the Present Day. Ed. by Isidore Singer. 12 vols., New York, 1901–6.

Joffe, J., "The Struggle between Burghers and Jews in Kurland during the Eighteenth Century" (Russian). *Evreiskaya Starina*, IV (1911), 568–80.

John of Antioch, *see* Mommsen, Theodor.

Jones, Arnold Hugh Martin, The Cities of the Eastern Roman Provinces. Oxford, 1937.

Joseph b. Moses (of Höchstadt), ed., ס' לקט יושר Collectaneen seines Lehrers Israel Isserlein. With an Introd. and Notes by Jakob Freimann. 2 pts., Berlin, 1903–4.

Josephus, Flavius, Opera. Ed. by Benedictus Niese. 7 vols., Berlin, 1887–95.

Josephus, Flavius, Works. An early English translation by William Whiston, 2 vols., in numerous editions.

———, Works. Greek text with English translation by H. St. John Thackeray and Ralph Marcus. Vols. I–VI. London and Cambridge, Mass., 1926–37. "Loeb Classical Library." Vols. VII–IX to be issued.

Jouguet, Pierre, La vie municipale dans l'Egypte romain. Paris, 1911.

Judah b. Barzilai al-Barceloni, ס' השטרות (Book of Deeds). Ed. with an Introd. and Notes by S. Z. J. Halberstam. Berlin, 1898.

Judah b. Samuel he-Ḥasid, ס' החסידים (Book of the Pious). Ed. by J. Wistinetzki. 2d ed., Frankfort, 1924.

Judah b. Yeḥiel Rophe, ס' נפת צופים (Rhetoric). Ed. by Adolf Jellinek. Vienna, 1863.

Judah, George Fortunatus, "The Jews' Tribute in Jamaica; Extracted from the Journals of the House of Assembly of Jamaica." *PAJHS*, XVIII (1909), 149–77.

Judeich, Walther, *see* Humann, Carl.

Judelowitz, Mordecai David *or* Morduch, "The Town of Sura" (Hebrew). *Sinai*, I, Pt. 1 (1937), 168–74, 268–75; Pt. 2 (1938), 156–62, 317–24, 411–22; II, Pt. 1 (1938), 130–32.

———, חיי היהודים בזמן התלמוד (Jewish Life in the Talmudic Period): The City of Pumbedita in the Days of the Amoraim. Jerusalem, 1939.

Jüdisches Lexikon; ein enzyklopädisches Handbuch des jüdischen Wissens. Ed. by Georg Herlitz and Bruno Kirschner. 5 vols., Berlin, 1927–30.

Julianus, Flavius Claudius, Apostata, Oeuvres complètes. Ed. and transl. by J. Bidez. Vol. I in 2 Pts. Paris, 1924–32. Vol. I, Pt. 2: Letters and Fragments.

———, Works. With an English translation by Wilmer Cane Wright. 3 vols., New York, 1913–23. "Loeb Classical Library." Vol. III includes Letters.

Juster, Jean, Les Juifs dans l'empire romain. Leur condition juridique, économique et sociale. 2 vols., Paris, 1914.

JUSTIN, MARTYR, Opera. *In* Migne's Patrologia graeca, Vol. VI.
———, Dialogue avec Tryphon. Greek text with French translation, notes and index, by G. Archambault. 2 vols., Paris, 1909.
———, Writings. English translation by M. Dods, Edinburgh, 1870. *In* Ante-Nicene Christian Library, Vol. II.
JUSTINIAN (Emperor), *see* Corpus Iuris Civilis.
JUVENAL, DECIMUS JUNIUS, Works. Latin text with English translation by G. G. Ramsay, London, 1920. "Loeb Classical Library."

KAHAN, I., "L'usage de se couvrir la tête." *REJ*, LXXXIV (1927), 176–78.
KAHANE *or* KAHANA, ABRAHAM, ספרות ההסטוריא הישראלית (Jewish Historical Literature: An Anthology). 2 vols., Warsaw, 1922–23.
KAHN, LÉON, Histoire de la communauté israélite de Paris: Le Comité de bienfaisance, l'hôpital, les cimetières. Paris, 1886.
KAHN, SALOMON, "Documents inédits sur les Juifs de Montpellier." *REJ*, XIX (1889), 259–81; XXII (1891), 264–79; XXIII (1891), 265–78.
KALLNER, H. D., and E. ROSENAU, "The Geographical Regions of Palestine." *Geographical Review*, XXIX (1939), 61–80.
KAPP, ARNO, "Elkan Herz, der Freund und Verwandte Moses Mendelssohns, der Vater der ersten Leipziger liberalen Judengemeinde." *ZGJD*, IV (1932), 198–202.
KARO, JOSEPH B. EPHRAIM, ס' בית יוסף (House of Joseph, Commentary). On Jacob b. Asher's *Ṭurim*. Printed with most editions of the latter work.
———, שלחן ערוך (Shulḥan 'Aruk). A Code of Laws. Venice 1564–65 and many subsequent editions. Follows the arrangement of Jacob b. Asher's *Ṭurim*.
KARPF, MAURICE JOSEPH, Jewish Community Organization in the United States: An Outline of Types of Organizations, Activities and Problems. New York, 1938.
KASSEL, KARL, "Zwei Schriftstücke zur Geschichte der Aerzte und Apotheker in Fürth." *MGWJ*, LXVI (1922), 233–35.

KATZ, BEN ZION, לקורות היהודים ברוסיא פולין וליטא (Excerpts to the History of the Jews in Russia, Poland and Lithuania in the 16th and 17th Centuries). Berlin, 1899.

KATZ, JOSEPH B. MORDECAI GERSHON, ס' שארית יוסף (Responsa). Amsterdam, 1767.

KATZ, SOLOMON, "Pope Gregory the Great and the Jews." *JQR*, XXIV (1933–34), 113–36.

KATZENELLENBOGEN, MEIR B. SAMUEL ISAAC OF PADUA, ס' שאלות והשובות (Responsa). Venice, 1553. Issued together with those of Judah Menz.

KAUFMANN, DAVID, Samson Wertheimer, der Oberhoffaktor und Landesrabbiner (1658–1724) und seine Kinder. Vienna, 1888.

———, "Letters Referring to the History of Palestine" (Hebrew). *Yerushalayim*, III (1889), 105–24.

———, "Une lettre de Josef Caro adressée aux Juifs de Carpentras." *REJ*, XVIII (1889), 133–36.

———, "Don Joseph Nassi, Founder of Colonies in the Holy Land, and the Community of Cori in the Campagna." *JQR*, O. S. II (1889–90), 291–97, 305–10.

———, "L'incendie de Salonique du 4 Ab 1545." *REJ*, XXI (1890), 293–97.

———, "Correspondance echangée entre les communautés juives de Recanati et d'Ancone en 1448." *REJ*, XXIII (1891), 249–55.

———, "Three Centuries of the Genealogy of the Most Eminent Anglo-Jewish Family before 1290." *JQR*, O. S. III (1891), 555–66.

———, "David Carcassoni et le rachat par la communauté de Constantinople des Juifs faits prisonniers durant la persécution du Chmielnicky." *REJ*, XXV (1892), 202–16.

———, "Die Schuldennot der Gemeinde Posen während des Rabbinates R. Isak b. Abrahams (1668–1685)." *MGWJ*, XXXIX (1895), 38–46, 91–96.

———, "Jewish Informers in the Middle Ages." *JQR*, O. S. VIII (1895–96), 217–38.

———, "The Minute-Book of the Community of Bamberg" (Hebrew). *Ḳobeṣ ʿal yad*, XII–XIII (1896–97), 1–46.

Kaufmann, David, "Rabbinic Diploma whereby Ezekiel Landau was Invited to Serve as Chief Rabbi of Prague" (Hebrew). *Ha-Eshkol*, I (1898), 177–84.

———, Gesammelte Schriften. Ed. by Marcus Brann. 3 vols., Frankfort, 1908–15.

Kaufmann, M., "Die erste israelitische Kleinkinder-Bewahranstalt in Europa errichtet im Jahre 1835 in Prag." *ZGJT*, I (1930–31), 247–52.

Kaufmann, Yehudah, ר' יום טוב ליפמן מיהלהויזן (R. Yom Tob Lipmann Mühlhausen), The Author of *Niṣṣaḥon*, Philosopher and Cabalist. Pt. I: His Life, Teaching and Actvity; Pt. II: Sefer ha-Eshkol and Sefer Kavvanat ha-tefillah. Ed. from unique manuscripts, with introd. and notes. New York, 1927.

Kayserling, Meyer, Die Juden in Navarra, den Baskenländern und auf den Balearen. Berlin, 1861.

———, Geschichte der Juden in Portugal. Leipzig, 1867.

———, "Ein Verein der jüdischen Schuhmacher in Saragossa." *Allgemeine Zeitung des Judentums*, LVI (1892), 438.

———, "Notes sur l'histoire des Juifs en Espagne." *REJ*, XXVII (1893), 148–49.

Kimḥi, David b. Joseph, פירוש רד"ק על התורה (Commentary on the Pentateuch [Genesis]). Ed. by A. Ginzburg. [With notes by Raphael Kirchheim]. Pressburg, 1842.

Kinkeldey, Otto, "A Jewish Dancing Master of the Renaissance (Guglielmo Ebreo)." *Studies in Jewish Bibliography . . . in Memory of A. S. Freidus*, New York, 1929, pp. 329–72.

Kirchheim, Raphael, ed., פירוש על דברי הימים (Commentary on the Book of Chronicles). By a Pupil of Saadia Gaon. Frankfort, 1874.

Kisch, Alexander, "Das Testament Mardochai Meisels. Mitgeteilt und nach handschriftlichen Quellen dargestellt." *MGWJ*, XXXVII (1893), 25–40, 82–91, 131–46.

Kisch, Guido, "Entwicklung und Verfassung der jüdischen Gemeinde zu Halle." *Sachsen und Anhalt; Jahrbuch der historischen Kommission für die Provinz Sachsen und für Anhalt*, VI (1930), 306–36.

KISCH, GUIDO, "Die Zensur jüdischer Bücher in Böhmen. Beiträge zu ihrer Geschichte." *JGJC*, II (1930), 456–90.

———, Die Prager Universität und die Juden. Mährisch-Ostrau, 1935.

———, "Studien zur Geschichte des Judeneides im Mittelalter." *HUCA*, XIV (1939), 431–56.

———, "The Jewry Law of the Medieval German Law-Books." *Proceedings of the American Academy for Jewish Research*, VII (1936), 61–145; X (1940), 99–184.

———, "The Landshut Jewry Oath." *Historia Judaica*, I (1939), 119–20. Supplemented ibid., III (1941), 41–45.

KLAUZNER, ISRAEL, קורות בית העלמין הישן בוילנה (A History of the Old Cemetery in Wilno). Wilno, 1935.

———, תולדות הקהלה העברית בוילנה (History of the Jewish Community in Wilno). Vol. I: Environment and Communal Organization. Wilno, 1938.

KLECZYNSKI, G., and FR. KLUCZYCKI, Liczba głów żydowskich w Koronie z taryf roku 1765 (The Number of Jews in Poland on the Basis of the Assessments of 1765). Cracow, 1898. Archiwum Komisyi Historycznej, Vol. VIII.

KLEIN, JULIUS, "Medieval Spanish Gilds." *Facts and Factors in Economic History* (in honor of E. F. Gay), Cambridge, Mass., 1932, pp. 164–88.

KLEIN, SAMUEL, Jüdisch-Palästinensisches Corpus Inscriptionum (Ossuar-, Grab- und Synagogenschriften). Vienna, 1920.

———, "Zur jüdischen Altertumskunde." *MGWJ*, LXXVI (1932), 545–57, 603–4; LXXVII (1933), 81–84, 180–98, 356–65. Pt. I has subtitle, "Das Fremdenhaus der Synagoge."

———, תולדות הישוב היהודי בארץ ישראל (A History of the Jewish Settlement in Palestine from the Conclusion of the Talmud to the Modern Colonization Movement). Tel-Aviv, 1935.

———, "R. Simon the Scribe of Tarbane" (Hebrew). מנחה לדוד (Jubilee Volume in Honor of David Yellin), Jerusalem, 1937, pp. 96–99.

KOBAK, J., ed., *see* Jacob b. Elijah.

Kober, Adolf, Grundbuch des Kölner Judenviertels, 1135–1425. Cologne, 1920. Publikationen der Gesellschaft für Rheinische Geschichtskunde, Vol. XXXIV.

———, "Rheinische Judendoktoren vornehmlich des 17. und 18. Jahrhunderts." *Festschrift des Jüdisch-Theologischen Seminars Fraenckelscher Stiftung*, 2 vols., Breslau, 1929, II, 173–236.

———, "Die deutschen Kaiser und die Wormser Juden." *ZGJD*, V (1935), 134–51.

———, [History of the Jews in] Cologne. Philadelphia, 1940. "Jewish Communities Series."

———, and Elisabeth Moses, Aus der Geschichte der Juden im Rheinland; Jüdische Kult- und Kunstdenkmäler. Düsseldorf, 1931. Publikationen des Rheinischen Vereins für Denkmalpflege, 1931, Heft 1.

קובץ פסקים (Ḳobeṣ pesaḳim; A Collection of Decisions). Columbia University Manuscript, X 893.19 K 79.

Koch, Charlotte, Wandlungen der Wohlfahrtspflege im Zeitalter der Aufklärung. Erlangen, 1933.

Koenen, Hendrik Jacob, Geschiedenis der Joden in Nederland. Utrecht, 1843.

Kohler, Kaufman, "Zum Kapitel der jüdischen Wohltätigkeitspflege." *Festschrift . . . A. Berliner*, Frankfort, 1903, pp. 195–203.

———, Hebrew Union College and Other Addresses. Cincinnati, 1916.

Köhler, Ludwig, "Die hebräische Rechtsgemeinde." *Bericht der Universität Zürich*, 1930–31, pp. 3–23.

Kohler, Max J., "The Jews in Newport." *PAJHS*, VI (1897), 61–80.

———, "Civil Status of the Jews in Colonial New York." *PAJHS*, VI (1897), 81–106.

Kohut, Alexander, "Les fêtes persanes et babyloniennes mentionnées dans les Talmuds de Babylone et de Jérusalem." *REJ*, XXIV (1892), 256–71.

———, Aruch completum sive lexicon, vocabula et res, quae in libris Targumicis, Talmudicis et Midraschicis continentur.

8 vols., 2d impression, Vienna, 1926. (Based upon Nathan b. Yeḥiel's '*Aruk*, frequently printed.)

כל בו (Kolbo; A Juridical Treatise). Venice, 1547.

KON, PINḤAS, "The Struggle of the Wilno Community Against Luxury in Dress in 1809" (Yiddish). *Yivo Bleter*, III (1932), 281–83.

———, "Organized Action of the Wilno Teachers Against Competition in 1822–23" (Yiddish). *Yivo Bleter*, IV (1932), 94.

———, "From the Wilno Archives" (Yiddish). *Yivo Studies in History*, II (1937), 605–14.

KÖNIG, JOHANN BALTHASAR, Annalen der Juden in den deutschen Staaten besonders in der Mark Brandenburg. Berlin, 1790. 2d impression, Berlin, 1912.

KOROBKOW, CH., "Jewish Population Statistics for Poland and Lithuania in the Second Half of the Eighteenth Century (On the basis of the Official Censuses)" (Russian). *Evreiskaya Starina*, IV (1911), 541–62.

KOSOVER, MORDECAI, "The Responsa of Rabbi Joel Sirkes (Sources for the History, Manners and Customs of the Jews in Poland in the 16th–17th Centuries)" (Yiddish). *Yivo Studies in History*, II (1937), 223–47.

KRACAUER, ISIDOR, "Rabbi Joselmann de Rosheim." *REJ*, XVI (1888), 84–105.

———, "Beiträge zur Geschichte der Frankfurter Juden im dreissigjährigen Kriege." *ZGJD*, O. S. III (1889), 130–56, 337–72; IV (1890), 18–28.

———, Geschichte der Juden in Frankfurt a. M., 1150–1824. 2 vols., Frankfort, 1925–27.

———, ed., Urkundenbuch zur Geschichte der Juden in Frankfurt a. M. von 1150–1400. Vol. I: Urkunden, Rechenbücher, Bedebücher. Frankfort, 1914.

KRAELING, CARL H., "The Jewish Community of Antioch." *Journal of Biblical Literature*, LI (1932), 130–60.

KRAFT, HILDEGARD, "Die rechtliche, wirtschaftliche und soziale Lage der Juden im Hochstift Paderborn." *Westfälische Zeitschrift*, XCIV (1938), Pt. 2, pp. 101–204. Non vidi.

KRAUSS, SAMUEL, Talmudische Archäologie. 3 vols., Leipzig, 1910–12.

———, Studien zur byzantinisch-jüdischen Geschichte. Vienna, 1914. XXI Jahresbericht der Israelitisch-Theologischen Lehranstalt in Wien.

———, "City, Town and Village" (Hebrew). *He-'Atid*, III (2d impression, 1923), 1–50.

———, Synagogale Altertümer. Berlin, 1925.

———, "חבר עיר, ein Kapitel aus alt-jüdischer Kommunalverfassung." *JJLG*, XVII (1926), 195–240.

Cf. also Horovitz, Jakob.

———, "Ancient Synagogues in Palestine and the Near East" (Hebrew). *Yerushalayim in Memory of A. M. Luncz*, Jerusalem, 1928, pp. 221–49.

———, "Beiträge zur Geschichte der Geonim." *Livre d'hommage . . . Poznanski*, Warsaw, 1929, pp. 133–46.

———, "Über Siedlungstypen in Palästina in talmudischer Zeit." *MGWJ*, LXXXII (1938), 173–90.

———, and ISIDOR FISCHER, Geschichte der jüdischen Ärzte vom frühesten Mittelalter bis zur Gleichberechtigung. Vienna, 1930.

KRAUTHEIMER, RICHARD, Mittelalterliche Synagogen. Frankfort, 1927.

———, "Die Synagoge in Worms." *ZGJD*, V (1935), 87–99.

KREMER, ALFRED VON, "Zwei arabische Urkunden." *Zeitschrift der Deutschen Morgenländischen Gesellschaft*, VII (1853), 219–23.

KREMER, M., "Study of Craft and Craft Guilds among the Jews of Poland in the 16th to the 18th Centuries" (Hebrew). *Zion*, II (1937), 295–325.

———, "The Participation of Jewish Artisans in Christian Guilds in the Old Republic of Poland" (Yiddish). *Bleter far Geshichte*, II (1938), 3–32.

KROCHMAL, MENAḤEM B. ABRAHAM, ס׳ צמח צדק (Responsa). Amsterdam, 1675.

KRONER, THEODOR, Die Geschichte der Juden in Erfurt. *In his* Festschrift zur Einweihung der neuen Synagoge in Erfurt am 4. September 1884 auf Wunsch der Gemeinde-Collegien verfasst. Erfurt, [1885].

KUHN, ARTHUR K., "Hugo Grotius and the Emancipation of the Jews in Holland." *PAJHS*, XXXI (1928), 173–80.

KURREIN, VIKTOR, "Kartenspiel und Spielkarten im jüdischen Schrifttume." *MGWJ*, LXVI (1922), 203–11.

KUTRZEBA, STANISLAW, "The Judiciary over Jews in the Cracow Palatinate" (Polish). *Przegląd prawa administracyjnego*, XVI. Non vidi.

———, Zbiór aktów (A Collection of Documents). Non vidi.

LAGUMINA, BARTOLOMEO, and GIUSEPPE LAGUMINA, Codice diplomatico dei Giudei di Sicilia. 3 vols., Palermo, 1884–95. Incomplete.

LALLEMAND, LÉON, Histoire de la charité. 4 vols., Paris, 1902–12.

LAMBERT, ELIE, "Les synagogues de Tolède." *REJ*, LXXXIV (1927), 15–33.

LAMPRIDIUS, AELIUS, [Biography of] Alexander Severus. London, 1924. *In* Scriptores Historiae Augustae, with an English translation by David Magie, II, 178–313. "Loeb Classical Library."

LAMPRONTI, ISAAC, ס' פחד יצחק (A Legal Dictionary). 6 vols. (א—ם), Venice, 1750–1813. 8 vols. (נ—ת), Lyck, 1864–74; Berlin, 1885–88.

LANDAU, EZEKIEL B. JUDAH, ס' נודע ביהודה (Responsa). With notes by Joseph Saul Nathansohn. 2 pts., Lwów, 1857–58.

———, דרושי הצלח (Homilies). Warsaw, 1899.

LANDSBERGER, BRUNO, Assyrische Handelskolonien in Kleinasien aus dem dritten Jahrtausend. Leipzig, 1925.

LANDSBERGER, FRANZ, Einführung in die jüdische Kunst. Berlin, 1935.

LANDSBERGER, J., "Zur Biographie des R. Baruch Wesel (Bendix Ruben Gumpertz), ersten schlesischen Landrabbiners, ca. 1690–1754." *JJLG*, V (1907), 182–205; VI (1909), 416; VII (1910), 380.

———, "Schulden der Judenschaft in Polen, zugleich ein Beitrag zur Geschichte der inneren Organisation." *JJLG*, VI (1909), 252–79.

LANDSBERGER, J., "Zur Geschichte des Sanitätswesens der jüdischen Gemeinde in Posen." *JJLG*, X (1913), 361–71.

LANDSHUTH, LESER (ELIEZER), תולדות אנשי שם ופעולתם בעדת ברלין (The Lives and Works of the Leaders of the Berlin Community from 1671 to 1871). Berlin, 1884.

LANE-POOLE, STANLEY, and J. D. JERROLD KELLEY, The Story of the Barbary Corsairs. New York, 1896.

LA PIANA, GEORGE, "Foreign Groups in Rome in the First Centuries of the Empire." *Harvard Theological Review*, XX (1927), 183–403.

LATTES, MOSES, "Documents et notices sur l'histoire politique et littéraire des Juifs en Italie." *REJ*, V (1882), 219–37.

———, ed. לקוטים שונים מס' דבי אליהו (Excerpts from Elijah Capsali's Chronicle). Padua, 1869.

LAUBERT, MANFRED, "Geleitszoll und Koscherfleischabgabe, zwei Sondersteuern der Posener Juden." *MGWJ*, LXVII (1923), 273–78.

———, "Die Schuldenregulierung der jüdischen Korporationen in der Provinz Posen." *MGWJ*, LXVIII (1924), 321–31.

LAUER, CH., "R. Meir Halevy aus Wien und der Streit um das Grossrabbinat in Frankreich." *JJLG*, XVI (1924), 1–42.

LAURIÈRE, E. J. DE, D. F. SECOUSSE, *et al.*, eds., Ordonnances des roys de France de la troisième race. 21 vols., Paris, 1723–1849.

LAUTERBACH, JACOB Z., "The Attitude of the Jew towards the Non-Jew." *Yearbook of the Central Conference of American Rabbis*, XXXI (1921), 186–233.

———, "The Name of the Rabbinical Schools and Assemblies in Babylon." *Hebrew Union College Jubilee Volume*, 1925, pp. 211–22.

LAZARD, L., "Les revenus tirés des Juifs de France dans la domaine royale (XIIIs.)." *REJ*, XV (1887), 233–61.

LAZARUS, FELIX, Die Häupter der Vertriebenen, Beitrag zu einer Geschichte der Exilsfürsten in Babylonien unter den Arsakiden und Sassaniden. Frankfort, 1890. *Jahrbücher für jüdische Geschichte und Literatur*, ed. by N. Brüll, Vol. X.

LAZARUS, FELIX, "Neue Beiträge zur Geschichte des Exilarchats." *MGWJ*, LXXVIII (1934), 279–88.

———, "Judenbefehlshaber, Obervorgänger und Landrabbiner im Münsterland." *MGWJ*, LXXX (1936), 106–17; LXXXI (1937), 444–45.

———, Die Judenbefehlshaber im Münsterland (Vorort Coesfeld)." *ZGJD*, VII (1937), 240–43.

LEACH, ARTHUR F., Educational Charters and Documents 598–1909. Cambridge, 1911.

LEBERMANN, J., "Das Darmstädter Landrabbinat." *JJLG*, XX (1929), 181–252.

LEHMANN, JOSEPH, "Assistance publique et privée d'après l'antique législation juive," *REJ*, XXXV (1897), pp. I-XXXVIII.

LEICHT, PIER SILVERIO, Corporazioni romane e arti medievali. Turin, 1937.

LENTSHITS, SOLOMON EPHRAIM B. AARON, ס' עוללות אפרים (Homilies). Amsterdam, 1710.

———, ס' עמודי שש (Homilies). Leyden, 1772.

LEO OF MODENA (Yehudah Aryeh di Modena), The History of the Present Jews Throughout the World. Engl. transl. by Simon Ockley from the Italian work, *Historia dei riti ebraici*. London, 1707.

———, ס' סור מרע (Turn Away from Evil; Against Games of Chance). Transl. into English by Hermann Gollancz. London, 1908.

LÉON, HENRY, Histoire des Juifs de Bayonne. Paris, 1893.

LESQUIER, JEAN, "L'arabarchès d'Egypte," *Revue Archéologique*, Ser. V, Vol. VI (1917), 95–103.

Letters of Certain Jews to Monsieur Voltaire containing an Apology for Their Own People and for the Old Testament with Critical Reflections, and a Short Commentary Extracted from a Greater, with Christian Notes and Additions on Various Parts of the Work [English transl. from the French]. 2 vols. in 1, 2d American ed., Paris (Ky.), 1845.

LÉVI, ISRAEL, "L'origine davidique de Hillel." *REJ*, XXXI (1895), 202–11; XXXIII (1896), 143–44.

LÉVI, ISRAEL, "Un recueil de consultations de rabbins de la France méridionale." *REJ*, XXXVIII (1899), 103–22.

———, "La lutte entre Isaie, fils d'Abba Mari, et Yohanan, fils de Matatia, pour le rabbinat de France à la fin du XIVe siècle." *REJ*, XXXIX (1899), 85–94.

———, "Le roi juif de Narbonne et le Philomène." *REJ*, XLVIII (1904), 197–207.

———, "Encore un mot sur le roi juif de Narbonne." *REJ*, XLIX (1904), 147–50.

LEVI, SALI, Beiträge zur Geschichte der ältesten jüdischen Grabsteine in Mainz. Mayence, 1926.

———, "Die Verbundenheit zwischen den jüdischen Gemeinden Worms und Mainz im Mittelalter." *ZGJD*, V (1934), 187–91.

LÉVI-PROVENÇAL, EVARISTE, "Les 'Mémoires' de 'Abd Allah, dernier roi Ziride de Granade: Fragments publiés d'après le manuscrit de la bibliothèque d'Al-Qarawiyin à Fês, avec une introduction et une traduction française," *Al-Andalus*, III (1935), 233–344; IV (1936–39), 29–145.

LEVITATS, ISAAC, "The Pinkas of the Dubno Community (Unpublished Statutes and Communal Documents)" (Yiddish). *Yivo Studies in History*, II (1937), 80–114.

LEVY, ARTHUR, Jüdische Grabmalkunst in Osteuropa. Berlin, 1923.

LÉVY, EMILE, "Un document sur les Juifs du Barrois en 1321–23." *REJ*, XIX (1889), 246–58.

LEVY, HANS *or* J. "Emperor Julian and the Rebuilding of the Temple at Jerusalem" (Hebrew). *Zion*, VI (1940–41), 1–32.

LEVY, JAKOB, Neuhebräisches und chaldäisches Wörterbuch über die Talmudim und Midraschim. 4 vols., Leipzig, 1876–89. 2d ed. by Lazarus Goldschmidt. 4 vols., Berlin, 1924.

LEVY, MORITZ, Die Sephardim in Bosnien. Ein Beitrag zur Geschichte der Juden auf der Balkan-Halbinsel. Sarajevo, 1911.

LEVY, REUBEN, An Introduction to the Sociology of Islam. 2 vols., London, 1929–31.

LEWENSTEIN, T., Uber die rechtliche Stellung der jüdischen Frauen." *Nachalat Z'wi*, VI (1935–36), 159–75.

LEWIN, BENJAMIN MENASSEH, ed., "Three Responsa by R. Sherira and R. Hai" (Hebrew), *Ginze Ḳedem*, I (1922), 73–80.

———, "A Letter by [Saadia] Al-Fayyumi, Head of the Academy" (Hebrew). *Ginze Ḳedem*, II (1923), 33–35.

———, "Letters of a Babylonian Gaon to the Yemen" (Hebrew). *Ginze Ḳedem*, III (1925), 14–23.

———, "Ancient Fragments from a *Maḥzor* of the Academy of Pumbedita" (Hebrew). *Ginze Ḳedem*, III (1925), 50–56.

———, אוצר הגאונים; Thesaurus of the Gaonic Responsa and Commentaries, following the Order of the Talmudic Tractates. Vols. I–X, Haifa-Jerusalem, 1928–41.

———, "Responsa by R. Hai Gaon concerning the Two Holidays in the Dispersion and a Responsum by R. Joseph" (Hebrew). *Ginze Ḳedem*, IV (1930), 33–37.

———, "A Letter of R. Hai Gaon to the Priests of Ifrikiya" (Hebrew). *Ginze Ḳedem*, IV (1930), 51–56.

———, "Genizah Fragments, I: Chapters of Ben Baboi" (Hebrew). *Tarbiz*, II (1930–31), 383–405.

———, "Differences in Customs between the Jews of Palestine and of Babylonia" (Hebrew). *Sinai*, I, Pt. 1 (1937), 116–31, 249–59, 351–60, 497–99; Pt. 2 (1938), 109–16, 251–56, 423–29; II, Pt. 1 (1938), 47–54, 193–200; Pt. 2 (1939), 140–45, 259–64, 386–91. A revised edition of the well-known geonic treatise first published by Joel Müller, Vienna, 1878.

LEWIN, ISAK, "Eine Urkunde der Vierländersynode aus dem Jahre 1699." *MGWJ*, LXVII (1933), 387–89.

LEWIN, LOUIS, Geschichte der Juden in Lissa. Pinne, 1904.

———, Neue Materialien zur Geschichte der Vierländersynode." Pts. I-III, *JJLG*, II (1904), 1–26; III (1905), 79–130; XI (1916), 141–208.

———, "Der Schtadlan im Posener Ghetto." *Festschrift . . . Wolf Feilchenfeld*, Pleschen-Grimm, 1907, pp. 31–39.

———, "Jüdische Ärzte in Grosspolen." *JJLG*, IX (1912), 367–420.

———, "Ein Bannfluch." *Festschrift . . . David Hoffmann*, Berlin, 1914, pp. 162–66.

LEWIN, LOUIS, "Ein Judenlandtag aus Süd- und Neuostpreussen." *MGWJ*, LIX (1915), 180–92, 278–300.

———, "Die jüdischen Studenten an der Universität Frankfurt a. d. Oder." *JJLG*, XIV (1921), 217–38; XV (1923), 59–96; XVI (1924), 43–86.

———, Die Landessynode der grosspolnischen Judenschaft. Frankfort, 1926.

———, "Nachträge." *Festschrift . . . Simon Dubnow*, Berlin, 1930, pp. 124–35.

LEWINSKY, A., "Zur Geschichte der Juden in Lublin." *MGWJ*, XLVI (1902), 170–76.

———, "Zur Statistik den jüdischen Bevölkerung in Stadt und Hochstift Hildesheim im 18. Jahrhundert." *Blätter für jüdische Geschichte und Literatur*, III (1902), 113–19, 150–53, 169–71.

———, "Sulla storia degli Ebrei in Italia durante il secolo XVIII." *Rivista israelitica*, IV (1907), 143–48; V (1908), 103–5, 211–16; VI (1909), 54–58.

———, "The Communal Statute of Hildesheim [of 1706]" (Hebrew). *Ha-Eshkol*, VI (1909), 236–40.

LEWIS, BERNARD, "The Islamic Guilds." *Economic History Review*, VIII (1937–38), 20–37.

———, "A Jewish Source on Damascus just after the Ottoman Conquest." *Bulletin of the School of Oriental Studies* (*University of London*), X (1939–40), 179–84. Refers to Moses Bassola's Pilgrimage to Palestine.

LIBANIUS, Opera. Ed. by Richard Förster. 12 vols., Leipzig, 1903–27. Bibliotheca scriptorum graecorum et romanorum Teubneriana. Vols. X-XI: Epistulae.

LIBER, MAURICE, "Un mot sur les consultations de Hayyim Or Zaroua." *REJ*, LIII (1907), 267–69.

LIBERMANN, KOPEL, "La découverte d'une synagogue secrète à Anvers à la fin du dix-septième siècle." *REJ*, XCIX (1935), 36–48.

LIBOWITZ, NEHEMIAH SAMUEL, "On the Venetian Ordinance" (Hebrew). *Ha-Zofeh*, XIII (1929), 88–90. A critique of A. Apfelbaum's essay ibid., XII, 268–70.

Lidzbarski, Mark, ed., Das Johannesbuch der Mandäer. 2 vols., Giessen, 1915.

Liebe, Georg, Das Judentum in der deutschen Vergangenheit mit 106 Abbildungen und Beilagen nach Originalen, grösstenteils aus dem fünfzehnten bis achtzehnten Jahrhundert. Leipzig, 1903. Monographien zur deutschen Kulturgeschichte, Vol. XI.

Lieben, Salomon Hugo, "Zur Charakteristik des Verhältnisses zwischen Rabbi Jecheskel Landau und Rabbi Jonathan Eibenschütz." *JJLG*, I (1903), 325–26.

———, "Handschriftliches zur Geschichte der Juden in Prag in den Jahren 1744–1754." *JJLG*, II (1904), 267–330; III (1905), 241–76, Hebrew section, pp. 31–59.

———, "Die von Maria Theresia projektierte Esrogimsteuer." *MGWJ*, LIII (1909), 720–22.

———, "David Oppenheim." *JJLG*, XIX (1928), 1–38.

———, "Beiträge zur Geschichte der Zensur hebräischer Drucke in Prag." *Soncino Blätter*, III (1929), 51–55.

Liebermann, Saul, "On the מעשים לבני ארץ ישראל" (Hebrew). *Ginze Ḳedem*, V (1934), 177–85.

Lincoln, F. Ashe, The Starra: Their Effect on Early English Law and Administration. London, 1939.

Lindeman, E. C., Community. New York, 1921.

Lindo, Elias Ḥayyim, The History of the Jews of Spain and Portugal, from the Earliest Times to Their Final Expulsion from those Kingdoms, and Their Subsequent Dispersion; with complete translations of all the laws made respecting them during their long establishment in the Iberian Peninsula. London, 1848.

Linfield, Harry Sebee, Communal Census of Jews: Methods Used in Recent Years. New York, 1938. Jewish Library of Facts, No. 2.

———, State Population Census by Faiths. Meaning, Reliability and Value. New York, 1938.

———, "Statistics of Jews and Jewish Organizations in the United States: A Historical Review of the Censuses, 1850–1937." *American Jewish Year Book*, XL (1938–39), 61–86.

Linfield, Harry Sebee, "The Jews of the United States: Preliminary Figures for 1937." *American Jewish Year Book*, XLI (1939), 181–88.

———, "The Jewish Communities in the United States: Number and Distribution of Jews of the United States in Urban Places and Rural Territory." *American Jewish Year Book*, XLII (1940–41), 214–66.

Lionti, Ferdinando, "Le magistrature presso gli Ebrei di Sicilia." *Archivio storico siciliano*, N. S. IX (1884), 328–71.

———, "I ministri della religione presso gli Ebrei di Sicilia." *Archivio storico siciliano*, N. S. X (1885), 130–36.

Lipschutz, M., "Un livre de compte du XVIIe siècle de la Confrèrie des Purificateurs et Fossoyeurs de Carpentras. פנקס מקופת מטהרים וקברים." *REJ*, LXXXII (1926), 425–30.

Loeb, Isidore, "Statuts des Juifs d'Avignon (1779)." *Annuaire de la Société des études juives*, I (1881), 165–275.

———, "Les Juifs de Strasbourg de 1349 à la Révolution." *Annuaire de la Société des études juives*, II (1883), 139–98.

———, "Un convoi d'exilés d'Espagne à Marseille en 1492." *REJ*, IX (1884), 66–76.

———, "Actes de vente hébreux originaires d'Espagne." *REJ*, X (1885), 108–22.

———, "Règlement des Juifs de Castille en 1432 comparé avec les règlements des Juifs de Sicile et d'autres pays." *REJ*, XIII (1886), 187–216.

———, "Les sacs des Juiveries de Valence et de Madrid en 1391." *REJ*, XIII (1886), 239–47.

———, "Histoire d'une taille levée sur les Juifs de Perpignan en 1413–1414." *REJ*, XIV (1887), 55–79.

———, "Le nombre des Juifs de Castille et d'Espagne au moyen âge." *REJ*, XIV (1887), 161–83.

———, "Notes sur l'histoire des Juifs en Espagne." *REJ*, XIV (1887), 254–68.

———, "Josef Haccohen et les chroniqueurs juifs." *REJ*, XVI (1888), 28–56, 211–35; XVII (1888), 74–95, 247–71.

Loevinson, Ermanno, "Le basi giuridiche della comunità israelitica di Livorno (1593–1787)," *Bolletino storico livornese*, I, Pt. II (1937). Non vidi.

LOEVINSON, ERMANNO, "Notizie e dati degli Ebrei entrati a Bologna nel sec. XV." *Annuario di studi ebraici*, II (1938), 125–73.

LOEW (LIWA *or* JUDAH) B. BEZALEEL, ס' נתיבות עולם (Ethical treatise). Zhitomir, 1867.

LOEWY, FRANZ, "Wie eine jüdische Gemeinde entstand. Zur Geschichte der Gemeinde Glatz." *Jahrbuch für jüdische Geschichte und Literatur*, XXXI (1938), 208–22.

LÖW, IMMANUEL, "Jardin et Parc." *REJ*, LXXXIX (1931), 147–63.

LÖW, LEOPOLD, Gesammelte Schriften. Ed. by Immanuel Löw, 5 vols., Szegedin, 1889–1900.

LÖWENSTEIN, LEOPOLD, Geschichte der Juden am Bodensee. Vol. I, Konstanz, 1879.

———, "Der Prozess Eisenmenger." *Magazin für die Wissenschaft des Judentums*, XVIII (1891), 209–40.

———, Geschichte der Juden in der Kurpfalz. Frankfort, 1895.

———, "Eine jüdische Notabelnversammlung in Hanau im Jahre 1659." *Israelitische Monatsschrift* (supplement to *Jüdische Presse*), 1897, no. 11, p. 43.

———, "Verzeichnis der israelitischen Einwohner von Karlsruhe im Jahre 1733." *Blätter für jüdische Geschichte und Literatur*, III (1902), 131–37, 154–57.

———, "Wormser Gemeindeordnungen." *Blätter für jüdische Geschichte und Literatur*, IV (1903), 145–50, 161–65, 177–79.

———, "Zur Geschichte der Juden in Fürth." 3 pts., *JJLG*, VI (1909), 153–234; VIII (1911), 65–213; X (1913), 49–192. Pt. I: Das Rabbinat; Pt. II: Rabbinatsbeisitzer und sonstige hervorragende Persönlichkeiten; Pt. III: Die hebräischen Druckereien in Fürth.

———, מפתח ההסכמות Index approbationum. Berlin, 1923.
Cf. also Wachstein, Bernhard.

LOWENTHAL, MARVIN, A World Passed By. Scenes and Memories of Jewish Civilization in Europe and North Africa. 3d ed. New York, 1938.

LUCE, SIMÉON, "Catalogue de documents du Trésor de Chartes relatifs aux Juifs sous le regne de Philippe le Bel." *REJ*, II (1881), 15–72.

LUDEWIG, J. P. DE, ed., Reliquiae manuscriptorum omnis aevi diplomatum ac monumentorum ineditorum. 12 vols., Frankfort, 1720–31; Halle, 1733–41.

LUNCZ, ABRAHAM MOSES, "The Ḥakam-bashi in Turkey" (Hebrew). *Yerushalayim*, IV (1892), 186–217.

———, "*Halukkah*, Its Origins, History and Ramifications" (Hebrew). *Yerushalayim*, VII (1906), 25–40, 181–201.

LURIA, SOLOMON B. YEḤIEL, ס' ים של שלמה (Novellae to various talmudic tractates). 7 pts., Prague, 1616, 1812; Lublin, 1636; Cracow, 1646; Altona, 1740; Berlin, 1766; Stettin, 1862.

———, ס' חכמת שלמה (On the Talmud). 2d ed. abridged, Amsterdam, 1691; also frequently in editions of the Talmud.

———, ס' שאלות ותשובות (Responsa). Fürth, 1788.

LURIE, ISAAC, "The Lithuanian Communities and the Karaites: The Assessment of Karaite Taxes and their Collection during the 16th and 17th Centuries" (Hebrew). *He-'Abar*, I (1918), 159–71.

LUTHER, BERNHARD, "Kahal und 'edah als Hilfsmittel der Quellenscheidung im Priester-Kodex und in der Chronik." *Zeitschrift für die alttestamentliche Wissenschaft*, LVI (1938), 44–63.

LUTZKY, ALEXANDER, "The 'Francos' and the Effect of the Capitulations on the Jews in Aleppo (from 1673 till the time of the French Revolution)" (Hebrew). *Zion*, VI (1940–41), 46–79.

LUZZATTO, SAMUEL DAVID, "Responsum of the Roman Scholars Addressed to the Scholars of Paris" (Hebrew). *Bet ha-Ozar*, I (1847), 57a–60a.

LYONS, JACQUES JUDAH, *see* Shearith Israel.

MAARSEN, ISAAC, De Amsterdamsche Opperrabbijn R. Saul Löwenstam (1755–1790) en zijn tijd. Amsterdam, 1921. Reprinted from *Nieuw Israël. Weekblad*, LVI, nos. 48, 49, 51, 52; LVII, nos. 1, 2.

———, "The Council of Four Lands and the Communities of Amsterdam in the Seventeenth Century" (Hebrew). *Ha-Zofeh*, VIII (1924), 289–300.

MAARSEN, ISAAC, "De Responsa als Bron voor de Geschiedenis der Joden in Nederland." *Bijdragen en Mededeelingen van het Genootschap voor de Joodsche Wetenschap in Nederland*, V (1933), 118–46.

McIVER, ROBERT M., Community, a Sociological Study. Being an Attempt to Set out the Nature and Fundamental Laws of Social Life. 3d ed., London, 1924.

MAHLER, EDUARD, Handbuch der jüdischen Chronologie. Leipzig, 1916.

MAHLER, RAPHAEL, "On the National-Social Character of the Karaite Movement in its Early Period" (Yiddish). *Yivo Bleter*, VIII (1935), 304–22.

———, "The National-Social Foundation of 'Anan's Religion" (Yiddish). *Yivo Bleter*, IX (1936), 31–62.

———, "Hebrew Documents relating to the Provincial Councils in Old Poland" (Yiddish). *Yivo Studies in History*, II (1937), 639–49.

———, "The Jewish Population in the Area of the Present Province of Lodz in 1764" (Yiddish). *Lodzer Visenshaftleche Shriften*, I (1938), 32–54.

———, "Women, Children and Adolescents as Members of By-Gone Associations: An Essay in the Cultural History of the Jews in Poland" (Yiddish). *Di Zukunft*, XLIII (1938), 163–66.

———, "The Austrian Government and the Hasidim during the Period of Reaction (1818–1848)," *Jewish Social Studies*, I (1939), 195–240.

———, "A Budget of the Council of Four Lands in the Eighteenth Century" (Yiddish). *Yivo Bleter*, XV (1940), 63–86.

———, דער קאמף צווישן השכלה און חסידות אין גאליציע (The Struggle between Haskalah and Hasidism in Galicia in the First Half of the 19th Century). New York, 1942.

MAIMON, SOLOMON, An Autobiography. English translation by J. C. Murray. London, 1888.

MAIMONIDES (Maimuni), ABRAHAM, ס' ברכת אברהם (Responsa and Polemics), ed. with the author's biography, by Ber Goldberg. Lyck, 1860.

MAIMONIDES (Maimuni), ABRAHAM, תשובות רבנו אברהם בן הרמב"ם (Responsa), Collected from Mss. and ed. with introduction and notes by A. H. (Alfred) Freimann. The Arabic Text revised and annotated by Solomon Dob [Fritz] Goitein. Jerusalem, 1937.

MAIMONIDES, MOSES (Moses b. Maimon), ס' משנה תורה (A Code of Jewish Law). Amsterdam, 1702.

———, פירוש המשנה (Kitab al-Siraj *or* Commentary on the Mishnah). *In* most editions of the Mishnah or Talmud. The various partial editions of the Arabic text are listed by A. Yaari in *Kirjath Sepher*, IX (1932–33), 101–9, 228–34. Supplemented ibid., XII (1935–36), 132. Partial Latin translations by E. Pococke in his Porta Mosis, Oxford, 1655, etc.

———, קובץ תשובות הרמב"ם ואגרותיו (A Collection of Responsa and Letters), ed. by A. L. Lichtenberg. 3 vols., Leipzig, 1859.

———, "A Responsum to His Disciple Joseph ha-Ma'arabi on the Objections Raised by Samuel b. 'Ali the Head of the Bagdad Academy." Ed. by A. H. (Alfred) Freimann. Transl. from the Arabic by D. Z. Baneth. (Hebrew). In *Lewin Jubilee Volume*, Jerusalem, 1939, pp. 27–41.

MALTER, HENRY, Saadia Gaon; His Life and Works. Philadelphia, 1921.

MALVEZIN, THÉOPHILE, Histoire des Juifs de Bordeaux. Bordeaux, 1875.

MANN, JACOB, "The Responsa of the Babylonian Geonim as a Source of Jewish History." *JQR*, VII (1916–17), 457–90; VIII (1917–18), 339–66; IX (1918–19), 139–79; X (1919–20), 121–51, 309–65; XI (1920–21), 433–71.

———, The Jews in Egypt and in Palestine under the Fatimid Caliphs. 2 vols., Oxford, 1920–22.

———, "Historical Survey of Capital Jurisdiction at the Present Day" (Hebrew). *Ludwig Blau Jubilee Volume* (*Ha-Zofeh*, X), Budapest, 1926, pp. 200–8.

———, "La lettre polémique de Jacob b. Elie à Pablo Christiani." *REJ*, LXXXII (1926), 363–77.

———, "The Exilarchic Office in Babylonia and its Ramifications at the End of the Geonic Period" (Hebrew). *Livre d'hommage . . . Poznanski*, Warsaw, 1929, pp. 18–32.

MANN, JACOB, Texts and Studies in Jewish History and Literature. 2 vols., Cincinnati, 1931; Philadelphia, 1935.

———, "Varia on the Gaonic Period" (Hebrew). *Tarbiz*, V (1933–34), 148–79, 273–304; VI(1934–35), 66–88, 238–42, 543.

———, "On the Time and Place of R. Jacob b. Elijah, the Author of a Polemical Letter against Fra Pablo" (Hebrew). *Alim*, I (1934–35), 75–77.

———, "The Journey of Ḥayyim ibn 'Aṭṭar and His Companions to Palestine and their Temporary Settlement in Acre" (Hebrew). *Tarbiz*, VII (1935–36), 74–101.
Cf. also Artom, Elija.

———, The Bible as Read and Preached in the Old Synagogue: A Study in the Cycles of the Readings from Torah and Prophets, as well as from Psalms, and in the Structure of the Midrashic Homilies. Vol. I: The Palestinian Triennial Cycle: Genesis and Exodus. Cincinnati, 1940.

MANSI, J. D., ed. Sacrorum conciliorum nova et amplissima collectio. 53 vols., Florence, 1757–Paris, 1927.

MARCUS, JACOB RADER, The Jew in the Medieval World: A Source Book, 315–1791. Cincinnati, 1938.

MARCUS, JOSEPH, "Studies in the Chronicle of Ahima'az." *Proceedings of the American Academy for Jewish Research*, V (1934), 85–93.

MARCUS, RALPH *or* RAPHAEL, "Main Educational Teachings of Philo Judaeus" (Hebrew). *Sefer Touroff* (Touroff Anniversary Volume), Boston, 1938, pp. 223–31.

MAREK, P., "Tax Assessors (Shammaim) in the Lithuanian Communities of the XVII and XVIII Centuries" (Russian). *Evreiskaya Starina*, I (1909), 161–84.

———, "Hasidism and the Crisis in Jewish Self-Government" (Russian). *Evreiskaya Starina*, XII (1928), 45–101.

MARGHARITA, ANTONIUS, Das ganze jüdische Glaub. Augsburg, 1530.

MARGOLIES, Ḥ. W. *or* Z., דובנא רבתי (A History of the Dubno Community), With Copies from Its Communal Pinḳas from 1715 on and from Tombstone Inscriptions of Its Rabbis and Leaders. Warsaw, 1910.

Margoliouth, George, "Some British Museum Genizah Texts." *JQR*, O. S. XIV (1901–2), 303–20.

Margoliouth, Moses, The History of the Jews in Great Britain. 3 vols., London, 1851.

Margulies, Mordecai, ed., חילוקים שבין אנשי מזרח ובני ארץ ישראל (The Differences between Babylonian and Palestinian Jews). Ed. from different versions with an introduction and notes. Jerusalem, 1938.

Margulies, Samuel Hirsch, "Il Talmud Torà di Firenze." *Rivista israelitica*, V (1908), 14–24, 48–54.

———, "Dall' archivio dell' Università israelitica di Pisa." *Rivista israelitica*, V (1908), 70–73.

Markon, Isaak Ber, "Wer ist der in einem Responsum des Natronai Gaon II erwähnte Karäer Daniel?" *Festschrift Moritz Schaefer*, Berlin, 1927, pp. 130–36.

———, "The Statutes of the Polish Community in Amsterdam of the Year 432 [1672]" (Hebrew). *Ṣiyyunim* in memory of J. N. Simḥoni, Berlin, 1929, pp. 159–80.

———, "Etwas über den Einfluss der Wilnaer Emigranten auf das geistige Leben der deutschen Judenheit im XVII Jahrhundert." *Jahrbuch für die jüdischen Gemeinden Schleswig-Holsteins*, I (1929–30), 111–18.

Markreich, Max, "Das Memorbuch der Judengemeinde in Emden." *Jahrbuch für die jüdischen Gemeinden Schleswig-Holsteins*, V (1933–34), 24–36.

Marmorstein, Arthur *or* Abraham, "La réorganisation du doctorat en Palestine au troisième siècle." *REJ*, LVI (1913), 44–53.

———, "Sur un auteur français inconnu du treizième siècle." *REJ*, LXXVI (1923), 113–29.

———, "L'acte de se couvrir la tête chez les Juifs." *REJ*, LXXXV (1928), 66–69.

———, "A Few Remarks on Seventeenth-Century Preachers" (Hebrew). *Alim*, II (1935–36), 37–41.

———, "The Synagogue of Claudius Tiberius Polycharmus in Stobi." *JQR*, XXVII (1936–37), 373–84.

MARMORSTEIN, ARTHUR *or* ABRAHAM, "The Economic Conditions of Galilean Jewry in the Generation of R. Johanan b. Nappacha and the Generation after Him," (Hebrew). *Festschrift Jakob Freimann*, Berlin, 1937, Hebrew Section, pp. 81–92.

MARX, ALEXANDER, "Italienische Statuten." *Zeitschrift für hebräische Bibliographie*, XI (1907), 112–21; XV (1911), 139–45.

———, "The Expulsion of the Jews from Spain. Two New Accounts." *JQR*, O. S. XX (1907–8), 240–71.

———, "Glimpses of the Life of an Italian Rabbi of the First Half of the Sixteenth Century (David ibn Yaḥya)." *HUCA*, I (1924), 605–24.

———, "Der arabische Bustanai-Bericht und Nathan ha-Babli." *Livre d'hommage ... Poznanski*, Warsaw, 1929, pp. 76–81.

———, "A Jewish Cause Celèbre in Sixteenth-Century Italy (the Pesaḳim of 1519)." *Abhandlungen zur Errinerung an Hirsch Perez Chajes*, Vienna, 1933, pp. 149–93.

———, "On Joseph Arli's Demotion from, and Restoration to, the Rabbinate" (Hebrew). *Tarbiz*, VIII (1936–37), 171–84.

———, Studies in Jewish History and Bibliography. To appear in 1942. Will include an essay on "Some Jewish Bookcollectors" and revised reprints of the "Jewish Cause Celèbre," etc.

MASSIGNON, LOUIS, "Enquête sur les corporations musulmanes d'artisans et de commerçants au Maroc (1923–24)." *Revue du monde musulman*, LVIII (1924), 1–250.

———, "Sinf." *Encyclopaedia of Islam*, IV (1924), 436–37.

———, "Etudes sur les corporations musulmanes Indo-Persanes." *Revue des études islamiques*, I (1927), 249–72.

———, "Compléments à l'enquète de 1923–1924 sur les corporations marocaines." *Revue des études islamiques*, I (1927), 273–93.

MAULDE, M. DE, Les Juifs dans les états français du Saint-Siège au moyen âge. Documents pour servir à l'histoire des Israélites et de la Papauté. Paris, 1886. The documents are reprinted from *REJ*, VII-X (1883–84).

MAY, JAKOB, "Die Steuern und Abgaben der Juden im Erzstift Trier." *ZGJD*, VII (1937), 156–79.

MAYER, LEO A., "The Status of the Jews under the Mamelukes" (Hebrew). *Magnes Anniversary Book*, Jerusalem, 1938, pp. 161–67.

MEDINA, SAMUEL B. MOSES DI, ס' שאלות ותשובות (Responsa). 4 pts., according to the arrangement of Jacob b. Asher's *Ṭurim*. Salonica, 1797–98.

MEIR B. BARUCH OF ROTHENBURG, ס' שאלות ותשובות (Responsa). 4 parts. Cremona, 1557; Prague, 1608; (With notes by J. S. Nathansohn) Lwów, 1860; (Ed. by M. Bloch, 2 sections), Berlin, 1891.

MEIR B. GEDALIAH OF LUBLIN, ס' שאלות ותשובות (Responsa). Venice, 1618.

MEIR HA-KOHEN, הגהות מימוניות (Haggahot Maimoniot) on Maimonides' Mishneh Torah. Printed with many editions of the latter.

MEIRI, MENAḤEM HA-, בית הבחירה (Commentary) on M. K., ed. by Simeon Strelitz and Benjamin Zvi Rabinowitz. *In* Harry Fischel Institute Publications, Section III, Vol. I, Jerusalem, 1937, Pt. III, pp. 1–158.

MEISL, JOSEF, Geschichte der Juden in Polen und Russland. 3 vols., Berlin, 1921–25.

MEISSNER, BRUNO, Babylonien und Assyrien. 2 vols., Heidelberg, 1920–25.

MELDOLA, DAVID B. RAPHAEL, ס' דברי דוד (Responsa). Amsterdam, 1753.

MELDOLA, RAPHAEL B. ELEAZAR, ס' מים רבים (Responsa). 4 vols., Amsterdam, 1737.

MENAḤEM B. ZERAḤ, see Ibn Zeraḥ, Menaḥem.

MENAḤEM OF MERSEBURG, ס' נמוקים (On Law). Appended to Jacob Weil's Responsa.

MENCZEL, J. S., Beiträge zur Geschichte der Juden von Mainz im XV Jahrhundert; eine quellenkritische Untersuchung mit Quellenabdruck. Berlin, 1933.

MENDELSOHN, ISAAC, "Gilds in Babylonia and Assyria." *Journal of the American Oriental Society*, LX (1940), 68–72.

MENDELSOHN, ISAAC, "Guilds in Ancient Palestine." *Bulletin of the American Schools of Oriental Research*, 80 (Dec. 1940), 17–21.

MENES, ABRAM, Die vorexilischen Gesetze Israels. Giessen, 1928.

———, "Tempel und Synagoge." *Zeitschrift für die alttestamentliche Wissenschaft*, L (1932), 268–76.

———, "Prophets and Popular Assembly. (Their Position in Jewish Public Life in the Biblical Period)" (Yiddish). *Yivo Bleter*, IX (1936), 199–217.

MENZ (Minz *or* Mainz), JUDAH B. ELIEZER, ס' פסקים ושאלות (Responsa). Venice, 1553.

MENZ (Minz *or* Mainz), MOSES B. ISAAC, ס' שאלות ותשובות (Responsa). Cracow, 1717.

MESSER LEON, *see* David b. Judah *and* Judah b. Yeḥiel.

MEYER EDUARD, Die Enstehung des Judentums. Eine historische Untersuchung. Halle, 1896.

———, and BERNHARD LUTHER, Israel und seine Nachbarstämme. Halle, 1906.

MEYERHOF, MAX, "Mediaeval Jewish Physicians from Arabic Sources." *Isis*, XXVIII (1938), 432–60.

MEZ, A., Die Renaissance des Islams. Heidelberg, 1923.

———, "The Renaissance of Islam." English translation by S. Khuda Bukhsh. *Islamic Culture*, II (1928), 92–121, 260–86, 414–48, 593–610; III (1929), 273–97, 427–51, 569–91; IV (1930), 130–43, 291–309, 430–51; V (1931), 118–41, 442–61; VI (1932), 131–52; (with D. S. Margoliouth) 431–59; VII (1933), 114–24, 309–23, 536–60.

MICHAEL SYRUS, Chronique de Michel le Syrien, Patriarche Jacobite d'Antioche (1166–1197), éditée pour la première fois et traduite en français par J. B. Chabot. 4 vols., Paris, 1899–1924.

MICZYŃSKI, SEBASTJAN, Zwierciadło Korony polskiej (The Mirror of the Polish Crown: Heavy Insults and Vexations of Jews). Lwów, 1618. Non vidi.

MIGNE, JACQUES PAUL, ed., Patrologiae cursus completus. Series latina, 221 vols., Paris, 1844–61. Series graeca, 161 vols., Paris 1857–66.

Milano, Attilio, "Documents pour l'histoire de la communauté juive d'Ancone." *REJ*, LXXXVII (1929), 166–76; LXXXVIII (1929), 51–58.

———, Ricerche sulle condizioni economiche degli Ebrei a Roma (1555–1848). Città di Castello, 1931. Reprinted from *Israel*, V-VI.

———, "La Pragmatica degli Ebrei romani nel secolo XVII." *Israel*, VII (1932–33), 176–88.

———, "I capitoli di Daniel da Pisa e la Communità di Roma." *Israel*, X (1935–36), 324–38, 409–26.

———, "Gli Ebrei in Italia nei secoli XI° et XII°. Loro distribuzione territoriale e attività economica." *Israel*, XIII (1938), 18–39. Was to be continued.

———, and Roberto Bachi, Università israelitica a Roma. Storia e riordinamento del archivio col catalogo del archivio e un saggio bibliografico sulli Ebrei di Roma. Rome, 1929.

Millas y Vallicrosa, José Maria, Documents hebraics de Jueus catalans. Barcelona, 1927.

———, Documentos hebraicos del Archivo del Pilar de Zaragoza. Madrid, 1930.

———, "Contratos de Judios y Moriscos del reino de Navarra." *Anuario de historia del derecho español*, X (1933), 273–86.

Mirsky, Samuel Kalman, "On the Organization of the Babylonian Academies in the Talmudic Period" (Hebrew). *Ḥoreb*, III (1936), 109–24.

Mishnah, The, Edition Lwów. 6 vols., Lwów, 1862. — Die Mischna. Text, Übersetzung und ausführliche Erklärung mit eingehenden geschichtlichen und sprachlichen Einleitungen. Herausgegeben von G. Beer, O. Holtzmann *et al.* Giessen, 1912 ff.— Mischnacodex Kaufmann. Faksimile Ausgabe, published by G. Beer, The Hague, 1929.— The Mishnah Translated with Introduction and Brief Explanatory Notes, by Herbert Danby. Oxford, 1933.

Mitteilungen des kaiserlichen deutschen archaeologischen Instituts. Athenische Abteilung, Vols. I-LXII. Athens, 1876–1937.

Mizraḥi, Elijah b. Abraham, ס' שאלות ותשובות (Responsa). Revised ed. by Michael Rabbinowicz, Jerusalem, 1938.

MOELLN, JACOB B. MOSES HA-LEVI, ס' מנהגים *or* ס' מהרי"ל (Custumal). [Johannesburg], 1858.

MOMIGLIANO, ARNALDO *or* M. A., "I nomi delle prime sinagoghe romane e la condizione giuridica delle communità in Roma sotto Augusto." *Israel*, VI (1931–32), 283–92.

———, "Severo Alessandro Archisynagogus. Una conferma alla Historia Augusta." *Athenaeum. Studii periodici di letteratura e storia*, XXII (1934), 151–53.

MOMMSEN, THEODOR, ed., "Bruchstücke des Johannes von Antiochia und des Johannes Malalas." *Hermes*, VI (1872), 323–83.

MONYPENNY, WILLIAM FLAVELLE, and GEORGE EARLE BUCKLE, The Life of Benjamin Disraeli Earl of Beaconsfield. Revised ed., 2 vols., London, 1929.

MOORE, GEORGE FOOT, Judaism in the First Centuries of the Christian Era. The Age of the Tannaim. 3 vols., Cambridge, Mass., 1927–30.

MORDECAI B. HILLEL HA-KOHEN *or* ASHKENAZI, ס' מרדכי (Halakic Commentary on Alfasi). Printed with many editions of the latter work.

MORET, A., "L'administration locale sous l'ancien empire égyptien." *Académie des inscriptions, Comptes rendus*, 1916, pp. 378–86.

MORPURGO, EDGARDO, "L'università degli Ebrei in Padova nel XVI secolo." *Bolletino del Museo Civico di Padova*, XII (1909), 16–25, 65–75.

———, "Bibliografia della storia degli Ebrei nel Veneto." *Rivista israelitica*, VII (1910), 180–90, 227–32; VIII (1911), 14–29, 68–81, 106–26, 215–29; IX (1912), 49–79, 127–52, 214–30 (incomplete).

MORPURGO, SAMSON B. JOSHUA MOSES, ס' שמש צדקה (Responsa). With additions by Moses H. S. Morpurgo. Venice, 1743.

MORRIS, NATHAN, The Jewish School from the Earliest Times to the Year 500 of the Present Era. London, 1937.

MORTARA, MARCO, "Die Censur hebräischer Bücher in Italien und der *Canon purificationis*." *Hebräische Bibliographie*, V (1862), 72–77, 96–101.

MORTARA, MARCO, "The Text of Rabbi Nathanel Trabotto's Will." *Magazin für die Wissenschaft des Judentums*, XIV (1887), Hebrew section, pp. 11–22.

MOSES B. JACOB OF COUCY, ס' המצוות [הגדול] (A Code of Laws). Venice, 1522.

MOSES B. MAIMON, *see* Maimonides, Moses.

MOSES B. NAḤMAN, *see* Naḥmanides.

MOSES, LEOPOLD, Die Juden in Niederösterreich. Vienna, 1935.

MOSSÉ, ARMAND, Histoire des Juifs d'Avignon et du comtat Venaissin. Paris, 1934.

MUELLER, EWALD, Das Konzil von Vienne 1311–12. Münster, 1934.

MÜLLER, DAVID HEINRICH, and JULIUS VON SCHLOSSER, eds., Die Haggadah von Sarajevo. Eine spanisch-jüdische Bilderhandschrift des Mittelalters, nebst einem Anhange von David Kaufmann. Vienna, 1898.

MÜLLER, JOEL, מפתח לתשובות הגאונים Einleitung in die Responsen der babylonischen Geonen. Berlin, 1891.
Cf. also Lewin, Benjamin Menasseh; Teshubot geone mizraḥ u-ma'arab.

MÜLLER, WALTHER, Zur Frage des Ursprungs der mittelalterlichen Zünfte. Leipzig, 1910.

MÜLLER, WILLIBALD, Urkundliche Beiträge zur Geschichte der mährischen Judenschaft im 17. und 18. Jahrhundert. Olmütz, 1903.

MUNK, L., "Die Constituten der sämmtlichen hessischen Judenschaft im Jahre 1690." *Jubelschrift . . . I. Hildesheimer*, Berlin, 1890, pp. 69–82; Hebrew section, pp. 77–85.

———, "Die Judenlandtage in Hessen-Cassel." *MGWJ*, XLI (1897), 505–22.

———, "Aus dem Constituten-Buch der sämtlichen hessischen Judenschaft." *Festschrift . . . Salomon Carlebach*, Berlin, 1910, pp. 339–50.

MUNK, SALOMON, Palestine, description géographique, historique, et archéologique. Paris, 1844.

MÜNZER, ZDENKA, "Die Altneusynagoge in Prag." *JGJC*, IV (1932), 63–105.

Naḥmanides, Moses (Moses b. Naḥman), ס' מלחמות ה' (Commentary on Alfasi). Printed in many editions of the latter work.

Nakawa, Israel ibn al-, ס' מנורת המאור (An Ethical Treatise). Ed. by Hyman G. Enelow. 4 vols., New York, 1929–32.

Nathan b. Yeḥiel, *see* Kohut, Alexander.

Nau, François, "Analyse de la seconde partie inédite de l'histoire ecclésiastique de Jean d'Asie." *Revue de l'Orient Chrétien*, II (1897), 455–93.

Nehama, Joseph, Histoire des Israélites de Salonique. Vols. I-IV, Salonique, 1935–36.

Nemoy, Leon, "A Tenth-Century Disquisition on Suicide According to Old Testament Law." *Journal of Biblical Literature*, LVII (1938), 411–20.

Netter, Nathan, "Die Schuldennot der jüdischen Gemeinde Metz (1791–1854)." *MGWJ*, LVII (1913), 591–619; LVIII (1914), 63–80.

———, Vingt siècles d'histoire d'une communauté juive (Metz et son grand passé). Paris, 1938.

Neubauer, Adolph, "Zwei Klagelieder." *Israelitische Letterbode*, VI (1880–81), 32–37.

———, "Documents inédits." *REJ*, IV (1882), 173–91; V (1882), 41–56, 246–49; IX (1884), 51–65, 214–30; X (1885), 79–107; XII (1886), 80–94.

———, Medieval Jewish Chronicles and Chronological Notes. 2 vols., Oxford, 1887–95. *In* Anecdota Oxoniensia. Documents, and Extracts Chiefly from Manuscripts in the Bodleian and Other Oxford Libraries. Semitic Series, Vol. I, Pts. IV and VI.

———, and M. Stern, eds., Hebräische Berichte über die Judenverfolgungen während der Kreuzzüge. With a German translation by S. Baer. Berlin, 1892. Historische Kommission für Geschichte der Juden in Deutschland, Quellen zur Geschichte der Juden in Deutschland, Vol. II.

Neubürger, Friedrich, Verfassungsrecht der gemeinen Judenschaft zu Fürth und in dessen Amt im achtzehnten Jahrhundert. Fürth, 1902. Reprinted from *MGWJ*, XLV (1901).

NEUFELD, SIEGBERT, Die Juden im thüringisch-sächsischen Gebiete während des Mittelalters. 2 pts., Berlin and Halle, 1917–27.

NEUSTADT, D., "Some Problems concerning the 'Negidut' in Egypt during the Middle Ages" (Hebrew). *Zion*, IV (1938–39), 126–49.

NEWMAN, J., The Agricultural Life of the Jews in Babylonia between the Years 200 C. E. and 500 C. E. London, 1932.

NISENBAUM, S. B., "Un manuscript de la 'Gueniza' de Lublin." *REJ*, L (1905), 84–89.

———, Evreiskie nagrobnyie pamiatniki goroda Liublina (Jewish Tombstones of the City of Lublin, XVI–XIX Centuries). St. Petersburg, 1913. Supplement to *Evreiskaya Starina*, Vol. VI.

NISSIM B. REUBEN OF GERONA (Gerondi), ס' שאלות ותשובות (Responsa). Rome, 1546.

———, חדושי הלכות (Commentary) on Alfasi's Halakot. Printed with many editions of the latter work.

NÖLDEKE, THEODOR, ed., *see* Ṭabari, Muḥammad.

NORDMANN, ACHILLE, Der israelitische Friedhof in Hegenheim in geschichtlicher Darstellung. Basel, 1910.

———, "Histoire des Juifs à Genève de 1281 à 1780." *REJ*, LXXX (1925), 1–41.

NOTH, MARTIN, Das System der zwölf Stämme Israels. Stuttgart, 1930.

NÜBLING, E., Die Judengemeinden des Mittelalters, insbesondere die Gemeinde der Reichsstadt Ulm. Ulm, 1896.

OBERMEYER, JULIUS, Die Landschaft Babylonien im Zeitalter des Talmuds und des Gaonats. Frankfort, 1929.

OESTERLEY, WILLIAM OSCAR EMIL, HERBERT MARTIN JAMES LOEWE and ERWIN I. J. ROSENTHAL, eds., Judaism and Christianity. 3 vols., London, 1937–38. I: The Age of Transition, ed. by W. O. E. Oesterley; II: The Contact of Pharisaism with Other Cultures, ed. by H. Loewe; III: Law and Religion, ed. by Erwin I. J. Rosenthal.

OPPENHEIM, SAMUEL, "The Early History of the Jews in New York, 1654–1664: Some New Matter on the Subject." *PAJHS*, XVIII (1909), 1–91.

———, "The Jews in Barbados in 1739." *PAJHS*, XXII (1914), 197–98.

———, "The Jewish Burial Ground on New Bowery, New York, Acquired in 1682, Not 1656." *PAJHS*, XXXI (1928), 77–103.

OR ZARU'A, ḤAYYIM B. ISAAC, ס' שאלות ותשובות (Responsa). Ed. by Judah Rosenberg. Leipzig, 1860.

OR ZARU'A, ISAAC B. MOSES, ס' אור זרוע (Halakic Treatise). 2 pts., Zhitomir, 1862.

ORDENAÇOENS . . . AFFONSO, *see* Affonso V.

ORIGEN (ORIGENES), ADAMANTIUS, ST., Opera omnia. *In* Migne's Patrologia graeca, XI–XVII.

———, Werke. Published by the Prussian Academy of Science. Vols. I–XI. Leipzig, 1899–1935.

———, Writings. Engl. transl. *In* Ante-Nicene Christian Library. Vols. X, XXIII. Edinburgh, 1869–72.

OSTERMAN, NATHAN, "The Controversy over the Proposed Readmission of the Jews to England (1655)." *Jewish Social Studies*, III (1941), 301–28.

OSTERSETZER, ISRAEL, "On the Investigation of the Spirit of Jewish Law" (Hebrew). *Sefer ha-Shanah li-Yehude Polonia* (Polish Jewish Yearbook), I (1937), 35–60.

OVADIAH, A., "R. Elijah Mizraḥi" (Hebrew). *Sinai*, III, Pt. 1 (1939), 393–413; Pt. 2 (1939–40), 73–80, 230–41.

OVIDIUS NASO, PUBLIUS, [Ars Amatoria]. The Art of Love, and other poems. With an English transl. by J. H. Mozley. London, 1939. "Loeb Classical Library."

PACIFICI, RICCARDO, "I regolamenti della Scuola italiana a Venezia nel secolo XVII." *Israel*, V (1930–31), 322–402.

PALANQUE, JEAN-REMY, Saint Ambroise et l'Empire Romain. Contribution à l'histoire des rapports de l'église et de l'état à la fin du quatrième siècle. Paris, 1933.

PARKES, JAMES, The Conflict of the Church and the Synagogue: A Study in the Origin of Antisemitism. London, 1934.

Parkes, James, The Jew in the Medieval Community. A Study of his Political and Economic Situation. London, 1938.

———, "Christian Influence on the Status of the Jews in Europe." *Historia Judaica*, I (1938), 31–38.

Pastor, Ludwig von, The History of the Popes from the Close of the Middle Ages. 32 vols., London, 1891–1940.

Pazdro, Zbigniew, Organizacya i praktyka żydowskich sądów podwojewodzińskich (Organization and Practice of the Jewish Palatinate Courts in the Years 1740–1772). Lwów, 1903.

Pedersen, Johs., "Masdjid." *Encyclopaedia of Islam*, III, 361.

Perles, Josef, "Geschichte der Juden in Posen." *MGWJ*, XIV (1865), 81–93, 121–36, 165–78, 205–16, 256–63.

———, "Urkunden zur Geschichte der jüdischen Provinzial-Synoden in Polen." *MGWJ*, XVI (1867), 108–11, 152–54, 222–26, 304–8, 343–48.

Perlow, Towa, L'éducation et l'enseignement chez les Juifs à l'èpoque talmudique. Paris, 1931.

Perugini, "L'Inquisition romaine et les Israélites." *REJ*, III (1881), 94–108.

Pesaro, A., Memorie storiche sulla communità israelitica ferrarese. Ferrara, 1878.

Philo Judaeus, Opera quae supersunt, ed. by L. Cohn and P. Wendland. 7 vols., Berlin, 1886–1930. Vol. VII consists of indices prepared by I. Leisegang.

———, Opera quae reperiri potuerunt omnia, edited and annotated by Th. Mangey. 2 vols., London, 1742. Contains fragments not included elsewhere.

———, Works. Greek text with English translation by F. H. Colson and G. H. Whitaker, Vols. I-VI. London and Cambridge, Mass., 1929–35. "Loeb Classical Library." Vols. VII-IX to be issued.

———, The Works of Philo Judaeus, the Contemporary of Josephus. An English translation by C. D. Yonge. 4 vols., London, 1854–55.

Picciotto, James, Sketches of Anglo-Jewish History. London, 1875.

Pines, S., "Une notice sur les Rech Galuta chez un écrivain arabe de IXe siècle." *REJ*, C (1936), 71–73.

Pinsker, Simḥah, לקוטי קדמוניות. Zur Geschichte des Karaismus und der karäischen Literatur nach handschriftlichen Quellen bearbeitet. Vienna, 1860.

Pinthus, Alexander, "Studien über die bauliche Entwicklung der Judengassen in den deutschen Städten." *ZGJD*, II (1930–31), 101–30, 197–217, 284–300. Appeared also as a dissertation of the Technische Hochschule in Hannover, under the title, *Die Judensiedlungen der deutschen Städte, eine stadtbiologische Studie*, Hannover, 1931.

Poland, Franz, Geschichte des griechischen Vereinswesens. Leipzig, 1909.

Pollack, A. N., "The Jews and the Egyptian Treasury in the Times of the Mamelukes and the Beginning of the Turkish Regime" (Hebrew). *Zion*, I (1935–36), 24–36.

Pool, David de Sola, The Mill Street Synagogue (1730–1817) of the Congregation Shearith Israel. New York, 1930.

———, "Early Relations between Palestine and American Jewry." *Brandeis Avukah Annual of 1932*, ed. by Joseph Shubow, New York, 1932, pp. 536–48.

Poppers, Helena, De Joden in Overijsel van hunne vestiging tot 1814. Utrecht, 1926.

Popper, William, The Censorship of Hebrew Books. New York, 1899.

Porges, Nathan, "Censorship." *Jewish Encyclopedia*, III, 642–50.

Porter, Josias Leslie, Five Years in Damascus, including an Account of the History, Topography and Antiquities of that City, with Travels and Researches in Palmyra, Lebanon, and the Hauran. 2 vols., London, 1855.

Porto, Moses b. Yeḥiel di, ed., ס' פלגי מים (Responsa, against Issac Gershon). Venice, 1608.

Posener, S., "Les Juifs sous le premier empire; les statistiques générales." *REJ*, XCIII (1932), 192–214; XCIV (1933), 157–66.

Poznanski, Samuel, Babylonische Geonim im nachgaonäischen Zeitalter. Berlin, 1914.

Preliminary Report on the Synagogue of Dura. New Haven, 1936.

PRENER, J., "Contrat d'engagement du rabbin d'Avignon en 1661." *REJ*, LXV (1913), 315–18.

PRIBRAM, ALFRED FRANCIS, Urkunden und Akten zur Geschichte der Juden in Wien. 2 vols., Vienna, 1918. Historische Kommission der israelitischen Kultusgemeinde in Wien, Quellen und Forschungen zur Geschichte der Juden in Deutsch-Österreich, Vol. VIII.

PRIEBATSCH, FELIX, "Die Judenpolitik des fürstlichen Absolutismus im 17. und 18. Jahrhundert," *Forschungen und Versuche zur Geschichte des Mittelalters und der Neuzeit, Festschrift Dietrich Schaefer*, Jena, 1915, pp. 564–657.

PRINZ, ISAAK, "De oud-hollandsche drukpersvrijheid ten opzichte van het joodsche boek." *Bijdragen en Mededeelingen van het Genootschap voor de Joodsche Wetenschap in Nederland*, V (1933), 147–76.

Privilegi e concessioni di S. S. R. M. e i suoi reali predecessori a favore dell' Università Generale degli Ebrei del Piemonte. Turin, 1744.

PROFIAT DURAN, *or* ISAAC B. MOSES HA-LEVI, ס' מעשה אפוד Einleitung in das Studium u. Grammatik der hebräischen Sprache. With an appendix by S. D. Luzzatto. Ed. by J. Friedländer and J. Kohn. Vienna, 1865.

PROU, MAURICE, Les registres d'Honorius IV, publiées d'après le manuscrit des archives du Vatican. 4 pts., Paris, 1886–88. Bibliothèque des Écoles françaises d'Athènes et de Rome, 2d ser., no. 7.

RABBINOVICZ, RAPHAEL NATHAN, ס' דקדוקי סופרים (Variae lectiones in . . . Talmud Babylonicum). Pts. 1–15, Munich, 1867–84. Pt. 16, ed. by H. Ehrentreu, Przemyśl, 1897.

RABBINOWITZ, SAUL PINḤAS, ר' יוסף איש רוסהים (R. Joseph of Rosheim). Warsaw, 1902.
Cf. also Graetz, Heinrich.

RABIN, ISRAEL, Die Juden in Zülz. Zülz, 1926. Reprinted from *Festgabe zur 700-Jahrfeier der Stadt Zülz OS.*

Rabinowitsch, Wolf (Zeeb), "Manuscripts from an Archive in Stolin" (Hebrew). *Zion*, V (1939–40), 125–32, 244–47.

Rabinowitz, Louis Isaac, "France in the Thirteenth Century." *Judaism and Christianity*. Ed. by W. O. E. Oesterley, Herbert Loewe and Erwin I. J. Rosenthal, 3 vols., London, 1935–37, II, 189–220.

———, "The Origin of the Canterbury 'Treaty' of 1266." *Miscellanies of the Jewish Historical Society of England*, III (1937), 76–79.

———, "The Medieval Jewish Counter-Part to the Gild Merchant." *Economic History Review*, VIII (1937–38), 180–85.

———, "The Talmudic Basis of the *Ḥerem ha-yishub*." *JQR*, XXVIII (1937–38), 217–23.

———, The Social Life of the Jews of Northern France in the XII–XIV Centuries as Reflected in the Rabbinical Literature of the Period. London, 1938.

Radin, Max, "A Charter of Privileges of the Jews in Ancona of the Year 1535." *JQR*, IV (1913–14), 225–48.

Raphael Joseph b. Aaron Ḥazzan, ס' חקרי לב (Halakic Discourses) on Joseph Karo's *Shulḥan 'Aruk*. 7 vols., Salonica, 1787–1832; Leghorn, 1794.

Rashi, *see* Solomon b. Isaac.

Recanati, Menaḥem b. Benjamin, ס' פסקי הלכות (Brief Decisions). Bologna, 1538.

Reglement voor de Broedershap van het Weesjongenshuis der Nederlandsche Portugeesche Israelietische Gemeente te Amsterdam, genaamd Aby Jetomim. Amsterdam, 1817.

Regné, Jean, "Étude sur la condition des Juifs de Narbonne du Ve au XIVe siècle." *REJ*, LV (1908), 1–36, 221–43; LVIII (1909), 75–105, 200–25; LIX (1910), 59–89; LXI (1911), 228–54; LXII (1911), 1–27, 248–66; LXIII (1912), 75–99.

Regolamento fatto dall' università degli Ebrei di Reggio per la continuazione delli accordi in essa rinovati l'anno 1757. Florence, 1758.

Reifer, Manfred, Ausgewählte historische Schriften. Dokumenten-Sammlung. Černauti, 1938.

REINACH, SALOMON, "Inscription grecque de Smyrne: La juive Rufina." *REJ*, VII (1883), pp. 161–66.

———, "Les Juifs d'Hypaepa." *REJ*, X (1885), 74–78.

———, "La communauté juive d'Athribis." *REJ*, XVII (1888), 235–38.

REINACH, THÉODORE, Textes d'auteurs grecs et romains relatifs au Judaïsme. Paris, 1895.

REISCHER, JACOB B. JOSHUA, ס' שבות יעקב (Responsa). 2 vols., Halle-Offenbach, 1710–19.

REMY, NAHIDA, The Jewish Woman. Authorized transl. by L. Mannheimer, with a Preface by Moritz Lazarus. Cincinnati, 1895.

RENNARD, J., "Juifs et Protestants aux Antilles françaises au XVIIe siècle. Préliminaires de la révocation de l'édit de Nantes." *Revue d'histoire des missions*, X (1933), 436–62.

REVEL, DOB (Bernard), "The Renewal of the Ordination Four Hundred Years Ago" (Hebrew). *Ḥoreb*, V (1939), 1–26.

REVERE, AMEDEO, "La confraternità israelitica 'Sovegno' di Padova." *Israel*, XII (1938), 277–86.

[REUMONT, ALFRED VON], "Die Juden im Kirchenstaate und in Toscana." *Der Orient*, II (1841), 247–48, 250–52, 257–60.

RIGG, J. M., Select Pleas, Starrs, and Other Records from the Rolls of the Exchequer of the Jews, A. D. 1220–1284. London, 1902. Publications of the Selden Society, Vol. XIV.

———, and H. JENKINSON, eds., Calendar of the Plea Rolls of the Exchequer of the Jews Preserved in the Public Record Office. 3 vols., London, 1905–29.

RINGELBLUM, EMANUEL, "The Minute-Book of the Płock Tailors' Guild (At the End of the 18th Cent.)" (Yiddish). *Yivo Studies in Economics*, II (1932), 20–31.

———, "Restrictions on the Importation of Jewish Books to Poland at the End of the Eighteenth Century" (Yiddish). *Yivo Bleter*, IV (1932), 149–58.

———, Żydzi w Warszawie (Jews in Warsaw). I: From the Origins to the Last Expulsion in 1527. Warsaw, 1932.

RINGELBLUM, EMANUEL, "The Stamp Tax on Jewish Books in Poland in the Eighteenth Century" (Yiddish). *Yivo Bleter*, V (1933), 123–36. Supplemented by B. Weinryb's remarks ibid., p. 408.

———, "The Census of Jewish Books in Poland in 1776" (Yiddish). *Yivo Bleter*, V (1933), 333–45.

RIOS, AMADOR DE LOS, Historia social, politica y religiosa de los Judios de España y Portugal. 3 vols., Madrid, 1875–76.

RITTER, BERNHARD, "Aus dem Frankfurter Gemeindebuche." *MGWJ*, XXVIII (1879), 36–38.

———, Philo und die Halachah. Breslau, 1879.

RIVKIND, ISAAC, "A Codex of Prague Ordinances" (Hebrew). *Reshumot*, IV (1926), 345–52.

———, "Contributions to the History of Gaming Among Jews; Its Influence on Family Peace" (Hebrew). *Ḥoreb*, I (1934), 82–91.

———, "Dice Tax in Connection with the Tax of Disgrace" (Hebrew). *Zion*, I (1935–36), 37–48.

———, "The Laws concerning Gamblers" (Hebrew). *Ḥoreb*, II (1935–36), 60–66.

RIVLIN, ELIEZER, "The Statute of the *Ḥalukkah* of the Perushim District in Palestine of 1823" (Hebrew). *Ṣiyyon*, II (1926–27), 149–70.

———, "The *Ḥazakah* of Real Estate in Jerusalem" (Hebrew). *Festschrift Jakob Freimann*, Berlin, 1937, pp. 149–62.
Cf. also Frumkin, Aryeh Leb.

RIXEN, CARL, Geschichte und Organisation der Juden im ehemaligen Stifte Münster. Münster i. W., 1906.

ROBERTS, COLIN, THEODORE C. SKEAT, ARTHUR DARBY NOCK, "The Gild of Zeus Hypsistos." *Harvard Theological Review*, XXIX (1936), 39–88.

ROCHETTE, JACQUELINE, La condition des Juifs d'Alsace jusqu'au décret du 28 septembre 1791. Paris, 1938.

RODOCANACHI, EMMANUEL, Le Saint-Siège et les Juifs. Le ghetto à Rome. Paris, 1891.

———, "La communauté juive de Rome au temps de Jules II et de Léon X." *REJ*, LXI (1911), 71–81.

Rokyčana, J., "Die militärische Dienstpflicht der böhmischen Juden." *ZGJT*, I (1930–31), 104–8.

Romanoff, Paul, "Onomasticon of Palestine." *Proceedings of the American Academy for Jewish Research*, VII (1936), 147–227. Also enlarged reprint.

Romanos, Johannes A., "Histoire de la communauté israélite de Corfou." *REJ*, XXIII (1891), 63–74.

Rönne, Ludwig von, and Heinrich Simon, Die früheren und gegenwärtigen Verhältnisse der Juden in den sämmtlichen Landestheilen des Preussischen Staates. Breslau, 1843. Die Verfassung und Verwaltung des Preussischen Staates, VIII, Pt. 3.

Rosanes, Salomon A., דברי ימי ישראל בתוגרמא (בטורקיה) (A History of the Jews in Turkey). Vols. I–III, 2d ed., IV–V, Jerusalem, 1931–38.

Rösel, Isert, "Die Reichssteuern der deutschen Judengemeinden von ihren Anfängen bis zur Mitte des 14. Jahrhunderts." *MGWJ*, LIII (1909), 679–708; LIV (1910), 55–69, 206–23, 333–47, 462–73. Also reprint.

Rosenberg, H., "Die Statuten der Gemeinden auf der Insel Candia." *Festschrift David Hoffmann*, Berlin, 1914, pp. 267–80.

Rosenthal, B., "Oberrabbiner Michael Scheuer als Kritiker seiner Zeit." *ZGJD*, III (1931), 72–75. Critique of I. Unna's article.

Rossi, Azariah de', ס' מאור עינים (Light of the Eyes). Supplemented by מצרף לכסף. Ed. by D. Cassel, Wilno, 1864–66.

Rost, Leonhard, Die Vorstufen von Kirche und Synagoge im Alten Testament. Stuttgart, 1938. Beiträge zur Wissenschaft vom Alten und Neuen Testament, 4th ser., No. 24.

Rostovtzeff, Michael I., and C. B. Welles, "A Parchment Contract of Loan from Dura Europus on the Euphrates." *Yale Classical Studies*, II (1931), 1–78.

Roth, Abraham Naftali Zevi, "The Law of the Kingdom is Law" (Hebrew). *Ha-Soker*, V (1937–38), 110–26. With notes by D. S. Löwinger.

Roth, Cecil, "Rabbi Menaḥem Navarra: His Life and Times. 1717–1777. A Chapter in the History of the Jews of Verona." *JQR*, XV (1924–25), pp. 427–66.

———, "An Association for the Redemption of Captives in the Seventeenth Century" (Hebrew). *Ha-Zofeh*, IX (1925–26), 232–35.

———, "The Forced Baptisms of 1783 at Rome and the Community of London." *JQR*, XVI (1925–26), 105–16.

———, "Une mission des communautés du Comtat Venaissin à Rome." *REJ*, LXXXIV (1927), 1–14.

———, "Sumptuary Laws of the Community of Carpentras." *JQR*, XVIII (1927–28), 357–83.

———, "A Seventeenth Century Library and Trousseau." *Studies in Jewish Bibliography . . . in Memory of Abraham Solomon Freidus*, New York, 1929, pp. 160–69.

———, Archives of the United Synagogue, Report and Catalogue. London, 1930.

———, [History of the Jews in] Venice. Philadelphia, 1930. "Jewish Communities Series."

———, "The Jews in Malta." *Transactions of the Jewish Historical Society of England*, XII (1931), 187–251.

———, A Life of Menasseh ben Israel, Rabbi, Printer and Diplomat. Philadelphia, 1934.

———, "Sumptuary Laws." *Jewish Chronicle Supplement*, April, 1934, pp. v–vi.

———, "An English Account of the Jews of Jerusalem in the Seventeenth Century." *Miscellanies of the Jewish Historical Society of England*, II (1935), 99–104.

———, "The Portsmouth Community and Its Historical Background." *Transactions of the Jewish Historical Society of England*, XIII (1936), 157–87.

———, "Forced Baptisms in Italy." *JQR*, XXVII (1936–37), 117–36.

———, "The Lesser London Synagogues of the Eighteenth Century." *Miscellanies of the Jewish Historical Society in England*, III (1937), 1–7.

ROTH, CECIL, Magna Bibliotheca Anglo-Judaica. A Bibliographical Guide to Anglo-Jewish History. London, 1937.

ROTHSCHILD, S., Die Abgaben und die Schuldenlast der Wormser jüdischen Gemeinde 1563–1854. Worms, 1925.

RUBIO Y LLUCH, ANTONIO, Documents per l'historia de la cultura catalana migeval. 2 vols., Barcelona, 1908–21.

SAALFELD, S., Das Martyrologium des Nürnberger Memorbuches. Berlin, 1898. Historische Kommission für Geschichte der Juden in Deutschland, Quellen zur Geschichte der Juden in Deutschland, Vol. III.

SACHAU, EDUARD, "Von den rechtlichen Verhältnissen der Christen im Sassanidenreich." *Mitteilungen des Seminars für orientalische Sprachen zu Berlin*, X, Pt. 2 (1907), 69–95.

SACKS, MORDECAI JUDAH LEB, and ELIJAH ISAAC PRISSMAN, eds., שיטה על מועד קטן (Comments on M. Ḳ.) by a Disciple of R. Yeḥiel of Paris [Yedidiah of Nuremberg], Pt. II. *In* Harry Fischel Institute Publications, Section III, Vol. I, Jerusalem, 1937, Pt. II, pp. 1–116.

SALTARO, JUDAH B. MOSES, ed., ס' מקוה ישראל (Polemical Treatise against Isaac Gershon). Venice, 1607.

SALZMAN, MARCUS, *see* Aḥimaaz.

SAMUEL B. DAVID HA-LEVI, ס' נחלת שבעה (A Juristic Treatise). Pt. I: Deeds; Pt. II: Responsa. Königsberg, 1865.

SAMUEL, WILFRED S., "The First London Synagogue of the Re-Settlement." *Transactions of the Jewish Historical Society of England*, X (1924), 1–147.

———, "Review of the Jewish Colonists in Barbados, 1860." *Transactions of the Jewish Historical Society of England*, XIII (1936), 1–111.

———, "The Jewish Oratories of Cromwellian London." *Miscellanies of the Jewish Historical Society of England*, III (1937), 46–55.

SARACHEK, JOSEPH, Faith and Reason: The Conflict over the Rationalism of Maimonides. Williamsport, Pa., 1935.

SARAL, SANCHO, El gremio zaragozano. Saragossa, 1925. Non vidi.

SASPORTAS, JACOB B. ABRAHAM, ס' אהל יעקב (Responsa). Amsterdam, 1797.

SASSOON, DAVID SOLOMON, "The History of the Jews in Basra." *JQR*, XVII (1926–27), 407–69.

———, *Ohel Dawid*, Descriptive Catalogue of the Hebrew and Samaritan Manuscripts in the Sassoon Library. 2 vols., London, 1932.

SCHAEDER, HANS HEINZ, Ezra der Schreiber. Tübingen, 1930.

SCHECHTER, FRANK I., "The Rightlessness of Mediaeval English Jewry." *JQR*, IV (1913–14), 121–51.

SCHECHTER, SOLOMON, "Notes sur Messer David Léon tirées de manuscrits." *REJ*, XXIV (1892), 118–38.

———, Studies in Judaism. 3 vols., New York, 1896–1924.

———, Fragments of a Zadokite Work. Edited from Hebrew Manuscripts in the Cairo Genizah Collection . . . and Provided with an English Translation, Introduction and Notes. Cambridge, 1910. *In* Documents of Jewish Sectaries, Vol. I.

SCHERER, J. E., Die Rechtsverhältnisse der Juden in den deutsch-österreichischen Ländern. Mit einer Einleitung über die Principien der Judengesetzgebung in Europa während des Mittelalters. Leipzig, 1901. Beiträge zur Geschichte des Judenrechtes im Mittelalter mit besonderer Bedachtnahme auf die Länder der österreichisch-ungarischen Monarchie, Vol. I.

SCHIAVI, L. A., "Gli Ebrei in Venezia e nelle sue colonie." *Nuova Antologia*, CXXXI (1893), 309–33, 485–519.

SCHIFF, MEIR B. JACOB, ס' חדושי הלכות (Juristic Novellae). 2 vols., Hamburg, 1737–41.

SCHIPPER, IGNAZ *or* ISAAC (Yiṣḥaḳ), "Beiträge zur Geschichte der partiellen Judenlandtage in Polen um die Wende des XVII und XVIII Jahrhunderts bis sur Auflösung des jüdischen Parlamentarismus (1764)." *MGWJ*, LVI (1912) 456–77, 602–11, 736–44.

———, געשיכטע פון יידישער טעאטערקונסט און דראמע (A History of Jewish Theatrical Arts and Drama from the Beginning to 1750). 4 vols., Warsaw, 1923–28.

SCHIPPER, IGNAZ *or* ISAAC (Yiṣḥaḳ), "The Composition of the Council of Four Lands" (Yiddish). *Yivo Studies in History*, I (1929), 73–82.

———, "Polish Regesta to the History of the Council of Four Lands" (Yiddish). *Yivo Studies in History*, I (1929), 83–114.

———, יידישע געשיכטע (An Economic History of Medieval Jewry). 4 vols., Warsaw, 1930.

———, "The Warsaw Committee; a Contribution to the History of Jewish Autonomy in Poland" (Polish). *Księga jubileuszowa* (Jubilee Volume in honor of) *Markus Braude*, Warsaw, 1931, pp. 145–55.

———, "The Financial Ruin of the Central and Provincial Autonomy of the Jews in Poland (1650–1764)" (Yiddish). *Yivo Studies in Economics*, II (1932), 1–19.

SCHIRMANN, JEFIM *or* ḤAYYIM, "Eine hebräisch-italienische Komödie des XVI Jahrhunderts." *MGWJ*, LXXV (1931), 97–118.

———, "The Life of Yehudah Halevi" (Hebrew). *Tarbiz*, IX (1937–38), 35–54, 219–40, 284–305; XI (1939), 125.

SCHLOESSINGER, MAX, "Hazzan." *Jewish Encyclopedia*, VI, 284–86.

SCHNEIDER, DAVID M., The History of Public Welfare in New York State 1609–1866. Chicago, 1938.

SCHOLEM, GERHARD *or* GERSHON, "Kabbala." *Encyclopaedia Judaica*, IX, 630–731.

———, "A Document of the Disciples of Isaac Luria" (Hebrew). *Zion*, V (1939–40), 133–60.

———, "Review of Mortimer J. Cohen's *Jacob Emden: A Man of Controversy*." *Kirjath Sepher*, XVI (1939–40), 320–38.

SCHÖNBAUER, ERNST, "Reichsrecht, Volksrecht und Provinzialrecht: Studien über die Bedeutung der Constitutio Antoniana für die römische Rechtsentwicklung." *Zeitschrift für Rechtsgeschichte*, LXX (Romanistische Abteilung, LVII, 1937), 309–55.

SCHORR, JOSHUA HESCHEL, "R. Nissim bar Mosheh of Marseilles" (Hebrew). *He-Ḥaluṣ*, VII (1865), 89–144.

SCHORR, MOSES, Organizacya Żydów w Polsce (Jewish Communal Organization in Poland until 1772). Lwów, 1899.

Schorr, Moses, Zydzi w Przemyślu (Jews in Przemyśl to the End of the Eighteenth Century). Lwów, 1903.

———, "A Cracow Collection of Jewish Statutes and Privileges [Sumaryusz przywilejów nadanych Żydom polskim]" (Russian). *Evreiskaya Starina*, I (1909), 247–64; II (1909), 76–100, 223–45.

———, Rechtsstellung und innere Verfassung der Juden in Polen. Berlin, 1917. Reprinted from *Der Jude*.

Schreiner, Martin, "Contributions à l'histoire des Juifs en Egypte." *REJ*, XXXI (1895), 212–21.

Schudt, Johann Jacob, Jüdische Merckwürdigkeiten. 4 vols., Frankfort, 1714–17.

Schuerer, Emil, Geschichte des jüdischen Volkes im Zeitalter Jesu Christi. 4th ed., 3 vols., Leipzig, 1901–11. I: Einleitung und politische Geschichte; II: Die inneren Zustände; III: Das Judentum in der Zerstreuung und die jüdische Literatur.

———, ———, A History of the Jewish People in the Time of Jesus Christ (English transl.). 2d ed. revised, 3 vols., New York, 1890–91.

Schwab, Moïse, "Une supplique de la communauté de Rome à Pie V." *REJ*, XXV (1892), 113–16.

Schwabe, Moshe, "The Letters of Libanius to the Patriarch of Palestine" (Hebrew). *Tarbiz*, I, Pt. 2 (1929–30), 85–110; Pt. 3, 107–21.

Schwalm, Jacob, "Ein unbekanntes Eingangsverzeichnis von Steuern der königlichen Städte aus der Zeit Kaiser Friedrichs II." *Neues Archiv der Gesellschaft für ältere deutsche Geschichtskunde*, XXIII (1897–98), 519–53.

Schwarz, Arthur Zacharias, "The Introduction of Jacob the Translator (cod. Paris 1173, 5)" (Hebrew). *Alim*, I (1934–35), 36–37, 77.

———, "Letters Concerning the Confiscation of Books in 1553" (Hebrew). *Alim*, II (1935–36), 49–52.

Schweinburg-Eibenschitz, S., "Une confiscation des livres hébreux à Prague." *REJ*, XXIX (1894), 266–71.

Schwerin, Ursula, Die Aufrufe der Päpste zur Befreiung des Heiligen Landes von den Anfängen bis zum Ausgang Innozenz IV. Ein Beitrag zur Geschichte der kurialen Kreuzzugs-propaganda und der päpstlichen Epistolographie. Berlin, 1937. Historische Studien, no. 301.

Schwöbel, Valentin, Die Landesnatur Palästinas. 2 pts., Leipzig, 1914.

סדר אליהו Seder Eliyahu rabbah *and* Seder Eliyahu Zuta. Ed. from MS. Rome with an introduction and notes by Meir Friedmann. Vienna, 1902.

Seeligmann, Siegmund, "Het Marranen-Probleem uit oekonomisch Oogpunkt." *Feestbundel . . . L. Wagenaar* (*Bijdragen en Mededeelingen*, III), Amsterdam, 1925, pp. 101–36.

———, Bibliographie en Historie. Een Bijdrage tot de geschiedenis der eerste Sephardim in Amsterdam. Amsterdam, 1927.

———, "De Gilden en de Joden." *De Vrijdagavond*, V (1928), 135–37.

———, "Ein Originalbrief der Vierländersynode nach Amsterdam aus 1677." *Livre d'hommage . . . Poznanski*, Warsaw, 1929, pp. 147–52.

Sefer Ḥasidim *see* Judah b. Samuel he-ḥasid.

ס' התקנות וההסכמות . . . ירושלים (Sefer ha-taḳḳanot ve-ha-haskamot . . . Yerushalayim; The Book of Ordinances in Jerusalem). 2d. ed., Jerusalem, 1883.

Segré, Arnaldo, "Note sullo *Status civitatis* degli Ebrei nell' Egitto tolemaico e imperiale." *Bulletin de la Societé royale d'archéologie d'Alexandrie*, N. S. VIII (1933), 143–82.

Senigaglia, O., "La condizione giuridica degli Ebrei in Sicilia." *Rivista italiana per le scienze giuridiche*, XLI (1906), 75–102.

Serrano y Sanz, Manuel, Origenes de la dominacion española en America. Vol. I, Madrid, 1918.

ס' שערי צדק (Sha'are Ṣedeḳ; A collection of geonic responsa). Ed. by Nissim b. Ḥayyim Modai. Salonica, 1792.

ס' שערי תשובה (Sha'are Teshubah; A collection of geonic responsa). Ed. by Moses Mordecai Meyuḥas. Salonica, 1802.

Shabbethai Beer, ס' באר עשק (Responsa). Venice, 1674.

Shalem, Nathan, "The Pilgrimage to Palestine in 1521 A. D." (Hebrew)." *Bulletin of the Jewish Palestine Exploration*

Society, VI (1939), 86–95. Refers to Moses Bassola's Pilgrimage to Palestine.

SHATZKY, JACOB, "Ducal Ordinances for the Jews of Sokołów" (Yiddish). *Yivo Economic Studies*, I (1928), 80–87.

———, "Drama and Theatre among the Sephardim in Holland" (Yiddish). *Yivo Bleter*, XVI (1940), 135–49.

———, "Cantors and Synagogue Music in Holland" (Yiddish). *Yivo Bleter*, XVII (1941), 146–56.

[SHEARITH ISRAEL, NEW YORK], The Earliest Extant Minute Books of the Spanish and Portuguese Congregation Shearith Israel in New York, 1728–1786" (Jacques Judah Lyon's transcript checked against the original). *PAJHS*, XXI (1913), 1–160.

SHERIRA GAON, אגרת ר' שרירא גאון (Epistle on the Chain of Tradition). Ed. by Benjamin Menasseh Lewin. Arranged in two Versions with Variations and Notes. Haifa, 1921.
Cf. also Lewin, Benjamin Menasseh.

SHOHET, DAVID MENAHEM, The Jewish Court in the Middle Ages. Studies in Jewish Jurisprudence According to the Talmud, Geonic and Medieval German Responsa. New York, 1931.

SHOHET, I., "The Synagogue on the Tomb of the Prophet Samuel (Hebrew)." *Bulletin of the Jewish Palestine Exploration Society*, VI (1938–39), 81–86.

Siete Partidas, Las, del rey Don Alfonso el Sabio. 3 vols., Madrid, 1807.

———, English transl. and notes by S. P. Scott . . . Introduction, Table of Contents and Index by C. S. Lobingier . . . Bibliography by J. Vance. Chicago, 1931.

SIFRE, *see* Friedmann, Meir.

SILBER, MENDEL, The Origin of the Synagogue. New Orleans, 1915.

SILVA ROSA, J. S. DA, Geschiedenis der Portugeesche Joden te Amsterdam, 1593–1925. Amsterdam, 1925.

SIMONSOHN, MAX, Die kirchliche Judengesetzgebung im Zeitalter der Reformkonzilien von Konstanz und Basel. Breslau, 1912.

SIMPSON, GEORGE, Conflict and Community: A Study in Social Theory. New York, 1937.

SIRKES, JOEL B. SAMUEL, ס' שאלות ותשובות הב"ח (Responsa). O. S., Frankfort, 1697.

SLONIK, BENJAMIN AARON B. ABRAHAM, ס' משאת בנימין (Responsa). Metz, 1776.

SLUYS, D. M., "Bijdragen tot de geschiedenis van de Poolsch-Joodsche Gemeente te Amsterdam." *Feestbundel . . . L. Wagenaar* (*Bijdragen en Mededeelingen*, III), Amsterdam, 1925, pp. 137–58.

SMITH, GEORGE ADAM, Historical Geography of the Holy Land. 25th ed., London, 1932.

SMOLENSKI, WLADYSLAW, Stan i sprawa Żydow polskich w XVIII wieku (The Status of the Jews and the Jewish Question in Poland in the Eighteenth Century). Warsaw, 1876.

SOBERNHEIM, MORITZ, and EUGEN MITTWOCH, "Hebräische Inschriften in der Synagoge von Aleppo." *Festschrift . . . Jakob Guttmann*, Leipzig, 1915, pp. 273–85.

SOFER (SCHREIBER), MOSES B. SAMUEL, ס' שאלות ותשובות חתם סופר (Responsa). Vienna, 1895.

SOLOMON B. ISAAC (Yiṣḥaḳi *or* Rashi), פירוש (Commentary on the Talmud). *In* most editions of the Talmud.

———, ס' האורה (On Law). Ed. by Salomon Buber. Lemberg, 1905.

SOMBART, WERNER, The Jews and Modern Capitalism. Engl. transl. with notes by M. Epstein. London, 1913.

S. DE B. [Sommerhausen, H.], "Les Israélites néerlandais — Reminiscences." *Archives israélites*, VI (1845), 276–84, 370–80, 644–51, 716–23.

SONNE, ISAIAH, "I congressi delle communità israelitiche italiane nei secoli XIV–XVI ed il sinodo dei quattro paesi in Polonia." *L'Idea sionistica*, I, Pts. 11–12 (1931), 5–9.

———, "Neue Dokumente über Salomo Molcho." *MGWJ*, LXXV (1931), 127–35.

———, "Documents" (Hebrew). *Sefer ha-Shanah li-Yehude Amerika* (American Hebrew Year Book), 5695 (1935), 218–25. Supplemented ibid., 5698 (1938), 154–62.

SONNE, ISAIAH, "Materials to the History of the Jews in Verona" (Hebrew). *Zion*, III (1938), 123–69; Pt. 2: "Verona, 1539–1653" (Hebrew). *Ḳobeṣ 'al yad*, N. S. III (XIII), Pt. 2 (1939), 145–91.

———, "An Appeal from Reggio for the Support of the Jerusalem Talmudic Academy (1698)" (Hebrew). *Zion*, IV (1938–39), 86–88.

———, "Contributions to the History of the Jewish Community of Bologna at the Beginning of the Sixteenth Century. With Unpublished Documents from a Pamphlet and from Collections of Responsa by R. Azriel Trabotto the Elder and R. Azriel Dayyena." *HUCA*, XVI (1941), Hebrew Section, pp. 35–98.

SONNINO, G., "Il Talmud Torà di Livorno." *Israel*, X (1935–36), 183–96.

SOSIS, I., "Social Conflicts in the Jewish Communities of the Sixteenth and Seventeenth Centuries according to the Rabbinic Responsa" (Hebrew texts with Yiddish translation). *Zeitshrift*, I (Minsk, 1926), 225–38.

———, "The Jewish Diet in Lithuania and White Russia in Its Legislative Activity (1623–1761), According to Its Minutes" (Yiddish). *Zeitshrift*, II–III (Minsk, 1928), 1–72.

SPANIER, MEIER, "Der Spruchdichter Süsskind von Trimberg." *Jahrbuch für jüdische Geschichte und Literatur*, XXXI (1938), 124–36.

SPARTIANUS, AELIUS, Hist. Aug. Pescennius Niger. London, 1921. *In* Scriptores historiae Augustae, with an English transl. by David Magie, I, 430–59. "Loeb Classical Library."

SPITZER, A. S. B., "The Torah Must Be Obeyed; an Analysis of the Law Concerning Woman Suffrage." *Jakob Rosenheim-Festschrift*, Frankfort, 1931, Hebrew section, pp. 1–43.

STARR, JOSHUA, The Jews in the Byzantine Empire 641–1204. Athens, 1939. Texte und Forschungen zur byzantinisch-neugriechischen Philologie, no. 30.

———, "Jewish Life in Crete under the Rule of Venice." *Proceedings of the American Academy for Jewish Research*, XII (1942).

Statuto della Pia Opera di Misericordia Israelitica in Verona. Verona, 1900.

Steinheim, Salomo Ludwig, Moses Mendelssohn und seine Schule in ihrer Beziehung zur Aufgabe des neuen Jahrhunderts. Hamburg, 1840.

Steinschneider, Moritz, "Die italienische Literatur der Juden." *MGWJ*, XLII (1898), 33–37, 74–79, 116–23, 162–69, 261–65, 315–22, 418–24, 466–72, 517–22, 551–57; XLIII (1899), 32–36, 91–96, 185–90, 266–70, 311–21, 417–21, 472–76, 514–20, 562–71; XLIV (1900), 80–91, 235–49.

———, "Miszellen und Notizen." *Zeitschrift für hebräische Bibliographie*, IX (1905), 186–89.

Steinthal, Fritz Leopold, Geschichte der Juden in Augsburg. Berlin, 1911.

Stern, Moritz, "Die Versammlung zu Worms im Jahre 1510." *ZGJD*, O. S. III (1889), 248–51.

———, "Der Hochverratsprozess gegen die deutschen Juden im Anfange des 17. Jahrhunderts." *Monatsblätter für Vergangenheit und Gegenwart des Judentums*, ed. by B. Koenigsberger, 1890–91, pp. 24–39, 80–90, 115–28, 154–62 (incomplete).

———, "Zur Statistik der Wormser Juden im 15. Jahrhundert." *Israelitische Monatsschrift* (Supplement to *Jüdische Presse*), 1897, nos. 1–2, 9–11.

———, König Ruprecht von der Pfalz in seinen Beziehungen zu den Juden. Kiel, 1898.

———, "Zur Geschichte der Fleischgebühren in der Berliner jüdischen Gemeinde." *Soncino-Blätter*, II (1927), 97–108.

———, "Jugendunterricht in der Berliner jüdischen Gemeinde während des 18. Jahrhunderts." *JJLG*, XIX (1928), 39–68; XX (1929), 379–80.

———, "Aus Regensburg. Urkundliche Beiträge." *JJLG*, XXII (1931–32), 1–123.

———, "Das Vereinsbuch des Berliner Beth Hamidrasch 1743–1783." *JJLG*, XXII (1931–32), 401–20; Hebrew section, pp. i–xviii.

———, Die israelitische Bevölkerung der deutschen Städte:

VII: Worms, Pt. I: Die Reichsrabbiner des 15. und 16. Jahrhunderts. Berlin, 1937.

Stern, Selma, Der Preussische Staat und die Juden. Pt. 1: Die Zeit des Grossen Kurfürsten und Friedrichs I. 2 vols., Berlin, 1925. Veröffentlichungen der Akademie für die Wissenschaft des Judentums, Historische Sektion. Vol. I: Darstellung; Vol. II: Akten.

Steuart, A. Francis, "Jews in Rome, 1704." *JQR*, O. S. XIX (1906–7), 398–99.

Stewart, H. F., "Casuistry." *Judaism and Christianity*, ed. by Oesterley, Loewe and Rosenthal, II, 299–331.

Stillschweig, Kurt, Die Juden Osteuropas in den Minderheitenverträgen. Berlin, 1936.

———, "Die nationalitätenrechtliche Stellung der Juden in der Tschechoslovakei." *Historia Judaica*, I (1938), 39–49.

———, "Die nationalitätenrechtliche Stellung der Juden in den russischen und österreichischen Nachfolgestaaten während der Weltkriegsepoche." *MGWJ*, LXXXII (1938), 217–48.

Stobbe, Otto, Die Juden in Deutschland während des Mittelalters in politischer, sozialer und rechtlicher Beziehung. 3d impression, Berlin, 1923.

Stöger, M., Darstellung der gesetzlichen Verfassung der galizischen Judenschaft. 2 vols., Lwów, 1833.

Stokes, H. P., Studies in Anglo-Jewish History. Edinburgh, 1913.

———, "Records of Mss. and Documents Possessed by the Jews in England before the Expulsion." *Transactions of the Jewish Historical Society of England*, VIII (1918), 78–94.

Strabo, The Geography of Strabo, with an English transl. by Horace Leonard Jones. 8 vols., London, 1917–32. "Loeb Classical Library."

Strassburger, B., Geschichte der Erziehung und des Unterrichts bei den Israeliten. Von der vortalmudischen Zeit bis auf die Gegenwart. Mit einem Anhang: Bibliographie der jüdischen Pädagogie, Stuttgart, 1885.

Straus, Raphael, Die Juden im Königreich Sizilien unter Normannen und Staufen. Heidelberg, 1910.

Straus, Raphael, Die Judengemeinde Regensburg im ausgehenden Mittelalter auf Grund der Quellen kritisch untersucht und neu dargestellt. Heidelberg, 1932. A documentary Appendix of 464 pages after reaching the page proof stage (one set has kindly been placed at the present writer's disposal) was suppressed by the German administration.

———, "Ein Landshuter Judeneid aus dem 14. Jahrhundert. *ZGJD*, V (1934), 42–49.

Strauss, Eli, "Zu einer Vermutung Jacob Manns." *Archiv Orientalni*, VIII (1936), 96–97.

———, "A Journey to India" (Hebrew). *Zion*, IV (1938–39), 217–31.

Strauss, Leo, "On Abravanel's Philosophical Tendency and Political Teaching." *In* J. B. Trend and H. M. J. Loewe, eds., *Isaac Abravanel: Six Lectures*, Cambridge, 1937, pp. 93–129.

Strickland, Reba Carolyn, Religion and the State of Georgia in the Eighteenth Century. New York, 1939.

Suetonius, Tranquillus, C., [Works], with an English transl. by J. C. Rolfe. 2 vols., London, 1924–30. "Loeb Classical Library."

Sukenik, Eliezer Lipa, The Ancient Synagogues of Palestine and Greece. London, 1934. "Schweich Lectures, 1931."

Sulzbach, A., "Ein alter Frankfurter Wohltätigkeitsverein." *JJLG*, II (1904), 241–66.

Szper, J., ed., Stary cmentarz żydowski w Łodzi (The Old Jewish Cemetery in Lodz). Lodz, 1938.

Ṭabari, Muḥammad ibn Jarir, al-, Annales. Ed. by M. J. de Goeje. 15 vols., Leyden, 1879–1901.

———, Geschichte der Perser und Araber zur Zeit der Sassaniden, aus der arabischen Chronik des Tabari übersetzt und mit ausführlichen Erläuterungen versehen, von Theodor Nöldeke. Leyden, 1879.

Taglicht, J., ed., Nachlässe der Wiener Juden im 17. und 18. Jahrhundert. Ein Beitrag zur Finanz-, Wirtschafts- und Familiengeschichte des 17. und 18. Jahrhunderts. Vienna,

1917. Historische Kommission der Israelitischen Kultusgemeinde in Wien, Quellen und Forschungen zur Geschichte der Juden in Deutsch-Oesterreich, Vol. VII.

תקנות הקהלה דק"ק אשכנזים באמשטרדם (Taḳḳanot Amsterdam, Statutes of the Ashkenazic Community) (Yiddish). 2d ed., Amsterdam, 1737.

תקנות מהחברה קדישא דביקור חולים חדשה (Taḳḳanot of the New Holy Society Biḳḳur Ḥolim in Fürth) (Yiddish). Fürth, 1818.

תקנות ק"ק המבורג בלונדון (Taḳḳanot Ḳ. Ḳ. Hamburg be-London. Statute of the Hambro Congregation in London). London, 1795.

TALMUD, BABYLONIAN, Edition Wilno, 1895; also uncensored edition, Amsterdam, 1644–48. — Der Babylonische Talmud. Hebrew text with German translation by L. Goldschmidt, Vols. I–VIII, 2d ed., Berlin, 1925. — The Babylonian Talmud, translated into English with notes, glossary and indices, under the editorship of I. Epstein. Series I–III in 24 vols., London, 1935–39. Another series in 8 vols. is to appear.

TALMUD, PALESTINIAN, Edition Krotoshin, Krotoshin, 1886. — Talmud de Jérusalem. Translated into French and annotated by M. Schwab. 11 vols., Paris, 1871–89.

TAM, JACOB B. MEIR, ספר הישר (Juristic Treatise). Vienna, 1811.

———, ——— (Responsa). Ed. by F. Rosenthal, Berlin, 1898.

TAQIZADEH, S. H., "The Iranian Festivals Adopted by the Christians and Condemned by the Jews." *Bulletin of the School of Oriental Studies* (*University of London*), X (1939–40), 632–53.

TCHARNO, SHALOM JONAH, לתולדות החנוך בישראל (A Contribution to the History of Education in Israel). Pts. I–II: The Biblical and Talmudic Periods. Jerusalem, 1939.

TEIMANAS, DAVID BENCIONAS, L'autonomie des communautés juives en Pologne aux XVIe et XVIIe siècles. Paris, 1933.

תשובות גאוני מזרח ומערב (Teshubot geone mizraḥ u-ma'arab; Responsa of Eastern and Western Geonim). Ed. by Joel Müller. Berlin, 1888.

תשובות הגאונים (Teshubot ha-geonim; Geonic Responsa). Ed. by A. Harkavy. Berlin, 1887.

תשובות הגאונים, Ed. and annotated by Jacob Musafiah. Lyck, 1864.

THEODOSIUS (Emperor), *see* Codex Theodosianus.

THOMAS AQUINAS, Summa theologica. Literally Translated by the Fathers of the English Dominican Province. 2d ed., 22 vols., London, 1920–25.

THOMPSON, JAMES W., An Economic and Social History of the Middle Ages (300–1300). New York, 1928.

THOMSEN, PETER, ed. (in collaboration with several scholars), Die Palästina-Literatur. Eine internationale Bibliographie in systematischer Ordnung mit Autoren- und Sachregister. 5 vols., Leipzig, 1908–38. The title of Vol. I was Systematische Bibliographie der Palästina-Literatur.

TILANDER, GUNNAR, "Documento desconocido de la aljama de Zaragoza del año 1331." *Studia neophilologica* (Uppsala), XII (1939–40), 1–45.

TOAFF, ALFREDO, "Il Collegio Rabbinico di Livorno." *Israel*, XII (1938), 184–95.

TOLAS, A., L'enseignement chez les Arabes: La Madrasa Nizâmiyyâ et son histoire. Paris, 1939.

TOLEDANO, JACOB MOSES, "Ancient Synagogues in Alexandria and Its Environs" (Hebrew). *HUCA*, XII–XIII (1937–38), 701–14.

TÖNNIES, FERDINAND, Gemeinschaft und Gesellschaft. 7 ed., Berlin, 1926.

Toratan shel rishonim, see Horowitz, Chajim Meir.

TORRE, LELLIO DELLA, Scritti sparsi. 2 vols., Padua, 1908.

TORREY, CHARLES C., Ezra Studies. Chicago, 1910.

תוספות (Tosafot; Commentary on the Babylonian Talmud and Rashi). Printed with most Talmud editions.

TOSEFTA, Edited by M. S. Zuckermandel. Pasewalk, 1881. Supplement enthaltend Uebersicht, Register und Glossar zu Tosefta, von M. S. Zuckermandel. Trier, 1882. — 2d ed. with "Supplement to the Tosephta" by Saul Liebermann. Jerusalem, 1937.

TOVEY, D'BLOSSIERS, Anglia Judaica, on the History and Antiquities of the Jews in England. Oxford, 1738.

Trachtenberg, Joshua, "Jewish Education in Eastern Europe at the Beginning of the 17th Century." *Jewish Education*, XI (1939), 121–37.

———, Jewish Magic and Superstition. A Study in Folk Religion. New York, 1939.

Trani, Joseph b. Moses, ס' שאלות ותשובות (Responsa). Pt. I, Constantinople, 1640; Pts. II and III, Venice, 1645.

Trexler, Gustav, "Das Gödinger Maskir-Buch." *ZGJT*, V (1938), 28–36.

Tscherikower (Tcherikover), Abigdor *or* Victor, Die hellenistischen Städtegründungen von Alexander dem Grossen bis auf die Römerzeit. Leipzig, 1927.

———, היהודים והיונים בתקופה ההלניסטית (Jews and Greeks in the Hellenistic Period). Jerusalem, 1931.

———, "On the History of the Jews of Fayyum during the Hellenistic Period" (Hebrew). *Magnes Anniversary Book*, Jerusalem, 1938, pp. 199–206.

Tsherikover, Elias, "The Commune of the Jerusalem Kabbalists 'Love of Peace' (Ahavat Shalom) in the Middle of the Eighteenth Century" (Yiddish). *Yivo Studies in History*, II (1937), 115–39.

———, "The Archives of Simon Dubnow" (Yiddish). *Yivo Studies in History*, II (1937), 565–604.

Tyan, Emile, Histoire de l'organisation judiciaire en pays d'Islam. Paris, 1938. Annales de l'Université de Lyon, 3e Série, Droit, Fasc. 4.

Tykocinski, H., "Bustanai, the Exilarch" (Hebrew). *Debir*, I (1923), 145–79.

———, Die gaonäischen Verordnungen (Takkanot). Berlin, 1929.

Uhlhorn, G[erhard], Die christliche Liebesthätigkeit. 3 vols., Stuttgart, 1882–90. Vol. III. Die Liebesthätigkeit seit der Reformation.

Ullmann, Salomon, "Geschichte der spanisch-portugiesischen Juden in Amsterdam im XVII Jahrhundert." *JJLG*, V (1907), 1–74.

———, Histoire des Juifs en Belgique jusqu'au 18e siècle (Notes et documents). Antwerp [1927].

ULRICH, JOHANN CASPAR, Sammlung jüdischer Geschichten, welche sich mit diesem Volke in den 13ten und folgenden Jahrhunderten bis auf 1760 in der Schweiz von Zeit zu Zeit zugetragen; zur Beleuchtung der allgemeinen Historie dieser Nation herausgegeben. Basel, 1769.

UNNA, ISAK, "Die Verordnungen für die Lemle Moses Klausstiftung in Mannheim." *JJLG*, XVII (1926), 133–45.

———, "Oberrabbiner Michael Scheuer als Kritiker seiner Zeit." *ZGJD*, I (1929), 322–28.

UNNA, JOSEPH, Statistik der Frankfurter Juden bis zum Jahre 1866. Frankfort, 1931.

UNNA, SIMON, Gedenkbuch der Frankfurter Juden nach Aufzeichnungen der Beerdigungs-Bruderschaft: bearbeitet und ins Deutsche übertragen. Vol. I., Frankfort, 1914.

URBACH, EPHRAIM E., "Aus der Geschichte der Juden in Italien im 18. Jahrhundert." *MGWJ*, LXXX (1936), 275–81.

———, "Die Staatsaufassung Don Isaac Abravanels." *MGWJ*, LXXXI (1937), 257–70.

VAJDA, GEORGES, "Les corps de métiers en Turquie d'après deux publications de V. Gordlevskij." *Revue des études islamiques*, VIII (1934), 79–88.

———, "Juifs et Musulmans selon le hadiṭ." *Journal Asiatique*, CCXXIX (1937), 57–128.

VAUX, R. DE, "Les decréts de Cyrus et de Darius sur la réconstruction du Temple." *Revue biblique*, XLVI (1937), 29–57.

VENETIANER, LAJOS, A zsidóság szervezete (Jewish Community Organization in European Lands). Budapest, 1901.

VIDAL, PIERRE, "Les Juifs des anciens comtés de Rousillon et de Cerdagne." *REJ*, XV (1887), 19–55.

VINCENT, "DR.," Les Juifs en Poitou au bas moyen âge. Paris, 1931. Reprinted from *Revue d'histoire économique et sociale*, Vol. XVIII.

VINOGRADOFF, PAUL, "Customary Law." *In* Legacy of the Middle Ages, ed. by C. G. Crump and E. F. Jacob, Oxford, 1926, pp. 287–319.

Virolleaud, Charles, "L'epopée de Kéret, roi des Sidoniens." *Revue des études sémitiques*, Vol. I, Pt. 1 (1934), pp. VI–XIV.

Voet, Elias, Jr., Haarlemsche goud- en zilversmeden en hunne merken. Amsterdam, 1928.

Vogelstein, Hermann, "Die Entstehung und Entwicklung des Apostolats im Judentum." *MGWJ*, XLIX (1905), 427–49.

———, "The Development of the Apostolate in Judaism and its Transformation in Christianity." *HUCA*, II (1925), 99–123.

———, and Paul Rieger, Geschichte der Juden in Rom. 2 vols., Berlin, 1895–96.

Vogt, Joseph, Kaiser Julian und das Judentum. Studien zum Weltanschaungskampf der Spätantike. Leipzig, 1939. Morgenland. Darstellungen aus Geschichte und Kultur des Ostens, no. 30.

Voll, Christoph, Von dem Armenrechte der Juden an dem Kaiserlichen Reichskammergerichte. Wezlar, 1787. Non vidi.

Volumina legum (Polish Statutes). 9 vols., St. Petersburg, 1859–89. Reprint of a collection of laws published in Warsaw in the years 1732–92.

Vopiscus, Flavius, of Syracuse, [Biographies of] Firmus, Saturninus, Proculus and Bonosus. London, 1932. *In* Scriptores historiae Augustae, with an English translation by David Magie, III, 386–415. "Loeb Classical Library."

Wachstein, Bernhard, Die Gründung der Wiener Chewra Kadischa im Jahre 1763. Leipzig, 1910. Revised reprint from *MGJV*, XXXII–XXXIII.

———, Die Inschriften des alten Judenfriedhofes in Wien. 2 vols., Vienna, 1912–17. Historische Kommission der Israelitischen Kultusgemeinde in Wien, Quellen und Forschungen zur Geschichte der Juden in Deutsch-Oesterreich, Vol. IV, Pts. I–II. With additional "Randbemerkungen" ibid., Vol. XI.

———, Urkunden und Akten zur Geschichte der Juden in Eisenstadt und den Siebengemeinden. Vienna, 1926.

Wachstein, Bernhard,, "Bemerkungen zu [Leopold] Löwensteins Index Approbationum." *MGWJ*, LXXI (1927), 123–33.

———, "The Prague Anti-Luxury Ordinances of 1767" (Yiddish). *Yivo Bleter*, I (1931), 335–54.

———, "Das Statut der jüdischen Bevölkerung der Grafschaft Wied-Runkel (Pinkas Runkel)." *ZGJD*, IV (1932), 129–49.

———, "A Jewish Community in the Eighteenth Century, Pinḳas Runkel" (Yiddish). *Yivo Bleter*, VI (1934), 84–116; VIII (1935), 187.

Wallach, Luitpold, "The Colloquy of Marcus Aurelius with the Patriarch Judah I." *JQR*, XXXI (1940–41), 259–86.

Walsh, James J., The History of Nursing. New York, 1929.

Walter, K., Das Judenbad zu Offenburg. Offenburg, n. d.

Waltzing, J. P., Etude historique sur les corporations professionelles chez les Romains depuis les origines jusqu'à la chute de l'Empire d'Occident. 4 vols., Louvain, 1895–1900.

Weber, Max, Gesammelte Aufsätze zur Religionssoziologie. 3 vols., Tübingen 1920–21. Vol. III: Die Wirtschaftsethik der Weltreligionen. Das antike Judentum; Nachtrag: Die Pharisäer.

Weil, Jacob, ס' שאלות ותשובות (Responsa). Hanau, 1610.

Weill, Julien, "Contribution à l'histoire des communautés alsaciennes au XVIIIe siècle." *REJ*, LXXXI (1925), 169–80.

Weinberg, Magnus, "Die Almosenverwaltung der jüdischen Ortsgemeinden im talmudischen Zeitalter," *Israelitische Monatsschrift* (Supplement to *Jüdische Presse*, Berlin), XXIV, 1893; no. 1, pp. 2–3; no. 2, p. 7; no. 3, p. 10; no. 5, pp. 18–19; no. 6, p. 23; no. 9, p. 35.

———, "Die Organisation der jüdischen Ortsgemeinden in der talmudischen Zeit." *MGWJ*, XLI (1897), 588–604, 639–60, 673–91.

———, "Untersuchungen über das Wesen des Memorbuches." *JJLG*, XVI (1924), 253–323.

———, "Memorbücher." *Menorah* (Vienna), VI (1928), 697–708.

———, Die Memorbücher der jüdischen Gemeinden in Bayern. Frankfort, 1937–38.

WEINREICH, MAX, די שווארצע פינטעלאך (The Black Dots). Wilno, 1939.

WEINRYB, BERNARD *or* DOB BER, "From the Communal Minute-Books in Cracow. Contributions to the History of the Communities and the Council of Four Lands in Poland at the Beginning of the Eighteenth Century" (Hebrew). *Tarbiz*, VIII (1936–37), 185–207. Supplemented by S. H. Kuk, *ibid.*, p. 368.

———, "Private Letters in Yiddish of 1588" (Yiddish). *Yivo Studies in History*, II (1937), 44–67.

———, על יחסן של הקהלות שבפולין לבעלי מלאכה ולפועלים (On the Attitude of the Polish Communities to Craftsmen and Laborers). Tel-Aviv, 1938. Reprinted from the *Yediot* [Bulletin] of the Archives and Museum of the Labor Movement.

———, "Beiträge zur Finanzgeschichte der jüdischen Gemeinden in Polen." *MGWJ*, LXXXII (1938), 248–63; Pt. 2, *HUCA*, XVI (1941), 187–214.

———, "Studies in the Economic and Financial History of the Jews in the Polish and Lithuanian Cities in the Seventeenth and Eighteenth Centuries" (Hebrew). *Tarbiz*, X (1938–39), 90–104, 201–31.

Cf. also Ringelblum, Emanuel.

WEISS, ISAAC HIRSCH, דור דור ודורשיו (A History of Halakah). 6th ed., 5 vols., Wilno, 1911.

WEISS, MEIR ZVI, "A Decision by R. Judah Muscato" (Hebrew). *Ha-Eshkol*, VII (1913), 202–7.

WELLESZ, J., "Ueber R. Isaak b. Mose's 'Or Sarua'." *JJLG*, IV (1906), 75–124.

———, "Ḥayyim b. Isaac Or Zaroua." *REJ*, LIII (1907), 67–84; LIV (1907), 102–6.

———, "Meir b. Baruch de Rothenbourg." *REJ*, LVIII (1909), 226–40; LIX (1910), 42–58; LX (1910), 53–72; LXI (1911), 44–59.

Wellesz, J., "Die Dezisionen R. Isaks aus Corbeil." *JJLG*, IX (1912), 490–97; Hebrew section, pp. 1–8.

Wellhausen, Julius, Israelitische und jüdische Geschichte. 4th ed., Berlin, 1901.

Wenisch, Rudolf, "Beziehungen Kommotaus zu den Juden der Umgebung im sechzehnten und siebzehnten Jahrhundert." *JGJC*, VII (1935), 37–198.

Wesseling, Peter, Diatribe de Judaeorum archontibus ad inscriptionem Berenicensem. Utrecht, 1738.

Wessely, Carl, "Das Ghetto von Apollinopolis Magna." *Studien zur Palaeographie und Papyruskunde*, XIII (1913), 8–10.

Westermann, William L., "Ptolemies and their Subjects." *American Historical Review*, XLIII (1938), 270–87.

Wettstein, Feiwel Hirsch, "Documents from Ancient Minute-Books (Ordinances of the Cracow Community in Various Matters)" (Hebrew). *Oṣar ha-Sifrut*, IV (1892), 577–642.

———, "From the Minute-Books of the Cracow Community." *Gedenkbuch . . . David Kaufmann*, Breslau, 1900, Hebrew section, pp. 69–84.

———, דברי חפץ מפנקסי ק"ק קראקא (Excerpts from the Cracow Minute-Books): Contributions to the History of the Jews in Poland, particularly in Cracow. St. Petersburg, 1902.

———, "Discourses on Ancient Matters Transcribed from Cracow Minute-Books, with Notes on the History of Polish Jewry and Its Scholars" (Hebrew). *Ha-Zofeh*, IV (1915), 166–86.

Wickersheimer, Ernest, "Lèpre et Juifs au Moyen Âge." *Janus, Archives internationales pour l'histoire de la médecine*, XXXVI (1932), 43–48.

Wiener, Meir, Regesten zur Geschichte der Juden in Deutschland während des Mittelalters. Vol. I, Hannover, 1862.

———, "Des Hof- und Kammeragenten Leffmann Berens Intervention bei dem Erscheinen judenfeindlicher Schriften." *Magazin für die Wissenschaft des Judentums*, VI (1879), 48–63. Cf. also Ibn Verga, Solomon.

Wigderman, S., "Donkey's Burial" (Hebrew). *Reshumot*, II (2d printing, 1927), 448–53.

Wilhelm, Kurt, Von jüdischer Gemeinde und Gemeinschaft. Aus Gemeindebüchern, Satzungen und Verordnungen ausgewählt und deutsch herausgegeben. Berlin, 1938.

Williams, A[rthur] Lukyn, Adversus Judaeos. A Bird's-Eye View of Christian *Apologiae* until the Renaissance. Cambridge, 1935.

Wischnitzer, Mark, "Die jüdische Zunftverfassung in Polen und Litauen im 17. und 18. Jhd." *Vierteljahrsschrift für Sozial- und Wirtschaftsgeschichte*, XX (1928), 433–51. Appeared also in Yiddish, with additional notes by the editors, in *Zeitshrift*, II–III (Minsk, 1928), 73–88.

———, "Handwerk. Vom Ausgang des Altertums bis zur Mitte des 19. Jahrhunderts." *Encyclopaedia Judaica*, VII, 951–70.

Wolf, Gerson, "Die Einladung der Wiener Chebra vom J. 1320 und der Satzbrief vom J. 1329." *Hebräische Bibliographie*, VI (1863), 118–19.

———, "Der Prozess Eisenmenger." *MGWJ*, XVIII (1869), 378–84, 425–32, 465–73.

———, Die alten Statuten der jüdischen Gemeinden in Mähren samt den nachfolgenden Synodalbeschlüssen. Vienna, 1880.

———, "Gemeindestreitigkeiten in Prag 1567–1678." *ZGJD*, O. S. I (1887), 309–20.

———, "Zur Geschichte der Juden in Böhmen." *ZGJD*, O. S. III (1889), 91–92.

———, Kleine historische Schriften. Vienna, 1892.

Wolf, Lucien, "Jews in Elizabethan England." *Transactions of the Jewish Historical Society of England*, XI (1929), 1–91.

Wolf, Sandor, "Die Entwicklung des jüdischen Grabsteines und die Denkmäler des Eisenstädter Friedhofes." *In* B. Wachstein's Die Grabinschriften des alten Judenfriedhofs in Eisenstadt. Vienna, 1922.

Worman, E. J., "The Exilarch Bustani." *JQR*, O. S. XX (1907–8), 211–15.

Wreschner, L., "R. Akiba Egers Leben und Wirken." *JJLG*, II (1904), 27–89; III (1905), 1–78, 312–15.

YAARI, ABRAHAM, באהלי ספר (In the Book Realm). Jerusalem, 1939.

YAFEH, MORDECAI B. ABRAHAM, ס' הלבושים (Vestments. On Jewish law, etc.). 10 pts. with individual titles. Lublin, 1594– Prague, 1603–9–10. Pt. 7 unpublished.

YAHUDA, ABRAHAM SHALOM, "The Synagogue of Samuel ha-Levi [Abulafia] in Toledo and its Inscriptions" (Hebrew). *Bitzaron*, III (1940–41), 101–9, 251–58.

YARḤI, ABRAHAM B. NATHAN HA-, ס' המנהגים (On Jewish Laws and Customs). Ed. with notes by Jacob Moses Goldberg. Berlin, 1855.

ZACUTO, ABRAHAM B. SAMUEL, ס' יוחסין השלם Liber Juchassin sive lexicon biographicum et historicum. Ed. by Herschell Filipowski. London, 1857. 2d ed., with an Introd. [and Indexes] by Abraham Ḥayyim Freimann. Frankfort, 1925.

ZACUTO, MOSES B. MORDECAI, שודא דדינא (The Judge's Discretion). Mantua, 1678.

———, אגרות הרמ"ז (Epistles). Leghorn, 1760.

ZAHALON, JACOB B. ISAAC, ס' אוצר החיים (A Medical Treatise). Venice, 1683. Incomplete.

ZARCHIN, MICHAEL M., "Tailor's Guild of Kurnik, Province of Posen." *JQR*, XXVIII (1937–38), 47–56.

———, "Studies in the Communal Records of the Jews in the Province of Posen during the Eighteenth and Nineteenth Centuries." *JQR*, XXIX (1938–39), 135–65, 247–315. Also reprint.

ZEITLIN, SOLOMON, "Rashi and the Rabbinate: The Struggle Between Secular and Religious Forces for Leadership." *JQR*, XXXI (1940–41), 1–58.

———, "The Opposition to the Spiritual Leaders Appointed by the Government." *JQR*, XXXI (1940–41), 287–300.

ZERAḤIAH B. ISAAC HA-LEVI, GERONDI, ס' המאור [הגדול] (Critical Commentary) on Alfasi's Halakot. Printed with most editions of the latter work.

ZHITLOVSKY, CHAIM, געזאמעלטע שריפטן (Collected Writings). 10 vols., New York, 1912–19.

ZIEBARTH, ERICH, Das griechische Vereinswesen. Leipzig, 1896. Preisschriften der Fürstlich Jablonowskischen Gesellschaft, Vol. XXXIV.

ZIMMELS, H. J., Beiträge zur Geschichte der Juden in Deutschland im 13. Jahrhundert, insbesondere auf Grund der Gutachten des R. Meir Rothenburg. Vienna, 1926. Veröffentlichungen des Oberrabbiner Dr. H. P. Chajes-Preisstiftung an der Israelitisch-Theologischen Lehranstalt in Wien, Vol. I.

ZIMMELS, H. J., "Erez Israel in der Responsenliteratur des späteren Mittelalters." *MGWJ*, LXXIV (1930), 44–64.

———, Die Marranen in der rabbinischen Literatur. Forschungen und Quellen zur Geschichte und Kulturgeschichte der Anussim. Berlin, 1932.

ZINBERG, ISAAC, "The Conflict between the Elders and the 'Last Rabbi' of Wilno" (Hebrew). *He-'Abar*, II (1918), 45–74.

———, "The Feud between the Heads of the Jewish Community and the Rabbinate in Wilno in the Second Half of the 18th Century" (Yiddish). *Yivo Studies in History*, II (1937), 291–321.

ZORAS, GIORGIO, Le corporazioni bizantine. Rome, 1931.

ZUCKER, HANS, Studien zur jüdischen Selbstverwaltung im Altertum. Berlin, 1936.

ZUNZ, LEOPOLD, Die gottesdienstlichen Vorträge der Juden, historisch entwickelt. Berlin, 1832; 2d ed., Frankfort, 1892.

———, Zur Geschichte und Literatur. Vol. I, Berlin, 1845.

———, Die Ritus des synagogalen Gottesdienstes geschichtlich entwickelt. Berlin, 1859.

ZURI (RZEZAK), JACOB SAMUEL, תולדות המשפט הצבורי העברי (A History of Hebrew Public Law): The Government of the Patriarchate and the Council. Vols. I–II, Paris, 1931.

———, ———, The Reign of the Exilarchate and the Legislative Academies, Period of Rab Nachman bar Jizchak (320–355). Tel-Aviv, 1938.

Zwarts, Jacob, De joodsche Gemeente van Amersfoort, Gedenkschrift, Amersfoort, 1927.

———, "De eerste Rabbijnen en Synagogen van Amsterdam naar archivalische Bronnen." *Bijdragen en Mededeelingen van het Genootschap voor de Joodsche Wetenschap in Nederland*, IV (1928), 147–271.

———, Hoofdstukken uit de Geschiedenis der Joden in Nederland. Zutphen, 1929.

INDEX

INDEX

(Italic numerals indicate main entries)

Aaron (high priest), I, 45, 60
Aaron b. Ephraim (Lwów bridegroom), II, 315
Aaron Berekiah of Modena, collection of prayers by, I, 353
Aaron of York, Jewish archpresbyter, I, 297; III, 69
Aaronide priesthood, *see* Priesthood, Israelitic
Ab (month), election days in, III, 116. *See also* Ninth of Ab
Ab bet din, I, 151; II, 95. *See also* Heads of the court; Judiciary
Abar Nahara, I, 64
Abasids (dynasty), and Jewish unity, I, 189. *See also* Caliphate
Abattoirs, Jewish: and Church segregation, II, 157; and taxation, II, 108, 256; III, 186; Christian leaseholders of, II, 159; in Erfurt, III, 107; institutional rank of, II, 124; Polish supervisors of, II, 63; Spanish rabbis at, III, 125. *See also* Meat taxes; Slaughtering
  municipal, exclusion of Jews from, II, 107–8
Abba Arika (amora), I, 130, 151-52, 154; II, 83; III, 23
Abbahu, R. (amora), II, 99
Abbaye (amora), I, 152
Abd 'Allah (king of Granada), III, 34
Abenafia, Joseph (Sicilian chief rabbi), I, 292–94; II, 304; III, 67
Abennuba, Juceff (Valencia rabbi), II, 74
Abenporath, S. (Teruel preacher), II, 82
Abiram (biblical rebel), I, 167; II, 37
Ablutions, ritual, and synagogues, I, 91. *See also* Baths
Abnadean, David, II, 14
Aboab, Isaac, III, 129
Aboab, Samuel b. Abraham, I, 306
Abortions, provisions against, II, 315
Abot de-R. Nathan, III, 16, 25
Abraham (patriarch), and charities, II, 320
Abraham b. Avigdor (arbiter in Bohemian controversy), I, 308–9
Abraham b. David of Posquières, III, 145
Abraham b. Eleazar ha-Kohen, III, 135
Abraham b. Joseph ha-Levi, I, 254; III, 58
Abraham ha-Kohen, defends Bologna ordinance, III, 182
Abraham Levi (ḥakam-bashi), I, 199
Abraham of Bohemia (Polish chief rabbi), I, 300–1
Abraham of Lissa (chairman of Polish Council), I, 328
Abraham of Lublin (chairman of Polish Council), I, 329
Abravanel, Don Isaac, I, 286; II, 172, 217; III, 21, 174
Absalom (biblical prince), I, 39–40
Absence: and majority vote, II, 282; and residence rights, III, 98
Absolutism: ancient, I, 35, 37; Arabian and *shtadlanim*. I, 187. *See also* Caliphs; Monarchy; Tyranny
  communal, *see* Dictatorship; Oligarchy
  modern (enlightened): and court Jews, III, 220; and ecclesiastical

power, II, 43; and Jewish community, I, 12–13, 338–39, 341; II, 36, 348, *355–58*, 364; and Jewish liturgy, III, 150; and Jewish taxation, II, 159–60; germs of dissolution in, II, 121
Abu Ḥanifa, An-Nu'man ibn Tabit, I, 178. *See also* Ḥanafite school
Abu Yussuf, Yaḳub b. Ibrahim, I, 171; III, 34
Abudirham, David b. Joseph ibn, III, 133-34
Abulafia, Don Samuel (rabbi of the court), I, 237; III, 66, 147
Abulafia, Meir ha-Levi, II, 171, 194, 276–77, 298; III, 52
Abulafia, Todros b. Judah ha-Levi, I, 289
Abun, R. (amora), on imagery, III, 146
Aby Jetomim (Amsterdam society), II, 332; III, 212
Academies, Jewish, ancient: I, 150–55; III, 23, 33, 161; admission to, I, 139; and democracy, I, 28; and Sanhedrin, III, 29; and Sepphoris conflicts, I, 135; influence of, I, 117; Pharisaic leadership of, I, 140
Babylonian: and communal uniformity, I, 206; and court organization, II, 241; and exilarchs, I, 149, 174, 177; and noble descent, III, 46; and Polish Council, III, 82–83; designation of, I, 202; *kallahs* at, 154–55, 180, 182, 184; III, 33; organization of, III, 33; revenue from titles of, I, 201; supremacy of, I, 207. *See also* Gaonate
eastern: III, 163; and exilarchate, I, 179, 206; III, 44; and negidim, III, 44; heredity in, III, 46; inquiries to, I, 165; in various regions (Egypt), I, 191, 194; (Kairowan), I, 193–94; (Palestine), I, 191–94, 201, 206; III, 44–46, 217; revenue from titles of, I, 201
medieval and modern: and capitalism, II, 362; and charitable legacies, I, 361; III, 60; and democracy, I, 28; and educational associations, I, 356; and private excommunications, III, 126; and professional judiciary, II, 73; and public opinion, I, 347; and recitation of Decalogue, III, 22; and Talmud editions, I, 325; II, 203; communal responsibility for, II, 172; III, 41–42; founded by students, II, 180–81; graduation from, and further study, II, 206; importance of, III, 165; in various regions (England) III, 60; (Germany), III, 126; (Italy), I, 210, 317; III, 166; (Lithuania), II, 189, 278; (Moravia), I, 339; II, 189–90; (Poland), I, 325; II, 203; (Portugal), I, 285; (Spain), I, 194; II, 114, 172; itinerant students at, II, 180, 187; leadership of, II, 94–95; maintenance of students at, II, 189–90; practical training at, III, 171–72; program for graduates of, II, 203; III, 168; rights to establishment of, II, 79
Academies, Soviet, Yiddish in, I, 15
Acceptance of office, obligatory features of, II, 53–54, 60; III, 119, 124
Accounting, communal: II, 64–66, 286–87; III, 122–23; and passive franchise, II, 44; by charity overseers, I, 133; II, 64, 348; limited by discretionary expenses, II, 65; of Palestinian messengers, II, 342
Accounts, commercial, and intermediaries, II, 238
Accusation, of informer, dispensed with, II, 241
Achaemenides (Persian dynasty), I, 138. *See also* Persia
Acquired rights (*Ḥazaḳah*): II, 7, *292–300*; III, 99, *197–200*; and anti-alien bias, II, 322–23; and Christian residence in ghetto, II, 296; and lay judiciary, II, 88; and private worship, II, 125–26; and residence rights, II, 234, 296;

and synagogue functions, II, 133; III, 145; communal control of, II, 6–7, 125–26, 131, 262; in synagogues, II, 131. *See also* Ban of settlement; Economic regulation;Residence rights

Acrostics, Hebrew, and Jewish judiciary, II, 214

Actio sepulchri violati, I, 109

Actio sequitur forum rei, I, 249; II, 242

Activism, Jewish: and character building, II, 190; and liturgical innovations, II, 143; and social welfare, II, 290

Adam and Eve, descent from, and peace, III, 174

Adaptability, communal: and force of tradition, II, 167–68; and Jewish survival, I, 55–56, 85, 156; II, 208, 245; and scholarly control, II, 244. *See also* Law, Jewish

Adar (month), maintenance of students during, II, 189–90

Addison, Lancelot, on absence of Jewish beggary, II, 347; III, 218

Addresses: exilarchic, preparation of, I, 154; prophetic, circularized in provinces, III, 8

Adelantadi, II, 55. *See also* Elders

Aden, Jews in, III, 43–44

Adenantatos, II, 40. *See also* Elders

Administration, communal: and banking prerogatives, I, 244; and neighborhood meeting, I, 74; and *shtadlanim*, I, 188; and taxation, I, 148, 160–61, 244. *See also* Taxation; and three-class system, II, 28–30; exilarchic control of, I, 147; laymen in, I, 129; of cemeteries, II, 151, 153, 155-56; of charities, II, 330; of education, III, 166; of ritual slaughtering, I, 107–10; of synagogues, II, 131, 134–35; III, 150; patriarchal control of, I, 142, 147; promoted by archives, I, 72–73; rabbinic supervision of, I, 151, 155, 285; II, 181, 330; share of poor in, II, 27; special buildings for, II, 24. *See also* Bureaucracy; Communal control; Elders; Financial administration; *and under* respective offices and functions

Administrative committees, and general board of elders, II, 55

Admission to membership, regulations on, I, 246; II, 4, 19, 112. *See also* Membership; Residence rights

Admissions, judicial, II, 112

Admonition of neighbors, rabbinic demand of, III, 180

Adolescents, as members of associations, III, 89–90. *See also* Children

Adonai (divine name), I, 77

Adribi, Isaac b. Samuel: on burial societies, III, 88; on elders, III, 110; on informers, II, 222; on plenary assembly, II, 30; on rabbis, III, 125; on Salonican Talmud Torah, I, 348; III, 88

Adult education, Jewish: I, 125; II, 206–7; and associations, I, 356; and business women, II, 179; and moneylending, II, 176; and parental responsibility, II, 174; and school age, II, 173–74; in synagogue, II, 144; responsibility for, II, 169. *See also* Education; Schools; Teachers

Adultery: denounced by Forli Conference, II, 312–13; disfigurement for, II, 223; offspring of, II, 315; vs. prostitution, II, 314. *See also* Sex morality

Adventuress, Jewish, medieval, I, 305; II, 107

Advocati, Jewish, Roman, I, 217; II, 59. *See also* Supervisors

Aegean Islands, synagogues in, I, 83

Aegina (Greece), archisynagogus of, I, 103

Aemilia (Marcus Tittius's mother), I, 100

"Affairs of the city," vs. "affairs relating to heaven," I, 134

Affidavits of support, and settlement rights, II, 11
Affonso III (Portuguese king), I, 285
Affonso IV (Portuguese king), I, 234
Affonso V (Portuguese king), I, 236, 241; II, 111
Africa, ancient, synagogues in, I, 83. *See also* North Africa; *and under* respective countries and cities
African Church, and Jewish witnesses, I, 229
Afternoon services, and interruption of prayers, II, 33–34
Age: and charitable support, II, 325; and educational responsibilities, I, 360; II, 169, 173–75, 198; and plenary assemblies, II, 23, 281–82; and public office, II, 54; III, 49, 119–20; and reverence for scholar, I, 140; and taxation, I, 159; II, 38, 172, 248–49, 251, 275; III, 184–85, 189; and transportation costs, II, 324; of marriage, II, 310–11, 333; specific (three), II, 173–74, 198; (six), II, 325; (eight), II, 251; (twelve), II, 251, 311, 333; (fifteen), II, 248–49, 251, 281–82, 311, 333; (eighteen), II, 251, 310–11; (twenty), II, 251, 310; III, 189; (thirty), II, 175; (sixty), II, 251
Age of buildings, and responsibility of tenants, II, 292
Agency of state power, Jewish community as, II, 358–61. *See also* Government intervention; State control
Agents, diplomatic, non-Jewish, I, 330; II, 116, 261, 297; III, 214. *See also* Diplomacy; Marriage brokerage; *Shtadlanim*
Aggada, importance of study of, II, 207; *novellae* on, III, 134
Agnosticism, Jewish, modern: and acceptance of office, II, 54; and communal control, I, 5, 7, 12; II, 361–62; and consistory, I, 14; and Prussian law of secession, III, 5; and public law recognition, I, 25. *See also* Atheism; Religion
Agobard of Lyons (archbishop), I, 295; II, 96; III, 67
Agoranomos, Jewish, I, 130. *See also* Markets
Agreements, communal: and price-fixing, II, 300; and tax immunities, II, 10; of Venetian rabbis, II, 87; on congregational mergers, II, 21; on elections, III, 115; on gaming, III, 207; on sale of synagogues, II, 128–29; revocation of, III, 200; with cities on wine, II, 162. *See also* Economic regulation; Ordinances
  mutual: and judiciary, I, 128, 212–14, 276; II, 214, 237; by families, II, 310, 344; on taxation, III, 38; professional, I, 364. *See also* Guilds
Agriculture *and* agriculturists, ancient: I, 31; III, 7
  Israelitic: and landowners, I, 44, 47; and prophets, I, 45; settlements of, I, 31–34, 42, 50; slaves of, I, 46; tithes on, I, 38; water supply of, I, 32
  Jewish: and distribution of *maṣṣot*, II, 320–21; and military service, I, 268; and mixed relations, III, 61; and patriarchal possessions, III, 33; and rabbis, I, 138; II, 253; III, 31, 33, 185; and taxation, I, 148, 159–61, 172; II, 253; and unfair competition, II, 297; charitable dues on, I, 132; II, 320–21; encouragement through taxation of, II, 253; III, 185; gradual elimination of, I, 274; II, 253; in various regions (France), III, 61; (Poland), I, 268–69; (Spain), II, 320–21. *See also* Colonization; Land
Agrippa, Marcus Vipsanius (Roman statesman), I, 81, 109
Aguesseau, D' (chancellor), I, 263
'*Agunah*, remarriage of, II, 91, 317
Ahab (Israelitic king), I, 57

Ahabat Shalom association, in Jerusalem, I, 355; III, 91–92
Aḥijah the Shilonite (Israelitic prophet), I, 36
Aḥima'az: chronicle of, I, 190; II, 75–76; III, 43, 121, 134; family of, II, 76
Aix (Provence), at Provençal assemblies, III, 75
Aḳabiah b. Alyoini, tombstone of, III, 31
Aḳiba, R. (tannai), I, 153; III, 46
Akko, siege of, III, 73
Al-Ghazali, Abu Ḥamid Muḥammad, I, 164
Al-Ḥakim Bi'amr Illah (Egyptian caliph), I, 165, 171
Al-Jaḥiẓ, Abu Othman 'Amr ibn Baḥr, of Baṣra, III, 41
Al-Kalkashandi, Aḥmad ibn 'Ali, I, 201; III, 39
Al-Kasim b. Ibrahim, I, 175
Al-Mamun (caliph), and exilarchic elections, I, 178–79
Al-Mawardi, Abul-Ḥasan 'Ali ibn Muḥammad, III, 35
Al-Mutadhid (caliph), I, 160, 188, 193
Al-Umari, III, 39
Alabarch, Egyptian, position of, I, 80, 106; III, 18–19, 31
Albedin, Saragossan, III, 125. *See also* Judiciary
Albrecht II (Holy Roman emperor), I, 315
Alcaldes: Jewish, *see* Judiciary; Spanish, to try Jews, I, 239, 241
Alcolea: cemetery in, II, 150; preparation of statute in, III, 110; privilege of, II, 303; synagogue in, 236–37
Alconstantin (Alfaquim), Solomon (Aragonese chief rabbi), I, 290; III, 65
Alderney Road, London, Jewish cemetery at, II, 147; III, 59
'*Alenu* (prayer), prohibited in Prussia, III, 150
Aleppo: capitulations in, III, 102; synagogues in, III, 35
Alessandria, community of, controlled by Turin, II, 22
Alexander the Great (Macedonian king), I, 75, 86; III, 13
Alexander (Polish king), I, 269
Alexander III (pope), I, 217; II, 59
Alexander (Yugoslav king), I, 13
Alexandria, ancient: archives of, I, 93; Claudius' letter to, I, 92; courts of, III, 178; Jerusalem's "sister," I, 78; Jewish council of, I, 99, 105–6; Jewish education in, III, 16; Jewish quarter in, I, 85–86, 93; Jewish settlement in, I, 75; III, 13–14; necropolis in, I, 93–94; III, 31; Palestinian letters to, I, 145; shipmasters in, I, 365; synagogues in, I, 81, 86, 88, 93–94, 105, 364
Muslim: and anti-Maimonidean controversy, I, 316; and election of *ḥakam-bashi*, III, 49; and synagogues, III, 35; marriage licenses in, II, 319
Alexandrians in Palestine, I, 120–21
Alfaquim, *see* Alconstantin
Alfasi, Isaac b. Jacob: and early traditions, II, 69; on chanting, II, 105; III, 136; on charities, II, 344; III, 211; substitutes for Talmud, II, 198
Alfonso (Infante of Aragon), I, 236; II, 71, 150, 227, 303
Alfonso V (Aragonese king), *also* Alfonso I (Sicilian king), I, 294, 316, 362; II, 309–10
Alfonso V (Castilian king), I, 368
Alfonso VIII (Castilian king), I, 234
Alfonso XI (Castilian king), I, 233; II, 253; III, 176
Algeria *and* Algiers: forbids shipment of wheat, III, 200; Jewish education in, III, 92; league of Jewish merchants in, 366; rabbis of, and Teruel deeds, II, 112; single Jewish chiefs

in, III, 50; Spanish immigration to, III, 50–51; statutes of, III, 208; synagogue order in, II, 129, 141
Algerian congregation in Nice, II, 19
Alguades, Don Meir (Castilian chief rabbi), I, 289; II, 276
Ali ibn Abi-Talab, succession of, I, 177–78
Alien groups in ancient world, I, 55, 76–77, 80, 82, 94, 110–11; III, 17
Aliens: disliked as chiefs in caliphate, III, 46; "Francos" as, III, 102; in ancient Orient, I, 72; in ancient Palestine, I, 46–48, 50, 120; Jewish attitudes toward, I, 85–86, 322; Jews as, I, 243; II, 9; Marranos favored as, I, 252

Jewish: and charities, II, 211, 323, 333–34, 345; III, 213, 216; and gaming, III, 207; and local rituals, III, 149; and marriage, III, 98, 204; and sumptuary laws, III, 202; as rabbis, I, 343; III, 100, 134; as students, I, 339; II, 173, 187; as teachers, II, 185; in various regions (Frankfort), II, 117; (Hesse-Cassel), I, 343; (Poland), I, 332–33; III, 134; (Turkey), I, 199; (Tuscany), II, 11; property taxes of, III, 188

Alimony, for wife beating suggested, II, 319
Aljaferia, in Saragossa, II, 24
Alkmar, Jews of, I, 253; III, 58
Allegiance, communal: and cemetery control, I, 283; and communal oligarchy, II, 357–58; of visitors, II, 12; vs. public law, II, 351. *See also* Loyalties
Alliance, of Jews and kings, I, 279, 281–82
Allufim, I, 183; II, 63. *See also* Elders
Almemar, II, 132, 138, 140–41, 145
Almeria, ransom of Christian captives in, III, 214
Al-minbar, II, 132. *See also* Almemar
Almosnino (family) in Salonica, II, 50
Almosnino, Baruch, III, 142
Almosnino, Moses b. Baruch, I, 348; II, 75, 202, 222, 263
Almunia de Dona Godina (Spain), Talmud Torah of, III, 92
Alphabet, Hebrew, in Greek inscriptions, I, 121; instruction in, II, 196
Alsace, Jews of: I, 262, 264; III, *62–63*; communal bureaucracy of, II, 117; III, 141; leadership of, II, 363; *Pletten* of, III, 209; population of, II, 117; III, 141; prohibition of dancing by, III, 206; regional community of, II, 185; III, 88; rabbis of, III, 128, 134; schools of higher learning of, II, 185
Alshech, Moses b. Ḥayyim (Safed preacher), II, 96
Altar, synagogue use of, II, 141
Altneuschule, Prague, II, 153, 226; III, 155
Altona, II, 23. *See also* Hamburg
Ambassadors: Jewish, *see* Deputations; Diplomacy; *Shtadlanim*; Portuguese, Marrano among, I, 255–56
Ambrose (Ambrosius) of Milan, Saint, I, 114, 219; III, 18, 21
Amen (responsorium), I, 78
America, and Menasseh ben Israel, I, 309; earliest rabbis in, III, 129; factors in communal growth in, II, 363–66; oldest Jewish community in, III, 129. *See also* United States; *and under* other countries and cities
American Revolution, and Jewish community, I, 21, 278; II, 351
Amersfoort, Jews of, III, 58
Amicable settlements, hasten procedure, II, 237. *See also* Agreements
'Amidah (prayer), I, 121, 192, 237; II, 89, 105
Amilmarduk (Evil-merodach, Babylonian king), I, 69

Amnesty, Aragonese, for new cemeteries, II, 149

Amora'im, Babylonian, *see* Academies; Rabbis

Amos (prophet), I, 45

"Amphictyony," Israelitic, I, 40

Amphitheater, in ancient synagogues, I, 100

Amram (Bagdad banker), I, 188

Amram b. Sheshna Gaon, I, 182; II, 100; III, 41–42

Amsterdam, Jews of: III, *57–58*; and Barbados, I, 262; and Brazil, I, 255; III, 59; and Emden-Eibeschütz controversy, III, 176; and Moravia, I, 306; and intercommunal controversies, II, 229; and Polish Council, I, 331; II, 243; III, 73; and Polish victims, I, 307; II, 336; and Venetian associations, I, 364; as model for other communities, I, 255; II, 31; Bordeaux wines of, II, 164; cemeteries of, I, 253; II, 148; III, 153; charities of, I, 363; II, 332, 344; III, 93, 104–5, 212; economic activities of, III, 58, 159; education of, I, 358, 363; II, 172, 175, 194; III, 166, 172; excommunication of, II, 243; oppose communal loans, II, 268; population of, I, 26, 253; II, 23; III, 108; rabbis of, I, 331; II, 243, 296; III, 127; salaries of, III, 127, 141; scholarly periodical of, III, 172; synagogues of, II, 21, 131, 141; III, 58, 117, 150; unification of, II, 21

Amulo of Lyons (archbishop), I, 244; III, 56

Amusements, Jewish, I, 147; II, 205, 302–3. *See also* Dancing; Games; Sports; Theater

Analphabets, *see* Illiteracy

'Anan (Karaite), I, 178

Anarchy, communal, Jewish: and anti-Jewish legislation, I, 281; and judges' discretion, II, 218; and provincial chief rabbinate, I, 303; in Germany, II, 22; in Poland, I, 281, 303, 353–54; stemmed by councils, I, 347

Anathema, *see* Excommunication

Anatoli, Jacob b. Abba Mari, III, 134–35

Anatomical Institute, of Padua University, II, 151

'Anav, Zedekiah b. Abraham, II, 97; III, 37, 133, 136, 169

Ancestors, visits to graves of, II, 154; III, 206

Ancestry of synagogue, often fictitious, II, 130

Anciens, controversy over meaning of, III, 120

Ancona, Jews of; III, *185*; and Azariah de' Rossi, I, 308; and conferences, III, 79; and Mt. Zion chapel, I, 320; charter of privileges of, III, 158; diplomatic intervention for prisoners among, III, 73, 214–15; *ḥazaḳah* legislation of, II, 293; III, 198; legacy for, III, 212; meat administration of, II, 158; III, 137, 158; rabbis of, III, 73; sumptuary laws of, II, 326; III, 201; taxation of, II, 254–56, 277; III, 193

Andalusia, Muslim, and eastern caliphate, III, 50. *See also* Spain, Muslim

Andernach, early bath in, II, 166

Andros, Sir Edmund (New York governor), I, 260

Anello of Girgenti, legacy of, III, 189

Angers, Jews of, III, 185

Anglican Church, and Jewish community, I, 20

Angora (Turkish capital), I, 349; III, 50

Animals, figures of, and synagogue art, II, 138

Anjou, Jews of, I, 312; III, 67–68, 185

Ankava, Abraham b. Mordecai, III, 203, 205

Annianus (Roman child), I, 104

Announcements, in synagogues, II, 24–26, 140

Annulment: of bans, II, 231–32; of marriage, II, 310; III, 204
Anonymity of artists, II, 145; III, 147–48
Ansbach, elector of, II, 91
Anselm (Ratisbon rabbi), III, 100
Anselm of Cologne (German chief rabbi), I, 299, 315; III, 69
Anti-alien bias: and acquired rights, II, 297; and marriage licenses, II, 311; and *Pletten*, II, 322–23; and visiting preachers, II, 99. *See also* Acquired rights; Aliens; Economic regulation; Residence rights
Anti-British orientation, Soviet, and Zionism, I, 16
Anti-Christian feelings, and Jewish prayers, II, 143; and preachers, II, 98–99. *See also* Disputations
Anti-defamation, *see* Apologetics; Defense of Jewish rights
Anti-heretical benediction, Castilian decree on, II, 143
Anti-luxury legislation, *see* Sumptuary laws
Anti-Maimonidean controversy, and interterritorial action, I, 223, 307, 315–16; II, 191; III, 71–73, 78
Antinomianism, I, 9
Anti-Polish bias, German, and Jewish education, III, 163
Anti-rabbinism, Jewish, III, 48, 138–39
Anti-Semitism, ancient: I, 80–82, 86, 88; and Jewish solidarity, I, 115–16, 136; and Jewish status, I, 93; defense against, I, 5, 25, 106, 165, II, 204–5, 270; III, 171; early Christian, I, 23, 96, 112–15, 117; III, 21; in various regions (Egypt), I, 71, 86; (Palestine), I, 119; (Persia), I, 63–64, 148–49; III, 36; (Rome), I, 12, 80; (Syria), III, 15; sources of, III, 15
Arabian, I, 17, 165, 170; contemporary, I, 13–19; III, 220
medieval and modern: III, 52; and burghers, I, 276–79, 281; III, 64; and charities, II, 339, 349; and Christian creditors, II, 270; and Christian servants, III, 61; and community, I, 14, 208, 211, 270; II, 65, 120, 354, 364; and conversion, I, 218; III, 77; and enlightened absolutism, II, 357; and guilds, I, 365; and Hebrew deeds, II, 111; and houses of ill-repute, II, 313–14; and informing, I, 235; and instruction of Gentiles, II, 177; and interterritorialism, II, 351, 354; and Jewish councils, I, 313, 320–21, 323–24, 326; and Jewish economy, I, 244, 365; III, 94–95; and Jewish segregation, I, 295; and Jewish settlement, I, 257–58; III, 99; and peace, III, 174; and prisoners, II, 338–39; and royal protection, I, 244; and religious disputations, II, 193; and scholarly control, II, 244; and sumptuary laws, II, 302–3; and synagogue restrictions, I, 220, 237; and tenant protection, II, 295–96; hindered by feudal divisions, I, 231; in legislative terminology, I, 269; in various regions (Byzantium), I, 365; (England), I, 276; (France), I, 295; III, 61; (Germany), I, 277–78, 280; (Italy), I, 279, 320–21; (Poland), I, 270, 280–81, 323–24, 326, 354; III, 64, 99; (Portugal), II, 111; (Russia), I, 14–15; (Spain), I, 220, 237, 276, 278–79; II, 111. *See also* Apologetics; Expulsions; Libel, ritual; Massacres; Persecutions
Anti-trust laws, Jewish, II, 301
Anti-usury laws: and charities, II, 186, 346; and communal loans, II, 269, 285. *See also* Interest; Usury
Antilles, French, Jews of, I, 265–66; III, 62
Antioch: Jewish community in, I, 105, 142; III, 15, 19; synagogues in, I, 91, 93–94, 105; III, 15

Antiochus III (Syrian king), I, 82
Antiochus IV Epiphanes (Syrian king), I, 62, 83, 88; III, 15
Antoninus (Roman emperor), identity of, III, 29
Antoninus Pius (Titus Aurelius, Roman emperor), I, 108, 141; III, 28
Antonio Vaz, island of, III, 59
Antonius, Lucius (Roman consul), decree of, I, 110
Antwerp: expulsion of Marranos from, I, 253; synagogues in, III, 58
Aosta, bishop of, as Jewish conservator, III, 68
Apion of Alexandria, I, 86
Apollinopolis Magna (Egypt), ghetto of, I, 85; III, 15
Apologetics, Christian: and Jewish liturgy, I, 192; III, 150; anti-Jewish arguments of, I, 216
Jewish: and communal mourning, III, 153; and education, I, 125; II, 207; and illicit relations, II, 313; and Spanish chief rabbinate, I, 290; III, 66; and "sponge" function, II, 246–47
Apostles: Christian, I, 103, 120; III, 29; patriarchal, I, 142–43, 151, 181; *III, 29*
Apostolé (impost), I, 144
Appeals, Jewish: interterritorial, I, 304–9; II, 135–36; III, 146. *See also* Interterritorial action; judicial, I, 115; II, 135, 241. *See also* Courts of appeal
Appointments: communal, regional control over, III, 182; governmental, I, 272; III, 113–14; rabbinic, II, 78–79. *See also* Bureaucracy; Elections; Government intervention
Appraisal of books, and booklending, II, 202
Apprentices, Jewish, I, 336, 370;II, 18, 299; III, 96
Approbations, of Hebrew books, II, 202–4; III, 83, 170–71
Apt (Provence), Jewish delegates from, III, 75
Apulia, Jewish economic history in, III, 148
Apulian congregation in Salonica, II, 75
Arabarch, not identical with Alabarch, III, 19
Arabia, French visitor in, III, 159
Arabian Nights, on Bagdad, I, 177
Arabic, *see* Languages; Literature
Arabs: ancient, I, 47, 158; II, 205; III, 18; history of, III, 31, 35; medieval (conquests of), I, 154; II, 67, 340; (deride Jews), II, 154, 200; (reinstate exilarchate), I, 148, 173; modern, I, 17. *See also* Caliphate; Islam
Aragon (kingdom): assemblies in, I, 234, 286–87; chief rabbinate in, I, 288–90; III, 66, 71; debt bondage in, I, 226–27; deeds from, III, 139; elections in, II, 102; emigration restrictions in, I, 278; II, 15–16; excommunication in, II, 232; growth of rabbinate in, II, 74; guilds in, I, 367, 370; informers in, I, 235; Jewish judiciary in, I, 235; II, 70, 85; Jewish serfdom in, I, 233, 278; Jewish taxation in, II, 153, 248–49, 286–87; obligatory acceptance of office in, III, 119; respects minority laws, I, 238; synagogues in, I, 236–37; III, 143; war with Castile of, III, 66; wedding attendance in, II, 303
Aragon (province), and general assemblies, I, 287–88
"Aragonese" congregation: in Rome, II, 20; in Salonica, I, 351
Aragonese dynasty (south Italian), and Jewish self-government, I, 232, 279; II, 76
Arama, Isaac b. Moses, II, 314; III, 134–35, 205

Aramean Empire, I, 35

Arbitrators, Jewish: and Palestinian courts, II, 214; fees of, II, 215; of royal dispute, I, 296; qualifications of, II, 214

Arca (Lebanon), Jews of, I, 82

Archaeology, Palestinian: and cities, I, 41; III, 6; and deportations, I, 58; and Dura synagogue, I, 91; and guilds, III, 94; and population, I, 46; III, 10. *See also under* respective sites

Arché, *see* Archives

Archeion, I, 93; III, 16. *See also* Archives

Archipherekitae, Justinian on, I, 154; II, 52; III, 32

Archisynagogus: I, 102–3, 105; hereditary status of, I, 105; invites readers, I, 122; marital preference for, I, 124; medieval, in Spires, I, 250; position of, I, 138; III, 15, 18; rabbi as, I, 124; Severus nicknamed as, I, 109; woman as, I, 94, 97

Architecture *and* architects: Israelitic, I, 41–42; Jewish, ancient, I, 78, 81, 84, 87, 90, 100, 112–13; III, 16; Jewish, medieval, I, 237; II, 136–41; III, 147–48; (Arabian influences on), II, 132; (bathhouses), II, 166; (royal palaces), I, 368. *See also* Art; Houses; Synagogues

Archives *and* archivists, Jewish: ancient, I, 72–73, 93–94, 102; III, 16, 24; medieval and modern, II, 110; III, 139–40; (geonic), III, 42; (London), III, 59–60; (Moravia), III, 218; (Palermo), II, 59; (Poland), I, 272; (Prague), III, 173; (private), III, 81, 92, 139; (validity of deeds), I, 127; III, 24. *See also* Aramaic papyri; Minute-books

non-Jewish: I, 32; III, 6; Dutch, III, 57–58, 129; notarial, II, 130; Roman, I, 127; Venetian, III, 179; Wilno, III, 97, 197

Archon alti ordinis, in Rome, I, 106

Archon pases times, in Rome, I, 102

Archontes, ancient, I, 96, 100; II, 146

Archpresbyters, *see* Presbyters

Ardingo Judaeus, of Modena, III, 185

Arendas, Polish, II, 6–7

Aristeas, Letter of, I, 77; III, 13

Aristocracy, Israelitic; I, 44–45, 48; allied with priesthood, I, 50; and monarchy, I, 35; and returning exiles, III, 11; slaves of, I, 46

Jewish: attitudes to, II, 217; not hereditary, I, 28

"of learning": I, 135; II, 51; and democracy, I, 28. *See also* Oligarchy; Patricians

non-Jewish, *see* Nobles

Aristotle, on group jurisdiction, III, 20

Arithmetic, Jewish instruction in, II, 191

Ark in synagogue: I, 104; II, 25, 135, 140; III, 145; and "altar," II, 141; and price of seats, II, 130; decoration of, II, 132; III, 147

Arles, Jews of: and French assemblies, III, 75–76; charitable societies of, III, 93; citizenship in, III, 54–55; communal indebtedness of, III, 190; educational foundation of, I, 358; II, 114, 186; III, 104; notarial archives on, II, 130; oath of elders of, III, 113

Arli, Joseph (itinerant rabbi): II, 87, 91; demotion of, III, 130

Armament production, Jewish, medieval, in Sicily, I, 368

Armenians: and *ḥazakah* legislation, II, 298; autonomy in Poland of, I, 267

Arminius, Jacobus, followers of, I, 254

Armistice, and Prussian law of secession, III, 5

Arms, chopping off, and Jewish penal procedure, II, 223

Army, *see* Military service
Arrab, title of, II, 67, 73
Arraby moor, I, 285, 365. *See also* Chief rabbinate
Arrears: charitable, and moral compulsion, II, 349; in salaries, III, 127–28, 140
Arrivals, new, Jewish, rights and duties of, II, 12, 19, 344. *See also* Ban of settlement; Residence rights; Visitors
Arrueti, Juce (royal cobbler), I, 367
Arsinoe (Egypt), district of, I, 130
Arson, of ancient synagogues, I, 114–15. *See also* Desecration
Art *and* artists: I, 142; II, 360; Jewish (ancient), I, 90–92; II, 137; III, 16; (capacity for) II, 137; (funerary), II, 155; III, 156–57; (of synagogue), III, 146; (Turkey), III, 49. *See also* Architecture; Manuscripts
Artaxerxes (Persian king), I, 64, 68
Aryeh Yehudah Löw b. Hirz, III, 145
Asceticism, Jewish: I, 195; and charities, II, 346; and flogging, II, 225; and sumptuary laws, II, 306
Asher b. Yeḥiel: biography of, III, 70, 76; encourages book lending, II, 201–2; III, 170; family agreement of, II, 344; on associations, I, 353; III, 89–90; on bans, II, 229; III, 112, 177; on cantors, II, 101, 103; III, 135–36; on capital punishment, II, 223; III, 175; on change of endowments, II, 186, 266; III, 165; on charities, II, 320–21; III, 209; on excessive severity, II, 212; on fines, III, 52; on judiciary, II, 214; III, 172; on "law of the kingdom," III, 52; on mourning for scholar, II, 147; on Passover flour, II, 320–21; III, 209; on physical punishments, II, 223; III, 176; on prayers, II, 142; III, 148; on rabbis, II, 74, 276–77; III, 193; on regional conventions, III, 65, 76; on Rindfleisch massacres, III, 76; on "sale" of members, III, 104; on scribes, III, 139; on size of classes, II, 196; on Spanish elders, III, 124; on synagogues, III, 147; (candles), II, 134; III, 146; (seats), II, 130; III, 144; on taxes, I, 211; III, 51; (arrests), II, 219; III, 174; (assessments), II, 282; III, 194, 196; (immunities), II, 276–77; III, 192–93
Asherah, lay judges as, II, 71–72
Ashi, R. (amora), I, 151–53, 155, 213
Ashkenazi, Bezaleel b. Abraham, I, 190; III, 71, 129, 134, 198
Ashkenazi, (Ḥakam) Zevi b. Jacob, II, 82, 93, 174, 194
Ashkenazic congregations in: America, III, 143; Amsterdam, III, 108, 117, 150; England, I, 20; II, 21; III, 59; Hamburg, III, 138, 144; Italy, I, 242, 306–7; III, 138, 149, 335; Paris, I, 264; Turkey, I, 205; II, 311, 340, 342. *See also* German congregations; Polish congregations; *and under* respective congregations
Ashkenazic ritual, I, 122; II, 142–43, 213; III, 138
Ashkenazim: and seizure of property, II, 233; and Sephardim, II, 18, 142, 172, 311, 365; III, 138; and Venetian confraternity, II, 335; concentration on Talmud of, II, 193; in Palestine, III, 215; (allocation of Palestine relief among), II, 340, 342; western, and Polish Council, I, 331
Asḥor, (Mibṭaḥiah's husband), I, 70; III, 12
Asia Minor, ancient: archives in, I, 93; Assyrian colonies in, I, 55; III, 10; collections for Temple in, I, 88; guilds in, I, 365; Jerusalem synagogue from, I, 120; Jewish quarters in, I, 85–86; Jewish settlements in, I, 82–84, 92, 95
medieval and modern: redemption of captives in, II, 337; synagogues

in, I, 230. *See also* Near East; *and under* respective countries and cities
Assault and battery: frequency among Jews of, III, 179; in synagogue, III, 150; part of civil law, II, 213–14
Assemblies: Israelitic, I, 46; III, 7–8; (character of), I, 127; III, 9
Jewish, ancient: I, 66, 86, 95; III, 27; and elections of officials, I, 101, 105; and municipal oligarchy, III, 9; and Roman law, I, 108, 110, 113; educational, I, 154–55; honoring member, I, 100; in various countries (Babylonia), I, 59, 61, 154–55; (Egypt), I, 70, 89; (Palestine), I, 42, 48, 51–53, 61, 65; (Persia), I, 70
interterritorial: I, 284, 304; and *kallah*, I, 182; III, 33; in Aragon, I, 287; in Constantinople, III, 48; in France, I, 305. *See also* Councils; Synods
medieval and modern: II, 23–24; III, *106–12*; and associations, I, 348–49; and communal controversies, II, 307; and exilarchic authorization, III, 44; and expulsion of new arrivals, II, 19; and provincial councils, I, 341; II, 49; and rabbis, II, 77, 87, 90; III, 129, 131–32; and sumptuary legislation, II, 303; and taxes, II, 257–58, 281–82; attendance at, II, 55; III, 114, 119; chairmen of, II, 55; discretionary powers of, II, 265, 285; III, 88; educational value of, II, 206; location of, II, 90, 144; obligatory convocation of, II, 62; Prussian supervision of, III, 220
Assembly of New York, and Jewish worship, I, 260–61
Assessores, Jewish, Polish, in mixed litigations, I, 272; II, 116
Assessors, lay, in professional courts, II, 215
Assimilation, Jewish: ancient, I, 67, 85–86, 116; medieval, I, 210; II, 167; modern (and Communism), I, 16; (and learning), II, 362; (and Reform Judaism), I, 9; (demanded by Prussian bureaucracy), II, 360; (in Palestine), I, 17
Polish, of Germans, and Jewish status, I, 280–81
Associations, Graeco-Roman: I, 77; *III, 19*; constitutions of, I, 95–96, 101–2, 116; III, 17; and Jewish community, I, 116; and Roman law, I, 107–8; exclusive jurisdiction of, I, 110–11; III, 20; medieval influences of, III, 91; officials of, III, 18
Holy, *see* Burial Societies
Jewish: I, *348–74*; III, *90-97*, 104; acceptance of office in, III, 119; and local community, II, 3; III, 96; and membership, I, 169; II, 17–20; and rabbinic sinecures, II, 81; and sextons, II, 106; and synagogues, II, 125, 129, 140; III, 143, 148; and Talmud, III, 90–91; and taxation, I, 109; and treaties of reciprocity, III, 102; as communal creditors, I, 372; II, 270, 272; attendance at, III, 119, 143
charitable: I, 6, 25, 349, *360–64*, 373–74; III, *89*; and free burial, II, 155–56. *See also* Burial associations; budgets of, II, 343; different ranks in, II, 148; for care of sick, II, 327–30. *See also* Sick; for free loans, II, 327. *See also* Loans, charitable; for Sabbath lights, III, 146; for the support of brides, II, 332. *See also* Brides; redemption of captives by, II, 336; III, 73. *See also* Redemption of captives; specialization of, I, 361; women in, II, 37
educational: I, 349, *356–60*, 373–74; III, 92, 119, 127; and clothing of pupils, II, 188; bequests for, I, 363; III, 104, 165; communal support of, II, 114, 169; family control of, III, 104; geonic responsa on, III, 94; in

Palestine today, I, 17. *See also* Education
professional: I, 12, 349–50, *364–74*; III, *94–97*. *See also* Guilds
religious: I, *348–56*, 373–74; III, *88–92*; and Roman law, I, 108; for synagogue illumination, II, 134, 146; leadership of, III, 13; of *ḥasidim*, Shabbetian, I, 355. *See also* Burial societies; Congregations; Ḥasidism
social, I, 12, 17, 25, 92; III, 16. *See also* Landsmannschaft
medieval and modern: (American), I, 101; (and state charities), I, 11–12; (influence of Crusades on), III, 93; (Muslim), III, 91
Assyria: I, 35, 41; deportations of, I, 50, 55, 57; guilds in, III, 11; invasions of, I, 47, 50; merchant colonies of, I, 55–57; III, 10; titles of officials in, III, 18; tributes to, I, 38
Astronomy, and calendar regulation, I, 143
Astrug b. Vidal, II, 100
Asylum, right of, in synagogue, I, 88; II, 11; III, 143
Atheism: a Roman crime, I, 12; Jewish, and Inquisition, I, 288; Soviet and Jewish community, I, 15
Athens (ancient), Jews in vicinity of, I, 103
Athribis, Jews of, I, 77; III, 13
Attendance: at meetings, obligatory nature of, II, 24–30; III, 119; (councils), I, 341; II, 41, 60, 62; at synagogue, III, 105, 143; interdenominational, of Jewish theater, III, 207; personal, at provincial assemblies, II, 41
Attestations, communal, of tenant rights, II, 294
Attorney General, English, stops indictment of elders, I, 258
Attorneys: and informers, II, 241; discouraged by Jewish law, II, 237; III, 180
Auctions: of synagogue functions, II, 133; of synagogues, II, 131
Auditing, of guardians' accounts, II, 330
Auditors of accounts, communal, II, 57, 58–59, 60–63, 65; III, 116. *See also* Accounting
Auerbach, Simon Wolf (Poznań chief rabbi), I, 333
Augsburg: diet of, and Jewish delegation, III, 71; Jewish assembly in, I, 314; III, 78; Jews in, II, 158; III, 107, 185; mixed courts in, I, 250
Augustians, Roman congregation of, I, 105
Augustine, Aurelius of Hippo, Saint, on captive women, II, 336; III, 213
Augustus III (Polish king), on Lwów chief rabbinate, I, 303
Augustus (Roman emperor), I, 80–81, 106–7, 109–10; III, 14, 18
Aurum coronarium, I, 129, 143, 145, 228. *See also* Taxation
Austerlitz (Moravia), minute-book of, III, 131
Austria, Jews of: and banking, II, 81; and Bohemia, I, 305, 309; and Bukovina, III, 105; and chief rabbinates, III, 85; (French), I, 308: (Galician), I, 303; III, 72; (German), I, 311; and communal debts, I, 337; and Cracow dictator, II, 64; and excommunication, II, 232–33; and German assemblies, I, 314–15, 341; and Ḥasidism, III, 220; and minority rights, III, 4; and Moravian Council, I, 338–39; II, 41; and Polish population, II, 354–55; III, 108; cemeteries of, II, 150, 153–54; censuses of, III, 108; communal legislation on, I, 18–20, 267; II, 354–55; III, 5; congregational divisions of, I, 352; II, 129–30; extradition treaty on, I, 246; family quotas of, II, 5; Germanization of, II, 192; scholarly women among,

III, 162; synagogues of, II, 129–30; taxation of, III, 197; (candles), II, 260; (citrons), II, 260; (funerals), II, 153–54; (immunities), II, 277; (*Leibzoll*), II, 264; (meat), II, 108, 159–60, 258, 260; wandering scholars among, II, 188
Austrittsgesetz, Prussian, III, 5
Autarchy: of Israelitic cities, I, 41–42, 53; III, 9; Jewish, medieval, I, 224
Authenticity of ancient records, I, 76
Authority: communal, extent of, I, 27, 208; II, 218. *See also* Communal control; spiritual vs. temporal, II, 217
Authorization of judges: ancient, I, 128, 155; II, 79; III, 24; (patriarchal), I, 142; exilarchic, I, 155; III, 41–42, 44; geonic, I, 193, 202; formula of, I, 202; medieval, II, 92, 241–42. *See also* Ordination
of books, I, 308, 331–32; of slaughterers, II, 84–85, 109; III, 137–38
Authors, Jewish, communal protection of, I, 331; II, 202–3
Autobiographies, Jewish, II, 329–30; III, 131
Autonomous regions, Jewish, in Soviet Union, I, 15
Autonomy, Jewish, *see* Self-government
Auxerre, and synod of Troyes, I, 312
Aversa, synagogue of, I, 232
Avignon, Jews of: III, 53, 106–7; and acceptance of office, II, 54; and Gentile tenants, II, 296; bans of, II, 232; birth records of, II, 84; charities of, II, 213, 321, 325, 328; communal revolts among, III, 114; constitution of, II, 30, 61, 321, 325, 328; III, 103, 137, 190; elections of, II, 36, 104; emigration restrictions by, II, 15; financial irregularities among, III, 122; indebtedness of, III, 190; officials of, II, 104, 114; III, 137, 140; pestilence among, III, 210–11; ritual of, II, 142; successive burial among, III, 155; synagogue illumination among, II, 134; taxation of, II, 251, 256, 275, 283; three-class system among, II, 39
Avignonese Jews, in Bordeaux, I, 262–64; II, 19
Ayutamichristo, Guilelmo (Sicilian banker), II, 285
Azariah b. Yehallelel (*nasi*), I, 186
Azulai, Ḥayyim Joseph David (Palestinian messenger): II, 216, 342; III, 216–17; as preacher, II, 96; III, 133, 168; disqualifies Bordeaux slaughterers, III, 138, 217; for local rituals, III, 149; on age discrepancy in marriage, III, 204; on aliens' property taxes, III, 188; on capital jurisdiction, III, 175; on cutting of beards, III, 203; on fellow messengers, III, 217; on *ḥazakah*, III, 198; on head covering, III, 202; on inquiry from Poland, III, 188; on intercommunal controversy III, 183; on Jewish censorship, III, 170; on lending communal funds, III, 195; on Mayence regional community, III, 88; on mourning, III, 153, 157; on ransom of captives, III, 213; on recitation of Decalogue, III, 22; on Venice finances, III, 190

Baba de-resh galuta, III, 31. *See also* Courts, royal
Babel (city), Jews in, I, 67
Babylonia, ancient: centralization of, I, 41; III, 7; documents from, I, 63; guilds in, I, 81; III, 11; Jewish policies of, I, 63; Jews in, I, 27, *55-74*; (courts) I, 71; (elders), I, 65, 77–78, 145; (Ezekiel), I, 58; Palestinian invasions of, I, 58; poets of, I, 36; publicans in, I, 38; III, 7; wool tax in, 7. *See also* Babylonian exile
medieval, Jews of: I, 27; III, 6;

and anti-Maimonidean controversy, I, 316; and European Jewry, I, 194, 212; II, 69; and Palestine, I, 167, 192; III, 45; districts of, I, 180; education among, III, 92; exilarchic supremacy over, I, 185; III, 39. *See also* Exilarchate; flogging by, II, 224–25; geonic control of, I, 203. *See also* Gaonate; "great ḥazzan" of, III, 136; hegemony of, I, 157, 167, 187, 192; III, 37; inquiries to, I, 165; interruption of prayers among, II, 33; letters of, III, 34; local judges among, I, 203; titles of rabbis of, I, 210. *See also under* respective cities

Sassanian, Jews in: against interrupting prayers, II, 33; agriculture of, III, 31; and calendar regulation, I, 122, 143–44; and European communities, I, 212, 242, 346; II, 142; and Greek language, I, 100; and Palestine, I, 118–19, 122, 147, 149-50, 152, 154-55; and Sephardic ritual, I, 242; II, 142; criminal law of, II, 220; democracy of, III, 27; flagellation among, II, 224; guilds of, I, 364; III, 94; historical records of, I, 146; judges of, I, 128; II, 241; preachers among, I, 122; II, 22-23; public law of, II, 217; rabbis of (ordination), I, 154; III, 24; (supremacy), I, 135–36, 151–52; II, 94; (title), II, 66; recitation of Decalogue in, III, 22; students' decisions by, III, 172; tax immunities of, I, 138. *See also* Academies; Exilarchate; Talmud; *and under* respective cities

Parthian and Seleucide: few extant sources from, III, 31; Hellenistic influence in, I, 118; Jewish emigrants from, I, 140; religious toleration in, I, 75

Babylonian congregation, in Fustat, II, 102

Babylonian Exile: I, 55–74; and Jewish survival, I, 73; and Palestinian municipality; I, 53–54, and Palestinian shrines, III, 9; doctrine of repentance in, II, 221; *gerim* in, III, 12; guild congregations in, I, 81; inscriptions on, III, 11

Bacharach, Ḥayyim Ya'ir b. Samson, II, 247; III, 103, 132, 136, 141, 183, 214

Bachelors, Jewish: and educational costs, I, 137; and prostitution, II, 314; available at academies, II, 81; barred from teaching, II, 179; electoral rights of, II, 23, 37–38; III, 106, 114; rare, II, 308

Baden, Jews of, I, 18, 315

Badge, Jewish, I, 161; II, 307; III, 61

Bagdad: courts of, I, 170; decline of, I, 184–86, 189; *dhimmi* chiefs in, III, 40; glamor of, I, 177. *See also* Caliphate

Jews of: academies of, I, 41, 179, 181, 184; III, 38; and Constantinople, I, 197; III, 49; appointment of gaon among, I, 203; bankers among, I, 160, 183, 188; III, 34; Benjamin on, I, 200; connection with Yemen of, III, 44; officials of, II, 67; Palestinian inquiries to, 193. *See also* Academies; Exilarchate; Gaonate

Bagohi (Bigvai, Persian governor), I, 71

Baḥur, traveling, *see*, Wandering scholars

Baḥya b. Asher, II, 171; III, 134–35

Bail, communal, of Jewish defendants, III, 176

Bailiffs: German, jurisdiction over Jews of, I, 248; *ḥazzanim* as, I, 104; sextons as, II, 106

Baiulo generale, Sicilian, I, 231. *See also* Chief rabbinate

Baiulus, Spanish, and search for stolen objects, II, 227

Bake-houses, communal, II, 167

Bakers: Basel guilds of, III, 198; Jewish, sales taxes on products of, II, 261
Balaban, Lewko (Lwów elder), III, 122
Balearic Islands, Jewish history in, I, 287–88; III, 65–66. *See also* Majorca
Balkan Peninsula: ancient, I, 83; (patriarchal influence on), III, 28; medieval, Jewish economy in, I, 243, 365
Turkish, Jews of: communal agreements among, III, 110–11; elections of, II, 36, 47–48; evolution of rabbinate of, II, 75, 352; Gentile landlords in quarters of, II, 295; hospices of, III, 211; parental interference in marriages of, III, 204; public education of, 172; redemption of captives among, II, 337; Spanish exiles among, I, 168, 197; II, 48, 338; III, 198; spread of Polish influences among, II, 355. *See also under* respective provinces and cities
Ball games, Jewish, history of, III, 207
Ballot boxes, communal, III, 115. *See also* Elections
Baltic areas, Soviet-occupied, I, 17
Bamah, and origin of synagogue, III, 9. *See also* Sanctuaries, local
Bambalo, Nissim, II, 243
Bamberg, Jews of: I, 344–45; III, 87; charities of, II, 332; III, 211; household employees of, II, 300; III, 200; marriage broker's fees among, III, 208; regional community of, I, 341, 344–45; shoeless worship of, II, 129; tax privileges of, III, 193
Ban, *see* Excommunication
Ban of settlement: history of, III, 98, 101; and guilds, I, 367, 370; III, 95; talmudic origin of, II, 5–6. *See also* Acquired rights; Residence rights
Banchi del ghetto, in Venice, II, 327
Banishment, Jewish: and educational responsibilities, II, 175; and judiciary, II, 70–71, 241; III, 178; and local customs, III, 203; for prohibited marriage, II, 319; for seeking tax immunity, II, 15; of itinerant beggars, II, 323; of unlawful residents, III, 99; Spanish laws on, II, 9, 70–71. *See also* Ban of settlement; Expulsion
Banking *and* bankers: ancient, I, 57, 63, 80; Byzantine guilds of, I, 365; Christian, for community, II, 285; Islamic (Christian), I, 365; (communal leadership), I, 183, 187–89, 197; (corrupt judges), I, 165; (oppression of poor), I, 166–67; (taxes), I, 159–60; (usury), I, 365
Jewish: and admission to cities, I, 275; and anti-Semitism, I, 244; and chirograph offices, II, 110–11; and communal loans, II, 270; III, 191–92; and communal oligarchy, I, 244, 297; II, 29, 48; III, 142; and congregational divisions, II, 18–19; and debt bondage, II, 226; and educational responsibilities, II, 176; and *ḥazakah* legislation, II, 298; and Jewish law, I, 210; and lay judiciary, II, 76; and rabbinate, II, 78, 80–81, 87; III, 125; and settlement restrictions, II, 10–11; and Shabbetian movement, II, 25–26; and taxation, I, 268, 296; II, 253, 261; associations of, I, 365, 368–69; II, 76; charitable contributions of, II, 335, 346; favored by England, I, 251, 297–98; in various regions (England), I, 251, 297–98; II, 110–11; (France), I, 296; (Germany), II, 25–26; III, 142; (Italy), I, 275, 368–69; II, 10–11, 29, 48, 76, 87, 298, 335; III, 125, 191–92; (Poland), I, 268, 329; III, 191; Polish Council's regulation of, I, 329. *See also* Anti-usury laws; Interest; Usury
Bankruptcy: communal, II, 350; III, 84; (and Jewish solidarity), I, 334; II, 352–53; (and royal taxation), I, 281; individual (and communal

debts), III, 191–92; (and sumptuary laws), II, 302; (communal ordinances on), II, 301, 338. *See also* Debts
Banquets: at exilarchic court, I, 147; communal, I, 95–96; restricted by synods, II, 303. *See also* Conviviality; Sumptuary laws
Baptism, *see* Conversion
Bar-Hebraeus, Gregory Abulfaraj, III, 40
Bar Kocheba, revolt of, I, 141, 143; III, 30; (*nasi* title), I, 141
Barbados, Jews in, I, 262; III, 61; (and New York), II, 136
Barbarian migrations, I, 114
"Barbarians," Europeans as, I, 210
Barbastro, lay judiciary in, II, 71
Barbers, Jewish: exempted from office, III, 119; guilds of, I, 369–70; III, 96
Barcelona: and Maimonidean Code, I, 240; banishment from, II, 9; communal conflicts in, II, 52; communal institutions in, III, 92, 143, 155, 211; conference of, I, 287–88, 291, 310; III, 65; (migrations), I, 234; (procedural latitude), II, 241; (revenue), I, 234–35; (royal permits), I, 322; constitution of, II, 58; courts in, I, 239; III, 211; early Jewish history in, I, 182; II, 67–68, 74; III, 100; rabbis in, I, 211; II, 67–68, 73; regional community of, I, 286–87; II, 20; synagogue right of asylum in, III, 143. *See also* Collectas
Bari, legislation of, I, 232, 279
Barrois, Jewish burials in, III, 153
Barsimson, Jacob (early New York settler), III, 60
Baruk she-'amar, prayer of, III, 22
Basel: Church council in, III, 77; craft guilds in, III, 198; faulty prayer-books from, II, 203; Jewish assembly in, I, 315; III, 77
Bashi = pasha, I, 196
Basque provinces, Jews of, III, 65–66
Baṣra, Jews of, III, 36
Bassano, Mordecai b. Samuel Ḥayyim, III, 51
Bassola, Moses, itinerant rabbi, II, 87; III, 215
"Bastards," Jewish definition of, II, 315
Bathmasters, Jewish, III, 160
Baths: Christian, exclusion of Jews from, II, 165; Jewish, I, 219; II, 165–66, 219; III, 160; (ancient), I, 120; (associational), III, 97; (rank of), II, 124; (women keepers of), II, 115
Baṭlanim, I, 133–34; II, 127; III, 26. *See also* "Ten men of leisure"
Batory, Stephen (Polish king), III, 64
Baumeister, Frankfort, II, 61. *See also* Elders
Bavaria: and Bamberg Council, I, 345; *memor*-books from, III, 152; regional cemetery in, I, 283; II, 154
Baylons du luminaire, II, 134
Bayonne, Jews of: I, 264; III, 62; assist Bohemian Jewry, I, 305; mourning customs of, III, 203; parental intervention in marriage among, III, 204; rabbis of, II, 296; tax ordinance of, II, 265
Bazaars, *see* Markets
Beadles, *see* Sextons
Beards, communal regulations on, II, 104, 109, 223; III, 203
Beaver St. (New York), synagogue at, I, 261
Bedershi, Abraham b. Isaac, I, 289
Bedinage, I, 238. *See also* Fees, judicial
Bedinaticum, I, 238
Bedouins, Palestinian: I, 33; and city walls, III, 8; and prophets, I, 45
Beds, Jewish delivery of, II, 268
Beer (drink), on Passover, I, 65
Beer (Frankfort family), III, 141–42
Beer, Shabbetai, III, 212, 216–17
Begging *and* beggars, Jewish: and Gentile opinion, III, 219; by charity overseers, II, 346; communal inves-

tigation of, III, 209; discouraged by rabbis, I, 132; II, 321, 323–24; effects of charities on, II, 347; itinerant, II, 322; modern spread of, I, 363. *See also* Pletten; Public charges
Behelfer, II, 115, 185. *See also* Teachers, assistants of
Beit-Mirsim, population of, I, 31
Bela IV (Hungarian king), I, 267
Belfrymen, Catholic, and Jewish sextons, II, 106
Belgium, modern, Jews of, I, 13, 25; III, 57–58
Belgrade, and Venetian associations, I, 364
Bell, as magic implement, III, 160
Belles-lettres, new Jewish appreciation of, II, 363
Belon, Pierre, III, 214
Bełz (city), Jews of, I, 301; III, 81
Ben-Hadad (Damascus king), I, 57
Ben-Meir, Aaron, I, 186, 193; III, 45
Ben Shushan (Salonican family), II, 50
Benallel, Solomon (Majorcan rabbi), II, 299
Benedict XIII (anti-pope), I, 220, 320
Benedict XIV (pope), II, 107–8, 158
Benedict of York, burial of, III, 153
Benedictine monks, and Bordeaux synagogue, III, 61
Benedictions, Hebrew: I, 121; and covering of heads, II, 306–7; III, 202; and women, II, 178; anti-heretical, I, 237. *See also* Liturgy; Priestly blessing
Benedikt, Markus (Benet, Mordecai b. Abraham, Moravian chief rabbi), II, 43
Benefit of counsel, *see* Attorneys
Benevolence, gradations of, II, 333; III, 210. *See also* Charities
Benjamin (tribe), III, 12
Benjamin b. Abraham of Rome, II, 150
Benjamin of Tudela, Itinerary of: I, 164, 175; on Byzantine community, I, 230; on craftsmen, I, 365; III, 94; on eastern chiefs, I, 175, 194; III, 40, 43; on Jehoiachin's synagogue, III, 12; on Lunel academy, II, 187; on "ten men of leisure," I, 200, III, 50; on title *rab*, II, 67; III, 123
Benjamin Ze'eb b. Mattathias, III, 206
Bensanchi, Israel, tax exemption of, II, 276
Bentifac, Jewish *procureur*, I, 295
Benveniste, Abraham (Castilian chief rabbi), I, 289, 291
Benveniste, Ḥayyim b. Israel, III, 22, 46
Benveniste, Isaac b. Solomon (?) Nasi, I, 305
Benveniste, Joseph, II, 303
Benveniste, Don Judah b. Abraham, II, 295
Bequests, Jewish: and officials' salaries, II, 81, 266; and welfare budgets, II, 265–66, 343; charitable, I, 353; II, 328–29, 340–41; III, 198; communal administration of, III, 189; diversion of, II, 266, 328–29, 344; III, 165, 213; educational, I, 348–49; II, 114–15, 185–87; III, 60, 165; intercommunal, I, 348–49; II, 332; III, 212–13; legal problems of, I, 361; III, 93, 217; parental, II, 201; III, 204; religious, II, 99, 132; (ancient), III, 19. *See also* Contributions; Wills
Berab, Jacob, I, 309; II, 220; III, 74
Bérats, I, 198–99; III, 47–49. *See also* Law
Berdiczew, Jewish guilds in, I, 371
Berdons, Jewish, III, 200
Berenice (North Africa), Jews of, I, 95, 100; III, 17
Berens, Leffmann (court Jew), and anti-defamation, III, 171
Berkamsted, obtains exclusion of Jews, I, 276
Berlin: and conversion of Roman boys, I, 306; and Kleve assembly, I, 343–

44; bans in, II, 312; charities in, I, 363; II, 349; education in, III, 119, 127, *166*; Egyptian papyri of, I, 93; elections in, II, 36; III, 113; enforced allegiance in, II, 358–59; government control over elders in, II, 358–59; III, 127, 220; *Haskalah* in, II, 360; marriages in, III, 107; meat taxes in, III, 186; population in, III, 107; private synagogues in, II, 125; rabbinic salaries in, II, 82
Bernard of Clairvaux, Saint, II, 138
Bernardino, Saint, III, 151
Bernstein, Aryeh Löb b. Issachar Ber (Galician chief rabbi), III, 72
Berthold of Ratisbon, II, 193; III, 151
Bertinoro, Obadiah Yare b. Abraham, I, 203; III, 50
Berure 'aberot, II, 57. *See also* Sex Morality
Berure tebio't, II, 71. *See also* Judiciary
Berurim, II, 55. *See also* Elders
Besht, *see* Israel Ba'al Shem Tob
Best men, communal, I, 133; II, 55; 63, 212; III, 111. *See also* Elders
Bet ha-keneset, I, 87. *See also* Synagogues
Bet-hamidrash, I, 155; II, 144; III, 151. *See also* Academies; Schools; Synagogues
Betchaim, London, II, 115. *See also* Cemeteries
Beth ha-midrash (Berlin association), statute of, III, 119, 127
Beth-Shan, population of, I, 31
Bethar, fall of, I, 117
Bethel, sanctuary of, I, 40; III, 7–8
Betrothals: and brokers' fees, III, 208; and communal control, II, 76, 112, 311; and parental consent, II, 310; and sumptuary laws, II, 303; behavior of couples during, II, 315; III, 206; forced, II, 311; synagogue rites at, II, 145. *See also* Bridegrooms, Brides; Marriage
Bianca (Sicilian queen), I, 293
Bible: and age of taxpayers, II, 251; and burial, I, 353; II, 147; and communal discipline, I, 203–4; and exilarchic genealogy, I, 146; III, 30–31; and frequent re-elections, III, 117; and Jewish dispersion, III, 10; and masquerades, II, 316; and origin of synagogue, III, 9; and polygamy, II, 308; and *Shema'*, I, 121; burning of, I, 109; III, 11; chronology of, I, 76, 146; debt bondage in, II, 226; doctrine of retaliation in, II, 221; expert writing of, I, 102; II, 110; flogging in, II, 225; III, 118; historicity of, I, 146; homilies on, II, 205; III, 16; instruction in, I, 104, 125–26, 142; II, 114, *192–95*; III, 24; (age), II, 174; (feminine), II, 178; (parental responsibility), II, 174; (public), II, 172; (Tiberian), I, 192; messianic prophecies in, I, 36; neglect of, and Jewish persecutions, II, 195; on censuses, III, 9, 184; on charity, I, 131, 353; II, 326, 330; on city walls, III, 8; on constitutional law, I, 37; II, 216–17; III, 7, 9, 12, 44; on fines, II, 234; on *gerim*, III, 12; on "house of the people," III, 11; on Jubilee year, III, 8; on landless Israelites, III, 11; on levirate marriage, II, 317; on local sanctuaries, I, 49; on necromancy, II, 154; on orientation in prayers, III, 13; on popular assemblies, III, 10; on professional associations, III, 94; on returning exiles, III, 11; on *Senaah*, III, 11–12; on seventy elders, III, 8; on suicide, III, 157; on Temple, I, 60; III, 10; on varieties of fish, II, 161; orientation of, I, 62, 69; III, 12–13; Philo's use of, III, 14, 20; rabbinic interpretation of, I, 73, 122–24. *See also* Bible exegesis; revelation of, and Inquisition, I, 288; taboos in, II, 297; III, 202, 206; use

in synagogue of, III, 21–22; vs. Talmud, II, 129; III, 167–68

individual Old Testament books: Genesis, I, 32, 36, 353; III, 7; (commentaries on), III, 15, 89, 164; Exodus, III, 8; Leviticus, III, 8; Numbers, III, 8, 14; Deuteronomy, I, 51, 53, 89, 121, 216; III, 7, 9, 10, 16; Joshua, I, 34; II, 177; III, 10; Judges, I, 42; III, 8, 10; Samuel, I, 37; III, 7, 9; Kings, I, 59, 69; III, 7, 9, 10, 12; Isaiah, I, 74; III, 7; (commentary), III, 40; Jeremiah, I, 59, 65; III, 7, 9–11; Ezekiel, I, 60, 65; III, 8, 10, 12; Hosea, I, 53; Amos, III, 7; Micah, I, 43, 166–67; Zechariah, III, 13; Malachi, III, 10; Psalms, I, 36, 42; III, 7, 11. *See also* Psalms; (commentary), III, 28; Proverbs, I, 134; II, 205; III, 26; Job, I, 131; III, 25; Ruth, I, 44; Esther, I, 63–64; II, 110; Daniel, III, 13; Ezra, I, 64–66, 68, 72; III, 8; Nehemiah, III, 8, 10–11, 94; Chronicles, I, 43, 141, 146; III, 7, 9–10, 12, 30–31, 94

Bible exegesis: I, 89, 146; III, 30–31, 40; and ancient preachers, I, 123; and Code of Justinian, III, 32; Babylonian divergences in, I, 150; instruction of Gentiles in, II, 177; of Ḳimḥi, III, 15; of Origen, III, 28; of Rashi, III, 86, 164

Bible recitation: I, 52, 59, 61, 67, 74, 89–92; and *almemar*, II, 140; and family events, II, 145; and *ḥazzan*, II, 100–1, 105; and interruption of prayers, II, 33–34; and *morenu* title, II, 91; and priests, III, 42; and reading of Decalogue, I, 121; III, 22; by all, I, 103–4, 124–25; (children), II, 189; (priests), I, 97; (women), I, 96; daily, I, 121–22; during flogging, II, 224–25; educational value of, II, 193; medieval developments in, I, 189; II, 141; rabbinic precedence in, II, 89–90; vows during, II, 103, 132, 188, 264, 344. *See also* Summonses to Torah

Bible versions: ancient, I, 122–23; Greek, I, 82, 90, 123, 141. *See also* Septuagint; Latin, I, 123; III, 152; Yiddish, II, 192

Bidache (France), Jewish boycott in, II, 295–96

Bielitz (Bielsko), taxation of merchandise from, II, 263

Biet, Antoine (French traveler), III, 62

Bigamy, and levirate marriage, II, 317. *See also* Polygamy

Biglietto d'oblazione, *see* Tax declarations

Bigvai (Persian governor), I, 71

Biḳḳur ḥolim societies, I, 362. *See also* Sick, care of

Billeting: and Jewish taxation, I, 138; II, 268; III, 189; in synagogues, I, 114; of poor, *see* Pletten

Bimah, II, 141. *See also* Almemar

Bing (Frankfort family), III, 141–42

Bingen am Rhein, Jews in: III, 69; conference of, I, 299; III, 77; tax district of, I, 341

Birds, figures of, and synagogue art, II, 138

Birobidjan, projected republic of, I, 15

Births, Jewish: and communal membership, II, 4; records of, I, 72, 198; II, 84; rites at, I, 25

Bishops, Catholic: and Jewish question, I, 216; and tithes, III, 185; jurisdiction over Jews of, I, 248, 250; II, 103, 273; III, 55, 151

Jewish, I, 249, 300; II, 55–56, 62, 78; III, 130. *See also* Elders

Bismarck, Prince Otto, on law of secession, III, 5

Bit Karun, Assyrian, I, 57

Bitonto (southern Italy), Jewish murderer in, II, 227

Bivar, Rodrigo Diaz de (Cid Campeador), III, 91

Black Death, massacre during: I, 288, 298; and distant cemeteries, II, 149; and rabbinic control, II, 78–79; reconstruction after, II, 70
Blacklist, communal, strength of, II, 319
Blackboards, of synagogues, III, 206
Blackmail: and levirate marriage, II, 318; by change of venue, II, 242–43
Blindness: and public office, II, 169; III, 136; as penalty, II, 223
Blood accusation, *see* Libel, ritual
Blood, consumption of, by heretics, I, 165
Blood-letting, Jewish, banquets after, II, 303
"Blue laws," *see* Sumptuary laws
Board, free, of students, II, 188–89. *See also* Students
Board of Deputies of British Jews, I, 20; II, 62
Boards of electors: gradation of, II, 44–45; restrictions on, II, 44, 46; size of, II, 39–40; III, 114–15. *See also* Elections
Boards of standards, Jewish, II, 291. *See also* Weights
Boaz (biblical leader), I, 44
Bobba, Marco Antonio (Piedmont conservator), III, 68
Bodensee, Jews at, III, 143
Bodyguard, royal, Palestinian, I, 39, 141
Bohemia, Jews of: III, *187*; chief rabbis of, I, 299, 339–40; II, 52; communal debts of, III, 192; Council of, I, 339–40; early rabbis of, II, 103; education of, III, 92, 161, 163; emigration restrictions among, I, 246; II, 16; expulsion of, I, 305; French assistance for, I, 305; guilds of, I, 366; II, 18, 88–89; III, 97; *ḥazakah* legislation of, II, 298–99; intercommunal controversies of, I, 308; interruption of prayers among, II, 34; in villages, III, 206; merchants' arbitration courts among, II, 89; privileges of, I, 267; sex morality of, III, 206; taxation of, II, 52, 153–54; (citrons), II, 260; (meat), III, 186; (military), III, 189
Bohemian Jews, in Poland, I, 300
Bolesław the Pious (Polish king), decree of, I, 267–68
Bologna, Jews of: III, 101, 107; against outside bans, II, 243; III, 110; and chair for Hebrew, III, 135; and Jewish conferences, I, 319–20; III, 79–80; ordinances of, III, 110, 179 182, 212; pro-alien trends among, II, 11; rabbi deposed by, II, 91
Bonafed, Solomon, on Jewish guild domination, I, 368; III, 95
Bonartino, Joshua (Sicilian chief rabbi), I, 294, 316; III, 67
Bonavoglia, Moses de (Sicilian chief rabbi), I, 293–94, 316
Bondage, personal: for seeking tax immunity, II, 15; of emigrés, I, 246. *See also* Debt bondage
Bonfils (Ṭob 'Elem), Joseph b. Samuel, II, 253, 284
Boni viri, II, 55. *See also* Best men; Elders
Book collectors, Jewish, II, 201; III, 171
Book of Creation, III, 123
Book of the Pious: against age discrepancy in marriage, II, 204; on admission of settlers, III, 99–100; on books, II, 200–1; III, 169; on education, II, 178, 186, 200; III, 170; on endowments, III, 165; on interruption of prayers, II, 34; on vows for cantors, II, 103
Book trade, Jewish: and Christian competitors, II, 204; and communal control, II, 200–5; and prices, III, 169; protection of, II, 200–1

Bookkeepers, Christian, of Roman community, II, 116

Books, Hebrew: II, *200–5*; and excommunication, I, 169; and Jewish councils, I, 324, 331–32; II, 83; and teachers' control, II, 180–81; anti-Christian attacks in, I, 237; as part of dowry, II, 83; bequests of, III, 166; burning of, I, 321. *See also* Talmud; censorship of, I, 223–24; III, 49, 54. *See also* Censorship; communal control of, III, 169–71; confiscation of, II, 98–99, 335; III, 134; reading during synagogue services, of; II, 141; shortage of, I, 224; II, 200, 335; III, 169; writing by scribes of, II, 110

Ladino, censorship of, II, 202; Latin, medieval prices of, III, 169–70

Books of Deeds, *see* Deeds; *and under* respective authors

Bordeaux, Jews of: II, 364; III, *61–62*; assist Bohemian Jewry, I, 305; examination of slaughterers among, III, 138, 217; meaning of *ancien* among, III, 120; patriotic prayers of, II, 143–44; petitions of, I, 266; Sephardic-Ashkenazic divisions among, II, 18–19; synagogues of, I, 262–64, 266; III, 151; wine exports of, II, 163–64

Borja (Aragon), emigration restrictions in, II, 15

Bosnia, Jews of, III, 36

Boston, Jews of, help New York synagogue, II, 136

Boucher, de (French intendant), I, 263

Boulé, Palestinian, and taxation, I, 134–35; III, 25, 27. *See also* Councils; Elders

Boundaries, local, of Jewish communities, I, 283; II, 4, 18

Bourg, Jewish leper in, III, 155

Bourgeois nationalism, Jewish, modern, II, 4. *See also* Middle class

Bourges, new synagogue in, I, 219–20

Bouzygian imprecations, and Jewish charities, III, 25. *See also* Curses

Boycott: and price control, II, 161; and tenant protection, II, 293, 295; as Church sanction, I, 234; of excommunicates, II, 230; of Helicz press, II, 204

Brandenburg, *see* Prussia

Brazil, Jews of, I, 255; III, 58–59, 129

Bread: excise taxes on, II, 260; "of the synagogue," II, 321. *See also* Unleavened bread

Bremen: exclusion of Jews from, I, 277–78; III, 63; guilds in, I, 372

Breslau: and Leipzig fairs, III, 149; and Polish Jewry, I, 324, 332; II, 63; Church Council of, I, 225; II, 125; III, 54; fairs of, II, 263; Jewish cemeteries in, III, 156; Jewish letter carrier in, III, 141

Bribery, *see* Corruption

Bricks, and Polish taxes, II, 273

Bridegrooms: and parental approval, II, 310; benediction of, III, 46

Brides: communal support of, I, 362–65; II, 265, 332–33; III, 212–13; dances with, II, 315; wigs of, III, 203. *See also* Betrothals; Marriage; Weddings

Bridges, communal surveillance of, II, 291

Briefs, legal, discouraged by rabbis, II, 238; III, 180. *See also* Attorneys

Briele, Judah b. Eliezer, on synagogue illumination, II, 144

Brihuega (Spain), fair at, I, 236

Bristol, Jews of, I, 259

British Empire, Jewish community in, I, 20–21. *See also* Colonies; England

Broadsides, Jewish, of sumptuary ordinances, II, 304

Brody, Jews of, II, 263; III, 149, 151, 209

Brokerage, *see* Marriage brokerage

Bronze Age, Palestinian, I, 31
Brotherhoods, Jewish, *see* Associations
Bruna, Israel b. Ḥayyim: and bans, II, 232; III, 178; controversy of, III, 100; incarceration of, II, 285–86; on cantors, II, 103; III, 136; on changes in endowments, III, 189; on charities, III, 218; on dancing, III, 206; on head covering, III, 202; on horse races, III, 207; on insults to scholars, II, 79; on Palestine pilgrimages, II, 339; III, 215; on preaching, III, 134; on taxation, III, 193–94
Brussa (Turkey), Jews of, I, 172; III, 49
Brussels, desecration of cemetery in, III, 154
Brześć, Jews of: and Councils, I, 325, 328; chief rabbinate of, II, 87; decrees on, I, 272; elections of, II, 47; Palestine pilgrims from, II, 341; quota of brides among, II, 333; settlement of, II, 22, 331
Budapest, Jews of: I, 26, 157, 349; Sephardic endogamy among, II, 311
Budgets, communal: and deficits, I, 172; II, 273; and donation of candles, II, 259; and entry fees, II, 262; and legacies, II, 114–15; and taxes, I, 171; II, 257; III, 187, 191; charitable, II, 343–49; educational, II, 114–15, 188, 196; III, 166; in various regions (Islam), I, 171–72; (Metz), III, 192; (Nice), III, 189; (Poland), II, 273; III, 191; (Rome), II, 257, 346; III, 190; of Polish Council, I, 326–27; III, 84. *See also* Financial administration
Bugia (North Africa), Jews of, I, 205
Building committee, in London, II, 62
Building trades, Jewish, medieval, in Sicily, I, 368
Buildings, *see* Houses
Buitrago (Spain), Jewish hospital in, II, 329
Bukovina; meat taxes in, III, 186; private synagogues in, III, 143–44; regional communities in, III, 105
Bulgaria, ancient synagogue in, I, 83
Bullion dealers, guilds of, I, 365
Bund (Jewish socialist party), III, 4
Bureaucracy, ancient: III, 7; Babylonian, I, 69; Egyptian, I, 77, 105; Israelitic, I, 35–36, 38, 51; (and big landowners), I, 44; (and monarchy), I, 43; III, 7; Persian, I, 63–64, 71, 78; (and Elephantine), I, 71–72; (and taxation), I, 148; (Jews in), I, 73, 146; III, 13; Roman (and Jewish community), I, 108, 142; III, 19, 25; (and Jewish law), I, 96, 115, 127; (and Jewish privileges), I, 93; (epistolary style of), III, 29; (rapacity of), I, 88
communal: II, *52–122*; III, *118–42*; ancient, I, 64, 68, 73, 95–107; III, 18; and communal stability, II, 121; and congregational divisions, II, 20; and councils, I, 318, 328–29, 342; and elections, I, 329–30; II, 45, 63–64; and governmental appointment, I, 292; and Greek associations, III, 18; and majority principle, III, 110; and Muslim corruption, I, 166; and preachers, II, 97; and property qualifications, II, 29; and residence rights, II, 119; at academies, I, 180; combination of offices in, III, 24; controlled by Portuguese chief rabbi, I, 285–86; in various countries (France), I, 296; (Germany), I, 342, 364; (Islam), I, 166, 180; (Italy), I, 318; II, 10; (Poland-Lithuania), I, 328–30; II, 45, 63–64, 259; (Portugal), I, 285–86; (Spain), I, 292; loyalty to Councils of, I, 331; priests in, I, 97; ranks in, II, 106, 108–9; revenue of, II, 132, 165, 266; III, 128, 210; statistics of, II, 23–24, 117; III, 141; women in, I, 96–97
medieval and modern: Alsatian,

III, 88; and billeting, II, 268; and communal control, II, 355; and corruption, II, 247; III, 133; and court Jews, II, 357; and fee system, II, 85; Austrian (debts), I, 337; (funeral tolls), II, 153; (Moravian autonomy), I, 338–39; II, 43; French, III, 88, 120; Italian (bans), III, 178–79; (communal affairs), I, 275, 293, 317; (tax distribution), II, 279–80; Papal (bans), II, 232; (communal archives), III, 139; (communal finances), II, 256, 272; III, 122; (congregational divisions), III, 149; (elders), II, 59; (fees for elections), II, 36; (Roman statute), II, 20; Polish (Councils), I, 327–28, 333; (payments to), I, 333, 353–54; Prussian (assimilation), II, 360–61; (Jewish self-government), I, 337; II, 36; III, 220; (migrations), III, 98; Russian (communal debts), I, 337; Spanish (communal banishment), II, 9–10; (Jewish councils), I, 287; (Jews in), I, 289–90

Muslim: III, 39, 46; and Jewish ban, I, 172–73; Jews in, I, 159, 187; Persian models for, I, 158; rapacity of, I, 159–60, 164, 166, 170; II, 247; Turkish, and religious minorities, I, 195–97; II, 298. *See also* Government; *and under* respective offices

Burggraf (Friedberg), share in Jewish fines of, I, 343

Burghers, *see* Cities

Burgos (Spain), Jews of, I, 288–89, 368; II, 271; (converts), III, 66

Burgundy, Jews of, II, 16; III, 128

Burial, Jewish: ancient, I, 80, 94, 121; III, 16–17; and residence rights, II, 234; and taxation, II, 152, 171–72, 263, 284; charitable, I, 132, 136; II, 147, 320, 329. *See also* Burial societies; ceremonies of, I, 94, 121; II, 264; despite illegality, I, 263; dishonorable, II, 148, 156; III, 177. *See also* Donkey's burial; in Christian cemeteries, III, 61; in Palestinian soil, I, 120–21, 149; II, 339–40; model for Christian, III, 17; private, II, 148, 157; refusal of, I, 169; II, 284; successive, III, 155–56. *See also* Catacombs; Cemeteries; Funeral procession; Mourning

Burial societies, Jewish: I, *352–54*; II, 147, 155–56; III, *89–91*; and congregations, III, 88; and enforced burials, III, 157; and free burials, II, 330; and Roman brotherhoods, I, 372; III, 90; and sextons, II, 106; and specialization in funeral rites, I, 350; as communal creditors, I, 372; II, 272; heredity in, II, 17; Spanish, I, 362; III, 91, 120. *See also* Holy Association

Burriana (Spain), Jewish officials in, II, 102

Busachi (Sicilian family), II, 274

Business accounts, settlement in synagogue of, II, 127–28. *See also* Commerce

Busrah (Transjordan), Jews of, I, 164; III, 24

Busseto (Italy), Jewish conference in, III, 80

Bustanai (exilarch), I, 177; III, 39–40, 46

Butchers, Christian: and Jewish slaughtering, II, 108, 158; III, 137–38; and Jewish taxes, II, 160; guilds of, II, 258; III, 198

Jewish: ancient, I, 120; and Christian guilds, II, 258; III, 187; and slaughterers, II, 109; III, 186; license fees of, II, 258; trade restrictions of, II, 158–59, 301

Byzantine congregations, in Constantinople, I, 205

Byzantine Empire: Jews in, I, 195, *228–30*; III, 52; and academy of

Tiberias, I, 191; and caliphate, I, 158, 162; and Jewish liturgy, I, 192; captives from, II, 336; executioners in, III, 175; expulsions from, I, 209; guilds in, I, 365, 368; III, 94; influence on Islam of, III, 36; Jewish officials in, II, 58; III, 32; Jewish taxation in, I, 282; III, 54; outside European unity, I, 227; ritual in, II, 142; segregates Jews, II, 165; suppresses Jewish judiciary, I, 213, 249; III, 52; synagogues in, I, 114, 162, 229–30

Cabala and cabalists: II, 207; and communal control, II, 168; and Jewish preaching, III, 134; and Palestinian messengers, III, 110; and Sephardic ritual, II, 142; and Spanish chief rabbinate, I, 289; associations of, I, 354–55; III, 91–92; suppressed by Tunis cadi, III, 170

Caceres (Castile), and Jewish taxation, II, 250

Cacicavalli (cheese), communal monopolies of, II, 261

Cadis, Jewish, III, 50, 170, 175. *See also* Judiciary

Caesar, Julius, I, 107–8, 140

Cagliari, Sicilian chief rabbi in, III, 67

Cairo, Jews of: III, 38; and *ḥakambashi*, I, 190, 197; III, 49; and separatism, I, 185; and talmudic community, I, 156; desecration of cemeteries of, II, 151; rabbis of, I, 190–91. *See also* Fustat

Calabria: Jewish assembly in, I, 317; II, 41–42; tax defaulters in, II, 284

Calabrian congregation, in Salonica, I, 351

Calatayud, Jews of: II, 9, 74, 133, 275

Calcarenses, Roman congregation of, I, 81

Calendar regulation: by academies, I, 153–54; controversies over, I, 192–93; III, 30; patriarchal regulation of, I, 143–45; III, 30; permanent, I, 145

Caligula, Caius Julius Caesar (Roman emperor), I, 99, 109

Caliphate and caliphs: and *dhimmi* chiefs, I, 174, 178–79, 203; III, 40; and communal hierarchy, I, 187, 207; and exilarchate, I, 176–77, 183, 185; III, 41; and inquiries from academies, I, 180–81; and Jewish advisers, I, 165; and Jewish decentralization, I, 167, 189, 207, 210, 212; III, 50; and profusion of titles, I, 201; characteristics of, I, 158; Fatimid, Jews under, III, 32; influence on Jewish law of, I, 211; poll taxes of, I, 171, 188; position of readers under, II, 100; religious authority of, I, 228; seizure of orphans' property under, II, 331; synagogues under, I, 162–65. *See also* Cordova; Islam; *and under* respective countries, cities and rulers

Calixtus I (pope), I, 113

Calixtus II (pope), privilege of, I, 217–18

Calixtus III (pope), II, 150

Calligraphy, Hebrew, instruction in, II, 117. *See also* Reading; Writing

Callings, Jewish: and study, I, 135, 151; dignity of, I, 132, 139–40, 151; free choice of, I, 321; Muslim legislation on, I, 170

Muslim, attire of, I, 161. *See also* Craftsmen; Labor

Callinicum (Mesopotamia), synagogue in, I, 114

Cambridge (England), Jewish community in, I, 259

Camondo, Count Abraham, I, 197

Campagna, Jews of, III, 216

Campenses, Roman congregation of, I, 81

Canaanites, I, 32, 41, 43, 46, 48; III, 9

Cancellation of debts, royal, and communal debts, II, 271

Candia, Jews of: against government appointments, III, 136; against marriage of strangers III, 204; and outside ordinations, III, 131; conferences of, I, 319; II, 293, 315; III, 79, 96, 143; desecration of cemetery of, III, 154; economic regulation by, II, 163, 293; III, 96, 159, 187; executioners among, III, 175; interruption of prayers by, 112; obligatory attendance of, II, 28; III, 106, 143; ordinances on morals of, II, 215; III, 206; quorum at weddings of, III, 47; ransom of captives by, III, 213

Candles: and diversion of tithe, II, 344; and patriotic illumination, II, 144; in synagogues, II, 61, 134, 144; III, 146; taxes on, II, 259, 261

Candlestick, ritualistic, I, 91

Canon law: administration of, and sacerdotal functions, III, 124; against mixed sex relations, II, 312; doctrine of bans in, II, 229-30; flaunted in Spain, I, 236; influence on Italy of, I, 275; on conversion of minors, I, 222; on divorce of converts, II, 317; on trust in charity supervisors, II, 64; relations with Jews of, I, 221, 224; (banking), I, 244; (bans) II, 229; (congregational divisions), II, 19; (funerals), II, 155; (holidays), I, 236; (interest on communal loans), II, 269; (judiciary), I, 226; II, 241; (law), III, 150; (synagogue), II, 125; III, 53; (tenant protection), II, 293; (tithe), II, 254; validity of, I, 226

Canon purificationis, III, 54

Canons, of African Church, I, 229

Canterbury: Jewish community in, I, 259; Treaty of, II, 6, 90; III, 98. *See also* Ban of settlement

Cantors, *see* Ḥazzan

Capi, Jewish, II, 77. *See also* Elders

Capistrano, John, anti-Jewish agitation of, I, 321; III, 77, 79

Capital: flight of, II, 340; III, 103; shortage of, and interest rate, I, 334–35; taxation of, II, 253, 256–57, 260, 279

Capital crimes, and warrants for arrest, II, 227

Capital punishment, Jewish: I, 109, 111, 126–27; II, *221–24*; III, 37–38, 174; and burial, II, 156–57; and communal councils, I, 133; and illegal return, II, 9; and "irrevocable" bans, I, 271, 301; II, 228; for arbitrary tax immunities, II, 15; for attack on rabbi, II, 74–75; infrequency of, II, 223; in various regions (Islam), I, 169; (southern Italy), I, 230; (Spain), II, 71, 74–75; judges' discretionary powers in, I, 213; II, 71, 218, 241; of informers, I, 169, 235–36; State indemnity for, II, 15, 232; vs. mutilation, II, 223–24

non-Jewish: medieval (anti-Christian blasphemies), II, 339; (mixed sex relations), II, 312; Persian, of exilarch, I, 149; Portuguese, for Hebrew deeds, I, 241; II, 111; Roman, for violation of patriarchal papers, I, 144; Spanish, for illegal Jewish emigration, I, 233–34; Turkish, for refusal of royal appointment, I, 198

Capitalism: ancient, I, 155, 211; Arabian, I, 158, 211; influence on Jewish law of, I, 211; III, 173

modern: and ban of settlement, II, 9, 11; and Christian unity, I, 227; and guilds, I, 371–74; and *ḥazakah*, II, 294, 298; and Jewish community, I, 4; II, *351–66*; III, 173, *220–21*; and Jewish education, II, 181–82, 184; and judiciary, II, 215; and Third Estate, I, 274; fosters tax evasions, II, 288

Capitalization: of earnings, II, 254–55; of hereditary leaseholds, II, 295; III, 198

Capitoli, *see* Statutes
Capitulations, Turkish, I, 199; III, 101–2
Capons, Spanish taxes on, II, 249
Cappadocia, Assyrians in, I, 57
Cappelanus, in Valencia, II, 74. *See also* Rabbis
Capsali, Elijah b. Elkana, I, 195; III, 46, 106, 207
Capsali, Moses b. Elijah, I, 195–96, 230, 351; III, 46–47, 89, 135, 198
Captives: Gentile, Jewish ransom of, III, 214; Jewish (ancient), I, 63, 69, 79–80; (Babylonian and decentralization), I, 194; Protestant, and Catholic ransom, 214. *See also* Redemption of captives
Caracalla, Marcus Aurelius Antoninus (Roman emperor), III, 19
Carcassoni, David (Turkish deputy), I, 307; III, 73
Carcassonne, Montpellier Jews from, III, 100
Carcer judaicus, Jewish, in Lwów, II, 226. *See also* Prisons
Card games, I, 320; II, 316; III, 207. *See also* Gaming
Carlo (Savoy duke), and Jewish meat, II, 159
Carnival festivities, and dancing, II, 316
Carolingian Empire, *see* Frankish Empire
Carpenters, Jewish, I, 368; III, 41–42
Carpentras: bachelors in, III, 114; charities in, II, 325; III, 89, 213; election days in, III, 116; deputies from, I, 305; II, 115; membership rights in, II, 13; ritual of, II, 142; sale of meat in, II, 158; sumptuary laws in, II, 305; III, 201; synagogues in, I, 220–21; taxation in, II, 283; III, 104; travel restrictions in, II, 15
Carpet weavers, Jewish, in Alexandria, I, 78
Carvajal, Don Antonio Ferdinando de, I, 256
Carvajal, Donna Esther, I, 256
Casa de la merced, Jewish, II, 329. *See also* Hospitals
Casale, Jews of, III, 203
Caschisi (Jewish master builder), I, 368
Case work, importance of in Jewish law, II, 244
Casimir the Great (Polish king), I, 268, 324
Casiphia (Ktesiphon), Jewish chief of, I, 68
Cassel (city), Jews not admitted to, I, 343. *See also* Hesse-Cassel
Cassella method of self-assessment, II, 283; III, 194–96
Cassettes, in Reggio taxation, III, 196
Castigation, ritualistic, of distinguished citizens, II, 226. *See also* Flogging
Castile: and Jewish holidays, I, 236; cantors in, II, 103; chief rabbinate in, I, 288–90; debt bondage in, II, 226; destruction of Jewish property in, II, 271; discourages Jewish emigration, I, 234; education in, I, 357–58; II, 171–72; elections in, II, 46; execution of informers in, II, 223; free sex relations in, II, 312; hospitals in, II, 329; Jewish craftsmen in, I, 367–68; II, 275; Jewish statute of, III, 67. *See also* Valladolid, synod of; Jewish population in, III, 108; Jewish tenant protection in, II, 293; luxury of dress in, II, 303; professional rabbinate in, II, 73–75; regional conventions in, III, 65. *See also* Valladolid; respects minority laws, I, 237–38; restrictions on Jewish meat in, II, 159; suppresses Jewish judiciary, I, 239; II, 111; synagogues in, II, 139; (attendance), II, 126; (government interference), II, 125, 143; taxation in, II, 250, 253, 283–84; (churches), III, 55; (immu-

nities), II, 13–14, 275; war with Aragon of, III, 66; witnesses in, I, 241; II, 114. *See also under* respective provinces and cities
"Castilian" congregations in: Fez, III, 47, 201; Rome, II, 20; Salonica, I, 351; II, 50
Casuistry: Jewish, vs. Jesuit, II, 195; III, 168; Muslim, on synagogues, I, 163. *See also* Dialectics, rabbinic
Catacombs, Jewish, in Rome, I, 80, 94, 106; II, 147, 155; III, 17
Catalan congregation, in Salonica, I, 351; II, 50, 75, 202; III, 74, 142
Cataloguing of books, Jewish, II, 201
Catalonia: and Aragonese assemblies, I, 287–88; lay judiciary in, II, 70–71; new cemeteries in, II, 149; rabbinic responsa from, III, 176. *See also under* respective cities
Catania: Jews in, I, 238; II, 309–10; III, 113; minority laws in, I, 238
Catechumens, Jewish, *see* Converts; Houses
Catherine the Great (Russian empress), communal legislation of, II, 355
"Catholic consent," in Islam, I, 165
Catholic rites, and Jewish marriages, I, 263
Catholic services, English, Jewish attendance at, I, 255–56, 258
Catholicism, *see* Church, Catholic
Catholicos, Nestorian, I, 173–74; III, 39–40
Cattaveri, Venetian, and Jewish self-government, I, 275
Cattle, *Leibzoll* likened to tolls on, II, 264
Cattle-raising, ancient Palestinian, I, 32, 35, 37, 42–43
Cattle trade, Jews in, II, 159, 297
Cavadores, Saragossa society of, I, 353. *See also* Grave diggers
Cavafuessas, Huesca society of, I, 352–53. *See also* Grave diggers
Cavalchini (cardinal), III, 72
Cavalleria, Gonzalo de la (Saragossan convert), II, 116
Caves, Palestinian, I, 32
Caviar, Jewish law on, III, 159
Cayenne, Jewish community in, I, 265; III, 59, 62
Cefalù, bishop of, and Syracuse cemetery, III, 155–56
Celebrations, *see* Family; Festivities
Cemeteries, interdenominational: medieval occurrence of, III, 61, 153
Jewish, ancient: I, 93–94; and supercommunity, I, 106–7; legal protection of, I, 94, 109; location of, I, 93; ritual of, I, 121; supervisors of, I, 133
medieval and modern: II, 146–57; III, 152–58; and associations, III, 97; and burial of Gentiles, II, 148; and cantors' immunities of, II, 277; and convents, III, 61; and government non-recognition, II, 363–64; and judiciary, II, 211; and regional control, I, 283–84, 344; III, 153–54; and Spanish Holy War, II, 135–36; bequests for, II, 329; desecration of, I, 109, 218; II, 150–51, 155; III, 154–55; (forbidden by popes), I, 218; (Polish decrees on), I, 270; funds of, and education, II, 186; institutional rank of, II, 124; keepers of, II, 115; in various regions (America), I, 260; III, 60; (Brussels), III, 154; (England), I, 256; III, 59; (France), I, 263–65; III, 61–62; (Germany), I, 344; (Holland), I, 253; (Poland), III, 97; (Resettlement areas), I, 24; (Spain), II, 135–36; neighborhood use of, I, 283; private, short duration of, II, 148–49; III, 153; regional, communal control by, I, 283–84; II, 153; III, 153–54; Sephardic separatism in, II, 365; status of, I, 236–37, 253, 256, 260,

263–65; III, 126; tombstone inscription on, III, 126. *See also* Inscriptions; Tombstones
Cennini (cardinal), II, 291
"Censors," Jewish, II, 61. *See also* Auditors of accounts
Censorship, Christian: and anti-heretical benediction, I, 237; and Jewish books, I, 223–24, 237; II, 204; III, 54, 171; and Jewish preaching, II, 98–99; III, 134
  rabbinic: I, 224; III, 170; and Azariah de' Rossi, I, 308; and communal control, II, 77, 202; and Inquisition, II, 202; Ferrara resolution on, I, 321; limitations of, III, 49
Censures: ecclesiastical, for shielding synagogue, I, 220; Jewish, II, 211, 224; III, 41; (tax immunities), II, 14. *See also* Excommunication; Interdict
Census, of American congregations, I, 6. *See also* Congregations
Censuses of population: II, 38, 117; III, 106–8; and capitation tax, II, 252; in various regions (ancient Israel), III, 9; (France), III, 185; (Islam), I, 171; (Poland), II, 252; III, 184–85; reliability of, I, 171; II, 252; III, 184–85. *See also* Land; Population
Central administration, in ancient Israel, I, 41, 46, 51, 54
Centralization, communal: alleged boycott of, III, 71. *See also* Chief rabbis, German; and communal control, I, 20, 290–91, 295; II, 241–42, 352; and court organization, II, 241–42; apex in Portugal of, I, 285
  of worship: and ancient synagogues, I, 81, 92; at Temple, I, 40–41, 50–54, 90–91; (and Babylonian exile), I, 59–60. *See also* Deuteronomic reformation; Sanctuaries
"Century of beggary," eighteenth century as, I, 363
Cerdagne, county of, Jews in, II, 103
Ceremonies, religious, Jewish: and Gentiles, I, 82; and judiciary, II, 211; and names, I, 63; banquets at, II, 303; persistence of, I, 67. *See also* Family celebrations
Certificates, communal: for Avignon beggars, II, 325; for Polish merchants, III, 191
Cervera (Spain), and Jewish funeral processions, II, 153
Chairman of council of elders, I, 99; II, 55
Chairs, monopolies in, II, 299
Chajes, Gerson b. Abraham (Moravian chief rabbi), III, 85
Châlons-sur-Marne, and Troyes synod, I, 312; III, 75
Châlon-sur-Saône, and Troyes synod, III, 75
Chamber of commerce, Jewish, in medieval Algiers, I, 366
Champagne: fairs of, and Jewish synods, I, 322; Jews in, I, 245; (ban of settlement), II, 6; (cemeteries), III, 154
"Chancellors," Jewish: French, II, 118; Portuguese, I, 285. *See also* Scribes
Change of venue, rabbinic teachings on, II, 242; III, 180
Chants, in synagogue, *see* Ḥazzan; Music
Chapels, Christian, of guilds, I, 369. *See also* Churches
Character building, Jewish, vs. intellectual training, II, 190
Charities, Christian: I, 5; III, 93, 218; and associations, I, 360–61; and Crusades, III, 93; and *monti di pietà*, I, 275; denominational character of, I, 9
  communal, ancient: I, 131; III, 17, *25–26*; and budgetary deficiencies, III, 18, 26; and burial societies, I,

353–54; and Graeco-Roman philanthropy, I, 80; III, 25; and support of scholars, I, 139; effectiveness of, I, 116

communal, medieval and modern: I, 7; II, *319–50*; III, 90, *209–19*; Alsatian statistics of, II, 117; and burial, II, 147, 154, 156–57, 264; and educational responsibilities, I, 360; II, 169, 173, 175, 185, 189; and migration of poor, II, 16–17; and new residents, III, 102; and property taxes, II, 280; and rabbinic salaries, II, 81; and support of scholars, I, 194; II, 81, 172; and synagogue quarrels, III, 150; and wedding fees, II, 119; contributions of poor to, I, 172; distribution of, II, 320; embrace transients and Gentiles, I, 136; excessive budgets for, II, 349–50; gradations in, II, 333; guild collections for, I, 370; idea of, I, 120, 131; in Paris, III, 62; Palestinian messengers' contributions to, II, 342; rabbinic restrictions on, II, 325, 345; share in fines of, II, 234–35; vs. individual begging, II, 321. *See also* Associations, charitable; Begging; Philanthropists; Public charges

intercommunal and interterritorial: I, 164, *305–7*, 313, 323, 333; III, 216; and branch societies, I, 364; and Polish councils, I, 331; and Salonican Talmud Torah, I, 348–49; and synods, I, 310. *See also* Palestine relief; Redemption of captives

Charity overseers, Jewish: I, 102, 133; II, 55; III, 209; accounting of, II, 64; III, 218; and congregational divisions, III, 88; and female domestics, II, 333; and legacies, II, 264; III, 212–13; and new arrivals, II, 12; and obligatory collections, I, 363; and *Pletten*, II, 322. *See also* Pletten; and revenue from burials, II, 154, 157. *See also* Burials; Cemeteries; arduous distribution by, I, 133; assign visitors for sick, II, 328; begging in person by, II, 346; discretion of, III, 210; effect of curses on, II, 348; election of, II, 47, 60, 63; establish mortgages, III, 196; in various regions (Alsace), II, 119; (Avignon), II, 61; (France), I, 305; III, 62; (Islam), I, 172, 194; (Italy), I, 363; III, 212–13; (Lithuania); II, 40, 47; (London), II, 62; (Poland), I, 331; II, 63; marital preferences for, I, 124; personal responsibility of, II, 348–49; III, 18; property qualifications of, II, 40; rabbinic supervision of, II, 330–31; single or three, II, 55, 57; women as, I, 349; II, 37; III, 114. *See also* Overseers

Charlemagne, and Narbonne Jewry, III, 68

Charles I (Sicilian king), III, 67–68

Charles II (English king), answers Jewish petition, I, 258

Charles VI (French king), maintains converts' property, I, 247

Charles of Valois (French prince), and Jewish procureurs, I, 296

Charles IV (Holy Roman emperor): against change of venue, II, 243; against free elections, II, 35; and excommunicate's property, II, 230–31; and regional community, I, 298; III, 71

Charles V (Holy Roman emperor): appoints chief rabbi, I, 299; expels Marranos, I, 253; penal code of, II, 235

Charters, *see* Constitutions; Ordinances; Statutes

Chastisement of children, rabbinic regulations on, I, 126; II, 198, 200; III, 169. *See also* Discipline, educational

Chatting: in churches, III, 151; in synagogues, II, 105, 141; III, 148. *See also* Decorum

Checks and balances, constitutional, II, 167–68. *See also* Communal control
Cheese, excise taxes on, II, 260–62
Chełm, Jews in, I, 301; III, 81
Chelm Segal, Abraham, rabbinic contract of, III, 131
Chess games, Jewish participation in, III, 207
Chest, communal (*Kuppah*), universality of, II, 320
Chests: electoral, II, 45; for Palestine relief, spread of, II, 340–41; for *Pletten*, II, 322; for taxes, III, 12, 195. *See also* Cassella; Korobka
Chicago, Jews in, I, 26
Chickens, Spanish taxes on, II, 249
Chief of Islam (Turkish), and synagogues, III, 36
Chief rabbinate *and* chief rabbis: and bankers, II, 81; and bans, II, 229, 231; and charities, II, 330; and congregational divisions, I, 336, 351; II, 20, 95; and control of academies, II, 95; and Councils, I, 332; II, 62; III, 85; and court Jews, II, 81; and dancing, II, 315–16; and education, II, 172, 194; and evolution of rabbinate, II, 74–75, 82, 244; and government appointments, II, 218–19; III, 135–36; and interterritorial action, I, 308; II, 229; and lay leadership, II, 76; and majority principle, II, 27–28; and price control, II, 161; and signatures of artists, III, 147–48; authority of, I, 236; II, 8, 352; Byzantine antecedents of, I, 230; controversies over, I, 310–11; III, 66, 68–69, 126; elections to, II, 42–43; exclusion of natives from, I, 333; influence of, I, 346–47.
in various regions: Austria, III, 126; Bohemia, I, 299, 339–41; II, 52, 81; III, 85–86; (Prague), I, 339–40; III, 127–28; England, I, 20, 245, 297–98, 311; II, 109; III, 69; France, I, 296–97, 308; III, 68–69; (controversy), III, 66, 68–69, 126; Galicia, III, 72, 85, 128; Germany, I, 245, 298–300, 310–11, 314, 341–45; II, 231; III, *69–71*, *86–88*, 127, 138; Hamburg, II, 48–49, 62, 229; Hesse-Cassel, I, 341–43; II, 330; Kairowan, I, 181; Kleve, I, 341–44; Lithuania, I, 300–2; III, 193; Mediterranean lands, I, 284–95, 346–47; Moravia, I, 300, 337–39, 341; II, 8, 27–28, 42–43, 81, 85, 95, 161, 268; III, 85, 147–48; Poland, I, 300–3, 332–33, 336; II, 42, 80, 82–83, 95, 194, 218–19; III, 71–72; Portugal, I, 236; II, 74; III, 65, 71; Sicily, I, 292–95, 316–17, 319; II, 76, 304; III, 67; Spain, I, 288–92; II, 75, 82, 218–19, 334; III, 65–66, 71, 182; (Aragon), I, 310; (Castile), I, 310; II, 172, 276; Turkey, I, 190, 195–99, 230, 351; II, 20, 75, 352; III, *46–50*, 135–36, 198; Wied-Runkel, II, 315–16
protect Jewish autonomy, III, 182, 198; provincial vs. central, I, 300–3, 337–45; prohibition of criticism of, II, 48–49; redemption of captives by, II, 334; replace *nagid*, I, 190; responsible for taxes, I, 245; II, 52, 268; (immunities), II, 80, 276; III, 193; revenue of, II, 82–83, 85; III, 127–28; sumptuary legislation by, II, 304; supervision of slaughterers by, II, 109; III, 138; vs. synods, I, 310–11, 314, 316–17, 319, 341. *See also* Rabbinate
Chiefs, *see* Elders
Chiefs, provincial, *see* Chief rabbinate; Elders; Exilarchate; *Nagid; Nasi;* Patriarchate; Provincial elders
"Child archon," I, 104
Childbirth: and gaming, II, 317; and sumptuary laws, II, 303

Childlessness: and divorce, II, 328; and inheritance of dowries, II, 318; and Palestine pilgrimages, II, 339–40; and polygamy, II, 309

Child marriages, half-hearted measures against, II, 310

Children, Israelitic: I, 42, 52, 65; in Babylonian exile, I, 63

Jewish: and collection of alms, II, 346; and membership rights, I, 104–5; II, 4–5, 7; III, 89; and mixed relations, II, 313, III, 61; and recitation of Decalogue, III, 22; and taxation, I, 159; II, 326; III, 103; blacklisting of, II, 185; conversion of, I, 306; III, 53; education of, I, 92; II, 144, 185, 205, 207; (age), I, 125–26; (associations), I, 356. *See also* Associations; (co-education), II, 178; (occupational training), I, 132; (responsibility for), II, 114, 169, 173, 175; (universal importance of), II, 170. *See also* Education; exilarchic rights on, I, 175; in *memor*-books, II, 146; legitimacy of, II, 240, 314–15; III, 206; limitations on chastisement of, III, 169. *See also* Chastisement; of Bustanai, I, 177; of excommunicates, II, 230; of rabbis, and local marriage, II, 86; payment for burial of, III, 158; position in synagogue of, I, 124; refugee, II, 337. *See also* Waifs; responsibility towards parents of, I, 127; support of, II, 325; testimony of, II, 297, 316

Chirograph offices, English, I, 251; II, 110–11; Jews at, II, 110–11. *See also* Scribes

Chmielnicki, Bohdan, revolt of, II, 8, 273; III, 73. *See also* Cossack revolts

Choirs, in synagogues, II, 105

Chorin, Aaron b. Kalman, I, 9; III, 159

Chorostków, Jewish burial society in, III, 90

Chosroes I Anushirvan (Persian king), I, 149; III, 36

Christ: passion of, and toleration of Jews, I, 220; universal body of, I, 227. *See also* Jesus

Christendom, western: apart from Byzantium, I, 227; concentration on land taxes in, II, 253; expansion of, I, 157, 225; Jewish interterritorial status under, I, 304; public education under, II, 171, 177–78

Christian education of youth, papal encyclical on, II, 170

Christian Hebraists: II, 177–78; and Jewish community, I, 304–5; and Jewish preaching, II, 98–99. *See also* Hebrew

Christiani, Fra Pablo, I, 186; III, 43

Christianity: and ceremonial law, I, 9; and charities, I, 5, 363; and Jewish magic, I, 237; and modern dictatorship, I, 13; and political power, I, 8; Jewish attacks on, forbidden, I, 222; teaching of, and suppression of synagogues, III, 53

Christians, medieval: alleged kidnapping of, II, 339. *See also* Libel, ritual; and chirograph offices, II, 110–11; and communal institutions, II, 157; and *ḥazakah* legislation, II, 298; and Jewish economy, II, 123, 299, 301; (loans), II, 248, 327. *See also* Banking; and Jewish wandering scholars, II, 187; and judicial biases, I, 250; as communal bookkeepers, II, 116; as customers of Jewish craftsmen, I, 367; as ghetto guards, II, 116; as landlords in ghetto, II, 295; as owners of Jewish slaves, II, 337; as owners of synagogue seats, II, 130–31; as slaves of Jews, I, 145; II, 309; associate with Jews, II, 316; III, 162, 316; attend synagogues and Jewish theatres, II, 130; III, 133, 207; hide banished Jews, II, 9–10; pilgrimages to Palestine by, II, 339. *See also* Church

Chroniclers: Christian, ancient, and Persian taxation, III, 32; Jewish (on redemption of captives), II, 334; (on Spanish chief rabbi), III, 66

Chronology, Jewish: and calendar regulation, III, 30; and decline of exilarchate, III, 32; and gaonate, III, 42; and higher criticism, III, 9; and Persian rule, I, 146; and synagogue ancestry, II, 130; of ancient records, I, 76; of Lithuanian Council sessions, I, 328

Chrysostom, John, Saint, I, 96, 112

Church, ancient: I, 87; III, 11, 21; and Hellenistic Jewry, I, 117; and Jewish burial, III, 17; and Jewish education, III, 16; and Jewish mission, I, 97, 145; and Jewish status, I, 107–8, *111–16*; and patriarchate, I, 144; and Persian festivals, III, 149; and Septuagint, I, 90; and synagogue attendance, I, 87, 103, 112; anti-Semitic trends in, III, 21; Fathers of, on Jews, I, 96, 112–14, 144, 216. *See also under* individual Fathers; in various regions (Egypt), III, 13; (Palestine), III, 27; (Persia), III, 31, 36, 149; (Rome), I, 12, 107; III, 14–15; separation from Judaism of, I, 87, 103, 111–12, 141

Catholic, medieval and modern, and Jews: autonomy, I, 13, 208, 222, 270; cemeteries, II, 150, 152; chief rabbinate, I, 289–90, 295; communal organization, I, 215–26; II, 74, 106; controversy with, I, 216–17, 224, 237; III, 58; councils and synods, I, 287, 309, 323–24, 333, 345; III, 208; economy (communal indebtedness), I, 334; II, 270–71, 273–74; III, 84, 190; (landownership), I, 234; II, 254; (tax farming), I, 235; education, I, 375; II, 170; Hebrew printing, III, 170–71. *See also* Censorship; heresies, I, 237, 288; II, 365; law, I, 156; II, 134, 210–11; III, 150; (deeds), I, 251; (Talmud), I, 305–6; III, 167–68; (wine), II, 161; legal status, I, 242, 244, 265, 275–76, 279, 282, 295; II, 254; III, 52, 77; preaching, II, 96, 98; rabbinate, II, 96, 98, 211, 239; III, 124; ritual meat, II, 107–8; 157–58; synagogues, II, 134; (attendance) II, 131; (height), I, 220; II, 139; III, 147; (illumination), II, 144; (loud prayers), II, 155; III, 148; (new) I, 219–20; II, 266; (private), II, 125; taxation, III, 55; (funeral tolls), II, 154; (immunities), II, 274; (tithes), II, 254; III, 185

and Marranos, I, 24; II, 364; and medieval uniformity, I, 216; and reconquest of Iberian peninsula, I, 157; and state, I, 8, 11, 114, 222; II, 43, 358; brotherhoods of, III, 93; charities of, I, 5, 360–61; II, 346; control of weddings by, II, 83–84; educational responsibilities of, II, 170; effects of Jewish practices on, I, 221; Enlightenment's attacks on, II, 360; interterritorial character of, I, 13; in various countries (America), I, 262; (England), I, 258–59, 276; (France), I, 265, 295; II, 254; (Germany), I, 323; II, 103; (Holland), I, 254–55; (Italy), I, 231, 275; (Poland), I, 220, 270, 323–24, 333–34; II, 271, 273–74; III, 84, 190; (Sicily), I, 295; (Spain), I, 157, 234–35, 279, 287, 289–90; II, 74, 150; requires testimony, I, 209; reverence for tradition of, I, 209. *See also* Censorship; Christianity; Clergy; Councils; Inquisition; Papacy; Papal states; Synods; *and under* respective countries

Eastern: and conversion of synagogues, I, 230; and Islam, I, 157–58; and Muslim bureaucracy, I, 187; and Muslim taxes, I, 170–71; and Turkish state, I, 197, 199; resents exilarchs, I, 176; III, 40–41; self-government of, I, 173–74, 178, 191; III, 40, 41

Protestant: and charities, I, 5; II, 347; and Christian unity, I, 227; and Jewish elections, II, 36; and Marrano communities, I, 24; and political power, I, 8; and Reform Judaism, I, 9; and state intervention, I, 11; Anglican, and British government, I, 20; Dutch (against synagogues), III, 58; (Jewish charities), II, 347; French in West Indies, III, 62; opposed to Jewish burial in America, III, 152

Churches (structures): I, 103, 162; converted from synagogues, I, 230, 237; III, 53, 151; height of, I, 112; imposts on Jewish burials for, I, 253; Jewish attendance in, I, 252, 255–56, 258, 260; III, 53; Jewish institutions removed for, II, 150; Jewish remainders in, II, 151, 155; III, 147; lack of decorum in, III, 151; not centers of private life, II, 144; tax immunities of, I, 11

Cid Campeador (Rodrigo Diaz de Bivar), III, 91

Cilicia, Jews in, I, 120

Cinque scuole, Roman, I, 350; III, 149

Circulating libraries, Jewish, II, 202. *See also* Libraries

Circumcisers, Jewish, II, 115

Circumcision: and excommunication, II, 234; III, 177; and mixed relations, II, 312; associations for, I, 362; attendance at, II, 90, 304; denounced by Dutch Reformed Church, I, 254; despite baptism, I, 263; imposts on, II, 171–72; of proselytes, I, 145; refusal of, I, 169; II, 14, 284; Roman prohibition of, I, 108; synagogue rites at, II, 115, 145

Citadels, Persian, and Palestinian city walls, III, 8

Cities, ancient, oriental: I, 31; Assyrian, III, 18; Babylonian, I, 119; Canaanite, I, 33, 41, 43; Egyptian, III, 7, 18; Persian, I, 148; III, 8

Graeco-Roman: I, 55; constitutional forms of, I, 75, 99, 118; councils of, I, 133; foundation of, III, 13; individualism in, I, 137; Jewish settlements in, I, 75; officials of, I, 102; III, 13; Palestinian, I, 119

Israelitic: I, *31–54*; administration of, I, 43, 48, 51, 62, 70, 86; III, 6–10. *See also* Elders; aliens in, I, 46–48; and Babylonian Exile, I, 59, 67; III, 11; and Babylonian synagogues, I, 66–67; and Jerusalem, I, 50; craftsmen's quarters in, I, 364; Deborah on, I, 45; gates of, I, 42; (assemblies), I, 48, 70, 86; (judicial proceedings), I, 48, 51; (synagogues), I, 61; migrations into, I, 50; slaves in, I, 46; social stratification in, I, 48; terminollogy of, I, 31; III, 8; walls of, I, 33–34, 42; III, 8

Jewish, ancient: I, 135; and Hellenistic cities, I, 119; III, 13; and Roman taxes, I, 129, 137–38; councils of, I, 133–34; courts of, I, 128–29. *See also* Judges; population of, I, 134; III, 27; religious functions of, I, 134; walls of, I, 137

medieval and modern: I, 7, 10, 22, 26, 270–71, *274–81*; II, 3; against mixed sex relationships, II, 312; and communal control, I, 299, 315, 323–24, 333; II, 24, 35, 62, 358; and craftsmen, I, 368–69, 371; III, 119; and equality, I, 231–32; and funeral processions, I, 253; II, 153; and judiciary, I, 238–39, 250, 279; II, 111, 208, 249–50; and legalization of Jewish worship, I, 253–55; and Marranos, I, 253; and notaries, II,

111; and real estate, II, 292; and ritual meat, II, 107–8, 158–59; III, 137–38. *See also* Butchers; and taxation, I, 235; II, 249–50, 257, 263; III, 184; (tax farming), I, 235; II, 284; and transfer of Jews, I, 231; and wine administration, II, 162; area of, and community, I, 283; charities in, I, 360; II, 347, 349; compete with Jews, I, 234; II, 204; contest royal power over Jews, I, 276; differing from Palestinian, I, 31, 42; economic concentration of, I, 274; II, 291, 301; extradition treaties of, I, 246; gates of, II, 291; houses of ill-repute in, II, 313–14; indirect elections in, II, 44

in various regions: America, I, 31, 42; II, 347; Baltic lands, III, 65; England, I, *276;* III, 63; Germany, I, 246, *276–78;* III, 57, 63–64, 69; (book trade), II, 204; (communal organization), II, 35, 62; III, 142; (ghetto architecture), III, 154; (massacres), I, 277; (meat), II, 158. *See also* Butchers; (real estate), I, 292; (regional community), II, 299, 315; (struggle for liberation), I, 276–77; (students), III, 166; (taxation), II, 250; III, 184; Italy, I, 231, *274–76*, 279; III, *63–64*; (equality), I, 231–32; (meat), III, 137; Lithuania, III, 186; Malta, III, 119; Moravia, I, 339; Netherlands, I, 253–55; III, 58; (cemeteries), I, 253; (Marranos), I, 253; Palestine (people's community), I, 17; Poland, I, *279–81*; III, 64–65, 186; (as creditors), I, 334; (controled by nobles), I, 269–70; (councils), I, 323–24, 333; (*de non tolerandis Judaeis*), II, 270–71; (German attitudes), I, 267, 270; (guilds), I, 369, 371; (mixed litigations), I, 272; (promote anti-Semitism), III, 64; (sales taxes), II, 263; Prussia, II, 358; Sicily, I, 238, 279; II, 111, 249; Spain, I, 234, 238, *278–79*; II, 24; III, 64; (communal gatherings), II, 24; (craftsmen), I, 368; (fairs), I, 236; (funeral processions), II, 153; (judiciary), I, 239; (meat), II, 159; (taxation), I, 235; II, 257; U. S. S. R., I, 15

Maimonidean terminology for, III, 160–61; mixed litigations in, I, 272; oligarchic trends in, II, 50–51; III, 142; opposed to massacres, I, 277; ordinances of, I, 215; promote anti-Semitism, III, 64; struggle for liberation of, I, 276–77; support students, III, 166; sumptuary laws in, II, 302; III, 202; walls of, II, 291; (Jewish defense), II, 267; (Jewish tombstones), II, 155; (location of cemetery), II, 149–50

Citizenship, Jewish: III, 54–55; in Italy, I, 228, 231–32, 243; of Turkish chief rabbis, III, 49; under Rome, I, 228. *See also* Emancipation

Citrons: communal administration of, II, 22, 164–65; proportionate contributions to, II, 101; III, 160, 187; rabbinic revenue from, II, 84–85; III, 126; taxes on, II, 260; III, 187

"City of origin," principle, I, 206. *See also* Landsmannschaft

Cives, Jews as, *see* Citizenship

Civil law, Jewish: II, *213–16*; adjustments of, II, 69; administration of, I, 126–27; II, 79, 211–12, 241; (lay judges), II, 70–72. *See also* Judges; Judiciary; and academy controversies, I, 152; and Commercial Revolution, II, 76; and "law of the kingdom," II, 210; and rabbinic ordination, I, 155; and Sicilian chief rabbis, I, 293; controled by Venice, I, 275–76; impersonal inquiries in, II, 238; Israelitic codes of, I, 52; neglected in Byzantium, I, 213, 229; Spanish respect for, I, 238; supremacy of

social interest in, II, 245, 331; systematic nature of, II, 219
Civil War: American, III, 4; Castilian, II, 271; Polish, II, 261
Clans, Israelitic: admission to, I, 47; III, 12; and Babylonian synagogues, I, 66; III, 11; and charity, I, 131; and sanctuaries, I, 49; congregational units of, I, 66; III, 11, 14; Deborah on, I, 45; dissolution of, I, 47, 50; elders of, I, 48; migrations of, 47; ownership of, I, 43
Class divisions: and differences in attire, I, 161; II, 307; (sumptuary laws), II, 302, 305; and charitable contributions, I, 360; II, 321–22; and incidence of taxation, II, 278–80, 287; and talmudic community, I, 119; in ancient Israel, I, 40, 45–46, 48; (Babylonian Exile), I, 59. *See also* Middle class; Oligarchy; Proletariat
Class struggle, Jewish: I, 16; ancient, I, 35–36, 38, 45, 50–52, 54, 135, 148; and billeting of soldiers, III, 189; and communal dissolution, I, 165–66, 168; II, 353–54; and communal oligarchy, I, 24; and fiscal inequalities, I, 148; II, 278–80, 287; III, 197; and guild system, I, 367–68, 371; III, 97; and majority principle, II, 27; III, 109; and massacres, I, 277; and Polish councils, I, 336; and preachers, II, 98; and statutes, II, 3; III, 111
Classes, educational, *see* Schools
Classis, *see* Church Council, Dutch
Claudios Tiberios Polycharmos (founder of synagogue), I, 84; III, 15
Claudius, Tiberius Drusus Nero Germanicus (Roman emperor), I, 80, 92, 106; III, 13–14, 18, 31
Clavarii, Spanish, II, 241. *See also* Elders
Cleanliness, provisions in ghetto for, II, 178; III, 197
Clement VI (pope), I, 233
Clement VII (pope), and Roman statute, II, 20
Clement VIII (pope), and meat taxes, II, 257
Cleopatra, I, 77
Clergy, Christian: and Church art, II, 137; and investiture of cantor, II, 103; and Jew-baiting, I, 244, 279. *See also* Anti-Semitism; and money-lending, I, 244; II, 273; and rabbinic functions, I, 361; III, 124–25, 151; and status of Jewish teachers, II, 184; competes with Jews, I, 234; familiarity with prayer-books of, II, 178; Jewish instructors of, II, 177; jurisdiction over Jews of, I, 216, 248, 250; (transfers of Jews), I, 231; III, 55; revenue of (fees), II, 85; (Jewish fines), III, 179; taxes mendicant friars, II, 254; vs. laity, I, 361; III, 151. *See also* Bishops; Church; Papacy; Patriarchate
Clerks, communal: and convocation of assemblies, II, 25; and legal procedure, II, 240; vs. beadle, III, 137. *See also* Shammash
Clothing: change of, and study, II, 177; charitable distribution of, I, 132, 136; II, 320, 324; (associations for), I, 362; (pupils), II, 187–90; (redemption of captives), II, 333; (refugees), II, 8; communal regulations on, II, 306–7; industry of, I, 365, 368. *See also* Tailors; of opposite sex, and masquerading, III, 206; sumptuary restrictions of, II, 302–4; III, 202; taxes on, II, 248–49, 261; under Islam, I, 161
"Clouds of locusts," Polish teachers as, II, 183–84
Clubhouses, communal, II, 167
Coal, Spanish taxes on, II, 249
Cobblers, Jewish, Spanish: as judges, I, 368; guilds of, I, 367; III, 95
Coblenz, Jews of, and regional community, III, 87

Code of Justinian: I, 115; and Bible recitation, I, 123; II, 52; III, 22–23, 150; and communal organization, III, 19; (courts), III, 21; (elders), II, 52; III, 32, 118; (price regulation), I, 130; III, 25; and Jewish ceremonies, I, 230; II, 143; and Jewish witnesses, I, 229, 251; and Theodosian Code, I, 229; discriminatory laws in, III, 54; influence on France of, I, 251; prohibits oral law, I, 191; II, 52; III, 45, 150

Code of Theodosius: I, *112–15*; against destruction of synagogue, I, 219; III, 21; and Code of Justinian, I, 229; and communal organization (Cologne), III, 27; (courts) III, 20–21; (guilds), I, 365; III, 94; (officials), III, 15; (price regulation), I, 130; III, 25; and Jewish shipmasters, I, 365; and Palestinian patriarchate, III, 30

Codes: Napoleonic, logical consistency of, II, 245; Portuguese, include tax laws, III, 183

rabbinic: and changing conditions, II, 208, 215–16; (local customs), II, 70, 213; and educational responsibilities, II, 170, 174; and preaching, II, 98; and ritual meat, II, 160; and sumptuary ordinances, II, 304; on accounting by elders, II, 348; section on family life in, II, 319. *See also* Jacob b. Asher; Karo, Joseph; Maimonides, Moses

Co-education, Jewish, prohibitions of, II, 177–78. *See also* Women

Coesfeld, Jews of, III, 87

Cofem, Don Judah (Portuguese chief rabbi), III, 65

Coffee, and Jewish sumptuary laws, II, 305

Cohen, B., Amsterdam bequests of, I, 363

Coins: communal ordinances on, III, 199; Maccabean, on *ḥeber ha-ʿir*, I, 134; Roman, and Palestinian paganism, III, 27

Cok Hagin, excommunication of, II, 230

Colbert, Jean Baptiste, for toleration of Jews, I, 265; III, 62

Coliseum, Jewish adornment of, III, 52

Collectas, Spanish: and dependent settlements, II, 20; and foreign assemblies, I, 319; III, 75; and right of asylum, III, 143; and tax declarations, II, 281; in Aragon, I, 286–87; III, 155. *See also* Colletta; Regional community

Collections, charitable: by associations, I, 363; for Palestine relief, II, 341; for redemption of captives, II, 334–35; monthly, II, 132, 341; of synagogue vows, II, 132; weekly, II, 335, 341

Colleges: and Jewish dormitories, II, 187; Jewish, Sicilian, I, 317. *See also* Academies; Universities

Collegia, Roman, I, 107–8. *See also* Associations

Collegium tenuiorum, I, 101

Colletta, Jewish, Sicilian, I, 317. *See also* Collecta; Regional community

Cologne, Jews of: ancient, I, 83; III, 15; and court of defendant, I, 250; and Frankfort assembly, I, 323; and government appointment of cantor, II, 103; III, 135–36; attestation of *ḥazaḳah* by, II, 294; elders of, III, 122; (bishops), III, 130; hospitals of, II, 329; (Christian), II, 327; household employees of, II, 299; interruption of prayers by, II, 34; quarter of, III, 63; rabbis of, I, 299; registry of real estate of, I, 277; II, 292; III, 63; stained glass windows of, II, 138; stone masons among, II, 145

Colon, Joseph b. Solomon: against lending synagogue ornaments, III,

145–46; against parental interference in marriage, III, 204; and lay leadership, II, 77; and Nuremberg synod, I, 313–14; II, 243; III, 77; and redemption of captives, II, 333; III, 213; on changes in endowments, II, 266; III, 189; on charitable tithes, III, 217; on excommunicate's property, II, 230–31; III, 177; on *hekdesh*, III, 211; on Jewish prisoners, III, 214; on obligations of new residents, III, 102; on quorum at weddings, III, 47; on private bans, II, 79; III, 126; on private worship, II, 125; III, 142; on status of rabbis, III, 126; on taxation, III, 195–96; (Gentile interference), II, 283; III, 195; threatens ban in Germany, II, 243

Colonies, American, Jews in: autonomy of, I, 374; II, 365; British, I, 23, 259–62; II, 365; Dutch, I, 255, 260; II, 347, 365; III, 58; French, I, 23, 265–66; II, 365; III, 62. *See also under* individual colonies

foreign, in ancient Orient, I, 55, 72, III, 10; (Jewish), I, 59, 69–73. *See also* Babylonian Exile; Dispersion; Elephantine; Exile; Migrations

Venetian, Jewish history in, III, 73, 154

Colonization: German, in Poland, I, 267; Jewish (Palestine), I, 17; III, 215–17; (U. S. S. R.), I, 15

Columbia University Library, manuscripts in, II, 200

Combination of offices, I, 126; II, 103, 111

Comedies, Jewish, Italian, II, 167, 207

Comes, Roman, I, 113

Comforting of mourners, communal responsibility for, II, 147

"Commander of Jewry," Josel of Rosheim as, I, 299. *See also* Chief rabbinate

"Commander of the Jews," in Münster, I, 345. *See also* Provincial elders

Commemorations: Exilic gatherings for, I, 61; synagogue rites at, II, 145

Commenda, Jewish, Spanish, II, 248

Commentaries, Hebrew: and Talmud, II, 216; vs. teachers' control, II, 180–81. *See also* Literature, Hebrew

Commerce, ancient: I, 31, 55; III, 10, 23; Assyrian, I, 57; Hellenistic, I, 55, 75; Israelitic, I, 40, 42, 46, 56–57; Jewish, I, 67, 126, 138–39; (Babylonian Exile), I, 63; (Elephantine), I, 70; (Palestinian synagogues), I, 120; (records of), I, 93

Jewish, medieval and modern: and burghers, I, 274–75, 281, 373; II, 253; III, 94; and cattle trade, II, 159; and communal indebtedness, III, 191; and communal control, I, 224–25, 248; II, 63; (license fees), II, 262; (restrictions), II, 14, 22; (support), II, 361; and communal office, II, 48, 64; and communal unity, I, 167; and educational responsibilities, II, 175; III, 162; and exclusion of aliens, II, 8; and excommunicate, I, 169; and fish, III, 159; and growth of population, I, 259; and judicial intermediaries, II, 237–38; and Iberian toleration, I, 241; and meat monopoly, II, 108–9; and migrations, III, 103, 215; and Palestine relief, II, 341; and Polish councils, I, 322, 324; and price-fixing, II, 301; and rabbinic privileges, II, 80, 278; III, 128; and redemption of captives, II, 335–36; and seizure of property, II, 234, 331; and taxation, I, 159, 175; II, 20–21, 253–54, 265; III, 188; and wine administration, II, 162–63; complexity of, and Jewish law, I, 200, 210; II, 76, 237–39, 362; familiarity with, and lay arbitrators, II, 215;

feminine participation in, II, 179, 314; insecurity of, and rabbis, II, 92; international aspects of, I, 168, 210, 275, 290, 324, 365; III, 188; in various regions (Caliphate), I, 159, 167–69, 175, 210; (England), I, 259; (French colonies), I, 266; (Germany), II, 25–26, 89, 164; (Italy), I, 275; II, 3–4, 6, 11, 48, 76, 298, 335–36; (Lithuania), II, 22; (Poland), I, 281, 324, 332–33; II, 6, 63, 80–82; (Sarajevo), II, 13; (Sicily), II, 162; (Spain), I, 241; II, 14, 20–22, 163; preferable to teaching, III, 42; rabbis' share in, II, 80–82; III, 42. *See also* Banking; Capitalism; Merchants

Commercial instruments, communal regulations on, II, 301. *See also* Deeds

Commercial Revolution: and charitable associations, I, 363; and Jewish judiciary, II, 215, 237–38, 362; and rabbinic position, II, 76, 89; and Resettlement, I, 242–43, 252; and synods, I, 323; and Jewish tenant protection, II, 295

Commercialization: of *ḥazaḳah*, II, 297; of learning (medieval protests), I, 181–82; (tax immunities), I, 138

Commissions of brokers, communal regulation of, II, 319. *See also* Marriage brokerage

Committees, communal: I, *99–100*; and drafting of statutes, II, 30, 55, 57; III, 110–11; educational value of, II, 206; of academies, I, 154; of Moravian lay judges, II, 88; of Salonican rabbis, II, 75; of tax assessors, II, 286; of Ten (Rome), II, 59; of Twelve (London), II, 62; of Twenty (Leghorn), II, 61. *See also* Warsaw Committee

governmental: on communal debts, II, 273; "Jewish," in Russia, I, 13–14; papal, II, 256

Common Council of New York, against Jewish worship, I, 260–61

Common sense, and law finding, I, 128; II, 209

Commonwealth, Second: academies under, III, 161; urban transformations under, III, 8. *See also* Palestine, ancient

Communal center, *see* Center; Synagogue

Communal control: I, 115–16; II, 351; and acquired rights, II, 131, 295–96, 298. *See also* Acquired rights; Tenant protection; and anonymity of artists, III, 147; and associations, I, 372; II, 3; III, 96–97; (guilds), I, 368–72; III, 96. *See also* Associations; Guilds; and book production, II, 200–5. *See also* Books; Censorship; and cantors, II, 103–5; and Catholic intolerance, I, 224. *See also* Church; and excommunicate's property, II, 231; and extra-talmudic studies, II, 207; and individual guarantees of debts, III, 191; and institutionalized religion, II, 167–68; and interruption of prayers, II, 32–33; and legal creativity, II, 216; and licenses (marriage), II, 311, 319; (scribes), III, 140; (trade), I, 332–33; and prayer-books, III, 42; and preaching, II, 98–99; and price-fixing, II, 300–1; and prisoners, II, 338; and professional judiciary, II, 214–16; and provincial chiefs, III, 123; and residence rights, II, 5–8; III, 101; and ritual food, II, 160–61. *See also* Meat, ritual; Wine, ritual; and royal appointment of judges, II, 218–19; and royal immunities, II, 13–14; and segregation, I, 161–62; and synagogue assemblies, II, 144; and taxation, I, 137, 282; II, 247–48, 283, 285, 289; and teaching profession, II, 180,

183–85, 196–97; self-imposed rules on, I, 259, 266; spiritual, of rabbis, I, 150; supported by Dutch government, I, 255. *See also* Administration, communal; Charities; Economic regulation; Education; Elders; Financial administration; Judiciary; Property; Religion; Responsibility; Social welfare; Synagogues; Taxation

Communism: Persian, and persecutions of Jews, I, 149; Russian, and Jewish community, I, 15–17

Community, meaning of term of, III, 3

Community chest, investigation by, I, 132. *See also* Charities

Community of goods, marital, II, 210

Company, military, as a Jewish communal unit, I, 71

Competence of courts, controversies over, II, 241. *See also* Judiciary

Competition, economic: and acquired rights, II, 293–94, 296–97; III, 198; and bachelors, II, 18; and ban of settlement, II, 5-7; and biblical taboos, II, 297; and communal control, II, 361; and guilds, I, 366, 368–69; and Hebrew printing, II, 202–4. *See also* Book Trade; and hiring of servants, III, 200; and Judeo-Christian relations, I, 274, 366, 368–69; II, 204, 265; (England), I, 276; (Poland), I, 281, 329; (southern Italy), I, 279. *See also* Anti-Semitism; Cities; Persecutions; and new members, II, 11–12; III, 98–100; and rabbinic license of scribes, III, 140; and sale of Jewish meat, II, 158; and scholarly merchants, I, 139; II, 180; and synagogue auctions, II, 133; and supply of fish, II, 160–61; and tax assessors, II, 287; and wine prices, II, 163; encouraged by governments, III, 199–200; in release from bans, III, 178; of charitable associations, I, 363; of marriage brokers, II, 81, 319; of rabbis, III, 100, 128–29; of slaughterers, II, 109; of teachers, II, 183–86, 196; III, 164; unfair, II, 293–94, 297, 319. *See also* Acquired rights; Economic regulation; Merchants

Compilations, legal, and academy controversies, I, 152. *See also* Codes

Compromises: communal, on taxation, II, 279–80; judicial, preferred, II, 208–9, 214, 237

Compulsion: and public education, II, 170–71; and expert judges, III, 173

Concealment of property, Jewish, and property taxes, II, 256

Condottas, Italian, I, 275; II, 10–11. *See also* Treaties

Conferences, Jewish, *see* Councils

Confession: of criminal, during flogging, II, 225; of dying, II, 328

Confiscation: of books, II, 204; III, 54; (preaching), III, 134; (smallness of libraries), II, 201; of electoral bribes, II, 93;

of property: II, 233–34; and communal indebtedness, III, 84; and excommunication, I, 271, 301; II, 230; III, 71, 177; and legal residence, II, 234; and popular assemblies, I, 66; and taxation, I, 148; II, 235, 281, 284–85; (for immunities), II, 15; of elders, II, 52–53; of synagogues, II, 135

Conflagrations: and tenant protection, II, 293; III, 199; destroy minute-books, I, 327

Conflicts, communal: and ambitious leadership, II, 52, 59; and baths, II, 166; and cantors, II, 105; III, 136–37; and capitulations, III, 102; and cemeteries, II, 148; III, 153, 156; and changes in legacies, III, 189; and class attire, II, 307; and demotion of rabbis, III, 130; and exilarchic heredity, I, 174; and fish, III, 159; and free elections, II, 359; and "gifts" to rulers, II, 21–22; and government interference, II, 36; and growth of western communities, II, 365; and guilds, I, 367–68, 371; III, 95, 97; and majority principle, II, 31, 48–49; III, 109; and mourning for leaders, III, 153; and Palestine relief, II, 341–42; and preaching, II, 96; and priests, III, 42; and private excommunication, II, 79; and rabbinic ordination, III, 132; and regional control, III, 106, 203; and residence rights, III, 101; and sanctions on burial, II, 157; III, 157; and sextons, II, 106; and slaughterers, II, 110; III, 137–38, 159; and social control, II, 352; and Spanish exiles, I, 205; and synagogues, I, 123; (attendance), III, 105, 143; (possession), III, 149; (seats), III, 145; and taxation, II, 289; III, 138, 192, 197; and teachers' status, III, 165; and trust in charity supervisors, II, 64; and variety of rituals, I, 123; II, 142; III, 138; and writs of divorce, III, 181; in various regions (ancient Alexandria), I, 78; (ancient Sepphoris), III, 26–27; (Babylonia), III, 42–45; (French chief rabbinate), III, 66, 68–69, 126; (Islam), I, 174; (Italy), III, 51, 130; (Prague), III, 86; (Prussian suppression of), II, 358–59; (Wilno rabbinate), II, 86. *See also* Class struggle; Controversies

intercommunal: I, 308–9; III, 73–74; and divergent traditions, I, 150, 152; and excommunication, II, 229; and French rabbinate, III, 66, 68–69, 126; and hospices, II, 329; III, 211; and Italian rabbinate, III, 130, 212; and Polish councils, I, 331; and taxation, III, 183, 196–97

private, in synagogues, II, 145; III, 150

Conformity, religious: and communal control, I, 108, 115; II, 210; and communal creativity, II, 168; and interterritorial action, I, 306–9; and Roman law, I, 108; and sumptuary laws, II, 302; despite Justinian, I, 123; vs. local variety, III, 149

Confraternities, *see* Associations

Confraternity for the Redemption of Captives, in Venice, II, 335–36

Congrega, Roman, II, 60. *See also* Council of elders (60)

Congregations, Jewish: and admission of members, I, 6; II, 18–20; and agnosticism, I, 5; and associational experience, I, 374; and burial societies, III, 88; and communal conflicts, II, 11–12, 148; and general assembly, I, 344; and High Holidays, I, 6; and separation of state and church, I, 11; and tax exemptions, II, 276; as communal units, I, 5; autonomy of, II, 75; III, 88–89; ḥasidic, II, 100, 125–26; importance of *ḥazzan* for, II, 101; in small settlements, I, 6; in various regions (America), I, 6, 11; (Graeco-Roman world), I, 11–12, 59, *75–84*; III, 13–15; (Holland), I, 253; II, 21; (Islam), I, 167–68, 200; (Kleve), I, 344; (Mantua), II, 21; (Turkey), I, 205, 348, 351; II, 75, 276; III, 88–89; mergers of, I, 253; II, 21, 29, 59; quorum of, I, 61; rabbinic control of, II, 75; ritual diversity of, I, 167–68; statistics of, I, 6, 348, 351; subdivisions of community, I, 200; vitality of, I, 6. *See also* Associations; Conflicts; Landsmannschaften

Congregations, sacred (papal), I, 221; II, 158; III, 185

Congress: of the United States, I, 45; of Vienna, III, 63, 98

Congressus generalis judaicus, see Councils, Polish

Connubium, and relatives of excommunicates, II, 230

Conquest, territorial, and new synagogues, I, 163

Conrad (German king), and chief rabbinate, III, 70

Conscientious objections: and communal discipline, III, 118; and juridical strictness, III, 172

Consciousness, operation of ban in, II, 229

Consent: of community (bans), II, 229. *See also* Excommunication; (rabbinic tenure), II, 88; of parties, and unqualified judges, II, 72. *See also* Compromises, judicial; of wife (divorce), II, 310; (polygamy), II, 309

Conservadori degli atti, II, 59. *See also* Archives

Conservatism, Jewish: and ancient academies, I, 152; and communal creativity, I, 12; II, 167–68, 353

Conservative Judaism, American, and community, I, 5

Conservators, of Jews: Piedmontese, III, 68; southern French, I, 264; III, 68, 76

Consistorial system, Jewish: allegiance to, I, 13–14; and agnosticism, I, 25; and England, I, 20; and Germany, I, 18, 344; in Belgium, I, 13; in France, I, 13–14, 18, 25, 344

Consistory, Prussian, and Jewish divorces, II, 211

Conspiracies, Jewish, outlawry of, II, 48–49. *See also* Conflicts, communal

"Conspiracy of traitors," prohibited by Lithuanian Council, II, 49

Constance, Church council in, III, 77

Constantine, Flavius Valerius Aurelius, the Great (Roman emperor), I, 12, 96, 111, 138, 225; III, 21, 27

Constantinople, Byzantine: and *ḥakam-bashi*, I, 230; Jewish craftsmen in, I, 365; III, 94; Jewish quarter in, I, 229; suppresses heresies, I, 288

Turkish, Jews of: I, 195; and Bagdad, I, 197; and Cologne precedent, III, 135–36; and customs duties, II, 263; and election of *ḥakam-bashi*, III, 49; and execution of informers, II, 222; and Greek patriarch, I, 196; and Hamburg community, I, 308; II, 26; and provincial communities, I, 190, 197; II, 352; and redemption of captives, I, 307; II, 335; III, 73; and talmudic community, I, 156; approval of Salonican ordinance by, II, 222; congregational divisions of, I, 168, 205, 351; II, 4, 20; constitutional reform of, III, 48; guilds of, I, 365; *ḳehayas* of, I, 198; population of, I, 26; II, 23; sumptuary ordinances of, II, 306; III, 201. *See also* Chief rabbinate

Constantius Flavius Valerius (Roman emperor), and Jewish judiciary, III, 21

Constitutio Antoniana, and Jewish community, III, 19

Constitutio Criminalis Carolina, II, 235

Constitution, Israelitic, adoption of, I, 48. *See also* Cities, Israelitic; Monarchy; Public Law

Constitutions, communal: and Graeco-Roman law, I, 107, 118, 136–37; and municipal statutes, I, 118, 255, 274; II, 3; preparation by committees of, III, 110–11. *See also* Committees; Law; Ordinances; Statutes

Consuetudines Palermitanae, on Hebrew deeds, II, 111

Consuls, European, and extraterritorial Jews, III, 101–2

Consulta, Roman, II, 60. *See also* Council of elders (60)

Consultation, mutual, and individual study, II, 206
Consumers, Jewish: and indirect taxation, II, 38; and meat (decline in Rome), II, 257; (prices), III, 187; and wine, II, 162–63
Continuity, *see* Historic continuity
Contractors, Jewish, rise of, II, 357. *See also* Court Jews
Contracts, Jewish: ancient Babylonian, I, 71; and Exchequer of Jews, I, 250–51; and relations among fiancés, III, 206; of diplomatic agents, II, 116; of preachers, II, 114; III, 134; of rabbis, II, 86–88, 126, 128–29; (commercial activities), II, 81; (Lwów controversy), II, 93; (preaching), III, 134; (texts), III, 129, 131, 140; of teachers, II, 114; III, 161; (hours of instruction), II, 197; (mostly private), II, 169, 173. *See also* Covenants; Deeds; Loans; Marriage; Writs
Contributions, communal: I, 349; for academies, I, 180–81, 184, 193, 201; for baths, II, 166; for Palestine, I, 74, 87–88, 157–58. *See also* Palestine relief; for rabbis, I, 151; II, 81, 97; III, 128; for synagogues, I, 95, 103, 164; II, 130–34, 136; (enforceable), I, 120; for Temple, I, 110; in Elephantine, I, 72; obligations to, I, 136–37; of Gentiles, I, 109; II, 347; revenue from, II, 265–66, 328, 345; voluntary vs. taxes, I, 247; II, 344. *See also* Bequests; Donors; Gifts; Taxation
Control: communal, *see* Communal control; Taxation; royal, *see* Law; Legal status; Monarchy
Controversies, legal: and growth of law, II, 212; and Palestine messengers, II, 342; III, 216–17; and pledges by parties, II, 214; over fish, II, 161; over taxation, II, 252–53, 260
Conventicle Act, British, and synagogues, I, 257–58
Conventicles: cabalistic, I, 354; III, 91. *See also* Associations, religious; Israelitic, and origin of synagogue, III, 9; Oxford students accused of, II, 187
Convents, French, and Jewish cemeteries, III, 61. *See also* Church; Clergy; Monasteries
Conversations, private, educational value of, II, 206
Conversion to Christianity: and communal conflicts, I, 112, 218–19, 222; II, 54; and communal membership, I, 247; II, 4, 17, 319; III, 104; and chairs for Hebrew, III, 135; and Hebrew printing, II, 204; and instruction of Gentiles, II, 177; and Jewish burial, III, 153; and Jewish status, I, 247; II, 124; III, 184; and missionary sermons, III, 135. *See also* Preaching; and political influence, I, 300; and problem of *'agunah*, II, 317; and Prussian law of secession, III, 5; and responsibility of elders, I, 53; entails loss of property, I, 247; III, 57; forced, I, 218, 228; III, 53–54; (interterritorial action against), I, 304–6; III, 72; (repudiated by popes), I, 218, 304; (Spanish chief rabbinate), I, 289–91; (Spanish massacres), I, 289; in various countries (Byzantium), I, 228; (France), I, 263; (Italy) I, 218, 304–6; (Poland) I, 300; (Prussia), III, 5; (Spain), I, 289–90; Jewish assistance in, I, 219, 222–23; of children, I, 263, 304–6. *See also* Minors; of criminals, II, 338; of Palestine messenger, II, 342–43; of rabbis, I, 220, 289–91; vs. modern assimilation, II, 360
to Islam; I, 158–59; and humiliation of infidels, I, 171; and Muslim guilds, I, 366; III, 94; and problem of *'agunah*, II, 317
to Judaism: ancient, I, 85, 97; and Babylonian exile, III, 11; and com-

munal control, I, 224; and Hellenistic Jewry, I, 90, 116–17; by patriarchs, I, 145; forcible vs. voluntary, I, 121; in various regions (Elephantine), I, 70; III, 12; (Martinique), III, 62; (Persia), III, 36; (Rome), I, 82; prosecution for, I, 218, 222. *See also* Proselytes; Semi-proselytes

to Paganism, in Elephantine, III, 12

Conversion loans, Jewish, in Rome, II, 272

Converts, Jewish: and burial, III, 153; and German-Jewish community, I, 19; and Hebrew letters, I, 338; and nationalism, I, 7; backsliding, I, 222; support of Jewish institutions by, II, 134, 347; testimony of, disqualified, I, 232. *See also* Marranos

Convicts, Jewish, Cotton Mather on, I, 261. *See also* Criminality; Prisons

Conviviality, Judeo-Christian, ecclesiastical condemnation of, I, 225

Copyright, Jewish, I, 331; II, 202–4; III, 83, 170–71

Corbeil, rabbis of, II, 318–19

Corcos, Solomon b. David, II, 20

Cordova: Caliphate of, and Jewish separatism, I, 185; Jewish officials in, I, 189; new synagogue of, I, 220

Cordovero, Moses b. Jacob, religious association of, I, 355

Corfû, Jews of: election of elders by, III, 121; levirate marriage of, III, 205; ordinances of synod of, II, 163, 310, 315; Palestine relief of, III, 213, 216; rabbis of, I, 205; ransom of captives by, III, 213

Cori, Jews of, and Palestine colonization, III, 216

Cornelia Salvia, Antioch legacy of, III, 19

Corners (charity), I, 132

Corporal taxes, *see* Tolls, personal

Corporal punishment: III, 175–76; of Jewish elders, II, 52

Corporate organization, and Roman law, I, 107–8

Corporate system, European: and Jewish community, I, 8, 22, 209, 357; (assimilation), I, 210; (associations), I, 372; (court Jews), II, 357; and new taxes, I, 215

Corpses, Jewish: and University of Padua, II, 151; removal in Nice of, II, 152. *See also* Burial; Cemeteries

Corpus of Jewish communal records, desirability of, III, 6

Correction, doctrine of, and criminal law, II, 221–22, 224

Correspondence, Jewish, medieval, orderliness of, III, 42, 72. *See also* Letters; Responsa

Corruption: communal, I, 142; II, 46, 72, 107, 132; III, 132, 189; of officials, II, 247; III, 133, 183; (and burials), I, 263; II, 151; (Muslim), I, 167, 170, 204; (Polish), II, 107, 353–54

Cortes, Spanish: III, 65; and debt bondage, III, 176; and Jewish councils, I, 287–88; and Jewish judiciary, I, 241; and luxury in dress, II, 303; and rabbinic tenure, II, 86; and tax immunities, II, 13; and tenant protection, II, 293; anti-Semitism of, I, 278–79

Corvée, see Labor, forced

Cossack revolts: I, 330, 333; and admission of aliens, II, 8, 324; and captives, I, 307; II, 334–35; III, 73; and communal debts, II, 273; and local autonomy, II, 335; and Palestine relief, II, 341; and sumptuary laws, II, 302; and tax immunities, II, 278. *See also* Chmielnicki; Warfare

Costs, judicial, *see* Fees, judicial

Costume, Jewish: communal regulations of, II, 307; III, 147; local variations in, II, 8. *See also* Class divisions

Council of elders, size of: I, 133–34; 2 (Frankfort), II, 61; 3 (Hamburg), II, 61–62; 6 (frequent), III, 121; (Hamburg), II, 61–62; 7 (frequent), III, 120; (Catalonia), II, 70; (Constantinople), III, 48–49; (London), II, 62; 10 (Barbastro), II, 71; 11 (Moravia), III, 120–21; 12 (frequent), III, 121; (Frankfort), II, 61; (Leghorn), II, 60; (Palermo), II, 58–59; (Worms), II, 35; 15 (Avignon), II,61; 20 (Rome), II,60; (Tudela), II, 58; 25 (Saragossa), II, 71; 30 (Spain), II, 58; 40 (Leghorn), II, 60; 42 (Tudela), II, 58; 60 (Leghorn), II, 60–61; (Rome, papal), II, 29, 48, 55, 60; 70 (ancient), I, 43–44, 99; III, 8, 17; (academies), I, 193; (Babylonian Exile), I, 68; (Galilee), I, 133; 71 (ancient), I, 78, 99; (academies), I, 151; (rare in Poland), II, 56. *See also* Sanhedrin; 72 (academies)

Council of Four Lands, *see* Councils, Poland

Council of [Jewish] Federations, American, I, 5

Council of the Provinces, *see* Councils, Lithuania

Council of Three Lands, *see* Councils, Poland

Council, royal, Jewish, ancient, and Sanhedrin, III, 29

Councils *and* synods, ecclesiastical: and Jewish deputies, III, 77, 80; and Jewish question, I, 216; and Jewish synods, I, 309; at Elvira, I, 225; at Narbonne, III, 23; at Piotrków, I, 220; at Trent, II, 83–84; at Vienne, III, 135; Lateran, III (Christian witnesses), I, 226, 251; (loss of converts' property), I, 247; (segregation of Jews), I, 225; III, 54

Jewish: I, *309–45*; III, *74–88*; and regional leadership, I, 284; and scholarly control, II, 244; election of representatives to, II, 41–43; personal attendance of members at, II, 24, 41–42; preferred to governmental chiefs, I, 347

regional: I, *310–13*; Alsace, III, 88; (school of higher learning), II, 185; Bohemia, I, 339–40; (*ḥazaḳah*), II, 298–99; France (Troyes), I2, 2,1 310–11; III, 74–75; (books), II, 200; (Christian influences), III, 208; (divorces), II, 240; (dowries), II, 318; (royal orders), I, 322

regional, Germany: I, 323, *337–45*; III, *86–88*; and bans, II, 230–32; and chief rabbinate, I, 300, 347; and Commercial Revolution, I, 323; and educational revenue, II, 188; and gaming, II, 317; and Gentile courts, II, 230; and governmental immunities, II, 15; III, 193; and levirate marriage, II, 318; and Palestine relief, II, 341; and rulers' suspicions, I, 322–23; and sumptuary legislation, II, 303; and synagogue decorum, II, 141; and tax declarations, I, 315; II, 281; at Frankfort, I, 313; (accusation of treason), I, 322–23; III, 74; (censorship), II, 202; (organization of German Jewry), I, 340–41; (outside bans), II, 243; (rabbis), II, 92, 128; (taxation), I, 313–14; II, 284; (training of slaughterers), II, 109; (wine), II, 161, 163; at Hesse-Cassel, I, *341–43*; III, *86*; (educational budgets), II, 115; (elections), II, 36–37; (new arrivals), II, 5, 12; (personal attendance), II, 24, 41–42; (regional jurisdiction), III, 105; at Kleve, I, *343–44*; III, *86*; (officials' expenses), II, 119; (personal attendance), II, 24; in Rhinelands, III, 74–75; (bans), II, 32, 230–31; (diversion of funds), II, 185–

86; (examination of slaughterers), II, 109; (wine), II, 161

regional, Italy: I, *315–23*; III, *78–81*, 139; and Commercial Revolution, I, 323; and communal scribes, II, 111–12; and sumptuary laws, II, 303–4; at Candia, I, 319; II, 293, 315; III, 79, 96, 143; at Corfù, I, 163, 310, 315; at Ferrara, I, 321; II, 238; III, 80; (censorship), I, 224; II, 202; (electoral rights), III, 114; (lay leadership), II, 77; (legal inquiries), II, 238; (outside bans), II, 243; (polygamy), II, 309; (quorum at weddings), III, 47; (rabbis), II, 92; III, 128, 130–31; (tenant protection), II, 293; at Forli, III, 79; (gaming), II, 317; (rabbinic ordination), II, 91; (sexual laxity), II, 312; at Sicily, III, 78; (adoption of statutes), III, 110; (chief rabbinate), I, 293–94; (communal elections), III, 113; (polygamy), II, 309; (tax immunity), III, 192

regional, Moravia: I, 323, *337–39*; III, *85–86*; against outside bans, II, 243; and expulsion from Zülz, III, 106; and German councils, I, 344; and talmudic studies, II, 203; and tax immunities, II, 278; election of members to, II, 41–43; limits vows, II, 133

regional, Poland-Lithuania: I, *323–37*; *III*, *81–85*; and aliens, II, 7–8, 323, 337; III, 209; (children), II, 331, 337; and attendance at sessions of, III, 158; and authorization of slaughterers, II, 109; and ban of settlement, II, 6–7; and brokers' fees, III, 208–9; and burial societies, I, 354; and business women, II, 314; and chanting, II, 105; and charity, II, 323, 326, 332–33; (redemption of captives), II, 335–36; and chief rabbinate, I, 302; (Wilno), II, 87; and Christian residents in ghetto, II, 296; and deserting husbands, II, 317; and education, II, 114–15, 189; (reforms), II, 194; and endorsement of communal debts, III, 191; and exposure in pillory, II, 224; and free elections, I, 328; II, 46; (corruption), II, 93; III, 132; (electors), II, 39–40; III, 114; and foreign councils, I, 288, 319; III, 79–81; and fugitives, III, 103; and funeral charges, III, 158; and guardians of orphans, II, 330; and hearings within 24 hours, II, 236; and Hebrew books, II, 203; III, 83; and household employees, III, 202; and investigation of marriage applicants, II, 311; and investment of endowment, III, 189; and irrevocable ban, II, 228–29; and judges' share in fines, II, 234–35; and Karaites, III, 185; and Mazovian settlement, III, 99; and Palestine relief, II, 341, 343; and parental approval of marriage, II, 310–11; and prosecution of criminals, II, 338; and rabbis, II, 87, 93; III, 128–29, 132; (tenure), II, 87; and regional control, II, 20, 23, 42; III, 115; (cemeteries), II, 149; (taxation), III, 153–54; and residence rights in major communities, II, 7–8, 22, 314, 323, 337; III, 99, 209; and scribes, II, 113; III, 140; and seven best men, III, 120; and Silesian expulsion, I, 307; III, 106; and sumptuary laws, II, 302, 305–6; and synagogue seats, II, 130; and taxation, II, 252; III, 153–54; (capitalization of property), II, 255; (evasions), II, 15–16, 283; (immunities), II, 278; (meat), II, 257–58; and tenure of cantors, II, 104; and visiting preachers, II, 99; and weights and measures, II, 291; and wine trade, II, 163; chronology of sessions of, III, 83; commercial borrowings of,

III, 191; composition of, II, 42; III, 81–83, 115; control nobles' moneylending to Jews, I, 272; decisions of, and sextons, II, 106; diplomatic representatives of, II, 116; disintegration of, I, 336; II, 352–53; III, 84–85; drafting of resolutions of, II, 31; excommunicate entire communities, II, 229; foreign relations of, I, 331–32, 337–38, 341; II, 116, 243; III, 72–74; imitated in Germany, I, 337–38, 344; influence of closing of, II, 352–53; mutual relations of, I, 327, 332, 341; III, 82; outlaw "conspiracies," II, 49; protect local institutions, III, 146, 182; provincial, III, 71; (and central councils), III, 82; (and partitionist powers), III, 85, (and *sejmiki*), I, 324; (appeals of), I, 333; (indebtedness of), I, 334–35; II, 273

regional, Spain: I, 310; and Aragonese taxation, I, 286–87; at Barcelona (Jewish migrations), I, 234; (mortgaging Jewish revenue), I, 234–35; at Valladolid, I, 310; III, 65, 67, 121; (chief rabbi), I, 289, 291–92; (defenders of statutes), III, 111; (forced betrothals), II, 311; (free elections), II, 46; (government intervention), I, 292, 322; (invitations to assemblies), II, 25; (judicial intermediaries), II, 237–38; (lay judges), II, 72; (preachers), II, 96; (public education), II, 171–72; III, 92; (rabbis), II, 73, 82; (sumptuary legislation), II, 303; (synagogue attendance), II, 126; III, 143; (tax exemptions), II, 276; (teachers), II, 114; (warrants of arrest), II, 227; (wine administration), II, 162–63. *See also* Chief rabbinate; Provincial elders; Regional control

Councils, imperial: Muslim, III, 38; religious minorities in, I, 173–74; Persian, exilarchs in, I, 146–47; Turkish, *ḥakam-bashis* in, I, 195–96, 198

Counsellors, Jewish, of Muslim rulers, I, 165. *See also* Diplomacy

"Counselor of evil," judicial intermediary as, II, 237

Counter-Reformation, Catholic: and communal debts, II, 272; and Jewish status, I, 322; II, 360; and sumptuary legislation, II, 303

Courland, Jews of, III, 64

Courses, academic, Jewish, and adult education, II, 206

Court Chancery, Austrian, II, 98–99, 159–60, 260; III, 85. *See also* Bureaucracy

Court clerks, and legal procedure, II, 240. *See also* Clerks; Scribes; Sextons

Court houses, communal, universality of, II, 167

Court Jews, Austro-German: II, 357; III, 126, 220; and anti-defamation, III, 171; and communal leadership, I, 345; II, 357–58; III, 142; and confiscation of books, II, 98–99; and synagogues, II, 130; and taxation, III, 123, 193; as rabbis and scribes, II, 81, 120; influence of, I, 187, 289–90

Court messengers, Jewish, and governmental appointment, I, 292. *See also* Clerks; Sextons

Court physicians, Jewish, medieval, I, 289–90, 293–94, 304

Court records, Jewish, preservation of, II, 113, 330; III, 211

Court witnesses, *see* Witnesses, communal

Courts of Appeal, governmental: ancient Israelitic, I, 39, 51; discouraged in Cassel, I, 343; Polish, and mixed

litigations, I, 273; Roman, and Jewish courts, I, 115; Spanish, I, 240, 290
Jewish: II, 241; ancient, I, 127–28; and chief rabbinate, I, 285, 290, 292; and judicial reversal, II, 242; and regional communities, I, 284; III, 182. *See also* Appeals; High Court; Judiciary; Supreme Court

Courts of arbitration, Jewish: I, 23; and communal controversies, III, 115, 133; and legal advances, II, 209; and professional judiciary, I, 114–15; II, 214–15. *See also* Arbitrators; Judiciary

Courts, royal: Babylonian, I, 63, 69; Israelitic, and Palestinian provinces, III, 7; Jewish billeting of, II, 268; of exilarchs, I, 147, 154, 182; III, 31; of patriarchs, I, 141; Persi n and Jewish status, I, 64. *See also* Monarchy

Courtyards, and synagogues, II, 127, 141

Cousins, second, ineligibility to office of, II, 40

"Covering of the dead," society for, I, 353

Covering the head, observance of, II, 69, 306–7; III, 202

Covenants: Israelitic, I, 47, 51; III, 12; of Abraham, II, 145. *See also* Circumcision; of Ezra and Nehemiah, I, 70; of Omar, I, 161, 163

Cracow, Jews of: III, 71, 194, 219; (population), I, 326; II, 23; and begging, II, 321–22; and John Capistrano, III, 77; and Helicz books, II, 204; and Palestine settlement, III, 215; and talmudic community, I, 156; and withdrawal of passive franchise, III, 177; as members of Polish Council, I, 325–26; II, 42; III, 81; communal indebtedness of, II, 273, 353; III, 191; confiscation of property of, II, 233–34; congregation in Leipzig of, III, 149; constitution of, II, 63, 321–22; III, 63, 127; dictator of, II, 64; educational foundation of, II, 186; guilds of, I, 369–70; III, 96; health officers of, III, 291; indirect elections among, II, 45; judicial fees of, II, 84; III, 127; Lithuanian Jews from, II, 7–8; minute-book of, III, 82, 195; palatin's ordinances in, I, 270; II, 46; payments to governors of, I, 269; periodic examination of pupils by, II, 197; pestilence among, II, 329; III, 211; physicians of, III, 140; police of, II, 291; private teachers of, II, 196–97; quotas for printers among, II, 203; rabbis of, I, 271, 300, 325; (Rovigo controversy), II, 166; regional control of, I, 302; II, 20; residence rights of, II, 234; synagogues of, I, 220; II, 130; talmudic tractates ordered from, II, 95; tax administration of, II, 261, 263, 273, 285; III, 188, 195; vocational training of, III, 96. *See also* Lesser Poland

Craftsmen and industry, Israelitic: concentrated settlements of, I, 364; slaves of, I, 46
Jewish, ancient: I, 31, 42; and economic regulation, I, 126, 364; and rabbis, I, 135, 138; in Babylonian Exile, I, 59, 66–67; in Graeco-Roman world, I, 75; (Alexandria), I, 78–79, 364–65; separate streets of, I, 130
medieval and modern: acquired rights of, II, 296–97, 299; and ban of settlement, II, 5–6; and burghers, I, 274, 281; and burial societies, I, 352–54; and communal license fees, II, 262; and communal monopolies, II, 262; and educational responsibilities, II, 176; and Polish councils, I, 324; and professional

training, II, 175; III, 96, 167; and rabbinic privileges, II, 80–81; and state encouragement, I, 367; II, 253; and sumptuary laws, II, 306; and teaching, III, 41–42, 96; attraction by tax exemptions of, II, 275; class attire of, II, 307; communal support of, II, 361; guilds of, *see* Associations; Guilds; inspectors of, II, 56; in various regions (Byzantium), III, 94; (Italy), III, 95–96; (Poland), I, 281, 324; II, 307; (Salonica), III, 199; (Spain), I, 352–54; (Turkey), II, 262; political power of, I, 373; regulation of, and membership restrictions, II, 16, 18, 299. *See also* Guilds; sales taxes of, II, 261

Crassus, Dives Marcus Licinius (Roman statesman), I, 88

Creation *ex nihilo*, Maimonidean proofs for, I, 307

"Creative élan of the masses," I, 116

Creativity: artistic, problem of, II, 137; communal, I, 85; II, 121; (vs. historic continuity), II, 167–68; legal, in early middle ages, II, 216; liturgical, and Hebrew printing, II, 143; rabbinic, and dialectics, II, 195

Credentials, of Palestine messengers, II, 341, 343

Credit economy, Jewish, and debt bondage, II, 226. *See also* Banking; Loans

Creditors, Christian: and communal interest, II, 269–70, 272; in Poland, III, 84, 191; in Rome, III, 191–92; in Spain, III, 145

Jewish: and acquired rights, II, 297; and charities, III, 209; and communal interest, II, 269–70; and orphans' property, II, 331; III, 212; and seizure of debtors' property, II, 232; and synagogue seats, II, 130–31; and tax liabilities, III, 196; elders as, II, 52, 64; risks of, II, 269; III, 212. *See also* Debts; Loans

Creechurch Lane, London, synagogue at, I, 256–57

Cremation, Roman, and Jewish burial, I, 94

Crémieux, Elijah (Avignon teacher), II, 114

Cremona, Jews of, I, 308; II, 188

Crescas, Don Ḥasdai (Aragonese chief rabbi and philosopher): I, 290–91; III, 66; and French controversy, I, 297; polygamy of, II, 309

Cretans in ancient Israel, I, 39, 76

Crete, Jews of, III, 175. *See also* Candia

Crimea, Jewish autonomous regions in, I, 15

Crime and punishment, doctrine of, II, 221

Crimes, Jewish: II, 220; and burial, II, 156; and capital punishment, II, 221; and prosecution of Polish fugitives, I, 331; and unproclaimed bans, II, 229; elders' responsibility for, II, 52–53, 71, 338; III, 214; Italian immunities of, II, 11; self-imposed fines for, II, 346. *See also* under respective crimes

Criminality, Jewish, lesser frequency of, II, 227–28

Criminal law: II, 156–57; Canon, I, 218; (hiding of Jewish children), I, 222–23; German, I, 277; Graeco-Roman, I, 109; (atheism), I, 12; (Christian synagogue attendance), I, 112; (desecration of sanctuary), I, 88; (protects patriarch), I, 144; Israelitic, I, 47, 49

Jewish: II, 213–14, *220–36*; III, 37–38, *174–80*; ancient, I, 87, 88, 100, 126–27; (safeguarded by Rome), I, 109, 111; and burial, II, 156–57; and care for prisoners, II, 338; and communal elections, I, 96; II, 41; and debasement of Polish metals,

I, 330; and defaulting taxpayers, II, 219; and judiciary, I, 249; II, 218; (lay), II, 71–72, 88; and non-Jewish aid, I, 213; and overstaying aliens, II, 10–11; and southern chief rabbis I, 285, 292–93; III, 66; continuity of, II, 216; Draconian penalties in, II, 221, 235; prohibits private deeds, I, 202; Spanish respect for, I, 238–39; supported by supernatural sanctions, I, 208; supremacy of social interest in, II, 245

Muslim, and tax frauds, I, 171; Polish, on desecration of Jewish institutions, I, 270; Soviet, and Hebrew, I, 16; Spanish, I, 278; (Jewish magic), I, 237. *See also* Law; Penalties

Crippled, exempted from taxation, II, 38

Crises, Jewish: and rabbinic position, II, 92; and welfare budgets, II, 350; visiting of graves during, II, 154

Criticism, biblical: and chronology, III, 9–11; on *ḳahal* and *'edah*, III, 10–11

Criticisms, rabbinic, of preachers, III, 134

Cromwell, Oliver, I, 255–57, 308; III, 59

Crops, agricultural: and taxation, II, 253; marketing of, and Polish nobles, I, 269. *See also* Agriculture

Crucifixion, and medieval taxation, III, 55

Cruelty of husbands, communal action against, II, 318

Crusades: and associations, I, 360; III, 93; and hospitals, II, 327; and interterritorial action, I, 306; and Jewish synods, I, 310; and Palestine, I, 157, 194; and spread of leprosy, III, 155; breakdown of imperial protection during, I, 277; III, 77

Crystallization: of law, and judge's discretion, II, 218; of synagogue functions, and auctions, II, 134. *See also* Petrification

Culture, Jewish: ancient diversity of, I, 85; and community, I, 3, 7–8; (contemporary Palestine), I, 17; and Islam, I, 167, 210; and Italian expulsions, I, 231; and Palestine messengers, II, 343; interterritorial features of, I, 304

Cumanus, Ventidius (Roman procurator), I, 109

Cuneiform tablets, on Babylonian Jews, I, 71

Curaçao, Jews of, help New York synagogue, II, 136

Curiae, electoral, *see* Three-class system

Curiosities, Jewish, history of, II, 305; III, 77

Curricula, educational: I, 16; II, 95, 190–200; III, 167–68

Curses: biblical, and oath of office, II, 37; Hellenistic, Oriental influences on, III, 25. *See also* Bouzygian imprecations; of mendicants, and charities, II, 348

Curtains, cover feminine lecturers, II, 178

Customs *and* customary law, Jewish, ancient: and patriarchs, I, 142; and synagogue ritual, I, 89; III, 22; and taxation, I, 110; Babylonian divergences in, I, 150, 192; funerary, I, 94

medieval and modern: III, 172; and adjustments of Jewish law, II, 208, 212; and break in historic continuity, II, 215; and charities, II, 320–21; and communal burial, II, 147; and communal elections, I, 285; III, 113; and communal interest, II, 269; and congregational charters, I, 12; and emigration, III, 37; and English toleration, I, 276; II, 116; and forced labor,

I, 218; and hours of instruction, II, 197; and interterritorial action, II, 357; and judges' discretion, I, 239; II, 202, 218, 242–43; and marital responsibilities, II, 175; III, 208; and obsolescence of endowments, II, 266; and officials, II, 290; and polygamy, II, 308; and preparation of deeds, II, 113; and public education, II, 173; and regional control, III, 203; and ritualistic neglect, III, 124; and shoeless worship, II, 129; and support of children, II, 325; and taxation, II, 214–15, 282, 288; (cantor's immunities), II, 277; and visiting of sick, II, 328; and wedding rites, II, 310; III, 46–47; and wine administration, II, 163; as sources of law, II, 245; as unifying forces, I, 62–63; created by timid decisions, II, 213; oriental models for, II, 306–7; plurality of, I, 167, 205, 323; II, 242; III, 44; (despite geonic control), I, 206; power of, I, 165, 214–15; III, 149, 172; Roman-Visigothic antecedents of, I, 286–87; II, 74; validity of, II, 69–70. *See also* Mores

Customs duties, communal: I, 38; II, 247, 262, 278–79; III, 19; anti-alien character of, II, 12–13; III, 102; for the redemption of captives, II, 335–36; in Leghorn, II, 13, 265

Custumals, Jewish, medieval: II, 70; and deeds, II, 240; and local precedents, II, 213; and luxury, II, 303; and synagogues, I, 236–37; (vows), III, 145; borrowings from, III, 172

Cycles in Bible recitation: annual, I, 122; triennial, I, 122; III, 21–22

Cyprus, Jews of, I, 64

Cyrenaica, ancient, Jews in, I, 76, 78–79, 83; III, 14

Cyrene, Jewish status in, III, 14

Cyrenians in Jerusalem, I, 120

Cyrus the Great (Persian king), I, 64, 80; III, 11

Czars, against Jewish bans, II, 233. *See also* Russia

Czechoslovakia, modern: and Moravian council, I, 339; Jews of, I, 19; (minority rights), III, 4

Da pecuniam, Roman proverb on, II, 246

Dadhisho (Nestorian patriarch), I, 244

Damages, civil: and criminal law, II, 213–14; in houses, tenants' responsibility for, II, 292

Damascus: Israelitic merchants in, I, 57; Jewish leaders in, I, 194; III, 73, 105; various rituals in, I, 167

Damascus sect, I, 95; III, 17

Damask garments, and sumptuary laws, II, 306

Damwah (Egypt), I, 164

Dan (city), sanctuary of, I, 40

Dan (tribe), I, 56

Dancing: communal ordinances on, II, 315; III, 202, 206; Jewish instruction in II, 191, 315–16; III, 206; ritualistic, with bride, II, 315

"Dancing-houses," communal, II, 167, 315; III, 206

Danger, personal: and denunciation of transgressors, II, 236; and redemption of captives, II, 333; and taxes for defense, II, 268

Daniel (exilarch), I, 178

Daniel (Karaite), III, 41

Daniel b. Hezekiah (exilarch), I, 185

Daniel b. Ḥisdai (exilarch), I, 175; III, 44, 46

Daphnae (Egypt), Jews of, I, 57

Darius I (Persian king), I, 64; III, 11

Darius II (Persian king), I, 65; III, 11

"Dark Ages": and lay judiciary, II, 209; Italian, and Counter-Reformation, I, 322; Jewish, mitigated by councils, I, 347

Darmstadt: chief rabbinate of, III, 86; illuminated *haggadah* of, III, 146
Daroca (Spain), rabbinic position in, II, 74
Darshan, II, 97. *See also* Preaching
Dathan (biblical rebel), I, 167; II, 37
Daughter, marriageable, and begging, II, 324
"Daughters," of cities, I, 34
David (king), I, 35, 39, 43, 68–69; bureaucracy of, III, 13; census under, III, 9, 184; election of, I, 45
David, Abraham (Cassel court Jew), II, 120
David b. Ḥayyim ha-Kohen, I, 205; III, 51, 124
David b. Hodaiah (*nasi*), I, 186
David b. Judah of Mantua (Messer Leon), I, 291; III, 66, 128
David b. Naḥmias, tax exemption of, II, 276
David b. Raphael, III, 196
David b. Samuel ha-Levi, III, 145, 210
David b. Yehudah (exilarch), I, 178–79
David b. Zakkai (exilarch), I, 183; III, 39, 42
David, "the confederate," II, 227
Davidic descent: I, 141; and academy leadership, III, 46; of Ben-Meir family, I, 193; of exilarchs, I, 145, 149, 175–77, 186; of medieval *nesi'im*, I, 194; III, 68; of *negidim*, I, 189; of Palestinian patriarchs, I, 140; III, 29. *See also* Descent; Genealogy
Day of Atonement: and flogging, II, 225–26; execution on, I, 166; sermons on Sabbath preceding, II, 97; synagogue services on, I, 6; II, 105; (candles), II, 134; (vows for Palestine relief), II, 341; visits to graves on eve of, III, 206. *See also* High Holidays
Day of Judgment, and students of Torah, II, 98
Dayyane di baba, III, 31
Dayyane golah, I, 147. *See also* Exilarchate; Judiciary
Dayyanim, position of, II, 74, 84, 95. *See also* Judiciary
Dayyena *or* Diena, Azriel b. Solomon, III, 80, 132
Dead, care of, associations for, II, 327, 362–63. *See also* Burial societies
Dead Sea, region of, I, 31
Death robe, bequest of, II, 329
Deaths: by burning, for mixed sex relations, II, 312. *See also* Capital punishment; Jewish rites at, *see* Burial; Funeral rites; records of, I, 72, 198; II, 84. *See also* Registration
Debasement of metals, prohibited by Polish councils, I, 330
Debates: legal, and systematic law, II, 219; theological, despite toleration, I, 216. *See also* Disputations
Deborah (prophetess), I, 45; Song of, I, 44, 56
Debt bondage, Jewish: and care for prisoners, II, 338–39; and responsibility for taxes, II, 155, 284; and Sabbath, I, 236; in various regions (Avignon), III, 190; (Germany), III, 176; (Palestine), II, 340; (Poland), II, 226, 273; III, 84; (Sicily), III, 176; (Spain), II, 53, 271, 284; III, 176; Jewish immunities from, III, 176; of elders, II, 53, 273; III, 190
Debtors, Jewish: and sumptuary laws, II, 302; and teachers' salaries, II, 173; prosecution of, I, 331; II, 233; oppression of, I, 166
Debts, communal: II, 268–74; III, 190–92; and associations, I, 372; III, 97, 196; and cemeteries, II, 152; and Christian creditors, I, 334–35; and councils, I, 333–34; III, 75, 81, 88; and educational foundations, I, 358; II, 186; and meat taxes, II, 257–58; and outside begging, II, 325; and rabbis, II, 82, 92; and right of

emigration, II, 15; III, 103–4; and seizure of property, II, 233; and suspension of worship, II, 229; and synagogue seats, II, 131, 135; and taxation, II, 247, 256–59, 279; III, 38; and welfare budgets, I, 363–64; II, 346, 350; immunities of, II, 11; in various regions (Alsace), III, 88; (France), I, 358; II, 186; III, 75; (Germany), II, 356; (Holland), II, 356; (Islam), III, 38; (Italy), II, 11, 356; (Poland), I, 334–35, 337; II, 271; III, 81, 83–84; (Rome), II, 256; (Spain), II, 82, 279; liquidation of, I, 337; responsibility of elders for, II, 53; safeguard Jewish status, I, 334
of charitable associations, III, 96; royal and Jewish excommunication, II, 230. *See also* Banking; Creditors; Loans

Decalogue: and oath of office, II, 37; and papal taxation, II, 246; recitation of, I, 121; III, 22

Decentralization, communal: ancient, I, 206; (and medieval rabbinate), II, 68; and financial administration, II, 20; and growth of associations, I, 372; and Polish councils, I, 326; and royal control, I, 231

Decisions, rabbinic, conflicting on *ḥazakah*, III, 199

Declaration of Indulgence, British, and synagogues, I, 258

Declarations for taxes, *see* Manifest; Tax assessment

Decoration, interior, of synagogues, I, 90, 221. *See also* Art

Decorum: and female lecturers, II, 178; in synagogue, III, 148, 150; (auctions), II, 133; (Church), III, 23; (interruption of prayers), II, 34; (visitors), I, 257

Decrees: geonic, formularies of, III, 37; of appointment (Muslim), I, 203; III, 39; (rabbinic), I, 204; III, 85. *See also* Contracts; of banishment, I, 169, 318. *See also* Expulsions; royal, medieval terminology of, III, 104. *See also* Law; Turkish, confirming *ḥakam-bashis*, I, 198. *See also* Bérats

Dedications: of ancient synagogues, III, 13; of churches from converted synagogue, I, 230; III, 53

Deductions, in property taxes, allowed, II, 255. *See also* Taxation

Deeds, Jewish: ancient, I, 93–94, 102; (Dura-Europos), III, 19; (Elephantine), I, 70–72; and intermediaries, II, 238; and land registers, I, 277; and mutual tax agreements, III, 38–39; books of, III, 50; communal regulations on, I, 329; II, 301; III, 200; English keepers of, II, 116; examination of, II, 239–40; formulas of, III, 139, 189, 196; governmental recognition of, I, 229; II, 110; in various regions (Byzantium), I, 229; (England), II, 116; (Germany), I, 277; (Islam), I, 202; (Spain), III, 189; judicial fees on, I, 202; of medieval endowments, II, 266; of mortgages, III, 196; preparation by scribes of, II, 110, 113; (exilarchic), I, 183; rabbinic signatures on, III, 130; reconstruction of, III, 165; reliability of, I, 241, 251
Muslim, validity of, I, 170; Roman, validity of, I, 127. *See also* Contracts; Writs

Defendants, Jewish: and change of venue, II, 242; and intermediaries, II, 238; courts of, preferred, II, 242, 249–50; law of, applied, I, 240, 249–50

Defenders of statutes, II, 31, 57, 60; III, 111

Defense in war, distribution of taxes for, II, 268. *See also* Taxation; War

Defense of Jewish rights: I, 106; II, 204–5; III, 171; and Christian

creditors, II, 270; and Muslim Jew-baiting, I, 165; in the United States, I, 5, 25
Deficits, communal; and free loan banks, II, 327; and indebtedness, I, 334. *See also* Debts; and social control, II, 352–53; and taxation, I, 172; II, 248; charity overseer's responsibility for, III, 18; in Palestine relief, II, 341. *See also* Budgets; Financial administration
Degel, of Elephantine soldiers, I, 71
Degrees of charity, rabbinic teachings on, II, 333; III, 210
Dejudaization, *via* assimilation, II, 360. *See also* Assimilation; Conversion
Dekaprotoi, I, 133. *See also* Council of elders; Elders
Delays, judicial, reduction of, II, 236
Delegates, Jewish, *see* Deputations
Delmonte, Jacob, private cemetery of, II, 148
Delos, synagogue of, I, 84
Delta region (Egypt), Jews of, I, 58
Delta (Alexandrian quarter), I, 85
DeLyon, family (Georgia), III, 152
Demagoguery, of preachers, censured by rabbis, II, 99
Demetrios (alabarch), I, 80
Demetrius I (Syrian king), I, 83
Demetrius II (Syrian king), I, 83
Democracy, in Jewish community: I, 4, 12, 27–29; II, 358; III, 50; ancient, III, 26–27; (Israelitic), I, 44–45, 50–53; (medieval heritage), I, 204; and associational autonomy, I, 349, 373–74; and Barcelona synod, I, 288; and decentralization, I, 207; and electoral rights, II, 26–28; (lots), II, 43. *See also* Majority principle; and excommunication, II, 32; and interruption of prayers, II, 32–34; and liturgical innovations, II, 143; and rabbinic supremacy, I, 28, 135–36; II, 170–71; and size of population, II, 121; and synagogue assemblies, II, 144; and victory of Third Estate, I, 274; of learning, I, 28, 135–36; III, 26–27; relative strength of, III, 38–39. *See also* Egalitarianism; Equality of rights; Liberty of conscience
Demons: and chastisement of pupils, III, 169; and study, III, 169
Demotion of rabbis, *see* Deposition
Denarii, Muslim, value of, I, 175
Denunciation: by informer, and capital punishment, II, 221; of informer, dispensed with, II, 241. *See also* Informing; of transgressors, obligatory, I, 320; II, 236, 281, 284, 314; (Prussia), II, 359
Departure, Jewish levies on, III, 103. *See also* Emigration
Deportations: ancient, I, 75; (Babylonian synagogues), I, 66; Jewish, of mendicants, II, 342. *See also* Banishment; Expulsions; Migrations
Depositario, Jewish, in Palermo, II, 286. *See also* Treasurers
Deposition from office: for use of Hebrew, I, 241; II, 111; of cantors, II, 104; of judges, I, 203–4; of notaries, II, 111; of rabbis, II, 86, 88, 91; III, 129–31; (communal controversies), II, 95; (corrupt elections), II, 93; of slaughterers, II, 110
Deposits, monetary: against repudiation of judgments, II, 214; against polygamy, II, 308
Depreciation of values, during wars, II, 271
Depression, American, and Jewish congregations, I, 6. *See also* Economic decline
Deputations *and* deputies, Jewish: and interterritorial relief, I, 333; at diet of Augsburg, III, 71; from Comtat de Venaissin, II, 61; (salaries), II, 115; from Sicily in Spain, I, 317–18;

in Rome, I, 106, 305; III, 19. *See also* Diplomacy; Interterritorial action

Derasha "presents," II, 97. *See also* Preaching

Descendants, of criminals, lose passive franchise, III, 177

Descent: and communal rights, I, 3, 5, 105, 119; III, 45–46; (elections), II, 47; (leadership), I, 140; (membership), II, 4–5; and guild control, I, 373; and interterritorialism, II, 351; and Messiah, I, 177; and religious functions, I, 134; appreciation in Babylonia of, I, 66; medieval emphasis on, II, 362. *See also* Aristocracy; Davidic descent; Families; Oligarchy

Desecration of shrines, Israelitic, and origin of synagogue, III, 9. *See also* Centralization; Synagogues; Temple, First

Desertion, marital, increase of, II, 317

Designation by retiring officers, communal statutes on, II, 47–48

"Despoiler of the Jews," patriarch as, I, 144

Despotism, communal, attacked by Weil, II, 66. *See also* Absolutism; Dictatorship; Oligarchy

Dessau: congregation in Leipzig from, III, 149; funeral tolls in, II, 154

Detention: of defendants, II, 226; of Meir of Rothenburg's body, III, 70. *See also* Debt bondage; Prisons

Deutero-Isaiah (prophet), I, 58, 74

Deuteronomic Reformation: I, 36, 50–53; and Babylonian Exile, I, 59, 62; and equality of rights, I, 45, 47–48; and monarchical weakness, I, 54; and synagogue, I, 62, 67, 73–74

Deuterosis, Justinian's outlawry of, I, 191, 230. *See also* Oral law

Deyan (Dayyan), III, 125. *See also* Judiciary

Dhimmis, exclusion from office of, I, 187. *See also* Minorities

Dialectics, rabbinic: and congregational autonomy, I, 206; and complex slaughtering, II, 107; and ritual bath, II, 165; and Sicilian chief rabbi, III, 67; and synagogue chanting, II, 105; censors' familiarity with, I, 223; value of, II, 195, 206, 245; III, 168. *See also* Casuistry

Dialects: Arabic, use in deeds of, II, 112; Romance, Jewish, III, 152. *See also* Languages

Diamonds, and household help, II, 305

Diaspora, Jewish, ancient: and Palestine, I, 74, 87–88, 95, 97, 110, 116, 120, 123, 129, 139, 151; II, 215, 220; III, 21; and Roman Empire, I, 76, 82; early growth of, I, 56–58; III, 10; effects of revolt on, I, 111; influenced by Deuteronomic Reformation, I, 50–51; Jewish education in, I, 92; patriarchal appointments in, I, 141; III, 18; uses Greek Bible, I, 123

medieval and modern: and medieval supercommunity, I, 346; and Palestine relief, I, 157–58; II, 340–43; (messengers), III, 216–17. *See also* Deportations; Dispersion; Migrations

Diaspora nationalism, and people's community, III, 3–4

Dice playing: and Jewish excommunication, I, 232; taxes on, III, 208. *See also* Gaming

Dictatorship, Jewish, communal: in Rome, II, 59; in Venice, II, 77

modern, and Jewish community, I, 12–13; Roman, and free associations, I, 107–8. *See also* Absolutism; Oligarchy

Dictionaries, talmudic, III, 16

Didrachmon, *see* Half-shekel

Dienchelele, III, 67. *See also* Chief rabbinate (Sicily)

Dietrichstein, Prince, and Moravian chief rabbi, II, 43
Diets: German, and Jewish assemblies, I, 314; III, 70–71; Hessian, against Jewish judiciary, I, 343; Lithuanian, restricts municipal courts, I, 280; Polish, I, 269, 281, 335–36; (capitation taxes), II, 252; (communal reform), II, 353; (communal indebtedness), I, 335; (Jewish councils), I, 323–24, 328, 333, 336–37; (official bribery), II, 247. *See also* Parliamentarism
Difensori dei capitoli, III, 111. *See also* Defenders of statutes
Differentiation, economic, and medieval cities, I, 274
Dijon, and synod of Troyes, I, 312
Dina de-malkuta dina, *see* Law of the Kingdom
Diocaesaria, *see* Sepphoris
Diocletian, Caius Aurelius Valerius (Roman emperor), I, 135, 143
Diplomacy *and* diplomats, Jewish: I, 317; III, 72–74, 141; ancient, I, 33, 63–65, 105–6; and Ancona prisoners, III, 214–15; and Benjamin Disraeli, II, 54; and communal leadership, I, 197; II, 57, 61; and Church, II, 115–16; III, 80; and court bankers, I, 188–89, 191, 296; and government officials, II, 115–16; and haircuts, III, 203; and Jewish councils, I, 288, 332; III, 78; and Marranos, I, 255–56; and nobles, II, 115–16; and Palestine messengers, II, 342; and polygamy, II, 309; and refugees, I, 320–21; and regional control, I, 295–96; and revocation of expulsion, III, 104; and Saadia Gaon, III, 43; and Salonican congregations, I, 348; and *shammash*, II, 106; and southern chief rabbinates, I, 291, 294–95; III, 66; and tax immunities, II, 274; III, 193; foster regionalism, I, 284; in various regions (Bohemia), III, 86; (England), II, 54; (France), I, 295–96; (Germany), III, 71, 78; (Islam), I, 187–89, 191; III, 43; (Italy), I, 320–21; II, 11; III, 80, 214–15; (Persia), I, 63–65; (Poland), I, 332; (Rome, papal), I, 304, 320–22; (Sicily), I, 294–95; (Spain), I, 288, 291; III, 66; (Turkey), I, 197–98, 348. *See also* Deputations
Diplomas, rabbinic, *see* Contracts
Direct election, Jewish, relatively rare, II, 43. *See also* Elections
Direct taxes, *see* Taxation; Taxes
Directors, as title of elders, I, 101
Dirhem, value of, I, 171
Diritto nazionale, in Leghorn, II, 13. *See also* Customs duties
Disability, physical, of officials, II, 86. *See also* Bureaucracy
Disasters, national, and sumptuary laws, II, 302. *See also* Crises
Disbursements, communal, rights of elders in, II, 60. *See also* Financial administration
Discipline, communal: II, 28; III, 118; and charities, II, 346; and excommunication, I, 198; II, 231; and rabbinic control of slaughterers, II, 109–10; and residence rights, II, 8; and synagogue assemblies, II, 144; and talmudic studies, II, 207; and voting, I, 211; geonic complaints of, I, 203–4; III, 37; self-imposed rules on, I, 259–66; supported by Dutch government, I, 255. *See also* Communal control
educational, I, 360; II, 198–99; III, 169; (teacher-pupil relations), II, 199; in household, and *ḥazaḳah*, II, 299–300; in synagogue, provisions for, III, 150. *See also* Quarrels; interterritorial, and Polish Council, I, 332, 337–38, 344; judicial, flaunted

and wife's consent, II, 310; fees on, I, 175, 202; II, 83; marriage stipulations on, II, 309; not in Noahidic commandments, I, 214; procedural law of, I, 214; II, 240; state control of, II, 211; writs of (aspersions prohibited), II, 318; (communal controversies), III, 164–65, 181; (in exilarch's name), I, 185; (levirate marriage), II, 328; (neglected by heretics), I, 165; (validity), I, 127; II, 240, 318. *See also* Marriage

Diwan, Muslim, *see* Councils

Djizia, Muslim, medieval heritage of, II, 250. *See also* Poll taxes

Dogmas, French Enlightenment's attacks on, II, 360. *See also* Religion

Dohm, Christian Wilhelm, and communal control, II, 363

Domains, owned by exilarchs, I, 175; royal in ancient Palestine, I, 43

Domenico Hierosolymitano (censor), I, 223

Domestics, *see* Servants

Dominicans; and Spanish chief rabbinate, I, 290; as creditors of Polish communities, III, 84

Domnos, inscription of, I, 101; III, 17

Domus conversorum, London, Jewish contributions to, I, 247; III, 184. *See also* Houses

Donat, price of textbook by, III, 170

Donativo, for king, voted by Sicilian assembly, I, 318. *See also* Gifts; Taxation

Dongan, Thomas (governor of New York), I, 260–61

"Donkey's burial," II, 156–57, 224, 331; III, 157

Donnolo, Shabbetai b. Abraham, II, 67; III, 123

Donors, charitable: and reserved annuities, II, 186; and tax exemptions, II, 275; control educational foundations, II, 186; restricted liberality of, II, 345–46; vanity of, and school buildings, II, 186. *See also* Charities; Gifts; Philanthropy

Doria, Andrea (Genoese naval commander), and Jewish captives, I, 306

Dormitories, Jewish, II, 187

Dortmund, under imperial ban, II, 229

Dosa b. Saadia Gaon, III, 46

Double standard of ethics, between faiths, I, 241

Double taxation, problems of, II, 287

Dowries: and brokers' fees, III, 208; and communal aid, II, 332. *See also* Brides; and inheritance laws, II, 318; and marriage quotas, III, 98; fees on, II, 83, 102, 119; in *ḥazaḳah*, II, 295; restrictions on, II, 306; III, 201; taxes on, II, 15, 188, 255. *See also* Marriage contracts

Drach, Abraham, feud of, III, 141

Draconian methods, *see* Criminal law

Draguignan (southern France), at Provençal assemblies, III, 75

Drama, Jewish, history of, III, 167, 207

Drohobycz: communal tyrants in, III, 122; privilege *de non tolerandis Judaeis* of, I, 280

Droughts, in ancient Palestine, I, 42. *See also* Water

Drunkenness: and church attendance, III, 151; and itinerant scholars, II, 323

Druya, "donkey's burial" in, III, 157

Dubno, Jews of: III, 96–97; against out-of-town weddings, III, 128; and billeting of soldiers, III, 189; and Christian ghetto residents, II, 296; communal baths of, II, 166; elect Council deputies, II, 42; emigrate to Palestine, II, 339–40; guilds of, I, 371; meat monopoly of, II, 108–9, 259; residents' oath of, III, 104; taxes of, II, 280; (meat), II, 259; (tenants), II, 252

Dubno *maggid*, II, 99. *See also* Kranz, Jacob
Dubnow, Simon M., as Diaspora nationalist, III, 3–4
Ducks, Spanish taxes on, II, 249
Due process of law, and insult of scholars, II, 180. *See also* Excommunication; Scholars
Duels, ordeal of, I, 251
Dues of guild members, regulation of, I, 371
Dungeons, medieval, and Jewish prisons, II, 226. *See also* Prisons
Dura-Europos: Jewish population of, I, 92; loan contract of, III, 19; synagogue of, I, 83, 91; III, 16
Duran, Profiat (Isaac b. Moses ha-Levi): advises loud study, II, 199–200; III, 169; on availability of books, III, 170; on night study, II, 176; on persecutions and neglect of Bible, II, 195; III, 167
Duran, Simon b. Zemaḥ: on educational associations, III, 91; on league of Jewish merchants, I, 366; on North-African elders, I, 205; III, 50–51; on scholarly women, III, 162; on status of wives, III, 208; on synagogue decorum, III, 148; on title of rabbi, II, 67; III, 123
Duran, Solomon b. Simon: on Marrano gifts, II, 134; III, 146; on sex morality, II, 311; III, 205; on shoeless worship, II, 129; III, 143; on synagogue schoolhouses, III, 151
Dutch Reformed Congregation, New York, and Jewish charities, II, 347
Dyers, Jewish: ancient guilds of, I, 365; in Sicily, I, 368
Dyhernfurth, Jewish cemeteries in, III, 156
Dynastic legitimacy, Muslim, and Bustanai's succession, I, 176
Dynasties: exilarchic, longevity of, I, 175, 186. *See also* Exilarchs; royal (and taxation), III, 183; (as patrons of synagogues), I, 77. *See also* Caliphs; Emperors; Monarchy

Eastern Empire, *see* Byzantine Empire; Roman Empire
'Ebed ha-melek, as Israelitic official, III, 7. *See also* Bureaucracy
Ecclesia, term of, I, 87
Ecclesiasticus, Book of, I, 131; III, 23, 25, 161
Ecija (Spain), educational foundation in, I, 357–58; III, 165
Economic activities, Jewish, ancient: I, 144; III, 26–27; and Babylonian academies, I, 152; and Persian persecutions, I, 148–49; and preservation of resources, I, 132; and rebellions, III, 24; and Roman taxation, I, 116; self-sufficiency of cities in, III, 9
medieval and modern: and boycott of excommunicate, II, 230; and charities, I, 360; II, 344–45, 349; and citrons, II, 164; and communal stability, I, 69; II, 26, 120; and confiscation of synagogues, II, 135; and corporal taxes, III, 188; and councils, I, 321, 347; and education, II, 71, 199, 205, 207; and expulsions, I, 231; and guild system, I, 369; III, 95; and Jewish self-government, I, 22, 208, 274–75; and lay leadership, II, 46, 70; and private worship, II, 125; and polygamy, II, 308; and right of substitution, III, 180; and Sabbath, III, 37; and scholars' privileges, II, 80; III, 25; and teaching profession, II, 183; and women, II, 179; communal safeguards for, II, 361. *See also* Economic regulation; devoid of slaves, II, 177; importance of Marranos in, I, 252; in various regions (Amsterdam), III, 58; (Germany), II, 164; (Islam), I, 157, 167; III,

38; (Italy), I, 231, 274–75, 321; III, 148, 185, 191–92; (modern Palestine), II, 340; (Paderborn), III, 87; (Poland), I, 329; II, 199, 324–25; III, 191–92; (Spain), II, 82; interterritorial features of, I, 304; II, 351; of Spanish exiles, successful, I, 204; state interest in, I, 234, 282; II, 123–24; III, 100. *See also* Class struggle; Taxation; *and under* respective activities

Economic decline, Jewish: and communal bankruptcies, III, 191–92; and corrupt elections of rabbis, II, 93; and Counter-Reformation, II, 272; and education, II, 199; and Polish hospitality, II, 324–25; and Polish taxation, I, 329; and rabbinic salaries, II, 82

Economic regulation, Jewish: II, *290–301*; III, *197–202*; ancient, I, 129–31; III, 17; and associational membership, I, 363; II, 17–18; and ban of settlement, II, 5–7, 9, 16; III, 95; and communal license fees, II, 262; and communal statutes, III, 200; and excommunication, I, 246; III, 178; and exilarchic control, I, 147–48, 169–70; and guilds, I, 366; and Hebrew printing, II, 203; and hospitality, II, 337; and idea of justice, I, 130; and international trade, II, 290; and Palestinian patriarchs, I, 144, 147–48; and price-fixing, II, 300; and private scribes, III, 140; and ritual food, II, 162; III, 187. *See also* Fish; Meat; Wine; and scholars' privileges, I, 139; II, 80; and teachers' competition, III, 164; and social welfare, II, 290; by Candia synods, III, 96; by Polish councils, I, 329–30, 332–33; capitalist attacks on, II, 361; outside influences on, II, 349. *See also* Acquired rights; Communal control; Financial administration; Law; Ordinances; Statutes

Economic status: of officials, II, 118, 120. *See also* Bureaucracy; Salaries; of parents, examined by schools, II, 185. *See also* Charities; Parents

Economic theory, Jewish: history of, III, 25; modern, and congregational divisions, II, 18–19. *See also* Liberalism

'Edah, I, 61, 66, 70, 86–87; II, 124; III, 110–11. *See also* Congregations

Edom, I, 50, 158. *See also* Christianity

Education, Jewish, ancien : I, 60, *124–26*; III, 16, 23; and priesthood, I, 53; and prohibited fees, I, 128; and synagogue, I, 89, 92; bachelors' contributions to, I, 137; communal responsibility for, I, 92, 129, 136; gratuitous, I, 126; *ḥazzan* in, I, 104; in Diaspora, I, 117; (Babylonia), I, 62, 154; open to all classes, I, 135; reforms in, II, 170

medieval and modern: II, 123, *168–207*; III, 92, *160–62*, 170; and assimilation, II, 360; and bankers' support, II, 78; and book lending, II, 201–2; and capitalism, II, 362; and charitable legacies, I, 361; and civil law inquiries, II, 238; and councils, I, 324, 339, 342; III, 146; and dancing, II, 315–16; and Emancipation, I, 8; and Hebrew printing, II, 203; and judiciary, I, 213; II, 73; and Muslim education, III, 163; and rabbinic salaries, II, 81; and ritualistic training, II, 211; and Salonican congregations, I, 348; and semi-annual assemblies, I, 182. *See also* Kallah; and Sicilian chief rabbis, III, 67; and slaughterers, II, 109; and Spanish Holy War, I, 362; and synagogue premises, II, 144; III, 151; and taxation, II, 246; and "ten men of leisure,"

II, 127; and threatening bankruptcy, II, 350; autonomy in, II, 349–50; Bagdad, as center of, I, 193; bequests for, II, 264, 329; communal responsibility for, I, 7, 28, 125–26, 356–58; II, 114–15; III, 42, 161, 164; diversion of funds from, II, 135; German influences on Poland in, I, 271; goals of, II, 190–200, 206–7; high evaluation of, I, 28; III, 161; interterritorial features of, I, 358; minor government interference in, II, 208; obligatory in Metz, III, 165; private, *see* Responsibility, individual; Teachers; occupational, I, 350; II, 190–91, 324; III, 96, 167; rabbinic control of, II, 95, 243–44; reforms in, II, 198–99, 360; vows for, II, 188. *See also* Reforms, educational; superior to Western, I, 210. *See also* Associations, educational; Scholars; Schools; Students; Study; Teachers; Training

Edward I (English king): and excommunication, II, 230; and property of converts, I, 247; outlaws usury, I, 244

Effendi, *ḥakam-bashi* as, I, 198

Egalitarianism, Jewish: and associational autonomy, I, 373–74; and communal bureaucracy, II, 121; and membership rights, II, 13; and modern democracy, II, 358; and supercommunity, I, 346. *See also* Democracy; Equality; Inequalities

Egea (Spain), private skin monopoly in, II, 299

Eger, Akiba b. Simḥah, III, 131; against acquired rights of functions, III, 145; against solemn oath, III, 181; and polygamy, III, 203; and real estate taxes, III, 187–88

Egypt, ancient: I, 47, 57–58, 66; centralization of, I, 41; control over Palestine of, I, 33; Exodus from, I, 56; Jewish intermarriage in, III, 12; leprosy in, III, 155; poets of, I, 36; royal officers in, III, 7; tax-farmers in, I, 38; warriors of, I, 33. *See also* Elephantine

Graeco-Roman, Jews of: I, *76–79*; III, *18*; and Imperial worship, I, 109; and Josephus, III, 31; and municipal administration, III, 18; bankers among, I, 80; Christians among, III, 13; communal dissensions among, I, 79; envoys to Rome of, I, 106; guilds of, III, 18; judiciary of, III, 20; legal status of, I, 75; III, 14; migrations of, III, 13–14; military organization of, I, 71; prayers of, I, 90; quarters of, I, 85–86; taxation of, III, 18; synagogues of, I, 81, 83, 89. *See also* Alabarch; Alexandria; Ethnarchs

Muslim: I, 189; III, 32, 39; academies in, I, 185; and anti-Maimonidean controversy, I, 316; and Babylonian geonim, I, 188–89; and Byzantine captives, II, 336; Babylonian captives in, I, 194; *dhimmis* in, III, 35; desecration of cemeteries in, II, 150–51; excommunication in, III, 178; exilarchic influences in, I, 185; fear of massacres in, I, 171; local judges in, I, 203; *negidim* in, I, 187, 189–90, 291; III, 43; rabbinic tax immunity in, III, 34; relations with Aden of, III, 43–44; synagogues in, I, 164–65; III, 35; various rituals in, I, 167

Turkish: I, 190; congregational divisions in, I, 351; III, 149; French visitor in, III, 159. *See also under* respective cities

Egyptians, ancient: pay *laographia*, I, 105; uprising in Elephantine of, I, 71

Eibeschütz, Jonathan b. Nathan: against lengthy chanting, II, 105; III, 136; against luxuries, III, 201; and behavior of fiancés, III, 206;

and Bordeaux wines, II, 163–64; and dancing, III, 206; and education, III, 163; (after marriage), II, 175; III, 161; (ethics), III, 168; (night study), III, 162; (rabbinic dialectics), II, 195; (Talmud vs. Bible), III, 167–68; and *excommunicatio latae sententiae*, III, 177; and papal intervention in Bohemia, I, 305; and rabbinic contracts, III, 131; and ritual fringes, III, 203; and southern French communities, I, 305; and support of scholars, III, 165; as academic teacher, II, 182; as preacher, III, 134–35; ban for slurs on, III, 178; demands admonition of neighbors, III, 180; letters of, III, 72; relation to Landau of, III, 178. *See also* Emden-Eibeschütz controversy

Eight (Otto) *di Guardia e di Balia*, I, 276

Eisenmenger, Johann Andreas, trial of, III, 171

Eisenstadt: cemetery in, III, 156; rabbinic diploma in, III, 131

El-Amarna period, I, 32

Elaians, congregation of, I, 81

Eldad the Danite, on female slaughterers, II, 107; III, 137

Elders, associational: I, 353; III, 88; election of, I, 359; of private synagogues, III, 144; statutory competences of, I, 356

communal, Israelitic: I, 34–41, 43–45, 48, 55, 68; III, 7, 9; and class struggle, I, 50; assemblies of, I, 46; at local sanctuaries, I, 49; hereditary, I, 50; in Jerusalem, I, 62; influence of, I, 53

Jewish, ancient: I, 98–107, 119, 134–35; III, 13, 21; and Greek associations, III, 18; and Palestinian municipalities, I, 43–44, 133–34; and rabbis, III, 26–27; and Roman law, I, 108–9; and synagogue patrons, I, 98; appointed by patriarch, I, 142; exclusion of relatives among, I, 136; in Babylonia, I, 59, 63–69, 117; in Egypt, I, 76, 89; (Alexandria), I, 78; III, 17; (Elephantine), I, 71–72; in Rome, I, 80, 106–7

medieval and modern: II, 4, *55–66*; III, *118–23*; administer marriages and divorces, I, 276; II, 319; III, 205; and administration of legacies, III, 189; and adoption of statutes, I, 261, 338; II, 30; III, 110–11; and anti-Christian blasphemies, II, 339; and appointment of cantors, III, 137; and archive administration, III, 139; and censorship, I, 321. *See also* Books; Censorship; and charities, II, 266, 322, 335; III, 210, 218; and communal citrons, III, 187; and communal debts, I, 333–34; II, 268–69, 273; III, 190–91; and councils, I, 309–12, 324, 329, 332, 340; II, 41–42; and elections, I, 271–72, 329–30, 342; II, 34–36, 39, 47, 58–59; III, 88, 116, 131–32; and Enlightenment, II, 359–60; and examination of slaughterers, III, 138; and excommunication, I, 246–47; II, 32, 75, 231–32; III, 126, 178–79; and exilarchic officials, III, 44; and foreign interventions, III, 74; and government control, I, 198, 246, 285; II, 34–36, 102, 359, 364; III, 220; and Great Sanhedrin, II, 56; and guilds, I, 371; II, 298; and judiciary, I, 270–71; II, 71–72, 239, 241–42; and law finding, II, 68–70, 290; and *memor*-books, II, 146; and migrations, III, 98; and Palestinian messengers, II, 343; and passive franchise, III, 177, 200; and permission to depart, III, 103; and pestilences, III, 211; and plenary assemblies, I, 316; II, 25, 30; and preachers, II, 99, 114; and price fixing, II, 300; and prisoners, II, 338; and prostitution, II, 314; and rabbinic control, I, 285, 333, 340; II, 74–75, 87; III, 129, 131–32; (ordination), II, 67; (salaries), II, 82; (tenure), III, 129; and residence rights, II, 8, 219, 234; III, 99; and revocation of expulsion, III, 104, 106; and ritual meat, II, 108; III, 137–38; and seizure of property, II, 233; and self-supporting refugees, II, 337; and sex relations, II, 312; and Shabbetian movement, II, 25–26; and signatures of artists, III, 147–48; and stolen objects, II, 227; and support of students, II, 177, 189; III, 166; and sumptuary laws, II, 306; and synagogues (attendance), III, 105; (illumination), II, 134; and taxation, I, 262; II, 246, 280–81, 287; III, 77, 196; and tenant protection, II, 296; and withdrawal of membership, II, 4

appeal to other Jewries, I, 224; appointed for life, III, 113; arrest defaulting taxpayers, II, 219; artisans among, II, 307; boards of, II, 55. *See also* Council; business interests of, II, 361; control economic relations, I, 272; discretionary powers of, I, 272; II, 28, 39, 102, 163, 216, 262, 266, 281, 285, 335, 363–64; III, 110–11; (funeral payments), II, 264; (license fees), II, 262; (loans), II, 268; (wine administration), II, 163; divisions among, III, 121; excluded from Fürth association, I, 364; imprisoned for taxes, II, 340; III, 84, 176, 190; indicted for synagogue, I, 258; intimidation of, I, 212; II, 52; in various regions (America), I, 261; (Alsace), III, 88; (Austria), III, 163; (Avignon), III, 190; (Bohemia), I, 340; III, 86; (Byzantium), II, 52; (Constantinople), III, 48; (Egypt), III, 178; (France) I, 246–47; II, 19, 114, 296; III, 103, 113, 138; (Frankfort), II, 287; (Fürth), I, 364; (Germany), II, 41–42, 48–49, 146, 177, 189; III, 77, 166; (Hamburg) II, 62; III, 187; (Hesse-Cassel), I, 342; (Holland), II, 268; (Islam), I, 200–6; II, 319; III, 43–44; (Italy), I, 276, 321; II, 41–42, 319, 322, 335, 359–60; III, 110–11, 129, 139, 196, 205, 210, 218; (Kingston, Jamaica), I, 262; (Lithuania), I, 333–34; II, 40, 47, 99, 114, 189, 268–69, 273, 337, 343; III, 129, 191; (Moravia), I, 338; III, 147–48; (Palestine, Turkish), II, 340; III, 178; (Poland), I, 270–72, 285, 309–12, 324, 329–30, 332–33, 340, 371; II, 8, 35–36, 42, 71–72, 74–75, 87, 273, 298; III, 43, 84, 86, 113, 122, 129, 131–32, 177, 191, 200, 211; (Portugal), I, 285–86; (Prague), III, 106; (Prussia), II, 312, 359, 361; III, 98, 200; (Rome), I, 222–24; II, 233; (Sicily), I, 316–17; II, 58–59, 102, 232, 280, 339–40; III, 84, 110, 113, 176; (Spain), I, 239, 353; II, 25, 36, 39, 44, 74–75, 82, 108, 227, 241, 281; III, 137–38; (Turkey), I, 198, 246, 285, 316; II, 25, 30, 34–36, 75, 102, 359, 364; III, 105, 220; (Venice), III, 179; (Worms), I, 248–49; lend borrowed money, III, 191; literacy test for, III, 163; local versus regional, I, 283–84; marital preference for, I, 124; number of, II, 55; III, 122. *See also* Council of elders; oath of office of, III, 113; oppressive government of, II, 44; prohibition of criticism of, II, 48–49; prosecuted in conversion of children, I, 222–23; regional, I, 333; II, 8, 71–72; III, 43, 84, 86, 191; resignation of, and tax strikes, II, 348; responsibility for debts of, II, 269, 273; variety of titles of, I, 201; III, 120; vs. ancient heritage, II, 244. *See also* Bureaucracy; Oligarchy

general, Polish, *see* Chief rabbinate; "of the month," II, 62; III, 99. *See also* Executive officers; "rebellious," and Polish Council, I, 332

Eleanor (English queen), and Jewish excommunication, II, 230

Eleazar b. Azariah, R. (tannai), III, 46

Eleazar b. Judah ha-Rokeaḥ, and Rhenish synods, I, 313

Eleazar b. Zadok (tannai), genealogy of, III, 12

Elections, communal, ancient: I, 96–97, 101, 104–5; III, 27; (Israel), I, 48; methods of, III, 27; Roman law on, I, 108–9; time limits of, III, 17–18; vs. appointments, I, 129

medieval and modern: II, 4, *34–50*; III, 98, 113–18; and accounting, II, 65; and associations, I, 350, 359, 362, 371; and congregational divisions, I, 336; II, 20; and councils, I, 328–29; and demagoguery, II, 94; and governments, I, 198, 244–46, 271–72, 301–2, 325; II, 103; and non-native rabbis, I, 333; and plenary assemblies, II, 24; and rabbinic supremacy, I, 135; II, 243–44; and *shtadlanim*, I, 188; and synagogue , II, 144; and unanimity, II, 102; annual (London), II, 62; by lot, I, 342; II, 43–44, 48, 58; by predecessors, II, 43; confirmed by Portuguese chief rabbis, I, 285; corrupt practices at, II, 41, 48, 92–94, 106–7; III, 127; days of, III, 115–16; for life, II, 41, 47; freedom of, II, 74, 359; independence of, II, 74; in private synagogues, III, 144; in various regions (Cologne), III, 130; (Germany), III, 127; (Gerona), II, 58; (Hessia), I, 342; (Huesca), I, 353; (Islam), I, 174, 176, 178–80, 188, 193, 203–4; (Lithuania), II, 39–40, 46; (London), II, 62; (Poland), I, 271–72, 301–2, 325, 328–29, 333; II, 45–46, 84, 92–93, 106–7; (Portugal), I, 285; (Prussia), II, 74, 359; (Rome), I, 336; II, 20; (Sicily), II, 58–59; (Spain), II, 44, 58, 71, 74, 86; (Turkey), I, 198; III, 48; (Worms), I, 248–49; methods of, I, 200, 342; II, 43–49, 61; III, 48; obligatory acceptance of, II, 53–54; of cantors, II, 102–3; of exilarchs, I, 174, 176, 178–80, 193; of fiscal officers, II, 57, 285–86, 288; of judges, II, 71, 84; of *negidim*, I, 193; of rabbis, II, 73–74, 78–79, 86, 92; III, 127; (tenure), II, 86, 92; III, 129; of sextons, II, 106–7; refund of costs of, II, 93; triennial, and demagoguery, II, 94. *See also* Assemblies; Franchise; Membership

Electoral qualifications, *see* Franchise

Electorate, Jewish, participation in ban by, II, 231–32

Eleemosyne, meaning of, I, 131

Elephantine, Jewish colony in: I, 58, *69–73*; and Persian authorities, I, 77–78; archives in, III, 16; communal divisions in, I, 97; III, 17; Darius II's circular to, I, 65; marriages in, III, 12; scribes in, III, 12–13; significance of papyri from, I, 93; III, 11. *See also* Papyri; temple in, I, 60, 71–72, 97

Eles, Mordecai Moses (Moravian chief rabbi), I, 338

Elias l'Eveske (arch-presbyter), I, 297

Elias of Weinheim (imperial tax collector), I, 298

Eliezer b. Hyrcanus, R. (tannai), I, 152

Eliezer b. Isaac (Bohemian rabbi), II, 103

Eliezer b. Joel ha-Levi; II, 348; III, 90, 110; and Rhenish synods, I, 313; as Cologne rabbi, III, 135
Eliezer b. Meshullam (cantor), II, 104
Eliezer b. Nathan of Mayence, I, 212
Eliezer b. Samuel of Metz, on communal decisions, II, 30
Elijah (prophet), I, 45
Elijah b. Moses Gershon, on citrons, III, 160
Elijah b. Samuel, of Lublin, III, 118; 143, 145, 156
Elijah b. Solomon Abraham ha-Kohen, II, 99; III, 218–19
Elijah Menaḥem of London, on preferential treatment of books, II, 200–1, 235; III, 169, 179
Elisha (prophet), I, 36
Elizabeth (English queen), Jews under, I, 255; III, 59
Ellul, maintenance of students during, II, 189–90
Elrin (Germany), anti-competitive ordinance in, II, 297
Elvira, Church synod of, I, 225; III, 54
Elyakim b. Asher Zelig, *see* Jacob Zelig's
Emancipation, Jewish: and communal status, I, 4, 7–8, 21; II, 123, 167, 351–52, 360, 363; (consistories), I, 14; (constitutions), II, 4; (debts), II, 274, 350; and corporal taxes, II, 264; and education, III, 163, 166; (estimate of teachers), II, 183–84; (general sciences), II, 192; and excommunication, II, 233; and secularism, I, 8; in various regions (Frankfort), II, 61; (Germany), I, 18; (Holland), III, 58; (Italy), II, 11; (Moravia), I, 339; (Palestine), I, 18; (Prussia), III, 220. *See also* Democracy; Equality of rights; Legal status
of slaves, Jewish, I, 88; of women, in Italy, II, 178–79
Embassies, Jewish, *see* Deputations; Diplomacy
Embezzlement, communal: II, 228; in Frankfort, III, 142; in Paderborn, III, 123
Emden (city): *memor*-book of, III, 152; rabbis of, III, 131
Emden, Jacob b. Zevi: against Katzenellenbogen, III, 128; as educational reformer, II, 194; (Hebrew grammar), II, 194; (neglect of Bible), III, 167; as school child, II, 174; autobiography of, III, 127; on charitable contributions of orphans, II, 331; III, 212; on Mantua organization, III, 196; on marriage, III, 204; on Polish Council, I, 331; III, 83; on wigs, III, 203
Emden-Eibeschütz controversy, I, 308, 331; III, 73–74, 176
Emendations, of talmudic text, question of, III, 30
Emesa (Syria), patriarchal messenger in, I, 143
Emigration, Jewish: and communal debts, II, 233; and double taxation, II, 287; and regional control, I, 313, 323; II, 20–23; and rights of settlement, II, 7; and Thirty Years' War, I, 307; from various regions (England), I, 297; (France), I, 313; (Germany), I, 245, 307, 323; (Italy), I, 318; II, 21; (Spain), I, 233–34; II, 10; levies on, III, 103; organized by Sicilian assembly, I, 318; restrictions on, I, 233–34, 245, 297; II, 10, 15–16; (communal fees), II, 264; threat in Italy of, II, 21; to Palestine, II, 339–40. *See also* Deportations; Migrations
Emilia (Italy), district of, financial institutions in, III, 196
Emir, Muslim, and Jewish taxpayers, I, 171
Emmerich (bishop of Worms), II, 35, 47

Emotionalism, and communal control, II, 168; vs. intellectualism, II, 198

Emperors: Byzantine, religious authority of, I, 228; Holy Roman (German), and Jewish community (book trade), II, 204; (chief rabbinate), I, 245; III, 70–71; (fiscal responsibilities), II, 154–55; (Frankfort oligarchy), III, 142; (French refugees), I, 313; (massacres), I, 306; (privileges), III, 69, 78; (*qua* judges of Jews), I, 249–50; (redemption of captives), II, 336; (ritual libel), I, 313; (synods), I, 313–15, 322–23; (vs. papacy), I, 183. *See also* Germany; Law (Germany); Roman, and Jewish self-government, I, 76, *107–16*; (diplomacy), I, 304; (ethnarchs), III, 18; (patriarchs), I, 144–45; (price regulation), I, 130. *See also* Law, Roman; Roman Empire; Rome

Emphyteusis: in Sicilian cemeteries, III, 155–56; in synagogue seats, III, 145

Employees, Jewish: and Cassel taxation, II, 12; and population, III, 107; educational opportunities of, II, 176. *See also* Labor; Servants

Employers, Jewish: protected by *ḥazaḳah*, II, 299; relations with employees of, I, 130. *See also* Commerce; Crafts; Guilds

Employment, private: as means of charitable rehabilitation, II, 326–27; legal tenure of, III, 129

Encyclopaedia, Horowitz's treatise as, III, 168

Encyclopedists, French, and communal control, II, 360

Endorsement of communal debts, enforced, III, 191

Endowments, charitable and educational: II, 265–66; III, 165–66; and anti-usury laws, III, 189, 195; and government confiscations, II, 135; obsolescence of, II, 266; III, 165, 189; of cemeteries, III, 152; of synagogues, II, 132, 135; tax exemptions of, II, 275. *See also* Bequests; Foundations

Engagements, *see* Betrothals

England, Jews of: I, 20, 23, *242–47*, 249–50, *255–62*; II, 116, 245, 363–66; III, *59–60*; and disfranchisement of public charges, II, 39; and ecclesiastical courts, II, 210; and excommunication, I, 230, 246; and loss of convert's property, III, 57; and Menasseh ben Israel, I, 309; and moneylending, I, 251; and overcrowded hospitals, II, 327–28; and unity, I, 227; ban of settlement of, II, 6; burghers' opposition to, I, 276; cemeteries of, II, 149; charitable societies of, III, 211; chirograph offices for, II, 110–11; debt bondage of, II, 227; deeds of, II, 111; III, 139; expulsions of, and vested interests, II, 120; families of, III, 123; judiciary of, I, 249; (mixed courts), I, 250. *See also* Exchequer of the Jews; parental interference in marriage among, III, 204; population of, III, 106; prohibition of gatherings of, III, 74; rabbinate of, II, 77; (responsa), III, 169; regional community of, I, 297–98; Sephardic-Ashkenazic divisions in, II, 18; slaughterers among, II, 109; status of women among, III, 163–64; synods of, I, 311; taxation of, II, 249–51; use of Torah in oath by, III, 181. *See also* Law; Monarchy; *and under* respective cities and rulers

Enlightenment, European: and charities, III, 93; and corporal taxes, II, 264; and Jewish education, II, 179, 182, 184; and Jewish university students, III, 167

Jewish: I, 14; II, *351–66*; III, 220; and communal responsibility for books, II, 204–5; and educational reform, II, 190; III, 92, 163; (feminine), II, 179; and ḥasidism, III, 220; and juridical strictness, III, 172; and opposition to Jewish bans, II, 233; and rabbis, II, 77; III, 168; (tax immunities), III, 194; and tax evasions, II, 288; in Galicia, III, 220; in Germany, II, 360–61; in Poznań, III, 131

public, *see* Education

Enmities, personal: and acceptance of office, III, 119; and lovingkindness, I, 132

Entry fees, communal: II, 9; and budgets, II, 262. *See also* Residence rights

Envoys, Jewish, *see* Deputations; Diplomacy

Ephraim b. Isaac the Elder, and synagogue decorations, II, 138

Epigraphy, *see* Inscriptions

Epiphanius, Saint, on Sepphoris Jewry, III, 27

Episcopus judaeorum, *see* Bishops, Jewish; Elders

Equality before the Torah, I, 136

of rights, Jewish: ancient, I, 96; III, 19; (Israel), I, 44–46, 48–49; and community, I, 8, 14, 21; and judicial administration, I, 49; and royal seizure of property, II, 276; in various regions (Byzantium), I, 228; (Italy), I, 232; (Poland), I, 280; (Ptolemaic Egypt), I, 76; (Roman Empire), I, 107; III, 19. *See also* Democracy; Egalitarianism; Emancipation; Inequalities

Equilibrium, communal, and scholarly control, II, 244

Equity, and law finding, I, 128

Eranoi, association of, I, 77

Erfurt, Jews of: III, 77, 107; charitable legacies of, I, 361; synod of, III, 77; transfer of synagogue of, II, 135; wandering scholars among, II, 188

Ergas, Joseph b. Immanuel: on art, III, 146; on expediting procedure, III, 180; on polygamy, III, 203; on tax ordinances, II, 265; III, 188

Errors, judicial, responsibility for, I, 128; II, 218–19

Eṣ ha-ḥayyim congregation, in Salonica, II, 18

"Escape" from reality, in Jewish education, II, 205

Eschatology, Jewish, and Turkish taxation, III, 183. *See also* Messianism

Escheator, Jewish, in England, II, 116. *See also* Exchequer, Jewish

Eschenbach, Wolfram von, II, 192

Eskeles, Bernhard Ritter von, II, 81

Eskeles, Berusch (Moravian chief rabbi), II, 81; III, 126

Eskeles, Gabriel (Moravian chief rabbi), I, 338; II, 8

Espionage, communal, encouraged by Prussia, II, 359

Essenes (sect), I, 87, 95; II, 128

Estates, administration of, and secular courts, II, 210

Estella (Spain), transfer of synagogue of, II, 135

Esther Kyra (Turkish intermediary), I, 197

Etampes, and synod of Troyes, I, 312. *See also* Evreux, Louis d'

Ethics, Jewish: and acceptance of office, III, 119; and admission of Jewish settlers, III, 99–100; and character building, II, 190; and charities, II, 320; III, 218–19; and commercial transactions, III, 200; and educational responsibilities, II, 170–71; and equitable taxation, I, 173; and legal procedure, II, 240; and preaching, II, 97–98, 100; and status of women, II, 318; importance of study of, III, 168; independent of politics, I, 29; liturgical position of, I, 121–24. *See also* Moral conduct; Moralists; Sex morality; Sumptuary laws

Ethiopia, I, 58

Ethiopians, Elephantine soldiers against, I, 69

Ethnarchs, Jewish: Egyptian, I, 106, 190; III, 18, 31; (and *nagid*), I, 190; Palestinian, I, 140–41; (patriarchs as), III, 28

Ethnic principle: Israelitic, superiority of, I, 54; Jewish, in Babylonian Exile, I, 73

Etroger, Lithuanian, II, 165. *See also* Citrons

Eugenius III (pope), I, 217

Eugenius IV (pope), I, 221, 320

Eunuchs, royal, and Israelitic administration, III, 7

Euphrates valley, Jews at, I, 83. *See also* Assyria; Babylonia

Europe: I, 3; III, 5–6, 52; ancient settlements in, I, 82–84; and eastern synagogues, I, 164; and modern dictatorship, I, 12–13; and Palestine relief, II, 340; and Palestino-Babylonian influences, I, 192, 194; and sectarian struggles in America, II, 365; and segregation in baths, II, 165; attacks on synagogues in, III, 36; constitutional experiments in, I, 156; II, 3; corporate organization in, I, 208; field synagogues in, I, 86; learning of, I, 194; ministries of cults in, I, 7; oligarchic trends in, I, 27; II, 50; pilgrimages to graves in, II, 154–55; rabbinic tax immunities in, III, 34; slavery in, II, 177; three-class system in, III, 115; use of Torah in oath in, III, 181. *See also under* respective countries and cities

central: congregational divisions in, I, 351–52; nexus between taxation and autonomy in, I, 282; *Pletten* system in, II, 322; rabbinate in, III, 123, 134; stained glass windows in, II, 138

eastern: I, 10; and nationalism, I, 7; III, 4; and secularism, I, 6; and socialism, I, 7; communal debts in, II, 353; covering the heads in, II, 307; heyday of rabbinate in, II, 89; interruption of prayers in, II, 33; Jewish education in, III, 169; Jewish population in, I, 26; modern importance of, I, 267; private congregations in, II, 125–26; rules of evidence in, I, 273; synagogue decorum in, III, 23

western: I, 4; associational autonomy in, I, 374; few Jewish guilds in, I, 366–67; Jewish resettlement in, I, 252; rabbinate in, III, 123, 134; spread of Polish communal influences in, II, 355; III, 134. *See also under* respective countries and cities

Eusebius Pamphilius: I, 80; and Palestinian patriarchs, III, 40; Philonic fragments preserved by, III, 16

Evangelists, Jewish, II, 97. *See also*, Preaching

Evening services: and flogging of criminals, II, 225; and interruption of prayers, II, 33–34. *See also* Liturgy; Synagogues; Worship

Everardus, *magister Judaeorum*, I, 295

Eviction, of tenant, and new leaseholds, II, 293. *See also* Acquired rights; Tenants

Evidence, rules of: II, 239; III, 177; and acquired rights, II, 297; and informing, II, 240–41; and insistence on clarity, II, 212; and mixed dancing, II, 316; and Polish mixed litigations, I, 273; complexity of, I, 128; variety of, I, 240, 251. *See also* Procedure

Evil-merodach (Babylonian king), I, 69

Evolution, communal, and modern stability, II, 121
Evora congregation, in Salonica, I, 351; II, 96
Evreux, Louis d', Count d'Etampes, I, 296; III, 75–76
Examination: of animals, and ritual slaughtering, II, 107; of slaughterers, and rabbinic authorization, II, 109–10; III, 138
Examiners, communal, periodic examination by, II, 197
Examples, setting of, and criminal law, II, 221, 224
Exarchon, Roman, position of, I, 106
Exchequer of the Jews (English): III, *56–57*; and mixed litigations, I, 250; and Jewish presbyters, I, 297; Christian officials of, II, 116
Excise taxes, communal: and class divisions, II, 278–79; and communal services, II, 257; and municipal taxation, II, 257; attacked in Emancipation era, II, 260. *See also* Candles; Meat; Wine
Exclusion of members, from private synagogues, II, 126. *See also* Membership
Exclusivity, congregational, Brazilian statutes on, III, 59. *See also* Regional control
Excommunicatio latae sententiae, II, 229; III, 177
Excommunication, European: for Christians living with Jews, I, 225; for Jews yielding to pressure, I, 235; for preferring Jewish witnesses, I, 226; of German communities, II, 229

Jewish: I, 169; II, *228–33*; III, *177–79;* abuses in, I, 298; II, 231–32; III, 178; ancient, I, 111, 115, 152; and associational expulsion, I, 349; and censorship of books, II, 202; and charitable contributions, II, 344; and communal statutes, II, 31; and confiscation of property, I, 271; and correction of criminals, II, 222; and disregard of local customs, III, 203; and "donkey's burial," II, 156; and enforced divorces, III, 204; and exilarchs, III, 41; and exploitation of poor, I, 166; and forbidden emigration, I, 246; and gaming, III, 207; and government safeguards, I, 111, 115, 172–73, 246, 271, 301; III, 71; (control), I, 275; (non-recognition), II, 364; (pressure), I, 198; II, 74, 102; (restrictions), II, 52; and *ḥakam-bashi*, I, 196; and interruption of prayers, III, 112; and loss of taxpayer, II, 232; and *negidut*, I, 190–91; and oath of office, II, 37; and price fixing, II, 300; and private cemeteries, II, 148; and residence rights, I, 314; II, 234; and Shabbetian movement, I, 308, 331; and sumptuary laws, II, 306; and taxation, II, 282–83; (declarations), II, 281, 283; (immunities), II, 14, 275; III, 34; (ordinances), II, 265, 282; and wine exports, II, 164; and women suffrage, III, 114

assures authority, I, 213; Catholic control over, I, 275; duration of, I, 228, 230–31, 271; elaborate ceremony of, II, 32; extent of, I, 331; failure of execution of, II, 85; for absence during Bible recitation, II, 141; for bi-sexual dancing, II, 316; for corrupt elections, II, 44, 46, 93; for criticism of leaders, II, 49; for derision of foreign rituals, III, 149; for enforced burial, III, 157; for illicit relations, II, 312–13; for inflicting losses on Christians, I, 272; for minor transgressions, I, 168–69; for private deeds, I, 202; for private synagogues, I, 256; III, 144; for re-election of elders, II, 41; for synagogue gossip, II, 141; for testimony against Jews,

I, 240; for unauthorized reprints, I, 331; formulas of, I, 169; II, 229–30, 233; III, 37, 177; fortifies communal ordinances, II, 31; III, 111–12, 179, 200. *See also* Ḥerem; foreign, contested validity of, I, 314; II, 92, 243; III, 110; geonic, types of, I, 168–69; interterritorial, I, 169; II, 198; in various regions (Byzantium), II, 52; (Candia), III, 112; (France), I, 246, 263; (Germany), I, 246, 298–99, 311; II, 92; (Islam), I, 168–69, 190–91, 202; III, 41; (Lithuania), II, 93; (London), II, 21; (Moravia), II, 41; (Poland), I, 271–72, 301, 330–31; II, 93; (Rome), I, 111, 115; II, 60; (Spain), I, 286; II, 71, 74, 85; (Venice), I, 275; (Turkey), I, 196, 198; of elders, III, 142; of entire communities, II, 170, 229; III, 177; of London New Synagogue, II, 21; of rabbis, I, 152, 298–99; III, 129; penalties for breaches of, II, 235; private promulgation of, II, 75, 79, 231; III, 124, 126; III, 178; (restricted), II, 32; promulgated by Gershom, and synods, I, 311; rabbinic vs. lay control of, II, 60, 71, 74–76, 79; III, 129; regional enforcement of, I, 286–87; restrictions on, I, 152; II, 32; revocation of, III, 112, 126; self-imposed, II, 238, 295–96; synagogue announcements of, II, 144; synodal sanction for, I, 212, 330–31

Execution of court sentences, Jewish: ancient, I, 109, 111, 115, 127; and excommunication, II, 228; and prisons, II, 226

Executioners, Jewish, III, 175

Executive committees, communal: II, 58–61, 111–12. *See also* Committees; Council of elders

Executive officers, communal: rotation of, II, 55, 58–59, 62; III, 99; sextons as, II, 106

Executors, and administration of legacies, III, 189

Exemptions, personal: and communal control, II, 13–14; from acceptance of office, III, 119–20, 164; from chief rabbis' authority, I, 293; from debt bondage, III, 190; from excommunication, I, 246; II, 232. *See also* Tax immunities

Exhumation, Jewish: and removal of cemetery, II, 152; for burial within city walls, II, 149; for profit, I, 218; papal prohibition of, II, 150

Exilarchate *and* exilarchs: I, 69, *145–50*, *173–86*; III, 30–32, 39, 41, 43; and ancient academies, III, 33; and advent of Messiah, I, 155; and court organization, II, 241; and Davidic descent, I, 68–69; and European supercommunity, I, 187, 191, 285, 346; and geonim, I, 174, 179–80, 183, 186; and government appointments, I, 173, 207; II, 218–19; (decrees), III, 39; and *ḥakam-bashis*, I, 195; and local elections, I, 203; and local judges, I, 128, 201, 203; III, 50; and *negidut*, I, 190–91, 193; III, 44; and Palestinian calendar, I, 192; and patriarchs, I, 68–69, 149–50; and rabbinic ordination, III, 24; and Rab's imprisonment, I, 130; and scholarly training, I, 154; and synagogue legends, III, 12; contributions to, denied, I, 181; control of, I, 27, 206; extinction of, and Spain, I, 210; local, in Damascus, III, 73; migrations of, I, 173, 189; monarchical features of, I, 27; respected by Maimonides, III, 43; succession in, III, 39; support scholars, III, 41–42

Exile, Jewish: and dangers of informing, II, 221; and redemption of captives,

II, 337; and symbols of mourning, II, 138; substitutes in, I, 209. *See also* Babylonian Exile; Diaspora; Spanish exiles
Exodus from Egypt: and *shabbat hagadol*, III, 134; significance of, I, 56
Expansion, Jewish, and prohibition of new synagogues, I, 112–13. *See also* Dispersion; Population
Expense accounts: of Palestinian messengers, suspect, II, 342; of *shtadlanim*, II, 115; of tax assessors, limited, II, 286. *See also* Accounting
Expenses, monetary, and denunciation of transgressors, II, 236
Experiences of students, and study for its own sake, II, 206–7
Experts: judicial, debated by rabbis, III, 173; ritualistic, and religious law, II, 211. *See also* Scholars
Expiation of sins, and flogging, II, 225
Exports: communal duties on, II, 262. *See also* Customs duties; from ancient Palestine, I, 42. *See also* Commerce
Expropriation: for taxes, rabbinic opinions on, II, 285; judges' discretionary powers in, II, 218; of Christian landowners, for ghetto, II, 291
Expulsion: associational, and excommunication, I, 349; from synagogue, as judicial penalty, III, 178; for unfair competition, II, 299; of Jewish heretic by ecclesiastical court, I, 221. *See also* Banishment
Expulsions of Jews: and ban of settlement, II, 6–7; and break in historic continuity, I, 209, 252; and burghers (agitation for), I, 276–79; (against), I, 279; III, 64; and charitable associations, I, 362; and Christian residents in ghetto, II, 296; and Church, I, 224, 279; and congregational conflicts, II, 19; and evolution of rabbinate, II, 75; and fiscal obligations, I, 235; III, 145; (citron taxes), I, 260; (departing members), III, 104; (payment for poor), II, 246; and foreign students, III, 166; and Jewish councils, I, 307, 313, 318, 327; and Jewish courts, III, 181; and liquidation of communal property, II, 186–87, 271; and organized exodus, I, 318; and prisoners, III, 176; and redemption of captives, II, 337; and Resettlement, I, 242; and royal power, I, 231; and small size of libraries, II, 201; and vested interests, II, 120; from various regions (ancient Rome), I, 80; (Bohemia), I, 305; II, 260; (Byzantium), I, 228; (England), I, 242, 276; III, 63; (France), I, 242, 296; II, 186–87; (French colonies), I, 266; (Germany), I, 277–78; (Italy), I, 231, 279; III, 64, 80; (Lithuania), I, 269; (Netherlands), I, 242; (Papal States), I, 221, 224; (Poland), I, 327; (Portugal), I, 235, 279; (Sicily), I, 318; (Spain), I, 235, 279, 318, 362; II, 75; III, 181; leave behind converts, I, 247; legality of, I, 215–16; prevented by Christian creditors, II, 270; threat of, as legal sanction, I, 263. *See also* Anti-Semitism; Persecutions
Expurgation of Hebrew books, I, 223. *See also* Censorship
Extortions, bureaucratic: and care for prisoners, II, 338–39; and Jewish funeral tolls, II, 153. *See also* Bureaucracy; Corruption; Gifts
Extradition treaties: French, and Jewish migrations, I, 245; Spanish, I, 234
Extraterritorialism, Jewish, and capitulations, III, 101–2
"Eye for an eye," doctrine of, II, 221
Eymeric, Nicholas (inquisitor), I, 221; III, 53
Ezekiel (prophet): I, 45, 52, 58–59, 61; as founder of synagogue, I, 164; confers with elders, I, 68; death of, I, 69; on *nasi*, I, 141; on priesthood,

I, 60; projected constitution of, I, 47–48; III, 12; reputed grave of, II, 154; Temple of, III, 10

Ezofowicz, Abraham (converted noble), I, 300; III, 71

Ezofowicz, Michael (Lithuanian chief rabbi), I, 300–1; III, 71

Ezra the Scribe: I, 61, 64–66, 70, 73, 89; and Babylonian inscriptions, III, 11; and meaning of "scribe," III, 11, 13; and Temple ministers, I, 68; as founder of synagogue, I, 164; reputed grave of, II, 154; types of exiles returning with, III, 11

FAILURE, economic, and teaching profession, II, 183

Fairs, Jews at: I, 236; and tax exemptions of visitors, II, 12; communal ordinances on, III, 199; French, and synods, I, 322; German, I, 324; III, 149; Lithuanian, and sale of citrons, II, 165; Polish (and Jewish councils), I, 322; (and Italian merchants), I, 332–33; (and supreme court), I, 325; (and taxes on merchandise from), II, 263

Faiseurs d'articles, II, 30. *See also* Defenders; Statutes

Fakers: among Palestine pilgrims, II, 341; loss of passive franchise by, III, 177

Falcona (Abenafia's widow), I, 293]

Falk, Jacob Joshua b. Zevi Hirsch: election of, II, 93; on marital relations, III, 208

Falk Kohen, Joshua b. Alexander: I, 329; II, 95; at Polish Council, III, 83; on majority principle, III, 109; on recitation of Decalogue, III, 22; personal responsibility for, II, 236

False denunciations, personal responsibility for, II, 236

False tax declarations, obligatory denunciation of, II, 281

Families, Israelitic: I, 42; and Babylonian synagogues, I, 66; and clans, I, 43; elders of, I, 48; feuds of, I, 47

Jewish, ancient: and communal office, I, 99, 103, 105, 136; and Palestinian pilgrimages, I, 120; purity of, I, 72

medieval and modern: III, 81, 123, 126, 142; and cloistered teachers and students, I, 357; and elections to Polish councils, I, 328–29; and funeral payments, II, 263; and hereditary rabbinate, III, 132; and identification of heirs, I, 248; and poll tax, I, 273; and rituals, I, 67; and scholarly prestige, I, 154; II, 181; and settlement restrictions, II, 10; as recipients of meat taxes, II, 259; average size of, II, 259; cemetery plots of, communal revenue from, II, 156; disfranchisement of, II, 47; heads of, and plenary assemblies, II, 23; instability of wealth of, I, 28; II, 50, 121; interterritorial features of, I, 168; in various regions (Austria), III, 126; (Frankfort), III, 142; (Italy), II, 10; (Islam), I, 168; (Poland), I, 273, 328–29; II, 80, 259; (Spain), II, 14, 126, 259; III, 132; (Worms), II, 47; names of, and titles of elders, III, 120; number of, and communal responsibilities, II, 73, 82, 96, 114, 126, 162–63, 172, 189; of diplomatic agents, allowances for, II, 116; of Polish rabbis, tax exempt, II, 80; support after marriage of, II, 175; synagogue seats of, II, 130; tax exemptions of, II, 14, 80, 274–76. *See also* Descent; Genealogy; Heredity; Inheritance

Family: educational responsibilities of, II, 170. *See also* Parents; Responsibility; peace of, and gaming,

III, 208; pride in (admission of new members), III, 99–100; (*Chronicle of Aḥima'az*), I, 190. *See also* Descent; Genealogy; solidarity of, and charitable obligations, II, 325
celebrations: and adult education, II, 206; and announcements in synagogue, II, 145; and hair cuts, III, 203; and sumptuary laws, II, 302–3; unrestricted number of guests at, II, 326
chapels, Austrian tax on, II, 130. *See also* Synagogues, private
control: and associational membership, II, 17; III, 107; and exclusion of native rabbis, III, 132; of educational endowments, I, 357–58; III, 166. *See also* Oligarchy
groups, Babylonian, and Restoration, I, 68; quotas, in German-speaking countries, II, 5, 16. *See also* Residence rights
relations, Jewish: and investigation of marriage applicants, II, 311; and moral laws, II, 307; and talmudic studies, II, 207; communal control over, II, 210, 291, 317–19. *See also* Divorce; Marriage; Parents; Wives

Famines: and Persian persecution, I, 148–49; in ancient Israel, I, 47; Muslim taxation during, III, 38

Fano, Menahem 'Azariah da: on acceptance of office, III, 119; on desecration of cemeteries, II, 151; III, 154; on fiscal obligations, II, 256; III, 145; on *ḥazakah*, II, 297; III, 199

Fano, Sabbato (Rome rabbi), III, 72

Farmers *and* farming, *see* Agriculture; Monopolies; Tax-farming

Fascism, and Jewish community, I, 13–14

Fashions: ancient, and Jewish burial, I, 94; modern, and *sha'atnez*, II, 297

Fasts, Jewish: I, 86; and imminent massacres, I, 306; before homage to popes, I, 217; games during, II, 317; of teachers, impair efficiency, II, 183

Fat, consumption of, by heretics, I, 165

"Father of orphans" Society, Dutch, II, 332

Fathers: as teachers, II, 174. *See also* Parents; in-law, educational responsibilities of, II, 175; of guilds, II, 88–89; "of orphans," communal supervisors as, II, 330; "of the court," position of, I, 151; II, 95, 258. *See also* Judiciary; Rabbis

Fatimids (dynasty), Jews under: III, 32; and local judges, I, 203; and provincial leadership, I, 189–90, 193–94. *See also* Egypt

Fattori, Roman: and communal indebtedness, II, 272; as name of derision, II, 53; election of, II, 60. *See also* Elders

Fatwas, Turkish, and synagogues, III, 36. *See also* Responsa, Muslim

Favoritism, communal: and charity overseers, II, 348; and Polish oligarchy, I, 336; III, 99; and *Pletten*, II, 345; checked by tax provisions, II, 286; III, 99
royal: and Jewish abattoirs, II, 159; and Jewish polygamy, II, 309–10; and taxation, II, 247, 288; (immunities), II, 13–14, 274; (meat), II, 259. *See also* Inequalities

Fayyum, Jews of, I, 130; III, 13–14

"Fear of the Master," vs. "fear of heaven," II, 180–81. *See also* Teachers

Feast of Tabernacles: I, 52, 100, 182; and election days, III, 116; and rabbinic revenue, II, 84; and sale of citrons, II, 164–65

Feathers, revenue from, and meat taxes, III, 186–87

Federations of Charities, American, I, 5–6

Fees, communal: and revenue of officials, II, 92, 101–3, 114, 117–19; III, 186; for administration of oath, II, 103; for funerals, I, 353–54; II, 103; for German emigration permits, II, 16; for release from ban, III, 178; for postal services, II, 115; for ritual slaughtering, II, 108; III, 186; for services, regulations of, I, 364, 370; (and taxation), II, 256–57; for settlement rights, II, 9; for weddings, II, 101–3

judicial: III, 177; and lay judiciary, II, 64, 215; Cracow statute on, III, 127; evasion of prohibition of, I, 128; for witnessing deeds, II, 113; reduction of, attempted, II, 236; revenue from, II, 84, 265; III, 51–52

of agents, and anti-competitive regulations, II, 297; of cantors, II, 101–3; of marriage brokers, III, 208; of rabbis, II, 83, 92; of slaughterers, III, 186; of teachers, II, 114

royal: for election of elders, II, 36–37; for private worship, II, 160

Felonies, Oxford students accused of, II, 187

Feminism, Jewish, and popular literature, II, 178. *See also* Women

Fences of the law, and judges' discretion, II, 218

Fenolet, Don Pedro, Viscount de Illa, III, 66

Ferdinand I (Aragonese king), I, 220

Ferdinand IV (Castilian king), III, 55

Ferdinand I (Holy Roman emperor), I, 299; II, 35

Ferdinand I (king of Naples), I, 232; II, 153

Ferdinand the Catholic (Spanish king): and cemeteries, III, 155; and craftsmen, I, 368; and Jewish judiciary, I, 239; III, 56; and Jewish taxpayers, II, 280; and rabbis, I, 289; II, 74–75; III, 182; and Spanish dependencies, I, 318; III, 64

Ferrara: and Azariah de' Rossi, I, 308; and Jewish conferences, I, 319–21; III, 80. *See also* Councils; bisexual dancing in, II, 316; congregational divisions in, III, 149; ghetto ordinances in, I, 226; II, 291–92; III, 197; in pre-censorship commission, I, 321; Jewish brotherhood in, III, 92; legacy for, III, 212–13; messianic movement in, III, 215; property taxes in, II, 256; statute of on electoral rights, III, 114. *See also* Councils; Statutes; Talmud Torah in, II, 191; tenant protection in, II, 293

Festivals: Israelitic, at local sanctuaries, I, 49, 52; private, II, 303. *See also* Family celebrations; Holidays

Festivities, communal: and donation of Pentateuch scrolls, II, 132; and sumptuary laws, II, 303

Fettmilch, Vincent, rebellion of, II, 61

Feudalism, ancient: influence on Jewish law of, I, 211; in Palestine, I, 33; in Persia, I, 147–48, 155; in Roman Empire, I, 117, 156

medieval and modern: and communal control, III, 104; and Jewish associations, I, 372; and Jewish status, I, 208, 269; (military service), II, 267; and migrations, I, 245; and oaths of residents, III, 104; and tolls, II, 153, 263; and transfer of Jews, I, 231; III, 55; hinders fiscal exploitation, I, 231; northern, vs. Mediterranean, I, 227, 243

Fez, Jews in: III, 47; and Muslim guilds, III, 94; sumptuary ordinances of, III, 201; taxation of (immunities), III, 193; (meat), III, 186

Fiancés, relations among, regulated, III, 206. *See also* Betrothals

Fickleness of cantors, proverbial, II, 104

Field synagogues, I, 86

Fields, taxes on, II, 253. *See also* Agriculture; Land; Real estate

Figo, Azariah b. Ephraim, as preacher, III, 134–35

Financial administration, communal: II, *246–89*; III, *183–97*; ancient, I, 72, 84, 87–88, 102–3, 110, 142, 148; (Persian taxation), I, 149; III, 31; (Roman taxation), I, 135; and appropriation of synagogues, II, 135; and charities, II, 343–49; and Christian creditors, II, 270; and confiscation of electoral bribes, II, 93; and congregational divisions, II, 11, 19–20; and debts, II, 271–72; and expenses of tax-farmers, II, 285; and education, II, 114–15, 171–72; and free loan banks for Christians, II, 327; and funeral processions, II, 152–54; and judiciary, I, 202; II, 283–84. *See also* Fees, judicial; and license fees, II, 262; and meat taxes, II, 257–59; III, 186–87; and new synagogues, I, 221; and obsolescence of endowments, II, 266; and oligarchy, III, 142; and regional community, I, 286; and responsibility of elders, and members, II, 52–53; III, 104, 176; and revenue from cemeteries, II, 149–50, 155–56; and ritualistic disparity, II, 19; and salary of *ḥazzan*, II, 101–2; and *shtadlanim*, I, 188; and state taxes, I, 105, 159, 187; and sumptuary laws, II, 302; and supervision of chests, III, 195; and synagogues (architecture), II, 136–37; (candles), II, 134; (seats), II, 130–31; (vows), II, 132; and trust in charity supervisors, II, 64; and welfare budgets, II, 290, 349–50; discretionary powers of, II, 285; III, 195; importance of, II, 57; in various regions (Alsace), III, 88; (Hamburg), II, 62; (Islam), I, 159, 169–73, 187–88; (Nice), III, 189; (papal Rome), II, 60, 256, 272; (Poland), I, 300–3, 326–27; II, 93; III, 184; (Spain), I, 286; (Venice), II, 327; irregularities in, II, 259; III, 122; reviewed by *tribunus populi*, II, 287; state interest in, I, 209; II, 123–24. *See also* Budgets; Economic regulation; Taxation; Treasurers

agents, Jewish, rise of, II, 357. *See also* Court Jews; status, *see* Wealth

Fines, governmental: Austrian on private synagogues, III, 143–44; English, from London community, I, 211; German (central collection), I, 298; (for Frankfort assembly), I, 323; (for non-attendance at Church), III, 53; inquisitorial, for Jewish magic, I, 237; papal, for burial within city walls, II, 149

Jewish: II, 228, *233–35*; ancient, I, 84, 94, 115, 127; II, 67; III, 16–17; and elders, II, 54; III, 99, 218; and Exchequer of the Jews, I, 250; and governmental approval, II, 232; and legal residence, II, 234; and prison terms, II, 226; and prostitution, II, 314; and rabbis, II, 74, 76, 85; (ordination), I, 127; II, 67, 214, 220; and regional control, II, 22; and Roman courts of arbitration, I, 115; assure authority, I, 213; communal revenue from, I, 330; II, 265; III, 51–52; division of, I, 343; III, 16–17; (charities), I, 330; II, 346; (education), II, 185; (governments), I, 99, 271, 330; (judges), I, 330; for absence from meetings, I, 341; II, 29, 62; for absence from synagogue, II, 126–27; for appeal to government, I, 343; for breaches of discipline, II, 304, 306; III, 118; for communal borrowing, I, 334;

for competition with burghers, I, 281; for criticism of leaders, II, 48–49; for debasing metals, I, 330; for errors in accounting, II, 348; for evasion of *ḥazakah*, II, 300; for failure to elect, III, 116–17; for illicit relations, II, 312–13; for insulting scholars, II, 75, 79; for interruption of prayers, II, 34; for private deeds, I, 202; for private synagogues, III, 143–44; for re-election of elders, II, 41; for refusals (to accept office), II, 54; III, 119; (to collect alms), I, 363; II, 346; (to lend books), II, 201–2; for Sabbath violations, III, 55; for summonses to Christian courts, I, 236; for support of beggars, II, 324; for synagogue assaults, III, 150; for unlawful return, I, 333; imposed by local associations, I, 349; in various regions (England), I, 250; (Germany), I, 343; (Hesse-Cassel), I, 341, 343; (Islam), I, 202; (Italy), I, 363; II, 29, 76; (Lithuania), I, 334; (Moravia), II, 41; (Poland), I, 271, 281, 330, 333; (Prussia), III, 218; (Rome, ancient), I, 94, 115; (Spain), I, 74; II, 85; III, 55; of free-masons, III, 175; replace physical retaliation, II, 221; III, 175; self-imposition of, and charities, II, 346. *See also* Penalties

Fire: as charitable gift, I, 132; ordeal of, I, 25. *See also* Conflagrations

First-born, redemption of, and exilarchs, I, 175

Firuz (Persian king), I, 148

Fiscal administration, *see* Financial administration; Taxation

Fischel, Franczko *or* Ephraim (Polish chief rabbi), I, 300–1

Fischel, Moses (Polish tax-farmer), I, 300

Fischel, Moses, Doctor (Polish chief rabbi), I, 301

Fish: and communal control, II, 160–61; III, 159; Spanish taxes on, II, 249

Five-year contracts, reasons for, II, 88

Fiscus judaicus, Roman, medieval heritage of, II, 250–51. *See also* Taxation

Flaccus, L. Valerius (Roman governor), I, 88, 109

Flaccus Pomponius (Roman governor), I, 99

Flanders, spread of poverty in, I, 363

Fleet, for Jewish refugees, and Capistrano, I, 321

Flight of capital: Polish, and Jewish council, II, 15–16; tax on, in Rome, III, 103–4. *See also* Emigration

Flirtation, verbal, prohibited by Prague ordinance, II, 314

Flogging, governmental: for Hebrew deeds, I, 241; II, 111; of ancient synagogue assailants, I, 113; of Jewish elders, II, 52–53; of Jewish heretics, I, 221

Jewish: III, 175–76; and asceticism, II, 225–26; and charitable contributions, II, 344; and eastern chiefs, I, 168–69, 191, 196, 203; III, 41; and rabbinic ordination, II, 220; assures authority, I, 213; by *ḥazzan*, I, 104; conversion of fines into, II, 227; for breaches of discipline, II, 307; III, 118; for private deeds, I, 202; judges' discretionary powers in, I, 168–69; II, 218, 241; legal adjustments in, I, 168–69; II, 224; of free-masons, III, 175. *See also* Penalties

Florence, Jews of: III, 63, 125; bankers among, III, 125; conference among, I, 320; III, 79; ghetto statutes of, III, 197; Hebrew manuscripts of, II, 143; judiciary of, I, 276; lay control of, II, 77; III, 125; legacies for, III, 212–13; Levant trade of, I, 275; sale of

meat among, II, 158; Talmud Torah of, III, 166
Florentin (Salonican family), II, 50
Flour, Jewish taxes on, II, 249, 260
Folk art, Jewish, and funerary arts, III, 156
Folklore: Arabian, and exilarchs, III, 40; Jewish, and burial, I, 94
Folkways, Jewish: American adjustments in, II, 365–66; medieval perseverance of, I, 210, 243; II, 69, 161. *See also* Customs; Mores; Traditions
Fondachi, Judeo-Italian, II, 11. *See also* Hostelries, Jewish
Food: ancient Palestinian, I, 42; and schoolchildren, II, 187–90, 199; and sumptuary laws, II, 302–4; III, 202; charitable distribution of, I, 131–32; II, 320, 322, 333. *See also* Kitchen; communal control over, II, 160–61; (taxes on), II, 249, 260, 262
ritual, and *corvée* labor, II, 267; and feminine education, II, 178; and judiciary, II, 211; and prisoners, III, 215; and Reform Judaism, I, 9; and talmudic studies, II, 207. *See also* Meat; Wine
"For the sake of peace": and burial of Gentiles, II, 148; III, 153; and Gentile poor, II, 320; III, 214
Forced conversion, *see* Conversion to Christianity
Foreign: accounts, and customs duties, II, 265; cattle dealers, agents of, and unfair competition, II, 297; Jews, *see* Aliens; languages, and Jewish diplomats, I, 187–88. *See also* Languages; mercenaries, in ancient Palestine, I, 39; nations, emulation of, I, 36
Forgeries, medieval, and reliability of deeds, I, 251
Forli, meeting of vigilance committee at, I, 320
Formalism, legal, and writs of divorce, II, 240. *See also* Law
Formulas, legal, and communal witnesses, II, 113. *See also* Contracts; Deeds
"Fortified cities," Palestinian, III, 8. *See also* City walls
Forty days lapse, and English excommunication, II, 230
Foundations: charitable, I, 361; II, 185–86; educational, I, 357–58; Moravian, I, 339
Founders: associational, and statutes, I, 356, 361; of synagogues, II, 145
Four captives, authenticity of story of, I, 194
Fourth son of *Haggadah*, defendant likened to, II, 238
Fowl, Spanish taxes on, II, 249
France, Jews of: I, 11, 13, 23, 25, 83, 242, *244–51*, *262–66*; III, *61–62*; agriculture of, II, 253; and anti-Maimonidean controversy, I, 307, 316; and burghers, I, 278–79; and burial societies, III, 90; and Emancipation, I, 14; and exilarchic glory, I, 176; and Jewish question, II, 353; and justices of the Jews, I, 250; and *Leibzoll*, II, 264; and oath *more judaico*, III, 181; and opposition to bans, II, 233; and overcrowded hospitals, II, 327–28; and transportation of poor, III, 209; and unity, I, 227; Babylonian heritage of, I, 212; basic privileges of, I, 268; bathhouses of, III, 160; cemeteries of, II, 149; III, 154; charitable tithes of, II, 344; citizenship of, III, 54–55; communal control of, I, 212; communal debts of, II, 274; Crusaders' threats to, I, 306; development of dialectics among, III, 67; early traditions of, II, 69; education of, I, 357–58; III, 92; elections by plenary assembly among, II, 43; *ḥazakah* legislation of, II, 293, 295–

96, 298; interruption of prayers among, II, 33; itinerant mendicants among, II, 323; judiciary of, III, 180; legalization of worship of, II, 143–44; Maimonides' appreciation of, III, 52; migrations of, I, 245; II, 15–16, 183; III, 103, 108; Palestine messengers among, II, 342–43; population of, III, 106, 108; powers of excommunication among, II, 32; prices of manuscripts among, II, 200; rabbis of, II, 77–78; III, 209; (no natives), III, 132; (salaries), II, 83; regional communities of, I, 295–97, 305; III, 75–76; (Alsace), III, 88; registry of deeds of, III, 139; scholarly women among, III, 162; Sephardic-Ashkenazic divisions among, II, 18–19; state revenue from, III, 68; sumptuary laws of, II, 305; synods of, I, 310–15. *See also* Councils; use of *scola* for synagogue by, III, 151. *See also* Frankish Empire; French; *and under* respective provinces and cities

southern, Jews of: and anti-Maimonidean controversy, I, 307; emigration restrictions on, II, 15; factors in communal growth of, II, 363–66; forced conversions among, I, 304; frequency of assault and battery among, III, 179; gravitate to Spain, I, 227, 242; guilds of, I, 370; less congregational separatism among, II, 19; officials' salaries among, II, 118; preaching of, II, 98; prostitutes among, III, 205; provincial assemblies of, I, 305; II, 41–42; III, 75–76; tenant protection among, II, 295–96. *See also* Provence; *and under* respective cities

Franchise, communal: I, 98; and minimum tax, II, 27–29; and public charges, II, 39; loss of, and penal procedure, II, 224; III, 177; passive, loss of, II, 29; III, 177; (for criticism of elders), II, 48–49; (of servants), III, 200. *See also* Assemblies; Elections; Membership

Franciscans: and charities, I, 360; II, 346; Palestinian, and papal taxation, I, 320

Franconia, admission of aliens to, II, 9

"Francos," Jewish, extraterritorial rights of, III, 101

Fränkel, Benjamin (Berlin charity overseer), II, 349; III, 218

Frankfort-on-the-Main, Jews of: III, 77; and admission of aliens, II, 8; (family quotas), II, 5; and city courts, I, 250; and Jewish conferences, I, 314–15; III, 78; and Kleve divorce, III, 181; and suppression of guilds, I, 372; and talmudic community, I, 156; as district center, I, 340–41; book trade of, II, 204; bureaucracy of, II, 117; burial society of, III, 90; cemeteries of, II, 150; III, 154, 157; charities of, III, 93, 209; communal elections of, II, 35; III, 113; communal examiners of, II, 197; communal oligarchy of, III, 141–42; conflict with Pfefferkorn of, I, 314; delegates to Vienna from, III, 78; education of, III, 166; (German instruction), II, 192; exclusion of relatives by, III, 115; height of synagogue of, II, 139; health officers of, II, 291; minute-books of, III, 78, 113; (judicial), II, 214; III, 173; population of, II, 117; III, 108; rabbis of, II, 91; III, *78*, 129; (contracts), III, 126; (salaries), II, 85; statutory accounting disregarded by, II, 65; successive statutes of, II, 61; sumptuary laws of, II, 305; support of foreign students by III, 166; suppression of prostitution by, II, 314; taxation of, II, 279, 287; three-class system of, II, 38

Frankfort-on-the-Oder: Jews at fairs of, II, 263; Jews at University of, III, 67
Frankish Empire, Jews of: I, 248, 295; and synods, I, 310; economic role of, I, 210; elders of, III, 15; expulsions of, I, 209; few records from, II, 78
Frankist movement, and Polish Council, I, 331, 336
Fraternity, Pharisaic, I, 135. *See also* Pharisaism
Fraud: and legal briefs, II, 238–39; and Polish Council, II, 338
Frederick II (Austrian marquess), privilege of, I, 267; (cemeteries), II, 150
Frederick I (Holy Roman emperor), privileges of, I, 248–49, 267–68
Frederick II (Holy Roman emperor): and Judeo-Christian witnesses, I, 240; checks transfers of Jews, I, 231; employs Jews, I, 235, 368; privileges of, I, 248–49, 267–68; taxation under, III, 184
Frederick III (Holy Roman emperor): and ritual libel, I, 313; appoints chief rabbi, I, 299; convokes Jewish diets, I, 315; exempts from excommunication, I, 246; II, 232; transfers synagogues, II, 135
Frederick (II) the Great (Prussian king), communal legislation of, II, 355
Frederick II (Sicilian king), I, 240; II, 262
Frederick William, Great Elector (of Prussia), II, 358; III, 98, 188
"Free cities," Polish communities as, I, 336
Freedmen, Jewish, ancient, I, 94. *See also* Slavery
Freedom: associational, and charities, I, 363; individual, and communal authority, I, 27. *See also* Democracy; in selection of teachers, and size of classes, II, 196; of movement, Jewish, II, 50, 233; III, 103; (restrictions on), II, 10, 15–16, 22, 30, 44; III, 104. *See also* Emigration; Migrations; of worship, American, and Jewish charities, II, 347. *See also* Liberalism; Liberty of conscience
French: Enlightenment, and communal control, II, 360. *See also* Enlightenment; exiles, liquidation of property of, II, 186–87; Jews, in Italy, II, 79; III, 69; (Roman congregation of), II, 20
Revolution: I, 278; and burning of prisons, III, 24; and Carpentras synagogue, I, 220–21; and communal control, I, 21, 264, 266, 351; II, 363; (debts), II, 272; and freedom of movement, II, 15; and regional communities (Alsace), III, 88; (Cassel), I, 341–42; (Moravia), I, 339
Frenchmen, among North African captives, III, 214; travel reports by, II, 294, 337
Frequency of litigations, and Jewish judiciary, II, 215
Frescoes, in Meissen synagogue, II, 138
Fridays: and court sessions, II, 211; and intensive study, I, 355; II, 177
Friedberg: and Hanau conference, III, 78; as district center, I, 341; early baths in, II, 166; III, 160; rabbis of, and Hessian Jewry, I, 343; restrictions on communal borrowing in, II, 269
Frontiers: medieval, and Jewish tolls, II, 263; Persian, and exilarchic jurisdiction, I, 150; Roman, and patriarchal jurisdiction, I, 150
Fueros, Spanish, on Jews: III, 56; and books, I, 237; and illicit relations, II, 312; and sale of meat, II, 159. *See also* Cities; Law
Fugitives, Polish councils' regulations on, III, 103. *See also* Bankruptcy

Fulda, Jews of: and Hanau conference, III, 78; rabbis of (and Frankfort elections), III, 115; (and Hessian Jewry), I, 343; regional community of, I, 341

Functions: communal, divisions of, I, 134; II, 246; (and titles of elders), I, 200; in synagogue, and ritualistic implements, III, 210. *See also* Division of functions; Miṣvot

Funeral: parlors, II, 156; processions, Jewish, imposts on, I, 253, 284; II, 153–54, 160, 263–64

rites: and burial societies, I, 25, 350, 353; II, 145; III, 90. *See also* Burial societies; and "donkey's burial," II, 156; and mourning for leaders, III, 153; Avignon supervisors of, II, 61; Church complaints of, III, 23; rabbis at, II, 90; refusal for tax immunities of, II, 14; sextons at, II, 106

Funerary: arts, Jewish, history of, II, 155. *See also* Art; inscriptions, I, 94, 98. *See also* Inscriptions; Tombstones

Furriers, guilds of, I, 369; III, 198

Furs, taxes on, II, 249, 261

Fürth, Jews of: III, 73, 99; charitable associations of, I, 364; II, 332; III, 93, 212; control over dependent settlements of, II, 22; electoral rights among, III, 115; height of synagogue of, II, 139; interruption of prayers among, II, 32–33; III, 112; physicians and pharmacists among, III, 212; prohibit mixed dancing, III, 206; prohibit attendance at theatres, III, 207; rabbis of, III, 100, 133; right of settlement among, III, 99; sumptuary laws of, II, 305

Fustat: fear of massacres in, I, 171; flogging in, II, 225; imprisonment of elders in, I, 171; "informing" cantor in, II, 102; Jewish academy in, III, 44; judges' discretion in, II, 225; *nesiim* in, I, 194; rabbis of, I, 194; synagogues in, I, 164; various rituals in, I, 167. *See also* Cairo

Gabba'e ha-mas, II, 57. *See also* Tax collections

Gabbai, as family name, III, 120

Gabba'im, II, 55. *See also* Elders

Gabelle, Jewish, in Bayonne, II, 265. *See also* Taxation

Gagin, Abraham Ḥayyim b. Moses (Jerusalem chief rabbi), III, 47

Gaiety, Italian, and sumptuary legislation, II, 303

Gainful employment, and school age, II, 175

Gaio, Maestro (Isaac b. Mordecai), III, 78

Galicia, Jews of: III, 219; chief rabbis of, I, 303; III, 85, 128; constitution of, III, 219; Enlightenment vs. ḥasidism among, III, 220; meat taxes of, III, 186. *See also* Lesser Poland; Red Russia; *and under* respective cities

Galilee, ancient: council of, I, 133; economic history of, III, 27

Galleries, in synagogues, for women, II, 140. *See also* Women

Galluf, Don Samuel, Saragossan settlement of, II, 10

Gamaliel (I or II, patriarch), I, 127

Gamaliel II (patriarch), I, 121, 141, 152–53

Gamaliel V (patriarch), I, 144 (?), 145

Gambling, communal ordinances against, II, 316; III, 208

Games: ancient, Jews participate in, I, 92; communal regulations on, III, 206–8; self-imposed fines for, II, 346

Gamrat (Cracow bishop), and Hebrew printing, II, 204

Gaonate *and* geonim, Babylonian: I, *173*, *179–86*; III, 6, 39; against use of Torah in oath, III, 181; and appointment of local judges, I, 202; III,

50; (impeachments), I, 203; and burial societies, I, 352; and Byzantine courts, I, 230; and decrees of appointment, III, 39; and economic privileges of scholars, II, 80; (tax immunities), III, 193; and Jewish education, II, 171; III, 92; and European supercommunity, I, 346; and excommunication, II, 229–30; III, 112, 177, 179; and exilarchs, I, 174, 179–80, 186; (appointments by latter), I, 174, 207; (combination of both offices), III, 41; (elections by former), I, 174, 193; and interruption of prayers, II, 33; and medieval rabbinate, II, 66; III, 83; and medieval ritual, II, 142; and Palestine, I, 191–92; and preaching, II, 97; and provincial leaders, I, 187; (*ḥakam-bashis*), I, 195; (Polish Council), III, 83; and synagogue schoolhouses, III, 151; and three-class system, III, 115; and Yemen, III, 45; chronology of, III, 42; correspondence of, I, 309; III, 41, 46; extinction of, and Spain, I, 210; meaning of title of, I, 179, 183, 193; permanence of ordinances of, II, 217–18; variations of later codes from, II, 216

in medieval Rome, I, 210

Palestinian: I, 193; and *negidim*, I, 193; control local judges, I, 203; independence of, I, 191–92. *See also* Academies; *and under* respective teachers

Gardens: communal, II, 167, 291; III, 197; Jewish ownership in Spain of, I, 160–61

Gardien général, French; I, 296; and Jewish synods, I, 310. *See also* Conservators

Gassengerichte (Swiss), I, 48

Gaul, ancient, synagogues in, I, 83. *See also* France

Gaulanitis, patriarch's possessions in, III, 33

Gaya (Moravia): II, 228; III, 160; adoption of statutes in, III, 111

Gaza, ancient, Jews of, I, 31; III, 18

Gebalene, patriarchal messenger in, I, 143

Gedaliah b. Ahikam, I, 58

Geese, Spanish taxes on, II, 249

Gehinnom, and *minhag*, II, 70

Geiger, Abraham, I, 9; II, 5

Gelasian Sacramentary, I, 230

Geleitszoll, Jewish, in Poznań, III, 186. *See also* Tolls, personal

Genarches, I, 106. *See also* Ethnarchs

Genealogy, Jewish: and *archisynagogi*, I, 103; and exilarchic distinction, I, 153. *See also* Davidic descent; and family lists, I, 145–46; and gaonate, I, 194; and heirless estates, II, 267; and patriarchal distinction, I, 153. *See also* Davidic descent; and priests, III, 12, 43; in Babylonia, I, 72; in England, III, 123; in Frankfort, III, 142. *See also* Aristocracy; Descent; Families

Generalization, anti-Jewish, and individual criminals, II, 338

General-Judenreglement für Süd- und Neuostpreussen, II, 93, 355

General Polizei-, Prozess-, und Kommerzialordnung für die Judenschaft des Markgraftums Mähren, I, 339. *See also* Statutes, Moravian

Generosity, in vows, often excessive, II, 132–33. *See also* Vows

Geneva, Jews of, III, 158

Genizah: of Cairo, texts from, III, 18, 38, 74, 94; of Lublin, III, 148

Genoa: Levant trade in, I, 275; proalien tendencies in, II, 11; projected conference in, I, 316

Gentiles: and communal taxation, I, 148; and interruption of prayers, II, 34; and Jewish business women, II, 314; and Jewish learning, II, 177; III, 162. *See also* Christian Hebraists; and *maṣṣot*, II, 321; and mourning for leaders, III, 153; and patriarchal courts, I, 145; and ransom of captives, III, 214; and sumptuary regulations, II, 302, 304; and tenant protection, II, 293, 300; (acquisition of houses of), III, 198; bread of, I, 169; burial of, commanded, II, 148; III, 153; "congregation" of, I, 87; exilarchic contacts with, I, 146–47; influence on Jewish education of, II, 191–92; legal discrimination against, I ,127; litigation with Jews of, I, 110. *See also* Litigations; sale of synagogues to, II, 129; supported by Jewish charities, I, 136; II, 320, 347; wine of, II, 161. *See also* Christians; Muslims; Pagans

Geography: European, and Jewish community, I, 242; of Palestine, III, 6–7

Geonim, *see* Gaonate

Georgia, Jewish burial ground in, III, 152

Geraci (Sicily), Jewish authorities protected in, III, 176

Gerim, Israelitic: I, 46–47; III, 9; and returning exiles, III, 11–12. *See also* Aliens

Gerlach, Stephan (der Ältere), III, 37

German congregations in: America, III, 143; Amsterdam, III, 117, 150; Ferrara, III, 114–15; Hamburg, III, 138, 144; unite with Polish, III, 145. *See also* Ashkenazic congregations

German-Jewish dialects, *see* Dialects; Languages; Literatures

Germans: colonization of Poland by, I, 267, 280; visit Turkey, I, 351

Germany, Jews of: I, 18–20, 25, *245–51*; III, 6; ancient community of, I, 83; III, 15; and anti-Maimonidean controversy, I, 316; and burghers, I, 276–78; and Crusades, I, 306; and foreign titles, II, 92; and French refugees, I, 313; and governmental system, II, 242–45, 268; (imperial tribunal), II, 239; and Italian intercommunal controversies, I, 308; and Jewish question, II, 353; and northern Italy, I, 242, 308; and Polish Jewry, I, 336; II, 16; (Council), III, 74; (mutual migrations), II, 183, 331, 337; III, 157; (teachers), III, 163–64; and support of Palestine Ashkenazim, II, 342; and visitors at fairs, II, 263; Babylonian heritage of, I, 212, 242; ban of settlement among, II, 5–6, 8–9; III, 99; bathhouses of, II, 166; III, 160; burial societies of, I, 352; III, 90; capitalist influences on law of, III, 173; cemeteries of, II, 148–49; changes in communal structure of, II, 356–63; charitable tithes of, II, 344; citron ritual of, II, 164; III, 187; communal control of, I, 212; II, 61–62, 120; (debts), II, 274; (oligarchy), I, 27–28; controversies over cantors among, III, 136; councils, assemblies and synods of, I, 310–15, 322–23; III, 76–78; "dancing-houses" of, II, 315; debt bondage among, II, 336; III, 176; deeds of, II, 111; duties of new arrivals among, II, 12; education of, II, 172–73, 193; III, 92; (associations), I, 357; elections of, II, 43, 47; III, 132–33; emigration of, I, 245, 307, 323; II, 231, 331, 337; III, 71; excommunication by, II, 32, 274; (abuses), II, 231; (foreign), II, 92, 243; expulsions from, and vested interests, II, 120; funeral tolls among, II, 153; *haggadahs* of, III, 149; *ḥazakah* legislation of, II, 293, 297–98; III, 199; hospitals of, III, 211; importation of *lulabs* by, III, 159–60; imprisonment of leaders of, I, 304; II, 336; interruption of prayers among, II, 32–34; itinerant mendicants among, II, 322; legal innovations among, II, 233; majority principle among, II, 26; marriage brokerage among, II, 319; meat sales of, restricted, II, 158; *memor*-books of, II, 145–46; mixed sex relations among, III, 205; *morenu* title among, II, 90; mutilation of criminals by, II, 223; neglect of Bible studies by, II, 194–95; oaths in synagogues among, II, 144–45; Palestinian influences on, I, 242; parental interference in marriages of, III, 204; preaching declines among, II, 97; prices of manuscripts among, II, 200; rabbinate of, I, 271, 304; II, 77–79, 81, 89; III, 90, 123; (corrupt elections), II, 92; III, 132–33; (decline), II, 215; (salaries), II, 82; Reform Judaism among, I, 9–10; regional control of, I, *298–300*, 340–41; II, 22, 148–49; III, 106; reverence for learning among, I, 271; II, 94; sanitary services among, II, 329–30; secession from community of, III, 5; seizure of property of, II, 233; Sephardic-Ashkenazic divisions among, II, 19; Shabbetians among, I, 355. *See also* Emden-Eibeschütz controversy; smallness of communities of, II, 23; social life of, III, 156; synagogues of, II, 136; (*almemar*), II, 141; (art), II, 138; (forced attendance), II, 126; taxation of, II, 22, 250–51, 284; (citrons), III, 187; (immunities), II, 15, 278; (strikes), II, 348; wandering scholars among, II, 188; wedding rites among, II, 303; (quorum), III, 46; wife-beating among, II, 318. *See also* Emperors; Law; *and under* respective states, provinces and cities

Gerona: and translation of Maimonidean code, I, 240; associations in, I, 353; III, 89; deed of endowment from, II, 266; desecration of cemetery in, II, 150; election by lot in, II, 43; emigration restrictions in, II, 16; III, 101; lay judges in, II, 71; new constitution of, II, 58; private monopolies in, II, 299; rabbis of, II, 73, 157. *See also* Nissim b. Reuben; restricted passive franchise in, II, 44

Gerousia, Jewish, I, 99, 100, 106; III, 18. *See also* Council of elders

Gerousiarches, I, 99

Gershom b. Judah, "the Light of the Exile": alleged ordinances of, II, 70; and early traditions, II, 69; and Jewish synods, I, 311; in German *memor*-books, II, 146; on ban of settlement, II, 5; on communal sovereignty, II, 218; III, 50, 174; on interruption of prayers, II, 33–34; on judges, III, 174; on *ma'arufia*, II, 80; on majority principle, II, 26, 219; on migrations, III, 98; on polygamy, II, 307–8; on rabbinic privileges, II, 80; on synagogues (candles), II, 134; (private), II, 126; on tenant protection, II, 293; on visitors' contributions, II, 12; restricts divorces, II, 310

Gerson, Johannes, on Jewish academies, II, 182; III, 163

Gerush Sefarad congregation, in Salonica, I, 351; II, 18, 75

Ghetto community: and Emancipation, I, 8; and people's community, I, 18; disintegration of, I, 155; II, 181; European originso f, I, 209. *See also* Quarters

Gibbore ha-ḥail, I, 38. *See also* Military service

Gideon (Israelitic judge), I, 44–45

Gieser, Feivish (Cracow dictator), II, 64

Gifts, private: as means of charitable rehabilitation, II, 326–27; deeds of, II, 111–12; litigations over, II, 215.

See also Bequests; Charities; Contributions
to rulers: I, 318; and appointment of chiefs, I, 174, 179; and communal conflicts, II, 21–22; III, 183; and fines, II, 235; and taxation, II, 162, 247; (immunities), III, 193; Israelitic, I, 38. *See also* Taxation
Giḳaṭilia, Joseph b. Abraham, manuscript of, II, 200
Gilead (Palestine), population of, I, 35
Giovanni de Agello (bishop), I, 238
Girgenti (Sicily): annulment of bans in, II, 232; exemption of teacher in, III, 164; legacy in, III, 189
Girls, *see* Brides; Women
Gizbar, proselyte as, II, 286
Gizze ha-melek, III, 7. *See also* Taxation
Glatz (Silesia), Jews in, I, 277–78; III, 63–64
Glaziers, Jewish, sales taxes of, II, 261
Gleanings (charitable), I, 132
Glückel of Hameln, II, 179
Gnesen (Gniezno), Archdiocese of, I, 225
Gnosticism, ancient, and religious associations, I, 354
God: and doctrine of repentance, II, 222; and Israelitic monarchy, I, 35; as judge, I, 39; communion with, I, 124–25; II, 168; divides the world, I, 158; irreverence for, objectionable, I, 139
"of Heaven," I, 78; "of Jacob," and Shabbetai Zevi, II, 26; "the Most High," I, 77–78; III, 13
Godfather, rabbi as, II, 90
Gödingen, *maskir*-book of, III, 152
Gold: embroidery of, and Jewish household help, II, 305–6; investments of captives' funds in, II, 335; ornaments of (in synagogue), II, 132, 135; (restricted by Mannheim ordinance), III, 202; stars of, prohibited in synagogue, III, 146; taxes on, II, 249, 255, 261
Goldsmiths: Dutch, and Jews, III, 96; Jewish, in Alexandria, I, 78; in ancient Palestine, I, 67; Polish guilds of, I, 369
Good-will, and support of Gentiles, II, 347. *See also* Toleration
Good works, and choice of cantors, II, 105
Goshen (Egypt), Jews of, I, 56
Goslar, Jewish privileges in, III, 64, 99
Götz, Elyakim b. Meir: on acceptance of office, III, 119; on music during half-holidays, III, 206; on sex morality, and dancing, III, 205–6; on tax distribution, III, 194
Government intervention: and admission of settlers, III, 99; and appointment of officials, I, 298; II, 34–35, 64–65, 108; III, 69–70, 123, 137; and bi-sexual dancing, II, 316; and book trade, II, 104; and burials, III, 157; and communal accounting, II, 64–65; and communal indebtedness, II, 269, 271; III, 190, 192; and communal statutes, III, 110; and control over sex relations, II, 313; and demotion of rabbis, III, 129–30; and disintegration of Poland, II, 354; and divorces, III, 204; and educational responsibilities, II, 170; and elections, I, 340; II, 34–36, 47, 62, 74, 102; III, 113–14, 123, 135–36; and emigration to Palestine, II, 340; and excommunication, I, 235, 246; II, 228–29, 232; and expulsion of poor, II, 323; and *ḥazaḳah*, III, 199–200; and heirless estates, II, 267; and Jewish customs service, II, 262; and Jewish diplomacy, I, 203–4; II, 115–16; and Jewish Enlightenment, III, 220; and lay judges, II, 72; and legacies, III, 189; and Mecklenburg Council, I, 345; and migrations, III, 132; and Polish guilds, I, 371; and polygamy, II, 309; and prisons, III, 176; and pros-

ecution of criminals, I, 330; II, 338; and rabbinic ordination, II, 91; and regional control, I, 287–92, 298, 312, 323, 329–31, 340–43; III, 84–85; and reliability of census, III, 184–85; and share in Jewish fines, II, 235, 265; III, 16–17, 52; and social welfare, I, 5; and synagogue worship, II, 143; and taxation (inequalities), II, 283, 285; III, 185, 197; (immunities), II, 274; III, 192–93; (self-assessment), II, 282; and uncharitableness, III, 209; appeal to (allowed), I, 213; II, 49, 87, 283, 353–54; III, 164; (repudiated), I, 212, 228–29, 235, 343; II, 15, 218–19; III, 99, 135–36; (Valladolid solution), I, 292; in various regions (Aragon), I, 287–88; (Berlin), II, 36; (Bohemia), I, 340; III, 192; (Cologne), III, 130; (France), I, 246; III, 69; (Germany), I, 298; II, 62; III, 70; (Hesse-Cassel), I, 341–43; II, 282; (Islam), I, 203–4; (Mecklenburg), I, 345; (Poland), I, 267, 323, 329–31, 371; II, 87, 353–54; III, 84–85, 184–85; (southern Italy), I, 232; (Spain), I, 288–92; II, 72, 74, 108; (Trapani), II, 47; (Troyes synod), I, 212, 312; (Valladolid synod), I, 292; (Venice), III, 190; (Wilno), II, 87; III, 164; personal responsibility for, I, 212; Polish peculiarities of, I, 267; sporadic decline of, I, 206–7, 346. *See also* Bureaucracy; Monarchy

Governors, Polish, *see* Palatins

Gozzo, redemption of captives in, I, 294; II, 334

Grades, educational, *see* Schools

Gradisca, disqualification of slaughterers in, III, 217

Graeco-Roman world: and mores of forefathers, I, 174; associations in, I, 354; (guilds), I, 372; III, 94; communal trends in, I, 11–12, *74–117*, 206; III, *13–21*; (democracy), I, 204; facility of travel in, III, 23; leprosy in, III, 155; medieval heritage of, I, 158; II, 3, 68, 199–200; synagogues in, I, 83; III, 15; variety of titles in, III, 120. *See also* Hellenism; Roman Empire; ***and under*** respective provinces and cities

Graetz, Heinrich, and Jewish education, III, 163

Grain, in ancient Palestine, I, 42

Grammar, Hebrew: instruction in, II, 192–95; Tiberian center of, I, 192. *See also* Languages

Grammar schools, Council of Valladolid on, II, 114. *See also* Education; Schools; Teachers

Grammateus, I, 102, 105; III, 13. *See also* Scribes

Granada: conquest of, I, 318; Jewish taxation in, III, 34; *negidim* in, I, 191

Grand jury, English, indicts elders, I, 258

Grand vizier, Turkish, and Jewish eschatology, III, 183. *See also* Bureaucracy

Grapes, private monopolies in, II, 299

Grave-diggers, Jewish, Huesca Society of, I, 352–53

Graves: graduated payments on, II, 264; of ancestors, visits to, II, 154; III, 206; outside cemetery, III, 157. *See also* Cemeteries; Tombstones

Great Britain, *see* England

"Great charity," Lithuanian, supervisors of, II, 63

"Great community," Rhodes, shares in *ḥazakah*, III, 198

"Great God," in Judeo-Persian correspondence, I, 78

"Great Sabbath," II, 97. *See also* Sabbath

"Great Synagogue": ancient, I, 124; at Saragossa, III, 125

in London: I, 20; III, 127; and

obligatory acceptance of office, III, 119; and women suffrage, III, 114; cemetery of, II, 147; constitution of, II, 62; III, 109; election days in, III, 116; encourages emigration of poor, II, 16; excommunicates New Synagogue, II, 21; *shammash* in, III, 137; statutes of, III, 60; teachers in, III, 164–65; wedding fees in, II, 119. *See also* Ashkenazic congregations

Greater Poland: III, 197; as member of Polish Council, I, 325; III, 81; chief rabbis in, I, 300–1; II, 42; communal constitutions in, II, 63; indebtedness of, I, 334–35; meat administration in, III, 158; physicians in, III, 140; privileges of, I, 271, 324; provincial council of, I, 332, 336, 345; II, 8; III, 71, 82; rabbinic salaries in, II, 82–83; residence rights in, II, 270–71, 273; tax farmers in, II, 285. *See also* Poznań; *and under* other cities

Greece: communal price agreements in, II, 300; French visitor in, III, 159; *ḥazaḳah* legislation in, II, 298. *See also under* respective cities

Greed, and desecration of cemeteries, II, 151

Greek-orthodox Christians, in Turkey, I, 196

Greeks: ancient colonies of, I, 55. *See also* Hellenism; autonomy in Catania and Poland of, I, 267; unified control in Turkey of, I, 196

Greenhalgh, Rev. John, I, 257; III, 59

Gregariousness, public, Forli ordinances against, I, 320

Gregory I, the Great (pope): I, 216; and forced conversions, I, 304; and Jewish religion, III, 53; and *Sicut Judaeis*, I, 217; and synagogues, I, 219; III, 53; (loud prayers), III, 23; intervenes for foreign Jews, III, 72

Gregory VII (pope), and synagogue, I, 216

Gregory IX (pope), II, 254

Gregory XIV (pope), I, 217; III, 52

Grimmelshausen, Hans Jakob Christoffel von, III, 205

Grodno: deeds in, II, 113; elections in, II, 47; privilege of, I, 268; quota of brides in, II, 333; regional control of, I, 328; III, 182; (chief rabbinate), II, 87; rights of settlement in, II, 22

Groet (Holland), Jewish cemetery in, I, 253

Gromnice, Polish fair of, II, 165

Grotius, Hugo, and Jewish status, I, 254–55; III, 58

Group: divisions, in synagogues, III, 42; jurisdiction, Aristotle on, III, 20; studies, Jewish, and individual effort, II, 206

Guadalajara (Spain), II, 280, 329

Guarantees, communal, for rents, II, 292

Guarantors: Christian, of communal loans, II, 270; Jewish, Worms privileges on, I, 249

Guard of honor, Roman, of Palestinian patriarchs, III, 28–29

Guardians, of orphans: and charitable responsibilities, II, 331; III, 216; and school attendance, I, 360; appointment of, II, 240, 330

Guards, Jewish: against refugees, II, 337; at cemeteries, II, 156; at ghetto gates, II, 116; III, 141; discipline of, III, 167–68; salaries of, II, 266

Guests: Palestine messengers as, II, 342; sumptuary restrictions on, II, 302–5, 326

Guglielmo da Pesaro (dancing master), II, 315; III, 206

Guide for the Perplexed, papal protection of, I, 308. *See also* Maimonides, Moses

Guiana, Jews in, III, 61

Guilds, general: and Jews, III, 94–96; (exclusion from), I, 369; (Jewish associations), I, 362, 364; and Polish councils, I, 324; and sale of Jewish meat, II, 158, 160, 258; III, 138, 187; as religious fraternities, I, 369; capitalist attacks on, II, 361; economic motivations for, I, 366; III, 95; in various regions (Byzantium), III, 94; (Graeco-Roman world), III, 18, 91, 94; (Holland), III, 96; (Islam), III, 91, 94; (Orient, ancient), III, 11; (Poland), I, 324; II, 160; III, 96; (Spain), I, 362; III, 91; membership restrictions in, I, 369; II, 18; price fixing by, II, 301

Jewish: I, 349–50, *364–74*; III, *94–97*; ancient, I, 81; III, 13; (Alexandria), 78; (Babylonian Exile), I, 67; (congregations of), I, 67, 81; agreements with Christian guilds of, III, 137–38, 141; and acquired rights, II, 9, 298; III, 198; and lay judiciary, I, 275; II, 88; and professional training, III, 167; and Roman-Jewish bankers, II, 76; jurisdiction of, I, 367; membership restrictions in, II, 17–18; of musicians, III, 141; of teachers, II, 164, 184–85; (and size of classes), II, 196; preachers at, III, 134. *See also* Associations; Craftsmen

Gulgolet (Polish poll tax), II, 251. *See also* Poll taxes

Gumbiner, Abraham Abele b. Ḥayyim, II, 102; III, 135

Gumpertz, Bendix Rubin (Baruch Wesel, Silesian chief rabbi), III, 87

Günzburg (Germany): as district center, I, 341; Jewish conference in, III, 77–78; rabbis of, and Rovigo controversy, II, 166

Gymnasia, Greek, Jews in, I, 92

Gymnastics, in ancient Jewish education, I, 92

HAARLEM, Jews in, III, 58, 96

Haas (Frankfort family), III, 141–42

Habdalah, public recitation of, II, 128, 133

Habeas corpus, Jewish, in Spain, II, 227

Ḥaber, title of: II, 68. *See also* Rabbis; and educational goals, II, 206; and electoral rights, I, 134; II, 28; III, 115; and examination of slaughterers, III, 138; and scholarly control, II, 244; conferring of, II, 84; III, 131; not attained by Joseph b. Moses, II, 188; use of, II, 90, 92

Habits, Jewish: American adjustments in, II, 365–66; and sumptuary laws, II, 306

Ḥaburah, I, 353; III, 94; geonic meaning of, III, 94. *See also* Associations; Burial societies

Hacohen, Joseph b. Joshua, I, 306; III, 66

Ḥad gadya, derision of, punished, III, 149

Hadiṭ, Muslim, on Jews, III, 35. *See also* Law

Hadrian (Roman emperor), I, 80, 106, 108, 127; III, 24, 27

Ḥadzan, II, 102. *See also* Ḥazzan

Hafṭarot, I, 74, 122; II, 198; III, 21–22. *See also* Liturgy

Hağas, *see* Hağis, Moses

Haggadah (Passover): derision of, punished, III, 149; fourth son in, II, 238; full recitation of, I, 168; illuminated manuscripts of, II, 138; III, 146. *See also* Passover

Hagiographa, liturgical sections from, II, 193

Hağis, Moses b. Jacob (Palestinian messenger): II, 342; III, 216; and drafting of statutes, II, 30–31; III, 110; and synagogue taxes, II, 135

Hague, The, Jews in, III, 58

Hahn, Joseph (Yuspa) b. Pinḥas Seligmann, II, 193–94

Hai b. Sherira Gaon: and academy students, III, 41; and *excommunicatio latae sententiae*, III, 177; and Jewish solidarity, I, 185, 193; and Judah b. Barzilai, III, 38; and judiciary, I, 166, 202; and North-African priests, III, 42; and Pumbedita's glory, I, 184; and second holidays, III, 30; Book of Deeds by, I, 204; II, 240; III, 38; Davidic descent of, III, 46; on breaches of bans, II, 235; on ceremony of flogging, II, 224–25; on cantors, and chanting, II, 105; III, 135–36; on Muslim courts, I, 170; III, 38; Palestinian inquiries to, I, 193; solicits contributions, I, 181
Haifa, population of, I, 17
Hair cuts, communal regulations on, III, 203
Ḥakam, meaning and position of, I, 151, 196; II, 67; III, 33, 125
Ḥakam-bashi, *see* Chief rabbinate
Ḥakam Zebi, *see* Ashkenazi, (Ḥakam) Zevi
Ḥalawa, Moses, of Tortosa, and French controversy, I, 297
Halberstadt, Jews of: III, 133; congregation in Leipzig of, III, 149; Palestine relief among, III, 216; preaching among, II, 97; rabbinic salaries among, II, 82
Halevi, Solomon (Salonican preacher), II, 96
Halevi, Yehudah b. Samuel: III, 34, 51; and Jewish taxation, III, 34; and motions during study, II, 200; III, 169
Half-holidays: as election days, II, 45; III, 115–16; music on, I, 168; shaving on, III, 206
Half-shekel, biblical: and Palestine relief, II, 340; and salaries of cantors, II, 101; paid to patriarchs, I, 87, 143–44. *See also* Aurum coronarium
Ḥalfon (Aden *nagid*), III, 43
Halicarnassus (Asia Minor), Jewish quarter in, I, 85
Ḥaliṣah: II, 317–18; and emigration to Palestine, II, 340; rabbinic control of, II, 71, 91; (fees), II, 83
Halle, Jews of: III, 122; and transfer of synagogue, II, 135
Ḥalukkah, II, 340, 343; III, 217. *See also* Palestine relief
Haman (biblical Jew-baiter), I, 63–64
Hambro Congregation (London): II, 148; and communal discipline, III, 109; and constitution makers, III, 110; and obligatory acceptance of office, III, 119; and *Pletten*, III, 209; election days in, III, 116; statutes of, III, 107, 110; wedding fees in, II, 119
Hamburg-Altona-Wandsbek, Jews of: admission of aliens by, II, 8–9; and charitable payment of *Schutzgeld*, II, 326; and Eibeschütz controversy, I, 308. *See also* Emden-Eibeschütz controversy; and obligatory acceptance of office, II, 54; and overcrowded hospitals, II, 327–28; and Polish Council, III, 74; and Shabbetian movement, II, 25–26; and Venetian associations, I, 364; II, 335; and Wandsbek excommunication, II, 229; arbitration among, II, 214; Bordeaux wines among, II, 163–64; censorship of, III, 170; communal archives of, II, 25–26; III, 107, 109, 139; communal indebtedness of, II, 356; elections of, II, 103–4; III, 16; import citrons from Italy, III, 187; judicial fees of, II, 84; limit vows, II, 133; marriage broker's fees among, III, 208; minute-books of, II, 25–26; III, 109; monopolies of, II, 299; officials' salaries among, II, 118; III, 128; Palestinian messengers among, II, 135; III, 110; *Pletten* system among, II, 322; population of, II, 23; III, 107; postal system of, II, 115; III,

141; prohibit "conspiracies," II, 48–49; rabbis of, III, 133, 178; (revenues), III, 128; (tenure), II, 86, rights of settlement among, III, 103; Sephardic-Ashkenazic agreement of, II, 19; slight poverty among, III, 218; statutes of, II, 30, 61; III, 99; sumptuary ordinances of, III, 20; synagogues of, III, 147; (discipline), III, 150; (private), III, 144; taxation of, III, 144; (distribution), II, 280, 344–45; III, 138; (immunities), III, 193; (secret assessments), II, 287; teachers of, II, 118

Hamburger, Marcus, private cemetery of, II, 148. *See also* Hambro congregation

Hamlets, ancient Palestinian, meaning of, I, 31, 34; III, 8. *See also* Cities

Hamm (Germany), as district center, I, 341

Hammurabi (Babylonian king), I, 41; III, 7, 94

Hamon, Moses (Turkish leader), I, 197

Ḥanafite school, of Muslim jurisprudence, I, 162–63

Ḥananel (Jeremiah's cousin), III, 11

Ḥananel b. Ḥushiel, I, 181; II, 277

Ḥananiah ('Anan's brother), I, 178

Ḥananiah (nephew of R. Joshua), I, 143, 150; III, 30

Ḥananiah Gaon, I, 203–4

Hanau, Jewish conference in, III, 78

Hanbalite school of Muslim jurisprudence, I, 163

Hand, loss of, for wife beating, II, 318

Handbooks: for conversionist sermons, III, 135; Hebrew, and teachers' control, II, 180. *See also* Textbooks

Ḥanina b. Dosa (tannai), alleged ancestor of Saadia, III, 45

Ḥaninai (exilarch), I, 173

Hannover (state): regional community in, I, 341; suppression of synagogues in, III, 53

Hannover, Nathan Neta: on number of Polish scholars, III, 130; on Polish hospitality, II, 189, 324; III, 209

Ha-noten teshu'ah (prayer), II, 143

Ḥanukkah: games during, II, 317; provisions for candles on, III, 146; tax collections during, II, 269; vows during, II, 103, 188

Hapsburg dynasty, and Jewish bankers, II, 81. *See also* Court Jews; Emperors; *and under* respective monarchs

Hardwicke, Philip Yorke (lord chancellor), on Jewish status, III, 60

Harems, Turkish, and communal leadership, I, 197

Harsha'ah, legal implications of, II, 238; III, 180. *See also* Intermediaries

Harun al-Rashid (caliph), I, 159, 165

Ḥasdai (rabbi of Oria), II, 67

Ḥasdai Nasi (Lerida rabbi), II, 68; III, 124

Ḥaṣer, meaning of, III, 8. *See also* Hamlets

Ḥasidism: and communal repasts, II, 128; and communal stability, II, 121, 168; and congregational divisions, I, 352, 355; III, 89; and Enlightenment, III, 220; and Galician government, III, 220; and Jerusalem cabalists, III, 92; and Polish councils, I, 336; and preachers, II, 100; and private congregations, II, 125–26; III, 143–44; and Sephardic ritual, II, 142; and Shabbetian movement, I, 335; and slaughterers, II, 110; III, 138–39

Haskalah, *see* Enlightenment

Haskamah, Salonican, on sumptuary legislation, II, 304. *See also* Ordinances; Statutes

Ḥatti-humayum, Turkish decree of, I, 163–64, 199

Hausvogt, Prussian, and Jewish elections, II, 36

Ḥayyim b. Bezaleel, attacks Isserles, III, 172

Ḥayyim di Mercado, and Jewish boycott of landlord, II, 295
Ḥayyim of Landshut (imperial adviser), I, 299
Ḥayyim Tyro Tschernowitzer, private synagogue of, III, 143–44
Ḥazaḳah, *see* Acquired rights
Ḥazzan: II, *100–5*; III, 18, *135–37;* ancient, I, 78, 123, 126; III, 24; and academies, III, 32; and Bible recitation, II, 141; and collection of meat taxes, II, 258; and communal hierarchy, I, 123, 126, 140; III, 178; and congregational separation, III, 149; and preparation of deeds, II, 113; and printed prayer-books, II, 143; as teacher, II, 197; III, 24; censured for favoritism, II, 132; decree of appointment of, I, 204; etymology of, III, 18; female, II, 140; in various regions (Alexandria), I, 78; (Alsace), II, 117; (Amsterdam), III, 150; (Babylonia), III, 136; (Bagdad), II, 67; (France), II, 118; (Frankfort), II, 117; (Germany), II, 48–49, 118, 140; III, 136; (Islam), I, 204; (Lithuania), II, 258; (Prague), III, 178; medieval transformations of, I, 200–1; necessity for, I, 123; prohibition of criticisms of, II, 48–49; provincial, III, 136; recites constitution, III, 109; replaced by celebrant or mourner, II, 145; revenue of, II, 118, 280; III, 141; (fees), II, 83, 118–19; substitutes for public, III, 127; tax immunities of, II, 277. *See also* Liturgy; Music; Synagogues
Head covering, postulate of, II, 69, 306–7; III, 202
Heads of academies, Jewish: II, *94–95;* and rabbinic authorization, II, 91; as judges, II, 73; as marriage brokers, II, 81; in Muslim Babylonia, I, 192; *morenu* qualified for, II, 91; tax immunities of, II, 277
of courts, Jewish: I, 151; II, 95; and anti-mendicancy proclamation, II, 323–24; at Babylonian academies, I, 183; communal mourning for, II, 147. *See also* Judiciary; Rabbis
of Elephantine congregation, I, 71–72; of families (oath of allegiance), III, 106; (plenary assemblies), II, 23–26, 30; "of fathers' houses," I, 65, 68; of *kallahs*, I, 182
Health, and educational responsibilities, II, 169, 174
Hearings of courts, early terms for, II, 236
Hearth taxes vs. poll taxes, II, 251. *See also* Households
Ḥeber ha'ir, I, 134; III, 26
Ḥebra de-nashim ṣadḳaniot, III, 89
Ḥebra Guemilut Ḥasadim, III, 90
Ḥebra Ḳadisha, I, 352–54. *See also* Burial societies
Ḥebrat reḥiṣah, I, 354
Hebrew alphabet: and Greek inscriptions, I, 121; and vernacular translations of prayers, II, 143; instruction in, II, 117. *See also* Books; Language; Literatures
renaissance, and Palestinian people's community, I, 17; slaves, I, 46. *See also* Slavery
"Hebrews," Roman synagogue of, I, 81; III, 15
Hebron: allocation of relief to, II, 342; messengers from, III, 217; Salonican legacy for, III, 165; Venetian debts to, III, 190
Ḥebrot: I, 348. *See also* Associations; *Shas*, I, 356. *See also* Education; Talmud
Hecataeus of Abdera, I, 85
Ḥeder, Polish, Maimon's description of, II, 198–99. *See also* Schools
Hegelians, and communal decline, II, 123

Hegenheim, Jewish cemetery in, III, 157
Hegmon parnas, II, 56. *See also* Elders
Hegoumenos, III, 13. *See also* Elders
Heidingsfeld, *memor*-book of, II, 146
Heinemann (Paderborn chief), III, 123
Heirless estates, communal inheritance of, I, 247–48; II, 267; III, 14, 35, 57
Heirs, Jewish, always identifiable, I, 248. *See also* Inheritance
Heisterbach, Caesarius von, III, 205
Hekdesh, use of term of, II, 328–29; III, 38, 210–11. *See also* Hospices
Hélias of Valence, foundation of, I, 358
Helicz family (Polish printers), II, 204
Hellenism: and Greek-Jewish relations, III, 18; (forcible assimilation), I, 83; (in Egypt), I, 76–77, 82; (in Parthia), I, 118; and rise of Christianity, I, 117; educational inferiority of, I, 125; influences on Jews of, I, 90, 156; (communal organization), I, 75, 85, 99, 107, 122; (law), I, 211; (synagogue), I, 86, 88, 95; (resistance to), I, 141–42; II, 167; Jewish influences on, I, 77–78; III, 25–26. *See also* Graeco-Roman world; Greeks; Languages; Literatures; Septuagint; *and under* respective provinces and cities
Heller, Yom Tob Lipmann b. Nathan: I, 338; against corrupt elections, II, 93; against judges' share in fees, II, 235; III, 179
Hendel Manoaḥ b. Shemarya, II, 192
Hengstfeld, *memor*-book of, II, 146
Henotheism, Graeco-Roman, and divine names, I, 77
Henry II (Castilian king): against Jewish debt bondage, III, 176; enormous tax load under, II, 271, 283–84
Henry IV (Castilian king), protects Jewish cemeteries, III, 155
Henry III (English king): and Jewish banking, I, 243; and Jewish excommunication, II, 230; and Jewish residence rights, I, 276; fiscal oppression of, I, 245, 297; forbids Jewish synods, I, 245, 311
Henry IV (Holy Roman emperor): and Crusades, I, 306; and rabbinate, II, 78; privileges of, I, 248–49, 267–68
Heredity: and associational membership, I, 353, 364; II, 17; III, 104–5. *See also* Mutual benefit societies; and educational foundations, I, 357–58; and European supercommunity, I, 346; III, 66; and electoral freedom, II, 50; and frequent re-elections, III, 17; and institutionalized religion, II, 168; and Muslim dynasties, I, 177–78; and tax arrears, II, 326; in academies, I, 194, 210; III, 46; in acquired rights, II, 297; (leaseholds), II, 294–95; (residence rights), II, 326, 342; in communal office, I, 84, 105; in Egyptian *negidut*, I, 190; in exilarchate, I, 145, 174, 176–77, 207; in Narbonne *nesi'ut*, III, 68; in patriarchate, I, 140–41; in rabbinic office, II, 81; III, 66, 132; in secretarial post, II, 113; (Elephantine), I, 72–73; in synagogue functions, II, 133; in Turkish leadership, I, 197–98. *See also* Descent; Inheritance; Oligarchy
Ḥerem: meaning of, I, 169; II, 228, 232–33. *See also* Excommunication; *ha-yishub*, talmudic basis of, III, 98. *See also* Ban of settlement; vs. *taḳḳanat ha-ṣibbur*, III, 111–12
Heresies *and* heretics, Christian: affected by Jews, I, 221; suppression of, I, 228; II, 210. *See also* Dissidents
Jewish: ancient, I, 52; III, 21–22; and communal solidarity, I, 165, 224; and established order, I, 237; and excommunication, II, 231; and Inquisition, I, 221, 237, 288, and prayers, I, 121; and recitation of Decalogue,

III, 21–22; and Spanish execution, II, 222; under Islam, I, 165, 168, III, 36–37
Heritage, ancient, vs. local leadership, II, 244
Hermandad de la caridad, Spanish, III, 91. *See also* Associations
Hermeneutics, Jewish, ancient, I, 123. *See also* Bible exegesis
Hermopolis Magna (Egypt), Jewish market in, I, 130
Herod (king), I, 67, 81
Herodians, and Palestinian patriarchate, I, 140
Heroes: biblical, and eastern synagogues, I, 164; national, in *memor*-books, II, 145–46
Herrings, excise taxes on, II, 260
Herz, Elkan (Leipzig merchant), III, 149
Ḥesed shel emet, I, 353. *See also* Burial societies
Hesse-Cassel: care for underprivileged in, II, 330; court Jews in, II, 120; III, 142; educational budget in, II, 115, 188; emigration restrictions in, II, 16; examination of slaughterers in, III, 138; honorary scribes in, II, 120; household employees in, II, 299–300, 305–6; oath of loyalty in, II, 36–37, 330; III, 133; obligatory denunciation of transgressors in, II, 236; Palestine relief in, II, 341; regional community in, I, 341–43; III, 86; rejects self-assessment, II, 282; sumptuary legislation in, II, 305; taxation in, II, 246–47; (new arrivals), II, 12; theologians of, II, 246–47. *See also* Councils
Hesse-Darmstadt, regional community in, I, 341; III, 86
Hesychius (Roman), executed, I, 144
Heterogeneity: of Graeco-Roman population, I, 111; of Hellenistic Jewry, I, 90
Hezekiah (exilarch and gaon), I, 179, 184; III, 41
Hezekiah (Israelitic king), I, 52; III, 13
Hezekiah b. David (exilarch), I, 179
Ḥezḳat ha-yishub, II, 6. *See also* Ban of settlement
Hides, revenue from, and meat taxes, III, 186–87
Hierapolis (Asia Minor), Jews of: I, 93; III, 16–17; guilds of, I, 364; III, 94
Hierarchy, communal: I, 140; and caliphs, I, 207; and European supercommunity, I, 346; cantors' position in, II, 103. *See also* Bureaucracy; Elders
Hierosolymitano, Domenico (censor), I, 223
"High Court," Jewish: academies as, I, 150, 202; and exilarchic appointment, I, 147; and Polish Council, I, 332. *See also* Supreme Court; control over communities of, I, 211; in Egypt, III, 44. *See also* Courts of Appeal
High Holidays: and synagogue attendance, I, 6, 283; (candles), II, 134; election of cantors for, II, 102. *See also* Day of Atonement; Holidays; New Year
High priesthood *and* high priests: I, 79, 117, 140; and Jewish education, III, 23; and rabbinate, II, 90. *See also* Priesthood
High treason, Frankfort conference accused of, III, 74
Hildesheim: communal controversies in, III, 119, 192; election day in, III, 116; Palestine relief in, III, 216; parental authority over marriage in, III, 204; population of, III, 107; rabbis of, III, 131; (Frankfort elections), III, 115; responsibility of elders in, II, 52; sex morality in, III, 205; slaughterers in, II, 109; text of statute of, III, 116

Hillel: I, 140; and patriarchate, III, 28; Davidic descent of, III, 29; school of, I, 152
Hillel II (patriarch): I, 144, 192; calendar proclamation of, III, 30
Hillel b. Naftali Hirz, on responsibility of elders, III, 118
Hillel b. Samuel of Verona, I, 315–16; III, 78
Hirsch, Samson Raphael, as Moravian chief rabbi, I, 338
Ḥisdai b. David (exilarch), III, 41
Historians: Arabic, I, 148; French, III, 151; Israelitic, I, 35–36, 40, 52, 60; III, 7. *See also* Bible
  modern: and communal organization, I, 29; III, 4–6; and interterritorial action, I, 306; and Jewish charities, III, 218; and Jewish status in ancient Rome, III, 19; and medieval guilds, III, 91; and Moses Isserles, II, 213; and public book approvals, II, 203–4; and Sicilian assemblies, I, 319; and "sponge" function, II, 246–47; on Roman Jewry, I, 107, 110–11; on Saadia's conflict with exilarch, III, 42; on "seven best men," III, 120–21
Historic continuity, Jewish: and American adjustments, II, 365–66; and communal organization, I, 9, 18, 81; (Graeco-Roman), I, 81, 95; (modern), I, 21; and legal status, I, 252, 268; and medieval associations, III, 91; and rabbinate, II, 77, 94, 244; despite expulsions, I, 243; medieval break of, II, 215, 241–42; medieval views on, II, 216; vs. communal creativity, II, 167–68; vs. legal elasticity, II, 245
Historical: background, and legal precedent, II, 245; events, and new prayers, II, 142; geography, of Palestine, III, 6–7; literature, *see* Historians; remains, of Polish Jewry, III, 53
History, Jewish: Abravanel's attitude to, III, 174; and Reform Judaism, I, 9; French Enlightenment's attacks on, II, 360
History-mindedness, and medieval belief in continuity, II, 216
Hitler, Adolf, I, 4
Hittite names in Palestine, I, 46
Ḥiyya, R. (amora), I, 155
Ḥiyya bar Abba, R. (amora), I, 122, 143; II, 99
Hoce Hece (*'Ose ḥesed*) society, I, 362
Hochmeister, I, 298. *See also* Chief rabbinate
Hohenstaufen dynasty, I, 235
Holdheim, Samuel, I, 9
Holidays, Jewish: abstention from courts on, I, 236; ancient liturgy of, I, 112, 121; and calendar regulation, I, 143; and itinerant beggars, II, 325; and Jewish debt bondage, II, 226; and prison terms, III, 176; and talmudic studies, II, 207; and vows for cantors, II, 103; Bible recitation during, II, 141; charitable distribution on, II, 320; consumption of meat on, II, 259; *hafṭarot* on, I, 122; in Babylonian Exile, I, 59, 62–63; local, perpetual celebration of, III, 106; musicians at, II, 115; protected by non-Jewish laws, I, 218, 232; school vacations during, II, 197; second days of, I, 145; III, 30; sermons on, III, 133; supply of fish for, II, 160–61; Torah summonses during, II, 132; visits to ancestors' graves on, II, 154; III, 206; visits to families on, I, 357. *See also* Festivals; High Holidays; *and under* respective holidays
  Persian, rejected by Jews, III, 149
Holland, Jews of: I, 242, *252–55*, 270; III, *57–59*, 61; and Dutch guilds,

III, 96; and emigrés, I, 307; II, 183; and Polish victims, I, 307; and Shabbetian movement, I, 308; bans of, II, 233, 243; cantors of, III, 137; capitalist influences on law of, III, 173; changes in communal structure of, II, 356, 360; communal stability of, II, 120; conflicts on taxes among, II, 289; education of, II, 172; (linguistic and Bible studies), II, 195; electoral procedure of, II, 43; growth of oligarchies among, I, 27–28; II, 50, 363; Hebrew printing of, III, 170–71; Marranos among, II, 364; oath *more judaico* of, III, 181; physicians among, III, 140; rabbis of, III, 133; sanitary services of, II, 329–30; Sephardic-Ashkenazic divisions among, II, 18, 365; traders in Memel from, III, 188; tax strikes impossible among, II, 348; theatrical arts among, III, 207; wealth of, I, 307. *See also under* respective cities

Holleschau, Joḥanan, on London controversy, III, 153

"Holy associations," importance of, II, 148. *See also* Associations

"Holy associations of lovingkindness," I, 353. *See also* Burial societies

Holy Roman Empire, *see* Germany

Holy War, Spanish: and destruction of Jewish quarters, II, 135–36, 329; and dissolution of societies, I, 362; and illicit relations, II, 313; and public education, II, 171; and synagogues, I, 220, 237; II, 135–36; communal reconstruction after, II, 58. *See also* Massacres; Persecutions

Homeland, Jewish, *see* Palestine

Homeless travelers, and Jewish hospitals, II, 327

Homes, Jewish: boarding of students in, II, 188; religious observances in, II, 210; symbols of mourning in, II, 138. *See also* Houses

Homiletics *and* homilists, *see* Preaching

Homogeneity of pre-Emancipation community, questionable, II, 351

Homotaphoi, Greek, and Jewish burial societies, III, 90

"Honest men": and lay judges, II, 72; participation in Lerida elections of, II, 47

Honesty, in balloting, constitutional provisions for, III, 116. *See also* Corruption; Elections

Honor, sense of: and execution of criminals, II, 223; and no accounting for charities, II, 64; and public mourning, III, 153; of girls, communal regulations on, III, 206

Honors conferred on members: I, 96–97, 100, 103; and exilarchs, I, 147, 149–50, 182, 189; and geonim, I, 183–84; and patriarchs (imperial), I, 144–45; III, 28–29; in academies, I, 149–50; in *memor*-books, II, 146; in synagogues, I, 124, 147; (functions), II, 132–33, 264. *See also* Functions; (loss of), II, 49, 224; rabbinic precedence in, II, 89

Honorius IV (pope), on Jewish neglect of Bible, II, 194–95; III, 167

Honorius I (Roman emperor), I, 144

Honorius III (Roman emperor), I, 219–20

Horowitz (Bohemian city), controversy with Prague of, I, 308–9

Horowitz, Isaiah b. Abraham: contract of, III, 126; declines fees, II, 85; on importance of education, II, 205; (Gentiles), III, 162; (night study), III, 162; (persecution), III, 171; study of treatise by, III, 168

Horses: in ancient Palestine, I, 57; Jewish attendance at races of, III, 207; pasture in cemeteries, II, 151; riding on, forbidden by Muslims, I, 161

Hosea (prophet), I, 35, 45

Hosha'ana Rabbah (holiday), charitable distributions on, II, 321
Hospices *and* hospitals, Jewish: I, 92; II, 327–30; III, 210–12; and Jewish segregation, II, 167; and synagogues, II, 128; in Frankfort, II, 61; in Paris, III, 62; in Spain, I, 361–62; staffs of, II, 115; supervisors of, I, 133; II, 61; term of *hekdesh* for, II, 328–29. *See also* Illness; Sanitation; Sick
  non-Jewish: Christian (Jewish funeral tolls), II, 154; (unsatisfactory conditions), II, 327–28; Muslim, and Jewish hospitals, II, 327
Hospitale pauperum, Christian, in Cologne, II, 327
Hospitality, charitable, Jewish, II, 322; III, 166, 209. *See also* Charities; Hospices; *Pletten*
Host, desecration of, and responsibility of elders, II, 53
Hosts, Italian, responsible for visitors, II, 10–11
Hotzenplotz (Moravia), and expulsion from Zülz, III, 106
Hours: of chastisement of pupils, III, 169; of instruction and study, I, 359–60; II, 118, 176, 197; III, 162; (and court sessions), II, 211–12; of work, I, 130; (educational responsibilities), II, 176. *See also* Education
House: "of mercy," I, 361. *See also* Hospices; "of the Council," II, 24; "of the people," I, 62, 87; II, 145; III, 11, 151
Household employees, *see* Servants
Household taxes: II, 251; and class divisions, II, 278–79; and *Pletten*, II, 345
Housekeeping, and feminine education, II, 178
Houses: ancient Palestinian, I, 41–42; communal, II, 24, 124–25, 128–29, 291; (and Roman law), I, 109; of catechumens, I, 219, 247; III, 184; of ill-repute, II, 313–14, 323; III, 205. *See also under* respective institutions
  private: and rabbinic salaries, III, 128; and schoolhouses, II, 186; and tenant protection, II, 292–94; III, 199; construction of, III, 147. *See also* Ḥazakah; height of, I, 91, 162–63; III, 147; non-Jewish, I, 261; II, 24; III, 197; synagogues in, I, 261; II, 127, 129; taxes on, I, 175; II, 248, 252; III, 187–88. *See also* Household taxes; Real Estate
Housewives, protected by *ḥazakah*, II, 299–300
Huesca (Spain), Jews of: burial society of, I, 352–54; III, 120; emulate Barcelona constitution, II, 58; inquisitorial proceedings against, I, 222; judiciary of, III, 125; (procedural latitude), II, 241; tax statutes of, II, 248–49, 251, 260, 281; (immunities), II, 14–15; (reduction), II, 274; women's synagogues of, III, 147
Ḥukke ha-Torah, statute of, I, 356–57; III, 92; on dormitories, II, 187; III, 126–27; on size of classes, II, 196
Ḥulaju (Mongol ruler), I, 186
Human figures, and synagogue art, II, 137
Humanism, and Catholic-Jewish relations, I, 304
Humanitarianism, modern: I, 9; and charitable associations, I, 363; and *Leibzoll*, II, 264. *See also* Enlightenment
Humility, and sumptuary legislation, II, 304
Huna, R. (amora), and Persian taxation, III, 31–32
Huna, R. (exilarch), I, 149
Huna, R. (gaon of Sura), III, 46
Huna Mari (exilarch), I, 149
Hungary, Jews of: I, 267; ancient, synagogues of, I, 83–84; chief rabbis

of, II, 81; combination of offices among, II, 103; intercommunal tax controversy of, III, 197; Reform Judaism among, I, 9. *See also* Austria-Hungary

Hussein (Mohammed's grandson), I, 175

Hyksos, land grants by, I, 33

Hypaepa (Asia Minor), Jews of, I, 92; III, 16

Hyperetes, position of, I, 102; III, 18. *See also* Ḥazzan

Hypsistos, dedication to, III, 13. *See also* God, the Most High

Hyrcanus II (high priest), I, 140

IBERIAN PENINSULA: apart from northern lands, I, 227; Christian reconquest of, I, 157; importance of Jewish taxation for, I, 235; Jewish banking in, I, 243. *See also under* respective countries, provinces and cities

Ibn Abbas, Judah, educational program of, II, 174

Ibn abi Zimra, David, b. Solomon: I, 191; on congregational divisions, I, 351; III, 89; on desecration of cemeteries, II, 151; III, 154; on *nagid*, III, 43

Ibn Adret, Solomon b. Abraham: III, 55; as preacher, II, 99; forced to condemn informer, II, 73; on age limits, III, 106, 184; on ban for tax defaults, II, 282; on cantors and chanting, II, 104–5; III, 136; on changes in endowments, II, 266; III, 189; on charities, III, 209; (begging), II, 321; (dues), II, 321, 344; III, 209; on communal debts, III, 190; (interest payments), II, 269; III, 190; on communal discipline, I, 211; II, 217–18; III, 51; on debt bondage and Sabbath, II, 226; on designation by retiring officers, II, 47; on duties of new arrivals, II, 12; on *hekdesh*, II, 329; III, 211; on judiciary, II, 71–72; III, 124, 173–74; (Gentile), I, 213; III, 52; on meat administration, II, 259; III, 158, 187; on plenary assemblies, II, 23; III, 106; on quorum at weddings, III, 47; on recitation of Decalogue, III, 22; on regional community of Barcelona, I, 286–87; III, 65; on seven elders, II, 55; III, 120; on Spanish agriculture, III, 185; on synagogues (attendance), III, 143; (called *midras*), III, 152; (founders' commemoration), III, 152; (seats), II, 130–31; III, 144; (vows), III, 145; on taxation, II, 15, 253; III, 102–3, 184; (as benefit), II, 246; III, 183; (assessments), III, 196; (immunities), III, 192; on teachers, II, 183; III, 163; (salaries), II, 117; III, 141; on women's suffrage, III, 114

Ibn 'Aḳnin, Joseph b. Judah, and academy of Bagdad, III, 41

Ibn al-Nakas, III, 35, 38

Ibn al-Nakava, *see* Nakawa

Ibn al-Shuwaich, Abu'l Fatḥ Isḥak (gaon), III, 38

Ibn Daud, Abraham ha-Levi, I, 184

Ibn Ezra, Moses b. Jacob, III, 51

Ibn Ḥabib, Jacob b. Solomon, on sanctity of synagogue, II, 127; III, 143

Ibn Ḥabib, Joseph, II, 215; III, 173, 177

Ibn Ḥabib, Levi b. Jacob: against preaching of cabala, III, 134; and rabbinic ordination, III, 74; on communal elections, II, 36; III, 113; on congregational divisions, III, 149; on *ḥazaḳah*, III, 198; on scholars' tax immunities, III, 193

Ibn Ḥabib, Moses (Valladolid rabbi), II, 74

Ibn Hajar, Aḥmed b. Muḥammad, and Jewish teachers, II, 184

Ibn Ḥamdun, Baha al-Din Muḥammad, III, 39

Ibn Hanbal, Abu 'Abdi Illah Aḥmed, I, 163

Ibn Ḥayyun, 'Ali, I, 190

Ibn Ḥazm, Abu Muḥammad 'Ali b. Aḥmed, III, 41

Ibn Ḥibad, Daniel b. Eleazar, I, 203

Ibn Kuraish, Judah, I, 146; III, 30–31

Ibn Laḥia, III, 39

Ibn Leb, Joseph b. David, on communal trade ordinances, III, 112, 200

Ibn Megas, Joseph b. Meir ha-Levi: and Jewish capital jurisdiction, III, 38; on *ḥazakah*, II, 298; on *hekdesh*, III, 211; on rabbinic tax immunities, I, 160–61; II, 80, 276–77; III, 34; on seven best men, III, 20

Ibn Sa'ad, al-Zuhri, Muḥammad, II, 35

Ibn Shaprut, Ḥisdai b. Isaac, I, 189

Ibn Tibbon, Judah b. Saul, library of, II, 201; III, 170; on teachers' salaries, II, 117; III, 141

Ibn Verga, Solomon: and redemption of captives, II, 334; on exilarchic installation, III, 39; on French controversy, III, 66; on music, II, 191; on Spanish morals, II, 313; III, 205

Ibn Yaḥya (Salonican family), II, 50

Ibn Yaḥya (Negro), David, I, 289

Ibn Yaḥya, David b. Joseph: biography of, III, 128; (as preacher), III, 133; educational program of, III, 167

Ibn Yaḥya, Gedaliah b. Joseph, III, 53

Ibn Yaish, Solomon (Alvaro Mendes), I, 197

Ibn Zeraḥ, Menaḥem b. Aaron: on synagogue decorum, III, 148; on teachers' salaries, II, 117–18; III, 141

Iconoclasm, religious, of Enlightenment, and communal control, II, 359–60

Iddo (Babylonian-Jewish chief), I, 68

Idealism: rabbinic, and public law, II, 216–17; Zionist, and reality, I, 17

Ideals of poverty, and charities, II, 346

Ideas, musical, rabbinic attitude to, II, 104

Identity, Jewish, continuity of, and legal adjustments, II, 245

Ideologies, and communal practice, I, 8, 119–20

Idolatry: and communal conflicts, II, 27; and elementary teachers, II, 182; and Gentile wine, II, 161; and imperial worship, I, 109; and lay judiciary, II, 71–72; and origin of synagogue, I, 60; III, 9. *See also* Worship, pagan

Idumeans, in Egypt, I, 76

Ifrikiyya: I, 190; priests of, III, 42. *See also* Kairowan; North Africa

Ijma, Muslim principle of, I, 165

'*Ikkub tefillah*, III, 112. *See also* Interruption of prayers

'*Ikḳul*, II, 233. *See also* Seizure of Property

Illiteracy *and* illiterates: ancient Israelitic, I, 48, 51; and concealing information, II, 177; and judiciary, II, 71–72, 113, 237; and marital preferences, I, 124; and rise of *ḥazzan*, II, 101; and translation of prayers, II, 143; condemned by Pharisees, I, 135; oppressed by learned, I, 166. *See also* Literacy

Illness: and hair cuts, III, 203; and vows for Palestine, III, 216; synagogue rites at, II, 145; visiting of graves during, II, 154. *See also* Hospitals; Physicians; Sick; Sanitation service

'*Illui*, Italian, II, 198

Image, "graven," in Israelitic Temple, III, 9

Imagery, prohibition of, and synagogue art, II, 137–38; III, 146–47

Imam, Muslim: and election of cadi, III, 50; and *ḥazzan*, I, 201
Immanuel b. Solomon of Rome, on cantors and choirs, II, 105; III, 136
Immediatstände, German and Polish communities, I, 336
Immunity: for debts and crimes, as bait to Jews, III, 100; judicial, and authorization, I, 149; of scholars, against demons, III, 169. *See also* Tax immunities
Impartiality, judicial: and courts of arbitration, II, 214; and rabbinic elections, II, 94; and taxpaying judges, II, 287–88. *See also* Judiciary
Impeachments of Jewish officials, II, 104; III, 48–49
Impediments, in marriage, and Jewish law, II, 210–11
Imperial worship, Roman, I, 99, 109
Imperialism: Graeco-Roman, and Jewish self-government, I, 76, 207; Persian, and Jews, I, 64, 206–7; Turkish, and religious toleration, I, 195. *See also* Politics
Importation, communal regulation of: and acquired rights, II, 296, 301; of citrons, II, 165; of Jewish books, I, 224; II, 203; III, 171; of meat, II, 108, 258–59; III, 187; of wine, II, 162–64
Improvements on real estate, and raising of rents, II, 292
Impoverishment, of families, and sumptuary laws, II, 302
Incense, allowed in Elephantine Temple, I, 60
Incest, prohibition of: II, 315; and registration of waifs, II, 331
Income taxes, Jewish, II, 13, 248–49, 254–55; and charitable tithes, II, 344; and electoral rights, II, 38; confused with excise taxes, II, 260; for redemption of captives, II, 335–36; methods of assessment of, II, 281–83
Incompetents, Jewish, become teachers, II, 183
Inconsistencies, constitutional, Jewish, and communal effectiveness, II, 122
Incorruptibility, Jewish, and local judges, I, 204. *See also* Corruption
Indemnities, communal: for delation, II, 236; for royal seizure of property, II, 276; of Christian owners of ghetto houses, II, 291–92; of state (for banishment), II, 9; (for capital punishment), II, 15, 71; (for excommunication), I, 246; II, 232
Independence: judicial, and division of fees, II, 84; local, in ancient Palestine, I, 32–34; scholarly, and patriarchal support, I, 151
Index, papal, and Hebrew books, I, 223. *See also* Censorship
India, I, 46, 58, 157, 200
Indifference, artistic, and synagogue art, II, 138
Indirect elections, II, 44–49, 61. *See also* Elections
Indirect taxation, *see* Taxes
Indispensability, of synagogue auctions, II, 133
Individualism: and adoption of statutes, III, 111; and agnosticism, I, 25; and associations, I, 372; and communal control, I, 3, 11, 14, 24–25, 116, 211; II, 361; and group study, II, 205; and historic continuity, II, 168; and responsibility for charity, I, 132; and seizure for communal debts, I, 334; and stamping out crime, II, 235; and synagogue candles, II, 134; despite basic uniformity, I, 156; in taxation, I, 137; (defense), II, 268; (education), II, 171; vs. majority principle, II, 26–27
Indoctrination, Jewish, and survival, II, 190
Industrial Revolution: I, 156; and charitable associations, I, 363

Industry, *see* Craftsmen
Inequalities: economic, in ancient Palestine, I, 35, 45, 47; fiscal, III, 196–97; regional, and dissolution of councils, II, 23. *See also* Class struggle; Egalitarianism; Equality
Infanticide, and communal regulations, II, 315
Infirmity, physical: and Muslim poll taxes, II, 259; as excuse from office, III, 124
Inflation, Polish, and rising meat taxes, II, 259
Influencing elections, statutory prohibitions on, II, 43, 45. *See also* Corruption; Elections
Informality, in synagogues, II, 128; of judicial proceedings, II, 239
Informing *and* informers, Jewish: III, 55; and appeal to Gentile courts, II, 102; and ban of settlement, II, 6; and capital punishment, I, 169; II, 221–23; and communal accounting, II, 65; and councils, I, 287, 330; II, 238; and criminals, II, 338; and doctrine of prevention, II, 221; and "donkeys' burial," II, 156; and forced condemnation, II, 73; and indirect actions, I, 212; and judiciary, I, 211; (lay), II, 71; and relaxation of procedure, II, 227, 240–41; and Spanish chief rabbis, III, 66; and seizure of property, II, 234; dangers of, II, 221–22; outlawed by Spanish kings, I, 235–36
Ingenuity, governmental, and Jewish taxation, II, 248
Inheritance laws, Jewish: and emigration to Palestine, II, 340; and endowments, II, 275; and heirless estates, I, 161, 247–48; II, 267; III, 35; and judges' discretion, II, 215, 331–32; and medieval dowries, II, 318; and preference for preaching, II, 98; and real estate (subdivisions), II, 292; (taxes), III, 188; and rights of husbands, III, 208; determined by religion, II, 210; discussed at Worms conference, III, 76. *See also* Heredity
taxes: and educational budgets, II, 185, 188, 275. *See also* Taxation
Injury to persons, and doctrine of repentance, II, 222
Innkeepers, Jewish: and congregational allegiance of visitors, II, 12; and Polish burghers, I, 281
Innocent II (pope), I, 217
Innocent III (pope): I, 217–18; against Jewish land ownership, I, 234; against loud prayers, III, 148; against reliability of deeds, I, 251
Innocent IV (pope): against Cordovan synagogue, I, 220; and liberation of Palestine, III, 215; and ritual libel, I, 218
Innovations, communal: and European supercommunity, I, 346–47; and habits of worshipers, II, 143; and mutilation of criminals, II, 223; via constitutional interpretation, III, 110
Inowrocław, Jews in, I, 269
Inquiries, legal: and public opinion, I, 347; and use of intermediaries, II, 238. *See also* Responsa
Inquiry, procedural, of informers, dispensed with, II, 241. *See also* Procedure
Inquisition, Catholic: and Barcelona synod, I, 288; and boycott of Ancona, III, 73; and censorship, II, 202, 335. *See also* Censorship; and heretical Jews, I, 221, 237; and Jewish assemblies, I, 322; and new synagogues, I, 219; and Sicilian chief rabbis, I, 294; and Spanish refugees, I, 253; and trial of Reuchlin, I, 304–5; handbook for, I, 221; in various regions (Portugal), I, 305; (Rome), I, 219, 221, 304–5, 322; (Sicily), I, 294, 317;

(Spain), I, 253, 288; Jewish exemptions from, I, 317; Marrano struggle against, I, 305; penal procedure of, II, 235. *See also* Church; Judiciary

Insaculation, II, 43. *See also* Elections (by lot)

Insanity of wife, and polygamy, II, 308

Inscriptions, Jewish, ancient: I, 76, 93, 121; III, *14*, *21*; and associations, I, 365; III, 16–17, 94; and cemeteries, I, 80, 94; and dispersion, III, 10–11; and elders, I, 98, *100–6*; III, 17; and priests, I, 98; and synagogues, I, 77, 83–84, 86, 88, 90, 100, 103–5; III, 13
medieval and modern: funerary, history of, III, 126, 156–57. *See also* Tombstones; in synagogues, III, 35, 148; (antiquity of), I, 164; (benefactors), II, 145; (dancers), III, 206; (Toledo), III, 147

Insecurity, Jewish: and aristocratic rule, II, 50; and charities, II, 319; and democracy, I, 28; and desecration of cemeteries, II, 151; and education, II, 171; and fee system, II, 85; and leadership, II, 52; and libraries, II, 201; and synagogue architecture, II, 136–37; mitigated by councils, I, 347. *See also* Legal status; Persecutions

Insolence of poor, and claims on charities, II, 347–48

Inspectors *see* Overseers

Installations of officials: exilarchs, I, 174, 176; III, 39; *geonim*, I, 180; *ḥakam-bashis*, I, 199; *negidim*, III, 43; popes, I, 217

Instigatores, Polish, in mixed litigation, I, 272; II, 116. *See also* Prosecuting attorneys

Institutionalized religion, dangers of, II, 168

Institutions, Jewish: and Roman law, I, 107; variety of, II, 157–67. *See also* under respective institutions

Instruments, commercial, legislation on, III, 200. *See also* Deeds

Insults: and deceased excommunicates, II, 231; of scholars, II, 180; prosecution for, II, 316

Intellectualism, Jewish: and book approvals, II, 203–4; and character building, II, 190; and communal control, II, 168; and emotional instability, II, 198; and Italian rabbinate, II, 77; and precocity of children, II, 198; and prolonged study, II, 176; vs. emotionalism, II, 198

Intercommunal cooperation: and banishment, II, 319; and hospices, III, 211; and Palestine colonization, III, 216; and rabbis, II, 323; III, 125, and sex relations, II, 313, 319. *See also* Charities; Conflicts; Councils; Interterritorial action; Synods

Interdict: ecclesiastical, and Jewish bans, II, 229; Jewish, Spanish privilege on, II, 14

Interest: on charitable loans, II, 326; and communal investments, III, 189, 191–92, 195; and communal loans, I, 334–35; II, 269, 271, 285; (*monti di pietà*), II, 257; and economic regulation, I, 130; and educational foundations, II, 186; and sale of citrons, II, 165; rates of (Assyrian colonies), I, 57; (Poland), I, 329, 334–35; II, 271, 273; (Rome, papal), II, 272. *See also* Banking; Usury

Interest of members, and associational variety, I, 350

Interior decorators, Jewish, prevailing anonymity of, III, 147. *See also* Art

"Interlopers," among rabbis, III, 128

Intermarriage, Judeo-Gentile: and responsibility of elders, II, 53; Christian condemnation of, I, 225; in Elephantine, I, 70; III, 12; in Soviet Union, I, 16; of a Palestinian mes-

senger, II, 342–43; outlawed by Ezra and Nehemiah, I, 70;
of Sephardim and Ashkenazim, II, 18–19, 365. *See also* Marriage
Intermediaries: before God, and visiting of graves, II, 154; legal, II, 237; III, 180. *See also* Attorneys
International relations: and decline of exilarchate, I, 185; and Jewish commerce, I, 168; and Jewish community, I, 10, 14; and Palestine, I, 18; and Persian churches, III, 36; and provincial leadership, I, 189; and *shtadlanim*, I, 187–88. *See also* Diplomacy; Interterritorial action
traders, Jewish: I, 210; in New World, II, 365; Turgot on, II, 290. *See also* Commerce; Merchants
Internationalism, Marxist, and Jewish minority rights, III, 4
Interpretations, juristic, Jewish: and constitutional law, II, 219; III, 110; and family life, II, 319; and growing severity, II, 212; and "law of the kingdom," I, 214–15; and legal adjustments, II, 216; and sumptuary laws, III, 202; of petition to Cromwell, I, 257; of Polish privileges, I, 268; repudiated by pope, I, 217; of talmudic legends by preachers, III, 134. *See also* Bible exegesis; Codes; Law
Interpreters, Jewish: ancient, I, 123–24; in Muslim bureaucracy, I, 188
Interruption of prayers: history of, II, 32–34, 145; III, 112; Spanish decree on, II, 14
Interterritorial action, Jewish: I, 10, 18, 208, *304–9*, 351; III, 72; ancient, I, 80, 174–75; and Ancona prisoners, III, 214–15; and branch societies, I, 364; and Capistrano's agitation, III, 77; and communal elections, III, 115, 123; and communal taxation, III, 104; and control over sex relations, II, 313; and educational borrowings, I, 358; and excommunication, II, 32, 98, 243; (of communities), II, 229; (private), II, 79; and expulsion from Zülz, III, 106; and Hebrew books, I, 224; II, 203; and Palestine relief, II, 343; and Polish Council, I, 331–32, 337–38, 341, 344; and rabbinate, I, 296–97; II, 77, 243–45; III, 129–31; and redemption of captives, II, 334, 336; and ritualistic controversies, II, 166; III, 138; and seizure of property, II, 233; and synagogue budgets, I, 164; II, 135–36; III, 146; and wine exports, II, 163–64
Intolerance, religious, *see* Anti-Semitism; Expulsions; Massacres; Persecutions; Toleration
Intonation, of cantors, controversies over, II, 105
Intoxication, state of, and judiciary, II, 211
Introductions, to Hebrew books, and approvals, II, 203–4
Inventories, and communal accounting, II, 65
Investigations, communal: for charities, limited, I, 132; of marriage applicants, II, 311; of Passover observance, I, 168
Investigators, Jewish, and government appointment, I, 292; and self-assessment, II, 283
Investment of funds: for redemption of captives, II, 335; of minors' funds, communal supervision of, II, 330
Invitations, royal, of Jewish settlers, III, 100
'Ir, meaning of, III, 8. *See also* Cities
Iran: Jewish settlements in, I, 66; influences on Judaism of, I, 46; III, 149. *See also* Persia
Iraq, *see* Babylonia
Ireland, dependent on London community, II, 21

Isaac (rabbi of Mannheim), II, 247
Isaac b. Abraham (Poznań rabbi), III, 83
Isaac b. Baruch, on preference for local poor, II, 323
Isaac b. David of Marseilles (Sicilian chief rabbi), I, 293
Isaac b. Elyakim, on hours of study, II, 176
Isaac b. Joel ha-Levi, rabbinic ordination of, II, 90–91
Isaac b. Joseph of Corbeil: legal decisions by, III, 179; on oath against gambling, III, 207; on seizure of informer's property, II, 234
Isaac b. Mordecai (Maestro Gaio), III, 78
Isaac b. Mordecai Gershon, and Rovigo bath, III, 160
Isaac b. Samuel of Dampierre (tosafist), on change of venue, III, 180
Isaac b. Sheshet Profet (Perfet *or* Barfat): against written briefs, II, 238; III, 180; and French controversy, I, 297; III, 66, 68; and Rimini conference, III, 79; on age discrepancy in marriage, II, 311; III, 204; on Algerian communities, III, 50, 118, 200; on associations, III, 89; on Barcelona conflicts, II, 52; on benefit of counsel, II, 241; III, 181; on cantors, II, 104; III, 136; on capital punishment, II, 221; III, 175; on communal indebtedness, III, 145; on deficient scribe, III, 139; on flogging, II, 225; III, 175; on French rabbis, II, 83; on gaming, III, 207; on government appointments, II, 218–19; on insults to scholars, II, 75; III, 124; on judiciary, I, 228; III, 56, 173–74; on liturgical controversies, III, 136; on preparation of statutes, III, 110; on private synagogues, III, 144; on rabbinic ordination, III, 126; on revenue from weddings, III, 127; on right of settlement, III, 100; on ritual slaughtering, II, 108; III, 137, 159; on Sicilian chief rabbi, III, 67; on synagogues (attendance), II, 143; (seats), II, 130–31; III, 144; on teachers' salaries, III, 140; on trade regulations, II, 162; III, 200; on wine administration, II, 162; III, 159
Isaac, Bezaleel's (German chief rabbi), III, 71
Isaac ha-Kohen, of Pinczów, rabbinic contract of, III, 131
Isaac of Oppenheim (imperial tax collector), I, 298
Isabella (Castilian queen): and rabbis, I, 239; II, 74–75; (chief rabbinate), I, 289; III, 182; protects Jewish craftsmen, I, 368; protects taxpayers, II, 280
Isaiah (prophet), I, 45, 51. *See also* Deutero-Isaiah
Isaiah b. Abba Mari of Savoy (French chief rabbi), I, 296; III, 68–69
Isaiah of Trani: and early traditions, II, 69; on medieval judiciary, II, 214; III, 173; on support of students, III, 166
Ishmael, I, 158. *See also* Islam
Ishmael, R. (tannai), I, 138–39
'Iska, and sale of citrons, II, 165. *See also* Interest
Islam: I, 157; II, 352; III, 6; ancient heritage of, I, 206; and charitable societies, I, 360; and desecration of cemeteries, II, 151; and Gentile wine, II, 161; and guild system, I, 365–66; III, 91, 94; and *ḥazakah* regulations, II, 298; and Jewish elections, II, 35–36, 50; and Jewish free-masons, III, 175; and Jewish population, I, 157–58; and mores of forefathers, I, 174; and papal taxation, I, 320; and polygamy, II, 308, 310; and public education, II, 171, 177–78, 187, 192–93; (elementary teachers), I, 182–83;

II, 184; and rabbinate, II, 67–68; 73–75; III, 124; (judiciary), III, 50, 124–25; (Mediterranean chief rabbis), I, 285, 346; and sextons, II, 106; and south Italian Jewry, I, 230–31; and synagogues, III, 36; (height), I, 162; II, 139; (new), I, 162, 219; (officials), III, 32; and synods, I, 310; and titles of elders, I, 200; III, 50; cabalistic conventicles under, I, 354; communal transformations under, I, 156, 206; II, 19; III, 68; emigration to Europe from, I, 209; *ḥazzan* under, III, 18; influences on Jews of, I, 232–33, 285, 346, 360; II, 35–36, 50, 67–68, 73–75; 129, 167; III, 25, 50; Jewish heresies under, III, 36, 38; Jewish rituals under, II, 142; Jewish views on, I, 195; representation by attorneys under, III, 180; sociology of, III, 35; taxation under, I, 228; II, 253; (immunities), II, 274, 277; III, 34–35, 80; Turkish chiefs of, I, 196; unity of, and Jewish uniformity, I, 167; vs. Christendom, I, 157, 227, 243; III, 91. *See also* Arabs; Caliphate; Mosque; Muslims; *and under* respective countries and cities

Isolation, physical, of tax assessors, II, 287

Isopoliteia, I, 107. *See also* Equality of rights

Israel, "in flesh," vs. "in spirit," I, 112. *See also* Church; Palestine, ancient

Israel Ba'al Shem Tob (Besht), and ḥasidic associations, I, 355

Israel Kohen, Palestine messenger, III, 217

Israel of Krems *or* Kremsier (German chief rabbi), I, 298; III, 69–70

Israeli, Isaac d', II, 54

"Israelites," in synagogue ritual, I, 97

Isserlein, Israel b. Petaḥiah: and German chief rabbinate, I, 311; consults wife on ritual, II, 178; III, 162; disciples of, III, 125–26; for free book lending, II, 201; on adherence to legal literature, III, 172; on bans, II, 233; III, 178; (private), II, 79; III, 126; on cantors, II, 277; (salaries), II, 101–2; III, 136; on cemeteries, II, 151; III, 153; (desecration), II, 151; III, 155; (regional control), III, 155; on changes in endowments, II, 266; III, 189; on citrons, II, 164; on insults to scholars, II, 79; on judiciary, II, 211–12; III, 172, 174; (competence), II, 242; III, 182; on majority principle, II, 27; III, 109; on marriage brokerage, III, 208; on private legal advice, III, 180; on quorum at weddings, III, 46; on rabbis, I, 311; III, 126, 132; on rights of minors, II, 331–32; III, 212; on taxation, II, 282; III, 185, 194; (immunities), II, 275, 277; III, 192–93; writ of ordination by, II, 90–91

Isserles, Moses b. Israel: and Ashkenazic customs, II, 213; and general sciences, II, 92; attacks on, III, 172; Cracow synagogue of, II, 130; on accounting of elders, III, 122; on cantors, III, 135; on charitable contributions, II, 344; on citrons, III, 160; on desecration of cemeteries, III, 155; on education, III, 161–62; on excessive severity, II, 212–13; III, 172; on expediting procedure, III, 180; on lending communal funds, III, 195; on majority principle, III, 109, 119; on physical penalties, III, 176; on private bans, III, 126; on rabbinic tenure, III, 129–30; on rights of minors, III, 212; on settlement of scholars, III, 100; on scholars' precedence in litigation, III, 180; on synagogues (*almemar*), II, 141; (candles), II, 134; III, 146; (height), III, 147; (private), II, 126; III, 142;

on tax collections, III, 174; on Vienna synod, III, 76

Istanbul, *see* Constantinople, Turkish

Italian congregations: in Constantinople, I, 205; in Corfù, and parental consent, II, 310; in Rome, vs. "Ultramontani," II, 20; in Salonica, II, 50; in Venice, statute of, II, 12; III, 121; mergers with "Germans" of (Ferrara), III, 114–15; (Verona), II, 19

Italian Jews: in medieval France, II, 98; in Poland, I, 332–33; II, 6; in Salonica, and local style of beards, III, 203; vs. Sephardim, II, 19

Italy, north-central, Jews of: I, 274–76; II, 120; III, 6, 185, 198; ancient, I, 108; (supercommunity), I, 106; (synagogues), I, 80, 83; and Bohemian controversies, I, 309; and Germany, I, 24; and Marrano communities, I, 24; and Roman appeal, I, 224; and unification of country, I, 322; assault and battery among, III, 179; associations of, II, 270; III, 102; (charitable), I, 362–63; (educational), I, 358–59; (guilds), I, 366, 368–69; (religious), I, 354; ban of settlement of, II, 9–12; bankers among, and right of settlement, II, 10–11; borrowing of synagogue ornaments among, III, 145–46; brevity of tenure among, II, 86; III, 121; cantors' salaries among, II, 101; capitalist influence on law of, III, 173; changes in communal structure of, II, 356, 359–60; censorship of books of, I, 223–24, 321; II, 204; III, 54; citron exports by, II, 164; III, 187; collections for foreign relief by, I, 306–7, 333; (Palestine), III, 216; conferences and synods of, I, 310, *315-23*; II, 42; III, *79–81*; (and Frankfort Conference), I, 313; (and Hebrew deeds), II, 111; congregational separatism of, II, 19–20; dancing masters among, II, 315; desecration of cemeteries among, II, 150–51; early traditions of, I, 242; II, *69*; education of, I, 242; II, 172; (Bible studies), II, 195; (general sciences), II, 191; (Hebrew studies), II, 193; (linguistic studies), II, 195; (precocity), II, 198; (teachers' salaries), II, 184; electoral procedures of, II, 43; expulsions of, I, 209; II, 120; freedom in selection of mates by, III, 204; *ḥazaḳah* legislation of, II, 293–95, 298; III, 198; (Gentile landlords), II, 295; Hebrew letters among, III, 125; illicit relations among, II, 312; immigration to, I, 242; III, 100; (from France), II, 79; (from Spain), II, 338; (invited), III, 100; intercommunal controversies of, I, 308; II, 229; judiciary of, I, 221; (lay), II, 70–71, 75–77, 215; *lulab* exports by, III, 159–60; masquerades among, II, 316; polygamy among, II, 308; population movements of, III, 108; projected university of, II, 191; quorum at weddings of, III, 47; rabbinate of, II, *75–77*; (mercenary ordinations), III, 132; (private patronage), II, 87; (secretarial services), II, 113; III, 139; (tenure), II, 86; redemption of captives by, I, 307; II, 334; sanitary services among, II, 329–30; status of women among, II, 178–79; (charity overseers), II, 37; (ritual slaughterers), II, 107; (scholars), III, 162; sumptuary laws of, II, 303–4; suppression of Talmud among, II, 191, 198; synagogues of, II, 136–37; (patriotic illumination), II, 144; taxation of, II, 246, 289; (*cassella* method), II, 283; theatrical arts among, III, 207; wandering scholars among, II, 188. *See also under* respective states and cities

southern, Jews of: ancient synagogues of, I, 83; and burghers, I, 279; and Egyptian *negidim*, I, 189–90; and Salonican congregations, I, 348; apart from northern, I, 227; appeal to Christian courts, III, 56; chief rabbinate of, I, 292–95; citizenship of, III, 54–55; communal legislation of, I, 230–32; II, 58–59; early judiciary of, I, 230; guilds of, III, 95–96; hospitality toward students of, III, 166; Muslim heritage of, II, 250; sale of meat by, II, 159; taxation of, II, 250; under Byzantium, I, 230. *See also* Naples; Sicily; *and under* respective provinces and cities

Itinerant: mendicants, II, 322. *See also* Begging; preachers, Jewish, I, 122; II, 97, 206. *See also* Preaching; rabbis, Italian, and private patronage, II, 87. *See also* Rabbinate; students, II, 180, 187, 323. *See also* Students

Iudice universale or *Judex universalis*, Sicilian, I, 231, 292; III, 67. *See also* Chief rabbinate (Sicily)

Iudices, Jewish, Roman, II, 59. *See also* Judiciary

Iugera, I, 138. *See also* Taxation, ancient

Ius Gazaga, papal, II, 293. *See also* Acquired rights

Iuxta murum, and location of cemetery, II, 150

JACOB (patriarch): blessing of, I, 141, 176; children of, non-Sephardim as, II, 19; God of, II, 26

Jacob Abraham b. Raphael, on position of rabbis, III, 130

Jacob b. Asher: and nullification of Jewish law, II, 208; and rise of rabbinate, III, 124; for judicial compromise, III, 173; on accounting of elders, II, 64; III, 122; on arbitrators, III, 173; on bans, III, 177; (private), III, 126; on begging, II, 321; on cantors, III, 135; on cemeteries, III, 156; on charitable obligations, III, 209, 217; (Gentile contributions), III, 218; on chastisement of children, II, 198; on congregational worship, III, 142; on concentration on Talmud, III, 167; on diversion of funds, III, 165, 189; on educational responsibilities, II, 169–70; III, 160–61, 165; (feminine study), III, 162; (size of classes), III, 168–69; on head covering, III, 202; on judiciary, III, 173, 182; on legacies, III, 93; on master-pupil relationships, III, 163; on mourning for leader, II, 147; III, 153; on obligatory acceptance of office, III, 119; on quorum at weddings, III, 47; on recitation of Decalogue, III, 22; on redemption of captives, III, 213; on ritual bath, III, 160; on successive burial, III, 155; on summonses to Torah, III, 42; on synagogue sanctity, III, 143, 151; on taxation, III, 194–95; (immunities), III, 126, 192; on visiting of sick, III, 211; on women slaughterers, III, 137; section on family life in code of, II, 319

Jacob b. Elijah, I, 186; III, 43

Jacob b. Ḥayyim of Worms (German chief rabbi), I, 299; III, 69

Jacob b. Meir Tam: and synod of Troyes, I, 212, 311–12; family of, III, 147; in German *memor*-books, II, 146; on aspersions against divorces, II, 318; on ban of settlement, II, 6; III, 98, 101; on binding communal decisions, II, 30; on change of endowments, II, 266; on concentration on Talmud, I, 193; III, 167; on disposition of legacies, I, 361; on height of synagogue, II, 139; III, 147; on local customs, II, 69–70; III, 51;

Jewish education), III, 23; (installation of popes), III, 52; (Jewish public law), II, 216–17; (Spanish Jewry), III, 34; officials of, I, 102; patriarchs of, I, 155; refugees from, I, 79; (Cotton Mather on), I, 261; restoration of, I, 60, 68; ritualistic diversity in, I, 67; Sanhedrin in, III, 29; (and Polish Council), I, 332; synagogues in, I, 67, 91, 120; walls of, III, 8. *See also* Temple, Second

medieval: and excommunication of Italian scholar, II, 98; controversy over synagogue in, I, 163; inquiries to, I, 193; *nesi'im* in, I, 194; pilgrimages to, II, 329; rabbinic tax immunities in, III, 34; visiting preachers from, II, 97–98. *See also* Messengers

Turkish: against renewal of ordination, I, 309; chief rabbis of, I, 197; III, 47–49; correspondence with other communities of, I, 169; III, 216–17; English account of, III, 215; excommunication of Pesaro by, II, 229; expulsion of bachelors from, II, 38; III, 114; *ḥazaḳah* legislation in, III, 198; messengers from, II, 30–31; III, 217; religious associations in, I, 355; III, 91–92; share in Palestine relief of, II, 342; III, 212; scholars of, III, 71

under Mandate, bi-national, I, 17

Jesse b. Hezekiah (exilarch), III, 73

Jesters, Jewish, and sumptuary laws, II, 305

Jesuits: against toleration of Jews, I, 265; and Jewish preachers, II, 98–99; as communal creditors, III, 84, 191; as synagogue owners, II, 129; dialectics of, and *pilpul*, III, 168; unfamiliarity with Bible of, II, 193–94

Jesus: alleged Jewish blasphemies against, I, 222; II, 339; and *archisynagogi*, I, 103; and Babylonian exilarchs, III, 31; crucifixion of, and medieval Jewry, I, 233; (taxation), III, 55; (witness), I, 279

Jewelry: sumptuary regulations on, II, 302; III, 200–1; taxes on, II, 248–49, 255, 261

"Jewish centers": and plenary assemblies, II, 24; and Salonican Talmud Torah, I, 348

Jewish city of Prague, and Bohemian council, I, 339–40. *See also* Quarters Jewish

Jewish question: medieval debates on, I, 216; (Church councils), III, 77; modern discussions on, II, 353; (England), I, 257–58; (Poland), III, 64; (Vienna Congress), III, 63. *See also* Anti-Semitism

Jews' bishop, *see* Bishops, Jewish

Joel b. Isaac ha-Levi of Bonn, on lending communal funds, III, 195

Joḥanan b. Mattathiah Trèves, I, 296–97; II, 83; III, 68–69

Joḥanan b. Nappaḥa, R. (amora): I, 89, 135, 151, 153–54; on *boulé*, III, 27; on continuous praying, II, 142

Joḥanan b. Zakkai, R. (tannai), I, 141 150; III, 29

Johannes Asiaticus, III, 16

John (Infante of Aragon): and excommunication, II, 232; and guilds, I, 370–71; and new synagogue, II, 140; and procedural latitude, II, 241; as spokesman of Jews, I, 291

John II (Aragonese king), confirms Gerona statute, II, 43

John (the Blind, Bohemian king), and synagogue treasures, II, 135

John I (Castilian king): against Jewish judiciary, I, 239; and synagogue worship, I, 237; II, 143

John II (Castilian king): I, 234; III, 65; against Jewish judiciary, I, 239; and guilds, I, 368

John I (English king), and Jewish tax collections, I, 245; appoints Jewish presbyter, I, 297
John II (French king), and excommunication, I, 246; and Jewish tax collectors, I, 244
John I (Portuguese king): centralization under, I, 285; and Hebrew deeds, I, 241; II, 111
John (Sicilian king), and Jewish *studium generale*, II, 185
John of Antioch, III, 17
John of Ephesus, I, 230
Jonah b. Abraham Gerondi, forced to condemn informer, II, 73
Jonathan (David's scribe), III, 13
Jordan, refuge at, I, 135
Jose, R. (tannai), I, 133, 145
Josel (Joseph) b. Gershon of Rosheim (German "chief rabbi"): I, 299; III, *69*, *74*; and German-Jewish conferences, I, 314; and intercommunal controversies, I, 308–9; threat to life of, I, 309
Joseph, R. (amora), I, 134
Joseph II (emperor): II, 355; abolishes *Leibzoll*, II, 264; against chief rabbinate, II, 43; III, 85; and Moravian communities, I, 339; II, 43; and obligatory instruction in German, II, 192
Joseph b. Eliezer (Palestine pilgrim), II, 341
Joseph b. Ephraim ha-Levi, foundation of, I, 358
Joseph b. Joḥanan Trèves, scholarly wife of, III, 162
Joseph b. Joshua ha-Kohen, *see* Hacohen
Joseph b. Moses of Höchstadt: as wandering scholar, II, 188; education of, III, 166; on book lending, III, 170; on formula of oath, III, 181; on Isserlein's wife, III, 162; on rabbinic ordination, III, 125–26, 130; on relations between moneylending and study, II, 78, 176; III, 162
Joseph Hama'arabi (Maimonides' pupil), III, 43
Joseph Isaac's, on Jewish beggars, III, 219
Joseph of Burgos (stone-mason), II, 275
Joseph of Schlettstadt (German rabbi), III, 69
Joseph *Rosh ha-seder*, on second holidays, III, 30
Josephus Flavius: and exilarchic tradition, III, 31; and Hellenism, III, 25–26; and Jewish embassies, III, 19; on charity, I, 132; III, 25; on common suppers, III, 17; on communal councils, I, 133; III, 26; on Cyrenaican Jewry, III, 13; on education, I, 125; III, 23; on Egyptian ethnarch, III, 18; on Herodians, III, 28; on Jewish quarters, I, 85–86; III, 15; on "Macedonian" Jews, III, 14; on Onias temple, I, 79; on origin of Jewish war, III, 24; on Roman decrees, I, 109; III, 19–20; on synagogues, III, 15–16; political theory of, II, 217
Joshua b. Gamala (high priest), educational reform of, II, 170, 174; III, 23
Joshua b. Ḥananiah, R. (tannai): I, 143, 152; nephew of, I, 143, 150; III, 30
Joshua b. Peraḥiah, and Jewish education, III, 23
Joshua Falk Kohen, *see* Falk Kohen
Josiah (exilarch), III, 40
Josiah (Israelitic king), I, 34, 36, 51, 89
Josiah b. Zakkai (anti-exilarch), I, 183
Joucet of Pontoise, and royal dispute, I, 296
Journeymen, Jewish: and wandering scholars, II, 187; competition in hiring of, III, 198; length of services as, II, 18; regulations on, I, 366. *See also* Craftsmen; Guilds
"Joy-killing" legislation, *see* Sumptuary laws

Juana (Castilian queen), and new synagogues, II, 125
Jubilee Year, and city walls, III, 8
Juceff (Joseph) Cohen, Tortosa endowment of, III, 166
Judaea, *see* Palestine
Judaeus (family name), III, 185
Judah, *see* Palestine
Judah (Jacob's son), sceptre of, I, 141, 176, 186–87
Judah I (patriarch): I, 141, 143–44, 149, 152–55; and calendar regulation, III, 30; Roman recognition of, III, 28–29; "writings" of, I, 213
Judah II (patriarch), I, 142
Judah, R. (amora), I, 154
Judah Aaron (Polish chief rabbi), I, 301
Judah b. Asher: ethical will of, II, 344; III, 127, 167; on Bible studies, II, 194; III, 167; on obligation to denounce criminals, III, 179; salary of, II, 82
Judah b. Barzilai, al-Barceloni: Book of Deeds by, II, 240; on formulas for appointments, I, 284; III, 50; on mutual tax agreements, III, 38–39; on rabbinic office, II, 67–68; on writ of ordination, III, 123
Judah b. 'Ilai (tannai), I, 123
Judah b. Samuel, the Pious, *see* Book of the Pious
Judah b. Titus (Roman elder), III, 17–18
Judah b. Yeḥiel Messer Leon, rhetoric of, II, 96; III, 133
Judah Löw b. Bezaleel (Moravian chief rabbi), I, 338
Judah's rod, and exilarchic glory, I, 141, 176, 186–87;
Judah, tribe of, Sephardim as descendants of, II, 18–19
Judenordnung, Austrian, II, 354
Judeo-Arabic records, Sicilian, III, 155–56
Judeo-Christians, and Roman synagogues, III, 15
Juderia, I, 239. *See also* Quarters, Jewish
Judex Judaeorum: German, I, 250; Polish, I, 272; II, 116. *See also* Judiciary; Justiciars
"Judges": Israelitic, I, 35; from small clans, I, 45; of assessment, in Mantua, III, 196; "of the Dispersion," I, 147; "of the gate," I, 174, 179
Judgments, judicial, Jewish: acceptance by parties of, II, 214; and clause on reversal, II, 242; and communal ledger, II, 112; fees for examination of, II, 84. *See also* Divine
Judiciary *and* judges, Jewish, ancient: I, *126–29*; III, 17, *24–25*; and academies, I, 151; and authorization, I, 135, 147, 149; (appointment), I, 128–29; III, 17–18; (ordination), I, 127–28, 155; and civil law, I, 110; and economic regulation, I, 129; and elders, I, 65, 99–100, 133; and exilarchs, I, 147, 149; III, 31; and learning, I, 127–28, 142; and patriarchs, I, 145, 147; and personal responsibility for errors, I, 128, 142; and Polish Council, I, 332; and Sanhedrin, III, 29; and synagogues, I, 87; and tax immunity, I, 138; appointed by Ezra, I, 64, 68; communal position of, I, 126; III, 20; exclusion of relatives from, I, 136; Ezekiel on, I, 60; gratuitous function of, I, 128, 181; in ancient Israel, I, 36, 39, 42, 48–49, 51, 53, 57; (Deuteronomy on), III, 7; in Babylonian Exile, I, 60, 65; in Egypt, III, 20; (Elephantine), I, 70–71, 73; indispensability of, I, 120; records of, I, 93; Roman legislation on, I, 23, 109–11, 114–15, 229; III, 20–21, 24; secre-

taries of, I, 102; sessions of, I, 128; used by Christians, I, 112

medieval and modern, eastern: and communal leadership, I, 179; (exilarchs), I, 174, 180, 207; III, 44; (*geonim*), I, 180, 183; III, 38; (*ḥakam-bashis*), I, 196; (*negidim*), I, 191; and teachers' authorization, II, 181; appointment of, I, 174, 180, 201–2, 204, 241; III, 44; (deposition), I, 166; at exilarchs' courts, I, 174, 179, 183; at *kallahs*, I, 182; geonic responsa on, III, 38; impeccability of, I, 195; (attacked), I, 166; lay, I, 202–4; Muslim law on, I, 161–62; power of, I, 165, 169; III, 50; prerogatives of, I, 202–3; promote business, I, 170; qualifications of, I, 204; rabbinic control of, in Turkey, II, 75

western: I, 211; II, *69–75*, 88–89, 123, *207–45*; III, *123–33*, *172–82*; against informers, I, 235; and ban of settlement, II, 5–6; and burial of criminals, II, 156; and capitalism, II, 362; and censorship, I, 224; and chief rabbinate (Polish), I, 300–3; (southern), I, 285, 289–90, 292–95, 347; II, 71–72; III, 66; and communal budgets, II, 65, 350; and communal conflicts, I, 323, 326; and creative law finding, II, 70, 290; and economic regulation, II, 290; and English presbyters, I, 297; and excommunication, II, 74, 231; and government appeal, I, 343; and government confirmation, II, 35; and guilds, I, 367–68; and intermediaries, II, 238; and interruption of prayers, II, 32–34, 145; and Jewish allegiance, II, 124; and legal briefs, II, 239; and majority principle, II, 26; and *morenu* title, II, 91; and opinions to single parties, II, 238; and Palestinian courts, II, 214; and plenary assembly, II, 31–32; and preachers, II, 100; and preparation of deeds, II, 113; and private ownership, II, 245; and protection of orphans, II, 330–32; and rabbinate, II, 95; (elections), II, 94; III, 132–33; (ordination), II, 68; and regional communities, II, 21, 241; (cemeteries), II, 148–49; and salaries, II, 63; III, 127; (fees), II, 64, 85; (fines), II, 234–35; (talmudic prohibition), II, 85; and social welfare, II, 290; and synods, I, 212, 312, 321; and taxation, I, 238, 282; II, 219, 246, 261, 287; (administration), II, 283–84; (dispute), II, 287–88; (immunities), III, 193; and witnesses, I, 226, 229; and writs of divorce, II, 318; combination with other offices of, II, 103; controled by Italian cities, I, 275–76; corruption of, II, 247; discretionary powers of, II, 84, 212, 215–16, 218, 225, 231, 238, 245, 331–32; educational importance of, I, 213–14; effects of centralized control on, III, 106; elections of, II, 58–59; III, 132–33; in various regions (Byzantium), I, 228; III, 52; (England), I, 249, 297; III, *69*; (France), I, 212, 312; (Frankfort), II, 117; (Germany), I, 247–49; II, 26; III, 70, 132–33; (Hessia), I, 343; (Italy), I, 275–76, 321; II, 59; (Lithuania), II, 40, 63, 330; (Moravia), II, 88; (Poland), I, 270–71, 300–3, 324, 326, 332; II, 21, 35, 84, 88, 100, 113, 214; III, 63; (Portugal), I, 285; (Sicily), I, 231–32, 292–95; (Spain), I, 238–41, 289–92; II, 58–59, 63–64, 71–72, 103; III, 66, 120, 124, 132–33; (Worms), I, 248–49; (Zurich), I, 277; lay vs. rabbinic, II, 57, 69–73, 88, 209, 215, 219, 243–44; III, 51–52, 124–25, 132–33; (favored by Reischer). III, 133; (fees), II, 64;

(religious law), II, 211; may reverse non-Jewish decision, I, 214; meet in synagogues, II, 144; membership of, I, 202; II, 117, 236; neighborhood use of, I, 283; outside influences on, II, 349; qualifications for, II, 71–72; (like "laymen"), II, 214; reliability of deeds of, I, 251; II, 240; repudiation of, I, 213, 238; scribes of, II, 110; State interest in, I, 343; II, 123; (protection of), I, 232, 238–41, 248–49, 270–71, 301; III, 56; (suppression of), I, 249, 277, 343; III, 52; vested interests in, III, 51

non-Jewish, ancient: Assyrian, I, 57; Graeco-Roman, and desecration of sanctuary, I, 88; in Elephantine, I, 71; Persian, use Aramaic, I, 71; Roman (Jews at), I, 110, 114–15, 127, 229; (prosecute Flaccus), I, 88

Islamic: III, *34*; and Jewish judges, III, 50; and Jewish parties, I, 162–63, 189; and *negidut*, I, 190; corruption of, I, 166, 170; geonic responsa on, III, 38; hinder Jewish business, I, 170; testimony at, suspected, I, 170; Turkish (and capitulations), I, 199; (Jewish capital punishment), II, 222; (*kehaya*), I, 198

medieval and modern: and enforcement of Jewish bans, II, 230; and execution of Jews, II, 223; and Jewish charities, III, 219; and Jewish *habeas corpus*, II, 227; and Jewish holidays, I, 236; and Jewish oaths, I, 262; II, 240. *See also* Oaths; and Jewish parties, I, 236, 238, 247–50; and lay judiciary, II, 71; and mixed litigations, I, 240, 250, 272–73, 276, 280, 297–98; II, 48; III, 69, 117; and synagogue contributions, II, 133; and tax-collectors, I, 245; appeal to, I, 232; III, 51, 56; (charities), II, 346; (councils against), I, 212–13, 302, 330; II, 77; (disqualification of cantor), II, 102; (excommunication), II, 228; (occasional permission), I, 213, 330; II, 285; ecclesiastical (and ancient courts), I, 114–15; (Barcelona synod on), I, 288; (books), I, 223. *See also* Censorship; (family relations), II, 210; (jurisdiction over professing Jews), I, 221–23, 272; (mixed litigations), I, 250, 276; II, 116; (Reuchlin's trial), I, 304–5; feudal, jurisdiction over Jews of, I, 278; in various regions (Byzantium), I, 229; (England), II, 210, 297–98, 364; III, 69; (France), I, 245; (Germany), I, 248–50; III, 219; (Italy), I, 232, 276; (Lithuania), I, 280, 330; (Poland), I, 272–73; II, 48, 116; III, *17*; (Sicily), I, 238; (Spain), I, 227, 240–41, 278; II, 73; (West Indies), I, 262; rabbinic counsellors in Spain of, II, 73; royal, for mixed litigation, I, 241, 250; slowness of procedure at, II, 239; universality of, I, 214. *See also* Arbitrators; Courts of Appeal; High Court; Law; Litigations; Procedure; Summonses; Supreme court

Julian, Flavius Claudius, the Apostate (Roman emperor): I, 144; and Jewish poor, II, 347; III, 218; and judiciary, III, 21; and patriarchs, III, 29–30; authenticity of epistles by, III, 29

Julius II (pope), Jewish community under, III, 109

Julius III (pope), and synagogue tax, II, 135

Juntas, Jewish, Castilian, III, 65. *See also* Councils

Jurisdictionalia, Hessian, and foreign judiciary, I, 343

Jurisprudence *and* jurists: Jewish, and rabbinic dialectics, II, 195; III, 124; Muslim, I, 165, 170; (and Jewish sectarianism), I, 178; (on exilarchic

revenue), I, 175; western, I, 269; (in English chirograph offices), I, 251
Justice, idea of: and economic regulation, I, 130; and lower land taxes, III, 185; and penal retaliation, II, 221; and prophetic-rabbinic ideals, I, 129–30; and Semites, I, 39
Justiciars of the Jews, English, for mixed litigations, I, 297–98; III, 69. *See also* Judiciary, non-Jewish
Justin Martyr, III, 18
Justinian (Byzantine emperor): I, 115; and Christian churches in Persia, III, 36; forbids African synagogues, I, 230; surpassed by Eugenius IV, I, 221. *See also* Code of Justinian
Jus ubique docendi, and rabbinic ordination, III, 130
Juvenal, Decimus Junius, on synagogue, I, 82

Ḳabbarim, association of, I, 352–53
Ḳabranim, Metz society of, III, 89. *See also* Burial societies
Ḳaddish, recitation of, II, 69
Kafnai (exilarch), I, 173
Ḳahal: biblical use of, III, 10–11; *qua* communal council, I, 280; II, 63. *See also* Communal control; Councils; Elders
Kairowan: and *geonim*, I, 181, 193, 202; and provincial leadership, I, 189; Babylonian captives in, I, 194; chief rabbis in, I, 181; Muslim courts of, I, 170; *negidim* in, I, 191
Kajdany, class distinctions in, II, 307
Kalisz, Jewish privilege of, I, 267
Kallah: I, 154–55, 180, 182, 184; (etymology), III, 33; heads of, I, 182
Kallistos (Venosa child), I, 105
Kalot of Rouen (*procureur général*), I, 296
Kann (Frankfort family), III, 141–42
Kann, Beer Löw Isaak zur (Frankfort leader), III, 142
Kanne, Isaak zur, Frankfort feud of, III, 141
Karaites: I, 178; III, 37; and exilarchate, III, 41; and title of rabbi; II, 67; controlled by Egyptian *nagid*, I, 191; elders of, I, 201; Lithuanian (conferences of), III, 83; (taxation of), III, 185; Sabbath observance of, I, 168; stir communal unrest, I, 166–67
Karga, Persian, medieval heritage of, II, 250–51
Karl Ludwig (Palatine elector), II, 247
Karlin, ḥasidic movement of, III, 92
Karlsruhe, Jewish population in, III, 107
Karmatians, Muslim propaganda of, I, 365
Karo, Joseph b. Ephraim: against Gentile courts, III, 52; and new customs, II, 213; and nullification of Jewish law, II, 208; on Bible studies, II, 194; on book lending, III, 170; on burial of Gentiles, II, 148; on cantors, III, 135; on Carpentras taxation, III, 104; on charities, II, 320; III, 209; on concentration on Talmud, III, 167; on desecration of cemeteries, III, 155; on elders (accounting), III, 122; ("seven"), III, 120; on excommunication (of scholars), III, 129; (private), III, 126; on *ḥazaḳah*, III, 199; on head covering, III, 202; on judges, III, 172, 174; (precedence of cases), III, 180; on "Law of Kingdom," III, 52; on majority principle, III, 109–10; on mourning for leader, III, 153; on obligations of new residents, III, 102; on quorum at weddings, III, 46–47; on rabbinic tax immunities, III, 126; on recitation of Decalogue, III, 22; on rights of minors, III, 212; on synagogues, III, 143; (height), III, 147; (lending ornaments), III, 146; (private), III,

142; (seats), III, 145; on tenure in private employment, III, 129; on women slaughterers, III, 137; section on family life in code of, II, 319

Kastenmeister (Frankfort), II, 61, 287. *See also* Tax assessments; Tax collections; Treasurers

Katz, Joseph b. Mordecai Gershon: against outside bans, III, 182; on Jewish prisoners, III, 214; on majority principle, II, 27; III, 109; on marital relations, III, 208; on Moravian debts, III, 192; on Palestine relief, III, 216; on ransom of captives, III, 213; on responsibility of elders, III, 118; on slaughtering, III, 159; on three-class system, III, 115

Katzenellenbogen, Ezekiel b. Abraham (Hamburg chief rabbi): II, 86; election of, III, 128; statute of, II, 30

Katzenellenbogen, Meir b. Samuel Isaac of Padua: and synod of Ferrara, III, 130; excommunicates community, II, 229; III, 177; on cantors, II, 101; III, 135; on civil-law inquiries, II, 238; on preaching, III, 134; on private synagogues, II, 126; III, 142; on rabbis (immunities), III, 193; (secretarial services), III, 139

Katzenellenbogen, Samuel Judah b. Meir, on rabbinic ordination, III, 130

Kazimierz, Jewish history in, III, 71. *See also* Cracow

Keepers: English, of deeds, II, 116; Jewish, of baths and cemeteries, II, 115

Kefar, meaning of, III, 8

Kehaya (Turkish), I, 197–98

Ḳehillah, New York, I, 26

Kemal Pasha Ghazi Mustafa (Turkish dictator), I, 13; III, 50

Keneset, I, 61, 87. *See also* Synagogues

Kenishta, I, 61. *See also* Synagogues

Kerak, meaning of, III, 8

Keri'ah, ha-, Roman, II, 60. *See also* Council of elders (60)

Kesut (medieval charity), II, 320. *See also* Clothing

Ketab masmik, II, 67. *See also* Decrees of appointment; Ordination

Ḳeṭeb meriri, III, 169. *See also* Demons

Keys, of tax chests, control over, II, 283

Khazana (Assyrian official), III, 18

Kiblah, and *negidut*, I, 191

Ḳiddush, public recitation of, II, 128

Kidnapping of child, Jews accused of, II, 339

Kiev, as member of Polish Council, III, 81

Ḳimḥi, David b. Joseph, I, 82; III, 15

Ḳimḥi, Raphael Israel (Palestine messenger), III, 217

Kimpolung (Bukovina), controlled by Suczawa community, III, 105

Kings, *see* Monarchy

Kingston, Jamaica, synagogue in, I, 262

Kitchen, communal, obligatory contributions to, I, 132, 136; II, 320

Klamen, II, 33. *See also* Interruption of prayers

Klaus: ḥasidic, II, 125; in Wilno, II, 107. *See also* Congregations; Synagogues

Klausrabbiner, III, 127.

Klausstiftung (Mannheim), statute of, III, 127

Kleiderordnung, Frankfort, II, 305. *See also* Sumptuary laws

Kleisdorf (Germany), anti-competitive ordinance in, II, 297

Kleparz (Poland), residence rights in, II, 234

Kleve: examination of slaughterers in, III, 138; household employees in, II, 299; officials' revenue in, II, 119–20; personal attendance at Council of, II, 28, 41–42; regional community in, I, 341, 343–44; III, 86–87; residence rights in, II, 119–20; revenue of provincial messenger in, II, 119–20; tax assessments in, II, 280, 287, 326; writ of divorce of, disqualified by Frankfort, III, 181. *See also* Councils

Knives of slaughterers, periodic examination of, II, 85, 109

Knocking at doors, by sextons, II, 106

Koblenz, Jewish hospital in, II, 329

Kobylin, election day in, III, 116

Kohen Zedek (gaon): I, 183–84, 188–89; on Babylonian superiority, III, 37

Kolbo: formula of ban in, III, 177; on burial imposts, III, 156; on mourning for leader, III, 153; on Passover flour, III, 209; on synagogue discipline, III, 150; on tenure of cantors, II, 104

Kolin (Bohemia), Jews of: III, 85; communal debts of, III, 192; meat taxes of, III, 186

Kol Nidre, prayer of, on Passover, I, 240

Kommotau (Bohemia), regional control of, III, 105–6

Königsberg: anti-communal *haskalah* in, II, 360; Jewish societies in, III, 90

Korah (biblical conspirator), II, 37

Korobka, II, 257, 278; III, 186, 195. *See also* Meat taxes

Kozienice, *maggid* of, II, 100

Kranz, Jacob b. Ze'eb (Dubno *maggid*), II, 99

Krems (Lower Austria), Jews of: I, 298; and German chief rabbinate, III, 70

Kremsier (Moravia): III, 200; and German chief rabbinate, III, 70; rabbis of, I, 298; III, 85; Swedish invasion of, I, 306

Krisshaber, Isaac, and sturgeon controversy, III, 159

Krochmal, Menahem Mendel b. Abraham (Moravian chief rabbi): and Moravian constitution, I, 338; on cantors' salaries, II, 101; III, 135; on fish, III, 159; on interior decorator, III, 147–48; on majority principle, II, 27–28; III, 109, 118; on synagogue seats, III, 145; on tax distribution, II, 268; III, 190, 194

Krotoszyn (Poland), passive franchise in, II, 40

Ktesiphon (Persia), Jewish chief of, I, 68

Kulp (brothers), and Frankfort controversy, III, 142

Kültepe, Assyrians in, I, 55; III, 10

Ḳuppah, I, 132, 136; II, 320. *See also* Charities

Kurnik (Poland), Jewish guilds in, III, 97

Kyrios (divine name), I, 77

Labadists (sect), legal position of, I, 261

Labor *and* laborers, Jewish: and associational variety, I, 350; and educational responsibilities, I, 360; II, 176; III, 162; and French wine exports, II, 164; and *ḥazaḳah*, II, 299–300; and mourning for scholars, II, 147; and Polish communities, III, 96; and relations with employers, I, 130; and repair of ghetto houses, II, 294; and study of law, I, 138; and synagogue attendance, III, 143; and taxation, I, 159; II, 253–54, 267–68; exchange of, in Alexandria, I, 78–79, 88, 364–65; forced (ancient), I, 38, 138, 365; (medieval), I, 218, 267–68; modern unions of, I, 17, 25; Roman appreciation of, I, 110. *See also* Apprentices; Craftsmen; Guilds; Servants; Slavery

Lace-makers, Jewish, Polish guilds of, I, 369

Ladies and girls, Roman association of, I, 372

Lambs, Spanish taxes on, II, 259

Lamentations, Jewish, decrees against noise of, II, 155

Lampronti, Isaac b. Samuel, II, 191; III, 192

Land *and* landownership, ancient: censuses of, I, 159; Israelitic, I, 33, 39, 42, 44; III, 8–9; (hereditary), I, 47; (in Babylonian exile), I, 63; III, 11; Jewish (of patriarchs), I, 141; III, 33; (riparian rights), I, 137; (taxes), I, 148; Persian, I, 148

medieval and modern, Jewish: and communal membership, I, 136; and *ḥazakah*, II, 297–98; of Narbonne *nasi*, III, 68; opposed by Church, I, 234; II, 254; taxes on, II, 248, 253; (Church), II, 254; (Muslim), I, 159–61, 172; III, 33; (rabbinic opposition to), III, 185. *See also* Agriculture; Tithes

Landau, Ezekiel b. Judah: affected by Enlightenment, III, 168; and Worms assembly, I, 314; as preacher, III, 134; contract of, III, 131; for Kleve divorce, III, 181; not Bohemian chief rabbi, I, 340; on Bohemian morals, III, 205–6; on charities, III, 209; on conflicting loyalties, III, 199–200; on education, III, 161–63; (study of ethics), III, 168; on financial irregularities, III, 122; on *ḥazakah*, III, 199–200; on imports of Vienna clothing, II, 297; III, 199; on lay judiciary, II, 89; on position of rabbis, III, 130; on rabbinic dialectics, II, 195; on synagogues (decorum), III, 148; (private), I, 352; III, 89; on taxation, III, 183, 196; (immunities), III, 194; relation to Eibeschütz of, III, 178

Landesmassafond, Moravian, I, 339; III, 85

Landesverband, Jewish, in Moravia, I, 339; III, 85

Landgraf of Hesse-Cassel, and admission of new members, II, 5

Landlords, urban: Christian (and ghettos), II, 291–92; III, 197; (of Jewish cemeteries), II, 152; (of synagogues), II, 129; Jewish (and interruption of prayers), II, 33; (and prostitution), II, 314; and real estate taxes, III, 188; and residence rights, II, 234; and tenant protection, II, 293. *See also* Acquired rights; Houses; Leaseholds; Tenants

"Land of Israel," Babylonia as, I, 154. *See also* Palestine

Landshut, Jews of: I, 299; oath of, III, 158, 181; sales of meat by, II, 159

Landsmannschaften, Jewish: ancient, I, 66, 81, 120; III, 11–12; in Caliphate, I, 167–68; in Turkey, I, 205, 348, 350–51; Italian, I, 350; rituals of, and congregational divisions, III, 149; vs. centralization, I, 206. *See also* Congregations; *and under* respective national groups

Landsofer, Jonah, will of, III, 168

Landteidinge, Teuton, and Israelitic assemblies, I, 48

Langobards, expel Jews, I, 209

Languages: Arabic, and Jews, II, 112, 132, 250.

Aramaic: Greek loan words in, I, 100; in Palestine, I, 81, 122–23; in Persia, I, 71; Jewish proficiency in I, 72

European: I, 242; and Jewish prayers, II, 143; control of Jewish books in, II, 202; familiarity of Jews with, I, 187–88; II, 192; (feminine), II, 178–79; French, and rabbinic registration, II, 84; German (and Jewish scribes), II, 112; (and Moravian chief rabbis), II, 43; (obligatory instruction in), II, 192; Greek (and Hellenistic Jewry), I, 90; (in Palestine), I, 121; (in Talmud), I, 130; III, 16; (influenced by Septuagint), I, 141; (studied in Soviet Union), I, 16;

Italian (and Jewish preachers), II, 96; (and scribes), II, 112; (Jewish study of), I, 359; II, 191; (translation of prayer-book into), II, 143; III, 149–50; Latin (and scribes), I, 241; II, 112; (in synagogue), I, 123; (Jewish instruction in), II, 191; (studied in Soviet Union), I, 16; Polish, scribes' unfamiliarity with, II, 112; Portuguese (in deeds), I, 241; (in Dutch ceremonies), I, 255; (term *arrab* in), II, 67; Spanish, term *arrab* in, II, 67

Hebrew: and Hellenistic Jewry, I, 90; and rabbinic registration, II, 84; and Reform Judaism, I, 9; and rise of *ḥazzan*, II, 100; and synagogue, I, 87, 125–26; and variety of rituals, I, 9; II, 142; and vernacular sermons, II, 96; cultivation of, and communal control, II, 359–60; equivocal translations from, II, 68; familiarity with (of censors), I, 223; (of scribes), II, 112; (of women), II, 178; Greek loan words in, I, 100; in deeds (forbidden by Portugal), I, 241; (not in Elephantine), I, 71; instruction in, I, 104; II, *191–95*; (in Soviet Union), I, 16; (Jewish ignorance), I, 122–23; (of Gentiles), II, 177; mixed with Yiddish, III, 164; philological studies of, II, 359–60; (Italy), I, 359; (Tiberias), I, 192; (universities), I, 16; III, 135; spoken, in religious associations, I, 355; used by Christians, I, 304; II, 177; III, 135. *See also* Christian Hebraists

Ladino, imposed by exiles, I, 197; Yiddish, II, 113; (German origin of), I, 267; (in Soviet community), I, 15

Languedoc, *see* France, southern

Laodicaea, patriarchal messenger in, I, 143

Laographia (Egyptian tax), I, 105

Larissa (Greece), communal price agreements in, II, 300

Lascari (papal nuncio), I, 334

Latins, judiciary in Catania of, I, 238

Lattes, Bonetto de (Jacob b. Immanuel Provinciale), I, 304–5

Lavadores, association of, I, 354. *See also* Burial societies

Lavatory, public, Jewish requirement of, I, 120

Law *and* legislation, Israelitic: and Hellenistic charities, III, 25–26; and justice, I, 39; and medieval Jewry, I, 238–39; and popular assembly, III, 9; and priestly schools, I, 60–61; and social unrest, I, 47; in Babylonian Exile, I, 60; popular reverence for, I, 36, 49; pre-exilic character of, III, 9; uniformity of, I, 51

Jewish: I, 119; II, 210–13; III, 172–73; adaptability of, I, 323; II, 69, 128, 168, 208, 245; and academy controversies, I, 152; and admission of settlers, II, 10; III, 99–100; and agricultural dues, I, 132; and banking prerogatives, I, 244; and burial, I, 94; and charities, I, 132; II, 346; III, 218–19; (contributions to), II, 321; and Christianity, I, 9, 216; and communal administration, I, 126–27, 129, 135; II, 6; and copyright, III, 171; and deeds, I, 73; and disfranchisement of bachelors, II, 37–38; and divorce, I, 70; (of converts), II, 317; and drafting of statutes, II, 31; and education, I, 124; II, 104–5, 172, 177, 197, 207; III, 174; (charges for), I, 126, 128; (marriage quotas), III, 98; (modern plutocracy), II, 362; (of orphans), II, 330; and elders, I, 99; and family life, II, 319, 325; and flogging, I, 168–69; and formulas of deeds, II, 112; and Gentile captives, III, 214; and Gentile witnesses, I, 226, 241; and Hellenistic statutes,

I, 77; and interest on communal loans, II, 269; and interruption of prayers, II, 32–34; and Italian assemblies, I, 320; and judiciary, I, 162, 202; II, 208; III, 124–25; (charges for), I, 126, 128; (of guilds), II, 89; and local precedents, II, 213; and obsolescence of endowments, II, 266; and Palestine relief, II, 341; and Philo, III, 20; and police regulations, III, 197; and Polish councils, I, 323; III, 82, 84–85; and preaching, I, 122–23; II, 100; III, 134; and rabbinic tenure, II, 86–87; and ritual bath, II, 165; and ritual slaughtering, II, 106–7, 160; and Sanhedrin, III, 29; and scribes, I, 64; II, 112; and seven best men, III, 120–21; and Sicilian chief rabbis, III, 67; and signatures on deeds, II, 113; and slaves, I, 177; II, 177, 308; and Spanish courts, I, 239; and suicide, III, 157; and sumptuary laws, II, 303; and synagogues, II, 127; (private), III, 142–43; and synods, I, 313. *See also* Ordinances, synodal; and taxation, I, 110; II, 252, 256; (equity of), I, 173; (immunities), II, 275–78; and teachers' control, II, 180–81; and variety of rituals, I, 150; II, 142; and visiting of sick, II, 328; and wedding rites, II, 310; autonomy of, I, 115; Babylonian hegemony in, I, 65, 150, 191–92; Barcelona synod on, I, 288; codes of, I, 52; defended by Mendelssohn, II, 360; distinguishes between visitors and residents, III, 102; divine character of, I, 126, 214; economic function of, I, 210–11; III, 173; elders' familiarity with, I, 205; exclusivity of, I, 212–15; geonic influences on, I, 185, 216; and government intervention, II, 208–9; liturgical position of, I, 89, 121; nature of, I, 102, 115, 124, 128; II, 219; papal interference with, I, 221; prohibited by Justinian, I, 191; rabbinic vs. biblical, II, 129; reluctance in formal application of, II, 209, 214; states' respect for, I, 282; III, 55; (ancient Rome), I, 111; (German cities), I, 277; (Poland), I, 301; (Savoy), I, 264–65; (Sicily), I, 317; (Spain), I, 238; (Venice), I, 275–76; studied by Romans, I, 127; students' decisions on, III, 171–72; supplemented by officials, II, 290; supremacy of social interest in, II, 245; universal familiarity with, I, 125; vs. ethics, III, 168

non-Jewish, ancient: I, 85, 107; and synagogues, I, 91; Egyptian, for Onias Temple, I, 79; Persian, I, 72; (and exilarchate), I, 147, 173; Roman, I, 80, 107–16; II, 245; III, 19–20; (and communal elders), III, 15; (and elections), I, 96; (and holidays), I, 236; (and judiciary), I, 115, 128; III, 20–21; (and patriarchate), I, 12, 140–45; (and synagogues), I, 91, 112–15; (influence of), I, 227, 243; (Jewish transgression against), I, 238–39; Syrian, I, 83

medieval and modern, eastern: I, *158–65*, 171; allows written briefs, III, 180; and *dhimmi* witnesses, I, 226, 241; on execution of informers, II, 222–23; and Jewish courts, I, 162; and Jewish slavery, II, 337; and rabbinic tax immunities, III, 34–35, 38; and synagogues, I, 162–63, 219; III, 35–36; (private), II, 125; personal principle in, I, 161–62; uniformity of, I, 167; validity of, I, 226; Turkish, I, 198; II, 222–23, 337; III, 36

western: I, 10, 22, 233, 252; and bi-sexual dancing, II, 316; and Catholic biases, I, 13, 222, 226–27; and change of venue, II, 242–43;

and communal budgets, II, 65, 269; and confiscation for tax-defaults, II, 284; and elections, III, 113–14; and exclusivity of Jewish law, I, 212–13; and funerals, II, 153–55; and heirless estate, I, 248; and judiciary, II, 208–9, 242; and new synagogues, I, 219–21; and rabbinate, III, 124–25; and Sunday rest, I, 11; and taxation, II, 57, 260; and tenant protection, II, 292–96; and uncharitableness, III, 209; enforce disposal of Christian slave, II, 309; in various regions (Austria), III, 219; [funeral tolls], II, 153; [*ḥazakah*], II, 298–99; [synagogues], II, 129–30; III, 143–44; (England), I, 20, 259; III, 56–57, 59, 61; [deeds], III, 139; [fiction of non-recognition], I, 276; II, 364; (France), III, 56–57, 67–68; [excommunication], I, 246–47; (Germany), I, 48, 243, 277; III, 56–57; [book trade], II, 204; [Church councils], III, 77; [excommunication], I, 230–31, 246–47; III, 71; [fines], II, 234; [law books], III, 57; ["law of aliens"], I, 243; [Nazi], I, 4; (Holland), I, 253–55; (Italy), II, 360; (Poland), I, 267, 270–72; III, 62, 64; [excommunication], III, 71; [German models], I, 267; [new synagogues], I, 220; [parliamentary defects], I, 335; (Portugal), I, 236; (Prussia), III, 219; [bans], III, 178; [family relations], II, 210–11; [immigration], III, 98; (Russia), III, 219; (Sicily), II, 210; (Spain), I, 236; II, 36, 232–41; III, 113; [funeral processions], II, 153; [tax collections], II, 283–84; [weddings], II, 303; Jewish recognition of, I, 127, 214–15. *See also* "Law of the kingdom"; uniformity of, I, 216; (contradictions), III, 113–14. *See also* Canon law; Church; Cities; Civil law; Codes; Customs; Criminal law; Emperors; Judiciary; Jurisprudence; Legal status; Literatures; Monarchy; Oral law; Ordinances; Papacy; Procedure; Public law; Religion; Responsa; Ritual; Statutes; Talmud; Traditions; *and under* respective countries and cities

Law enforcement, Jewish: **I, 20, 26;** II, *207–45*; III, *172–82*; and excommunication, I, 169; II, 243; and flogging, II, 226; and state, I, 22–23, 111, 166; and supernatural sanctions, I, 208; and talmudic studies, II, 207; and tax assessors, II, 283–84; nonpolitical, I, 150. *See also* Communal control; Judiciary; Police; *and under* respective penalties

Law: finding, Jewish, advanced by laymen, II, 209; merchant, II, 215; of concealment, I, 330; II, 200–1

"of the Kingdom": I, 214; II, 218–19; III, 52; and break in historic continuity, II, 215; and family relations, II, 210; and government's share in fines, II, 235; and royal tax immunities, II, 14

Layers, successive, in Jewish cemeteries, II, 152–53

Laymen, Jewish: ancient, I, 134; (and medieval rabbinate), II, 68; and Christian laity, III, 151; and tax immunities, I, 138; distinctions from rabbis of, II, 168; inarticulateness of, II, 78, 193; role at councils of, I, 309, 315, 322, 328. *See also* Judiciary

Lazarowicz, Ḥayyim (Lwów rabbi), II, 93

Leadership *and* leaders, communal: and capitalism, II, 362; and communal mourning, II, 147; III, 152; and consistory, I, 14; and liturgical innovations, II, 143; and public law recognition, I, 24; and synagogue minorities, II, 143; authority of, II,

136; III, 51; conservatism of, II, 167–68; intellectual interests of, II, 203–4. *See also* Bureaucracy; Councils; Elders; Rabbis

Leap year, Palestinian control of, I, 143, 192; (and Babylonia), I, 150. *See also* Calendar regulation

Learning, Jewish: and associational membership, I, 353; and cantors, II, 100, 104–5; and chief rabbinates, I, 347; (Bohemian), I, 340; (German), I, 298–300; III, 71; (Spanish), I, 291; and communal leadership, I, 98, 204; II, 46, 50, 75–76, 78; and democracy, III, 27; and guild control, I, 373; and legal procedure, II, 239–40; and moneylending, II, 176; and *morenu* title, II, 90; and Palestine messengers, II, 342; III, 217; and patriarchate, I, 141; and Polish teachers, II, 183–84; and priests, III, 42; and rabbinic position, II, 94, 244; III, 126; (demotion), III, 130; and religious functions, I, 134; and scribes, II, 111–12; and visiting of graves, II, 154; ancient traditions in, I, 242; changes in meaning of, II, 362; medieval emphasis on, II, 72, 173, 176, 362; social evaluation of, II, 94, *179–90*; women's attainments in, II, 178. *See also* Education; Jurisprudence; Professionalization; Rabbis; Teachers

Leaseholds, Jewish: and communal license fees, II, 262; and tenant protection, II, 292; on baths, II, 166; on ritual slaughtering, II, 108–9; on synagogue seats, II, 130–31; II, 264; quasi-ownership rights of, II, 294; taxes on, III, 188. *See also* Landlords; Tenants

Lebanon: I, 31; Jewish settlements in, I, 82

Lecce (southern Italy), burghers of, against Jewish autonomy, I, 279

Lecturers, Jewish, female, II, 178. *See also* Preaching; Teachers

Łęczyca, communal debts in, II, 34; III, 191

Ledesma (Spain), *fuero* of, III, 55

Ledgers, communal, Mantua conference on, II, 111–12. *See also* Minutebooks

Legacies, *see* Bequests

Legales Christiani et Judaei, I, 250. *See also* Judiciary; Jurisprudence

Legal status, Jewish, ancient: I, 93; and academies, III, 33; and gymnastic training, I, 92; and Josephus, III, 31; and patriarchate, I, 143–44; and sextons, II, 106; and synagogues, III, 14; in Cyrenaica, I, 78; in Egypt, I, 76–78; III, 14; in Roman Empire, I, 23, 116, 143–44; III, 14, 19–20

medieval and modern: and ban of settlement, II, 9; and Bible studies, II, 194–95; and charities, II, 349; and communal stability, II, 69, 120; (debts), I, 334; and Crusades, I, 306; and guild system, I, 369; and ownership of cemeteries, II, 149–51; and right of settlement, III, 99; and synagogues (architecture), II, 136–37; (confiscation), II, 135; and taxation, I, 235; influence of Church on, III, 52; interterritorial features of, I, 304; in various regions (America), III, 60; (England), III, 59–60; (Germany), I, 306; (Islam), I, 158–65; (Lithuania), III, 63; (Paderborn), III, 87; (Poland), I, 334; III, 99; (Rome, papal), I, 217–18, 228; (Spain), I, 235. *See also* Equality; Law; Persecutions

Legends, Jewish: and Byzantine prohibitions, I, 192; and eastern synagogues, I, 164; and exilarchate, III, 31; and long-term teachers, III, 161; and Narbonne *nasi*, III, 68; and regional allegiance, I, 283; interpretation by preachers of, III, 134. *See also* Aggada

Leghorn, Jews of: II, 11, 23; constitutional experiments of, II, 3–4, 56, 60; customs duties of, II, 13, 263, 265; *ḥazaḳah* legislation of, III, 198; elections by lot among, II, 43; income taxes of, II, 255; legacies for, III, 212–13; public education in, II, 172; Talmud Torah of, III, 166; taxation of visitors by, III, 102; visitors in Tunis from, III, 175

Legislature, Jewish, ancient, and academies, I, 151

Legitimacy of children, and technicalities in divorce, II, 318

Leibzoll, see Tolls, personal

Leicester, obtains exclusion of Jews, I, 276

Leipzig: congregational divisions in, III, 149; funeral tolls in, II, 154; Jews at fairs of, II, 263; III, 149; Polish visitors in, I, 324

Leisure, low medieval estimate of, II, 197

Leḳeṭ Yosher, a book of student's notes, II, 188. *See also* Joseph b. Moses

Lelezmuroz (*lel ashmorot*), association of, I, 354

Lemberg, *see* Lwów

Lemburger, Moses (Moravian chief rabbi), I, 339

Lemle, Moses, III, 127

Lending of books, Jewish regulations on, II, 201–2. *See also* Books

Leniency, excessive, condemned by rabbis, II, 212

Lenin, Nikolai, *see* Ulyanov

Leningrad, Jews of, I, 17

Lent, Christian, and supply of Jewish fish, II, 160–61

Lentshits, Solomon Ephraim b. Aaron: against fee system, II, 85; against interruption of prayers, II, 34; as preacher, III, 134–35; on demagoguery of rabbis, III, 133; on education, II, 176; III, 162; on marriage, III, 162, 204; on peace, III, 174; on rabbinic salaries, III, 127; subsidized by Polish Council, II, 203

Leo VI (Byzantine emperor), guild ordinances of, I, 365; III, 94

Leo X (pope): III, 109; drops Pentateuch scroll, I, 217

Leo XII (pope), and Jewish flight tax, III, 104

Leo (Yehudah Aryeh b. Isaac) of Modena: and Rovigo bath, III, 160; as preacher, III, 133; dialogue on gaming by, III, 207; family of, II, 191; III, 131; on dictatorial elders, II, 77; on position of rabbis, III, 125; on visitors' allegiance, II, 12

Leonore (Aragonese queen), I, 235–36; II, 74

Leontopolis (Egypt), I, 60, 79. *See also* Onias, temple of

Leopold I (Holy Roman emperor), and Hanau conference, III, 78

Lepanto, visitors in Patras from, III, 202

Lepers, Jewish, quarantined in cemeteries, III, 155

Leprosy, medieval prevalence of, III, 155

Lerida (Spain): acceptance of judgments in, II, 214; and dependent settlements, II, 21; and wine administration, II, 162; communal debts in, II, 272; distribution of Passover flour in, III, 209; early rabbis of, II, 68; elections in, II, 39, 44, 47; III, 117; judiciary in, III, 124; re-established community of, II, 272; synagogues in, II, 135; III, 151

Lèse-majesté, crime of, and Christian synagogue attendance, I, 112

Lesser Poland: as member of Polish Council, I, 325; chief rabbis of, I, 300–1. *See also* Cracow; Lublin

Leszno, II, 63, 273; III, *121*. *See also* Lissa

Letter carriers, Jewish, II, 115; III, 141

Letter: exilarchic, in Maimonides' home, I, 185; "of Aristeas," on recitation of Septuagint, III, 16; "of leave," ducal, in Hesse-Cassel, II, 16

Letters: Graeco-Roman, style of, III, 29; Hebrew, medieval: III, 66; (written by Reuchlin), I, 304; Jewish (ancient, writing of), I, 102; III, 29; (medieval, preservation of), III, 40; of authorization, geonic, I, 202; of Polish Council, III, 73; of recommendation, II, 324; III, 72; of solicitation, geonic, I, 181, 193; private, III, 211; (on Palestine relief), III, 216. *See also* Correspondence; Inquiries; Responsa

Lettres patentes, French, I, 264

Leṭuta, writ of, II, 228. *See also* Excommunication

Leucius (Roman Jewish dictator), II, 59

Levant: and boycott of Ancona, III, 73; Jewish role in trade of, I, 275; II, 11; Marrano communities in, I, 24. *See also* Turkey; *and under* respective provinces and cities

Levantine congregation in Venice, II, 335

Levayat metim, association of, I, 354. *See also* Burial societies

Levées, modern, and Jewish military service, II, 267

Levi b. Sissai (amora), I, 126, 128

Levi, Berend (Paderborn chief), III, 123

Levi, Bonaiuolo Isaac (Mantua secretary), III, 139

Levi, Isaac (Leo of Modena's grandson), ordination of, III, 131

Levirate marriage: and levir's exactions, II, 317–18; and professional judges, II, 73; communal regulations on, II, 317; rabbis attendance at, III, 205; precautionary writs of divorce against, II, 328

Levites: and Bible recitation, I, 189; and Israelitic priesthood, I, 49; and returning exiles, III, 12; at Israelitic assemblies, I, 61; Ezekiel on, I, 60; synagogue position of, I, 97, 124; III, 17

Lewin, Hirschel (German rabbi): as preacher, II, 97; salary of, II, 82

Lex Pappia, against aliens in Rome, I, 80

Lexicography, Jewish, medieval, I, 192, 219

Leyes del Estilo, on Jewish judiciary, II, 74

L'ḥolim, Arles society of, III, 93

Libanius, and Palestinian patriarch, I, 142; III, 29

Libel, ritual: and care of prisoners, II, 339; and Jewish synods, I, 313; and Polish Council, I, 324; and Poznań rabbinate, I, 303; papal condemnation of, I, 218, 305

Libellarius, private, functions of, I, 102, 120; III, 140. *See also* Scribes

Liberalism: and equality, I, 9; and Reform Judaism, I, 9; and religion, I, 9; (Grotius), I, 254–55; Arabian, and Hellenism, I, 158; economic, medieval reasons for, III, 94–95; French, and Jewish toleration, I, 265; Italian (and *ḥazakah* legislation), II, 298; (and Jewish judiciary), I, 276; Jewish, Talmud on, III, 27; Polish, and communal reform, II, 354. *See also* Capitalism; Democracy; Equality; Toleration

Liberties, personal, and long-term contracts, III, 161

Libertines, synagogue of, I, 120

Liberty of conscience, Jewish: I, 8; ancient, under Seleucidae, I, 83; Dutch, beginnings of, I, 254; (Surinam), III, 61; English, evolution of, I, 258–59; French, Colbert on, I, 265; in Resettlement areas, I, 266; North-American advocated by Roger Williams, I, 261–62. *See also* Democracy; Equality; Toleration

Liberum veto, Polish, and Jewish councils, I, 335. *See also* Unanimity

Libraries: Arabian, models for Jewish, II, 201; III, 170; Jewish, II, 200–5; III, 170; (ancient), I, 93; (Italian), I, 360; western, communal records in, III, 6

Licenses, communal: fees for, II, 262; of private scribes, III, 140; of slaughterers, periodic renewal of, II,, 109. *See also* Authorization

governmental, for Jewish bans in Venice, III, 178–79; of university graduates, and rabbinic ordination, III, 130

Lichtzündesteuer, Austrian, II, 260

Lida, David (Amsterdam rabbi): I, 331; and Polish Council, II, 243; work of, III, 182

Liebmann (Anspach rabbi), II, 91

Liepmann (Berlin family), private synagogue of, II, 125–26

Life: protected by medieval legislation, I, 218, 282; saving of, and swimming, II, 198; tenure, rabbinic, II, 86, 94

Light of the Eyes, *see* Rossi, Azariah de'

"Light of worship," association of, II, 134

Lime-kiln workers, Jewish, in Rome, I, 81

Limestone, Palestinian, I, 32, 41

Limoges, rabbis of, II, 284

Linen: prohibited mixing with wool of, III, 202; Spanish taxes on, II, 249

Liquidation of communal debts, attempts at, II, 274; III, 191–92. *See also* Debts

Liquor, sales taxes on, II, 261

Lisbon (Portugal): as regional community, III, 65; elders of, III, 65

Lisbon congregation, in Salonica, I, 351; II, 30, 50

Lissa, Jews of: II, 63; III, *121*; as members of Polish Council, I, 329; communal debts of, II, 273; indirect elections among, II, 45; guilds of, I, 369

Literacy: ancient Israelitic, I, 51; and passive franchise, II, 44; in Elephantine, I, 72; of Polish teachers, II, 183. *See also* Illiteracy; Writing

Literatures, Arabian: I, 148; II, 192–93; on exilarchs, I, 175; III, 33, 39–40; on Jewish physicians, III, 140; on Jewish teachers, II, 184; on synagogues, III, 35

European: English (on Palestine relief), II, 340; III, 215; (on Roman converts), I, 247; French, Jewish familiarity with, II, 192; German, III, 205; (Jewish part in), II, 192; Greek, I, 76; III, 15; (and Onias temple), I, 79; (on synagogues), I, 83; Italian, and Jewish authors, II, 191; III, 167; Latin, I, 80; III, 15; Polish, golden period of, II, 192

Hebrew: and chief rabbinates, I, 290–91; III, 66, 71–72; and communism, I, 16; and enactment of bans, II, 231–32; and Italian Renaissance, III, 167; and Jewish migrations, III, 51; and Jewish persecutions, III, 73; and judiciary, II, 215; and local customs, II, 213; III, 124; and Marranos, III, 58; and rabbinic control, II, 78; and sale of Jewish meat, II, 160; and sanctity of cemeteries, III, 156; and synagogue seats, III, 145; charitable treatises in, III, 218–19; Israelitic, educational use of, I, 53; rabbinic (and attacks on synagogues), III, 36; (and Portuguese chief rabbis), I, 286; (binding force of) III, 172; (censors' familiarity with), I, 223; (influence of), I, 347; (instruction in), II, 114, 172–74; (on deeds), II, 240; (orientation of), I, 97; sidelights on, III, 171; silent on guilds, I, 366. *See also under* respective disciplines, books and authors

Yiddish, and communism, I, 16; and general studies, II, 192; and letters, III, 211; and printing, III, 171

Lithuania, Jews of: I, *267–73*; III, 108; "alien" mendicants among, II, 323; III, 209; and capitalism, II, 352; and Karaites, III, 185; and Palestine relief, II, 341; as members of Polish Council, I, 325, 329; basic privileges of, I, 280; burial societies of, I, 354; chief rabbis of, I, 300–2; communal constitutions of, I, 280; II, 63–64; communal debts of, III, 191; economic history of, III, 186; elections among (provincial deputies), III, 115; (re-election), II, 40; (relatives), II, 40; guilds of, I, 371, 373; III, 96; *ḥazakah* legislation of, III, 199; hospices of, III, 210; influences on other countries of, II, 355; III, 117; interruption of prayers among, III, 112; itinerant preachers and scholars among, II, 99, 188; judiciary of, III, 63; (Gentiles repair to), II, 239; position of sexton among, II, 106–7; rabbis of, III, 123; redemption of captives by, II, 335; refugees in Amsterdam from, III, 117; relations with Christians of, I, 272; scribes' monopoly among, II, 113; supply of textbooks for, II, 203; support of brides by, II, 333; sumptuary laws of, II, 302, 305–6; synagogues of (architecture), II, 137; (seats), II, 130; taxation of, II, 257–58; III, 195; (immunities), III, 193–94. *See also* Councils; Poland; *and under* respective cities

Litigations, Jewish: over inheritance, and protection of orphans, II, 331–32; over responsibility of tenants, III, 199; over taxes, and local judges, II, 287

Judeo-Christian: and debt bondage, II, 226; and meat monopolies, III, 187; and states' fiscal interest, I, 282; and *ṭobim*, II, 63; in synagogue courtyards, II, 144; in various regions (Byzantine Empire), I, 228; (England, and presbyters), I, 297–98; (France, and *gardien général*), I, 296; (Germany), I, 249, 277; (Islam, and *negidut*), I, 191; (Lithuania), I, 280, 330; (Poland), I, 272; II, 48, 116; (Spain), I, 240, 278; variety of laws on, I, 249–51. *See also* Judiciary; Law; Procedure

Liturgy *and* prayers, Christian: clergy's familiarity with, II, 178; on converted synagogues, I, 230

Israelitic: I, 40, 52; and origin of synagogue, III, 9; at local sanctuaries, I, 49; of Solomon, date of, III, 13; replacing sacrifices, I, 53

Jewish: III, 21; and burial societies, I, 353; and Byzantine prohibitions, I, 192; and Decalogue, III, 22; and exilarchs, I, 180; III, 41; and *ḥazzan*, I, 101, 104, 201; II, 100; III, 127; and *negidut*, I, 191; and position of rabbis, I, 123; and recognition of Jewish worship, I, 263; and study, II, 193, 197, 207; and synagogue vows, II, 132; and threatening massacres, I, 306; Babylonian emphasis on, I, 60, 67; before homage to pope, I, 217; Candia statutes on, III, 112; covering the head during, II, 306–7; excessive zeal in, III, 148; for academies, I, 180, 183; for benefactors, I, 358; for criminals, II, 225; for dead, and private worship, II, 125; for rulers, I, 109; II, 143–44, 365; in German *memor*-books, II, 146; in

Hellenistic Jewry, I, 90; (Alexandria), I, 78; (Book of Tobit), I, 90; (Pharos), I, 86; Italian translations of, III, 149–50; local variations of, II, 69; loud recitation of, III, 23, 148; of elementary teachers, slighted, II, 182; of judges, II, 225; Palestinian, and diaspora Jewry, II, 340; priestly, I, 60; rabbinic precedence in, II, 89; Spanish legislation on, I, 236–37; II, 14; standardization vs. improvisation in, I, 67, 103, 121–23; II, 142; III, 42; women's familiarity with, II, 178. *See also* Ḥazzan; Interruption of prayers; Prayer-books; Ritual; Synagogues

Living wages, *see* Salaries

"Living waters," II, 188. *See also* Education, Jewish; Torah

Livyat ḥen congregation in Salonica, II, 75

Loans, charitable: provisions for, II, 326–27; III, 210; (associations), III, 93

communal: and charitable funds, II, 335; collectibility of, III, 191–92; interterritorial, I, 318; pledge not to contract new, II, 268–69, 272

private: and taxation, II, 247–48, 253, 261; (discounts), II, 255; contracts of (governmental registration), III, 139; (scribes' income), II, 261; on acquired rights, II, 297; on books, II, 204. *See also* Banking; Creditors; Debts; Interest

Local: communities, Jewish: and associations, I, 348–49, 352, 354; and Egyptian clan organization, III, 14; and Polish poll taxes, II, 252; and regional communities, I, 286–87, 342; II, 3, 20–23; III, 51; and talmudic charities, III, 26

diversity vs. uniformity, I, 206; II, 60. *See also* Customs; marriages, (and brokers' fees), III, 208–9; (and guilds), I, 370; (and rabbi's children), II, 86; poor, preferential treatment of, II, 323; (and Palestine relief), III, 216; (and redemption of captives), II, 333–34; prayer-books, and new prayers, II, 142; units, Israelitic, and returning exiles, III, 11. *See also* Landsmannschaften

Location of cemeteries, legislation on, III, 154

Locke, John, on powers of taxation, II, 57

Lodging, free, and Polish hospitality, II, 324

Lodz, Jews of: cemetery of, III, 157; population of, III, 108

Loew (Liwa *or* Judah) b. Bezaleel: as educational reformer, II, 190; on rabbinic elections, II, 94

Logic: and legal consistency, II, 244; Jewish instruction in, II, 192

Lombardy, and Jewish conferences, III, 80

London, Jews of: I, *255–59*, 262; and immigration restrictions, II, 16; and parental approval of marriage, II, 310; and redemption of captives, I, 307; and Roman baptism, I, 306; III, 72; and tenant protection, II, 300; bandits among, II, 338; begging outlawed by, II, 321–22; Bordeaux wines used by, II, 164; burial society of, III, 89–90; cemeteries of, II, 147, 149; III, 152–53; censorship of, II, 202; communal centralization of, I, 20; II, 21; communal solidarity of, I, 211; III, 51; confiscation of excommunicate's property by, II, 230; *domus conversorum* of, III, 184; election days of, III, 16; help New York synagogue, II, 136; household help of, II, 300; judicial minute-books of, III, 173; Marranos among, I, 255–57; obligatory acceptance of office by, II, 54; III, 119; orphan asylum of, II, 332; population of, I, 26; preaching among, II, 96; presbyters of, I, 297–98; rabbis of, II, 200, 235; III, 169; (salaries), II, 82; ritual slaughtering among, III, 138; ritualistic controversies among, II, 148; III, 137; synagogues of, III, 59; (assemblies), II, 28, 144; (discipline), III, 150; (officials), III, 137; (private), III, 144; status of teachers among, III, 164–65; wedding fees of, II, 119; women's suffrage among, III, 114. *See also* Great Synagogue; Hambro congregation; Spanish-Portuguese congregation

"Lord of the land," Asher b. Yeḥiel as, III, 70

Lorraine, Jews of: I, 262, 264; and synod of Troyes, I, 312; rabbis of, I, 305. *See also* Metz

Lost objects, synagogue announcements of, II, 144

Lot: assignment of bridal support by, II, 333; assignment of visitors of sick by, II, 328; distribution of communal citrons by, III, 187; elections by, I, 342; II, 43–44, 48, 58

Louis IX (French king): forbids Jewish emigration, I, 245–46; outlaws usury, I, 244

Louis XI (French king), disqualifies Jewish witnesses, I, 251

Louis XIV (French king): against foreign rabbis, III, 132; and charities, I, 363

Louis XVI (French king): I, 264; abolishes *Leibzoll*, II, 264

Louis the Bavarian (Holy Roman emperor), and *fiscus judaicus*, II, 250–51

Loving-kindness, importance of, I, 124; II, 319–20. *See also* Charities; Ethics

Löw, Leopold, I, 9

Löwenstamm, Saul (Amsterdam rabbi), III, 150

Lower Austria: III, 87; and German chief rabbinate, III, 70; funeral tolls in, II, 160; meat tariffs in, III, 158; regional community in, I, 341, 344. *See also under* respective cities

Loyalties, Jewish: and associational autonomy, I, 349, 374; conflict of (and *ḥazaḳah*), III, 199–200; (and judiciary), II, 208–9. *See also* Allegiance; Patriotism

Lübeck, Jewish exclusion from, I, 277–78; III, 63

Lublin, Jews of: and Italian merchants, I, 332–33; and Palestine relief, II, 341; appeal for assistance, III, 84; as members of Polish Council, I, 325; III, 81–82; (minute-book, destroyed), I, 327; academies of, II, 95; cantors of, III, 150; cemetery of, III, 157; Hebrew printing of, II, 203; Lithuanian delegates among, I, 326; outside provincial council, I, 336; rabbis of, I, 271, 301, 325; II, 95; III, 118, 143; synagogues of, III, 146; (decorum), II, 141; III, 148

Polish Diet of, confirms Lwów ordinance, I, 271; regional fairs of, and Polish Council, I, 327; rulers' ordinances of, I, 270; "Union" of, and Lithuanian judiciary, III, 63

Lubomirski, Michael (prince), III, 104

Lubomirski, Stanisław (Cracow palatin), ordinance of, II, 46

Lubomla, Christian residents in ghetto of, welcomed, II, 296

Lucca, academy of, I, 242

Lucena (Spain), Jews in, I, 160–61; III, 34, 38

Łuck, synagogue in, I, 220, 270

Lulab, communal administration of, III, 159–60

Lull, Raymond, III, 135

Lunel, Jews of: I, 194; alien students among, II, 187

Luria, Isaac b. Solomon: and recitation of Decalogue, III, 22; and Sephardic ritual, II, 142; disciples of, III, 92

Luria, Solomon b. Yeḥiel: and bans' effects on relatives, III, 177; and general sciences, II, 192; on cantors, III, 136; on dancing, II, 316; III, 206; on government appointments, II, 218–19; on *ḥazakah*, III, 199; on head covering, III, 202; on Meir of Rothenburg, II, 336; III, 213; on physical penalties, III, 175–76; on recitation of Decalogue, III, 22; on sex morality, II, 316

Lusitanus, Amatus, against night study, III, 162

Lutherans, American, and Jewish charities, II, 347

Luxury: and display of candles, II, 134; and eastern chiefs, I, 176–77; and funerary arts, II, 155; communal regulations against, I, 320; II, 301. *See also* Sumptuary laws

Luzzatto, Moses Ḥayyim: III, 92; religious association of, I, 355

Luzzatto, Simone (Simḥa) b. Isaac, mercantilistic arguments of, II, 298

Lwów, Jews of: III, 62; academies of, II, 95; anti-Semitic municipality of, III, 64; as members of Polish Council, I, 325, 329; communal debts of, II, 273–74, 353; communal tyrants among, III, 122; criminals among, II, 227; distribution of Purim collections by, III, 210; elections among, II, 40, 45; (crooked), II, 48; forced to purchase Helicz books, II, 204; guilds of, I, 369; judiciary of, II, 35; III, 173; minute-books of, III, 81, 173; musicians among, III, 141; neglect of Bible studies by, II, 194; official recorder among, II, 113; outside provincial council, I, 336; III, 115; payments to governor of, I, 269; pillory of, extant, II, 224; pledges of betrothed among, II, 315; prisons of, II, 226; prohibit importation of meat, II, 258; rabbis of, I, 325; II, 83, 95; III, *71*, 145; (conferring of titles), II, 92; (elections), II, 93; (immunities), II, 80; (provincial chief rabbinate), I, 303; III, 72; regional community of, III, 115; rulers' ordinances for, I, 270–72; II, 35; suburban community of, I, 303; II, 83, 226; synagogue decorum of, II, 141; III, 148; Talmud Torah of, II, 196; tax administration of, III, 195; (and aliens), III, 188; (meat taxes), II, 258–59. *See also* Red Russia.

Lwów (Lemburger), Moses (Moravian chief rabbi), I, 339

Lynching, Jewish: for tax immunities, II, 15; of informers, recommended, II, 221, 241

Lyons (France), Jews of: and Venetian association for orphan girls, I, 364; Christian attendance at sermons of, II, 96; propaganda against, I, 295

MAʿARIB SERVICES, and flogging of criminals, II, 225. *See also* Liturgy; Worship

Maʿarikim, II, 57. *See also* Tax assessors

Maʿarufia, and rabbinic privileges, II, 80

Maʿase bet din, Frankfort, III, 173

Maʿaseh ha-geonim: on clothing, III, 200; on criminal jurisdiction, III, 176

Maccabeans: I, 90; and Hellenism, I, 118; and Roman alliance, I, 76; III, 15; and Temple services, I, 79; as leaders of world Jewry, I, 140; as *negidim*, I, 190; III, 13; communal councils under, I, 134; revolt of, I, 60, 79, 118; use *nasi* title, I, 141

Maccabees, Books of, III, 15–16

Macedonians: I, 75; Jews as, III, 14

Macerata, Jews in, III, 79–80

Madrid: no record of Jewish hospitals in, II, 329; pillage of Jewish quarters in, III, 211
Madrigal, Cortes of, II, 86
Magdeburg law, and Polish Jewish autonomy, I, 267. *See also* Judiciary
Maggid, II, 97. *See also* Preaching
Magians, *see* Zoroastrians
Magic, Jewish: III, 156; and *archisynagogi*, I, 103; and burial, I, 94; and Christian magic, I, 103; and education, III, 169; fear of, and charities, II, 348; implements of, III, 160; inquisitorial prosecution for, I, 237; Jewish prohibitions of, II, 154
Magister: and *morenu* title, II, 90; *Judaeorum*, Frankish, I, 295, 310
Magistrates, Jewish, Byzantine, Justinian's threats against, II, 52. *See also* Elders; Judiciary
Magnus, Marcus (Berlin elder), III, 220
Mahalalel Halelujah of Ancona, III, 73
Mahamad, London, *see* Council of Elders; Spanish-Portuguese Congregation
Maḥanot, Italian, II, 11. *See also* Hospices
Maharil, *see* Moelln, Jacob
Maḥzor, Babylonian, fragments of, III, 41
Maimon, Salomon, on Polish *ḥeder*, II, 198–99; III, 169
Maimonides (family), as *negidim*, I, 190
Maimonides, Abraham b. Moses: against professionalization of learning, I, 42; against titles, I, 201; III, 50; on abuses of bans, III, 178; on charitable will, III, 217; on exilarchs, III, 43; on investment of orphan's funds, III, 195; on marriage licenses, III, 208; on prayers, III, 148; on provincial officers, III, 43; on quorum at weddings, III, 47
Maimonides, Moses (b. Maimon): and professionalization of learning, I, 181; III, 41–42, 124; and rabbis of Lunel, I, 194; and Yemenite Jewry, III, 44–45; as *nagid*, questionable, I, 190; Catalan translation of code by, I, 240; doctrine of resurrection of, III, 44–45; economic views of, III, 25; on ancient public law, II, 217; on Bagdad chiefs, I, 184; on capital punishment, II, 222; III, 175; on charitable obligations, II, 320, 344; III, 209; (begging), II, 321; (eight degrees), II, 326–27; III, 210; (loans), II, 326–27; on chastisement of children, II, 198; on communal sovereignty, II, 218; on congregational worship, III, 142; on educational responsibilities, II, 161, 169–70, 197; III, 160–61, 169; (concentration on Talmud), III, 167; (feminine), II, 178; III, 162; (hours of study), III, 162; (loud study), II, 199–200; (night study), II, 176; (size of classes), III, 168–69; on flogging, I, 168; II, 225; III, 175; on government appointments, II, 218–19; on *ḥeber ha-'ir*, I, 134; on *hekdesh*, II, 329; III, 211; on identifiable heirs, I, 248; II, 267; III, 57, 189; on independence of Jewish law, II, 208; on irrevocable bans, II, 228; III, 177; on judiciary (extreme discretion), III, 174; (lay), III, 52; (priorities), II, 236–37; III, 180; (responsibility), III, 174; on "law of the kingdom," III, 52; on mourning for suicide, II, 156; on music, II, 191; III, 167; on negative commandments, III, 37; on quorum at weddings, III, 47; on redemption of captives, II, 333; III, 213; on scholars' tax immunities, I, 160–61; II, 80, 276–77; III, 34, 193; on synagogue decorum, III, 148, 151; on "ten men of leisure," I, 200; on

titles, I, 201; III, 50; on use of Torah in oath, III, 181; on western Jewry, I, 194, 213; III, 52; on wine of libation, III, 159; rationalism of, III, 73; respects exilarchs, III, 43; study groups for works of, III, 91; teachings of, praised by pope, I, 307; world leadership of, I, 185. *See also* Anti-Maimonidean controversy

Main Street, Israelitic gates like, I, 42

Maintenance of students, and Cassel budget, II, 188

Majorca, Jews of: and designation by retiring officers, II, 47; judiciary of, I, 238–39, 249; private monopolies of, II, 299; privileges of, III, 56; rabbinate of, II, 299; redemption of captives by, II, 336–37; ritual slaughterers among, II, 108; taxation of, I, 278. *See also* Balearic Islands

Majorcan congregation, in Salonica, I, 351

Majority principle: I, 286–87; II, 26–28; and absent members, II, 282; and adoption of statutes, II, 25, 30; III, 111; (modification), II, 265; and appeal to courts, II, 219; and communal bathhouses, II, 166; and congregational divisions, III, 149; and construction of synagogues, II, 126; and education, II, 173; and elections (of cantors), II, 102; (of rabbis), III, 129; and expulsion of new arrivals, II, 19; (naturalization), II, 11; and price fixing, II, 301; and taxation, II, 27; Aragonese decree on, II, 71; in ancient academies, I, 152; in Roman Council of Sixty, II, 60; Surinam elders against, II, 87; Talmud on, III, 27; upheld by Ibn Adret, I, 211; Valladolid synod on, II, 46. *See also* Democracy

Makkat mardut, II, 224. *See also* Flogging

Makkot, *see* Flogging

Malachi (prophet), I, 58

Malaga, redemption of captives of, I, 290; II, 334

Malikite school of Muslim jurisprudence, I, 163

Malḳot, *see* Flogging

Malsin, II, 241. *See also* Informing

Malta: III, 213; Jewish barbers in, III, 119; redemption of captives in, I, 294; II, 334

Mamelukes (dynasty), Jews under, I, 163, 203; III, 35, 39

Mamran (deed), II, 301

Management, agricultural, Jewish, and Polish nobles, I, 269

Mandeans: I, 62; scriptures of, III, 11

Manecier of Vesoul, as tax collector, I, 296

Manifest method, in tax assessments, II, 281–82. *See also* Tax assessments

Manipulation of elections, II, 41, 48, 92–93, 106–7; III, 127. *See also* Elections

Mannheim: Jewish bribes in, II, 247; rabbinic salaries in, II, 82; research rabbis in, III, 127; restricts Jewish luxuries, III, 202

Manslaughter, Oxford students accused of, II, 187

Mantua, Jews of: II, 29–30; and Azariah de' Rossi, I, 308; and communal scribes, II, 111; and conferences, I, 313–14, 321; II, 111, 236, 238; III, 80; and hearings within 24 hours, II, 236; and judicial intermediaries, II, 238; and rabbis' attendance at weddings, III, 205; and redemption of captives, I, 307; II, 335; and Roman refugees, I, 320–21; and taxation of visitors, III, 102; charitable associations of, III, 93; communal archives of, III, 139; elders of, II, 335; III, 121, 210; in pre-censorship commission, I, 321; Italian writers among, II, 191; legacy for, III, 212; obligatory attendance at meetings of, II, 28; police of, II, 291; preaching among, II, 96; quarter of (Christian guards), II, 291; (crash), II, 294; restricted settlement of, II, 10–11; sumptuary laws of, II, 304; tax administration of, III, 196; treaty with Modena association by, III, 102

Manuel Comnenus (Byzantine emperor), suppresses Jewish judiciary, I, 229; III, 52

Manufacturing rights, and immigration restrictions, II, 16

Manumission of slaves, Jewish: and Bustanai's marriage, I, 177; validity of deeds of, I, 127

Manuscripts, Hebrew: catalogues of, III, 73, 131; expurgation of, I, 223; female copyists of, III, 162; high costs of, II, 200; illumination of, II, 138, 141; of statutes (Candia), III, 47, 79, 112; (educational), I, 357; (Moravian), III, 85; of translated prayers, II, 143; on authorization of slaughterers, III, 138; on communal debts, III, 191; on provincial councils, III, 84; on synagogue decorum, III, 148; preservation of, III, 78. *See also* Books; Libraries; Literatures; Papyri

Maqueda (Spain), synagogues of, I, 220

Marana, and *magister*, II, 90

Marbiṣ torah, in Turkish communities, II, 75. *See also* Rabbis

Marches, The (Italy), Jews in, III, 79–80

Marcus Aurelius (Roman emperor), and Judah I, III, 29

Marcus Cuyntus Alexus (Roman child) I, 105

Margharita, Antonius, on synagogue candles, II, 134; III, 146

Margins of books, use of, II, 200

Margolies, Samuel (Poznań chief rabbi), I, 301

Maria Theresa (Holy Roman empress): and Jewish taxation, II, 160; III, 183; (citron tax), III, 187; (tolerance tax), III, 197; communal legislation of, II, 355; (Bohemia), I, 305; III, 183; (Galicia), III, 85; (Moravia), I, 338–39; II, 41; III, 85. *See also* Joseph II

Marital relations, *see* Family relations

Mark (Prussia), regional community in, I, 341, 344

Market prices, and Jewish cemeteries, II, 152

Markets, Jewish: ancient, I, 96, 130; and preaching, II, 98; and Spanish burghers, I, 278; communal surveillance of, I, 130, 170; II, 63, 291; exilarchic taxes on, I, 175

Spanish, and sale of Jewish meat, II, 159

Marks, distinguishing, on ritual meat, III, 158

Marranos: and Amsterdam societies, III, 104–5; and boycott of Ancona, III, 73; and communal disunity, I, 24, 205; as spearheads of resettlement, I, 243, 252, 255, 262, 264; II, 120, 363; contributions to synagogues by, II, 134; economic problem of, III, 58; expulsion of, I, 253; honorable burial of, II, 156–57; in rabbinic literature, III, 58; public profession in England of, I, 256; Roman envoys from Portugal of, I, 305. *See also* Conversion; Inquisition; Spanish exiles

Marriage, Jewish: ancient records of, I, 72; and educational responsibilities, II, 175; and execution of criminals, II, 223; and guild membership, I, 370; II, 18; and *negidut*, I, 191; and parental arrangements, II, 310; III, 203–4; and peace, III, 174; and qualification of cantors, II, 104; (salaries), II, 101–2; and rabbinic titles, II, 91–92; and rabbinic vs.

lay control, I, 276; II, 76–77, 81, 83–84, 90–91; III, 128, 205; and students, II, 175, 181, 187–88, 362; III, 163; and taxation, II, 15, 171–72, 255; (annulment for default), II, 284; (exemptions), II, 275, 278; charitable support of, I, 132, 362; childless, and polygamy, II, 308–10; children of rabbis barred from local, II, 86; communal regulations on, II, 7, 210–11; III, 208–9; (limitations of numbers), III, 98; duration of, as qualification for office, II, 38, 40, 45, 91–92, 104, 175; early age at, II, 23, 175, 198, 310–11; educational value of, III, 162; intercommunal controversies over, II, 229; in various regions (Berlin), III, 107; (Elephantine), I, 70; (France), I, 263; (Germany), II, 192; (Hesse-Cassel), I, 342; (Holland), I, 255; (Islam), I, 165, 175, 191, 202; (Italy), I, 276; II, 76–77; (Poland), II, 86; III, 98; (Spain), II, 15; (Turkey), I, 196; laws on, I, 214; (and sex morality), III, 205; (not in Noahidic commandments), I, 214; legitimacy of, and writs of divorce, II, 240; preferences in, I, 124; restrictions of, I, 342; III, 98; (family quotas), II, 5; rites at, I, 25, 196, 284; II, 145; III, 128; (Catholic, in France), I, 263; (confirmed by Dutch cities), I, 255; (fees for), I, 175; II, 83, 101–2, 118–19; statistics of, in Berlin, III, 107; synagogue announcements of, II, 144. *See also* Wedding rites

brokerage *and* brokers: III, *208–9*; and rabbis, II, 81; and teaching, II, 184; communal ordinance on, II, 319; taxation of, II, 261

contracts *and ketubot*: III, 208; and communal records, II, 112; and educational responsibilities, II, 175; and judiciary, II, 215; (fees of), I, 202; II, 83; and polygamy, II, 308; and synagogue seats, II, 131; and terms for divorce, II, 309; and use of vernacular, I, 255; II, 192; in Elephantine, I, 70; neglected by heretics, I, 165; of elders, and communal debts, II, 53; procedural law of, II, 240. *See also* Divorce

licenses, communal: II, 319; preliminary investigations for, II, 311

Marsala, Jews of: and Sicilian Council, III, 78; bigamy among, II, 309; designation by retiring officers among, II, 47; election days of, III, 116

Marseilles, Jews of: and southern French assemblies, I, 316; III, 75; citizenship of, III, 54–55; redemption of captives by, II, 334–35; ritual meat administration of, III, 137; Sicilian chief rabbi from, I, 292–93

Marshals, communal: collect vows, II, 132; deliver summonses, III, 182; employed in mixed litigations, I, 272; of councils, I, 328

"Marshals," provincial, Polish, I, 332

Martenne, Dom, on Bordeaux Jewry, III, 61

Martin, Don (Aragonese and Sicilian king): and adoption of statutes, III, 110; and communal debts, II, 272; and disfranchisement of smaller taxpayers, II, 39, 279–80; appoints Jewish officials, I, 292–93

Martin V (pope), and Italian synods, I, 320; and Mt. Zion chapel, I, 320

Mar Zutra (amora); I, 129; as itinerant preacher, III, 23

Maskilim, North-African association of, III, 91

Maskir-book, III, 152. *See also* Memorbooks

Masonic lodges, Italian, Jewish members of, III, 175

Masons, Roman, and repair of ghetto houses, II, 294
Masquerades, Jewish: and clothing of opposite sex, III, 206; on Purim, restricted, III, 207
Massacres of Jews: and anti-alien laws, II, 7; and Asher b. Yeḥiel's departure, III, 76; and communal debts or assets, II, 135–36, 271; and conversion, I, 289; III, 153; and dissolution of societies, I, 362; and Polish councils, I, 330, 333–34; and redemption of captives, II, 337; and regional communities, I, 298; (Barcelona synod), I, 288; and sumptuary laws, II, 302; and waifs and strays, II, 330–31, burghers' reaction to, I, 277; interterritorial action against, I, 306–7; in various regions (England), III, 153; (Germany), I, 277, 298; III, 76; (Poland), I, 307, 330–31, 333–34; II, 7; (Spain), I, 288–89, 362. *See also* Anti-Semitism; Persecutions; Riots
Masseur, Jewish, ancient, I, 120
Master artisans, contracts with parents by, III, 96. *See also* Craftsmen
Mata Meḥasia, *see* Sura
Mater synagogae, I, 97, 101
Materialism, capitalistic, and Jewish education, II, 181–82, 184
Mather, Cotton, I, 261
Mattanah, II, 235. *See also* Fines; Gifts
Matteo of Agrigento, Fra, I, 295
Mattathiah b. Joseph Trèves (French chief rabbi), I, 296
Ma'uziah (Elephantine scribe), I, 72
Maximilian I (Holy Roman emperor): and Josel of Rosheim, I, 299; and Moravian chief rabbinate, I, 338; convokes Jewish assembly, I, 314; delimits excommunication, I, 247
Maximilian II (Holy Roman emperor), I, 299; III, 70–71
Mayence, Jews of: III, *63*, 107; and archbishops, I, 245, 322; III, 142; and burial societies, I, 352; and councils, I, 313, 322; III, 76, 78; and Crusades, I, 306; and Jewish emigration, I, 245; cemetery of, III, 154; elders of, I, 245, 306; massacres of, and burghers, I, 277; rabbis of, I, 299; regional community of, I, 341; III, 88; synagogue decorations of, II, 138; unity with Worms of, III,154
Mayorales, II, 58. *See also* Council of elders; Elders; Executive Committees
Mayor of New York (colonial), against Jewish worship, I, 260–61
Mazdak (Zoroastrian reformer), I, 148–49
Mazovia: chief rabbis in, I, 300–1; rights of settlement in, III, 99; royal charters of, I, 271
"Meal offering," in Elephantine Temple I, 60
Meals, communal, and itinerant poor, II, 322
Means of study, and educational responsibility, II, 169–70
Meat, ritual, *see* Abattoirs; Slaughtering
Meat taxes, communal: II, 108, 256; III, 186–87; and cities, II, 257; and public education, II, 171–72; and royal favoritism, II, 159; private monopolies of, II, 299
Mecca, as place of refuge, I, 163
Mecklenburg: III, *87*; rabbinic salaries in, III, 127; regional community in, I, 341, 345
Mediation before God, and position of cantors, II, 102, 105
Medical school, Jewish, project for, II, 191
Medici (dynasty), and Jews, II, 3
Medicine, Jewish: ancient and magic, I, 103; and flogging, I, 169; and ritual wine, II, 109; and treatises, III, 211–12. *See also* Physicians

Medievalism, of northern Jewish communities, I, 243

Medina, *see* Samuel b. Moses

Medina (city), I, 164

Medinah (term), Maimonides' use of, III, 160–61

Mediterranean areas: I, 116; ancient oligarchies in, III, 8–9; ban of settlement in, II, 9–12; citron exports from, II, 164; elections in, II, 35–36, 102; governmental chief rabbis in, I, 346; greater liberalism of, III, 101; Greek colonies in, I, 55; growth of plutocracies in, II, 50–51; heterogeneity of, and "alien" Jews, I, 243; Jewish executioners in, III, 175; libraries in, II, 201; peculiarities of, I, 227, 242; piracy of, and redemption of captives, II, 334; position of Jewish women in, III, 89; (polygamy), II, 307–10; preaching in, II, 95–96; rights of settlement in, III, 101; seizure of property in, II, 233; study of general sciences in, II, 191; taxation in (declarations), II, 281; (no funeral tolls), II, 153; university life of, III, 167; wine administration in, II, 162; (taxes), II, 259. *See also under* respective countries and cities

Mediterranean coast of Palestine, I, 119

Meetings, *see* Assemblies

Megapolensis, Domine, and New York Jewish charities, II, 347

Megiddo, size of, I, 41

Megillot Yuḥasin, I, 72. *See also* Families; Genealogy

Mehler Reutlingen, Juda (Rhenish rabbi), III, 87

Meḥmet II (sultan), I, 195

Meir, R. (tannai), I, 153

Meir b. Baruch ha-Levi of Vienna: and French controversy, I, 296; III, 69; as banker, II, 80–81; III, 126

Meir b. Baruch of Rothenburg: III, 70; and German chief rabbinate, III, 69–70; and *morenu* title, II, 90; burial place of, II, 154–55; flight of, III, 70; imprisonment of, I, 304; II, 336; (retention of body), II, 154–55; on accounting of charity overseers, II, 348; on cantors, II, 101–2; III, 135–36; on cemeteries (control by), II, 149; III, 153; (honorable burial), III, 157; (pilgrimages to), III, 156; on change of endowments, II, 266; III, 189; on change of venue, III, 180; on charitable tithes, II, 344; III, 217; on citrons, II, 101; on communal debts, III, 190; on competence of courts, III, 182; on dance halls, III, 206; on education, II, 172, 175; III, 161; on excommunication, III, 112; on exposure in pillory, II, 224; on *hekdesh*, III, 211; on heredity in rabbinate, III, 132; on illuminated prayer-books, II, 138; III, 146; on majority principle, II, 30; III, 110; on marital relations, II, 317; on meat administration, III, 158; on ritual bath, III, 160; on safeguards, for books, III, 169; on seizure of property, II, 233; on synagogues (art), III, 146; (attendance), II, 126; III, 142; (functions), II, 145; (oaths), II, 145; III, 150; on taxation, II, 246–47; III, 135, 183; (immunities), III, 192–93; (lower on land), III, 185; (rates), III, 184–85; on teachers, II, 183; III, 161, 163–65; (tenure), III, 161; on wife beating, II, 318; III, 208; students of (books by), III, 145; supported by master), II, 187; III, 166

Meir b. Gedaliah of Lublin: II, 95; on Moravian taxation, III, 106; on prisoners, III, 214; on professional ransom of captives, III, 214; on synagogue attendance, III, 143

Meir b. Saul (Wahl) of Brześć (chairman of Lithuanian Council), I, 328

Meir ha-Kohen: on educational responsibilities, III, 161–62, 167; on height of synagogue, III, 147

Meiri, Menaḥem b. Solomon, III, 152–53

Meisel, Mordecai: Prague synagogue of, II, 130; will of, III, 144

Meisel synagogue in Prague, II, 130

Meissen: justices of the Jews in, I, 250; synagogue frescoes in, II, 138

Meister, and *morenu* title, II, 90

Meisterlein (Wiener-Neustadt rabbi), on Cracow appeal, III, 77

Mekilta, on Jewish judiciary, III, 24

Melammed, David (Palestine messenger), III, 217

Melarchontes, ancient, children as, II, 146

Meldola, David b. Raphael: on parental approval of marriage, III, 204; on tax assessments, III, 196

Meldola, Raphael b. Eleazar: on Bayonne ordinance, III, 203; on mourning for leader, III, 152; on redemption of captives, III, 213; on tax ordinances, II, 265; III, 188; on Porto's will, III, 212–13

Melun: and synod of Troyes, I, 312; convention of, I, 245–46

Membership *and* members, associational: I, 5, *354–56*; collection of dues of, I, 362; mutual benefits of, I, 364; of burial societies, I, 353; III, 90; of guilds, I, 370–71

congregational: ancient, I, 89–90; and assignment of seats, II, 131; attendance of, I, 6; in London Great Synagogue, II, 16; in private synagogues, II, 126; voluntary, I, 11

communal: II, *4–17*, 123; III, *98–106*; ancient, I, 89–90, 95; (in Babylonian Exile), I, 68; and anti-alien bias, II, 322–23; and *archisynagogus*, I, 103; and constitutional changes, III, 109, 111; and education, II, 205–6; and interest payments, II, 269; and plenary assemblies, II, 23–24; and private worship, II, 126; and sale of synagogues, II, 128–29; and visiting of sick, II, 328; intracommunal, II, 17–20; lists of, I, 102; rights of, II, 20; III, 110; talmudic requirements for, I, 136

of Councils: Bohemian, I, 340; Polish-Lithuanian, I, 327

Memel, corporal taxes in, III, 188

Memor-books, medieval, II, 145–46, 329; III, 152

Memorial services, in Salonican Talmud Torah, I, 348

Memphis (Egypt), Jews of, I, 58, 77

Menahem (Israelitic king), I, 38

Menaḥem of Merseburg: on elders' discretion, III, 174; on physical penalties, III, 175–76; on tax immunities, III, 192

Menasseh (Israelitic king): I, 37; III, 9

Menasseh ben Israel: III, *74*; as preacher, III, 133; negotiations with Cromwell of, I, 256–57, 298, 309

Mendelssohn, Moses: II, 183; and communal control, II, 360; and educational reform, III, 163–64; defense of traditional law by, II, 360

Mendes, Alvaro (Solomon ibn Yaish, Duke of Mytilene), I, 197

Mendicancy, *see* Begging

Mental instability, and women slaughterers, II, 107

Mental reservations in oaths, validity of, III, 104

Menz (Minz *or* Mainz), Judah b. Eliezer ha-Levi: on communal baths, II, 166; on masquerading, II, 316; III, 206; on orphans' support of poor, II, 331; III, 212; on *Pletten*, II, 322; III, 209

Menz, Moses b. Isaac ha-Levi: on cantors, III, 136; on citrons, III, 160; on charities, III, 212; on Cracow appeal, III, 77; on intercommunal tax controversies, III, 196; on lay judiciary, III, 173; on regional control, II, 22, 42; III, 106, 115; on rights of absentee members, III, 103; on ritual baths, III, 160; on shoeless worship, II, 29; III, 143; on synagogue art, III, 146

Mercantile records, procedural law on, II, 240

Mercantilism, European: and communal control, II, 359, 364; and *ḥazakah*, II, 298; and Jewish elections, II, 36; and toleration of Jews, I, 265–66; III, 62

Mercenaries: foreign, in ancient Palestine, I, 39; Greek, I, 55; Jewish, in Egypt, I, 57–58. *See also* Elephantine; modern, and Jewish military service, II, 267

Merchants: ancient, and Jewish dispersion, III, 10; Christian guilds of, and Jewish commerce, III, 94–95; Italian (and Jewish mediators), I, 275; (repair to Jewish courts), III, 180

Jewish: ancient, (protected against competition), I, 126; (rabbis as), I, 138–39; and Bordeaux wines, II, 164; and citron monopoly, II, 165; and education, II, 175; III, 162; and franchise, II, 48, 64; and *ḥazakah*, II, 296–99; and luxury in dress, II, 302–3; and scholars' tax immunities, II, 278; and Shabbetian movement, II, 25–26; as lay judges, II, 89; guilds of, I, 366, 373; III, 94–95; in various regions (Bohemia), II, 89; (Bordeaux), II, 164; (Germany), II, 25–26; (Hamburg), II, 164; (Italy), I, 332–33; II, 6, 11, 298; (Poland), I, 322, 324, 332–33; II, 6; (Sarajevo), II, 13; (Sicily), II, 162. *See also* Banking; Commerce

"Merciful descendants of merciful sires," Jews as, II, 320

Mercy: acts of, and begging, II, 324; divine, invoked for criminals, II, 225

Mergers, congregational, and rights to functions, III, 145

Meshullam b. Kalonymus of Narbonne, decisions of, III, 179

Mesopotamia, ancient, destruction of synagogue in, I, 114

"Messenger of the people," I, 201; II, 100–1. *See also* Ḥazzan

Messengers, Jewish: and calendar regulation, I, 192; and local administrations, I, 142–43, 181; and search for deserting husbands, II, 317; dispatched to Shabbetai Zevi, II, 26; sent by leaders (geonim), I, 181; (Polish Council), II, 317; (patriarchs), *see* Apostles

Palestinian: II, *341–43*; III, 88; and drafting of statutes, II, 30–31; III, 110; and examination of slaughterers, III, 138; and local controversies, III, 216–17; and Western tax ordinances, II, 265; as preachers, II, 96; objections to, II, 342; III, 216; rivalries among, III, 216. *See also* Palestine relief

provincial, in Kleve, revenue of, II, 119–20; royal, Frankish, protect Jews, I, 295

Messer Leon, *see* David b. Judah *and* Judah b. Yeḥiel

Messianism, Christian, and medieval legislation, I, 282

Jewish: III, 215–16; and charities, II, 346; and communal control, II, 168; and communal survival, I, 158, 209; and communism, I, 16; and exilarchate, I, 155; and nationalism, I, 9; and Palestine relief, II, 339; III, 216; and patriarchate, I, 155;

and purity of descent, I, 177; and Reform Judaism, I, 9; and renewal of ordination, I, 309; and Shabbetianism, II, 25–26. *See also* Shabbetian movement; biblical prophecies on, I, 36; revolutionary nature of, II, 168
Messina (Sicily), Jews of: and chief rabbinate, I, 293–94; and Council, III, 78; change of venue among, II, 243; elders of, punished for bans, II, 232; elections of, III, 113; taxation of, III, 192
Mestre (Italy): formula of Jewish oath in, III, 181; wandering scholars in, II, 188
Metakne takkanot, III, 110–11. *See also* Committees; Ordinances; Statutes
Metal trades, Jewish, medieval, in Sicily, I, 368. *See also* Craftsmen
Metal utensils, and non-ritual meat, II, 110
Methods, educational, history of, II, 190–200. *See also* Education; electoral, history of, II, 43–49. *See also* Elections; fiscal, *see* Tax assessments
Metropolitan areas, modern: congregations in, I, 6, 25, 27; effects on Jewish community of, I, 17; II, 244; III, 5. *See also* Cities; Population
Meturgeman, talmudic, I, 123–24; III, 23
Metz (Lorraine), Jews of: III, *62*, 108; and Bordeaux wines, I, 164; burial society of, III, 89; cemeteries of, II, 152; (funeral tolls), II, 154; Christian notaries for deeds of, III, 139; communal debts of, III, 192; judiciary of (lay), III, 132–33; (reforms), III, 180; legal status of, III, 108; ordinances of (educational), II, 175, 185; III, 165; (on chanting), II, 105; (on coat vents), III, 203; (on relations of fiancés), III, 206; rabbis of, I, 305; III, 89, 132, *180*; (and Frankfort elections), III, 115; (contracts), III, 131; restrictions on butchers of, II, 159; sumptuary laws of, II, 304; III, 201; supply of fish for, II, 161
Mezerich, II, 100. *See also* Międzyrzecze
Mezuzot: and excommunication, I, 169; and licensed scribes, II, 110; III, 140; and prisons, II, 226; and teaching, II, 184; in Germany, II, 187; protracted neglect of, II, 69
Mibṭaḥiah (Elephantine Jewess), marriage contract of, I, 70; III, 12
Michael Syrus, on *dhimmi* chiefs, I, 176; III, 40
Miczyński, Sebastjan, III, 64
Middle class, Jewish: and billeting of soldiers, III, 189; and charitable contributions, II, 321; and economic status of officials, II, 120; dependent on Israelitic landowners, I, 44; electoral rights of, II, 29; hostility to competition of, II, 297, 299; tax burdens of, I, 159; II, 278–79. *See also* Class struggle; Conflicts; Social relations
Midras or *Midrash* (term), used for school and synagogue, I, 357; II, 67; III, 151–52
Midrash (literature): III, *21–22*; and Byzantine prohibitions, I, 192; educational value of quotations from, II, 206; on importance of education, II, 182, 205; III, 23; on strictness of judges, II, 212; used by preachers, II, 97–98. *See also* Preaching
Gen. Rabbah, III, 28–29, 33, 89; Kohelet Rabbah, III, 23
Midwives, Jewish, communal provisions for, II, 115, 329
Międzyrzecze: cemetery in, III, 157; *maggid* of, II, 100
Migrations: Israelitic, I, 47, 50, 53–57; III, 12. *See also* Diaspora
Jewish, ancient: and Alexandrian labor exchange, I, 365: and com-

munal creativity, I, 85; and Hillel, I, 140; and love for Palestine, I, 149–50; and new synagogues, I, 112; and Persian anarchy, I, 173; and preachers, I, 122; under Hellenism, I, 75; (to North Africa), I, 78; (to Spain), I, 233

medieval and modern: and abuses in bans, II, 231; and anti-Jewish legislation, I, 281; and associations, I, 348; and bureaucracy, II, 119–20; and care of refugees, II, 337–38; and communal control, I, 209; III, 98; and congregational divisions, II, 18; III, 149; and decentralization, I, 197; and electoral rights, III, 114; and English presbyters, I, 297; and enlightened absolutism, II, 357; and entry fees, II, 262; and family quotas, I, 196; II, 4–5; and foreign rabbis, III, 132; and growth of western communities, I, 209; II, 364; and heirlessness, II, 267; and interterritorial Jewish action, I, 307, 309; and itinerant begging, II, 324; and Marranos, I, 24; and militarism, II, 357; and Nazism, I, 19; and new synagogues, I, 219; and Palestine, I, 18, 157–58; II, 329, 339; and Polish councils, I, 302, 332–33; and preaching, III, 134; and status of bachelors, II, 38; and talmudic adjustments, II, 69; and taxation, I, 172, 273; III, 70; (double), II, 287; and varieties of dishes, II, 161; eastern direction of, I, 267; encouraged by kings, I, 233; in various regions (Algeria), III, 50; (England), I, 297; (France), I, 263; (Germany), I, 19; III, 70; (Islam), I, 172; (Palestine), I, 18, 157–58; II, 329, 339; (Poland), I, 273, 281, 300, 302, 332–33; III, 71; (Spain), I, 233; III, 50; (Soviet Union), I, 16–17; (Turkey), I, 196; limitations on, I, 263; II, 10, 15–16; III, 108; opposition of exiles to, I, 205; overcome local isolation, I, 167–68; II, 355; sufferings during, II, 338; III, 214. *See also* Emigration; Resettlement

Miḳvah, controversies over, II, 166. *See also* Baths; Ritual

Milan: I, 114; at Padua conference, I, 321; expulsion from, and fiscal obligations, III, 145

Mile-End (London), Jewish cemetery at, I, 256

Military service, Jewish, ancient: in Palestine, I, 33, 37–39, 45, 69–73; (and Rome), I, 109; under Egypt, I, 71, 77; under Persia, I, 146; III, 32

medieval and modern: II, *267*; and Jewish billeting, II, 268; and migrations, II, 357; and new synagogues, I, 233; and religious sanctions, I, 208; Jewish exemptions from, I, 268; taxes in lieu of, I, 268; III, 189

Milk, sales taxes on, II, 261

Mill Street Synagogue, New York: I, 261; III, 60; outside contributions to, III, 146. *See also* Shearith Israel

Miltenberg (Germany), burial society in, I, 352

Mines, Roman, criminals sent to, I, 113

Minhag, and *gehinnom*, II, 70. *See also* Customs

Ministry of Cults, and people's community, I, 7

Minorities, religious: ancient, I, 55, 75; (in Sassanian Persia), I, 149; and dangers of informing, I, 235; II, 221; Caliphate's policy on, I, 158, 173–74; in Turkey, I, 195–96. *See also* Law; Legal status

Minority groups, communal: and secession from associations, I, 349; and size of taxation, II, 250; growth of rule of, III, 117. *See also* Oligarchy

Minority rights, Jewish: agitation for, I, 7–8; III, 3–4; and State, I, 8; in Soviet Union, I, 14; Turkish disregard of, III, 50. *See also* Nationalism; Self-government

Minors, Jewish: ancient status of, I, 46; as associational members, II, 17; conversion of, I, 218, 222–23; protection of rights of, III, 212; taxation of, II, 275; III, 192. *See also* Children; Orphans

Minsk, Jews of: anti-alien legislation of, II, 7; guilds of, I, 371; III, 97; rulers' ordinances on, I, 270; social conflicts among, III, 97

Minute-books, Jewish: and court judgments, II, 84; and education, III, 166; and guild agreements, I, 369–70; and pledges of betrothed, II, 315; and rabbis, II, 90, 113; (diplomas), III, 131; and synagogue seats, III, 144–45; and taxation, I, 173; II, 257–58; in various regions, (Bamberg), III, 87; (Bayonne), II, 265; (Carpentras), III, 89; (Chorostków), III, 90; (Dubno), III, 97; (Frankfort), II, 214; III, 78, 90; (Hamburg), II, 25–26; (Islam), I, 173; (Italy), II, 113; (Kleve), III, 86; (New York), III, 61; (Lithuania), I, 327–28; III, 81–82, 158; (Paderborn), III, 86–87; (Poland), I, 327; II, 84; III, 81–82, 190–91, 195; (Rome, papal), II, 181; judicial, III, 173; (include pledges by parties), II, 214; preparation of, II, 113. *See also* Archives

Minutiae: legal, and growing severity, II, 212; ritualistic, women's familiarity with, II, 178

Minyan, ḥasidic, II, 125–26. *See also* Congregations; Synagogues

Miracles: biblical, and *shabbat ha-gadol*, III, 134; ḥasidic performance of, and preaching, II, 100; historical, and growth of western communities, II, 364

Miscarriage of justice, judicial delay as, II, 236. *See also* Procedure

Miserabiles personae, widows and orphans as, II, 330

Mishnah: II, 193–94; compilation of, I, 141, 153; Ibn Adret on, I, 213; meaning of, I, 125–26; on group divisions, III, 17; on position of women, III, 17; on quorum of ten, III, 10; on Roman judiciary, III, 24; on "ten men of leisure," I, 133–34; on vernacular Bible reading, III, 22–23; on world's foundation, III, 23

Ber., III, 17; Demai, III, 94; Meg., III, 17, 22–24, 26; Soṭah, III, 28; Ket., III, 174; Giṭ., III, 17; B. M., III, 28; B. B., III, 27; Sanh., III, 10, 27; Abot, III, 23, 25; (commentaries on), III, 34, 123

Mishpaḥot, *see* Clans

Mishpaṭim, acrostic of, II, 214

Misinformation, and communal control of preachers, II, 98

Mismanagement, communal, and welfare budgets, II, 350

Mission, religious, *see* Conversion; Preaching; Proselytes

Miṣvot, in synagogue, sale of, II, 132–33; III, 145–46. *See also* Synagogues

Mitanni names, in ancient Palestine, I, 46

Mixed courts, *see* Judiciary; Litigations

Mizraḥi, Elijah b. Abraham, I, 197; III, 47

Mob, vs. majority principle, II, 27

Mobility, individual, I, 26

Modena: associations in, I, 358–59; III, 92–93, 102; church tithe in, III, 185; collection of prayers in, I, 353; in pre-censorship commission, I, 321; Jewish settlers in Palestine from, III, 215; legacies for, III, 212–13; obligatory acceptance of office in, III, 119

Moderation in living, demanded by rabbis, I, 132

"Modernity," and state control over family relations, II, 210–11

Moelln, Jacob b. Moses ha-Levi: against lengthy chanting, II, 104–5; III, 136; and chief rabbinate, I, 299; as itinerant scholar, II, 188; as preacher, II, 96; III, 133; disposes of salary, II, 81; III, 126; on contributions for citrons, III, 160; on sale of synagogue functions, III, 145; on Torah summonses, II, 132; on use of tithes, II, 344. *See also* Custumals

Mohammed: and "people of the book," II, 205; belief in, I, 171; successors of, I, 175. *See also* Caliphate; Islam

Mohel, II, 115. *See also* Circumcision

Molina (Castilian city), surrender of, III, 66

Molko, Solomon, documents on, III, 80

Monarchy *and* monarchs, Israelitic: and bureaucracy, III, 7; and judiciary, I, 39–40; and medieval oligarchies, III, 117; and *negidut*, III, 13; and patriarchate, I, 140; and prophets, I, 45; Deuteronomic constitution of, I, 51; court of, I, 35, 38; in Exile, I, 63, 69; influence of, I, 117; population under, III, 6; taxation under, III, 7; weakness of, I, 34–41, 48, 53, 54; III, 8. *See also* Palestine

Jewish: and exilarchate, I, 27, 145–47, 175–76, 179, 187; III, 40; and Narbonne *nasi*, III, 68; and rabbis, I, 140; Christian resentment of, I, 144; constitutional rights of, I, 215; II, 216–17; (superfluous in dispersion), I, 179; in Sassanian Persia, I, 149

non-Jewish: absolutism of, and modern oligarchies, II, 50–52, 357; and abattoirs, II, 108; and ambiguities of communal statutes, II, 3, 31; and betrothals, II, 311; and burghers, I, 276, 279; II, 51; and cemeteries, II, 146, 150–51; III, 155; and chief rabbis, I, 285, 292–95, 346; II, 87; III, 66; and communal debts, II, 271–72; and communal leadership, II, 24, 50–52, 57, 74; and councils, I, 287–88, 310, 323–24; III, 75; and craftsmen, I, 368; and ecclesiastical tithes, II, 254; and elections, II, 35, 74; III, 113–14; and excommunication, II, 230, 232; III, 178; and ghettos, III, 197; and individual monopolies, II, 299; and Jewish "serfdom," I, 215; II, 218; III, 104; and judiciary, I, 216; II, 73–79; III, 125; and levirate marriage, II, 318; and migrations, I, 233–34, 267; III, 68, 132; and mixed litigations, I, 272–73; and oath *more judaico*, I, 273; and rabbis, I, 271, 333; II, 73–74; III, 125; and redemption of captives, II, 336–37; and share in confiscated property, II, 281; (in fines), III, 179; and taxation, I, 215, 243–44, 246–47; III, 68; (exemptions), II, 274–75; (meat), II, 259; (wine), II, 162. *See also* Taxation; coercion by, I, 212; disparaging decrees of, I, 269; in various regions (Aragon), I, 279, 287–88, 292–95; III, 125; (Castile), III, 66, 155; (Egypt, Ptolemaic), I, 77; (England), II, 230, 276; III, 75; (France), I, 296; III, 68, 132; (Germany), I, 341. *See also* Emperors; (Mediterranean countries), I, 346; (Persia), III, 8; (Poland), I, 267, 269, 271–73, 323–24, 333; II, 87; III, 64, 197; (Portugal), I, 285; (Prussia), III, 178; (Sicily), I, 231, 292–95, 368; II, 249, 274–75; III, 68, 113–14; (Spain), I, 233–34, 310; II, 24, 73–74, 108, 162, 259, 271–72, 274–75, 281, 299, 311, 336–37; Jewish alliance with, I, 279; prayers in honor of, II, 143; synagogue illumination for, II, 144;

whimsies of, and Jewish community, II, 351. *See also* Government intervention; Law; Legal status; State; Viceroys
Monasticism *and* monasteries, Catholic: and charities, I, 360; and communal credit, I, 334; II, 271, 273; III, 84; and ecclesiastical taxes, II, 254; and *Ḥukke ha-Torah*, I, 357; and Jewish institutions, II, 150; (baths), II, 166; (cemeteries), II, 152; and Jewish sermons, II, 96; III, 133. *See also* Church; *and under* respective orders and monks
Mondays: announcement of assemblies on, II, 25; Bible recitation on, II, 141; court sessions on, I, 128; proclamation of bans on, II, 228
Mondovi, controlled by Turin, II, 22
Money: and assault and battery, II, 213–14; and intellectual achievement, II, 181; capitalist emphasis on, II, 362; charitable distribution of, II, 320. *See also* Chest, communal; loss of, and court sessions, II, 212; transfer of, and patriarchal tax, I, 144; tax discounts on, II, 255. *See also* Banking
Mongol dynasties, religious minorities under, I, 186. *See also* Mamelukes
Mongolian invasions: I, 157; and Jewish separatism, I, 186
Monmouth, Earl of, on synagogue, I, 257
Monogamy, Christian, and Jewish polygamy, II, 308. *See also* Marriage; Polygamy
Monopolies, communal: II, 261–62; and rabbinic revenue, II, 84–85; farming of, II, 261–62; in citrons, II, 165; in meat and wine, II, 108, 162
of guilds (and Jewish converts to Islam), I, 366; (and ritual meat), III, 138, 187; private, in Spain, II, 299; royal (and *ḥazakah*), III, 199–200; (and Jewish abattoirs), III, 186; (Jewish collaborators in), I, 235, 368
Monotheism: and education, I, 92; II, 174; and exilic names, I, 63; and Jewish nationalism, I, 9; liturgical profession of, I, 121. *See also* God; Religion
Montblanch, and Barcelona *collecta*, I, 286–87
Monti di pietà, Italian: and toleration of Jews, I, 275; as communal creditors, II, 257, 272. *See also* Banking; Pawnbroking; Usury
Montpellier, Jews of: III, *75*; and burning of the *Guide*, I, 223; bathhouses of, III, 160; cemetery of, III, 154; royal invitation of, III, 100
Monzon (Spain): synagogues in, III, 151; Talmud Torah in, III, 92
Moors, Spanish: conversionist sermons among, III, 135; derision of Jewish worship by, II, 129; freedom of movement by, I, 234; guilds of, I, 367; judiciary of, I, 239; play dice with Jews, II, 232; taxation of loans to, II, 248. *See also* Arabs; Islam; Muslims
Moral conduct, Jewish: and associational membership, I, 353; and interruption of prayers, II, 145; and state, I, 11; II, 123; communal regulations on, II, *307–19*; III, *203–9*; supervisors of, II, 55, 57. *See also* Ethics; Ordinances; Sex morality; Sumptuary laws
Morale, maintenance of, and charitable contributions, II, 326
Moralists, Jewish: against luxuries, III, 201–2. *See also* Sumptuary laws; against new educational approaches, II, 181–82; legalistic emphases of, III, 134; on acceptance of office, III, 119; on charitable contributions

by poor, II, 326; on sex relationships, II, 312. *See also* Ethics; Preaching
Moratorium, on Polish communal debts, III, 191
Moravia, Jews of: III, *98*; adoption of statutes by, I, 339; III, 111; and German chief rabbinate, III, 70; and Palestine relief, II, 341; and Swedish invasion, I, 306; archives of, III, 218; (minute books), III, 144; bathhouses of, III, 160; burial societies of, III, 90; citron administration of, II, 164–65; (taxes), II, 260; communal debts of, III, 192; education of, I, 339; II, 175, 189–90; (district academies), I, 340; II, 95; (teachers), II, 114, 184–85; elections among, II, 40–43; III, 116; elders of, II, 40–41; III, 120–21; excommunicate for appeal to Gentile courts, II, 228; faulty prayer-books of, II, 203; few emigration restrictions among, II, 16; guilds of, I, 366; III, 97; household employees of, II, 300; interior decorators among, III, 147–48; *Landesmassafond* of, I, 339; III, 85; judiciary of (lay), II, 88; (courts of appeal), II, 241; majority principle among, II, 27–28; rabbis of, II, 89–90; (control academies), II, 95; (oath of loyalty), III, 133; (revenue), II, 85; rights of settlement in, III, 103; (family quotas), II, 5; sumptuary ordinances of, III, 201; supply of fish for, II, 161; synagogue vows limited among, II, 133; taxation of, II, 263; (collectors), II, 40; (immunities), II, 278. *See also* Chief rabbinate; Councils; Statutes; *and under* respective cities
Mordecai b. Hillel ha-Kohen: III, 76; on accounting of charity overseers, II, 348; III, 218; on fines, II, 235; on "law of the kingdom," III, 179; on marriage brokerage, III, 208; on obligatory acceptance of office, III, 119; on opinions for single parties, II, 238; III, 180; on seven elders, II, 55; III, 120; on synagogues, II, 127; III, 143; (art), III, 146; (attendance), III, 142; (inheritance of functions), II, 133; on tax collections, III, 174, 194; (court appeals), II, 219; (land taxes), III, 185; on teachers, III, 140; on trade regulation, III, 200; on visiting of sick, III, 211
Mordecai b. Judah ha-Levi, III, 34–35
Morenu, degree of, II, 84, 206, 214, 244; (origin of), II, 90–92; III, 130
Mores, of forefathers: and Roman law, I, 108, 110–11, 145; under Islam, I, 174. *See also* Customs
Moritz (Hessian landgraf), decree of, I, 343
Morning services, and interruption of prayers, II, 33–34. *See also* Liturgy; Worship
Morocco, Jews of: I, 157, 200; and Fatimid conquests, I, 190; and *ḥakam-bashi's* authority, II, 352; and Muslim guilds, III, 91, 94; ordinances of, III, 47; taxation of, III, 186; (immunities), III, 193. *See also under* respective cities
Morpurgo, Samson b. Joshua Moses: on communal interest payments, II, 270; III, 190; on diversion of educational funds, II, 135; on expediting procedure, III, 180; on fish, III, 159; on gaming, III, 207; on growing beards, III, 203; on levirate marriage, III, 205; on rabbi's attendance at wedding, III, 205; on real estate *ḥazakah*, III, 199; on restrictions in Palestine relief, III, 216; on sex morality, III, 203, 205; on synagogues (lending ornaments),

III, 146; (patriotic illuminations), II, 144; III, 150; (taxes), III, 146; on tax assessments, III, 146, 195–96
Morteira (Veronese family), II, 113
Morteira, Saul Levy, as preacher, III, 133
Mortgages, Jewish: on communal charities, III, 196; on *ḥazakah*, II, 295; on synagogue seats, II, 130; taxes on, II, 248. *See also* Creditors; Debts; Loans
Mosaic tradition, and local sanctuaries, I, 49. *See also* Pentateuch; Religion
Moscheta, used for synagogue, I, 232
Moscow, Jews of, I, 17, 26
Moselle wines, compete with those of Bordeaux, II, 164
Moses (biblical lawgiver): I, 45, 53, 56, 89; alleged influence on Hellenism of, III, 25–26; as founder of synagogue, III, 10; as model for elections, II, 35; invoked in oath of office, II, 37
Moses b. Jacob of Coucy: as preacher, II, 98; on degrees of charity, II, 327; III, 210; on height of synagogue, III, 147; on *hekdesh*, II, 329; III, 211; on minimum requirements of study, II, 177; III, 162; on use of Torah in oaths, III, 181
Moses ha-Kohen (Asher b. Yeḥiel's nephew), III, 70
Moses the Chirographer, II, 111
Mosque: and Jewish private worship, II, 125; and synagogue height, I, 162; as center of private life, II, 128, 144–45; in converted synagogues, I, 163. *See also* Islam
Mosul, local exilarchs in, I, 185, 194; III, 40
Moszko, "the extortionist," II, 227
Motions, during study, recommended by rabbis, II, 199–200; III, 169
Mourning *and* mourners, Jewish: I, 168; II, 138; and burial societies, I, 353–54; and cutting of hair, III, 203; and private worship, II, 21, 124–25; and synagogue candles, II, 134; communal, and individual burial, II, 147; for excommunicates and suicides, restricted, II, 156, 231; III, 157; for leaders, III, 152–53; national, and chastisement of pupils, III, 169. *See also* Burial; Funeral
Movables, and *ḥazakah*, II, 297–98
Muezzins, Muslim, and Jewish sextons, II, 106
Mühlhausen, Yom Tob Lipmann, biography of, III, 77
Munich, Jews of: hospital of, II, 329; supply of fish for, II, 161
Municipalities, *see* Cities
Münster, Jews of: III, *87*; rabbinic salaries of, III, 127; regional community of, I, 341, 345
Murad III (sultan), and feminine luxuries, III, 200–1
Murashu, Babylonian house of, I, 63, 71
Murcia (Spain): and Christian captives, III, 214; complaint against chief rabbi in, III, 182
Murderers, Jewish, occasional preference to, II, 227; Oxford students accused as, II, 187
Muscato, Judah (Leo) b. Joseph, as preacher, III, 134–35; on head covering, III, 202
Muschmann, exempted from bans, I, 246; II, 232
Music *and* musicians: ancient Israelitic, I, 52; and exilarchic court, I, 147; and Gentile music, II, 104; and half-holidays, III, 206; and *ḥazzan*, I, 201; II, 104–5; and sextons, II, 106; and sex relationships, II, 312; and sumptuary laws, II, 302, 305; at Christian ceremonies, III, 141; in Frankfort, II, 115, 117; in synagogue, history of, I, 236; II, 100–1; III, 135–37, 148; Jewish instructors of, II, 191;

Maimonides' attitude to, III, 167. *See also* Ḥazzan; Liturgy
Muscovite War: and Polish councils, I, 333; and redemption of captives, II, 335. *See also* Russia
Muslims: as landlords in Jewish quarters, II, 295; as owners of Jewish slaves, II, 337; judiciary in Catania of, I, 238; pilgrimage to Palestine by, II, 339; protected by Egyptian *nagid*, I, 191. *See also* Arabs; Caliphate; Islam; Moors
Musselimlik, Turkish, and Jewish customs duties, II, 263
Mussolini, Benito, I, 13
Mustarab congregation in Damascus, III, 105
Mutawakkil (caliph), I, 165
Mutilation of criminals, medieval, II, 223–24, 241
Mutual: benefit societies, and charities, I, 364; III, 90, 213; insurance, and charities, II, 337, 349; support, and communal solidarity, I, 165
Mysia, Roman Jews from, I, 81
Mysticism and mystics: and communal control, II, 168; and communal repasts, II, 128; and preaching, III, 134; and religious associations, I, 354; and strictness of judges, II, 212. *See also* Cabala; Ḥasidism
"Mystic urge," and Jewish community, I, 21; (councils), I, 310, 323
Mytilene, Duke of, I, 197. *See also* Mendes, Alvaro

NAAMAN, leprosy of, II, 37
Nagid and *negidim*: I, *189–91*, 194; III, *43–45*; and central authorities, I, 206; and government appointments, II, 218–19; III, 39; and Narbonne *nasi*, III, 68; and Palestinian elections, I, 193; and rabbinic tax immunity, III, 34; and Spanish chief rabbinates, I, 291; functions of, I, 191, 203; III, 43; title of, I, 187, 190; (Septuagint translation), III, 13
Naḥman b. Isaac, R. (amora), III, 32
Naḥman b. Jacob, R. (amora), I, 154
Naḥmanides (Moses b. Naḥman): on honorable burial, III, 157; on "law of the kingdom," III, 52; on state criminals, II, 156; on tax immunities, II, 277
Naḥshon b. Zadok Gaon, II, 276–77; III, 34, 46
Nahum, Ḥayyim (Turkish chief rabbi), I, 198
Nakawa, Israel, Ibn al-: for judicial compromise, III, 173; on degrees of charity, III, 210; on education, II, 197, 205; III, 169, 171; (self-instruction), II, 174; III, 161; on obligatory acceptance of office, III, 119
Names: divine, I, 77–78; foreign, in ancient Palestine, I, 46; Israelitic, I, 45; Jewish, in Babylonian Exile, I, 63; of elders, I, 200
Naples (city), status of rabbis in, III, 128
Naples (kingdom), Jews of: and all-Italian conferences, III, 80; and confiscation for tax defaults, II, 284; and growth of minority rule, III, 117; dependence on Spain of, I, 232; expulsion of, III, 64; judiciary of, III, 56; regional communities of, I, 292; taxation of, I, 235; (no funeral tolls), II, 153. *See also under* respective provinces and cities
Napoleon I (French emperor), and Jewish community, I, 12–14, 18; III, 88
Napoleonic era, and western German assemblies, I, 342, 344-45
Narbonne: Church council of, I, 225; *nasi* in, III, 68; old Jewish tomb-

stone in, II, 155; schoolhouses in, II, 187

Naro (Sicily), constitution of, II, 59

Nasi: and Fatimid Caliphate, I, 194; control over communities of, I, 211; decrees of appointment of, I, 204; in Narbonne, III, 68; in Rome, I, 210; poems in honor of, III, 40; title of, I, 186–87; III, 28; (exilarch), III, 73; (*nagid*), III, 43; (patriarch), I, 141
  of Holy Land, II, 341. *See also* Overseers; Palestine relief

Nasi, Don Joseph (Duke of Naxos), I, 197; III, 216

Nasli (Asia Minor), *synodos* in, I, 95

Nassy, David (Surinam), privilege of, I, 255

Nathan b. Ananiah (Elephantine scribe), I, 72; III, 12

Nathan b. Isaac ha-Kohen, the Babylonian (geonic period): III, 38–39; on Jewish education, III, 42; on exilarchic taxation, I, 175; on local judges, I, 202; III, 50; on Mar Uḳba, III, 43; on semi-annual assemblies, I, 182

Nathan b. Yeḥiel: on inexpensive shrouds, II, 150–51; synagogue of, I, 219; III, 53

Nathan the Babylonian (tannai): I, 153; on recitation of Decalogue, III, 22

Nathan Uḳban (exilarch), I, 145

National Assembly, French, and communal control, II, 363

National Council of Palestine, I, 17

National heterogeneity, and Jewish status in Persia, I, 64

Nationalism, Jewish: I, *3–10*; III, 3–4; and Babylonian Exile, I, 59; and second fall of Jerusalem, I, 110; and tenant protection, II, 295; in eastern Europe, I, 7, 14–17; in Turkey, III, 50; independent of politics, I, 28–29. *See also* Minority rights

Naṭronai b. Hilai Gaon, III, 41–42; on heresies, I, 168; on study of Bible, II, 193

Naturalization, communal, of Leghorn Jews, II, 11. *See also* Ban of settlement; Residence rights

Navarra, Menaḥem b. Isaac (Verona rabbi), II, 96; III, 129

Navarre, Jews of: III, 65–66; board of standards of, II, 291; chief rabbinate of, I, 288, 290; III, 66; deeds of, III, 139; Sicilians from, II, 329; synagogue oath of, II, 144

Navicularii, Jewish, ancient, Theodosian Code on, I, 365

Naxos, Duke of, I, 197; III, 216

Nazarenes, I, 121. *See also* Christians

Nazism: I, 3–4, 20; and German legal system, II, 245. *See also* Anti-Semitism

Near East: abuses of bans in, II, 32; III, 178; against use of Torah in oath, III, 181; ancient guilds in, III, 11; and Ashkenazic ritual, III, 149; modern capitulations in, III, 101–2; Sephardim in, II, 365; slavery in, II, 177; spread of Polish influences to, II, 355; synagogues in, III, 35–36. *See also under* respective countries and cities

Nebuchadrezzar (Babylonian king), I, 41, 59, 62

Necromancy, and visiting of graves, II, 154

Necropolis, Jewish, in Alexandria, I, 86. *See also* Cemeteries

"Needy" population, Italian, and Jewish moneylenders, I, 275

Ne'emanim, II, 55. *See also* Elders

Negid 'am el, I, 190

Negidut, see *Nagid*

Negro, David, *see* Ibn Yaḥya

Negroponte, Jews in, III, 73

Nehardea: I, 156; ancient synagogues around, III, 12; as seat of exilarchs,

III, 12; recitation of Decalogue in, III, 22; teachings of, I, 152
Nehemiah b. Hachaliah (governor), I, 64–65, 67, 70; III, 11
Nehemiah b. Kohen Zedeḳ Gaon, I, 181
Neighborhood, importance of: I, 26, 74; and ancient synagogue, I, 74, 91; and congregational divisions, I, 351
Neḳiṭat ḥefeṣ bi-, III, 181. *See also* Oaths; Pentateuch
Nemine exempto, in Sicilian tax statutes, II, 275. *See also* Tax immunities
Neoi, Jewish association of, III, 16
"Neolog," *see* Reform Judaism
Neo-orthodoxy, and community, I, 5
Ner tefillah, associations, II, 134
Nestorians: moneylending among, I, 244; Muslim decrees on, III, 39; self-government of, I, 173–74
Nethaneel ha-Levi, authorized by exilarch, III, 44
Netherlands, Spanish: Marranos in, I, 242, 253. *See also* Holland
Neṭira (Babylonian banker), I, 160, 188–89, 211; III, 34
Neutrality, Jewish, Turgot on, II, 290
New Amsterdam, *see* New York
New Bowery, New York, Jewish burial ground in, III, 152
"New European order," and Jewish community, I, 20. *See also* Anti-Semitism; Nazism
New Moon: I, 100; III, 116; and calendar regulation, I, 143; and installation of elders, II, 306; Israelitic worship on, I, 52; Palestinian announcement of, I, 192
New Synagogue, London, excommunicated by German community, II, 21
New Testament: Luke, III, 18; Acts, III, 16, 18, 21, 29; Corinthians, III, 24
New Year, Jewish: and calendar regulation, I, 192; and election day, III, 116; change in date of, I, 96; charitable contributions on, II, 345; rabbis at services of, II, 105; sermons on Sabbath preceding, II, 97; visits to graves on, III, 206; vows for Palestine relief on, II, 341. *See also* High Holidays
New York *or* New Amsterdam, Jews of: III, 4, *59–61*; communal responsibility for poor of, II, 347; III, 218; "donkey's burial" by, II, 156; first cemetery of, II, 147; III, 152; oldest synagogue of, II, 136. *See also* Shearith Israel; population of, I, 26; worship of, I, 6, 255, 260–61
Newbury (England), obtains exclusion of Jews, I, 276
Newcastle, medieval, obtains exclusion of Jews, I, 276
Newlyweds, tax exemptions of, II, 275; III, 209
Newport, R. I., Jewish community in, I, 261–62; III, 61; (cemetery), II, 147; III, 152
Newspapers, and community today, I, 26
Nibrarim, *see* Council of elders
Nice, Jews of: III, *62*; against Turin control, II, 21–22; automatic ban of, III, 177; communal indebtedness of, III, 190; congregational divisions among, II, 19; constitution of, II, 30, 175, 342; III, 110, 164; *conservators* of, III, 68; controversy over cemetery of, II, 152; rabbinic salaries among, III, 128; restricted passive franchise of, II, 44; school age among, II, 175; suppression of prostitution by, II, 314; sumptuary laws of, II, 305; synagogue of, I, 264; (feminine quarrels), II, 146; (Jesuit owners), II, 129; taxation of, III, 189; (denunciation of tax defaulters), II, 284; (royal exemptions), II, 13; tuition fees among, III, 164

Nicholas III (pope), on missionary sermons, I, 219
Nicholas IV (pope): intervenes for Meir of Rothenburg, I, 302; on Maimonides, I, 37
Nicholas V (pope), and Jewish assemblies, I, 321
Nicosia (Sicily), Jewish hospital in, II, 329
Nidḥe Israel congregation, in Barbados, I, 262
Nieto, David (London chief rabbi), II, 96
Nidduy or *niddui*, meaning of, I, 169; II, 71, 228, 232–33. *See also* Excommunication
Night: closing of ghettos, and houses of ill-repute, II, 314; study, differences of opinions on, I, 169, 176–77, 197; III, 162; watchmen, communal, in Frankfort, II, 117
Nikolsburg (Moravia): academy of, I, 339; and Frankfort Conference, I, 341; and Palestine settlement, III, 215; rabbis of, and defense taxes, II, 268; teacher's guild in, II, 185, 196; III, 164
Nineteenth century, antecedents of communal evolution during, II, 355
Ninth of Ab: and Palestine relief, II, 341; charitable collections on, I, 363; cutting of hair before, II, 203; prohibition of gaming on, III, 207; vacations during, II, 197
Niort (France), Jewish cemetery in, II, 149
Nippur (Babylonia), Jews of, I, 66–68
Nissim (of Trapani), designates candidates, II, 47
Nissim b. Jacob, I, 181
Nissim b. Moses, of Marseilles, on exilarchs, III, 40
Nissim b. Reuben of Gerona (Gerondi): on associations, I, 353; III, 89; on burial, I, 353; III, 157; on cantors, III, 135, 137; on communal separatism, II, 157; on taxation, III, 194; (ban on tax defaulters), II, 282; (immunities), II, 277
Nizamiya, academy of, III, 163
"Noahidic commandments," I, 214; II, 210
Nobles, European: and absolutism, II, 358; and Jewish tax exemptions, II, 274; and military training, II, 267; as communal creditors, II, 270; as Jewish overlords, I, 234, 248; Aragonese, and Barcelona synod, I, 288; English (appropriate Hebrew books), II, 200–1; (as justiciars of Jews), I, 298; French, and Jewish freedom of movement, II, 16; German (and Bamberg Council), I, 344–45; (and Prussian residence rights), II, 270–71; (have jurisdiction over Jews), I, 248; (indebted to court Jews), III, 142; Maltese, use Jewish barbers, III, 119
Polish: against burghers, I, 280; III, 64; and Jewish councils, I, 323–24, 327–30; and elders, I, 272; II, 53; and guilds, I, 369, 371; and Jewish status, I, 269, 280; III, 64, 186; and real estate taxes, III, 188; and tax-farming, II, 6–7, 285; as communal creditors, I, 334–35; II, 270; III, 84; as judges of Jews, I, 272; II, 116; compete with Jews, I, 329; Jewish ransom of, III, 214; repair to Jewish court, III, 180. *See also* Aristocracy; Feudalism
Nolle prosequi, royal decrees of, I, 258–59
Nomadism, ancient Palestinian, I, 32, 35
Non-conformity, religious, *see* Dissidents; Heresies
Non-political aspects of Jewish community, I, 28–29
Non-recognition, legal: and associational experience, I, 374; and com-

munal growth, II, 363. *See also* Government intervention; Legal status
Non-residents, Jewish, taxes of, II, 219, 263
Noph (Egypt), Jews of, I, 58
Normandy, and synod of Troyes, I, 312
Normans in Italy, Jews under, I, 231
North Africa: ancient, Jewish settlements in, I, 81, 100; Byzantine, tolerates no synagogues, I, 230
  Muslim: and Marranos, I, 24; and Nathan the Babylonian, III, 38; anti-polygamous marriage contracts in, II, 308; Babylonian influence on, I, 167, 189; educational associations in, III, 91; governmentally appointed elders in, I, 203; local rituals in, I, 192; mixed sex relationships in, II, 311–12; Jewish envoys of, I, 188; Palestinian residents from, III, 37; redemption of captives in, II, 334; III, 214; Spanish exiles in, I, 168; 204, 238; II, 13, 338. *See also under* respective countries and cities
North America, early Jewish history in, III, 60. *See also under* respective countries, states and cities
Northampton (England), Jews of, II, 230
Norwich (England), rabbis of, and Jewish debt bondage, II, 227
Noses, cutting of, and Jewish penal procedure, II, 223
Notaries, Jewish, ancient: I, 102; III, 24; in Elephantine, I, 72–74
  medieval and modern: III, *139–40*; Dutch, Grotius on, I, 254–55; in Frankfort, II, 117; preservation of records of, II, 113; reliability of, I, 241; II, 112; restricted in Iberian countries, I, 241; II, 111; salaries of, I, 202; scribes as, II, 110. *See also* Deeds; Scribes
Notarius, meaning of, III, 139
Notes, of wandering scholars, II, 180, 188
Novellae of Justinian, *see* Code of Justinian
Nuremberg, Jews of: association for orphans of, III, 212; exclusivity of city courts for, I, 250; feminine cantors among, II, 140; *memor*-book of, II, 329; III, 152; population of, III, 107; rabbis of, II, 147; supply of fish for, II, 160–61; synods of, I, *313–15*; III, *77*; (Colon's proclamation), II, 243; (desertion of husbands), II, 317; (ritual libel), I, 313
Nurses, Jewish, communal, II, 115, 117, 329

OATHS, Christian: and Jewish ceremonial, I, 112; validity of, I, 249
  Jewish, judicial and administrative: administration of, procedural law on, I, 273; II, 144–45, 239–40; and attestation of poverty, II, 326; and size of population, I, 171; and tax assessments, II, 282, 286; (declarations), II, 12, 281, 283; and uncovered heads, III, 202; and Zurich judiciary, I, 277; formula of, III, 181; *more judaico*, II, 240; III, 57, 180–81; (in Barbados), I, 262; (in Poland), I, 273; (texts of), III, 158; of writer of legal brief, II, 238; rabbinic fees for administration of, II, 83; taken by Christians, I, 112; validity of, I, 349
  of loyalty: and admission to membership, II, 5; and mental reservations, III, 104; of Avignon Jewry, III, 106; of Jewish elders, II, 35–37; III, 113; of rabbis, formulas of, II, 330; III, 133
  of office: II, 37; of accounting officers, II, 65; of charity overseers, not required, II, 348; of Lithuanian elders, and loyalty to Councils, I,

331; of Polish electors, II, 45–46; of sextons, II, 106; of tax assessors, II, 286; of teachers, concerning qualifications, III, 164–65; of Trapani elders, on elections, II, 47; of wine administrators, II, 163; of Wilno chief rabbi, on restrictions, II, 87
private, *see* Vows
Obernai (Alsace), regional sessions in III, 88
Oberältester, Berlin government control over, III, 220. *See also* Elders
Oberstarši, of Prague guilds, II, 89. *See also* Elders; Guilds
Obituaries, Jewish, in German *memor*-books, II, 146
Obituary sermons: and state criminals, II, 156–57; for scholars, II, 147; Italian, II, 96. *See also* Mourning; Preaching
Object of history, Jews as, I, 22
Objects, sacral, and redemption of captives, II, 334
Observance, religious: and growing severity, II, 212; laxity under Islam of, I, 147, 165; of Passover, communal control of, I, 168. *See also* Orthodoxy; Ritual
Occupancy, lapse in, and *ḥazaḳah*, III, 198
Occupational: changes, and aristocratic rule, II, 50; statistics (and bureaucracy), III, 141; (in Rome), III, 95–96; training, demanded by rabbis, I, 132. *See also* Education
Octogenarians, tax exemption of, II, 275
Offenburg, early bathhouses in, II, 166; III, 160
Offerings to synagogues, and government confiscations, II, 135. *See also* Donors; Gifts; Vows
Oil, expenditure for, and night study, II, 176
Old age, of officials, few provisions for, II, 86
Old Testament *see* Bible
Oligarchy, communal: I, 27; II, 50–51; III, 117–18, 141–42; ancient Israelitic, I, 44; III, 8–9; and accounting, III, 122–23; and administration of charities, II, 348; and ambiguity of statutes, II, 3; (defies them), II, 46, 50, 62–63; and associational democracy, I, 349, 373–74; and capitalism, II, 362; and communal stability, I, 24; II, 121–22, 353–54; and Councils, I, 328, 336, 347; II, 47; and court Jews, II, 357–58; and education, II, 362; and excommunication, II, 32; and fee system, II, 84–85; and officials, II, 120; and Polish nobles, I, 270; and preachers, II, 99–100; and public-law recognition, I, 24; and rabbinate, II, 76, 181; III, 26, 132; (tenure), II, 86–87, 94; III, 132; and re-election, II, 40–41, 50; and sextons, II, 106–7; and size of communal boards, II, 56; and size of population, II, 23; and sumptuary laws, II, 305; and synagogue assemblies, II, 144; and taxation, II, 27–28, 288–89; (immunities), II, 278; and three-class system, II, 28–30, 39; and wedding fees, II, 119; attacked by Jacob Weil, II, 66; checked by exclusion of relatives, I, 136; disobeys courts, I, 165; in various regions (France), II, 39; (Germany), II, 62, 66; (Islam), I, 165; (Italy), II, 76; (Lithuania), II, 47, 278; (Poland), I, 270, 328, 336; II, 63, 84, 86–87; (Rome, papal), II, 29; (Spain), II, 32. *See also* Bureaucracy; Elders; Patricians
"Olive tree," Roman synagogue of, III, 15. *See also* Elaians
Olkusz, and Cracow pestilence, II, 329; III, 211
Omar I (caliph), I, 157, 164, 177; alleged covenant of, I, 161, 163

Omar II (caliph), and heirless estates, III, 34
'Omedim al tikkune ha-medinah, *see* Defenders of statutes
Omri (Israelitic king), I, 38, 45
Oña, Abbot of, II, 139
Ona'ah, principle of, I, 130–31. *See also* Economic regulation
One-fifth of fortune, and charities, II, 345
One hundred rabbis, divorce dispensation by, II, 308
One-month's sojourn: and charitable tithe, II, 344; and fiscal duties, II, 12
One-sixth of cost, as maximum profit, I, 130–31. *See also* Economic regulation
One-year contracts of cantors, II, 104
One-year residence, and marriage, III, 204
Onias III (high priest), I, 60, 79, 110; III, 14. *See also* Temples
Onomasticon, Palestinian, III, 8
Opatów: and Cracow chief rabbinate, I, 302; communal banishment from, II, 8, rabbinic tenure in, II, 86
Opferpfennig, golden: II, 250–51; and regional control, I, 298; II, 148
Ophir, Israelitic merchants in, I, 56
Oppenheim, David b. Abraham: III, *85*; as chief rabbi, I, 338, 340; as overseer of Palestine relief, II, 341; revenue of, III, 128
Oppenheim, Emilie, II, 5
Oppenheim, Samuel, collection of, III, 59
Oppenheim, Seligmann, of Bingen (German chief rabbi), I, 299, 310–11
Opposition, *see* Conflicts, communal; Controversies
Optional, vs. compulsory organization, I, 25
Orabuena, Joseph (Navarrese chief rabbi), I, 290
Oral exchanges between parties, encouraged, II, 238–39; III, 180. *See also* Attorneys
Oral Law: and feminine education, II, 178; and Philo, III, 20; divine character of, I, 119–20; Justinian's prohibition of, II, 52. *See also* Talmud; Tradition
Oral testimony of witnesses, required, II, 240
Oranese (Algerian) congregation, in Nice, II, 19
Oratories, private, in London, I, 256. *See also* Synagogues
Orchards: ancient Palestinian, I, 32, 42–43; Spanish, Jewish ownership of, I, 160–61
Ordeals, medieval, Jewish exemption from, I, 251
Order of Redemption, Catholic, and Protestant captives, III, 214
Ordinances, communal: against dancing, III, 206–7; against gaming, III, 206; against informing, II, 222; against residence outside ghetto, II, 296; against membership turnover, II, 18; against private bans, III, 124; against private synagogues, III, 144; against prostitution II, 314; against rabbinic competition, III, 128; and charities, II, 320–24, 332–33, 335, 344–46; and class attire, II, 307; and customs duties, II, 263; and discharge of cantors, II, 104; and economic regulation, I, 170; II, 162, 200, 290; and exclusion of members, II, 19, 126; and fugitives, III, 103; and Gentile tenants, II, 296; and *ḥazakah*, III, 197–99; and hours of instruction, II, 176, 197; and interruption of prayers, III, 112; and judicial fees, II, 84; and majority principle, II, 25–27; and marital status, II, 75, 318; III, 208; and opinions to single parties, II, 238; and ritual meat, II, 160; III, 138, 159;

and ritual wine, II, 162–63; and school age, II, 175; and scribes, II, 113; III, 140; and secret marriages, III, 204; and shoeless worship, II, 129; and sumptuary legislation, II, 301–7; and synagogues (attendance), III, 143; (seats), III, 145; and taxation, II, 12, 14–15, 219, 252–55, 260, 275–76, 281–82, 285–86, 288; III, 194–95; and tenant protection, II, 292–96; and tuition fees, III, 164; and visitors' contributions, II, 12; disqualify private witnesses, II, 114; enhanced by synods, I, 309–14, 316–19, 322; foster regionalism, I, 284; issued by ancient academies, I, 151; issued by Asher b. Yeḥiel, III, 70; issued by Councils, I, 329–33, 338–39; III, 83–85, 103; issued by geonim, II, 97; III, 37–38; issued by Gershom, II, 70; issued by *ḥakam-bashi*, I, 196; issued by majority vote, II, 265; revocation of, III, 112; sanctions of, III, 99, 179; vs. Jewish law, II, 6. *See also* Constitutions; Law; Statutes; *and under* respective functions

Ordination, rabbinic: II, 90–91; III, 130–31; ancient, I, 154–55; III, 24, 33; (and medieval rabbis), II, 79; (and penal procedure), II, 220; (Berab's renewal of), I, 309; II, 220; III, 74; and exilarchs, I, 179; and judiciary, I, 127–28; II, 242; and *morenu* title, II, 90; and reverence for teachers, II, 180; and ritualistic training, II, 211; and Roman Council of Sixty, II, 60; and scholarly control, II, 244; ceremony of, II, 67; criticism of, II, 85; Ferrara resolution on, I, 321; formula of, II, 90–91; in Babylonian academies, I, 182; medieval changes in, II, 67–68. *See also* Authorization; Rabbis

Oria, rabbis of, II, 67

Orientation toward Jerusalem: I, 74; and synagogue art, II, 140

Origen (Origenes) Adamantius, Saint: I, 144; honored by Romans, III, 29; on Jewish patriarchs, III, 28

Originality of cantors, and Gentile music, II, 104

Orléans: III, 132; and synod of Troyes, I, 312; schoolhouse in, II, 187

Ornaments: of synagogues, II, 132; restricted by sumptuary laws, II, 304

Orphans, Jewish: and judiciary, II, 216; (priority), II, 237; and parental interference, III, 204; charitable provisions for, I, 131–32; II, 330–31; III, 212; (asylums), II, 331–32; (societies), I, 362, 364; II, 175; communal responsibility for education of, II, 169; eligible for marriage, III, 163; guardians of, and Palestine relief, III, 216; investment of funds of, III, 195; supported by duties, II, 265; tax immunities of, II, 275; III, 192–93. *See also* Children

Orthodoxy: Christian, (affected by Jewish practices), I, 221; (endangered by Jews), I, 225; Islamic, I, 164–65

Jewish: I, 19; and associational membership, I, 353, 355; and community, I, 4, 14, 29; and meat taxes, I, 237; and Prussian law of secession, III, 5; and scholars' tax immunities, III, 194; and synagogue decorum, III, 23; and wigs, III, 203; and Polish Council, I, 307; use of bans by, II, 233. *See also* Heresies; Ritual

Or Torah association, in Padua, I, 355

Or Zaru'a, Ḥayyim b. Isaac: and Mayence synod, III, 76; on communal baths, II, 166; III, 160; on enactment of bans, III, 112; on fiscal responsibilities, III, 103; on frequent re-elections, III, 117; on majority principle, II, 160; III, 110, on marital relations, II, 317; on synagogue oaths, III, 150; on *sha'atnez*, III, 202; on size of German communities, II, 23; III, 106; on tax immunities, III, 192

Or Zaru'a, Isaac b. Moses: against inheritance of synagogue functions, II, 133; and synagogue art, II, 138; favors scholars in renting houses, III, 199; on cantors, III, 136; (beards), II, 104; (elections), II, 102; III, 135; on lending communal funds, III, 195; on marriage brokerage, III, 208; on mendicants, II, 322; III, 209; on *morenu* title, III, 130; on rabbinic office, II, 67; (title *rab*), III, 123; on ritualistic neglect, III, 123–24; on settlement of scholars, III, 100; on synagogues (appeals), II, 136; (sales), III, 146; on wedding fees, II, 83; III, 127

'Ose ḥesed society, I, 362

Osnabrück, synagogue discipline in, III, 150

Ossuaries, Jewish, ancient, III, 17. *See also* Cemeteries

Ostracism, social, of bachelors, II, 37–38. *See also* Public opinion

Ostrog, as member of Polish Council, I, 326; III, 81

Ostrogoths, new synagogues under, I, 112

Otranto, position of rabbis in, III, 139

Ottensen, controversy over cemetery of, III, 156

Ottoman Empire, *see* Turkey

Ouderkerk an den Amstel, Jewish cemetery in, I, 253; III, 157

"Our property and our treasure," royal, Jews as, I, 233

Outside marriages, and brokers' fees, III, 209

Ovens, communal, II, 167

Overijsel (Holland), Jews in, III, 58

Overseers *and* supervisors, communal: I, 101; II, 55; and Portuguese chief rabbis, I, 285; obligatory acceptance by, III, 119; of cantors in Babylonia, III, 136; of charities, II, 55, 62, 333. *See also* Charity overseers; of education, II, 114, 173; of industry, Polish, II, 56; of merchants, I, 170. *See also* Agoranomos; of morals, II, 55, 313, 315; of Palestine relief, II, 340–43; of ritual meat, and wine, II, 60, 162, 164; of streets, II, 55; of treasuries, II, 62. *See also* Councils; Elders; Treasurers

Ovid (Publius Ovidius Naso): on synagogues, I, 88; III, 16

Oviedo: bishop of, II, 125; Church Council of, I, 225; III, 54

Ownership rights, of tenants, and *ḥazaḳah*, II, 294. *See also* Leaseholds; Property

Oxford, medieval: prices of books in, III, 169–70; student bandits in, II, 187; university of, III, 135, 165

PABLO, FRA, *see* Christiani

Pacifism, Jewish, I, 179; II, 179. *See also* Peace

Paderborn (bishopric), Jews of: III, 87; regional community of, I, 341; III, 86–87; salaries of provincial chiefs of, III, 122–23

Padua, Jews of: III, 54; and Azariah de' Rossi, I, 308; and synods, I, 319–21; III, 80; association of (charitable), III, 93; (religious), I, 355; III, 91–92; cantors of, II, 101; contributions to Venetian taxes of, III, 190; election of elders of, III, 121; in pre-censorship commission, I, 321; legacies for, III, 212–13; local ordinances of, and synod of Ferrara, III, 131; (and civil law inquiry), II, 238; (and intercommunal bans), II, 229;

quarter of, I, 225; university of (and Jewish corpses), II, 151; (Jewish students at), III, 167

Pagans, ancient: I, 12; and patriarchs, I, 142; at Jewish services, I, 82; conversion of, I, 112; deride Jewish magic, I, 103; in Roman Palestine, III, 27. *See also* Syncretism

Palaeography, of ancient inscriptions I, 84. *See also* Inscriptions; Writing

Palatinate, German, II, 153; III, 156

Palatin's decrees (Lwów): and importation of meat, II, 258; and official recorder, II, 113; and rabbinic position, II, 80, 83; and titles, II, 92

Palatins, Lithuanian: ordinances of, III, 197; of Wilno, and merchant visitors, II, 263

Polish: I, 271; and confirmation of rabbis, II, 93; III, 133; and Jewish elections, II, 35; courts for mixed litigations of, I, 271–72; II, 48; III, 117; (ṭobim at), II, 63; share in fines, II, 234

Palatinus, Polish, I, 271

Palermo, Jews of: and chief rabbis, I, 293–94; and conferences, I, 317–18; III, 78; and taxation, II, 279, 286; archives of, III, 155–56; burghers' protest against expulsion of, I, 279; III, 64; carpenters' guild of, I, 368; communal indebtedness of, III, 190; condemned for blasphemies, II, 339; constitution of, II, 58–59; disqualification of testimony of, I, 279; elections of, II, 44; III, 113, 116; equality of, I, 232; excise taxes of, II, 260; imprisonment of, III, 176; monopolies of, II, 261–62; *negidut* of, under Islam, I, 189–90; recognition of deeds of, II, 111; silk workers among, I, 368; sumptuary laws of, II, 304; transferred to Church, I, 231; wine administration of, II, 162

Palestine, ancient Israelitic and Achaemenide: agriculture in, I, 45; and Elephantine, I, 70–72; and Persian authorities, I, 77–78; and royal bureaucracy, III, 7; and Spain, I, 233; care of widows and orphans in, II, 330; democratic heritage of, III, 27; deportations from, I, 57–59; III, 10; elders of, III, 7; fortified cities in, III, 8; freedom from leprosy of, III, 155; influenced by Deuteronomic Reformation, I, 50–51; municipal organization of, I, 31–54; occupation of, I, 56; physical characteristics of, I, 31–32; III, 6–7; "princes of," III, 7; reconstruction by exiles of, I, 74; restoration to, and Jewish names, I, 63; settlement of craftsmen in, I, 364; small townships in, III, 9; suspension of sacrifices in, I, 79; synagogue as substitute for, I, 89; under Persia, I, 71–72, 77–78, 173; unity of, I, 58

Graeco-Roman: III, *217*; academies in, III, 29; and Ashkenazic ritual, I, 242; II, 142, 215, 220; and Babylonia, I, 118–19; 147, 149–50, 152, 154–55; and Byzantine guilds, III, 94; and calendar regulation, I, 143; and competence of courts, II, 241; and Diaspora, I, 74, 87–88, 95, 97, 110, 123, 129, 139, 151; II, 215, 220; III, 17–18, 21. *See also* Patriarchate; and European supercommunity, I, 346; and judiciary, I, 127; II, 214; III, 24; (authorization of), I, 128; and Spain, I, 233; III, 34; archives in, III, 16; burial in, I, 120–21; charities in, I, 131; III, 26; Christians in, I, 139; clan-life in, I, 43; communal functions in, III, 17; divisions of, I, 31–33, 41; educational reform in, III, 161; effects of revolt on, I, 111; elders in, I, 65; envoys to Rome of, I, 106; exilarchic leadership in, I, 149; guilds in, III, 11; hegemony of, I, 117, 123, 143; Hellenistic influences in, I, 100, 118; historical geography of, III, 6–7; importance of archives in, III, 24; interruption of prayers in, II, 33; III, 112; languages spoken in, I, 100, 122–23; market supervision in, I, 130; ossuaries in, III, 17; patriarchal appointees in, I, 142; Pharisaic leadership of, I, 140; population of, III, 27; preaching in, I, 122; II, 99; (itinerant), III, 22–23; rabbinic ordination in, I, 154; II, 66–67; III, 24; rabbinic supremacy in, I, 135; recitation of Decalogue in, III, 22; Roman army and officials in, I, 81, 109; scholarly residences in, I, 151; scribes in, I, 102; synagogues in, I, 120; III, 15; tax collections in, I, 129; III, 25; triennial cycle in, I, 122; under Seleucidae, I, 82–83; women's position in, I, 96–97

medieval: III, 6, 32; and Babylonia, I, 167, 192; III, 37, 45; and Diaspora, I, 157–58, 194; II, 340; (European divergences), II, 69; (model for Italy), I, 210; II, 59; (views of medieval rabbis on), III, 215; and Egyptian *negidim*, III, 43; burial in, desired, II, 339; calendar regulation in, I, 192; destroyed by Crusades, I, 194; Fatimid hegemony of, I, 193; few inquiries from, III, 45–46; Jewish records from, III, 45; local judges in, I, 203; *negidut* in, I, 189–90; papal appeals on, III, 215; pilgrimages to, II, 15, 329, 339; III, 37; suppresses private ban, III, 178; synagogues in, III, 35–36

Turkish: and Hamburg community, II, 26; and papal taxation, I, 320; II, 135; capitulations in, III, 102; conflicts among settlers in, II, 342; European visitors from, III, 88. *See also* Messengers; famines in, II, 340; French visitor in, III, 159; Sephardic ritual in, II, 142

under British mandate: and Jewish secularism, I, 6; and Zionism, I, 9; III, 4; area of, I, 31; as center of Jewry, I, 12; people's community in, I, 17–18. *See also under* respective cities

Palestine relief: II, *339–43*; III, *215–17*; and Cassel assembly, I, 342; and parental anger, III, 204; and sermons, II, 96; and Venetian indebtedness, III, 190; distribution in country of, III, 212; supervisors of, II, 57, 61; Zechariah of Porto's legacies for, II, 332; III, 212–13. *See also* Messengers

Palestinian congregation, in Fustat, II, 102

"Palestinian *halakot*," on women slaughterers, II, 107

Palma (Majorca), and Jewish taxation, I, 278

Palmyra, invades Babylonia, I, 152

Palṭiel (leader under Fatimids), I, 189.

Pamphleteering, Jewish, I, 193; II, 166. *See also* Public opinion

Panzieri, Shabbetai (Roman rabbi), II, 282

Papacy *and* popes: III, 89; and cemeteries, II, 150–51, 155; and Christian attendance at Jewish theaters, III, 207; and divorce of converts, II, 317; and expulsions of Jews, I, 221, 320–21; II, 270; and government of Papal States, I, 216–17; (Avignon oath), III, 106; (Roman greetings), I, 217; and guilds, I, 368; and Jewish law, I, 216; and Jewish status, I, 216, 228, 287–88, 304–5; III, 52–54; and loud prayers, III, 23; and Marranos, III, 73; and medieval Hebrew literature, I, 307; and

Palestine, III, 215; and Polish Jewry, I, 334; III, 72; and ritual libel, I, 305; and ritual meat, II, 158; III, 137; and reciprocity in toleration, I, 233; and spiritual leadership of Christianity, I, 216; and synagogues, I, 221, 233, 237, 350; and synods, I, 310, 319–20; III, 80; and Talmud, I, 305–6, 321; II, 191, 194–95, 198; and taxation, II, 135, 246, 254–56, 265; (flight tax), III, 103–4; (Roman poverty), II, 272; and tenant protection, II, 262, 293; and usury, I, 321; decrees of, I, 217, 268–69; II, 150; evasion of law of, III, 137; ghetto ordinances of, II, 291–92; international position of, and Jewish action, I, 304–6; II, 57; legend of Jew in See of, III, 207; sporadic intolerance of, I, 221; vs. empire, I, 183. *See also* Canon law; Church; Clergy; Rome, papal

Papal States: III, 208; and ecclesiastical tithe, II, 254; and foreign Jewry, I, 304; expulsions of Jews from, I, 221, 320–21; Jewish assemblies in, I, 319–20; III, 80; Jewish flight taxes in, III, 103–4; meat sales restricted in, II, 158; synagogue taxes in, II, 135, 265; tombstones prohibited in, II, 155. *See also* Church; *and under* respective cities and districts

Papists, *see* Catholics

Papyri, Aramaic, I, 69–73, 93; III, 11–13. *See also* Elephantine

Greek: and Jewish archives, III, 16; on associational officials, III, 18; on electoral rights, I, 98; on gymnastics, III, 16; on legal transactions, I, 93; on markets, I, 130; on synagogues, I, 83, 86–87; III, 15–16

medieval, on *negidim*, III, 43. *See also* Archives; Manuscripts

Paradise, Muslims in, III, 183

Parchment: price of, II, 200; production of, and literary output, III, 170; scrolls of, in Salonica, II, 202

Pardo, David b. Joseph, and Amsterdam Talmud Torah, I, 358

Parents, Jewish: and conversion of minors, I, 218, 222; and inheritance of dowries, II, 318; approval of marriages by, II, 310–11; III, 203–4; demands on children of, I, 127; educational responsibilities of, II, 114, 125–26, 169, 171, 174; III, 161; (chastisement), II, 198; III, 169; (choice of teachers), II, 196; III, 164–65; (duration of), II, 175–76; (school attendance), I, 360; II, 175–76; (vocational training), II, 185; III, 96; living, and recitation of *ḳaddish*, II, 69; reverence for, I, 139

Paris: I, 264, 266; II, 364; III, 62, 106; and synod of Troyes, I, 312; as creditor of Alsatian Jewry, III, 88; ban of settlement in, III, 101; burning of Talmud in, I, 223; exclusivity of city courts of, I, 250; overcrowded hospitals in, II, 327–28; parliament of, against Jewish bans, I, 247; II, 233; poverty in, I, 363; rabbis of, and Rome, III, 101; suppression of guilds in, I, 372; university of, III, 165; (chair for Hebrew), III, 135; (rabbinic ordination), III, 130

Parks, communal, history of, III, 197

"Parliament," French, against excommunication, I, 247; II, 232–33

Parliamentarism *and* parliaments: I, 20; and minority rights, I, 8; English (and student bandits), II, 187; (and Jewish status), I, 258–59; III, 60; Jewish, at Worcester, I, 297, 311, 315, 319. *See also* Councils; Polish, vices of, I, 335–36; Sicilian, abolishes Jewish *colletta*, I, 317. *See also* Diets

Parma (duchy), Jews in, III, 80
Parnas, as family name, III, 120
Parnasim, II, 55. *See also* Elders
Paros: Jews of, I, 95; Roman decree to, I, 108; stone of, I, 100
Parsees, *see* Zoroastrians
Parthia: I, 27, 146; closed frontiers of, I, 122; continues Seleucide policies, I, 83; Hellenism in, I, 118
Parties, judicial: bans on recalcitrance of, II, 228; division of fees among, II, 84
Partitions of Poland, and communal disintegration, I, 337, 354–55. *See also* Austria; Prussia; Russia
Partnerships, Jewish: II, 136; and anti-trust laws, II, 301; and guilds, I, 370; and income from educational funds, II, 186; as means of charitable rehabilitation, II, 326–27; silent, of scholars, I, 139
Pascal, Blaise, on Jesuit casuistry, II, 195
Passivity, congregational, and synagogue decorum, II, 141
Passover: and Poznań synagogue, I, 336; before Easter, Justinian's prohibition of, I, 230; charitable distributions on, II, 320–21; III, 209; Darius II's order on, I, 65; elections during, II, 45; III, 115–16; *Kol Nidre* on, I, 240; minute observance of, I, 168; sermons on Sabbath preceding, II, 97. *See also* Haggadah
Passport fees, and *Leibzoll*, II, 264
Pastures, ancient Palestinian, I, 42–43
Pateressa, title of, I, 97
Pathros (Egypt), Jews of, I, 58
Patras (Greece), sumptuary laws in, III, 202
Patres synagogae: freed from taxes, I, 138; Theodosian Code on, III, 15; title of, I, 101
Patriarchal society, and clan admission, I, 47
Patriarchate *and* patriarchs, Christian: and *ḥakam-bashis*, I, 196; and *negidim*, I, 191; Jacobite, and exilarchs, III, 40; Nestorian, and money-lending, I, 244; Venetian control bans, III, 178–79. *See also* Church; Clergy
  Israelitic: I, 32, 35, 43, 89; as founders of synagogue, III, 10
  Palestinian, I, *140–45*, 153; III, *28–30*; (etymology), I, 141; and academies, I, 151–53; III, 133; and advent of Messiah, I, 155; and authorization of judges, I, 128; and Babylonian leap year, I, 150; and courts of arbitration, I, 114–15; and democracy, I, 27; and diaspora elders, III, 18; and European supercommunity, I, 346; and exilarchs, I, 68–69, 149–50; and ordination, I, 154; III, 24, 33; and prayers, I, 121, and preachers, I, 122; and Rome, I, 12; and synagogue honors, I, 147; diaspora contributions for, I, 84, 87–88, 110, 129; extinction of, I, 23, 145, 152; Jerome's criticism of, I, 176; medieval heritage of, I, 186, 206; position of, I, 153; III, 33; provincial, question of, I, 107; III, 19, 28; support scholars, I, 151
Patricians: Canaanite, I, 41; German, protect Jews, I, 277. *See also* Cities
  Jewish, and ancient academies, III, 27, 46; and electoral manipulations, II, 46; and exilarchic authorization, III, 44; and Italian conferences, III, 79–80; and Polish Council, I, 328. *See also* Aristocracy; Oligarchy
Patrimonium pauperum, Church property as, I, 360
Patrios nomos, I, 145, 174. *See also* Customs; Mores
Patriotism: English, and anti-Spanish feeling, I, 256
  Jewish: and execution of criminals,

II, 156–57; and *ḥazakah* in monopolies, III, 199–200; and prayers for rulers, I, 262–63; II, 143; and self-accusations, III, 183; in various regions (ancient Persia), I, 64; (Egypt), I, 77; (France), I, 262–63; (Prague), II, 98–99; III, 199–200; (Prussia), III, 220; (Turkey), I, 196; III, 49; provincial, of Councils, I, 332–33, 339. *See also* Allegiance; Loyalties

Patrons, Italian, of Christian teachers, II, 184
 Jewish: of academies, exaggerated titles of, I, 201; of arts and letters, feminine, II, 178; III, 163; of Italian rabbis, II, 87; of synagogues, I, 77, 81, 84, 90, 98, 103, 109; II, 145

"Patrons," of Jewish guilds, and judiciary, II, 88–89

Paul IV (pope), on Jewish quarter, I, 225

Paul of Burgos (bishop), Messer Leon against, III, 66

Paul of Tarsus, Saint: I, 87; on judicial self-government, III, 20, 24

Paula (Hebrew copyist), III, 162

Pauw, Reinier van, on Jewish status, I, 254–55

Pawnbroking *and* pawnbrokers, Jewish: and educational responsibilities, II, 176; and Italy's admission of Jews, I, 275; and luxury in dress, II, 302–3; of books, II, 200; taxes on, II, 261. *See also* Banking; Money-lending

Payments of substitutes, and visiting of sick, II, 328

Paz, Elias de, bequest of, III, 60

Peace, international, Jewish teachings on: I, 179; II, 217; and charitable support of Gentiles, II, 320; and judicial decisions, II, 212–13; and marriage, III, 174

Pearls, Jewish, Spanish taxes on, II, 249

Peasants, East-European, repair to Jewish courts, II, 239. *See also* Agriculture

Pechno (Poznań chief rabbi), I, 300

Pedagogy, Jewish, ancient, I, 125–26. *See also* Education; Programs

Pedaiah (Sheshbazzar?), I, 69

Peddling and peddlars, Jewish: and refugees, II, 8; feminine, among Christians, II, 314; in ancient Rome, I, 80; sales taxes of, II, 261

Pedro (Aragonese infante), on private Jewish monopolies, II, 299

Pedro II (Aragonese king): and interruption of prayers, II, 33–34; revokes tax immunities, II, 14–15

Pedro III (Aragonese king): against desecration of cemeteries, II, 150; condemns informer, I, 235; II, 73; on lay judiciary, II, 70–71; forbids tax immunities, II, 13; on obligatory acceptance of office, II, 53–54

Pedro IV (Aragonese king): and acceptance of office, III, 119; and appointment of rabbis, III, 125; and cobblers, I, 367; and elections of officials, II, 102; and Jewish serfdom, I, 233; and judiciary, I, 239; and magic, I, 237; and Majorcan slaughterer, II, 108; and new cemeteries, II, 149; and synagogue seats, II, 130; and taxation, I, 278; II, 274–75, 281; appoints noble spokesman of Jews, I, 291; confirms associational statutes, II, 248; III, 95; grants dispensation for polygamy, II, 309; grants permission to depart, III, 103; orders translation of Maimonidean Code, I, 240; protects favorite against censure, II, 14; protects wedding guests, II, 303

Pedro I (Castilian king): against Jewish luxuries, II, 303; and judiciary,

I, 241; and tenant protection, II, 293

Pedro, Maestro (Toledan chief rabbi), I, 289

Penalties, Jewish: and parental consent for marriage, II, 310; and school age requirements, II, 175; and worship, I, 263; for breaches of discipline, II, 28; (government interference), II, 219; for house owners, and legal residence, II, 234; for mixed dancing, II, 316; for refusal to collect alms, II, 346; for support of beggars, II, 324; for use of judicial intermediaries, II, 237; relative mildness of, II, 227–28, 235–36; purposes of, II, 220–22; supernatural, and ritual law, II, 211. *See also* Capital punishment; Excommunication; Fines; Flogging; Prisons

"Penitential Sabbath," II, 97. *See also* Sabbath

Penitentiaries, modern, and Jewish prisons, II, 226. *See also* Prisons

Pensions, rabbinic: and tax exemptions, II, 276; slight provisions for, II, 86. *See also* Salaries

Pentateuch: I, 61; and homage to Pope, I, 217; annual vs. triennial cycle of, I, 74. *See also* Cycles; instruction in (and liturgy), II, 193; (papal permission), I, 221; (parental responsibility), II, 174; (size of classes), II, 196; Philo's commentary on, III, 20; recitation of, I, 121–22

scrolls of: and Catholic processions, II, 53; and greeting of new popes, III, 52; belonging to Carvajal, I, 256; brought to exilarch, I, 147, 189; donated to synagogue, II, 132; enforced acquisition of, I, 120; in Salonica, II, 202. *See also* Bible; Scroll

Pentecost, reading of constitution during, III, 109

"People of the Book," Arab designation of Jews as, II, 205

"People of the land," I, 124, 136, 140. *See also* Illiteracy

People's community: I, 7; in Palestine, I, 17–18; in Soviet Union, I, 15–17; propaganda for, I, 29

People's courts: gradual disappearance in antiquity of, I, 127; in ancient Israel, I, 49; in Soviet Union, I, 15

People's parliaments, agitation for, I, 8

Pepys, Samuel, on visit to synagogue, I, 257

Per capita taxes: and charitable tithes, II, 344–45; and payment for citrons, III, 187; vs. property assessments, II, 279–80; III, 194

yield: and price of meat, III, 187; Polish, estimates of, III, 191

"Perdition," Jewish, I, 216

Perera, Moses (Musa Effendi), III, 47

Perez b. Elijah, on wife-beating, II, 318–19

"Perfidy," Jewish, I, 217

Perfumers, Jewish, in ancient Palestine, I, 67

Peri eṣ ḥayyim (Amsterdam periodical), III, 172

Perjury: denounced by Forli Conference, II, 312–13; fear of, and preference for assessment, II, 282; in tax declaration, and disqualification of testimony, II, 281; inquest of, and oath of office, II, 37. *See also* Oaths

Perosino, Rafaele, I, 232

Perpetuation in office, extreme in Worms, II, 47–48

Perpignan, Jews of: and translation of Maimonidean Code, I, 240; emigration of, III, 103; guilds of, I, 370–71; "house of council" of, II, 24; rights of settlement of, III, 101; tax administration of, III, 196

Persecutions of Jews: ancient, I, 113–14, 127; and economic depression, I, 148–49; in Egypt, I, 56; in Rome, I, 80–81

medieval and modern: and academy of Tiberias, I, 191; and badge, I, 161; and Bible studies, II, 195; and break in communal evolution, I, 209; and Christian residents in ghetto, II, 296; and communal accounting, II, 65; and communal solidarity, I, 165; II, 69; and deputations to Rome, I, 305; and education, II, 205; III, 161; and law enforcement, I, 166; and rabbis, II, 67, 78; and synagogues I, 163; and taxation, I, 160; in various regions (Byzantium), I, 191; (France), I, 305; (Islam), I, 165–66; (Italy, southern), I, 231; (Resettlement areas), I, 252; records of, III, 73. *See also* Anti-Semitism; Expulsions; Massacres

Persia, Achaemenide: I, 70; III, 32; administration of, I, 58; (Jews in), I, 64; and Palestine's reconstruction, I, 74; and priestly tax immunity, I, 138; Aramaic language in, I, 71; communal patterns of, I, 116–17; decrees of, I, 63–64, 72; exilarchate in, I, 69; influences on Palestine of, I, 46; III, 149; minorities in, I, 64; rabbinic chronology of, I, 146; religious toleration in, I, 58; urban transformations under, III, 8

Sassanian: I, 27; III, 31; and Caliphate, I, 158; III, 36; and European community, I, 212; and non-Parsee churches, III, 36; Arab conquest of, I, 148, 173; communal trends in, I, 206–7, 228; difficulty of travel in, III, 23; economic regimentation in, I, 129; elimination of Hellenism from, I, 18; exilarchate in, I, 69, 146–47, 173–74, 177; (execution of), I, 173; (judges of), III, 31; guild system under, I, 364–65; heritage of, I, 157–58; influence on Jewish law of, I, 156, 211; rabbinic tax immunities in, II, 80; semi-feudalism of, I, 147–48; vs. Rome, I, 157. *See also* Zoroastrianism

Muslim: I, 148, 173; exilarchic supremacy in, I, 185

Personal: appearance at court, required by Jewish law, II, 237–38; principle, and medieval laws, I, 161–62; relations and funeral payments, II, 263; services, Jewish, and taxation, II, 267–68. *See also* Labor; taxes, and scholars' immunities, II, 277. *See also* Income taxes; Poll taxes; Property taxes; Tolls

Personalities, biblical, national influence of, III, 7

Personality, juristic: of medieval community; I, 108–9; II, 136; and interest payments, II, 269

Perugia: Jewish conference in, I, 320; III, 79; Toledan bookseller in, II, 201

Perushim, Palestinian congregation of, III, 217

"Perversion," Jewish, I, 112, 216

Pesaro, Jews of: and Azariah de' Rossi, I, 308; dancing master of, III, 206; excommunication of, II, 229; letter from Rome to, II, 233; III, 179, 218; officials' salaries among, II, 118

Pescennius Niger (Roman emperor), I, 129; III, 25

Pestilences: and changes in endowments, III, 189; and distant cemeteries, II, 149; and hospitals, III, 210–12; high mortality in Verona during, II, 17; in ancient Israel, I, 47; struggle against, II, 329–30. *See also* Illness; Sick

Petach Tikvah, municipality of, I, 17

Petaḥiah b. Jacob of Ratisbon: and Jewish education, III, 92; on eastern chiefs, I, 184, 186, 194

Petiḥah, writ of, II, 228. *See also* Excommunication

Petitions, Jewish, in England, I, 256–58

Petrification, communal: and modern stability, II, 121; dangers of, II, 167. *See also* Crystallization

Pews, in Alexandrian synagogue, I, 78

Peyrehorade (France): III, 62; early cemetery in, I, 264; II, 146–47; officials' salaries in, II, 118; Palestine messengers in, II, 342

Pfefferkorn, Johannes (Joseph): and Jewish synods, I, 314; controversy with Reuchlin of, I, 304

Pharisaism *and* Pharisees: against mutilation of criminals, II, 223; and doctrine of retaliation, II, 221; and education, I, 125; and Palestinian leadership, I, 140; modern heritage of, I, 156; separatism of, I, 135–36

Pharmacy *and* pharmacists, Jewish, III, 112, 140

Pharos (island), festival of, I, 82, 86

Philadelphia (Pa.), Jews of: I, 26; forced synagogue attendance in, II, 126–27

Philanthropic societies, *see* Associations, charitable

Philanthropy *and* philanthropists, Jewish: and moral compulsion, II, 348–49; and Palestine relief, II, 340–43; and synagogue records, II, 145; and tax exemptions, II, 275; and Torah summonses, II, 132. *See also* Charities; Donors

Philip II Augustus (French king), Jews under, I, 245–46, 251; III, 151

Philip le Bel (French king), Jews under III, 165

Philipp (Hessian landgraf), II, 246–47

Philippopolis, Jews in, III, 48

Philistines, and Israelitic monarchy, I, 35, 39

Philo Judaeus: and Hellenism, III, 25–26; and judiciary, III, 20; on Alexandrian quarters, III, 14–15; on charities, III, 25; on *'edah,* III, 15; on education, I, 92, 125; III, 16, 23; on elders, III, 17; (councils), I, 100; III, 17–18; on embassies, III, 19; on ethnarchs, III, 18, 31; on festivals, I, 86; III, 15; on Jewish worship, III, 16; on markets, I, 130; III, 25; on Onias temple, I, 79; on *phyle,* III, 14; on population, I, 78; on position of women, I, 96; III, 17; on synagogues, I, 86–87, 89

Philomène, on Narbonne *nasi,* III, 68

Philosophy *and* philosophers: Christian, differ on Jewish question, I, 216, 269; Islamic, and synagogues, I, 164. *See also* Religion

Jewish: and rabbinic dialectics, II, 183, 195; and Spanish chief rabbinates, I, 290; III, 66; new appreciation of, II, 363; protected by pope, I, 307–8; study of, in Poland, II, 192. *See also* Anti-Maimonidean controversy; Ethics; Literatures; *and under* respective philosophers

Phoenicia *and* Phoenicians, I, 55–56, 58, 64, 79, 83

Phrontistes, Jewish in Rome, I, 102. *See also* Financial administration

Phrygians, *politeuma* of, I, 76

Phylacteries, commandment of: III, 124; and licensed scribes, I, 102; II, 110; III, 140; donned by children, II, 198; neglected in Germany, II, 69

Phyle, Jewish, Egyptian, I, 71; III, 14

Physical: defects, and cantors, III, 136; exercises, neglected in Jewish schools, II, 197–98; weakness, and women slaughterers, II, 107

Physicians, Jewish: ancient, I, 120, 135; and chief rabbinates, I, 289–90, 293–94, 301; III, 67; and communal leadership, I, 135, 197, 304–5; II, 67; and education (foundations), I, 358; (Gentile teachers), II, 191; (night study), III, 162; and polygamy, II, 309; communal provisions for, II, 115, 117, 329; III, 140–41; in various regions (Germany), III, 212; (Islam), I, 159, 187–89; (Italy), I, 304–5; III, 162, 211–12; (Poland), I, 301; (Sicily), I, 293–94; II, 275; III, 67; (Spain), I, 289–90; (Turkey), I, 197; influence of, I, 187–89; taxes of, I, 159; (exemptions), II, 275. *See also* Hospitals; Medicine; Sanitation; Sick

Physiocratism, French, and growth of community, II, 364

Pi (Mibṭaḥiah's husband), III, 12

Piarists, Lithuanian, as communal creditors, II, 273

Piazza, Jewish, communal control of, II, 291

Picho, Joseph, assassination of, I, 239

Piedmont, Jews of: III, 203; at Padua conference, I, 321; *conservators* of, III, 68; meat sales of, II, 158–59; privileges of, and Jewish capital flight, III, 103; regional control of, II, 21–22. *See also under* respective cities

Piety *and* pietists, Jewish: ancient, Philo on, I, 89; and cantors, II, 104–5; and chief rabbinates, I, 291, 347; and growing severity, II, 212; and local judges, I, 202, 204; and *morenu* title, II, 190; and numerous prayers, II, 142; and Palestine messengers, II, 342; and scholarly control, II, 244; and slaughterers, II, 109–10; and symbols of mourning, II, 138; and visiting of graves, II, 154; excesses of, condoned, III, 172–73; medieval emphasis on, II, 362; of illiterates, respected, I, 136

Piła (Schneidemühl), real estate tax in, III, 188

Pilgrimages and pilgrims, Jewish: ancient, I, 120; and Palestine, I, 157–58; II, 341. *See also* Palestine relief; to cemeteries, II, 154; III, 156; (and regional allegiance), I, 283. *See also* Migrations

Pillory, exposure of, in Jewish legal procedure, II, 224

Pilpul, of cantors, II, 105. *See also* Dialectics

Pilsudski, Józef, I, 13

Pinaxes, II, 113. *See also* Minute-books

Pinczów: and Cracow chief rabbinate, I, 302; rabbinic contracts in, III, 131; statute of, on tax chest, III, 195

Pinḳasim, II, 113. *See also* Minute-books

Pińsk: as seat of Lithuanian Council, I, 328; chief rabbinate in, II, 87; elections in, II, 47; quota of charity brides in, II, 333; rights of settlement in, II, 22

Pinto, Isaac de, II, 18–19, 36

Pioneering, Western, and Jewish community, II, 363–66

Piotrków: Church council of, I, 220; Jewish burial society in, III, 90

Pirates: Jewish, occasional references to, II, 227; modern, and redemption of captives, II, 334–37

Pirḳe de-R. Eliezer, III, 18

Pirḳoi b. Baboi (Babylonian leader), I, 167

Pisa, Jews of: and Leghorn elections, II, 43; and Leghorn taxation, III, 102; and Venetian associations, I, 364; archives of, III, 102; conference among, III, 79; legacy for, III, 212

Pisa, Daniel da, constitution of, II, 20, 29; III, 109

Pisa, Yeḥiel Nissim da, and Bologna ordinance, III, 212

Pitḳa de-dayyanuta, I, 202

Pius II (pope), against sale of Jewish meat, II, 107–8, 158

Pius IV (pope), Jewish prisoners of, III, 214–15
Pius V (pope), application to, III, 199
Pius VI (pope), and Roman indebtedness, III, 190
Pius XI (pope), educational encyclical of, II, 170
Piyyuṭim: I, 192; and rise of *ḥazzan*, II, 100. *See also* Poetry
Plagiarism, avoidance of, and dialectics, III, 168
Plaintiffs, Jewish: allowed use of judicial intermediaries, II, 237–38; choice of courts by, II, 242
Planning, communal, today, I, 27
Pledges: of English slaughterers, formula of, II, 109; of parties, and medieval judiciary, II, 214
Plenipotentiaries, of female voters, II, 37. *See also* attorneys
Pletten: history of, II, 322–23; III, 209; property taxes for, II, 345. *See also* Tickets, communal
Płock, Jewish guilds in, I, 369
Plumbers, Jewish, Polish guilds of, I, 369
Plutocracy, *see* Oligarchy
Plymouth, Jewish community in, I, 259
Podole (Polish province): and Lwów chief rabbinate, I, 303; as member of Polish Council, III, 81
Padwojewoda, as judge of Jews, I, 271–72. *See also* Palatins
Poetry *and* poets: French, and German Jews, II, 192; German, Jewish participation in, II, 192

Hebrew: ancient Israelitic, I, 36; and Byzantine prohibitions, I, 192; and communal control, II, 76, 78; and desecration of cemeteries, II, 150; and exilarchs, III, 40; and preaching, II, 97–98; and Spanish massacres, I, 362; III, 93; feminine, II, 178–79. *See also* Liturgy
Pogłówne, II, 251. *See also* Poll tax
Pogroms, *see* Massacres
Poitou *and* Poitiers, Jews of: *III, 75*; and synod of Troyes, I, 312; cemeteries of, II, 149; III, 154
Polak, Jacob (Cracow chief rabbi), I, 271, 300; II, 69
Poland, Jews of: I, 13, 20; III, 6, 62–64, 191–92; and Bohemian controversies, I, 308; and capitalism, II, 352; and Frankfort Conference, I, 313; and German emigrés, I, 307; (transplantation of learning), III, 71; and Jewish unity, I, 227; and Palestine Ashkenazim, II, 342; (cabalists), III, 92; and Polish independence, II, 353–54; and Polish society, I, 267; (burghers), I, 278–81; (Christians at courts of), II, 239; III, 180; and Shabbetian movement, I, 308; and Soviet occupation, I, 17; appeal for support, I, 307; Ashkenazic Haggadah among, III, 149; ban of settlement among, I, 307; II, 6–8; III, 98; bi-sexual dancing among, II, 316; book trade of, II, 203–4; III, 171; burial societies of, I, 354; cantors' salaries among, II, 101–2; chief rabbis of, I, 300–3; citron administration of, II, 164–65; combination of offices among, II, 103; commercial instruments of, II, 301; communal indebtedness of, I, 271, 273–74; III, 190–91; communal stability of, II, 120; communal witnesses among, II, 113; constitutions of, II, 63–64; corruption among, II, 93–94, 247; costume of, II, 307; courts of appeal among, II, 241; Councils of Twenty-three of, II, 55; debt bondage of, II, 226; deputation to Rome from, I, 305; III, 72; early traditions of, II, 69; economic history of, III, 186; (of teachers), II, 184; educational attainments of, II, 173, 189; (boarding of students), II, 189;

(neglect of Bible), II, 193; (Padua students), III, 167; (teachers), II, 163–64, 183–85; elections among, II, 35, 40, 43; (corrupt), II, 93–94; (days), 116; (relatives), II, 40; growth of oligarchies among, I, 27–28; II, 50; guilds of, I, 364, 366, 369–73; II, 18, 88–89; III, 95–97; ḥasidic congregations among, I, 352; *ḥazaḳah* among, III, 199; historical remains of, III, 53; hospitality of, II, 324–25; influence on other countries of, II, 355; interruption of prayers among, II, 33–34; itinerant preachers among, II, 99; judiciary among, II, 88–89, 215; "king" among, I, 328; legal status of, III, 62–63; majority principle among, II, 27; marriage brokerage among, II, 319; III, 208–9; marriage quotas among, III, 98; meat sales of, II, 159–60; migrations of, I, 307; II, 331; III, 71; (and burial in Poland), III, 157; (and Lithuanian Council), II, 324; (mendicants), III, 209; (teachers and rabbis), II, 183, 188; III, 134, 163–64; mixed courts for, II, 116; oath of betrothed among, II, 315; partitions of, effects on, II, 354–55; III, 85; population of, I, 281; III, 108; prisons of, II, 226–27; rabbis of, II, 77; III, 123, 134; (control of academies), II, 95; (dialectics), II, 195; (salaries), II, 82–83; redemption of captives by, II, 335; III, 214; Reform projects for, III, 219; reverence for learning of, II, 94; rural settlements of, I, 281, 336; sanitary services of, II, 329–30; scribes of, II, 112; segregation of, demanded, I, 225; seizure of property of, II, 233; self-government of, I, *267–74*; (compared with Spain), I, 233; Sephardic ritual among, II, 142; sextons of, II, 106; sumptuary laws of, II, 302, 305–6; synagogues of, I, 220; (architecture), II, 137; III, 147; (endowments), II, 132; (forced attendance), II, 126; (new), III, 53; (seats), III, 145; taxation of, II, 204, 251–52, 258–61, 280, 348; III, 184; (communal conflicts on), II, 287, 289; (farmers of), II, 285; (funeral tolls), II, 263; (immunities), II, 278; (meat taxes), II, 108, 258–59; III, 186; (per capita load), III, 191; title holders among, II, 90–91; visitors at fairs from, II, 263; women's status among, III, 89; (charity overseers), II, 37. *See also* Councils, Polish; *and under* respective provinces and cities

Polemics, Christian, medieval, I, 216; III, 40

Police: II, 116, 291; (and talmudic law), III, 197. *See also* Communal control; governmental (and Cassel assembly), I, 341; (and variations in costume), II, 8; Prussian, and communal control, II, 358–59

Policies, deeds of, and communal ledger, II, 112

Polis, Greek, and Maimonidean *Medinah*, III, 160–61

Polish congregations: in Amsterdam, elections of, III, 117; unite with German, III, 145. *See also* Ashkenazic congregations

Politeuma, Jewish community as, I, 76–77, 100; III, 19

Political theory, Jewish, medieval, II, 217; III, 174

Politics *and* political status: I, 22, 27–28; II, 121; ancient Palestinian, I, 31, 36; and Antiochus Epiphanes, I, 83; and capital punishment, II, 222; and charities, I, 360; II, 349; and Christianity, I, 8; and communal rights, I, 28, 98, 119; II, 121; and education, II, 190, 199, 205; and exilarchate, I, 207; and Iberian toleration, I, 241; and manipulations of assemblies, II, 25; and Oriental Jewry, III, 38; and Palestinian city, I, 31; and Polish councils, I, 331; and public law, II, 217; of Spanish exiles, I, 204; and synods, I, 310, 313

Politikon archeion, I, 93. *See also* Archives

Poll taxes, Jewish: ancient, medieval heritage of, II, 250; and Christians, I, 170–71; III, 32; and class divisions, II, 278–79; and community (collections), I, 273; (compromises), II, 280; (debts), I, 335; and councils, I, 320, 325; and population figures, III, 184–85; and tax defaults, I, 148; in various regions (France), III, 185; (Germany), III, 185; (Islam), I, 159–60, 170–72, 202; (Italy), I, 320; (Persia), I, 148; III, 32; (Poland), I, 269, 273, 329, 335; II, 87; III, 34; (Spain), II, 248–49; rabbis' influence on, I, 102; II, 87; (immunities), II, 277; III, 34

Polycharmos, Claudios Tiberios, III, 15

Polygamy: and Bustanai's succession, I, 177; communal regulations against, II, 307–10; III, 203

Pomerium, Roman, and synagogues, III, 14

Ponentine congregation, Venice: Palestine relief in, II, 344; provision for brides in, III, 213

Pontifical state, *see* Papal States

Pontius Maximus, homily of, I, 96

Poor, Jewish: ancient rabbis as, I, 135; and billeting of soldiers, III, 189; and sumptuary laws, II, 302; III, 201; and taxation, II, 246, 250–52, 278–79; III, 196; charitable burial of, II, 264; data on, III, 218; departure of, encouraged, II, 16–17; education of children of, II, 114, 169, 173, 175; III, 164; invade house of renitent contributor, II, 349; questionable reduction by charities of, II, 347; right to charities of, I, 131, 361; II, 344, 347–49; share in communal administration of, II, 27–28; supported by Jewish community alone, II, 347. *See also* Begging; Charities; Donors; Philanthropy; Pletten

Popper, Joachim, expulsion from Prague of, II, 298–99

Popularity: of cantors, II, 105; of preachers, Talmud on, II, 99; of rabbinic dialectics, shortcomings of, II, 195; of sextons, II, 106

Population, Israelitic: I, 31–32, 37, 40; III, *6*, 10; and Assyrian invasions, I, 50; and cities, I, 34, 43–44; III, 8; and oligarchy, I, 43–44; III, 9; proportion of *gerim* in, III, 9

Jewish, ancient: and cities, III, 27; and Palestinian Greeks, I, 134; and returning exiles, I, 74; III, 11; and rise of Christianity, I, 117; censuses of, I, 159; in various regions (Alexandria), I, 93; (Babylonia), I, 118–19; (Dura), I, 92; (Egypt), I, 75, 78; (Elephantine), I, 72; (Palestine), I, 74, 118–19, 134; III, 11; (Rome), I, 80–81; (Seleucide Empire), I, 82

medieval and modern: I, 26; II, 23–24; III, *106–10*; and cemeteries, I, 284; II, 147, 152–53; and citrons, II, 164; and collegiate bodies, II, 62; and combination of offices, II, 103; and communal cohesiveness, I, 20, 27, 55; II, 352; and congregational membership, I, 68, 350; and crowding of hospices, III, 210; and education, II, 114; (Soviet schools), I, 15; (teachers) II, 184; and elections, II, 43; and expansion of Islam, I, 157; and expulsions, I, 247, 281; and height of synagogues, II, 139; and guilds, I, 366–67, 369; and housing shortage, II, 292; and judiciary, II, 72–73, 82; and lay preponderance, II, 68; and meat sales, II, 159; and migrations,

II, 337–38, 357; and mortality, II, 17; and plenary assembly, I, 344; II, 121; III, 106; and polygamy, II, 308; and poverty, III, 218; and private worship, II, 125; and provincial rabbinate, I, 302; and quorum at weddings, III, 46; and scholarly control, II, 244; and support of brides, II, 332; and synagogues, I, 5–6; and taxation, I, 171, 273, 316–17, 329; II, 108, 249–50, 259, 276, 288; III, 184–85; and tenant protection, II, 295; and three-class system, II, 38; and Zechariah of Porto's will, III, 212; concentration of, I, 261; in various regions (Alsace), II, 117; III, 141; (Altona), III, 107, 218; (America), I, 6, 261; III, 3; (Amsterdam), III, 108; (Augsburg), III, 107; (Avignon), III, 106–7; (Bagdad), I, 184; (Berlin), III, 107; (Bologna), III, 107–8; (Constantinople), I, 195; (Egypt), I, 189; (England), I, 258–59; II, 249–50; III, 106; (Erfurt), III, 107; (France), III, 106, 108, 132; (Frankfort), III, 108; (Germany), II, 38, 62; III, 69; (Hesse-Cassel), I, 341; (Hildesheim), III, 107; (Islam), I, 157, 159, 171, 184, 189; III, 46; (Italy), I, 231, 320; II, 201; III, 108, 212; (Karlsruhe), III, 107; (Kleve), I, 344; (Lithuania), III, 108, 210; (Lodz), III, 108; (Mantua), II, 30; (Mayence), III, 107; (Metz), III, 108; (New York), I, 6; (Nuremberg), III, 107; (Orléans), III, 132; (Poland), I, 273, 302, 329, 334; III, 108; (Prague), III, 107; (Prussia) II, 359; (Ratisbon), III, 111; (Rome), III, 108, 218; (Sicily), I, 316–17; (Spain-Portugal), I, 232, 238; II, 58, 72–73, 82, 159, 334; III, 34, 108; (Venice), III, 107; (Verona), III, 107; (Vienna), III, 199; (Worms), III, 107

Portaleone, Samuel, on games of chance, III, 207

Portella, Ismael de (Aragonese chief rabbi), I, 290

Porters, Jewish, sales taxes on revenue of, II, 261

Porto, Moses b. Yeḥiel di, and Rovigo bath, III, 160

Porto, Zechariah b. Ephraim di, will of, II, 332; III, 212–13

Portsmouth, Jewish community in, I, 259

Portugal, medieval: III, 53; and Christian witnesses, I, 240–41; and Marranos, I, 24, 305; associations in, III, 89; burghers' attitude to Jews in, I, 278–79; discourages Jewish emigration, I, 234; expulsions from, and vested interests, II, 120; growth of professional rabbinate in, II, 73–75; Jewish hierarchy in, II, 74; (chief rabbinate), I, 285–86; III, 71; legislation on Jewish community of, I, 232, 234–36, 238, 240–41; meat sales of, II, 159; respects courts of defendants, I, 240; suppression of Hebrew deeds in, II, 111; tax law in, I, 241. *See also under* respective cities

Portuguese congregations in exile: and evolution of rabbinate, II, 75; and marriage with Ashkenazim, II, 365; in Amsterdam, I, 253; III, 58; in Bordeaux (and wine exports), II, 163–64; in Hamburg (and Shabbetian movement), II, 25–26; (censorship in), III, 170; (share in meat taxes), III, 138; in Nice, II, 19; in Salonica, I, 351; (rabbinic control), II, 75; in southern France, I, 262–64; in Turkey, and local associations, I, 348, 350–51; in Venice, and redemption of captives, II, 335. *See also* Sephardim; Spanish exiles; Spanish-Portuguese congregations

Possession: of Hebrew books, danger of, I, 223; of ritual meat, local ordinances on, III, 138

Postal system, Jewish, II, 115; III, 141
Potestas, reshut as, I, 128
Pottery, and non-ritual meat, II, 110
Poznań (city), Jews of: III, *120*, 132, 197; against alien mendicants, II, 325; III, 209; and councils, I, 300, 303, 324–25, 332, 336–37, 345; III, 97; and excommunication of entire community, II, 229; and hours of study, II, 176; anti-Maimonidean controversy in, III, 71–72; blood accusation of, I, 303; communal examiners of, II, 197; communal debts of, I, 334–35; II, 273, 353; III, 83, 191; deputies from, II, 116; elections of, II, 45, 56; enlightened movements in, III, 131; expulsions of "aliens" by, I, 325, 332–33; II, 6; III, 209; forced to purchase Helicz books, II, 204; formula of ban by, III, 177; guilds of, I, 369, 371; marriage quotas of, III, 98; physicians among, III, 140; rabbis of, II, 92; (at supreme court), I, 325; (chief rabbis), I, 271, *300–3*; II, 83; (non-native), I, 333; III, 100, 132; records of, III, 81, 98; rulers' ordinances on, I, 270; *shtadlanim* of, III, 141; sumptuary laws of, II, 306; supported by Italian charities, I, 333; taxation of, II, 252; III, 186
Poznań (province), Jews of: council of, I, 300, 303, 324, 332; II, 83; guilds of, III, 97. *See also* Greater Poland; *and under* respective cities
Practice: daily, and talmudic studies, II, 207; vs. theory, in reverence for scholars, II, 180
Praefectura honoraria, of Palestinian patriarchs, I, 144–45
Praetorian generals, Roman, I, 45
Pragmaticas, Italian, texts of, II, 301, 304; III, 201. *See also* Sumptuary laws
Prague, Jews of: and Bohemian Council, I, 339–40; and Frankfort Conference, I, 341; and Josel of Rosheim, I, 299; architects among, III, 147; at local university, III, 167; bans of, III, 178; cemetery of, II, 153; III, 155; (successive layers), III, 155; charities of, III, 209; confiscation of books of, III, 134; controversy with Horowitz of, I, 308–9; education of, III, 161; (hours of study), II, 176; III, 162; (reforms), II, 190; elections among, II, 35, 94; guilds of, II, 89; III, 134; importation of Vienna garments to, II, 297; in Breslau, III, 141; judicial minute-books of, III, 173; orphan asylum of, III, 212; population of, II, 23; III, 107; preachers of, III, 134; prison of, II, 226; III, 176; rabbis of, I, 339–40; II, 94; III, 134; (chief rabbis), II, 52, 81, 89; III, *85–86*; (contracts), III, 131; (salaries), III, 127–28; sex morality of, III, 205–6; sumptuary ordinances of, III, 201; suppress prostitution, II, 314; synagogues of, II, 130; (private), I, 352; talmudic tractates ordered from, II, 95; scholars' tax immunities among, III, 194; tenants' responsibility among, III, 199; three-class system among, III, 114; youth burial society of, III, 90. *See also* Chief rabbinate; Councils
Prayer shawl, bequest of, II, 329
Prayer-books, Jewish: and new prayers, II, 142; Castilian expurgation of, I, 237. *See also* Censorship; compiled by geonim, III, 42; illumination of, II, 138; Polish Council on, II, 203; printing of, III, 142, 170–71; spread of, and position of cantors, II, 102
Prayers, *see* Liturgy
Preaching *and* preachers, Christian: II, *95–100*; III, *133–35*; among Jews, I, 96, 219; III, 135; and medieval

anti-Semitism, III, 77; conversionist, I, 219; III, 53, 135; (enforced attendance), I, 260; II, 53; (Sicilian exemption), I, 317; (southern chief rabbis), I, 290, 295

Jewish, ancient: I, 53, 59, 89, 103; and Bible, III, 21–22; and burial societies, I, 353; and Christian listeners, I, 112; and class divisions, I, 119; and exilarchs, I, 155; and patriarchs, I, 142, 155; and synagogue ritual, I, 122; and support of scholars, I, 139; communal position of, I, 122–23, 126, 140; itinerary of, III, 22–23; popularity of, II, 99

medieval and modern: II, 76, *94–100*; III, 133–35; against luxuries, III, 201; against tax evasions, III, 196; and cantors, I, 200–1; II, 105; and charities, III, 218; and class distinctions, II, 27; and communal appointments, III, 74; and congregational divisions, III, 89; and corrupt elections, II, 93; and denunciation of criminals, III, 179–80; and education, II, 181–82, 188; III, 163; (adult), II, 206; (night study), III, 162; and fee system, II, 83, 85; and libraries, II, 202; and mourning for leaders, II, 147; III, 153; and Palestine relief, II, 341–42; and rabbis (censures), II, 99; (demotion), III, 130; (tenure), II, 86; and sex relationships, II, 312; and synagogue decorum, II, 140–41; and teaching positions, II, 114; in various regions (Islam), I, 200–1; (Italy), II, 76–77, 118; (Poland), II, 93; (Spain), II, 78, 82; itinerant, I, 122; II, 97, 206; (accusations), II, 323; (billeting), II, 323; (transportation costs), II, 324; lay, II, 77, 98; protect women, II, 318; salaries for, II, 82, 118; and students' attendance at, I, 360; Valladolid synod on, II, 73. *See also* Obituary sermons

Precedents, legal: and communal self-government, II, 217; and constitutional law, I, 268; II, 217, 219; and court sessions, II, 211; and Gentile ordinances, I, 215, 268; and inquiries from academies, I, 180–81; and legal advances, II, 209; and ritual slaughtering, II, 107; and scholars' salaries, I, 181; binding force of, I, 128, 165; II, 244; created by timid decisions, II, 213; in ancient Israel, I, 39; use of, I, 93; II, 236

Precentors, *see Ḥazzan*

Precious stones, rabbinic discourses likened to, II, 99

Precocity, Jewish, social advantages of, II, 198

Pre-emption, right of, and synagogue seats, II, 131; III, 145

Preissler, Wolfgang (Prague Jesuit), II, 98

Přemysl II Ottokar (Bohemian king), privilege of, I, 267

Presbyteros, meaning of, I, 99; III, 13

Presbyters, Jewish: II, 55, 76; Justinian's threats against, II, 52. *See also* Chief rabbinate; Elders

President of the United States, I, 45

Pressburg, rabbis of, II, 90

Pressure groups, communal, and tax exemptions, II, 275

Prestige: of Church, and ritual meat, II, 158; of schools, II, 180

Prevention: doctrine of, and criminal law, II, 221, 224; individual cooperation in, II, 235

Price control, communal: I, 130–31; II, 300–1; III, 200; and guilds, I, 370; and municipal price fixing, II, 301; and wine administration, II, 163; of citrons, II, 164; of fish, II, 161; of meat, II, 157–59, 258. *See also*

Communal control; Economic regulation

Prices: of books and teachers' salaries, II, 200; of captives, II, 336; of ritual vs. non-ritual meat, II, 157–58, 258

Priesthood and priests: Canaanite, I, 41; Catholic, and church decorum, III, 151. *See also* Church; Clergy

Israelitic: and Aaronides, I, 60–61; and cantors, III, 136; and class struggle, I, 50; and Exilic community, I, 54, 59–60, 65; III, 12; and monarchy, I, 35; and Mosaic tradition, I, 49; and prophets, I, 45; at local sanctuaries, I, 40–41, 45, 49; (disestablished), I, 52–53; III, 12; influence of, I, 53, 117; slaves of, I, 46

Jewish, ancient: and Ezra, I, 64; and laymen, III, 12; and marriage with proselytes, I, 97; and synagogue honors, I, 97, 124; III, 17; decline of, I, 28, 119; in Egypt, I, 79, 89; (Elephantine), I, 71–72; purity of, I, 72; tax exemptions of, I, 138; Theodosian Code on, III, 15

medieval and modern: and Bible recitation, I, 189; genealogy of, III, 42; honorary position of, III, 42. *See also* Kohen; Levites

Priestly blessing, I, 97, 104, 121–22; III, 136–37

Priestly Code: I, 60–61; on *nasi*, I, 141; terminology of, III, 10. *See also* Bible; Pentateuch

Primogeniture, in Islam, I, 178

"Prince," Jewish, Ezekiel's constitution on, III, 12. *See also* Nasi

"Prince of captivity," *see* Exilarchate

"Prince of Spanish captivity," chief rabbi as, I, 289

Princes: in ancient Israel, I, 44; communal mourning for, II, 147. *See also* Aristocracy

Princess, Persian, as Bustanai's wife, I, 177

Principles of Judaism, and feminine education, II, 178

Printing *and* printers, Hebrew: III, *170–71*; and associational statutes, I, 356; and cantors, II, 102; and censorship, I, 223; and Christian printers, II, 204; and circulating libraries, II, 202; and interterritorial competition, II, 203; and prayers, II, 142–44; and preaching, II, 96; and regulated studies, II, 95; and teachers' control, II, 180; and women, II, 178; III, 163; Ferrara resolution on, I, 321; influence on Jewish culture of, III, 170; Polish, and councils, I, 325, 331. *See also* Books; Censorship

Priorities, judicial, regulation of, II, 236–37

Priscianus (Roman official), I, 142

Prisons *and* prisoners, Jewish: II, 226–27; III, 176; ancient Israelitic, I, 49; and communal discipline, III, 144; and communal indebtedness, II, 273; III, 84; and elders' responsibility, I, 171; II, 52–53, 64, 273; and exilarchs, III, 41; and French Revolution, III, 24; and funeral tolls, II, 154; and *ḥakam-bashis*, I, 196; and judiciary (lay), II, 70–71; (mixed courts), I, 272; (writ of), II, 227; and Meir of Rothenburg, III, 70; and *negidim*, I, 191, 203; and modern penitentiaries, III, 215; and Portuguese chief rabbis, I, 236, 285; and private worship, III, 144; and redemption of captives, II, 338; and Sabbath observance, I, 236; III, 55; and school attendance, II, 199; and suicides, III, 157; and tax defaulters, I, 171; II, 219, 284, 286; communal attitudes to, III, 214; in various regions (Germany), III, 70; (Islam), I, 191, 203; III, 41; (Leipzig), II, 154; (Poland), I, 272; II, 64; III, 84; (Portugal), I, 236, 285;

(Poznań), II, 273; (Spain), I, 236; II, 70–71; III, 55; (Turkey), I, 196; surveillance of, II, 226. *See also* Criminal law; Penalties

Privacy, lack of, and tax evasions, II, 288

Private: initiative, capitalistic, and communal control, II, 361; life, and moral laws, II, 307

ownership: and judicial discretion, II, 245; and synagogue seats, II, 130; of endowments, and tax exemptions, II, 275. *See also* Property, private

Privileges, Jewish, ancient: I, 12, 76; and *patrios nomos*, I, 145; collections of, I, 93; negative character of, I, 107; revoked by Justinian, I, 229

medieval and modern: and diplomatic agents, II, 116; and funerals, I, 284; and holidays, I, 236; and lay preponderance, II, 68; and meat sales, II, 158–59, 258; and membership rights, I, 246; and property qualifications, II, 38; and taxation, I, 319; II, 246, 286; and term *ḥerem*, III, 179; *de non tolerandis Christianis*, I, 280; (vs. *de non tolerandis Judaeis*), I, 276, 278, 280–1; III, 99; enormous variety of, I, 248; fictitious nature of, I, 278

promulgated in various regions: Aragon, (against government intervention), II, 102; (on Jewish settlement), III, 100; England, and cities, I, 276; France, and Narbonne *nasi*, III, 68; Germany, I, 267, 278; II, 78; III, 78; (cities), III, 64; Islam, unclarified, I, 165; Italy, texts of, III, 158; (and equality of rights), I, 231–32; Lithuania, Disne's exception from, I, 280; Papal States, I, 217–18, 319; Poland, II, 270–71, 280–81; III, 99; (and councils), I, 324-25, 329–30; II, 22; (and free elections), I, 325; (and non-native rabbis), I, 333; (and taxation), II, 160; (German models for), I, 267; Sicily (and assemblies), I, 316–18; (and chief rabbinate), I, 294–95; (and lay leadership), II, 76, 102; (and tax equality), II, 249; Spain, I, 236; (and associations), I, 362; (and communal banishment), II, 9–10; (and communal indebtedness), II, 271–72; (and ecclesiastical censures), II, 14; (and judiciary), I, 239; II, 241; (and land taxes), II, 253; (and rabbis), II, 68; (and regional communities), I, 286–87; (and search warrants), II, 227; (and tax immunities), II, 13–14. *See also* Decrees; Law; Legal Status; Monarchy

Procedure, legal, Jewish: II, *236–43*; III, *180–82*; ancient, I, 39, 127; and calendar regulation, I, 143; and courts of arbitration, II, 215; and family life, II, 319; and illiteracy of witnesses, II, 114; and lay judiciary, II, 214–15; and Mantua Conference, III, 80; and Polish Council, I, 329; and private excommunication, II, 75; attempts at expediting of, II, 215, 236; foreign influences on, I, 211; II, 223–25; neglected for compromises, II, 237; Palestinian, and diaspora crimes, II, 220; records of, I, 93; relative mildness of, II, 235; scribes' position in, II, 110. *See also* Attorneys; Judiciary; Law; Litigations; Oaths; Parties; Witnesses

Muslim, and tax frauds, I, 171

Processions: Catholic, Jewish attendance at, II, 53; (papal), III, 52; Jewish, I, 86. *See also* Funeral processions

Proclamations in private synagogues, obligatory, III, 144

Procreation, duty of, and age discrepancy in marriage, III, 204

Procuradores: Christian, of Castilian Jewry, III, 155; Jewish, of Lisbon, III, 65

Procuratores, royal, of Jews, I, 295. *See also* Conservators

Procureur général, for Provençal Jewry, I, 296

Production, changing methods of: and charitable societies, I, 360; and communal control, II, 361; and Jewish migrations, II, 357; guild regulation of, I, 366; of books, II, 201. *See also* Manuscripts; Printing; of ritual wine, II, 162

Profane use of cemeteries, prohibited by Jewish law, III, 156

Profession of faith, Christian, and Marrano communities, I, 252

Professionalization of learning: and opposition to, I, 126; III, 41–42; and tax immunities, II, 80, 277; of judiciary, I, 128; of rabbis II, 78, 277; III, 100; (against preachers), II, 99; of slaughterers, II, 108; of teachers, I, 128; II, 182

Professions, hereditary in Elephantine, I, 72–73. *See also* Occupational; *and under* respective occupations

Profit: and hours of study, II, 176; vs. capital value, in communal taxation, II, 260

Programs, educational, *see* Curricula

Progressivism of Jewish law, and communal control, II, 168

Proletarian nationalism, Jewish, modern, III, 3–4

Proletariat, Roman, ancient, Jews among, I, 80

Pronunciation, of cantors, controversies over, II, 105

Propaganda: Christian, anti-Jewish arguments of, I, 216. *See also* Anti-Semitism; Apologetics; Mission; Karaite, and communal unrest, I, 166–67; Muslim, and trade associations, I, 365; Shabbetian, and religious associations, I, 355

Property, communal, ancient: I, 43; administrators of, I, 102; and Roman law, I, 108–10

medieval and modern: academies' accumulation of, I, 180; and destruction of synagogues, I, 165; and juristic personality, II, 136; and Muslim law, I, 161; III, 38; confiscation of, for tax frauds of elders, I, 171; destroyed by expulsion, I, 362; II, 186–87, 271. *See also* Financial administration

private: and charitable tithes, II, 344–45; (bequests), III, 218; and desertion of husbands, II, 317; and franchise, I, 98; II, 29, 38–40; III, 114–15. *See also* Three-class system; and freedom of movement, I, 234, 245; II, 16; III, 104; and judiciary, II, 215; and payment for citrons, III, 187; and *Pletten*, II, 322; and redemption of captives, II, 336; confiscation of, II, 233–34; III, 25; (and excommunication), I, 246; (and worship), I, 263; literary, communal protection of, II, 202–3; lost (after conversion), I, 247; (for Persian tax defaults), I, 148; protected by legislation, I, 218, 282; of illiterates, under Islam, I, 166; safeguarding of, and taxation, I, 137; seizure of, II, 233. *See also* Seizure of property; Torah's compassion with, II, 212–13. *See also* Private ownership

Property taxes, Jewish: II, 252–54; III, 185–86; and aliens, III, 188; and communal loans, II, 270; and exemption of poor, II, 252; and exilarchs, I, 175; and franchise, II, 38; and *Pletten*, II, 322; and purchase of citrons, III, 160; and scholars' tax immunities, II, 277; downward progression in, II, 279; in various regions

(Germany), II, 251; III, 185; (Islam), I, 172, 175; (Italy), I, 320; (Poland), III, 188; (Spain), II, 248–49; methods of assessment of, II, 281–83; unbearable rates of, II, 255–56; vs. *per capita* distribution, II, 279–80; III, 194. *See also* Taxation

Prophets, Israelitic: and local sanctuaries, I, 49; and monarchy, I, 35–37, 40; and popular assemblies, III, 9; and provincials, III, 7–8; and sex ethics, II, 313; and social unrest, I, 35–36, 47, 50; and synagogue, I, 61; idea of justice of, I, 129–30; in Babylonian Exile, I, 59, 65; "true" vs. "false," I, 36–37; writings of, I, 52; (enforced acquisition of), I, 120; (in liturgy), I, 74, 120, 122; II, 193

Proportional representation, absent from communal elections, II, 43. *See also* Elections

Prosecuting attorneys: absence in Jewish community of, II, 235; in Polish courts, I, 272. *See also* Attorneys

Proselytes, Jewish: and *connubium* with priests, I, 97; descent from, I, 134, 193; passive franchise of, II, 286; position in synagogue of, I, 97; III, 36. *See also* Conversion to Judaism; Semi-proselytes

Proseuché, I, 77, 84, 86; meaning of, III, 15–16. *See also* Synagogues

Prosperity, economic: and communal cohesiveness, II, 352, 356; and welfare budgets, II, 349–50. *See also* Wealth

Prossnitz (Moravia), Jewish interior decorators in, III, 147–48

Prostitutes, Jewish: betrothal of, III, 205; communal regulations on, II, 314; III, 205–6. *See also* Sex morality

"Protected Jews": in Altona, few poor among, III, 218; in Prussia, enforced communal allegiance of, II, 358–59

"Protection money," *see* Schutzgeld

Protection, royal, medieval, and Jewish taxation, I, 281; III, 107. *See also* Law; Privileges; Serfdom, Jewish

Protectors, male, of Jewish women, required, II, 314

Protestantism, *see* Churches, Protestant

Proti, *see* Elders

Provençal congregation in Salonica, II, 96

Provençale, David, appeals for Jewish college, II, 191

Provençale, Jacob b. David, on status of teachers, III, 164

Provence, Jews of: III, 67–68; cabalistic conventicles of, I, 354; III, 91; *conservateurs* of, I, 295–96; III, 68; interruption of prayers by, II, 33; rabbinic responsa of, III, 176; study of general sciences by, II, 191; teachers' position among, II, 117. *See also* France, southern; *and under* respective cities

Proverbs, medieval: on poverty of teachers, II, 184; on taxation, II, 247

Provinces, Palestinian, importance of, I, *34–41*, 53; III, 7–8

Provincial elders: German, salaries of, III, 122–23; Kleve, and residence rights, II, 119–20; Lithuanian (and redemption of captives), II, 335; (and rights of settlement), II, 6–7; Moravian (and elections), II, 41–43; (and rabbis), II, 85, 89–90; (property qualifications of), II, 40; Münster, I, 345; Spanish, fees for election of, II, 36; under Islam, I, *187–94*; vs. central authorities, I, 206. *See also* Councils; Elders; Regional control

Provincial rabbis, *see* Chief rabbinate

Provincialism, Lithuanian, and Polish hospitality, II, 324–25. *See also* Anti-alien bias; Ban of settlement

Prussia, Jews of: I, 18; III, 219–20; and Kleve assembly, I, 343–44; and Polish Jews, II, 354–55; III, 85, 108, 131, 188; and prohibition of *'alenu*,

III, 150; bans of, II, 232, 312; III, 178; charity administration of, II, 348; III, 218; communal debts of, I, 337; II, 356; communal legislation of, I, 352; II, 354–55, 358–59; family relations of, II, 210–11; leadership of, II, 363; III, 119; private synagogues of, III, 142; rabbinate of, II, 91, 93–94; residence rights of, II, 270–71; III, 98; secession from community of, III, 5; southern and new-eastern, III, 85; taxes of, II, 108, 280; III, 188. *See also under* respective cities

Przemyśl, Jews of: III, *53*; as members of Polish Council, I, 336; III, 81; control dependent settlements, II, 22; guilds of, I, 369, 371; judicial minute books of, III, 173

Przykahałki, controlled by regional communities, II, 22. *See also* Regional control

Psalms *and* psalmists, Israelitic: I, 36, 42; III, 7, 11; and depths of synagogues, II, 139; in Babylonian Exile, I, 60; in Jewish liturgy, I, 74, 122; (and "ten men of leisure"), II, 127; types of, III, 13. *See also* Bible

Psammetichus I (Egyptian king), I, 69

Psammetichus II (Egyptian king), I, 69

Psephisma, I, 100

Psychological factors, and artistic creativity, II, 137

Psychology, medieval, and historic continuity, II, 216

Ptolemies (dynasty): I, 75–76; and local government, III, 18; censuses under, I, 159; totalitarian economy under, I, 105–6

Ptolemy V Epiphanius [?] (Egyptian king), I, 77

Ptolemy, son of Epikydos, I, 77

Publicans: ancient oriental, III, 7; Israelitic, apparent absence of, III, 7. *See also* Tax-farming

Public charges: and educational responsibilities, II, 169, 172; and settlement rights, II, 11; and tax exemptions, II, 38–39, 251; and wandering scholars, II, 187; in Alsace, II, 117; influence on elections by, II, 39; "ten men of leisure" as, II, 127. *See also* Begging; Charities; Poor

charities, modern growth of, I, 363. *See also* Charities; education, evolution of, II, 170–77. *See also* Education; Responsibility; finance, communal, II, *246–89*; III, *183–97*. *See also* Financial administration

law, Jewish: II, 216–19; III, 23, 173–74; and lay judiciary, II, 88; and local associations, I, 349; and Moravian chief rabbinate, I, 338; and Palestine messengers, II, 343; community as organ of, II, 363; supremacy of social interest in, II, 245; vs. Gentile, I, 215; vs. voluntary allegiance, I, 12, 19, *21–27*, 374; II, 351; III, 19–20. *See also* Constitutions; Ordinances; Statutes

office, Jewish, proselytes' eligibility to, II, 286. *See also* Bureaucracy; *and under* respective offices

opinion, Gentile: and bi-sexual dancing, II, 316; and cutting of hair, III, 203; and mendicancy, III, 219; and mourning for leaders, III, 153; and tax-farming, II, 285; Graeco-Roman, I, 108; (and desecration of sanctuaries), I, 88; (and Sabbath), I, 110

opinion, Jewish: and allegiance, I, 25, 29; and communal indebtedness, I, 337; and diverse procedural laws, II, 243; and effectiveness of penalties, II, 235; and interruption of prayers, II, 33; and judiciary, II, 209, 218; III, 180; and juridical strictness, III, 172–73; and moralistic sermons, II, 97, 99–100, 105; and

private excommunication, II, 79; and rabbinic authority, I, 347; and *shtadlanim*, I, 188; and synagogue ancestry, II, 130; and tax evasions, II, 288; as source of law, II, 245. *See also* Constitutions; Law; Statutes
order: communal responsibility for, II, 223, 291; (and judiciary), I, 249; state responsibility for, I, 282; II, 220. *See also* Criminal law; Massacres
school, and Jewish education, II, 171; III, 161. *See also* Education; Schools; works, Jewish participation in, II, 267. *See also* Labor
Publicists, Jewish: I, 29; and redemption of captives, II, 334
Polish, on Jewish communal reform, II, 353–54
Publicity: and marriage quorum, I, 196; as checks to wrongdoings, I, 166
"Public's messenger," *see* Ḥazzan
Publishing *and* publishers, Hebrew: and women, III, 163; communal protection of, I, 331; II, 202–3. *See also* Book trade; Copyright
Pumbedita, academy of: I, 152, 179–81; III, 33; and Bagdad bankers, I, 183; and Sura, I, 183; exilarch as gaon of, III, 41; imitates Palestine, I, 193; *maḥzor* from, III, 41; recitation of Decalogue at, III, 22. *See also* Academies
Punishment and crime, doctrine of, II, 221. *See also* Criminal law; Penalties
Purification of sins, and flogging, II, 225
Purim: and vows for cantors, II, 103; charitable collections on, I, 363; II, 12, 321, 345; III, 210; games during, II, 317; masquerades on, II, 316; III, 207
"Purim Syracuse," in Salonica, II, 53
Puritanism, Jewish: and co-education, II, 177–78; and Prague ordinance, II, 314; and sex relationships, II, 312; and theater, III, 207
Purity, laws of: I, 72; in Diaspora, I, 97; Levitical, and Jerusalem societies, III, 90
Purpose of punishment, lack of clarity in, II, 220–21
Pursuer, Jewish, capital punishment of, II, 221
Pyrenees, I, 242

QUADRENNIAL DIET, Polish, and Jewish question, I, 337; II, 354; III, 219
Quakers, legal position of, I, 261
Qualifications: of teachers, evidence for, III, 164–65; of judges, II, 95
Quality of production, Jewish, medieval regulation of, I, 366. *See also* Production
Quarantine: of lepers, in cemeteries, III, 155; of tax assessors, II, 287
Quarta pauperum, ecclesiastical, I, 360
Quarters, Jewish: ancient, I, 85–86; III, 14–15; (in Alexandria), I, 93–94; III, 14–15; (in Rome), I, 80–81; (of Palestinian craftsmen), I, 364; and craftsmen, I, 364, 368; and economic regulation, II, 291; and houses of ill-repute, II, 313; and judiciary, I, 239; and location of cemeteries, II, 149–50; and military service, II, 267; and oriental foreign quarters, I, 161; and outside political conflicts, I, 282; and real estate registers, III, 63; and tax evasions, II, 288; architecture of, II, 294; III, 154; banishment from, II, 9; child conversions in, I, 222–23; class divisions in, I, 353; III, 114; conflagrations in, II, 293; court sessions in, I, 272; crowdedness of, II, 205, 295; eastern vs. western, I, 161, 209; elections in, I, 330; II, 44; gates of, II, 116, 291; (guards), II, 291; III, 141; Gentiles in, II, 295–96; in various regions (Bari), I, 279; (Breslau synod), I, 225;

(Constantinople), I, 195, 229; (Frankfort), II, 150; (Germany), III, 154; (Islam), I, 161; (Italy), II, 291–92, 294; III, 197, 207; (Poland), I, 225, 272, 330; II, 234; III, 140; (Prague), I, 339; (Rome, papal), I, 222–23, 291–92; (Sicily), II, 44; (Spain), I, 239; II, 9, 329; III, 211; ordinances of, II, 116, 291–92; III, 197; overcrowded hospices in, II, 327; propaganda for, I, 225, 279; resemble cities, I, 283; residence in, II, 234, 296; reverence for learning in, II, 94; sex morality in, II, 312; theaters in, III, 207; tragedies of, III, 140; walls of, resemble city walls, I, 283. *See also* Segregation

"Queen Sabbath," and religious associations, I, 355

Quinquennial division, in Palestinian education, III, 161

Quorum: at assemblies, requirements of, II, 26; at Palestinian academies, I, 151; at weddings, regulation of, I, 196; III, 46–47; of synagogue, I, 155; (exclusion from), I, 169; (forced attendance), II, 126–27; (and "ten men of leisure"), II, 127

Quotas for printers, assigned by Polish Council, II, 203

Rab, *see* Abba Arika

Rab, title of, II, 66–68, 90

Rab de la corte, *see* Rabbis of the court

Rab, *ha-gadol*, *ha-*, in Oria, II, 67

Rab mubhaḳ, II, 180. *See also* Teachers

Raba (amora), I, 152

Rabbana, exilarchic title of, I, 145, 155

Rabbanan di-metibta, III, 41. *See also* Academies

Rabbanan tena'e, III, 41

Rabbanites, Polish, and Karaites, III, 83

Rabbi, title of, II, 66–68

Rabbinate *and* rabbis, ancient: I, 150; III, 33; accusations of, III, 26–27; and Alexandria, I, 78; and *archisynagogi*, III, 18; and calendar regulation, III, 30; and choice of residence, I, 120; and education, I, 125–26; and emulation of Temple, I, 90–91; and exilarchate, I, 27, 145, 147, 154; and flagellation, II, 224; and idea of justice, I, 129–30; and imagery, II, 137; and judicial responsibility, I, 128; and local customs, III, 149; and marital preferences, I, 124; and medieval rabbinate, II, 66; and ordination, III, 24; and patriarchate, I, 145, 153; (messengers), I, 143, 153–54; and Persian executions, I, 149; and proselytism, I, 97; and Roman Jewry, I, 106; and status of women, I, 96; and synagogue art, III, 146; and tax immunities, I, 109, 138; III, 33; communal teachings of, I, 119; educational position of, I, 124–25; modern heritage of, I, 156; position in synagogue of, I, 122–24; public support of, III, 28; supremacy of, I, 119, 133–40; vs. lay leaders, III, 26–27. *See also* Mishnah; Talmud

medieval and modern: II, *66–94*; III, *123–33*; and academies, II, 95, 189; and adoption of ordinances, II, 30–31; III, 110–11; and agriculture, II, 253; III, 185; and appointments, I, 271; II, 73; (for life), III, 113; and *archisynagogi*, I, 103; and assemblies, I, 284; II, 28; (synods), I, 309–10, 312, 315; II, 73; III, 75, 79–80; and attorneys, II, 237–38; III, 180; and authorship of records, II, 78; and ban of settlement, II, 5–6, 323; III, 98; and bankers, II, 10, 80–81; and briefs, III, 180; and burial, II, 147, 152; (luxury), II, 155; (of Gentiles), II, 148; III, 153; (of suicides), III, 157; and capital punishment, II, 222; and capitalism, III, 173; and charitable responsibilities, II, 320, 323, 325–26, 330, 344–46; (for local poor), II, 323; (support of brides), II, 332; III, 212; and chief rabbinates, I, 196–99, 285–86, 296, 298–300, 308, 310–11; III, 66–67, 70; and civil disobedience, II, 231; and conversion to Christianity, I, 220; II, 134; and debt bondage, II, 227; and deeds, II, 112; and democracy, I, 28; and demotion, II, 86, 88, 91; III, 129–31; and desecration of cemeteries, II, 151; and education, II, 171, 173, 177, 179, 206; III, 161, 163, 171; (general sciences), II, 191; (of poor), II, 324; (of women), II, 178–79; (size of classes), II, 196–97; (teachers), II, 183, 199; and elections, I, 235–36, 325, 329–30; II, 39–40, 47, 103–4, 285; III, 115–17, 123; (fees), II, 36; (outsiders), III, 100; (relatives), III, 115; and Enlightenment, II, 359–60; and excessive severity, II, 142, 212; and excommunication, I, 246; II, 32, 74, 231–32, 282; III, 177, 179; (entire communities), II, 229; (outside bans), II, 243; and exilarchs, III, 41; and exploitation of poor, I, 166; and financial administration, II, 87, 270, 300–1, 334; III, 195; (of legacies), I, 361; II, 328; III, 189; and "Francos," III, 101–2; and freedom of movement, II, 16; III, 104; and Gentile wine, II, 161; and governmental appointment, I, 271, 292; II, 102–3; III, 113; and *ḥazzan*, II, 101, 103; and heresies, II, 231; and informers, I, 234–35; II, 222; and intercommunal controversies, I, 205, 308; II, 77, 166; III, 69, 212–13; and interterritorial action, I, 306; III, 75; and Jewish criminality, II, 227–28; and judiciary, I, 239, 275–76, 327–28; II, 211, 214–15, 236–37; (fees), III, 51–52; (lay), II, 57, 71, 89, 283; III, 124; (single), II, 236; and "law of the kingdom," I, 214; and lay leadership, I, 340; II, 40, 53, 57, 71, 74, 77, 89, 181, 283; III, 124; and legal creativity, II, 216; and local customs, III, 124, 149; and majority principle, II, 173, 282; and marital separation, II, 319; and marriage brokerage, III, 208; and masquerades, II, 316; and meat sales, II, 160; and mendicants' curses, II, 348; and Muslim corruption, I, 170; and nexus between moneylending and learning, II, 78, 176; and nobles, I, 345; and obligation to denounce transgressors, II, 236; and ordination, I, 309, 321; II, 192; III, 131; and Palestine, II, 59; III, 88, 215–16; and parental approval of marriage, III, 204; and personal slurs, II, 75, 79, 225–26, 231; III, 126, 148, 177–78; and pledges of betrothed, II, 315; and polygamous mock-marriages, III, 203; and prayers (continuous), II, 142; (loud), III, 148; (printed), II, 143; (various rituals), II, 70; III, 149; and preachers, II, 97–100, 206; III, 134; and prisoners, II, 226; (*mezuzot* of), II, 226; and private patronage, II, 87; and public registration, II, 83–84; and quorum at weddings, III, 46; and redemption of captives, II, 335–36; and regional communities, I, 284, 327–28; II, 22; III, 82–83; and ritual bath, II, 165; and settlement of scholars, III, 100; and sex relations, II, 311–13; (prostitution), II, 314; III, 205; and status of women, II, 318; (education), II, 178–79; (suffrage), III, 114; (support of brides), II, 332; III, 212; (synagogues), III, 147; and synagogues, II, 136, 141; III, 147; (art), II, 137–38; III, 146; (attendance), III, 105; (chanting), II, 104–5; (height), III, 147; (illumination), II, 134, 144, 259; (private), III, 144; (seats), II, 131; III, 145; and taxation, II, 148–49, 246, 260, 279–80, 282, 285–86; III, 135, 153, 196; (expropriation), II, 284–85; (immunities), II, 80, 219, 249, *276–78*, 331; III, 193–94; (imprisonment for), II, 340; (meat taxes), II, 258–59; and tenant protection, II, 292–96; III, 199; and uncovering of heads, III, 202; and visiting of graves, II, 154; and wandering scholars, II, 87, 187, 324; and wine exports, II, 164; and Zechariah of Porto's will, III, 212–13; as counter-weight to plutocracy, II, 66, 121, 123; III, 142; as governmental agents, II, 359; as teachers of Gentiles, II, 177; bound by legal literature, III, 172; combination with other offices of, II, 103; III, 140; control of, II, 41, 77, 360; (and social welfare), II, 290; (of cantors), II, 103–5; (of marriages), I, 263, 276; II, 83; (of scribes), II, 111–12; III, 140; (of sextons), II, 106; (of slaughterers), II, 109–10; degrees of, I, 125; II, 60. *See also* Ḥaber; Morenu; differences among, I, 215; divorce dispensations by, II, 308; functions of, II, *80–94*; III, 140; (ecclesiastical vs. judicial), II, 105; III, 124; honorary position of, II, 90;

in various regions: Alsace, II, 117; Austria, I, 308; Avignon, II, 104; Bohemia, I, 340; III, 178; Cologne, II, 102–3; England, I, 297; France, I, 246, 263, 305–6; II, 16, 83–84, 161, 164, 323; III, 75, 205, 209; Frankfort, II, 117; III, 78; Germany, I, 298–300, 308, 310–12, 315, 345; II, 66, 80–81, 85, 193–94; III, 69, 75, 79, 115, 123, 142, 161, 163, 216; Hamburg, II, 103; Hessia, I, 343; Holland, III, 57–58; Islam, I, 166, 170; Italy, I, 275–76, 308, 321; II, 10, 58–59, 77, 87, 113, 118, 135, 144, 151, 166, 179, 316, 359–60; III, 79–80, 110, 139–40, 146, 203, 212–13; Lithuania, II, 39–40, 47, 99–100, 189, 258, 335; III, 140; Moravia, II, 41; Palestine, I, 210, 309; II, 340; III, 82–83, 88; Poland, I, 271, 308, 325, 327–28; II, 53, 86–88, 95, 99–100, 226, 259, 315; III, 116–17; Portugal, I, 285; Prague, II, 98–99; Prussia, II, 211, 359; Rome, papal, I, 305; II, 60; Sicily, III, 67, 113, 121; Spain, I, 235–36, 239, 292, 296; II, 36, 72–75, 79, 103, 226–28, 249; III, 66, 69, 124–25, 147, 161; Turkey, I, 196–99, 205; II, 28, 36, 222; III, 48–49, 101–2, 105, 110–11, 196; Venice, III, 179

influence of teachers on, II, 182; investigation of, II, 98–99; itinerant, II, 87; III, 67; mourning for, II, 147; III, 152–53; mutual independence of, II, 77; neglect of Bible by, II, 193–94; non-native, II, 86; Palestinian titles of, I, 210; patriotism of, III, 183; present at functions (divorces), I, 276; II, 211; (elections), II, 36; (weddings), I, 276; II, 311; III, 205; revenue of, II, 36, 85, 117–19, 280; III, 51–52; royal intervention for, I, 271; III, 125; secretarial functions of, II, 113; III, 139; vs. laity, I, 340; II, 40, 53, 57, 71, 74, 77, 89, 168, 181, 283; III, 124. *See also* Chief rabbinate; Contracts; Judiciary; Law; Literatures; Scholars

Rabbinus, in Valencia, II, 74. *See also* Rabbis

"Rabbis," of guilds, as lay judges, II, 88–89

"Rabbis of the court," I, 289, 291. *See also* Chief rabbinate

Rabi, as Sicilian title, III, 67

Rabina (amora), I, 213

Raby mayor de toda Castella, I, 289. *See also* Chief rabbinate

Race: and artistic creativity, II, 137–38; and community, I, 3, 4, 13; in ancient Israel, I, 46
Radio, and community today, I, 26
Raḥmim, Modena association of, III, 102
Rains, in Palestine: I, 31–32; invocation of, I, 86
Rais al-yahud, III, 39. *See also* Nagid
Rais of Ragusa (Sicilian chief rabbi), I, 293
Ramleh (Palestine), I, 167
Ransom of captives, *see* Redemption of captives
Rap, title of, II, 73. *See also* Rab; Rabbis
Rapaport, Baruch (Wilno rabbi), II, 278; III, 129
Rape, Oxford students accused of, II, 187
Raphael Joseph b. Aaron Ḥazzan, on sanctity of synagogue, III, 143
Rappolstein, County of, Jewish elders in, III, 122
Ras Shamra, municipal council in, I, 134; III, 26
Rashi, *see* Solomon b. Isaac
Rashi chapel in Worms, II, 130
Rashim, II, 55, 63. *See also* Elders
Rationalism, Jewish: and communal control, I, 4, 25, 165; II, 362; and visiting of graves, II, 154. *See also* Enlightenment; Philosophy
Rationalizations, of depth of synagogues, II, 139
Ratisbon, Jews of: III, *111*; conferences of, III, 77; (and German taxation), III, 77; hospital of, II, 329; *judex Judaeorum* of, I, 250; meat sales of, II, 158; mixed relations among, II, 313; new statutes of, III, 111; no execution of, II, 223; III, 174; population of, III, 107; rabbis of, II, 91; (controversy), III, 100; regional cemetery of, I, 283; II, 154; rights of absentee members among, III, 103; supply of fish for, II, 160–61. *See also* Petaḥiah of Ratisbon
Ravaka (Elephantine commander), I, 71
Ravenna, Jews of: I, 95; assembly among, I, 320–21; III, 79
Raysius (Syracuse elder), I, 293. *See also* Rais
Reab, as Sicilian title, III, 67
Reader, *see* Ḥazzan
Reading and writing, instruction in: and feminine teachers, II, 179; contractual provisions for, II, 114, 117
Readmission of Jews to England, controversy over, III, 59
Real estate, Christian, tithes of Jewish owners of, II, 254
  Jewish: *ḥazakah* in, II, 292, 297; registration of, I, 277; (Cologne), III, 122; (Turkey), I, 198; (Vienna), III, 126; prices of, II, 292, 295; taxes on, I, 175; II, 248, 252–53; III, 38, 187–88. *See also* Houses; Land
"Rebellion," of Jewish craftsmen, I, 371. *See also* Class struggle; Revolutions
Recanati (city), Jews of: III, 79; assembly among, I, 321
Recanati, Menaḥem b. Benjamin: on lending communal funds, III, 195; on strictness of judges, II, 212; III, 172
Receivership, Jewish, Polish councils' regulation of, I, 329
Rechtsgemeinde, Israelitic, and Palestinian democracy, III, 27
Recife, Brazil, Jews of: III, 59; status of rabbi among, III, 129
Reciprocity: Christian-Muslim, and treatment of Jews, I, 233; Jewish (communal customs duties), II, 13; (regional control), II, 22; treaties of, in Italy, III, 102

Recognition of scholarly achievement, soundness of, II, 245
Reconquista, Spanish, and Jewish self-government, I, 238
Recorders, official, I, 173; II, 110, 113. *See also* Scribes
Records: communal, on charities, III, 218; Judeo-Arabic, in Sicily, III, 156; medieval, state orientation of, II, 78. *See also* Archives; Manuscripts; Papyri; Sources
Recreation, and concentration on study, II, 205
Recusancy, British laws of, I, 259
Red Russia: as member of the Polish Council, I, 325; III, 81; forced to purchase Helicz books, II, 204; Lwów's control over, I, 303; III, 115. *See also* Lwów; *and under* other cities
Redemption: Israelitic law of, I, 48
of captives: II, *233–39*; III, 212–14; and chief rabbis, I, 290, 294; and communal chests, I, 132; II, 335; (supervisors of), II, 57; in Babylonian Exile, I, 63, 69; interterritorial action for, I, 306–7; III, 73, 80; Italian associations for, I, 362; III, 73; limits of, I, 307; orphans' contributions to, II, 331; Zechariah of Porto's legacy for, II, 332. *See also* Captives; Charities
Redemptionists, Catholic, and Lutheran captive, III, 214
Re-elections: frequency of, and growth of oligarchy, III, 117; prohibited by Polish ordinance, II, 46. *See also* Elections
Reform Judaism: and assimilation, I, 9; and communal organization, I, 5, 29; III, 4; and Hebrew, I, 9; and history, I, 9, 29; and political liberalism, I, 9; and Protestantism, I, 9; and ritual, II, 142; in Hungary, I, 19
Reformation, Christian: and charities, III, 93; and Jewish Resettlement, I, 242–43, 252. *See also* Church, Protestant
Reformed Church, Dutch, against legalization of Jewish worship, I, 254
Reforms, communal: discussions in Poland on, II, 353–54; III, 219; of Palestine relief, III, 217; of rabbinic elections, II, 94
educational: ancient, III, 23; and degradation of Hebrew letters, II, 359–60; and Enlightenment, III, 163; and *Ḥukke ha-Torah*, I, 356–57; and Moravian Council, I, 339; and programs, II, 190; and rabbinic dialectics, II, 195; and size of classes, II, 196. *See also* Education
judicial (Lithuanian), III, 63; (under pressure), III, 180; social, and overcrowded hospices, II, 327
Refugees, Israelitic, I, 57. *See also* Exiles
Jewish: and associations, I, 348; and congregational divisions, I, 350; and councils, I, 320–21, 332–33; II, 7–8; and criminal prosecutions, I, 331; and extradition, II, 10. *See also* Extradition; and growth of western communities, II, 364; and interterritorial action, I, 307, 313; and itinerant mendicancy, II, 324; and redemption of captives, II, 337–38; and tenant protection, II, 295; from various regions (Germany), II, 331; (Lithuania), II, 324; (Poland), II, 7–8; (Rome, papal), I, 320–21; (Spain-Portugal), I, 348, 350; II, 10. *See also* Spanish exiles; in various regions (Frankfort), II, 8; (Lithuania), II, 7, 8; (Poland), I, 332–33; II, 331; (Rome, papal), I, 350. *See also* Migrations; Waifs
Regalia, Hessian, and foreign judiciary, I, 343. *See also* Taxation
Reggio, Jews of: and Palestine relief, III, 217; formula of ban in, III, 177;

in pre-censorship commission, I, 321; legacies for, III, 212–13; *Pletten* of, III, 209; tax provisions of, III, 196

Regidores, II, 58. *See also* Elders

Regimentation, *see* Economic regulation

Regional control: I, *283–347*; ancient, I, 105–6, 346; and associations, I, 372; and cemeteries, II, 148–49; III, 154; and congregational exclusivity, III, 59; and dependent communities, I, 319, 322; II, 3, 20, 22, 42, 296; III, 65, 115, 182; (bans on local communities), II, 229; and distribution of communal citrons, III, 187; and illicit relations, II, 313; and enlightened absolutism, I, 338–39, 341; and judiciary, II, 71–72; III, 182; and sumptuary regulations, II, 302; and synods, I, 309–10, 312; and tax assessments, II, 283, 288; in various regions (Brazil), III, 59; (Castile), III, 65; (eastern lands), III, 43; (France), I, 312; (Germany), I, 19; II, 42; III, 86–88; (Italy), II, 313; (Lithuania), II, 22; (Poland), II, 229, 283; (Rome, papal), I, 319, 322; (Spain), II, 71–72. *See also* Chief rabbinate; Councils; Ethnarchs; Nagid; Provincial elders

differences, in marriage brokers' fees, III, 208; schools, Alsatian, budgets of, II, 185. *See also* Academies; Schools; taxes, intercommunal controversies over, III, 196–97. *See also* Taxation

Regions, geographic: and Jewish ritual, I, 121; in Palestine, III, 6–7

Registration *and* registers, communal: of assemblies in Rome, I, 108; of deaths, I, 72, 198; II, 84; of guardians' accounts, II, 330; of immigrant children in Lithuania, II, 331; of marriages, and Church control, II, 83–84; of real estate, III, 63; (and municipal registers), I, 277; II, 292; of synagogue seats, III, 144; of unmarried girls in Lithuania, II, 338

governmental, and Jewish deeds, I, 277; II, 292; III, 139. *See also* Archives; Chirograph offices; Deeds

Rehabilitation, economic, rabbinic teachings on, II, 326–27

Reḥash, II, 83. *See also* Weddings

Reichsacht, imperial, and Jewish bans, II, 229

Reichskammergericht, and Jewish charities, III, 219

Reichsvertretung der deutschen Juden, I, 19

Reinstatement, of Jewish officials, I, 142

Reinterpretation, medieval, and talmudic law, II, 69. *See also* Commentaries; Interpretation

Reischer, Jacob b. Joshua: on change in endowments, III, 165, 189; on circumcision of child of mixed parentage, III, 205; on corrupt election of rabbis, III, 132–33; on desecration of cemeteries, III, 154; on execution for mixed relations, II, 312; on gaming, III, 207; on judicial reforms, III, 180; on majority principle, III, 109; on Prague conflagration, III, 199; on polygamy, III, 203; on preaching, III, 134; on resignation of cantors, III, 136; on seven constitution makers, III, 110; on synagogue decorum, III, 148; on tax immunities, III, 193

Rejoicing with the Law, festival of: and synagogue auctions, II, 133; memorial prayers on, I, 358

Relatives: and congregational allegiance of visitors, II, 12; and excommunication, I, 169, 230–31; III, 157, 177; and judicial intermediaries, II, 237; and mixed dancing, II, 315; and passive franchise, I, 136; II, 40–41, 45–46, 50, 285; III, 115, 117; (corrupt election of rabbis), III, 132–33; and polygamy, II, 309; and rabbinic tenure, II, 88; and size of population, III, 132; charitable obligations of, II, 323, 325, 331–32; III, 210; (redemption of captives), II, 336; identification of, II, 267; mourning for (and private worship), II, 124–25; (for excommunicates), II, 231; (for suicides), II, 156; of scribes, and communal ledgers, II, 112; presence at weddings of, II, 304–5, 311. *See also* Families; Genealogy

Release from ban, III, 178

Relief activities today, I, 5, 19. *See also* Charities

Religio licita, I, 107, 112

Religion, Jewish: American adjustments in, II, 365–66; and activism, I, 208; II, 141; and associational divisions, I, 352, 354–55. *See also* Associations, religious; and burial, II, 156–57; and changes in bequests, II, 266; and charitable responsibilities, I, 5; II, 320; and communal control, I, *3–10*, 115; II, 124, 349–50, 361–62; and communism, I, 16; and confiscation of synagogues, II, 135; and educational responsibilities, II, 170–71; and emigration to Palestine, II, 15; and equality of rights, I, 8; and fall of Jerusalem, I, 110–11; and Gentiles, I, 82; and geonim, I, 185; and guilds, I, 366–67; III, 95; and Hebrew, I, 16; and hostility to art; II, 138; and individual responsibility, II, 168; and interruption of prayers, II, 34; and judiciary, I, 162; II, 73; and law, I, 39; II, 210; (procedure), II, 240; and Maccabeans, III, 15; and magic, I, 237; and municipal functions, I, 134; and Palestinian peoples' community, I, 17; and provision for prisoners, III, 215; and Prussian law of secession, III, 5; and silence during prayers, II, 141; and synagogue activities, I, 89; II, 141; and taxation, II, 246, 288; and threatening bankruptcy, II, 350; attacks on, and censorship, III, 49; expansion of, I, 85; Graeco-Roman toleration of, I, 12, 107, 112, 229; in ancient Palestinian provinces, I, 40; in Babylonia, I, 62, 210; in Elephantine, I, 71–73; in Sicily, I, 232; in Soviet Union, I, 15; independent of politics, I, 28–29; institutionalization of, II, 168; interterritorial features of, II, 351; ministration of, excluded by ban, II, 230. *See also* Excommunication; scholarly control of, II, 243–44; state interest in, II, 123, 208, 252. *See also* Conversion; Law; Rabbis

Religionsgenossenschaft, I, 7

Religious denominations, censuses of, III, 3. *See also under* respective denominations

Religious scruples: and arbitrary leadership, II, 143; and forgotten tax ordinance, II, 265; and Prussian law of secession, III, 5; and wish for assessment, II, 282

Remonstrants, Dutch, against Jewish worship, I, 253–54

Remoshul, Cracow, II, 130

"Removal of a neighbor's boundaries," and *ḥazaḳah* legislation, II, 298

Renaissance, Italian: III, 63; and *ḥazaḳah* legislation, II, 298; and instruction of Gentiles, II, 177; and polygamy, II, 308; and preachers, II, 96; controversial responsa during, II, 166; sexual laxity under, II, 312–13; position of teachers during, II, 184. *See also* Italy

of Islam: III, 35; and business control of community, I, 165; and instruction of Gentiles, II, 177. *See also* Caliphate; Islam

Rentiers: and educational responsibilities, II, 176; and tax immunities, II, 278. *See also* Wealth

Rents, Jewish: II, 248–49, 252; and cemeteries, II, 152; and charities, III, 209; and synagogue seats, II, 130–31; and tenant rights, II, 294; arrears of Nice community in, II, 152; as source of communal revenue, II, 254, 262; purchase of, and usury, II, 270; regulation of, II, *291–96*. *See also* Ḥazaḳah; Tenant protection

Reorganization, communal, tasks of, I, 29

Repairs: of houses, and tenant protection, II, 294; of synagogues, controversial, I, 113, 163

Repasts, Jewish, in synagogue precincts, II, 128

Repentance: and correction of criminals, II, 221–22; of converts, and burial, III, 153; of excommunicates, II, 231; of tax defaulters, and effects of ban, II, 282

Representative bodies, and size of population, II, 23–24. *See also* Councils

Republic, Jewish: in Soviet Union, I, 15; Turgot on, II, 290

Republicanism, in ancient Palestine, I, 35. *See also* Monarchy

Repudiation of communal debts, rare, II, 271. *See also* Debts

Reputations, scholarly, rare ephemerality of, II, 244

Res judicata, and clause on reversal, II, 242. *See also* Procedure

"Research" position of rabbis, III, 126–27

Resettlement areas, Jews of: I, 20–21, *252–66*; associational autonomy of, I, 374; growth of, II, 364; nexus between taxation and autonomy of, I, 282; settlement of, ignored or forbidden, I, 23; vs. Middle Ages, I, 242. *See also under* respective countries and cities

Resettlement of refugees, in Lithuania, II, 337–38

Resh dukna, II, 115, 185. *See also* Teachers, assistants of

Resh kallah, in Rome, I, 210

Reshut, judicial, I, 128. *See also* Authorization

Residence rights: II, *5–12*; and charitable payments of *Schutzgeld*, II, 326; and Cassel assembly, I, 342; and communal debts, II, 233; and communal obligations, II, 344; III, 102; (educational responsibilities), II, 175; III, 166; and franchise, II, 29, 119–20; III, 115; and marriage, II, 5, 7; and membership, I, 136; II, 4; and taxation, II, 20–21, 251; (double), II, 287; and temporary absences, II, 7; III, 98; and tenant protection, II, 292; communal control over, II, 234; dues on, II, 9, 262, 264; (and settlement of aliens), II, 7–8; duration of (and elders), III, 120; (and marriage), III, 204; economic considerations for, I, 274–75; loss of, as penalty, III, 178. *See also* Banishment; noble champions of, II, 270–71; of itinerant beggars, restricted, II, 323–25; permits for (restrictive nature of), II, 10; (withdrawal of), II, 8; royal control of, I, 215; II, 10; vs. immigration restrictions, II, 16. *See also* Ban of settlement; Family quotas; Migrations

Residences: of children, and schoolhouses, II, 199; of scholars, and academies, I, 151; talmudic choice of, I, 120

Resident aliens, Marranos as, I, 252

Resignation: from office, often unlawful, III, 119; of cantors, opposed, III, 136

Resolutions, communal, adopted in synagogues, II, 144, 163

Responsa, exilarchic, I, 180

geonic: III, 42; and prayer-books, III, 42; antecedents of, I, 180–81; as a source of history, III, 38; deposited in archives, III, 42; discussed at *kallahs*, I, 182; few from Palestine, III, 45; interterritorial features of, I, 193; on academies, III, 43; on calendar regulation, III, 45; on communal discipline, I, 203–4; III, 37, 169; on educational associations, III, 94; on flogging, II, 224–25; III, 175; on *ḥazzan*, I, 200–1; III, 136; on heterodox currents, I, 165–66, 168; III, 36–37; on inadequacy of correspondence, I, 309; III, 74; on judiciary, I, 202; III, 38, 50; (Byzantine), I, 230; III, 54; on Palestine vs. Babylonia, III, 37; on rabbis' tax immunity, III, 34; on ritualistic diversity, III, 37; on Sabbath rest, III, 37; on scribes, III, 139; on second holidays, III, 30; on tax collections, III, 38; on teaching of slaves, III, 162; style of, III, 42. *See also* Geonim; *and under* respective authors

Muslim, on synagogues, III, 36; of Amsterdam students, III, 171–72

rabbinic: and lay leadership, II, 77; as Renaissance pamphlets, II, 166; bibliography of, III, 137; from various regions (Austria), I, 296–97; (Egypt), I, 351; (England), III, 169; (Germany), II, 233; (Holland), III, 58; (Italy), II, 77, 166; (Poland), II, 53, 317; III, 53; (Spain), I, 296–97, 353; on adoption of statutes, III, 109–11; on ban of settlement, III, 98, 101; on burial societies, I, 353; on charitable contributions, II, 320; on congregational divisions, I, 351; on debt bondage, III, 176; on deeds, II, 240; on Dutch Jewry, III, 58; on excommunication, III, 112; on French controversy, I, 296–97; on interruption of prayers, III, 112; on majority principle, III, 109–11; on music, III, 167; on new synagogues, III, 53; on search for deserting husbands, II, 317; on scribes, II, 112–13; on seizure of elders, II, 53; on seizure of property, II, 233; on tax ordinances, I, 171; II, 265; (aliens), III, 188; (defense), II, 268; (disadvantages of manifestation), II, 282; (real estate), III, 187–88. *See also* Rabbis; *and under* respective authors

Responsibility, communal: and individual criminals, II, 338; and Jewish printing, II, 201, 204–5; and rabbinic life tenure, II, 94; enhances control, I, 224; for baths, II, 165–66; for burial, II, 147, 157; for charities, I, 132; II, *319–50*; for congregational worship, II, 126; for education, I, 92, 125–26, 129; II, 114–15, *169–79*; III, 161, 164; for supplying executioners, III, 175; for taxes, I, 129; (evasions), II, 288; (exemptions), II, 274; (fiscal individualism), I, 137

individual: and breaches of bans, II, 235; and communal control, II, 168, 235; for acts of fellow Jews, III, 179–80; for charities, II, 320, 325; for education, II, 169, 177; (feminine for husband's), III, 162; for taxation, physical, II, 154–55; in synagogue functions, II, 134; of elders, I, 135; II, 52–54, 60, 64; III, 70, 176; of exilarchs, I, 147; of judges (and government appointment), II, 218–19; (eliminates laymen), I, 128; (rabbinic teachings on), III, 174; of parents, guild regulations on, II, 185. *See also* Parents; of patriarchs, I, 147

Responsoria, in ancient synagogues, III, 23

Restoration, of stolen objects, II, 200
Restoration to Palestine, ancient: *bamah* under, III, 9; characteristics of, I, 66
Resurrection: and burial in Palestine's soil, II, 339; Maimonidean doctrine of, III, 44–45
Retail trade, Jewish, American, I, 260. *See also* Commerce; Merchants
Retaliation, doctrine of, II, 221, 224
Retiring elders, rights of, II, 60, 65
Retribution, penal, individual cooperation in, II, 235
Reubeni, David, in Rome, I, 305
Reuchlin, Johannes, trial of, I, 304; III, 72
Reutlingen, *see* Mehler
Revenue, associational, and size of membership, II, 17
Reverence: for scholars, regulations on, III, 163–64; for synagogue, and shoeless worship, II, 129
Reversal of judgment, by single rabbi, II, 242
Revisers, *see* Censorship
Revolts, ancient: I, 36, 110; and archives, III, 24; and patriarchate, I, 140–41, 144; III, 28; under Persia, I, 149; III, 32; (and Palestinian city walls), III, 8. *See also* Maccabeans
communal: against authorities, III, 111, 114, 117–18, 123; anti-dictatorial in Cracow, II, 64; of Avignon electorate, II, 39; of Kajdany craftsmen, II, 307
Revolutions: Dutch, and Jewish toleration, I, 253; medieval (and heresies), I, 237; (and Jewish allies of kings), I, 281–82; Russian, I, 14; III, 4. *See also* Commercial Revolution; French Revolution
Rheims, and synod of Troyes, I, 312; III, 75
Rhenish communities, Jews of: III, 87; academies of, and Italy, I, 242; and ban of settlement, II, 5–6; and synods, I, 311, 313, 315; III, 75; election of cantors by, II, 102; early traditions of, II, 69; fast against Crusades, I, 306; physicians of, III, 140; tax immunities among, II, 277; vows of, II, 132; wandering scholars among, II, 188. *See also under* respective cities
Rhetoric, Italian, and Jewish preachers, II, 96
Rhine wines, compete with those of Bordeaux, II, 164
Rhineland, *see* Rhenish communities
Rhodes, Jews of: III, 198, 204; against marriage of aliens, III, 204; against wine imports, II, 163; bequests for academy of, III, 204; sumptuary ordinances of, III, 201
Rich: and educational responsibilities, II, 169; humiliation of, and flogging, II, 225–26. *See also* Wealth
Richard I, "the Lion-Hearted" (English king), appoints Jewish judges, I, 297–98
Richelieu, Duke de, and Bordeaux conflict, II, 18–19
Richenza *or* Richeza (Nuremberg female cantor), II, 140
Righteousness, idea of, and charity, I, 131
Rimini, Jews of: bequest for harbor by, II, 267; synod of, I, 319; II, 267; III, 79
Rindfleisch (German butcher or noble), anti-Jewish massacres of, III, 76
Ring, at wedding rites, II, 310
Riot, accusation of London elders for, I, 258
Riots, anti-Jewish: ancient, I, 109, 113; and badge, I, 161; and burial, I, 253, 263; II, 150–51; and councils, I, 287–88; and synagogues, I, 163, 218, 230; in Muslim Egypt, I, 171; Oxford

students accused of, II, 187. *See also* Massacres
Riparian rights, and public ownership, I, 137
Ritual, Israelitic, I, 40; and Deuteronomic Reformation, I, 52
Jewish, ancient: I, 12, *120–25*; and burial, I, 94; and Church art, II, 137; and new synagogues, I, 113; and Roman ritual, I, 82; experts of, I, 65; local diversities in, I, 67, 79, 89–90, 97, 150; persistence of, I, 67; progressive standardization of, I, 74, 103
medieval and modern: II, 210; American adjustments in, II, 365–66; and acquired rights, II, 297; and adjustment of talmudic law, II, 69; and Christianity, I, 9, 221; and clothing, III, 203. *See also* Sha'atnez; Show fringes; and communal price fixing, II, 300; and congregational divisions, I, 350, 352, 356; III, 148–49; and controversies over cantors, II, 105; and court sessions, II, 211–12; and French patriotism, I, 263; and Hebrew, I, 9; and Marrano chapels, I, 256; and *memor*-books, II, 146; and migrations, II, 11–12; III, 37; and private scribes, III, 140; and rabbis, II, 67, 89; and Reform Judaism, I, 9; and state legislation, I, 264–65; II, 160, 363; and synagogue candles, II, 134; and synagogue functions, III, 210; and trade promotion, III, 159, 187; and women, III, 162; (education), II, 178; (use of citrons), III, 187; communal control of, II, 79, 89, 167; III, 149; European, and Palestine-Babylonia, I, 205, 210, 242; French Enlightenment's attacks on, II, 360; Justinian on, I, 123; local divisions in, I, 167–68, 192, 205, 350, 352, 356; II, 11–12, 19, 69; III, 37, 148–49; Polish, German origin of, I, 267; relative finality of, II, 142–43; Sephardic, imposed by exiles, I, 197; simplicity of, II, 70. *See also* Customs; Food; Law; Libel; Liturgy; Prayer-books; Religion; Slaughtering; Worship
Rivers: ancient synagogues on banks of, I, 91; European, Jewish exclusion from, II, 165; riparian rights on, I, 137
Roads: charitable guidance on, I, 132; public ownership of, I, 137
Robberies *and* robbers: Jewish, occasional references to, II, 227–28; (and tax evasions), II, 282; Oxford students accused of, II, 187
Rodale (scroll), in Polish Jewish oath, I, 273. *See also* Pentateuch; Scroll of Law
Rodeph Shalom congregation, Philadelphia, forced attendance at, II, 126–27
Rodfe Ṣedeḳ, Spanish association of, I, 362
Rodfe Zedaḳah, Frankfort association of, III, 93
Rodphea Sholom Society, London, III, 211
Roger I (Sicilian grand count), transplants Jewish craftsmen, I, 368
Romagna (Italian province), and Jewish conferences, III, 80
Romances, Yiddish, medieval, II, 192
Roman Empire: I, 23, 107–11, 156; and communal charters, I, 12, 76; and Maccabeans, I, 76; III, 15; and new synagogues, I, 162–63; III, 36; and Persian Christians, III, 32; and scholars' tax immunities, I, 138; censuses in, I, 159; communal trends in, I, 167, 206–7; continues Seleucide policies, I, 83; decline of, I, 23, 139; eastern cities in, III, 27; facility of travel in, III, 23; early feudalism in, I, 129, 147–48; influence on Jewish law of, I, 211; Jewish fiscal tax in, I, 228; Jewish judiciary in, III, 20–21;

medieval heritage of, I, 209, 227, 243; (Barcelona), II, 74; (Byzantium), I, 228; (Islam), I, 157–58, 162; (supercommunity), I, 346; patriarchal supremacy in, I, 140; III, 28; (suppression of), I, 152; supports rabbis, III, 33; tax collections under, I, 38, 148; vs. Persia, I, 157; (closed frontiers), I, 122. *See also* Byzantine Empire; Emperors; Law; *and under* respective provinces, cities and rulers
Holy, *see* Germany
Roman Jews in Jerusalem, I, 120
"Romanesque" cloth, Judeo-Christian agreement on, I, 368–69
Romania *or* Roumania, II, 142; III, 52. *See also* Byzantine Empire
Romanos, Benjamin (Sicilian deputy), I, 317
Romans, ancient: and burial customs, I, 94; and Hellenistic cities, III, 13; attend synagogues, I, 82; deride rabbis' poverty, III, 28; Jews among, I, 81
Rome, ancient, Jews of: I, *79–82*; III, 14, 21; among alien groups, III, 17; and diplomacy, I, 304; III, 19; and Palestinian authorities, I, 143; III, 17–18; and praetorian generals, I, 45; art of, III, 16; catacombs of, and medieval cemeteries, I, 80, 94, 106; II, 147, 155; III, 17; education of, III, 16; elections among, I, 104–5; III, 17–18; elders of, I, 101–2, 105, 151; III, 19; ritual of, I, 67; scribes of, I, 102–3; synagogues of, I, 84; III, 14–15; (children in), I, 104–5; II, 146
papal, Jews of: I, 210; III, 109, 139–40; and Azariah de' Rossi, I, 308; and conferences, I, 319–20; III, 80; and diplomacy, I, 304–6; II, 57, 72–73; (convert), II, 116; and expulsion from Sicily, I, 318; and Inquisition, III, 63; and Palestine, I, 210; III, 51; and Paris, III, 101; archives of, III, 139–40; basic privilege of, I, 268; brevity of tenure among, III, 121; cemeteries of, II, 149–50, 155; capitalization of leaseholds among, II, 295; charitable associations of, I, 362–63; III, 89, 93, 146; (alms collection), II, 346; (bequests), II, 267; chastisement of pupils among, III, 169; Christian clerks of, II, 116; Christian teachers of, II, 192; Christians at courts of, III, 180; communal indebtedness of, II, 269, 272, 356; III, 190; (for social welfare), II, 346; (to associations), I, 372; III, 97; confiscation of books of, I, 224; congregational divisions among, I, 350; II, 19–20; III, 149; constitution of, II, 29, 47, 59–60; III, 109; (Council of Sixty), II, 55; controversy over priestly blessing of, III, 136–37; conversions of, I, 222–23, 306; III, 72; (loss of property), I, 247; III, 57; craftsmen among, I, 368; defenders of statutes of, III, 111; deterioration of houses of, II, 294; early bathhouse of, II, 166; economic conditions of, II, 262, 272; III, 185, 190, 218; elections of, II, 36, 40; III, 116; elders of, II, 53; III, 129; ghetto of, I, 225–26; greet new popes, I, 217; health officers of, II, 291; Hebrew records of, III, 79, 173 in pre-censorship commission, I, 321; legacies for, III, 212–13; letter to Pesaro of, III, 179; meat sales restricted among, II, 158; mercantilist arguments for toleration of, II, 298; memorials and appeals of, I, 224, 305–6; III, 190, 199; new synagogues of, I, 219; no ban of settlement among, III, 101; obligatory attendance in, II, 28; occasional polygamy among, II, 308; officials' salaries among, II, 118; papal congregations

on, III, 185; parents as teachers among, III, 161; pestilence among, II, 329–30; police of, II, 291; population of, II, 23; III, 107; rabbis of, II, 76, 282; III, 101, 129; real estate *ḥazakah* among, II, 293; III, 198; rent reduction for community among, II, 262; Reuchlin's trial among, I, 304–5; rituals of, II, 142; seizure of property for debts of, II, 233; sumptuary laws of, II, 304–5; III, 201; support of brides by, II, 332; synagogues of, I, 350; (taxes on), II, 135, 265; (termed *scolae*), III, 151; Talmud Torah for girls of, II, 179; taxation of, II, 135, 246, 254–57, 265, 282; (age), II, 251; (flight taxes), III, 103–4; (revenue declines), II, 280; III, 190; Toledan bookseller among, II, 201; tenant protection among, II, 293; III, 198; Venaissin deputies among, II, 61. *See also* Church; Papacy; Papal States

Roofs, of synagogues, and height, II, 139

Rosh bet din, II, 95. *See also* Judiciary

Rosh ha-golah, I, 186. *See also* Exilarch

Rosh ha-keneset, I, 103. *See also* Archisynagogus

Rosh ha-pereḳ, Palestinian, exilarch as, III, 32

Rosh ha-rabbanim, I, 181

Rosheim, Jews in, I, 299. *See also* Josel

Rossi, Azariah b. Moses de': and Leone da Sommi, II, 191; as patient, III, 162; attitude to life of, III, 174; controversy over orthodoxy of, I, 308; III, 73; on peace, II, 217

Rostock, early cemetery in, II, 146

Rotation in office: statutory provisions for, II, 55; in England, II, 62; in Germany, II, 61; in Gerona, II, 58; in Italy, II, 59, 61; in Poland, II, 63. *See also* Elders; Elections

Rotfecedi (*Rodfe Ṣedeḳ*), Spanish association of, I, 362

Rothenburg an der Tauber, Jews of: III, 77; rabbis of, I, 298. *See also* Meir b. Baruch

Rotterdam, Jews in, III, 58

Roussillon, County of, Jews of: III, 103; and Aragonese assemblies, I, 287

Rovigo, controversy over bath in, II, 166; III, 160

Rudolf I of Hapsburg (Holy Roman emperor): and Mayence synod, III, 76; and Meir of Rothenburg, III, 69–70; confiscates property of emigrants, I, 245

Rudolf II (Holy Roman emperor), and tax immunity of synagogue, II, 130

Rufina (Smyrna patroness), I, 94

Ruin, economic, and communal discipline, II, 231; III, 84. *See also* Debts

"Ruler of Jewry in the Empire," Josel of Rosheim as, I, 299. *See also* Chief rabbinate

Rumania, Jews of: I, 20; Soviet-occupied, I, 17

Runkel, *see* Wied-Runkel

Ruprecht von der Pfalz (German king): III, 69–71; and abuses in bans, II, 231; and Jewish tax farmers, II, 284–85; and regional communities, I, 298–99; (cemeteries), II, 148; collects Jewish fines, II, 235

Rural Jews, Polish: and anti-Jewish legislation, I, 281; and revolutionary currents, I, 336. *See also* Agriculture; Land

Russia, Czarist, Jews of: I, 13; III, 4, 62–63; class struggle among, I, 16; combination of offices among, II, 103; congregational divisions of, I, 352; communal debts of, I, 337; Diaspora nationalism among, III, 3–4; Gentiles repair to courts of, II, 239; incorpora-

tion of Polish communities by, II, 354–55; legislation of, II, 354–55; III, 219; meat taxes of, II, 108, 258; III, 186; prohibition of bans of, II, 233
Soviet, *see* U. S. S. R.
Russo-German war, I, 17
Ruth, biblical story of, I, 44, 48
Rzeszów: as member of Polish Council, I, 336; cantors in, II, 104

SAADIA B. JOSEPH GAON, al-Fayyumi: and calendar regulation, I, 192; and Egyptian communities, I, 188–89; and Jewish solidarity, I, 185; and Judah b. Barzilai, III, 38; and supremacy of Sura, I, 184; Book of Deeds by, I, 204; II, 240; III, 38; on Bagdad bankers, I, 188–89; on contacts with caliphs, III, 43; parentage of, I, 193; III, 46; prayer-book of, III, 42; struggles of, I, 183; III, 42, 45–46
Saar asamaim, congregation of, I, 256. *See also* Spanish-Portuguese congregation in London
Sabbateion, synagogue as, I, 89
Sabbath: and *corvée* labor, II, 267; and court sessions, I, 236; II, 212; and debt bondage, II, 226–27; and medieval heretics, III, 37; and names, I, 63; and Palestine relief, II, 341; and postmasters, III, 141; and prisoners, III, 55, 215; and plenary assemblies, II, 24–25; and Reform Judaism, I, 9; and synagogues, I, 89, 112; (auctions), II, 133; (Bible recitation), I, 122; II, 141, 193; (candles), III, 146; (chanting), II, 105; (*haftarot*), I, 122; (repasts), II, 128; (services on), I, 52, 180; II, 126–27; and talmudic studies, II, 207; announcement of, I, 104; II, 106; as election day, III, 116; at exilarchic court, I, 180, 182; attire during, II, 307; consumption of meat and fish on, II, 160–61, 259; executions on, I, 166; in Babylonian Exile, I, 59, 61; in Martinique, III, 62; interruption of prayers on, II, 34; neglect of, under Islam, I, 165; occasional bans on, II, 228; III, 124; rabbinic sermons during, II, 95–97; III, 133; reading of ordinances on, II, 222; state legislation on (France), I, 264; III, 62; (New York), III, 60; (Poland), I, 270; (Rome, ancient), I, 110; (southern Italy), I, 232; time limits of, III, 18; vacations during, II, 197; visit to families on, I, 357; vows during, II, 132, 188; warm dishes on, I, 168. *See also* Holidays
"Sabbath, the Great," meaning of, III, 133–34
Sabbatical year, I, 52, 132
Sabionetta, Jews of, III, 80
Sacerdos, English presbyter as, I, 297
Sacramentaries, Christian, on dedication of churches, I, 230; III, 53
Sacraments, absence in Jewish religion of, II, 168
"Sacred edifices," synagogues as, I, 109
Sacrifices, Jewish, ancient: I, 40–41, 49; and Deuteronomic Reformation, I, 52; and education, I, 53; and origin of synagogue, II, 101; III, 9; and priestly blessing, I, 121; by laymen, I, 49; Ezekiel on, I, 60; for emperors, I, 109; in Egypt, I, 79; (Elephantine), I, 60, 71–72; law of, I, 61; local suppression of, I, 54; none in Babylonia, I, 60; spread of, I, 58. *See also* Ritual; Temple; Worship
Sacrilege: and medieval *hekdesh*, III, 211; and synagogues, I, 109, 114; and Temple contributions, I, 110
"Sacrilegious assemblies," synagogues as, I, 112
Ṣaddiḳim, ḥasidic: and congregational divisions, I, 362; and preaching, II, 100

Sadduceeism: and education, III, 23; decline of, I, 119
Sadekin, of Northampton, excommunication of, II, 230
Sadism: and chastisement of children, II, 198; and desecration of cemeteries, II, 150
Safed, Jews of: allocation of Palestine relief among, II, 342; and renewal of ordination, I, 308; and Salonican congregation, III, 74; and Venetian Association for Orphan Girls, I, 364; independent of Turkish chief rabbis, I, 197; messengers of, II, 343; III, 216–17; preaching among, II, 96; religious associations among, I, 355; III, 91–92. *See also* Palestine relief
Safra, III, 13. *See also* Scribe
Sagas, Israelitic, I, 52, 60
Sahagun (Spain), rabbis of, I, 289
Sahl b. Maṣliaḥ, I, 166–67
Sa'id b. Ḥasan (Muslim theologian), III, 35
Saint Esprit (France), Jewish community in, I, 264. *See also* Bayonne
St. Edmond (England), demands exclusion of Jews, I, 276
St. Francis de Sales, monastery of, II, 152
St. Nicholas Hospital in Metz, II, 154
St. Paul's Church (London), to become synagogue, I, 257
Saints, Jewish: among rabbis, II, 94; among teachers, II, 183–84; and religious associations, I, 355
Salamanca, university of, and chair for Hebrew, III, 135
Salaries of communal officials: I, 102, 123, 292; II, *117–20*; III, 141; and charitable bequests, II, 266; and honorary functions, II, 132; and regional control, I, 292; III, 105; and tax distribution, II, 249, 260, 277, 280; and unemployed officials, I, 285; of ancient *archisynagogi*, III, 18; of cantors, II, 101–4; of elders, II, 64; III, 119; (provincial), I, 294, 328; III, 122–23; of judges, II, 73; of *negidim*, I, 191; of rabbis, II, *81–85*, 92; III, *126–27*; (and citron sales), III, 126; (and election costs), II, 93; (and meat taxes), II, 259; (charitable use of), II, 81; (taxation of), II, 249, 277; of secretaries, I, 202; of sextons, II, 106–7; of *shtadlanim*, II, 115; of Sicilian chief rabbis, I, 294; of teachers, I, 126; II, 114, 117–18, 171–72, 183–84, 186, 188; III, 140, 164; (and prices of books), II, 200; III, 170; (guaranteed by community), III, 164; (in Italy), I, 359; (in Spain), II, 114; (medieval *midrash* on), III, 161; Valladolid synod on, I, 292
Salerno, privilege of, on Jewish abattoirs, III, 186
Sales: deeds of, and communal ledgers, II, 111–12; of acquired rights, II, 297; of books, II, 200; (and public approvals), II, 203; of citrons, II, 164–65; of *ḥazaḳah*, II, 295; of members by community, III, 104; of ritual meat, III, 138; of ritual wine, II, 162; of synagogue equipment for captives, III, 213; of synagogue seats, II, 130, 264; of synagogues, legal requirements for, II, 128–29; synagogue announcements of, II, 144; taxes on (confused with excise taxes), II, 260; (in Poland), II, 261; (in Spain), II, 248–49. *See also* Commerce; Excise taxes; Merchants
Salman, of Worms, II, 78
Salon (Provence), at provincial assemblies, III, 75
Salonica, Jews of: adoption of statutes by, III, 110; and boycott of Ancona, III, 73; and *ḥakam-bashis*, I, 197; III, 49; and interterritorial Jewish charities, I, 348–49; and Italian

beards, III, 203; burial societies of, III, 88; central committees of, II, 20; charitableness of, II, 345–46; circulating library of, II, 202; communal hospice of, III, 210; communal monopolies of, II, 262; congregational divisions among, I, 348, 351; II, 4, 18, 242; III, 51; customs duties of, II, 262–63; education of, II, 172; (teachers' control), II, 180–81; (Talmud Torah association), I, 348; II, 24, 48; III, 88; frequent conflagrations among, II, 293; III, 73; *ḥazaḳah* ordinances of, II, 293–95; III, 198; industries of, III, 94, 199; legacies for Hebron of, III, 165; majority principle among, II, 27; meat monopoly of, II, 108; ordinances against gaming and dancing of, III, 206; ordinances against informers of, II, 222; oligarchic rule among, II, 30, 50; preaching among, II, 96; private synagogues of, III, 142; quorum at weddings of, III, 47; rabbis of, II, 75; (and pilgrimages to Palestine), II, 340; (and statutes), III, 110; (and tenant protection), II, 295; real estate boom among, II, 295; redemption of captives by, I, 306; II, 337; Safed intervention in affairs of, III, 74; secret cemeteries under Byzantium of, II, 147; sumptuary laws of, II, 304; tax assessments in, II, 286; III, 195–96; (immunities), II, 276

Salt, Jewish excise taxes on, II, 260

Saltaro, Judah b. Moses, and Rovigo bath, III, 160

Samaria: I, 35, 50; fall of, I, 50, 57; population of, I, 37; royal influence on, I, 37; slaves in, I, 46

Samaritans: and Elephantine, I, 71–72; Egyptian, controlled by *nagid*, I, 191; medieval manuscripts of, III, 47; Palestinian, and Sepphoris, III, 27

Samatha, meaning of, II, 233. *See also* Excommunication

Samaya (Castilian chief rabbi), I, 289

Sambari, Joseph b. Isaac, III, 34, 43

Sambor, privilege *de non tolerandis Judaeis* of, I, 280

Samuel (seer): I, 45; on monarchy, I, 37; synagogue on tomb of, III, 35

Samuel b. 'Ali Gaon: I, 172, 200; and Maimonides, III, 43–45; diploma by, III, 41; letters of, I, 184; III, 40; messenger of, I, 181; on late gaonate, III, 43

Samuel b. Avigdor (Wilno rabbi), II, 86; III, 129

Samuel b. 'Azariah [?] (exilarch), I, 186

Samuel b. David ha-Levi: on charities, III, 210; (Palestine relief), III, 212; on feminine contributions for citrons, III, 187; on *ḥazaḳah*, III, 199; on marital relations, III, 208; on rights of settlement, III, 99; on ritual slaughtering, III, 159; on synagogue attendance, III, 143

Samuel b. Eliezer (German chief rabbi), I, 299; III, 69

Samuel b. Ḥofni Gaon: and Jewish solidarity, I, 185; priestly descent of, III, 46; solicits contributions, I, 181

Samuel b. Meir, at synod of Troyes, I, 212, 311–12

Samuel b. Moses di Medina: against parental interference in marriage, III, 204; as rabbi of two congregations, II, 75; for local autonomy, III, 74; on burial (in Palestine), III, 215; (of suicide), III, 157; on changes in endowments, III, 165; on defendants' courts, II, 242; III, 182; on emigration to Palestine, II, 340; on gaming, III, 207; on *ḥazaḳah*, II, 292, 295; III, 197; on *heḳdesh*, III, 211; on informers, II, 222; on intercommunal controversies, III, 213; on majority principle, II, 27;

III, 109; on master-pupil relations, III, 163; on meat administration, III, 159; on private bans, III, 124; on provisions for brides, III, 213; on real estate boom in Salonica, III, 198–99; on sumptuary laws, III, 202; on synagogue ownership, III, 142; on teachers' control, II, 180–81; on trade ordinances, III, 199; on wine administration, III, 159; renounces tax immunities, II, 277

Samuel b. Nathan ha-Levi, bequest of, II, 329

Samuel ha-Kohen (gaon), I, 186

Samuel Ḥayyim (*ḥakam-bashi*), I, 199

Samuel of Mosul (exilarch), I, 185

Samuel Yarḥina'ah, Mar (amora): I, 152, 154; calendar computation of, I, 143; on price regulation, I, 131

San Marco, excuse from office in, III, 119–20

Sanaa, descent from III, 12

Sancho IV (Castilian king), extradition treaty of, I, 234

Sancho VII (Navarrese king), on oath in synagogue, II, 144

"Sanctification of the Name," II, 146. *See also* Martyrs; *Memor*-books

Sanctions, communal, and bans, III, 179

Sanctity: of cemeteries, regulations on, III, 156; of schools, III, 151; of synagogues (and decorum), III, 148; (and term *Schule*), III, 151; (legal problems of), II, 127–30; III, 143

Sanctuaries, ancient: desecration of, I, 88; Graeco-Roman (as depositaries), I, 88; (called *proseuchai*), I, 87

Israelitic, local: I, 40, 49, 61, 86; and Deuteronomic Reformation, I, 52–53; and idolatry, I, 60; and religious universalism, I, 54; and synagogues, I, 53, 62; survival of, I, 59. *See also* Centralization of worship; Temple

Sanctuary, "little," and synagogue: I, 60, 351; and private worship, II, 129–30; Talmud on, III, 10

Sandals, Jewish, and sanctity of synagogue, II, 129

Sandomierz: and Cracow chief rabbinate, I, 302; as member of Polish Council, III, 81

Sanguinetti, Abraham Ishmael Ḥayyim, letters of, III, 215

Sanhedrin, Great: and academies, I, 150–51, 182; and medieval community, III, 51; and penal procedure, II, 220; and Polish Council, I, 332; III, 82–83; composition of, I, 99; officials of, I, 102; (patriarchs), III, 29; Pharisaic leadership of, I, 140; position of, III, 29; rare emulation of, II, 56

"little": I, 127, 182; and Polish Councils, II, 55, 63; III, 82–83; Paris (Napoleonic), and Jewish community, I, 14

Sanitation, communal: II, 115, 291; III, *140*; and overcrowded hospitals, II, 327; in Poland, III, 197. *See also* Medicine; Physicians; Sick

Saracens, *see* Arabs; Islam; Moors; Muslims

Saragossa, Jews of: associations of, I, 354, 361–62; (for burial), I, 353; (guilds), I, 367–68; III, 93, 95; (synagogues of), II, 140; communal statutes of, II, 10, 284; III, 64, 183; communal use of Moorish palace in, II, 24; convert, as diplomatic agent of, II, 116; domination by craftsmen of, I, 368; exiles from, and Salonican "Syracuse" congregation, II, 53; elections of officials in, II, 102; (rabbis), III, 125; lay judges of, II, 71; meat payments by, II, 259; new synagogues of, II, 140; obligatory acceptance of office by, II, 53–54; procedural latitude of, II, 241;

sales of synagogue seats by, II, 130; tax ordinances of, I, 278; II, 15, 251, 257, 284; III, *183*, 194; (confiscation for tax defaults), II, 284; (denunciation of tax evaders), II, 281; (prohibition of seeking immunities), II, 14; wedding guests among, II, 303

Sarajevo (Bosnia), Jews of: chief rabbis of, III, 47; illuminated *haggadah* of, III, 146; obligatory acceptance of office by, II, 54; outsiders preferred, III, 100; prohibit departure by members, II, 28; reciprocity towards foreign merchants of, II, 13; responsibility of elders of, II, 53; synagogues of, III, 36; taxation of new arrivals by, II, 12

Saraval, Jacob Raphael (Mantuan preacher), II, 96

Sarbanut, writ of, II, 228

Sardes, Jews of, I, 85–86, 95, 110

Sargon (Assyrian king), inscription of, I, 57; III, 10

Sarim, significance of, III, 7. *See also* Nobles; Princes

Sasportas, Jacob b. Abraham: and Jewish boycott of landlord, II, 296; on associational membership, III, 105; on excommunication, II, 229; III, 177–78; on franchise of proselytes, II, 286; on *ḥazaḳah*, III, 198–99; on tax administrators, III, 195; on trade ordinances, III, 199

Sassanians (dynasty), religious policies of, III, 36. *See also* Persia; *and under* individual rulers

Sassoon library, catalogue of, III, 47

"Satan, Synagogue of," I, 216

Satanów: chief rabbinate in, I, 303; electoral controversy in, III, 116–17

Satin garments, and sumptuary laws, II, 306

Satires: Hebrew (on cantors), II, 105; (on guilds), III, 95; Roman on Jews, I, 80, 82; (synagogues), III, 15. *See also* Literatures; Poetry

Saul (Israelitic king), election of, I, 45

Saurau, Franz Joseph von, Count (Austrian court chancellor), II, 260

Savannah, Georgia, Jewish cemeteries in, III, 152

Savoy, Jews of: I, 264; conservators of, III, 68; continued toleration of, I, 264; French chief rabbi from, I, 296; settlement rights of, II, 10; Turin's control over, II, 21–22

Saxony, Jews of: III, *77*; and Basel assembly, I, 315

Scales, private monopolies in, II, 299

Schaffhausen, synagogue in (sale), II, 129; (womens' compartment), II, 145

Scheuer, Michael (Mannheim rabbi): III, 202; on Mannheim morals, III, 205

Schiff, Meir b. Jacob: against synagogue chatting, II, 141; III, 148; on educational neglect, III, 163

Schlettstadt, Jews of, III, 67

Schneidemühl, real estate tax in, III, 188. *See also* Piła

Schneitach, as district of German taxation, I, 341

Schola, II, 144. *See also* Schools; Synagogues

Scholars, Jewish, ancient: and exilarchate, I, 27, 145, 147, 154; and informality of synagogues, II, 128; occupational activities of, I, 135; II, 169. *See also* Academies; Mishnah; Talmud

medieval and modern: admitted on preferential basis, III, 100; and interterritorialism, II, 243–45; and Italian Talmud Torahs, I, 359; and judicial priority, II, 237; and Palestinian calendar, I, 192; and private synagogues, III, 144; and Torah summonses, II, 132; as courts of appeal, II, 241–42; electoral rights of, II, 40;

III, 115; esteemed above Portuguese chief rabbis, I, 286; exempted from renting restrictions, III, 199; feminine, II, 178–79; "fewer than books," in Spain, II, 201; German, in Palestine, III, 215; itinerant, II, 82; III, 67; leadership of, II, 181; marital preference for, I, 124; mourning for, II, 147; III, 152–53; numerical strength of, II, 277; prestige of (and slaves), II, 177; (talmudic injunctions on), II, 179–80; protection against demons of, III, 169; salaries of, attacked, I, 181; self-help by excommunication of, II, 231; III, 126, 178; slurs on, punished, II, 75, 79, 225–26, 231; III, 126; (and synagogue decorum), III, 148; support of (vs. building funds), II, 186; (vs. synagogue donations), III, 165; tax immunities of, II, 249, 276–78; III, 193–94; (and court action), II, 219; (and fiscal downgrade), II, 288; (definition), II, 80, 276–77; treatment of, as captives, II, 336; wealth of, II, 277. *See also* Education; Law; Learning; Rabbinate

Scholasticism, Christian, influence on Jewish political theory of, II, 217

Schools, Jewish, ancient: III, 23–24; academies as, I, 151; and adult education, II, 206; and Christians, II, 199; and survival, I, 155; curricula of, I, 125–26; location of, I, 92, 125; obligatory contributions to, I, 136; position of, I, 120; reforms in, II, 170; sanctity of, I, 125; size of classes in, I, 126; supervisors of, I, 133

medieval and modern: associational, II, 185–86; and communal responsibility, II, 169; and educational foundations, I, 358; II, 186, 266; (Salonican legacy for Palestine), III, 165; and government non-recognition, II, 363–64; and Polish Talmud edition, I, 325; and seizure for communal debts, III, 90; and synagogues, II, 144; and teachers' salaries, II, 186; classes in (Italian division of), I, 359; (rabbinic regulations of), II, 185, 196–97; contributions of Polish councils to, III, 146; denounced by Dutch Reformed Church, I, 254; erection of, and *Seder Eliyahu*, III, 125; exclusion of excommunicates' relatives from, II, 230; funds for, II, 185–86; (Hesse-Cassel), I, 342; II, 188; geonic responsa on, III, 94; in Soviet Union, I, 15; in Spain, II, 114; institutional rank of, II, 124; Italian uses of, I, 359; janitors of, sextons as, II, 106; neighborhood pupils in, I, 283; Polish, description of, II, 198–99; research students at, III, 126–27; Sicilian privileges on, I, 316–17; supervisors of, II, 57, 61, 63; (and Polish Council), I, 331; Surinam privilege on, I, 255; synagogue used as, II, 144; III, 151; universality of, II, 167; vs. jail, modern humanitarians on, II, 190; years of, and maintenance of students, II, 189

of jurisprudence, Jewish: I, 128, 152; Franco-German foundation of, II, 69. *See also* Associations; Budgets; Curricula; Education; Endowments; Law; Students; Teachers

Schudt, Johann Jacob, on Jewish sumptuary laws, II, 305; III, 201

Schule, designation of, II, 130, 144; III, 151–52. *See also* Schools; Synagogues

Schulklopfer, rise of, II, 106, 117; III, 137

Schutzbrief, Jewish, and family quotas, II, 5. *See also* Residence rights

Schutzgeld, German: and charities, II, 325–26; and poll taxes, II, 251

Schutzjuden, Prussian, and communal allegiance, II, 358–59

Schwarzenfels, controlled by Cassel council, III, 105
Schwerin (city), and Mecklenburg Council, I, 345
Schwersenz: excommunication of, II, 229; financial irregularities in, III, 122
Sciacca (Sicily), bi-sexual dancing in, II, 316
Sciences, cultivation of: and agnosticism, I, 25; and Babylonian rabbis, I, 143; and Christian unity, I, 227; and communal control, I, 4, 156; II, 360; and Hellenism, I, 158; and Polish Jewry, II, 192; and Turkish Jewry, III, 49; feminine education in, II, 179; Jewish attitudes to, II, 191–92, 363. *See also* Education; Learning; Medicine
Scina (North Africa), Jews of, I, 81
Scola Judaeorum, III, 151. *See also* Synagogue
Scotland, dependent on Spanish-Portuguese community in London, II, 21
Scribes, Jewish, ancient: I, 73, 102–3, 119, 126; III, 11–13; as teachers, I, 129; in Achaemenide Persia, I, 64; in Babylonian Exile, I, 65; in Elephantine, I, 72–73; III, 12–13; in Transjordan, III, 24; rank below scholars, I, 140
  medieval and modern: II, *110–14*; III, 139–40; appointment of, II, 59, 102; (decree of), I, 204; (governmental), I, 292; in various regions (Frankfort), II, 117; (Germany), II, 251; (Hesse-Cassel), II, 120; III, 86; (Islam), I, 204; (Italy), II, 59; (Kleve), II, 119–20; (Sicily), II, 102; (Spain), I, 292; provincial, III, 86; (and residence rights), II, 119–20; (court Jews as), II, 120; salaries of, III, 141; taxation of, II, 251, 261. *See also* Archives; Libellarius; Manuscripts; Papyri; Secretaries
Scrinarii, I, 217; II, 59. *See also* Scribes
Scriptures, *see* Bible
Scroll of Law: and oaths, I, 273; III, 113, 181; and licensed scribes, II, 110; III, 140; in synagogue section, II, 140; silver ornaments on, II, 271. *See also* Pentateuch
Sculpture, and synagogue art, II, 137
"Sea of the Talmud," displaces Bible, II, 193
Seashores: public ownership of, I, 137; synagogues on, I, 91
Seats, in synagogues: I, 103; III, *144–45*; and communal budget, II, 264; and position of *almemar*, II, 140–41; private ownership of, II, 130–31
Secession from community: and taxation, I, 24–25; Prussian law on, III, 5
Second: days, of holidays, I, 145; generation, in Palestine, I, 18; marriages, of women, and juristic technicalities, II, 318. *See also* 'Agunah
Secrecy: cabalistic, and religious associations, I, 355; Marrano, and communities of Resettlement, I, 252, 255, 262; II, 363; of London synagogue, I, 257; synods suspected of, I, 322
Secret ballots: and election of rabbis, III, 129; in modern Turkey, III, 48–49; relatively rare, II, 43, 47
Secretaries, communal: and chief rabbis, I, 285; and guild agreements, I, 369, 371; combination with other offices of, III, 140; in various regions (Elephantine), I, 73; (Islam), I, 202; (Italy), II, 118; (Poland), I, 272, 328; (Portugal), I, 285; (Spain), I, 202; of councils, I, 328; position of, I, 102–3; salaries of, I, 202; II, 118; selection of, I, 272; II, 58; scribes as, I, 73. *See also* Scribes
"Sect," Judaism as I, 113

Sectarianism, Christian: and American communities, I, 261; II, 365; and Dutch legalization of Jewish worship, I, 253; and Marrano communities, I, 252

Jewish: ancient, I, 12, 85, 95, 121, 136. *See also* Pharisaism; Sadduceeism; and congregational divisions, I, 85, 165; III, 89; and exilarchic succession, I, 178; and judiciary, I, 162; and Muslim jurists, I, 178; and *negidut*, I, 191; and Prussian law of secession, III, 5; and ritual, I, 121; and synagogues, I, 95; strength in Caliphate of, I, 158, 165, 178, 191; talmudic elimination of, I, 136. *See also* Heresies

Secularism, modern: and associational experience, I, 374; and communal institutions, I, 4, 6–7; II, 157; and education, II, 192. *See also* Sciences; and Emancipation, I, 8; and municipal functions, I, 134; and scholars' tax immunities, II, 277; and Soviet community, I, 15; and synagogue sanctity, II, 127–28; vs. Jewish religion, II, 290. *See also* Agnosticism

Security: for borrowed books, II, 202; for tax defaults, demanded, II, 219

Sedaca, communal (London): care for sick by, II, 115; share in fines of, II, 300

Ṣedaḳah, meaning of, I, 131

Seder Eliyahu Rabba, III, 34, 36–37; III, 125

Seder 'Olam Zuṭṭa: I, 145; and exilarchic genealogy, III, 30

Sefer ha-Ma'asim, III, 45

Sefer Ḥasidim, *see* Book of the Pious

Sefer Yeṣirah, III, 123

Segovia (Spain): payments to bishopric of, III, 55; Seneor's intervention in, I, 290

Segregation, Jewish: ancient, Josephus on, I, 86; and bathing, II, 165; and Bible studies, II, 194–95; and Byzantine guilds, I, 365; and communal control, I, 224–26; and economic regulation, II, 291; and instruction of Gentiles, II, 177; and Jew-baiting, I, 64; and lepers, III, 155; and meat sales, II, 157; and social welfare, II, 167; and sumptuary legislation, II, 303; Agobard on, I, 295; linguistic, and communal control, II, 359–60; slight in Italy, II, 360. *See also* Badge; Quarters

Seizure of property: II, 233; and communal taxes, II, 276; and corrupt judges, I, 166; by creditors, and orphans, II, 331; for charities, II, 344; of books, limited, II, 201; of cemeteries by Gentiles, II, 151; of synagogues and accumulated property, II, 135. *See also* Property

personal, *see* Bondage

Sejanus (Roman dignitary), I, 80

Sejm and *sejmiki*, I, 324. *See also* Diets, Polish

Seleucidae (dynasty): I, 75–76; Hellenism of, I, 118; Jewish leaders under, I, 146; population under, I, 82; synagogues under, III, 15

Self-accusation, Jewish, and tax burdens, III, 183

Self-assessment, Jewish: II, 281–82; and new arrivals, II, 12. *See also* Manifest; Tax assessments

Self-government, communal, in ancient Orient, I, 55; III, 7

Jewish, ancient: III, 7; and Josephus, III, 31; and Palestinian homeland, I, 74; and professional scribes, I, 73; in Damascus, I, 57; in Egypt, I, 56, 105; promoted by Persia, I, 63–64; Roman legislation on, I, 107; under Hellenism, I, 75–77; under Seleucidae, I, 83

medieval and modern: and corporate decline, II, 357; and Emanci-

pation, II, 360; and European associations, I, 372; and Hebrew deeds, II, 111; and interterritorial cooperation, I, 304; and local community, II, 3; despite government control, I, 342; heyday of, II, 120; oligarchic effectiveness of, II, 121–22; promoted by Church, I, *215–26*; under Islam, I, *158–65*; universally accepted, I, 208. *See also under* respective autonomous functions and institutions
congregational, and mutual toleration, I, 205. *See also* Congregations; judicial (and taxation), II, 209; (limited in criminal law), II, 220. *See also* Judiciary; Law; religious, Jewish insistence on, II, 210. *See also* Religion; Ritual
Self-help, popular, and anti-social individuals, II, 349. *See also* Lynching
Self-instruction, and parental responsibility, II, 174. *See also* Education
Self-interest, communal, and denunciation of tax farmers, II, 285
Self-support, economic, demanded by rabbis, I, 132. *See also* Charities
Seliḥah, on desecration of cemeteries, II, 150
Seliḥot services, sexton's announcement of, II, 106
Semi-proselytes, Jewish, in Graeco-Roman world, I, 82, 90, 97, 116. *See also* Proselytes
Semiatichi, excommunication of community of, II, 229
Semikah, II, 67–68, 79. *See also* Ordination
Semites: communal property of, I, 43; law of, I, 39
Senaah, children of, III, 11–12
Senate of Frankfort, and refugee peddling, II, 8
Senators, Piedmontese, as Jewish conservators, III, 68
Seneor, Abraham (Spanish chief rabbi): and redemption of captives, II, 334; functions of, I, 289–90; Judah Messer Leon against, III, 66; protects Jewish courts, III, 182
Senigallia, Jews of: legacies for, III, 212–13; officials' salaries in, II, 118
Seniores, II, 55, 63. *See also* Chief rabbis; Elders
Sennacherib (Assyrian king), I, 50, 57; III, 8, 10
Sens, and synod of Troyes, I, 312
Separation, marital, for wife-beating, suggested, II, 318–19
Separation of state and church, and communal divisions, I, 11, 20, 24
Separatism, congregational: I, 348, 351; and Al-Mamun's decree, I, 179; and differences in ritual, III, 148–49; and local autonomy, I, 205–6, 348, 351; and meat monopoly, II, 108; and Pharisaism, I, 135; and *Pletten*, II, 322–23; and right of burial, II, 157; and rival caliphates, I, 185; forbidden in London, I, 256; of heterodox groups, I, 165; talmudic restrictions on, I, 205–6. *See also* Conflicts; Heresies; Sectarianism
denominational, and burial of Gentiles, II, 148; Sephardic, local variations of, II, 18–20, 335, 365; III, 138; (endogamy), II, 311; tribal, in ancient Palestine, I, 32, 34
Sephardim: and interterritorial relief, I, 305–7; II, 136; and literacy tests, III, 163; and meat administration, III, 138, 159; and rabbinate, I, 196; II, 75; III, 125; and redemption of captives, II, 334–35; and Talmud Torah in Venice, I, 358; and theatrical arts, III, 207; centralized control of, II, 21; education of, II, 172; in various regions (America), II, 136; (Amsterdam), I, 253; III, 108; (Austria), III, 163; (Bosnia), III, 36;

(Constantinople), I, 205; (England), I, 20–21; III, 59; (France, southern), I, 305; (Holland), I, 253; III, 57–58, 108, 207; (Italy), I, 242; II, 75; (London), III, 59; (Near East), I, 197, 205; III, 311, 342; (Palestine), II, 342; (Paris), I, 264; (Sofia), III, 159; (Turkey), II, 311; (Venice), I, 358; preaching among, II, 95–96; ritual of (adopted by ḥasidim), II, 142; (and Babylonia), II, 142; (and Bible recitation), I, 122; (prayers for rulers), II, 143; separatism of, II, 18–20, 311, 335, 365; III, 138; synagogues of, II, 127; (position of *almemar* in), II, 141. *See also* Spanish exiles; Spanish-Portuguese Congregation

Sepphoris, Jews of: communal conflicts among, I, 135; III, 26–27; rabbis of, and recitation of Decalogue, III, 22

Septuagint: I, 82, 122–23; Justinian's decree on, II, 52, 143; on charity, I, 131; on elders, III, 13; on synagogue, I, 61, 86–87; recitation of, I, 90; III, 16; use of designations by (*ethnarches*), I, 190; (*nagid*), III, 13; (*patriarch*), I, 141. *See also* Bible versions

"Serfdom," Jewish, medieval: I, 14; and economic liberalism, III, 95; and English presbyters, I, 297; and French *procureurs*, I, 296; and German synods, I, 314; and heirless estates, II, 267; and self-government, I, 233–34; and Spanish residence rights, II, 10; and taxation, I, 241; II, 253; and transfers of Jews, III, 55; Barcelona synod on, I, 291; doctrine of, I, 215, 245; III, 104; equivocal in Poland, I, 268–69; more pronounced in north, I, 243; under Normans, I, 231. *See also* Legal Status

Sermons, *see* Preaching

Servants, Christian, employment of: denounced by non-Jews, I, 254; III, 61; and conversion of minors, I, 222

Jewish: ancient, I, 46; (of exilarchs), I, 147; and bridal support, II, 333; and *ḥazaḳah*, II, 299–300; and sex morality, III, 205; at early age, II, 333; care in illness of, III, 211; communal status of, III, 200; discharge of, II, 300; poll taxes of, II, 251; restriction on employment of, III, 202

Services, royal, and tax immunities, II, 13–14

Sessions of Lithuanian Council, chronology of, I, 328

Settlement rights, *see* Residence rights

Settlements, Jewish: ancient Palestinian, types of, III, 8; and congregational divisions, II, 4; III, 149; new, and religious institutions, II, 124; small (congregations in), I, 6; (regional academies for), II, 189–90; (regional control of), I, 283; II, 288. *See also* Regional control

"Seven best men": I, 133, 212; III, 27; and sale of synagogues, II, 128–29; medieval interpretations of, II, 55–56, 63; III, 120–21

Seven days: of mourning, and private worship, II, 124–25; preliminary excommunication for, II, 228

Seven men, summoned to Torah: II, 100–1; and professional reader, II, 141

Seven Years' War, and growth of charities, I, 363

Severus, Alexander (Roman emperor), I, 82, 96, 109; III, 17, 20

Seville: new synagogue in, I, 233; restrictions on ritual meat in, II, 159

Sex morality, Jewish: II, *311–15*; III, *205–6*; and loss of residence

rights, II, 8; of heretics, I, 165; supervisors of, II, 57. *See also* Moral conduct
Sex relations, Judeo-Christian: general condemnation of, I, 225, 254; II, 311–15; III, 61
Sexes: prohibition of interchange of attire of, II, 316; separation of, I, 91; II, 139–40; and feminine education, II, 177
Sextons, Jewish: I, 104; II, 100, 106–7; III, 137; administer flogging, II, 225; and billeting of soldiers, III, 189; and elders, II, 53, 102; and meat taxes, II, 257–58; and preparation of deeds, II, 113; and sumptuary laws, II, 306; and synagogue decorum, II, 141; and visitors, II, 12; calling children to examinations, II, 197; deposition of, II, 104; in various regions (Germany), II, 118; (Poland), II, 45, 141; (Sicily), II, 102; (Spain), II, 249; (Venice), II, 12; participate in elections, II, 45; revenue of, II, 118–19; tax immunities of, II, 249. *See also* Shammash
Sextus (in Berenice inscription), I, 100
Sha'atnez, biblical prohibition of: III, 202; and acquired rights, II, 297; and Jewish needle trades, III, 96
Shabbat ha-gadol, III, 133–34
Shabbetai Zevi, hailed by Hamburg, II, 25–26
Shabbetianism *and* Shabbetians: III, 91–92; and associations, I, 354–55; and communal control, II, 25–26, 121, 168; and interterritorial action, I, 308; and Palestine relief, II, 343; III, 216; and Polish Council, I, 331; and support of scholars, III, 165
Shafi'ite school of Muslim jurisprudence, I, 163
Shalom: community, Rhodes, shares *ḥazaḳah*, III, 198; in Greek inscription, I, 121
Shalom b. Isaac Sekel, III, 125–26
Shalom of Vienna, conference under, III, 76
Shalom Shakna b. Joseph (Polish chief rabbi), I, 301, 325
Shammai, school of, I, 152
Shamma'im, II, 56; III, 195. *See also* Tax assessments
Shammash: as beneficiary of wedding fees, II, 83; in Kleve, II, 119; Lithuanian, oath of office of, I, 331; variety of meanings of, II, 106. *See also* Diplomacy; Sextons; *Shtadlanim*
Shapur II (Persian king), arrests Nestorian chief, III, 32
Shaving, dishonorable, of criminals, II, 223
Shealṭiel (Turkish *kehaya*), I, 197–98
Shearith Israel congregation, New York: I, *261*; III, *60*; and "donkeys' burial," II, 156; appeal of, II, 136; III, 146
Sheaves, charitable, I, 132
Shebna (Hezekiah's scribe), III, 13
Sheftall family (Georgia), III, 152
Sheftall, Mordecai, cemetery of, III, 152
Sheḥitah, *see* Slaughtering, ritual
Sheikh: Jewish, in North Africa, I, 203; *al-Islam*, I, 96. *See also* Cadi
Sheitel, *see* Wigs
Shela (son of Judah), alleged ancestor of Saadia, III, 45
Sheliaḥ ṣibbur: II, 100–1; as opposed to *ḥazzan*, I, 201
Shema', recitation of: I, 121; and Decalogue, III, 22; and educational responsibilities, II, 177; and rabbi's precedence, II, 89; Byzantine prohibition of, I, 192
Shemoneh 'esreh (prayer), I, 121, 192, 237; II, 89, 105
Sheriffs, Jewish: and Portuguese chief rabbis, I, 285; *ḥazzanim* as, I, 104
Sherira b. Ḥanina Gaon: I, 185; Davidic descent of, III, 46; on exilarchic venality, III, 39; on flogging, II,

224–25; on Jehoiachin's synagogue, III, 12; on *kallah*, I, 184; on Mar Uḳba, III, 43; on students, I, 166; III, 41; solicits contributions, I, 181
Sheshbazzar (exilic leader), I, 69
Sheshna (Mesharsheia) b. Taḥlifa Gaon, on excommunication, I, 172–73
Sheṭar, II, 111. *See also* Starrs
Shetikah yafah bi-she'at ha-tefillah, II, 141
She'urim, in Jewish adult education, II, 206
Shi'a taḳḳanot, *see* Statutes, Moravian
Shiloh, sanctuary of, I, 40
Shipmasters, Jewish, ancient, association of, I, 365
Shipping, Jewish: ancient, I, 56–57, 364–65; and customs duties, II, 13; of funds, interterritorial I, 18; of wine, and communal controversies, II, 164
Shoeless worship, Muslim, and Algerian Jews, II, 129
Shoes, Spanish taxes on, II, 249
Shoḥetim, *see* Slaughtering
Sholal, Isaac ha-Kohen (Egyptian *nagid*), III, 34, 43–44
Sholal, Jonathan ha-Kohen (Egyptian *nagid*), III, 43–44
Shomerim labboḳer, associations of, I, 354
Shopkeepers, Jewish: and educational responsibilities, II, 175–76; and participation in burial, II, 147; and unfair competition, II, 297; attestation of tenant rights of, II, 294. *See also* Commerce; Merchants
Shops, Jewish, location of, under Islam, I, 163. *See also* Commerce; Merchants
Shortages: of books, and accumulation of libraries, II, 201; of household help, and taxation, II, 299
Shoṭerim, I, 51. *See also* Bureaucracy
Show-fringes: III, 203; and excommunication, I, 169; manufacture of, and teaching, II, 184
Shrines, ancient, worship at, I, 164
Shrouds, inexpensive, and desecration of cemeteries, II, 151
Shtadlanim: I, 27, 187–89; II, 57; on Warsaw Committee, I, 326; position of, II, 115–16; III, 141. *See also* Diplomacy
Shtubels, ḥasidic, I, 355; II, 125–26. *See also* Associations, religious; Congregations; Synagogues
Shum (abbreviation for Spires, Worms and Mayence), I, 313
"Sicilian" congregation, in Salonica, I, 348, 351
Sicily, Jews of: III, 53–54, 67; ancient, synagogues of, I, 83; and burghers, I, 278–79; and Christian bankers, II, 285; and respect for minority laws, I, 238; III, 117; and Valladolid synod, III, 67; as witnesses, I, 240; banking among, I, 243; "blasphemies" by, II, 339; bureaucracy of, III, 119–21; cemeteries of, III, 155–56; chief rabbis of, I, 292–95; 316–17, 319; II, 76, 304; III, 67; citizenship of, II, 242; communal debts of, II, 272; communal monopolies of, II, 261–62; debt bondage of, II, 226; III, 176; dependence on Spain of, I, 232; Diet of, I, 316–19; II, 249, 309; III, 78; elders of, II, 53, 102; elections among, III, 113–14; emigration to Palestine of, II, 340; expulsions of, III, 64; guilds of, I, 368–69; III, 95–96; hospitals of, II, 329; Muslim heritage of, I, 189–90, 209–10; III, 156; *negidut* of, I, 189–90; notaries of, II, 111; obligatory acceptance of office by, III, 119–20; polygamy among, II, 309; Provençal Jews among, I, 293, 295; redemption of captives by, II, 334;

respect for family laws among, II, 210; rights of settlement of, III, 103; ritual abattoirs of, III, 158; (Gentile payments to), III, 186; schools of, I, 317; (*studium generale*), II, 185; III, 165; (teachers), III, 164; statutes of, III, 103; sumptuary legislation of, II, 304; taxation of, I, 235; (equality), II, 249; (immunities), II, 274; (meat taxes), III, 158; (no funeral tolls), II, 153; wine administration of, II, 162. *See also* Italy, southern; Viceroys; *and under* respective cities

Sick, care of: II, *327–30*; and transportation costs, II, 324; associations for, I, 362–64; (Arles), III, 93; (Fürth), III, 93; (Königsberg), III, 90; (London), II, 115; visits during, III, 210–11; (comforting of mourners), II, 148; (gaming), II, 317. *See also* Hospitals; Illness; Physicians; Sanitation

Siculus Sabinus (Roman child), I, 104

Sicut Judaeis, bull of: I, 217; against desecration of cemeteries, II, 150; and Polish privileges, I, 268

Siena, Jews of: and Azariah de' Rossi, I, 308; legacy for, III, 212

Siete partidas, Las, code of: on communal elections, III, 113; on government fees for elders, II, 36; on Jewish holidays, I, 236

Sifre: III, 27, 33; on educational responsibilities, II, 169–70; on judiciary, III, 24

Sigismund (Holy Roman emperor): and chief rabbinate, III, 70; and Jewish conferences, I, 314–15; III, 77; and regional community, I, 299

Sigismund I (Polish king): and Hebrew printing, II, 204; and regional chiefs, I, 300; confirms all-Polish court, I, 325; convokes Włocławek assembly, I, 324

Sigismund II Augustus (Polish king), communal decrees of, I, 271

Signatures: of artists, refused by rabbis, III, 147; of elders, in merged congregations, II, 21; of parties, unimportance of, II, 113; of sextons, II, 106; of witnesses, II, 113; of writers of legal briefs, required, II, 239

Silano (Italian poet), II, 97–98

Silence: at funeral processions, demanded, II, 155; during prayers, *see* Chatting; Decorum; Discipline; during study, and forgetfulness, II, 199; in face of crime, responsibility for, III, 179–80; on acceptance of office, like refusal, III, 119

Silesia, Jews of: chief rabbinate of, II, 81; III, 87; cemeteries of, III, 156; expulsions of, I, 307; III, 106; (partial exclusion), I, 277–78; postal system of, II, 115; regional community of, I, 341; III, 87; synagogue remainders of, III, 147. *See also* under respective cities

Silk: manufacture of, established in Sicily, I, 368; Spanish taxes on, II, 249; thread of, and coat vents, III, 203

Silver ornaments: and servants, II, 305–6; in synagogues, II, 132, 135, 271; restricted by Mannheim ordinance, III, 202

wares: investment of charitable funds in, II, 335; taxes on, II, 249; (discounts), II, 255

Silversmiths: Dutch and Jews, III, 96; Jewish, in Alexandria, I, 78

Simḥah b. Samuel of Spires, on status of cantors, II, 102

Simḥat Torah, see Rejoicing with the Law

Simon (Nestorian chief), III, 32

Simon, Abraham, De La (early New Yorker) I, 260

Simon b. Gamaliel II (patriarch): I, 153; and calendar regulation, III, 30; Roman recognition of, I, 141; III, 28
Simon b. Lakish, R. (amora), designates officers, III, 24
Simon b. Mattathiah, the Maccabean, as *hegoumenos* or *nagid*, I, 190; III, 13
Simon b. Sheṭaḥ, R. (tannai), educational reform of, III, 23
Simon b. Yoḥai, R. (tannai): I, 125; on Roman judiciary, III, 24
Simon (son of Onias) the Just: I, 124; and Jewish education, III, 23
Simon the Scribe, dismissal of, III, 22
Simonias, community of, I, 126, 128
Sinai, revelation on, III, 22. *See also* Decalogue
Sinecures, communal: II, 57; and support of rabbis, II, 81
Sing-song study, justification for, II, 199–200; III, 169
Sinior, Solomon, distributes entire fortune for charities, II, 346
Sins: and their wages, doctrine of, II, 221; denounced by Forli Conference, II, 312–13; purification of, and flogging, II, 225; tax arrears as, III, 196. *See also* Ethics; Moral conduct; Sex morality
Sirach, Book of, I, 131; III, 23, 25, 161
Sirkes, Joel b. Samuel: blames Rashi for neglect of Bible, II, 193; III, 167; on contribution for citrons, III, 160; on head covering, III, 202; on mourning for leader, III, 153; on ransom of Polish nobles, III, 214; on responsibility of elders, III, 118; (judges), III, 174; on rights of minors, III, 212; on synagogues (attendance), II, 126; III, 142; (height), II, 139; III, 147
Sixtus V (pope): and assemblies, I, 321; and Hebrew books, I, 321
Skins: communal ordinances on, III, 199; private monopolies in, II, 299
Slabs, on synagogue roofs, II, 139
Slaughtering *and* slaughterers, Jewish: II, 63, *107–10*, 117, *157–60*; III, *137–39*, 199; and appointments (decree of), I, 204; (governmental), I, 292; and combination with other offices, II, 103; and ḥasidism, II, 110; III, 138–39; and heretics, I, 165; and meat imposts, II, 297; and orthodoxy, I, 237; and payment of salaries, III, 186; and prices of meat, II, 258; (communal price fixing), II, 300–1; and private monopolies, II, 299; and professional rabbis, II, 73, 76, 211; and sales to Christians, II, 107–8; by children, II, 198; by women; II, 107; III, 137; distinguishing signs on, III, 158; fees from, II, 258; (exilarchic), I, 175; (geonic), I, 180; (rabbinic), I, 202; II, 84–85; in various regions (Cracow), II, 63; (Erfurt), III, 107; (Frankfort), II, 117; (Islam), I, 165, 175, 180, 202, 204; (Poland), II, 63, 110; III, 138–39; (Spain), I, 292; II, 103, 159; III, 125; private, permissibility of, II, 107–8; refusal of, and tax defaulters, II, 284. *See also* Abattoirs; Meat taxes
Slavery *and* slaves, Jewish, ancient: I, 37, 46, 88; and royal administration, III, 7; in Rome, I, 79–80; and education, II, 177; III, 162; and illegitimate children, I, 175; and Muslim slavery, I, 177; and polygamy, II, 308; and prices, II, 336; and prohibited cohabitation, I, 177; II, 308; and redemption of captives, II, 336–37; for illegal emigration, I, 233–34; for tax defaults, I, 148; II, 284; in Babylonian Exile, I, 63; in Castile, II, 271; of exilarchs, I, 147; of Palestinian patriarchs,

I, 141; small among Jews, II, 177. *See also* Debt bondage
Slaves, "Hebrew," and rabbinic tenure, II, 88
Sleeping, in synagogues, II, 128; III, 151
Slonik, Benjamin Aaron b. Abraham: on failure of electorate, III, 116–17; on ownership of synagogue seats, III, 145; on scholars' tax immunities, III, 193
Slums, modern, and ghetto housing, II, 199
Smiths, Jewish, I, 78
Smyrna, Jews of: ancient, I, 94, 97; *ḥazakah* ordinance of, III, 198; preaching among, II, 99; III, 218–19; and election of *ḥakam-bashi*, III, 49
"Soaking the rich," and government taxation, I, 173; II, 280
Soap, private monopolies in, II, 299
Sobieski, Jan (Polish king), anti-communal privilege of, I, 280
Social factors: and ancient stratification, I, 85, 116; and artistic creativity, II, 137; and legal evolution, II, 217; III, 173–74. *See also* Class struggle
Social justice: and adaptability of Jewish law, II, 124, 245; and doctrine of repentance, II, 222; and economic regulation, I, 129–30; II, 290; and criminal law, II, 221; and Israelitic religion, III, 8–9; and popular self-help, II, 349; and psychological transformations, II, 362; and rabbinic theory, III, 200; and sumptuary laws, II, 302; conflicts in, II, 331. *See also* Communal control
Social relations, Jewish: and boarding of students, II, 189; and communal control, II, 361–62; and educational programs, II, 190; and excommunication, II, 230; and *ḥazakah* legislation, II, 298; and neighborhoods, I, 74; and scholarships, II, 89, 92, 181–82, 198; and wine administration, II, 162; between Sephardim and other Jews, II, 18–19. *See also* Separatism
Judeo-Gentile: III, 162; and communal control, I, 248; II, 24, 362; and contempt (Muslim), I, 171; (of Polish nobles), I, 270; and *corvée* labor, II, 267; and diplomacy, II, 115–16; and education, II, 177; (interest in Bible), II, 192–93; (familiarity with languages), II, 192; and exilarchs, I, 147; and Forli ordinances, I, 320; and gaming, II, 232; and height of synagogues, II, 139; and judicial adjustments, II, 208; and ritual meat, II, 158; and sex relations, II, 312–13. *See also* Christian Hebraists; Segregation
Social welfare, Jewish: II, *290–350*; III, *197–219*; ancient, I, 116, 129–33; and Cassel assembly, I, 342; and communal allegiance, II, 124; and courts, I, 129; and economic regulation, I, 129–30; II, 290; and government recognition, I, 5; II, 364; and Maimonidean degrees of charities, II, 326–27; and Polish councils, I, 324; and taxation, II, 248; associations for, I, 362. *See also* Associations, charitable; variety of institutions of, II, 167. *See also* Charities; Economic regulation
Socialism, Jewish: in eastern Europe, I, 7; interest in communal history of, I, 29
Societies, Jewish, *see* Associations
Society for the Marrying off of Orphan Girls in Amsterdam, III, 104
Society for the Raising of Orphans, in Amsterdam, II, 175
Sociology, Jewish: and community, I, 28–29; and evolution of rabbinic law, III, 174

"Sodom," judges of, II, 166

Sofer, meaning of, I, 102; II, 110; III, 13, 24. *See also* Scribes

Sofer (Schreiber), Moses b. Samuel, on rabbinic position, II, 88, 90; (outsiders), III, 100; (tenure), III, 129

Sofia: communal mourning in, II, 147; meat administration in, III, 159

Sokołów, Jews of: III, 186; meat taxes of, II, 258

Soldiers, Polish, enforce burial, III, 157

Solidarity, Jewish: and Al-Mamun's decree, I, 179; and anti-Semitism, I, 115–16; and burial, II, 147; and care for prisoners, II, 338; and communal responsibility, I, 211; II, 319, 347; and councils, I, 326–27, 331–32; II, 347; and criminal prosecution, II, 235; III, 179; and decline of Caliphate, I, 185, 189; and geonim, I, 180; and local customs, I, 192; and Muslim discrimination, I, 161, 165; and outside conflicts, I, 282; and redemption of captives, II, 335, 337; and talmudic compilations, I, 136, 153; and tax conflicts, II, 289; undermined by migrations, I, 197. *See also* Class struggle; Conflicts

Solomon (Israelitic king), I, 35–36, 38, 46, 56; III, 9. *See also* Temple, First

Solomon b. Isaac (Yiṣḥaḳi *or* Rashi): and legal uniformity, II, 69; and medieval rabbinate, III, 123; and production of parchment, III, 170; and synods, I, 311; and Troyes, III, 74; and use of Torah in oath, III, 181; disciples and teachers of, II, 100; III, 154, 170; family of, I, 311; in German *memor*-books, II, 146; on ban of settlement, II, 5–6; on Bible vs. Talmud study, II, 193; III, 167; on burial societies, III, 90; on cantors, II, 100; III, 135; on communal discipline, III, 118; on excommunication, III, 112; on family laws, I, 214; II, 210; on flogging, II, 225; III, 175; on *ḥakam*, II, 67; on "law of the kingdom," II, 210; on loving-kindness, III, 89; on migrations, III, 98; on Noahidic commandments, II, 210; III, 52, 172; on parental responsibilities, II, 174; on scholars' protection against demons, III, 169; on teachers, II, 184; III, 164; on women slaughterers, III, 137

Solomon b. Yehudah (Palestinian gaon), I, 193

Solomon de Moneurchan (southern French leader), III, 75

Sombart, Werner, discussions on work of, III, 220–21

Sommi, Leone da, works of, II, 191; III, 167

Sonnenfels, Alois von, I, 338

Sons of families, Sicilian, tax assessment of, III, 192

"Sons" of God, kings as, I, 36

Sorcery, *see* Magic

Soup, and sumptuary laws, II, 305

Sources, medieval: articulateness on taxes of, II, 250; as sources of law, II, 245; educational, texts of, III, 164; historical, *memor*-books as, II, 146; on titles of elders, III, 120; rabbinic orientation of, II, 78, 244. *See also* Archives; Literatures; Manuscripts; Papyri; Records

Southhampton, exclusion of Jews from, I, 276

Sovereignty, communal: I, 10, 95, 214–15; and minority rights, I, 8; medieval doctrines of, II, 217–18; "of the people," electoral safeguards of, II, 50

municipal, and Jews, I, 274; (synods), I, 310, 315, 319; in Germany, I, 276–77, 315; in Italy, I, 310, 319. *See also* Cities

papal, and meat legislation, III,

137; royal, and burghers' competition with Jews, I, 274
Soviet Union, Jews of, I, 15–17
Soviets, local, and Jewish community, I, 15
Sowhide, and oath *more judaico*, I, 273
Spain, ancient and Visigothic: alleged Israelitic settlements in, I, 56–57, 233; Israelitic commerce with, I, 56; Jewish expulsions from, I, 209; synagogues in, I, 83
  Islamic, Jews of: I, 200, 209–10; and Muslim guilds, III, 91; capital jurisdiction of, III, 38; collegiate bodies of, III, 50; contacts with Orient of, I, 209–10; III, 50; dependence on Babylonia of, I, 210, 242; III, 41; democracy of, I, 204; III, 38–39; leadership of, I, 189; rabbinic office among, II, 67; taxation of, III, 34
  medieval, Christian, Jews of: III, 6, 53; Abravanel's flight to, I, 286; agriculture of, I, 160–61; and burghers, I, 278–79; and conquest of Granada, I, 318; and French chief rabbinate, I, 308; and influence of Teuton law, I, 243; and Jewish unity, I, 227; and Marrano communities, I, 24; and Muslim courts, I, 170; and southern France, I, 242, 262–64; III, 75; and synods, I, 310; and wheat imports from Algiers, III, 200; Asher b. Yeḥiel's settlement among, III, 76; associations of, I, 352, 361, 366–70; III, 89–91, 95; ban of settlement among, II, 9–10; III, 95; bathhouses of, III, 160; burial societies of, I, 352; III, 89–91; capital punishment by, II, 221–23; charities of, I, 361; II, 320, 344; cemeteries of, II, 149–50; communal witnesses among, II, 113; constitutions of, II, 57–58; council of elders of, II, 55; (responsibility of), II, 53; courts of appeal of, II, 241; criminality of, II, 227–28; controversies over cantors among, III, 136; conversionist sermons among, III, 135; debt bondage of, II, 226–27; III, 176; deeds of, II, 111; III, 189; (use of Arabic), II, 112; duties of new arrivals among, II, 12; early traditions of, II, 69; education of, II, 114, 171–72; (Bible studies), II, 194–95; (diversification of Hebrew studies), II, 193; (general sciences), II, 191; (instruction in music), II, 191; (size of classes), II, 196; (Talmud Torahs), I, 356; (teachers' control), II, 180, 183; (teachers' salaries), II, 117–18, 184; electoral procedure among, II, 43, 47; (ineligibility of relatives), II, 40–41; excommunication by, II, 32; (irrevocable), II, 228; expulsions from, and vested interests, II, 120; guilds of, I, 366–70; III, 95; *habeas corpus* of, II, 227; *ḥazaḳah* legislation of, II, 298–99; hospitals of, III, 211; houses of ill-repute of, II, 313–14; illicit relations among, II, 313; (Judeo-Christian), II, 311–12; III, 205; interruption of prayers among, II, 33–34; III, 112; judiciary of (fees), II, 215; (lay), II, 64, 70–71; (papal suppression), I, 221; legislation on community of, I, 232–41; III, 155; meat sales of, II, 159; migrations of, I, 168, 197; III, 51. *See also* Spanish exiles; mutilation of criminals by, II, 223; notaries of, II, 111; polygamy of, II, 308; population of, II, 23; III, 108; prisons of, II, 226–27; quorum at weddings of, III, 47; rabbis of, I, 215; (salaries), II, 82; redemption of captives of, II, 334; III, 214; regional communities of, I, 286–92; royal confirmation of statutes of, II, 31; scribes' monopoly among, II, 113; supply of fish for, II, 161; synagogues of, II, 136–37, 139; III,

151–52; (*almemar*), II, 141; (appeals), II, 135–36; (attendance), II, 126; III, 143; (endowments), II, 132; (new), I, 220; (seats), II, 130–31; (transfers of), II, 135; taxation of, II, 276; (age), II, 248, 251; (antecedents of *cassella* method), II, 283; III, 195; (communal conflicts), II, 289; (farming), II, 285; (personal tolls), II, 264; (privileges to attract settlers), II, 13; (royal exemptions), II, 13, 274. *See also* Iberian Peninsula; *and under* respective kingdoms, provinces, cities and rulers

Spaniards, Catholic, Marranos as, II, 364

Spanish dependencies, vs. mother country, III, 64

Spanish exiles: and associations, I, 348, 350–51; and education, II, 172; and electoral rights, II, 48; and *ḥazakah* legislation, II, 295, 298; III, 198; and informing, II, 222; and North-African elders, I, 203; and rabbinate, I, 196; II, 75; III, 125; and redemption of captives, II, 334–35; and secret synagogues, II, 127; and Turkish decentralization, I, 197; cemeteries of, II, 147; congregation of (in Algiers), III, 208; (in Damascus), III, 105. *See also* Spanish-Portuguese congregations; hospitable reception of, II, 338; in various regions (Balkans), II, 48; III, 198; (England), I, 255–56; (Marseilles), III, 213; (North Africa), I, 203; II, 13; III, 50–51; (Rome, papal), I, 350; (Turkey), I, 197, 348; 350–51; II, 48, 127, 147, 295; III, 125, 198; (Verona), II, 19; judiciary of, III, 125; losses during migrations of, II, 338; III, 214; Marranos as, I, 255–56; superiority feeling of, I, 204–5. *See also* Sephardim

Spanish-Portuguese Congregation, in Amsterdam: III, *105*, 141; against communal loans, II, 268; and assignment of seats, II, 131; expropriates private cemetery, II, 148; orphan asylum of, II, 332; rabbinic salaries in, III, 127

in Hamburg, minute-book of, III, 109

in London: I, 20–21, 256; accounting in, II, 65; against begging, II, 321–22; against public criticism of elders, II, 48; and care of sick, II, 327; and communal discipline, II, 144; and hiring of household help, II, 300; and Isaac d'Israeli, II, 54; and parental approval of marriage, II, 310; and synagogue assemblies, II, 144; and tenant protection, II, 300; and visitors, I, 257; control in Barbados of, I, 262; election days in, III, 116; exclusivity of, I, 256; II, 21; pre-censorship by, II, 202; statutes of, I, 256; II, 21, 48, 144, 202, 300, 310, 321–22, 327; III, 60; (recited in synagogue), III, 109–10. *See also* Sephardim

in New York, *see* Shearith Israel

Spartianus, Aelius (Roman historian), III, 25

Speculation: in *ḥazakah*, II, 295; in synagogue seats, II, 130–31; restrictions on, I, 130

Speech: correctness of Polish teachers in, II, 183–84; freedom of, restricted in Cassel, I, 342

Spending, unnecessary, discouraged by rabbis, I, 132

Speyer, *see* Spires

Spira-Wedeles, Isaac b. Yeḥiel Michael (Prague chief rabbi): I, 340; Eibeschütz's father-in-law, III, 163

Spira-Wedeles, Simon (Prague chief rabbi): I, 339–40; III, 85–86; salary of, III, 127–28

Spires, Jews of: and courts of defendants, I, 250; and Rhenish synods, I, 313; bathhouses of, II, 166; III, 160; cantors of, II, 102; early cemetery of, II, 146; emigration of, I, 245; rabbis of, II, 78
Spirits, *see* Demons
"Spiritual judges," Jewish, Italian, laymen as, II, 76
Spiritual transgressions, prison terms for, III, 176
"Spokesmen," aristocratic, Spanish, of Jewish communities, I, 291
"Sponge," Jewish taxation as, II, 247
Sports: ancient Jews in, I, 92; III, 16; low rabbinic estimate of, II, 198
Stability, social: and professional judges, III, 173; modern, growth of, II, 120. *See also* Insecurity
Stables, and sale of synagogue, II, 129
Stamp tax, Polish, and Jewish books, II, 204–5; III, 171
Standard of life: and accumulation of libraries, II, 201; and charitable associations, I, 360
Standardization of prayers, and rise of *ḥazzan*, II, 100
Starrs, Hebrew, in England, II, 111; III, 139. *See also* Deeds
State control, and Jewish community: I, 10–11, 13, 21–22, 111–16, 208, 222; II, 3, 123, 157, 353–54; and admission to communal membership, II, 4; and charities, II, 349; and Church, I, 11, 114. *See also* Separation; and control of weddings, II, 84; and court Jews, II, 357; and criminal law, II, 220; and deeds, II, 112; and Egyptian economy, I, 41, 105; and elections, II, 36; and establishment of cemetery, II, 147, 149; and guild autonomy, I, 371; and Hebrew printing, III, 170–71; and heresies, I, 237; and informers, II, 223; and interterritorial cooperation, I, 304; and Judeo-Christian sex relationships, II, 312; and judicial independence, I, 114; II, 144, 208, 239, 283; and minority rights, I, 8; and morals, I, 11; and price fixing, II, 301; and public order, I, 11; and rabbinate, II, 78; and religious associations, I, 354; and religious law, II, 11, 210; and Resettlement, I, 252; and sumptuary laws, II, 302; III, 202; and synagogues, II, 144; (adornment), II, 138; (Christian attendance), II, 131; and taxation, I, 209; II, 246; (farming), II, 6–7, 284; and Turkish churches, I, 197, 199. *See also* Government; Law; Legal status; Monarchy
Israelitic, religious view of, I, 54, 59. *See also* Monarchy
papers, medieval forgeries of, I, 251; "within the state," complaints of, I, 8, 208; and corporate decline, II, 358; and ghetto, I, 226; in ratio to taxation, I, 282
Statehood, features in community of: I, 8, 29, 208–9, 226, 282; II, 190, 358; and exilarchs, I, 150; and social welfare, II, 290–91; modern, I, 12–13
States of the Church, *see* Papal States
Statistics, Jewish: American, methods of, III, 3; congregational, of Constantinople, I, 168; educational, in Frankfort, III, 166; occupational, I, 368; (and Jewish bureaucracy), II, 117; population, and three-class system, II, 38
Stättigkeit, Frankfort, on Jewish musicians, II, 115
Status quo community, in Hungary, I, 19
Statutes, associational: III, 90; and community, I, 116; and membership rights, II, 17; and synagogue attendance, III, 143; and taxation, I, 109–10; availability of, I, 356–59,

362, 364; charitable, II, 332; III, 90, 92–93, 102, 104; (burial societies), I, 352; (Palestine relief), III, 217; (visiting of sick), III, 211; educational, III, 89, 92–93; enforcement of, I, 349; in various regions (Cracow), III, 96; (Frankfort), III, 93; (Fürth), III, 93; (Graeco-Roman world), I, 77, 108–10; (Italy), III, 92–93; (Metz), III, 89; (Modena), III, 102; (Moravia), III, 90; (Padua), III, 92; (Prague), III, 90; (Saragossa), III, 95; (Verona), III, 104; (Vienna), III, 89–90; of guilds, I, 366–67, 369–70; III, 95–96, 164

Statutes, communal, and congregational: I, 11–12; II, 3–4, 30; adaptability of, II, 290–91; adoption of, I, 261; II, 20, 35, 57; and acceptance of office, II, 54; III, 119; and bachelors, III, 114; and begging, II, 321–22, 324; and censorship, II, 202. *See also* Books; Censorship; and communal debts, III, 190. *See also* Debts; and communal discipline, I, 259; II, 12, 219; III, 109; and denunciation of transgressors, II, 236; and elders, I, 204; II, 71, 76; (elections), II, 40–41; (responsibility), II, 53; (share in ordination), II, 92; and government approval, I, 232, 264, 316; II, 364; and *ḥerem*, III, 179; and household employees, II, 300; III, 200; and membership, II, 13, 16, 19; and modern reforms, III, 48; and new arrivals, II, 12–13; and new synagogues, II, 21; and oath of office, III, 113; and Palestine relief, II, 342; III, 216; and passive franchise, II, 39; and plenary assembly, II, 28–31; (obligatory attendance), II, 28; and *Pletten*, II, 322; and polygamy, II, 307–10; and Portuguese chief rabbis, I, 285; and preaching, II, 97; and property qualifications, II, 38–40; and quorum at weddings, III, 47; and rabbis, II, 75; III, 71–72, 129; (as merchants), II, 81; (attendance at weddings), III, 205; (ordination), III, 130–31; (registration), II, 84; (tenure), II, 86; and regional control, I, 286–87, 331, 345; II, 22, 42; III, 87; and remuneration of deputies, II, 115; and rotation in office, II, 55; and sale of synagogues, II, 136; and synagogue decorum, III, 150; and talmudic law, II, 69; III, 27; and teachers, II, 114, 118, 185; and textbooks, II, 203; and treasurer's accounting, II, 65; and use of *morenu*, II, 92; communal demand for, III, 65; contradictions in, II, 3; dictated by middle class interests, II, 299; enforcement of, I, 211; III, 118, 179; (sextons), II, 106; imitation of, II, 31; in various regions (Amsterdam), III, 105; (Aragon), I, 287; (Avignon), II, 39, 84; III, 103, 190; (Bamberg), I, 345; II, 300; (Brazil), III, 59; (Carpentras), II, 13, 115; (Cracow), II, 234; III, 63; (France), I, 264; II, 15–16; (Fez), III, 47; (Frankfort), III, 129; (Germany), II, 15, 35, 236; (Graeco-Roman world), I, 95, 108; III, 27; (Hamburg), II, 54, 118; (Hesse-Cassel), III, 86; (Holland), I, 255; (Islam), I, 173, 204, 206; (Italy), I, 232; II, 10–12; III, 197; (Kleve), III, 86; (Lithuania), I, 331; (London), II, 16, 19, 21, 31, 202; III, 60, 109; (Moravia), I, 338–39; II, 40–41, 114, 175, 189–90, 300; III, 85, 120–21; (New York), I, 261; III, 60–61; (Poland), I, 332–33; II, 86; III, 71–72, 122; (Portugal), I, 285; III, 65; (Rome, papal), II, 20; (Salonica), II, 295; (Saragossa), II, 12; (Sarajevo), II, 12, 54; (Sicily), I, 316;

II, 76, 309–10; (Spain), I, 286–87; II, 14, 53; (Sugenheim), II, 65; (Turkey), I, 196; II, 75; III, 48; (Wied-Runkel), I, 345; III, 87; Italian ghettos, III, 197; preservation of, II, 31; quick succession of, II, 3–4, 60–61; recited in synagogue, III, 109; restrict travel facilities, II, 15–16; vagaries of, II, 122. *See also* Constitutions; Law; Ordinances; Public Law; *and under* respective cities and functions

Steg, Joseph Samuel (Warburg rabbi), papers of, III, 117, 144

Steinheim, Solomon Ludwig, on Polish teachers, II, 183–84; III, 163

Stephen, Saint (apostle), I, 120

Stern (Frankfort family), III, 141–42

Stobi (Yugoslavia), synagogue of, I, 84; III, 15, 28

Stolen property: privileges on search for, II, 227; purchase of, prohibited, I, 330; II, 200–1; taxation of, II, 256

Stolin, private archive in, III, 92

Stone-masons, Jewish, medieval, II, 145

Stones: precious, in synagogue adornment, I, 78; throwing of, at deceased excommunicate, II, 231

Stool, three-legged, and oath *more judaico*, I, 273

Strabo, Caius Fannius (Roman geographer): III, 13–14; on Egyptian ethnarchs, III, 31; on Jewish quarters, III, 15

Stradom, residence rights in, II, 234. *See also* Cracow

Strangers, Jewish, synagogue accommodations for, I, 92; II, 128; III, 15

Strasbourg, Jews of: III, 63, 88, 182; and Josel of Rosheim, I, 299; III, 69; and municipal courts, I, 250; change of venue among, II, 243

Strategia, Palestinian, and taxation, III, 25

Strategos, Byzantine, I, 229

Stratores, I, 217; II, 59. *See also* Elders

Straw, Spanish taxes on, II, 249

Streets: ancient Israelitic, in Damascus, I, 57; communal surveillance of, II, 55, 57, 167, 291; (set aside for crafts), I, 130; dirt of, and shoeless worship, II, 129; level of, and synagogue foundations, II, 139; ownership of, I, 135, 137

Strictness, juridical: differences of opinion on, III, 172; excessive, condemned by rabbis, II, 212; of Talmud vs. Bible, III, 167–68

Stripes vs. sticks, in flogging, II, 225

Struggle for liberation, Jewish-German, and collegiate bodies, II, 62

Students, Jewish: ancient, gathering of, III, 33; (at academies), I, 151; (at exilarchic courts), I, 147; and banditry, II, 187; and book lending, II, 201–2; III, 170; and class distinctions, I, 166; and day of judgment, II, 98; and educational goals, II, 206–7; and gaming, III, 207; and marriage quotas, III, 98; and redemption of captives, II, 336; and renting restrictions, III, 199; and synagogue attendance, I, 360; and Wilno chief rabbinate, II, 86; at academies, I, 151, 183–84, 193; II, 173; at Italian universities, III, 167; communal support of, I, 339; III, 166; (by bankers), II, 78; (billeting of), II, 323; (legacies for), I, 361; (taxes for), I, 181; exempted from office, III, 119; independence of, II, 180–81; number of, and teachers' salary, II, 118; participate in legal decisions, III, 172; provisions for textbooks of, II, 203; qualifications of, II, 79; relations to masters of, I, 139–40; II, 180; III, 163–64; residence of, I, 180; segregation of, I, 357; sex morality of, II, 315;

substitute for public, III, 127; synagogue accommodations for, II, 128; tax immunities of, II, 277–78. *See also* Scholars; Schools

Studium ad opus scolarium Judaeorum pauperum, in Tortosa, III, 166

Studium generale, Jewish, in Sicily, II, 185; III, 165

Study: abstention from, and mourning for scholars, II, 147; for its own sake, and living experiences, II, 206; in Palestine, and diaspora Jewry, II, 340; individual obligation to, II, 169, 177; lends immunity against demons, III, 169; and synagogue chanting, II, 104–5; of philosophy, protected by popes, I, 307–8. *See also* Anti-Maimonidean controversy; power of, and sex morality, II, 315; rabbinic concentration on, I, 135. *See also* Education; Rabbis; Scholars; Teachers

Sturgeon, legal controversy over, II, 161; III, 159

Style: architectural, and Gentile surroundings, II, 137; of cemeteries, I, 94. *See also* Architecture; Art; of letters, I, 102, 182–83; III, 29

Sub-conservators, Jewish, Franco-Italian, III, 68

Subdivisions, of Jewish real estate, II, 292

Subject of history, Jews as, I, 22

Subjection, physical, Jewish, demanded by Church, I, 217

Subsidies, for Hebrew printing, II, 203

Subterfuges, legal: and communal interest payments, II, 269–70; and height of synagogues, II, 139

Suburenses, congregation of, I, 81

Succession, geonic, history of, III, 46

Succoth, elders of, I, 44

Suczawa (Bukovina), regional community of, III, 105

Suetonius, Caius Tranquillus (Roman historian), III, 19

Sufferings, Jewish, in Babylonian Exile, I, 63. *See also* Massacres; Persecutions

Sugenheim (Franconia), Jews of: admission of aliens by, II, 9; communal accounting by, II, 65; Purim masquerades of, III, 207; statute of, on reading of constitution, III, 109; taxes for poor of, II, 345; III, 209

Suicide: and burial, III, 157; Jewish prohibition of, II, 156; of Jewish leader, III, 100

Suleyman the Magnificent (Turkish sultan), and papal prisoners, III, 214–15

Sultans, *see* Mamelukes; Turkey

Summonses, judicial: and marshals, I, 104, 272; and prisons, II, 226; enforced by excommunication, II, 228; fees from, II, 83; informality of, III, 182; refusal of, and charities, II, 346

to assemblies, II, 25; to prayers, by sextons, II, 106

to Torah: and *archisynagogi*, I, 103, 122; and excommunication, I, 169; and exilarch, I, 189; and *ḥazzan*, II, 100–1; and vows, II, 132; favoritism in, II, 132; of geonim, I, 184; of priests, III, 42; and refusal to accept office, II, 54. *See also* Bible recitation; Pentateuch

Sumptuary laws, Jewish, history of, II, *301–7*, 326; III, *200–2*

Sunday: as election day, III, 116; as legal holiday, I, 11, 260, 270

Super-assessors, II, 58, 63. *See also* Tax assessments

Supercommunity, Jewish, *see* Regional control; *and under* respective chiefs

Superintendents, *see* Overseers

Supply and demand, law of, and *ḥazaḳah*, II, 294

Superstitions, religious: III, *156*; and Polish censuses, III, 184; identification of Judaism with, I, 112
Supreme Court, Jewish, Polish: and Councils, I, 327; and drafting of statutes, II, 31. *See also* Courts of Appeal; High Court
Supremus magister, Meir of Rothenburg as, III, 69–77
Sura (Babylonia), academy of: I, 151–53, 155, 179–83; III, 33; imitation of Palestine by, I, 193; recitation of Decalogue at, III, 22; supremacy of, I, 183, 185; III, 46
Surgeons, Jewish, I, 120; II, 115; III, 157. *See also* Medicine; Physicians
Surinam, Jews of: III, 58; chief rabbis of, II, 87; freedom of worship of, I, 255; III, 61; help New York synagogue, II, 136; immigration from Cayenne of, I, 265; lay control over, II, 87
Surtaxes, communal, and elders' discretion, III, 196
Survival, Jewish: and ancient dispersion, I, 54, 67, 73, 75; and charities, II, 349; III, 218; and Christian anti-Semitism, I, 117; and communal control, I, 21–22, 209; II, 167; (self-discipline), II, 365; and congregational divisions, I, 67; and Hellenism, I, 118; and indoctrination of youth, II, 190; and medieval legislation, I, 282; and modern trends, I, 21–22; II, 363, 365–66; (Emancipation), II, 351; (in Soviet Union), I, 16; and rabbinate, II, 77, 94; and synods, I, 310; and talmudic consolidation, I, 155–56; and taxation, II, 246; and tenant protection, II, 295
Susannah, story of, I, 61; III, 10
Süsskind von Trimberg, II, 192; III, 167
Swedish-Polish Wars: and communal debts, III, 191; and interterritorial action, I, 306; II, 355; and Polish councils, I, 333; and tax immunities, II, 278
Swimming, educational requirement of, II, 198; III, 169. *See also* Sports
Switzerland: courts of, I, 48; Jews of, I, 315; III, *63*. *See also under* respective cities
Synagogé, Greek term of, I, 61, 86–87; III, 15–16
Synagogues, ancient, I, *55–74*; III, *9–13*, 21–22; (origins), I, 89; III, 9–10, 21; acquisition of, I, 135; and *archisynagogi*, I, 103; and artistic creativity, II, 137; and "House of the People," I, 62; and imperial worship, I, 109; and "Israel in flesh," I, 112; and Jewish survival, I, 155; and Palestinian sanctuaries, I, 53; and popular assemblies, I, 95; annexes of, I, 91–93; announcements from roofs of, I, 104; II, 106; as depositaries, I, 88; as substitutes for Palestine, I, 89; III, 16, 21; assaults on, I, 113; (desecration of), I, 62, 109, 113–15; attract Gentiles, I, 88, 112; dedications of, I, 77, 109; disposal of, I, 135; educational functions of, I, 124–25; enforced contributions to, I, 120; flogging in, I, 104; for all people, I, 74; functions of, I, *89–93*; height of, I, 91, 112, 162; in various regions (Alexandria), I, 78, 364–65; (Babylonia), I, 61, 66–67; (Dura-Europos), I, 92; III, 16; (Egypt), I, 76; (Graeco-Roman world), I, *75–117*; III, *13–16*; (Palestine), I, 120–25; (Rome), I, 80–82; III, 14–15; indispensability of, I, 120; legal erection of, I, 112; location of, I, 84, 86, 91; III, 14–15; meaning of, I, 61, 86–87; III, 15–16; and patriarchate, I, 145; non-territorial, I, 73–74; number of, in larger communities, I, 66; oath in, I, 112; "of Severus," I, 82; Persian

legislation on, III, 36; private, I, 61, 87; professional sections in, I, 364–65; ritualistic diversity in, I, 79, 121; Roman attitude to, I, 109; romances in, I, 88; seating order in, III, 16; size of, I, 92; support scholars, I, 139; tax immunity of, I, 109; traditions on, III, 12; transformation of, I, 86, 88

medieval and modern: II, *123–46*; III, *142–52*; administration of, II, 124–36; Adribi's definition of, III, 125; alleged antiquity of, I, 164–65; allegiance to, I, 5; and bathhouses, II, 166; and charitable funds, II, 328; (collections), I, 363; III, 210; (diversion of tithe), II, 344; (for captives), II, 334–35; III, 213; (Palestine relief), II, 341; (refugees), II, 8; and communal debts, II, 273; III, 190; and contributions of candles, II, 259; and dancing, III, 206; and dependent communities, II, 22; and education, I, 357; II, 186, 206; III, 32, 165; and exilarchs, I, 189; and Franciscan chapel, I, 320; and judiciary, I, 272; II, 211; and Kleve assembly, I, 344; and population, I, 5–6, 350; and rabbinic control, II, 75–76, 167; III, 125; (ordination), II, 67; and Spanish exiles, I, 197; II, 365; and suppression of Polish councils, I, 336–37; and tax immunities, I, 11; II, 277; as centers of private life, I, 6; II, 144–45; as houses of assembly, II, 24, 48, *136–46*; as houses of worship, I, 9; II, *136–46*, 210; as regional centers, I, 286; as security for loans, I, 334; assigned to rabbis, I, 199; associational, I, 349–50; III, 88, 97; attacks on, I, 270; II, 135; III, 36; attendance at, I, 25, 283, 352; (of children), I, 360; II, 198; built of wood, II, 137; III, 147; chanting in, II, 105; (and Gentile music), II, 104. *See also* Music; class attire in, II, 307; closing of, III, 112; (for debts), III, 84; consumption of food in, II, 128; controversy over possession of, III, 149; converted into churches, I, 220, 232, 237; III, 151; decoration of, II, 61. *See also* Art; distribution of citrons in, III, 187; elections in, II, 102; erection of, II, 328; III, 125, 153; (and imposts on books), II, 204; (and sale of seats), II, 130–32; (outside assistance for), II, 136; exclusion from (by ban), I, 169; II, 230; (for tax immunities), II, 14; (of rabbi), II, 85; exposure of criminals in, II, 224; flogging in, II, 225; for women, II, 249; height of, I, 162, 220, 270; II, 139; III, 147; honors of (lost for refusal to accept office), II, 54; (payments for, collectible), II, 133; in various regions (America), I, 25, 255, 260; III, 153; (Aragon), II, 140; (Austria), II, 160; (Avignon), II, 61; III, 190; (Byzantine Empire), I, 229–30; (Candia), III, 112; (Egypt), III, 149; (England), I, 256–60; II, 21, 48; (France), I, 262–64; (Germany), II, 8, 42; III, 107, 187, 206; (Hamburg), III, 187; (Holland), I, 254; II, 21; III, 57–58, 117; (Islam), I, 162, 169, 189; III, 35–36; (Italy), I, 232, 307–8, 360; II, 10–11, 19, 76; (Kleve), I, 344; (Lithuania), I, 280; II, 273, 335; III, 190; (London), II, 21; (Palestine), I, 320; (Poland), I, 270, 272, 330, 334, 336–37; II, 22, 46, 307; III, 84, 97, 147, 210; (Prague), I, 352; (Resettlement areas), I, 24; (Rome, papal), I, 218; (Sicily), I, 232, 316–17; (Spain), I, 233, 236–37, 286; II, 14, 102, 163, 249; III, 125, 135, 151, 155; (Turkey), I, 197, 199; II, 75, 127, 222; III, 36, 125; interruption of prayers in, II, 14, 34. *See also*

Interruption; location of, I, 86; (secretiveness of), II, 127; III, 58, 61; missionary sermons in, III, 135; new, prohibition of, I, 219, 229–30, 270, 280; II, 140; III, 35–36; (abrogated), I, 232–33, 236–37; (and changes of endowments), II, 266; (and congregational divisions), II, 19, 125; III, 149; of defendants, and choice of courts, II, 242; "of Satan," I, 216; Palestine messengers preach in, II, 96, 342; possession of, and fiscal control, III, 153–54; private, II, 124–25; III, 142–44; (and congregational divisions), I, 350–52; (prohibited in London), II, 21; proclamation of ordinances in, I, 330; II, 222, 306; III, 109–10; (anti-alien), II, 10–11; (on taxes), II, 257–58; (papal), I, 307–8; (regional), II, 42, 163; promulgation of bans in, II, 32, 46, 228; proximity to churches of, II, 150; quarrels in, II, 28; removal of, III, 23; repairs of, Christian legislation on, I, 219; research students at, III, 126–27; revenue from, and communal budgets, II, 264; right of asylum of, II, 11; ritualistic variations in, I, 9; II, 19, 69; (reformers on), II, 360; secessions from, III, 117; sexton's position in, II, 106–7; single, Canon law on, II, 125; state legislation on, I, 162–65, 219, *254–60*, 270, 316–17; II, 160, 363–64; III, 35–36, 52–53, 155; supervisors of, II, 57; taxes on, II, 130, 135, 265. *See also* Ḥazzan; Liturgy; Rabbis; Worship

Syncretism, religious, ancient: and burial, I, 94; and charities, III, 25; and communal divisions, I, 85; and religious associations, I, 354; Jewish resistance to, I, 97; II, 167. *See also* Pagans; Religion

Syndic (godfather), rabbi as, II, 90

Syndici, Jewish, Polish, I, 326, 328; II, 116. *See also* Diplomacy; *Shtadlanim*

Synodoi, ancient, and synagogue repasts, I, 95; II, 128

Synods, *see* Councils

Syracuse (Sicily), Jews of: and all-Sicilian conferences, I, 317; and Judeo-Christian witnesses, I, 240; cemetery of, III, 155–56; customs duties of, II, 262; lay leadership of, I, 293; II, 76; III, 121; (miraculous escape), II, 53

"Syracuse congregation," in Salonica, II, 53

Syria, ancient: climate of, I, 31; communal dissensions in, I, 79; controlled by Ezra, I, 64; Jewish emigration from, III, 14; Roman literature in, I, 142; religious toleration in, I, 75; synagogues in, I, 83

Muslim, various rituals in, I, 167; Turkish, capitulations in, III, 102

Ṭabari Muḥammad ibn Jarir al-, I, 148; III, 31–32

Tabeel (Persian-Jewish official), I, 64

Tables, monopolies in furnishing of, II, 299

Taboos, biblical, and Jewish needle trades, III, 96

Tahpanhes (Egypt), Jews of, I, 57

Tailors, Jewish: guilds of, I, 368–69, 371; III, 97; and leaseholds on baths, II, 166; and *sha'atnez*, II, 297; III, 96; and teachers, III, 41–42; as magistrates, I, 368; responsibility for sumptuary laws of, II, 306; sales taxes on products of, II, 261

Taitaṣaḳ, Samuel, and Salonica ordinance against informers, II, 222

Taḳḳanah, vs. *ḥerem ha-ṣibbur*, III, 111–12

Taḳḳanot, I, 170; II, 12, 30; III, 179. *See also* Ordinances; Statutes

Talbot, Charles, Duke of Shrewsbury, III, 57

Tallages, Jewish, medieval, and Exchequer of Jews, I, 245, 250. *See also* Taxation

Talmud, Babylonian: achievement of, I, 146; and ancient Diaspora, I, *117–56*; and ban of settlement, II, 5–6; III, 98; and European supercommunity, I, 346; and legal evolution, II, 211; III, 173–74; (criminal law), II, 219–20, 226; (public law), II, 216–17; and Maimonidean teachings, III, 25; and medieval adjustments, II, 69, 220; (rabbinate), II, 79; and medieval societies, I, 352, 354; III, 90–91; and polygamy, II, 308; anti-competitive laws of, II, 5–6; III, 98; as a source of communal history, I, 118–19; burning of, I, 223–24, 305–6; II, 191, 198; compilation of, I, 153; III, 217; educational heritage of, II, 199–200; (value of quotations from), II, 206; exegesis of, Franco-German, III, 90; Greek loan words in, I, 130; III, 16; Ibn Adret on, I, 213; includes Bible, II, 193–94; individualistic basis of tax laws of, II, 26–27, 268; large size of communities in, II, 23; meaning of term of, I, 125–26; on Alexandrian synagogue, III, 13; on *archisynagogus*, III, 18; on *boulé*, I, 134; on burial of Gentiles, II, 148; on burial societies, III, 90; on capital punishment, II, 221; on charities, I, 102; II, 320–22, 326, 345; (against begging), II, 321; (Gentile contributions), II, 347; (preference for local poor), II, 323; (supervisors), II, 64; III, 18; on childless marriage, II, 309; on class conflicts, I, 135; on communal hierarchy, I, 140; on communal property, II, 136; on covering the head, II, 307; on customs, II, 70; on cutting of beards, III, 203; on denunciation of criminals, II, 235–36; on diversion of legacies, II, 328; on education, I, 135–36, 142, 182, 356; II, 95, 170–71, 174, 207; III, 23–24, 151, 169; (feminine), II, 178; (night study), III, 162; (school age), II, 174; (size of classes), II, 195–96; (teachers), II, 182, 184; III, 85; (teaching of Gentiles and slaves), II, 177; on elders, I, 140, 200; III, 17–19; on electoral democracy, III, 27; (franchise of proselyte), II, 286; (majority principle), II, 126; III, 126; on embassies, III, 19; on exilarchs, I, 145–46, 176; on flogging, II, 220; on gambling, II, 316; on Gentile wine, II, 161; on group divisions, III, 17; on guilds, I, 364; III, 94; on *ḥazaḳah*, II, 292; III, 197–99; on *ḥeber ha'ir*, I, 134; on "house of the people," III, 11; on illicit cohabitation, I, 177; on indispensable institutions, III, 21; on inquiries from academies, I, 180–81; on investment of orphans' funds, III, 195; on Ishmael, I, 195; on judiciary, III, 24; (lay), II, 71–72; (mediators), II, 237–38; (priorities), II, 236–37; (qualifications of judges), II, 214; (tax disputes), II, 288; on *keneset*, III, 15; on "law of the kingdom," I, 214; on "little sanctuary," III, 10; on marital relations, II, 317, 319; (preferences in choice of spouse), III, 23; on necromancy, II, 154; on non-conformity, I, 168; on obligations of new residents, III, 102; on Palestinian cities, III, 8; on Persian holidays, III, 149; on preachers, II, 99; on private excommunication, II, 75; on prohibition of imagery, II, 137; on property of illiterates, I, 166; on position of princes, III, 44; on quorum at weddings, III, 46; on recitation of Decalogue, III, 21–22; on redemption of captives, II, 333, 336; on rights of cities, I, 135; on ritual bath, II, 165; on ritual slaughtering, II, 106–7; on robbery, II, 228; on scribes, II, 110; III, 12–13; on status of scholars, II, 80, 179–80; III, 28; on swimming, II, 198; III, 169; on synagogues, II, 127–29, 136; III, 151; (height), II, 138; (origins), III, 10–11; (substitutes for land), III, 16; on taxation, II, 252, 279; III, 31; (farming), I, 38; (immunity), II, 331; on Temple emulation, III, 16; on varieties of fish, II, 161; orientation of, I, 150; III, 12–13; outlawry of, and general sciences, II, 191, 198; printing of, I, 321, 325; II, 203; III, 170–71; semi-canonical position of, I, 119–20; II, 207–8; study of, I, 142; II, 95, 174, 177, 196, 207; (associational), I, 356; (at *kallah*), I, 182; textual variants in, III, 81; variations of later codes from, II, 216; vs. Bible, II, 193–94; III, 167–68

individual tractates: Ber., III, 16, 21–22, 33; Shab. III, 11, 26; ʽEr. III, 28; Pes., III, 18–19, 23, 26; Sukkah, III, 13; R. H., III, 30; Meg., III, 10, 17, 23, 27, 33, 146, 169; M. Ḳ., III, 90, 153; Ḥag., III, 94; Yeb., III, 51; Ket. III, 46; Soṭah, III, 28, 33; Giṭ., III, 24, 28–29, 52, 153; Ḳid., III, 17, 26, 28, 33, 161, 169; B. Ḳ., III, 24, 31, 94; B. M., III, 15, 25, 31, 94, 195; B. B. III, 18, 25, 27–28, 31, 34, 98, 122; Sanh., III, 21, 24, 28, 31–32; Shebuʽ, III, 76; ʽA. Z., III, 32–33, 149; Hor., III, 28, 33; Men., III, 16; Ḥul., III, 30

Palestinian: compilation of, I, 153; fragments of, III, 146; medieval continuation of, III, 45; on Alexandrian synagogue, III, 13; on ancient homiletics, III, 23; on assemblies, III, 17; on combination of offices, III, 24; on elders, II, 55; III, 17–19; on Hadrianic persecution, III, 24; on imagery, III, 146; on judiciary, III, 24; on *keneset*, III, 15; on proselytes, III, 17; on recitation of Decalogue, III, 22; on women's compartment, I, 91

individual tractates: III, 29; Pe'ah, III, 17, 24, 27–28, 120; Kil., III, 32; Sheb., III, 24; Bikk., III, 18, 28–29; ʽEr., III, 30; Sukkah, III, 13; R. H., III, 33; Meg., III, 17, 22, 27; Ḥag., III, 23, 29; M. Ḳ., III, 19, 26, 33; Yeb., III, 17; Soṭah, III, 31–32; B. Ḳ., III, 24; B. B., III, 15, 25; Sanh., III, 24, 29–30, 33, 76

Talmud Torah associations: I, *348–56*, 358–59; III, 92; of Arles, re-establishment of, II, 186; of Frankfort, administration of, III, 166; of Ferrara, II, 191; of Lwów, size of classes in, II, 196; of Rome, papal (as communal creditor), I, 372; (for girls), II, 179

of Salonica: I, 348; and communal administration, II, 24; III, 88; and rabbinic control, II, 75; and legacy for Hebron, III, 165; as communal hospice, III, 210; circulating library in, II, 202; elections in, II, 48

of Spain: revenue from wine of, II, 163; of Verona, compulsory school age in, II, 175; of Wilno, supported by teachers, III, 164

Tam, *see* Jacob b. Meir

Tamḥui, charitable institution of, I, 132; II, 320

Tammuz, election days in, III, 116

Tanna'im: and medieval legal evolution, III, 174; and penal procedure, II, 220; on fines, II, 234; on majority principle, III, 27; traditions of, compiled, I, 153

Tanners: French, and production of parchment, III, 170; Jewish, guilds of, I, 369

Taormina (Sicily): elections in, III, 113; removal of Jewish institutions in, II, 150

Tarascon (southern France), Jews of, I, 295; III, 75

Tarbane (Palestine), recitation of Decalogue in, III, 22

Tariffs: for shipment, talmudic regulation of, I, 364; on funerals, III, 158; on ritual meat, III, 158

Tarragona: and Barcelona *collecta*, I, 286; appeals to outside communities, II, 135–36

Tarsus (Asia Minor), Palestine Jews from, I, 121

Tartars: and redemption of Jewish captives, II, 334; autonomy in Poland of, I, 267

Tartessus (Spain), Israelites in, I, 56

Tax assessments *and* assessors, communal: I, 148, 172; II, 268, *280–88*; III, *195–96*; and cantors' salaries, II, 101; and charitable contributions, II, 325; and communal indebtedness, II, 269; and elections, I, 342, 344–45; II, 48, 58–61, 63; (electoral manipulations), II, 48, 64; and government tax rates, II, 252; and new arrivals, II, 12; III, 102; and oath of office, II, 36–37; and Polish councils, II, 352–53; and population, III, 108; and property qualifications, II, 40; and reduction, II, 286; III, 196; and synagogue deficits, II, 133; and tax discounts, II, 277; and terminological confusion, II, 260–61; and three-class system, II, 28; communal ordinances on, II, 282, 286–87; different from collections, II, 286; discretionary powers of, II, 255, 282, 285; (on immunities), II, 278; importance of, II, 57; in various regions (Austria, lower), I, 344–45; (Avignon), II, 61; (Cracow), II, 64; (Hesse-Cassel), I, 342; II, 36–37; (Islam), III, 38; (Lithuania), II, 40, 255, 278; (Persia), I, 148; (Poland), II, 48, 87, 352–53; III, 108; (Reggio), III, 196; (Sicily), II, 280; (Spain), I, 286; II, 12; legal controversies on, II, 252; III, 102, 194; methods of, III, 38, 194; ("taxation vs. manifestation"), I, 286–87; II, 12, 61, *281–83*; III, 196; periods of, II, 286; III, 195–96; rabbis' share in, II, 87; regional control of, I, 286–87; II, 22, 288; secretiveness of, II, 287

Tax collections *and* collectors, communal: II, *281–88*; III, *195–96*; ancient, I, 38–39, 111, 129; (patriarchs), I, 142; and censuses, III, 184; and communal control, I, 198, 244, 273; and communal indebtedness, II, 269, 272; and discretion of elders, I, 197–98; II, 53; III, 174, 195; (tax strike against), II, 348; and elections, II, 41; and excommunication, I, 172–73; and forgotten ordinance, II, 265; and judiciary, II, 88, 219; and Kleve messenger, II, 119; and meat taxes, II, 257; and medieval legislation, I, 282; and mourning, II, 282; and *Pletten*, III, 209; and Polish nobles, I, 269; and pressure groups, II, 275; and property qualifications, II, 40; and regional control, I, 284, 296, 298, 319, 322; (chief rabbis), I, 288–89, 291–92, 347; (councils), I, 317, 323–24, 329–30, 332–33, 340, 342, 352–53; II, 15–16; (English presbyters), I, 297; (exilarchs), I, 175; and residence rights, II, 326; III, 102; and Sabbath, I, 236; and sanctions on tax defaults, I, 148; II, 219, 284; and sextons, II, 106; and supervision of chests, III, 195; and tax arrears, I, 236; II, 272,

326; and talmudic theory of taxation, I, 137; and terminological confusion, II, 260–61; and validity of testimony, II, 219; centralization of, I, 245; different from assessments, II, 286; for state, I, 148, 228, 247; importance of, II, 57; in various regions (Bohemia), I, 340; (Byzantine Empire), I, 228; (England), I, 244–45, 297; (France), II, 265; (Germany), I, 298; (Hesse-Cassel), I, 342; (Islam), I, 172–73, 175; III, 38–39; (Italy), I, 317; (Kleve), II, 119; (Moravia), II, 40–41; (Persia), I, 148; (Poland), I, 269, 273, 323–24, 329–30, 332–33; II, 15–16, 87, 252, 352–53; III, 184; (Portugal), I, 347; (Provence), I, 296; (Roman Empire), I, 129, 142; III, 25; (Rome, papal), I, 319, 322; II, 272; (Sarajevo), II, 53; (Sicily), I, 317; (Spain), I, 288–89, 291–92, 347; (Turkey), I, 197–98; methods of, II, 252; III, 25, 38–39; (combatting evasions), II, 281, 288; III, 196; rabbis' share in, II, 87; III, 196; tax farmers' share in, II, 285; vs. evasions, I, 137; II, 15–16, 88, 275, 282; III, 102, 209

Tax-farming *and* tax-farmers, Jewish: II, 284–85; ancient, I, 38, 129; (not in Egypt), I, 105; and aliens, II, 6–7; and chief rabbinates, I, 289–90, 300–1; and councils, I, 314, 324; and false declarations, II, 281; and meat prices, III, 187; and Polish nobles, I, 329; and Roman taxes, I, 129; and share in confiscated property, II, 281; controlled by elders, I, 272; III, 182; influence of (in Caliphate), I, 187; (in Germany), I, 314; (in Poland), I, 272, 300–1, 324, 329; II, 6–7; III, 182, 187; (in Spain), I, 235, 289–90; II, 281

Tax immunities *and* exemptions: II, *274–81*; III, 103, *192–94*; and attendance at wedding, II, 303; and class distinctions, II, 303; and communal control, II, 13–15; (loans), II, 269–70; and fiscal downgrade, II, 288; and judiciary, II, 219; and right of settlement, II, 10, 13; and salaries, II, 119; III, 128; and Saragossan burial societies, I, 353; and Sicilian chief rabbis, I, 293; and taxation, II, 247, 274; (corporal taxes), III, 188; of cantors, II, 103–4; of churches and synagogues, I, 11; II, 130; of diplomatic agents, II, 116; of orphans, II, 331–32; of poor, and charities, I, 172; II, 325–26; of scholars and rabbis, II, 80; III, 34–35, 38, 128; (in Caliphate), I, 160–61; (in Roman Empire), III, 33; (in Spain), II, 249; of servants, II, 299; of visitors to fairs, II, 12; of wealthy tax collectors, III, 122–23; penalties for, II, 14–15; rabbinic teachings on, I, 138–39; II, 80; restricted by Polish Council, I, 330–31

Taxation, communal, ancient: and electoral rights, I, 98; and landowners, I, 136; and Roman law, I, 109–10; and talmudic theory of taxation, I, 136–39; II, 26–27; for patriarchs, I, 142; III, 29–30; for religious institutions, I, 120; Israelitic antecedents of, questionable, I, 37–39; III, 7

medieval and modern: I, 20; II, 57, *246–89*, 344; III, *183–97*; and admission of aliens, II, 6–7, 9; and baths, II, 166; and boarding of students, I, 189; and cantors' salaries, II, 101; and charities, II, 325–26, 346; and cemeteries, II, 155–56; III, 153–54; and citrons, II, 165; III, 160; and communal institutions, II, 157; and congregational membership, II, 18; and eastern "Francos," III, 101–2; and economic regulation, II, 290; and educational budgets,

II, 171, 185, 188; and electoral rights, II, 27–28; III, 114–15; and emigration, II, 15; III, 103; and expulsions, III, 145; and guilds, I, 372–73; and immunities, II, 277–78; and irrevocable bans, II, 229; and length of residence, II, 12; III, 102; and local associations, I, 349, 353; and majority principle, II, 27; and Mantuan bankers, II, 29; and modern secessions, I, 24–25; III, 5; and orphans, II, 331; and Palestine relief, II, 341; and pressure groups, II, 215, 280; and property qualifications, II, 38; and public law, II, 219; and raising of rents, II, 293; and redemption of captives, II, 335; and regional control, I, 180, 284–85; II, 20–22, 105; III, 65; and ritual meat, II, *107–10*, 258–59; III, 138, 158; and ritual wine, II, 162; and salaries, III, 105; and servants, II, 299; and state interest in community, I, 23; II, 123; and support of scholars, I, 181; and three-class system, II, 28–30; and titles, I, 201; collections of alms for, II, 326; commissions on, III, 122–23; communal ordinances on, I, 353; II, 248–49, 277–78, 280, 282, 286–87; (practicability of), II, 261, 265; Frankfort Conference on, I, 341; in various regions (Castile), III, 65; (Cracow), II, 261; (England), II, 21; (France), II, 185; (Germany), I, 341; II, 66, 188; III, 185; (Islam), I, 180–81, 201–2; (Italy), I, 279; II, 21–22, 29; (Lwów), III, 115; (Nice), III, 189; (Portugal), I, 285; (Prussia), III, 5; (Rome, papal), II, 255; (Saragossa), I, 353; (Spain), II, 20–21, 248–49; (Turkey), II, 18; III, 101–2; oligarchic rule of, II, 66; outside influences on, II, 349; rabbinic share in, III, 129; rates of, II, 252, 255, 258–59, 280; III, 185; (tax-free minima), II, 251; retroactive, II, 157; role in self-government of, I, 282; unified control of, II, 19; voluntary, I, 279

Jewish, for states, ancient: and exilarchic control, I, 147–48; and problem of synagogues, III, 36; and patriarchal contributions, I, 129, 142–43; and rabbinic immunities, I, 109; II, 80; III, 33; and Roman fiscal tax, I, 228; communal responsibility for, I, 129, 148; Greek, and talmudic tax system, I, 137; in Palestine, III, 25; in Ptolemaic Egypt, I, 105; III, 18; medieval heritage of, II, 250; oppressive nature of, in Rome, I, 23, 116, 129, 142; Talmud on Persian taxes, III, 31

Islamic and Turkish: I, 159–61, 171–72; and forced excommunication, I, 172–73; and Jewish leadership, I, 196–98; and migrations, I, 172; and rabbinic immunities, II, 80; and religious controversies, III, 183; and religious minorities, I, 176, 196; humiliating features of, III, 38; in Palestine, II, 340; medieval heritage of, II, 250; records of, III, 38

medieval and modern: I, 25; II, 250; and banking, I, 243; and book trade, II, 204; and burial, I, 253; II, 153; and Church, I, 244; and election fees, II, 36; and excommunication, II, 232; and feudal divisions, I, 231; and houses of catechumens, I, 219; and judiciary, II, 209, 211; (impartiality of Christian judges), I, 250; and "law of the kingdom," I, 214; and migrations, I, 245; III, 100; and new synagogues, I, 233; and rabbinic immunities, II, 80; and ritual wine, II, 162; and toleration of Jews, I, 282; III, 100; and welfare budgets, II, 349–50; communal responsibility for, I, 211;

(personal, of elders), II, 52; leaders in favor of, III, 34; records of, II, 250; severity of, I, 281

under various regimes: America, I, 262; (West Indies), III, 61

Austria: II, 160; and enlightened absolutism, II, 160; and family chapels, II, 130; and funeral tolls, II, 153–54; in Bohemia, and self-accusation, III, 183; in Galicia, III, 186

Byzantine Empire, problematic, I, 228; III, 54; Church (and assemblies), I, 319; (and cemeteries), II, 152; Holland, and communal indebtedness, II, 356

England: II, 249–51, 254; and regional community, I, 297; and staff of Exchequer, II, 116

France: and assemblies, I, 295–96; III, 75–76; and excommunication, I, 246; and *gardien général*, I, 296; and royal domain, III, 68; in Alsace, III, 88; in Provence, I, 295–96; III, 189

Germany: I, 277; II, 250–51; III, 184; and leaders' physical responsibility, II, 154–55; III, 70; and population, III, 107; and redemption of captives, II, 336; and regional control, I, 342, 344; II, 148–49; III, 87; (synods), I, 313–14, 322; III, 77; and support of students, III, 166; in Hesse-Cassel, I, 342; in Kleve, I, 344; in Trèves, III, 87; rates of, III, 185; records of, III, 107, 184

Italy (including Sicily): I, 274–76, 279; and abattoirs, III, 186; and chief rabbinate, I, 294–95; and customs duties, II, 262; and Jewish equality, I, 317; and synods, I, *315–23*; III, 80

Poland-Lithuania: I, 273, 326, 329; II, 273; III, 186; and book trade, II, 204–5; III, 171; and chief rabbinate, I, 300–1; and councils, I, 323–24, 326–29, 332–33; II, 352–53; (districts), III, 81; (provincial), I, 332; and elections, II, 35; and Karaite conferences, III, 83; and rabbinic control, II, 87; and regional community, II, 20; and royal privileges, I, 268–69

Spain: I, 233, 235; II, 248–50; and abattoirs, II, 108; and assemblies, I, 287–88; III, 75; and communal banishment, II, 9–10; and exemptions, I, 241; II, 13–14; and marriage restrictions, II, 15; and migrations, I, 234; and noble spokesmen for Jews, I, 291; and personal tolls, II, 264; and regional control, I, 286–87, 291; II, 20; and ritual meat, II, 159, 259; and ritual wine, II, 163; and sale of synagogue objects, II, 271; and separation of Jews, I, 278; extant records of, I, 235; III, 55; transfer to nobles of, I, 235

Taxes, direct: II, *248–56*; III, 197; and communal compromises, II, 280; "of disgrace," and dice taxes, III, 208; universality of, II, 38. *See also* Household taxes; Income taxes; Inheritance taxes; Poll taxes; Tolls; extraordinary in Spain, II, 278–79

indirect: II, *256–65*, 278–80; III, 187; and property qualifications, II, 38; on books, II, 204–5; III, 171; on candles, II, 259, 261; on synagogues, II, 130, 135, 265. *See also* Customs duties; Excise taxes; Houses; Land; Meat taxes; Property taxes; Real estate; Sales; Stamp tax; Tithes; Tolls; Wine taxes

Taxpayers, Jewish: age of, II, 251; and assemblies, II, 25; and English chirograph offices, II, 111; and feminine franchise, II, 37; and fiscal administration, II, 57; and judiciary, II, 219, 287–88; and *Pletten*, II, 345; and provincial chiefs, III, 122–23; and sumptuary laws; II, 302, 305; and teachers, II, 114; loss of, when excommunicated, II, 232; number of, and educational responsibilities, II, 114, 189; often prefer assessment to declaration, II, 282; rabbis on conflicting interests of, II, 268; statistics of, III, 111; terms for payments of, II, 286

Tchelebi (Turkish chief), I, 190

Tea, and sumptuary laws, II, 305

Teachers, Jewish: II, 114–15, 117; III, *23–24*, 140; ancient, I, 120, 124, 139, 155; III, *23–24*; and appointments (by exilarchic officials), III, 44; (governments), I, 292; (Portuguese chief rabbis), I, 285; and associations, I, 356; II, 88–89; and Bible studies, II, 194; and Christian teachers, II, 191–92; and competition, I, 126; II, 299; and Enlightenment, II, 359–60; and exchange for work, I, 139; and itinerant students, II, 180; and long-term contracts, III, 161; and masters' authorization, II, 181; (rabbinic ordination), II, 67, 91; and parental responsibility, II, 169; and school age, II, 175; and synagogue premises, III, 151; as marriage brokers, II, 81; assistants of, I, 359; II, 114–15, 185, 196, 199, 299; at Italian universities, III, 167; combine several offices, II, 103; III, 140; employment of, in *Seder Eliyahu*, III, 125; in various regions (Alsace), II, 117; (France), II, 186; (Germany), II, 251; (Islam), III, 44; (Italy), I, 359; II, 179, 359–60; III, 167; (Poland), II, 186, 194; (Portugal), I, 285; (Spain), I, 292; II, 73, 82, 103, 249; III, 151; influence of, I, 120, 155, 197; III, 163–65; (reverence for), I, 139; II, 180–81; legal requirements for, I, 126; low estimate of, II, 182–83; marital preference for, I, 124; of dancing, III, 206. *See also* Dancing masters; poll taxes of, II, 251; private, II, 117, 175; qualifications of, I, 126; residence at school of, I, 359; responsibility of, II, 79, 183; salaries of, II, 82, 85, 171–72, 186; III, 141; segregation of, I, 357; seizure of books by, II, 201; tax immunities of, II, 249; Valladolid synod on, II, 73; women as, I, 359; II, 179. *See also* Academies; Contracts; Education; Rabbis; Schools; Scholars; Students

Technicalities, juristic, and writs of divorce, II, 318

Technique, juristic, and medieval evolution, III, 173–74

Tefillah, I, 121. *See also* 'Amidah

Tekoites, among returning exiles, III, 11

Tel-Aviv, all-Jewish town of, I, 17

Tell el-Amarna, archives of, I, 32. *See also* El-Amarna period

Temple, First: I, 35; and Babylonian Exile, I, 59–60, 74; and holy places, I, 40; and religious universalism, I, 54; destruction of, I, 54; (and eastern synagogues), I, 164; idolatrous worship in, I, 9; mountain of, I, 61; pilgrimages to, I, 52. *See also* Centralization of worship; Priesthood; Sanctuaries

Second: and cantors, III, 136; and Church art, II, 137–38; and liturgy, I, 121; as depository, I, 88; attendance at, I, 92; building of, I, 60, 67; III, 10; despoliation of, III, 15; destruction of, I, 110; (and biblical genealogy), I, 146; (and symbols of mourning), II, 138. *See also* Jerusalem, fall of; Diaspora contributions towards, I, 87–88, 110, 143; II, 197; III, 165; mountain of, I, 120; Persian decrees on, I, 64; III, 11; priests at, I, 61, 68, 97; (tax immunities of),

I, 109, 138. *See also* Priesthood; reconstruction of (donations for), III, 165; (inferior to teaching), II, 197; (Julian's attempt at), III, 30; ritual of, I, 88; size of, I, 92; under Maccabeans, I, 79; use of *hekdesh* for, II, 328; womens' compartment in, I, 91

Temples, Jewish: of Elephantine, I, 60, 71–72, 97; of Ezekiel, III, 10; of Onias, I, 60, 79, 110; III, 14; of Zerubbabel, III, 10. *See also* Temple, Second

Temptations, and power of study, II, 315

Ten adult worshipers: I, 121, 155; and congregational divisions, I, 350; and private worship, II, 124–25. *See also* 'Edah; Quorum

"Ten foremost men," I, 133

"Ten men of leisure," I, 89, 133–34, 200; II, 127; III, 26, 50

Tenants, Jewish: and Christian landlords, II, 291–92; and interruption of prayers, II, 33; and lay judiciary, II, 88; and Persian tax defaults, I, 148; protection of, II, 292–96; III, 198; (and communal fees), II, 262; (of guilds), III, 198. *See also* Acquired rights; tax assessments on, II, 252

Tent tax, Turkish, alleged origin of, III, 183

Tenure of office: of cantors, gradual improvement in, II, 103–5; of Cologne elders, III, 130; of rabbis, II, 85–88, 94; III, 129; of teachers, medieval *midrash* on, III, 161

Ṭerefah, consumption of, by heretics, I, 165

Termini (Sicily), imprisonment of elders in, III, 176

Terminology, fiscal, indiscriminate use of, II, 260–61

Terms (scholastic), intermissions between, II, 189–90

Terms of service, and refusal to accept office, III, 119

Territory, Jewish: appreciation of, I, 54, 59, 62, 73–74, 89; communal substitute for, I, 209

Terror, and Cracow dictator, II, 64

Teruel (Spain): and dependent settlements, II, 20; *fuero* of, III, 56; Judeo-Arabic deeds in, II, 112; mixed litigations in, I, 240; prohibition of private synagogues in, III, 144; rabbinic salaries in, II, 82

Testators, respect for wills of, II, 186

Testimonials, for itinerant mendicants, II, 322

"Testimonies," Yabneh compilation of, I, 153

Testimony, idea of: and Jewish self-government, I, 209; and papal privileges, I, 217. *See also* Witnesses

Tetrastoon, in Stobi synagogue, I, 84

Textbooks: communal provisions for, II, 180, 203; in Italian schools, I, 360; scholarly authorship of, II, 244

Textile industry, Jewish, Turkish, communal monopoly in, II, 262

Theater, Jewish, history of, III, 207

Theatrical arts, Jewish writers on, II, 191

Thebes (Greece), Jewish craftsmen in, I, 368; III, 94

Thefts *and* thieves: and desecration of cemeteries, III, 154; and tax evasions, II, 282; discovery by magic of, I, 237; prosecution of, and Polish Council, II, 338

Theocracy, Jewish, promoted by Persia, I, 64. *See also* Priesthood

Theodorus (Aegina elder), I, 103

Theodosian Code, *see* Code of Theodosius

Theodosius I, the Great (Roman emperor), I, 114, 130, 144; II, 229

Theodosius II (Roman emperor), and Jewish quarter, I, 229
Theodotos, son of Vettenos, synagogue of, I, 91, 105, 120; II, 128
Theology, Jewish, doctrine of repentance in, II, 221–22. *See also* Religion
Theomim, Jonah (Lithuanian scribe), III, 209
Theory vs. practice, in reverence for scholars, II, 180
Therapeutai, sect of, I, 95; II, 128
Theudas (Roman elder), I, 106, 151; III, 19
Thiasoi, association of, I, 77, 101, 108
Thibaut (count of Champagne), I, 245
"Third Estate," struggle for liberation of, I, 274; II, 358. *See also* Cities
"Third meal" of the Sabbath, II, 128
Third Republic, *see* France
Thirty Years' War: and Bohemian Council, I, 339–40; and Cassel Assembly, I, 341–42; and Frankfort Jewry, III, 108; and migrations, I, 307, 331
Thomas Aquinas, Saint, on burial, II, 147; III, 152
Thought, derogatory of teachers forbidden, II, 180
Three-class system: II, 28–29, 38–39, 44–45, 59–60, 279; III, 110, 114–15; and tax assessments, II, 248, 286, 288; III, 196
Three-year concessions, Bohemian, and *ḥazakah*, III, 199–200
Three-year contracts, reasons for, II, 88, 104; III, 161
Thuringia, Jews of: III, 77; and Basel assembly, I, 315
Thurn and Taxis Company, II, 115
Thursdays: announcement of assemblies on, II, 25; Bible recitation on, II, 141; communal examinations on, II, 197; court sessions on, I, 128; proclamation of bans on, II, 228
Thutmes III (Egyptian king), I, 34
Tiber (river), I, 80
Tiberias: academy of, I, 149, 153–54, 156, 191–92; III, 32; (inquiries to), I, 193; ancient synagogue of, I, 87; and Massorah, I, 192; and Roman taxation, I, 135; climate of, I, 31; exilarchs in, I, 149, 173; III, 32; modern colonization of, III, 216; *nasi* in, I, 186; preachers in, I, 142; rabbis of, and recitation of Decalogue, III, 22; share in Palestine relief of, II, 342
Tiberius Claudius Nero Caesar (Roman emperor), I, 80, 106
Tickets, communal, for itinerant poor, II, 322. *See also* Pletten
Tiktin, *see* Tykocin
Times Square, New York, I, 26
Timidity of rabbis, and growing severity, II, 212–13
Tips, officials' revenue from, II, 118–19
Tithes: agricultural (ancient), I, 38, 132; III, 7; (and scholars' tax immunities), II, 277; charitable regulations on, I, 132; II, 343–44; III, 217; ecclesiastical, and Jewish landownership, I, 234, 254; III, 185
Titles: of elders, variety of, I, 101, 104–5, 200–1; II, 55–57; III, 120; (and Muslim mania for), III, 50; Palestinian, used in Rome, I, 210; rabbinic, III, 131; (limitations of), II, 91–92; (revenue from conferring of), II, 84. *See also under* respective titles
Tittius, Marcus (Berenice elder), I, 100
Titus Arch (Rome), Jewish adornment of, III, 52
Tivoli, assembly in, I, 320–21; III, 79
Ṭob Elem (Bonfils), Joseph, II, 253, 284
Tobacco: and Polish teachers, II, 199; excise taxes on, II, 260
Ṭobim, *see* Best men; Seven
Tobischau (Moravia), minute-books of, III, 144–45, 218
Tobit, Book of, I, 90, 131; III, 25

Toledo (Spain): archbishop of (and fairs), I, 236; (appoints chief rabbi), I, 289; bathhouse in, II, 166; booksellers from, II, 201; burial societies in, I, 353; charitable associations in, I, 362; control over dependent communities of, II, 71–72; hospital in, II, 329; lay judiciary in, II, 71–72; massacres in, III, 93; rabbis of, II, 171; (hereditary), III, 132; (salaries), II, 82; synagogues in, I, 237; III, 147; (in district of), I, 220; tax ordinance in, Draconian, II, 284

Tolerance edict, Austrian, II, 354

Tolerance tax, Austrian, distribution of, III, 197

Toleranzjuden, Vienna, and textile exports, III, 199

Toleration Acts, British, little effect on Jews of, I, 259

Toleration, Jewish, of divergent traditions, I, 150

religious: and communal stability, I, 8, 108; II, 120; and imperial interests, I, 195–96; and Jewish judiciary, I, 241; and Jewish solidarity, I, 165; and Marranos, I, 252; and Resettlement, I, 266; and synagogues, III, 53; and taxation, II, 246; and treatment of Christians abroad, I, 233; and Treaty of Utrecht, I, 253; despite polemics, I, 216–17; doctrine of, limited, I, 217–19, 228; economic arguments for, II, 298; in Graeco-Roman world, I, 12, 75–76, 107, 111; (and early Christianity), I, 113; (and Maccabeans), III, 15; (in Ptolemaic Egypt), I, 75–76

medieval and modern (Austria), II, 354; III, 197, 199; (England), I, 259; III, 60; (Holland), I, 260; (Islam), I, 158–65, 233; (Italy), I, 274–75; (Spain), I, 241; (Turkey), I, 195–96. *See also* Law; Legal status

Tolls: communal, II, 247; (anti-alien character of), II, 12–13; funeral, history of, I, 253, 284; II, 153–54, 160, 263–64; personal, history of, II, 263–65; III, 188; (and Spanish wedding guests), II, 303

Tombstones, Jewish: III, 156–57; ancient, I, 121; (and exilarchic genealogy), III, 31; and art, II, 155; III, 156–57; communal revenue from, II, 156; from Mayence, III, 154; inscriptions on, III, 126, 156–57; preservation of, II, 155; III, 156; trade in, and desecration of cemeteries, II, 151. *See also* Catacombs; Cemeteries; Inscriptions

Tongues, cutting of, and Jewish penal procedure, II, 223

Torah: admired by Romans, I, 127; compass of, I, 115, 124, 126; instruction in, II, 78, 174. *See also* Education; Scholarship; in the ark, II, 25. *See also* Pentateuch; Scroll; neglect of, and heavy taxation, III, 183; priestly teaching of, I, 53, 61. *See also* Law

Torat ḥaṭat, by Isserles, pun on, III, 172

Torches, processions with, restricted, III, 207

Tortosa: disputation of, I, 220; III, 66; educational endowment in, III, 166; old tombstone in, II, 155; rabbis of, I, 297; suppresses Jewish judiciary, I, 278

Torture: and suicide of prisoners, III, 157; of elders, for communal actions, II, 53; of tax defaulters, II, 284

Tosafot *and* Tosafists: on burial societies, III, 90; on cantors, III, 135; on cemeteries, III, 154; on change of venue, III, 180; on changes in endowments, II, 266; III, 189; on charitable imposts, II, 344; III, 217;

on Eleazar b. Zadok, III, 12; on excommunication, III, 177; on intensive studies, II, 177; on judiciary (disqualification of), II, 211; (intoxication of), III, 172; on marital obligations, II, 184; III, 164; on migrations, III, 98; (freedom of movement), II, 16; III, 103; on parental approval of marriage, III, 204; on rights of settlement, III, 98, 101; on size of classes, II, 196; on synagogues (art), II, 138; (decorum), III, 148; on teaching profession, II, 184; on women slaughterers, III, 137. *See also* Solomon b. Isaac; *and under* respective tosafists

Tosefta: on Alexandria (court), III, 20; (synagogue), III, 13; on homiletics, III, 23; on position of women, III, 17; on indispensable institutions, III, 21; on swimming, III, 169

individual tractates: Pe'ah, III, 20; Sukkah, III, 13; Meg., III, 17, 23; Ket., III, 20; B. M. III, 21; Sanh., III, 27–28, 33; Oholot, III, 33

Totalitarianism: communal, and education, II, 170; modern, I, 208; II, 170–71; (Turkish), III, 50

Totenzoll, Austrian, II, 160. *See also* Tolls

Toulouse, Jewish community in, I, 264

Tourists, modern: and "Rashi" chapel, II, 130; in Nice, and controversy over cemetery, II, 152

Tournaments, medieval, Jewish attendance at, III, 207

Tours, Jewish cemetery in, II, 149; III, 154

Towns, Palestinian, *see* Cities

Trabotto, Nethaneel b. Benjamin, will of, II, 133; III, 145

Trabotto, Yeḥiel b. Azriel, III, 79–80

Tractates, talmudic, and educational programs, II, 203, 207

Trade morals, communal ordinances on, II, 301. *See also* Economic regulation

Trade secrets: and tax assessments, II, 287; protected by Polish Council, I, 330

Trading rights, and immigration restrictions, II, 16, 337

Tradition, force of, ancient: I, 23, 76, 85, 111; and calendar regulation, I, 143; and charities, II, 319; and Palestinian city, I, 31; and visiting of graves, II, 154; Babylonian divergences in, I, 150; in Alexandria, I, 78–79; medieval heritage of, I, 227; III, 111

medieval and modern: I, 10, 18–19, 209, 211, 248; and ancient heritage, I, 227; III, 111; and associational autonomy, I, 374; and communal creativity, II, 167–68; and drafting of statute, II, 31; and excessive welfare budgets, II, 349–50; and interterritorialism, II, 351; and legal adjustments, II, 216; and medieval uniformity, I, 216; and popular self-help, II, 349; and Reform Judaism, I, 9–10; and residence outside ghetto, II, 296; and Resettlement areas, I, 23; II, 363; and ritual diversities, I, 121; and salaries of scholars, I, 182; as sources of law, II, 245; attacked by Enlightenment, II, 360; European variations in, II, 68–69

Training: legal, of exilarchs, I, 147; occupational, I, 350; II, 190–91, 324; III, 96, 167; of judges, II, 95; of rabbis, II, 95; III, 171–72; of slaughterers, rabbinic checks on, II, 109. *See also* Education

Trajan, Marcus Ulpius (Roman emperor), I, 78

Tramping, and wandering scholars, II, 187

Trani: and Judeo-Christian witnesses, I, 240; synagogues of, III, 148
Trani, Joseph b. Moses: and hereditary rabbinate, III, 132; on communal agreements, III, 111; on diversion of funds, II, 186; III, 165, 189; on *ḥazaḳah*, III, 198; on plenary assemblies, II, 23; III, 106; on polygamy, III, 203; on preaching, II, 98; III, 134; on taxation, III, 194, 196; on validity of will, III, 204; on vows for Palestine, III, 216
Transfer of residence, Jewish, medieval, freedom of, I, 234
Transfer taxes, communal, instances of, III, 187
Transfers of Jews, feudal: III, 55; and cities, I, 277; and regional control, III, 106; Barcelona synod against, I, 234–35, 288; by Normans, I, 231; in various regions (Aragon), I, 278; (France), I, 278; (Germany), I, 277; (Poland), I, 269; (Spain), I, 234–35
  of synagogues, by rulers, II, 135
Transit duties on merchandise, II, 265
Transjordan: I, 31; Bedouins in, I, 45; Greek cities in, I, 119; Jewish officials in, III, 24; medieval settlements in, I, 164
Translation, difficulties of, I, 122–23
Translations: biblical, and Jewish dialects, III, 152. *See also* Bible versions; Catalan, of Maimonidean Code, I, 240; vernacular, of Hebrew prayers, II, 143
Transportation of poor, communal provisions for: II, 323–25; and illness, III, 211
Transtiberian quarter in Rome, I, 80–81
Trapani, Jews of: elections among, II, 47; equality of, I, 232; power of elders of, II, 102
Traveling expenses: of Jewish officials, II, 115, 119; of Palestine pilgrims, II, 341
Travelogues, Hebrew: of medieval travelers, III, 43; of Palestinian messengers, II, 342
Travels *and* travelers, Jewish: ancient, I, 42; III, 29; and accommodation at hospices, II, 327; and corporal taxes, III, 188; and eastern synagogues, I, 164; and education, I, 193; and Sicilian chief rabbis, III, 66; and synagogue seats, II, 130; and women slaughterers, II, 107; in Byzantium, I, 230; in Rome, I, 210; insecurity of, II, 339–40; (and synods), I, 322; overcome isolation, I, 167. *See also* Messengers; *and under* individual travelers
  non-Jewish: ancient, mobility of, III, 23; English, on Roman converts, I, 247; German, on Turkey, I, 351; III, 37; in Nice, and controversy over cemetery, II, 152
Treasurers, communal: II, 62; authority of, II, 286; combine other offices, III, 140; election of, II, 58, 60; (obligatory acceptance by), III, 119; freed from accounting, II, 65; ignorant of tax assessments, II, 287; of councils (Hessian), I, 342; (Polish), I, 328; (Sicilian), I, 318. *See also* Financial administration; Elders
Treasures, in ancient synagogues, I, 87–88
Treasuries, European: mismanagement of, and Jewish taxation, II, 247; Muslim, *dhimmis* in, I, 187. *See also* Bureaucracy; Taxation
Treaties: Arabian, and new synagogues, I, 163; French, with West India Company, I, 265; Jewish, with Polish cities, I, 281; of extradition of Jews, I, 234, 245–46; of Utrecht, I, 253. *See also* Diplomacy; International relations; Interterritorial action
Treatise on the art of dancing, II, 315
Trebitsch, lay preaching in, II, 98

Trees, on cemeteries, sale of, II, 151
Trent: Church council of, III, 80; ritual libel of, I, 313
Trésor de Chartes, Jewish documents in, III, 165
Trèves, Electorate of, regional community in, I, 341; III, 87
Trèves (family), *see* Johanan; Joseph; Mattatiah
Treviso: bathhouse in, II, 166; *Pletten* in, II, 322
Trial: imperial, of Frankfort Conference, I, 323, 341; Jewish, detention for, II, 226; of Jeremiah, I, 49
Tribes: Israelitic, I, 40–41, 44; III, 7; (elections by), II, 35; (migrations of), I, 32, 47; Jewish, modern, French official on, I, 263; Teuton, prevalence of fines among, II, 234
Tribunal, imperial, slowness of procedure at, II, 239. *See also* Judiciary
Tribunus populi, Jewish, in Poland, II, 287
Tributes: Israelitic, to foreign monarchs, I, 38, 42; Jewish, and caliphate, I, 159. *See also* Taxation
Trieste: III, *100*; cemeteries in, II, 152; combination of offices in, III, 140; ghetto guards in, III, 141; private synagogue in, III, 144; residence restrictions in, II, 11
Trikkala (Greece): adoption of statutes in, III, 110–11; communal price agreements in, II, 300
Triklinion, in Stobi synagogue, I, 84
Trinitarian doctrine, and Jewish liturgy, I, 192
Tripolis, Jews in, I, 81, 163
Tripolitans, Roman congregation of, I, 81
Trito-Isaiah (prophet), I, 74
Troki, Karaite hegemony in, III, 83
Troubadours, Jewish, II, 192
Trousseaus: communal provisions for, II, 332; Italian, III, 170; rabbinic fees on, II, 83; restrictions on, III, 201
Troyes: as background for Rashi, III, 74; cemeteries in, II, 149; confiscation of tax-defaulted property in, II, 284; flogging in, II, 225; synagogues in, III, 147; synods in, I, 311–12; tanners of, III, 170
Truck gardens, in ancient Palestine, I, 42
Trumpets, use in synagogue of, I, 104
Trustees, I, 101; II, 55; III, 166. *See also* Elders
Tszur Israel, Recife congregation of, III, 59
Tuberculosis, leprosy compared with, III, 155
Tudela: constitution of, II, 58; early cemetery in, II, 146; Jewish settlers in, II, 15
Tuition fees: and seizure of books, II, 201; communal contributions to, II, 185; ordinances on, III, 164. *See also* Education; Schools; Teachers
Tulln, Lower Austria, meat tariff in, III, 158
Tunis: capital jurisdiction in, III, 175; dialectical discussions in, III, 168; interruption of prayers in, II, 33; preaching in, II, 96; suppression of cabalistic books in, III, 170; visitors from Leghorn in, III, 175
Turgot, Anne Robert Jacques: on Jewish republic, II, 290; opposition to guilds of, I, 371
Turin: controls dependent settlements, II, 21–22; restricted Jewish settlement in, II, 10
Turkestan, Jews of, I, 200
Turkey, Jews of: I, 13; III, 6, 25; and boycott of Ancona, III, 73; and capitulations, III, 101–2; and Carpentras taxation, III, 104; and country's expansion or disintegra-

tion, I, 157, 303; III, 352; and Egyptian *negidut,* I, 190; and guilds, III, 94; and local associations, I, 348, 350–51; and misrule in Palestine, II, 340; and Polish Jewry (appeals for captives), I, 307; (Council), I, 331–32; (Lwów chief rabbinate), I, 303; and Shabbetian movement, I, 308; and synagogues, I, 163–64; II, 127; III, 36; anti-trust laws of, II, 301; chief rabbinate of, I, *195–99*; III, *46–50*; communal control of, II, 20; (agreements), II, 300; III, 110–11; (monopolies), II, 262; congregational divisions of, III, 37; customs duties of, II, 263; envoys of, I, 188; execution of informers by, II, 222–23; failure of centralization of, I, 206; growth of oligarchies among, II, 50; *ḥazaḳah* legislation of, II, 298; imperial decrees on, III, 36; physicians among, III, 140; population of, II, 23; III, 108; rabbinic dialectics of, II, 195; rabbinic judiciary of, III, 125; redemption of captives by, I, 307; II, 334; III, 214; sanitary services among, II, 329–30; Sephardic separatism among, I, 204; II, 311; sumptuary laws of, III, 200–2; taxation of, I, 171; III, 184; (immunities), II, 277; (poll tax), I, 171; (tent tax), III, 183. *See also under* respective provinces, cities and rulers

"Turkish" chambers, in Jewish baths, II, 165

Turkish congregation, in Vienna: literacy test in, III, 163; status of servants in, III, 200

Tuscany, Jews of: III, 208; and attraction of merchants, II, 3–4; at Bologna synod, I, 319–20; communal naturalization of, II, 11; taxation of visitors by, III, 102. *See also under* respective cities

Two children, minimum of, and polygamy, II, 309

"Two worlds," and Jewish excommunication, II, 234

Tykocin: and ban on local community, II, 229; as member of Polish Council, I, 326; minute book of, III, 82; regional control by, III, 153–54, 182

Typography, Hebrew, *see* Printing

Tyranny *and* tyrants, communal: and Polish nobles, I, 270; and tax strikes, II, 348; in ancient Antioch, I, 142; in Frankfort, III, 141–42; Polish, sketches of, III, 122. *See also* Absolutism; Oligarchy

Tyre, ancient: Jewish judge in, III, 18; patriarchal messenger in, I, 143

UḲBA, MAR (exilarch), conflict with gaon of, I, 183

Ukraine: Jewish autonomous regions in, I, 15; Jewish emigration from, I, 16; Yiddish in, I, 15

Ullmann, Wolff (Leipzig cantor), III, 149

Ulm, Jews in, III, 152

"Ultramontani," vs. "Italians" in Rome, II, 20, 60

Ulyanov, Vladimir Ilyich (Lenin, Nikolai), I, 15

Unanimity, requirement of: II, 26, 335–36; and adoption of statutes, III, 111; and binding force of enactments, II, 30, 44; and election of cantors, II, 102; III, 135; in price fixing demanded, II, 301. *See also* Majority principle

Underground movement, Western communities as, II, 363

Underprivileged, communal protection of, II, 290. *See also* Charities; Social justice

Unemployed: free from Muslim poll tax, I, 159; must accept Portuguese appointments, I, 285

"Ungaros," and Sofia meat administration, III, 159
Unification, communal: and rabbinic control, II, 75; in Ferrara, III, 114–15
Uniformity: communal, despite medieval transformations, I, 156; educational (and Hebrew printing), II, 203; (difficulties in), II, 173; legal (and academy controversies), I, 152; (and judges' discretion), II, 218; III, 173–74; (absence in procedure of, and public opinion), II, 243; ritualistic (and standardization of prayers), II, 142; (and toleration of customs), III, 149; of leadership and scholarly control, II, 244; of medieval legislation, I, 216, 227; talmudic, vs. local diversity, I, 206; III, 149
Uniformity Acts, British, gradual repeal of, I, 259
Union of Moravian communities, I, 339; III, 85
Unitarians, English, toleration of, I, 259
United communities, Castilian, demand protection, III, 155
United Kingdom, *see* England
United States of America: associations in, I, 101, 374; bans in, II, 233; cemeteries in, II, 147; III, 60, 152; charities in, II, 347; churches in, I, 11; congregational censuses in, I, 6; III, 3; Dutch Jewish settlements in, I, 255; III, 129; legal system of, I, 45; II, 245; Jewish communal organization in, I, 4–5, 11, 21, 25, 259–62; III, 3; oldest synagogue of, II, 136. *See also* Shearith Israel; Palestine relief in, III, 217; Polish communal influences in, II, 355; Reform Judaism in, I, 9–10; Sephardim in, III, 61; synagogue attendance in, III, 143. *See also under* respective states and cities
United Synagogue, English: I, 20; ancestry of, III, 59; archives of, III, 59–61
"Universal body of Christ," and European legislation, I, 227
Universalism, religious, Israelitic: and Exilic community, I, 54, 59; and synagogue, I, 62, 74; prophets on, I, 58. *See also* Religion
Universe, maintained by schoolchildren, II, 170
Universitas, ancient, Jewish community as, I, 108; III, 19
Universities, western: admission of Jewish students to, III, 167; and Jewish academies, II, 182; and rabbinic ordination, III, 130; and *studium generale*, III, 165; degrees from, and further study, II, 206; of Oxford, student bandits at, II, 187; of Padua, and Jewish corpses, II, 151; of Prague, and Christian censorship, II, 98; of Soviet Union, Hebrew and Yiddish in, I, 15–16
University, Jewish; I, 317; projects for, II, 185, 191–92; III, 167
Unleavened bread: charitable distribution of, II, 320–21; Darius II's order on, I, 65
Unmarried mothers, stigma on, II, 314
Unoccupied buildings, communal rent payments for, II, 292
Unterfarrnbach, controlled by Fürth, II, 22
Untershammash, III, 137. *See also* Sextons; *Shammash*
"Untidy guests," Polish teachers as, II, 183–84
Ural, Jews at, I, 17
Urania (Worms female cantor), II, 140
Urban VIII (pope), and Jewish tenant protection, II, 294
Urbanization, Jewish: ancient, and synagogue, I, 86; medieval, and relations to cities, I, 274; modern,

and community, I, 25–26. *See also* Cities; Metropolitan areas
Urbino, Jews of, legacy for, III, 212
Urge, inner, Jewish, and self-government, I, 209, 211
Ursuline convent in Rome, and Jewish tenant protection, II, 294
U. S. S. R., Jewish community in, I, 15–17
Usury, Jewish: and burghers' anti-Semitism, I, 276; and communal control, I, 167; and loss of converts' property, I, 247; and Muslim prohibition, I, 365; and popes, I, 365; III, 185; communal ordinances on, I, 244, 320; II, 301; (Augsburg assembly), I, 314; (Falk Kohen's compilation), III, 83. *See also* Banking; Interest
Utilitarianism, Jewish, modern, and learning, II, 362
Utrecht, Treaty of, I, 253

Va'ad: *see* Councils, regional; *arba' araṣot*, *see* ibid. Poland-Lithuania; *ha-medinah*, *see* ibid.
Vacation, medieval, limitations of, II, 197
"Vagrants," among Spanish cantors, II, 103
Valence, France, physicians in, I, 358
Valencia, Jews of: and Aragonese assemblies, I, 287–88; communal banishment by, II, 9–10; control dependent settlements, II, 20–21; elders of, excommunicated, I, 235; electoral statute of, II, 40, 44; emulate Barcelona constitution, II, 58; government interference in elections of, opposed, II, 74; litigations with Christians of, I, 240; no records of hospitals of, II, 329; physicians among, II, 309; pillage of quarters of, III, 211; polygamy among, II, 309; redemption of captives by, II, 336–37; scholars among, I, 186; of tax assessments by, II, 279, 281; three-class system among, II, 28, 279
Valladolid: as Castilian capital, III, 65; Cortes of, II, 13; (and Jewish judiciary), I, 241; lawsuit in, II, 74; rabbis of, II, 74. *See also* Councils, regional, Spain
Vanity, of cantors, proverbial, II, 104
Vatican Library, manuscripts of, III, 79
Vellum books, prices of, II, 100
Velvet caps, and class distinctions, II, 307
Venaissin, County of, Jews of: III, 53, 68, 107; constitution of, II, 61; delegation from, III, 72; threatened expulsion of, II, 270. *See also* Carpentras
Venality of exilarchs, accusation of, I, 174; III, 39. *See also* Corruption
Venice, Jews of: III, 63, 154; and Azariah de' Rossi, I, 308; and Candia executioners, III, 175; and conferences, I, 316; III, 80; and London statute, II, 31; and Mt. Zion chapel, I, 320; associations of, I, 358, 364; II, 335–36; III, 93, 213; Christian attendance at sermons of, II, 96; communal indebtedness of, III, 190; congregational allegiance of visitors among, II, 12; election of elders by, III, 121; free-loan banks for Christians of, II, 327; in pre-censorship commission, I, 321; judiciary of, I, I, 275–76; Levant trade of, I, 275; lay dictatorship among, II, 77; legacies for, III, 212–13; oath in district of, III, 181; ordinances of, III, 101; Palestine relief of, II, 341; III, 190; population of, III, 107; rabbinate of (and outside rabbis), III, 131; (and Polish relief), I, 333; (solidarity of), II, 87; restrictions on bans of, III, 178–79. *See also* Colo-

nies; *and under* respective cities and colonies
Venosa: child *archisynagogus* in, I, 105; Jerusalem preacher in, II, 97
Vents in coats, and show-fringes, III, 203
Vernaculi, Roman congregation of, I, 81
Verona, Jews of: III, *105*; and Azariah de' Rossi, I, 308; and Moravia, I, 306; associations of, I, 358; II, 17; III, 92, 104; *cassella* method among, II, 283; communal indebtedness of, III, 190; congregational divisions in, II, 19; III, 51; enforced local ritual of, III, 149; exports of *lulabs* from, III, 159–60; ghetto of, I, 226; hereditary secretaries among, II, 113; legacies for, III, 212–13; population of, III, 107; preaching of, II, 96; (for Palestine), II, 341; rabbis of, III, 78; school age among, II, 175; statute of (on outside ordination), III, 131; (on position of rabbi), III, 129; taxation of, III, 102, 190
Vespasian, Titus Flavius Sabinus (Roman emperor), I, 79, 140–41, 150
Vested interests, Jewish: modern growth of, II, 120; of teachers and size of classes, II, 196. *See also* Bureaucracy; Oligarchy
Vestry (London), II, 62. *See also* Council of elders
Vettenos (Theodotos's father), I, 91
Vetus Latina, and Jewish dialects, III, 152. *See also* Bible versions
Vicar general, papal, and Jewish elections, II, 36
Vice, *see* Prostitutes; Sex relations
Viceroys, Sicilian: and Jewish blasphemies, II, 339; and sumptuary laws, II, 304; and tax immunities, III, 192; and united communities, III, 192; convoke assemblies, I, 317–18; exempt teachers from office, III, 164; permit polygamy, II, 309. *See also* Sicily
Victoria (queen of England), legalizes Jewish worship, I, 259
Vienna: and French controversy, III, 69; and support of Moravian Jewry, I, 306; communal indebtedness in, II, 356; conference of, date of, III, 76; Congress of, and Jewish question, III, 63; court Jews of, II, 81, 98–99; emigrés from, electoral rights of, III, 114; Frankfort delegates in, III, 78; holy association of, III, 89; Jewish privilege in, I, 267–68; Jewish quarter in, III, 63; literacy test in, III, 163; Lower Austrian assembly in, I, 344; nobles of, and preference for Talmud, III, 167–68; rabbis of, I, 296; II, 67, 80–81; real estate records in, III, 126; status of servants in, III, 200; taxation in, II, 159–60; textile exports from, II, 297; III, 199; tombstone inscriptions in, III, 126; wandering scholars in, II, 188
Vigilance committee, Italian, elected by Bologna synod, I, 320
Vilification: and Muslim-Jewish letters, I, 193; in geonic pamphlets, I, 183
Villafranca (Aragon), and Barcelona *collecta*, I, 286
Villafranca (Provence), *see* Villefranche
Villagers, Jewish, dependent on neighboring synagogue, II, 134
Villages, ancient, Palestinian, I, 31, 34; III, 8; (of single crafts), I, 364; medieval, itinerant slaughterers in, II, 108. *See also* Cities
Villefranche, permission for synagogue in, I, 264
Villeins, Polish, Jewish control of, I, 269
Vilna, Jacob (Palestine messenger), III, 216–17

Vindication of ownership, II, 200
Vineyards: ancient Palestinian, I, 32, 37, 42–43; medieval taxes on, II, 253, 284. *See also* Agriculture; Land; Real estate
Violante (Aragonese queen): and chief rabbis, III, 66; permits Tarragona's appeal, II, 135–36
Virgin Mary, alleged blasphemies against, I, 222
Viri clarissimi et illustres, patriarchs as, I, 144
Visa fees and *Leibzoll*, II, 264
Visconti, Cigala, and Jewish captives, I, 306
Visigoths, traditions in Barcelona of, II, 74
Visitations: annual, of Portuguese chief rabbis, I, 286; patriarchal, I, 142; rabbinic (and training of slaughterers), II, 109; (of academies), II, 95
Visiting, of fiancés, communal regulations on, II, 315; of graves, and rabbinic law, II, 154; III, 206; of sick, II, 328; III, 210–11; (societies of), I, 362, 364
Visitors: and communal membership, I, 136; II, 11–12; (tax assessment), III, 102. *See also* Ban of settlement; Residence rights; at ancient academies, I, 151; in English synagogues, I, 257; in Rome, find no Talmud, I, 305–6; obligation to observe local customs of, III, 203; protection of, by Austria, III, 168; to Leipzig fairs, and funeral tolls, II, 154; to Spanish fairs, exempt from taxes, II, 12
Vital Calabrese, Ḥayyim b. Joseph, III, 92
Vitalis, son of David Abnadean, II, 14, 333
Vitautas (Lithuanian grand-duke), privilege of, I, 268
Volga, Jewish migrations to, I, 17
Volhynia, as member of Polish council, I, 326; III, 81
Volksgemeinde, ideology of, III, 3–4. *See also* People's community
Voll, Christoph, on Jewish charity laws, III, 219
Voltaire, François Marie Arouet de: and communal control, II, 360; letters of Jews to, II, 365; III, 221
Volumnians, Roman congregation of, I, 81, 104–5
Volumnius (Roman procurator), I, 81
Vopiscus, Flavius, of Syracuse (Roman historian), III, 18
Voting, rights of: II, 26–28; of chairmen, II, 55. *See also* Elections
Vows, Jewish: against acceptance of office, validity of, II, 112–13; III, 119; against communal ordinance, validity of, III, 118; ancient, I, 84; at Bible recitation, II, 103, 132–33, 264; III, 145; charitable (and self-discipline), II, 346; (obligatory nature of), II, 344; for Palestine relief, II, 341; III, 216; not to gamble, III, 207; release from, I, 240; III, 207. *See also* Oaths
Vox psallentium, Jewish, Church complaints of, III, 23

WAGES: and sin, doctrine of, II, 221; of laborers, I, 130; (and educational responsibilities), II, 176; of scholars, preferred to building funds, II, 186
Wahl, Saul, as "king" of Poland, I, 328
Waifs and strays, communal provisions for, II, 330–31, 337. *See also* Orphans
Wallerstein, as district center of German Jewish taxation, I, 341
Walls, in synagogue, partially unplastered, II, 139
"Wandering scholars," Jewish, *see* Itinerant students
Wandsbek, *see* Hamburg

Waqfs, I, 161, 163; III, 35, 38. *See also* Property, communal
Warburg: rabbis of, III, 117; suppression of private synagogues in, III, 144
Wardens, obligatory acceptance by, III, 119
Warfare, ancient: I, 75; in Palestine, I, 33, 39, 47, 51, 57; (and monarchy), I, 35; Jewish, unnecessary in dispersion, I, 179; Persian (and non-Parsees), III, 32; (and persecutions), I, 148
medieval and modern: and charitable associations, I, 363; and destruction of communal assets, II, 271; and individual contributions, I, 137; and Polish councils, I, 330, 333; and taxation, II, 247, 267; and waifs and strays, II, 330–31; Jewish participation in, I, 189, 233; II, 267; of religion, I, 8; (and idea of peace), III, 174; (and Marrano communities), I, 252; (and rise of court Jews), II, 357
Warrants, Jewish, Polish, and tax evaders, II, 15–16
Warsaw, Jews of: III, 99; and councils, I, 326; and privilege *de non tolerandis Judaeis*, I, 280; congregation in Leipzig from, III, 149; deputies of, I, 337; rights of settlement of, III, 99; smallness of community of, I, 326; state archives of, on Polish Council, III, 81. *See also* Mazovia
"Warsaw Committee," I, 326, 337; III, 81. *See also* Committees; Diplomacy; *Shtadlanim*
Water: as charitable gift, I, 132; ordeal of, I, 251; pouring of, as sign of contempt, I, 169; regulation of, for baths, II, 165; supply of, in Palestine, I, 31–32
Water-carriers, ancient sages as, II, 169
"Water-gate," in Jerusalem, I, 61
Wazirs, Muslim, Jewish advisers of, I, 187
Wealth, Jewish: I, 165; ancient, and communal leadership, I, 45, 119, 134–35; and abuses of excommunication, II, 231; and assimilation, II, 360; and billeting (of poor), II, 322; (of soldiers), III, 189; and boarding of students, II, 189; and burial society, I, 353; and cantors' salaries, II, 101–2; and change of venue, II, 242–43; and charities, I, 305, 321; II, 344–45; and communal control, I, 98, 105; II, 39; (debts), II, 274; and division of communal functions, II, 94; and education, II, 171; (associations), I, 356; (parental responsibility), II, 117, 174; (teaching of own children), III, 161; and elders, I, 204; and electoral rights, II, 29; III, 114–15. *See also* Property qualifications; Three-class system; and funeral charges, II, 264; III, 158; and guilds, I, 373; and hereditary leaseholds, II, 295; and household employment, II, 333; III, 202; and judiciary, I, 195, 204; (fees), II, 84; and marriage (family quotas), III, 98; (selection of mates), III, 204; and *Pletten*, III, 209; and rabbinic control, II, 78, 81, 92–93, 245; and residence rights, II, 11; III, 100; and revenue from burials, II, 157; and sumptuary laws, II, 302, 305–6; and support of refugees, II, 337–38; and synagogues (ornaments), II, 132; (seats), II, 130–31; and taxation, I, 171–73; III, 196; (evasions), II, 283; (defense taxes), II, 268; (immunities), II, 274, 276–80, 288; III, 34, 122–23, 192–93; (meat taxes), II, 259; (of poor), II, 246, 250–52, 326; (wine taxes), II, 162; and Torah summonses, II, 132; and widespread poverty, III, 218; aristocracy of, II, 27–30, 51; III, 142;

attitude to learning of, II, 181; concentration in few hands of, II, 279; ratio of indebtedness to, II, 356; shifts in, I, 28; II, 121, 287; varying estimates of, II, 256. *See also* Oligarchy; Property
Weather, magic for, III, 160
Weavers: ancient, in Alexandria, I, 78; and teachers, III, 41–42; guilds of, I, 365, 369; low Muslim estimate of, II, 183; sales taxes on products of, II, 261
Wedding: gifts, restrictions on, II, 306; halls, medieval, dancing in, II, 167, 315; III, 206
Weddings, Jewish: and brokers' fee, II, 81, 184, 319; III, 208–9; and forced betrothals, II, 311; and polygamy, II, 308–10; and sumptuary laws, II, 302–4; at "dancing-houses," II, 167; dancing permitted at, III, 206; musicians at, II, 115; officials' fees from, I, 175; II, 83, 101–2, 118–19; private monopolies in supplies for, II, 299; private worship vs. synagogue rites at, II, 21, 145; rabbinic control of, II, 83–84; (presence at), II, 90; III, 128, 205; taxes on, II, 15, 171–72, 255. *See also* Family celebrations; Marriage
Wedeles, *see* Spira-Wedeles
Wednesday, as election day, III, 116
Weekly lessons, recitation of, and exilarchs, I, 147
Węgrów, as member of Polish Council, III, 81
Weights and measures, Jewish supervision of, I, 130; II, 57, 291
Weil, Jacob: favors scholars in renting houses, III, 199; on *almemar*, II, 141; on cemeteries, II, 151; III, 155; on communal accounting, II, 64–65; III, 122; on elders, III, 118, 122, 174; on fiscal responsibilities, III, 103; on insults to scholars, II, 79; on lay judiciary, II, 89; III, 130; on legacies, I, 361; III, 93; on Nuremberg synod, III, 77; on obligation to denounce criminals, II, 236; III, 179; on oppressive oligarchy, II, 66; on physical penalties, III, 175–76; on private bans, III, 126; on rabbis, III, 126, 173; (corruption of), II, 92; III, 132; on settlement of scholars, III, 100, 199; on synagogue candles, II, 134; III, 146; on tax evasions, III, 102; on tax immunities, III, 192,
Weil, Samuel Sanvil (Alsatian rabbi), III, 88
Weimar Republic, I, 18; III, 5. *See also* Germany
Weiss, Isaac Hirsch, and legal strictness, III, 172–73
Weissenfels, Jewish conference in, III, 76–77
Welfare budgets, Jewish, history of, II, 343–49. *See also* Budgets; Charities
Weli worship, II, 154. *See also* Ancestors
Weltanschauung, Christian, and European legislation, I, 227
Wenceslaus (Holy Roman emperor and Bohemian king), extradition treaty of, I, 246
Wertheimer, Samson: III, 126; as Prague chief rabbi, II, 81; rabbinic diploma of, III, 131
Wesel, Baruch (Bendix Reuben Gumperz, Silesian chief rabbi), III, 87
Wessely, Hartwig, as educational reformer, III, 163
West India Company, Dutch: and Cayenne Jewry, I, 265; and communal responsibility for poor, II, 347; and Jewish worship, I, 255, 260
West Indies, growth of Jewish communities in: II, 365; British, I, 262; III, 61; Dutch, III, 61; French, I, 265–66; III, 62. *See also* Colonies; *and under* respective areas

Western Empire, *see* Roman Empire
Western Hemisphere *see* America
Westphalia: medieval, Jewish history in, III, 150; modern, suppresses regional assemblies, I, 342, 344
Wet nurses, married women allowed as, in Prague, III, 205–6
White Russia: "alien" mendicants in, II, 323; Jewish emigration from, I, 16; Yiddish in, I, 15
Widowers: inheritance rights of, II, 318; investigation before remarriage of II, 311; residence rights of, II, 234
Widows: and judicial priority, II, 237; and parental selection of mates, III, 204; and plenary assemblies, II, 23; and rabbinic fees, II, 83; charitable provisions for, I, 131; II, 330–31; III, 212; contributions to *Pletten* by, II, 322; of rabbis, slight provisions for, II, 86; Palestinian, and famines, II, 340; residence rights of, II, 234; tax immunities of, II, 275–76; III, 192–93. *See also* Family relations
Wied-Runkel, regional community of: I, 341, 345; III, 87; ordinance on dancing of, II, 315–16; *Pletten* system of, II, 322; sumptuary laws of, II, 305
Wiener-Neustadt, rabbis of, I, 311
Wigs, rabbinic attitude to, III, 203
William (abbot), II, 137
William III (English king), Toleration Act of, I, 259
William the Wise (Hessian landgraf), and Cassel assembly, I, 341–2
Williams, Roger, I, 261–62
Wills: against public mourning, III, 153; ancient, and use of cemetery, I, 94; and communal ledgers, II, 112; and discretion in charities, II, 331; and intercommunal legacies, II, 332; and *lulab* exports, III, 159–60; and Palestine pilgrimages, II, 340; and secular courts, II, 210; and visitors, II, 328; Austrian texts of, III, 126; charitable, validity of, III, 217; ethical texts of, III, 127; obligatory nature of, I, 361; rabbinic, and educational programs, III, 168
Wilno, Jews of: III, *64*; and associational property, III, 97; appeal to government in tax inequalities, III, 197; archival materials on, III, 81, 97; as members of Lithuanian Council, I, 327, 331; II, 116; III, 82; board of electors of, III, 114; burial society of, III, 89–90; cemeteries of, II, 149; III, 157–58; communal debts of, II, 273, 353; III, 191; elders' responsibility among, II, 52; emigrés from, and education, III, 163–64; establishment of ghetto of, III, 197; hospice of, III, 210; judicial fees of, II, 84; population of, III, 210; rabbinate of, II, 87; (controversy over), III, 129; (lay control over), II, 87, 89, 92; (tenure of), II, 86–87; rulers' ordinances on, I, 270; sextons of, II, 106–7; sumptuary ordinances of, III, 201; suppression of private synagogues of, III, 144; taxes of, II, 255, 263; III, 186–87; (immunities), II, 278; teachers' guild of, III, 164
Wimpfen, Süsskind Alexander, II, 155
Wine: and synagogue repasts, II, 128; charitable distribution of, II, 321; communal administration of, II, 63, *161–64*, 300; III, 159; expenditure for, and night study, II, 176; for *habdalah*, auction of, II, 133; importation of, and acquired rights, II, 297
"of libation": I, 169; III, 159; and communal monopolies, II, 161; and excommunication, I, 169; and qualification of slaughterers, II, 109
taxes on: communal, II, 162 (and education), II, 171–72; (and orthodoxy), I, 237; municipal, II, 257; state (in Austria), II, 160; (in Bor-

deaux), II, 164; (in Mediterranean countries), II, 259
Wiśniowiecki, Jeremy (Polish king), decree of, I, 272
Witnesses, Jewish: ancient, I, 48–49; (and Sabbath), I, 110; and informing, II, 241; and prison terms of murderers, II, 226; appeals in synagogues for, II, 145; at weddings, III, 47; (penalized for parental disapproval), II, 310; communal, position of, II, 113, 240; III, 139; credibility of, I, 226, 249, 251; discrimination against, and Jewish judiciary, I, 226; disqualification of (after conversion), I, 232; (for criticism of leaders), II, 49; (for false tax declaration), II, 281; (for gambling), II, 316; (of relatives), II, 112; examination of, II, 239–40; (fees for), II, 84; local, and tax disputes, II, 288; of levirate marriage, exactions by, II, 318; of new moon, I, 143, 154; refusing summonses, II, 228; sign judges' writs, II, 227; single, and unfair competition, II, 297; state laws on (Byzantium), I, 229; (Castile), I, 241; II, 113–14; (Italy, including Sicily), I, 232, 240, 279; (Poland), I, 273; (Portugal), I, 241; (Spain), III, 181–82; tax collectors as, II, 219
non-Jewish: and Jewish family relations, II, 210; credibility of, I, 170, 226, 251; in Jewish courts, III, 181–82; (state laws on), I, 240–41
Witzenhausen, as seat of Cassel chief rabbi, I, 343
Wives, Jewish: and community of goods, II, 210; and membership of husbands, II, 5, 7; and payments for baths, II, 166; as guarantors of absentees' taxes, III, 103; beating of, communal action against, II, 318; consent of, and polygamy, II, 308–9; financial status of, III, 208; left by wandering scholars, II, 187–88; of elders, and communal debts, II, 53; of excommunicates, penalized, II, 230; of teachers, as business-women, II, 184; redemption of, as captives, II, 336; rights in synagogue seats of, II, 131. *See also* Brides; Women
Władysław IV (Polish king), against new synagogues, I, 270; III, 53
Włocławek, Jewish assembly in, I, 324
Włodzimierz (Vladimir): as member of Polish Council, III, 81; rabbis of, III, 71
Wolfowicz, Zelman, III, 122
Wollstein, congregation in Leipzig from, III, 149
Women, Jewish, in antiquity: communal position of, I, 46, 52, 65, 70, 96–97, 104–5; in synagogue, I, 91–92, 123–24; (compartments of), I, 91; III, 16; support scholars, I, 139
medieval and modern: access to cemeteries of, II, 155; and associational membership, I, 349, 354, 361; III, 89; and Christian women, II, 318; III, 151; and citron taxes, III, 187; and execution of criminals, II, 223; and judicial intermediaries, II, 237; and judicial priorities, II, 237; and plenary assemblies, II, 23; and polygamy, II, 308; and ritual baths, II, 165–66; and ritual slaughtering, II, 107; III, 137; and sumptuary laws, III, 200–2; and taxation, II, 251; (immunities of), I, 159; III, 193; and translation of prayers, II, 143; as household help, II, 300; as keepers of baths, II, 115; as teachers, in Italy, I, 359; II, 179; as visitors of sick, II, 328; as witnesses in unfair competition, II, 297; communal charities for, I, 362; II, 332–33; exclusion from education of, II, 177–79; financial status of, III, 208; in synagogues, I, 257;

II, 249; III, 147; (attendance of), II, 140; (compartments of), II, 139–40, 145; III, 147; (ornaments, contributed by), II, 132; (quarrels of), II, 145; Lithuanian supervisors of, II, 63; low Muslim estimate of, II, 183, 318; luxury of, and Turkish sultan, III, 200–1; married, and household employment, III, 205–6; prohibited from entering Gentile houses, II, 314; residence rights of, II, 234; riots by, II, 98; strolls of, prohibited in Prague, II, 314; status of, I, 132; II, 179, 318; III, 114; studies of, III, 162–63; suffrage of, II, 37; III, 106, 114. *See also* Brides; Wives

Wood, Spanish taxes on, II, 249

Wood-pickers, ancient sages as, II, 169

Wool: ancient oriental taxes on, III, 7; communal ordinances on, III, 199; mixing with linen of, III, 202. *See also* Sha'atnez; price agreements on, II, 300

Worcester, Jewish parliament at, I, 245, 297, 311, 315, 319

Workers, *see* Labor

World conquest, ancient dream of, I, 41

World Jewish Congress, project of, I, 316

World-to-come: and excommunication, II, 234; denied to elementary teachers, II, 182; rewards of business women in, II, 179

World War: First (and minority rights), III, 4; (and New York community), I, 26; Second, and Jewish community, I, 17, 20

Worms, Jews of: and city courts, I, 250; and government appointment, II, 35; and Hanau conference, III, 78; and Rhenish synods, I, 313–14; III, 76–78; as district center of German Jewry, I, 341; bathhouse of, II, 166; cemetery of, III, 154; communal bail for defendants of, II, 339; communal debts of, II, 274, 356; III, 192; elders of, III, 113, 121–22; (cooptation of), II, 47; emigration of, I, 245; examiners of, II, 197; fees for elections of, II, 36; female cantors among, II, 140; illuminated prayer-books of, II, 138; interruption of prayers by, III, 112; *memor*-book of, III, 148; population of, III, 69, 107; privileges of, I, 248–49, 267–68; rabbis of, I, 299; II, 78; (authorization of), II, 91; (exclusion of natives), III, 132; (German chief rabbis), III, 69; "Rashi" chapel of, II, 130; rotation of office among, II, 55; statutes of, III, 112; synagogues of, II, 146–47; (decorum), II, 141; III, 148; (of women), II, 140; taxation of, III, 192; unity with Mayence of, III, 154

Worship, Jewish, congregational, ancient: I, 40–41, 52–53, 124; adaptability of, I, 74; and community, I, 12; and "House of the People," I, 62; and neighborhood meeting, I, 74; and origin of synagogue, III, 9; and public assembly, I, 66; attracts Gentiles, I, 82; Decalogue in, III, 22; in Babylonian Exile, I, 61; in Elephantine congregation, I, 70; rabbinic concentration on, I, 135; suppressed in Rome, I, 80

medieval and modern: III, 17; accusation of riot for, I, 258; and age of worshipers, II, 100, 145; (conducted by children), II, 198; and associations, I, 354–56; and communal control, II, 24, 168; and education, II, 178, 206; and Emancipation, I, 8; and *ḥazzan*, II, 100; and interruption of prayers, II, 32–34. *See* Interruption; and patriotic prayers, II, 143–44; and synagogues (candles), II, 134, 259; (depth of), II, 139;

communal responsibility for, II, 126; function of laymen in, III, 151; meaning of, I, 124; II, 210; rabbinic precedence in, II, 89; state legislation on (Brazilian censure), III, 58; (Dutch), I, 253–55; (guaranteed by popes), I, 218; (in Martinique), III, 62. *See also* Toleration; summoning by sextons to, II, 106; suspension for debts of, II, 229; tranquillity of, demanded, I, 253, 260; III, 23; use of *morenu* at, II, 92. *See also* Ḥazzan; Liturgy; Synagogues

Jewish, private: and communal cemetery, II, 146; and communal synagogue, II, 124–25; (candles), II, 134; (chanting), II, 105; and congregational divisions, I, 350–52; and Dutch legalization, I, 254; and recitation of Decalogue, III, 22; authorization of, I, 256; in London, I, 255

non-Jewish: Christian, function of clergy in, III, 151; pagan, Jewish exemption from, I, 109. *See also* Imperial worship

"Worthy men," Jewish, German, and majority principle, II, 26. *See also* Elders

Writing, Hebrew: expertness in, I, 102; spread in ancient Israel of, I, 51

Writs: "of cursing," preliminary to excommunication, II, 228; "of insubordination," preliminary to excommunication, II, 228; judicial, and arrest, II, 227; texts of, II, 211; III, 130–31. *See also* Contracts; Deeds

Wulfowicz, Simon, II, 354

Württemberg: and Basel assembly, I, 315; consistorial influences in, I, 18

Würzburg, Jews of: and Hanau conference, III, 78; and litigations with Christians, I, 250; supply of fish for, II 160–61

Wycombe (England), obtains exclusion of Jews, I, 276

Xambell, Jacob, exempted from bans, II, 232

Xerez de la Frontera, Jewish hospital in, I, 361; II, 329

Yabneh, academy in, I, 150, 153; III, 29

Yafeh, Mordecai b. Abraham, on arbitrators, II, 214; III, 173

Yahwism, and local sanctuaries, I, 49

Yaḳubi, Aḥmad ibn Abi Yaḳub, III, 34

Yarḥi, Abraham b. Nathan ha-, I, 189; III, 43

Yedidiah b. Israel of Nuremberg, on mourning for scholar, II, 147; III, 152–53

Yedidiah of Spires, on marital relations, II, 317

Yedoniah (Elephantine priest), I, 71

Yeḥiel b. Joseph, of Paris, disciples of, III, 152

Yeḥiel Michael b. Nathan (Amsterdam cantor), III, 150

Yehudai Gaon, on physical defects of cantors, III, 136

Yekel of Rzeszów (cantor), II, 104

Yeḳum purḳan, prayer of, I, 180; III, 41

Yemen, Jews of: and Babylonia, III, 44–45; *negidim* of, I, 191, 194; III, 43–44; rituals of, II, 142

Yeruḥam b. Meshullam, on Bible studies, II, 194

Yeshibah, used by Ecclesiasticus, III, 161. *See also* Academies

Yiddish Scientific Institute, archives of, III, 81

Yiḥus, Jewish, communal, importance of, II, 362. *See also* Descent; Families; genealogy

Yoeṣ beliya'al, judicial intermediary as, II, 237

Yom Tob b. Abraham: on burial of repentant excommunicate, II, 231;

on judicial priority for scholars, II, 237; III, 180
Yom Tob b. Isaac, of England, on marital relations, III, 204
Yor edes, II, 113. *See also* Witnesses, communal
York (England), Jews of, I, 297; III, 69
"Young Jews," ancient association of, I, 92
Yugoslavia, Jewish community in, I, 13, 83–84. *See also* Stobi

Zabludowo, dependent of Tykocin, III, 153–54, 182
Zacuto (brothers), expelled from Poznań, I, 332–33; II, 6
Zacuto, Abraham b. Samuel, on Spanish morals, II, 313; III, 205
Zacuto, Moses b. Mordecai: against gaming, III, 207; and Mantua conference, III, 80, 139; and plight of Poznań Jewry, I, 333; III, 83; and rabbis' presence at weddings, III, 205
Zadok, priestly house of, I, 60
Zadok b. Levi ha-Levi, letter of, III, 37
Zadokites, *see* Damascus sect
Zahalon, Jacob b. Isaac: on Roman pestilence, II, 329–30; III, 211–12
Zaḳen and *Zeḳenim*, I, 99; II, 55; III, 13. *See also* Elders
Zamość, as member of Polish Council, III, 81
Zechariah b. Berekel (Bagdad teacher), I, 181
Zechariah of Porto, *see* Porto
Zeeb Wolf of Dubno, pledge by, III, 104
Zemaḥ (judge of the gate), I, 182; III, 42
Zemaḥ b. Ḥayyim Gaon, and prayer-book, III, 42
Zenon (Roman emperor), and Antioch Jewry, I, 93
Zeraḥiah b. Isaac ha-Levi Gerondi, on preaching, III, 134
Zerubbabel (biblical prince), I, 60, 65–66, 68–69, 145; temple of, *see* Temple, Second
Zhitlowsky, Chaim, as Diaspora nationalist, III, 3–4
Zion, Mt.: I, 117; Franciscan chapel on, I, 320. *See also* Jerusalem; Temple
Zionism: and Hebrew, I, 16; and people's community, I, 17; III, 4; in Soviet Union, I, 16; interest in communal history of, I, 29. *See also* Nationalism; Palestine, under British Mandate
Zirides (dynasty) in Granada, III, 34
Ziyad ibn Abihi (governor), I, 159
Zohar, misinterpretation by preacher of, II, 98
Żółkiew, Jews of: III, *116*; chief rabbis of, I, 303; interruption of prayers by, II, 34; minute books of, III, 81; printers' quotas among, II, 203; residence outside ghetto of, II, 296; synagogues of (quarrels), III, 150; (seats), III, 145; tax rates of, II, 280; *tribunus populi* of, II, 287
Zoroastrianism: ancient, I, 148–49, 156, 158; III, 31; medieval (and Muslim bureaucracy), I, 187; chiefs of, I, 176, 178–79; III, 40. *See also* Persia
Zu farheren, *see* Examiners
Zülz (Silesia), Jewish history in, III, 106
Zurich, Jews of: III, 63; suppression of judiciary of, I, 277
Zutra, Mar, I (exilarch), rebellion of, III, 32
Zutra, Mar, II (exilarch), I, 149, 173
Zutra, Mar, III (exilarch), I, 149, 173, 191
Żywiec (Saibusch), privilege *de non tolerandis Judaeis* of, I, 280